E/MJ Operating Handbook of Mineral Processing

- Concentrating
- Agglomerating
- Smelting
- Refining
- Extractive Metallurgy

Edited by

RICHARD THOMAS

ASSOCIATE EDITOR, Engineering and Mining Journal

Vol. I — E/MJ Library of Operating Handbooks

E/MJ MINING INFORMATIONAL SERVICES

McGraw-Hill, Inc.

1221 Avenue of the Americas, New York, N.Y. 10020 U.S.A.

E/MJ OPERATING HANDBOOK OF MINERAL PROCESSING

Library of Congress Catalog Card Number 77-85374.

07-019551-3

FOREWORD

In the past few years, mineral processing technology has been advancing energetically as part of a purposeful, planned response to such diverse stimuli as increasing costs, new environmental requirements, declining ore grades, energy shortages, and financing difficulties.

The pressing need to increase productivity and provide even more product values from today's raw mineral wealth has motivated a constant state of technological change and a quiet, but nonetheless potent, revolution by the processing sector of the worldwide mining industry. Process management, engineers and metallurgists are actually expanding the world's mineral resources through their efforts. In fact, advanced designs and progressive techniques—some already in commercial production and others yet developing—are literally building new reserves from ore that was once considered worthless.

This handbook, compiled from recent issues of *Engineering and Mining Journal,* presents a varied, yet detailed body of data on the development and application of contemporary mineral processing technology. In addition to source material gathered by E/MJ Editors during visits to processing plants, research establishments, technical symposiums, and other worldwide investigation, there are numerous articles contributed by top processing authorities.

The material in this reference has been organized into seven basic chapters, accompanied by an index prepared to provide quick access to available data. Included are 179 flowsheets, 96 tables, and 129 charts.

The *E/MJ Operating Handbook of Mineral Processing* is the first of a series of books planned to cover key areas of mining operations, including open-pit mining and reclamation, underground mining, labor and management. The Editors of E/MJ welcome all comments and suggestions that may help make future volumes more valuable to readers.

Richard Thomas

Contents

Chapter 1
General Processing Reviews

The quiet revolution in the wide world of mineral processing

Stan Dayton, Editor-in-chief

MINERAL PROCESSING IS UNDERGOING a state of planned, purposeful change in response to the needs and demands of society. The stimulus has come from a number of cascading forces: the drive for environmental compatibility, problems with energy supplies, inflation and financing difficulties, minerals nationalism, the pressing need to increase productivity, and an exponential increase in knowledge and communications.

When these dynamics interact with the irreversible necessity of mining ever-lower grades of ore, the challenge is great, but the response has been even more remarkable. To attribute the trend to lower grade ores solely to exhaustion of easily findable and mineable near-surface deposits of higher grade is actually a disservice to the processing fraternity of the mining industry. The advanced designs and progressive techniques employed in mineral processing are literally creating new reserves out of rock once considered worthless. Process engineers are making it possible to mine leaner ores at a profit.

One need look only as far as Cleveland Cliffs Iron Co.'s Tilden operation in Michigan for an example to illustrate this point. Here, selective flocculation of slimes and cationic flotation of silica made ore out of a fine-grained martite-hematite that grades roughly 37% iron. This mineralized zone had previously defied attempts at commercial recovery.

Mineral process developments range from the spectacular to those so esoteric that they are really understood only by a handful of insiders with highly specialized knowledge. The 10-ft cone crushers, 36-ft-dia autogenous mills, 600-cu-ft flotation cells, and thickeners 3 acres in size can fire the imagination. They are highly visible. Sharing in the impact of progress, however, are any number of less visible developments that provide a gain in recovery or grade.

It is the extractive end of the process industry that is showing the most fundamental change. New continuous smelting systems are gaining ground, and hydrometallurgy has burst into full bloom. The successful application of selective ion exchange reagents—particularly the LIX brands (a trademark of General Mills Chemicals Inc.)—have equipped process engineers with powerful tools that are non-intensive in consumption of energy.

Today, energy economics must be equated into the return-on-investment analyses for any processing system. Since energy is no longer cheap and abundant, all recovery systems will have to be evaluated carefully against the energy investment. For the first time, some meaningful energy consumption figures have become available for a wide spectrum of the mining and processing industry. Recently developed by the US Bureau of Mines, some of these statistics appear at the end of this chapter.

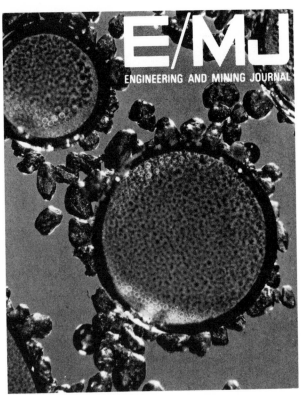

Dynamics of a process system are well illustrated in this photomicrograph of an air bubble and mineral suite reagentized with an amine acetate. Included in this system are principles involving surface chemistry, hindered settling, free settling, energy, ionization, and mass flow. (Photo courtesy of General Mills Chemicals Inc.)

This issue is the product of a two-part effort. The first 22 pages and the portfolio of flowsheets and diagrams were produced by E/MJ. The US Bureau of Mines prepared the text in the mid-section of this issue. While space is too limited to treat adequately all the important work now taking place in the mineral process field, this issue zeroes in on major aspects of a truly impressive panorama.

Instrumentation and control is finally beginning to mature in the mineral process industry. Texasgulf, for example, instrumented its Ecstall concentrator with ARL on-line analyzers and then put its flotation plant under a computer-controlled reagent feeding system. The computer programs utilized optimum seeking methods and smelter contract terms. Copper recovery has improved by 0.8%, zinc recovery by 1.6%, and reagent costs have been reduced by 12% at Ecstall. Although not anticipated, copper and zinc concentrate grades were improved modestly. Some Finnish mines have used computer control for reagents and pulp levels in flotation cells. Cities Service is moving stepwise into a computer-controlled grinding and flotation system, and as discussed later in this section, Cyprus Pima has a semi-autogenous grinding system under computer control and expects to put one of its flotation plants under computer control.

Cyprus Pima: computer control of grinding

Cyprus Pima Mining Co. is now using a computer-based control system, custom designed by Industrial Nucleonics Corp., for the grinding circuit of a nominal 14,000-tpd expansion of its facilities south of Tucson,

Cyprus Pima Flowsheet — Mill 2
With Computer-Based, Semi-Autogenous Grinding Circuit

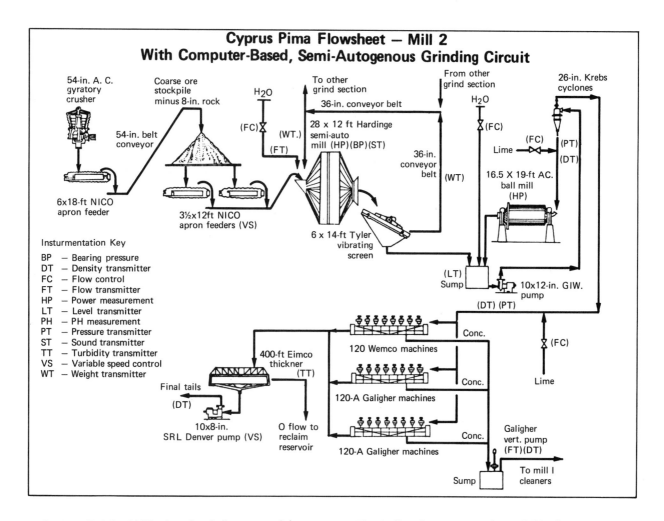

Instrumentation Key

BP — Bearing pressure
DT — Density transmitter
FC — Flow control
FT — Flow transmitter
HP — Power measurement
LT — Level transmitter
PH — PH measurement
PT — Pressure transmitter
ST — Sound transmitter
TT — Turbidity transmitter
VS — Variable speed control
WT — Weight transmitter

Ariz. Installed in 1972, the circuit is arranged in two parallel lines, each consisting of a 28 x 12-ft semi-autogenous Hardinge mill in closed circuit with a Tyler vibrating screen, followed downstream with a 16.5 x 19-ft ball mill in closed circuit with 26-in. cyclones. The schematics of Mill 2, which produces a rougher concentrate for finishing in Mill 1 facilities, are shown in the accompanying flowsheet.

The control system, which started as a data logging project in the latter half of 1973, has since blossomed into full automatic control of the twin grinding lines of Mill 2. In the future, flotation and any additional grinding circuits can be added to the system. Excellent discussions of the test work and decision making that led to adoption of semi-autogenous grinding appeared in the December 1973 TRANSACTIONS of AIME, written by J. H. Bassarear and H. W. Sortokke, and more recently in an AIME paper presented by Fred Pena. Jack Bailey of Cyprus Pima and Harry Carson of Industrial Nucleonics discussed the control package at the 1975 annual meeting of AIME.

At Cyprus Pima, major control loops are used to stabilize the semi-autogenous mill power draw and to balance the loading between the semi-autogenous mills and the ball mills. Also included is the control of flotation particle feed size, which is calculated from several process variable measurements. Tonnage variations at Cyprus Pima may range from 200 to 1,200 tph and changes in the Bond Work Index can vary from 12 to 26 kwh per ton with the five different types of ore processed. These gyrations complicated the satisfactory operation of the original analog system.

The Bailey-Carson paper is available from AIME as preprint 75-B-22. While it is impossible to capsulize the paper here, a few observations are worth repeating.

To establish a correlation between semi-autogenous mill power and mill inventory, bearing pressure proved more reliable than sound. A major campaign during the data logging period was to develop a measurement of flotation particle feed size. An on-line particle size analyzer was used extensively to provide continuous measurement of the primary cyclone overflow feed size. This information was then used to establish inferential particle size, based on ore hardness and density of the cyclone feed.

The horsepower hours of power consumed in the semi-autogenous mills could be related to hardness, but several other variables in this mill also influenced the throughput-hardness relationships. To arrive at a final relationship, it was necessary to combine the effects of cyclone feed density, power consumption, and the semi-autogenous mill discharge density.

The grinding circuit control system consists of two levels of control—the first incorporating three local loops. The first local loop regulates the new feed rate to maintain a given horsepower set point. In this loop, the operator may override the computer-generated horsepower set point and input any desired operating level. Alternatively, the control-system-generated set point may be used.

The second local loop is used to control the particle size of the flotation feed. The measurement of the flotation feed particle size is regulated by the addition of dilution water to the cyclone feed sump. However, water addition is not used entirely for size control. The control loop monitors the cyclone feed sump level which acts as an override on the water addition. As long as the sump level is within limits, size control alone is used. If the sump level approaches either the top or bottom limit, the water will shift from size control alone to size plus sump level, and finally sump level control alone as the sump level passes the maximum or minimum limit. Thus it is possible to utilize size control and at the same time keep the sump from either overflowing or running empty.

In practice, a particle size set point (in terms of cumulative plus 65 mesh) is entered by the operator. The water addition control loop operates from this set point only if the sump level is near neither the bottom nor top limits. If the sump level approaches either extremity, the control system requests the operator to add or subtract cyclones and to switch over to sump level control alone.

The third local loop maintains the pH of the flotation feed by primary lime additions to the ball mill feed. While all three of the first-level local loops are operated through the computer, there is no coordination among these loops. The purpose of the second level of control is to accomplish such coordination. □

Energy requirements of the US minerals industry totaled 1.3 × 10¹² kwh in 1973

(million kwh)

Energy source	Mining	Bene-ficiation	Smelting	Other	Total
Electricity (purchased)	13,100	18,000	78,400	16,100	126,000
Heavy fuel oils	2,650	9,100	20,300	28,600	60,700
Diesel or light fuel oils	34,800	3,890	954	9,550	49,200
Gasoline	4,420	811	122	2,230	7,580
Other petroleum products	1,010	901	2,910	2,040	6,860
Natural gas	18,400	61,800	40,000	194,000	314,000
Coal	1,570	9,900	12,500	104,000	128,000
Coke	—	148	490,000	2,540	493,000
Other energy	31	759	48,100	63,800	113,000
Total*	76,000	105,000	694,000	423,000	1,300,000

Source: US Bureau of Mines preliminary estimates.
*Data may not add due to independent rounding. Data was collected by a nationwide canvas and covers mines, pits, quarries, mills, coal preparation plants, and smelters (including base metal, aluminum, ferroalloys and iron blast furnaces).

Where energy was consumed in US minerals industry during 1973

(million kwh)

Consuming sector	Mining	Bene-ficiation	Smelting	Other	Total
Aluminum (largely estimated)²					
Bauxite (includes calcining, etc.)	99	1,350	—	—	1,450
Alumina	—	40,000	—	—	40,000
Aluminum	—	—	92,100	47,500	140,000
Blast furnace³	—	—	547,000	—	547,000
Cement	—	—	—	150,000	150,000
Clays	1,150	1,730	—	54,100	57,000
Coal (bituminous and lignite)	24,200	5,720	—	1,360	31,300
Coke and coal-chemical materials	—	—	—	69,000	69,000
Copper					
Ore and concentrate	5,200	6,630	—	1,450	13,300
Smelters	—	—	18,000	230	18,300
Ferroalloys	—	481	21,300	10,400	32,200
Gypsum	474	106	—	14,600	15,200
Iron ore	3,080	22,500	—	5,100	30,700
Lime	—	—	—	41,900	41,900
Phosphate rock	1,730	2,540	—	3,830	8,090
Salt	385	2,420	—	2,770	5,570
Sand and gravel	8,350	1,510	—	2,530	12,400
Stone (crushed and broken)	9,790	2,360	—	1,040	13,200
Sulfur (Frasch)	16,400	—	—	—	16,400
Zinc					
Ore and concentrate	314	208	—	56	578
Smelters	—	487	10,800	—	11,200
Other	4,900	17,800	4,990	17,300	44,800
Total¹	76,000	105,000	694,000	423,000	1,300,000

Source: US Bureau of Mines preliminary estimates.
1) Data do not add because of independent rounding. 2) Includes estimates of fuels used by aluminum industry to generate electricity, as well as purchased electricity. 3) Final data expected to be slightly lower when verified to eliminate duplicate reporting.

Cu-Mo recovery: a flowsheet study at Pinto Valley

ONE OF THE NEWEST PRODUCERS among the southwestern US porphyry coppers—the 40,000-tpd plant of Cities Service Co., 6 mi west of Miami, Ariz.—incorporates a number of progressive design features, all compatible with proven technology. Among them are:

■ Secondary and tertiary crushing circuits that automatically adjust feed rates according to the power draw at the crushers, although these commands can be overridden by high level signals at suitable surge points.

■ A system for adding makeup 3-in. balls for the six large primary mills directly to a cushion of ground ore on the ball mill feed belts.

■ Selection of large but proven equipment such as the 18 x 21-ft ball mills and 300-cu-ft flotation cells.

■ A near skin-to-skin arrangement of the rows of flotation cells, with walkways over them rather than between them, a feature which reduced the width of the flotation bay about 20%. Adjacent rows of cells share common launders.

■ A 10.7-mi concentrate pumping system, equipped with a test loop, which delivers copper concentrate to a filtering plant.

■ A set-point supervisory mill control system built around a computer. The system, scheduled to go on line this month, will be developed stepwise through data logging, using process display schematics, and finally to fully programmed systems and process modeling in the future.

Half of the new Pinto Valley concentrator was put into service last fall, and the plant was worked up to full capacity in the first quarter of 1975. It processes a quartz monzonite prophyry containing chalcopyrite and a little molybdenite. Mine reserves in the current open-pit design are 350 million tons of 0.44% sulphide copper. The mill is designed for three-stage crushing to minus ⅜ in., single stage primary ball milling to 15% plus 65 mesh, and a bulk copper-molybdenum float followed by depression of copper concentrate and flotation of molybdenum disulphide. The copper concentrate filter plant is located at a rail siding next to a smelter which was to have treated the copper concentrate.

Current reagent practice is to use Aerofloat 238, Z-14, and Dowfroth 250 for the bulk Cu-Mo float. The ore is pH-sensitive. Roughing of the bulk float is carried out at a pH of 10.0 to 10.5, and the pulp is adjusted to a pH of 11.5 to 11.9 for cleaning. For moly flotation, additives include Nokes reagent, sodium cyanide, ammonium sulphide, and fuel oil. Mixing of the Nokes reagent (water, caustic soda, and phosphorous pentasulphide) takes place in a well ventilated section of the reagent room. The mixing tank area is equipped with an H_2S detector. A concentration of H_2S above the set point triggers a dump mechanism that adds more caustic soda and stops the flow of P_2S_5.

The mill is equipped with an ARL on-line analyzer that reads out copper, iron, and molybdenum on the feed, tails, two concentrates, and several intermediate products.

Crusher feed adjusted to power draw

Run-of-mine ore is delivered from the open pit in 150-ton Wabco trucks to a 60 x 89-in. Traylor gyratory set to deliver a nominal 7-in. product. The crusher setting is adjusted hydraulically from the control panel.

The trucks discharge directly into the crusher, which is set in the bottom of a nominal 300-ton dump pocket. The dump pocket is equipped with automatic dust suppression sprays actuated from an ultrasonic truck dump detector.

Primary Crushing Plant

1. Throughput:	Design - 3,500 stph at 71% availability
2. Feed:	Maximum size of ore—60-in.
3. Product:	90% minus 8-in.
4. Equipment:	Primary crusher—Traylor gyratory Size 60 x 80-in. Hydraulic mantle adjustment Motor 500 hp Crusher setting open side 8-in.
	Discharge Feeder—Stephens-Adamson Type—Apron, Steel pans Size 84 in. Speed—Multiple: 30 fpm, 22.5 fpm, 15 fpm, 11.25 fpm
	Coarse ore storage conveyor—Continental Conveyor Type—Belt Size 60-in. wide Belt Grade—27% Conveyor length one way—1,400 ft. Design speed—510 fpm Motors—two 400 hp & one 600 hp
5. Coarse ore storage pile:	Total storage capacity—159,000 tons Live storage capacity—33,000 tons
6. Surge pocket in crusher building:	Live capacity 360 tons Level controlled by Nuclear Chicago Instruments
7. Dust control in primary crusher plant:	Spray nozzles in dump pocket Dust duct work throughout building with Krebs Elbair wet scrubber Spray nozzles at discharge end of coarse ore storage conveyor

Fine Crushing Plant

1. Throughput:	Design—1,962 stph at 85% availability Future—2,943 stph at 85% availability Note: Future throughput requires expansion of tertiary crushing and screening section but not the secondary crushing section.
2. Feed:	90% minus 8-in.
3. Product:	80% minus ½-in.
4. Equipment:	Secondary crushers—Nordberg Type—7-ft. Standard cone crusher Number of crushers—3 Motor hp—300 Hydraulic rams for adjusting cone setting Crusher setting close side 1½-in.
	Tertiary crushers—Nordberg Type—7 ft. Shorthead cone crushers Number of crushers—6 Motor hp 300

Primary crusher, Pinto Valley (Cities Service Co.)

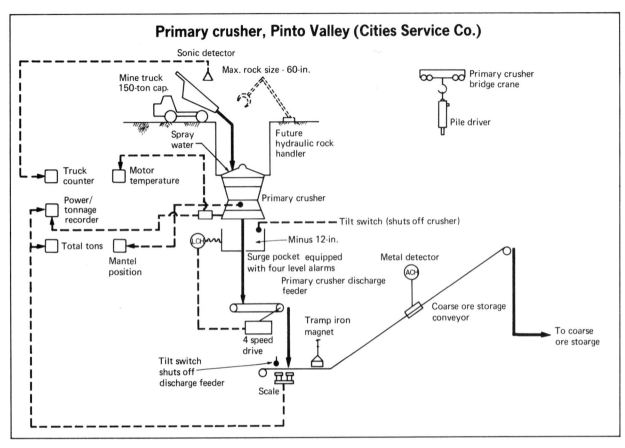

Secondary and tertiary crushing, Pinto Valley (Cities Service Co.)

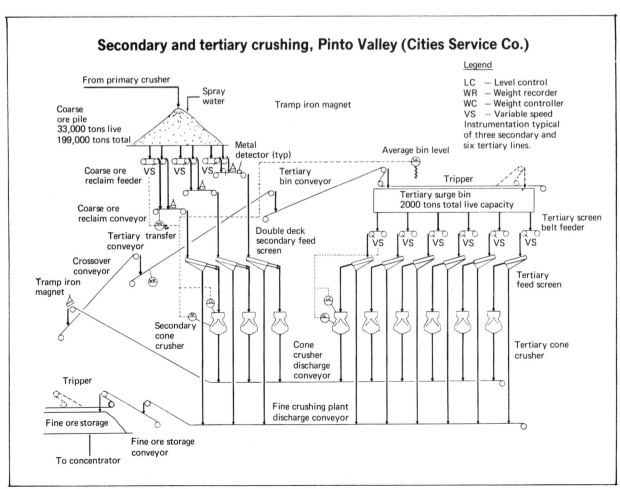

Legend

LC — Level control
WR — Weight recorder
WC — Weight controller
VS — Variable speed
Instrumentation typical of three secondary and six tertiary lines.

Grinding circuit, Pinto Valley (Cities Service Co.)

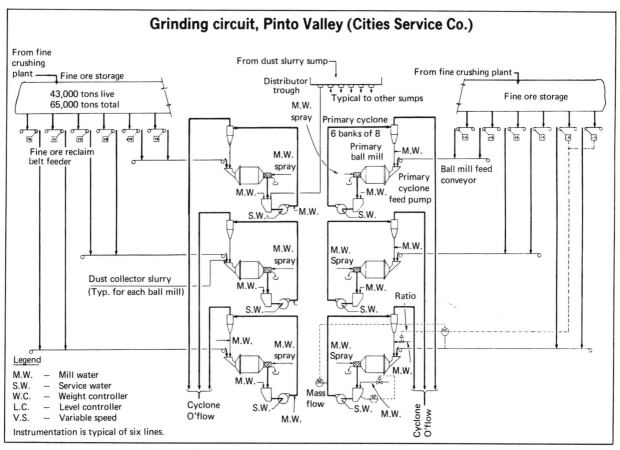

From fine crushing plant
Fine ore storage
43,000 tons live
65,000 tons total

Fine ore reclaim belt feeder

From dust slurry sump
Distributor trough
Typical to other sumps
M.W. spray

Primary cyclone
6 banks of 8
Primary ball mill
M.W.
Primary cyclone feed pump

From fine crushing plant
Fine ore storage
Ball mill feed conveyor

M.W. spray
M.W.
S.W.

Dust collector slurry
(Typ. for each ball mill)

M.W. spray
M.W.
S.W.

M.W. Spray
M.W.
S.W.

Ratio

M.W. spray
M.W.
S.W.

M.W. Spray
M.W.

Cyclone O'flow

Mass flow
S.W.
M.W.

Cyclone O'flow

Legend
M.W. — Mill water
S.W. — Service water
W.C. — Weight controller
L.C. — Level controller
V.S. — Variable speed
Instrumentation is typical of six lines.

Rougher flotation, Pinto Valley (Cities Service Co.)

Legend
M.W. — Mill water
S.W. — Service water
L.C. — Level controller

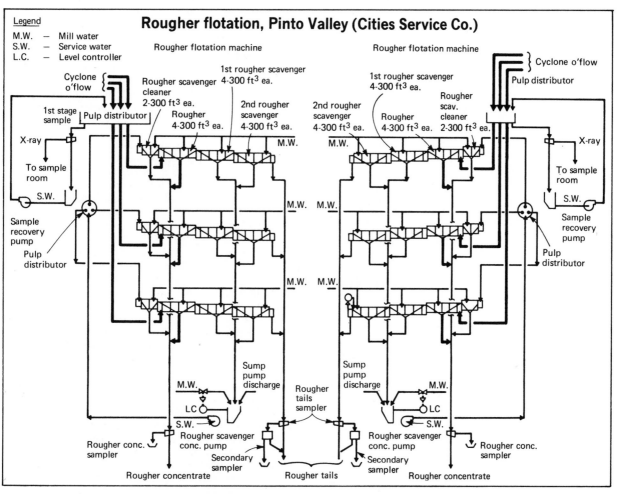

Rougher flotation machine

Rougher flotation machine

Cyclone o'flow
Pulp distributor

1st rougher scavenger 4-300 ft³ ea.
Rougher scavenger cleaner 2-300 ft³ ea.
2nd rougher scavenger 4-300 ft³ ea.
Rougher 4-300 ft³ ea.

1st rougher scavenger 4-300 ft³ ea.
2nd rougher scavenger 4-300 ft³ ea.
Rougher 4-300 ft³ ea.
Rougher scav. cleaner 2-300 ft³ ea.

Cyclone o'flow
1st stage sample
Pulp distributor

X-ray
To sample room
S.W.
Sample recovery pump
Pulp distributor

M.W.
M.W.
M.W.
M.W.

X-ray
To sample room
S.W.
Sample recovery pump
Pulp distributor

Sump pump discharge
M.W.
LC
S.W.

Rougher conc. sampler
Rougher scavenger conc. pump
Secondary sampler
Rougher concentrate

Rougher tails sampler

Sump pump discharge
M.W.
LC
S.W.

Rougher tails

Rougher scavenger conc. pump
Secondary sampler
Rougher conc. sampler
Rougher concentrate

Hydraulic rams for adjusting
  cone setting
Crusher setting close side—½-in.

Secondary feed screens—Tyler
  Type—vibrating double deck; top
    deck grizzly with bottom
    deck slotted screen
  Size—7 ft x 16 ft long
  Number of screens—3

Tertiary feed screens—Tyler
  Type—Vibrating single slotted
    screen deck
  Size 8 ft x 20 ft long
  Number of screens—6

Coarse ore reclaim feeders—
  Stephens-Adamson
  Type—apron, steel pans
  Size—42-in. wide
  Number of feeders—6
  Speed—variable, 15 fpm to 30
    fpm

Fine crushing plant feed
  conveyors—Continental Conveyor
  Number of conveyors—3
  Type—belt
  Size—42-in. wide
  Design speed—368 fpm

Fine crushing plant conveyors—
  Continental Conveyor
  Type—belt
  Size—60-in. wide
  Design speed—630 fpm
  Number of conveyors—6

Crushing plant discharge conveyor—
  Continental Conveyor
  Type—belt
  Size—60-in. wide
  Design speed—435 fpm

Fine ore storage conveyor—
  Continental Conveyor
  Type—belt with tripper
  Size—60-in. wide
  Design speed of belt—435 fpm

Tertiary screen feeders—Continental
  Conveyor
  Type—belt
  Size—84-in. wide
  Speed variable—16 fpm to 31
    fpm
  Hydraulic drive motor
  Number feeders—6

Fine ore reclaim feeders—
  Continental Conveyor
  Type—belt
  Size—48-in. wide
  Speed variable, 16 fpm to 60
    fpm
  Hydraulic drive motor
  Number feeders—12

Mill feed conveyors—Continental
  Conveyor
  Type—belt
  Size—30-in.
  Design speed—231 fpm
  Number of conveyors—6

5. Dust control at fine crushing plant: Dust duct work throughout buildings
with Krebs Elbair wet scrubbers

Concentrator

1. Primary ball mills (6 each)	—Allis-Chalmers
Feed rate per mill:	125 stph minimum, 375 stph maximum
Cost for 6 mills:	$3.5 million (not incl. installation)
Mill size:	18 x 21 ft long, overflow
Mill speed:	12.28 rpm
Ring gear:	Single helical, split, alloy cast steel, 281 hobbed teeth, Mfg.—Falk Gear
Pinion:	Forged alloy steel, 23 teeth (mill No. 4—24 teeth); capable of operating with 22, 24, 25 tooth future pinions. Pinion bearings by SKF.
Lube systems:	2 ea—Farval piston seal ring system 1 ea—Farval gear spray system 2 ea—A-C trunnion bearing system (Hi press & Lo press pumps) 1 ea—A-C pinion bearing system
Air clutch:	Wichita Clutch
Motor:	Allis-Chalmers, 4,000 hp synchronous motor, 150 rpm, 4,160 volts
2. Primary cyclone feed pumps; (7 each, including 1 spare)	—Warman Equipment 8,000 gpm; 370 rpm; 400 hp motor (A-C)
3. Pulp distributors: (2 each)	—Denver Equipment Co. Each has 3 feed compartments to 3 rougher circuits One 9,500 to 12,350 gpm pump per distributor 3 hp motor for rotating distributor

These sprays can also be operated manually if necessary. The entire stream of ore passes through the crusher, as no grizzly is provided to separate the fines. Below the crusher is a nominal 360-ton bin which receives the crushed product. Bin capacity is sufficient to empty the crusher in case of a downstream failure in the primary crusher conveyor equipment. Four level sensors are located in the bin. Lights on the control panel advise the operator of the bin level. Crushed ore is withdrawn from the surge pocket by a four-speed, 84-in.-wide x 20-ft Stephens-Adamson apron feeder. The speed is adjusted to compensate for the rate of delivery of ore from the mine.

The apron feeder discharges to a 60-in. x 1,450-ft steel cable conveyor which carries the ore to an open coarse ore storage of 33,000 live tons. The belt is driven by two 400-hp motors and one 600-hp motor. The primary crusher capacity, a nominal 3,500 tph, is used during all three shifts to accommodate the capacity of the mine shovels.

The fine crushing plant contains three 7-ft Nordberg Standard secondary crushers and six 7-ft Nordberg Shorthead tertiary crushers, plus associated equipment. All nine crushers are equipped with hydraulic adjustments. The three secondary screens are 7 x 16-ft Tyler double deck units. The upper deck contains grizzly bars set 2 in. apart. The tertiary screens are 8 x 20-ft Tyler equipment. All of the conveyor belts are 60 in. wide.

Coarse ore is reclaimed by six 42-in. x 15-ft Stephens-Adamson apron feeders. Two feeders discharge to one 42-in. conveyor belt that feeds one standard crusher. The speed of the apron feeders is adjustable to maintain a constant power draw on the secondary crushers. Each feeder can supply the full feed to a crusher. The coarse ore reclaim belt discharges onto a 7 x 16-ft double deck screen. Each screen has a 2-in. grizzly top deck and ⅜-in. bottom deck. Oversize from both decks discharges into a 7-ft Standard cone crusher. Screen undersize is collected on the fine crushing plant discharge conveyor. The crushed product is collected from all nine crushers and returned to the feed bin ahead of the tertiary crushers.

Distribution of ore in both the tertiary bin and the fine ore storage is maintained by belt trippers that are automatically operated from ultrasonic level detectors. Tripper location and direction of travel is displayed in the control room. Each bin level is also displayed. The trippers can also be locked into any bin or bins from the control room. Both trippers can also be operated manually.

Ore is drawn from the tertiary surge bin by six 84-in.-wide feeder belts. Each feeder belt is driven by a hydraulic motor that takes its signal from the crusher motor to maintain a steady motor load. Each belt feeds an 8 x 20-ft single deck vibrating screen with ⅜ x 5-in. openings. The oversize is fed to a 7-ft Shorthead crusher. The undersize is collected on the fine crushing plant discharge conveyor, along with the screened undersize from the secondary crushers. The tertiary crusher discharge is recycled back to the tertiary surge bins.

The secondary crushers are protected from tramp metal by both magnets and metal detectors on the coarse ore reclaim conveyors. The tertiary crushers are protected by a metal detector on the crusher discharge conveyor that prevents metal from entering the tertiary surge bin.

Eight wet-scrubber-type dust collectors serve all crushing, screening, and ore transfer points. All effluent from the dust collectors is delivered to a distribution box that feeds the primary cyclone feed sumps in the mill.

Feed to the secondary crushers is regulated by crusher power. The power signal adjusts the variable speed motor driving the reclaim feeders. This signal can be overridden by a high average level signal in the tertiary bin, which re-

Molybdenum flotation, Pinto Valley (Cities Service Co.)

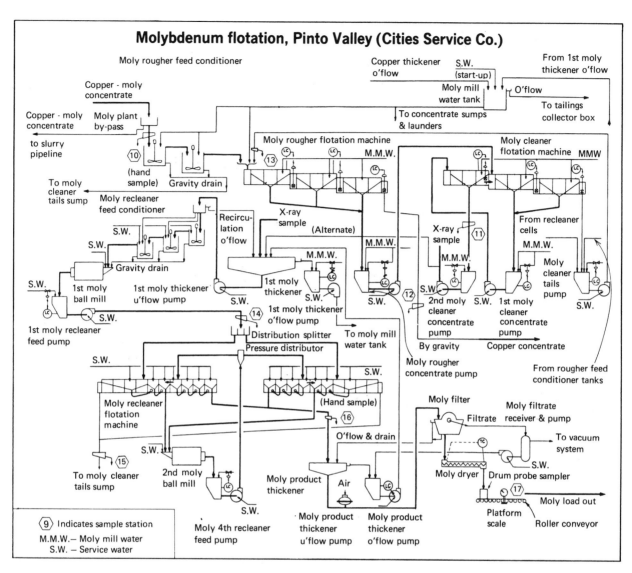

4. Flotation machines:

WEMCO
6 ea—rows of rougher flotation machines; 300 cu ft volume, 14-cell, arranged 2-4-4-4; complete with skimmers, automatic level controls, feed boxes, connection boxes and discharge boxes

Each cell—1,200 rpm—30 hp A-C motor

5. Regrind ball mills: (2 each)
   Mill size:

—Fuller Co.
11 x 15 ft long, overflow
One—left hand drive
One—right hand drive

Motor:

800 hp, 277 rpm, 4,160 volts

Moly Plant

1. Moly rougher flotation machines (2 rows)

WEMCO
300 cu ft volume, 18 cells total, 3-3-3 arrangement per row, complete with skimmers, automatic level controls, feed boxes, connection boxes, and discharge boxes

Each cell—1,200 rpm, 30 hp A-C motor

2. Moly recleaner flotation machines (2 rows)

Denver
50 cu ft volume, 2 ea. 10-cell units, self-aerating

Feed preparation:

Copper-moly concentrate, cleaned for moly and reground

Pulp level control:

Handwheel adjustable weir plus lever operated sand relief gates.

Drive:

2 mechanisms driven by 1 each, 15 hp motor

3. Moly ball mills: (2 each)

Denver Equipment Co.
5 ft by 7 ft long, wet overflow ball mill

4. Moly dryer

Denver Equipment Co.

Includes one thermal fluid heater complete with fuel oil burner and booster pump; thermal fluid recirculating pump; thermal fluid expansion tank; automatic lube system; CO_2 smothering device for thermal fluid expansion tank; venturi scrubber dust collector for vapor exhaust

Material

85% MoS_2 concentrate filter cake

Initial Moisture
Content:

15%

Final Moisture
Content:

3% nominal; 5% maximum

Feed Rate Solids:
(Dry basis)

334 lb per hr nominal; 1,250 lb per hr max. design

duces the secondary crusher feed regardless of the crusher power. Feed to the tertiary crushers is also regulated by crusher power. The power signal is used to adjust a variable-speed hydraulic drive on the tertiary feeds, but this input can be overridden by a level signal from a tilt switch located in the crusher bowl. Feed is automatically reduced until the ore level in the chute falls below the detection point. A second, higher-positioned tilt switch in the crusher and a third tilt switch in the feed hopper are interlocked with the feeder and activate a high level alarm.

All belt conveyors are equipped with zero speed switches, belt side travel switches, and emergency pull cords. The reclaim belts also have torn-belt detectors. All of this equipment is interlocked to the belt drive to protect the belt from damage, or to protect the equipment following the belt in the circuit. All belt discharge chutes are equipped with tilt switches to shut down the conveyor when the discharge chute becomes plugged.

Single-stage primary grinding

The primary grinding circuit consists of six 18 x 21-ft Allis-Chalmers ball mills driven by 4,000-hp motors

Equipment	
Type of dryer:	Indirect hollow screw
Heat Transfer agent:	Thermal Fluid: Therminol 0.66 (Monsanto)
Fuel:	No. 2 fuel oil
Material of const:	316SS
Type of drive:	Variable speed—1.5 hp

Thickeners

1. Copper-moly thickeners:	Dorr-Oliver
Type:	CableTorq
Tank dia:	90 ft
Number thickeners:	2
Feed:	15% solids
Underflow:	50% solids
2. Copper concentrate thickeners	Dorr-Oliver
Type:	CableTorq
Tank Dia:	90 ft
Number thickeners	2
Feed:	17% solids
Underflow	60% solids
3. First moly thickener	Dorr-Oliver
Type:	CableTorq
Tank Dia:	40 ft
Number thickeners:	1
Feed:	24% solids
Underflow:	50% solids
4. Moly product thickener	Dorr-Oliver
Tank dia:	26 ft
Number Thickeners:	1
5. Tailing thickeners	Dorr-Oliver
Type:	Center pier; compacted earth bottom
Tank dia:	350 ft
Number thickeners:	3
Feed:	29% solids
Underflow:	45% solids

through air clutches. Each mill is in closed circuit with eight 26-in. cyclones. The mill discharge is pumped to the cyclones by a 14 x 12-in. Warman pump driven by a 400-hp motor.

The fine ore for each mill is reclaimed by two belt feeders that discharge to a conveyor feeding the ball mill. Feed to each ball mill is weighed on a belt scale. Each feeder belt has a variable-speed hydraulic drive controlled from the concentrator control room. The set point of the controller is either manually adjusted to maintain a constant feed rate or automatically regulated to maintain a constant mass flow to the cyclones. Water is automatically ratioed to the rate of new feed to the mill.

The open overflow mills are spout fed with minus ⅜-in. ore. The new 3-in. grinding balls are added as necessary, directly on the mill feed belts. The final grind is 15% on 65 mesh. The circulating ball mill load is about 500%.

The ball mill discharge is pumped by a fixed speed pump to a cluster of eight 26-in. cyclones. Five cyclones are normally used at any time. Underflow density is 75-80%, with an overflow density of 30%. The cyclone overflow goes to flotation, while the underflow is returned to the ball mill.

Control of the grind can be done either by a manual set of the new feed to the ball mill or by a manual set of the mass flow to the cyclones. When controlling by the mass flow, the original feed is varied to maintain a constant mass flow.

Copper-molybdenum flotation

The copper-moly flotation circuit contains six rows of roughers, each having fourteen 300-cu-ft Wemco cells. The cleaners are arranged in two 14-cell rows of 300-cu-ft Wemco machines. The flotation circuit is divided into two sections, each fed by three ball mills. The rougher concentrate is reground in two 11 x 15-ft mills.

Primary cyclone overflow from three grinding mills feeds the rougher distributor, which divides the pulp equally to three rougher flotation rows. Each row is in a 2-4-4-4 cell arrangement with the new feed entering at the third cell. Scavenger concentrate from the last eight cells in the row is recirculated, with the cleaner tails sent to the head of the rougher row through a rotating distributor. Concentrate from the first six cells of each row is combined with regrind ball mill overflow and pumped to a bank of four 20-in. regrind cyclones to remove any plus 65-mesh material that might adversely affect the operation of the concentrate slurry pipeline. The second stage overflow feeds the cleaner cells. The underflow from both stages of cycloning feeds the regrind mill.

Recleaners, cleaners, and cleaner scavengers are combined in one row of 300-cu-ft flotation machines in a 4-6-4 cell arrangement. New feed enters the first of the six cleaner cells and is pumped to the four recleaners. The recleaner concentrate flows by gravity to a 90-ft Cu-Mo concentrate thickener. The concentrate from the four cleaner scavengers is recycled back to the regrind system.

Flotation reagents are distributed by metering pumps, fed from head tanks above the control room. Any of the reagents can be added to any feed box of any bank through a system of rotating distributors. Distribution systems have been provided for two collectors and two frothers to the flotation cells. In addition, one collector and fuel oil can be added to the primary cyclone underflow launder to the ball mills.

Rougher pH is maintained by lime addition to the ball mills. Final rougher pH adjustment is made in the rougher cells from a pH signal originating in the first rougher cells.

Copper concentrate handling, Pinto Valley (Cities Service Co.)

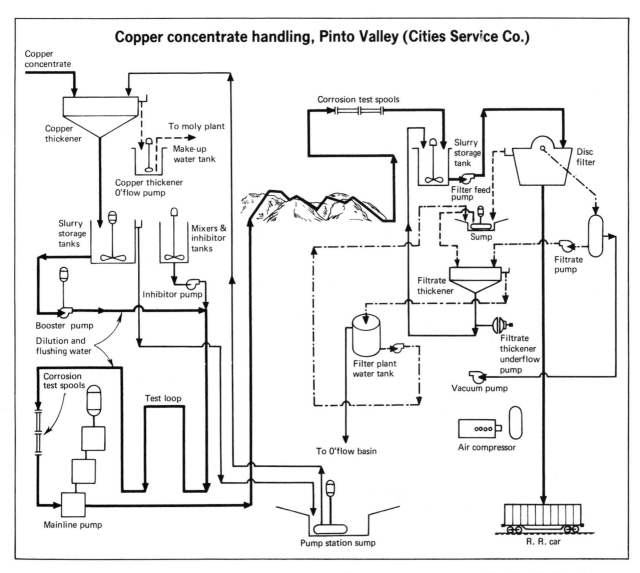

Reagent Facilities

1. Lime Ball Mill	Denver Equipment Co. 6 x 10 ft, wet overflow ball mill

Main Pumphouse

1. Mainline slurry pumps:	(2 each—including 1 standby) Ingersoll-Rand
	Heavy Duty, reciprocating, plunger-type, skid-mounted, variable capacity output
Main components:	Ingersoll-Rand Aldrich Triplex pump
	Gear Pak unit combining a speed reducer gear with a variable speed drive (Philadelphia Gear); flush water pump for plug location; suction and discharge pulsation dampeners; Allis-Chalmers motor, 350 hp, 1,750 rpm, 4,000 volts
Maximum pressure:	2,300 psi
Maximum flow:	190 gpm
Slurry:	Slurry concentrate 55% to 65% solids by weight
2. Mill water pumps:	(4 each including 1 standby) Goulds 6,500 gpm, 223 ft head, 1,800 rpm, 500 hp motor

3. Service water pumps:	(3 each including 1 standby) Goulds 2,500 gpm, 395 ft head, 1,800 rpm, 350 hp motor

Copper-molybdenum separation

The molydenite flotation circuit contains eighteen 300-cu-ft Wemco flotation cells and twenty 50-cu-ft Denver flotation cells. There are two 5 x 8-ft Denver polishing mills in the circuit. The rougher molybdenite concentrate is thickened in a 40-ft thickener. The final molybdenite concentrate is thickened before filtering in a 26-ft thickener. The concentrate is filtered in 4-ft, three-disc Denver filter. The concentrate is dried in a Denver 14-ft Holoflite screw drier.

The thickened copper-molybdenum concentrate is pumped to two conditioners in series, where the copper depressants are added. The conditioned concentrate is fed to a nine-cell row of 300-cu-ft cells, which make a rougher concentrate. The rougher tailing is the final Cu concentrate, which goes to two 90-ft thickeners. The moly rougher concentrate is cleaned twice in another row of nine 300-cu-ft Wemco cells. The tailing is returned to the head of the rougher circuit, while the concentrate goes to a 40-ft thickner. All thickeners at the plant were supplied by Door-Oliver. Concentrate thickeners are mostly of the

Tailing disposal, Pinto Valley (Cities Service Co.)

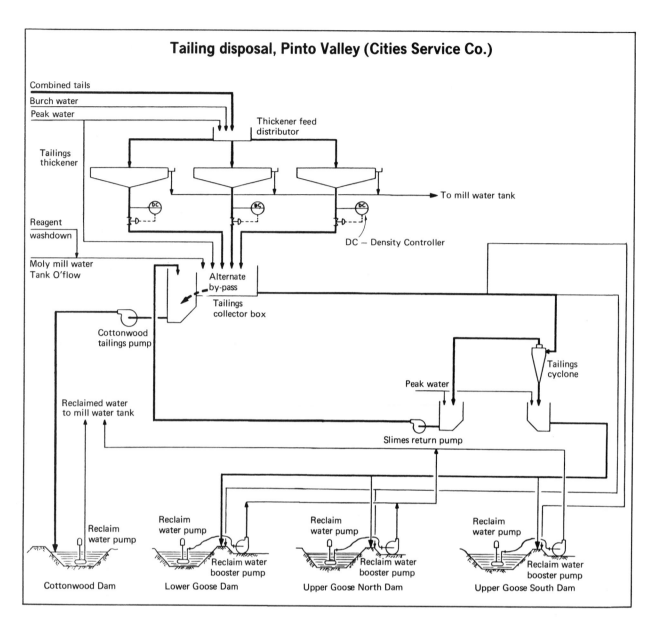

CableTorq type, while the tailing units are of the center-pier type.

The thickened molybdenite rougher concentrate is pumped to three conditioners in series, to which reagents are added. From the conditioners, the concentrate passes through a 5 x 8-ft ball mill and then to the recleaner row of cells. The recleaners are two parallel row of 10 cells, 50-cu-ft Denvers. The cells are arranged 4-1-1-1-1-1-1. Concentrate from the sixth cell passes through another 5 x 8-ft ball mill. The recleaner tailings are returned to the head of the rougher circuit. The final concentrate is thickened in a 26-ft thickener, filtered on a disc filter, and dried in a Holo-flite screw drier.

Concentrate handling

The copper concentrate handling system consists of two 238,000-gal slurry storage tanks, two ASH 3 x 3-in. centrifugal pumps, two I.R. Aldrich positive displacement pumps, one 476,000-gal slurry storage tank, two Denver nine-disc 8-ft 10-in. disc filters, two Nash vacuum pumps, and one 26-ft thickener.

The Cu concentrate flows by gravity at 60% solids from the copper thickeners to two slurry storage tanks. The slurry is pumped by a centrifugal from the storage tank through a test loop to determine its pumpability. If the density and viscosity are correct, the flow is diverted to one of two positive displacement pumps, which transfer the concentrate 10.7 mi to the filter plant storage tanks. Total pressure developed is 1,500 to 1,600 psi. At the filter plant, two disc filters are set above railroad cars to allow discharge of filtered concentrate directly into cars for movement to the smelter.

Tailings from copper-moly flotation go to three 350-ft thickeners through a 42-in.-dia pipe. At the thickeners, the tailings can be directed to all or any one of the three thickeners. Water is reclaimed from the thickeners and returned to the mill water supply. Thickened tailings can be sent to any one of four dam areas. Water is reclaimed from all tailing disposal areas.

Lime is received in a 240-ton bin and then ground in a 6 x 10-ft ball mill. The slurry is stored in two 100,000-gal agitated storage tanks. The lime slurry is pumped in a loop through the mill and back to the slurry storage.

Liquid reagents are received in 9,000-gal tanks and diluted as needed or used at full strength. Reagents are pumped to head tanks in the mill and distributed by metering pumps to the point of usage. □

Duval Sierrita adds flexibility with ferromoly plant

RESOURCEFULNESS IN PROCESSING is well demonstrated at a new $2 million ferromolybdenum plant added to Duval Sierrita Co.'s copper-molybdenum mining installation, 20 mi south of Tucson, Ariz.

A wholly owned subsidiary of Duval Corp., Duval Sierrita utilizes a silicothermic reduction of roasted molybdenum sulphide concentrates to ferromoly—a product that not only diversifies the internally produced molybdenum line, but also makes the company less dependent on toll smelting arrangements with competitors. Duval now markets molybdenum as a ferroalloy, as molybdenum trioxide, or as MoS_2 concentrate in a wide variety of packaged forms. The company is in an approximate standoff with Kennecott Copper Corp. as the No. 2 source of domestic molybdenum. In 1974, Sierrita produced 11.5 million lb of molybdenum, while Duval's neighboring Esperanza copper-molybdenum unit recovered about 3.7 million lb of molybdenum.

Sierrita, the largest of three Arizona properties operated by Duval, was originally equipped with a 60,000-tpd copper-molybdenum concentrator, placed in production in 1970. This plant was expanded to 72,000 tpd the following year, and capacity has subsequently been raised to 88,000 tpd. Exploration and preliminary development at Sierrita delineated an orebody of 414 million tons with an average grade of 0.35% copper and 0.036% molybdenum, but subsequent work continues to add to this total.

Started up in February 1975, the new ferromoly plant was designed for a nominal capacity of 2.5 million lb of molybdenum contained in a 60-64% ferroalloy. The add-on facility at Sierrita's copper-moly concentrator receives its trioxide feed by air conveyor from stored calcines produced by roasting molybdenite concentrate in multiple hearth units. The plant was designed by Mountain States Engineers. The batch process takes place in a sand mold as a series of exothermic reactions, in a grand display of controlled pyrotechnics lasting about 5 min. During the process, molybdenum is reduced by silicon contained in ferrosilicon, with an assist from powdered aluminum.

Copper-moly separation

The ore is open-pitted from 50-ft benches for a three-stage coarse and fine crushing system that yields a minus ½-in. product. This feed is ground to about 33% on 100 mesh in sixteen 16½ x 19-ft primary ball mills, each in closed circuit with four of five 26-in. cyclones overflowing at about 230 tph. The primary mills carry an approximate 500% circulating load, which is returned as cyclone underflow. The bulk copper-moly float takes place in 100-cu-ft cells using Aerofloat 3302, Z-6, fuel oil, and MIBC.

The rougher concentrate is reground in two 11 x 15-ft mills in closed circuit with cyclones for flotation cleaners and recleaners. Finished tailing is settled to about 50% solids in four 350-ft-dia center pier thickeners and then piped about 6 mi to the tailings pond. The Cu-Mo concentrate is thickened to 52% solids. The feed to Cu-Mo separation is about 25% Cu and 2-3% Mo, and this section produces a final tail of 0.15% Mo.

The bulk Cu-Mo concentrate is steamed to destroy adhering flotation reagents and conditioned with a reagent suite considered proprietary. The cooked concentrate goes through roughing and scavenging stages, where copper is depressed and a 7-9% moly concentrate is skimmed from the cells. The float is thickened for the cleaner circuits. The copper concentrate in the rougher and scavenger moly flotation tailing is thickened, filtered, and loaded in gondola cars for shipment to custom smelters.

Ferric chloride leach cleans moly

The thickened moly rougher and scavenger concentrate is stage-cleaned and recleaned several times in a circuit that includes a regrind mill. During flotation the final concentrate is upgraded to 47-48% Mo, and this product is dewatered on a belt filter and a Holoflite drier to 2% moisture. The molybdenite concentrate then goes through a ferric chloride leach to remove an approximate 2.5-3% copper content and further upgrade the product to 53-54% Mo. The leached concentrate is filtered, dried, and roasted in a pair of 23½-ft-dia, 11-hearth furnaces, each fed at a nominal 1.5-tph rate. The calcine produced by the roasters contains 60-61% Mo and less than 0.10% S. The offgases are treated in a train of dust cyclones and electrostatic precipitators before being lime-scrubbed in a UOP turbulent scrubber and vented to the atmosphere.

Fe-Mo theoretics

According to a Soviet article, translated and published for the National Science Foundation, the silicothermic reduction has proved to be the simplest method of producing ferromolybdenum. The article states that the reduction of molybdenum oxides with silicon proceeds according to the following reactions with the release of free energy:

$$\frac{2}{3} MoO_3 + Si \rightarrow \frac{2}{3} Mo + SiO_2$$
$$MoO_2 + Si \rightarrow Mo + SiO_2$$

The reaction of aluminum with molybdenum oxides proceeds more completely with an even greater release of free energy:

$$\frac{2}{3} MoO_3 + 4/3\ Al \rightarrow \frac{2}{3} Mo + \frac{2}{3} Al_2O_3$$
$$MoO_2 + 4/3\ Al \rightarrow Mo + \frac{2}{3} Al_2O_3$$

In the silicothermic reduction of molybdenum oxides, iron slag or oxide is usually added to the charge. The reduction of iron oxides proceeds partly to iron and partly to ferrous oxide.

According to the article, it has been calculated that the quantity of heat generated in such processes is sufficient to melt the metal and the slag and to cover the heat losses. The reactions, therefore, may be carried out without supplying outside heat. To improve the precipitation of metal droplets from the viscous high-silica slag, a part of the silicon in the charge may be substituted by aluminum.

The siliocothermic method of smelting ferromolybdenum, according to the Soviet article, has found wide use.

Batching for burns

Process schematics at Sierrita are shown in the accompanying diagram. Major unit operations at the plant consist of: 1) charge preparation; 2) charge mixing; 3) mold preparation; 4) mold charging; 5) charge ignition and reaction, which takes place under a movable hood; 6) mold cooling; 7) discharge of a solid cake of metal and slag from a casting ring; 8) quenching of the solidified cake; and 9) separation of the metal and slag, and crushing.

For a typical 1,500-kg charge of moly trioxide, the following ingredients are added: 465 kg of 75% ferrosilicon, 355 kg of 15% ferrosilicon, 300 kg of ferrous oxide, 225 kg of lime, 70 kg of aluminum powder, 50 kg of powdered iron, and 45 kg of CaF_2.

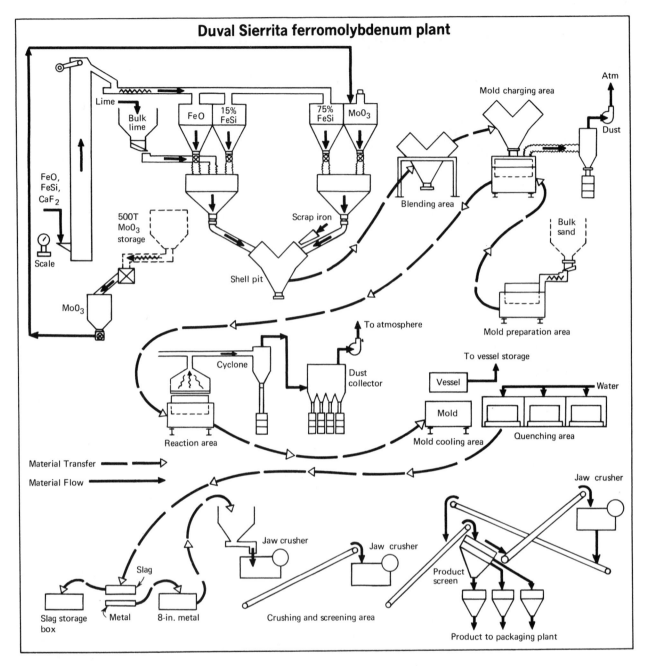

Duval Sierrita ferromolybdenum plant

Some of these charge materials are weighed in the warehouse and bucket-elevated to a screw conveyor that distributes iron oxide, lime, and the two grades of ferrosilicon to storage bins over the shell pit. Moly trioxide is air-conveyed to a fifth bin over the shell pit area. These materials are weighed into a Patterson Kelly blender—a bottle-type mixing device that is moved into a rotary drive apparatus after it is charged. Powdered aluminum and iron and fluorite are manually added to the blender.

The mold boxes, measuring about 8 x 8 x 3 ft high, are two-thirds filled with bulk sand at the mold preparation area. A refractory-lined 6-ft-dia ring about 18 in. high is then placed on the sand bed in the mold. The blender and mold box with casting ring are moved separately to a charge area where the mix is emptied into the casting ring and leveled. The mold and ring are then moved to the reaction area, where the movable hood assembly is positioned over the casting ring and locked into a flue system. An ignition charge of powdered aluminum, magnesium, iron oxide, and potassium nitrate is broadcast on top of the

charge. When all is ready, the charge is ignited manually using a railroad flare attached to the end of a 20-ft pole. The reaction flashes to life and the ideal burn lasts 5 min.

The combustion gases are drawn from the hood to the dust collector train, consisting of a Buell cyclone and baghouse. The mold box is then moved by crane to an area next to a series of three quench tanks for an approximate 12-hr cooling period at ambient temperatures. The solidified metal and slag cake is then quenched. On removal from the quench tanks, the slag and metal easily part into two layers when hit with a heavy sledge hammer. The metal cake is then hammered into 8-in. chunks for a three-stage Kue Ken and Tyler screening circuit, which produces a sized 1-in., ¾-in., and ⅝-in. product.

The product is delivered to a sophisticated packaging plant where the full moly product line can be placed in bags, barrels, or cans of varying weights. Sulphide concentrates or technical grade molybdic oxide can even be briquetted, packed in cartons, and wrapped with a heat-shrunk polyethylene seal. ☐

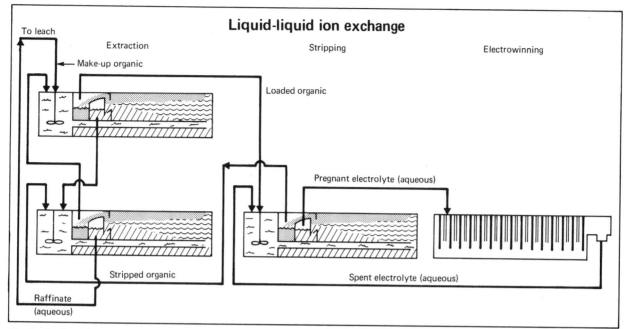

Liquid-liquid ion exchange

Extraction — Stripping — Electrowinning

To leach

Make-up organic

Loaded organic

Pregnant electrolyte (aqueous)

Stripped organic

Spent electrolyte (aqueous)

Raffinate (aqueous)

Idealized solvent ion exchange circuit always involves a closed solvent loop although the aqueous loops may be open-circuited.

Ion exchange: the new dimension in copper recovery systems

SOLVENT ION EXCHANGE is fast maturing as an important unit operation in large scale recovery of base metals from ores. By this time next year, liquid-liquid ion exchange systems will play a major role in well over 200,000 stpy of primary copper production capacity. Beyond this capacity, as shown in the accompanying table, are additional plants now in preliminary planning stages or under consideration in such locations as Zaire, Zambia, Chile, Peru, Europe, Japan, and the US.

Solvent ion exchange (SIX) functions as a highly versatile mechanism for purifying leach liquors and for concentrating metal values into smaller, more manageable solution volumes for recovery by electrowinning, precipitation, or crystallization.

Because the reactions taking place in SIX systems are ionic in nature, the solution matrix can be changed completely. For example, the copper contained in the ammoniacal leach liquors of the Arbiter process can, under cer-

tain conditions, be evacuated down to the parts-per-million level and pulled into an organic liquid phase containing a suitable ion exchange reagent. This occurs during the extraction stage, as shown in the above diagram. The copper can then be transferred from the loaded organic phase by a sulphuric acid solution in the stripping stage of the flowsheet shown.

In this example, the pregnant copper sulphate (an aqueous phase of the stripping circuit) is electrolyzed in a tankhouse, regenerating acid as spent electrolyte for return to the stripping circuit. The pregnant aqueous copper solution of the stripping circuit, however, could be processed through chemical steps other than electrowinning to precipitate the copper.

Similarly, the input solution to an SIX circuit could be an acidic base-metal-bearing solution of copper, as in the more commonly employed non-Arbiter processes. In such SIX reactions, ions are transferred across the interface of two immiscible liquids, according to the following general formula for copper:

$$Cu^{++} + 2HR \rightleftarrows CuR_2 + 2H^{++}$$

The active extractant (represented by HR) is dissolved in a carrier liquid of kerosene or some other liquid that does not mix with water.

While solvent ion exchange has been widely used in the recovery of uranium and certain other metals, the concept faced a struggle for recognition and acceptance among copper producers despite its simplicity and obvious advantages. General Mills spokesmen capsulize some of the inherent advantages of SIX for copper as follows: in electrowinning, the electrolyte copper content is divorced from the leach circuit; because SIX purifies, the system can tolerate higher impurities in the leach liquors, and higher current densities can be maintained in the tankhouse; electrowon copper cathodes from SIX systems are of high quality, and the concentration and purification characteristics of the system could improve the performance of current copper vat leach systems. □

New and planned liquid ion exchange plants for copper

Company	Location	First year of operation	Capacity (cathodes, tpy)
Ranchers Exploration and Development	Miami, Ariz.	1968	7,000
Cyprus Bagdad	Bagdad, Ariz.	1970	7,000
Nchanga	Zaire	1973	90,000
Anaconda[1]	Anaconda, Mont.	1974	36,000
Cyprus Johnson	Johnson Camp, Ariz.	1975	5,000
Anamax	Twin Buttes, Ariz.	1975	30,000
Minero Peru	Cerro Verde, Peru	1976	30,000
Cities Service	Miami, Ariz.	1976	7,000
Codelco	Chuquicamata, Chile[2]	1977	36,000

1. Operates on Arbiter process liquors. 2. A first-stage plant to treat ores from the Exotica mine.

Bluebird: a bold step into commercial liquid ion exchange

RANCHERS EXPLORATION AND DEVELOPMENT CORP. was the first to go commercial with copper liquid ion exchange and electrowinning. The Ranchers plant at Miami, Ariz., having a nominal 30,000 lb per day capacity, was inaugurated in 1968. This remarkable company—a financial pigmy among mining giants—bases its Bluebird operation on heap leaching of an oxidized ore zone containing a copper mineral suite that is predominantly chrysocolla, with minor amounts of malachite and azurite. There is little iron of consequence in the orebody.

Ranchers put the deposit into production in 1964 using a cementation recovery system. The company began investigating LIX-64 (a trademarked product of General Mills Chemicals Inc.) when the reagent was introduced in 1965, and then acted on feasibility studies when it became apparent that it would be increasingly difficult for an independent producer of precipitate to smelt and sell copper. Ranchers ran its first solution into the plant in March 1968, pioneering a pathway that others were to follow. While the operation experienced a year of teething problems in reaching rated output, capacity of the plant has since been pushed as high as 45,000 lb per day of cathode copper. Ken Power, manager of Bluebird, says appreciatively, "It's fun to run this plant."

Ranchers collects pregnant leach solution from the heaps in a butyl rubber-lined pond. The pond serves a five-vessel liquid ion exchange train in which three vessels are on extraction and two on stripping—all have a countercurrent flow of organic and aqueous phases.

The organic-to-aqueous flow ratio on the extraction side is about 1:1, whereas in the stripping circuit it is about 2.0:1, counting an aqueous recycle. The organic is composed of 12% LIX-64N and 88% kerosene, which carries the reagent. The tankhouse is operated at a high current density—up to 32 amps per sq ft—adjusted according to the amount of copper input to the system, to maintain the desired concentration of copper in electrolyte. Acid consumption amounts to about 5 lb per pound of copper extracted.

Dumps leveled in 90,000-sq-ft surface area

The mining rate is 12,000 to 14,000 tpd of 0.4% to 0.45% copper ore and about 1.5 times that amount of waste. Most of the ore is ripped and pushloaded into scrapers for a ¾-mi haul to one of the leach areas. A new leach area is readied by grading and sloping the natural surface, after which it is compacted with standard road equipment.

About 11 or 12 heaps out of a total of 21 or 22 are undergoing active leach at any one time. The heaps, built up in 20-ft lifts, are rotated as necessary through leaching, drying out, addition of new ore, and repiping of the surface area. The surface area of the dumps is prepared for leaching by laying a network of 2-in. PVC pipes on 8-ft centers. The pipes, fed from a 4-in. PVC header, are equipped with small needle valves on 8-ft centers. The valves drip an acidified raffinate (the aqueous off-solution from the final extraction vessel, to which makeup acid is added if necessary) at a rate of 200 gpm per heap. The acidified raffinate carries about 20 gpl H_2SO_4 and 0.2 gpl copper.

The heaps in the leaching cycle receive raffinate at about 2,400 gpm. The solution percolates through the dumps and is collected at about 2,200 gpm in the surge sump. Roughly 200 gpm are lost through evaporation and absorption. Recovered pregnant leach solution piped to the pond con-

tains about 1.9 gpl of copper and 3-4 gpl H_2SO_4.

Ken Power described the Bluebird operation at an International Solvent Extraction Conference at The Hague in 1971. It is essentially the same today as then, although solution volumes and concentration have undergone small variations.

The feed to the plant is heated to 80°F in a heat exchanger to assist in phase disengagement of organic and aqueous layers in the solvent extraction train.

Each of the five mixer-settlers in the solvent extraction system consists of an approximately 8-ft-dia cylindrical tank equipped with a turbine-type impeller at one end of the settler—a covered tank of rectangular surface dimension. Aqueous and organic phases enter the mixer, which is sized for a retention time of about 2 min for the approximate 4,200-gpm flow of the two immiscible liquids in the extraction circuit. A propeller pump moves the mixed phases through a distributor pipe to the far end of the settler. The mixed phases begin to separate and flow back toward the mixer—an overflow weir drawing off the top 2 in. of the 9- to 12-in. organic layer, and an underflow baffle tapping the bottom aqueous phase into their separate launders. The settlers are designed for a phase disengagement rate of about 2 gpm per sq ft of surface area.

The pregnant aqueous leach solution advances downstream through three extraction stages countercurrently to the organic, and is drawn off the third extraction unit for recycle to the heaps. Stripped organic moves upstream through the three extractors. The active ion exchange reagent in the organic phase exchanges its hydrogen ion for the copper ions in the aqueous phase according to the reaction:

$$2HR_{org} + CuSO_{4aq} \leftrightarrows R_2Cu_{org} + H_2SO_{4aq}$$

The direction of the reaction proceeds according to the concentration of the reactants in the system.

Copper-loaded organic recovered from the first extractor is advanced to the stripping circuit, where copper is transferred back to the aqueous phase from the organic. Here, the loaded organic from the extraction circuit moves upstream against a downstream advance of spent electrolyte returned from the tankhouse. Copper is stripped from the organic in a reversal of the previous reaction. Solution volumes in the stripping circuit consist of about 2,100 gpm of organic and 450 gpm of aqueous electrolyte, and a significant concentration of copper in the aqueous phase results. Typical solution flows and concentrations through the system are shown in an accompanying table.

Pregnant electrolyte is pumped through a six-cell flotation circuit for removal of small amounts of entrained organic before electrowinning. The presence of organic in the electrolyte can cause a poor deposit of copper on the cathodes, particularly in the top 2 or 3 in. of the cathode. The organic froth is returned to the stripping circuit after dewatering. The electrolyte tailing from the flotation cells is pumped at 450 gpm to a head tank at the electrowinning plant. Raffinate from the third extractor stage goes through a separate air-cell flotation circuit to recover a small amount of organic, which is returned to the system.

The barren raffinate, taken as tailing from the flotation cells, is pumped to a surge tank equipped with level controls for the addition of makeup water to adjust for small losses in the system. The leach solution returned to the dumps consists of raffinate, recycled heap underflow solution, and makeup water. It is prepared by drawing off so-

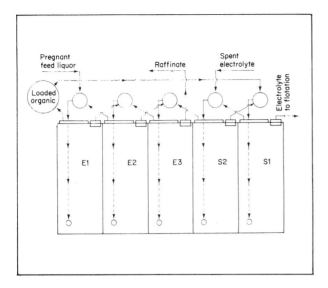

lution from the raffinate surge tank to a set of 12 sumps and pumps. Concentrated sulphuric acid is added to the sump boxes as necessary.

Acid is added to the solution going on a new lift during the first 60 days of a leach cycle, and straight raffinate is then dripped on the heap, which has an average life of about 120 days. The normal pattern of acid addition during the first 60 days is 20 gpl, followed by 60 days of raffinate acidity of 5 to 7 gpl of H_2SO_4. Power estimates the average residence time for new solution in a lift at about one week. The leach is controlled by monitoring the copper concentration of the underflow solutions.

The electrolytic tankhouse contains 48 cells arranged in four quadrants of 12 cells connected in series. Each cell has 40 cathodes and 41 anodes of 8% antimonial lead. The 96-v dc current is distributed evenly as a 2-v drop across each cell. The current density is varied to maintain an approximate 40-gpl copper content in the spent electrolyte. The power consumption is about 1.1 kwh per lb of copper deposited. Bluebird has traditionally purchased its starter sheets but is now setting up an assembly line to produce the 36 x 36-in. starter sheets.

In commenting on the plant operation, Power reports that the LIX-64N reagent has a laboratory maximum loading ability of 0.25 gpl for each percent of ion exchange reagent in the organic. In operation, the flow rates are adjusted so that the reagent is loaded only to about 60-70% of capacity, maintaining an aggressive organic solution throughout the extraction circuit.

The most serious problem in early operation, he states, was the occasional uncontrolled movement of sludge in the organic stream. At times, some change of operation would activate the normally quiescent sludge, which collected at the organic-aqueous interface, and it would rise and flow with the organic. This movement led to transfer of iron-laden leach liquor into the electrolyte and of electrolyte back into third stage extraction, as well as other transfer problems in the circuits.

The sludge consists primarily of fine air-borne particles that are simultaneously wetted by both aqueous and organic phases. To control the sludge problem, the organic layers were carried a little deeper to lessen the likelihood that sludge would be carried over the overflow weirs. Two mixers were also changed from aqueous-continuous to organic-continuous operation, since aqueous-continous seemed to make the sludge more mobile. Baffles were installed in the settlers to retard the flow of both the aqueous and organic streams in the vicinity of the distributing pots at the back of the settlers.

A sludge removal system was then devised to periodically remove some of the sludge from the circuit. The sludge is decanted from the second-stage stripping settler, where it tends to accumulate, and is pumped to a 30,000-gal holding tank. After a suitable settling period, clear organic can be decanted and returned to the circuit and the aqueous drained to a recovery sump. The concentrated sludge is then pumped through a plate-and-frame filter press using diatomaceous earth as a filter aid, to recover clean recycle organic.

Before the problem was controlled, organic losses of 0.30 gal per 1,000 gal of raffinate were common. Today these losses are on the order of 0.12 to 0.16 gal per 1,000 gal. ☐

Typical solution concentrations at Bluebird reveal a concentration ratio of over 20:1

	Flow rate (gpm)	Gm per liter Cu	Gm per liter H_2SO_4
Leach solution	2,400	0.25	5-20
Solvent extraction feed	2,100	1.9-2.1	3-4
Pregnant electrolyte	450	46-48	140-150
Spent electrolyte	450	40	150-160
Raffinate	2,100	0.2	20
Loaded organic	2,100	2.0-2.1	
Stripped organic	2,100	0.25	

Anamax to grind oxide ore for LIX*-electrowin plant

THE NEWEST COPPER SOLVENT extraction and electrowinning plant in the US will soon be started up by Anamax Mining Co. at Twin Buttes, Ariz. Scheduled for initial operation at mid-year and full capacity in 1976, the approximately $75 million Anamax installation will process 26 million st of stockpiled oxide ore accumulated during development and mining of the sulphide section of the Twin Buttes orebody. At capacity, the plant will treat 10,000 tpd of oxide ore carrying about 1% acid-soluble copper, with an anticipated yield of about 36,000 tpy of cathode copper.

The Anamax flowsheet will involve three-stage crushing, with the ore moving progressively through a 48 x 60-in.

Allis-Chalmers primary, a 7-ft Symons Standard secondary, and finally, a pair of 7-ft Symons Shorthead tertiaries—the last in closed circuit with two 8 x 20-ft vibrating screens. The minus ½-in. product will be stored on a conical surge pile of 15,000-live-ton capacity and reclaimed via two conveyor-equipped underground tunnels. The belts will feed two parallel lines of open circuit rod and ball mills—each line consisting of one 11½ x 18½-ft rod mill and one 12½ x 30-ft ball mill. This equipment is expected to produce a 15% plus 65 mesh grind for the acid leaching circuit.

The significant lime content of the Anamax ore leads designers to anticipate an acid consumption rate of 250 lb per ton of ore. On the other hand, this ore characteristic

---

*LIX is a registered trademark of General Mills Chemicals Inc.

will be utilized to adjust the pH of the clarified leach liquor prior to solvent extraction. The acidity of the pregnant solution will be lowered by agitating it with a bleed stream of freshly ground ore (see flowsheet). Makeup acid will be supplied from a large add-on acid plant at Magma Copper Co.'s San Manuel smelter, about 50 mi northeast of the Twin Buttes plant.

The ore will be leached in five rubber-lined, mechanically agitated tanks, each having a 147,000-gal capacity, in a concurrent flow of pulp and acid. The pregnant pulp enters a countercurrent decantation system of four 400-ft-dia thickeners. The sands will advance through successive washings to tailing disposal at the sulphide concentrator pond. The pregnant leach liquor overflowing the first thickener is ready for pH adjustment, which takes place in three mechanical agitators where the liquor and fresh ore will be contacted. This slurry will be clarified in a 400-ft-dia thickener, which overflows to a 400-ft clarifier reservoir serving filters at the solvent extraction circuit. The underflow from the pH adjustment thickener will then be recycled to the leach agitators.

The clarified liquor is passed through a series of sand filters and then pumped to the solvent extraction plant. The filtered liquor entering the circuit will contain about 2.5 gpl of copper, which will be concentrated for electrowinning to about 50 gpl in the mixer-settler solvent extraction circuit.

Solvent extraction will be carried out in two sections with four stages of mixer-settler vessels in each section. Stripping will take place in two sections of two stages each. In the extraction circuit, the filtered leach liquor flows countercurrently to the extractant—LIX 64N, carried in kerosene. In the final two vessels, copper in the organic phase is transferred back to the aqueous phase for electrowinning. The electrowinning plant, equipped with a starter sheet section, will have a capacity of about 100 tpd of commercial cathodes.

Anamax is a 50-50 joint venture of Amax Inc. and Anaconda Mining Co. The mine, equipped with a sulphide concentrator that was recently expanded to 40,000 tpd from 30,000 tpd, went into production in 1969, following one of the largest pre-production stripping programs in mining history.

The sulphide plant was inactivated for a six-month period starting in March, to allow advance development in the pit, which suffers from poor ground conditions. Completion of the mine development and expansion program should lower costs, raise productivity, and hike capacity to 90,000 tpy of copper in concentrates and 36,000 tpy of cathode copper from stockpiled oxide ore. The new hydrometallurgical plant is being built by a joint venture of Arthur G. McKee's Western Knapp Engineering Div. and Davy Powergas Inc. □

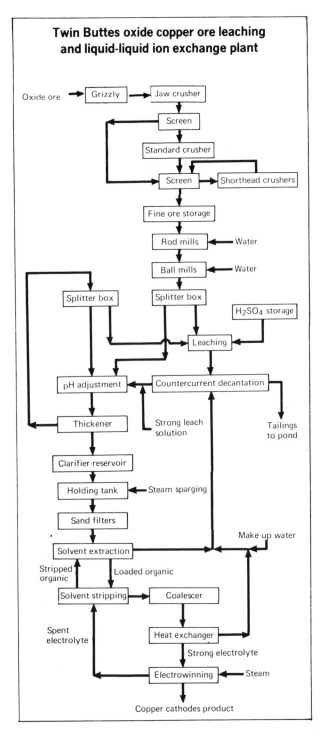

Twin Buttes oxide copper ore leaching and liquid-liquid ion exchange plant

Cities Service to join solvent extraction circle

THE COPPER CEMENTATION FACILITIES at Cities Service Co.'s Miami, Ariz., unit will be replaced by a new solvent extraction and electrowinning plant scheduled for completion in July 1976. This plant will enable the company to produce cathode copper directly from leach solutions recovered from the inactive Maimi underground mine—eliminating the need for toll smelting of precipitate.

The Cities Service unit will be sized for the production of about 1 million lb per month of cathode copper. It may have the distinction of taking the lowest grade leach liquor into a liquid ion exchange circuit. The planned installation will process leach liquors of about 0.85 gpl copper in two solvent extraction trains, each with five mixer-settlers. Three of the vessels in each train will be on extraction, and two will strip copper from the loaded organic phase into the aqueous phase.

It is planned to take a copper solution of 35 gpl into the electrowinning plant, which will be equipped with 60 cells. Of these, 16 cells will make up the starter sheet section, and the commercial section will consists of 44 cells. The electrolytic plant will be designed to operate at a current density of 22 amps per sq ft. □

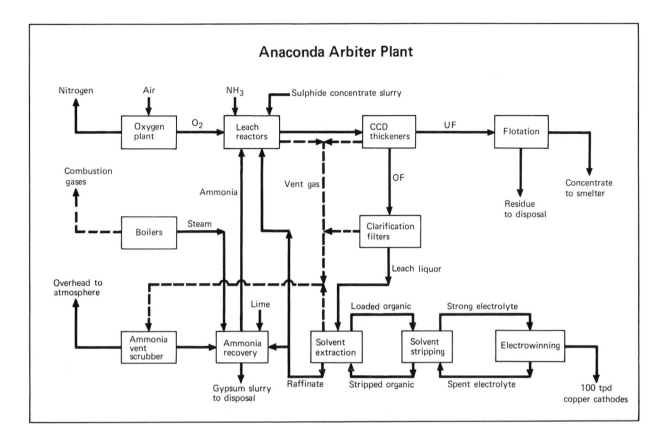

Anaconda Arbiter Plant

Copper hydrometallurgy: the third-generation plants

OF THE NEW GENERATION of copper extraction plants, the Anaconda Co.'s Arbiter plant is in operation, Duval Corp.'s Clear process is nearing completion, and the Cymet process, developed by Cyprus Metallurgical Processes Corp., is in a pilot demonstration stage. All were designed to treat copper sulphide concentrates in hydrometallurgical systems. The Arbiter process opens with an ammoniacal leach, while Clear and Cymet take up copper in ferric chloride solutions.

Arbiter: ammonia solutions with alternatives

Anaconda's Arbiter plant went on line at Anaconda, Mont., in September 1974 with an installation capable of 36,000 tpy of copper cathodes. The process takes its name from Nathaniel Arbiter, group consulting metallurgist of Anaconda's Natural Resources Group and leader of the team that launched this pioneering effort. The system strikes off in new creative directions in an attack on the problems of winning metals from ores while eliminating air pollution.

The Arbiter process offers a number of options, depending on the characteristics of the feed, the market for sulphur compounds, and the cost of energy or other supplies. For example, the system presents several alternatives for treating mixed concentrates containing appreciable amounts of zinc, nickel, and cobalt or lesser amounts of other metals. The process is also open ended as to recovery of precious metals, which could be cyanided—a step that would compensate for the traditional weakness of base metal hydrometallurgical systems in recovering precious metals. Sulphur can be handled in several different ways.

The Anaconda plant is based on a moderate-temperature, low-pressure leach of concentrates in an oxygen/ammonia/ammonium sulphate system. The leach is carried out at temperatures of 65° to 80°C and near-ambient pressure. Copper is solubilized as a copper amine sulphate $(CuNH_4SO_4)$. Pyrite is unaffected by the leach. The leach is followed by a solvent ion exchange (SIX) circuit, which yields an electrolyte of copper sulphate for electrowinning of copper. The tankhouse returns an acidified spent electrolyte to the SIX stripping stage. The residues of the ammonia leach circuit are washed with raffinate of the SIX train and processed through flotation to recover small amounts of undissolved copper and precious metals.

Most of the processing options for other metals and for sulphur fixation have been piloted, with interesting results. The most significant piece of ongoing work now involves precipitation of copper from its soluble tetra amine sulphate state using an SO_2 gas stream, to be followed by briquetting, melting, and reverberatory refining to a quality product.

This step would eliminate the solution ion exchange and electrowinning stages and could be of importance where power costs are high. Of the 1.4 to 1.5 kwh of energy per lb of cathode copper produced by electrowinning, 1.1 kwh is consumed in the tankhouse, while the remainder is used for agitation and pumping. Arbiter says preliminary studies indicate that an Arbiter process plant of the size built in Montana could be placed in operation at about two-thirds the capital cost of the already attractive $22 million installation cost of the Anaconda plant if the SO_2 precipitation system were used.

From easily to slowly soluble, the general order of

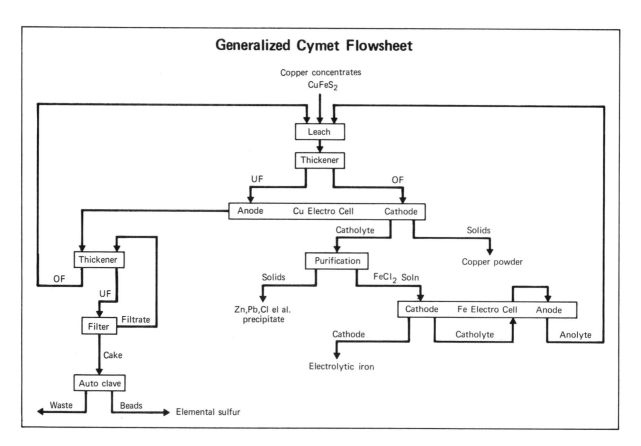

Generalized Cymet Flowsheet

Copper concentrates
$CuFeS_2$

Leach → Thickener

UF → Anode — Cu Electro Cell — Cathode ← OF

Catholyte → Purification

Solids → Zn,Pb,Cl el al. precipitate

$FeCl_2$ Soln → Cathode — Fe Electro Cell — Anode

Solids → Copper powder

Cathode → Electrolytic iron

Catholyte / Anolyte

Thickener — OF / UF → Filter — Filtrate

Cake → Auto clave

Waste / Beads → Elemental sulfur

---

response of copper sulphides to leaching systems reads: chalcocite, covellite, bornite, chalcopyrite, and enargite. The leaching of copper sulphides in the ammonia system depends on agitation well beyond the conventional range. For example, Arbiter reported that power intensities of about 0.15 hp per cu ft are used at the Montana plant.

The mixing design speeds reaction rates and helps counteract to some extent the formation of insoluble ferric hydroxide films on mineral surfaces. Pilot plant work indicated that continuous monitoring and control of temperature and pressure and of the ammonia and oxygen partial pressures were sufficient to gain reproducible results.

Pregnant ammoniacal solution from the wash circuit is processed through vacuum precoat filters in preparation for the solvent ion exchange train. In the SIX circuit, LIX-65N is used in a high-flash-point carrier of distillate.

Several alternatives are available for handling sulphur. The Anaconda plant uses recovery of ammonia and discard of gypsum by steam stripping of the raffinate bleed (an ammonium sulphate solution) with lime. Further work indicates that addition of lime directly to the leach appears equally practical. Others alternatives include crystallization of ammonium sulphate (potentially a salable product in some areas); thermal reduction of ammonium sulphate to sulphur with recovery of ammonia; or possibly a bacterial decomposition of ammonium sulphate solution to yield sulphur and ammonia.

Cymet: a venture in chloride electrochemistry

The Cymet process is being piloted in a plant capable of treating 25 tpd of chalcopyrite concentrates. Developed jointly by Paul R. Krusei, Hazen Research Inc., and Cyprus Mines Corp., the Cymet process is one of several ferric chloride processes now under study. Duval is about ready to start a commercial size plant, but few details

are available. Cominco and South Africa's National Institute of Metallurgy have also investigated ferric chloride leach systems. The NIM process uses a solvent ion exchange step employing LIX-64N (a registered trademark of General Mills).

One major attraction of ferric chloride processes is that they take place at atmospheric pressures. As the Cymet process prefers a feed of 95% minus 200 mesh, concentrates may or may not require regrinding. The heart of the system is based on electro-oxidation of sulphide sulphur to the elemental state at the anode of diaphragm cells, solution of metal ions, and reduction of copper at the cathodes. The ground slurry of sulphide concentrate is leached countercurrently with a ferric chloride anolyte returned from the iron cells.

A thickener stage provides a clear overflow for feeding the cathodes of the cells. The underflow is distributed to the cell anodes, where the attack on chalcopyrite is continued at a high current density (up to 200 amps per sq ft). Copper is recovered from the leach and anolyte solutions in the cathode compartment of the cell as a powder precipitate. The solids from leaching are autoclaved for about 2 hr at 135°C to form globules of sulphur that can be screened off. The screen undersize can be subjected to flotation.

The spent catholyte of the electro-oxidation cells then undergoes a purification step: cementation with iron, to further deplete copper. This solution is further purified by zinc cementation to remove residual traces of copper and other impurities such as lead, antimony, bismuth, and arsenic. Zinc occurring in the feed and added for purification is removed by solvent extraction with a tertiary amine.

The purified ferrous chloride solution is sent to the electrolytic iron cells, which plate high purity iron on iron starter cathodes. Ferric chloride is regenerated at the anodes and recycled to the leach. □

Automatic starter sheet stripping at Outokumpu

MECHANIZED STRIPPING OF STARTER SHEETS from mother blanks has been in continuous operation at the Pori copper refinery of Finland's Outokumpu Oy since the spring of 1974, in an effort to reduce heavy manual work and operating costs.

Consisting of three conveyors and a stripping station, the system occupies about 85 sq m (925 sq ft), as shown. At peak capacity, the machine has handled 900 starter sheets per hour, although the practical capacity is 600 per hour. A pair of sheets can be stripped from a mother blank in 8 sec, including auxiliary operations of recoating the blanks and transferring the blanks into and out of the system. While the unit illustrated here was developed for copper, Outokumpu reports that the same machine, with minor modifications, could be used for stripping nickel and zinc.

The process starts on conveyor No. 1, where the mother blanks with copper deposits grown on both sides are washed free of electrolyte by warm water sprays. The mother blanks are then transferred one by one to the hooks of conveyor No. 2, which marches them stepwise in a vertical single file through the stripping station.

At the stripping station, a mother blank is locked in the correct position. Blades open the upper edge of the sheets, and pneumatically operated jaws on each side of the blank grip the opened upper edges. The copper sheets are then peeled and drawn to a pile that rests on an adjustable hydraulic table. A controller maintains the pile at a constant level. When a pile of 500 sheets has been accumulated, an overhead crane transfers the sheets to the feed end of an electrode looping and preparation area, for the commercial section of the refinery.

Stripped mother blanks move through a spray coating unit where both surfaces are coated with a chemical. From the stripping conveyor, the blanks are collected on conveyor No. 3, where they are positioned with the required spacing for the stripper cells. Faulty mother blanks can be removed from the stripping conveyor line for maintenance.

Mother blanks of rolled copper have been used in daily production. Titanium blanks have also been tested on a stripping machine and found suitable for the process. The edges and solution line of the mother blanks are protected by narrow plastic strips.

In operation, the stripping blades open only the upper edges of the starter sheets, leaving the blanks undamaged. The piles of starter sheets are said to be well formed and easy to transfer and handle in the commercial cathode preparation area. □

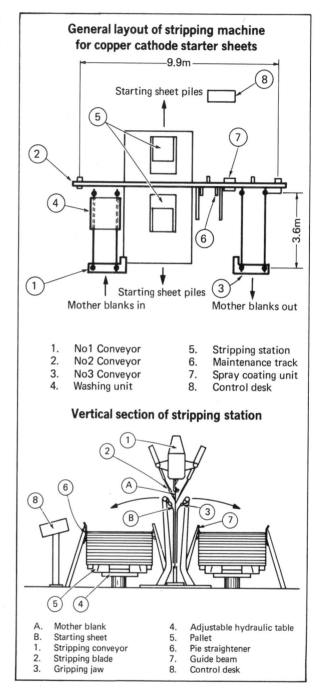

General layout of stripping machine for copper cathode starter sheets

1. No1 Conveyor
2. No2 Conveyor
3. No3 Conveyor
4. Washing unit
5. Stripping station
6. Maintenance track
7. Spray coating unit
8. Control desk

Vertical section of stripping station

A. Mother blank
B. Starting sheet
1. Stripping conveyor
2. Stripping blade
3. Gripping jaw
4. Adjustable hydraulic table
5. Pallet
6. Pie straightener
7. Guide beam
8. Control desk

Lakeshore to use roast-leach-electrowinning and cementation

WHEN HECLA MINING CO. STARTS UP the 15,500-tpd Lakeshore project near Casa Grande, Ariz., later this year, one of North America's most diverse sets of processing subsystems will be locked into the recovery of copper from oxide and sulphide ores. The company will link time-tested metallurgical processes for the production of both cathode and cement copper. The feed will originate from an underground mine developed in a large, complex deposit containing both oxide and sulphide ores.

Located about 30 mi south of Casa Grande, the Lake shore project is a joint venture of Hecla (the operator) and

El Paso Natural Gas Co., which originally drilled out the deposit. The recovery installation consists of separate but interlocked sulphide and oxide plants to be fed independently from separate sections of the mine.

Hecla will sulphate-roast the concentrate from a new 9,150-tpd sulphide mill in slurry-fed, fluid-bed reactors for an agitation leach circuit. After clarification, the pregnant leach liquor will be pumped to an electrowinning tankhouse containing 164 cells (including a 16-cell starter sheet section). Spent electrolyte will be divided between the agitation leach circuit and the oxide leach plant in a ratio that balances the solution needs and copper recovery of the two plants. The roaster offgas will be converted to a sulphuric acid. The washed leach residue in the sulphide plant will be directly reduced in a kiln with coal to sponge iron. This product, a hematite concentrate containing minor amounts of unrecovered copper but most of the precious metals, provides most of the iron units needed for cementation in the oxide plant.

The 6,450-tpd oxide plant is based on vat leaching of the feed and precipitation of copper on roll-crushed pellets made from sponge iron. About 80% of the total acid requirements of the system will be supplied by a 270-tpd Chemico acid plant treating the roaster gas stream and by regeneration in the tankhouse. The remaining acid will be purchased.

Since iron recovered from the leach residue of the sulphide plant will be insufficient for copper precipitation in the oxide circuit, the flotation concentrator is equipped with a magnetite recovery section. Here the flotation tailing will be cycloned to recover an underflow for two stages of magnetic separation. This additional iron concentrate will produce more than enough feed for the sponge iron plant to offset internal requirements.

The RLE (roast-leach-electrowinning) section has been described in detail at several local meetings by the Hecla metallurgical staff and in an article recently published in the JOURNAL OF METALS. The RLE process was extensively piloted in a 5-tpd plant, first using a "stand-in" concentrate from Cyprus Pima Mining Co. and then Lakeshore concentrate as it became available for testing.

The authors point out that although the RLE process is not new, it has not previously been used commercially in North America. Large installations in Zambia and Zaire produce several hundred thousand tons annually by this method. RLE limitations are well known, they say. Copper recovery is lower than in reverberatory smelting, converting, and electrolytic refining. Precious metals in sulphide concentrates are lost in the leach residue. Relatively large volumes of copper-bearing, acidic, spent electrolyte must be disposed of, since more acid is generated during electrolysis than is required in leaching sulphated calcines.

The authors also state that although roaster gases are strong enough for autothermal conversion to acid, the SO_2 content is near the lower limit for autothermal operation.

In the Lakeshore operation, relatively simple means are available to overcome these deficiencies. All of the concentrated sulphuric acid produced from the roaster gases will be used in vat leaching of oxide ore. The vat leaching operation will also absorb the spent electrolyte bleed from

electrowinning, utilizing the acid for recovery of copper by cementation. The hematitic leach residue in the sulphide treatment section, containing unrecovered copper and precious metals, will be converted to sponge iron. Since the sponge iron is used for cementation, it compensates well for the inherent weakness of RLE in recovering copper and precious metals.

The sulphide concentrator has one rod and two ball mills, which will produce a product for rougher flotation using lime for pH control, potassium amyl xanthate collectors, and MIBC as a frother. A regrind circuit will yield an 80% minus 325-mesh product for flotation cleaning from rougher scavengers. The concentrate will then be thickened and/or filtered to control the density of the slurry fed to the fluid bed reactors. The cake is to be repulped for the two Lurgi fluid bed roasters. Pilot plant test work indicated fluid bed space rates of 1.5 to 2.0 ft per sec.

The roaster calcines will be leached in a multiple-stage agitation circuit, and the residue washed in a CCD system. The electrowinning circuit contains 148 cells in the commercial section and 16 cells in the starter circuit. The cells, connected in series, contain 73 anodes and 72 cathodes. Made of concrete and lined with Barber Webb "Paraliner," each cell measures 3 ft 8 in. wide x 4 ft 5 in. deep x 22 ft 6 in. long.

As it enters the starter sheet section, the pregnant electrolyte will contain about 55 gpl of copper and 14 gpl of acid. This solution will flow next to the commercial section, which is arranged in four rows. Depletion of copper during electrolysis in the starter sheet section will adjust the solution concentration to about 45 gpl of copper and 28 gpl H_2SO_4 for the commercial section. It is expected that the electrowinning plant will operate at a current density of 15 to 20 amps per sq ft.

The oxide plant is equipped with 10 vats, a conveyor loading bridge, and a bucket excavator span, also equipped with a conveyor line terminating at a truck bin. Each vat will function in a cycle of approximately 10 days, including bedding the ore in the vat, leaching, washing, draining, and excavation. The oxide leach residue will be used to further build the tailing dam berms.

The leach residue and magnetite of the sulphide treatment circuit will be balled on discs for a Dravo straight grate pelletizer. This indurated product will then be converted to sponge iron in a rotary reduction kiln, using coal from New Mexico. The pellets are to be broken to about 20 mesh for feed to the cementation plant. Pelletized cement copper, containing gold and silver values, will be trucked to Casa Grande for shipment to a smelter. □

Gold and silver: a mix of old and new technology

US PRECIOUS METALS are undergoing a mini-revival with construction of two processing plants, one in Nevada and the other in Idaho. The first plant is based on recently developed heap leaching, charcoal adsorption, desorption, and electro-winning techniques, and the other uses conventional cyanidation and zinc dust precipitation. Planned recovery from this pair will amount to more than 95,000 oz of gold and at least 2.2 million oz of silver per year, according to engineering estimates.

Smoky Valley keyed to low-grade gold ore

Copper Range Co., along with Felmont Oil Corp., Essex Royalty Corp., and the Ordrich interests, recently awarded an engineering and construction contract for a 2 million

tpy gold processing facility at Round Mountain, Nev., to Mountain States Mineral Enterprises Inc., of Tucson, Ariz. The operating entity will be Smoky Valley Mining Co.

An extensive metallurgical testing program, including a pilot plant campaign by Mountain States Research and Development over the past two years, has proved the suitability of the cyanide heap leaching concept for Round Mountain gold ore.

Such a process is effective in leaching the values from finely crushed Round Mountain ore because the gold occurs in fracture fillings and pores. Gold is liberated from the abrasive, acid volcanic rock (a rhyolite) for solution contact at a relatively coarse size. Although part of the gold was probably originally emplaced in sulphide minerals, the gold is now largely free and the sulphides are converted to oxide except in some small veinlets.

The general flowsheet encompasses heap leaching on permanent watertight pads, with subsequent excavation and disposal of leached tailings, carbon adsorption of the gold and minor silver values, and desorption and electro-winning of values. Smelting produces doré bullion containing approximately two-thirds gold and one-third silver. The cycle of heap emplacement, leaching, washing, and tailings disposal will require approximately one month. The lime-cyanide leaching solution will be 0.5% NaCN at a pH of 11 to 11.5. Reagent consumption is expected to be 1 lb of cyanide and 2 lb of calcined lime per ton of ore. At current gold prices, heap leaching is the only process that is economic for the low-grade Round Mountain ore. The simplicity of such a system provides a good production rate at minimum capital cost.

New life for an old mining district

The general technique of heap leaching of relatively coarse rock, followed by carbon adsorption and electro-winning of precious metal values, was developed at the Salt Lake City Metallurgy Research Center of the US Bureau of Mines. The process has been applied commercially at Newmont Mining Co.'s Carlin operation and at Cortez Gold Mines, both in Nevada. Homestake uses parts of the system at Lead, S. Dak.

The production history of the Round Mountain gold mining district dates back to 1910. Most of the output originated from detrital placers eroded from Round Mountain itself, a landmark in the region. Some higher-grade vein material has also been mined by underground methods from the lode. The new operation will be based on lower grade ore surrounding the high grade lode areas already mined.

The new plant will incorporate many recent but proven technological advances in gold recovery and is designed to achieve minimum ecological disruption and maximum safety for plant personnel. Operations are scheduled for September 1976 startup at an estimated annual rate of 82,000 oz.

Earth Resources launches silver-gold project

The second new operation is a 1,400-tpd silver-gold plant sited on the Idaho side of the tri-state corner of Idaho, Washington, and Oregon. Earth Resources plans to carve out an open pit in the rugged, mountainous terrain of the De Lamar mining district, 15 mi east of Jordan Valley, Ore. This $8 million plant will incorporate standard cyanidation, CCD washing, and Merrill-Crowe precipitation for a doré smelter; all in a carefully planned setting compatible with the environment.

The mine will be contoured as excavation continues. Waste material will be hauled from the pit area and continuously leveled. The ground cover and overburden removed before the start of mining and mill construction will be used for reclamation and revegetation as plant operation continues. A total reclamation plan has been approved by the Idaho Land Commission.

Scheduled for first production in the final quarter of 1976, the De Lamar operation is expected to produce about 2.2 million oz of silver and 13,400 oz of gold a year. The plant and support facilities will be built by Mountain States Mineral Enterprises.

A run-of-mine ore storage pad will be benched from a mountain side. The ore will be delivered to the crusher area by a 7½-yd front-end loader and apron-fed to a 36 x 48-in. jaw crusher. Crushing will produce a minus 8-in.

product for a semi-autogenous grinding circuit. The coarse crushing plant is sized for a 360-tph rate, so that 6 hr of crushing five days per week will meet the 1,400-tpd grinding requirement based on a 24-hr, seven-day week. An electromagnet downstream in the crusher product conveyor line provides tramp iron protection.

An air-inflated structure will encase the fine ore storage pile, protecting it from the hostile winter climate, while also controlling any fugitive dust generated. The enclosure will measure 190 x 190 x 80 ft high. The ore will be reclaimed from a tunnel equipped with several vibrating feeders controlled from an electronic scale on the mill feed belt.

Cyanide to be dry fed

Selection of semi-autogenous grinding in an 18 x 9-ft mill, driven by a 1,000-hp wound-rotor motor, was determined from physical characteristics of the ore and evaluation of grinding tests. The semi-autogenous mill discharges through an integral end trommel to a cyclone feed sump. The cyclones split an oversize for a 9½ x 15-ft re-grind ball mill and an overflow for the leaching circuit.

Reagent dosage starts early in the De Lamar flowsheet. Lime for protective alkalinity purposes is added to the mill feed conveyor of the semi-autogenous mill in an amount adjusted by a pH recorder-controller with a sensing probe on the mill discharge. Dry calcium cyanide will be fed to the regrind mill to start the leaching process as soon as possible. The dry feeding system for the active leaching reagent was selected to eliminate the handling problems normally associated with cyanide solutions.

Bulk quantities of the two primary reagents will be handled by pneumatic conveying arrangements. Lime is to be delivered directly to a 50-ton bin next to the semi-autogenous mill conveyor line by pneumatically equipped trucks. Cyanide will be shipped by rail to a siding 65 mi from the plant and then trucked in bulk transports for pneumatic discharge to a pair of 100-ton storage bins.

Leaching is done in four 50-ft-dia x 40-ft-high tanks, each equipped with a turbine impeller and an air sparge system. The pulp advances in series to a CCD (countercurrent) washing circuit composed of five 125-ft thickeners. Here the underflow advances downstream against a return flow of reclaimed liquor decanted from the tailing pond and returned to the fifth thickener. The overflow of the second thickener is pumped to a steady head tank, which overflows for gravity return to thickener No. 1. No. 1 thickener overflows a pregnant solution that is pumped to a 100,000-gal solution tank.

All fresh process water and barren solution recovered during precipitation is added to thickener No. 5 underflow. The addition of these solutions at this point maximizes the recovery of precious metals by simulating a sixth CCD stage through the use of the decant from the tailing pond.

All tailing will be contained in a pond of about 140 acres. The dam will have an impervious core and is to be about 1,600 ft long and 150 ft high on completion of the total project. Since liquor will be reclaimed from the pond and none allowed to escape, the only fresh water makeup is that required to offset evaporation losses.

Pregnant solution will be processed in a standard Merrill-Crowe precipitation and filtering system. The filter cake will be converted to doré metal in a gas-fired furnace.

The De Lamar district was the scene of mining starting in 1863 and active until the early 1900s. It has been dormant since about 1930. □

Processing gains chalked up on many fronts

US Bureau of Mines metallurgy research staff

EVERY SECTOR OF THE FIELD of minerals processing is subject to change, and the pressures for change have intensified in recent years. Rising costs of raw materials, labor, and equipment spur plant operators to look for more efficient ways of using long-established processing technology. Environmental controls force changes in old technology and inspire a search for new, cleaner processing techniques. Rising costs and shortages of fuel call for adaptation of both old and new plants to previously unused energy sources. Declining ore grades pose a continuing challenge to operators trying to build new, economic processing facilities.

Both processing equipment and process chemistry get close scrutiny in the search for better technology. Equipment in general grows larger, and occasionally a change in equipment shape is found that yields a more economic process flow. Process chemists continue a never-ending search for better recoveries at higher concentrate grades.

The relative merits of pyrometallurgy and hydrometallurgy are debated, and new, economic applications of both types of extraction processes are eagerly sought. In the field of minerals processing, continuing change will characterize the years to come. ☐

> **Editor's note**
>
> Material for this report was supplied by staff members at the US Bureau of Mines' eight metallurgy research facilities. Additional information relating to secondary recovery and recycling of metals and to materials research was also compiled, and some of this information appears in the July 1975 issue of E/MJ.

Grinding: the search for increased efficiency

AT A TIME OF RISING COSTS and energy shortages, a major goal of the minerals industry is higher production rates at lower unit costs. In crushing and grinding, the need to process ever-larger tonnages of lower grade ores has spurred a continuing evolution of larger and more efficient size-reduction machinery.

To realize potential cost savings, throughput in new large mills must be maintained at optimum levels, with a minimum of downtime for repairs and maintenance. Such demands have prompted development of automatic control systems, improved mill drives, longer-wearing grinding media, and more efficient maintenance procedures.

Size is being scaled up both in conventional rod and ball mills and in autogenous mills, with some especially notable new units being designed into grinding lines at new and expanded iron ore projects in northern Minnesota and

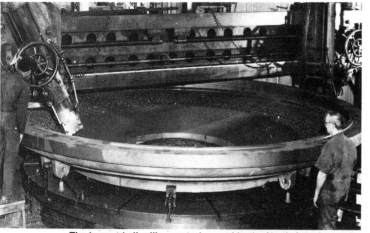

The largest ball mills ever to be used in the North American mining industry are being built by Rexnord Inc. for Eveleth Expansion Co.'s iron ore concentrator at Fairlane, Minn. The mill head above has an 18-ft 9-in. OD and weighs 40 tons.

Michigan. In some expansion programs, practice has been to more or less duplicate existing lines but to employ larger equipment.

Autogenous mills offer advantages in eliminating grinding media costs and in grinding intergranularly rather than transgranularly, to produce minimum fines and slimes. Disadvantages of autogenous grinding are the generally higher capital costs and the higher net power consumption, which in the case of primary mills may be 25% to 50% above consumption for conventional units. (Despite this lower kilowatt-hour efficiency, planning is in progress for primary autogenous mills at feed sizes up to 5 ft dia.) Autogenous mills are not usable when grinding-media-size material is ground away so fast that finer sizes are not adequately ground. Semi-autogenous mills are the alternative.

Flow capacity may be a problem with larger conventional mills, but in autogenous mills a peripheral discharge arrangement behind the grates overcomes any difficulty. Flow limitations may arise with wet or dry rod mills, and as rod mills increase in size, rod diameter must be increased to avoid rod breakage. Similarly, an increase in ball mill size calls for increased ball size.

Hibtac to install 36-ft autogenous mills

The world's largest autogenous mills to date have been specified for the new Hibbing Taconite Co. pellet project 6 mi north of Hibbing, Minn. Designed and built by Allis-Chalmers, the six mills measure 36 x 15 ft and will be driven by two 6,000-hp motors for a total of 12,000 hp per mill. The mills, weighing 2.5 million lb each, will be supported on 150-in.-dia babbitted bearings. Mill drive for the six Hibtac units will be supplied through speed reducers driving pinion gears meshed with a 39-ft-dia x 30-ft-wide girth gear that is about the maximum pitch diameter that gear manufacturers can now cut.

The mills will take a feed of nominal 8-in.-dia and discharge via trunnion overflow through 3/16-in. grate openings. Discharged material will be screened on trunnion-mounted trommels to return the plus ⅛-in. material to the mill. After passing a first stage of magnetic concentration, minus ⅛-in. concentrates will be sized by a hydrocyclone, with plus 325-mesh material to be reintroduced to the autogenous mill. With this circuiting, a single mill will grind a final product to about 85% minus 325 mesh.

Already installed are two 34½ x 7½-ft autogenous mills at Iron Ore Co. of Canada's Carol Lake operations and six 27 x 14½-ft mills at The Cleveland-Cliffs Iron Co.'s new Tilden Project on Michigan's Upper Peninsula.

Driving power increases from 5,720 hp for the 27-ft mills to 6,000 hp for the 34½-ft mills, and, as noted above, 12,000 hp for the 36-ft mills. Still larger units having up to 35,000-hp drives are contemplated.

At the Tilden Project, each of the primary autogenous mills is followed by two 15½ x 30-ft pebble mills. Screening after the primary mills produces a minus 3-in. plus 1¼-in. fraction used as grinding media in the pebble mills. A minus 1¼-in. plus ½-in. fraction reports to an intermediate crusher, along with excess pebbles, and the crushed product is returned to the primary mills. Minus 2-mm material reports directly to the pebble mills, which are operated in closed circuit with 15-in. cyclones.

At the National Steel Pellet Plant on the Mesabi Range, dry, semi-autogenous, 26 x 7-ft mills are being converted to operate wet and fully or nearly autogenously. As dry mills, the units had required a charge of up to 120,000 lb of 5-in.-dia balls. New mills for the planned expansion from a nominal 2.4-million-tpy capacity to 5.8-million-tpy capacity will also be wet and fully or nearly autogenous.

In another Mesabi Range conversion, one of the five 26 x 7-ft dry, semi-autogenous mills at Butler Taconite is being retrofitted as a 26 x 18-ft wet mill.

At the Fairlane concentrator near Eveleth, Minn., Eveleth Expansion Co.'s new plant will have the largest rod and ball mills in use on iron ores in the US. The three 15-ft-dia x 20-ft rod mills will each feed a 17-ft-dia x 41-ft ball mill. The ball mills will draw 6,000 hp and are driven by dual 3,000-hp motors.

In an application on copper ores, Cyprus Bagdad Copper Co. is building a 40,000-tpd concentrator incorporating another variation of an autogenous grinding circuit. The

A line of six 27-ft-dia primary autogenous mills (shown here during installation in 1974) is one of the many mammoth features at Cleveland-Cliffs' $200 million Tilden Project.

system utilizes a cone crusher to crush critical-size material produced in the autogenous mill. Products from the cone crusher are screened, with oversize returned to the mill and undersize fed to a conventional ball mill for fine grinding. The system reportedly allows close control of the autogenous mill while reducing consumption of metal and power.

Pima Mining Co. is using a semi-autogenous circuit to reduce wet, sticky copper ores. Problems in treating these ores in a conventional crushing and grinding circuit are avoided by eliminating fine crushers and related screens and ore storage facilities.

Bougainville Copper Pty. Ltd., in the South Pacific, grinds through eight 18-ft-dia x 21-ft, single-stage Allis-Chalmers overflow ball mills. Power is provided by 4,250-hp synchronous motors through air clutches, gear reducers, and pinion and ring gears. Each mill is spout fed and in closed circuit with Krebs cyclones.

Eight 18-ft-dia x 21-ft-long ball mills grind ore at the Panguna minesite of Bougainville Copper. The Allis-Chalmers mills are each powered by a 4,250-hp motor.

A Symons 10-ft cone crusher, the largest ever built, is being assembled in the Johannesburg, South Africa, shops of Rexnord. The main shaft and head assembly are shown above.

At the St. Lawrence Cement Co. a 17-ft-dia x 56-ft ball mill driven without gears by an 8,700-hp wraparound motor has been in operation for more than a year. The wraparound motor has variable speed capabilities.

Shell-mounted ring gear dominates drive systems

The shell-mounted ring gear driven by single or dual pinions is the most common mill drive in use today. Gear manufacturers can cut gears to a 39-ft pitch diameter, which limits shell-driven mills now to about a 36-ft maximum diameter.

Other drives in use are wraparound, low-frequency electric motors and foot-mounted trunion coupled drives. The wraparound design appears to be preferred for large mills at this time; however, one manufacturer is offering a shaft-mounted drive driven by dual low-starting-torque synchronous motors capable of delivering up to 50,000 hp. The drive system, adapted from BOF furnace tilt drives, uses hydroviscous clutches to couple the motors to primary reduction gears that drive the single trunion-mounted bull gear. The hydroviscous clutches permit motor load sharing and starting, jogging, braking, and variable speed operation of the mill.

Development of wraparound variable speed motors was made possible by application of thyristors. Electric circuits using these devices can convert 60-Hz current to lower frequencies for running mills at lower operating speeds.

Media wear and other milling advances

Compensation for media wear—a major grinding problem—has been achieved to some extent by introduction of new cylindrical-type grinding media. These media are cast in special chill molds. Heat treatment then produces a perlitic matrix in which fine needles of iron carbide are embedded, oriented at right angles to the wear surface. Although the Brinell hardness of these media is 530, the structure makes wear resistance just as high as that of high-alloy grinding media having a hardness above 600 Brinell. The new media conserve special alloying metals and do not introduce these metals as interfering elements into froth flotation mill water.

Rubber liners and lifters in ball mills have now been in use long enough to permit an evaluation of their effectiveness. In most cases, wear has been reduced, but one mill has reported an approximate 30% increase in ball consumption.

Centrifugal milling has received a new impetus from a 2- to 4-tph-grinding-capacity prototype design installed at a mine where it operates in closed circuit grinding. The unit can tolerate a 500% circulating load.

(In centrifugal milling, a grinding mill is rotated on its own axis, while the axis is rotated about an axis of gyration that is parallel to the mill axis.)

The prototype centrifugal mill is constructed with three 35-cm-long, 20-cm-dia tubes, oriented vertically and mounted symmetrically about a circle of gyration having a diameter of 33 cm. Acceleration in this mill is greater than nine times the acceleration of gravity. First cost of the mill is about 15% that of a conventional mill, and the centrifugal mill is easier to drive, with its higher speed of rotation. The mill may open new opportunities for autogenous grinding, and its compact size should facilitate mobile crushing, milling within pit operations, and milling in deep underground mines. Underground milling would permit rejected mill material to be used directly as backfill.

New single-toggle jaw crushers with feed openings of 83 x 66 in. and feed rates as high as 3,000 tph have been installed by LKAB in Sweden.

A new 10-ft-dia cone crusher having a capacity of more than 300 tph has been installed at an iron ore project.

And in hammer mills, a new double rotor type has been developed that reduces power requirements and wear costs in the grinding of lime.

A reduction in power requirement for grinding cement clinker has been achieved by replacing a dry-grinding ball mill with a roller mill. The roller mill accepts 3½-in. feed, against 1-in. feed for the ball mill, and the volume of air drawn through the roller mill during operation is lower than that required for a ball mill. Roller mill power draw ranges from 57% to 83% of the requirement for a comparable ball mill—depending on the type of material being ground. From an average of 22 samples, a 20% to 30% power saving is anticipated.

Ring and ball-type mills similar in construction to a roller mill are established in coal grinding, and recent tests have demonstrated that such mills might be adaptable to grinding very hard materials. Mill installations of this type are now grinding limestone, sandstone, and manganese ore. Advantages are low noise and vibration levels, low power consumption, and an integral classifier. □

Large cells and improved agitation reduce flotation costs

TWO TRENDS have been prominent in recent flotation practice: increased cell volume to handle greater throughput and reduce capital and operating costs, and improved agitation and aeration of ore pulps. In both cases, the stimulus for new development is a need for increased efficiency.

A review of recent installations, including results of a recent Canadian mill operations survey, underscores the importance of these trends in recent flotation plant design.

Cominco Ltd. has installed cells varying in size from 150-300 cu ft for zinc, potash, coal, and copper-lead separation, to 1,200-cu-ft Maxwell cells for lead-zinc and zinc roughing separation. There has been a tendency to "sand up" at high pH, but operational service has been very good.

A unique treatment of relatively high grade nickel-copper ore at the Manibridge mill in Canada employs a 10-ft-dia x 10-ft Maxwell cell (700 cu ft) and three 12-ft-dia x 12-ft tank cells (1,350 cu ft) in the rougher and scavenger circuits. Three 8-ft-dia x 8-ft tank cells (400 cu ft) clean and reclean concentrates from the larger tank cells. The tank cells are arranged in a cell-to-cell configuration with a 1-ft difference in elevation between the cells, so no pumps are needed to transfer slurry from one cell to the next. Froth depth is an important variable, and all cells are operated with a froth bed of 12 to 15 in.

Other recent large-cell installations include Maxwell flotation cells at Falconbridge Copper's Opemiska division, ranging in size from 2,000 cu ft for roughing and 700 cu ft for scavenging to 170-300 cu ft for cleaning. At the Nacimiento copper mine in New Mexico, additional capacity was gained by adding two 2,000-cu-ft Maxwell cells, 14 ft dia x 14 ft high. A 1,200-cu-ft cell at Magmont serves as a lead scavenger or as a zinc rougher, and a 1,200-cu-ft cell at Greenex is operating as a zinc rougher.

For these large cell installations, advantages claimed include a low number of units, reduced floor space, simplified instrumentation, lower capital and operating costs, and better concentration results.

In a review of scale-up principles for froth flotation cells, published in the March 1974 INTERNATIONAL JOURNAL OF MINERAL PROCESSING, C. C. Harris reported experimental and operational data and flotation criteria and compiled this information in a chart offering details for various types of flotation machines.

The present state of knowledge of the attachment of a mineral particle to a bubble was reviewed by S. R. Rao in MINERAL SCIENCE AND ENGINEERING, January 1974. Three types of active forces are recognized: van der Waals forces of attraction, electrical forces resulting from overlapping double layers in the liquid around the particle, and hydration of any hydrophilic groups on the surface of the particle. Attractive forces are measured in terms of the Hamaker constant, which is an excellent indicator of the degree of floatability of the mineral.

In Finland, Outokumpu Oy has developed a new flotation machine based on a rotor/stator design that achieves an unchanged air pressure over the whole rotor surface. Pulp and air are introduced alternately in the direction of motion, and the pulp is drawn from below the rotor. With only a moderate energy consumption, the machine permits greater amounts of air to be dispersed through the whole cell volume while increasing the amount of pulp held in suspension. The OK 16 flotation machine (16 cu m) has four cells in sequence, with slight differences in height that prevent sanding during emergency shutdowns. In normal operation, each cell requires 20-30 kw per motor and 20-25

cfm of air. According to Outokumpu, results from the OK 16 have been so encouraging that the company has initiated partial replacement programs for existing cells.

In the handling of frothy pulps and slurries from flotation circuits, Warman International Ltd., of Sydney, Australia, achieved a major advance with development of outsized froth pumps. By means of a tangentially fed cyclone hopper chamber, the froth is either wholly or partially deaerated before it enters the pumping head. The pumps are available in capacities up to 3,000 Imperial gpm.

New technology for higher recoveries and grades

A number of innovative flotation techniques have been investigated to improve product quality, recover values lost in current practice, improve beneficiation economics, and treat refractory ores. Among them:

■ The US Bureau of Mines and Great Salt Lake Minerals and Chemicals Corp. have developed a froth flotation process for concentrating potassium salts from Great Salt Lake solar evaporites containing about 5% K. A 15-tph pilot plant constructed by GSLM&C has been operating without major difficulty since October 1974. The crude evaporites are conditioned in a saturated brine solution to convert nonfloatable kainite to floatable schoenite, which is then selectively floated with a medium-molecular-weight fatty acid. Pilot plant results indicate that 80% of the potassium can be recovered from crude evaporites as concentrates assaying about 11% K. Based on these results, construction of a 120- to 150-tph plant is anticipated.

■ Mitsui Mining & Smelting Co. has developed and piloted a combined segregation-flotation process for copper oxide ores. The ore is charged with powdered salt and coke into a rotary-type reaction furnace at 800°C, and the copper minerals react with the salt to form copper chloride, which is vaporized and then reduced by the coke to metallic copper. The metallic copper deposited on the coke particles is concentrated in three flotation stages. Pilot plant results have produced concentrates containing 53-58% Cu, with 75-80% recoveries from ores assaying 5-5½% Cu. Pilot plant results have been excellent, and Mitsui is

Flotation tests for separation of non-magnetic taconites are being run in US Bureau of Mines laboratory flotation cells.

Single-spindle impeller and four-spindle impeller models of Galigher Agitair 400-cu-ft flotation machines are in use at large mills. Four-spindle model 120 x 400 installations include 56 cells at Atlas Consolidated in the Philippines and 60 cells at Brenda Mines in Canada. Single-spindle model 120A x 400 installations include 152 cells at Sar Cheshmeh in Iran and 66 cells at INO in the Philippines.

planning a larger plant for the Katanga mine in Peru.

■ Flotation schemes for separating molybdenite from other minerals are based on the inherent hydrophobicity of molybdenite. However, talc is also a naturally floatable mineral that causes serious problems in treating talcose moly ores. From flotation of "pure" samples of molybdenite and talc, a technique has been developed using ligno-sulphonates to depress moly without affecting the talc float. Flotation of talc was accomplished with a light alcohol-type frother, and the moly was subsequently reactivated with kerosene, pine oil, and frother and floated. Applied to a high-talc ore sample, the dual flotation procedure has yielded talc concentrates relatively free of moly, and moly concentrate. Similar tests were repeated successfully in both pilot and full-scale plant evaluations.

■ A combined chemical treatment-flotation process to recover relatively high grade moly concentrates from off-grade sulphide materials has been patented. Off-grade moly sulphide materials containing other metal sulphides and non-sulphide impurities are roasted with sulphuric acid and leached with an aqueous solution to remove the solubilized constituents. The molybdenite remains unaltered and is concentrated in a subsequent flotation step. The technique has been successfully tested at a pilot plant at Kennecott's Nevada Mines Div.

■ V. M. Lepetic has developed a process for concentrating chalcopyrite without using a collector. In bench-scale tests, chalcopyrite from a thermal vein deposit was successfully concentrated by employing dry autogenous grinding and a small amount of frother. Comparison tests showed that the simplified flotation treatment yielded higher copper recoveries and concentrate grades than a conventional modifier-collector-frother system. The process has potential for lower flotation costs, because of its simplicity and its lower reagent consumption.

■ Titanium impurities have been floated from kaolin by intensive conditioning of an acidic kaolin dispersion with tall oil or other anionic, oleo-type collectors for titanium minerals and lead acetate. The conditioned pulp is adjusted to pH 8.0, and the titanium minerals are floated.

■ Texada Mines, on Texada Island, B. C., is operating a mill on 100% sea water. The sea water gives the mill a very stable, easily controlled flotation circuit, and reagent consumption was greatly reduced and reagent feeding greatly simplified when the use of 100% sea water was incorporated into the flowsheet. The flotation circuit at the Black Angel Mine in Greenland also uses sea water instead of fresh water. Because salt water resulted in valve corrosion, nearly every valve in the plant was replaced with rubber

diaphragm valves. Some minor problems have occurred in controlling pulp densities.

Flotation recovers growing percentage of iron

Cationic flotation of magnetic iron concentrates to bring silica content within specifications is becoming more commonplace. Approximately 9.5 million ltpy of magnetic concentrates received such treatment in 1974. When the Iron Ore Co. of Canada's plant at Sept Iles and The Cleveland-Cliffs Iron Co.'s Tilden plant reach design capacity, their production and that of Cleveland-Cliff's Republic mill will total more than 12.6 million ltpy of hematite-goethite concentrate, produced with flotation as a primary means of beneficiation. Additionally, as much as 4.4 million ltpy of concentrates are produced at Groveland, in Michigan, and Meramec Mining, in Missouri, from mixed magnetite-hematite ores using flotation as one step in the beneficiation sequence.

At the Tilden plant, a number of innovative features may find future utilization in processing the considerable known resource of fine grained, nonmagnetic, hematitic-goethitic taconites. Designed to treat 10 million ltpy of crude ore averaging 36% Fe, this plant grinds ore to 85% minus 25 microns, followed by selective flocculation desliming in preparation for cationic flotation of silica. The Tilden plant is the first commercial application of the selective flocculation-desliming process developed by the US Bureau of Mines for ores of this type. Initial design capacity calls for production of 4 million ltpy of concentrates containing 65% Fe. Future expansion may raise capacity to 12 million ltpy.

Emphasizing the trend toward bigness, the Tilden plant has six lines of 25 flotation cells each (cell capacity 500 cu ft). The plant's grate-kiln pelletizing line is the largest single line in the industry: its grate is 18½ ft wide and 210 ft long, and its rotary kiln is 25 ft dia x 160 ft long.

In filtration of the Tilden concentrate, live steam is injected into enclosed filter disks. The steam treatment is needed to lower the moisture content of the high-surface-area concentrates to a level suitable for balling.

Elsewhere, at IOC's Sept-Iles flotation plant, other difficult-to-filter concentrates are filtered to about 16% moisture. The filter cake is then dried in a heated kiln and the dried product is passed through hammermills prior to being fed to the balling circuit.

Another iron ore beneficiation trend is the increasing use of fine rapped screen panels to remove plus 325-mesh low grade fractions from magnetic concentrates. Over half of Mesabi Range production from such concentrates is now treated this way, and even wider application is planned. Instead of cam-actuated hammers, the newer screen panels are rapped by air-actuated devices mounted on the screen underside, delivering about 10 raps or less per minute.

In some applications in taconite processing, urethane screen surfaces for sieve bends are claimed to have outworn stainless steel by 10 to 1, plus being lighter in weight and requiring screen reversals less frequently.

Also in iron ore processing, improved pole design and new magnetic materials are combined to give better field configurations on magnetic separators. Separators 10 ft long and 36-in. dia are becoming standard. Magnetic separators are also being substituted for thickeners as dewatering devices in applications such as thickening magnetic products ahead of grinding mills or prior to filtration.

Hydroseparators, which in the past have commonly been 30- or 40-ft dia, are now being installed in diameters up to 75 ft to elutriate fine silica from intermediate magnetic concentrates. Hydrocyclones up to 30-in. dia are successfully being used in taconite processing, where the accepted standard had been 26-in. dia.

In Missouri, fine screening (DSM screens) of magnetic concentrates by Meramec Mining continues to produce a high grade iron product containing less than 2.7% silica. An increasing fraction of the production is required to meet the needs of the heavy media market. A relatively small tonnage of a specialty material for use in ceramic magnets is produced by flotation upgrading of the magnetic concentrate to yield magnetite containing less than 0.25% SiO_2. Pyrite and apatite flotation circuits produce marketable products of each commodity.

Pilot Knob Pellet Co. has installed a regrind and flotation circuit to reduce silica content of the magnetic concentrate to less than 5%. Alkali content is reduced simultaneously with the silica. Flotation cells of 500- and 300-cu-ft capacity are being used.

Improved reagents contribute to flotation efficiency

The continuing search for new and better-functioning reagents is an essential part of the improvements in flotation systems. Some recently developed reagents of interest:

■ For flotation of molybdenite from copper sulphide ores, choline xanthate was used as a depressant for copper and iron sulphide minerals, while fuel oil or kerosene was used to float the molybdenite. The choline xanthate is also claimed to suppress sulphide minerals in the flotation of fluorspar, barite, silica sand, or feldspar. (M. F. Werneke, US Patent No. 3,788,467.)

■ An aliphatic sulphate having a 16-18 carbon chain and at least one molecule each of ethylene and propylene oxide was developed for the flotation of chalcopyrite or other copper sulphides from pyrite. The collector is effective in the pH range of 7.0 to 11.5. The sulphides of copper, molybdenite, zinc, and lead are floated, while almost all of the pyrite is depressed. The bulk concentrate can then be treated by differential flotation. (E. Fisher, US Patent No. 3,827,557.)

■ A collector for use in flotation of copper oxides was prepared by reacting nonylphenol with tetraethylene pentamine. (D. R. Weimer, US Patent No. 3,819,048.)

■ A product trade-named "Teefroth" is used in flotation of mixed copper-iron sulphide ores. Teefroth—a polyglycol ether of methanol containing both polypropylene and polyethylene glycol in its molecule—is a molecularly designed product that provides bubbles of a consistent size

and texture. The reagent can also be used in flotation of lead, zinc, and gold ores.

■ An improved amine reagent was developed for use in flotation of phosphate rock or other siliceous ores. A monofunctional diamine was condensed with reconstituted tall oil having an acid number of 150 to 165 and containing 72-77% fatty acids, 11-16% rosin acids, and 10-13% unsaponifiables. The reagent may be used either alone or in conjunction with other reagents and is effective in separating acid-insolubles from phosphate minerals. (E. A. Grannen, US Patent No. 3,817,972.)

Advances in nonmetallics beneficiation

While no outstanding technical breakthroughs have been recently recorded for improved recovery or quality of feldspar production, most producers have devoted research to achieving these goals. The increased use of high attrition scrubbers prior to froth flotation has had a marked effect on recoveries in plants using flotation. Recovery of 50% or more of the ore feed is becoming the rule.

High intensity magnetic separation has been a major technical advance in the kaolin industry. Thiele Kaolin Co. has placed a large magnet on stream—the fourth operating magnetic separator in the industry. Magnetic separators make possible the production of new grades of high-brightness kaolin and the exploitation of marginal or previously unprofitable clays for standard filler or coating grades. Magnetic separation removes TiO_2 and Fe_2O_3 impurities and often reduces the chemical cost of leaching.

In another recent development, the Minerva Co. has started recovering barite from fluorite mill tailing. The tailing is thickened to about 32% solids and the barite floated with sodium cetyl sulphate.

Beneficiation of barite in mill tailings using an agglomeration technique has been demonstrated by the National Research Council of Canada. Barite was selectively absorbed from a conditioned aqueous slurry into a collector oil by mechanically mixing slurry and oil. The resulting oil-bonded, barite-containing agglomerate was washed to remove gangue material and further mechanically contacted with dilute sulphuric acid. This treatment resulted in transfer of barite to the aqueous phase. Grades as high as 97% $BaSO_4$ with recoveries of 80% have been achieved.

The Canadian National Research Council has also applied the spherical agglomeration process to beneficiating an ilmenite concentrate containing finely disseminated silicate minerals. The results obtained were close to the apparent physical limits of separation. The agglomerates were suitable for subsequent processing to titanium dioxide via the chlorination route.

Selective agglomeration has also been applied to the beneficiation of a phosphoric ferrous iron ore. The iron ore, which had proven refractory to beneficiation by conventional technique, responded well to the selective agglomeration process.

The Bureau of Mines is sponsoring a grant to be given this fiscal year to the University of Alabama to investigate the feasibility of selectively agglomerating a ferruginous bauxite to produce a refractory grade bauxite material.

Basic research focuses on mathematical models

Interest in mathematical modeling of the froth flotation process remains high as a result of the trend toward more complete automation of flotation plants. Kinetic modeling of the performance of single conventional flotation cells in either batch or continuous operation has reached an advanced stage. However, *a priori* prediction of all of the required model parameters remains a problem, especially for larger cells of new and different design.

Greater emphasis is being placed on extending or modifying existing models to predict the performance of a complete, continuous, multicelled flotation circuit having a complex flow configuration. The work of R. P. King at the National Institute for Metallurgy, South Africa, is a notable example of efforts along these lines. Integration of grinding operation and flotation operation models to achieve a quantitative description of a complete plant is also an investigative area of increasing importance.

Fundamental research on surface phenomena relevant to froth flotation is also expanding, both in scale of effort and sophistication of experimental technique. As in the past, the primary emphasis is on gaining an understanding of the adsorption mechanism of reagents at the solid-liquid interface and of their subsequent role in enhancing or diminishing hydrophobicity. Electrochemical techniques are being used by researchers at laboratories of the Commonwealth Scientific and Industrial Research Organization in Australia, for fundamental studies of interaction of xanthates with sulphides and of the mechanism of oxygen reduction at a metal sulphide electrode.

Several experimental techniques formerly associated mainly with basic research and the solid state physics of surfaces are now complementing more traditional flotation research techniques. This trend reflects increased awareness of the importance of the electro-physical properties of solids and their surfaces in moderating phenomena occurring at the solid-liquid interface. R. K. Clifford, at the University of Missouri-Rolla, reported on the use of the electron spectroscopy chemical analysis technique for investigating the surfaces of copper, lead, zinc, molybdenum, and iron sulphide minerals before and after treatment with a variety of flotation reagents. The role of electronic properties and crystal defects in important surface phenomena in both flotation and leaching is an especially active area of investigation, particularly for the sulphides of copper, lead, zinc, and nickel. In sulphide flotation research at the US Bureau of Mines' College Park Metallurgy Research Center, work is focused on determination of semiconductor properties using techniques based on galvanomagnetic effects and surface photovoltage measurements, in conjunction with electrochemical studies. Investigations of the solid state aspects of the reactivity of minerals, especially the role of lattice defects in leaching and flotation of sulphides, are being started at the National Institute for Metallurgy, South Africa.

A special Symposium on Interfacial Phenomena at the 78th National Meeting of AIChE, Salt Lake City, Utah, in August 1974 included several papers pertinent to fundamental flotation research. These contributions were summarized by Smith and Somasundaran in MINING ENGINEERING, February 1975. □

Wet high-intensity, high-gradient magnetic separation

SHORT SUPPLIES AND HIGHER COSTS of flotation reagents have heightened interest in using high-intensity wet magnetic separation to process non-ferromagnetic iron ores. In the largest application to date, Cia. Vale do Rio Doce has installed 28 separators at its Itabira, Brazil, plant, each machine having a capacity of 120 tph, or 1 million tpy. Research has shown that a superconcentrate grading less than 1.5% SiO_2 can be produced from minus 100-mesh Itabira fines by high-intensity wet magnetic separation, and a plant incorporating the concept is scheduled to come onstream in 1975. Superconcentrate produced at the plant will be processed into iron by direct reduction.

In Canada, Sidbec-Dosco Co. plans to construct a plant by 1976 in Port Cartier to produce 3 million ltpy of superconcentrates. Jones high-intensity wet magnetic separators will reprocess minus 14-mesh Fire Lake spiral concentrates, and the superconcentrates will be pelletized and shipped to the Sidbec-Dosco direct reduction plant at Contrecoeur, Que. Single-pass pilot plant tests with recirculating wash water show a 96.3% Fe recovery in a superconcentrate of 68.7% Fe and 1.45% SiO_2.

Wabush Mines, also in Quebec, has installed high-intensity wet magnetic separators to recover iron values from the tailings of an existing spiral plant.

All of the applications cited above involve specular hematite ores that tend to liberate without excessive grinding. As a consequence, there is no production of large quantities of submicron particles or slimes. The specular hematite ores tend to carry traces of residual magnetite that give them an apparent magnetic susceptibility much greater than that of reagent grade hematite.

The largest reserves of non-ferromagnetic iron ore in the US—the oxidized taconites and semitaconites of northern Minnesota. and similar ores in Michigan's Upper Peninsula—pose a more difficult problem. The ores usually require fine grinding for liberation, and the iron is usually present as earthy hematite and goethite. The grinding process tends to produce large quantities of slimes. Minute traces of magnetite may be present in the hematite, but the goethite is largely free of ferromagnetics.

Attempts to concentrate the oxidized taconites by high-intensity wet magnetic separation alone have generally not yielded a high grade concentrate at an acceptable recovery. However, experiments conducted at the Mines Experiment Station of the University of Minnesota, beginning in 1964, indicated that high-intensity wet magnetic separation might be of value in preparing a preconcentrate as feed for subsequent flotation. Silica and slimes rejected during magnetic separation do not consume valuable reagents in the subsequent flotation stage.

In a pilot investigation, Hanna Mining Co. has tested this concept. A continuous "Carousel" separator was used, with the magnetic field produced by a variation on an iron-clad solenoid design. High field gradients were produced by a matrix of stainless steel wool or expanded metal. Preliminary flotation tests indicated only marginal reductions in flotation reagent consumption after first producing magnetic preconcentrate.

The Twin Cities Metallurgy Research Center of the US Bureau of Mines has begun an extensive research program on high-intensity wet magnetic separation.

There has been recent interest in new designs for high-intensity wet magnetic separators having application not only to iron ores but also to other mineral separations. Original Carpco and Jones designs used conventional magnetic circuits. However, while such designs use electrical energy efficiently to produce a field, they result in very massive machines, because the volume of iron required to complete the magnetic circuit is many times greater than the gap volume. To produce the same field volume with less iron mass, iron-clad solenoid designs have been developed and successfully applied to the removal of paramagnetic impurities from kaolin clay. These separators work on a batch basis, with feed, rinse, and flush periods over an operating cycle of about 20 min. The Magnetic Corp. of America recently built a clay separator with an internal diameter of 76 in. for J. M. Huber Corp. A field of 20 kilogauss is developed over the 20-in. length of the separating zone, with a power input of 400 kw. At 30% solids, the capacity of the 250-ton machine is 50-60 tph.

For iron ore processing, the Carousel represents an attempt to design a continuous separator based on an iron-clad solenoid. Separator weight for the SOL dense-field magnetic separator developed by Krupp Industrie und Stahlbau of Rheinhausen, West Germany, is reduced to a minimum by using solenoids without any iron cladding.

The decrease in separator weight achieved by using a solenoid rather than a conventional iron magnetic circuit is offset by an increase in the quantity of copper wire and electric power required. If the copper coil were replaced by a superconducting coil, the electric power requirement could be greatly reduced. However, a helium refrigerator would be necessary to maintain the coil in the super-conducting state. At present, capital investment for a large (internal diameter greater than 6 ft) superconducting coil, including the refrigerator, is about equal to that for an iron-clad solenoid having a power supply that would yield the same working volume. Presumably, operating costs of the superconducting system would be lower, although some of the energy advantage would be lost because of the necessity of turning the magnetic field on and off in a cyclic operation.

Development of a superconducting separator with a constant magnetizing current and continuous feed is clearly desirable. Operating under a US Bureau of Mines grant, the University of Wisconsin has developed a conceptual design for a continuous superconducting magnetic separator that eliminates the need for a ferromagnetic matrix. In this concept, 100 kilogauss is to be produced in a single busbar of superconducting material encased in a cryogenic container. The slurry flows would be either parallel to the bar or in a helical channel around it, with the magnetic material being attracted toward the bar and removed with a splitter. The concept has not yet progressed to the point where 100-kilogauss fields are employed, but it has been tested with fair success on a system using a copper conductor and a magnetite slurry to simulate the behavior of hematite in a superconducting system. □

Mills seek greater water recycle, better discharge quality

FOLLOWING GOOD INDUSTRIAL PRACTICE, most mills recycle as much process water as possible, both to save reagents and power and to conserve water and prevent water pollution. Strong government regulations for discharge water quality have made knowledge of water supply and disposable effluent increasingly important.

The rapid development of Missouri's new lead belt into the world's largest lead producing region has been accompanied by a number of local alterations in the Ozark stream environment. The sulphide concentrators and their reagents, products, and wastes have been studied in detail. The reagents that remain in the concentrator tailings are a potential hazard to aquatic life, and considerable effort is necessary to maintain tailings ponds and adequate residence times to permit complete degradation of toxic chemicals prior to release into streams. In some cases, complete or rapid degradation may be aided by micro-biological activity.

Because the amount of sulphydryl collectors used in sulphide flotation is large and the pollution potential is high, the toxicity hazards to aquatic life have been carefully evaluated. Data for xanthates, dithiophosphates, and ethylthionocarbamate have been reported on a 96-hr median lethal concentration (LC50-96) for rainbow trout. Xanthates with chain lengths of three or fewer carbons gave median lethal concentrations of less than 20 ppm. Isopropyl ethylthionocarbamate was in the range of 40-50 ppm. Amyl xanthate showed a range of 70-80 ppm. Diethyl and dibutyl dithiophosphates produced LC50-96 at concentrations greater than 300 ppm. The temperature, which ranged from 8° to 20°C, had a pronounced effect on toxicity limits. As the temperature increased, LC50-96 level decreased.

A recent case history of Cleveland-Cliffs' water quality laboratory has been compiled by R. J. LaBelle. Subjects of water quality studies included the Humboldt, Republic, and Empire iron ore mines. A water-oriented analytical section of the case history details types and costs of equipment, types and costs of chemical analyses performed, and benefits accrued in non-water-related research.

Cleveland-Cliffs' Tilden plant is noteworthy for the extraordinary attention to water quality. Through careful control of process and water treatment reagent additions, pH is held at about 10.5 to 11.0, and the total water hardness is maintained in the range of 40-50 ppm. If these limits are not maintained, both the selective flocculation and flotation circuits may be impaired at the plant.

An excellent review of water recycling experience at Canadian mills was authored by D. E. Pickett and E. G. Joe in SME/AIME TRANSACTIONS, September 1974. Present recycling practices were evaluated as a basis for improved plant design and operating procedures.

A water treatment process consisting of ion precipitation and ultrafine-particle flotation has been developed for a sulphide system using Nagahm flotation machines. The Nagahm cell has a very great aeration rate, produces very fine and evenly dispersed air bubbles in all parts of the cell, and froth volume removal is high. About 2,700 cu m per day of effluent containing cyanides and residual suspended sulphides is treated with sulphuric acid at a zinc concentrate thickener at the Kamioka concentrator. All ingredients in the overflow except CN^- are floated and separated from the water. The treated water, containing 30 ppm CN^-, is recycled to the Pb-Zn differential flotation circuit. The method has markedly improved the quality of effluent and has also generated a profit by recovering copper, zinc, and cadmium formerly lost in the thickener overflow.

Magnetic Engineering Associates Inc., of Cambridge, Mass., a subsidiary of Sala Magnetic Inc., has developed a barge-mounted high-gradient magnetic separator system to remove pollutants from river waters—a system that could be applicable to mineral and metal stream problems. The design represents a pioneering application of advanced magnetic technology to environmental pollution control.

Removing selenium from waste water

The method generally used for purifying acidic waste water containing dissolved metals is lime neutralization. When metal complexes are not involved, lime treatment effectively precipitates many of the more common metals, including iron, zinc, copper, manganese, and nickel. However, selenium occurring as either anionic selenate or selenite is only partly precipitated by liming. It frequently occurs in waste water from scrubbing sulphurous zinc smelter gases prior to acid making.

Effective technology for lowering soluble selenium to an acceptable level was demonstrated by the US Bureau of Mines in cooperation with a major zinc producer, in a unit treating 1 gpm. Gas scrubber waste containing 6 ppm of soluble selenium was first treated with zinc powder to precipitate insoluble elemental selenium. The water next was limed to neutralize acidity and precipitate iron, zinc, cadmium, and other metals, and the solids were allowed to settle. Treatment with 0.4 lb of zinc per 1,000 gal of waste, followed by liming to pH 9.5, produced water containing less than 0.1 ppm of selenium—pure enough to permit discharge to public waters. □

Progress sought in tailings stabilization

MORE STRINGENT FEDERAL AND STATE legislation and pressure from environmental groups have led to major changes in industrial waste disposal. The US Bureau of Mines started work in this field in 1966 and soon developed two techniques that are applicable to a wide variety of tailings.

One technique—the chemical-vegetative method—calls for preparation of the site by contouring, fertilizing, adding the necessary soil conditioning agents, seeding, and spraying with a chemical agent to form a temporary crust, stabilizing the area long enough to allow a cover of vegetation to grow. The method is applicable if the tailings do not contain an excessive amount of plant poisons and if there is sufficient rainfall for plant growth.

The second technique attempts only to form a hard, durable crust on areas where vegetation is not feasible.

Both techniques have been used by USBM in cooperation with industry to stabilize abandoned tailings sites. The chemical method was first used to stabilize uranium tailings in an acid area in Arizona, and the chemical-vegetative method was first used on copper tailings in Nevada. The latter method, which has proved extremely versatile, has been tested by USBM on 12 sites in eight states and has been adopted by industry in several areas.

Other tailings stabilization techniques include hydroseeding, drip irrigation, furrow grading for moisture retention, use of matting for steep slopes, and mulching with various materials.

The Pima Mining Co. combined hydroseeding with chemical stabilization on a test plot at the Pima mine, 20 mi southwest of Tucson, with excellent results.

Another area of research is aimed at discovery and use of special varieties of plants having high tolerances for the metal content of tailings and/or for areas having unusually high or low pH.

One commercial chemical—"Chemfix"—has been developed by Environmental Services Inc., of Pittsburgh, Pa., and licensed by Powell Duffryn Pollution Control Ltd., of the United Kingdom, for transformation of toxic aqueous wastes into inert solid material. The process has been successfully used in the UK on more than 4 million gal of liquid and sludge wastes and on effluents from mining and mineral processing. However, the process cannot handle certain liquids and sludges.

The physical characteristics of solids produced by the Chemfix process and the process costs vary, depending on the quantities and composition of reagents used and the chemical composition of the waste product. However, the cost is claimed to be less than for other treatment methods now used.

Even a liquid without suspended solids can be "Chemfixed" into a solid. However, if the suspension contains 5% solids, the amount of reagents required is considerably less. The Chemfixed solids can generally support weight within one to two days after production and can be left in situ or excavated for use as a landfill. □

Mill instrumentation finds increasing favor

SOME SPECTACULAR SUCCESSES have been achieved in the past few years with automated process controls, in terms of both large unit operations and sophisticated instrumentation. Indications point to a generally positive attitude toward increasing automation in process controls, for which two opposing trends are evident.

In some cases, large, centralized, computer-controlled circuits are being designed for new mills and for supplementary circuits at existing mills. One example is the Pyhasalmi concentrator of Outokumpy Oy, where the whole process except for crushing is under the control of one operator per shift in the central control room.

An opposite trend at small unit operations was identified in a survey of major aspects of instrumentation and control at copper concentrators. At these installations, the most successful procedure for achieving automation seems to be gradual introduction in existing mills. In such circumstances, mill operators are able to learn to work with the instrumentation without being overwhelmed by batteries of control panels, awesome computers, and flashing red lights.

In either case, the key to successful automation may well be in overcoming resistance by plant personnel and in more concerted backup efforts by the vendors, rather than in the technological capability of the instrumentation itself.

At the Kloof and East Driefontein gold mines in South Africa, an effective combination of remote control and decentralized operations has reportedly been achieved by breaking down individual operations into simple components and providing instrumentation for each basic function, while maintaining centralized monitoring and control. Process analysis in these plants also seems to be trending toward decentralization. Rather than delivering samples for process control to a central laboratory, on-line instrumentation provides continuous analysis within the circuit.

Submersible X-ray probes using radioisotopes have been successfully introduced at a number of Australian mills. At New Broken Hill Consolidated, lead and zinc are continuously monitored in flotation feed, flotation circuits, tailing and residue streams, and classifiers. Immersion probes to monitor copper and iron content and process stream density are being installed at Katmantoo mines.

Mills have used X-ray analyzers for many years, and considerable effort has gone into applying them to on-stream operation. The plumbing to bring samples to a central facility represents a considerable investment, and the lineup of samples causes a time lag in analysis. However, large turnkey X-ray fluorescence systems are a proven technology and are still being considered for new plants. At least two dozen large systems have been installed in concentrators in the US and Canada within the past three years.

Texas Nuclear Corp. recently installed several neutron activation analysis systems for monitoring silica in taconite and iron ore processing streams, and nuclear analytical devices are gaining wider acceptance. Properly and safely used, radioactivity is no longer a frightening concept.

The US Bureau of Mines is developing a multi-element analyzer based on a Cf 252 neutron source that produces a prompt gamma spectrum for analysis. This instrumentation will permit determination of many elements in bulk streams with a minimum of residual activity and will offer many possibilities for application in on-line processing.

A variety of sensors have been installed in automated grinding circuits to feed information to central computer facilities. These real-time particle size analyzers have stimulated considerable effort to apply computers to the mathematical modeling of metallurgical processing.

A possible increase of 5-10% in grinding capacity can be obtained with a well-designed automatic mill control system.

To improve grinding efficiency, Autometrics, of Boulder, Colo., tested a continuous particle size analyzer at Minntac. The system uses attenuation of ultrasonic energy transmitted at two different frequencies through the slurries to give particle size and slurry solids. The unit reportedly performed satisfactorily on feeds of 90% minus 325 mesh, having specific gravities of less than 4.8. Magnetic slurries required demagnetization at 400 Hz for satisfactory operation of the system.

In the iron ore industry, there has been a gradual increase in instrumentation. Computer data-logging and inventory control systems are in use, and in some cases computer-based alarm functions operate in parallel with older analog systems. However, digital control is not yet a general trend in the industry, and except for pelletizing, very little instrumentation is in use and control loops tend to be local.

However, some newer sensors have found applications in iron ore. The capacitive level detector is rapidly replacing both the point and continuous-pressure types for sump level control, and ultrasonic sonar detectors for bin level control are also coming into use. In at least one plant, a nuclear level detector monitors the crusher screen for plugging.

A number of mineral sorting devices are on stream, mostly for special-purpose uses. At Doornfontein in South Africa, a system based on a laser-light source in a scanning system optically sorts gold ore. Light reflected from rock surfaces is detected, and an air-blast rejection device is activated to remove certain particles from the stream.

Other recent developments in sorting instrumentation include sensors of magnetic properties of minerals, magnetic eddy currents, metal detection devices, and infrared sensors. An infrared scanner at Belgium's Metallurgie Hoboken-Overpelt detects short circuits in copper electrodeposition cells.

Developments in automation for pollution-control monitoring have been significant in recent years. Intelligence terminals based on minicomputers are in use at remote sampling stations, where the immediate detection of any deterioration in effluent quality is processed over telephone lines to a central facility.

On-line moisture measurement, particularly in magnetite, has long been a problem. Numerous moisture determinators have been developed—for example, Republic Steel's neutron moisture meter. In Europe, S.I.C./LKAB recently announced development of a moisture meter based on infrared reflectance. However, particle size effects and sensitivity problems with this instrument have not been fully resolved.

Accurate measurement of slurry mass flow is still a problem because of changes in slurry density. One pellet producer, as part of its in-house development of a direct digital control system, is attempting to measure mass flow using a magnetic flowmeter, a pulp density gauge, and a Ramsey flow-through coil. The signals from the flowmeter are corrected for magnetic density changes occurring in the magnetic field through the use of empirical relationships based on the incoming solids density and the bulk magnetization. The same company is also evaluating a Doppler-effect ultrasonic flowmeter.

One major prerequisite—even with good sensors and instrumentation systems—is extensive development work on control concepts before such systems can be applied in iron ore agglomeration. A case in point is a grind control concept developed in Australia and recently tested by Erie Mining Co. The system did not achieve enough economic benefit to encourage its use, and there has been no apparent follow-through on the program. It is not known whether the control concepts were inadequate or whether the process sensitivities were generally too low for iron ore. However, specialists in the pellet industry generally feel that size-based grind control will be practical within the next few years, and that it will probably permit increased throughput. □

Alternative fuels are getting a second look

A SURVEY OF PYROMETALLURGICAL PLANTS reveals that most, if not all, systems now in operation are closely tied to conventional fuels. However, worsening shortages and higher costs of natural gas and fuel oil have focused attention on alternate, coal-derived energy sources, especially at iron ore pelletizing plants in the Lake Superior district, where the outlook for natural gas supplies is uncertain.

In the past, a switch from natural gas to oil might have been expected, but now even the capability of converting from gas to oil will not guarantee an uninterruptible fuel supply.

One method of direct coal utilization for pellet induration is being tested in a 800-lb-per-hour grate-kiln module at the US Bureau of Mines' Twin Cities Metallurgy Research Center. In a system similar to that used to fire cement and lime kilns, coal is pulverized to about 60-80% minus 200 mesh and transported in an air stream through a simple pipe or gun-type burner into the kiln hood. There, it is ignited and mixed with preheated secondary air to achieve complete combustion. While the system is uncomplicated and recovers the maximum amount of thermal energy, it introduces ash and other deleterious elements into the kiln and onto the pellet bed. The system may also be limited to coals having an ash softening temperature above 2,500°F. Coals with ash softening temperatures much below this level can cause serious "ring buildup" in the kiln interior, which could interfere with pellet throughput if not periodically removed. Also, accretions from fly ash deposition in the grate-to-kiln transfer occurred with certain Western coals, both in the USBM tests and in a commercial kiln trial conducted by private industry.

Dravo Corp. research in progress during the last half of 1974 has suggested at least one mode of an external combustion chamber for firing a straight-grate pelletizing system. One concept would place two coal combustion chambers, about 28-30 ft high, on either side of the grate stand. A PCF gun-type burner would be mounted on either side of the grate chamber with the flame directed downward. Combustion temperatures would be kept high enough to slag a substantial portion of the ash constituents. The molten slag would be discharged through the bottom of the chamber, water quenched, and discarded. The hot gas, still containing some suspended ash and volatile constituents, would be vented to the grate hood, where streams of gas would be tempered and routed to various points along the pellet bed.

Since no known coupling of the combustion chamber to an actual pelletizing machine has yet been made, there is no available information on how much ash or volatile constituents would be carried over in the gas stream to the pellet bed. Another unknown is the possible effect of these constituents on the operation and on pellet quality. However, it is logical to assume that the problems would be less acute than if no ash had been removed.

The traveling-grate pelletizing furnaces at Inland Steel's Minorca plant—scheduled to start up in April 1977 near Virginia, Minn.—will incorporate external combustion chambers and are expected to start up with pulverized coal firing for pellet induration. Traveling grates at Hibbing Taconite's new plant will be similarly equipped, but are expected to use oil at first.

The USBM Twin Cities Metallurgy Research Center is also evaluating a cyclone-type slagging reactor for use in pelletizing systems. The small cyclone combustion chamber is a replica of the German Babcock and Wilcox cyclone furnace in use at coal-fired power plants in Western Europe. The compact, horizontal, cylindrical furnace is water cooled to freeze a thin slag layer on its interior surfaces. Finely crushed coal and primary air are introduced tangentially into the burner and pass into the cyclone in a whirling motion. High velocity preheated secondary air, also introduced tangentially, burns the coal particles rapidly and completely to reach temperatures of about 3,000°F. Molten slag is discharged through a tap hole at the rear of the burner, removing about 75% of the total ash. Ash input to the system and contamination of the pellet are minimized but not entirely eliminated. Heat is lost in the molten slag and to the cyclone-cooling water.

In contrast to gun-type burners, the cyclone burner requires coal that is only fine crushed, not pulverized. However, the accrued energy saving is probably offset by the higher capacity fans needed to deliver secondary combustion air to the cyclone.

The compact configuration of the cyclone burner may offer advantages, especially at existing installations where space for modifications is limited. Barring other considerations, the burner might be adaptable to grate, grate-kiln, or shaft systems. Testing of USBM's small cyclone combustion chamber on its grate-kiln module was scheduled to begin during the first half of 1975.

Base metal smelters seek to maximize energy use

The need to conserve environmental quality and optimize the use of energy reserves is also ushering in changes and modifications in conventional copper, nickel, and lead pyrometallurgical processes. A new way of reducing use of petroleum fuels, as well as eliminating costly electric power input, has been developed by Outokumpu Oy at Harjavalta, Finland, for use in copper and nickel smelting. Exothermic heat from flash smelting of copper sulphide and/or nickel sulphide concentrates is used to sustain the oxidation reaction, while smelter heat makeup is provided by oxygen-enriched combustion air in lieu of heat supplied from burning petroleum fuel. A total of 16 copper plants and two nickel plants have been licensed by Outokumpu to use the process.

The high cost and increasing scarcity of metallurgical grade coke has also compelled lead producers to investigate fuel alternatives and fuel economy measures for lead smelting. A process for injecting a continuous stream of air mixed with powdered coal, lead concentrate, and silica flux into a 1,200°C bath of fused lead-rich slag shows promise of replacing the conventional lead blast furnace. Violent agitation of the lead-rich slag—produced as a consequence of submerged coal combustion—provides the intimate contact needed between the liquid lead and melted slag to maintain the reaction in spite of fluctuations in the feed. The heat of coal combustion provides the thermal balance makeup.

Calculations indicate that a smelting rate of 33.2 tph of concentrate would produce 24.6 tons of lead metal and consume 1.5 tph of coal. A conventional smelter of similar capacity would consume about 5.5 tph of metallurgical coke. Such savings are significant enough to warrant further study of the submerged smelting process.

The shortage of prime coking coals has inspired steel producers to investigate the use of formed coke (carbonized coal briquettes), made partly or entirely of non-coking coals. The British Steel Corp. has reported two small blast furnace tests on "green" formed-coke briquettes made of British coals by the German Bergbau Forschung-Lurgi Process and on calcined, formed-coke briquettes made of low-ash US coals by the FMC Process. These short-duration tests established that both formed-coke products can replace conventional coke.

With the BBF-Lurgi "green" formed coke, an increase of 3-10% in gross carbon requirements was observed, along with a decrease in output relative to coke used during the base period. With calcined FMC formed coke, a decrease of 3-6% in the gross carbon rate was realized, along with improvements in efficiency and potential production levels.

A recent test in an Inland Steel Co. blast furnace with FMC formed coke made of Western subbituminous coals demonstrated that formed coke can be used in blends of at least 50% with acceptable results. There are no commitments for commercial production of the formed coke, but licensing is available through FMC.

Coal gasification may in the future provide an alternate fuel source for pyrometallurgical operations. However, coal gasification processes are either still in the development stage or warrant further improvement to increase the Btu content of their product. With few exceptions, the prospect of large scale commercial production via coal gasification seems unlikely before 1980.

Tapping nuclear energy for steelmaking is also receiving consideration. A conference of European steelmakers and nuclear plant manufacturers met in London in June 1973 for discussion of practical ways to use nuclear energy in steelmaking. The agenda included outlines of the latest methods of direct reduction of iron ore, current nuclear reactor technology, and the evaluation of research programs for the project. A nuclear steelmaking consortium was formed as a result of the meeting. □

Capacity surge slated for direct reduced iron

INTEREST IN THE DIRECT REDUCTION of iron ore, which in the past has reflected increases or decreases in the price of scrap, remains strong in 1975. In the US, two Midrex plants—one at Georgetown, S.C., and the other at Portland, Ore.—and one Armco plant at Houston, Tex., are producing at a combined capacity of 980,000 mtpy. World direct reduction capacity was 5.2 million mtpy at the end of 1974, and an additional 13.7 million mtpy of capacity is due onstream during the next three to four years. Over 70% of the plants producing this capacity will be Midrex or HyL installations.

At present, 13,775,000 mtpy of direct reduction capacity is on order throughout the world. Additionally, 6,150,000 mtpy of capacity is covered by letters of intent, 6,790,000 mtpy is in advanced planning, and 15,120,000 mtpy is under study. Completion of all these plants would lift world capacity for direct reduced iron to 47,035,000 mtpy.

The HyL process, commercially successful in Mexico since 1957, is a static bed process that uses gaseous reduction. Three plants at Monterrey have combined capacity of 775,000 mtpy. A 220,000-mtpy plant is operating at Tamsa/Vera Cruz, and a 315,000-mtpy plant is in production at Hylsamex/Pueblo. A 630,000-mtpy plant on order for Hylsamex is slated for a 1976 startup. In Brazil, a 220,000-mtpy plant came onstream in 1974, and six other plants having a combined capacity of 5.4 million mtpy are on order outside Mexico, with startup dates scheduled for 1976 and 1977.

Midrex, Armco, and Purofer shaft furnace processes also use gaseous reduction. At the end of 1974, Midrex had four plants in operation, Armco one, and Purofer a large pilot plant. Midrex's first plant started up at 300,000 mtpy in 1969 at Gilmore Steel in Portland, Ore. In 1971, two additional facilities—a 300,000-mtpy plant at Korf Steel in Georgetown, S.C., and a 350,000-mtpy plant at Korf Stahl in Hamburg, Germany—were brought onstream. A 350,000-mtpy plant started up in 1973 at Sidbec operations in Contracoeur, Que. Midrex had five plants on order at the end of 1974, with a combined capacity of 4,980,000 mtpy.

In January 1974, Korf Industries acquired the former Midrex Div. of Midland-Ross Corp., and Midrex is now a wholly-owned Korf subsidiary. A 500,000-tpy mini-steel plant being built by Korf at Beaumont, Tex., will be fed by barge shipments of sponge iron produced at Georgetown.

Armco Steel is operating a 330,000-mtpy plant at Houston, Tex., and has announced plans to build another unit there.

Four 175-ton electric arc furnaces are operating at Armco's Houston installation. Processing varies from standard procedure by using two submerged tuyeres to blow oxygen under the bath at rates up to 2,000 cfm during the refining period. The charge to the furnace consists of 40-50% hot metal, 25% prereduced 92% iron, and the remainder scrap. During melting, the 22-ft-dia furnaces are tipped back about 5° from the horizontal to allow slag to dribble from the door. The tuyeres abet slag removal.

Armco stated in September 1974 that its process is producing prereduced pellets at $50.00 per ton. Included in this total is the cost of either high-grade lump ore or pelletized iron ore, natural gas, electric power, on-site labor, and repayment of invested capital. The conversion cost is given at $8.24 per mt. Estimated cost of a new 330,000-mtpy plant is $25 million.

The rotary kiln process has not advanced as fast as the shaft furnace and static bed. Incorporated in the SL-RN, Krupp, and Kawasaki processes, the rotary kiln uses non-coking coal as fuel and reductant.

An SL-RN plant at Sudbury, Canada, designed to produce 300,000 mtpy of pellets with 1.6% nickel-bearing iron ore, was closed at the end of 1974 for economic reasons. The principal deficiency was the failure of key process equipment to produce at rated capacity or to achieve continuous operation in accordance with guarantees.

The Steel Co. of Canada is building a 400,000-mtpy plant at the Griffin mine to produce 92% iron pellets. The kiln will be 1,150 ft long—the largest of its kind in the world—and is scheduled for completion by mid-1975. Seven rotary-kiln direct reduction plants now in operation throughout the world have a combined capacity of 1,540,000 mtpy.

The only operating plant utilizing US Steel's HIB fluidized bed process is a 350,000-mtpy facility at Puerto Ordaz, Venezuela, where expansion to 700,000 mpty is planned. The product is formed into dense briquettes that ship and store well. Because they are made without a binder, they provide a furnace feed having a minimum of gangue. The briquettes are 75% reduced and have an iron content of 86%. The HIB plant has experienced some mechanical, electrical, and instrument problems. However, there have been no major process problems with fluidization, scale-up, or agreement with pilot plant predictions for productivity and utilization of reducing gas. The plant has.operated near design production rate.

The Fior process developed by Esso Research has been piloted at Baton Rouge, La., in a 5-tpd plant. Following the pilot test, an experimental plant of 300-tpd capacity was installed at Dartmouth, Nova Scotia, by Imperial Oil Enterprises, Ltd. The first commercial Fior plant, with a capacity of 400,000 mtpy, is being built for Corporacion Venezolana de Guayana in Venezuela by Arthur G. McKee and Co. McKee, the exclusive licensee of the Fior process, is offering single-module plants up to 2 million tpy in capacity. □

US steel producers adding new capacity

US CAPACITY FOR BASIC OXYGEN STEELMAKING increased by a modest 4.1 million tons last year, to 87.8 million tons; however, a number of planned expansions were announced during the year. Jones & Laughlin Steel, at Aliquippa, Pa., and Bethlehem Steel, at Burns Harbor, Ind., are planning BOF expansions. And Youngstown Sheet & Tube and Bethlehem Steel plan to convert open hearth shops to BOF operations at Youngstown, Ohio, and Johnstown, Pa., respectively.

The bulk of the 1974 increase in US BOF capacity was attributable to Inland Steel's new 2.2 million-tpy shop at Indiana Harbor, Ind. This second-generation shop applies some of the latest technology, including a closed-hood "OG" system for converter gas recovery, scrap preheating, and extensive fume collecting at metal transfer points.

An additional 1 million tons of capacity will come onstream with the forthcoming startup of a single basic oxygen furnace at Sharon Steel. Two old Kaldos will be placed on standby when the new furnace becomes operational.

Elsewhere, US Steel has started up two 200-ton Q-BOP converters at Fairfield, Ala.—the company's second Q-BOP shop. Three 200-ton converters—the world's first large-scale use of the Q-BOP process—started up in early 1973 at Gary, Ind. The Q-BOP process, in which oxygen, lime, and other additives are blown through the bottom of the vessel, reportedly yields more metal at lower operating and capital investment costs than the conventional top-blown BOF process.

Electric furnaces coming on line at rapid pace

For the first time in 1974, more steel was produced worldwide in electric furnaces (20% of the total) than in open hearth furances (17%). Seventy-five new electric steelmaking furnaces are due to start up over the next few years. These furnaces are able to process greater tonnages of scrap and to efficiently utilize direct reduced iron, which is becoming more important as a raw materials source.

Most of the new production will be in ultrahigh-power (uhf) electric furnaces made possible by the development of premium-grade graphite electrodes. With power ratings between 350 and 400 kva per ton, 75 electric furnaces now operating have 100-ton capacities, and 16 top the 200-ton mark. Northwestern Steel & Wire Co. is installing a second 400-ton electric arc furnace rated at 150 mva.

In ferroalloys production, Union Carbide Corp.'s 55-mva silicon furnace at Alloy, W. Va., and its 75-mva ferrosilicon furnace at Ashtabula, Ohio, typify furnace installations completed over the last two years. Although the new units are larger and represent a substantial increase in ferroalloy capacity, the shutdown of many older furnaces is keeping the industry's production capacity about the same.

The new furnaces emphasize pollution abatement with little change in energy requirements. Sealed furnace designs are the ultimate in offgas control; however, valuable versatility is lost by virtue of the fixed electrode spacing and the charging difficulties inherent in a sealed electric furnace. Producers favor open furnaces for production of alloys containing more than 75% silicon, as opposed to the restricted access of a sealed system.

A new Japanese electric furnace design is attracting the attention of US ferroalloy producers. The furnace includes a second taphole, located above the furnace hearth. The use of the upper taphole during normal operations leaves a molten heel in the furnace after each tap. Retention of the molten heel reduces thermal cycling enough to increase refractory life and reduce net power consumption.

The trend is still to bigger blast furnaces

Bigger size and better operating efficiency are emphasized in recent blast furnace technology. Among the newer large units is the Fukuyama No. 4 blast furnace of Nippon Kokan's Fukuyama works, which was blown in during September 1971. Furnace hearth diameter is 45.3 ft and working volume is 127,282 cu ft. In November 1971, the furnace was producing 11,042 tpd of metal.

By way of contrast, in June 1955, Great Lakes Steel Corp. blew in the then-largest furnace, a unit having a 30-ft 3-in. hearth and a 55,300-cu-ft working volume.

Inland Steel has awarded a contract for a new furnace, scheduled for completion in 1978, in which hearth diameter will be 45 ft and working volume 130,000 cu ft. Initial iron production capacity will be 7,000 tpd, with a potential of more than 10,000 tpd. The furnace will be conveyor-fed. Two 150,000-cfm turbo blowers will supply wind.

The No. 13 furnace of US Steel at Gary, Ind., has a hearth diameter of 40 ft, working volume of 100,100 cu ft, and planned capacity of about 10,000 tpd.

Sumitomo Metal Industries is planning a 5,000-cu-m (176,550-cu-ft) blast furnace at its Kashima Works, with completion scheduled for June 1976.

All large furnaces in Japan blown in since 1964 are equipped for high pressure operation. The Fukuyama No. 4 furnace can operate at a top pressure of 35.5 psig.

In the US, US Steel's No. 6 Duquesne Works furnace is designed to operate at 30 psig, as is its No. 13 furnace at Gary.

Increased blast furnace efficiency is based on a number of factors. Among the most important are: effective use of prepared burdens, improved blast furnace coke, screening and sizing of the burden, humidity control of the blast, oxygen injection, auxiliary fuel injection, high wind rates, high blast temperature, and high top pressure.

Beneficiated burdens promote an even distribution of ascending gases. Improved gas-solid contact permits higher blast temperatures, oxygen enrichment, and moisture additions—increasing the driving rates of blast furnaces and lowering the coke rates. □

Hydrometallurgy makes advances in copper processing

THE COPPER INDUSTRY CONTINUES to search actively for economic hydrometallurgical processes, for both sulphide and oxide concentrates. For sulphides, US copper companies pilot-tested two acid ferric chloride leaching processes, one ammoniacal leach, and one roast-leach during 1974. Two trends are evident in oxide leaching: a greater tonnage of ore is being processed by this method, and solvent extraction-electrowinning technology is being used to a greater degree to recover metallic copper from the leach solution.

Arbiter process advances to commercial production

The Anaconda Co. made its first Arbiter process commercial copper cathodes on October 2, 1974, at Anaconda, Mont. The plant, designed to produce 36,000 tpy of electrolytic copper, was built in 18 months and will employ 120 people.

The Arbiter process extracts copper from sulphide concentrates by oxygen-ammonia leaching below 100°C. After dissolving the copper, a liquid-solids separation is performed, and the residue is floated to recover residual copper and silver values. The copper in solution is recovered by solvent extraction and electrowinning.

The Montana plant is receiving initial concentrate feed from the Anaconda concentrator at Weed Heights, Nev., and is scheduled to receive additional feed from the 1,000-tpd concentrator at the Victoria mine, also in Nevada. The Victoria concentrate contains quantities of bismuth that make it unsuitable for conventional smelting, but it is treatable by the Arbiter process.

Anaconda's Tucson laboratory will also test the Arbiter process on concentrate from Centrala Handler Zagranicznego (Centrozap), in Poland. If the method proves feasible, Poland may be licensed to build a commercial plant.

At the Lakeshore mine of Hecla and El Paso Natural Gas, near Casa Grande, Ariz., construction is underway on a commercial plant that will use a roast-leach-electrowinning process. Completion is planned for July or August 1975. The process calls for fluid-bed roasting of sulphide flotation concentrate to a sulphate. The calcine will be leached with dilute sulphuric acid, and the copper electrowon directly from the aqueous solution. Acid manufactured from the roaster offgas will be used to vat-leach the oxide ores. Planned capacity is about 32,500 tpy *each* of electrolytic copper and cement copper.

Duval and Cyprus testing ferric chloride leaches

At plants near Tucson, Ariz., Duval Corp. and Cyprus Mines Corp. are each testing ferric chloride leach processes.

Duval Corp. operated a pilot plant for its CLEAR process for two years and has begun construction of a 32,500-tpy plant at its Esperanza mine. Startup was scheduled for 1975. The CLEAR process extracts copper and iron from copper sulphides by ferric chloride leaching, forming elemental sulphur in the process. Electrolysis of the ferrous and cuprous chlorides recovers the copper. The iron chloride is further oxidized to regenerate ferric chloride and precipitate the excess iron as hydroxides.

Cyprus Mines is operating a Cymet process pilot plant at a feed capacity of 25 tpd, producing 7 tpd of copper powder. The process, like the CLEAR process, utilizes ferric chloride to leach iron from chalcopyrite and also forms elemental sulphur. However, ferric chloride is regenerated by electrolysis, both during copper electrowinning and in the production of electrolytic iron. Cyprus will submit data from the plant to an outside engineering firm for independent analysis. The company expects costs to be competitive with conventional smelting and has plans for licensing the Cymet process to other companies.

Laboratory research has developed a number of hydro- or combination pyro-hydro metallurgical processes for copper sulphides. Two roast-leach copper recovery processes have emerged from work by the US Bureau of Mines, as well as a unique procedure for altering chalcopyrite to chalcocite or metallic copper in aqueous acid solution by using metal reductants.

Processes for leaching copper sulphides with nitric acid and recovery of copper from the solution have been reported by Prater and Habashi.

Use of acid-dichromate solutions to oxidize copper sulphide has been reported by the University of Arizona and Inspiration Consolidated Copper Co. The process electrowins copper and concurrently regenerates dichromate in a diaphragm cell, produces elemental sulphur, and precipitates iron as sodium jarosite.

Copper industry expands oxide leach capacity

A new leaching plant was started up at Asarco's San Xavier mine early in 1973. Vat leaching extracts the copper, which is recovered by cementation. Capacity is 12,000 tpy of copper. About 15% of the acid produced as part of air-pollution-control operations at Asarco's Hayden, Ariz., smelter will be utilized at the San Xavier leach plant.

At Kennecott Copper Corp.'s Ray Mines Div., a 40% expansion of the silicate leach plant has been completed, lifting ore throughput from 10,000 to 14,000 tpd. Grinding and sizing units were added, and 12 new 10 x 50-ft pachuca tanks were installed for leaching. The project uses acid from the company's Hayden, Ariz., smelter.

A leaching plant recently completed by Phelps Dodge at Morenci, Ariz., recovers copper from tailings, using acid produced as part of the air quality control program at PD's Morenci smelter. The leaching and precipitation plant will

process tails from the Morenci and Metcalf concentrators. The plant, the first of three planned units, will treat about half of the tails (30,000 tpd) produced at the Morenci concentrator. Construction of the second and third units is dependent on satisfactory operation of the first.

Solvent extraction gaining wider acceptance

A new low-grade copper leaching plant at Nchanga Consolidated Mines' Chingola operation in Zambia will produce 80,000 mtpy of copper from the tailings of current operations and from reclamation and treatment of old tailings. The plant includes solvent extraction and electrowinning sections that are about 10 times bigger than the Bluebird operation at Miami, Ariz.

At Johnson Camp, about 70 mi southeast of Tucson, Ariz., Cyprus Mines was planning startup of a new mine and leaching operation during the first quarter of 1975. Established reserves of about 0.5% copper ore total 15 million tons. Open-pit mining methods, dump leaching, and solvent extraction-electrowinning techniques will extract 5,000 tpy of cathode copper. Increased supply of low cost acid and improvements in electrowinning procedures were partly responsible for the attractive economics of the venture.

A new 10,000-tpd oxide leach plant under construction at the Twin Buttes mine of Anamax Mining will process overburden from a copper sulphide deposit. A solvent extraction circuit and electrowinning circuit will recover 30,000 tpy of cathode copper.

Cities Service Co. plans to build a solvent extraction-electrowinning plant at its Miami operation in Miami, Ariz. At present, leaching operations are extracting copper from old mine workings for cementation on scrap iron. The new plant will recover copper directly from the leach solution and replace cementation, eliminating the necessity of smelting.

Minero Peru has announced plans to exploit the oxide portion of the Cerro Verde-Santa Rosa deposit. The process will include heap leaching and solvent extraction-electrowinning. A change in plans from vat leaching to heap leaching reduced construction costs and will permit rapid cleanout of the oxide ore and faster access to the underlying sulphides.

Native copper getting a closer look

A recent development in copper that may be a forerunner of a trend is the increased interest in the native copper deposits of Michigan's Upper Peninsula. These ores cost more to mine than the porphyry copper deposits of the Southwest, but processing the ores would avoid the extra expense and air pollution control problems experienced by smelters of sulphide concentrates.

A joint venture of Homestake Copper Co. and the International Nickel Co. is dewatering and reopening the Centennial Mine near Calumet, Mich. Efforts are being made to develop new orebodies and to determine economic mining methods. Milling and smelting methods are also being studied for possible use if the mine is reactivated. A pilot mill has been constructed and startup was planned for first-half 1975.

Early mining methods in the Keweenaw Peninsula left substantial copper values in low grade rock used as stope fill, and an in-situ ammonia leach process has been proposed to exploit this resource. Essentially, the process would leach the broken ore with dilute ammoniacal ammonium carbonate solution, pump the pregnant solution to the surface, and process part of the solution by solvent extraction for recovery of copper. The remainder of the solution would be aerated to oxidize the copper complex, combined with barren raffinate and returned to the mine to leach additional copper.

Theoretically, 1.07 lb of ammonia and 0.94 lb of CO_3^{--} are needed to leach 1 lb of copper. But because only copper is recovered in the solvent extraction step, only a first charge and small make-up quantities of reagents would be needed.

Simulated in-situ leaching tests conducted by the US Bureau of Mines have shown that a solution containing only 2.2 gpl of NH_3 and 1.9 gpl of CO_3^{--} is a suitable solvent for native copper capable of producing solutions containing 1.4 gpl of copper. However, in solvent extraction tests using conventional agitation-type mixers, a voluminous emulsion formed, interfering with phase separation. Replacement of the agitated mixer by a packer tower containing ½-in. ceramic saddles, and percolation of both the pregnant solution and organic mixture downward through the tower resulted in nearly complete copper extraction—and the troublesome emulsion was not formed. Research is continuing to further define the parameters of the process and to obtain engineering data for process design. □

New copper processes move to commercialization

WITH A VIEW TO MORE EFFICIENT ENERGY USE and production of offgases rich enough in SO_2 for sulphuric acid manufacture, copper producers have been evaluating new copper smelting systems for several years. At this time, it is too early to determine which of the new processes will become dominant: flash smelting, electric furnace smelting, direct conversion, or continuous smelting.

Reverberatory furnaces still produce the most Cu

"Conventional" reverberatory furnace-converter technology is still producing most of the world's copper, but the pressures of antipollution regulations have forced curtailments at some smelter operations. Research efforts have focused on upgrading the percentage of SO_2 in exhaust gases for easier processing to sulphuric acid or other nonpolluting product.

In a report on oxygen utilization in copper reverberatory furnaces, Wrampe and Nollmann of Union Carbide's Linde Div. state that enrichment of combustion air and/or use of oxy-fuel roof burners economically increase smelting rates by 25-50%. Oxygen use reduces metal losses in slag and cuts down on specific fuel consumption and dust losses. Effluent flue gas can be upgraded to acid plant strength of 3½% to 5% SO_2, making it possible to feed reverberatory offgases to an acid plant either directly or blended with converter or roaster gases. Limiting factors for oxygen use are roof temperatures and materials handling capacity.

At the Onahama smelter and refinery in Japan, two auxiliary burners have been installed vertically through the reverberatory furnace roof. High-pressure, pure oxygen atomizes and burns the fuel on the furnace's fettling slope. The very short, high-temperature flame melts the charged concentrate at an extremely high rate. Use of the oxygen-oil burners has increased the furnace capacity and boosted the SO_2 content of the offgas to 2-3%.

Effluent flue gases from the two Onahama reverberatory furnaces are cooled and washed before treatment in MgO and gypsum plants. Half the gas stream is treated at the MgO plant to concentrate the SO_2 to 10-13% for subsequent sulphuric acid manufacture. The gypsum plant fixes the balance of the gas stream as gypsum for use in the manufacture of wallboard.

Flash smelters now operating worldwide

During the past 25 years, the flash smelting method has advanced further, both metallurgically and technically, than any of the other new copper smelting concepts. The process, developed by Outokumpu Oy of Finland, has established itself both economically and environmentally, and Outokumpu has sold more than 20 flash smelting licenses for treating various types of copper and nickel concentrates.

The main attractions of flash smelting are efficient use of energy and high sulphur recovery. The process combines the roasting and smelting stages of conventional copper smelting with some converting. Dried concentrate, preheated air, and fuel are charged through concentrate burners and blasted into the reaction chamber. Heat generated by the exothermic oxidation reactions aids in smelting, and deficiencies in the heat balance are supplemented by additional fuel or by the use of oxygen in combustion air. The process produces a higher grade matte than other furnaces and reduces the load on the converters. It yields a steady flow of strong SO_2 that is not only excellent acid plant feed but can also be reduced to elemental sulphur.

Disadvantages of flash smelting are the formation of high-copper-content slag and dust problems. At the Tamano smelter in Japan, installation of electrodes in the settler of the flash furnace permitted elimination of a separate electric furnace for slag cleaning. The electrodes maintain the heat in the settler and facilitate slag cleaning.

To alleviate the dusting problem, a strong soot-blowing system with a hammering device has been installed in many flash furnaces. At the Kosaka smelter in Japan, where the copper concentrate may contain high lead and zinc values, hand lancing is periodically resorted to when soot blowing and hammering do not remove the dust.

Recent developments in flash smelting include adoption of oxygen-enriched air, use of electronic instrumentation that includes an on-line computer for process control, a high-temperature SO_2 reduction method for production of elemental sulphur, and production of blister copper directly in flash smelting furnaces.

The first flash smelter in the US will be Phelps Dodge's new Hidalgo copper installation in southwestern New Mexico. Startup is scheduled for third-quarter 1975.

Mitsubishi process uses multi-furnace system

A commercial-scale plant having a capacity of 4,000 mtpm of blister copper has been constructed at the Naoshima, Japan, smelter of Mitsubishi Metal Corp. The plant incorporates the company's continuous copper smelting and converting process. A second commercial Mitsubishi continuous plant is planned for Texasgulf's Timmins, Ont., operations, with a projected capacity of 130,000 tpy scheduled for 1978 startup. The multi-furnace system employs a separate furnace for each reaction stage, which allows each stage to be controlled and optimized independently, minimizing slag loss and efficiently removing impurities in the blister copper. On-line computer control has facilitated production of a 65% copper matte, saving fuel and holding down slag formation in the converter.

The Mitsubishi system provides separate furnaces for three metallurgical stages; concentrates are smelted in the first, slag cleaned in the second, and matte converted to blister copper in the third. Raw materials are charged to the smelting and converting stages through lances in the tops of the furnaces. Continuous converting avoids cooling of converter linings, and the transfer of matte and slag by launder avoids "reverts" formation. At Naoshima, the continuous smelter is integrated with the reverberatory smelter. The rich continuous smelter SO_2 gas is combined with the lean reverberatory furnace gas to yield a 5% SO_2 feed to the acid plant.

Electric furnaces attract US interest

The electric furnace, developed by Norwegian and Swedish producers for smelting copper concentrates, has recently been gaining a bigger role in the US copper industry. In 1972, Cities Service installed at Copperhill, Tenn., the first electric furnace for smelting copper to be built in the US in recent years. Inspiration Consolidated Copper has just completed a $54 million electric smelter and double absorption sulphuric acid plant. And The Anaconda Co. is presently installing an electric furnace at its smelter in Anaconda, Mont.

Among the attractions of electric furnaces: high smelting rates, low gas generation, negligible dust carryover, flexibility of charging sulphide and oxide concentrates, and furnace offgases containing 4-7% SO_2 that are suitable for acid plant feed.

TBRC based on oxygen steelmaking

Developed by The International Nickel Co. and Dravo Corp., the top blown rotary converter (TBRC), based on oxygen steelmaking technology, is now in use for smelting nickel concentrates at Copper Cliff, Ont., and has been demonstrated in full-scale autogenous smelting tests on copper concentrates. These tests demonstrated that a single TBRC can smelt and convert 200 to 300 tpd of copper concentrate.

The TBRC can produce high-SO_2 exhaust gases to facilitate production of sulphuric acid, liquid SO_2, or elemental sulphur. When using pure oxygen, chemical heat from the oxidation of iron and sulphur in the concentrate can be used for converting cold concentrate to molten blister copper at 2,350°F.

WORCRA process uses single continuous furnace

In the WORCRA continuous copper smelting process being developed by Conzinc Riotinto of Australia, smelting to matte, conversion of matte to metal, and slag cleaning all take place in communicating zones of an elongated hearth-type furnace. All of the SO_2 generated in these operations can be concentrated in a single gas stream high enough in SO_2 to be used in production of acid or elemental sulphur. A siliceous flux is added to the converting zone, and the slag formed flows countercurrent to the matte and metal. As the slag moves through the smelting zone to the slag settling zone, it undergoes both chemical reduction and "washing" effects that result in low metal losses in slag.

During semi-commercial tests of the WORCRA furnace, its developers evolved a large, rugged lance that represents a major technical achievement. Other features established for commercial plant design during subsequent semi-commercial operations include: a straight-line rather than a "U"-shaped furnace, higher intensities of feeding and lancing in the converting zone, multiple points of concentrate injection, use of supplemental oxygen to provide greater flexibility, simplified controls and advantages in lancing, and use of low pressure oxidizing air in the converting zone to react with the falling and burning concentrate lumps and with the shower of matte droplets above the lancing region. Because of rapid absorption of fine material, use of micro-pelletized concentrates will not be necessary to minimize dusting in commercial operation.

Noranda process commercial plant started in 1973

A commercial Noranda process continuous smelter came onstream at Noranda, Que., in March 1973 at a design capacity of 800 tpd of copper concentrate. Concentrates and silica flux are introduced onto the surface of a reactor bath in a single 17 x 70-ft reactor. The bath is maintained in a turbulent state by air introduced through a series of tuyeres. Exothermic oxidation provides part of the heat for smelting, and a burner at the feed end of the reactor supplies the balance.

In the smelting and converting zone, copper and slag coexist with high-grade matte under a partial pressure of SO_2. Copper tapped from the reactor contains 1-2% sulphur and needs more oxidation than conventional blister copper in processing to anode copper. The highly-oxidized slag contains 20-30% Fe_3O_4 and 8-12% Cu.

The slag is tapped from the end of the reactor into ladles, cooled, and treated in a flotation plant. Slag concentrate is recycled to the reactor, and low-copper tailings are discarded. Offgases leave the reactor through a water-cooled hood and pass through an evaporative, water-spray cooler, an electrostatic precipitator, and on to an acid plant.

The Noranda process can also be used to produce copper matte. Such an operation requires additional converting capacity to produce blister copper, but it permits greater throughputs and prolongs the life of the reactor refractory lining.

Blister copper produced by the Noranda process contains about the same amounts of minor elements as copper after conversion in conventional processing.

During testing with oxygen enrichment, the Noranda process smelting rate was more than doubled, and a continuous high-strength offgas was produced that contained about 12% SO_2.

Kennecott Copper Corp. is installing the Noranda process at its Garfield, Utah, smelter. □

Smelters seek economic emissions control

STRINGENT AIR QUALITY STANDARDS have forced the smelting industry to increase its control of plant offgases. The standards have most directly affected primary copper, lead, and zinc smelters. So far, proven technology, especially conversion of SO_2 to sulphuric acid, has been the basis of most pollution controls installed.

To meet ambient air standards, a number of smelters have installed taller stacks for better SO_2 dispersion, thereby reducing SO_2 concentrations at ground level. To meet acid plant requirements for at least 3½% to 4% SO_2 in the feed gas, smelters are modifying existing equipment or installing new smelting processes. Even with extensive modifications and equipment installations, some smelters do not claim 90% control of SO₂ emissions.

The Smelter Control Research Association (SCRA), an organization of US primary copper smelters, is seeking better methods for removing sulphur oxides and particulates from smelter smoke. The first SCRA pilot plant study, at the McGill smelter of Kennecott Copper Corp. in Ely, Nev., examined the effectiveness of wet-limestone scrubbing on low-strength gas streams. After an intensive pilot program and review of all available information from pilot-scale studies and commercial prototype systems in other industries, SCRA concluded that "at its present state of development, wet-limestone scrubbing is not a reliable process for removal of sulphur dioxide from copper reverberatory furnace gas," and that "it would be more productive to devote future efforts to other processes that avoid the problems inherent in the limestone system and that offer promise of greater reliability and better sulphur dioxide recoveries."

Subsequently, SCRA and the US Bureau of Mines jointly sponsored an engineering evaluation by the Lummus Co. of several of the more promising high-efficiency SO₂ control systems. Five processes were evaluated: the sodium sulphite scrubbing process (Wellman-Lord), the sodium double-alkali process, the ammonium bisulphite process, the ammonia double-alkali process, and the Bureau of Mines' buffered SO₂-H₂S process. Partly as a result of this engineering evaluation, SCRA selected the ammonia double-alkali process for a pilot plant study at the Magma smelter of Newmont Mining Corp. at San Manuel, Ariz. Pilot testing was scheduled to begin in the spring of 1975.

SCRA reported the results of the Lummus study in March 1974, including process economics that indicated a cost of about $200 per ton of sulphur removed. Since copper sulphide concentrate averages about 1 ton of sulphur per ton of copper and since 10-30% of the sulphur is removed in the reverberatory furnace operation, the increased cost of smelting copper would be about 5¢ per lb.

In Japan, smelters have been required by stringent SO₂ emission regulations to install flue gas desulphurization units (FGD). Units either planned or operating include the lime scrubbing process, the Dow aluminum sulphate process, and the magnesia scrubbing process. The first two processes produce gypsum, which is generally used to make wallboard, while the third process produces a strong SO₂ gas that is used to make sulphuric acid or to produce elemental sulphur in a Claus furnace.

Power plants process weak offgases

The US power industry has been making progress toward SO₂ emissions control using the Wellman-Lord process, the Combustion Engineering lime slurry process, and the soda ash solution process. The soda ash solution process is a once-through method having limited applicability. Other processes now starting up at power plants are the Chemico MgO slurry process, the Monsanto Cat-OX process, the limestone slurry process, and the limestone injection process. The two limestone processes have exhibited many mechanical and operational problems, and Combustion Engineering no longer advocates the

The USBM buffered SO₂-H₂S (citrate) pilot plant is testing removal of SO₂ and recovery of elemental S from lead smelter stack gas.

limestone injection process. Processes under development at power plants include the Wellman-Lord/Allied Chemical process, the Stone and Webster ionics process, the Envirotech sodium hydroxide lime double-alkali process, the Atomics International molten carbonate process, the Atomics International aqueous carbonate process, the US Bureau of Mines buffered SO_2-H_2S process, the Westvaco fluidized-bed activated-carbon process, the Monsanto-Calsox organic liquid-lime double-alkali process, the General Motors sodium-lime double-alkali process, and the SCRA ammonia double-alkali process. Of these processes, only two are being studied at US metal smelters: the US Bureau of Mines buffered SO_2-H_2S process, under development at a lead smelter, and the SCRA ammonia double-alkali process, scheduled for development at a copper smelter.

The US Bureau of Mines buffered SO_2-H_2S process comprises cleaning and cooling of the flue gas, absorption of the SO_2 from the flue gas by a buffered citric acid solution, reaction of the absorbed SO_2 with hydrogen sulphide to produce sulphur, separation of the sulphur from the regenerated citrate solution, and conversion of two-thirds of the sulphur to H_2S for recycling. The process removes better than 95% of the SO_2 contained in the flue gas and produces an elemental sulphur product that may be stored or sold.

In the SCRA ammonia double-alkali process, ammonium sulphite solution is used for SO_2 absorption, and the spent liquor (containing ammonium bisulphite, sulphite, and sulphate) is regenerated by reaction of limestone and precipitation of calcium sulphite and sulphate. This process removes better than 95% of the SO_2 contained in the flue gas and produces a relatively inert, throwaway calcium sulphite and sulphate product. ☐

Higher current density sought for copper deposition

SUBSTANTIAL INCREASES are clearly desirable in the current density—and therefore the rate—at which copper is electrodeposited in both refining and winning cells. Slow mass transport through the cathodic and anodic diffusion layers normally limits the current density to 15 or 20 amps per sq ft. The remedy, basically, is to reduce the thickness of the diffusion layers. Several changes in tankhouse practice are being investigated to achieve this objective.

Periodic reverse current techniques have received the most attention to date. Gecamines used periodic reverse at a current density of 44 amps per sq ft to electrowin copper in full-size cells, and the Ronnskar Works in Sweden and Nippon Mining Co. in Japan used the same technique to electrorefine copper at current densities up to 37 amps per sq ft. Canadian Copper Refiners Ltd. has reportedly been operating a periodic reverse current plant since 1972. And IMI Refiners Ltd., of Walsall, England, presented a paper at the 1975 AIME annual meeting describing operation of a copper refinery at 34 amps per sq ft, using periodic reverse techniques.

The US Bureau of Mines' College Park Metallurgy Research Center has been investigating high-current-density electrorefining of copper with electrolyte moving rapidly past the electrode surfaces. First experiments were done with small rotating discs and cylinders. More recently, satisfactory deposits were made at current densities up to 300 amps per sq ft, with the electrolyte pumped at high velocities through a narrow channel formed by an anode of crude copper and a titanium cathode.

Kennecott Copper Corp. has used air agitation in experimental electrowinning cells, with satisfactory deposits obtained at 60 amps per sq ft in cells equipped with perforated bubbler tubes placed between the bottom edges of the cathodes and anodes. Recently, the company also applied air agitation to electrorefining cells. The upper limit of current density to copper concentration was about 5 amps per sq ft for each gram per liter, higher by a factor of 10 than in conventional practice.

The International Nickel Co. of Canada obtained good deposits at 90 amps per sq ft in experimental electrowinning cells using air agitation.

Another approach is improved electrolyte circulation, with the electrolyte flowing up over the anode surfaces and down over the cathode surfaces to win copper at 60 amps per sq ft.

High frequency sound has been used in England to electrodeposit copper at 45 to 90 amps per sq ft.

Minera de Cananea has conducted pilot plant studies on electrowinning copper in the form of continuous sheet at high current density on a rotating drum cathode. ☐

Aluminum research targeted at alternatives to bauxite

AFTER ALMOST A DECADE OF STABLE BAUXITE PRICES, aluminum producers now have to cope with a drastic increase in the price of their basic raw material. During the past year, Jamaica raised royalties and taxes on bauxite nearly seven-fold and tied them to the price of aluminum. In short order, Guyana, the Dominican Republic, and Surinam took similar action or simply bought up the bauxite mining operations.

This increase in bauxite cost has spurred new interest in developing an economic substitute for bauxite. Eight aluminum companies and the US Bureau of Mines are operating a mini-plant using a nitric acid process for producing alumina from clay; a second mini-plant is being constructed for treating clay by a hydrochloric acid process; and a third mini-plant is planned to study a lime-soda sinter technique to process anorthosite. Companies involved in the project include Aluminum Co. of America; Alcan Aluminium Ltd.; Amax Aluminum Co. Inc.; Anaconda Aluminum Co.; Consolidated Aluminum Corp.; Kaiser Aluminum and Chemical Corp.; Martin Marietta Aluminum Inc.; and Reynolds Metals Co.

The Bureau of Mines had been evaluating possible alternatives to the use of bauxite for several years, and construction of the nitric acid plant was begun two years ago.

At the nitric acid mini-plant, 60 to 70 lb per hr of clay are leached with nitric acid, dissolving alumina, iron, and other minor impurities. After a solution-residue separation, the solution passes through an ion exchange step that removes the iron, and a concentration step that crystallizes the alumina as aluminum nitrate nonahydrate. Following separation from the mother liquor, the crystals decompose in a molten salt bath that contains potassium nitrate as the heat transfer media. The alumina thus formed is separated from the molten salt, washed to remove potassium nitrate,

The USBM alumina mini-plant in Nevada includes a leach section (center) and sand-liquid separation section (lower left).

sulphuric acid to form aluminum sulphate. After separation from the residue, the aluminum sulphate solution is saturated with hydrogen chloride to form sulphuric acid, hydrochloric acid, and aluminum chloride hexahydrate precipitate. The precipitate is separated from the mother liquor and decomposed to alumina and hydrogen chloride, which is recovered for recycle within the process. Most of the hydrochloric acid in the mother liquor is removed from the sulphuric acid by boiling. Both sulphuric acid and hydrogen chloride are recovered for reuse. Impurities such as iron and potassium are removed from the recycle solution by treatment with chlorine.

A 1-tpd pilot plant has been operated in France to test the H-Plus process, and construction of a 20-mtpd plant is planned. It is claimed that the process will work with other raw materials as feed.

New aluminum processes receive consideration

Alumina is converted to aluminum in the Hall-Heroult cell, which has been in use since 1900. Over the years, attempts to eliminate the Hall-Heroult cell have included methods designed for direct reduction of aluminum from its ores and variations in cell design. None have proved commercially viable. Several processes now being actively investigated may eventually become viable.

One of these, the Alcoa smelting process, will be used in a 15,000-tpy semi-commercial plant. Alumina obtained by any known technique is chlorinated to form anhydrous aluminum trichloride, which is fed into a molten salt electrolytic cell, where it decomposes into aluminum and chlorine. The chlorine is recovered for reaction with additional alumina. The process is claimed to use 20% less energy than the conventional Hall-Heroult cell.

Other processes involve a more direct approach for recovery of aluminum. The Toth process reacts clay or other alumina material with chlorine and coke at high temperature to volatilize anhydrous aluminum trichloride. The aluminum trichloride is separated from impurities by fractional condensation and reacted with manganese to form manganese dichloride and aluminum.

In the monochloride process, bauxite and coke react with aluminum trichloride to form aluminum monochloride and carbon monoxide. In addition, impurities such as silica may react to form their chlorides. This mixture of gases passes into a decomposer, where molten lead is sprayed into the hot gases so that aluminum monochloride and silicon dichloride disproportionate to form aluminum, silicon, and their respective higher chlorides. The lead-aluminum mixture cools in a separation unit, where molten aluminum containing small amounts of lead and silicon floats to the top.

In December 1974, patents were issued describing another chloride technique for producing aluminum. Ore is reacted to form aluminum trichloride and then converted with additional ore to aluminum monochloride at temperatures above 1,000°C. Flash cooling produces aluminum metal by direct contact with liquid aluminum trichloride or a solution of aluminum trichloride and a metal chloride above aluminum in the halide affinity series.

Another technique, the Alcan process, reached semi-commercial plant stage. However, after about $40 million had been spent over 12 years to develop the process (including construction of a 5,000-tpy pilot plant), work was discontinued in 1968. The process smelts bauxite and coke in an electric furnace to produce a crude alloy of aluminum, silicon, iron, etc. This alloy is reacted with aluminum trichloride vapor to form aluminum monochloride at about 1,300°C. The gas is then cooled to about 700°C in a

and calcined to α-alumina. Nitric acid vapor from decomposition is recovered for subsequent recycle in the process.

Besides the cooperative agreement with the Bureau of Mines, aluminum companies are also searching individually for alternate sources of alumina. In March 1974, processing of a laterite ore from the Washington-Oregon area was demonstrated in a standard Bayer operation that had been processing Jamaican bauxite. The laterite yielded lower alumina output because its alumina content is lower, but the technical feasibility of the operation was dramatically demonstrated.

In Golden, Colo., a pilot plant is recovering alumina from Utah alunite. The process treats the alunite to form alumina and potassium sulphate, which is subsequently recovered for possible use in fertilizer manufacture.

Another technique under development is the H-Plus process, which leaches a shale that contains lignite with spray of molten aluminum. At this temperature, the aluminum monochloride decomposes to form aluminum and aluminum trichloride.

Kaiser develops red mud disposal system

Kaiser Aluminum and Chemical Co. has started up a red mud disposal system that eliminates undesirable environmental conditions. At the company's Gramercy, La., alumina plant, a new 200-acre combination filtration and storage system for waste red mud has stopped discharge of the mud into the Mississippi River.

The red mud is dewatered and stored in a pond enclosed by levees and having a sand bottom that incorporates a French-type drainage system. Separated water is returned to the plant for further processing. A similar system will treat waste red mud at Kaiser's Baton Rouge plant.

The Bureau of Mines has been pursuing a research program for red mud disposal over the past two years. Research initially centered on conventional methods of dewatering and disposal and is now focusing exclusively on sand and static filtration techniques. □

Pyrometallurgy still dominant in lead-zinc processing

CONVENTIONAL TECHNOLOGY—blast furnace production for lead, and electrolysis of calcined concentrates for zinc—has dominated production of these metals in recent years. Within a few months after passage of the 1970 Clean Air Act, a rash of "pollution-free" processes were proposed, many of which simply substituted water pollution for air pollution. But just as the Clean Air Act seemed to tip the balance in favor of hydrometallurgical lead and zinc processes, the energy crisis tipped it back, because most of the proposed new processes needed more energy input than conventional pyrometallurgy.

In the future, processes for extracting lead and zinc will of necessity take advantage of the autogenous nature of the pyrometallurgical treatment of sulphide ores.

The Imperial Smelting Process is one of the few significant advancements in lead-zinc metallurgy in recent years, but plants using the technique appear to be experiencing difficulties. The increasing cost of metallurgical coke and high-cost labor have forced closures of ISP plants at Swansea, Wales, and Belledune, N.B., having a combined capacity of more than 100,000 tpy.

The rising cost of metallurgical coke has also been a matter of concern to operators of conventional smelters.

Suggestions for new primary lead production methods include the Q-S process, which combines autogenous smelting with direct reduction in a single furnace to produce a concentrated SO_2 gas, with localized gas recovery helping to minimize air pollution. St. Joe Minerals Corp. has an option for exclusive use of the process from its developers, Dr. Paul E. Queneau and Dr. Reinhardt Schuh-

mann, Jr. Work on the process is awaiting clarification of the patent position. The process is said to eliminate sintering and blast furnace operations by continuously converting PbS mill concentrates to lead bullion using oxygen in a single bottom-blown reactor.

At its Trail, B.C., operations, Cominco Ltd. is conducting a pilot plant study of a process that could replace its conventional lead smelter. Technical and cost data for the process have not been released.

The US Bureau of Mines is developing a leach-electrolysis procedure to produce corroding-grade lead from galena concentrate without lead or sulphur emissions. The concentrate is leached with hot $FeCL_3$-$NaCl$ solution to obtain a filtrate containing more than 99% of the lead and a residue of elemental sulphur and gangue material. Pure $PbCl_2$ crystallizes out of the leach solution on cooling and is electrolyzed in a low-temperature, fused-salt cell to yield lead metal and chlorine gas, the gas being used to regenerate the leach solution.

The Bureau of Mines is also developing a chlorine-oxygen leaching technique to treat complex lead-zinc-copper sulphide concentrates. During leaching, zinc, copper, cadmium, silver, and gold are solubilized as chlorides, while lead and iron are converted to insoluble sulphate and oxide, respectively. More than half of the sulphide is converted to elemental sulphur. Metal recoveries are higher than 99%. The metal values are recovered from solution by conventional methods such as solvent extraction, zinc precipitation, and brine leaching. The zinc and lead chlorides produced are treated by fused-salt electrolysis to produce molten metals and chlorine for reuse.

NL undertakes major secondary expansion

Secondary production of lead in the US now totals about 600,000 tpy and exceeds primary production. NL Industries, the world's largest secondary lead producer, plans a major expansion program over the next 10 years to greatly increase its secondary lead capacity. The main feature of the plan is a network of technologically advanced plants with capacities ranging from 50,000 to 100,000 tpy—three to six times the capacity of the average existing US secondary lead smelter.

The new NL Industries plants are also being designed to meet all current and expected environmental regulations. With an intensifying concern about the toxic effects of heavy metals, secondary smelters are finding pollution control more difficult.

New methods of recycling batteries are receiving more emphasis. The trend toward Ca-Pb batteries may have a significant impact on the secondary smelter of the future, and modification of processing techniques will have to be worked out to accommodate larger tonnages of these new materials.

USBM leach electrolysis for galena concentrates

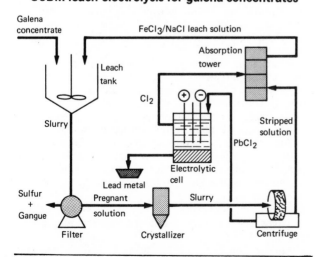

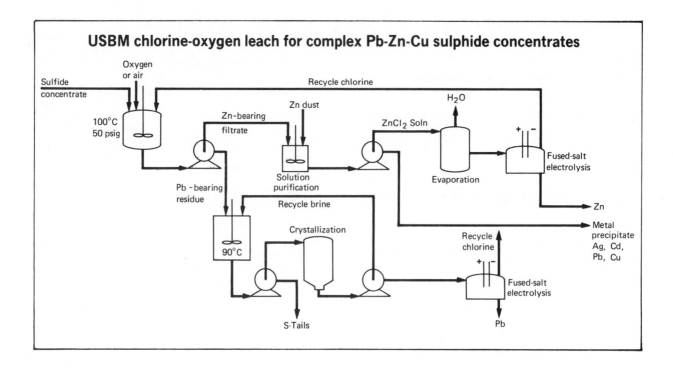

USBM chlorine-oxygen leach for complex Pb-Zn-Cu sulphide concentrates

Zinc producers seek to improve existing technology

It seems clear that most future world zinc production will be via the established pyro-hydro-electrowinning process. The current trend in zinc production, as described by G. M. Meisel, is to improve on existing practice.

Recent improvements include the use of a dilute sulphuric acid preleach to remove dolomitic magnesium, and the jarosite and goethite processes for recovery of ferritic zinc. While automatic cathode handling and stripping is being incorporated to a greater degree in overseas operations, no US plant is yet automated. However, new US plants will include automation for cathode handling and stripping.

New electrolytic zinc smelters are planned for Clarks-ville, Tenn., and Stephensport, Ky. A new electrolytic zinc refinery is also planned for construction at Bartlesville, Okla. The Clarksville plant of New Jersey Zinc will have a capacity of 160,000 tpy of zinc metal, making it the largest electrolytic refinery in the US. Concentrate feed will come from New Jersey Zinc mines in Virginia and eastern Tennessee and from the new Elmwood operation in central Tennessee.

Much of the zinc now produced in the US is a byproduct of the lead industry in southeast Missouri and contains nickel and cobalt. Amax has reportedly found a way to remove some of the deleterious elements, and is presently processing southeast Missouri concentrates as a "significant percentage" of the total feed at the Sauget, Ill., electrolytic refinery. ☐

Nickel development focuses on laterite ores

ALTHOUGH MOST NICKEL has in the past been produced from sulphide ores, the trend now is toward exploitation of extensive world laterite deposits. Most of these new developments employ hydrometallurgical processing techniques that are extensions or modifications of proven technology.

The Cuban government will invest $350 million to $450 million to upgrade its Nicaro and Moa Bay operations and to open a new mine and plant having a capacity of 30,000 mtpy of nickel in nickel oxide sinter pellets (77% Ni, 3% Co). The renovation at Nicaro is intended to raise capacity to 21,000 mtpy. The Nicaro process first reduces laterite ore and then leaches nickel from the reduced ore with an aerated ammoniacal-ammonium carbonate solution. Nickel carbonate precipitated from the liquor is calcined to yield nickel oxide. Streamlining is planned for the Moa Bay operation, but no capacity increase is contemplated. Moa Bay utilizes high pressure leaching with sulphuric acid.

Some newer installations elsewhere in the world incorporate procedures similar to those at Cuban plants, usually with improvements that increase the nickel recovery and also recover cobalt. In the early stages of the Ni-caro operation, cobalt was considered a contaminant.

New nickel operations at Greenvale in Queensland, Australia, and at Marinduque Mining and Industrial Corp. on Nonoc Island, Philippines, are also using reduction-ammoniacal leaches. At both locations, cobalt and some nickel are removed from the leach solution by sulphide precipitation.

The process at Greenvale, developed by Freeport Minerals Co., is targeted for a peak production of about 54 million lb per year of nickel and 2.75 million lb per year of cobalt. About 46 million lb of nickel production will be nickel oxide, and the remainder sulphide. About 2.5 million lb of annual cobalt production will be as sulphide.

The Marinduque plant, incorporating a process developed by Sherritt Gordon Mines Ltd., is scheduled for an annual capacity of 68.4 million lb of pure, refined nickel, 6.6 million lb of nickel, and 3.3 million lb of cobalt as sulphides.

P. T. Pacific Nickel has been evaluating a 60- to 100-million-ppy nickel project in Indonesia that would also use the Sherritt Gordon process.

Amax is continuing development work on a high-pres-

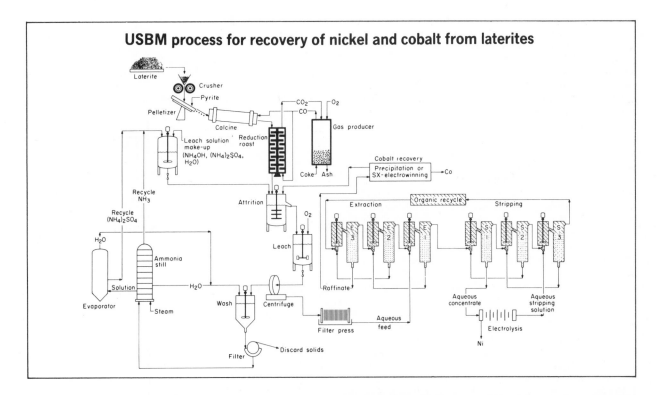

USBM process for recovery of nickel and cobalt from laterites

sure sulphuric acid leaching process for use on New Caledonian laterites.

In addition to the hydrometallurgical processes now applied to laterite ores, several new smelters are being built to treat such materials. Majority-owned subsidiaries of International Nickel Co. plan a 1976 startup for smelters in Indonesia and Guatemala, producing 75% nickel matte by a reduction-smelting process. On the Indonesian island of Sulawesi, P. T. International Nickel plans to produce 35 million ppy. In Guatemala, Exmibal expects to produce 25 million ppy.

A new process developed by Universal Oil Products incorporates ore reduction followed by conventional ammoniacal leaching. UOP has obtained greater than 90% recovery of nickel from laterites by adding sulphur and/or hydrogen halides to the reducing gas stream. The company claims even greater recoveries if the ore is pretreated with a dilute acid. Treating undissolved residue with dilute acid also improves extraction. UOP and the Puerto Rican government are negotiating a possible joint venture to use the UOP process to treat Puerto Rican laterites, with plans for a two-year technical and economic study, including operation of a pilot plant.

The US Bureau of Mines has developed a process for recovery of nickel and cobalt from US laterites utilizing reduction-ammoniacal leaching. However, the reduction is

performed at only 350° to 600°C (ideally at about 500°C). The reduction occurs in the presence of pyrite and with pure carbon monoxide rather than producer gas. The nickel and cobalt dissolve in an oxidizing ammonium hydroxide-ammonium sulphate leach and are separated by solvent extraction with LIX-64N. Following recovery of nickel as cathode and cobalt as sulphide precipitate, the leach solution is recycled. There are no effluents other than normal operating losses.

Reduction in the Bureau of Mines process is ideally autogenous and requires only 15 min. Ore enters the reduction chamber at 500°C following dehydration, and carbon monoxide produced from recycled carbon dioxide enters at 1,100°C.

Heat for production of carbon monoxide is provided by burning coke, so only coke and oxygen are consumed in the process. Enough excess carbon monoxide is produced to provide fuel for dehydration and drying.

The Bureau of Mines process is being evaluated in a continuous circuit having a capacity of 20 lb per hr of laterite. Recoveries from a laterite containing 1% Ni and 0.2% Co have been as high as 90% for Ni and 85% for Co, while 85% of the Ni and 76% of the Co were extracted from laterite containing only 0.53% Ni and 0.06% Co. A technical and economic evaluation of the process is being undertaken by an industrial contractor. □

Silver and gold: heap leaching exploits low grade feed

HYDROMETALLURGICAL DEVELOPMENTS in gold processing show a definite trend toward treating lower grade ores and mine waste material by heap-leach cyanidation, followed by precious metal recovery from solution by carbon adsorption or zinc precipitation. There is also renewed interest in carbon-in-pulp cyanidation techniques for treatment of slimy ores that do not respond to conventional liquid-solids separation. These trends, spurred by record high prices for gold and silver, are the fruits of research and development for improved methods of precious metal recov-

ery from resources previously considered submarginal.

The Carlin Gold Mining Co. in Nevada started heap leaching mine cut-off material in 1971, treating about 10,000 tpm of ore. The ore is crushed to ¾ in., dumped on an asphalt pad, and leached by sprinkling with dilute cyanide solution for seven days. About 70% gold extraction is achieved. The pregnant effluent is fed into the mill stream from the company's conventional cyanide plant for gold recovery by zinc precipitation.

Cortez Gold Mines in Nevada has been heap leaching

approximately 2 million tons of run-of-mine waste material for three years, in conjunction with conventional cyanidation treatment of oxide gold ore. About two years ago, Cortez Gold Mines started a cyanide heap-leaching carbon-adsorption electrowinning operation at its Gold Acres property, about 8 mi from the main cyanide plant. Over 2 million tons of mine cut-off material is being leached at this site. A low pressure stripping method developed by the US Bureau of Mines is employed to desorb gold from activated carbon.

Several companies are conducting pilot heap leaching studies on lean gold ores from deposits too small to warrant construction of a cyanide mill or too low grade for economic treatment involving fine grinding and agitation. In one such study, Idaho Mining Corp. in Nevada is heap leaching 20,000 tons of gold-bearing sandstone that reportedly contains approximately 0.05 oz gold per ton. Summa Corp. is conducting a similar study on ore containing about 0.1 oz gold per ton in the old mining camp of Manhattan, Nev.

The application of granular activated carbon in gold extractive metallurgy is getting new attention. The simplicity of the carbon adsorption process, which requires a low capital outlay, makes this technique very attractive for processing slimy cyanide pulps and unclarified effluents from heap leaching. After extensive testing in cooperation with the US Bureau of Mines, Homestake Mining Co. adopted the carbon-in-pulp process in 1973 for treating 2,250 tpd of slimes at its cyanide plant at Lead, S. Dak. Former practice recovered about 60% of the gold by amalgamation with mercury in the ball mill grinding circuits, but this technique was discontinued because of pollution problems. The carbon-in-pulp operation at Lead costs 68¢ per ton of slimes treated. Soluble gold losses in the tailings have been reduced to about 0.0002 oz per ton of solution.

Based on these favorable results, Homestake and the Bureau of Mines are conducting pilot plant studies to determine the feasibility of extending the carbon-in-pulp cyanidation treatment to silver-bearing flotations at Homestake's operation at Creed, Colo. The trend toward using granular activated carbon (6 x 16 or 12 x 30 mesh product manufactured from coconut shells) for recovery of gold and silver is prevalent at most of the commercial heap leaching operations in Nevada and Colorado.

Two new procedures for stripping gold from activated carbon have been reported by the Bureau of Mines. One method uses a 150°C temperature and 52-psig pressure to reduce the time and reagent required in stripping the carbon. The other method employs alkaline alcohol solutions to increase the rate of gold and silver recovery.

Current high prices for gold and silver have stimulated a re-evaluation of mine waste and tailings at old mining camps in the West, and several new projects have evolved. In 1974, Sierra Mineral Management went into production, cyaniding the old silver-bearing dumps around Tombstone, Ariz. Gold Hills Mesa Corp. announced plans to reprocess old tailings at Cripple Creek, Colo. Yuba Goldfields Inc. has obtained a permit from the State of California to resume dredging of the gold placer deposit at Marysville. Golden Cycle Corp. has reopened its Ajax mine at Cripple Creek, Colo., and is constructing a mill to treat gold telluride ores from the Ajax mine. The proposed flowsheet calls for flotation followed by oxidation of the concentrate to liberate gold. The gold is then dissolved by cyanidation and recovered by Merrill-Crowe precipitation. Tails from flotation are to be cyanided by the carbon-in-pulp method.

Laxen, of the National Institute for Metallurgy in South Africa, has reported an improved extraction of gold values from Witwatersrand ores as a result of a reverse leaching

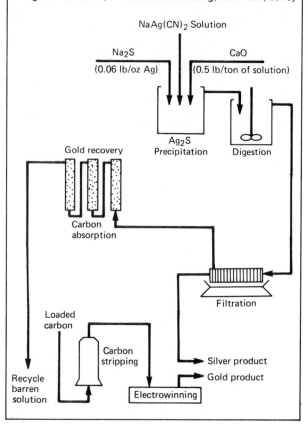

Silver recovery from pregnant cyanide solution

(Reported by Heinen and Lindstrom, "Silver Extraction from Marginal Resources," AIME annual meeting, New York, 1975)

method that leaches acid-soluble uranium prior to gold recovery. Because of the poisonous nature of mercury, the trend is to eliminate amalgamation in favor of direct smelting of flotation concentrates.

Two methods have been developed for processing carbonaceous gold ores. Oxidation agents—either chlorine or sodium hypochlorite generated in situ by electrolysis of a brine-containing ore pulp—destroy the activated carbonaceous material in refractory gold ores.

In 1972, Carlin Gold Mining introduced the first commercial cyanide plant to use chlorine for oxidation treatment of carbonaceous ores prior to cyanidation. Plant design was based on results of a cooperative pilot plant study conducted by Carlin Gold Mining and the Bureau of Mines. Gold extractions averaged 83% from carbonaceous ore, in contrast to only 33% extraction by conventional cyanidation without the oxidation pretreatment. Chlorine consumption was 28 lb per ton of ore. However, recent increases in the cost of chlorine have prompted Carlin Gold Mining to take a second look at the Bureau of Mines' electrooxidation technique, which features low operating costs.

Early work on heap leaching of gold ores reported by the Bureau of Mines was supplemented by a recent study, in which heap leaching of silver-gold ores was followed by precipitation of silver values with sodium sulphide and recovery of residual gold values on activated carbon. The technique reportedly eliminates the large inventories of activated carbon required to process pregnant cyanide solutions rich in silver, as well as providing for separation of silver and gold values. □

Uranium R&D directed to low-grade ores

RECENT YEARS HAVE PRODUCED RELATIVELY FEW CHANGES at US uranium operations, with available processing technology doing a good job on ores now fed to mills. In 1974, US uranium mill feed grade averaged about 0.18% U_3O_8—down from an average of about 0.20% U_3O_8 in 1973.

Anticipation that lower grade resources will provide a significant portion of future uranium production is reflected in much current research and development work in the industry. In exploration programs of the US Geological Survey and ERDA (formerly AEC), a major objective is identification of areas that may contain uranium mineralization in the 0.01% to 0.1% U_3O_8 range. Process development has focused on in-situ and heap leaching and countercurrent ion exchange of both slurries and clear solutions.

Sandstones are target of in-situ leaching

The unconsolidated sandstone deposits of Wyoming and Texas have been the prime target for in-situ leaching development. Initial investigations were primarily acidic leaching operations, but applications of carbonate leaches have recently been expanded. Both fixed-bed and continuous expanded-bed ion exchange systems have been investigated for recovery of uranium from the recirculating leach solutions. Patterns for injection and recovery wells have been the subject of a number of patents.

In early 1974, a $7 million operation started up near George West, Tex., utilizing in-situ leaching to feed a plant rated at 250,000 lb per year of yellow cake. Atlantic Richfield holds a 50% interest in the new project and is serving as operator for the other participants, US Steel and Dalco (a subsidiary of Sabine Royalty), each holding a 25% interest.

Heap leaching of lower grade uranium ores is being applied or considered mostly for treatment of sub-mill-feed-grade ores at operating mines or mills. However, some consideration is being given to heap leaching as an extraction method for relatively small, lower grade deposits.

A significant number of moderate-scale heap leaching operations and experiments have been performed, but relatively little information on the results has been published. The Bureau of Mines is initiating studies to gather fundamental and comparative data on the heap leaching characteristics of ores from different uranium districts.

Earlier studies acknowledged the influence of bacterial activity on uranium leaching when sulphide minerals are present in uranium ores. More recent studies are evaluating the direct effect of bacteria on uranium minerals, and the possible formation of uranium-enzyme complexes has also been investigated.

Phosphoric acid is new uranium source

Both Gulf Research and Development Co. and United Nuclear Corp. have announced plans for recovering uranium from wet-process phosphoric acid. The processes are apparently based on modifications of the octylphenyl-phosphoric acid solvent-extraction technique developed by the Atomic Energy Commission at the Oak Ridge National Laboratory.

Gulf built a $500,000 mobile pilot plant to demonstrate its process at Agrico Chemical Co.'s Fort Pierce, Fla., operation. United Nuclear has announced both construction of a plant for W. R. Grace and Co. and a tentative agreement for construction of an $8 million operation at the International Minerals and Chemical Corp. plant near Mulberry, Fla.

Continuous ion exchange draws interest

Both multiple-compartment columns and multiple-contactor tank arrangements of continuous ion exchange equipment have been studied during the past several years, and new commercial installations are in the planning or construction stages. Projections indicate that this equipment can offer both lower capital costs and the advantages of continuous operation on unclarified solutions.

The continuous ion exchange systems can also be used on slime slurries, but specific applications depend on the type of equipment and the mineralogy of the ores being processed. For example, the presence of swelling clays may produce viscosity effects that severely limit applicable slurry densities. For most conditions, however, continuous ion exchange systems appear to offer particular advantages in treating lower grade ores.

Multiple-compartment ion exchange columns are being considered for use in conjunction with processing gold-uranium ores in South Africa and with recovery of uranium from the low grade solutions produced by in-situ mining ventures in the US. An adaptation of the multiple-tank contactor system is reportedly planned for installation at the Rossing plant being constructed in Southwest Africa. This plant is scheduled to treat 20,000 tpd or more of 0.03-0.04% U_3O_8 ore.

Ion exchange is also being used to recover uranium from mine waters in both the US and Canada. At Grants, N. Mex., recoveries exceeding 90% are achieved on mine waters containing only 5 to 7 ppm U_3O_8.

Yellow cake specs are more demanding

Over the years, specifications for yellow cake uranium concentrates have gradually become more restrictive. As a result, many mills have installed multi-stage precipitation flowsheets to control product contaminants such as molybdenum, phosphorus, sulphate, vanadium, and sodium. A number of uranium operations have also used modifications of the hydrogen peroxide precipitation technique. This procedure is especially effective in controlling the phosphorus, vanadium, and sodium contents of yellow cake concentrate. Future recovery of lower grade ores may require even more selective recovery techniques.

In another milling development, autogenous or semi-autogenous grinding has been adapted to uranium operations. At Shirley Basin, Wyo., Utah International Inc. uses a cascade mill in closed circuit with a 20-mesh DSM screen in place of the more conventional multi-stage crushing and grinding circuits. Run-of-mine ore is fed directly to the mill by an apron feeder. At Jeffrey City, Wyo., the operations of Western Nuclear Inc. were temporarily suspended during the early part of 1974 while a similar grinding circuit was installed.

Preconcentration of uranium ores has been investigated over the years, but except in isolated instances, results have not met the necessary uranium recovery and cost criteria. Recent investigations at Elliot Lake, Ont., encountered the same problems. However, an increasing number of uranium ores contain discrete carboniferous fractions that are not treatable by currently operating flowsheets. Past work and some work in progress indicates possible application of froth flotation to such refractory material, either on the feed or tails streams at conventional acid-leaching uranium operations.

As in most mining and milling operations, closed circuit tailings disposal has become an operating criterion at uranium mills, with most using some form of impoundment technique for disposal of liquid and solid wastes. Appreciable quantities of tailings solutions are recycled to mills, with most operations relying on solar evaporation for disposal of excess water.

X-ray spectroscopy has become a standard analytical technique for control of uranium mining and milling operations. Initially the technique was used primarily on ore samples, but now almost all mill control analyses are possible by X-ray technique. Several operations are installing or considering installation of second generation X-ray hardware, and a number of plants will integrate such analytical units with automated data acquisition and analysis equipment. □

Phosphate booming, on strong fertilizer demand

BURGEONING DEMAND FOR PHOSPHATE ROCK in fertilizer manufacture has prompted a wave of expansion activity at phosphate operations in the US and throughout the world. In Washington, N.C., the North Carolina Phosphate Co. is planning to mine and process 4 to 5 million tpy of phosphate rock, and Texasgulf is expanding its Lee Creek, N.C., operation to about 1 million tpy of ore. Conventional processing technology will be used in these new facilities.

In the Florida pebble rock field, major expansions are planned by Agrico Chemical (8.5 million tpy), Brewster Phosphate (2 to 3 million tpy), Belser Industries (3 million tpy) and Hooker Chemical (2 million tpy). Additional expansions are also planned by International Minerals and Chemical and by Occidental Chemical.

In processing, the recently demonstrated recovery of 85% plus 65-mesh phosphate rock at Brewster Phosphate in Bradley, Fla., indicates potential for feeding roughing and scavenging flotation circuits coarser grinds than have conventionally been employed. The coarse concentrates could then be upgraded by regrinding and cleaning.

At conventional grind sizes, improved selectivity can be obtained in roughers by using less collector, followed by scavengers, with improved recovery because of greater ability to pull more free and locked particles. The improved flotation results derive from better circulation of pulp, which increases the opportunity for a particle to float.

Local land usage groups have strongly opposed expansion of mining into new areas in the Florida central pebble field. In numerous instances, approval to mine phosphate deposits has been granted only after detailed plans and commitments have been made for environmental control and reclamation.

In most cases, new Florida phosphate operations will use conventional concentration technology. However, mining practice and waste slime disposal technology planned by Brewster Phosphate will probably utilize a sand-slime compaction system developed by the company. Brewster has demonstrated that this system can consolidate waste slime and tailing sands from phosphate rock processing into about the same volume in mined pits as was originally occupied by the ore in place. After final replacement of overburden, Brewster expects to reclaim land at or near original ground level.

The Brewster method for consolidating slime and sand wastes is being tested on plant wastes of other Florida operations by the Phosphatic Clays Research Project.

In recognition of the environmental problems created by phosphatic slime wastes, Florida mining companies and the US Bureau of Mines started cooperative research in June 1972 to develop satisfactory slimes dewatering methods. Research under the agreement has been directed at methods that had not previously been examined. Characterization studies of products from all active mines indicated a wide variability in slimes mineral composition

from mine to mine, and even within a single mine. The research also found that dewatering of the slimes becomes more difficult as attapulgite clay content in the slimes increases.

Extensive studies were also conducted using a wide variety of reagents, including flocculants and compounds not usually considered to be flocculants. Lab tests with long chain polymer flocculants produced initial rapid settling of slimes, but ultimate settling volumes were not favorable. The reagents used were also expensive.

Flocculating reagents have been used with sand tailings and slimes to dewater and consolidate the combined waste products. Although preliminary tests were favorable, results from small-scale continuous field tests indicate that the process would be costly.

In another processing development, Davy Powergas, Inc. demonstrated an energy saving in wet grinding of phosphate product followed by acidulation. The method was effective in holding down dusts and reducing energy requirements for drying in processing the rock to fertilizer.

Western phosphate production rising

A major percentage of US phosphate reserves are in the West, and if increasing fertilizer demands are to be met, these reserves must be developed. In 1973, about 5 million tons of phosphate were mined in southeastern Idaho.

The Departments of Interior and Agriculture have organized an interagency task force under the leadership of the US Geological Survey to prepare an environmental impact statement and to provide for orderly development of phosphate resources in the area. Production from western areas is expected to double in the next five years, and a four-fold increase is projected by the year 2000.

A new phosphate mine and beneficiation plant on a 3,000-acre site about 35 mi northeast of Soda Springs, Ida., will mine and process about 2.5 million tpy of phosphate rock. A panel mining method will extract ore from areas about 500 yd wide to reach the sloping ore beds. When one panel is depleted to a maximum overburden-to-ore ratio of 10:1, the mined-out trench will be filled with overburden from the next panel.

In September 1972, Beker Industries Inc. reactivated the El Paso Products Co. fertilizer plant near Conda, Ida., and its mine 20 mi away at Dry Valley. Beker also took over Mountain Fuel Supply Co.'s rock beneficiation plant. A $10 million expansion of the fertilizer plant was slated for early 1975 to double capacity for diammonium phosphate.

Under an agreement with Earth Sciences Inc., the Canadian firm Western Co-operative Fertilizer Ltd. will advance $1.25 million for feasibility studies for an Idaho phosphate rock development. The studies are expected to be completed this year. Early planning indicates production at a rate of 1 million tpy of calcined, beneficiated rock, to begin in the 1977-1978 fertilizer season.

J. R. Simplot Co. plans to install a Fluo-Solids reactor at

its open-pit phosphate mine at Conda, Ida., to burn organic materials from the phosphate rock prior to processing. The calciner will be located near the beneficiation plant. Storage and loading facilities will be included in the construction program.

In addition, Simplot has installed several pipe reactors under license from the Tennessee Valley Authority at major distribution centers at Pocatello and Twin Falls, Ida., and Brandon, Man., Canada. Another is being installed at Scotts Bluff, S. Dak. Pipe reactors permit production of liquid fertilizer, such as 11-37-0 and 11-34-0, at the distribution centers. The pipe reactors can generate a liquid having a high-polyphosphate content from wet-process acid. Relatively inexpensive, easily handled feed acid containing only 15-30% polyphosphate can be used.

With the exception of the Kerr-McGee plant at Soda Springs, Ida., which is recovering vanadium from ferrophosphorus, there is no significant byproduct recovery at western phosphate operations. Fluorides evolved and recovered as fluosilicic acid during the production of wet-process phosphoric acid are not being used to any extent, presumably because the phosphate content in the fluosilicic acid makes it unattractive to aluminum producers.

Recent Bureau of Mines research indicates that precisely controlled neutralization of impure byproduct fluosilicic acid with lime produces a precipitate that could be substituted for natural fluorspar as a slag conditioner during steelmaking. Under proper conditions, the contained phosphorous remains in the slag and does not contaminate the steel. □

Potash production moves to lower-grade ores

POTASH PRODUCTION IS BEING BOOSTED substantially to meet fertilizer demand. Because of the deleterious effect of chlorides in some agricultural areas, production of potassium sulphate is on the upswing. Potash is also being used to produce complex potassium phosphate or nitrated potassium phosphate fertilizers, which offer savings in shipping costs and certain advantages in application.

As high-grade potash reserves in the Carlsbad, N. Mex., district are diminishing, the alternative there is to recover muriate of potash from low-grade sylvinite ores containing large amounts of clay slimes. Duval Corp. and Kermac Potash Corp. have been treating such materials for several years. Duval uses countercurrent decantation to remove clay slimes prior to flotation, while Kermac uses a heat-consuming leach-crystallization procedure.

Mississippi Potash Co. has been remodeling the old Teledyne flotation plant to treat low grade Carlsbad area ores, and startup was schedule by mid-1975.

The clay slimes, especially from the Duval operation, contain entrapped soluble salts that reduce overall potash recovery and can eventually cause pollution problems in natural water courses when the soluble salts are leached during wet periods. Available technology for treating the high-clay ores has not been entirely satisfactory. Selective flocculation and flotation of the clays prior to potash flotation appears to offer encouraging possibilities, and Cominco Ltd. has reported successful application of a similar technique for removing fine clays.

Texasgulf has converted the Cane Creek saline potash deposits near Moab, Utah, from conventional underground mining to solution mining followed by solar evaporation of the brines. Cationic flotation separates the sylvite from the crude evaporites. Mill and product treatment circuits are similar to those used prior to the conversion. The plant, which treats about 150 tph, is expected to produce a premium-grade muriate of potash (61% K_2O).

At Great Salt Lake Minerals and Chemicals Corp., solar evaporation pond areas are being expanded, and a commercial-scale pilot plant is testing a flotation method developed by the US Bureau of Mines and GSLM&C. The flotation circuit is designed to produce suitable feed material for the K_2SO_4 chemical refinery from low-grade evaporites assaying less than 7% K, which are normally discarded. The crude evaporites are ball milled and conditioned with chemical plant end-liquor (saturated brine) to convert epsomite and kainite to schoenite. The schoenite is froth floated using medium-molecular-weight fatty acid. Test results show about 80% potassium recoveries in concentrates averaging 12% K and halite rejection of about 85%.

In February 1975, Pennzoil Chemical Inc. started shakedown tests at a new potassium phosphate plant at Hanford, Calif. Although no details are available, company officials report that results have been very encouraging. The process converts potassium chloride to potassium bisulphate with sulphuric acid at 125°C to evolve HCl, and then contacts the remaining slurry with phosphate rock at 70°C to form monopotassium phosphate, phosphoric acid, and gypsum. After removal of gypsum by filtration, the monopotassium phosphate is crystallized with methanol and removed by centrifuging. Methanol is separated by distil-

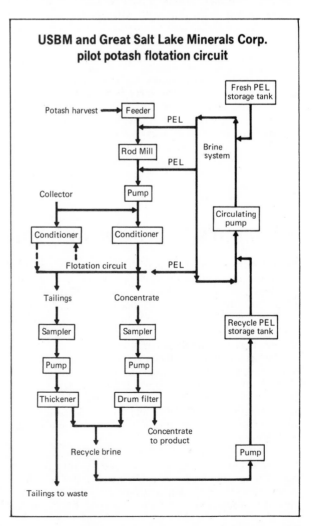

USBM and Great Salt Lake Minerals Corp. pilot potash flotation circuit

lation for recycle, and the phosphoric acid is withdrawn and used as raw material for liquid fertilizers, superphosphoric acid, dicalcium phosphate, detergents, or food-grade acid.

Superfos A/S, a Danish fertilizer manufacturer, has developed a process for making a chlorine-free complex nitrogen-phosphorus-potassium fertilizer. The German engineering company, Uhde, offers the process under the tradename "KC Ion Process." The technique acidulates phosphate rock with nitric acid to produce a slurry containing nitrate, phosphate, and calcium ions, and the slurry is contacted with a potassium-loaded cation exchanger to replace calcium ions with potassium ions. Potassium chloride is used to regenerate the ion exchanger. ☐

Brines are source for iodine, bromine, and other minerals

US PRODUCTION OF BROMINE is believed adequate to meet projected domestic needs at least through the year 2000, but iodine demand greatly exceeds production. More than 90% of US iodine supply is imported, most of it from Japan. The US iodine supply-demand balance could be reversed if economic means were available to extract iodine from domestic oil well brines—which contain enough iodine as waste to supply double the world demand. Treatment of these brines to recover both iodine and other values, such as bromine, would produce a strategically valuable resource and at the same time alleviate disposal problems in petroleum production.

Some oil field brines in Oklahoma having high iodine levels (300-500 ppm) are now being developed as sources of iodine, but most oil well brines are too low in iodine content for economic recovery.

In one Oklahoma joint venture, Amoco will be responsible for field development and Houston Chemical Co. for operation and marketing at a plant scheduled for startup in second-half 1976. The plant will operate in a closed loop system, with the only two effluents being iodine and spent brine to be reinjected into the field to push fresh brine toward the producing wells. This approach will minimize air pollution in processing oil well brines.

Another Oklahoma venture, by Ethyl Corp., is not as advanced as the Amoco-Houston Chemical project.

The Oklahoma oil field brines contain even greater quantities of bromine than iodine, but the lower price of bromine—about one-half that of iodine—and the cost of added plant facilities for a dual process make dual recovery uneconomical at this time. Moreover, the oil well brines have only one-tenth the bromine content of natural brines in Arkansas.

Both Oklahoma ventures expect to use a standard oxidation-blow out procedure in which sulphuric acid, chlorine, and sodium nitrate are mixed with the brine.

Total Oklahoma iodine production is expected to be about 2 million lb per year, approximately one-third of US demand. Too great a domestic production of iodine could prompt the Japanese to lower their prices so that recovery from US oil well brines would no longer be economic. (Japanese production has leveled off recently because of problems with pollution and subsidence, but renewed growth is anticipated.) Recovery of iodine from brackish waters in Indonesia could also alter world supply.

US bromine supply in 1973 came from 10 plants in three states—Arkansas, Michigan, and California. Arkansas continues to be the leading supplier and is increasing its share of US production.

In California, bromine is extracted from Searles Lake brines, while in Arkansas and Michigan, bromine is separated from well brines. Bromine is usually separated from brines by using chlorine to oxidize bromide to bromine, removing the bromine with steam, and then, after condensation, separating the water and the bromine.

Searles Lake brines are also treated industrially to recover soda ash, salt cake, and borax. Tungsten is present in these brines in low concentrations but is not extracted commercially. The US Bureau of Mines has developed several ion-exchange resins that extract tungsten, but commercially available resins have proven ineffective. In laboratory testing, tungsten and coextracted boron are eluted from the resin with water for subsequent separation and recovery. Because process development is in its infancy, commercialization depends on continuing research and development. ☐

Titanium's future lies with ilmenite

ENVIRONMENTAL AND ENERGY CONSIDERATIONS, coupled with a pending worldwide shortage of rutile, are the major problems facing the titanium industry. Best estimates place world rutile reserves (95-98% TiO_2) at less than 10 million tons. With annual TiO_2 production for pigments running close to 2.5 million tons, industry will obviously exhaust the rutile supply in fairly short order.

Alternate sources of titanium include high-grade alluvial deposits and titaniferous magnetites, disseminated throughout the world, which will provide a source of TiO_2 far into the future. Known pigment-grade ilmenite reserves (more than 45% TiO_2) total about 165 million tons. Inclusion of lower grade ilmenite resources would add 225 million tons.

The shortage of rutile has stimulated an intensive search for new deposits of high grade ilmenite and for new methods of upgrading ilmenites to synthetic rutiles containing more than 95% TiO_2. Pigment producers prefer synthetic rutile for production via the chloride route, because pollution problems are minimized and higher reactor throughputs can be achieved.

A wide variety of approaches are being studied to upgrade ilmenite materials to a suitable TiO_2 content. Among them: smelting of ilmenite concentrates to recover pig iron and high-titania slag; reduction of ore to form pig iron and TiCl; roasting followed by leaching with hydrochloric or sulphuric acid; partial reduction and acid leaching; and selective chlorination with removal of iron as $FeCl_2$ or $FeCl_3$ vapor to be treated for recovery of chlorine. Some of these upgrading methods have progressed to plant scale operation in India, Australia, and Japan.

At present there are no upgrading plants in the US. However, Kerr McGee has reportedly investigated the Benilite process—partial reduction followed by HCl leach with acid recycle—to produce synthetic rutile. And Sherwin-Williams, New Jersey Zinc, and other pigment producers are also reportedly interested in plants for synthetic rutile production, with some in the planning stage.

Increasing energy costs may adversely affect installation of upgrading facilities and stimulate interest in direct chlorination techniques. However, certain environmental and technological problems remain to be solved before low-grade ilmenite materials can be processed commercially by direct chlorination.

The sulphate process produces TiO_2 from low grade ilmenites and slags, but generates large quantities of ferrous sulphate and dilute sulphuric acid waste.

Production of TiO_2 by the chloride route depends on a high-grade feed material, preferably containing more than 95% TiO_2, because use of lower feed materials (65-75% TiO_2) generates large quantities of $FeCl_3$ that pose serious environmental problems and also result in a chlorine loss, adversely affecting costs.

Du Pont converts ilmenite to $TiCl_4$ and $FeCl_3$ by a direct chlorination process; however, the company has encountered considerable difficulty in disposing of the highly corrosive acid-forming $FeCl_3$ byproduct. Du Pont is reportedly operating a small pilot plant using a 3-ft-dia fluidized-bed dechlorinator to convert $FeCl_3$ to Fe_2O_3 and Cl_2 by reaction with oxygen. Successful operation of this project could resolve the pollution problems and enhance the economics of the chloride process. Chlorine produced by the process would be recycled, and the iron oxide product could be used in steelmaking.

Direct chlorination of both high- and low-grade ilmenites obtained from alluvial, rock-type ores and slags has been investigated by the US Bureau of Mines for the past three years, and dechlorination of $FeCl_3$ in a fluidized bed reactor has been studied intensively during the same period. Although work has not progressed beyond the laboratory stage, the procedures look promising. About 98% of the TiO_2 content of all ores tested was recovered as $TiCl_4$, and almost total conversion of $FeCl_3$ to Fe_2O_3 and Cl_2 was effected. Pilot plant development is needed to further evaluate the method.

Future trends in titanium production will depend on the economics and energy consumption of direct chlorination, as opposed to the costs of upgrading ilmenite to 95%-plus TiO_2 and subsequent conversion of upgraded material to $TiCl_4$. The trend toward use of the chloride process for pigment production rather than the sulphate process will probably continue; however, pollution problems confronting the industry must be resolved, regardless of which process is used. □

Rare earths: new production processes based on oxides

PRODUCERS OF RARE EARTH METALS are making technological strides both in working out new production processes and in developing new markets. Misch metal has proven effective in controlling sulphur morphology in plate and sheet steel, and the growing demand for this special type of steel in large diameter pipelines for natural gas and oil—particularly in Arctic environments—has created a major new market for misch metal. In production of misch metal, a new process based on research by the US Bureau of Mines has recently entered the commercial stage. The process electrowins misch metal directly from mixed rare earth oxides dissolved in a fluoride electrolyte.

Rare Earth Metal Corp. of America, a joint venture of Alcoa and Molycorp, has successfully completed operation of a pilot electrolytic cell using mixed rare earth oxides, and has begun construction of a 20,000-amp cell for a production rate of about 250,000 lb of misch metal per year.

Santoku Metal Industry Co. of Japan has changed its method of producing misch metal from the use of chlorides to oxides and is operating several 20,000-amp cells.

Permanent magnets using rare earth and cobalt metals to achieve previously unattainable properties are now commercially available. This new class of magnet materials, consisting of Sm-Co and Sm-Co-Cu-Fe alloys, has already replaced Pt-Co in microwave devices and in electric watches and clocks. However, the high cost of samarium metal has severely restricted the use of Sm-Co magnets to critical applications where material cost is secondary to performance. Lower cost magnets in which samarium has been partially replaced by cerium and misch metal are now being produced by Colt Industries, General Electric Co., and others. Misch metal-cobalt magnets containing no samarium are under development at the US Bureau of Mines.

The use of yttrium in alloys appears to be leveling off, but lanthanum-containing alloys are a growing business. A mixture of Gd_2O_3 with U_3O_8, pelletized for nuclear fuel elements, is out of the laboratory stage and entering production. Demand is also good for rare earths as cracking catalysts. □

Bibliography

The following source material was used by the US Bureau of Mines in compiling this report.

Alumina and aluminum
Maurel, Pierre, "Alumina From Schist Ores," French Pat. 1,558,347, Feb. 28, 1969, Chem. Abs., v. 72, 1972, p 22976.

Othmer, D. F., "Method for Producing Aluminum Metal Directly From Ore," US Pat. 3,853,541, Dec. 10, 1974.

Parkinson, Gerald, "Golden Pilot Plant Points Way to 500,000-tpy Alumina-From-Alunite Mine and Plant in Utah," E/MJ, August 1974, pp 75-77.

Peacey, J. G. and W. G. Davenport, "Evaluation of Alternative Methods of Aluminum Production," Jour. of Metals, July 1974, pp 25-28.

Smith, Gene, "Reynolds Begins Tests of Laterite to Obtain Alumina," The New York Times, March 7, 1974, pp 55, 60.

Blast furnaces
Coulis, J. L., and W. M. Malone, "The Rebuild of Republic's No. 5 Furnace," AIME, Ironmaking Proceedings, v. 31, 1974

Greenawald, Ralph A., and Edward L. Auslander, "Burns Harbor High Top Pressure Operation—Its Problems and Rewards," AIME, Ironmaking Proceedings, v. 33, 1974, pp 167-173.

Higuchi, Masaaki, Tsunenori Sugawara, and Seiji Matsui, "The

Design and Operation of Fukuyama No. 4 Blast Furnace," AIME, Ironmaking Proceedings, v. 31, 1972, pp 35-51.

Hollingsworth, W. W., and H. W. Finney, "Design of No. 13 Blast Furnace, Gary Works," AIME, Ironmaking Proceedings, v. 33, 1974, pp 401-415.

Copper electrometallurgy
Balberyszski, T., and A. K. Andersen, "Electrowinning of Copper at High Current Densities," Proc. Australian Institute Min. Met., No. 244, December 1972.

Cooper, J. R., and R. Stern (Cia. Minera de Cananea), "High Current Density Deposition of Continuous Sheet Copper," Annual Meeting, AIME, New York, February 1975.

Eggett, G., W. R. Hopkins, T. W. Garlick, and M. J. Ashley, "High Current Density Electrowinning of Copper from Ultrasonically Agitated Solutions," Annual Meeting, AIME, February 1975.

Ettel, V. A., A. S. Gendron, and B. V. Tilak (International Nickel Co. of Canada), "Electrowinning of Copper at High Current Densities," Annual Meeting, AIME, Chicago, Ill., February 1973.

Harvey, W. W., M. R. Randlett, and K. I. Bangerskis (Kennecott

Copper), "Exploratory Development of Air-Agitation Copper Electrorefining," Annual Meeting, AIME, Dallas, Tex., February 1974.

Harvey, W. W., M. R. Randlett, and K. I. Bangerskis (Kennecott Copper), "Elevated Current Density Electrowinning of Superior Quality Copper from High Acid Electrolyte with Lead/Antimony Anodes," Annual Meeting, AIME, February 1973.

Imai, C., "Application of Periodic Reverse Current for Electrolytic Refining of Copper," EMD Symposium on Electrometallurgy, Cleveland, Ohio, December 1968.

Liekens, Henry A., and Philippe D. Charles, "High Current Density Electrowinning," World Mining, April 1973.

Lindstrom, R., "Production Unit with Current Reversal at the Ronnskar Works of Boliden Aktiebolag, Skelleftehamn, Sweden," Annual Meeting, AIME, February 1975. (Paper was withdrawn.)

Lindstrom, R., and S. Wallden (Boliden AB, Ronnskar Works), "Reverse Current Copper Electrolysis," International Symposium on Hydrometallurgy, AIME, Chicago, Ill., 1973.

McCawley, F. X., P. B. Needham, and G. R. Smith (USBM, College Park), "Electrodeposition of Copper at Current Densities Ranging from 100 to 270 asf in a Channel Cell," Annual Meeting, AIME, February 1975.

Owen, M., and J. S. Jacobi (IMI Refiners Ltd.), "High Intensity Refining of Copper at James Bridge," Annual Meeting, AIME, February 1975.

Schlain, David, Frank X. McCawley, and Gerald R. Smith (USBM, College Park), "Electrodeposition of Copper at High Current Densities," Annual Meeting, AIME, February 1974.

Copper oxide hydrometallurgy

Engineering and Mining Journal, "Copper Leaching Expansion Slated for Kennecott's Ray Mines Div.," March 1974, p 38.

——. "Large Chingola Copper Solvent Extraction Plant Seen As Major Advance," July 1973, p 21.

——. "Cyprus Steps Up Expansion and Exploration," July 1974, pp 26-29.

Groves, R. D., T. H. Jeffers, and G. M. Potter. "Leaching Coarse Native Copper Ore with Dilute Ammonium Carbonate Solution," Proc. of the Sol. Mining Symp., 103rd Ann. Meeting, AIME, Dallas, Tex., Feb. 23-28, 1974, Ch. 26, pp 381-389.

Pay Dirt (Bisbee, Ariz.), "ASARCO's New Leaching Plant at Mission in Operation," March 26, 1973, pp 1-3.

——. "Construction Under Way at Twin Buttes Leach Plant," Oct. 29, 1973, p 8.

Shoemaker, R. S., "Ammonia Revival for the Keweenaw," Min. Eng., March 1972, pp 45-47.

Copper smelting technology

Bailey, J. B. W., R. R. Beck, G. D. Hallett, C. Washburn, and A. J. Weddick, "Oxygen Smelting in the Noranda Process," Annual Meeting, AIME, New York, February 1975.

Cole, R. C., "Inspiration's Pollution Controls are First Using Separately Proven Components," Pay Dirt, May 27, 1974, pp 3-19.

Daniele, R. A. and L. H. Jaquay, "Full Scale TBRC Smelting Tests on Copper Concentrates," Annual Meeting, AIME, Dallas, Tex., February 1974.

Dayton, S., "Inspiration's Design for Clean Air," E/MJ, June 1974, pp 85-96.

Ethem, M. Y., "Black Sea Copper Operates Mines, Mills, and Smelter," World Mining, September 1974, pp 52-55.

Fujii, T., M. Ando, and Y. Fujiwara, "Copper Smelting by Flash Furnace at Saganoseki Smelter and Refinery," MMIJ-AIME Joint Meeting (Tokyo), May 1972.

Harkki, S. U. and J. T. Juusela, "New Developments in Outokumpu Flash Smelting Method," Annual Meeting AIME, February 1974.

Itakura, K., H. Ikeda, and M. Goto, "Double Expansion of Onahama Smelter and Refinery," Annual Meeting, AIME, February 1974.

Juusela, J., S. Harkki, and B. Andersson, "Outokumpu Flash Smelting and Its Energy Requirement," Instit. of Gas Technol. Symp., Chicago, Ill., December 1974.

Kitamura, T., T. Shibata, and S. Tanaka, "Flash Smelting at Tamano Smelter, Hibi Kyodo Smelting Co. Ltd.," Annual Meeting, AIME, Chicago, Ill., February 1973.

Mackey, P. J., G. C. McKerrow, and P. Tarassoff, "Minor Elements in the Noranda Process," Annual Meeting, AIME, New York, February 1975.

Mining Magazine, "Smelting at Harjavalta," May 1973, pp 368-377.

Ogura, T., K. Fukushima, and S. Kimura, "Process Control with Computer in Toyo Copper Smelter," Sumitomo Metal Mining Co. Ltd., 1974, 26 pp.

Okazoe, T., T. Kato, and K. Murao, "The Development of Flash Smelting Process at Ashio Copper Smelter, Furukawa Mining Co. Ltd.," Pyrometallurgical Processes in Nonferrous Metallurgy Symp., AIME, November 1965.

Pay Dirt (Bisbee, Ariz.), "Construction on Phelps Dodge's Hidalgo Copper Smelter Passes Half-way Mark," Sept. 23, 1974.

Suzuki, T., Mitsubishi Metal Corp. Continuous Copper Smelting Project, Manager; private communication in November 1974 with G. Potter and M. Hayashi.

Suzuki, T., I. Ohyama, and T. Shibazaki, "Computer Control in Mitsubishi Continuous Copper Smelting and Converting Process," Annual Meeting, AIME, Dallas, Tex., February 1974.

Torii, T., J. Minoura, and K. Sata, "Development and Improvement of the Flash Smelting Furnace Operation at the Kosaka Smelter of the Dowa Mining Co., Ltd.," First Internat. Flash Smelting Cong. (Finland), October 1972.

Treilhard, D. G., "Copper—State of the Art," E/MJ, April 1973.

Worner, H. K., and B. S. Andrews, "Integrated Smelting-Converting-Slag Cleaning in a Single Furnace," Annual Meeting, AIME, February 1974.

Wrampe, P., and E. E. Nollmann, "Oxygen Utilization in the Copper Reverberatory Furnace: Theory and Practice," Annual Meeting, AIME, February 1974.

Yasuda, M., "Recent Developments of Copper Smelting at Hitachi Smelter," Annual Meeting, AIME, February 1974.

Copper sulphide hydrometallurgy

Dresher, W. H., "Chemical Processing," Min. Eng., v. 27, No. 2, pp 58-60.

Engineering and Mining Journal, "Hecla Zeroes in on Lakeshore Copper Project's Completion Date," August 1973, pp 21-22.

——. "Inspiration Aids in Development of Dichromate Leach Processing Steps," May 1974, pp 73, 90.

Griffith, W. A., H. E. Day, T. S. Jordan, and V. C. Nyman, "Development of the Roast-Leach-Electrowinning Process for Lakeshore," Int. Symp. on Hydrometallurgy, AIME, Chicago, Ill., Feb. 26-March 1, 1973.

Habashi, F., "Action of Nitric Acid on Chalcopyrite," Trans. Soc. Min. Eng., AIME, v. 254, No. 3, 1973, pp 224-228.

Haskett, P. R., D. J. Bauer, and R. E. Lindstrom, "Copper Recovery From Chalcopyrite by a Roast-Leach Procedure," TPR 67, March 1973, 12 pp.

Kruesi, P. R., "Cymet Copper Reduction Process," Min. Cong. J., September 1974, pp 22-23.

Kruesi, P. R., E. S. Allen, and S. L. Lake, "Inventor Developers Explain How Cymet Process Works," Pay Dirt, Oct. 23, 1972.

Kuhn, M. C., and N. Arbiter (Anaconda Co.), "Recovery of Copper From Sulfide Minerals," Ger. Offen 2,311,285 (C1 C22b), Sept. 13, 1973. US Appl. 232,454, March 7, 1972, 42 pp.

Pay Dirt (Bisbee, Ariz.), "Arbiter Plant, First of Its Kind, Begins Production," Oct. 28, 1974, p 26.

——. "Schedule Arbiter Tests for Polish Copper Concentrates," Oct. 28, 1974, p 26.

Prater, S. D. and P. B. Queneau, "Nitric Acid Process for Recovering Metal Values From Sulfide Ore Materials Containing Iron Sulfides," U.S. Pat. 3,793,429, Feb. 19, 1974.

Shanz, R., and T. M. Morris, "Dichromate Process Demonstrated for Leaching of Copper Sulfide Concentrates," E/MJ, May 1974, pp 71-72.

Shirts, M. B., P. A. Bloom, and W. A. McKinney, "Double Roast-Leach-Electrowinning Process for Chalcopyrite Concentrate," BuMines RI 7996, 1975, 33 pp.

Shirts, M. B., J. K. Winter, P. A. Bloom and G. M. Potter, "Aqueous Reduction of Chalcopyrite Concentrate with Metals," BuMines RI 7953, 1974, 18 pp.

Crushing and grinding

Amsden, M. P., "Review of Recent Developments in the Field of Mineral Processing," Can. Min. Met. Bull., September 1974,

Atkins, A. R., A. L. Hinde, P. J. D. Lloyd, and J. G. MacKay, "The Control of Milling Circuits," Journ. S. Af. Inst. Min. Met., June 1974, pp 388-395

Australian Mining, "Outsize Froth Pumps for Bougainville Copper," October 1974, p 6.

Bradley, A. A., A. J. Freemantle, and P. J. D. Lloyd, "Developments in Centrifugal Milling," Jour. S. Af. Inst. Min. Met., June 1974, pp 379-387.

Dannenbrink, W. C., "The Status and Potential of Large Grinding Mills," Australian Mining, November 1974, pp 38-41.

Dinsdale, J. D., and Y. Berube, "A Characterization of Hydrodynamics in 700-cu-ft Maxwell Flotation Cell," Can. Metallurgical Quarterly, July-September 1972, pp 507-513.

Engineering and Mining Journal, "Scully Mine—No. 1 Supplier to Canadian Steel Industry," December 1974, p 79.

Harris, C. C., "Impeller Speed, Air, and Power Requirements in Flotation Machine Scale-Up," Int. Jour. Min. Processing, March 1974, pp 51-64.

Hellyer, W. C., "Crushing and Grinding," Mining Eng., February 1974, pp 66-67.

Ironman, R., "Double-Rotor Hammer Mill Doubles Lime Production," Rock Products, July 1974, pp 71-76.

Keys, N. J., R. J. Gordon, and N. F. Peverett, "Photometric Sorting of Ore in a South African Gold Mine," Jour. S. Af. Inst. Min. Met., September 1974, pp 13-21.

Klovers, E. J., "Energy Crisis Spurs Use of Roller Mills," Rock Products, October 1974 pp 47-80.

Lawver, J. E., and D. M. Hopstock, "Wet Magnetic Separation of Weakly Magnetic Minerals," Mineral Science and Engineering, July 1974, pp 154-172.

Lepetic, V. M., "Flotation of Chalcopyrite without Collector After Dry, Autogenous Grinding," Can Min. Met. Bull., June 1974, pp 71-77.

Mining Magazine (London), "Balls or Pebbles for Grinding," September 1974, pp 239-240.

——. "Chrome Mining in Finland," October 1974, pp 287-293.

——. "Euboean Magnesite Mining and Deadburning in Greece," February 1974, pp 111-117.

——. "Nacimiento," April 1973, pp 226-235.

——. "Large Volume Flotation Cells," September 1974, p 229.

——. "Ring and Ball Type Mills Show Increased Usage in Hard Ore Grinding Installations," November 1974, pp 387-389.

Pickett, D. E., and E. G. Joe, "Water Recycling Experience in Canadian Mills," Trans. Soc. Min. Eng. AIME, September 1974, pp 230-234.

Rao, S. R., "Surface Forces in Flotation," Mineral Science and Engineering, January 1974, pp 45-53.

Schwedes, W. H., and E. L. Owen, "How to Choose Electric Drives for Large Grinding Mills," E/MJ, December 1973, pp 86-91.

Shoemaker, R. S., "Mineral Processing in 1973," Min. Cong. Jour., February 1974, pp 24-29.

Skillings, D.N., "C.V.R.D.'s Iron Ore Mining and Processing Operations at Itabira," Skillings' Min. Rev., Nov. 30, 1974, pp 6-12.

Skillings' Mining Review, "Wet and Dry Grinding Topic of Technical Meeting," May 4, 1974, pp 18, 19.

Smith, R. W., and N. Trivedi, "Variation of Point of Zero Charge of Oxide Minerals as a Function of Aging Time in Water," Trans. Soc. Min. Eng. AIME, March 1974, pp 69-74.

Spencer, A. G., "Electric Drives for Large Grinding Mills," Can Min. Met. Bull., October 1972, pp 73-79.

Direct reduction of iron ore

American Metal Market, "Cost Figures for Armco Plant," Sept. 12, 1974, p 3.

Brown, J. W., D. L. Campbell, A. J. Saxton, and J. W. Carr, Jr., "FIOR—The Esso Fluid Iron Ore Direct Reduction Process," AIME, Ironmaking Proc., v. 24, 1965, pp 61-66.

Engineering and Mining Journal, "McKee Awarded Contract to Build First FIOR Plant," October 1973, p 38.

Journal of Metals, "Armco's Innovative Electric Furnace Practice," November 1974, pp 43-44.

Rollinger, R., "Steel Via Direct Reduction Iron and Steel-making," I&SM, January 1975, pp 10-17.

Skilling, David N., Jr., "Korf Industries and Midrex Dedicate New Facilities," Skillings' Min. Rev. Dec. 28, 1974, pp 1, 8-11.

Electric furnaces and electro-slag refining

Astier, J. E., and J. Antoine, "Developments in Electric Steelmaking," Ironmaking and Steelmaking Quarterly, No. 1, 1974,

Brown, J. W., editor, Electric Arc Furnace World Wide Newsletter, December 1974.

Duckworth, W. E., and G. Hoyle, **Electro-slag Refining**, Chapman and Hall Ltd., London, 1969, 178 pp.

Iron and Steel Engineering, "Developments in the Iron and Steel Industry During 1974," January 1975, pp D34-36.

Klein, H. J., and J. W. Pridgeon, "Effective Electroslag Remelting of Superalloys," Superalloys-Processing, Proc. of Second Internat. Conf., Metals and Ceramics Inf. Center Report 72-10, Battelle Columbus Laboratories, 1972, pp B1-B26.

McManus, George J., "Electric Steelmaking Assumes New Role," Iron Age, April 1, 1974, pp 45-56.

Wooding, P. J., and J. M. Mowat, "An Approach to the Production of Large Forging Ingots by Electroslag Refining," Steel Times, January 1973, pp 67-70.

Froth flotation

Canadian Mining Journal, "Flotation Machines . . . The Bigger the Better," June 1974, pp 59-62.

Kennecott Copper Corp, "Combined Chemical Treatment and Flotation Process for Recovering Relatively High Grade Molybdenite From Off-Grade or Low-Grade Ore Materials," US Patent. Abs. in E/MJ, October 1974, p 125.

Fisher, E., "Froth Flotation Beneficiation of Chalcopyrite or Other Copper Sulfide Ore Associated With Pyrite," US Patent No. 3,827,557, Aug. 6, 1974.

Fuerstenau, M. C., B. M. Wakawa, R. K. Price, and R. D. Wellic, "Toxicity of Selected Sulfhydryl Collectors to Rainbow Trout," SME/AIME Trans., December 1975, pp 337-341.

Gale, N. L., M. G. Hardie, J. Whitfield, and P. Marcellus, "The Impact of Lead Mine and Mill Effluent on Aquatic Life," Proc. Univ. of Minn. 35th Ann. Min. Symp., Duluth, Minn., Jan. 17-18, 1974.

Grannen, E. A., "Froth Flotation Beneficiation of Phosphate Rock," US Patent No. 3,768,646, Oct. 30, 1973.

Grannen, E. A., "Improved Amine Reagent For Use in Froth Flotation Beneficiation of Phosphate Rock or Other Siliceous Ores," US Patent No. 3,817,972, June 18, 1974.

Haig, L. D., "Sea Water Flotation," Can Min. Jour., June 1974, pp 68-70.

Huiatt, J. L., G. M. Potter, and R. B. Tippin, "Potassium Salt Flotation From Great Salt Lake Evaporites," AIME Preprint 75-B-33.

Kaneko, M., "Mitsui Segregation Process Treats Peruvian Copper Oxides," E/MJ, December 1974, pp 61-64.

LaBelle, R. J., "Recent Cleveland-Cliffs Experience in the Monitoring Analysis and Control of Effluent Water Quality," Proc. Univ. of Minn. 35th Ann. Min. Symp., Duluth, Minn., Jan. 17-18, 1974,

Lepetic, V. M., "Flotation of Chalcopyrite Without Collector After Dry Autogenous Grinding," CIM Bull., June 1974, pp 71-77.

Mathieu, G. I., and R. W. Bruce, "Getting the Talc Out of Molybdenite Ores," Can. Min. Jour., June 1974, pp 75-77.

Mikkelborg, E., "Looking Over the Black Angel's Shoulder," Can. Min. Jour., August 1974, pp 30-36.

Mining Journal (London), "Development of Larger Flotation Cells," July 19, 1974, p 55.

—— "Flotation at Limni," Feb. 22, 1974, p 136.

—— "Pollution Fine Particle Removal Process," July 5, 1974, p 11.

—— "Solidifying Harmful Effluents," Dec. 14, 1973, p 491.

Mining Magazine, "Large Volume Flotation Cells," September 1974, p 229.

—— "Liquid Waste Into Solid Fill," March 1974, p 221.

Nahahama, T., "Treatment of Effluent From the Kamioka Concentrator by Flotation Techniques, Including the Development of the Nagahm Flotation Machine," CIM Bull., April 1974, pp 79-89.

Pickett, D. E., and E. G. Joe, "Water Recycling Experience in Canadian Mills," SME/AIME Trans. September 1974, pp 230-235.

Smith, S. J., "Froth Flotation of Kaolin," US Patent No. 3,744,630, July, 1973.

Veith, D. L., "Superconcentration of Commercial Magnetic Taconite Concentrates by Cationic Flotation," BuMines RI 7852, 1974

Weimer, D. R., "An Improved Collector Reagent For Use in the Froth Flotation of Copper Oxide Ore," US Patent No. 3,819,048, June 25, 1974.

Werneke, M. F., "Froth Flotation Recovery of Molybdenite From Copper Sulphide Ore," US Patent No. 3,788,467, Jan. 29, 1974.

Fuel substitutes

American Metal Market, "Formed Coke From Subbituminous Coal," Dec. 30, 1974, p 16.

—— "Republic Mill Likely Site of Coal Gasification Plant," Feb. 5, 1975, p 3.

Frommer, Donald W., and John C. Nigro, "The Bureau of Mines Looks at Coal Firing for Induration of Iron Ore Pellets," 48th Ann. Meeting, Minn. Section, AIME, Duluth, Minn., Jan. 15, 1975.

—— "Practical Aspects of Coal Firing in the Induration of Iron Ore Pellets," Iron Making Conf., AIME, Toronto, Ont., April 1975.

Holgate, J. K., and P. H. Pinchbeck, "Use of Formed Coke: BSC Experience 1971/1972," Jour. of the Iron and Steel Inst., August 1973, pp 547-566.

Journal of the Iron and Steel Institute, "A Strategy for Nuclear Steelmaking," August 1973, p 11.

Leighton, G. P., and M. A. deKlaver, "Coal Firing of Dravo-Lurgi Traveling Grates," Annual Meeting, Minn. Section, AIME, Duluth, Minn., Jan. 15, 1975.

Mining Magazine, "Smelting at Harjavalta," May 1973, pp 368-377.

Quarm, T. A. A., "Submerged Smelting of Lead Merits Longer Look," E/MJ, July 1974, pp 60-61.

Skillings' Mining Review, "Iron Ore Pellet Shipments in North America 1955 to 1980," Aug. 24, 1974, pp 1, 6-9.

Gold and silver metallurgy

Aplan, F. F., W. A. McKinney, and A. D. Pernichele, "Heap Leaching Practice at the Carlin Gold Mining Co., Carlin, Nev.," Solution Mining Symp., AIME, 1974.

Guay, W. J., and D. C. Peterson, "Recovery of Gold from Carbonaceous Ores at Carlin, Nevada," SME-AIME Trans., March 1973,

Hall, Kenneth B., "Homestake Carbon-In-Pulp Process," Annual Meeting, AMC, Las Vegas, Nev. 1974.

Hall, Kenneth B., "Homestake Uses Carbon-In-Pulp to Recover Gold from Slimes," World Mining, November 1974.

Heinen, H. J., D. G. Peterson, and R. E. Lindstrom, "Silver Extraction from Marginal Resources," Annual Meeting, AIME, 1975.

Heinen, H. J., and Bernard Porter, "Experimental Leaching of Gold from Mine Waste," BuMines RI 7250, 1969.

Laxen, P. A., "Some Developments in Gold Extraction from Witwatersrand Ores," Annual Meeting, AIME, 1975.

Merwin, R. W., G. M. Potter, and H. J. Heinen, "Heap Leaching of Gold Ores in Northeastern Nevada," Annual Meeting, AIME, Washington, D.C., February 1969. Preprint No. 69-AS-79.

Potter, G. M., "Recovering Gold from Stripping Waste and Ore by Percolation Cyanide Leaching," BuMines TPR-20, December 1969.

Potter, G. M., and H. B. Salisbury, "Innovations in Gold Metallurgy," Min. Cong. Jour., July 1974, pp 54-57.

Ross, J. R., H. B. Salisbury, and G. M. Potter, "Pressure Stripping Gold from Activated Carbon," Annual Meeting, AIME, Chicago, Ill., 1973.

Salisbury, H. B., S. J. Hussey, F. M. Howell Jr., and G. M. Potter, "Silver Recovery from Flotation Tails by Carbon-In-Pulp Cyanidation," Annual Meeting, AIME, 1975.

Scheiner, B. J., R. E. Lindstrom, W. J. Guay, and D. G. Peterson, "Extraction of Gold from Carbonaceous Ores; Pilot Plant Studies," BuMines RI 7597, 1972.

Scheiner, B. J., R. E. Lindstrom, and T. A. Henrie, "Processing Refractory Carbonaceous Ores for Gold Recovery," Jour. of Metals, March 1971, pp 37-40.

High intensity magnetic separation

Bartnik, J. A., W. H. Zabel, and D. M. Hopstock, "Production of Iron Ore Superconcentrates by High Intensity Wet Magnetic Separation," to be published in Internat. Jour. of Miner. Processing (1975).

Hein, R. A., "Superconductivity: Large-Scale Applications," Sci., v. 185, No. 4147, 1974, pp 211-222.

Kelland, D. R., and E. Maxwell, "Pilot Investigation of High Gradient Magnetic Separation of Oxidized Taconites," Annual Meeting, AIME, 1975.

Lawver, J. E., "Iron Ore Beneficiation Process," US Patent No. 3,337,328, 1967.

Lawver, J. E., R. R. Beebe, and R. M. Hays, "New Methods for Beneficiating Semitaconite," Min. Cong. Jour., April 1968.

Lawver, J. E., and D. M. Hopstock, "Wet Magnetic Separation of Weakly Magnetic Minerals," Miner. Sci. Eng. v 6 No. 3. 1974.

Lawver, J. E., J. L. Wright, and H. R. Kokal, "The Behavior of Mesabi Iron and Silicate Minerals in 20-Kilogauss Magnetic Fields," SME-AIME Trans., v. 241, 1968, pp 194-203.

Stekly, Z. J. J., G. Y. Robinson, Jr., and G. J. Powers, "Magnetic Processing: Commercial Supercon?," Cryogenics and Industrial Gases, July-August 1973.

Iron and steelmaking

Daellenbach, C. B., W. M. Mahan, and J. J. Drost, "Utilization of Automobile and Ferrous Refuse Scrap in Cupola Iron Production," Proc. of 4th Mining Waste Utilization Symp., Chicago, Ill., May 7-8, 1974, pp 417-423.

Foundry Management and Technology, "1975 Outlook: 4.2 Percent More Castings," January 1975, pp 26-30.

—— "Recuperator Reduces Cupola Costs," October 1974, pp 88-89.

—— "Technical Highlights of 78th Casting Congress," June 1974, pp 36-42.

Heine, J. J., AFS/CMI Electric Melting Conference, Foundry Management and Technology, January 1975, pp 44-52.

Journal of Metals, "Foundry Arc Furnace," November 1974, pp 47-49.

Kaiser Engineers L-D Process Newsletter, "Six Hundred Million Tons of L-D Capacity by 1980," Jan. 20, 1975, pp 1-8.

Ostrowski, E. J., "Recycling of Solid Waste Ferrous Scrap in the Blast Furnace," 35th Ann. Min. Symp. and 47th Ann. Meeting of Minn. Sec. AIME, Jan. 16-18, 1974, pp 58-64.

Scrap Age, "Tin Cans—New Scrap Source for Foundries," August 1974, p 48.

Iron ore beneficiation

Bartlett, R. W., and T. H. Chin, "On-Stream Particle Size Analyses from Continuous Measurements of Pulp Density with Nuclear Gages," Trans. SME-AIME, December 1974, p 323.

Engineering and Mining Journal, "North American Iron Ore: Launching a Rescue Mission for a Steel-Short Economy," November 1974, pp 83-162.

—— "North American Iron Ore (Part 2); Target: New Technology to Improve Economics of Iron Ore Beneficiation," December 1974, pp 65-90.

Hall, A. W., J. L. Konchesky, and R. F. Stewart, "Continuous Monitor of Coal by Neutron Moisture Meter," BuMines RI 7807, 1973.

Krukienicz, R., and J. Laskowski, "Development of Magnetizing Alkali Leaching Process for Concentration of Siderite Ores," Proc. 10th Internat. Min. Processing Cong., London, 1973.

Mining World (London), Mining Annual Review—1973, "Minerals Processing," June 1973, p 207.

—— Mining Annual Review—1974, "Iron Ore," June 1974, p 75.

Rao, S. R., and L. L. Sirois, "Study on Surface Chemical Characteristics in Gravity Separation," Annual Meeting, CIM, Vancouver, B.C., April 1974.

Rice, D. A., and R. I. Stone, "Influence of Plant Water Chemistry on the Strength of Unfired Pellets," Trans. SME-AIME, March 1972, pp 1-6.

Veith, D. L., "Superconcentration of Commercial Magnetic Taconite Concentrates by Cationic Flotation," BuMines RI 7852, 1974.

Weigel, R. L., Mineral Resources Research Center, State Research Program, Proc. 35th Ann. Min. Symp. and 47th Annual Meeting of Minn. Sec., AIME, January 1974, pp 116-118.

Lead and zinc metallurgy

Kellogg, H. H., "New Copper Extraction Processes," Jour. of Metals, v. 26, No. 8, p 21, 1974.

Meisel, G. M., "New Generation Zinc Plants, Design Features and Effect on Cost," Jour. of Metals, v. 26, No. 8, pp 25-32, 1974.

Queneau, P. E. and R. Schuhmann, "The Q-S Oxygen Process," Jour. of Metals, v. 26, No. 8, pp 14-16, 1974.

Potash milling and refining

Brogoitti, W. B., and F. P. Howald (American Cyanamid Co.), "Selective Flocculation and Flotation of Slimes from Sylvinite Crude Salt," US Pat. 3,805,951, April 23, 1974.

Huiatt, J. L., R. B. Tippin, and G. M. Potter, "Potassium Salt Flotation from Great Salt Lake Evaporites," Annual Meeting, AIME, New York, February 1975. SME Preprint 75-B-33.

Jackson, Daniel Jr., "Solution Mining Pumps New Life into Cane Creek Potash Mine," E/MJ, July 1973, pp 59-69.

Knudsen, K. D. (Superfos A/C), "Ion Exchange Makes Chlorine-Free NKP Cheaper," Phosphorus and Potassium, January-February 1973, pp 42-43.

Phosphorus and Potassium, "Pennzoil Near to Commercial Production of Potassium Phosphates," November-December 1973, pp 44-49.

Smelter gas cleaning technology

Ando, Jumpei, "Status of Flue Gas Desulfurization Technology in Japan," Symp. on Flue Gas Desulfurization, sponsored by Control Systems Laboratory, US Environmental Protection Agency, Atlanta, Ga., November 1974, 24 pp.

—— "Utilizing and Disposing of Sulfur Products from Flue Gas Desulfurization Processes in Japan," Symp. on Flue Gas Desulfurization, 1974, 14 pp.

Beychok, Milton R., "Coping with SO^2," Chem. Eng., Oct. 21, 1974, pp 79-85.

McKinney, W. A., W. I. Nissen, D. A. Elkins, and J. B. Rosenbaum, "Pilot Plant Testing of the Citrate Process for SO_2 Emission Control," Symp. on Flue Gas Desulfurization, 1974, 19 pp.

Pay Dirt (Bisbee, Ariz.), "Test Plant Nears Operation," Jan. 27, 1975, p 46.

Smelter Control Research Association Inc., "Engineering Evaluation of Possible High-Efficiency Soluble Scrubbing Systems for Removal of Sulfur Dioxide from Copper Smelter Reverberatory Furnace and Like Flue Gases," BuMines Contract No. SO133044, March 25, 1974, 100 pp.

—— "The Removal of Sulfur Dioxide from Copper Reverberatory Furnace Gas by Wet-Limestone Scrubbing," 77 pp.

Uranium processing

Aplan, F. F., et al eds, Solution Min. Symp., Annual Meeting, AIME, Dallas, Tex., February 1974.

Catopreso, F. E. and W. P. Badger, "Hydrogen Peroxide Precipitation of Uranium," Trans. AIME-SME, December 1973, p 285.

Chiu, Y. S., "Recovery of Heavy Metals by Microbes," Thesis (PhD), Univ. of Western Ontario, London, Ont. Nat. Library of Canada, Ottawa, 1973.

Fitch, J. L., and B. C. Hurd, "Method of Leaching Subsurface Minerals In Situ," US Pat. 3,309,141, March 14, 1967.

Gardner, J., and M. I. Ritchie, "Leaching of Uranium Ore In Situ," US Pat. 3,309,140, March 14, 1967.

Grimes, M. E., "Rio Algom Investigations into the Preconcentration of Uranium Ores," Trans. AIME-SME, 1973.

Himsley, A., "Separation of Metals in Aqueous Solutions," Annual Meeting of Can. Miner. Producers, Ottawa, Canada, January 1975.

Mining Engineering, "Hydrometallurgy is Key in Winning U_3O_8," August 1974, pp 26-27.

Rhodes, V. W., "Uranium Solution Mining Process," US Pat. 3,792,903, Feb. 19, 1974.

Schwartz, W., "Use of Microorganisms in the Leaching Process," Metallurgy (Germany), 1973, v. 27, No. 12, pp 1202-1206.

Shabbir, M. and K. E. Tame, "Hydrogen Peroxide Precipitation of Uranium," BuMines RI 7931, 1974, 12 pp.

Traut, D. E., I. L. Nichols, and D. C. Seidel, "Design Criteria for Uranium Ion Exchange in a Fluidized System," Annual Meeting, AIME, New York, February 1975. SME preprint 75-B-116.

Processing: Responding to new demands

Lane White, Managing editor

Pressures for change have intensified at minerals processing operations in recent years, and processing engineers have responded by developing a continuing stream of new technnology. Some of this technology has already moved into commercial production. Some of it is still advancing in that direction.

The stimuli for change in minerals processing comprise a familiar list of ongoing concerns: environmental controls, declining ore grades, inflation, energy shortages, and financing difficulties. Strategies to cope with these problems range from truly new processes to scale-ups in equipment size to. modifications of long-established processes, motivated by a desire for increased efficiency.

The extractive side of minerals processing has experienced the sharpest changes. In copper, reverberatory-and-converter technology still accounts for the bulk of US smelter production. However, Kennecott is installing a new continuous Noranda-process reactor at its Utah smelter, Phelps Dodge has adopted flash furnace technology for its new smelter in New Mexico, and three other US copper smelters have installed electric furnaces. Also in copper, hydrometallurgical processes account for an increasingly important share of US production and further gains can be expected. In zinc, a number of US smelters were shut down over the past several years because they could not be brought into compliance with pollution control laws. Now, National Zinc is bringing a new electrolytic zinc plant into production in Oklahoma, and New Jersey Zinc and Union Miniere are jointly building a plant in Tennessee.

At beneficiation plants, changes have generally been less dramatic. Equipment scale-up has not yet peaked. advances are regularly reported in instrumentation, and more economic materials handing systems are sought. Cleveland-Cliffs' new Tilden iron ore operation on Michigan's Upper Peninsula is an important exception — incorporating a new process that opens the way for development of large nonmagnetic iron reserves.

Rising costs dictate changes in mill design

CONTINUING EFFORTS to maintain profitable operations in spite of rising costs have influenced recent mill design more strongly than any changes in process methodology. The introduction of ever larger milling and flotation equipment and the development of simplified flowsheets are the most prominent cost-cutting trends, along with increasing use of process instrumentation.

A Bechtel study, "Mill Design for the Seventies," presented at the AIME Centennial meeting in 1971, suggested that a mill incorporating the largest available proven equipment and the latest improvements in plant design (Fig. 1) can be built at 68% of the constructed cost of a more conventional mill.[2] The capital cost estimates were based on a hypothetical 20,000-tpd copper concentrator in the southwestern US. The modern mili would use two 4,500-hp ball mills and 500-cu-ft rougher and scavenger flotation cells, while the more conventional mill would incorporate six 1,500-hp mills and 100-cu-ft rougher scavenger cells. Cleaner and recleaner cells in the modern mill would be 120-cu-ft units, while 50-cu-ft cells would be used in the conventional mill.

"Older plants of comparable size were forced to use multiple processing lines because of limitations imposed by the equipment available," the Bechtel study noted, "but there is no justification for continuing this practice in a modern plant. The commonly held idea that multiple mill lines will increase plant availability is simply not true; the fact is that a 20,000-tpd plant is a 20,000-tpd plant regardless of the number of process lines employed.

"The use of large equipment reduces the plant capital cost, both in terms of process equipment cost and in reduced costs for foundations, buildings, piping, electrical requirements, and instrumentation. It also will reduce operating costs, although perhaps less dramatically."

Other design innovations suggested by the study included elimination of unnecessary building structures and mounting of large flotation cells on grade (Fig. 1). By the 1980s, the Bechtel study speculated, "We can expect to be faced with grinding mills drawing tens of thousands of horsepower, flotation cells of several thousand cubic feet capacity and other equipment of commensurate size."

US manufacturers are now experimenting with prototype 1,000-cu-ft flotation cells, and grinding mills drawing 3,500 hp are reported to be on the drawing boards.

Simplicity and compactness in mill design are emphasized in a report by R. L. Bullock on the mine-plant design philosophy of St. Joe Minerals at its New Lead Belt operations in Missouri.[3] Furthermore, St. Joe design engineers have not forgotten the elementary principles of ore flow: "Namely, 1) whenever possible utilize gravity to move the ore; 2) when it is moving, keep it moving; 3) move it as few times as possible." The importance of these principles is emphasized in Fig. 2, which illustrates the ore flows of two mills handling the same type of ore and producing the same type of products. The simplified ore flow represents St. Joe's Fletcher or Brushy Creek mills; the other flow is characteristic of mills built 50 years ago.

The St. Joe report outlines these advantages in its compact, simple flow design:

1) Since there is less material and machinery in use, less space is wasted and first cost is less.

2) With less operating machinery and less rehandling and recycling of ore, the costs of maintenance, power, and cleanup are reduced.

3) All parts of a compact plant can be run and seen from the operating floor, and only one man is required to monitor the milling operation.

4) The mill can be automated more cheaply and its operation more easily supervised; therefore, the cost of supervision is less.

Process controls can cut costs, boost recovery

The desire to reduce mill labor costs and improve process economics has prompted installation of a variety of computer-controlled instrumentation in new minerals processing plants. (See Fig. 3 for a simplified flotation control system.) Dr. Harold W. Smith of Coopers & Lybrand Associates Ltd. cites the development of X-ray fluorescent spectrometers to continuously measure the chemical composition of flotation process streams and reliable, relatively inexpensive minicomputers as key developments enabling mill superintendents to achieve better operating results.[5] While process control systems represent a significant investment, Smith states, returns on the investment can take various forms:

■ Reduced costs and/or lower capital investment for ore blending.

■ Improved recovery of ore values and/or improved product grade, resulting in reduced shipping and smelting costs.

■ Increased process throughput.

■ Reduced operating costs through savings in reagents and through more productive employment of mill personnel.

"In the project's execution, strong coordination between the mill personnel, designers, and supplies is needed," Smith cautions. "Careful attention must be paid to adequate documentation and to operating and maintenance training. Special care in scheduling must be taken to ensure that an accurately calibrated X-ray spectrometric system is achieved at an early point in the project. Otherwise, the technology is sufficiently mature that no unusual technical problems will arise."

However, automation is not always accepted readily by operating personnel. In a survey of the reaction to automation at a number of mills, both in the US and at Canadian and overseas operations, James W. White of the University of Arizona found that "there is an explicit feeling of dissatisfaction in some quarters where system performance has not met contractor and vendor promises."[6] Some problems have arisen from design oversights, White found, while others seem to occur because of improper and inadequate attention to operations after startup. Lack of vendor support after startup can also lead to problems. However, when asked to rate specific control loop performance, the majority of respondents in the survey gave their instrumentation "excellent" marks. (See table.)

Texasgulf keeps instrumentation simple

Texasgulf's highly automated Ecstall concentrator near Timmins, Ont., is the site of successful process automation, as reported by M. P. Amsden, C. Chapman, and M. G. Reading in 1975, at the 13th International Symposium on the Application of Computers and Mathematics for Decision Making in the Mineral Industries, Clausthall-Zellerfeld, West Germany.[7] The Texasgulf ores are processed by selective flotation in three circuits. The plant's on-stream X-ray analysis system was recently automated further by the addition of computer control of reagents for two copper-zinc flotation circuits. The computer programs, utilizing optimum seeking methods and smelter contract terms, have increased copper recovery by 1.1% and zinc recovery

Fig. 1—Mill design for the 1970s

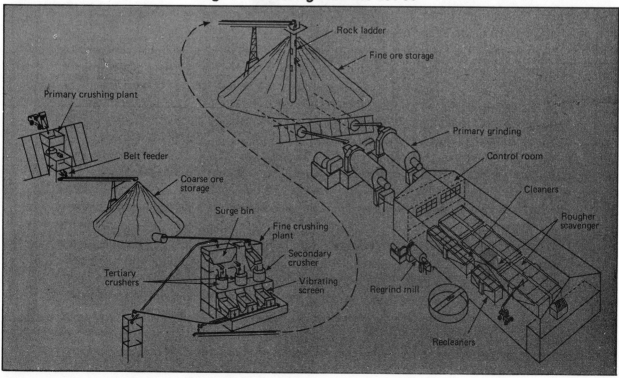

by 1.4%, and have reduced reagent costs by 16%. Although not expected, copper and zinc concentrate grades were improved slightly as well. The company's basic approach to computer control has been "to keep it simple."

The Texasgulf control system was outlined as follows:

"The operation is controlled closely in all sections of the concentrator. Most of the crushing, grinding, and flotation equipment is started from individual operating panels in central control. Crushing is monitored by closed circuit television, and nuclear gauges are used to indicate bin and chute levels. Set-point control is used to regulate rod mill feed rates. Cyclone overflow pulp densities are controlled by nuclear gauges. Flotation pulp levels are regulated automatically. Assays of flotation products are provided by two ARL on-stream X-ray analyzers and a Honeywell model H-21 computer. The H-21 computer also monitors mill bearing temperatures and provides logs of shift and daily tons crushed and milled and of concentrate loaded out. . . .

"Of prime importance to flotation control is the sam-pling system incorporating the on-stream X-ray analyzers and the H-21 computer. The process streams to be sampled pass through conditioners equipped with powerful 'Lightnin' mixers. Vertical pumps mounted on top of the tanks deliver approximately 50 gpm of slurry to small constant-head tanks located in a sample room above the X-ray analyzers. The head tanks overflow through Denver samplers, which take cuts every 20 min. These cuts are filtered continuously and collected every 24 hr for chemical assay. Where required, pH is sensed by electrodes immersed in

Fig. 2—Comparative mill flows

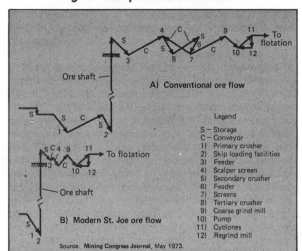

Source: Mining Congress Journal, May 1973.

Fig. 3—Simplified flotation control system

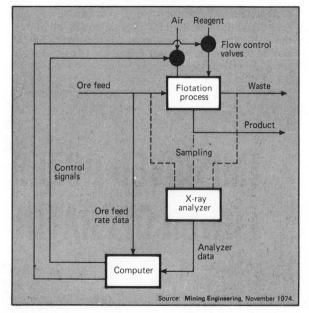

Source: Mining Engineering, November 1974.

General criteria for a large concentrator

In a review of "Basic Design Problems for a Large Concentrator," Wayne D. Gould, metallurgical superintendent at the Miami operations of Cities Service Co., notes: "Material handling is the basic problem for a large concentrator. A 40,000-tpd plant requires the processing of nearly 28 tons per min of ore with the use of 20,000 gal of water per min. The combined pulp flow [per minute] is a stream 36 in. in diameter by 425 ft long. Planning should therefore minimize the lifting of material, minimize the distance between steps in the process, and use the highest possible pulp density in every step following the introduction of water."[4]

The first step on a new project, Gould states, is to lay out the general processing criteria. His impressively long listing of criteria for Cities Service's Pinto Valley project included:

Primary crushing
Daily feed rate
Operating hours per day
Operating days per year
Feed size
Product size

Coarse ore storage
Live storage
Total storage

Fine crushing
Daily feed rate
Operating hours per day
Operating days per year
Feed size
Product size

Fine ore storage
Live storage
Total storage

Concentrator
Hourly feed rate
Yearly feed
Service factor
Feed size
Product size
Work index
Grinding energy per ton
Speed of grinding unit
Classification method
Rougher feed, % solids
Rougher flotation time, minimum
Rougher flotation time, design
Regrind circuit product
Speed of regrind unit

Cleaner circuit feed
Cleaner flotation time, minimum
Cleaner flotation time, design
Recleaner flotation time, minimum
Recleaner flotation time, design
Scavenger flotation time, minimum
Scavenger flotation time, design

Thickener
Tailings thickener underflow, % solids
Tailings thickener design area, tons per 24 hr
Copper-moly thickener feed, % solids
Copper-moly thickener underflow, % solids
Copper-moly thickener area, tons per 24 hr
Copper thickener feed, % solids
Copper thickener underflow, % solids
Copper thickener area, tons per 24 hr
Copper filter cake, % H_2O
Copper filter loading, lb/sq ft/24 hr maximum
Copper filter loading, lb/sq ft/24 hr design

Copper slurry pipeline
Slurry pipeline daily tonnage
Slurry pipeline length
Slurry pipeline, % solids pumped
Slurry pipeline, ft per sec

Control criteria
Local start-stop of equipment or remote start-stop from a control room
Electrical or pneumatic actuations
Manual or automatic set points
Analog or digital instruments
Human or computer optimization

the head tanks. Approximately 4 gpm flow to the X-ray analyzer.

"Assay data are generated by the H-21 computer from X-ray voltage readings and presented on IBM No. 11C logging typewriters at the central control operator's desk. Copper, lead, zinc, silver and iron assays are available on 15 process streams. For each of three flotation circuits, heads, copper-lead concentrates and tailings, and zinc concentrates and tailings are analyzed. A complete set of assays, ratios of concentrations and recoveries is presented every 12 min for the two copper-zinc circuits and once every 6 min for the silver-lead-zinc circuit. The computer also provides shift and daily averages of these data. Assay type-out availability exceeds 95%."

Cost of implementing the system was expected to total about $122,000.

The Texasgulf presentation included a discussion of the evolution of its control strategies for copper and zinc and a review of metallurgical costs.

ISA sponsors annual instrumentation meeting

Continuing interest in mining process controls has generated an annual symposium on Instrumentation in the Mining and Metallurgy Industries, sponsored by the Instrument Society of America. At the organization's fourth symposium, held in Milwaukee in October 1975, the focal topic was instrumentation and control for crushing and grinding. A second group of papers delivered at the same meeting was directed at "National Concerns and Instrumentation," and covered instrumentation problems in monitoring liquid effluents and gaseous and particulate emissions.[8] The ISA plans to develop symposia programs over the next several years that will provide instrumentation technologists with a working library of technical papers focused on a series of application themes. □

Mills seek ways to hold down comminution costs

RISING ENERGY COSTS and the need to process growing tonnages of declining ore grades provide incentives for more efficient size-reduction machinery. Size is being scaled up both for conventional rod and ball mills and for autogenous mills, with some very large units being installed at new and expanding iron ore projects in Minnesota and Michigan.[9] Automatic control systems, improved mill drives, longer-wearing grinding media, and more efficient maintenance procedures are the subject of efforts to increase crushing and grinding productivity.

Autogenous mills have carved out an important niche in the grinding equipment market over the last 10 years. On suitable ores, these mills eliminate grinding media costs. Depending on ore characteristics, autogenous mills may also produce lower percentages of slimes and fines than conventional rod and ball mill units. However, the comparative economics of autogenous and conventional milling must be closely examined in light of the grinding characteristics of individual ores. In one notable instance, Anaconda converted from autogenous to steel grinding at its C. E. Weed concentrator in Butte, Mont., after metallurgical evaluation indicated that tonnage throughput could be increased at a finer flotation feed size by using steel ball mills. Moreover, initial tests showed that the improved grind yielded slight recovery gains in subsequent flotation processing.[10]

Nordberg bills its new Symons 10-ft cone crusher as a major breakthrough in crusher design. The crusher is rated at 3,000 tph in either Short Head or standard models, and two units have been installed in a South African iron ore plant. Advantages cited include lower capital cost per unit of capacity and reduced requirements for building and foundations, power drives, and spare parts inventory.

How to optimize grinding capacity

Optimization of grinding and regrinding capacity in mill design was outlined in a paper by R. J. Brison and R. A. Campbell at the 1972 annual meeting of AIME.[11] These Parsons-Jurden engineers suggest that in future computer-controlled plants, blending of ore to produce a uniform mill feed may be unnecessary if each type of ore can be processed efficiently at its optimum feed rate. The greater the variability of the ore, the greater the potential advantage in such an approach.

In the specific examples used in the paper, it was calculated that optimum grinding of a blended 1% copper ore would cost 6% more and would result in a recovery of 0.6% less copper than separate grinding under optimum conditions of the same total tonnage of 0.5% and 2.0% ores containing the same total amount of copper. In cases where the low grade ore is harder to grind than the higher grade

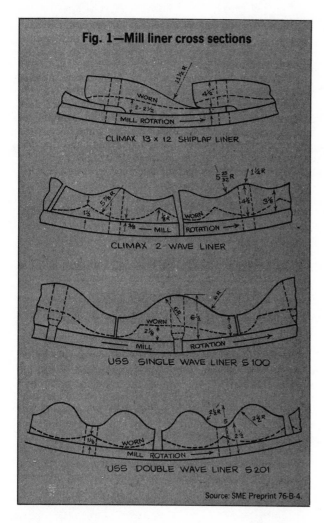

Fig. 1—Mill liner cross sections

CLIMAX 13 x 12 SHIPLAP LINER

CLIMAX 2-WAVE LINER

USS SINGLE WAVE LINER S 100

USS DOUBLE WAVE LINER S 201

Source: SME Preprint 76-B-4.

ore, the advantage of separate processing would be enhanced, suggesting that design should be optimized on a dynamic basis to respond to continuously changing conditions. "Where nature has provided a partial preconcentration of the ore," the authors point out, "perhaps we should take advantage of it, not spend money to undo it."

Such a concept runs somewhat counter to the commonly accepted idea that a steady, smooth, easily controlled operation is the best kind. The authors feel the ultimate resolution of this conflict will depend largely on process control. Improved control systems might allow mill design and operation to take greater advantage of ore variations and equipment flexibility.

"Autogenous and Semi-Autogenous Mill Selection and Design" was discussed by C. A. Rowland Jr. and D. M. Kjos of Allis-Chalmers at the September 1974 meeting of SME.[12] The authors note that many of the first autogenous grinding installations in the US and Canada were used to grind iron ores and produced fewer fines than more conventional circuits. This led to the general belief that autogenous grinding produces less extreme fines than conventional grinding. However, as more autogenous grinding mills were installed for nonferrous ores—especially low-grade copper ores—this idea was found to be incorrect. For some nonferrous ores, autogenous grinding produces an excess of fines and greater surface area than conventional grinding. The explanation may be that production of fines is a function of the grain structure in the ore.

In autogenous grinding, breakage occurs principally along grain boundaries, with little transgranular breakage. So, when studying the feasibility of using autogenous

grinding, the key questions are: 1) will the product be suitable for the next processing step, 2) will the power consumption be economical, and 3) what other considerations (such as abrasiveness of the ore, metal wear reduction, and material handling) are significant?

"In conventional grinding, the size of product can be changed by changing medium size, feed size, feed rate, classifier cut size, etc. The grinding circuit responds to these changes. In autogenous grinding, the ore 'says' how it wants to be ground and the product size that it will produce, and does not change in response to the same factors. With some ores, there are two possible products from an autogenous grinding circuit—a coarse product or a fine product. With other ores, there may only be one product."

Basic operating parameters for autogenous and semiautogenous mill design include mill charge, mill power, total feed conditions (including total mill volumetric flow rate and recirculating load), and the milling circuit flowsheet. Experience indicates that the ball charges used in semiautogenous grinding have generally been most effective in the range of 6% to 10% of the mill volume, including the void spaces between the balls—i.e., ball charge volume based on 290 lb per cu ft.

For fully autogenous grinding, mill drives are usually selected with a slightly oversized rating to allow for variations in ore specific gravity and charge level. For example, if an ore is quite uniform and normal operation is expected to be at a 30% charge, a drive is selected at, perhaps, a 35% charge.

For semiautogenous grinding, the drive is usually selected for both a higher total charge and a higher ball charge than normally expected.

"If a mill is run on a 'constant power' concept, the tonnage will vary depending on the autogenous quality of the ore," the Allis-Chalmers paper states. "It will sometimes be average, sometimes higher and sometimes lower than average, but because of the control concept, this scheme will generally average a higher daily tonnage than the constant tonnage concept because controls are always pushing for maximum tonnage."

Build a better mill liner

Mill liners are a major cost factor in mill operation, and efforts to prolong liner life have met with some success. Rubber liners and lifters have supplanted steel in some operations, and in most cases wear has been reduced. However, one mill reported an approximate 30% increase in ball consumption.

A good mill liner should grind ore to optimum size for liberation, with net tonnage maximized and power cost and ball consumption minimized, Climax Molybdenum Co. materials engineer David J. Dunn told a meeting of the National Western Mining Conference in 1973. The liner should be cheap, long lasting, easy to install, easy to remove, and it should be worn paper-thin when it is scrapped.[13]

"Mill liners are expensive," Dunn notes. "They are really finished metal products of some precision. They cost two to four times the basic cost of steel shapes such as rails, rods, and balls, and 25% of the new weight is thrown away when they are worn out."

Once the best grinding contour is determined, design should minimize foundry costs. Liners of greater length, width, or thickness reduce the number of castings to be molded. Holes and complex configurations require special sand core molds and may unnecessarily increase liner costs.

"Labor is a large part of milling cost and increases in

proportion to liner cost. A crew of 10 men at $5 per hr plus time-and-a-half costs $700 to change a mill shell liner in 12 hr. Double up on liner length, simplify liner installation pattern, give these men one of the power-hoisted or hydraulic lift-and-placing systems to work with, and maybe you can cut that time to 8 hr and reduce the crew by one or two men. That could cut labor costs by $380 and save you 4 hr of mill downtime. If you have 20 mills, that's $7,600 a year and 80 hr of downtime saved, assuming shell liners last a year."

In "Optimizing Ball Mill Liners for Production and Economy," presented at the 1976 AIME annual meeting, Dunn described testing of four mill liner profiles at Climax for 13 x 12-ft overflow primary ball mills (Fig. 1). The tests showed that improved design increased mill tonnage by 3 tons per hr, reduced finish grind by 1.7% plus 100 mesh, reduced liner wear, and almost doubled liner life.[14] The improvements—using S-201 double wave liners—were attributed to reduced sliding of balls across the higher, more abrupt wave profile, the greater thickness and abrasion resistance of the alloy, and a fortuitous wave migration that caused wave peaks to end up centered above liner bolt holes at the end of liner life. This allowed liners to be worn through completely without loss of liner bolts, extending the life two to three months beyond that of the earlier Climax design, with worn wave valleys centered over the bolt holes.

Controlling comminution

Rapid developments are taking place in modeling and control of both crushing and grinding operations. A review of such developments was presented by R. K. Wood of the University of Alberta at the Instrument Society of America Mining and Metallurgy Symposium in 1975.[15] Although the Wood survey is restricted to articles published in the last 10 years, it still includes 64 references. Wood cites his references in pointing out that the trend is toward more sophisticated and extensive control units and instrumentation, and that "there is a clearly visible progress path charted for digital computers in minerals processing plants."

Wood offers the following summary of recent control experience at one plant as an example of current operating practice and problems:

"Brown has discussed the development of the grinding circuit of the Island Copper mine from the original six autogenous mills to six semiautogenous mills operating in partial or fully open circuit followed by three secondary ball mills. The original control scheme employed two principal control loops. One loop was designed to control cyclone overflow density by manipulating water addition to the cyclone feed sump. Although satisfactory density control was possible using a nuclear density gauge, it did not provide control of product particle size. It is stated that a particle analyzer is presently being tested for possible utilization. The other loop was designed to maintain constant mill power draw by utilizing the control signal from the mill load controller as a cascaded set point to the ore feed rate controller. Mill water was ratioed to ore feed rate by means of a cascaded loop with set point from a ratio controller. Experience showed that cascade control of feed rate based on power draw set point was not possible because the instrumentation could not differentiate between decreasing power drawn due to mill overload vs. an increase in ore amenability to grinding. However, back pressure on the mill trunnion lubrication system was found to be a reliable indicator of actual mass loading, and use of the reading in conjunction with mill power draw allowed

the operator to determine if a decrease in power draw was due to mill overload or improved ore amenability. Operation was further complicated by the fact that optimum mass loading changed with changes in ore characteristics. Mill sound level was also tried as a cascaded set point signal but was found to be unsatisfactory. The optimum sound level also varied with ore type. The author states that the three measurements allow the operator to provide manual control and speculates that the signals 'could provide the basic elements necessary for a digital-computer-based control strategy.' "

Energy consumption vs. fineness in comminution

R. T. Hukki of the Technical Research Center of Finland presented an analytical summary of comminuting relationships—weight, grind size, specific surface, size distribution, energy consumption, classification, and operating efficiency—in E/MJ, May 1975. To obtain a sensible correlation between energy consumption and fineness of grind, he states, the comminution process must be considered over the full range from primary crushing to the production of ultrafine micropowders. Hukki's basic formulation of the energy-to-size relationship is indicated in Fig. 2, with the entire range of comminution subdivided into five internal ranges:

1) The crushing range, covered by the basic law of Kick. The slope m of the cumulative curve varies from

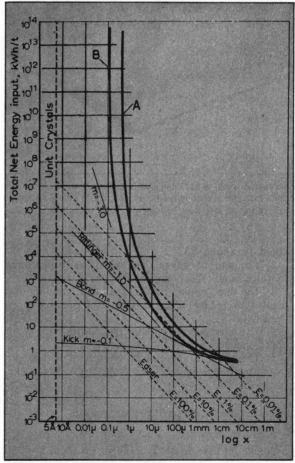

Fig. 2—Overall energy consumption vs. fineness in comminution. Curve A is for an open circuit, curve B for the same material in a closed circuit. The series of parallel lines at slopes $m = -1$ represent comminution efficiencies of 100%, 10%, 1%, 0.1%, and 0.01%, based on Edser's specific surface energy of quartz.

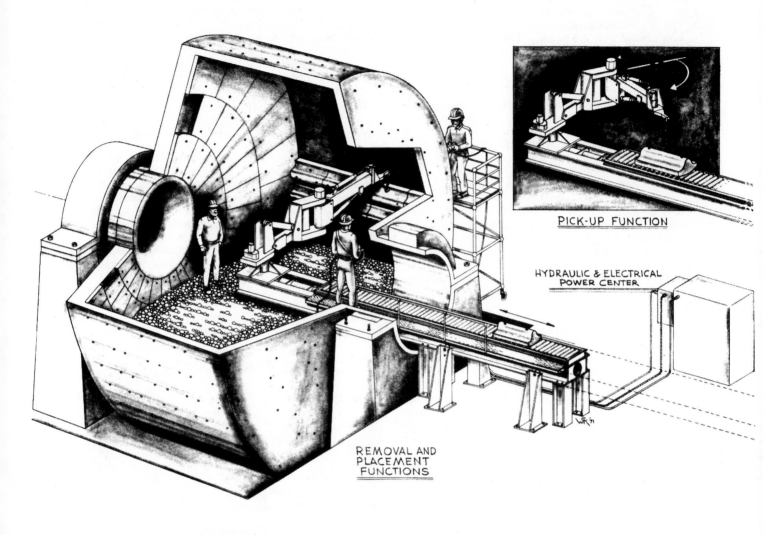

PICK-UP FUNCTION

HYDRAULIC & ELECTRICAL POWER CENTER

REMOVAL AND PLACEMENT FUNCTIONS

Servocontrolled "robot" mill-liner handlers can cut downtime, reduce manpower requirements, and eliminate safety hazards in mill relining. The PaR handler of Moog Inc. incorporates six servovalves to receive electrical signals from the operator's remote control (worn at waist level) and translate them to hydraulic flows that manipulate the machine's power cylinders.

about 0 to about –0.1.

2) The range of conventional rod and ball mill grinding, to which Bond's theory applies. Slope m is about –0.5.

3) The fine grinding range—such as the grinding of cements—covered by the law of Rittinger. Slope m is approximately –1.

4) The micropowder grinding range, with slope m from approximately –1 to –3.

5) The range of approaching grind limit, with slope m from about –3 to infinity. This range has no practical applications.

Second generation particle size analysis

On-stream particle size analyzing equipment has been available for base metals applications for about five years. At the 1975 annual general meeting of CIM, Robert E. Hathaway and Donald L. Guthals of Autometrics Co. described their company's PSM System-200, a second generation unit, and revealed some results of prototype tests.

The "200" transmits two beams of ultrasonic energy across a slurry sample. The frequency attenuation of one beam is highly sensitive to changes in particle size. The frequency of the other beam is such that changes in particle size have very little effect on the amount of ultrasonic energy transmitted through the slurry. Electronic comparison of the two separate output signals yields particle size and percent solids.[16]

Installations outlined in the Autometrics paper include:

■ US Steel's Minntac plant, where the objective is to develop an automatic grinding circuit control system to maintain a nearly constant particle size in final concentrate. The system is complex and utilizes a GE 4010 computer. Major benefits are expected to be better filter and agglomerator performance.

■ Craigmont Mines, which produces a magnetite concentrate that is used for heavy media separation and has strict particle size specifications. The new particle size monitor will hold sizes within these limits and keep particles from becoming so fine that they cause problems in filtering. The unit is calibrated to read from 95% to 85% minus 325 mesh. □

Flotation: the No. 1 beneficiation process

FLOTATION, often called the single most important metallurgical development in the 20th century, continues to process ever larger tonnages and to find new applications. A 1970 Bureau of Mines survey reported a record 405 million tons of ore processed by flotation, up from 279 million in 1965 and 198 million in 1960.[17] Figures for 1975 (the survey is made every five years) were still being processed as this issue of E/MJ was being prepared. When the new statistics become available, they should show another significant increase.

Sulphide ores continue to dominate flotation statistics, but other ores have recently had higher growth rates. Reagent suppliers report increasing interest in flotation of industrial minerals, and because only a small percentage of the total industrial minerals tonnage is now processed by flotation, these products represent an area of great potential. In the Midwest, one plant is floating carbonates out of foundry sand, and other plants are floating low grade limestones for upgrading and use as cement rock. Such applications might not have been economic in the past. But as high grade deposits are depleted, processing of lower grade materials by flotation becomes more feasible.

Another significant trend in flotation is the greater number of reagents available to mill operators. One reagent supplier estimates that total reagents on the market have doubled in the last 10 years. The mining industry tends to be conservative in its choice of reagents. However, with a wider selection now available, mill engineers are looking more closely for combinations of reagents that yield even small increases in recovery or concentrate grade.

Flotation cells continue to increase in size, and the upward limit of this growth curve is not yet in sight.[1,9,18] Cells in the range of 300-500 cu ft are not uncommon, and circular Maxwell cells have been installed at capacities up to 2,000 cu ft. Two such Maxwell cells are used as copper roughers at the Nacimiento copper mine in New Mexico. Pamour Porcupine Mines' Pamour Div. gold mine in Ontario uses a 2,000-cu-ft Maxwell cell as a pyrite rougher, followed by a 700-cu-ft Maxwell scavenger.

Cationic flotation of magnetic iron concentrates to bring silica content within specifications is becoming more commonplace. At Cleveland-Cliffs' Tilden plant on Michigan's Upper Peninsula, a fine grained, nonmagnetic hematitic-goethitic taconite is prepared for cationic flotation of silica by selective flocculation and desliming. The Tilden plant, designed to process 10 million ltpy of crude averaging 36% Fe, utilizes six lines of 25 flotation cells, each cell having a capacity of 500 cu ft.

Copper concentrators in the southwestern US have reported recent successes in flotation research directed at separating talc from molybdenum. At Anamax's Twin Buttes property, a new system uses lignin sulphonate in combination with a high pH milk-of-lime to depress molybdenum; it has increased the production of salable byproduct molybdenum concentrates. A process developed at Cyprus Pima treats a moly-talc float product from the copper concentrator with a water-soluble metallic salt of a weak base and a strong acid (aluminum sulphate), and then with a water-soluble salt of a weak acid (sodium silicate) to depress talc, permitting a moly float.

Interest in mathematical modeling of the froth flotation process remains high, and the advantages of establishing successful models are obvious. However, problems are posed by the large number of variables in the process—not the least of which is plant feed. Kinetic modeling of the performance of single cells either in batch or continuous operation has reached an advanced stage, but prediction of behavior for all the required model parameters remains a problem.

Other fundamental flotation research is directed at gaining an understanding of the adsorption mechanism of reagents at the solid-liquid interface and its role in enhancing or diminishing hydrophobicity.

In an "Analysis of Technology for Improved Beneficiation of Ultrafine Mineral Particle Systems," Battelle Laboratories notes that industrial flotation is rarely applied to particles below 10 microns in size because of lack of control of air bubble size. With ultrafine particles, extremely fine bubbles must be generated to improve attachment.[19]

Such bubbles can be generated by in-situ electrolysis in a modified flotation cell by a method called electroflotation, according to the Battelle researchers. Preliminary experiments at Battelle in a modified Denver flotation cell and in a specially designed cell achieved a dramatic increase in ultrafine particle recovery.

Among the advantages of the process:

■ Electroflotation can produce bubbles less than 0.1 mm in diameter, and bubble density can be controlled by both the current density and external air to yield optimum distribution of ultrafine bubbles as well as adequate froth control. Conventional flotation processes produce bubbles ranging from 0.6 to 1 mm in size, and there is considerable variation in bubble size.

■ The organic reagents required for processing may be reduced because electroflotation may increase surface activity of ultrafine particles and bubbles. This phenomenon may allow use of lower concentrations of surfactants.

■ The method does not require extensive modification of existing equipment.

Big cells boost Kennecott float plant results

Kennecott Copper Corp. replaced 100-cu-ft Forrester air cells with an arrangement of 500-, 300-, and 200-cu-ft cells at its Nevada Mines Div. The first 500-cu-ft machines went on line in August 1973 (Fig. 1). With fully one-half the concentrator converted and getting metallurgical results that compared favorably with earlier lab, pilot plant, and plant-scale test results (Table 1), Kennecott engineers reported on the conversion project at the 1975 annual meeting of AIME.[20]

The Nevada Mines Div. concentrator at McGill processes 21,500 tpd. Before the modernization program, it used modified Forrester cells throughout the mill except for twenty-four 200-cu-ft Booth mechanical cells in the scavenger circuit. Readily floatable chalcopyrite is the dominant mineral in the concentrator feed. However, recovery was being reduced to marginal levels by higher tonnages of limestone ore (requiring increased flotation efficiency), increased chalcocite mineralization (requiring longer flotation time), and tarnished chalcopyrite mineralization. In early 1970, the Nevada Mines Div. and Kennecott's Metal Mining Div. Research Center began to develop a program to improve copper recovery at the Nevada concentrator.

Extensive pilot plant testing produced favorable results using 300-cu-ft cells, and a plant-scale test run for 92 shifts

Table 1—Mechanical cells vs. air cells, metallurgical comparison

(Kennecott, Nevada Mines Div.)

	Completed South half: 500-cu-ft mechanical cells	North half: Forrester air cells
Head		
Percent Cu	0.594	0.594
Percent NS Cu	0.04	0.04
Concentrate		
Percent Cu	16.39	14.03
Percent MoS$_2$	0.58	0.48
Percent insol	16.9	21.0
Tail		
Percent Cu	0.108	0.146
Plus 100 mesh	35.5	35.9
Recovery		
Percent Cu	82.4	76.2
Percent MoS$_2$	41.0	40.1

Source: SME Preprint 75-B-77.

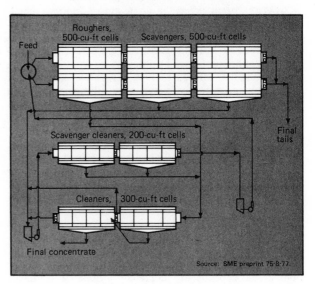

Fig. 1—Large-cell flowsheet at Kennecott's Nevada Mines Div.

(after 50% completion of renovation)

Source: SME preprint 75-B-77.

using nonsalaried employees averaged 75.8% copper recovery, against a 69.1% recovery in a control section and 69.6% in the general mill. Preliminary engineering and economic studies for renovation of the flotation plant began in 1972. Thirteen arrangement and equipment schemes were evaluated, of which nine were rejected on the basis of costs required for building modifications. Evaluation considerations included a 17-min retention time in the cells, pumping requirements, building modifications, maintenance accessibility, cost, and physical layout. After considerable study, a decision was made to design the modernization around cells larger than 300 cu ft. The decision was based on the number of units required, cubic feet of capacity vs. square feet of floor space occupied, connected horsepower, operational control, equipment costs, electrical costs, and power consumption. Accordingly, 500-cu-ft machines were selected.

The Kennecott engineers note: "During plant-scale testing, several problems arose that served to limit test effectiveness. The most severe problem was that of froth transport in launders. The 300-cu-ft machines removed a large volume of froth over a relatively short cell length. Launders 10 in. wide and 1-2 ft deep could not handle the volume of froth produced. The modernization includes rubber launders 2 and 3 ft wide with depths from 4 to 8 ft. The plant is currently handling voluminous froths caused by underground mine timbers.

"Froth pumping presented the second most severe problem. Abandoning conventional pump sizing techniques, large 12-in. x 14-in. pumps were selected, running at the lower end of their efficiency curves. Experience with these pumps has indicated minimal wear over a period of eight months, with 12 to 18 months more life expected on the wetted parts.

"In order to conserve floor space, all walkways are supported on the cell superstructures."

The construction and demolition projects were carried out in a way that permitted continued full production at all times. The modernization included installation of new sampling units, instrumentation to monitor circuit pH, indicator lights on all pumps and flotation machines, and reagent piping to insure proper addition rates of collectors and frothers. Pulp level is controlled through a combination of a conventional bubble tube, pneumatic controller, air motor, and dart valve. Retention time evaluations have been a nominal 15-17 min for the rougher scavenger circuits. In early 1975, copper recoveries were running at 82.4% in the completed section of 500-cu-ft cells, against 76.2% in remaining Forrester cells, and the new flotation sections had so far met all of Kennecott's expectations.

Large cells float Florida phosphates

A number of expansion and new plant construction projects in central Florida's phosphate fields have adopted 300-cu-ft flotation cells for recovery of both coarse (minus 20 mesh to plus 35 mesh) and fine (minus 35 mesh to plus 150 mesh) fractions in flotation plant feed. One plant has installed 500-cu-ft cells. U. K. Custred of Brewster Phosphates and V. R. Degner and E. W. Long of the Wemco Div. of Envirotech described early test work using the large cells at the SME fall meeting in 1974, noting that a nine-month test demonstrated good rougher performance on both coarse and fine feed. Product grade and phosphorite recovery equaled or exceeded those of existing smaller air cells, and the performance was achieved at a solids fraction significantly above that employed in the smaller cells.[21]

Among the specific conclusions drawn from the tests:

"The rougher circuit tonnage capacity for a given plant (i.e., fixed floor area) can be increased significantly. For example, this program demonstrates that a "specific capacity" (feed rate per flotation circuit area) of 0.65 tph per sq ft and 0.59 tph per sq ft was achieved by the large flotation cell rougher circuit with fine and coarse feed, respectively. This represents a 50% increase over the smaller cell circuit capacity.

"The power requirements of the rougher flotation circuit can be significantly reduced. Test results indicate that a "specific power requirement" between 0.27 and 0.36 hp per tph can be achieved with fine feed and 0.42 hp per tph can be achieved for coarse feed conditions.

"The pulp dilution for the rougher flotation circuit can be greatly reduced. Large-cell rougher circuit grade and recov-

ery comparable to the smaller air cell performance was achieved at a solids fraction of 30% for fine feed and 25% for coarse feed conditions. This dilution is much less than that practiced for the smaller air cells, where a solids fraction of 18% and 16% is maintained for fine and coarse rougher feed, respectively. The reduced water flow rate associated with the lower dilution of the large flotation cell will result in an additional power saving of approximately 0.35 hp per tph."

Testing at the Brewster plant in three Wemco 120 cells followed the "double float" procedure that is typical of Florida phosphate plants. In this procedure, phosphate is floated away from the silica in the rougher circuit using crude fatty acid, ammonia, and fuel oil or kerosene for conditioning. Rougher conditioning is accomplished at 60-70% pulp solids, and sufficient ammonia is added to raise the pH to 9-9.5. After coarse and fine rougher flotation, concentrate (overflow) streams join and are cleaned with sulphuric acid and washed before entering the cleaner circuit, where an amine float (cationic reagent and kerosene added in the feed box, pH 7.3 to 7.8) removes silica as the phosphate concentrate reports as underflow.

Flotation feed preparation is accomplished without comminuting devices, so the feed contains a relatively coarse particulate fraction not seen at other mineral beneficiation operations. The tests emphasized recovery of this coarse size fraction. To this end, cell modifications included connecting the false cell bottoms of the three test cells to form a single continuous false bottom, thus improving particle circulation and suspension, and adjustments in rotor submergence and speed. These modifications were then satisfactorily applied to the fine flotation circuit.

USBM tests flotation of high-clay potash ores

Concentration characteristics of high-clay sylvinite ores from the Permian basin near Carlsbad, N. Mex., have been investigated by the US Bureau of Mines Tuscaloosa Metallurgy Research Laboratory, and flowsheets have been developed to produce commercial grade products from these ores. The potash ores tested grade 14-19% K_2O and contain 3-5% clay slimes, which prevent processing by current commercial flotation methods.

Commercial plants in the Carlsbad district now process ores containing 1% clay slimes or less and grading 18-25% K_2O. However, vast tonnages of these ores have been mined during the past 40 years, and reserves are being rapidly depleted. The low grade, high-clay deposits in the district constitute a resource estimated to exceed 735 million tons. Interest in this resource stepped up recently, reflecting uncertainty about future Saskatchewan potash supply under the policies of the Socialist provincial government. The Carlsbad deposits occur with montmorillonite clays imbedded between crystals. The clays must be removed before flotation because they are strong absorbants of the amines used as flotation reagents. Clay particles are also locked inside the crystals, imparting a red color to concentrates due to associated hematite. These clays are released only when the crystals are dissolved.

The two high-clay, low grade sylvinite ores used in the USBM investigation were obtained from National Potash Co. and Duval Corp. The National sample contained 14.8% K_2O, 50.4% Cl_2, and 6.1% water insolubles; the Duval sample contained 18.8% K_2O, 51.4% Cl_2, and 3.7% water insolubles.

After preliminary studies, the researchers assembled a 300-lb-per-hr flotation plant for pilot testing and mounted it on a 33-ft-long trailer. The plant included equipment for

Fig. 2—USBM pilot plant flowsheet for high-clay potash ores from National Potash

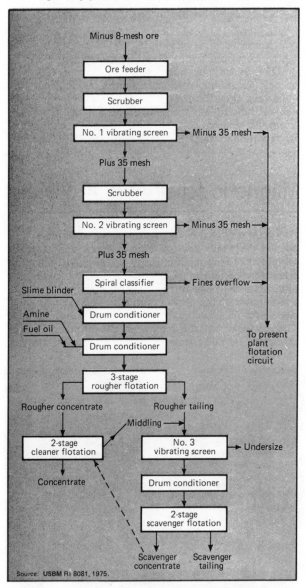

Source: USBM RI 8081, 1975.

Table 2—Reagents for flotation of potash ore*

(lb per ton of ore)

	Conditioner, First	Conditioner, Second	Rougher	Conditioner, Third	Scavenger
National Potash Co.					
Armeen HTD........	–	0.44	–	0.20	–
Phillips 66 fuel oil No. 5..........	–	1.75	–	0.50	–
Stein-Hall MLR-201 (blinder)..	0.60	–	–	0.10	–
Methyl isobutyl-carbinol	–	–	0.16	–	0.08
Duval Corp.					
Armac C..............	–	0.60	–	0.22	–
Barretts oil..........	–	1.80	–	0.60	–
Guar gum (blinder)	0.50	–	–	0.20	–
Nethyl isobutyl-carbinol	–	–	0.16	–	0.16

* Reagent consumption calculated on basis of total ore.　　Source: USBM RI 8081.

scrubbing, screening, classification, conditioning, and flotation and was designed to allow circuit changes with a minimum of effort. The rougher circuit used No. 7 D-R Denver cells, and the cleaner flotation circuit used No. 5 D-R Denver cells. The plant was moved to the Carlsbad area in March 1971 and operated intermittently until May 1973. Results were reported in 1975.[22]

After numerous tests, a flowsheet incorporating double scrubbing in saturated brine at 50-55% solids proved to be the best for producing coarse grained potash from National ores (Fig. 2). The flowsheet developed for Duval ores was substantially the same as the National flowsheet, except that screening was at minus 100 mesh, with undersize reporting to waste. Reagent schedules are indicated in Table 2.

The National cleaner concentrate contained 59.8% K_2O with a recovery of 62.9% of the total flotation feed; the scavenger concentrate contained 44.7% K_2O with a recovery of 18.5% and was suitable for leach crystallization.

The Duval cleaner concentrate contained 58.8% K_2O with a recovery of 59.7%; the scavenger concentrate contained 47.8% K_2O with a recovery of 10.0% and was suitable as leach crystallization circuit feed.

While they were not satisfactory in all aspects, the USBM report concludes, the continuous flotation processing tests did demonstrate the possibility of producing "premium" and "coarse" grade potash products meeting commercial specifications. □

Magnetic separators find wider use

GREATLY INCREASED FIELD STRENGTHS have effectively opened the whole field of mineral dressing to magnetic processing.[23] Jones high-intensity wet magnetic separators manufactured by Humboldt can separate feebly magnetic minerals such as hematite, pyrrhotite, siderite, ilmenite, or concentrates of the ores of chromium, manganese, tungsten, zinc, nickel, tantalum-niobium, and molybdenum. The machines can also remove magnetic impurities such as biotite, hornblende, tourmaline, garnet, iron silicates, and iron-stained particles from nonmagnetic materials including glass sand, apatite, clay, talc, kaolin, barite, graphite, bauxite, and cassiterite.

Cia. Vale do Rio Doce's iron complex at Caue, Brazil, is the site of the world's largest commercial wet high-intensity separation plant. The system was pioneered by CVRD for treating the itabirite fraction of its mine production. The concentrator, which started up in 1972, now recovers about 1 million tpy in 28 processing lines. CVRD also plans to install Jones separators at its $120 million Conceicao concentrator, now under construction.[24]

In Canada, Sidbec-Dosco is building a plant in Port Cartier to produce 3 million ltpy of superconcentrates using Jones high-intensity wet magnetic separators. The plant will reprocess minus 14-mesh spiral concentrates from Fire Lake, producing a superconcentrate to be pelletized and shipped to the Sidbec-Dosco direct reduction plant at Contrecoeur, Que. Single-pass pilot plant tests with recirculating wash water recovered 96.3% of the iron in the plant feed in a concentrate grading 68.7% Fe and 1.45% SiO_2.[9]

Magnetic separators filter kaolin clays

Since 1973, the Georgia kaolin industry has commercialized magnetic filtration of kaolin clays and now has a magnetic filtration capacity approximating the entire annual tonnage of water-washed coating and filler kaolin produced in the US.[25] The five large magnetic filters now on stream each process more than 1,000 gpm of kaolin slurry and 65 tph of kaolin on a dry basis.

The kaolin development brings together for the first time four concepts: retention time, extreme gradients, high-intensity fields, and efficient design for high-field magnets, according to J. Iannicelli, president of Aquafine Corp. of Brunswick, Ga.

The key breakthrough for commercialization was the discovery that separations of micron and submicron kaolin suspensions required very slow transit velocities and maximum exposure to collecting elements to allow capture of paramagnetic particles. Velocities of less than 1 cm per sec are used through 84-in.-dia separators at Georgia kaolin operations. The equipment consists of a filter canister packed with a matrix of compressed magnetic stainless steel wool. The canister is surrounded by hollow conductor copper coils that energize the entire canister volume to a field of 20 kilogauss. Coils are surrounded by a boxlike enclosure of steel plate that completes the magnetic circuit of the iron-bound solenoid. The units operate at 400-500 kw.

Jones high-intensity wet magnetic separators require a thoroughly mixed slurry as feed, with particles 100% minus 1 mm, although this upper size limit may vary. Degree of liberation, dispersion, pulp density, feed rate, type of plates and gap in the machine, wash water quality, field intensity, and the number of separation stages all influence performance.

The magnetic filters brighten kaolin by extracting submicron, feebly magnetic contaminants. Removal of only 1-2% of such material may brighten kaolin by 2-4 General Electric brightness units, permitting the mining of lower grade crude kaolin and reducing the consumption of leaching chemicals.

Iannicelli feels that kaolin separation is the most diffi-

cult application of magnetic separation ever commercialized. "The technology now can be applied advantageously to beneficiation of other industrial minerals, concentration of metallic ores, desulphurization of coal, and cleanup of effluent streams," he states. Such programs are now being studied at Indiana University under the direction of Dr. H. H. Murray. □

Photometric sorting concentrates gold ore

A HIGH-THROUGHPUT, MULTISTREAM PHOTOMETRIC sorting machine developed for South African gold mines is thought to have potential for a variety of sorting tasks.[26] The machine employs a laser light source and a sensitive photomultiplier in a scanning system to detect light reflected from the surfaces of rocks passing through the sorting zone. Electronic circuitry analyzes the photomultiplier signal, which changes with the varying intensity of the reflected light, and responds to "positive" signals by actuating air blasts that remove the selected particles from the ore stream. (See accompanying diagram.) Typical throughput per machine ranges from 50 tph for a minus 2½-in. plus 1¼-in. feed to 200 tph for minus 6-in. plus 2¾-in. material.

A machine at the Doornfontein gold mine "accepts" rocks having white or gray quartz pebbles in a darker matrix, but rejects quartzite ranging from light green through olive green to black. Most of the gold occurs in rocks in the "accept" category.

The scanning system incorporates a helium neon laser light source, an octagonal mirror drum, and a photomultiplier fitted with a lens system, field stop, polarizing filter, and red-light-sensitive photomultiplier tube. Typically, the system can detect a spot as small as 1 mm in diameter if there is a sufficient difference in reflectance between the spot and the background. In the unit at Doornfontein, the scan rate is 400 per sec over a conveyor belt moving about 80 in. per sec, resulting in a scan interval of 3/16 in. A 1¼-in. rock would be scanned five or six times.

Recent higher gold prices may make the machine applicable for sorting large quantities of low grade rock dumps at the South African mines, according to Keys, Gordon, and Peverett:[26] "Take, for example, the following conservative case. If one assumes a dump containing 4% reef (ore grade material) at 0.643 oz per ton (0.026 oz per ton

Mechanical layout for photometric sorter

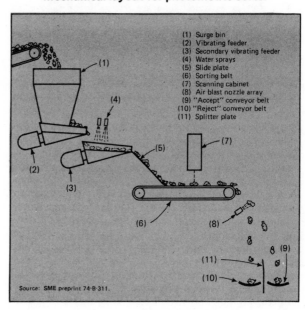

(1) Surge bin
(2) Vibrating feeder
(3) Secondary vibrating feeder
(4) Water sprays
(5) Slide plate
(6) Sorting belt
(7) Scanning cabinet
(8) Air blast nozzle array
(9) "Accept" conveyor belt
(10) "Reject" conveyor belt
(11) Splitter plate

Source: SME preprint 74-B-311.

overall), a treatment rate of 170 tph (1 million tpy), a 20% [rate of] accept when passed through a sorter (200,000 tons), with 80% metal recovery in the sorting and 90% metal recovery in milling, 18,522 oz of gold worth $3 million at $162 per oz would result. Assuming reclamation, sorting, and milling costs of $750,000 ($3.75 per ton of sorter 'accept' sent as feed to the mill), a gross working profit of some $2.25 million could be expected." □

New interest focuses on gravity separation

THE LAST 20 YEARS HAVE SEEN SIGNIFICANT ADVANCES in gravity separation technology: high-feed-density, high-capacity separators such as the Reichert Cone have been developed to treat particles in the 3-mm to 50-micron size range, spiral separators have been refined and modified to increase capacity within a given space, mechanical improvements have been made on jigs, and the Bartles Moseley concentrator has been successfully tested at high recovery on fine tin and tungsten ores at rates around 5 tph per unit. These developments, along with improved pumping and instrumentation technology, have provided new tools for designing efficient, compact gravity circuits.

Using recent plant designs and installations as examples, I. J. Terrill and J. B. Villar of Mineral Deposits Ltd. sum-

marized the state of the art of gravity separation at the 1974 meeting of CIM.[27]

Pinched sluices of various forms have been used for heavy mineral separations for centuries, the authors note, but major developments have been achieved during the last 20 years, especially in the Australian mineral sands industry, where many high capacity (100-1,500 tph) plants have been established. The most widely used unit is the Reichert Cone developed by Mineral Deposits, which is incorporated in a number of large circuits for primary, secondary, and tertiary upgrading, with spirals providing a finished concentrate.

Success in the mineral sands industry led to applications of cone circuits in other fields: preconcentration of tin in grinding circuits, scavenging of urania and zirconia from flotation tailings at the Palabora mine, and concentration of magnetite in New Zealand. Cone separators have also been designed into iron ore fines beneficiation circuits in the Australian Pilbara, and a pilot plant was to be commissioned for recovery of fines in Quebec.

Spirals have been widely used for several decades and are still excellent concentrators. The use of fiberglass and plastic construction with rubber lining has significantly improved the weight-capacity ratio: a twin spiral capable of treating 2-3 ltph of feed now weighs less than 150 lb. Up to 14 twin spirals can be incorporated into a light pipe framework and installed as a module capable of treating 40 tph; the modules are supplied complete with integrated feed distribution systems, water galleries, and product hoses.

The Bartles Moseley separator, capable of recoveries down to 10-15 microns, is a significant advance in fine gravity separation hardware. Relatively high throughputs of 4-6 tph can be achieved. Effective application requires effective fine screening, but good results have been achieved in pilot operations using well-classified cone concentrate.

Terrill and Villar state: "It is apparent that cone concentrators, Bartles units, and conventional slime tables can be effectively integrated to concentrate large, low grade flows containing fine valuable mineral."

Precise fine classification permits far better control of gravity circuit feed now than was possible 20 years ago, the authors note. Hydrocyclone technology, coupled with improved pumping systems, allows compact classification at each pulp transfer stage and can easily provide the high density feed necessary for cone concentrator circuits. Fine trommel screening, rubber screen cloths, sieve bends, and other high capacity improvements in classification technology all contribute to better control and economics in gravity circuits. □

Screens, cyclones, and thickeners

MINERAL PROCESSING REQUIRES A WIDE VARIETY of sizing and liquid-solid separating equipment, and suppliers to the industry are continually upgrading these products.

Nordberg has introduced a double-frequency vibrating screen that will reportedly increase throughput up to 40%. Motion is imparted to the screen by two vibrator motors, one mounted at the feed end and running with high amplitude at low speed, the other mounted at the discharge end and running at low amplitude and high speed. The two screening motions offer the action of a normal inclined screen at the feed end and of a high speed sizing screen at the discharge end. The screen has a high capacity per square foot, according to Nordberg, and reduces the cost of salable product.

Introduction of a new 18-in. lightweight cyclone designed for highly abrasive applications has expanded Dorr-Oliver's Dorrclone line. The new cyclone handles 300-1,300 gpm, making separations in the range of 270-140 mesh. A ¾-in. natural gum rubber liner extends wearability. The unit weighs only 160 lb (one-sixth the weight of some competitive models) and can be installed by two workers.

A new heavy media process for beneficiating fines is offered by Minerals Separation Corp. The Dyna Whirlpool Process (DWP) sets up a vortex in a cylindrical vessel, which operates at an inclined angle. Feed enters the vessel through a pipe at the higher end, while a medium enters the unit tangentially under pressure at the lower end. The medium rises and creates an open vortex at the feed end, with separation taking place on the inner face of the vortex. Light particles ride downward on the face and are discharged as tailings through a pipe at the end opposite the feed pipe. Heavy particles sink into the rising medium and are discharged with the medium through a discharge pipe near the feed end.

DWP vessel capacities range from 10 to 100 tph, according to the manufacturer, and through manifolding of several units, very high plant capacities can be achieved.[28]

The US Bureau of Mines has developed a prototype particle size analyzing system incorporating a series of hydrocyclone elutriation steps followed by weight-sensing nuclear attenuation techniques.[29] The unit is applicable in the range of 74 mm to 7 microns. Particle elutriation is accomplished through five cyclones in series, with the largest particles deposited in the closed apex chamber of the first cyclone and the smallest particles retained in the final cyclone.

Density of the solids-water slurry in each apex chamber, and ultimately the weight of the sized solids, is determined by the relative attenuation of a gamma ray beam to the suspended mineral particles. Particle size distribution can then be presented in terms of the Gaudin-Schuhmann function or by some other means such as a histogram or a percent passing of some limiting size.

The system was developed for iron ore beneficiation and for monitoring particle distributions of homogeneous materials, but its developers feel it could be adapted for processing heterogeneous materials.

Thickener diameters grow in size

Dorr-Oliver's "Superthickeners" are finding increasing use. The first was installed at Eveleth Mining in Minnesota about 10 years ago. Since then, Texasgulf has installed a large diameter caisson unit near Timmins, Ont., and Agrico has installed a 500-ft-dia unit for phosphate. The Anamax plant in Arizona uses five 400-ft-dia thickeners, and Cleveland-Cliffs has ordered a 450-ft unit for iron ore tailings.

The Superthickener drive mechanism rides on a hydrostatic bearing that wears much longer than ball bearings and is more resistant to unbalanced load conditions and torque surges.

In the past, the limiting factor on thickener sizing was the enormous torque load on the rake arm, combined with the load-carrying requirements of the center mechanism support system. Dorr-Oliver has also introduced a "Cable-Torq" design for process situations where surges occur, where intermittent operation is common, or where scaling is a maintenance problem. The system incorporates a mechanism that allows the rake arms to automatically override high torque loads and keep raking.

New screening materials last longer

Service life 10 to 30 times that of traditional wire cloth screening surfaces is projected by C-E Tyler for its new polyurethane "Tyrethane" screen sections. Among the advantages cited for the new product:

- The tapered apertures and resilience of Tyrethane

Five 400-ft-dia 'Superthickeners' clarify solutions for the Anamax oxide leaching plant 20 mi south of Tucson. (This photograph was taken before the tank was filled.) A sixth 400-ft-dia thickener at the site is equipped with a conventional drive.

eliminate blinding and pegging.
- The new screening does not stretch or lose dimensional stability during operating life.
- Wire reinforcement permits the same tensioning given wire cloth sections.
- Noise is reduced at the screen deck surface.
- Tyrethane has excellent resistance to mineral oils and grease, alcohol-free gasoline, ozone and oxygen, and most common solvents.

- Tyrethane does not blind in heavy media applications.

Important applications for the new screening surface are expected in copper, iron, and other beneficiation operations, crushed stone, sand and gravel, and coal processing. The screens are available in 84 apertures from 0.006 in. to 4.921 in.

A life of 500,000 to 1 million tons is reported for Tyrethane on dry round or crushed materials and 750,000 to 1.5 million tons on wet round or crushed materials. In marketing the product, C-E Tyler guarantees that it will not exceed the customer's current screening cost per ton, factoring in both materials and labor expense.

"Dur-elast" is another new screen surface offered for mining applications. Cast of Du Pont's "Adiprene" urethane rubber, the surface offers exceptional resistance to abrasion and impact, while effectively dampening noise. Supplied by Durex Products, the patented surface design reportedly offers more open area than other currently available synthetic screens; it has tapered holes wider at the bottom than at the top. The screening material is easy to install and will fit any size vibrator without modification of the vibrator itself. It is lighter in weight than wire cloth, contributing to vibrator efficiency. Durex warrants its product to provide an economic wear life equivalent to whatever screen surface it replaces.

Trelleborg Rubber Co. offers a new reinforced rubber screening product, "Trellcord." Having an embedded cord reinforcement, the Trellcord screen cloths can be installed using high tensile force, preventing the sagging between support members that sometimes occurs with rubber screen cloths. Trellcord rubber screens generally last up to eight times longer than conventional steel screen decks, according to Trelleborg. □

Belts still carry the main materials load

MATERIALS HANDLING can account for 30% to 60% of the total delivered price of raw materials, and conveyor belts remain the backbone of most materials handling systems.[30,31] A. T. Yu, now president of Orba Corp., reviewed 75 years of belt development at the AIME centennial meeting in 1971, noting that gradual evolutionary changes had produced belt conveyors with capacities up to 20,000 tph and single flight lengths exceeding 16,000 ft. Practical belt widths have grown to 120 in., and tests have indicated feasible speeds of more than 2,000 fpm.

Belt system flexibility has increased, and there are now hundreds of miles of extensible wire rope stringer systems in underground mines and shiftable and portable systems in open pits, Yu noted. By using unitized deck stringer sections mounted on rail ties, belt conveyors several thousand feet long can be shifted laterally into new positions. Such conveyors can follow the advance of a mine face or fill a valley with a crawler-mounted stacker in a waste dump operation. Installations using shiftable conveyors include the Nchanga copper operation in Zambia, the Neyvelli operation in India, the lignite fields in Germany, and Anaconda's Twin Buttes operation in Arizona.

The reliability of belt systems has been enhanced by advances in control technology, making possible a high degree of fail-safe automation. Sophisticated electrical, pneumatic, and hydraulic circuits have been widely employed to replace all but a few manual operations. Baffles in transfer chutes to guide material flow can now be remotely controlled by hydraulic cylinders, and hydraulics

have also been used extensively in belt training and in belt tension take-up. When more refined belt tension control is required, especially in starting and stopping long conveyors, load cell controlled electrical tensioning devices are used.

"Nearly foolproof protection of personnel and equipment is achieved by an assortment of devices such as motor overload and switchgear overheat detectors, over- and under-speed switches, chute-plugged switches, emergency pull-cord switches, brake trouble detection, lubrication monitors, and the like," Yu said. "With all these up-to-date protective devices, an availability of 80-90% in a normal 20-shift week is quite realistic."

'Handling Concentrates—A Sticky Problem'

The difficult handling characteristics of flotation concentrates—abrasiveness, sluggishness when moist, or fluidity when dry—were the subject of a review by Robert M. Abrams, head of Treadwell Corp.'s materials handling section, at the 1976 AIME annual meeting.[32] Wet concentrates tend to dry out and harden after extended storage, and they freeze in extremely cold weather. When bone dry, fluidization caused by air entrainment occurs readily, and dustiness can be a special problem.

Other exotic handling characteristics include a possible tendency to spontaneously form balls when rolling down the slope of a stockpile. And sulphide concentrates may be subject to slow oxidation or even spontaneous combustion

Long-distance slurry pipelines around the world

Material	System	Location	Service date	Length, mi	Diameter, in.	Throughput, million tpy
Coal	Consolidated Coal*	Ohio	1957	108	10	1.3
	Black Mesa	Arizona to Nevada	1970	273	18	4.8
	Wytex	Montana to Texas	Planned	1,260	42	30
	Energy Transportation Systems Inc.	Wyoming to Arkansas	Planned	1,030	38	25
	Houston Natural Gas Co.	Colorado to Texas	Planned	1,100	18	15
	Northwest Pipeline Corp.	Wyoming to Oregon	Planned	778	30	16
	Nevada Power Co.	Utah to Nevada	Planned	180	24	10
	—	Poland	—	125	10	—
	—	Soviet Union	—	38	12	108
	—	Soviet Union	1964	6	—	—
	—	France	—	5	15	1.5
Iron ore concentrate	Savage River	Tasmania, Australia	1967	53	9	2.3
	Waipipi	New Zealand	1971	6	8-12	1.0
	Pena Colorada	Mexico	1974	30	8	1.8
	Samarco	Brazil	Under constr.	250	20	12
	Las Truches	Mexico	Under constr.	17	10	1.5
	Sierra Grande	Argentina	Under constr.	20	8	2.1
	—	Africa	Planned	350	18	6.6
	Kudremukh	India	Planned	36	20-22	10.0
Copper ore concentrate	Bougainville	Papua-New Guinea	1972	17	6	1.0
	West Irian	Irian Jaya	1972	69	4	0.3
	Pinto Valley	Arizona	1974	11	4	0.4
	KBI	Turkey	—	38	5	1.0
	—	Japan	—	38	8	1.0
Limestone**	Calaveras	California	1971	17	7	1.5
	Rugby Portland Cement	England	1964	57	10	1.7
	Rugby Portland Cement	Trinidad	1959	6	8	1.0
Phosphate	Valep	Brazil	Planned	62	9	2

*Out of service. **Not listed here: several Colombian lines, one dating back to 1944; unknown if still in service. Sources: Slurry Transport Association, Battelle Memorial Institute, Bechtel Inc., British Hydromechanics Association. (Compiled by CHEMICAL ENGINEERING.)

under certain conditions.

For concentrate chute design, Abrams offers two important "don'ts": 1) don't place dead beds of rock or other material in the chutes in an attempt to prevent abrasive wear or diminish free fall impact, because the concentrate will pack in such dead beds and eventually plug the chute, and 2) avoid sliding wet concentrate down an inclined chute whenever possible, because concentrate-plate adhesion is usually excellent. Direct free fall is the ideal way to transfer concentrate from one belt to the next.

For dry concentrates, chute slopes can be reduced somewhat, and if the concentrates are also abrasive, chute surfaces can be protected by using stone boxes, liner plates, and bottom angles or riffle bars.

The ideal belt speed for discharging moist concentrates from one belt to another is about 200 fpm, according to Abrams, although such a low speed increases the cost of conveyors: 1) slower belt speed requires wider belts to handle a given capacity; 2) there is generally an increase in the cost of the required speed-reducing gearbox; and 3) lowering the belt speed *increases* the maximum tension level in a conveyor belt, influencing not only the cost of the belt but also the pulleys, pulley shafts and pillow blocks, and various supporting structures.

If weather conditions are mild, as in the southern US, the use of higher belt speeds, coupled with a deflector plate in front of the discharge pulley to limit material "throw," should be considered as a possible alternative to reduce capital costs.

Pneumatic conveyors are proving successful for concentrate handling, Abrams reports, primarily as a result of the mining industry's adoption of spray drying of concentrates, which produces the bone-dry material needed for pneumatic transport. Spontaneous combustion of sulphide concentrates is also prevented by spray drying, since the presence of free moisture is necessary for such reactions to proceed.

"The pneumatic handling of concentrates appears to be a very attractive alternative method of conveying, especially where waste heat is available for spray drying," Abrams suggests. "All chute and bin hangups are eliminated, along with freezing and dust problems. However, the abrasiveness of the concentrate or of any impurities or additives present, such as silica, may require special consideration, especially if continuous trouble-free operation is a must."

Long-distance slurry transport may boom

In the last 20 years, only a handful of lines for carrying slurried minerals have been completed—the most notable example being the 273-mi coal-slurry pipeline that crosses the Black Mesa desert of Arizona. However, companies around the world are now planning or constructing several ore-concentrate lines, including one 250 mi long, according to a recent CHEMICAL ENGINEERING report.[33] In the US, coal slurry pipelines are attracting keen interest. (Most of these lines are described in the accompanying table.)

A 250-mi Brazilian pipeline rates as the most ambitious slurry transport project now under construction. A joint venture of Utah International and Brazil's SA Mineracao

E/MJ OPERATING HANDBOOK OF MINERAL PROCESSING

da Trindade, the 20-in. Samarco line will carry some 7.7 million tpy of iron concentrates from a mine about 180 mi north of Rio de Janeiro to coastal pelletizing and shipping facilities.

Also in Brazil, a 62-mi phosphate rock slurry line is planned by Mineracao Vale do Parnaida—the first of its kind. Until now, phosphate slurry lines have served only short, in-plant applications.

In terms of sheer length, the Wytex project of Brown & Root and Texas Eastern Transmission Corp. takes top honors. The pipeline would stretch 1,260 mi from the Powder River basin in southeastern Montana to the Houston area. Capital costs are projected to top $1 billion.

New applications sought for Marconaflo

Since 1968, Marconaflo Inc. has been developing slurry transport systems, which originated in a successful search for a way to load slurries onto and off ships. A number of commercial applications for the process have been developed, and work is under way for applications in hydrometallurgy, underground mining, in-plant transfer, and tailings reclamation.[34] Mineral commodities now handled by Marconaflo include iron ore concentrate, copper tailings, tar sand tailings, petroleum coke, phosphate feed, lead and zinc tailings, and pyrrhotite.

Reclaiming large areas of loosely consolidated materials, such as tailings in ponds or overburden, often requires equipment that can operate at great depths and reslurry at great distances. One Marconaflo system available for such applications is a caisson unit, with a jet and slurry pump mounted at the bottom and the necessary power supply and control instruments at the top. Four large systems of this type are in commercial use for recovery and subsequent transport of tailings, the largest at a lead and zinc tailings reclamation project in Morocco, utilizing three caissons. The Moroccan system is designed to reclaim 1.8 million mtpy at pulp densities of 40% solids by weight, using 450 psig water through each Marconajet. Two of the caissons are mounted on skids and one is fixed. The skid-mounted caissons were designed to reclaim at depths to 30 ft in a single pass, through an arc of 270° and out to a minimum 40-ft radius. Power consumption varies between 2¢ and 4¢ per ton of material removed. □

Environmental impacts focus attention on waste handling

ENACTMENT OF A WIDE VARIETY of environmental controls during the past several years has wrought significant changes in the handling of mill tailings and mine and mill effluents. Environmental engineers have joined the staffs of many mine and mill operations, and the arrows pointing "to waste" at the corners of mill flowsheets have drawn much attention.

An International Tailing Symposium was sponsored by WORLD MINING in Tucson, Ariz., in late 1972, drawing registrants from 21 countries. Harris H. Burke, manager of soil engineering for Bechtel Inc., outlined the "Structural Characteristics Resulting from Construction Methods" for tailings dams, emphasizing that the separation of tailings into a coarse and a fine fraction and use of the coarse fraction in dam construction enhance the structural properties of dams.[35]

While the physical properties of tailing materials are quite variable, Burke said, milling processes often produce tailings that are excellent material for dam construction. (Exceptions include the black mud residues from cryolite recovery and the clay fines washed out of coal.) However, the hydraulic transportation and deposition processes generally used in moving tailings to storage ponds may leave a loose, saturated mass subject to liquefaction, especially under the dynamic stress conditions generated during an earthquake. Of less importance, but still a major factor, may be continued heavy blasting in a nearby open-pit mine.

Use of only coarse tailings fractions in dam construction and compaction of dam materials after emplacement increase dam stability. In addition, provision for adequate internal drainage, thus ensuring low seepage lines, can enhance dam strengths.

The two most common means for separating coarse tailings fractions are natural sedimentation of flat beaches or tailings ponds or mechanical separation by cyclones.

Designing safe tailings structures

Safe maximum embankment height and associated slope, along with the physical controls to be placed on the movement of water associated with a tailings structure, are among the basic questions to be addressed in designing safe tailings systems, USBM mining research engineer Dan Kealy said in a 1973 MINING CONGRESS JOURNAL report. Some answers to these questions are available in USBM publications.[36,37]

Some form of instrumentation should be used for monitoring the status and safety of every embankment at various time intervals, Kealy stated, especially tailings embankments that are under continual construction. Piezometers and slope indicators are the only instruments needed.

Rate of tailing deposition (annual rise) is important because it affects the phreatic surface (elevation of the "water table" within the tailings structure) and the pore water pressure. A large annual rise causes a high phreatic surface and therefore a high pore pressure. Higher embankments are more susceptible to failure; a rising dam that is safe now may be in a failure condition in five years.

Abandonment is another design criteria. In preparation for abandonment:

1) Tailings structures must be capable of handling 50-to 100-year storm conditions without adverse effect.

2) Decant systems must provide access to internal drainage for inspection monitoring and for potential leach operation. (The decant system is the key to design for abandonment.)

3) Consideration must be given to embankment geometry and esthetics relative to surrounding natural terrain.

4) Maintenance-free structures are desirable.

5) Exploration drilling prior to construction is a must to avoid construction over an unknown orebody that might require subsequent removal of the dam.

Reclamation at Climax, Urad, and Henderson

Most active mining operations in the US conduct ongoing tailings and waste dump reclamation programs. At its Climax mine near Leadville, Colo., Amax Inc. began tailings revegetation research in 1965. Subsequent development of the company's reclamation program was described by Amax environmental control engineer Larry F. Brown at the 1975 AMC convention in San Francisco.[38]

Amax's three molybdenum mines—Climax, Urad, and Henderson—operate at elevations ranging from 10,300 to 11,300 ft above sea level. Winters are severe, and growing seasons are very short. Native grass seeds are not commercially available, so much of Amax's research has been directed at finding commercially available seed species adaptable to its harsh operating environment.

At Climax, most of the tailings area is still being used for tailings deposition; however, overburden from an open-pit mine started up in 1973 is being used to reclaim a tailings area no longer in use. At Henderson, which will produce its first concentrate in 1976, reclamation will be easier than at Climax because extensive environmental planning has been part of the development of the mine.

Urad shut down at the end of 1974 after seven years of production, and a comprehensive reclamation program is under way. Two tailings areas covering about 125 acres pose the major reclamation problem, and three major waste products are being used to accomplish the job: mine-development rock from Henderson, sewage sludge from Denver, and wood chips from a nearby sawmill. Test plots begun in 1974 indicated that the most economical and beneficial tailings area treatment would be an initial application of 20 tons per acre of both sewage and wood chips, followed two or three years later by 10 tons per acre of sewage. Even with this application of 50 tons per acre of organics, inorganic fertilization will be necessary.

The revegetation process will follow these steps: cover with development rock, build up hills to break the flat contour; haul in and stockpile sewage and wood chips; spread P_2O_5 fertilizer and wood chips; rip wood chips and fertilizer into the surface with a dozer; spread sewage sludge; scatter dead timber on the surface; plant trees (both transplants and seedlings); seed with grass; irrigate (first year only); replant failures; and follow up with inorganic fertilizers.

The Urad reclamation project is expected to cost about $8 million. It will be essentially complete by 1982 but will require annual inorganic fertilization through 1996. By that time, a soil mature enough to support vegetation without additional fertilization should develop.

Complying with effluent guidelines

The Environmental Protection Agency has promulgated a number of mill and tailings pond effluent guidelines, with phase 1 deadlines coming due July 1, 1977. Dr. David E. Hyatt, manager of analytical services at the Colorado School of Mines Research Institute, reviewed these guidelines in some detail and examined available technologies and costs of application in a paper presented at the Western Mining Conference in Denver early in 1976.[39]

The first stage at which to consider technology bearing on the quality of final mill effluent is the mill processing circuit, Hyatt observed. He suggested the following steps in handling internal mill water to improve effluent quality:

1) Beneficiation processes in some cases can be designed so that process streams containing reagents such as cyanide, ammonia, and organic solvents are separated from tailings streams. The reagent-bearing streams can be recycled or treated to decompose the pollutants.

2) Reagents can in some cases be selected on the basis of recoverability and decomposability, as well as for their primary processing functions.

3) Tailings thickeners are now almost a necessity to obtain maximum clarification from ponds.

4) In instances where waste heat and excess water coexist in a mill, waste streams may be treated by segregation and selective evaporation to reduce their volume. If weather conditions are favorable, evaporative ponds may be feasible for controlling impurity bleed streams.

5) Physical modification of processing modules or of waste water handling systems to enhance aeration, solids-liquids contact, and exposure to ultraviolet radiation may promote the removal of some pollutants. Complexed cyanide ion, free cyanide ion, ammonia, oxidizable organic and metallic species, sulphide ion, and other waste water constituents are potentially influenced by this type of design modification.

6) Control of ore constituents or accessory minerals entering the mill may be practical to eliminate or sharply reduce particular pollutant levels in the mill waste streams. In most instances, however, the geology of the ore deposit will make this option impractical.

Hyatt also suggested that tailings ponds be sited in areas of limited or controllable runoff from natural water courses, because once such water enters the tailings system, it is subject to effluent regulations.

The large surface area of most ponds is conducive to evaporative loss of water and may either assist or aggravate plant water balance. In the southwestern US, evaporation rates may exceed 4 gpm per acre of surface.

Chemical treatment of waste water entering the pond may include oxidation, sorption, precipitation of soluble species, microbial degradation, and a variety of other potentially useful phenomena. Oxidation of cyanide, sulphide, ferrous iron, and other soluble species may render them less toxic or less soluble. Sorption of soluble metals on tailings, native soils, or on precipitation complexes of metals may provide an excellent opportunity to remove such soluble species as zinc (II), arsenic (III), cadmium (II), copper (II), and others. Precipitation of hydrous oxides or hydroxides of many transition metals may require a rather prolonged time, as more stable, soluble complexes are degraded and insoluble forms begin to predominate. Lime precipitation is perhaps the most common approach to metal hydroxide formation and, given adequate time and control of pH levels achieved, it may be satisfactory in many cases. Complexes of metals with cyanide and ammonia, however, are especially prone to stabilization and solubilization in caustic solution and may require special treatment. Microbial assimilation of such species as cyanide, sulphide, iron, copper, and zinc has been utilized at various levels from laboratory to full scale plant operation. Tailoring the environment of some or all of the tailings pond to accommodate beneficial organisms may prove highly successful in some instances.

Hyatt listed ion exchange, reverse osmosis, ultrafiltration, electrodialysis, electrooxidation and electroreduction, chemical oxidation and reduction, and activated carbon sorption systems among those available for treating pond effluent. While such systems are usually expensive to construct and operate, they may be justified by requirements to produce drinking-quality water.

"In the final analysis," Hyatt said, "we are forced to consider water as a real raw material in the ore dressing process. We may either use and reuse this water, or we may use it once and pass it on to the next user. In the first case, the quality demands placed on the water are largely of our own definition. In the latter case, 'the next user' is generally spoken for by regulatory agencies and our effluent quality is set by criteria outside the mill flowsheet. Under these conditions, the desirability of zero discharge and water recycle becomes appealing and plant design and operation to achieve this goal appears highly recommended." □

Pyrometallurgy: smelters pressured for emissions control

THE DRIVE FOR AIR QUALITY CONTROLS in the US since the passage of the Clean Air Act of 1970 has been the strongest recent influence for change in nonferrous smelting practice. Several US zinc smelters have been shut down because they could not economically be brought into compliance with pollution control laws, and existing copper smelters are struggling to install pollution controls that will allow them to operate in compliance with these laws without driving them into bankruptcy.

Reverberatory furnace and converter technology still accounts for the bulk of US copper production. Emissions control systems installed at such plants include acid plants, a liquid SO_2 plant, tall stacks, and closed loop monitoring systems that trigger production cutbacks if SO_2 levels in the air around a smelter reach prescribed levels. However, given the current state of copper technology, there is little likelihood that another reverb-and-converter smelting operation will ever be built again.

Several newer copper technologies are now available that have a single factor in common: more economic control of SO_2 emissions than reverb-and-converter technology.[40] Electric furnaces have been installed at Cities Service Co.'s Copperhill, Tenn., property, at Inspiration Consolidated in Arizona, and at the Anaconda plant in Anaconda, Mont.

Phelps Dodge has installed the first flash furnace smelter in the US, developed by Outokumpu Oy of Finland, at its new Hidalgo smelter in southwestern New Mexico. Principal attractions of the flash furnace are efficient energy use and production of a strong SO_2 gas stream suitable for conversion to sulphuric acid. The Hidalgo gas stream is expected to contain up to 15% SO_2—sufficient to permit conversion to elemental sulphur by a high-temperature catalytic conversion technology developed by Asarco Inc. In this process, sulphur dioxide is converted to sulphur vapor in catalytic reactors with hydrocarbon gas. The sulphur is then condensed to a liquid for recovery.

The most important new commercial smelting developments are the Mitsubishi and Noranda continuous smelting processes, which avoid the batch processing that is characteristic of reverb-and-converter operations. Each process has now been demonstrated on a commercial scale: the Mitsubishi process in Japan, and the Noranda process in Canada. Texasgulf has signed an agreement with Mitsubishi for use of its continuous copper smelting technology at a 130,000-tpy plant to be built at Timmins, Ont. Kennecott Copper is replacing reverberatory furnaces at its Utah copper smelter with three Noranda continuous reactors, each capable of treating 1,600 tpd of concentrate.

Mitsubishi's multifurnace continuous system

Mitsubishi started up a 4,000-mtpm commercial continuous copper smelting and converting plant in March 1974

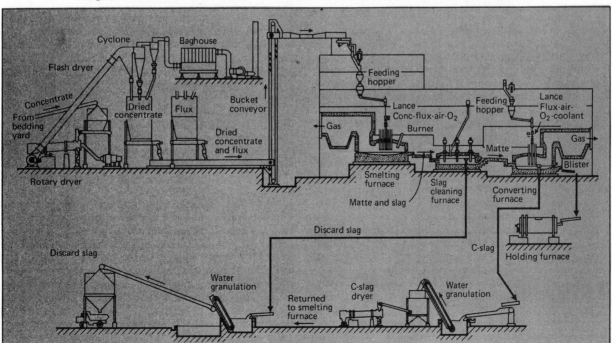

Fig. 1—Mitsubishi continuous copper smelting process at Naoshima

on Naoshima island in Japan. Three stationary furnaces—for smelting, slag cleaning, and converting—process melts flowing through launders by gravity from one furnace to the next (Fig. 1). A detailed discussion of the new plant was offered by Mitsubishi personnel at the International Symposium on Copper Extraction and Refining in Las Vegas, February 1976.[41]

Simplicity of design, construction, and operation was cited by Mitsubishi as one of the most important features of the process. No driving mechanisms, such as tilting mechanisms for the furnace, tuyere punches, or hood driving mechanisms, are needed. Gravity transfer of molten products from one furnace to the next eliminates the need for big ladles or a crane system, and the continuous overflow of molten products through the outlet hole of the furnace eliminates such operations as matte tapping and slag skimming, which are inevitable in conventional copper smelting practice.

The furnaces are compact: the oval-shaped smelting furnace 7 x 10½ m, the oval slag cleaning furnace 4 x 7 m, and the oval converting furnace 6 x 9 m. Hearth efficiencies are high and fuel requirements are low when compared with Mitsubishi's No. 1 and No. 2 reverberatory furnaces. The Mitsubishi continuous process requires 34.9 liters of fuel per mt of concentrate in the furnaces, 6.2 liters per mt in the preheater, and 9.2 liters per mt in the dryer, while the No. 1 Naoshima reverberatory takes 150 liters per mt of concentrate and the No. 2 reverberatory, 115 liters per mt. The Mitsubishi process consumes 41 kwh per mt of concentrate in generating oxygen for injection into the continuous furnace, and 21 kwh per mt in slag cleaning. (The slag cleaning furnace is an electric unit rated at a transformer capacity of 1,200 kva and having three 350-mm-dia prebaked graphite electrodes.)

The low fuel requirement, coupled with the addition of oxygen, makes possible a reduction of gas volume, which thus reduces the sizes of boilers, precipitators, flues, and the acid plant.

In discussing the rationale of its multifurnace system, Mitsubishi notes that sulphide copper ores are normally treated in two steps—matte making and converting. Although the chemical reactions in both steps are oxidations, there is a significant difference in the required level of oxi-

dation. The first stage is less oxidizing so that a low-copper slag can be produced; the second is strongly oxidizing so that iron and sulphur can be sufficiently removed from the blister. These two conditions can be maintained most efficiently if they are conducted in separate vessels, Mitsubishi states.

Moreover, Mitsubishi asserts, its process is distinct from conventional smelting methods in that the matte grade can be raised to 65% while maintaining copper loss in the discard slag at a low level. This feature has reduced the amount of slag formed in the converting furnace to less than 10% of the initial charge of concentrates. The reduced amount of converting furnace slag has greatly simplified slag return to the smelting furnace.

Feed materials for the smelting furnace consist of dry concentrates (the Naoshima smelter treats more than 20 different kinds of custom concentrates), silica flux, limestone flux, and granulated converting furnace slag. Blended feed materials are distributed to five pressurized hoppers, from which they are pneumatically discharged to the furnace through Mitsubishi-developed lances above the bath.

"The slag layer in the furnace is extremely thin and the molten bath consists mostly of matte, thus making possible a high-oxygen-efficiency top-blowing operation with relatively low pressure blast," Mitsubishi states. The slag contains 30-34% SiO_2 and 7-8% CaO. The matte-slag product of the smelting furnace advances by launder to the slag cleaning furnace, where small amounts of reducing agents—pyrites and/or coke breeze—are added to further reduce the copper in the slag. Slag grading 0.5% to 0.6% Cu is continuously tapped through an overflow hole located opposite the inlet hole and granulated with water. The matte is siphoned out and advances to the converting furnace by launder. In the converting furnace, matte is continuously converted to blister copper by blowing air and limestone flux (and cement copper as a cooling material when required) through lances. Converter slag grades 10-20% Cu, 10-20% CaO, and the balance mainly Fe_3O_4. Sulphur in the blister can be controlled by adjusting the slag content; when copper in the slag is low, sulphur is high, and vice versa. Slag is returned to the smelting furnace.

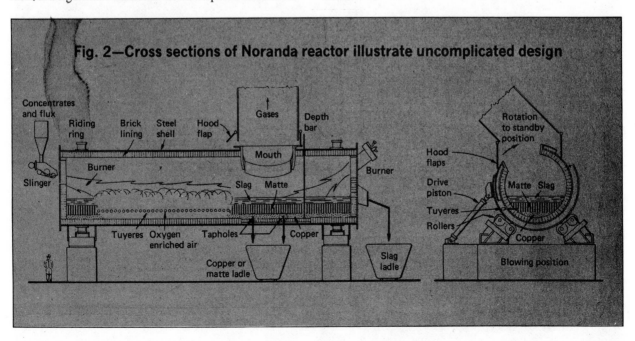

Fig. 2—Cross sections of Noranda reactor illustrate uncomplicated design

An IBM System/7 computer provides process control, including blast air and flux ratio regulation, temperature control, and feedback control of matte and slag compositions.

For acid plant feed, the high-strength SO_2 offgases at the Mitsubishi continuous plant are combined with low-strength gases from reverberatories still in use, sharply reducing overall sulphur emissions at the Naoshima plant.

Continuous Noranda reactor on stream since '73

Built at a cost of $12 million, the 800-tpd Noranda Process continuous smelter at Noranda, Que., produces either copper metal or high grade copper matte directly from sulphide concentrates in a single vessel fired from both ends (Fig. 2). Operational data and experience acquired during the first 30 months of reactor operation were reviewed by Noranda engineers at the International Symposium on Copper Extraction and Refining in early 1976.[41]

At the Noranda reactor, feed preparation for both incoming copper concentrates and recycled slag concentrates includes pelletizing on an 18-ft disk pelletizer. Pellets and dust then discharge to a conveyor belt, and flux feeds onto the pelletized mixture. A slinger throws the charge into the reactor through a port in the feed-end wall, and the charge is melted and oxidized by air introduced through tuyeres. Copper metal or matte is tapped through a taphole in the reactor barrel, and slag is skimmed through a taphole at the slag end. After slow cooling and milling, slag reports to a flotation circuit that produces a low copper tailing and a slag concentrate, which is recycled back to the reactor.

Reactor fuels include natural gas and oil and solid fuels such as coal and coke, which are added to the charge. A Gulf Vortometric burner at the feed end of the reactor is designed to burn 140 million Btu per hr of natural gas or heavy oil or any mixture of the two. At the slag end, a 20-million-Btu-per-hr Vortometric burner counters radiation losses from the shell and mouth. Until solid fuels were added to the charge, the capacity of the reactor was limited by burner capacity and efficiency, and there was considerable spare converting air capacity. Using part of the spare converting air for burning solid fuels has raised reactor throughputs while reducing burner firing rates and improving refractory life and fuel efficiency. It has also increased the ability of the converter to treat low-energy-content materials such as revert slags and purchased secondaries with low contents of oxidizable sulphur and iron.

The Noranda reactor's cylindrical shell measures 70 ft long x 17 ft in diameter. It is constructed of 515 Gr 55 steel selected for its low-creep characteristics and is supported on two riding rings 60 ft apart. The reactor can rotate through 48° to bring the tuyeres above the bath (standby) position.

An electrically driven 35,000-scfm, 17-psig Rootes-Connersville multistage blower delivers air to the reactor via a bustle pipe. Steel piping 2½ in. in diameter, coupled with Victaulic joints, links the bustle pipe to the tuyere adapters. Sixty tuyeres are installed, but those near the feed end of the reactor are generally not used because of splashing in the feedport. The tuyeres are of 2⅛-in.-ID stainless steel pipe, spaced 6¼ in. apart. The average blowing rate in the first run of the reactor was 19,000 scfm. During an oxygen testing period, it was 26,000 scfm, and the last run before the Noranda paper was presented averaged 38,500 scfm.

During copper production, copper, matte, and slag layers coexist in the reactor, and the air-to-concentrate ratio is used to adjust the levels of the three products. Product levels are determined by using a 1¼-in.-dia mild steel bar counterweighted over a porthole at the slag-end side of the

hood. The bar is lowered into the bath for 15-20 sec and then removed. The high thermal conductivity of the copper layer heats the bar to a red or yellow heat. The lower conductivity of the matte heats the bar to a dull red, and the slag sticks to the bar. Levels are accurate to within an inch and are checked hourly. No analyses of feed or molten contents are required for control.

When producing matte, only matte and slag phases exist, and the stoichiometric air requirement varies with different matte grades. The matte is sampled regularly and analyzed for copper and iron.

Tapped slag is analyzed for iron and silica every 2 hr during both copper and matte production.

Copper or matte produced in the Noranda reactor is tapped into 130- or 200-cu-ft ladles, which are then transported on a rail-mounted ladle car to the existing converter aisle. Copper has been finished in an anode furnace, but the usual Noranda practice is to pour reactor copper into any converter during the copper finishing blow. This saves transfer from one end of the converter aisle and gives a standard air blowing time in the anode furnace. The reactor copper contains about 2% sulphur, which would need several hours of blowing in the standard Noranda anode furnace fitted with only one air tuyere.

Offgases leave the reactor through a 12 x 8-ft mouth in the barrel. A water-cooled hood covers the mouth whether the tuyeres are in or out of the bath, avoiding gas spill common in converter operation. An evaporative cooler is bolted to the reactor hood, and 16 air-atomizer water sprays cool the gas to 700°F. (In other installations, a waste-heat boiler may be used.) An electrostatic-precipitation section consists of three parallel units and has an operating efficiency exceeding 98%. The reactor produces a constant-volume, high-strength SO_2 gas stream.[42]

Wanted: cost-effective emission controls

When Congress passed the Clean Air Act in 1970, it set a deadline of five years for cleaning up polluted air. EPA then established air quality standards, and the states embarked on an effort to develop and apply regulations for complying with the standards. EPA rejected many state plans and adopted a policy of stringent regulation based on the criteria of best available control technology, with the definition of such technology resting with the regulatory agency.

This drive for emissions controls has sharply affected nonferrous smelter operation and has required heavy investment in SO_2 emission controls. Smelter operators charge that much of the government's rule making has failed to consider realistically the economics of emissions controls, and nonferrous smelting companies have been in almost continuous confrontation in the courts with regulatory agencies for the past several years. A number of steps that could be taken to achieve more economic air quality improvement programs were suggested by Frederick E. Templeton of Kennecott Copper Corp.'s Metal Mining Div. at the 1975 AMC mining convention.[43] First, it is essential that environmental control programs be made cost effective, Templeton said: "That is, every dollar or Btu of environmental investment must produce a defined benefit, or it shouldn't be made."

Development of cost-effective air pollution control will involve: 1) an evaluation of air quality improvement to be gained from each of the control measures applicable at each source, 2) evaluation of the total cost of each of these control measures, and 3) selection of the combination of measures that produces the most improvement for the least total cost.

"To date, there has not been any meaningful effort to approach air pollution control from a cost-effective standpoint," Templeton asserted. "In fact, many regulators, in their zeal to apply controls, skip these steps—imposing controls on the basis of control technology rather than environmental improvement, a practice that can lead to waste of economic and energy resources on efforts of little significance. State or Federal regulatory agencies cannot possibly prescribe cost-effective environmental control strategies if they don't bother to assess the improvement and costs on a case-by-case basis."

There are several ways by which air quality can be improved, including: reducing the amount of pollutants emitted, limiting the number of sources that emit pollutants, selecting environmentally advantageous locations for emission discharge through such measures as tall stacks or source siting, and selective timing of emissions. A systematic approach can combine these methods to achieve environmental goals in the most cost-effective manner.

SCRA seeks means for SO$_2$ control

Commercial systems for limiting the amount of SO$_2$ emitted during nonferrous metals smelting have centered on SO$_2$ recovery and conversion to sulphuric acid. However, unless there is a market for the acid—not always the case—sulphuric acid is a byproduct that is not easily discarded.

In 1971, US copper producers formed the Smelter Control Research Association to investigate processes for removing sulphur oxides and particulates from copper reverberatory furnace gases. To date, SCRA efforts have focused on processes that produce environmentally acceptable, throwaway byproducts. Results of this research were reviewed by SCRA technical director Ivor Campbell at the 1975 AMC mining convention.[44]

The most extensive pilot scale and demonstration scale SO$_2$ control investigations so far have been devoted to throwaway processes using limestone or lime slurry scrubbing. A 4,000-scfm pilot plant for such processes was built at Kennecott Copper Corp.'s McGill, Nev., smelter. However, after about 18 months of tests, SCRA concluded that, at its present state of development, wet-limestone scrubbing is not reliable for removing SO$_2$ from copper reverberatory furnace gas. Negative test results included higher downtime than other processes, lack of reliable criteria for scale-up to commercial scale modules, lower SO$_2$ recoveries than with other scrubbing media, and the risk that limestone scrubbing might become obsolete before remaining development problems are resolved.

SCRA also found that with wet-limestone scrubbing, SO$_2$ recoveries decrease as SO$_2$ concentration in the feed stream increases, dropping from 85% recovery in feed streams containing 0.5% SO$_2$ to about 72% recovery in feed streams containing 1.5% SO$_2$. Extrapolation of these results indicated that a system employing six TCA contact stages in addition to a venturi scrubber would be needed for 90% removal of SO$_2$ on a sustained basis from rever-

beratory furnace gas containing 1% SO$_2$.

Subsequently, SCRA directed its attention to other soluble systems providing high SO$_2$ removal efficiencies and adaptable to either throwaway or regenerative processes. A further requirement was that the products could be discarded in an environmentally acceptable way.

Two processes based on ammonia scrubbing were selected as having potential for meeting SCRA's stated objectives: a regenerative closed-loop ammonium bisulphate process and a throwaway ammonia double-alkali process. Should both processes prove viable, ammonia scrubbing would have the added attraction of permitting the user to produce a throwaway product initially and then to substitute a regenerative process for acid or sulphur production at a later date, with little or no modification of the scrubbing system.

In both processes, ammonium sulphite scrubbing liquors react with SO$_2$ in the feed stream to form ammonium bisulphite.

After preliminary investigations, SCRA elected to build a 4,000-scfm pilot plant to test the ammonia scrubbing processes at the Magma copper smelter at San Manuel, Ariz. As of September 1975, when the plant had been on stream five months, results indicated that high SO$_2$ recovery efficiencies were attainable.

Limestone utilization rates have been significantly higher in ammonia scrubbing than in limestone scrubbing tests, and under favorable conditions, the total cost of alkali (limestone plus ammonia) could be lower for the ammonia double-alkali process than for the limestone process.

The calcium sulphite-sulphate precipitate formed is difficult to wash, however, and further work will be required to determine whether the ammonium ion content of the filter cake can be reduced to acceptable levels to avoid excessive ammonia makeup requirements and to minimize the soluble salt content of the throwaway product. Early testing showed no evidence of ammonia double salt formation, which, if it occurred, would complicate removal of ammonia from the filter cake.

Further work will be required to determine whether the formation of sulphates can be restricted to an acceptable level and if sulphate can be removed at a rate that avoids sulphate buildup. Additionally, a heavy plume forms at the plant stack under certain conditions, for reasons which are not yet well established.

An obvious major drawback of all throwaway processes is the generation of large tonnages of sludge.

While results of testing on the ammonia scrubbing processes are encouraging, Campbell concluded, the energy and raw material requirements are tremendous. The magnitude of these requirements dictates that scrubbers be employed only when alternative methods are not available for meeting air quality standards. Consideration must also be given to the interaction of all strategies in use for achieving acceptable water quality, air quality, and land usage, he said, to be certain that the cure is not worse than the disease. □

Hydrometallurgy: new processes move to commercialization

HYDROMETALLURGICAL PROCESSING has received increasing attention over the last several years, with the copper industry in particular devoting a major effort to developing commercial processes, for both sulphide and oxide

concentrates. Duval and Cyprus are developing ferric chloride leach processes for sulphides, and Anaconda has built a 36,000-tpy Arbiter process plant at Anaconda, Mont., to extract copper from sulphide concentrates by oxygen-ammonia leaching below 100°. Greater tonnages of oxide concentrates are being processed by a variety of leaching techniques, and solvent extraction-electrowinning technology is increasingly being used to recover metallic copper from leach solutions.[9]

Early in 1976, Anamax started up a 10,000-tpd oxide leach plant at its Twin Buttes mine in Arizona to process oxide ores that cap its sulphide deposit. A solvent extraction circuit at the plant is designed to yield 30,000 tpy of copper, which will be processed to cathodes in an electro-winning circuit.

Cities Service plans to build a solvent extraction-electrowinning plant at its Miami, Ariz., mine to recover copper directly from solution, replacing a current operation in which copper is extracted by cementation on scrap iron.

Cyprus pilots Cymet process

Cyprus Mines' Cymet process is being piloted in a plant capable of treating 25 tpd of chalcopyrite concentrates. The process is based on electrooxidation of sulphide sulphur to elemental sulphur at the anode of diaphragm cells; solution of metal ions; and reduction of copper at the cathodes. The ground slurry of sulphide concentrate is leached countercurrently with a ferric chloride anolyte returned from the iron cells.[1]

Paul R. Kruesi, president of Cyprus Metallurgical Processes Corp., offered the following description of the Cymet flowsheet at the 1973 meeting of the American Mining Congress:[45]

"Incoming feed is slurried using a 'Marconaflo' system. This system permits highly automated feed handling and control. In certain cases, the feed may require grinding. A 90% minus 270-mesh grind is desirable. The feed slurry is countercurrently attacked in a series of four contacts, of which one is the anodes of the cells. These leaches are conducted under relatively mild conditions of 70°-90°C except the final leach, which is more vigorous and produces a gangue-sulphur tails. Elemental sulphur may be recovered from this gangue.

"The cuprous-ferrous chloride solution from leaching is contacted with copper coming from Stage II and III cells to reduce any cupric ion present and to recover silver and gold.

"The solution is then sent to Stage I cathode, where copper powder is plated. The powder is recovered by thickening, centrifuging, and washing, and then briquetted for electrorefining into pure copper.

"The ferrous chloride solution, depleted in iron, is purified to remove other trace metals. In case of high zinc content, this may be removed by solvent extraction and separately recovered. The purified ferrous chloride is sent either to iron cells for the plating of iron or to iron hydrolysis for the removal of hydrated iron oxide. Either method regenerates the ferric chloride required in leaching.

"Water required in washing waste products is evaporated in cooling the electrolytic cells, which, as they are operated at high current density, produce a substantial amount of heat."

Duval building 32,500-tpy CLEAR process plant

After piloting its ferric chloride CLEAR process over a two-year period, Duval Corp. is now scaling it up to a 32,500-tpy commercial operation in Arizona. The process recovers metallic copper from chalcopyrite and other copper-containing materials by ferric chloride oxidation to produce cupric chloride. The cupric chloride is reduced to cuprous chloride and copper is recovered by electrolysis. Ferric chloride is regenerated by oxidation, with a concurrent purge of iron, sulphate ions, and other impurities from the process solution.

"By combining the ferric chloride oxidation and the ferric chloride regeneration, an advantageous reduction in iron content of the process solution is effected, along with significant retardation of scaling," according to a Duval patent description of the process.[45] "The desired chloride molal concentration is maintained by the addition to the process solution of sodium chloride, potassium chloride, and/or magnesium chloride. Potassium chloride is a preferred source of chloride ions as a means of purging substantially all sulphate ions from the process solution."

SIX: a new option for Cu recovery

Solvent ion exchange has in the past 10 years become an important system for recovery of copper. Plants now operating or under construction worldwide have a combined capacity of more than 200,000 tpy.[1] Solvent ion exchange (SIX) plants concentrate metal in solutions to strengths that permit recovery by electrowinning, precipitation, or crystallization. While the technique has been well established in recovery of uranium and some other metals, the concept was slow to catch on with copper producers. Now, companies operating SIX plants for copper extraction in the US include Ranchers Exploration and Development at Miami, Ariz., Cyprus at Bagdad and Johnson Camp, Ariz., Anamax at Twin Buttes, Ariz., and Anaconda at Anaconda, Mont. The Anaconda plant operates on Arbiter process liquors. Cities Service has built a plant at Miami, Ariz., that is slated to startup this year.

Because the reactions taking place in SIX systems are ionic in nature, the solution matrix can be changed completely. For example, the copper contained in the ammoniacal leach liquors of the Arbiter process can under certain conditions be evacuated down to the parts-per-million level and pulled into an organic liquid phase containing a suitable ion exchange reagent. This occurs during the extraction stage. The copper can then be transferred from the loaded organic phase to a sulphuric acid solution in the stripping stage.

In this example, pregnant copper sulphate in the stripping circuit is electrolyzed in a tankhouse, regenerating acid as spent electrolyte to be returned to the stripping circuit. The pregnant aqueous copper solution of the stripping circuit, however, could be processed through chemical steps other than electrowinning to precipitate the copper.

A General Mills spokesman capsulizes some of the inherent advantages of the SIX process for copper as follows: in electrowinning, the electrolyte copper content is divorced from the leach circuit; because SIX purifies, the system can tolerate higher impurities in the leach liquors, and higher current densities can be maintained in the tankhouse; electrowon copper cathodes from SIX systems are of high quality; and the concentration and purification characteristics of the system could improve the performance of current copper vat leach systems.

San Xavier leaching 4,000 tpd

Installation of a substantial number of new acid plants at US copper smelters as part of smelter operators' SO_2 emissions control programs is generating significant tonnages of sulphuric acid, which in turn has prompted development of new copper leaching operations based on sulphuric acid. One of the more recent new leaching operations, Asarco's 4,000-tpd San Xavier plant 20 mi south of Tucson, started up in March 1973 using acid from the company's smelters at Hayden, Ariz., and El Paso, Tex. Rollin W. Roberts, foreman at the leach plant, described the operation in MINING CONGRESS JOURNAL, December 1974.[47]

The San Xavier leaching section has nine vats, each 70 x 70 x 22 ft deep and each having a capacity of 4,000 dry tons of ore and 300,000 gal of solution. The vats operate on a nine-day cycle, during which one vat is always being loaded, one excavated, one washed, and five to six leached, depending the need for vat repair.

At the beginning of each leaching cycle, a high copper-bearing solution is advanced from the vat filled the previous day by upward percolation. The vat is topped off by downward filling and placed on recirculation for 8 hr.

The solution is then removed as a "pregnant" bleed to a 400,000-gal storage tank. The vat is refilled by downward percolation with a second advance solution, which is allowed to recirculate for 6 hr before being advanced into the next new vat of ore. Acid is added during the recirculation periods, with the acid profile maintained at a minimum of 30 gpl for the first three days of leach and 40 to 60 gpl during the last two days.

Vats are leached for an average of 5½ days, after which a vat's contents are washed for 39½ hr with a combination of dilute leach solutions (vat drains), barren solutions, and fresh water. The solution filling and advancing process is done simultaneously among the five to six vats in the circuit and requires 4-5 hr to complete using an 8-in. air lift system. The air lift system is operated by two 750-cfm blowers.

Present vat recovery at San Xavier ranges between 78% and 82%. Acid consumption ranges between 75 and 80 lb per ton of ore leached per day, or 18,000 to 21,000 gpd of 96% sulphuric acid.

Pregnant liquors produced in the leaching section assay 12 to 18 gpl copper and 8 to 12 gpl acid. This solution is advanced to a cementation section of 12 conventional iron precipitation launders. The precipitation material is a burnt, shredded, and detinned can product supplied from El Paso, Tex.

Phosphoric acid is new uranium source

Most of the world's phosphate rock production derives from marine phosphorites that generally contain 50 to 200 ppm uranium. Although such concentrations are only 5% to 10% of the content of commercially mined uranium ores, the vast extent of such phosphate deposits has made them targets of considerable interest for uranium for many years. Now, at least four uranium-from-phosphate extraction programs are moving toward commercialization, and one plant is nearing completion. Richard C. Ross, a technical specialist for United Nuclear Corp., provided an update on these uranium-from-phosphate developments in E/MJ, December 1975.

All of the new processes are based on liquid-liquid solvent extraction, in which uranium-bearing phosphoric acid is contacted with an organic liquid carrying a uranium extractant. Uranium Recovery Corp., a United Nuclear subsidiary, is using a module concept at Florida phosphate operations, the most obvious feature of which is the splitting of the process into two parts. Only initial extraction and stripping take place at the phosphoric acid plant site. The concentrated strip solution is then trucked to a central processing plant a few miles away. Using this approach, a simplified module can be erected at each phosphoric acid plant. Each module incorporates only the larger scale front-end processes, while more complex but smaller scale downstream processes (including all yellowcake handling) will be concentrated in a single, centrally located plant.

URC has completed its first full scale module at the W. R. Grace & Co. plant near Bartow, Fla., and the module was slated for full scale operation during the first quarter of 1976. URC has also contracted to install two modules at a new phosphoric acid plant owned by a subsidiary of International Minerals and Chemical Co., which came on line recently about 10 mi west of Mulberry, Fla. Another module will also be installed at the Grace plant as part of an expansion planned for completion during 1977. When all four modules are on line, production capacity of the URC operation should be about 1.3 million tpy of yellowcake.

In addition to the URC work, three other programs to recover uranium have been conducted in the Florida phosphate rock district. Westinghouse has worked on a cooperative pilot plant program with Gardinier Inc. at Gardinier's Tampa plant. The work is complete, but no definite commitments for a commercial plant had been announced as of last December.

Gulf Oil Chemicals has been operating a mobile pilot plant at the Agrico Chemical Co. phosphoric acid plant in South Pierce, Fla. The project was scheduled for completion during the third quarter of 1975, but again no commitment was made for construction of a commercial plant.

Freeport Minerals is in the advanced stages of a uranium pilot plant program at its phosphoric acid plant at Uncle Sam, La. Freeport feels its process is economically feasible, but it has not released plans for a commercial operation.

The total uranium content in wet process phosphoric acid produced annually in the US is estimated at 5.5 to 6 million lb of U_3O_8. Commercialization of recovery processes for this material will add substantially to US uranium reserves. □

Processors seek ways to hold down energy costs

MOST PYROMETALLURGICAL PLANTS ARE CLOSELY TIED TO conventional fuels; however, fuel shortages and higher costs for natural gas and fuel oil have focused attention on alternate energy sources.

In the Lake Superior iron mining district, coal is attracting growing interest for firing pelletizing plants—the subject of a number of test projects at the US Bureau of Mines Twin Cities Metallurgy Research Center.[9]

In the Southwest, Newmont Mining's 1975 annual report notes, supplies of natural gas have "become increasingly uncertain and limited at best." Newmont's Magma Copper subsidiary installed equipment in 1975, including storage facilities, that permits greater use of oil as smelter fuel during periods of natural gas scarcity. However, the cost of oil has risen to such an extent that Magma has also found it necessary to consider coal as an alternative, cheaper fuel, and the company has initiated engineering of installations for using coal as a primary smelting fuel. Magma also has a source of coal under investigation.

The high cost and increasing scarcity of metallurgical grade coke has compelled lead producers to investigate fuel economy measures for lead smelting, a USBM report notes.[9] A process for injecting a continuous stream of air mixed with powdered coal, lead concentrate, and silica flux into a 1,200°C bath of fused, lead-rich slag shows promise of replacing the conventional lead blast furnace. Violent agitation of lead-rich slag produced by submerged coal combustion provides the intimate contact between the liquid lead and melted slag needed to maintain the reaction in spite of fluctuations in feed. Calculations indicate that 1.5 tph of coal could produce 24.6 tph of lead metal from 33.2 tph of concentrates by this process, whereas a conventional smelter operating at the same rate would require 5.5 tph of metallurgical coke.

Coal gasification may in the future provide an alternate fuel source for pyrometallurgical operations. However, coal gasification processes are either still in development stages or warrant further improvement to increase the Btu content in their product. With few exceptions, the prospect of large scale commercial production via coal gasification seems unlikely before the 1980s.

How emission controls boost energy use

A study by University of Texas researchers reveals that a 56% reduction in SO_2 emissions from Asarco's El Paso copper smelter by conversion of converter gases to sulphuric acid raised overall plant energy consumption by about 6%.[48] Additional SO_2 controls on lower concentration reverberatory and roaster gas streams would increase that figure to about 11%. (See graph.) Controlling 98% of SO_2 emissions from the plant would increase the energy requirement to about 15% of the plant's total energy demand and 30% of its electricity use. Particulate controls now installed take only about 1% of the plant's total energy demand but 10% of its electricity requirement. Emissions controls now installed add 0.1¢ to 0.3¢ per lb to the cost of copper production, and future controls are expected to increase this burden to 0.5¢ to 1.0¢.

SO_2 controls implemented as of late 1975 at the El Paso smelter included a 550-tpd sulphuric acid unit for the converter flue gases from the copper smelter. Capital investment in air pollution control equipment totaled about $19 million for the acid plant and $6 million for particulate

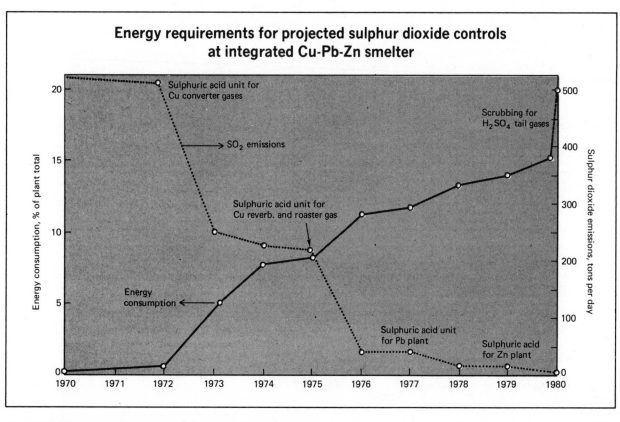

Energy requirements for projected sulphur dioxide controls at integrated Cu-Pb-Zn smelter

control equipment. The acid plant achieved a 56.4% reduction in total SO_2 emissions, for a capital expenditure effectiveness of $65,500 per ton of SO_2 removed per day. Operating costs for the sulphuric acid plant averaged $300,000 per month or $22 per ton of acid produced—equal to about $34 per ton of SO_2 removed from the converter gases. Future plans call for an additional capital expenditure of $40 million to $60 million, primarily for additional SO_2 controls through sulphuric acid manufacture.

For the copper industry as a whole, the University of Texas researchers conclude, capital expenditures exceeding $100,000 per tpd of capacity will be necessary to meet SO_2 emissions restrictions of 90% or greater. Overall economic impact on the copper industry will be an increase of more than $500 million in capital costs and increased fuel bills of $10 million to $25 million annually for air pollution controls.

Byproduct recovery and reuse of SO_2 as sulphuric acid, elemental sulphur, or ammonium sulphate is, of course, necessary to provide an effective solution to the problem of SO_2 emissions. Sulphuric acid is useful if nearby markets exist, but elemental sulphur is preferable if byproduct material must be shipped extensive distances. Development of markets for sulphuric acid products adjacent to smelters is necessary to minimize overall costs.

While installing emissions controls has raised the cost of nonferrous metals smelting, the report concludes, smelters may reap a major benefit from design improvements that minimize air flow and heat loss through tighter ducting, fewer leaks, water-cooled hooding, and oxygen enrichment of gas streams. Operating personnel may also become more cognizant of the need to minimize fuel usage as well as pollutant generation. However, training programs will be necessary to implement energy conservation activities. An additional benefit of extensive implementation of air pollution controls may be found in the shift from reduced use of natural gas to greater use of electricity.

Whatever the case, the amount of energy required to produce a pound of copper is expected to increase. From 1963 to 1973, this per-pound total rose by 22%, according to a US Bureau of Mines report, with the increased energy requirement attributable to declining ore grades as well as strict environmental controls. For the foreseeable future, these trends will continue, and the US energy investment in copper will grow.[49] □

References

1) "The Quiet Revolution in the Wide World of Mineral Processing," E/MJ, June 1975, p 87.
2) Shoemaker, R. S., and Taylor, A. D., "Mill Design for the Seventies," AIME Centennial Meeting, February 26-March 4, 1971.
3) Bullock, R. L., "Mine-Plant Design Philosophy Evolves From St. Joe's New Lead Belt Operations," MINING CONGRESS JOURNAL, May 1973, p 20.
4) Gould, W. D., "Basic Design Problems for a Large Concentrator," AIME Annual Meeting, New York City, February 16-20, 1975.
5) Smith, Dr. H. W., "Application of Mill Process Controls Can Slash Operating Costs and Improve Mineral Recovery," MINING ENGINEERING, November 1974, p 33.
6) White, J. W., "Survey of Automated Controls Generates Both Negative and Positive Feedback," E/MJ, February 1974, p 59.
7) Amsden, M. P., Chapman, C., and Reading, M. G., "Computer Control of Flotation at the Ecstall Concentrator," 13th International Symposium on the Application of Computers and Mathematics for Decision Making in the Mineral Industries, Technical University of Clausthal, Clausthal-Zellerfeld, West Germany, October 6-11, 1975.
8) Instrument Society of America, "Instrumentation in the Mining and Metallurgy Industries," Vol. 3, Proceedings of the 4th Annual Mining and Metallurgy Group Symposium and Exhibit, Milwaukee, October 6-9, 1975.
9) USBM Metallurgy Research Staff, "Processing Gains Chalked up on Many Fronts," E/MJ, June 1975, p 109.
10) Rovig, A. D., and Fisher, T. J., "Anaconda Converts from Autogenous to Steel Grinding at the C. E. Weed Concentrator, Butte, Mont.," SME Fall Meeting, Acapulco, Mexico, September 1974.
11) Brison, R. J., and Campbell, R. A., "Optimizing Grinding and Regrinding Capacity in Mill Design," AIME Annual Meeting, San Francisco, February 20-24, 1972.

12) Rowland, C. A. Jr., and Kjos, D. M., "Autogenous and Semi-Autogenous Mill Selection and Design," SME Fall Meeting, Acapulco, Mexico, September 1974.
13) Dunn, D. J., "Build a Better Mill Liner," National Western Mining Conference and Exhibition, Denver, Colo., February 7-10, 1973.
14) Dunn, D. J., "Optimizing Ball Mill Liners for Production and Economy," AIME Annual Meeting, Las Vegas, February 22-26, 1976.
15) Wood, R. K., "Modeling and Control of Crushing and Grinding Circuits," 4th Annual Mining and Metallurgy Symposium, ISA, Milwaukee, October 6-9, 1975.
16) Hathaway, R. E., and Guthals, D. L., "The Continuous Measurement of Particle Size in Fine Slurry Processes," CIM, Toronto, May 4-7, 1975.
17) US Bureau of Mines, "Technologic Trends in the Mineral Industries," Mineral Yearbook, 1970 (preprint).
18) "Annual Review," MINING MAGAZINE, June 1975.
19) Goldberger, W. M., Faulkner, B. P., and Thiers, E. A. (Battelle Columbus Laboratories), "An Analysis of Technology for Improved Beneficiation of Ultrafine Mineral Particle Systems," CIM Annual Meeting, Vancouver, April 15-18, 1973.
20) Anderson, M. A., Wilmot, C. I., and Jackson, C. E., "A Concentrator Improvement and Modernization Program Utilizing Large-Volume Flotation Machines," AIME Annual Meeting, New York City, February 16-20, 1975.
21) Custred, U. K., Degner, V. R., and Long, E. W., "Recent Advances in Coarse Particle Recovery Utilizing Large Capacity Flotation Machines," SME Fall Meeting, Acapulco, Mexico, September 22-25, 1974.
22) Browning, J. S., McVay, T. I., and Johnson, A. B., "Continuous Flotation of High-Clay Potash Ores," US Bureau of Mines Report of Investigations 8081, 1975.
23) Gaudin, A. M., "Progress in Magnetic Separation Using High-Intensity, High-Gradient Separators," MINING CONGRESS JOURNAL, January 1974, p 18.
24) Dayton, S. H., "CVRD: Charging into the Future with a Bundle of New Projects," E/MJ, November 1975, p 110.
25) Iannicelli, J., "High Extraction Magnetic Filtration of Kaolin Clay," AIME Annual Meeting, Las Vegas, February 22-26, 1976.
26) Keys, N. J., Gordon, R. J., and Peverett, N. F., "Photometric Sorting of Ore at a South African Gold Mine," SME Fall Meeting, Acapulco, Mexico, September 22-25, 1974.
27) Terrill, I. J., and Villar, J. B., "Elements of High-Capacity Gravity Separation," CIM Annual Meeting, Montreal, April 1974.
28) "Heavy Media Ore Dressing Tool," MINING MAGAZINE, March 1975, p 227.
29) Daellenbach, C. B., Mahan, W. M., and Armstrong, F. E., "Rapid Particle Size Analysis by Hydrosizing and Nuclear Sensing," US Bureau of Mines Report of Investigations 7879, 1974.
30) Yu, A. T., "Bulk Handling—A Three-Quarter Century Survey and Outlook," AIME Centennial Meeting, New York City, February 26-March 4, 1971.
31) Yu, A. T., and Kinneberg, D. A., "Handling of Smelter Feed—A Purpose-Oriented Approach," AIME Annual Meeting, Las Vegas, February 22-26, 1976.
32) Abrams, R. M., "Handling Concentrates—A Sticky Problem," AIME Annual Meeting, Las Vegas, February 22-26, 1976.
33) "Long-Distance Slurry Transport—Finally in the Pipeline?", CHEMICAL ENGINEERING, April 12, 1976, p 67.
34) Anderson, A. K., "Marconaflo Systems—State of the Art," National Western Mining Conference, Denver, January 1976.
35) "Tailing Disposal Today," Proceedings of the International Tailing Symposium, C. L. Aplin and G. O. Argall Jr., eds., Miller Freeman Publications Inc., San Francisco.
36) Kealy, D., "Safe Design for Metal Tailings Dams," MINING CONGRESS JOURNAL, January 1973, p 51.
37) US Bureau of Mines Information Circular 8410 and Report of Investigations 7477.
38) Brown, L. F., "Reclamation at Climax, Urad, and Henderson Mines," American Mining Congress Convention, San Francisco, September 28-October 1, 1975.
39) Hyatt, D. E., "Effluent Guidelines Compliance—Technology and Cost Elements," Western Mining Conference, January 29, 1976.
40) Rampacek, C. and Dunham, J. T., "Copper Ore Processing—US Practices and Trends," MINING CONGRESS JOURNAL, February 1976, p 43.
41) "Extractive Metallurgy of Copper—Pyrometallurgy and Electrolytic Refining," Vol. 1, Yannopoulos, J. C. and Agarwal, J. C., eds., Proceedings of an International Symposium sponsored by the Metallurgical Society of AIME, February 1976.
42) Hallett, G. D. (Noranda Mines), "Continuous Copper-Smelting Process Uses Single Vessel," CHEMICAL ENGINEERING, April 26, 1976, p 62.
43) Templeton, F. E., "Environmental Trends—Air," American Mining Congress Convention, San Francisco, September 29, 1975.
44) Campbell, I. E., "Developments in Sulphur Dioxide Control," American Mining Congress Convention, San Francisco, September 29, 1975.
45) Kruesi, P. K., "The 'Cymet' Copper Process," American Mining Congress, Denver, September 1973.
46) Duval Corp., US Patent 3,879,272, April 22, 1975.
47) Roberts, R. W., "San Xavier Vat Leach Plant Operation," MINING CONGRESS JOURNAL, December 1974, p 53.
48) Cooper, H. B. H. Jr., and Ledbetter, J. O. (University of Texas Department of Civil Engineering), "Energy and Economic Effectiveness of Air Pollution Control Systems at Southwestern US Nonferrous Metal Smelters," Annual Meeting of the Pacific Northwest International Section of the Air Pollution Control Association, Vancouver, November 19-21, 1975.
49) Rosencrantz, R. D., "Energy Consumption in Domestic Primary Copper Production," USBM Information Circular 8698.

A collection of flowsheets illustrating some of the latest innovations and modifications in mineral processing

CURRENT TRENDS IN MINERAL PROCESSING are capsulized here in E/MJ's 1975 flowsheet portfolio, a collection of processing schemes for aluminum, copper, lead/zinc, iron, nickel/cobalt, and assorted other products.

Among the highlights of this section:

■ Earth Sciences' alumina-from-alunite process, which will serve as a model for a commercial-scale 500,000-tpy alunite plant to be built in Utah.

■ Toth process, based on chlorination of kaolin, followed by a reduction of aluminum trichloride by manganese.

■ Mexico's alunite process, which has yielded 99% pure metallurgical grade alumina in pilot plant runs.

■ Continuous smelting processes such as the Noranda and Worcra methods, both of which have been pilot-plant tested and have evolved into commercial or semi-commercial sized plants.

■ Jarosite leach process used by Texasgulf, which not only improves zinc recoveries by several percent above the 90-93% range, but also boosts recoveries of cadmium, copper, silver, and lead.

■ Outokumpu Oy's process for the sulphatizing roasting of nickel-, copper-, and zinc-bearing cobaltiferous pyrite concentrates at its Kokkola works in Finland.

■ Liquid ion exchange, used in a unique operation combining pollution control and metal recovery at the El Paso, Tex., plant of SEC Corp.

■ Coming of age of the Midrex and the HyL processes, the two most prominent and successful direct reduction methods.

■ Inco's new nickel refinery at Copper Cliff, Ont., which makes use of both its TBRC and Carbonyl processes.

■ Pressure leaching of cobalt mattes in the USSR.

■ Sherritt Gordon's process for leaching nickel-cobalt sulphide concentrate at Fort Saskatchewan.

■ Computer control of pyrite flotation at Outokumpu's Pyhasalmi plant. □

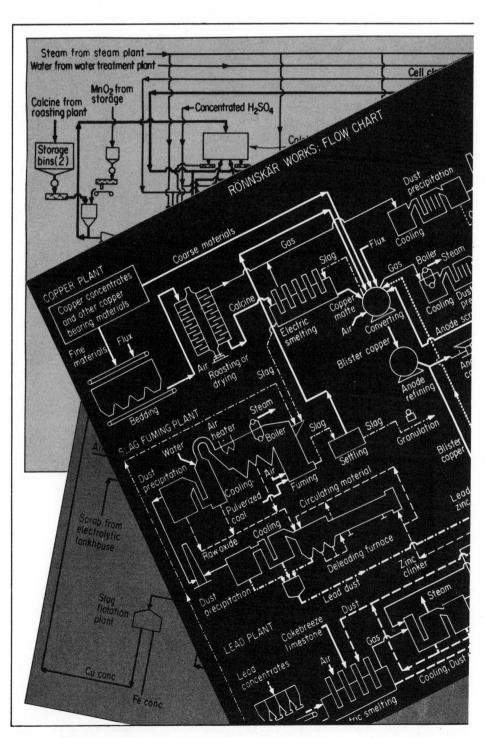

ALUMINUM

Alunite process

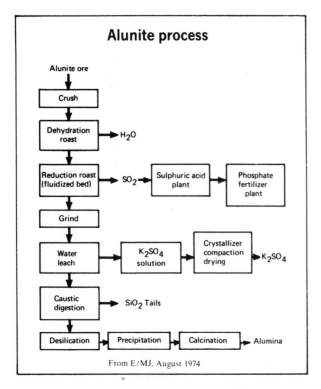

From E/MJ, August 1974

Alcoa fluid-flash calcination process

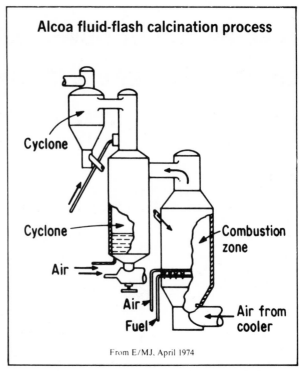

From E/MJ, April 1974

Mexican alunite process

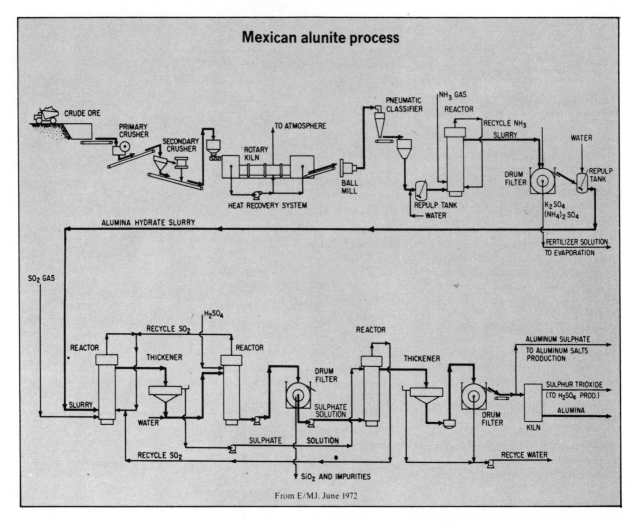

From E/MJ, June 1972

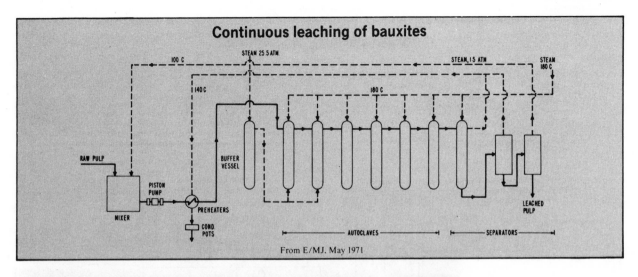

Continuous leaching of bauxites

From E/MJ, May 1971

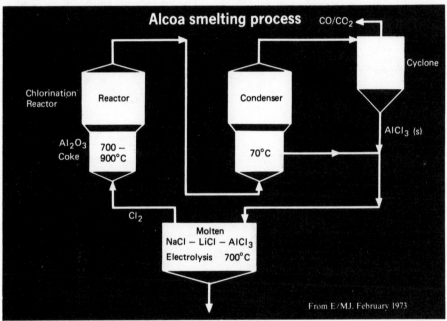

Alcoa smelting process

From E/MJ, February 1973

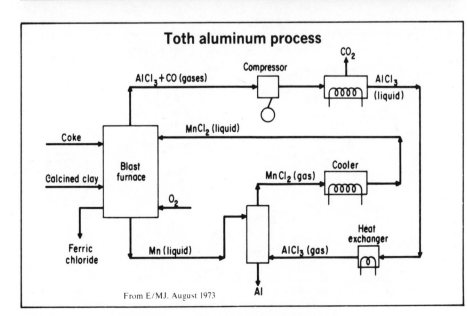

Toth aluminum process

From E/MJ, August 1973

Alumina from alunite is being produced at a $3 million, 10-tpd pilot plant in Golden, Colo., by a joint venture of Earth Sciences, National Steel, and Southwire. The process, yielding by-product fertilizers, is caustic-based, with the latter part being a modification of the Bayer process. Startup of a commercial plant is slated for mid-1975.

Alcoa's fluid flash calcining process, which drives off water of crystallization from precipitated aluminum hydroxide in the Bayer process, is said to reduce fuel requirements by 30-40%.

Mexico's alumina-from-alunite process—developed at the University of Guanajuato—will be used in a commercial plant being built at Salamanca.

Continuous leaching of bauxites offers the possibility of more extensive plant automation. The process uses low-speed, 370- to 500-psi piston pumps to push the bauxite pulp into the autoclaves.

Alcoa's smelting process is expected to reduce by as much as 30% the electricity requirements of the conventional Hall process. The first commercial unit, which is due on stream this year, will have an initial capacity of 15,000 tpy of primary aluminum.

The Toth process is based on a chlorination of kaolin clay, followed by a reduction of the resultant aluminum trichloride by manganese metal.

COPPER

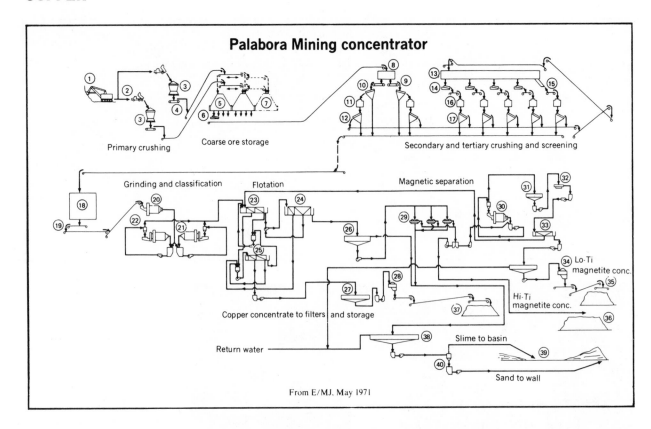

Palabora Mining concentrator

From E/MJ. May 1971

1. Electric shovels
2. Dump trucks
3. 2 - 54-in. primary gyratory crushers, Allis-Chalmers
4. 2 - 72-in. apron feeders, Fraser-Chalmers (AMSCO)
5. 2 - 30,000-ton coarse ore stockpiles
6. 8 - 60-in. vibratory feeders, Jeffrey Galion
7. Future stockpile area
8. Secondary ore bin
9. 2 - 60x14-in. apron feeders, Fraser-Chalmers (AMSCO)
10. 2 - 6x14-ft double-deck vibrating screens, Tyler
11. 2 - 7-ft Standard Symons crushers, Nordberg
12. 2 - 8x20-ft double-deck vibrating screens, Hewitt-Robins
13. Tertiary ore bin
14. 4 - 42x78-in. vibrating feeders, Jeffrey Galion
15. 1 - Langlaagte chute
16. 5 - 7-ft Shorthead Symons crushers, Nordberg
17. 5 - 8x20-ft single-deck vibrating screens, Hewitt-Robins
18. 6 - 10,000-ton fine-ore bins
19. 52 - Belt feeders
20. 6-12x16½-ft rod mills, Allis-Chalmers
21. 12 - 12x12-ft ball mills, Marcy
22. 12 - 27-in. cyclones
23. Agitair roughers and scavengers, Galigher
24. 300-cu-ft Fagergren cells, Wemco
25. Agitair cleaner cells, Galigher

26. 6 - 23-ft 6-in. Hydroseparators, Eimco
27. 2 - 75-ft copper thickeners, Eimco
28. 3 - 6-ft 9-in. x 7-ft disk copper filters, Eimco
29. 18 - 36x72-in. rougher, magnetic separators, Krupp
30. 2 - 22x12-ft regrind ball mills, Allis-Chalmers
31. 2 - Desliming Hydroseparators, Eimco

32. 8 - Cleaner magnetic separators, Dings
33. 28 - Agitator flotation cells, Galigher
34. 3 - 6-ft 9-in. x 8-ft disc filters, Eimco
35. Low-TiO₂ magnetite stockpile
36. High-TiO₂ magnetite stockpile
37. Copper concentrate storage bay
38. 3 - 300-ft tailings thickeners, Dorr Oliver
39. Tailings dam
40. Cyclone station

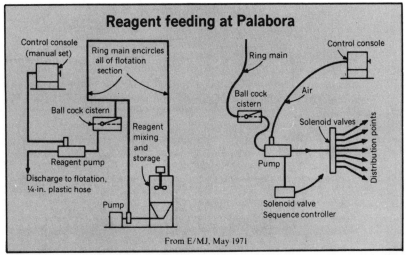

Reagent feeding at Palabora

From E/MJ. May 1971

Circulation of most reagents in the Palabora concentrator is handled by a small 0.16- to 8.23-gpm precision pump with micrometer-screw capacity control.

Noranda process

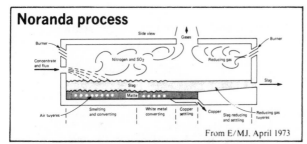

From E/MJ, April 1973

Noranda's continuous smelting process combines reverb and converter functions. SO_2 offgases can permit H_2SO_4 synthesis.

WORCRA furnace

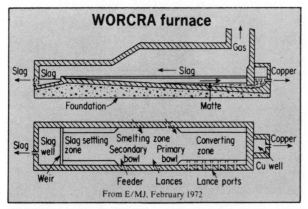

From E/MJ, February 1972

WORCRA process uses heat from converting reaction to smelt fresh charge. It delivers a steady gas stream of 8-10% SO_2.

TBRC process

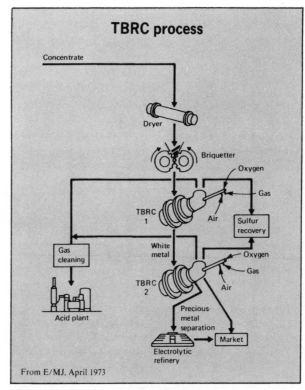

From E/MJ, April 1973

TBRC process, though not yet fully tested for copper production, was built into a 275-tpd nickel plant by Dravo for Inco.

At Palabora Mining (opposite page), current milling rate is more than 50,000 mtpd, with an average running time of 97%. (See E/MJ, May 1971, p 80.) Ore supplied to the mill is segregated into high-titania and low-titania to meet Japanese contract specifications. Even though the cutoff grade of the South African ore mined was reduced from 0.4% copper to 0.2% copper during the 1967-70 period, and the grade of mill feed dropped from 0.71% to 0.54% copper during the same period, mill recovery has increased from 81.90% to 84.39%.

Various reagents have been tested, but the best to date continues to be potassium amyl xanthate. Reagent 425 (Cyanamid) was used at startup as a froth modifier, but early in 1969 it was replaced by 41G, a product made locally by National Chemical Products SA. This reagent has contributed substantially to recovery, as it was found that 425 had a depressing effect on sulphides. A frother also made locally by National Chemical has replaced the mixer frothers previously used—pine oil, Aero 65, and MIBC.

Uranium and thorium, present in tailings from the concentrator, are recovered in Palabora's uranium oxide plant.

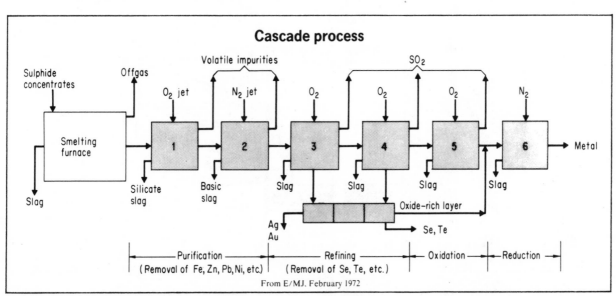

Cascade process

From E/MJ, February 1972

Cascade process—which can also be adapted to recover high-purity copper from scrap materials—consists of a reverb-type smelting furnace for copper sulphide concentrates, followed by a series of at least six treatment vessels.

COPPER

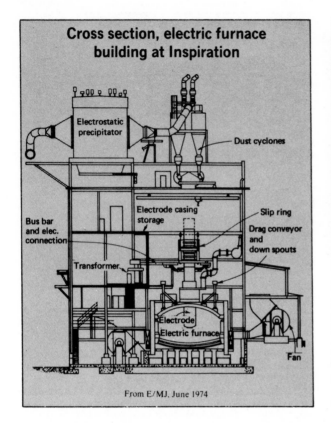

Cross section, electric furnace building at Inspiration

Electrostatic precipitator

Dust cyclones

Bus bar and elec. connection

Electrode casing storage

Slip ring

Drag conveyor and down spouts

Transformer

Electrode

Electric furnace

Fan

From E/MJ, June 1974

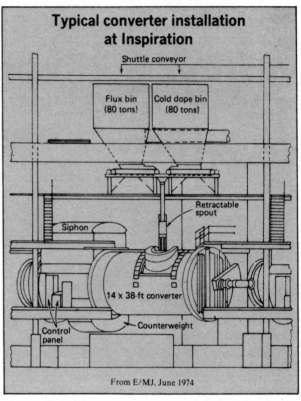

Typical converter installation at Inspiration

Shuttle conveyor

Flux bin (80 tons)

Cold dope bin (80 tons)

Siphon

Retractable spout

14 x 38-ft converter

Counterweight

Control panel

From E/MJ, June 1974

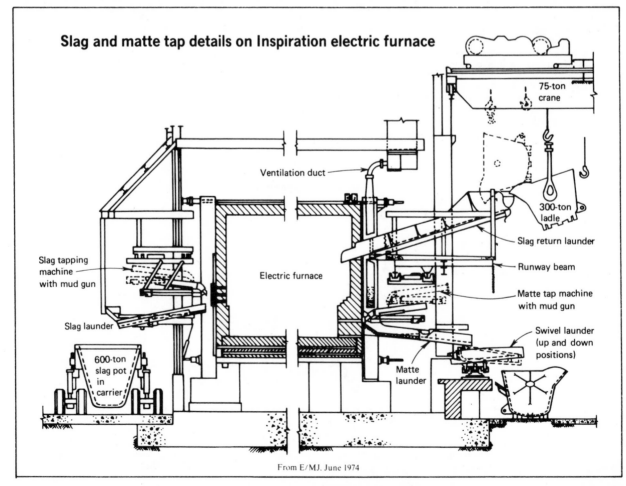

Slag and matte tap details on Inspiration electric furnace

75-ton crane

Ventilation duct

300-ton ladle

Slag return launder

Runway beam

Electric furnace

Matte tap machine with mud gun

Slag tapping machine with mud gun

Swivel launder (up and down positions)

Slag launder

Matte launder

600-ton slag pot in carrier

From E/MJ, June 1974

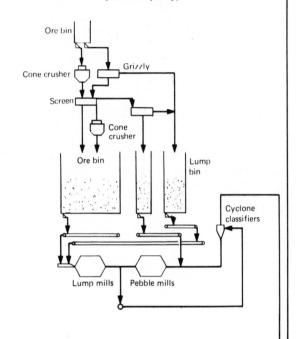

Pyhasalmi flotation scheme

(Outokumpu Oy)

Inspiration Consolidated Copper (opposite page) recently took a major step forward in the realm of air pollution abatement with equipment that included: a Norwegian-designed electric furnace and five Belgian-designed siphon converters; a hot gas cleaning system designed and made in the US; a cold gas cleaning system incorporating German and US equipment; a US-supplied rotary dryer; and an acid plant of West German design, which was assembled with German, UK, and US equipment.

Outokumpu Oy, Finland's biggest mining and smelting company, operates by computer control one of the largest pyrite flotation mills in the world, at the Pyhasalmi plant. The Pyhasalmi concentrator treats about 800,000 tpy of complex sulphide ore (chalcopyrite, sphalerite, and pyrite averaging 0.7% Cu, 2.2% Zn, and 38% S) to produce 20,000 tpy of copper concentrate, 30,000 tpy of zinc concentrate, and 500,000 tpy of pyrite concentrate.

Still the object of continuous development, the instrumentation of the flotation circuits now consists essentially of pulp, water, air, and reagent flow-meters; pump density meters; pH meters; and pulp level controllers in the cells. All these instruments are essential for stabilizing control. However, the key element of flotation control is the X-ray analyzer, which makes it possible for the company to optimize flotation operations.

The new Courier on-stream X-ray analyzers at Pyhasalmi are assaying copper, zinc, and iron in 13 slurries. The primary sample for each analyzer is about 200 liters per min, and the secondary sample 20 liters per min. Analyzing time for one slurry is 25 sec.

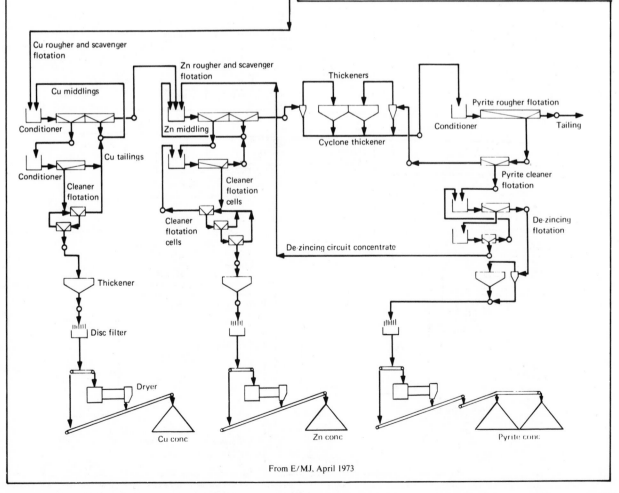

From E/MJ, April 1973

Bougainville's copper concentrator

Crushing & Ore Storage

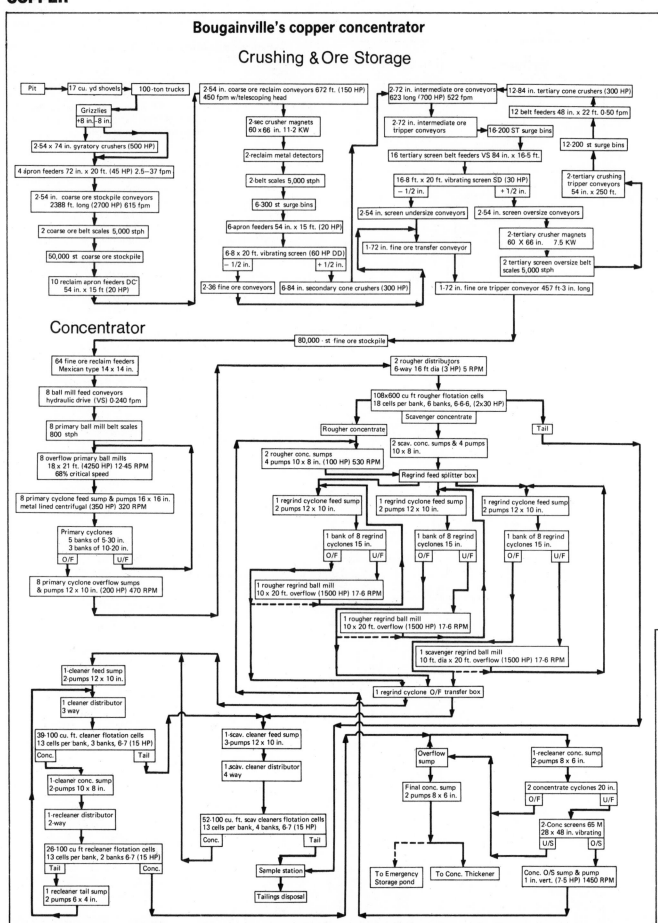

Concentrator

Concentrate Handling

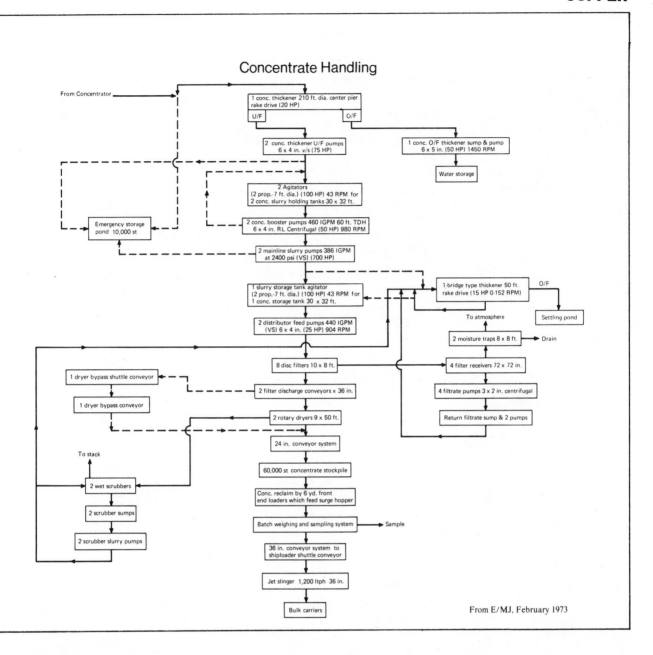

From E/MJ, February 1973

Bougainville Copper is exploiting a deposit estimated at 900 million lt of 0.48% copper and 0.36 dwt of gold per ton. The $400 million project is geared to mine and process ore at a rate of 90,000 stpd.

The operation was established on a production plan that called for an annual output in initial stages of 150,000 st of copper and 500,000 tr oz of gold in concentrate.

Bougainville ore has proved harder to grind than predicted by metallurgical testing. As a result, the plant has undergone modifications, including addition of a ninth grinding mill and changes in the fine crushing and screening plant.

Instrumentation at the primary crushers includes truck dump light controls, annunciators, and crusher power and mantle position indicators. Downstream from the primaries, instrumentation includes indication and control of apron feeder speed, coarse ore conveyor feed rates, and horsepowers. In the fine crushing sections, instrumentation includes flow rate recording of weight on the coarse ore reclaim conveyors and remote manual control. In addition, sensors provide tramp material detection; indication of surge bin tripper position and level; control of feed rate to all crushers by power draw; measurement of tertiary screen feed conveyor weight; remote manual control of tertiary

screens; and alarm indication for electrical and conveyor malfunctions and blocked chutes.

Instrumentation in the grinding circuit includes feed rate measurement by belt scale with chart recording and totalizers, mill feed-water measurement and ratio control, cyclone feed and overflow density measurement, cyclone feed pump sump level measurement and control, mill power draw, pump amps, and annunciators.

In the flotation circuit, instrumentation includes air-operated cell level controllers, pH recording and control, reagent addition timers for percent-of-time pulse feeders, reagent tank levels and total flow rate, and annunciators.

Final concentrate must be cycloned and screened to about 99% minus 100 mesh to meet requirements for pipeline delivery of concentrates to the filter plant at Anewa Bay.

Accessory items in the pumping plant include two booster pumps to provide the required intake head to the mainline pumps and the test loop. Instrumentation includes thickener torque, level, and meter amps indication; underflow density controller; holding tank level indication; pipeline density, flowrate, pH, test loop differential pressure; and pump discharge pressure and amps. The latter is used as a guide to pump wear.

COPPER

Magma's electrolytic copper refinery

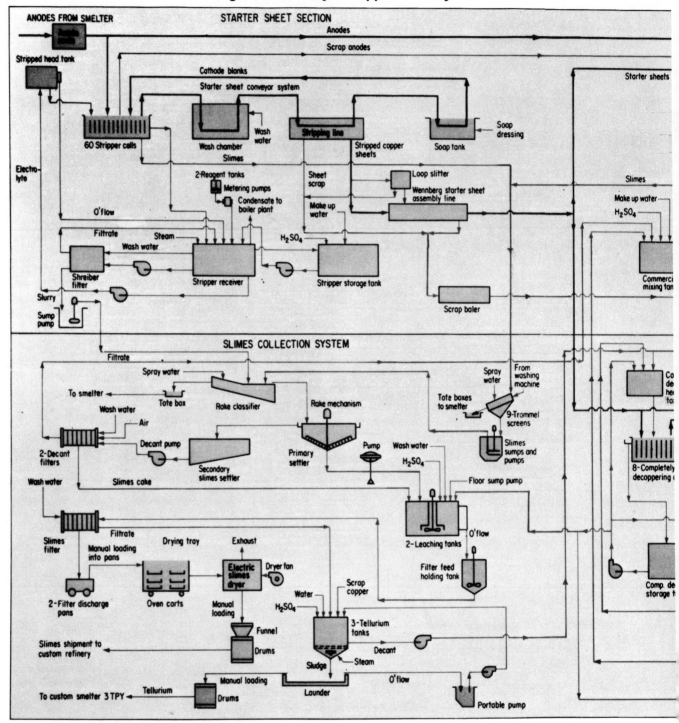

Magma Copper Co. topped off its $250 million expansion program in January 1972 with the dedication of what it termed an environmentally pure 200,000-tpy electrolytic copper refinery (see above) and a 100,000-tpy Southwire continuous rod (SCR) plant at the San Manuel Div. near Tucson, Ariz.

Highly automated, the new refinery was designed with a safety valve to permit 50% expansion without disrupting production, at some future time when it is economically and practically sound to expand.

The Magma refinery was given a realistic design rating of 200,000 tpy based on a current density of 20.35 amps per sq ft at a current efficiency of 85%.

The starter sheet or stripper section of the refinery is equipped

with a custom-designed mechanical trolley conveyor system that delivers full starter cell lots of 45 plated copper blanks (finished starter cathode) through a closed loop cycle that washes the load; sends it through a manual stripping line to remove the plated deposit; assembles and dips the stripped blanks in a soap tank; and returns the soaped blanks to the cell floor, where they are marshalled in a conveyor holding line for pick up and re-delivery to the starter cells.

This installation is credited with being a great saver of manpower, requiring a crew of only six men per shift to handle the plant requirements. Manpower requirements of an ordinary refinery for accomplishing the same routine may approximate four times the level of the new Magma plant.

Katanga ore processing

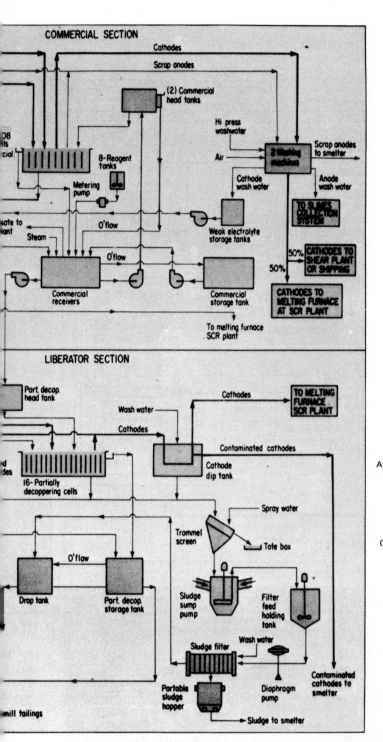

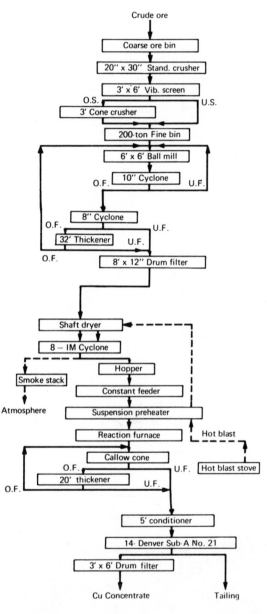

While stripping is now done manually, an automatic system figures prominently in future plans. Magma uses a Mitsubishi-licensed, metallized soap solution on the starter blanks to condition the surfaces for easy removal of the electrodeposit. A mechanical device employing suction cups and a vacuum system will probably be designed in the future to strip the metal layer.

Another important feature built into the refinery is a unique cell monitoring system for detection of short circuits—a rather common occurrence caused by bridging of the gap between the anodes and cathodes of a cell at localized spots of imperfect metal deposition. The heart of the system is a No. 7100 digital data system furnished by Westronics.

Cia. Minera Katanga, a Peruvian subsidiary of Mitsui Mining & Smelting Co., is operating a 150-tpd pilot plant that is doing a creditable job of extracting copper concentrates of 53% to 58% Cu from oxide ores with an average grade of 5% to 5½% copper. The Mitsui Segregation Process has been in operation since December 1973, recovering an average of 75% to 80% of the copper in the ore. After the first six months of trial operation, the process was stabilized, and the operators are now trained, leading to expectations of achieving 90% recovery and 60% Cu concentrates in the near future.

Ore discharged from the Kawasaki reaction furnace in the Mitsui segregation plant is immediately quenched, thickened, and pumped to the flotation section (see above). Flotation of the metallic copper deposited on cokes is done in three stages. Reagents used are KAX, pine oil, and a small amount of Z-200. Final froth is filtered, weighed, and bagged before storage.

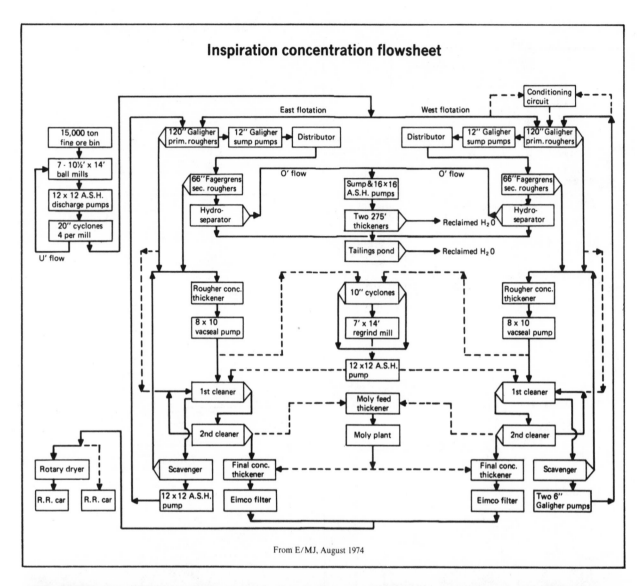

Inspiration concentration flowsheet

From E/MJ, August 1974

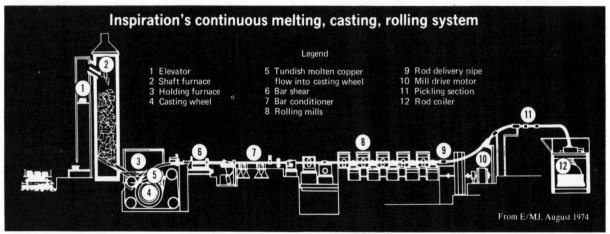

Inspiration's continuous melting, casting, rolling system

Legend

1 Elevator
2 Shaft furnace
3 Holding furnace
4 Casting wheel
5 Tundish molten copper flow into casting wheel
6 Bar shear
7 Bar conditioner
8 Rolling mills
9 Rod delivery pipe
10 Mill drive motor
11 Pickling section
12 Rod coiler

From E/MJ, August 1974

Inspiration concentrator's most notable feature is two identical circuits downstream from grinding. Rod plant utilizes Asarco continuous melting furnace and Southwire (SCR) process.

Vihanti handles record underground ore production achieved by Outokumpu Oy. Zinc and iron sulphides are depressed with lime and cyanide; a xanthate is used as collector, with copper and lead floated. Chalcopyrite is floated in alkaline circuit. Sphalerite is floated with copper sulphate and xanthate.

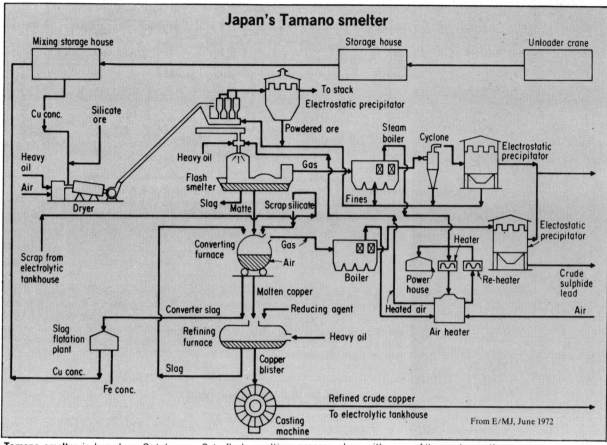

Japan's Tamano smelter

From E/MJ, June 1972

Tamano smelter is based on Outokumpu Oy's flash smelting process, along with some of its own innovations.

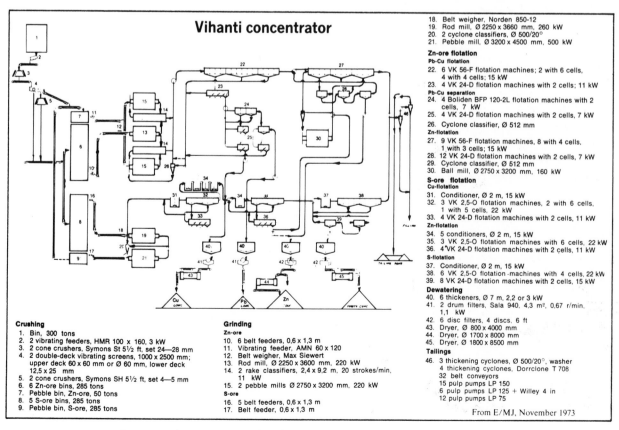

Vihanti concentrator

18. Belt weigher, Norden 850-12
19. Rod mill, Ø 2250 x 3660 mm, 260 kW
20. 2 cyclone classifiers, Ø 500/20°
21. Pebble mill, Ø 3200 x 4500 mm, 500 kW

Zn-ore flotation
Pb-Cu flotation
22. 6 VK 56-F flotation machines; 2 with 6 cells,
    4 with 4 cells; 15 kW
23. 4 VK 24-D flotation machines with 2 cells; 11 kW
Pb-Cu separation
24. 4 Boliden BFP 120-2L flotation machines with 2
    cells, 7 kW
25. 4 VK 24-D flotation machines with 2 cells, 7 kW
26. Cyclone classifier, Ø 512 mm
Zn-flotation
27. 9 VK 56-F flotation machines, 8 with 4 cells,
    1 with 3 cells; 15 kW
28. 12 VK 24-D flotation machines with 2 cells, 7 kW
29. Cyclone classifier, Ø 512 mm
30. Ball mill, Ø 2750 x 3200 mm, 160 kW

S-ore flotation
Cu-flotation
31. Conditioner, Ø 2 m, 15 kW
32. 3 VK 2,5-O flotation machines, 2 with 6 cells,
    1 with 5 cells, 22 kW
33. 4 VK 24-D flotation machines with 2 cells, 11 kW
Zn-flotation
34. 5 conditioners, Ø 2 m, 15 kW
35. 3 VK 2,5-O flotation machines with 6 cells, 22 kW
36. 4 VK 24-D flotation machines with 2 cells, 11 kW
S-flotation
37. Conditioner, Ø 2 m, 15 kW
38. 6 VK 2,5-O flotation machines with 4 cells, 22 kW
39. 8 VK 24-D flotation machines with 2 cells, 15 kW

Dewatering
40. 6 thickeners, Ø 7 m, 2,2 or 3 kW
41. 2 drum filters, Sala 940, 4,3 m², 0,67 r/min.
    1,1 kW
42. 6 disc filters, 4 discs, 6 ft
43. Dryer, Ø 800 x 4000 mm
44. Dryer, Ø 1700 x 8000 mm
45. Dryer, Ø 1800 x 8500 mm

Tailings
46. 3 thickening cyclones, Ø 500/20°, washer
    4 thickening cyclones, Dorrclone T 708
    32 belt conveyors
    15 pulp pumps LP 150
    6 pulp pumps LP 125 + Willey 4 in
    12 pulp pumps LP 75

From E/MJ, November 1973

Crushing
1. Bin, 300 tons
2. 2 vibrating feeders, HMR 100 x 160, 3 kW
3. 2 cone crushers, Symons St 5½ ft, set 24—28 mm
4. 2 double-deck vibrating screens, 1000 x 2500 mm;
   upper deck 60 x 60 mm or Ø 60 mm, lower deck
   12,5 x 25 mm
5. 2 cone crushers, Symons SH 5½ ft, set 4—5 mm
6. 6 Zn-ore bins, 285 tons
7. Pebble bin, Zn-ore, 50 tons
8. 5 S-ore bins, 285 tons
9. Pebble bin, S-ore, 285 tons

Grinding
Zn-ore
10. 6 belt feeders, 0,6 x 1,3 m
11. Vibrating feeder, AMN 60 x 120
12. Belt weigher, Max Siewert
13. Rod mill, Ø 2250 x 3600 mm, 220 kW
14. 2 rake classifiers, 2,4 x 9,2 m, 20 strokes/min,
    11 kW
15. 2 pebble mills Ø 2750 x 3200 mm, 220 kW
S-ore
16. 5 belt feeders, 0,6 x 1,3 m
17. Belt feeder, 0,6 x 1,3 m

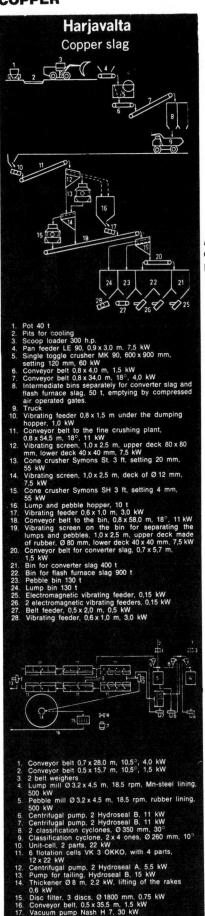

Harjavalta
Copper slag

1. Pot 40 t
2. Pits for cooling
3. Scoop loader 300 h.p.
4. Pan feeder LE 90, 0,9 x 3,0 m, 7,5 kW
5. Single toggle crusher MK 90, 600 x 900 mm, setting 120 mm, 60 kW
6. Conveyor belt 0,8 x 4,0 m, 1,5 kW
7. Conveyor belt 0,8 x 34,0 m, 18°, 4,0 kW
8. Intermediate bins separately for converter slag and flash furnace slag, 50 t, emptying by compressed air operated gates.
9. Truck
10. Vibrating feeder 0,8 x 1,5 m under the dumping hopper, 1,0 kW
11. Conveyor belt to the fine crushing plant, 0,8 x 54,5 m, 18°, 11 kW
12. Vibrating screen, 1,0 x 2,5 m, upper deck 80 x 80 mm, lower deck 40 x 40 mm, 7,5 kW
13. Cone crusher Symons St. 3 ft, setting 20 mm, 55 kW
14. Vibrating screen, 1,0 x 2,5 m, deck of Ø 12 mm, 7,5 kW
15. Cone crusher Symons SH 3 ft, setting 4 mm, 55 kW
16. Lump and pebble hopper, 10 t
17. Vibrating feeder 0,6 x 1,0 m, 3,0 kW
18. Conveyor belt to the bin, 0,8 x 58,0 m, 18°, 11 kW
19. Vibrating screen on the bin for separating the lumps and pebbles, 1,0 x 2,5 m, upper deck made of rubber Ø 80 mm, lower deck 40 x 40 mm, 7,5 kW
20. Conveyor belt for converter slag, 0,7 x 5,7 m, 1,5 kW
21. Bin for converter slag 400 t
22. Bin for flash furnace slag 900 t
23. Pebble bin 130 t
24. Lump bin 130 t
25. Electromagnetic vibrating feeder, 0,15 kW
26. 2 electromagnetic vibrating feeders, 0,15 kW
27. Belt feeder, 0,5 x 2,0 m, 0,5 kW
28. Vibrating feeder, 0,6 x 1,0 m, 3,0 kW

1. Conveyor belt 0,7 x 28,0 m, 10,5°, 4,0 kW
2. Conveyor belt 0,5 x 15,7 m, 10,5°, 1,5 kW
3. 2 belt weighers
4. Lump mill Ø 3,2 x 4,5 m, 18,5 rpm, Mn-steel lining, 500 kW
5. Pebble mill Ø 3,2 x 4,5 m, 18,5 rpm, rubber lining, 500 kW
6. Centrifugal pump, 2 Hydroseal B, 11 kW
7. Centrifugal pump, 2 Hydroseal B, 11 kW
8. 2 classification cyclones, Ø 350 mm, 30°
9. Classification cyclone, 2 x 4 ones, Ø 260 mm, 10°
10. Unit-cell, 2 parts, 22 kW
11. 6 flotation cells VK 3 OKKO, with 4 parts, 12 x 22 kW
12. Centrifugal pump, 2 Hydroseal A, 5,5 kW
13. Pump for tailing, Hydroseal B, 15 kW
14. Thickener Ø 8 m, 2,2 kW, lifting of the rakes 0,6 kW
15. Disc filter, 3 discs, Ø 1800 mm, 0,75 kW
16. Conveyor belt, 0,5 x 35,5 m, 1,5 kW
17. Vacuum pump Nash H 7, 30 kW
18. Filter fan HBDT—102 x 22, 2,2 kW

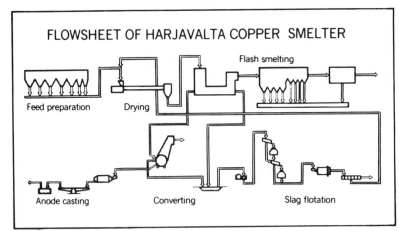

FLOWSHEET OF HARJAVALTA COPPER SMELTER

Feed preparation — Drying — Flash smelting — Anode casting — Converting — Slag flotation

At Harjavalta, in Finland, the flash furnace produces copper matte grades of 45% to 65% copper, a slag of 0.8% to 1.9% copper that is cleaned by flotation to 0.3% to 0.6% copper, and a furnace gas of 10% to 14% sulphur dioxide.

Cyprus-Pima Mining's new copper-molybdenum circuit, developed for Expansion 4, is a flexible mill, adaptable to a wide range of ore types and hardnesses. However, management feels there is still room for improvement. With experience gained during full scale operation of the additional circuit, a better design could be worked out using similar equipment in different or larger sizes and configurations, to improve the advantages of semi-autogenous circuits.

Legend, Cyprus-Pima flowsheet

1. 54-in. x 74-in. Allis-Chalmers gyratory
2. 3 - 5-ft x 14-ft Tyler
3. 3 - 7-ft Symons Standard
4. 7 - 6-ft x 14-ft Tyler
5. 7 - 7-ft Symons Shorthead
6. 10-ft x 16-ft Allis-Chalmers
7. 3 - Krebs D20B
8. 3 - Krebs D20B
9. 10½-ft x 13-ft Allis-Chalmers
10. 10½-ft x 13-ft Allis-Chalmers
11. 40 rows - 10-cell No. 66 Fagergrens
12. 8 rows - 10-cell No. 66 Fagergrens
13. 3 - Krebs D20B
14. 9-ft x 18-ft Allis-Chalmers
15. 6 rows - 10-cell No. 24 Denvers
16. 4 rows - 10-cell No. 24 Denvers
17. 2 rows - 10-cell No. 24 Denvers
18. 150 ft dia
19. 150 ft dia
20. 12-ft dia x 14-ft face - Eimco
21. 8-ft 10-in. x 10-ft disc - Eimco
22. 15-cell No. 120A Agitair
23. 3 - Krebs D20B cyclones
24. 9-ft x 18-ft Allis-Chalmers
25. 16 - No. 48 Agitairs
26. 10 - No. 48 Agitairs
27. 16 - No. 36 Agitairs
28. 16 - No. 48 Agitairs
29. 4 - Krebs D6B
30. 8 - No. 36 Agitairs
31. 5-ft x 5-ft Marcy
32. 6 - No. 36 Agitairs
33. 6 - No. 15 Denvers
34. 6 - No. 55 Denvers
35. 6-ft x 3-ft disc - Denver
36. Holoflyte
37. 54-in. x 74-in. Allis-Chalmers gyratory
38. 28-ft x 12-ft Hardinge
39. 28-ft x 12-ft Hardinge
40. 6-ft x 14-ft Tyler
41. 6-ft x 14-ft Tyler
42. 4 - Krebs D26B
43. 4 - Krebs D26B
44. 16½-ft x 19-ft Allis-Chalmers
45. 16½-ft x 19-ft Allis-Chalmers
46. 3 rows:
    15 cells No. 120 Fagergrens
    24 cells No. 120A Agitair

Flotation reagent consumptions (1973)
Copper Circuit

Reagent	Consumption (lb per ton ore)
Lime	2.75
Potassium amyl xanthate	0.019
Frothers—Shell 1638, Aerofroth 65, R-17 and R-23	0.043
Fuel oil—Shell aromatic T-54	0.010
NaCN	0.003

Cyprus-Pima flowsheet, with flexible new circuit (Mill 2)

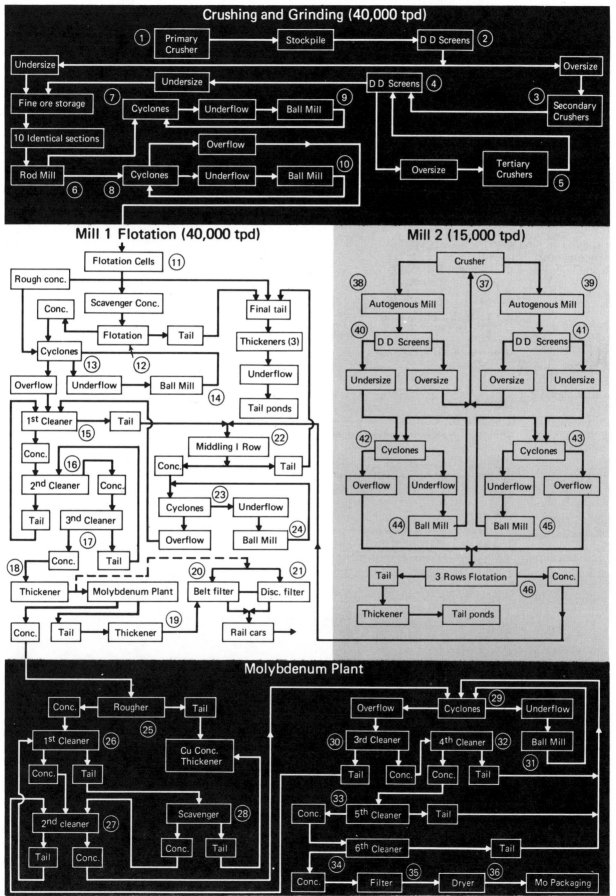

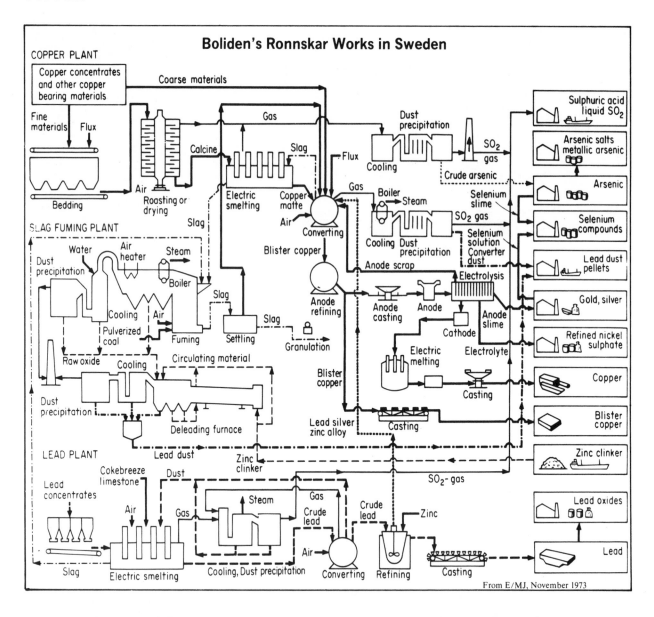

Boliden's Ronnskar Works in Sweden

COPPER PLANT

Copper concentrates and other copper bearing materials

Coarse materials

Fine materials | Flux

Bedding

Roasting or drying

Air

Calcine

Electric smelting

Slag

Gas

Slag

Flux

Copper matte

Air

Converting

Gas

Boiler

Steam

Cooling

Dust precipitation

Dust precipitation

Cooling

SO₂ gas

SO₂ gas

Crude arsenic

Selenium slime

Selenium solution Converter dust

Sulphuric acid liquid SO₂

Arsenic salts metallic arsenic

Arsenic

Selenium compounds

SLAG FUMING PLANT

Dust precipitation

Water

Air heater

Steam

Boiler

Cooling

Air

Pulverized coal

Fuming

Settling

Slag

Slag

Blister copper

Anode refining

Anode scrap

Blister copper

Anode casting

Anode

Electrolysis

Electric melting

Cathode

Electrolyte

Anode slime

Casting

Lead dust pellets

Gold, silver

Refined nickel sulphate

Copper

Granulation

Raw oxide

Cooling

Circulating material

Dust precipitation

Deleading furnace

Lead silver zinc alloy

Casting

Blister copper

LEAD PLANT

Lead dust

Zinc clinker

Zinc clinker

SO₂- gas

Zinc clinker

Lead concentrates

Cokebreeze limestone

Dust

Air

Gas

Steam

Gas

Crude lead

Crude lead

Zinc

Air

Slag

Electric smelting

Cooling, Dust precipitation

Converting

Refining

Casting

Lead oxides

Lead

From E/MJ, November 1973

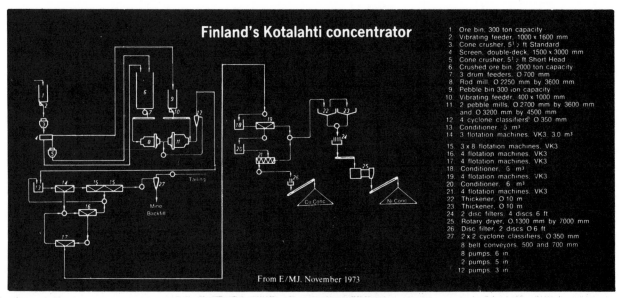

Finland's Kotalahti concentrator

1. Ore bin, 300 ton capacity
2. Vibrating feeder, 1000 x 1600 mm
3. Cone crusher, 5½ ft Standard
4. Screen, double-deck, 1500 x 3000 mm
5. Cone crusher, 5½ ft Short Head
6. Crushed ore bin, 2000 ton capacity
7. 3 drum feeders, Ø 700 mm
8. Rod mill, Ø 2250 mm by 3600 mm
9. Pebble bin 300 ton capacity
10. Vibrating feeder, 400 x 1000 mm
11. 2 pebble mills, Ø 2700 mm by 3600 mm and Ø 3200 mm by 4500 mm
12. 4 cyclone classifiers, Ø 350 mm
13. Conditioner, 5 m³
14. 3 flotation machines, VK3, 3.0 m³
15. 3 x 8 flotation machines, VK3
16. 4 flotation machines, VK3
17. 4 flotation machines, VK3
18. Conditioner, 6 m³
19. 4 flotation machines, VK3
20. Conditioner, 6 m³
21. 4 flotation machines, VK3
22. Thickener, Ø 10 m
23. Thickener, Ø 10 m
24. 2 disc filters, 4 discs 6 ft
25. Rotary dryer, Ø 1300 mm by 7000 mm
26. Disc filter, 2 discs Ø 6 ft
27. 2 x 2 cyclone classifiers, Ø 350 mm
   8 belt conveyors, 500 and 700 mm
   8 pumps, 6 in
   2 pumps, 5 in
   12 pumps, 3 in

Tailing

Mine Backfill

Cu Conc.

Ni Conc.

From E/MJ, November 1973

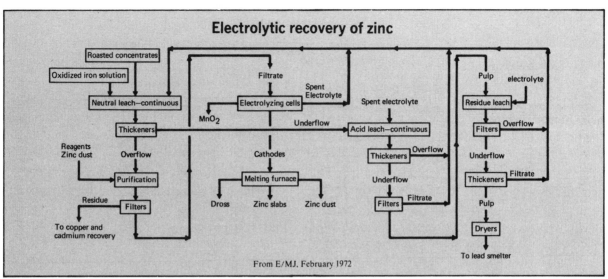

Electrolytic recovery of zinc

From E/MJ, February 1972

Electrolytic recovery of zinc continues to account for an increasing share of primary metal production in the US and abroad.

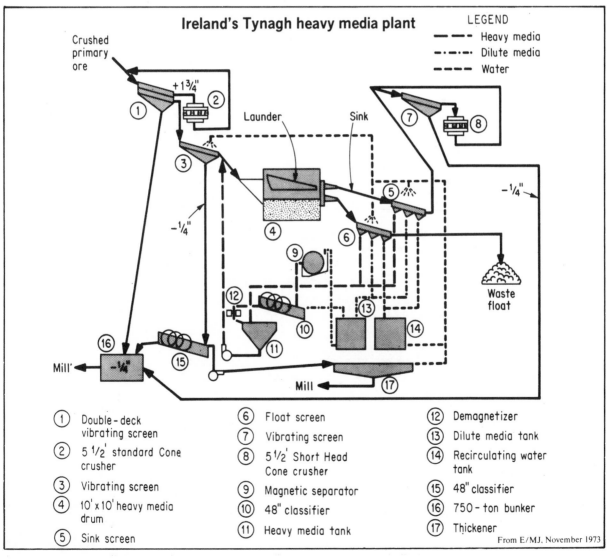

Ireland's Tynagh heavy media plant

LEGEND
— · — Heavy media
— · · — Dilute media
— — — Water

① Double-deck vibrating screen
② 5 ½' standard Cone crusher
③ Vibrating screen
④ 10' x 10' heavy media drum
⑤ Sink screen
⑥ Float screen
⑦ Vibrating screen
⑧ 5 ½' Short Head Cone crusher
⑨ Magnetic separator
⑩ 48" classifier
⑪ Heavy media tank
⑫ Demagnetizer
⑬ Dilute media tank
⑭ Recirculating water tank
⑮ 48" classifier
⑯ 750-ton bunker
⑰ Thickener

From E/MJ, November 1973

Japan's Akita zinc smelter

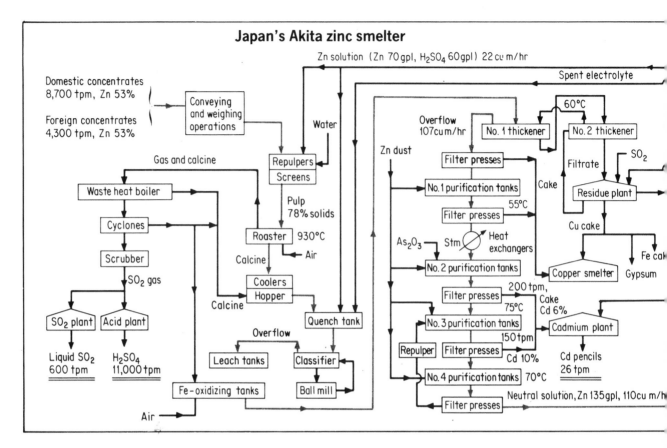

Texasgulf's zinc plant: first in North America to use

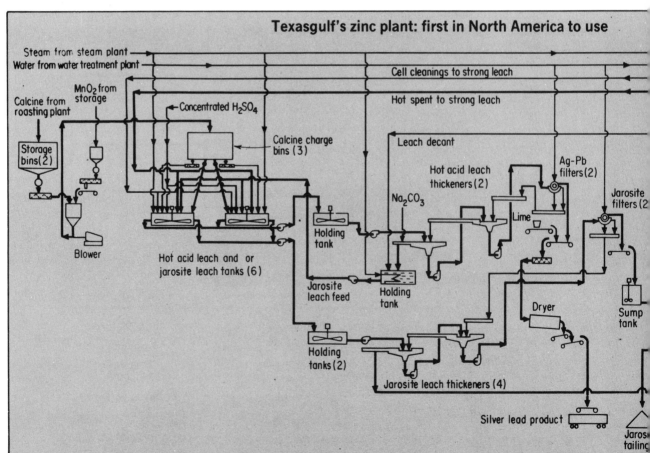

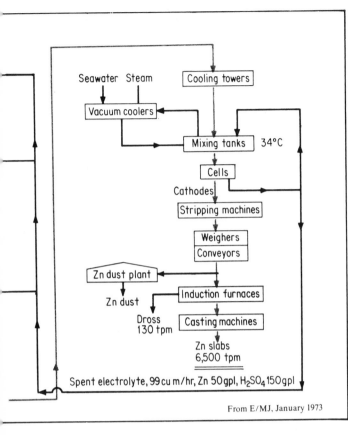

From E/MJ, January 1973

The Akita zinc plant, which started up in January 1972, was more than two years in the planning stages. The operating company, Akita Zinc, was formed by a group of six Japanese firms: Dowa, Nippon Mining, Sumitomo Metal Mining, Mitsui Metal Mining, Mitsubishi Metal Mining, and Toho Zinc.

The $36 million smelter features many types of equipment to eliminate manpower and ease the transportation of various concentrates to their processing points. Concentrates are mixed and routed to conveyors by automatically controlled machines. Automatic strippers in the zinc electrolytic plant require only occasional monitoring.

The main operations at the smelter are roasting, leaching, purification, and electrowinning of zinc from purified solution. The smelter is designed to produce 6,500 mtpy of slab zinc and 26 mtpm of cadmium.

Leaching at the Ecstall Mining (Texasgulf) zinc plant is a two-step procedure. A hot acid leach first dissolves zinc oxides and ferrites, leaving a lead-silver residue. After thickening and filtration, the hot acid leach solution becomes feed for the jarosite leach, with sodium carbonate added as the jarosite-forming reagent. After jarosite precipitation, thickening, and filtering, the jarosite is disposed of as tailings and the zinc-bearing solution is pumped to the purification plant.

jarosite precipitation to remove iron from solution

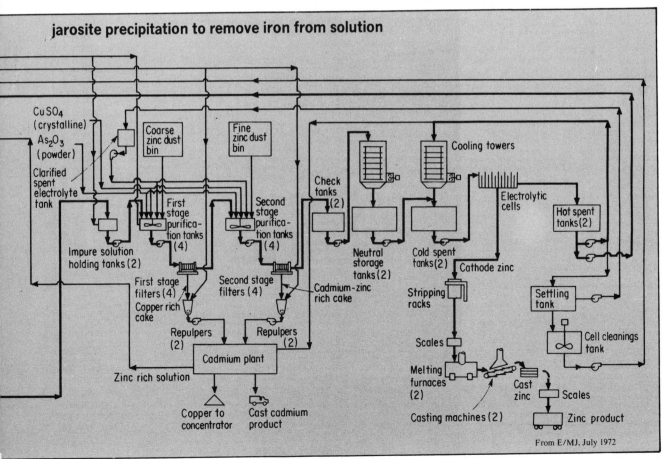

From E/MJ, July 1972

IOC's Carol Lake concentrator

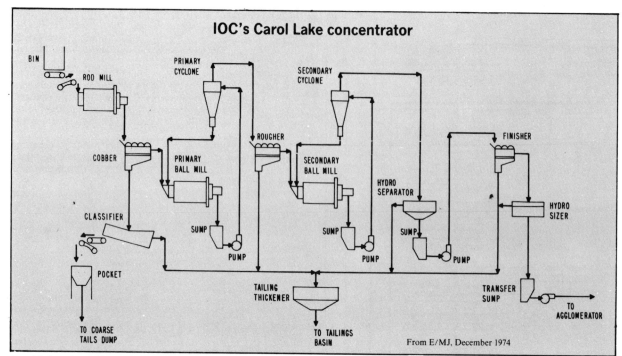

From E/MJ, December 1974

Carol Lake mined 30 million lt of crude specularite and magnetite averaging 38.4% Fe in 1973. Reserves are placed at more than 2 billion lt of open-pit ore. Concentration yields a product at 65.7% Fe, with weight and iron unit recoveries of 46% and 72%, respectively. Ore concentration takes place in 7,056 Humphrey gravity spirals arranged in 30 lines. Rougher tailings of 25 million tpy are magnetically beneficiated to produce 1.8 million tons of magnetic concentrate.

Typical concentrator section at US Steel's Minntac mine

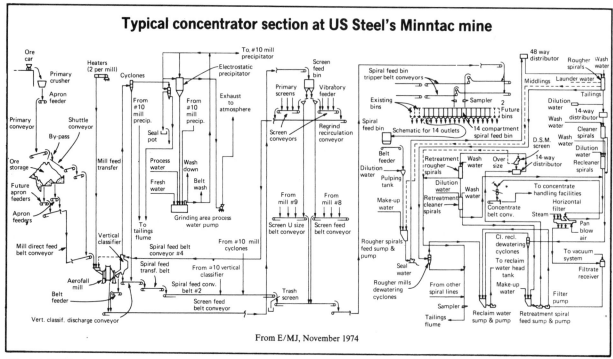

From E/MJ, November 1974

Minntac, US Steel's mammoth 12.5 million ltpy iron mine, is now preparing for its second major expansion program—designed to lift production to more than 18 million ltpy of 65% Fe pellets. Minntac's concentrator will stretch close to ½ mi long upon completion of the Step 3 expansion. It is fed from a three-stage crushing plant which receives run-of-mine crude. Crushing plant (not shown) consists of two 60 x 110-in. primary gyratories that deliver minus 6-in. material to the fine crushing circuit. The concentrator consists of six sections, each with two identical lines. Each section incorporates two rod mills, two primary ball mills, two secondary ball mills, eight sets of finisher magnetic separators, four sets of cobber magnetic separators, two spiral tailing classifiers, four secondary cyclones, two hydrosizers, two primary cyclones, four sets of magnetic separator roughers, two hydroseparators, and one tailing thickener.

Midrex direct reduction process

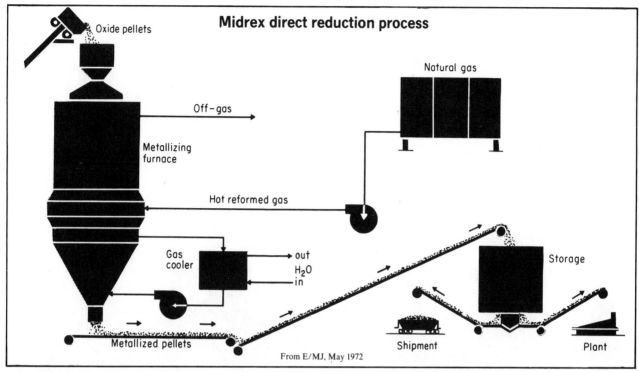

From E/MJ, May 1972

The Midrex direct reduction process produces 92-95% metallized material from cold indurated oxide pellets as they pass down a shaft furnace in a countercurrent flow of heated reformed gas. The reducing mixture of H_2 and CO is obtained from natural gas by reforming. A good system for offgas recovery and recirculation has evidently been developed. Efficient use of energy inputs may partly explain the unusually rapid acceptance of the Midrex process.

HyL direct reduction process

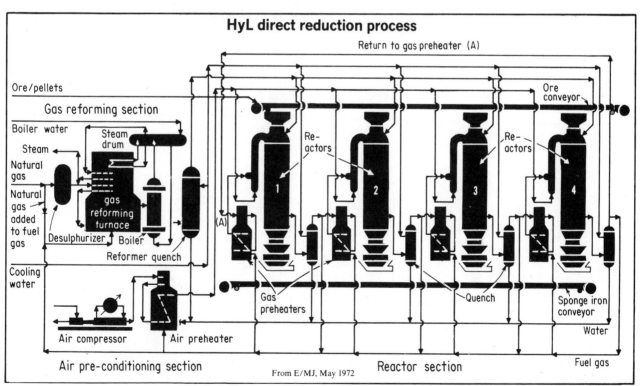

From E/MJ, May 1972

The HyL technique involves a static bed in which batches of ore remain stationary in a chamber through which hot reducing gases are circulated. The core of an HyL plant is a gas reforming section and a reduction section of four reactors. Desulphurized natural gas and steam are mixed, preheated, and processed in the presence of a nickel catalyst. The reformed product, after cooling, includes about 74% H_2, 13% CO, and a balance of CO_2 and CH_4. The mixture is passed to the reactors, each of which contains a fixed charge of ¼-in. to ½-in. iron ore lumps. Each reactor is operated in staged sequence: preheating raw ore by spent gas; reducing ore to sponge iron by fresh gas; cooling the sponge; discharging sponge and charging raw ore.

Nickel-cobalt process used by Freeport at Port Nickel

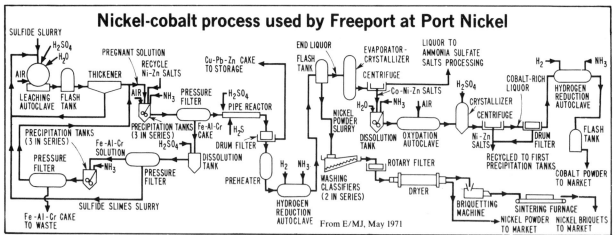

When Freeport owned Port Nickel, La., refinery, ores from Moa Bay, Cuba, were leached in autoclaves in the presence of H_2SO_4, yielding a solution of $NiSO_4$ and $CoSO_4$. Metals were precipitated by pressurized H_2. Amax now owns Port Nickel refinery.

Pressure leaching of nickel-cobalt mattes in USSR

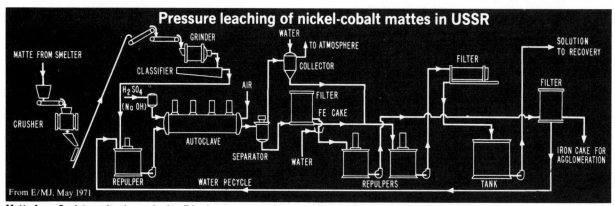

Matte from Soviet smelter is crushed to 74 microns, pumped into autoclaves at 130-160°C and 150-225 psi. Exiting the autoclave, iron hydroxide is filtered out. After solution is neutralized with soda, recovery of metals amounts to 95-97%.

Inco's Copper Cliff nickel refinery

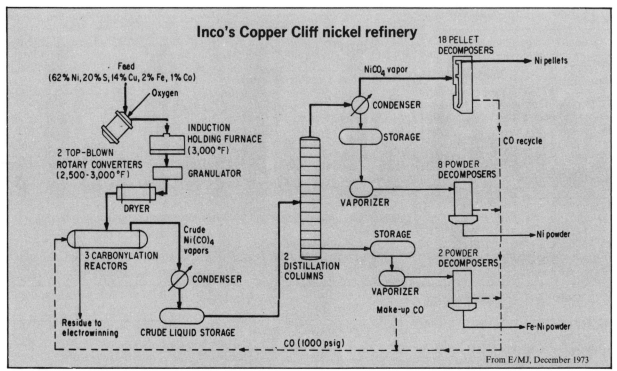

Inco's new $140 million refinery is versatile in its ability to produce high purity nickel from a wide range of nickel-bearing materials—such as nickel sulphide crudes, mattes, process dusts, and precious-metal-bearing intermediates.

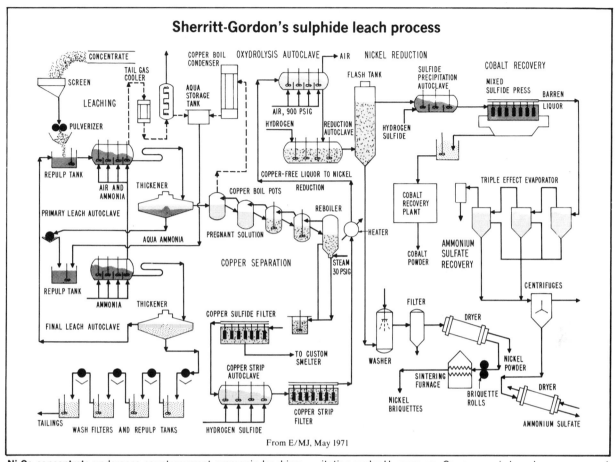

Sherritt-Gordon's sulphide leach process

From E/MJ, May 1971

Ni-Co concentrate undergoes countercurrent ammonia leaching in autoclaves at 80°C and 60 psi. Ni recovery proceeds by precipitation under H_2 pressure. Co recovery is based on aqueous oxidation of NiS-CoS precipitated at pH 2, 140°C, and 100 psi.

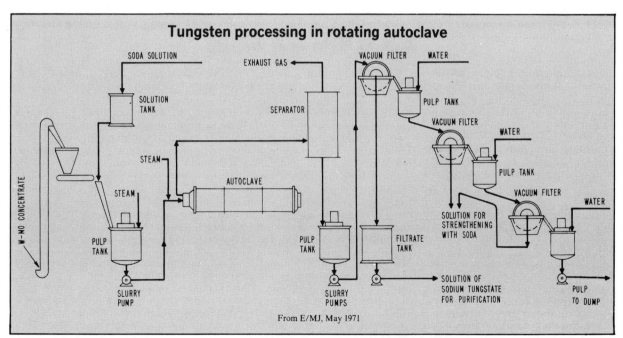

Tungsten processing in rotating autoclave

From E/MJ, May 1971

Extraction of tungsten and molybdenum is based on a one-stage leaching of low-grade materials inside a rotating autoclave. The concentrate, containing 8-12% tungsten and 1-6% moly, is initially mixed in a recycle solution and is slurried into the autoclave. Leaching occurs at 200°C over 4 to 6 hr. Slurry is forced in a separator and then on to filtration. The first filtrate is recycled for pressure leaching of high-grade scheelite concentrates.

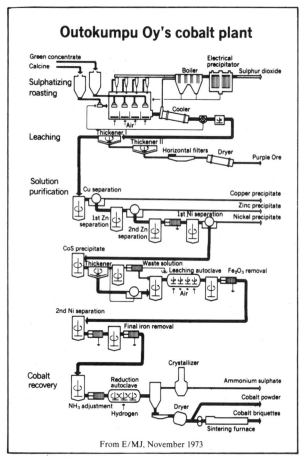

Outokumpu Oy's cobalt plant

From E/MJ, November 1973

Outokumpu Oy's process at Kokkola uses sulphate roasting to produce water-soluble metal sulphates, followed by leaching, solution purification, and cobalt recovery (1,200 mtpy).

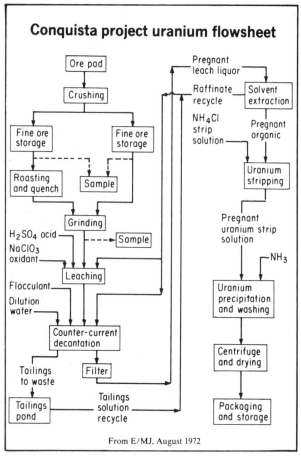

Conquista project uranium flowsheet

From E/MJ, August 1972

Conquista (Tex.) flowsheet for 2,000-tpd mill calls for H_2SO_4 leach. Solvent extraction is by the tertiary amine, Alamine 336. Project is owned jointly by Conoco and Pioneer Nuclear.

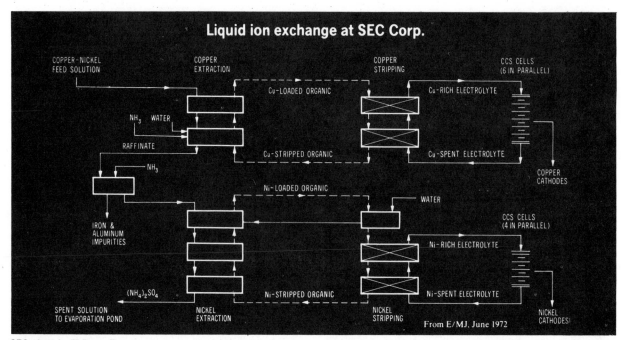

Liquid ion exchange at SEC Corp.

From E/MJ, June 1972

SEC plant in El Paso, Tex., treats a copper-nickel stream from a copper refinery containing about 80 gpl copper and 25 gpl nickel. Copper is separated by liquid ion exchange and electro-won after the loaded organic is stripped. After pH adjustment to remove Fe and Al, nickel is similarly separated and electrowon. Daily production rate is 4,000 lb Cu, 1,000 lb Ni.

Survey of automated controls generates both negative and positive feedback

James Wm. White, associate professor, College of Mines, University of Arizona

A PERSPECTIVE ON MINERAL ORE BENEFICIATION[1] published recently shows clearly that the trend in the mining industry is toward larger unit-operations equipment and more sophisticated instrumentation and process control. But, at the same time, there is an explicit feeling of dissatisfaction in some quarters where system performance has not met contractor and vendor promises.

"Do you see all these control loops? I can't remember ever seeing more than one or two of them on automatic," says one general foreman in the Southwest. And a mill superintendent at another operation claims: "We run our mill by the seat of our pants. If these blue-sky PhDs in instrument and control research had some operating experience, they wouldn't make a lot of the suggestions they do."

Although the evolution of process control in the mining industry has been investigated[4] and successful operations have been reported,[7, 10] the unfortunate fact remains that operating problems get little publicity—for obvious reasons. And, whereas recommended practices in instrumentation and control are available from the Instrument Society of America (ISA) for chemical and petrochemical plants, no such documentation exists for mineral processing plants.[5]

Not surprisingly, the instrument engineer in the mining industry feels isolated and must rely on his own inventiveness to make his installations work.

"We design with a minimum of instrumentation as we have found that it is the most troublesome phase of construction and run-in procedures," observes one survey respondent. Another says: "Our magnetic flowmeters were unreliable as installed and remain unreliable now—even after calibration and certification by an independent testing laboratory—which means that our mass flow indications are useless. The vendor has not been very helpful."

Negativism is by no means universal. In a special report which outlines the structure of the mining industry and its process control characteristics,[16] the Stanford Research Institute has found that attitudes in the mining industry toward automatic control are generally positive—even though many of the plants seem crude when compared to modern chemical refineries and power plants in their use of process control.

Since an identification and interpretation of some troublesome areas would prove helpful to operating personnel, I conducted a survey of the status, effectiveness, and support of installed instrumentation and process control in nonferrous ore concentrators, chiefly copper, in the summer of 1972. This survey, sponsored by the Primary Metals Div. of The Anaconda Co., summarizes the operating experience in more than two dozen mills, ranging from those with little installed instrumentation and controls to fully instrumented modern plants.

Following are highlights of how the survey was conducted and some of the results obtained.

Table 1—Qualitative evaluation of instruments and controls

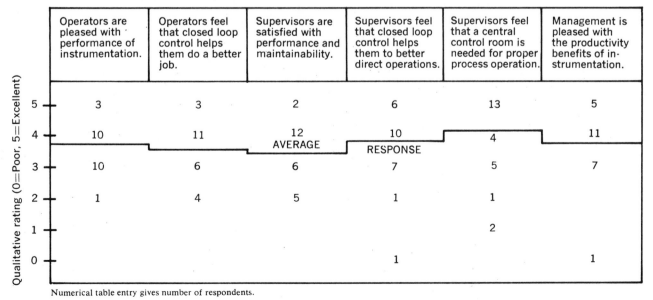

Qualitative rating (0=Poor, 5=Excellent)	Operators are pleased with performance of instrumentation.	Operators feel that closed loop control helps them do a better job.	Supervisors are satisfied with performance and maintainability.	Supervisors feel that closed loop control helps them to better direct operations.	Supervisors feel that a central control room is needed for proper process operation.	Management is pleased with the productivity benefits of instrumentation.
5	3	3	2	6	13	5
4	10	11	12	10	4	11
3	10	6	6	7	5	7
2	1	4	5	1	1	
1					2	
0				1		1

AVERAGE RESPONSE

Numerical table entry gives number of respondents.

General observations and recommendations

As a whole, the survey indicates that while some current problems are the result of design oversights, others seem to occur because of improper and inadequate attention to operations after startup. Vendor support, after an installation is completed, varies widely—and it's hard to generalize on this point, except to say that poor support can and does lead to serious problems.

To our surprise, the most successfully instrumented installations seemed to be those where instrumentation was gradually installed in *existing* mills. "We prefer to gradually install automatic controls so that the men on the property grow up with them and are not overwhelmed by flashing lights and pushbuttons," notes one vice president of operations.

Some of the most serious problems, on the other hand,

Survey objectives

In scope, the survey described in this article covered only those concentrator process variables which are measured or controlled by instrumentation either continuously or at periodic intervals. The specific goals of the survey were: to examine current philosophies and preferences of operating personnel in instrument and control strategy selection and modification; and to examine current operating practices in calibration, use and maintenance of instrumentation and process control, and in the training of plant personnel. Process logic, safety mechanisms, and alarms were not considered in this survey.

The survey was conducted by mailing a questionnaire covering the major aspects of instrumentation and control, and then complementing the questionnaires with visits by the author and one or two Anaconda research personnel to 11 copper concentrators in the Southwest area of the US. The 26 participating companies are as follows, with Group 1 being the area mills that were personally visited, and Group 2 responding only through the questionnaire:

Group 1: American Smelting and Refining (Mission and Silver Bell mills); Anaconda (Twin Buttes); Duval (Sierrita); Inspiration Consolidated (Inspiration); Kennecott (Ray and Chino mills); Magma (San Manuel); Pima Mining; Phelps Dodge (Morenci and Tyrone mills).

Group 2: Anglo American (Nchanga); Bethlehem Copper; Brunswick Mining and Smelting; Ecstall Mining; Falconbridge; Gaspe Copper; Hanna Mining; Mount Isa Mines; Newmont Mining (Granduc); Palabora Mining; Placer Development (Craigmont and Endako); Outokumpu Oy (Pyhasalmi); Sherritt Gordon Mines; St. Joe Minerals; and Union Miniere.

Many of the tabulated responses in this article are given as Group 1/Group 2.

Originally, we had hoped to obtain independent responses from a manager, an engineer, an instrument foreman, and an operator because we felt that they would have different ideas regarding instrumentation and process control. Almost without exception, the Group 1 mills submitted only one response per question, while about half the Group 2 mills submitted multiple responses which, as expected, did indicate differing points of view. Where possible, averages were computed and used in the tabulated responses.

---

were reported by personnel in mills with a large instrumentation and control complement designed and installed by contractors and vendors from user specifications. In our on-site visits, we often encountered some very bitter feelings: "There isn't a single automated mill that can't be run more effectively under manual control," was the reaction of one disgruntled respondent.

Nevertheless, it should be noted that the large added expense of installation in an existing mill, when compared with the cost of installation as part of an original design, argues strongly against the former choice for new operations.

What would actually lead to greater overall productivity and satisfaction would be to plan for adequate on-site staffing with well-defined responsibility and accountability in the instrument and controls area as soon as vendor and contractor leave the site. This should be obvious. And yet, proper engineering supervision of instrument maintenance policies and procedures seems woefully lacking even in some plants that have a large instrumentation and controls inventory.

We would recommend that an industry committee, perhaps under the AIME, should assemble and issue a quarterly design digest made up of members' contributions citing successful solutions to unique industry problems. Through the ISA Mining and Metallurgy group, these solutions should be classified, and other generally accepted practices should be added. Our survey, in effect, suggests that official ISA recommended practices should be developed for the mining and metals industry to parallel those already in existence for the chemical and petrochemical industries.[5]

Personnel attitudes, turnover, and related problems

"What is the overall impression of instrumentation control?" This question asked respondents to evaluate qualitatively their feelings and the feelings of others in the operating staff regarding the effectiveness and utility of installed instrumentation and process control. The results are summarized in Table 1. In most cases where multiple responses were obtained, the operator invariably had a lower opinion of equipment utility than did supervisory personnel.

Many supervisors, of course, are aware of the situation. According to one mill manager, "Instrumentation will be a complete failure unless you have complete operator cooperation, and so we spend a tremendous amount of time on operator acceptance of procedures for using instrumentation and automatic controls and for submitting routine maintenance work."

It is not uncommon for central control rooms in automated mills to be nerve centers that sometimes become sore spots for management, says the superintendent of a copper concentrator. He adds: "Management is determined to see its pet project succeed, but the operators don't trust the controls—usually because they don't work—so the operators essentially use the control room as a gathering place for coffee breaks."

Annual turnover of instrumentation and control technicians is another problem that plagues supervisors. With annual turnover rates approaching or exceeding 50%, continuity is difficult to maintain, and maintenance and performance suffer. Geography and poor management support are at least two of the reasons for the high turnover. According to some supervisors, "It is impossible to get the highly qualified men necessary to install and service this equipment out in the bush," and "More and more instrumentation is being installed, but we have trouble convincing management to provide the additional technicians to maintain it."

On-the-job training and outside contract maintenance are partial solutions to the turnover problem. "We hope our new apprentice program will give men in the labor crew a chance to advance, provide trained instrument men when we need them, and cut down our technician turnover," reports a plant manager. At another mill, the superintendent explains: "We don't have an instrument group as such and will probably continue to rely on vendor contract maintenance for much of our electronics support. This is inconvenient and expensive, but necessitated by the current personnel."

In addition to inadequate staffing in the instrument department, there is also the problem of obtaining on-site in-line engineering expertise to make effective use of instrumentation and process control, and to improve strategies as milling conditions or operating objectives change.

"There are few experienced metallurgical engineers in instrumentation and control, so we hire fresh graduates who lack the background or basic training in even the simplest concepts. Then we have to train them ourselves. Why can't the schools do some of this for us?" asks one mill manager.

Unfortunately, about one school or college of mines per year has closed during the last decade. This factor—combined with decreasing engineering enrollments nationwide, down some 40% since 1967—has led to such a shortage of new metallurgical engineering graduates that chemical engineers are being used instead. Moreover, many metallurgical engineering curricula are moribund. Concepts in instrumentation and process control are not covered in the undergraduate curriculum at all—or, at most, covered very briefly.

As to the type and extent of company-sponsored instruction and training provided to engineers, instrument crews, and operators, our survey indicates that companies rely heavily on their on-the-job training programs, but that Group 2 respondents provide a rather larger amount of classroom instruction (from 10 to 50 hr) than Group 1 respondents. (Of the 26 companies surveyed, only two provide any kind of simulator-aided instruction or training.)

Since most respondents provide on-the-job training only, operator and technician training programs need to be upgraded. Otherwise, foreman and operator apathy toward (and distrust of) instrumentation and process control will continue as a major obstacle to improving an already bad situation.

Other manpower and organization problems

Engineering-and-instrument manpower and organization vary so widely from one operation to another that a tabular presentation is not feasible. Of course, the more heavily instrumented mills have larger staffs of instrument technicians and foremen.

In Group 1 mills, the instrument foreman usually reports to the mechanical or electrical superintendent or, occasionally, directly to the concentrator superintendent. Surprisingly, the Group 1 mills have much less on-site instrumentation and control engineering support than Group 2 mills.

One Group 1 respondent with a heavy instrumentation commitment has no instrument department as such—and depends upon journeymen electricians and expensive vendor contracts for maintenance. In another heavily instrumented Group 1 mill, there are no on-site technical crews concerned with the inevitable problems of instrument and control support and improvement. This lack, which is apparent during site inspections, usually shows up in the form of unused or misused equipment, poorly maintained instrument shop records, operator distrust of control gear, and inadequate or nonexistent documentation of preferred operating policies.

In Group 1 we found one respondent which provides a loose-leaf "Control Center Guidebook" in the central control room as an aid in operator training and for operator reference. As operating policies and procedures change, the guidebook is updated; its outline includes the following:

Supervisor	Control procedures (start, stop)
Control system	Control notes
Feed conveyors	Cyclone pumps
Rod mills	Lube system
Ball mills	Tons/hour
Control panel design	Water/ore ratio
Control panel lights	By-pass water
Control panel instruments	Pumps (well, thickener, etc.)

Table 2—Responses to the survey question 'Who did what?'*

	Internal				External			
	Central research	Central engineering	Plant site personnel	Special project team	Engineering contractor	Equipment vendor	Consultant	Not applicable
Who did the preliminary study of instrumentation and process control?	1/3	1/3	**5/9**	0/3	4/2	**1/4**	0/2	
Who specified the process variables to be measured by instrumentation?	1/2	2/1	**9/10**	0/2	2/1	0/2	0/1	
Who developed the control loop functions?	1/0	2/4	5/4	**0/4**	5/1	1/3	**0/3**	
Who selected the transducers and controllers?	1/0	1/5	7/4	**0/4**	5/3	1/3	0/2	
Who checked out process control effectiveness in similar plants before approval?	0/1		7/4	**0/4**	2/1		0/2	1/1
Who checked out control loops by computer simulation before approval?	0/1			0/2		0/1	0/1	**10/5**
Who supervised installation of instrumentation and controls?		1/3	**6/9**	0/2	5/5	4/1	0/1	
Who now checks and recalibrates process transducers?		0/2	**9/13**	0/2		0/1		
Who supervises operators' use of estab. procedures?			**10/13**	0/1				
Who now provides technical support to improve strategy?	1/3	0/5	**9/7**	0/2		2/0	0/1	

*Table entry gives number of respondents, Group 1/Group 2. Some respondents indicated a shared responsibility in some areas. Numbers in bold face indicate response peaks.

The same respondent has developed and now uses a "work-order" procedure under which the operators report instrument malfunctions to the instrument shop.

Our survey indicates that very few respondents assign definite areas of responsibility to each instrument technician (with rotation to provide back-up)—which is common practice in the chemical industry.[11] In most cases, the technicians available are simply assigned to current problem areas; this practice, according to some mill technicians, does nothing to promote "pride of workmanship" in an area and contributes to overall inefficiency of operation.

In the area of custom-instrument development by operating units, we have found that all too frequently the excessive costs are hidden as "instrument maintenance," instead of being done by contract. One respondent, for example, reported in-house development of several dozen special-purpose printed circuit boards; the manual etching procedure required more than 30 min per board—with total fabrication, mounting, and check-out running several hours. This, in effect, removed one instrument technician from routine maintenance and instrument repair for several weeks.

In another case, however, the instrument foreman was ordered to cease all special-purpose instrument manufacture and instead submit his requirements to plant engineering, which then handled specification preparation and competitive job bidding. Falconbridge Nickel Mines is one of the companies which has rejected in-house special-purpose instrument development in quantity.[6]

Our survey found that the best staffed and most thoroughly supported mill, at all personnel levels, is run by Mt. Isa Mines, in Queensland, Australia. The thoroughness of MIM's approach to instrumentation and control is typified by its published calibration procedures for on-line X-ray analysis.[14, 15] Furthermore, the company's excellent work on digital computer control of wet grinding circuits has been widely publicized. Mt. Isa Mines is especially fortunate in having continuing management support, access to expert consultants, a low artificer (instrument technician) annual turnover of about 10% (some US mills have an annual turnover rate in excess of 50%), and excellent on-site support of instrumentation and control.

Now for a closer look at some of the specific questions asked by the survey:

'Who did what?'

In asking this question, we were interested in identifying which plant personnel had responsibility for 10 different functions ranging from preliminary studies to the upgrading of process control strategies. The responses in Table 2 are reported in the form of Group 1/Group 2, and the numbers in boldface represent response peaks.

Note than none of the Group 1 respondents used consultants for aid or advice, while several of Group 2 respondents did. Note also that none of the Group 1 respondents employed a special project team. Several Group 2 respondents used computer simulation to check out control effectiveness before approval, while none of the Group 1 respondents did. Both groups relied heavily on existing operations for strategy selection.

'How important is automatic process control?'

When technical personnel want to justify instrumentation and process control either for a new mill or for expanding or upgrading an existing operation, they usually base their arguments on a combination of "hidden benefits" (those aspects of control which have no economic incentive) and "economic benefits" (those aspects of control on which a cost-benefit analysis can be made). These "benefits" and respondents'

Table 3—Importance of 'hidden benefits' of process control*

	Very important	Moderately important	Of little importance
More complete operating data ...	4/6	6/2	0/5
More frequent operating data ..	4/7	5/5	1/3
More accurate operating data ..	6/5	3/6	1/3
Better control	10/13	0/1	0/0
Smoother operation	10/14	0/1	0/0
Safer operation	4/6	4/4	2/3

*Table entry gives number of respondents, Group 1/Group 2.

Table 4—The value of 'economic benefits' of process control*

	Very important	Moderately important	Of little importance
Higher recoveries	7/11	1/4	0/0
Increased throughput	7/12	2/3	0/0
Lower ore cutoff grade	2/0	2/6	5/6
Lower downtime	2/2	1/4	5/6
Lower net manpower	4/2	1/6	4/4
Lower reagent consumption	1/4	3/5	5/4

On justification:
1. The return on capital investment was less than 12 months due to 10% increase in throughput with no loss in recovery.
2. Even the current modest recovery increase warrants investments already made.
3. Higher production and hence greater returns were achieved by keeping the circuits "balanced" with the aid of instrumentation.

*Table entry gives number of respondents, Group 1/Group 2.

subjective estimates of their importance are summarized in Tables 3 and 4.

As for the actual or objective benefits of automatic process control, however, it should be noted that few quantitative analyses have been performed and still fewer have been published. In the abstract, it is fairly easy to make a convincing argument in favor of automatic process control. But there are exceptions.

For instance, consider a concentrator processing 32,000 tpd of ore averaging 0.83% Cu in sulphide form, and producing 722 tpd of concentrate at 32% Cu as sulphide, giving a recovery of 87%, with the remaining 34.4 tpd Cu lost with tailings that assay 0.11% Cu. Each 1% daily increase in tonnage throughput yields an additional 4,620 lb per day of elemental Cu. After allowing for current mining and milling costs, the incremental daily profit could be at least $1,000. As a combined profit and mineral resource incentive, each 0.001% decrease in tailings assay yields an additional 626 lb per day elemental Cu. Thus, a profit incentive is clearly present.

Still, a control system which can achieve impressive increases most of the time but which cannot handle a rapid change in ore work index from high to low (and indeed which responds to such a change by "sanding up all the way to flotation," as reported by one respondent) is hardly economical in the long run.

'How well do control loops function?'

Table 5 summarizes the respondents' overall impression of the effectiveness of control loops in crushing, grinding, and flotation, while Table 6 reports specific evaluations of some of the more important concentrator loops. (The last three entries in Table 6 were write-in options—hence the small number of responses.)

Some of the respondents' comments are also included. Comments No. 3 and 6, in Table 6, refer to the rather common problem that occurs when pulp level surges in flotation cells kept under automatic level control. One respondent, who had had a similar problem earlier, reported that the redesign of the dart valve (see Fig. 1) in the tailings box provided truly superior performance.

With the conventional design, surging is unavoidable when the dart valve approaches its seat due to the hydrostatic head acting on top of the dart—a situation that occurs frequently over the normal range of operating conditions. The improved design overcomes this problem, but a pneumatic amplifier has to be inserted between the controller output (which has a maximum 15 psi pressure available) and the valve diaphragm (which needs a maximum of 30 psi).

Problems were also reported in level-sensing. The most common complaint was the fouling tendency of the conductivity probes usually used for this application. To overcome this problem, another respondent used bubble tubes instead of conductivity probes.

(For some very interesting comments on flotation reagent measurement and control, see the recent report by Brailey.[6])

A typical problem in instrument calibration

Our survey indicates that the frequency of instrument calibration varies widely from one plant to another, and that it runs the entire gamut from daily to yearly frequency. A plurality of respondents reported that instrument calibration is done on a monthly basis.

For measurement of pulp density, the pipe-mounted density gauge was invariably the transducer of choice, and most respondents indicated that monthly standardization in line with manufacturer's recommendations was adequate. But our survey discovered that a number of respondents had more frequent or even daily standardization procedures, especially for high density slurries of, say, 60% to 75% solids by weight.

For instance, one of these respondents reported that, ever since installation, the wide-range (about 50%) high-density units exhibited such "severe drift" that daily standardization became necessary; furthermore, since the equipment seemed unreliable in the control room, additional floor operators had to be assigned to monitor pulp densities using Marcy scales—and density gauge readouts were largely ignored. At this respondent's plant, incidentally, the control objective was always a specified percentage solids by weight. An engineering analysis by off-site personnel indicated that the problem seemed to be caused by: (1) the failure to account for the inherent non-linearity of gauge transmittance vs. slurry specific gravity (the primary process variable) in original planning, design, installation, and maintenance; and (2) the failure to account for the effect of dry-ore specific gravity on slurry percent solids (the secondary process variable) when standardizing against a Marcy scale.

Let's examine this problem more closely.

Fig. 2 shows the true gauge transmittance vs. slurry specific gravity for ore specific gravity values of 2.6 and 3.0, as well as a typical straight-line approximation similar to that suggested by the vendor and used by the operations staff since startup. Now, assuming manual operation with a true known ore specific gravity of 2.6, let's standardize the instrument along line AB at a true 70% solids; without changing the density gauge settings, let the percent solids go to 80. The true transmittance is found at the intersection of line CD with the 2.6 ore specific gravity curve; the indicated percent solids, however, is found by reading vertically from the intersection of line EF with the calibration line. This procedure indicates 76% for a 4% error.

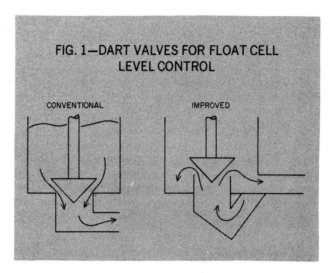

FIG. 1—DART VALVES FOR FLOAT CELL LEVEL CONTROL

CONVENTIONAL   IMPROVED

Table 5—Normal status of control loops

	Crushing Plant	Concentrator Grinding	Concentrator Flotation
Always in "automatic" mode	1	5	8
Usually in "automatic" mode	1	13	8
Rarely in "automatic" mode	1	2	1
Never in "automatic" mode	1	1*	3

Some general comments:
- Crusher control gear is available but time lags make it difficult to use.
- Automatic controls on ball mill circuits can only be used when conditions are ideal. This is rarely the case.
- *A matter of economics.
- Froth changes due to changing ore types make automatic control impossible.
- Reagents are proportioned using positive displacement pumps. There seem to be no other useable control functions.

Table 6—Evaluation of some common concentrator control loops*

	Average loop performance is:		
Controlled variable:	Excellent	Fair	Poor
Circulating load	2	5	1
Density of mill discharge	4	3	2
Density of cyclone feed	6	7	—
Collector flow rate	7	3	1
Cell pulp level	3	8	3
Cyclone feed sump level	10	4	1
Ore feed rate	17	5	1
Cyclone o'flo particle size	2+1**	1	1
pH of rougher feed	9	5	—
pH of cleaner feed	5	7	—
Water ratio to ore feed	14	2	1
Thickener u'flo density	1	—	—
Concentrate metal analysis . . . . —		1	—
Density of flotation feed	3	—	—

*Table entry gives number of respondents.
**Measurement only.

Some comments:
- Lack of direct cyclone feed density measurement makes calibration difficult.
- Ore feed rate system still suffers from basic design errors.
- Pulp level controls only work for small changes in load.
- Conductivity probes continually foul and give false readings.
- Sumps overflow on rod mill shut-down/start-up if loops on automatic.
- Pulp level surges in automatic mode regardless of controller settings.
- Ore feed rate problems continue due to freezing of fine ore bins.
- Magnetic flow meter calibration hard to maintain due to precipitation.

FIG. 2—TRANSMITTANCE VS. WEIGHT PERCENT SOLIDS INTERPRETATION PROBLEMS

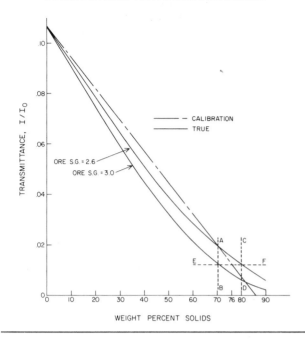

Fig. 3a—Companion gamma density gauge amplifier scale.

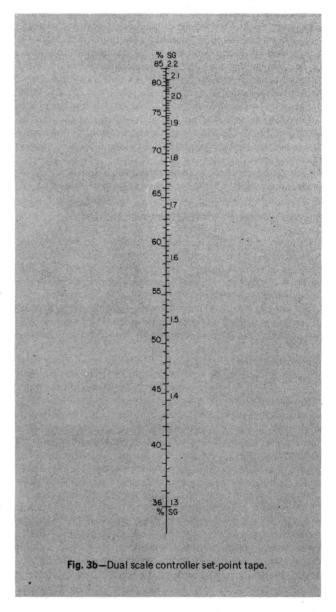

Fig. 3b—Dual scale controller set-point tape.

An alternative case: let the ore specific gravity vary from 2.6 to 3.0, while holding the true percent solids constant at 70. Here, the true transmittance is found at the intersection of line AB with the 3.0 ore specific gravity curve. The indicated percent solids is obtained as before from line EF and is 76%, indicating a 6% error. These effects may combine or cancel—depending on circumstances—and explain the erratic behavior in the course of daily standardization.

The proposed solution to this problem is straightforward and inexpensive.

A non-linear scale for slurry specific gravity (Fig 3a) would replace the dimensionless linear scale provided by the vendor for the standardization meter. And the density units would be calibrated by the instrument shop against Marcy scale slurry specific gravity. A dual-scale controller set point tape (Fig. 3b) would then replace the original vendor-supplied set point tape. With this dual-scale feature, the operator can read true slurry specific gravity, as well as an indicated weight percent solids, which would be valid as long as the specific gravity of the ore remains at the assumed value used in set-point tape design.

This problem could have been rectified much earlier had proper on-site engineering support been provided. As things stand, however, with the apathy and distrust for instrumentation, operator acceptance is not likely to be achieved even after the problem has been rectified.

'What about on-line X-ray analysis?'

This question elicited sharply diverse answers. Some respondents referred to their on-line X-ray unit as "invaluable as a guide to process control by the operator," and as very helpful "to spot and correct problems before they get too severe." Others said that their on-line X-ray unit "just costs too much to maintain," or that "we couldn't justify it for routine assay work and couldn't use it for process control." And, finally, in the words of another respondent, "Our on-line X-ray sampling system is a mechanic's nightmare. Besides, even when the sampling system is working, we can't get reliable assays though we do get trends. This information wasn't accu-

rate enough for metallurgical accounting, so we shut down the system."

Such severe problems, of course, are due to poor judgment in assessing the difficulties inherent in buying some components and doing system design, installation, calibration, documentation, and support in-house with inadequate or inexperienced personnel and an inadequate budget.

Perhaps the most thorough and impressive work in process instrumentation has been done by the Finnish company Outokumpu Oy, which has invested heavily in the development of its Courier 300 on-line X-ray analysis system. One Group 1 respondent recently purchased a Courier 300 system, but a report on its installation and use is not yet available.

Mixed opinions about on-line particle size analysis

Control of particle size distribution to flotation is possibly the single most important control variable in the concentrator. Since manual screening methods are inadequate for control purposes, much work has been done in the last decade on development of continuous on-line particle size monitors (PSM).

The most impressive advances have been made by Autometrics.[8] This company's units have been extensively tested in operating mills[3] and have worked out well with mean-time between failure reported by several respondents at about 2,000 hr. Weekly calibration seems adequate. Other direct measuring units available[12] have not been tested thoroughly in operating mills and show less promise than the Autometrics PSM.

An alternative to direct measurement is the on-line digital computer-based inferential technique developed by Lynch and coworkers,[10] used at Mt. Isa Mines in Australia—and now being installed in one of the Group 1 mills, where opinions range from hopeful ("We fully expect a 10-15% throughput increase by going to particle-size inference and control in a test grinding circuit"), to skeptical ("These inferential tech-

niques aren't worth a damn unless you have relatively constant work index and specific gravity").

Grinding circuit control in the Southwest

Because of its large effect on plant throughput, grinding circuit instrumentation and control is one of the most important areas of concern in a modern concentrator.

Simplified grinding circuit schematics are shown in Fig. 4 for three area mills. The differences in control strategy are intriguing.

Fig. 4a shows a rather interesting concept in feed forward control. The absence of compensating circuits in the feed forward path is surprising. Notice that no level control is provided on sump level and that a fixed speed pump is used. The absence of a cyclone-fed sample port makes calibration of the velocity and density transmitters difficult. Reportedly, this strategy is effective only when the circuit operates at or near design conditions. The circuit must be run manually when tonnage is reduced.

At another plant, density control is used to achieve the desired grind (Fig. 4b). Screen analyses are run periodically at this plant. As the work index of the ore decreases, the circu-

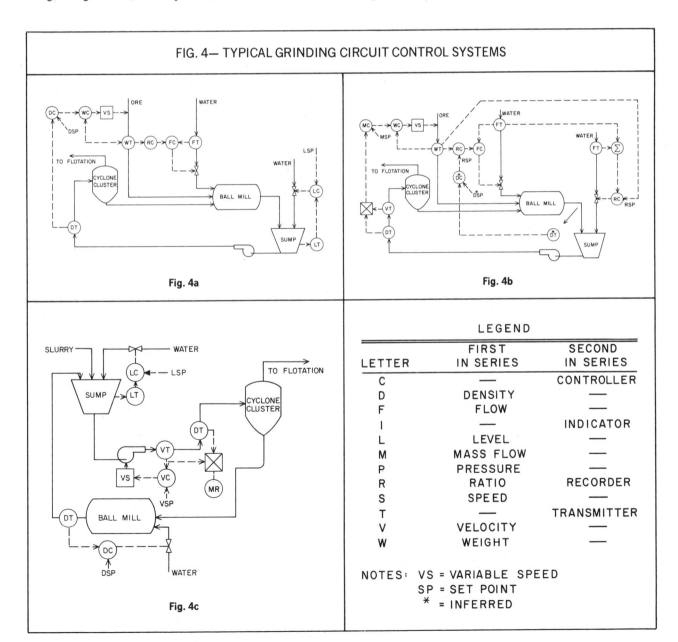

FIG. 4— TYPICAL GRINDING CIRCUIT CONTROL SYSTEMS

Fig. 4a

Fig. 4b

Fig. 4c

LEGEND

LETTER	FIRST IN SERIES	SECOND IN SERIES
C	—	CONTROLLER
D	DENSITY	—
F	FLOW	—
I	—	INDICATOR
L	LEVEL	—
M	MASS FLOW	—
P	PRESSURE	—
R	RATIO	RECORDER
S	SPEED	—
T	—	TRANSMITTER
V	VELOCITY	—
W	WEIGHT	—

NOTES: VS = VARIABLE SPEED
SP = SET POINT
* = INFERRED

Table 7—Some items of control equipment removed

Item	Comment
1. Sonics grinding control on ball mill	Frequent recalibration needed due to varying ore hardness and ambient sound levels. Little vendor support available; parts hard to get.
2. Density control on ball mill discharge launder	Removed due to sanding in launders and inability to obtain adequate flow characteristics past gauge.
3. Magnetic flow meters and gamma density gauges in grinding circuits	Both meter types inaccurate with high maintenance.
4. Gamma gauge density control to primary cyclone	The overflow density of the primary cyclone turned out to be unimportant in this circuit.
5. V-ball control valves on ball mill water lines	Excessively rapid wear in seats led to high maintenance costs.
6. All flotation cell pulp level controllers	Surging and continued probe fouling made use impossible.
7. Control loops for frother addition based on measurement of rougher froth flow	The quantity of rougher froth was not directly related to frother requirements.
8. Residual xanthate meter and redox potential meter	Measured variables had no observable correlation with flotation results.
9. Buoyancy type density control on tailings thickener	Measurements unreliable and inaccurate.
10. On-line X-ray analysis system	Cost too much to keep unreliable X-ray unit going; couldn't justify high maintenance costs.
11. On-line X-ray analysis system	Unit was unreliable and wouldn't hold calibration; couldn't justify high maintenance costs.

lating load should decrease—leading to a density decrease which in turn should call for more feed. In practice, this system overcompensates and reduces the feed rate too much on hard ores though not necessarily increasing it too much on soft ores.

The strategy shown in Fig. 4c fails if throughput is pushed. Since cyclone feed velocity, rather than mass flow rate, is controlled by varying the pump speed, the sump becomes a point for accumulation of solids, if the ore work index increases, as the level controller cuts back on water addition. The cyclone underflow density and, hence, the mill discharge density increase to the point where the density control loop around the ball mill moves the water valve to its full open condition. Only the pump speed-control loop continues to function and the strategy breaks down. The operator must then compensate by observing the cyclone feed density and cutting back on raw slurry feed to the sump.

'What equipment has been removed or modified?'

Among the most common problems with instrumentation and control equipment (Table 7) are difficulties with sonic-probes for level control in fine ore bins reported by respondents. Some modified the original systems to include contact probes to cover "blind spots" in sonic coverage; others developed air purge systems to combat dust interference.

Also mentioned were a number of special problems in pH control, particularly the difficulties caused by probe fouling

and incorrect probe placement.

According to one respondent, back-pressure air purge bubble tubes for level sensing in sumps must be used with caution in rod- and ball-mill circuits. Since sump level is an inferred variable in this type of system, rod mill shutdown leads to a density decrease that has the appearance of a falling level; then, as the control system compensates by increasing water addition, the density decreases even further—and the problem becomes more serious, frequently leading to sump overflow. This problem may be corrected by dividing the bubble pressure signal by cyclone feed density if a density gauge is available. Alternately, a capacitance probe may be used instead of a bubble tube for level sensing. In fact, another respondent who uses such capacitance probes for sump-level control reported that little difficulty was encountered in calibration and maintenance. ☐

References

1) Arbiter, N. "Mineral Ore Beneficiation: A Perspective." AIME Centennial Volume, pp 88-118, 1971.
2) Baker, A. L. "Process Simulators Build Operator Knowhow" Cont. Engr., pp 42-43, Oct. 1972.
3) Basarear, J. H. and G. McQuire "On-Stream Analysis of Particle Size," Mining Congress J., pp 36-42, May 1972.
4) Behrend, G. M. "The Evolution of Process Control in the Mining Industry." CIM Trans., *LXXIV*, pp 14-17, 1971.
5) Behrend, G. M. "The Installation of Instruments in Mineral Processing Plants." presented at ISA Symposium—Min. & Met. Group, April 1972.
6) Brailey, R. J. "Flotation Reagent Control." Presented at ISA Symposium—Min. & Met. Group, April 1972.
7) Fowler, H. B. and Kay, K. R. "Process Instrumentation and Control at Frood-Stobie Mill." Can. Min. J., pp 49-56, June 1971.
8) Hathaway, R. E. "A Proven On-Stream Particle Size Monitoring System for Automatic Grinding Circuit Control." presented at ISA Symposium—Min. & Met. Group. April 1972.
9) Kvaska, F. "Evaluating Instrument Maintenance" Elect. Constr. and Maint. pp 102-104, July 1970.
10) Lynch, A. J. and G. G. Stanley, "Automatic Control in Australian Mineral Processing Plants." World Min., pp 24-29, May 1971.
11) Martin, F. D. "Techniques in Analytical Instrument Maintenance." Presented at 4th Annual Instru. Maint. Symp., Detroit, 1969.
12) Osborne, B. F. "A Practical On-stream Particle Size Analysis System." ISA Trans., *10*, pp. 379-385, Oct. 1971.
13) Schubert, L. F., "The Organization and Operation of an Effective Instrument Maintenance Department." presented at Annual AIME Mtg., New York, Feb. 1966.
14) Stacey, G. S. and W. A. Bolt, "Developments in Instrument Design and Calibration Procedures for X-Ray Fluorescence 'On-Stream' Analysis of Mineral Processing Systems." Mt. Isa Mines Ltd., Queensland, Australia.
15) Stacey, G. S. and W. A. Bolt, "Multistream X-Ray Fluorescence Analysis of Mineral Slurries in No. 1 Copper Concentrator at Mt. Isa." Mt. Isa Mines Ltd., Queensland, Australia.
16) Anon.. "Process Control in the Minerals Processing Industry." Chapter 12. Stanford Research Institute Report. January 1, 1969.

Acknowledgement

The author wishes to express his deep appreciation to Nathaniel Arbiter, director of metallurgical research of The Anaconda Co., for suggesting this project, providing financial and technical support, and obtaining the cooperation of the survey participants; to C. Arentzen, Dr. M. Jansen, and S. Low of Anaconda Research, who helped in questionnaire preparation and local site surveys; and to all the employees of the participating companies.

The dollars and sense of selecting wear materials

Richard A. Thomas, Assistant editor

AT A TIME WHEN THE GROWING COMPLEXITY of process technology and the dictates of a pinched economy create many questions and few answers, a fresh look at structural materials used in minerals processing can be helpful. This review highlights consumable materials that are significant factors in plant operating costs on a month-to-month (or in some cases day-to-day) basis.

Cost/wear ratios, downtime, material availability, and a host of other factors influencing material usage demand particular attention when viewed against the backdrop of inflation, the need for increased efficiency in existing processes, and the dearth of standardized, accepted "how to" guides for materials assessment and selection. Materials designed for "sacrificial wear" through mechanical abrasion or chemical corrosion are especially important in this context.

The greatest wear logically comes in the comminuting phase of processing, when ores are mechanically reduced in size by primary and secondary crushing and by grinding in various types of mills. The material properties of greatest concern are abrasion resistance (influenced strongly by carbon content in ferrous materials) and toughness (a measure of resistance to impact). Complications arise from the almost inversely proportional relationship between the two properties. Materials with higher carbon volumes, such as white irons, have greater abrasion resistance, but they are more brittle and thus more subject to fracture than low-carbon materials such as steels. Likewise, martensitic (heat treated) structures generally have greater hardness and compressive strength than austenitic (as-cast) structures, but they are more subject to spalling and breakage.

The engineer must determine the optimum combination of these and other properties for each service—a job sometimes made difficult by variations in experts' opinions on the "best" material for a particular need. There are also substantial differences between laboratory data reported for a given material and that material's performance in a commercial scale operation.

Last year's Amax-sponsored Symposium on Materials for the Mining Industry, held on July 30 and 31 at Vail, Colo., aired numerous opinions about the relative merits of several standard alloys and pointed up the gaps in objective evaluation caused by non-standardized testing and reporting. Data here were taken in part from the symposium preprints, which are now available through Climax Molybdenum Co.

The demands of crushing service

Although low- and medium-alloy steels and several specialty alloyed irons have enjoyed some popularity gains in crushing service, high-alloy (10-18%) austenitic manganese steels continue to predominate, especially where severe crushing is required (Table 1). Toughness is frequently a must for mantles, bowl liners, segmental concaves in gyratory and cone crushers, and the movable and stationary plates of jaw crushers. A high degree of fracture toughness, coupled with adequate abrasion resistance, gouging resistance, and moderate cost, make austenitic Mn steels popular where repeated and severe impact occurs.

Hardenability (not to be confused with hardness) is another property that establishes the 100-year-old dominance of austenitic Mn steels (often called Hadfield steels). Under repeated impact, these steels tend to work-harden, with plastic deformation of the microstructure. Hardness increases of 300 HB and more can be achieved by work-hardening. Although several other alloying elements besides manganese—including Mo, Cr, Si, and Ni—can change the hardenability of steels, manganese is still the most potent (Fig. 1). Although carbon very strongly influences the maximum hardness of a given steel, it has only a minimal effect on hardenability.

As with all other structural materials, Mn steel does have drawbacks. Although its abrasion and gouging resistance are adequate, they are not great. Molybdenum and/or chromium are often added in 1-3% amounts to improve the abrasion resistance of Mn steel. Hardfacing of the ore-contacting surfaces with weld material is frequently necessary, especially when the ores processed are highly abrasive. (Taconites and high-silica ores are good examples.) Mn steel also lacks machinability and has a generally lower yield strength.

Photo credit: Amax Inc.

Wear scars form on the Mn steel mantle of a gyratory crusher.

Table 1—Typical compositions of cast austenitic manganese steels

| | Percentages | | | | |
	Mn	C	Cr	Mo	Other
Standard grade.........	12.0-14.0	1.0-1.4	–	–	–
Chromium alloyed.....	12.0-14.0	1.0-1.4	1.5-2.5	–	–
1% Mo alloyed..........	12.0-15.0	0.8-1.3	–	0.8-1.2	–
2% Mo alloyed..........	12.0-15.0	1.0-1.5	–	1.8-2.2	–
1% Mo lean alloy[1]	5.0-7.0	1.1-1.4	–	0.8-1.2	–
High yield strength[2]..............	12.0-15.0	0.4-0.7	2.0-4.0	1.8-2.2	2.0-4.0 Ni 0.5-1.0 V
Machinable[3]	18.0-20.0	0.3-0.6	–	–	2.0-4.0 Ni 0.2-0.4 Bi

1) US Patent No. 3,113,861.
2) US Patent No. 3,057,838.
3) US Patent No. 3,010,823.

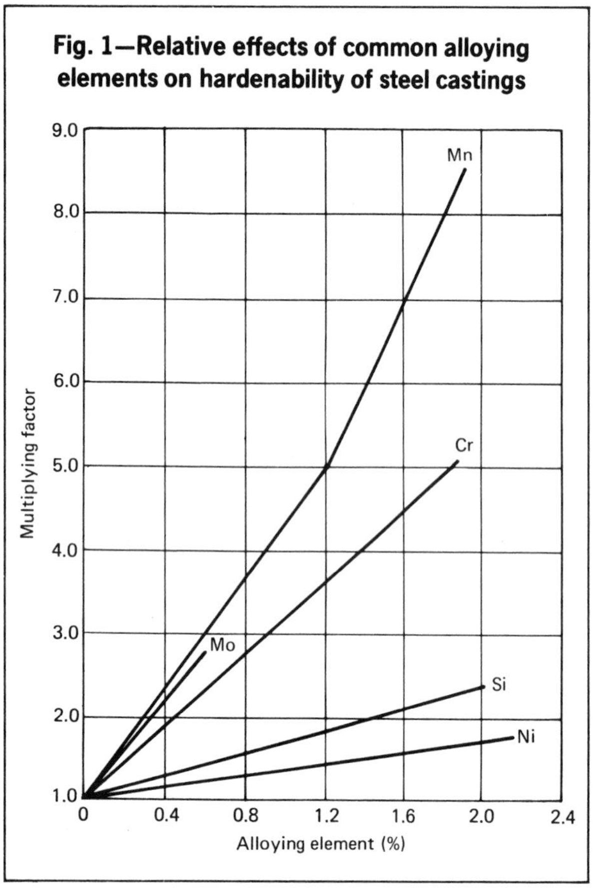

Fig. 1—Relative effects of common alloying elements on hardenability of steel castings

Availability is a critical factor in material selection. Orders for Mn castings have recently been backlogged because of the shortfall in foundry capacity, and customers are being advised to plan for longer lead time when ordering manganese alloy crushing equipment. Average lead time for new crushers has already stretched out from 7½ months to 18 months over the last year. A general awareness of the difficulty in obtaining replacement parts for processing and mining equipment is dictating an increase in the use of hard facing alloys to prolong the life of components in wear service.

Milling service—a very different animal

The milling stages of comminution commonly use a much wider variety of materials. There are three major divisions of candidate materials for mill liners: 1) ferrous alloys, both cast and wrought, 2) rubber and other elastomers, and 3) ceramics and natural stone materials. Although the elastomers are gaining popularity, particularly in double stage and fine grinding operations, ferrous alloys are still the principal lining materials in ball, rod, and autogenous mills. Ceramic liners are now largely restricted to the cement and pigment industries.

While toughness is the keynote in crushing service, abrasion resistance is the most important factor in milling operations. Large-grained martensitic structures provide much greater hardness and low-stress abrasion resistance than smaller-grained austenitic or pearlitic structures. Abrasion resistance is also a function of carbon volume percentage. Higher-carbon steels and white irons (more than 2% C) are generally more abrasion resistant—and less tough—than low-carbon steels. Martensitic Cr-Mo white irons, which incorporate chromium carbides (Cr_7C_3 type) in a martensitic matrix, are now billed as the most abrasion resistant materials commonly used.

While abrasion resistance is primary, toughness in mill liners is also important. Impact in mills is a function of service conditions (mill speed, bell diameter, interior lift contour, etc.) that may be varied as necessary; however, spalling and breakage continue to occur, even in the most expensive liners. One trend in liner upkeep is use of liner plates with fewer bolt holes, speeding up removal and replacement.

Cost factors in mill lining have a high priority because

A relatively new trend is the use of "lean manganese" steels in crushing service. Some of the extreme toughness in Hadfield 12-13% Mn steels is being sacrificed for improved abrasion resistance by reduction of the manganese content to 5-7%. This reduction still allows the high degree of toughness characteristic of Mn steels.

If crushing severity is mild (small particle size and/or favorable ore friability characteristics), a less tough material with greater abrasion resistance can be used. Oil-quenched low-alloy steels and alloyed cast irons appear suitable under certain well defined operating conditions.

Table 2—Typical costs of materials used for mill linings*

Material	Cost per lb	Installation cost per lb[1]	Installed cost per lb	Relative weight of complete lining	Relative installed cost of lining[4]	Toughness rating[5]
Martensitic Cr-Mo white iron	$0.38	$0.04	$0.42	100	42	6
Martensitic Ni-Cr white iron	0.30	0.04	0.34	100	34	7
Martensitic Cr-Mo steel	0.36	0.04	0.40	100	40	5
Austenitic 6Mn-1Mo steel	0.32	0.04	0.36	100	36	3
Austenitic 12Mn steel	0.30	0.04	0.34	100	34	2
Pearlitic Cr-Mo steel	0.28	0.04	0.32	100	32	4
Pearlitic white iron	0.22	0.04	0.26	100	26	8
Rubber	1.17	0.10	1.27	23[2]	29	1
Ceramic	0.37	0.18	0.55	44[3]	24	9

* Costs and weights are based on averaged data from several large milling operations in the western US in December 1973.
1) Installation cost includes cost of bolts plus labor, except for rubber, where bolt cost is included in cost per lb, and for ceramic, where cement was used in place of bolts.
2) Relative weight of rubber lining includes weight of bolts and metal reinforcement.
3) Ceramic assumed to have same lining volume as the ferrous materials.
4) Relative installed cost of lining does not include cost of lost production during shutdown for relining.
5) Highest order of toughness = 1, and lowest = 9.

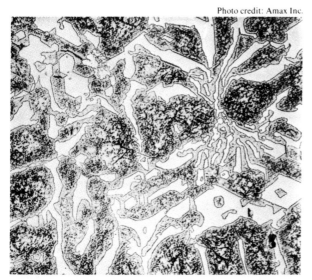

Typical microstructure of a mill liner made of martensitic Cr-Mo white iron. The section shows Cr_7C_8-type carbides in a martensitic matrix. Magnification is 500 x.

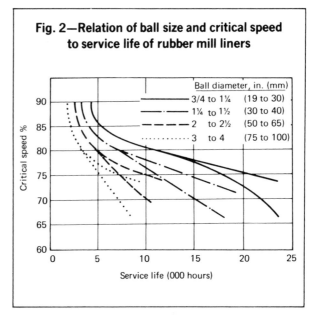

of the increasing necessity to process lower grade ores. Most of these ores contain high percentages of silica and other abrasive gangues that increase liner wear. *Total* cost of a given lining differs substantially from its *installed* cost. Total cost includes costs of the material, the installation, and the shutdown time for relining, which in turn is measured in terms of lost production. Although the value of lost production varies considerably from mill to mill, it can account for more than 50% of the installed cost. However, the installed cost is traditionally considered the major cost factor in liner selection, and it has risen rapidly over the last 30 years.

It cannot be overemphasized that today's technology has not produced a singular "best" mill liner. Widely varying mill and ore conditions, plus fluctuations in the availability and price of materials, make it unlikely that any material will merit such a designation in the near future.

Although literally hundreds of ferrous materials have been tested as mill liners since the 1930s, only a few have survived to dominate in milling service (Table 2):

Martensitic Cr-Mo white irons. These are the most abrasion resistant of the popular materials; unhappily, they are also highest in cost per pound. Tungsten carbides are even harder, but their first cost makes them prohibitively expensive in most applications. Cr-Mo white iron liners are surprisingly resistant to spalling and breakage, although some high-impact mills will cause them to break. They are enjoying increased use in the taconite industry, where abrasion levels are very high. Chromium improves abrasion resistance of the iron, while molybdenum fosters formation of the martensitic matrix and increases the amount of carbon that may be used.

Martensitic Ni-Cr white irons. Frequently known as "Ni-Hard" irons, these materials exhibit good-to-excellent abrasion resistance, frequently coupled with marginal toughness. Although nickel acts much like manganese on the transformation of steel, recurrent spalling and breakage has largely restricted chill-cast Ni-Hards to medium- and low-impact ball mills, and to rod mills where a high pulp level sufficiently cushions impact.

Martensitic Cr-Mo steels. Low alloying costs and the potential for a variety of applications are promoting quite rapid growth in this group. A number of recently developed wrought and cast compositions capable of full hard-

ening by air quenching may replace conventional oil-quenched types. Good-to-excellent hardness and relatively good toughness, especially in the medium-carbon range, will provide substantial competition for the white irons in the future. These steels are already being used in high-impact service where Cr-Mo irons and Ni-Hards are not feasible.

Austenitic Mn steels. These very tough steels, once the "workhorses" of milling, are falling into disuse because of their lower abrasion resistance. The 12% Mn steels so popular in crushing have been largely displaced by the harder 6% "lean" steels developed in 1959, which in turn are being displaced by martensitic irons and steels. An additional problem with austenitic Mn steels is the plastic deformation that accompanies work-hardening. Material flow and volume expansion make liner removal difficult and sometimes cause bolt breakage.

Pearlitic steels and irons. Pearlitic (lamellar) materials offer comparatively low first cost and good accessibility—they are easily castable by most foundries. Pearlitic "Chrome-Moly" steels, favored over pearlitic white irons and high-carbon unalloyed steels, are popular in high-impact service as liners, clamp and lifter bars, and grates. Several engineers and metallurgists project trends away from pearlitic materials because of the availability of more wear-resistant martensitic substances and the recent tendency toward narrowing of the cost differences between various candidate materials.

This narrowing of the range of installed costs, due to increasing labor and liner production rates, has created a trend toward selection of the more expensive longer-wearing liners. For mill liners, total cost considerations are becoming more important than installed cost.

Pro's and con's of nonferrous liners

Rubber and other elastomers offer several advantages over ferrous alloys under certain conditions. Since their advent in grinding back in 1921, elastomers have undergone significant technological development and have become considerably more popular, especially in the fine grinding mills. Light weight, noise-dampening properties, high resistance to impact, and lower installed cost compared with an equal volume of ferrous lining make elasto-

Table 3—Corrosion effects on common plastics

Material	Acids Weak	Acids Strong	Alkalies Weak	Alkalies Strong	Organic solvents	Water absorption (% per 24 hr)	Oxygen and ozone	Ionizing radiation	Temperature resistance (°C) High	Temperature resistance (°C) Low
Fluorocarbons	Inert	Inert	Inert	Inert	Inert	0.0	Inert	P	550	G-275
Polyethylene (low density)	R	A-O	R	R	G	0.15	A	F	140	G-80
Polyethylene (high density)	R	A-O	R	R	G	0.1	A	G	160	G-100
Polypropylene	R	A-O	R	R	R	Less than 0.01	A	G	300	P
Polyvinyl chloride (rigid)	R	R	R	R	A	0.10	R	P	150	P
Polystyrene	R	A-O	R	R	A	0.04	SA	G	160	P
Nylon	G	A	R	R	R	1.5	SA	F	300	G-70

Note: R = resistant, A = attacked, SA = slight attack, A-O = attacked by oxidizing acids, G = good, F = fair, P = poor.

mers popular where mill feed is relatively free of highly abrasive materials that tend to cut into the lining.

Notable restrictions on the use of elastomers include

Photo credit: Amax Inc.

Incorrect selection of materials can quickly sabotage system performance. These two pump impellers, made of different alloys, were in caustic slurry service for the same time span.

their working temperature and the critical mill speed. For the most part, working temperatures for rubber linings are restricted to a maximum of approximately 200°F. In addition, manufacturers report a strong link between mill speed and rubber's service-life expectancy. Rubber liners are reported to be suitable only when critical speed is below roughly 75% of maximum speed, making them inappropriate for many primary grinding mills (Fig. 2).

Because ceramics and natural stone ("Silex") liners have exceedingly low toughness, they are restricted to fine grinding plants, where impact and spalling are reduced by low critical speeds and high pulp densities. Advantages claimed for these materials include excellent resistance to heat and chemical attack, light weight, and relatively low installed cost. Ceramic bricks containing 85% alumina have largely supplanted other materials in this group because of their greater abrasion resistance.

Corrosion can be a big problem

Corrosion, simply defined as erosion by chemical rather than mechanical means, is a very significant factor in the selection of many wear materials. This is especially true in hydrometallurgical processes, where slurry-contacting and reagent-contacting surfaces are subjected to highly reactive environmental conditions, such as pH extremes and high temperatures. Abrasion and corrosion often act together in these environments: microspalling induced by slurry particles can remove the protective surface films of some ferrous materials (such as stainless steels), accelerating corrosion of the less resistant material underneath the films.

Proper design is of high priority in corrosion control, frequently taking precedence over material characteristics. A well designed piping system that uses cheaper, less corrosion-resistant material will sometimes outlast by many times a poorly designed system made of highly corrosion-resistant materials. Fig. 3 illustrates selected examples of design influences on corrosion.

The scope of materials for corrosion service is far too broad to be presented in any detail here. However, the following discussion of broad categories may help to improve upon the frequent "guesses" in material selection.

According to IRON AGE, corrosion experts in the high-alloy castings field agree that the five alloys shown in Fig. 4 can handle about 90% of the conditions encountered in the chemical processing industry. Mild steel has been included only for comparative purposes. (Detailed property data and design considerations for the alloys are available from the Steel Founders Society of America, Rocky River, Ohio.)

Stainless steel use in the processing industry is both popular and growing. Numerous applications of AISI stainless steel in copper recovery operations, as well as details on the types and chemistry of corrosion, are presented in E/MJ, May 1975, p 117.

Two categories of nonmetallics are very widely used for corrosion protection in mineral processing: natural and synthetic rubbers, and plastics. (Many other nonmetallic materials are candidates for corrosion service, such as acid brick, ceramics, glass, wood, and concrete, and the economics of a particular application is the final criterion for selection.) A major disadvantage of rubber appears to be its inability to resist the high abrasion levels that often accompany corrosion. A common mistake, made because of "metals-oriented" thinking, is the use of harder rubber for erosion-corrosion environments. Soft rubbers are reported to be best for abrasion resistance. Rubber is frequently used to line pipes, tanks, and centrifugal slurry pumps, and has been considered a standard material in corrosion service for many years.

Industry use of plastics has increased tremendously over the last 20 years, but certain drawbacks still keep plastics from overtaking the ferrous materials. The main disadvantage of plastics is their price, which may be three to 175 times that of mild steel per pound. In addition, certain heat limitations generally restrict the maximum service temperatures of plastics to well below the service temperatures of metals (Table 3). Polyvinyl chloride (PVC), probably the most common industrial plastic, has a maximum service temperature only slightly above the boiling point of water.

Fluorocarbon plastics, such as "Teflon" and "Kel F," have much higher service temperatures and are highly corrosion resistant (inert), but their price substantially limits their use; however, TFE components are widely used in corrosion-resistant valves, and as linings for some pipes, expansion joints, and heat exchangers. Other common industrial plastics include high-density polyethylenes, polypropylene, and recently, polybutylene (see E/MJ, April 1975, p 108).

Corrosion-resisting materials for transporting ore slurries in pipelines have merited much research, with considerable data generated in recent years. Short-distance piping systems provide in-plant transportation for liquid/solid mixtures in such common operations as filtration, pulp handling, sludge transport, and tailings disposal, while long-distance slurry systems, though fewer in number, transport numerous materials as far as 270 mi. The economics of such systems could be seriously affected by erosion-corrosion problems, since even a pinhole (resulting, say, from pitting corrosion) in such a line could be enlarged catastrophically in minutes by the outflow of high-pressure, abrasive slurry.

Tests have shown that two factors very strongly influence slurry pipeline corrosion: slurry linear velocity, and slurry concentration (percentage solids). In general, increases in either factor will sharply increase the corrosion rate through disruption of surface films that normally hinder the diffusion of oxygen to corrodible surfaces. (In certain cases, the material transported will form a protective scale on the inside pipe wall; however, this scale normally requires periodic "pigging" to prevent excess buildup that could clog the line.) Slurry abrasiveness is also obviously important. More abrasive materials, such as iron, induce corrosion faster than less abrasive materials, such as coal. The role of proper design should be re-emphasized here, since factors like particle settling velocity and slurry turbulence influence the effectiveness of even short lengths of slurry piping. For example, vertical piping

Fig. 3—Typical design considerations for wear resistance

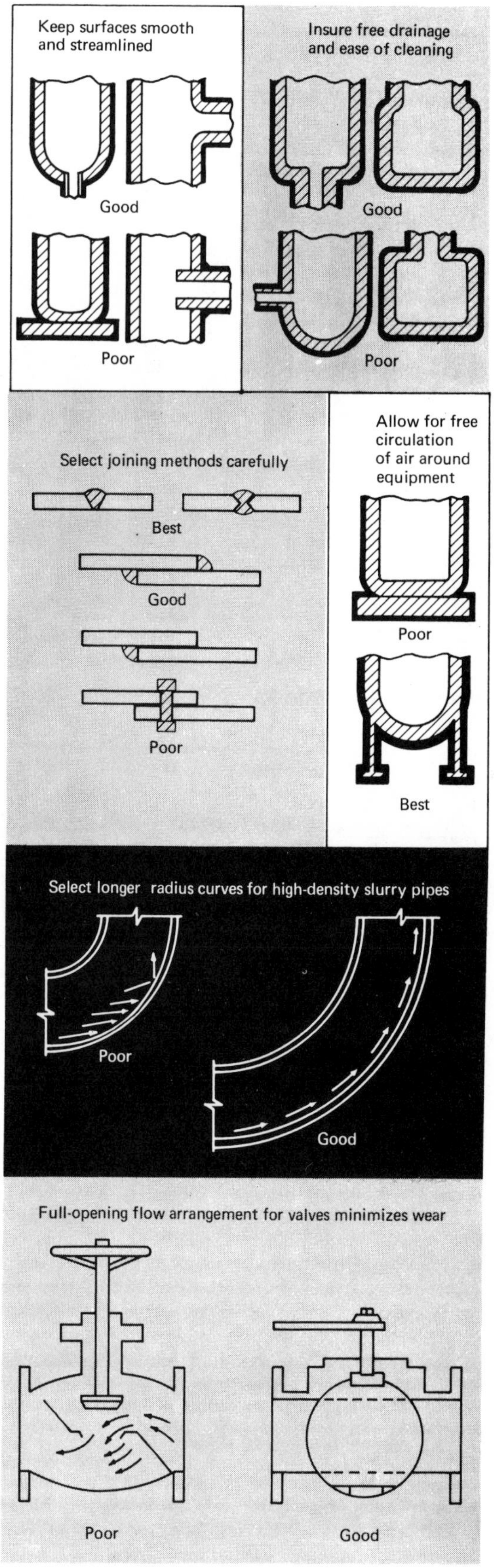

Keep surfaces smooth and streamlined
Good
Poor

Insure free drainage and ease of cleaning
Good
Poor

Select joining methods carefully
Best
Good
Poor

Allow for free circulation of air around equipment
Poor
Best

Select longer radius curves for high-density slurry pipes
Poor
Good

Full-opening flow arrangement for valves minimizes wear
Poor
Good

Fig. 4—Alloy selection charts for chemical processing industry

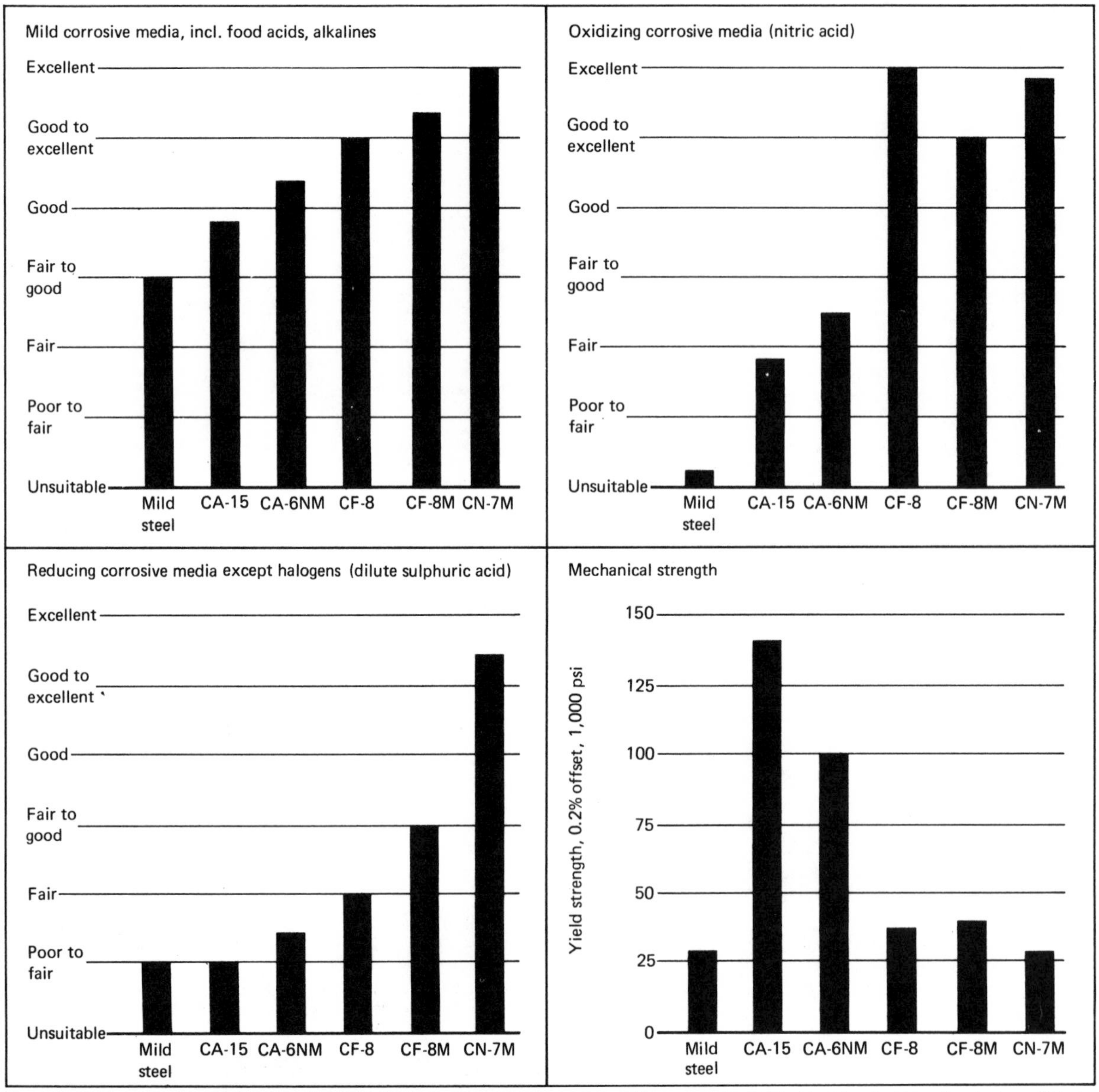

If corrosion resistance is primary, select alloys with high ratings in the medium to be encountered. Then consult the last chart to determine those alloys having sufficient mechanical strength. If mechanical strength is primary, reverse the procedure, starting with the required strength. Alloys shown are: Mild steel, annealed; CA-15, annealed at 1500° F; CA-6NM, air cooled from above 1750° F, tempered at 1100-1150° F; CF-8, CF-8M and CN-7M, solution annealed at 2000° F.

is often less subject to corrosion than horizontal piping, since solids are not deposited as readily on pipe walls.

Corrosion in scrubbers, resulting from high-velocity, hot corrosive gas streams, often represents another costly maintenance problem in · processing plants. Although stainless steel alloys are reportedly preferred for handling corrosive gases, they may be readily attacked in the more severe gas-liquid environments. Where the risk of steel alloy construction is unacceptable, brick linings frequently substitute. Acid brick, carbon brick, or silicon carbide brick is used to partially or completely line the scrubber interior, supported by an outer carbon steel structure.

Wear-resistant materials have numerous other applications in mineral processing. Leach tanks, classifying screens, mill discharge grates, grizzlies, loading buckets, and other ore- and slurry-contacting equipment are all subject to erosion and/or corrosion. Even excluding all nonmetallics, global use of steel in wear applications is conservatively estimated at 3 million tpy. "Calloy," a recently developed alloy reported by its originators to be "the best compromise between . . . manganese steels and . . . the cast iron alloys" is good evidence that wear materials are the subject of active research in the industrial sector. □

References

1) "Symposium: Materials for the Mining Industry," Climax Molybdenum Co., 1975.
2) Anon., "Proper Use of Materials Reduces Scrubber Corrosion," IRON AGE, Sept. 30, 1974, pp 54-55.
3) Wilson, C. L., and J. A. Oates, Corrosion and the Maintenance Engineer, Hart Publishing Co. Inc., 1968.
4) Fontana, M. G., and N. D. Greene, Corrosion Engineering, McGraw-Hill Book Co., 1967.
5) Aude, T. C., and others, "Slurry Piping Systems: Trends, Design Methods, Guidelines," CHEMICAL ENGINEERING, June 28, 1971, pp 74-90.
6) Postlethwaite, John, and others, "Erosion-Corrosion in Slurry Pipelines," CORROSION, Vol. 30, August 1974, pp 285-290.
7) Kopecki, E. S., "Stainless Steel: Effective Corrosion Control for Copper Recovery Operations," E/MJ, Vol. 176, May 1975, pp 117-121.

Chapter 2
Beneficiation

Wet grinding of phosphate rock holds down dollars, dust, and fuel

Samuel V. Houghtaling, senior process engineer, Davy Powergas Inc.

At wet grinding installation, conveyor reclaims rock from wet

A WET ROCK GRINDING PROCESS developed for the phosphate industry by Davy Powergas Inc. of Lakeland, Fla., can reduce capital costs, eliminate dust emissions, and save fuel and power consumption, thereby reducing operating costs. Total savings achievable through wet rock grinding are presently estimated at $3 to $4.25 per ton of P_2O_5.

An estimated 1 million bbl of fuel oil could be saved annually by phosphoric acid producers in Florida alone if wet phosphate rock grinding were utilized throughout the industry. Florida's phosphate industry accounts for more than 60% of the phosphoric acid produced in the US.

The advantages of wet rock grinding include: a 30-40% reduction in horsepower in the grinding area, with a corresponding reduction in mill size; elimination of rock drying (for a savings of about 2.5 gal of fuel oil per ton of rock, or 8-9 gal of fuel oil per ton of P_2O_5); open wet storage for all rock; and the elimination of all air classification equipment and its housing. The result is a reduction in operating costs in the grinding and attack areas.

The elimination of rock drying saves 60¢ to $1 per ton of rock or $2.10 to $3.50 per ton of P_2O_5. With the new process, power in the grinding and attack area is reduced by 35 kwh per ton of P_2O_5. At 1.2-mill power, this is equivalent to a savings of 42¢ per ton of P_2O_5. Overall operating costs at a Florida location can be reduced by a total of $3 to $4.25 per ton of P_2O_5.

The Davy Powergas wet rock grinding process incorporates a number of improvements and modifications of the highly successful Soc. de Prayon process, which is licensed by Davy Powergas.

The new process has been demonstrated in a pilot plant that Agrico Div. of Williams Brothers Inc. has been operating for several months at one of its production centers in central Florida. The pilot plant is a 60-tph wet rock grinding mill for phosphoric acid production. On the basis of performance at this installation, Agrico has decided to build a full scale plant using the Davy Powergas technology at Faustina, La.

C. F. Industries Inc. is converting an existing 800-tpd phosphoric acid plant in central Florida to the new process, and is building an identical plant alongside it. The firm expects to save $2.5 million in capital costs and approximately $1.5 million per year in energy costs, on the basis of current world oil prices.

W. R. Grace & Co. has also decided to base a new phosphoric acid plant on wet grinding, and several phosphoric acid producers are considering converting dry grinding systems to wet grinding.

The initial step of the wet rock grinding process is rock preparation in a wet ball mill. Screening may or may not be used, depending on sizing. Slurry from the ball mill is pumped via pipeline to the Prayon attack system.

Attack system: simple, two-step operation

The attack system is a simple one-stage process incorporating two successive operations. In the first step, phosphate rock and sulphuric acid react with recycled phos-

storage for mill, located up to 1,100 ft from phosphoric acid   plant. Dryer, enclosed mill, dry feed system are eliminated.

phoric acid to produce gypsum and phosphoric acid simultaneously. The phosphoric acid is in its most ideal form with respect to P_2O_5 content and free sulphuric acid. The calcium sulphate is in a form of dihydrate crystals of suitable size.

During the second step, the gypsum-phosphoric acid slurry is filtered, with the gypsum washed countercurrently to collect phosphoric acid and to wash the dihydrate crystals. This procedure maximizes P_2O_5 recovery before removing gypsum from the plant.

As each operation treats the principal product (acid) and the secondary product (gypsum) simultaneously, a compromise must constantly be made between the conditions of treatment required to promote one or the other. For example, raising the P_2O_5 strength of the phosphoric acid and limiting the free sulphuric acid content stops the development of highly filterable gypsum crystals. On the other hand, the amount of water required for thorough washing of the gypsum cake affects the plant water balance and limits the possible increase of P_2O_5 concentration of the product acid.

In the Davy Powergas process, the total reaction volume has been reduced by 10% and is divided into about 66% attack volume and 33% digestion volume.

The attack volume is composed of four to eight compartments in series, constructed of reinforced concrete with rubber and carbon brick lining. Phosphate rock, added to either the No. 1 or No. 2 compartment, is attacked by acid. High strength sulphuric acid is added to recycled acid through a specially designed mixing tee into ei-

ther compartment No. 1, 2, or 3, depending on the rock processed. The sulphuric dilution cooler is eliminated in the Davy Powergas process.

The agitation system has been modified to provide pitched blades on the bottom and flat blades on top. The top blades act as foam breaker and disperser and impart a high shear action, while the bottom blades provide uniform slurry throughout each compartment. Agitation is especially applicable to treating less finely ground phosphates that might contain a large percentage of carbonates and organic matters, with a minimum amount of defoamer usage. Agitation promotes quick, uniform dispersion of materials by preventing supersaturation pockets of calcium ions and sulphate ions which impede homogeneous crystallization.

The amount of slurry corresponding to the production flow or the filter feed flows from the attack area into the digestion area. Slurry is fed into digestion tanks for stabilization—the balancing of the slurry fluid, liquid and solid phases, and the maturing of crystallization.

Total installed horsepower of the agitation area in the attack and digestion systems has been reduced approximately 30% from the classical Prayon system.

Flash cooler serves twin function

Reaction heat and dilution of the sulphuric acid is removed by the slurry vacuum flash cooler, which has been improved in the new process. Capacity of the slurry flash cooler has been increased to allow for additional heat of

Rock slurry pumps feed phosphoric acid plant, replacing the entire dry feed system in a conventional rock grinding plant.

dilution of the sulphuric acid, which previously was diluted and cooled before addition. The flash cooler internals have been redesigned to minimize entrainment, with a corresponding reduction in the size of the flash cooler but with no decrease in heat removal.

The flash cooler not only cools the slurry, but also functions as a vacuum degasifier. When the slurry leaves the flash cooler, it is completely freed of occluded carbon dioxide, and danger of foaming has been reduced. Degasified slurry flowing out of the flash cooler is collected in a seal tank, where it is divided into two streams. One stream goes to the digestion section and feeds the filter. The other returns to the No. 6 or No. 8 compartment (depending on plant size), where it is mixed with fresh slurry. This procedure reduces the occluded carbon dioxide content, making the slurry easier to pump and preventing pulsations in the flow.

The slurry is recirculated to the No. 1 compartment of the attack tanks. The recirculated flow through the attack tank is about 2.5 times the volume of previous systems, or about twice the flow through the present flash cooler. Increasing the slurry recirculation rate to the reaction section is important to maintain homogeneous physical and chemical conditions (temperature, calcium, and sulphate concentration). Dispersing the raw material and evolved carbon dioxide in an increased flow also helps to facilitate control of the operation.

Recirculation through the attack tank is via side openings rather than the conventional over-and-under system previously used. The amount of recycle flow must be varied according to the type of phosphate rock used to feed the system. The increased recirculation flow and uniformity of the slurry make it possible to operate at a lower given sulphate level with a given rock.

Adjustments to the sulphate level can be made in the digestion area with the addition of a slight amount of sulphuric acid. Reduction of sulphate can be achieved by the addition of a slight amount of rock. The new process is expected to improve recovery of P_2O_5 by 0.5-1.0%. Recovery

and capacity are related to the type of rock which is fed to the system.

The Davy Powergas process uses a conventional Bird-Prayon filtration system. The acid strength is unchanged at 28-31% (depending on the rock feed). Since energy for evaporation of acid is generally available in the form of steam from sulphuric acid plants, raising the acid strength is not important.

Processing parameters

The rock grinding specification has been modified to 0.5% plus 35% mesh, 70% minus 100 mesh, and 40% minus 200 mesh. Before modification, the Prayon system required 60% minus 200 mesh grind.

The fine rock found in northern Florida and in some areas of central Florida yields a considerable amount of material that is minus 35 mesh. The rock can be pre-classified to remove the minus 35 mesh material and to reduce the required grinding capacity.

As the new process does not require sulphuric acid dilution to 55% before addition to the attack system, maintenance of the water balance calls for a stream equivalent to the water of dilution of the sulphuric acid.

The water can be replaced in several forms, such as pond water, which may be used as additional filter wash or as a direct addition to the recycle acid if additional wash is not required on the filter. Since pond water can now be used instead of process water, the pond balance has been altered. It should never be necessary to neutralize water from the pond for disposal.

In a well-run phosphoric acid plant with a properly designed cooling and gypsum pond, the water balance is such that water treatment should not be required even when diluting the sulphuric acid. Therefore, a stream of about 400 gal of additional water per ton of P_2O_5 is available for use as pond water.

Wet grinding is much more reliable

Since the wet grinding system has a much higher degree of reliability than a dry grinding system, the required amount of surge of ground rock can be reduced. If the chemical plant is located near a mine, a rock slurry can be pumped directly to the plant from the mine, eliminating rail transportation or belt conveyors.

(One negative aspect of wet grinding is that ball consumption will be about tripled, and the mill liner will wear out about three times faster—having a normal life of three to five years. Another possible disadvantage would be a plant water balance which makes treatment necessary, since process water is required in the mill due to corrosion properties of normal pond water.)

The new process eliminates the dry rock feed system. The rock is now pumped, with proper instrumentation, to any point necessary in the attack system. Distribution is now much simpler since rock can be piped into the openings in the attack tank.

The absence of dry rock anywhere in the system eliminates the air pollution which is generated in drying, transferring, storing, grinding, and weighing dry rock. There is no possibility of carrying rock into the scrubber through the attack system. In a large plant, the wet grinding process will eliminate about 1,000 lb of particulates per day.

The Davy Powergas wet grinding process with a Prayon dihydrate plant promises a high on-stream factor and adaption to treating all types of phosphate using high strength sulphuric acid, plus open wet rock storage which reduces dust pollution. These advantages can be significant in reducing the cost of processing phosphate. □

The principles of comminution: an analytical summary

R. T. Hukki, professor, Technical Research Center of Finland

COMMINUTING RELATIONSHIPS based on weight, grinding size, specific surface area, distribution of grind size, energy consumption, classification, and operating efficiency have been the subject of many years of research. This article, a summary and analysis of the principles of comminution, presents some conclusions that contradict earlier work. This analysis is the product of more than 30 years of special effort to make the basic theoretical aspects of comminution match the cold facts of grinding experience—both laboratory-scale experimental and large-scale industrial—across the entire range of size reduction, from coarse crushing to the production of micropowders of utmost fineness.

Weight distribution vs. fineness in ground products

Experimental weight-vs.-size data obtained in analyzing crushed and ground products is customarily plotted on graph paper for further examination. On log-log paper, the well known Gates (1915)-Gaudin (1926)-Schuhmann (1940) relationship plots as a straight line. As early as 1909, a similar straight-line relationship was presented by Rich-ards in *Ore Dressing*, Vol. 3. Rosin, Rammler, and Sperling formulated another straight-line relationship plotted on a log-log vs. log paper (1930-1934). Still other straight-line plots have been proposed. With minor modifications, the G-G-S and R-R-S straight-line relationships have been widely accepted, although the original authors did not discuss limitations relative to the particle size range over which the relationships are valid.

One of the practical advantages cited in support of these straight-line relationships is that they provide a basis for mathematical estimates of the specific surface area of a ground product. (The specific surface area is the ratio of surface area of a number of particles to their weight, usually expressed in square centimeters per gram.) Equations for such estimates have been derived, and examples of applications recorded.

Such estimates should be expected, within reasonable limits, to agree with surface areas measured experimentally. However, they usually do not, because the mathematical estimates do not incorporate values for a sample's lower particle size limit. In fact, they cannot, because the information does not exist, and no reasonable recommen-

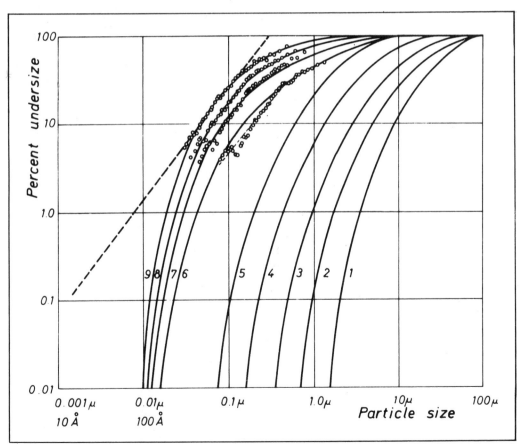

Fig. 1—Overall weight distribution vs. fineness. Sub-sieve size distribution for samples 1 to 5 and sub-experimental size distribution for samples 6 to 9 have been evaluated mathematically to obtain a sum of fractional surface areas converging toward the surface area measured on the original sample.

dation has been proposed for establishing its value. By arbitrarily setting the lower particle size limit far down in the submicron range, estimated specific surface areas may be increased several times. If a series of decreasing numerical values for the lower particle size limit is applied to the straight-line estimates, the result will be a nonconverging series of estimated surface areas increasing in numerical value.

Contradicting the widely accepted straight-line relationships is a proposal put forth in 1971 that the cumulative weight-vs.-size plot on customary logarithmic graph papers might instead be a smooth continuous curve.[1] In the coarse range, the curve of course follows data obtained experimentally. In the fine range, for which there is no experimental evidence, the curve is drawn so that the resulting $\sqrt{2}$ sequence of size fractions produces a sum of fractional surface areas. This sum converges toward the surface area measured on the original sample. Each fractional surface area is obtained by multiplying the specific surface area of the fraction by the weight of the fraction.

Details of the above method, with manual and computer evaluations of the sub-sieve size distribution, have been published,[1] and the results are illustrated in Fig. 1. Curves 1, 2, and 3 in the figure show the resulting overall size distribution for cements with specific surface areas of 1,500, 2,500 and 4,500 sq cm per gram, respectively; curves 4 and 5 are for calcite micropowders with specific surface areas of 11,500 and 25,000 sq cm per gram, respectively; and curves 6 through 9 are for albite powders originally studied by Gaudin and Kondo.[2] Curve 5 is fairly representative of the very finest micropowders that can currently be produced on an industrial scale. Curves 6 through 9 may represent the finest laboratory grinding products results ever evaluated and reported.

The following conclusions may be drawn from Fig. 1:

■ On a log-log paper, the overall cumulative weight-vs.-size distribution of a comminuted product plots as a smooth curve, not as a straight line.

■ In the customary coarse range normally covered by the conventional sieve analysis, and in that range alone, the curve may be approximated by a straight line, such as proposed by the Gates-Gaudin-Schuhmann principle. The slope of this part of the curve is normally less than 1.0.

■ In the sub-sieve range, the slope of each size distribution curve increases gradually with decreasing particle size.

■ In the finest size range, each curve apparently approaches asymptotically a vertical line whose abscissa is the grind limit.

■ For all practical purposes, the grind limit is reached when the cumulative amount of material passing a "screen" is less than 0.01% of the weight of the test sample.

■ The grind limit is not a constant figure, but decreases in numerical value with increasing specific surface area of the particular test material.

The lower parts of the Rosin-Rammler-Sperling plots behave essentially as the curves described above and lead to equivalent values for the grind limits. On R-R-S paper, the overall cumulative weight-vs.-size plot is again a curve, not a straight line.

For cements and similar materials, the grind limit seems to be from 0.25 to 0.5 microns. Particles finer than that can naturally be found in all such materials, but their relative total weight is too small to be of practical significance.

In industrial fine grinding, the grind limit usually falls within the range of 0.1 to 1 micron. Under laboratory conditions, the lowest grind limits so far obtained seem to approach 0.01 micron.

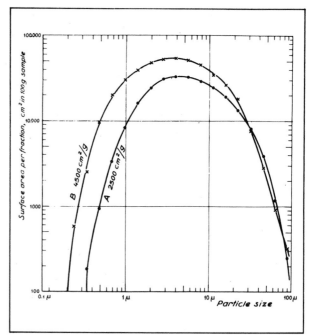

Fig. 2—Overall surface distribution vs. fineness. Curves A and B correspond to samples 2 and 3, respectively, in Fig. 1.

Surface distribution vs. fineness in ground products

The novel weight-vs.-size relationship described above calls for a correspondingly novel overall surface-vs.-size distribution—defined as the relative distribution of the total surface area available in the original sample between successive true and imaginary $\sqrt{2}$ screen fractions.

This relationship for two cement samples of different fineness was analyzed and tabulated in an earlier paper[1] and is illustrated in Fig. 2. The same materials are represented by curves 2 and 3 in Fig. 1. Curve A represents a cement having a specific surface area of 2,500 sq cm per gram; data for the curve were obtained from a computer. Curve B corresponds to a cement having a specific surface area of 4,500 sq cm per gram; these data were generated manually. Many other samples of ground products have produced surface distributions substantially the same as those shown.

The following conclusions can be drawn:

■ The overall fractional surface-vs.-size distribution in comminuted products can be represented by a bell-shaped curve resembling the Gaussian probability distribution.

■ The symmetric shape of the ideal probability distribution is more closely approached by products obtained in open circuit reduction processes, without outside size control.

■ Screened and classified fine and coarse products yield asymmetric surface distribution plots.

■ In the range where the industrial grind limit is approached (0.1 to 1 micron), the fractional surface areas fall to infinitesimal values.

Probability of crushing in comminution

The overall probability of a particle being crushed in comminution is represented by Fig. 3. (Under conditions where all particles are broken, the probability of breakage is 1.0. If one-half of the mass of particles is broken, the probability factor is 0.5. If none of the particles are broken, the probability factor is 0.)

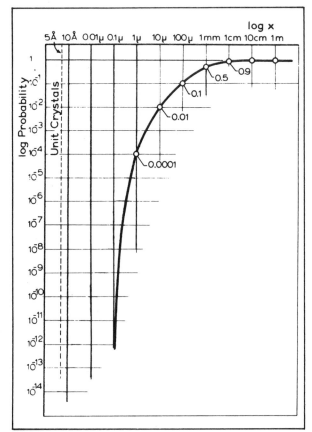

Fig. 3—A basic logarithmic curve plots probability of breakage for any given particle against the size of the particle.

In crushing large material, the probability factor is high. In fine grinding, it is low. In submicron grinding by conventional means, it approaches 0. Even in the micron size range, the coarsest particles lose their individuality, and the charge, both wet and dry, behaves on the whole rather like a homogeneous, fluid mass.

The nature of the phenomena encountered in grinding micropowders is demonstrated in Table 1. The hypothetical mill in line one represents about 1% of the volume of a base mill measuring 100 cm dia by 100 cm. The ball charge is 5,000 10-mm-dia balls weighing about 20 kg, and the hypothetical batch to be ground is about 1,325 grams (or 500×10^3 individual particles) in 1-mm "cubes." Comparable size reduction figures and mill dimensions are represented in decreasing decadic steps down to 0.1-micron "cubes."

The 10-mm-dia steel balls and 1-mm grind material are obviously of reasonable relative size. If the material is reduced to 1 micron, the relative size of the 10-mm-dia balls

Table 1—Comparison of theoretical statistics for a grinding mill magnified in decadic steps

Size class	Theoretical number of cubes	Number of 10-mm-dia balls	Number of cubes per ball	Magnification	Magnified Cube	Magnified Ball dia	Magnified Mill dia
1 mm	500×10^3	5,000	1×10^2	$1 \times$	1 mm	10 mm	26.8 cm
100 μ	500×10^6	5,000	1×10^5	$10 \times$	1 mm	10 cm	2.68 m
10 μ	500×10^9	5,000	1×10^8	$100 \times$	1 mm	1 m	26.8 m
1 μ	500×10^{12}	5,000	1×10^{11}	$1,000 \times$	1 mm	10 m	268 m
0.1 μ	500×10^{15}	5,000	1×10^{14}	$10,000 \times$	1 mm	100 m	2,680 m

is magnified 1,000 times, and the situation is drastically different. The laboratory-size mill becomes comparable to a 268-m-dia mill charged with 10-m-dia balls grinding 1×10^{11} 1-mm cubes. The probability of producing further efficient size reduction under these conditions within a reasonable grinding period is indeed small.

In the 0.1 micron range, the situation becomes simply hopeless.

Energy consumption vs. fineness in comminution

To obtain a sensible correlation between required energy and fineness of grind in comminution, it is essential that the process be considered over the full range from primary crushing to the production of ultrafine micropowders.

In the classic experiments of Gross and Zimmerley (1930), the maximum energy concentration applied was 1.27 kwh per ton. In other well known investigations, the energy concentrations applied have been similarly limited to startlingly narrow ranges. It is surprising in view of such limitations that conclusions of general validity have been proposed and the proposals widely accepted.

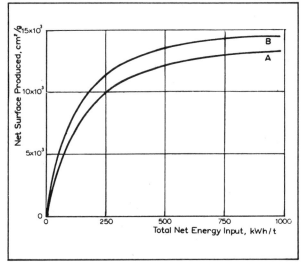

Fig. 4—Examples of development of new surface area are plotted as a function of energy consumption in grinding. Curve A indicates the trend for open circuit grinding. Curve B shows the trend for the same material in closed circuit grinding.

The production of new specific surface area as a function of net energy input in grinding is shown in Fig. 4, which demonstrates that with increasing energy input, the maximum specific surface area that can be obtained under any given set of conditions asymptotically approaches a certain upper limit. This limit is higher with wet grinding conditions than with similar dry grinding conditions. In closed circuit grinding, wet or dry, the limit is higher than in open circuit grinding. An increase in the energy input beyond the indicated 1,000 kwh per ton does not essentially alter the trend.

Mean particle size can be readily calculated from the specific surface area. For the finest powders graphed in Fig. 3, mean particle size is on the order of 2 to 3 microns.

Worldwide evidence, both small-scale experimental and large-scale industrial, supports a basic formulation of the fundamental energy-vs.-size relationship for comminution that is substantially as shown in Fig. 5. In open circuit processes, more energy is needed to produce a product than in closed circuit processes.

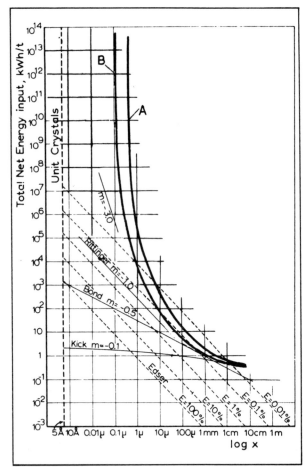

Fig. 5—Overall energy consumption vs. fineness in comminution. Curve A is for an open circuit, Curve B for the same material in a closed circuit. The series of parallel lines at slopes m = –1 represent comminution efficiencies of 100%, 10%, 1%, 0.1% and 0.01%; based on Edser's specific surface energy of quartz.

The entire range of comminution can be subdivided into five internal ranges:

1) The crushing range, covered by the basic law of Kick. The slope *m* of the cumulative curve varies from about 0 to about –0.1.

2) The range of conventional rod and ball mill grinding, to which Bond's theory applies. Slope *m* is about –0.5.

3) The fine grinding range—such as the grinding of cements—covered by the law of Rittinger. Slope *m* is approximately –1.

4) The micropowder grinding range, with slope *m* from approximately –1 to –3.

5) The range of approaching grind limit, with slope *m* from about –3 to infinity. This range has no practical applications.

Energy consumption vs. fineness in classification

Until now, very little if any attention has been paid to the relative energy requirement for sizing in size reduction operations, especially in classification. While the energy consumption in certain closed circuit sizing steps (such as screening of crushed products and rake or spiral classification of ground products in flotation plants) may seem of minor importance, this energy factor rapidly increases in closed circuit processes related to the production of finer and finer powders.

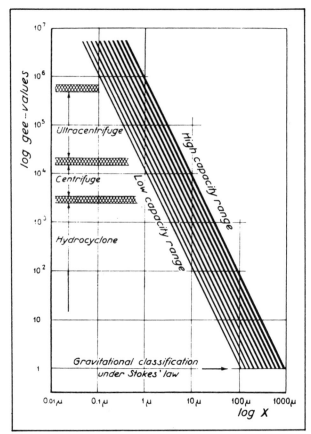

Fig. 6—Gee-values used in hydraulic classification vs. fineness for equal settling velocities; plot based on Stokes' law.

The fundamental relationship between the product fineness and the gee-values of the field applied in classification is shown in Fig. 6 (1968).[5] (Gee-values are for gravitational field or the comparable centrifugal field.) Originally, the figure was conceived for hydraulic classification. Under conditions of 1 gee, gravitational rake classifiers are commonly used to produce a fine overflow product of 95% minus 100 to 300 microns—and as high as 1 mm. The slope of the lines (*m* = –2) in Fig. 6 is derived from Stokes' law, so that gee-values in the centrifugal field multiplied by particle size raised to the second power (gees · x^2) yields a constant settling velocity.

It is obvious from Fig. 6 that increasing fineness of the classified product requires increasing energy consumption for classification (in kwh per ton). Furthermore, this fundamental relationship should be valid not only for hydraulic classification but for pneumatic classification as well.

The relationship between energy consumption and fineness in pneumatic classification is shown in Fig. 7 (1973).[6] The curve presents the range of optimum energy values obtained in pilot scale tests. In conventional practice, energy consumption may be several times higher.

(It should be pointed out that there seems to be no industrial classification process, wet or dry, in which a ground mineral product can be classified by any means to produce a product finer than 95% minus 2 or 3 microns. This seems to be the present lower size limit, independent of any reasonable increase in the amount of energy used in classification.)

In summary, maximum energy consumption in industrial mechanical size reduction processes is in the range of 100 to 1,000 kwh per ton, while in industrial classification, maximum energy consumption appears to be on the order

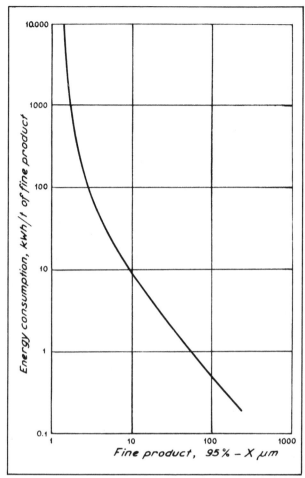

Fig. 7—Overall minimum energy consumption plotted against fineness in pneumatic classification.

The graph axes:
- Y-axis: Energy consumption, kwh/t of fine product (0.1, 1, 10, 100, 1000, 10,000)
- X-axis: Fine product, 95% – X μm (1, 10, 100, 1000)

ciency of the mechanical size reduction processes based on the surface energy of quartz of Edser is on the order of 0.2%.

■ This optimum efficiency range corresponds to conventional grinding operations, with the efficiency falling gradually as grinding moves toward the coarser and toward the finer reduction operations.

■ In the coarse (10 cm to 1 m) range, the overall efficiency of crushing seems to fall below 0.01%, in spite of relatively high figures which have been obtained in laboratory investigations.

■ In the micron range, the efficiency also falls below 0.01%.

■ In the range approaching the industrial grinding limit (0.1 to 1 micron), the efficiency approaches infinitesimally small values.

It is evident that efficiency figures based on the specific surface energy of solids are purely academic and of no practical value in the evaluation of industrial comminuting operations.

Testing the validity of this analysis

The validity of the statements made in this article should be judged against the following evidence:

■ All the statements are in good common sense agreement with each other.

■ In all of the relationships discussed, the practical industrial lower grind limit is reached within the same range.

■ The numerical value of this lower grind limit depends on the application and on the definition, but in broad terms, it falls in the 0.1- to 1-micron range.

■ The curves as presented agree with the following data from worldwide practical applications:

a) In coarse crushing, energy consumption is usually 0.1 to 1 kwh per ton.

b) In fine crushing, on the order of 1 kwh per ton.

c) In open circuit rod mill grinding, 2 to 4 kwh per ton.

d) In conventional grinding to flotation fineness, 5 to 15 kwh per ton.

e) In grinding cement clinker to cement, from 25 to 35 kwh per ton for the coarser grinds and up to 50 to 100 kwh per ton for the very finest cement grinds.

f) In production of micropowders, more than 100 kwh per ton.

g) Grinding and classification on an industrial scale have not been able to produce mineral powders finer than 95% minus 2 to 3 microns.

h) In production of the finest powders by jet milling, energy consumption ranges from 100 kwh per ton up to several thousand kwh per ton. □

of 100 kwh per ton of final fine product. Laboratory experiments have been carried out at energy concentrations up to 10,000 kwh per ton, while the classification of the finest powders obtained on the laboratory scale has apparently used energy ranging from 100 to 1,000 kwh per ton.

This experience leads to the tentative conclusion that in the production of the finest industrial mineral powders by comminution, the energy requirement for classification increases in relative importance with the increasing fineness of the product. And this energy requirement may ultimately amount to more than 10% of the final overall energy consumption figure. Furthermore, all evidence indicates that the increasing energy share for classification is economically beneficial.

Efficiency of comminution operations

In a classic investigation, Gross and Zimmerley found that the efficiency of the crushing process—as they performed it—was 1.65%, based on Edser's value (1922) of the specific surface energy of quartz (920 ergs per sq cm). This efficiency is often cited as being characteristic of the low efficiency of comminution operations in general. Fig. 5 also shows overall efficiencies, based on Edser's value, which is given the reference efficiency value of 100%. On the log-log paper used for Fig. 5, the efficiency lines are a series of parallel lines at slopes of $m = -1$. From the characteristic overall energy-vs.-size curves, the following conclusions can be drawn:

■ In practical industrial operations, the optimum effi-

References

1) Hukki, R. T., and J. E. Venho, "Evaluation of Sub-Sieve Size Distribution of Ground Products by Computer," Third European Symposium on Comminution, Cannes, 1971. DECHEMA-MONOGR., 69, 1972, pp 491-507.
2) Kondo, Yoshio, and A. M. Gaudin, "Sizing Comminution Products in Extremely Fine Range," TRANS. AIME, 229, 1964, pp 292-299.
3) Hukki, R. T., and I. G. Reddy, "The Relationship Between Net Energy and Fineness in Comminution," Second European Symposium on Comminution, Amsterdam, 1966. DECHEMA-MONOGR., 57, 1967, pp 313-339.
4) Hukki, R. T., "A Proposal for a Solomonic Settlement between the Theories of Von Rittinger, Kick and Bond," TRANS. AIME, 220, 1961, pp 403-408.
5) Hukki, R.T., "Hydraulic Classification in Gravitational and in Centrifugal Fields," Paper C-1, VIII International Mineral Processing Congress, Leningrad, 1968.
6) Hukki, R. T., "Construction and Performance of a Precision Gravitational Pneumatic Classifier and of Corresponding Gravitational-Centrifugal Classifiers," Paper No. 5, Tenth International Mineral Processing Congress, London, 1973.
7) Gross, John, and S. R. Zimmerley, "Crushing and Grinding I-III," TRANS. AIME, 1930.

How to optimize life of crusher wear parts through proper selection and use

Paul E. Hegmegee Jr., product manager, wear materials, Nordberg equipment, Rexnord Inc.

THOUGH THE RECESSIONARY TREND in the US economy during the past year has tended to ease acute materials shortages that prevailed only a year ago, many in the mining industry and among mine equipment suppliers have become accustomed to coping with short supplies. One of the more serious shortages has been in crusher wear liners.

The reasons for the wear liner shortage are primarily economic. Prior to 1971, capacity to supply the US market with wear resistant castings exceeded demand, and competitive marketing forced the shutdown of a substantial tonnage of casting capacity. (See graph.) Since 1971, demand for wear castings has outstripped supply, and casting capacity has yet to catch up with demand. If the laws of supply and demand work their usual results, we can anticipate that the two curves graphed here will eventually change trajectory, and shortages will disappear.

However, the problem today is time. Most foundry men agree that if plans for a new foundry or expansion of facilities were approved immediately, it would probably be at least 18 to 24 months before an actual production increase could be realized. In the meantime, users of crusher liners should look for ways to conserve wear material. A campaign to prolong wear-part life must emphasize proper material selection, maximum material utilization, well supervised maintenance and operation, and good forecasting and inventory control.

Of the materials used for crusher liners, Hadfields manganese is still the most popular alloy. However, other available alloys that may give improved efficiency and service in proper applications should be considered in meeting the challenge of the present materials shortage. Close liaison and consultation with crusher liner suppliers is important in selecting materials for extended service.

Maximum liner productivity with minimum throw-away weight can be obtained through proper selection of crusher cavity configuration, which is determined by liner design. A careful analysis of production throughput during the life of the liner should be coupled periodically with an analysis of the worn profile. Such a practice is especially important after a change in crusher location or product.

How to match the liner with the crushing job

For **cone crushers,** intelligent selection of crushing cavity design is of prime importance in maintaining maximum production through a crushing plant. Cone crushers are usually lined with two or three replaceable castings—crusher liners—that come into direct contact with the aggregate. The liners wear away in direct proportion both to the abrasiveness of the aggregate and to the amount of reduction that takes place in each crushing stage.

In most cone crushers the mantle is a single casting, but larger crushers incorporate an upper mantle and a lower mantle. In evaluating and selecting the cross section profile for the crushing cavity of a new or existing cone crusher, the liner designs normally available to mine operators include types for extra coarse, coarse, medium, and fine grinding. Variations within these designations involve cross section changes to optimize metal utilization and productivity.

The crushing cavity must be carefully designed to permit the top feed size to enter the crusher throughout the entire wear life of the liners. Because the most efficient crushing action takes place when the feed is reduced in a series of four or five blows as it passes through the crusher cavity, the crusher design should provide for some reduction to take place in the upper portion of the crushing cavity as well as in the lower or parallel sizing zone. In other words, too large a feed opening will allow feed to pass the upper zone without crushing and will probably develop excessive power draw. Since crusher feed rate is governed by power draw, an incorrect cavity cross section can reduce crusher capacity and occasionally create unnecessary maintenance.

If the crushing cavity design is not right for the job, cone crusher liners will wear more at the bottom than at the top. As the operator screws the bowl assembly down to maintain the closed side setting for product size, the opening in the upper zone is narrowed. This inhibits the feed rate and crushing activity in the upper area.

The fact that no two rock types or crushing applications are exactly the same has led to the availability of a large number of cavity designs through the years. The optimum in cavity design for a given service is one that draws close to the rated power draw throughout the entire liner wear life and that results in a liner scrap loss of 25% to 40%. If a crushing plant is not meeting rated capacity or if increased capacity is wanted, a crushing cavity investigation is frequently warranted.

As a guide, the initial liner selection for a cone crusher should be made on the basis of feed analysis, abrasiveness of the rock, and crusher product required. Feed should generally be no larger than 80% of the liner open side dimensions. Subsequent observation of the cone crusher in operation will help to determine optimum liner design.

For **jaw crushers,** cavity design considerations are similar to those for cone crushers. Curved jaws should be considered along with conventional straight types. Tooth design can be an important factor, depending on the size and shape of the material to be crushed.

For **impact and roll-type crushers,** maintenance of crushing dimensions is especially important. Wear parts should periodically get a careful weld buildup and hardfacing to help meet crusher throughput requirements while prolonging wear-part life.

Gyratory crushers by nature develop localized wear zones that require partial concave replacement to obtain maximum liner metal life. An established pattern of partial liner replacement helps conserve material; however, sometimes such a pattern still does not fully utilize the manganese. Judicious use of several different wear materials may promote more complete metal utilization. Hardsurface and buildup on gyratory liners is possible but less desirable and less economical than the use of an alloy-iron material.

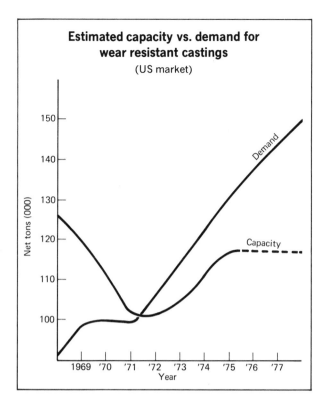

Estimated capacity vs. demand for wear resistant castings
(US market)

Net tons (000) vs. *Year* (1969–'77), showing curves labeled **Demand** and **Capacity**.

How to prolong liner life

For **cone crushers,** correct first installation is important for full crusher-liner utilization. During installation, make sure that the contact areas between the crusher non-wearing assembly (the head and bowl in the case of the cone crusher) and the liner are clean and sound. Then assemble the liner tightly in the crusher, so it cannot move during crushing operation. If bolts are used to hold the liner in place, make sure the bolts are torqued to give proper holding force. A loose nut is obviously dangerous, while an over-tightened nut may overstress the bolt and cause premature failure. Finally, make certain the liner is properly backed with an epoxy resin recommended by the manufacturer—or use zinc in operations where an epoxy resin cannot be used.

Allow for expansion of the liner as it wears. Manganese steel has the unique characteristic of flowing as it work hardens. In cone crushers, the mantle usually "grows" at the bottom, and the bowl liner "grows" at the top. Nordberg recommends that nothing be welded or assembled in the crusher to prevent the expansion of these parts.

Keep records of adjustments for wear. Most crusher manufacturers can advise on the allowable amount of wear before crusher liners should be replaced. For cone crushers, allowable wear is usually expressed in terms of either vertical travel of the bowl assembly or in terms of "x" number of notches that the bowl assembly is rotated. Contact a crusher manufacturer representative for information on how to get maximum use from any particular style of liner. The important thing is to record adjustments as they occur, which can be done effectively by requiring the crusher operator to keep a daily operations log for each crusher. The log should record power draw, crusher closed side setting, lube oil pressure, lube oil temperatures and any significant changes in the daily operational routine, such as making adjustments for wear.

Proper recording of all adjustments for wear should insure that liners are not removed from the crusher before maximum utilization.

Another way to determine maximum cone crusher liner use is to paint a red stripe around the bowl hopper to indicate to the operator the need for visual checks into the crushing cavity. Such checks may locate areas where liners have completely worn through or identify cracks in the liner when the cross section becomes too thin. The method obviously requires some daily attention by the crusher operator.

Records should be kept for all liners to permit comparisons of past and present performance.

Consult an expert. Let him know *routine* requirements for size of crusher feed and size of product. Advise him if for any reason a change is made in feed or product. Chances are he has recently handled a similar problem and can give you the benefit of his experience.

For **jaw crushers,** the following operating procedures should prolong wear-part life:

- Keep crusher jaws tight and centered.
- Reverse jaws more than once to even out wear.
- Repositioning of the toggle to a lower setting may minimize abrasion of jaw liners.
- Weld manganese bars to high-wear areas to prolong life.
- Utilize hardsurfacing wherever feasible. (A consultation with weld rod suppliers may be advisable.)

For **dynapactors and impactors:**

- Hardsurface frequently to minimize distortion or metallurgical problems.
- Maintain sleeves in dynapactors to allow distribution of wear.
- Consult the manufacturer on the lowest speed consistent with obtaining desired product and minimum wear for impactors.
- Reposition sleeves as necessary to obtain maximum metal utilization.

For **gyratory crushers:**

- Install and back mantles and concaves properly and completely to insure good support and maximum life.
- Install metal detectors to minimize introduction of tramp metal.
- Scarf manganese to minimize excess metal flow.
- Hardsurface concaves to prolong wear if the more wear resistant irons are not used. However, use of the irons should be very carefully considered as the better solution to minimizing wear.

Advise manufacturers of inventory requirements

All types of wear materials—or any other item in short supply—can be most advantageously distributed by setting up good demand forecasting and inventory control. Proper forecasting of requirements by users minimizes stock levels and reduces unnecessary production time.

Excessive stocks held by users tend to encourage premature removal of parts that have not been utilized to their fullest extent. Anticipation of changes in needs for wear materials can also aid suppliers in redistributing material, if possible, to maximize utilization of available parts. If demand changes are not anticipated far enough in advance to alter production schedules smoothly, manufacturers' efficiency is reduced and total availability is lowered, contributing to higher costs for producer and consumer alike.

A mine operator has a number of options to get the most out of crusher liners. The more methods used, the greater the liner utilization is likely to be—helping to maximize the operational and profit potential of the crusher. □

E/MJ OPERATING IDEAS

THOSE WORKING WITH WATER SLURRIES are interested in the solids specific gravity (S), the percent solids by weight (W), the specific gravity of the slurry mixture (M), and the percent solids by volume (V). The relationships are shown on the nomograph here, prepared by F. Caplan, a professional engineer, of Oakland, Calif. If any two properties are known, the other two are fixed. The nomograph gives a rapid simultaneous solution to the equations. Example: What are M and V if $S = 2.5$ and $W = 62.5\%$? Align the S and W values and read $M = 1.60$ and $V = 40.0\%$. ☐

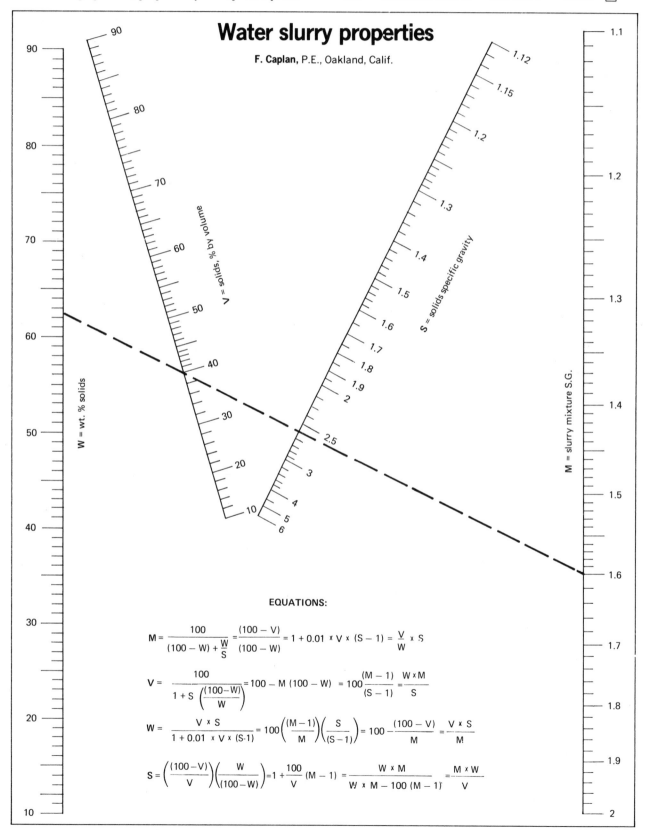

Water slurry properties

F. Caplan, P.E., Oakland, Calif.

V = solids % by volume

W = wt. % solids

S = solids specific gravity

M = slurry mixture S.G.

EQUATIONS:

$$M = \frac{100}{(100 - W) + \frac{W}{S}} = \frac{(100 - V)}{(100 - W)} = 1 + 0.01 \times V \times (S - 1) = \frac{V}{W} \times S$$

$$V = \frac{100}{1 + S\left(\frac{(100 - W)}{W}\right)} = 100 - M(100 - W) = 100\frac{(M - 1)}{(S - 1)} = \frac{W \times M}{S}$$

$$W = \frac{V \times S}{1 + 0.01 \times V \times (S - 1)} = 100\left(\frac{(M - 1)}{M}\right)\left(\frac{S}{(S - 1)}\right) = 100 - \frac{(100 - V)}{M} = \frac{V \times S}{M}$$

$$S = \left(\frac{(100 - V)}{V}\right)\left(\frac{W}{(100 - W)}\right) = 1 + \frac{100}{V}(M - 1) = \frac{W \times M}{W \times M - 100(M - 1)} = \frac{M \times W}{V}$$

How to choose electric drives for large grinding mills

Various power transmission arrangements are evaluated in terms of the drive requirements for optimizing grinding operations

W. H. Schwedes and **E. L. Owen,** General Electric Co.

ORE GRINDING MILLS are really just slowly rotating barrels, but barrels that are growing in size so fast that the application of electric drives for them is rapidly approaching a technology like that for wind tunnels or pumped storage drives. Ore grinding mills are particularly worthy of careful consideration because some 40% of the 75 Mw of power used by a large copper ore concentrator, or some 60% of the 200 Mw supplied to a large iron ore concentrator, is for grinding. Such ore plants are located where the ore is, not where a utility happens to be. Thus the challenge is not only to choose a drive and power transmission for reasonable cost, high performance, reliability and minimum maintenance, but also to afford the interface between mill drive and power distribution and source systems to minimize the whole ore plant's monthly power bill, or costs of self-generation.

Optimizing a drive selection requires a study of each particular ore plant's set of parameters. But by identifying the criteria for selection and then weighting each type of drive according to these criteria, general yardsticks for final choice become apparent.

Grinding action takes place inside the barrel, where the ore charge is ground with the aid of balls, mill length rods, or large chunks of ore—as in autogenous grinding.

Ore grinding mills in present use have been built as large as 32 ft in diameter and up to 40 ft in length, are rated as slow as 11 rpm, and are powered up to 9,200 hp. Envisioned for the immeidate future are diameters of 40 ft, lengths of 50 ft, and power levels of 35,000 hp at as low as 9 rpm. This presents quite a challenge in drive selection.

Mill power transmission arrangements

Fig. 1, in plan view, shows the basic power transmission arrangements.[1]

Arrangements *A, B, C, D, G,* and *H* on the left are semi-enclosed-ring-gear (RG) connected to the mill at either the shell or trunnion diameter; *D* and *F* on the right are trunnion connected (TCGB) enclosed gear sets; *I* is gearless, direct connected (D) to the mill shell or trunnion. There is a limit to the torque that can be transmitted from a pinion to a bull gear for long reliable tooth life, at reasonable cost, taking into account the high-torque burden on the drive and its rough grinding ambient. Therefore, as the mill size increases, the number of low-speed pinions is increased (top to bottom of Fig. 1) until confidence is lost in long, low-cost life of geared parts, and they are then omitted. This may happen when the electromechanical system becomes so complex or so subject to resonant torque amplification that continuous steady-state or transient load sharing by the parts is not assured.

The one-pinion arrangement *A* can be powered by a low-speed, high-torque synchronous motor. Thousands of these

W. H. Schwedes is manager of engineering-mining industries, and E. L. Owen is the mining industry application engineer at GE's Industry Sales and Engineering Operation, Schenectady, N.Y.

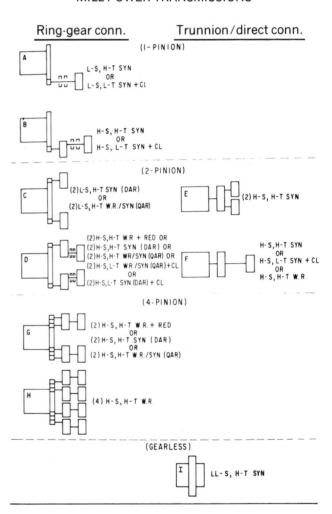

FIG. 1—BASIC ARRANGEMENTS OF MILL POWER TRANSMISSIONS

Ring-gear conn.   Trunnion/direct conn.

(1- PINION)

A   L-S, H-T SYN
OR
L-S, L-T SYN + CL

B   H-S, H-T SYN
OR
H-S, L-T SYN + CL

(2- PINION)

C   (2)L-S, H-T SYN (DAR)
OR
(2)L-S, H-T W.R./SYN (QAR)

E   (2) H-S, H-T SYN

D   (2)H-S,H-T W R + RED OR
(2)H-S,H-T SYN (DAR) OR
(2)H-S, H-T WR/SYN (QAR) OR
(2)H-S, L-T WR/SYN (QAR) +CL
OR
(2)H-S,L-T SYN (DAR) + CL

F   H-S, H-T SYN
OR
H-S, L-T SYN + CL
OR
H-S, H-T W.R.

(4- PINION)

G   (2) H-S, H-T W.R. + RED
OR
(2) H-S, H-T SYN (DAR)
OR
(2) H-S, H-T W.R./SYN (QAR)

H   (4) H-S, H-T W.R.

(GEARLESS)

I   LL-S, H-T SYN

are in use. An alternate choice is a low-speed, low-(starting and pull-in) torque synchronous motor with a clutch added to accelerate the mill on the motor's pull-out torque. There are scores of these in use.

Another one-pinion arrangement, *B,* is powered through a speed reducer by a high-speed, high-torque synchronous motor for a reduction in first cost; it can be used if efficiency is not paramount. There are several hundred of these in use. A clutch can also be added for softer start and some reduction in cost.

The two-pinion arrangement *C* can be powered by two low-speed, high-torque synchronous motors, equipped with a direct-axis load-share regulator (DAR). Several of these are being considered today. Alternatively, this arrangement is powered by two low-speed, high-torque synchronous motors with wound-rotor soft-starting windings and rheostats, and is equipped with a quadrature-axis, load-share regulator (QAR) for higher frequency response. Two of these at 9,200 hp each are just being put into service.

Another two-pinion arrangement, D, is powered through speed reducers by two high-speed, high-torque wound-rotor motors with soft-starting rheostats. Load-sharing is inherent with this type of motor. The speed reducers lower the first cost at the expense of efficiency. At this time, 11 of these are in use on this continent—one in Missouri, two in Ontario, two in Arizona, and six in British Columbia. Ten more have just been ordered.

Alternatively, this arrangement can be powered by two high-speed, high-torque synchronous motors, equipped with a direct-axis load-share regulator. A score of these are being considered today. As another alternative, these high-speed, high-torque synchronous motors can be furnished with wound-rotor soft-starting windings with rheostats, and equipped with a quadrature-axis load-share regulator. Either of these arrangements can be fitted with clutches for soft start and clutch control for initial load angle matching.

The two-pinion arrangements E and F are trunnion-connected, enclosed gear sets to help protect the gearing against cement mill or other very adverse ambients if the fairly high gear premium may be justified.

Arrangement E uses two high-speed, high-torque synchronous motors with a mechanical arrangement for initial, steady-state load sharing. Extra speed reduction is built into the gear set. Some 30 of these are in use, but they have presented problems in maintaining load balance and in transient stability. They can be equipped with a direct-axis load-share regulator.

Arrangement F is powered by a single high-speed, high-torque synchronous motor. There are hundreds of these in use. One alternative, a high-speed, low-torque synchronous motor with clutch, has been incorporated in dozens of installations. Another alternative is a high-speed, high-torque wound-rotor motor with starting rheostat, which is used in many mills.

The four-pinion arrangement G would require two reducers, each with two low-speed output pinions, and only two high-speed, high-torque wound-rotor motors with starting rheostats. As in arrangement F, the two low-speed pinions on each side of the ring gear are permanently paralleled and depend on mechanical design to achieve steady-state and transient load sharing. Alternatively, this arrangement could be powered by a pair of high-speed, high-torque synchronous motors with a direct-axis load-share regulator (DAR), or by high-speed, high-torque wound-rotor/synchronous motors with soft-starting rheostats and a quadrature-axis load-share regulator (QAR).

An alternate four-pinion arrangement, H, would be four reducers and four high-speed, high-torque wound-rotor motors with starting rheostats. Load sharing is inherent in this type of motor. The size of mills purchased to date has not required either variation of the basic four-pinion drive, but they might be considered in the future.

Finally, in arrangement I no gears are used.[2,4,5] The high-torque synchronous motor may be wrapped around the mill shell, or secured to a mill trunnion. It is large in diameter and operates directly at the low mill speed. Since its field pole design would not be practical at 50 or 60 Hz, an order-of-magnitude frequency converter must be used. An added benefit of frequency adjustment is that it affords soft start and mill speed adjustment at no extra equipment cost. An 8,400-hp drive is in use in a LeHavre, France, cement plant; three 8,400-hp units are used in the UNICEM cement plant in

Table 1—Characteristics of mill drive arrangements

DRIVE ARR	MILL CONN	# PIN.	# REDCRS.	# CL	MOTORS #	TYPE	SP	TQ
A	RG	1			1	S	L	H
A^I	RG	1			1	S	L	L
B	RG	1	1		1	S	H	H
B^I	RG	1	1		1	S	H	L
C	RG	2			2	S*	L	H
C^I	RG	2			2	WR/S*	L	H
D	RG	2	2		2	WR	H	H
D^I	RG	2	2		2	S*	H	H
D^{II}	RG	2	2		2	WR/S*	H	H
D^{III}	RG	2	2	2*	2	S*	H	L
D^{IV}	RG	2	2	2*	2	WR/S*	H	L
E	TCGB	(2)	**		2	S*	H	H
F	TCGB	(2)	**		1	S	H	H
F^I	TCGB	(2)	**	1	1	S	H	L
F^{II}	TCGB	(2)	**		1	WR	H	H
G	RG	4	2		2	WR	H	H
G^I	RG	4	2		2	S*	H	H
G^{II}	RG	4	2		2	WR/S*	H	H
H	RG	4	4		4	WR	H	H
I	D				1	S***	LL	H

* WITH LOAD SHARE REGULATOR
** MULTIPLE REDUCTION IN GEAR BOX
*** WITH FREQUENCY CONVERTER

Guidonia, Italy; one 6,560-hp unit is going into service in Germany; and an 8,750-hp drive has just been ordered for a Canadian cement plant. All these drives are just under 15 rpm and were operationally compared and economically evaluated against drive arrangement F, as well as other arrangements.

This total array of mill power transmission arrangements is certainly a tribute to design ingenuity, but it dictates a major screening process when making a selection for a specific mill drive. (There are actually a few more arrangements, such as squirrel-cage induction motors with clutches, not discussed here.)

Table 1 lists the characteristics of the 20 mill drive arrangements described above. Focusing on these arrangements, this article will consider the basic transmission and drive requirements for a successful mill installation, compare the 20 drive arrangements against each performance criterion, summarize findings and, finally, choose one or two arrangements most applicable to a given size of mill. This process is essential in

Table 2—Mill power transmission and drive requirements

1) Speed
2) Torque
3) Thermal (horsepower) margin
4) Starting effect on mechanical parts
5) Starting effect on power system
6) Running power factor high enough
7) Running efficiency high
8) Simplicity of installation, adjustment, maintenance
9) Reasonable initial cost
10) Risk assessment

designing a modern day ore plant and helps to minimize overall plant costs.

As evident from Table 2, there is no one single requirement for a mill drive arrangement. Any one requirement affects others. The first three requirements in Table 2 may be considered together and the remainder separately.

Speed requirements for mill drives

The mill operating speed of a geared drive is usually fixed by a constant speed motor and must be preselected. That speed decreases as the mill diameter increases, thereby increasing the transmission and drive problem. Since speed has such a great effect on grinding, production, mill wear, and resultant costs, it must sometimes be changed after installation by changing gears. At present, there is little interest in the mining industry in adjustable speed drives, but as process control strategies are further developed, and as mills in a plant become larger and fewer, the use of adjustable speed drives may emerge.

A geared drive implies at least one speed ratio between the mill and the low-speed pinion shaft(s). This pinion speed may yet be too low for a motor speed when balancing motor cost against motor and extra reducer installation cost and an assumed extra 2% losses per extra reduction. A 3,000-hp, 180-rpm synchronous motor will cost about 20% more than a 720-rpm motor plus a 4:1 reducer. The same sized 180-rpm wound rotor induction motor will cost about 50% more by comparison. The first cost saving seems evident, but other factors may outweigh it.

Torque requirements for mill drives

During starting, the mill charge action may be brought up through cascade to the equilibrium state of motion. The drive's load torque curve is shown in Fig. 2 for a rod mill or for a ball or autogenous mill, with the cascade peak occurring somewhere between one-third and two-thirds speed, depending on acceleration rate and gearing. Once running speed is reached, the ball or autogenous mill load torque smooths out, but the rod mill load torque does not. Jackstrawing of worn rod pieces and other characteristics cause it to continue surging.

While mill inertias are high at the mill, they are reasonably low referred to the drive motor(s) through the gearing. However, appreciable acceleration torque should be sustained during starting to minimize high-torque heating on the drive and to pass quickly through any resonant modes in this electro-mechanical system. An acceleration time of 8-12 sec is normal, except for clutch drives, where 6-10 sec is preferable.

Thermal (horsepower) margin

The performance of a mill is predicted in advance from theory and from pilot plant experience with a particular ore. These conclusions are then scaled up and the mill drive sized. Two years and millions of capital dollars later, its true performance is observed—showing whether or not its targets of production, grinding, power consumption, and consumption of wearing parts have been met.

After startup, more charge may have to be added. This requires torque and thermal (horsepower) margin in the transmission and drive, beyond that for worn liners and lifters. Past practice in this area has been inconsistent. Overload capability or "service factor" of 10% or sometimes 15% has been specified. Sometimes thermal margin has been specified, but none for torque. Sometimes no margin has been specified, but a vendor has volunteered it in whole or in part, leading to later confusion or disappointment in the drive purchased. The only correct practice is to specify a drive's maximum thermal (horsepower) rating, allowing margin in choosing that horsepower. Torque is then correct in proportion.

In other cases, speed may have to be increased after start-up. For a given charge over a small speed range, the average load in a mill is essentially constant torque. An increase in speed by gear change requires both torque and thermal margin. In practice, many mill operators have changed gears, which is difficult with multi-pinion transmissions. As mills increase in size, optimum speed becomes more important to plant profit. So far, adequate total drive margin has been discussed.

In multi-pinion drives, there is a requirement for equal sharing of total load by the drive parts. This means both steady-state and transient load sharing of both gears and motors in parallel. Mine hoist drive paralleling experience is not sufficient for calibration, since the larger mine hoist drives are essentially direct current, with armatures in series, or with special load-sharing regulators. This load-sharing requirement will be discussed specifically in Part 2 of this article, under the heading "Risk Assessment." At this point, though, the reliability of load sharing means should be predicted and torque and thermal margins should be added with this as a consideration.

Starting effect on mill mechanical parts

The control of net motor torque while starting the mill is built into the design of the high-torque, constant-frequency synchronous motor, with allowance made for the calculated loss of torque due to voltage dip. Fig. 3 shows the increase in this average motor torque if switched capacitors are used to reduce the voltage dip. Note also the comfortable accelerating torque margin over the load torque. A clever designer can shape this motor torque curve to reduce initial shock. As Fig. 3 also indicates, however, there are undesirable salient pole pulsations at twice slip frequency that will be related to transient stability a little later on.

The adjustable-frequency, high-torque synchronous motor would first be synchronized and then accelerated at controlled volts-per-cycle and regulated to constant acceleration. This is truly a soft start. Note the absence of salient pole pulsations in Fig. 3.

The high-torque wound-rotor motor starts the mill under control of a resistor-contactor secondary or a stepless liquid rheostat. The latter can be regulated for constant torque or constant acceleration, or some combination as indicated. The liquid rheostat is preferable, but a little more expensive for smaller drives. Individual secondary rheostats are required, but pairs have matched servos.

The low torque synchronous motor-with-clutch drive (not shown in Fig. 3) accelerates on motor pull-out torque under

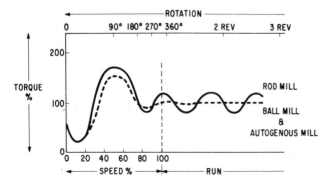

FIG. 2—MILL LOAD TORQUE AS A FUNCTION OF SPEED AND ROTATION

clutch control on a characteristic similar to that of a wound-rotor motor with liquid rheostat, set for initial ramp, then constant torque. Ten seconds of slip is about all the clutch will take.

These are the average torques impressed on the mill drive train parts, some being softer than others. Only the clutch or adjustable frequency or the wound rotor rheostat can actually soften initial torque shocks. In addition, these average torques can be greatly magnified should electro-mechanical resonant modes be excited during acceleration.

Starting effect on mill power supply

Soft start of a large mill drive is a must for either utility or self-generation source of power. At new ore locations, power system stiffness doesn't seem to be increasing as fast as mill sizes are increasing. Fig. 4 compares the alternate drive types against the selection criteria of power system disturbance when starting a mill. High starting current (usually of low power factor) drawn through the utility system, plant transformers, and plant distribution networks causes voltage dips. A utility often limits that dip at the point of purchase to 3% or less. A dip at the motor in excess of 20% causes excessive loss of starting torque and exposes plant contactors and relays to drop-out, loss of control sequence, or instrument malfunction. The high reactive content must be generated by the utility and transmitted, with resultant transmission losses. This cost will appear in the power contract.

The conventional high-torque synchronous motor stands out as having the highest inrush current at start. This can be reduced to half, or less, by capacitors switched onto the motor bus during starting and switched back off in steps. The low-torque synchronous motor requires less inrush, since its clutch accelerates the mill on the motor's pull-out torque, not its starting torque. The wound rotor motor with a ramp-torque-programmed liquid rheostat can afford the softest start of all, matched only by the adjustable frequency system.

When the ore plant has more than two grinding mill drives of the same rating, it is economic to consider time-sharing of a single set of soft-start equipment, either rheostat or capacitor type, since they are both expensive.

Running power factor

Similarly, the running power factor of each mill in a plant has a deciding effect on the utility power contract, particularly since grinding is 40% to 60% of the load and the remainder is mostly a lagging load. Synchronous motors rated 0.8 leading power factor have historically been used for grinding to improve the plant power factor to an acceptable level. When both primary and secondary grinding are involved, a load flow calculation for the entire plant load may show that leading power factor motors are required for only part of the grinding, perhaps just for the secondary mills. Table 3 compares the alternate drive types; the installed costs are estimated at 8,000 hp to correct the power factor of the last three types to that of the conventional synchronous type. In the case of the wound-rotor drive, it should be mentioned that static (unregulated) power factor correcting capacitors do not aid at all in achieving soft start. With voltage dip they collapse, and costly synchronous condensers must then be used.

Power factor correcting capacitors can be switched with an induction motor to the extent of about 0.95 lag corrected PF. Beyond that they must be switched separately. Of course, synchronous motor reactive capability can be increased at a premium design cost. The adjustable frequency synchronous motor PF can be improved, if needed, by capacitors switched with the system.

Running efficiency

Each mill in a plant will run some 7,500 hr per year. Since

FIG. 3—MILL DRIVE STARTING TORQUE CHARACTERISTICS

Wound rotor drive

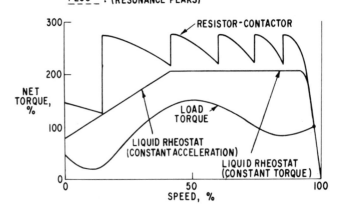

Synchronous drive

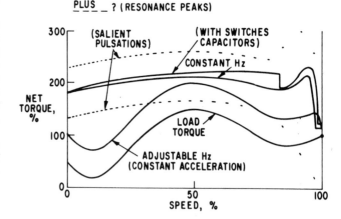

FIG. 4—POWER SYSTEM DISTURBANCE IN STARTING A LARGE MILL DRIVE

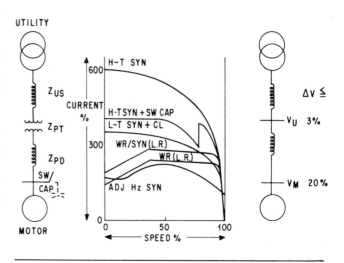

Table 3—Comparison of power factor by drive type (8,000 hp to mill shell) and costs to correct to 0.8 PF lead

MOTOR TYPE	TYPE DUAL DRIVE REGL.	TOTAL # RED.	COS Θ	TAN Θ	EFF CORR	TAN' Θ	REQD KVAR	COST TO CORRECT 8000 HP DRIVE TO 0.8 PF CAP'S (@ $5)	COST TO CORRECT 8000 HP DRIVE TO 0.8 PF S. COND (@ $17)
S	–	1	0.8	0.75	–	0.75	–	–	–
S	–	2	0.8	0.75	1.01	0.76	–	–	–
WR/S	QAR	1	0.8	0.75	1.00	0.75	–	–	–
WR/S	QAR	2	0.8	0.75	1.01	0.76	–	–	–
S	DAR	1	0.9	0.49	0.995	0.49	1,560	8,000	27,000
S	DAR	2	0.9	0.49	1.005	0.49	1,560	8,000	27,000
WR	–	2	(-)0.88	(-)0.54	1.015	(-)0.55	7,800	39,000	133,000
S (lf)	–	–	(-)0.8	(-)0.75	1.04	(-)0.78	9,200	46,000	156,000

(Diagram between TAN' Θ and REQD KVAR columns showing vectors from 1.0: LEAD 0.76, 0.49; LAG 0.55, 0.78)

grinding will cause 40% to 60% of the ore plant's energy bill, high efficiency is a must. Table 4 compares the alternate drive types for efficiency and cost of losses. Speed reducer losses at 2% per reduction are included because the first cost of a wound-rotor motor requires it to be high speed. The most efficient is the conventional high-torque, low-speed synchronous motor, run at 0.9 PF to accommodate dual drive load sharing by means of direct axis regulator (DAR). The extra annual cost of the losses of the others at 8,000 hp for 7,500 hr is indicated for both purchased power (at an assumed rate of 7 mils per kwh) and self-generation (at an assumed rate of 11 mils per kwh). The capital cost to self-generate these extra losses is also indicated (at an assumed $250 per kw). Note that these are on a *per mill* basis.

Motor efficiencies, published generically as indices, can be improved somewhat at a premium that rises exponentially.

Simplicity of installation, adjustment, maintenance

The expected wear parts in a mill are the liners and the lifters that inhibit slipping. The maintenance parts are bearings, gearing, reducers, couplings, motors, exciters, regulators, and control.

Besides being mechanically rugged, the mill drive system should be as simple as possible to install, adjust, operate, and maintain. One design objective is to achieve the fewest number of moving and wearing parts. Load-sharing schemes must be kept in adjustment. Maintenance of liquid rheostats and their servos, exciters and regulators, and frequency converters must all be considered, though the latter have static components today. Maintenance of power factor correction or soft-starting equipment, where required, must also be taken into account.

Table 4—Comparison of drive and transmission losses, and their penalty cost per mill

(8,000 hp to mill shell for 7,500 hr/yr)

MOTOR TYPE	TYPE DUAL DRIVE REGL	TOTAL # RED.	EACH DRIVE'S TOTAL LOSSES %	EACH DRIVE'S TOTAL LOSSES KW	PURCHASED PW. (@ 7 MIL/KW HR)° $/MILL/YEAR	SELF-GENERATED PW. (@ 11 MILS/KW HR)° $/MILL/YEAR	SELF-GENERATED PW. (@ $250/KW) CAP'T.$/MILL
S	DAR	1	7	450	–	–	–
S	DAR	2	8	520	3,600	5,700	+ 17,500
WR/S	QAR	1	7.5	485	1,800	2,800	+ 8,800
WR/S	QAR	2	8.5	560	5,800	9,100	+ 27,500
S	–	1	7.5	485	1,800	2,800	+ 8,800
S	–	2	8.5	560	5,800	9,100	+ 27,500
WR	–	2	9	595	7,600	11,900	+ 36,200
S (lf.)	–	–	11	740	15,200	24,000	+ 72,500

° ASSUME 7500 HOUR YEAR

Initial costs of mill drives

The relative installed costs of each type of mill drive system are roughly estimated in Table 5, ranging today from $60 per mill horsepower for the dual high-speed, high-torque, four-pinion, synchronous motor drive (less soft start) to over $100 per mill horsepower for three of the trunnion-connected systems and the gearless drive. The others are weighted in between, at about $5 per horsepower increments.

The relative first costs have been estimated based on the following assumptions:

    hp = 6,000-8,000/mill
    rpm = 720 (HS), 180 (LS), 10 (mill)
    Torques = 200 - 140 - 200% (types LR - PI - PO)
    Motor voltage = 4,000 v
    Motor enclosure = drip proof, guarded.
    Primary and secondary control included.
    Soft start optional.

In general, a motor voltage of 6,600 is practical if that distribution level is required for other plant loads. But a motor voltage of 13,200 is considerably more expensive than 4,000 (even including unit transformation between the two levels.)

Optional motor enclosures are also practical for severe ambients, such as totally enclosed, forced ventilated for an additional $1-$2/hp, or totally enclosed, air-water cooled for an additional $3-$4/hp (synchronous-wound rotor adders, respectively).

Soft-starting equipment has been shown to be optional for the following reasons. Synchronous (S) motors up to about 5,000 kva per mill can usually be started full-voltage across the line, depending on utility stiffness. Ore plants with mills larger than that and with two or more mills can profit by time-sharing the capacitor starting equipment. The plant's soft-starting cost then would be $20/hp divided by the number of mills sharing the starter. Wound rotor (WR) motors usually require soft-starting liquid rheostats. Again, these (one per motor on multiple motor mills) can be shared at a plant cost of $15/hp divided by the number of mills served.

Alternatively, seven-point contactor-resistor starters at $8/hp can be time-shared. Wound-rotor starting windings on synchronous (WR/S) motors also need soft starters per above. Clutch drives and gearless drives do not need soft starters.

Load sharing

Whenever more than one torque path exists between the driving motor(s) and the driven load, the designer needs to give special attention to assure proper division of load between the parallel torque paths. Motors are exposed to overload to the extent that one motor at a multiple-motor drive may be required to produce beyond its rating while other motors carry only a fraction of their rated load. Gears and couplings are designed to American Gear Manufacturers Association standards, which afford marginal continuous overload, plus greater momentary overload capacity for system dynamics such as load pulsations, drive starting torques, and even an occasional mild abuse.[3]

There are two principal areas of concern about gear load sharing, which must be dealt with separately. The first concern is with average load balance between the separate halves of a dual torque path drive train. The second concern is with transient torques as a result of torque pulsations and electromechanical resonances both when starting and while running.

Provision to achieve a load sharing capability on an average basis is quite different between drives with synchronous motors and drives with induction motors. Induction motors accept load as a function of rotor slip. If both induction motors are identical and run at the same slip, they carry identical loads. Since the geared mechanical connection between the

Table 5—Estimated relative installed costs

ARR	MILL CONN	# PIN.	# REDCRS.	# CL	#	TYPE	SP	TQ	$/HP
A	RG	1			1	S	L	H	68
A^I	RG	1		1	1	S	L	L	64
B	RG	1	1		1	S	H	H	64
B^I	RG	1	1	1	1	S	H	L	61
C	RG	2			2	S*	L	H	72
C^I	RG	2			2	WR/S*	L	H	85
D	RG	2	2		2	WR	H	H	73
D^I	RG	2	2		2	S*	H	H	68
D^{II}	RG	2	2		2	WR/S*	H	H	77
D^{III}	RG	2	2	2*	2	S*	H	L	66
D^{IV}	RG	2	2	2*	2	WR/S*	H	L	73
E	TCGB	(2)	**		2	S*	H	H	100
F	TCGB	(2)	**		1	S	H	H	95
F^I	TCGB	(2)	**	1	1	S	H	L	91
F^{II}	TCGB	(2)	**		1	WR	H	H	103
G	RG	4	2		2	WR	H	H	65
G^I	RG	4	2		2	S*	H	H	60
G^{II}	RG	4	2		2	WR/S*	H	H	69
H	RG	4	4		4	WR	H	H	68
I	D				1	S***	LL	H	120

6000 - 8000 HP
720 - 180 - 10 RPM
200 - 140 - 200% TORQUE
4000V, DP GUARDED ENCL.

*WITH LOAD SHARE REGULATOR
**MULTIPLE REDUCTION IN GEAR BOX
***WITH FREQUENCY CONVERTER

INCLUDES PRIMARY & SECONDARY CONTROL
SOFT START OPTIONAL @ $16/HP/MILL - WOUND ROTOR LIQUID RHEOSTATS
@ $20/HP/MILL - SYNCHRONOUS SWITCHED CAPACITORS

two motors in a dual drive insures that both run at precisely the same average speed (slip), identical motors will carry identical loads. Synchronous motors accept load as a function of the angle between the rotor and the magnetic flux rotating on the stator. Again, the geared mechanical connection between the two motors in a dual drive insures that both motors run at precisely the same average speed, but attention must be given to design of the system if they are to have the same average rotor angles with respect to the stator flux.

Design of the dual synchronous motor drives requires special attention to achieve satisfactory load balance between the two motors. Accurate positioning of the paralleled rotors during installation of the drive is essential (except for clutch versions) and must be maintained despite foundation movement, unequal mechanical wear, etc. Manual mechanical means of adjusting rotor angle have been used on dual synchronous drives—for example, rotor shift with respect to the shaft, gear type couplings with a differential modification, or stator rotation equipment. The stator rotation equipment can be made to operate while the drive is running; the other two methods require that the drive be stopped. Manual and automatic electrical means of adjusting apparent rotor angle have been used on dual synchronous drives, such as modulating the magnetic flux in the main field (d-axis regulator), or shifting the magnetic flux about the field pole center line in the air-gap (q-axis regulator). A third electrical means of adjusting apparent rotor angle which has been studied, but not applied, is the shifting of magnetic flux in the air-gap of a synchronous-induction motor (dq-axis regulator). Each of these three electrical methods has its advantages and disadvantages, as will be shown in Part 2 of this article. □

References

1. W. N. Thomas, G. J. Dickman, "The Selection of Drives for Large Grinding Mills," SME Paper 69-B-21, February 1969.
2. E. A. E. Rich, "Concepts of Gearless Ball Mill Drives," IEEE Cement Conference Paper, May 1968.
3. AGMA, "AGMA Standard Practice of Helical, Herringbone and Spur Mill Gears," (AGMA 321.05) American Gear Manufacturers Association, Washington, D.C., June 1968.
4. H. U. Würgler, "The World's First Gearless Mill Drive," IEEE, Trans. Industry and General Applications. Vol. IGA-6, p. 524-527, Sept./Oct. 1970.
5. D. Riehlein, "Gearless Drive for a Cement Mill," SIEMENS REVIEW, Vol. XXXVIII, No. 9, p. 398-401, September, 1971.

Part 2 of this article follows immediately.

This autogenous mill, successfully designed and installed at an iron plant in Ontario, is equipped with ring gear and two pinions which are driven through two reducers by two 3,400-hp (720-rpm) high-torque wound rotor motors with liquid rheostats.

Part 2 of a two-part article

How to choose electric drives for large grinding mills

The selection of a good mill design ultimately depends on assessing the risks involved, after minimizing various thermal and mechanical overstresses

W. H. Schwedes and **E. L. Owen,** General Electric Co.

THERE ARE THREE ELECTRICAL METHODS for achieving satisfactory load balance between the two motors of a dual synchronous motor drive system. As noted at the conclusion of Part 1 of this article,* the three methods are: 1) modulating the magnetic flux in the main field (d-axis regulator); 2) shifting the magnetic flux about the field pole center line in the air-gap (q-axis regulator); 3) shifting the magnetic flux in the air-gap of a synchronous-induction motor (dq-axis regulator). Each of these methods has its advantages and disadvantages, of which the following seem most pertinent:

The d-axis system has the compelling advantage of lower first cost and utilization of standard (non-special) equipment. Among its disadvantages, it is limited to torque disturbances of 2 or 3 Hertz or less; it is limited to about 50% change of electrical load angle or less (load angles vary from 15° to 35°

*Part 1 of this article appeared in the December 1973 issue of E/MJ.

electrical); it depends on power factor and torques, such that this limit varies from ±7° to ±17° electrical or 1° to 3° mechanical at 720 rpm; it is fully effective only at rated load with decreasing effectiveness until at no load it is ineffective; and it is subject to changing power factor of the drive as the flux is modulated.

The q-axis system has the advantage of higher frequency of response (8 to 10 Hertz) for dealing with torque pulsations, and it is fully effective over its entire normal load range and not nearly so subject to changing power factor, since the total magnetic flux is barely changed as it moves about the center line. However, it has a higher first cost and it requires a special q-axis winding in the otherwise standard motor. This technique is sometimes called "cross-axis" excitation.

The dq-axis system offers higher frequency of response (8 to 10 Hertz); it is fully effective over any apparent rotor angle shift (without limit); it is not at all subject to changing power factor unless desired; and it offers adjustable speed operation (d-axis and q-axis are constant speed only). It has the disadvantages of highest first cost and lower total efficiency than d-axis or q-axis. (The latter two are about the same in efficiency but they are both slightly lower in efficiency than a standard synchronous motor with constant excitation.)

The use of clutches with dual synchronous motor drives requires special design considerations as well. When the clutch operates as a slip device (like the induction motor), load sharing is relatively straightforward by means of a closed loop regulator using motor input power as the controlled variable and clutch friction pressure as the control variable. Load sharing will be adequate as long as the clutches slip, but if they are ever "locked up" to run without relative motion between input and output members, load sharing is a function of angular alignment. The change from sliding motion to non-sliding motion between the two engaging surfaces finally occurs in a random and abrupt manner. This means the clutches require a special control strategy to overcome the possible effects of "slip-stick" behavior (sometimes called "chatter" or "grabbiness"). The ratio of static to sliding friction would ideally need be 1.0 to minimize the slip-stick behavior, with ratios of 1.3 or greater making the problem very difficult.

Experience has shown that dual wound-rotor motor grinding mill drives can be made to share, on an average, load within 3% between the two motors. Load sharing is inherent in the motors without special regulators or mechanical modifications. Inherent thermal margin in these motors insures that each motor can be operated at rated load without overloading the other motor.

Limited experience has shown that dual synchronous motor grinding mill drives can be made to share load on an average within 1% by electrical means as long as the mechanical alignment is in range of the electrical adjustment. This load sharing capability is limited only by the accuracy of measuring devices, with 1% being more than adequate. Of special concern is the security of the mechanical means of adjusting rotor angle. It must be rugged enough to resist forces induced in mechanical parts by short circuit currents which may flow in the motor windings.

Risk assessment

Once a good mill design has been worked out, the designer must then consider what could happen to make that design fail. A mill is not considered to have failed if it shuts down because of normal protective devices or process sequencing. Rather, failure occurs when some part is so thermally or mechanically overstressed that it has to be repaired or replaced before operation at normal levels can be resumed.

Motor-protective functions have been developed to reduce exposure to failure from the following sources:

■ Voltage quality. Relays can sense poor voltage quality resulting from under- (or perhaps over-) voltage, reversed-phase-sequence, or phase voltage imbalance. Surge capacitors and lightning arrestors are commonly used to protect motor end-turns against lightning and switching surge overvoltages.

■ Frequency quality. Although this is seldom of concern, underfrequency or overfrequency relays can be used to protect against line frequency changes. Harmonics of line frequency seldom cause problems in the motors.

■ Overload protection. Phase overcurrent, thermal overload, and/or stator winding temperature detectors can be used to sense motor overload. The amortisseur winding of a synchronous motor can be protected during starting by a graduated squirrel-cage protective relay plus incomplete sequence shutdown. Temperature detectors can protect the external secondary resistors used with wound-rotor motors from thermal overloads.

■ Fault protection. Phase overcurrent, ground fault, and differential protection are commonly used measures for both synchronous and wound-rotor drives. Wound-rotor motors may, in addition, be provided with secondary flashover protection.

■ Motor pull-out. For synchronous motors, a normal full-voltage pull-out torque of 200% is decreased in proportion to the decrease in stator voltage (with constant field current), and in proportion to the decrease in field current (with constant stator voltage). More simply, the pull-out torque is proportional to the product of stator voltage and field current. A motor field excitation system which produces main field current in proportion to applied voltage results in a motor-excitation system which is relatively sensitive to voltage dip. A relay which can sense impending pull-out (in time to avoid the very high torques associated with slipping a pole) is commonly supplied as a part of the motor controller. Unlike the synchronous motor, the induction motor cannot "pull-out" of synchronism. It normally runs below synchronous speed, but it is as sensitive to voltage dip as the synchronous motor. The motor's maximum torque capability, called "break-down" torque, is proportional to the square of the stator voltage. For an induction motor capable of 200% breakdown torque, a voltage dip of 30% would allow rated load to stall the motor. Hence, wound-rotor motors require stall protection.

■ Reclosing protection. The utility which supplies power to the drives occasionally experiences a fault in its system. That fault can produce damaging torque levels in the drive equipment for two reasons:

1) Voltage snapback when the fault is cleared, allowing the

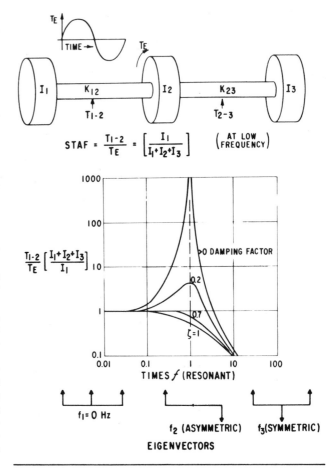

FIG. 1—RESONANT MODES OF SPRING-MASS SYSTEMS

$$STAF = \frac{T_{1-2}}{T_E} = \left[\frac{I_1}{I_1+I_2+I_3}\right] \quad \text{(AT LOW FREQUENCY)}$$

EIGENVECTORS

system generation which remains connected to the system to restore the voltage to its prefault level. This will result in a 5-7 cycle notch in the system voltage and two abrupt shifts in voltage transmission angle while the fault is attached to the system.

2) Fast reclosing of faulted circuits, which is a practice of many utilities. The risk is that while the drive is still running, should the power supply open and then be quickly reclosed, the motor-induced voltage may be out of phase with system voltage, resulting in very large torque shocks to the drive parts.

Transfer tripping of the motor starter or high-speed underfrequency tripping backed up by high-speed undervoltage relaying provides the best currently available protection against these contingencies of snapback and fast reclosing. This protection should be adjusted before plant startup.

Coping with torsional vibrations and drive failures

During the last 20 years, over 4,000 applications of single-pinion, ring gear mill drives have been made without undue incidence of drive failure. Since this base of application knowledge is largely empirical, trying to extrapolate with innovative drive types raises many questions about transient torque pulsations. Many years of experience have shown that torsional vibrations cause a complex problem and are a real engineering concern.[1]

Torsional vibrations are very elusive because deflections of springy members are twists in a shaft. It is possible for a severe torsional vibration to exist without the usual symptoms of vibration and distress being evident until some part fails. The failure, therefore, often seems quite mysterious. Lateral vibrations are conducted by bearings and supports into the floor, and it is easy to "feel" the presence of these vibrations. Torsional vibrations in large grinding mills are made even more difficult to sense without special instruments by the very small deflections involved (typically less than one degree). Finally, the analysis of torsional vibrations is usually more difficult than for lateral vibrations because the latter usually involve only two or three degrees of freedom, whereas torsional vibrations quite frequently involve five to fifteen degrees of freedom. The American Gear Manufacturers Association recognizes the risk of torsional vibrations by assigning the responsibility for analysis to the purchaser of the gears. (See AGMA 321.05, page 5, paragraph 2.1.1).[2]

It is rational to be concerned about the type of electric drive applied to the dual motor configuration.[3] The electrical drive is part of an electro-mechanical system with the majority of the connected masses and springs external to the motor. The peak (transient) torques in various mill drive system parts are a function of the ability of the electro-mechanical system to respond (resonant modes) to excitations existing within the system.

Mechanical members such as shafts, gears, and couplings are designed for some rated torque capability. That design will involve various safety factors to account for transient loads. If the design conditions are exceeded, the parts may fail in any of several different ways, of which the four most common are:

1) Breakage—where a single impact at very large value (10-30 times normal) results in an immediate fracture of the part.

2) Fatigue—where a repeated or cyclic stress exceeds the endurance limit of the material. Low-level fatigue is characterized by stress cycles on the order of a million or more before failure.

3) Creep—where prolonged loading causes a gradual plastic flow of material which destroys the shape of the part to such an extent that it is no longer functional.

4) Wear—where removal of material from the part changes its shape until it is no longer functional.

The American Society for Metals finds that many gear fail-

FIG. 2—DYNAMICS OF MILL DRIVE ELECTRO-MECHANICAL SYSTEM

(Ring gear is connected to two pinions, two reducers, and two motors)

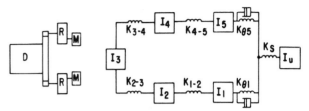

(2) HI-SPEED, HI-TORQUE <u>SYNCHRONOUS</u>: (4 RESONANT MODES STARTING, 5 RUNNING)

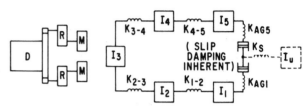

(2) HI-SPEED, HI-TORQUE <u>WOUND ROTOR WITH REDUCER</u>: (4 RESONANT MODES STARTING AND RUNNING)

ures are initiated by one very heavy or sharp overstress followed by continued consistent low stress for a long period of time, even though the latter would be called "normal" during operation.[4] Grinding mill experience seems to agree with these findings, as most known instances of gear failure have not occurred as a result of a single large impact or catastrophic event, but rather can be anticipated by a gradual deterioration of parts. Our application experience does not allow us to determine to what extent these gear failures have been caused by a sharp overstress which did not immediately fracture the part but which established an incipient failure (such as a small crack), which then allowed the otherwise normal cyclic stresses to fail the part by fatigue early in its expected life.

How to solve torsional resonance problems

The problem of torsional resonance is illustrated by the three-wheel, two-shaft (axle) mechanical system shown at the top of Fig. 1. Rigid body mechanics would allow each wheel six degrees of freedom (x, y, z, a, b, c), but to simplify the analysis, it is assumed that bearings and mountings will allow motion only about the shaft in a rotational direction (a axis). Each wheel is now constrained to only one degree of freedom so that the connected system is free to move in three degrees of freedom (a_1, a_2, a_3). Each wheel has its own rotational moment of inertia about the shaft (I_1, I_2, I_3) and each shaft has a torsional spring constant or force to twist the shaft by some angle (K_{12}, K_{23}).

Differential equations could be written for the system and solved to relate shaft torques to applied torque (Te). Assuming no damping, the equations would be satified without externally applied forces under three kinds of motion: 1) all wheels rotating in the same direction, at the same speed (with no relative motion); 2) the center wheel stationary relative to the two outside wheels, but the outside wheels rocking in opposition such that their shaft torques just balance each other at the center wheel; and 3) the center wheel rocking in opposition to the two outside wheels, which are themselves rocking

FIG. 3—TORSIONAL VIBRATION MODE SHAPES (EIGENVECTORS)

(for a five-mechanical mass,
one-electrical mass grinding mill system)

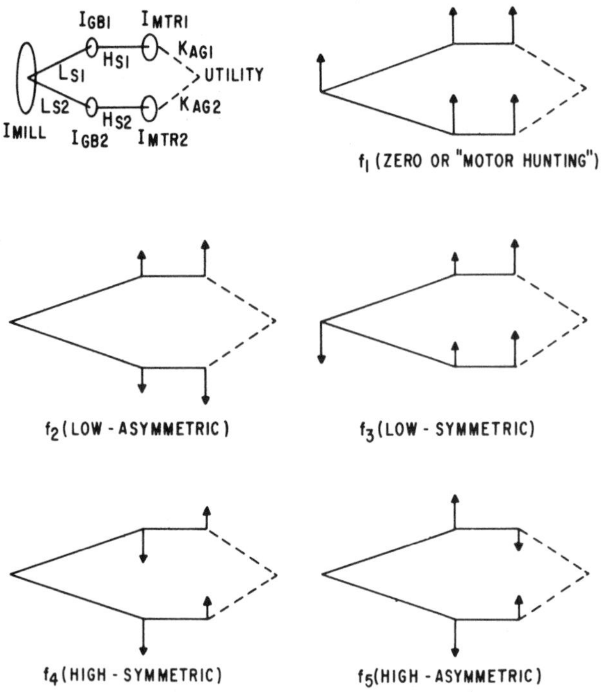

f_1 (ZERO OR "MOTOR HUNTING")

f_2 (LOW - ASYMMETRIC)

f_3 (LOW - SYMMETRIC)

f_4 (HIGH - SYMMETRIC)

f_5 (HIGH - ASYMMETRIC)

in concert or together to balance the forces which are twisting the shafts.

These three kinds of motion are each satisfied at only one unique frequency of vibration or so-called resonant frequency. The mode of vibration where all wheels turn with no relative motion can only be satisfied by uniform motion (no change in speed); hence there is no oscillation. Since the speed is constant, the frequency is zero and the mode is degenerate or not of much interest. The remaining two modes are of vital interest as they can produce resonant amplification of torques.

The chart in the middle of Fig. 1 shows the effect on shaft torque (left wheel to center wheel) as a result of the exciting torque (Te) applied to the rim of the center wheel at various frequencies and for various internal shaft damping ($I_1 = I_3$). For ordinary steel shafts, internal damping is so slight that Sinusoidal Torque Amplification Factors (STAF) of 200 or more are common. (The label STAF should not be confused with the term TAF as used in the analysis of rolling and slabbing mills. STAF refers to the amplification of a continuously applied, periodic signal, while TAF refers to the amplification of an impact or step change in load.) The chart at the bottom of Fig. 1, labeled "eigenvectors," shows the pattern of relative motion between masses, the so-called modal patterns or characteristic mode shapes.

In analyzing grinding mill systems to date, advantage has been taken of the symmetry of the drive parts in dual torque paths. The characteristic mode shapes are either symmetric (true mirror images) about the wheel representing the mill shell, or they are asymmetric (mirror images except out of phase). The excitation forces can then be divided according to whether they affect the torque paths in an in-phase (symmetric) or an out-of-phase (asymmetric) manner. This greatly simplifies the task of determining to what extent an exciting force is capable of coupling to a resonant mode.

Computer programming of numerical solutions

For large grinding mills, the mechanical drive train may have to be molded into many discrete lumped inertias interconnected by springy shafts. A differential equation is required for each inertia and as many as 10 to 15 differential equations may be necessary to describe the system. This presents an extremely complex problem if it is to be solved manually. In the past, various types of numerical methods have been employed, such as the Holzer Method, Matrix Iteration, Stodola Method and the Mechanical Impedance Method, which produce the first two or three lowest or highest modal frequencies with a considerable amount of work. Obtaining the remaining modal frequencies is exceedingly difficult due to complex mathematics.

The application of digital computer techniques has greatly simplified this burden on the engineer. Several numerical methods are easily programmed for the digital computer in solving these "eigenvalue" problems.

Fig. 2 shows mechanical one-line diagrams and simplified (five degrees of freedom) spring-mass diagrams for dual high-speed grinding mill drives, the top with synchronous motors and the bottom with wound-rotor motors. The difference in load-sharing capability between the two drive types shows up in these diagrams as the difference between a mechanically equivalent series connection and parallel connection of springs and dash pots to represent the air gap magnetic flux. These electrical effects emphasize the fact that the system is truly an electro-mechanical system and not just a mechanical system. Even more emphatically, not only are the resonant frequencies different with the motors connected to the electric power system than when the motor starter is open, but in the case of the synchronous motor, the utility adds one more resonant mode.

Fig. 3 is a chart of the characteristic mode shapes for either of the two spring-mass diagrams shown in Fig. 2. The top left-hand diagram identifies the mechanical elements as they relate to the five mode-pattern diagrams shown in Fig. 3. Since the inertia of the mill is frequently on the order of twice one individual motor's inertia, it is shown as the largest wheel, while the gear wheels in the speed reducer, being usually about one-tenth the inertia of a motor, are depicted as the smallest wheels. The relative lengths of lines representing the low-speed shafts ($LS1$ and $LS2$) and the high-speed shafts ($HS1$ and $HS2$) are intended to convey a sense of the relative compliance between those shafts. The compliances which are equivalent to magnetic forces in the motor are shown as dotted lines, as they are of interest primarily with synchronous motors.

The mode pattern for frequency (f_1) is greatly different between the synchronous and induction motor drives, and also between the motors energized and de-energized. With the motors de-energized (whether synchronous or induction), f_1 equals zero, and the pattern is degenerate and of little interest. But with the motors energized, f_1 is no longer zero but equal to the so-called "motor natural hunting frequency." For grinding mill drives, this is usually around 2 Hz. The induction motor has such high inherent damping at 2 Hz that this mode cannot be made to amplify disturbances. The synchronous motor does not necessarily have such high inherent damping and this mode can be very important. Generally, synchronous motors designed for relatively high damping never approach the performance of the induction motor. This mode would manifest itself as a 2-Hz torque pulsation in all shafts which are in-phase between the two parallel torque paths. With synchronous motors, it is possible to improve the damping of the mode by modulation of the main field excitation (d-axis system) or by main field flux shifting (q-axis system).

The mode patterns for frequencies f_2 and f_3 are slightly dif-

FIG. 4—CHART OF EXCITING AND RESPONDING FREQUENCIES

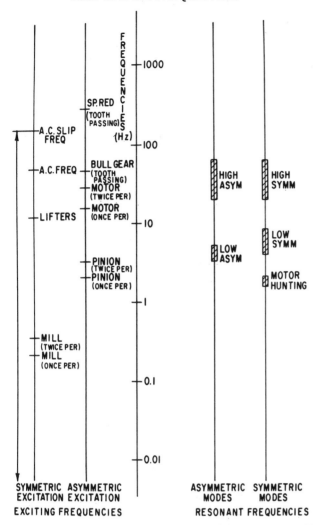

ferent between synchronous and induction motor drives, and between the motors energized and de-energized. The inherent motor damping of the induction motor or a specially designed synchronous motor can have an appreciable effect in reducing the severity of torque amplification due to these modes. Frequency f_2 for grinding mill systems usually falls in the range of 3 to 15 Hertz while frequency f_3 usually falls in the range 5 to 25 Hertz. The dual synchronous-motor drive system with the q-axis load-share regulator has a good chance of imparting beneficial damping to both of these modes, while the d-axis load-share system is not at all likely to impart any damping to either of the modes.

The mode patterns for frequencies f_4 and f_5 are least affected by choice of electric motor and by the state of the motor starter, but the excitation available to cause these modes to respond is greatest with the synchronous motor, as will be explained later. Frequencies f_4 and f_5 for grinding mill systems are usually almost the same frequency and tend to fall in the range 20 to 100 Hertz. There is very little any motor can do to provide damping for these modes.

The mode patterns are useful in understanding the nature of a particular vibration problem, but the eigenvalue-eigenvector base is of practically no value in obtaining a numerical estimate of peak torques. The eigenvalue problem assumes that the system being modeled is linear, but that assumption is generally not satisfied. The couplings frequently have a

non-linear torsional compliance, the gear backlash allows "lost motion" between adjacent wheels, and the motor electrical dynamics are highly non-linear. In addition, unless the eigenvalue problem is stated in terms of state vectors (and unless the eigenvalue computer subroutine can solve for eigenvectors with complex number components), the problem of damping cannot be handled very satisfactorily.

A final drawback to the eigenvalue approach is that it makes no allowance for the length of time the excitation frequency coincides with a resonant mode. Both excitation and resonant frequencies are changing with time. Since they do not coincide for prolonged periods of time, the torque amplifications predicted by the frequency analysis approach are far too pessimistic. It is a common practice to bring drives such as the steam turbine up to speed quickly, so that the exciting frequencies pass by the resonant frequencies quickly and cannot excite the resonant mode to damaging levels.

The need for analog simulation

The analog computer system simulation has been found to be the most effective, lowest-cost method of deriving these estimates of peak torque and the number of cycles to given stress levels. Recent studies of typical dual motor grinding mill drive systems have required hundreds of amplifiers for satisfactory modeling detail. Analog equivalents solved on digital computers impose such a tremendous computational load that the expense of using the computer is prohibitive.

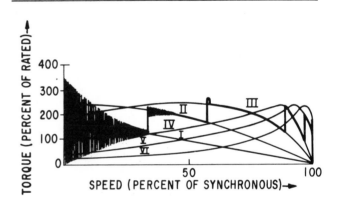

Fig. 5 a—Developed air-gap torque typical of wound-rotor motor with contactor-resistor secondary control during a normal start.

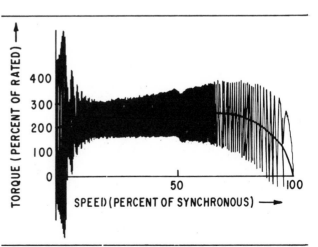

Fig. 5 b—Developed air-gap torque typical of salient pole synchronous motors during a normal start.

Table 1—Mill drive comparison summary (criteria rated from 1 to 10)

DRIVE ARR	MILL CONN	# PIN	# REDCR.	# CL	MOTORS #	TYPE	SP	Y	SP ADJ	SOFT START MECH	START ΔV	RUN PF	RUN EFF	SIMPL INSTL	COST MAINT	1ST COST****	LOAD SHARE	TRANS RISK
A	RG	1			1	S	L	H	–	8	10	1	2	1	1	4	–	2 ◄
A^I	RG	1		1	1	S	L	L	–	5	4	1	2	3	3	3	–	2
B	RG	1	1		1	S	H	H	–	8	10	1	4	3	2	3	–	3
B^I	RG	1	1	1	1	S	H	L •	–	5	4	1	4	3	4	2	–	3
C	RG	2			2	S*	L	H	–	10	6	3	1	5	5	6	5	8
C^I	RG	2			2	WR/S*	L	H	–	3	3	1	2	8	6	7	4	7
D	RG	2	2		2	WR	H	H	–	2	2	8	5	8	5	5	1	4 ◄
D^I	RG	2	2		2	S*	H	H	–	10	6	3	3	8	6	5	6	9
D^II	RG	2	2		2	WR/S*	H	H	–	3	3	1	4	9	7	6	5	8
D^III	RG	2	2	2*	2	S*	H	L	–	5	4	3	3	9	9	3	10	10
D^IV	RG	2	2	2*	2	WR/S*	H	L	–	5	6	1	4	9	10	5	9	9
E	TCGB	(2)	**		2	S*	H	H	–	10	6	3	3	10	10	8	8	9
F	TCGB	(2)	**		1	S	H	H	–	8	6	1	4	2	3	10	5	6
F^I	TCGB	(2)	**	1	1	S	H	L	–	5	4	1	4	3	4	8	5	6
F^II	TCGB	(2)	**		1	WR	H	H	–	2	2	8	5	2	4	10	5	4
G	RG	4	2		2	WR	H	H	–	2	2	8	5	9	8	3	7	6
G^I	RG	4	2		2	S*	H	H	–	10	6	3	3	8	10	3	10	10
G^II	RG	4	2		2	WR/S*	H	H	–	3	3	1	4	9	10	5	9	9
H	RG	4	4		4	WR	H	H	–	2	2	8	5	10	10	5	3	8
I	D				1	S***	LL	H	X	1	1	10	10	4	1	10	–	1 ◄

* WITH LOAD SHARE REGULATOR
** MULTIPLE REDUCTION IN GEAR BOX
*** WITH FREQUENCY CONVERTER
**** INCLUDES SOFT START (C THRU I) TIME SHARED OVER 3 MILLS

Simulations have been made recently for dual wound-rotor motor and dual synchronous motor grinding mill drives. The simulated electrical effects include electric power distribution system parameters, stator currents, rotor currents, magnetic fluxes (including saturation), instantaneous developed torque, and main field excitation for synchronous motors or secondary control for wound rotor motors. The simulated mechanical effects include inertias, linear and non-linear compliances, gear backlash, gear deviations (which give rise to non-uniform motion), solid and viscous damping, speeds, deflections, and torques (instantaneous). The simulated process effects include lifters, rigid charge, and cascading charge. Not included are secondary effects which experience has shown to cause variation in detail of individual computer trace but which do not affect the conclusions to be drawn. (Magnetic hysteresis, motor winding slots, current harmonics, process [charge] kinetics, and gear tooth meshing dynamics are typical of these secondary effects).

These simulations are accurate, but it would be unrealistic to expect to discriminate between torque peaks of 350% and 375% based on design data which are not experimentally verified. The simulation is operated over ranges of parameters to obtain an estimate of the sensitivity of the system to changes in parameters and inaccuracies to date. This sensitivity analysis helps to establish the band of confidence about the projected peak torques.

Fig. 4 is a chart of resonant modes and exciting frequencies plotted as a function of frequency. The resonant modes shown are those for the mechanical system in Fig. 3. The frequencies are shown as a band rather than a discrete value because there is no single frequency which applies under all conditions; the value changes as load conditions change, etc. The motor hunting frequency is not even on the chart if the motor starter is not closed. The excitation frequencies span a very wide range of values.

Most excitations show up as "once per something" or "twice per something." The "once-per-mill revolution" could be due to mill unbalance or perhaps an elliptic ring gear. The "twice-per-mill revolution" excitation can also arise from an elliptic ring gear, but since gear radial run-out generally has a repeat cycle of once per revolution, this twice-per-mill revolution excitation is generally not a problem.[5] The pinion once-per-revolution and twice-per-revolution (and motor once-per-revolution and twice-per-revolution) excitations are similar to the mill once-per-revolution and twice-per-revolution excitations.

It was discovered in an experimental program on a dual drive mill that lifters do contribute an excitation and must be accounted for in the analysis.[6] The tooth passing frequencies occur because of individual tooth engagements in a gear mesh. Certainly, tooth-to-tooth spacing deviations give rise to non-uniform motion between mating gear wheels. It is important to recognize that these gear deviations are not poor quality on the part of the gear vendor but normal manufacturing tolerances. Mills analyzed to date have involved gear sets with tolerances per AGMA quality level 8 or better.[5] (The tolerances given in AGMA 390.02 are not directly useful in torsional analysis but must be related in some way to angular deviations from uniform motion between input shafts and output shafts.)

The important excitations arising from the electric drive motors are the 60 Hz ac line frequency and the twice slip frequency component, which varies from 120 Hz down to 0 Hz. It is impossible just by looking at Fig. 4 to understand what excitations will couple to what resonant frequencies and how much resonant amplification can occur—hence the need for analog simulation.

The polyphase ac motor has the important advantage of being able to run without a pulsating torque under most conditions, but Fig. 5 reminds the analyst that an appreciable pulsation does exist during starting. For engineering purposes, it is customary to draw smooth speed-torque curves, which can be recognized in Fig. 5a for the wound-rotor motor and Fig. 5b for the synchronous motor. These smooth curves represent the average torque at a particular speed—not the instantaneous torque, which can be appreciably different. Superimposed over those average curves is a pulsating torque as shown by the oscillating curve. This developed torque is that which exists at the motor air-gap, not the motor shaft, although the shaft torque is greatly influenced by air-gap torque. There are two principal excitation frequencies:

1) ac line frequency, which arises because of an effect similar to dc offset in the motor. The ac motor starter applies all three phases of ac voltage simultaneously. At the instant of closure, at least two phase voltages must be non-zero, which is equivalent to imposing a dc voltage. This line frequency component exists in all ac motors which are switched by a motor starter, either induction or synchronous. It is a constant frequency and decays to zero quickly.

2) Twice slip frequency, which arises because of two principal construction properties of synchronous motors: the salient pole construction and the main field discharge circuit. This component varies from 120 Hz with the synchronous motor at rest to 0 Hz with the motor synchronized. Its frequency has to equal that of each resonant mode at some point during starting acceleration. The extent to which it will be amplified can best be determined by simulation.

The simulation for either the synchronous or induction motor is similar to the approach documented by Krause and Thomas.[7]

Simulation results have shown that in a grinding mill driven by wound-rotor motors, the shaft torques would be quite different from those in the same mill driven by synchronous motors. The pulsating torque from synchronous motors can excite mechanical resonance frequencies to respond with torques several times greater than normal rated torque.

According to correlations between experimentally derived data on actual installations[6] and analytically derived predictions from simulation, there is little doubt that simulation can be of real value in reducing the risk of failure in grinding mill drives because of torsional resonance.

It is natural to ask why simulation of single pinion drives is not as important as for the new innovative drives. Although single pinion drives are not immune to torsional resonance, the risk of failure is considerably reduced because of the relative simplicity of the system (two or three degrees of freedom rather than five or more). Also, the cost of failure is not usually severe (since the loss of one mill in a line of 20 is not as serious as the loss of one mill in a line of three). Finally, past experience has provided a reliable gauge of the safety factors required to avoid those problems that may occur with single pinion drives.

Evaluation and selection

In Table 1, the 10 selection criteria discussed in this article are compared against the 20 generic mill drive arrangements. Each drive system is weighted from one (first choice) to 10 (last choice), according to each criterion. Only one of these drive systems is *adjustable speed*. The criterion of *soft start mechanically* can be appraised from the drive's speed-torque curve and the rate of application of torque to the parts. *Start-*

Table 2—Choice of mill power transmission and drive

DRIVE ARR	MILL CONN	# PIN.	# REDCRS.	# CL	#	TYPE	SP	TQ	MILL MAX HP / RPM	CHOICE	REASON
A	RG	1			1	S	L	H	600	1	<MAINTENANCE
A^I	RG	1			1	S	L	L		2	<$, <ΔV
B	RG	1	1		1	S	H	H			
B^I	RG	1	1		1	S	H	L			
C	RG	2			2	S*	L	H		2	>EFF, >PF
C^I	RG	2			2	WR/S*	L	H			
D	RG	2	2		2	WR	H	H		1	SIMPLEST, STABLE
D^I	RG	2	2		2	S*	H	H			
D^{II}	RG	2	2		2	WR/S*	H	H	1200		
D^{III}	RG	2	2	2*	2	S*	H	L			
D^{IV}	RG	2	2	2*	2	WR/S*	H	L			
E	TCGB	(2)	**		2	S*	H	H			
F	TCGB	(2)	**		1	S	H	H			
F^I	TCGB	(2)	**	1	1	S	H	L			
F^{II}	TCGB	(2)	**		1	WR	H	H			
G	RG	4	2		2	WR	H	H			
G^I	RG	4	2		2	S*	H	H	(2000)		
G^{II}	RG	4	2		2	WR/S*	H	H			
H	RG	4	4		4	WR	H	H			
I	D				1	S***	LL	H		1	<MAINTENANCE, <ΔV$_1$ ADJ. SPEED

* WITH LOAD SHARE REGULATOR
** MULTIPLE REDUCTION IN GEAR BOX
*** WITH FREQUENCY CONVERTER

Ball mill featuring a wrap-around, gearless, 8,750-hp mill speed (14.5 rpm), high-torque adjustable-frequency synchronous motor.

ing voltage dip can be absolutely defined and its value calculated, and so can running *power factor* and *efficiency*. The latter two are extremely important to operating cost and can be related to first cost (in energy cost units) over any planned period. *Simplicity of installation* is an opinion, based on number and types of parts and on necessary adjustments. *Maintenance* is weighted partly on experience (based on life and failure) and partly on opinion (based on number and type of moving or wear parts).

Reasonable first cost is definable for a known size and speed of mill and plant layout. Cost of space and foundation have been averaged by others, and installation can be estimated. Costs of parts are known. Weighting this criterion will naturally vary, but it is an estimate through the mill hp/rpm and, hence, through the entire drive spectrum. In this first cost comparison, soft start was included for drives 6,000 hp and larger that did not use a clutch or adjustable frequency. Either a 15-MVAR capacitor bank or a pair of wound-rotor liquid rheostats was time-shared by three mills in a plant.

Load sharing is partly self-evident from calculation, partly based on experience, and partly on engineering judgment. *Transient risks*, starting and running, are based on experience, field tests, ability to predict by modern analog analysis techniques, and to some extent on personal opinion. The early assessment of risk of ownership is vital to the realization of income from mill investment and is just as important as first-cost or any operating cost. As a matter of fact, the risk may ultimately determine all costs.

A very conservative limit should be set on mill torque per pinion, particularly when despite all precautions the mill low-speed gear teeth are subject to transient overloads, starting torque shocks, overloads due to load-sharing schemes out of adjustment, fast reclosing torque shocks, and normal load oscillations—and if all are based on the very high, steady-state tooth stresses commensurate with very high horsepower and very low-speed mill ratings and competitive industrial gear standards. It is presently believed that tooth loadings should not exceed a limit of 150,000 lb per low-speed pinion. Quality ring gears of over 40 ft in diameter can be cut. The torque transmitted per pinion can then reach 3 million ft-lb or 600 mill hp/rpm. At 1,200 mill hp/rpm, two-pinion drives might

stress that limit, and that limit should perhaps be reduced to 2,000 mill hp/rpm for four-pinion drives, if used.

Each of the performance criteria in Table 1 has been weighted independently and not on any absolute scale. To make a final choice of drive arrangement for a given mill type, size, and speed in a given plant design, all these criteria must be weighted with respect to each other. In a particular plant, for example, experience may heavily emphasize one particular criterion.

Each prospective mill owner will thus have to do this weighting for his own operation. The criteria weights will then be added horizontally (as in Table 1) and the high sums eliminated, so that what stands out in each group is related to mill hp/rpm size—namely number of low-speed pinions. This is a mill operator's first cut at decision-making. The arrows on the right side of the table indicate the low sums (first choices) in each pinion category.

If these low sums—"First Choice" in that pinion or mill hp/rpm range—are supported by outstanding reasons, and if an "Alternate Choice" in each range can be selected on the basis of other strong, different reasons, then certain sound rules of thumb apply in the mining industry:

To date, the industry has chosen mill drives from three pinion categories: one, two, and none (gearless). Table 2 presents these decisions and the reasons (weighting of criteria) that have guided them.

Table 2 shows that up to 600 mill hp/rpm or so, the first choice has been the conventional single-pinion, low-speed, high-torque synchronous drive for highest efficiency and power factor and low maintenance. When it was important to save a few dollars per horsepower, or when soft-start was needed, the choice was the low-torque equivalent with starting clutch.

From 600 to 1,200 mill hp/rpm or so, the predominant first choice has been the two-pinion, wound-rotor drive with reducers, as the simplest and most inherently stable dual drive with soft start. When greater efficiency and power factor have been very important, the dual, low-speed, high-torque synchronous drive with load-share regulation has been chosen.

From 1,200 to about 2,000 mill hp/rpm, no decisions have been made for choosing four-pinion drives. Instead, the gearless drive has been chosen in cement plants even below this torque category, to obtain lower maintenance costs, greater up-time, softer start, and adjustable speed.

From about 2,000 mill hp/rpm on up, the gearless drive would appear to be the only choice.

Conclusion

To choose from the drives discussed here, which are all available on the market, analog simulation techniques, as predesign insurance, can be of help in the selection of size or configuration. Specific decisions can then be made based on the job to do and the costs of doing it. □

References

1) P. B. Thames, T. C. Heard, "Torsional Vibration in Synchronous Motor-Geared-Compressor Drives," American Institute of Electrical Engineers, *Power Apparatus and Systems*, Vol. 78, pp 1053-1056, December 1959.
2) "AGMA Standard Practice of Helical, Herringbone and Spur Mill Gears," (AGMA 321.05), American Gear Manufacturers Association, Washington, D.C., June 1968.
3) A. R. Olds, Jr., K. E. Olsen, I. Watson, "More on Large Grinding Mill Drives, Background, and Tests," Institute of Electrical and Electronics Engineers, *Proceedings of Cement Industry Technical Conference*, April 1964.
4) L. E. Alban, "Gears, Failure Analysis," American Society for Metals Failure Analysis Conference, June 1968.
5) "Gear Classification Manual for Spur, Helical and Herringbone Gears," (AGMA 390.02), American Gear Manufacturers Association, Washington, D.C., September 1964.
6) E. L. Owen, D. W. Nelson, H. F. Florkiewicz, W. H. Schwedes, "Dynamic Torque Measurements on a Twin Drive Aerofall Mill," Vol. 1-April 1968, Vol. 2-April 1969; (not published).
7) P. C. Krause, C. H. Thomas, "Simulation of Symmetrical Induction Machinery," Institute of Electrical and Electronics Engineers, *Transactions on Power Apparatus and Systems*, Vol. PAS 84, No. 11, pp 1038-1054, November 1965.

Modern plant aids St. Joe processing of elusive Balmat ores

ST. JOE'S BALMAT-EDWARDS DIV. has been successfully mining the complex, varied, elusive zinc orebodies of upper New York state's Balmat-Edwards district since 1926, when St. Joe bought the small but profitable Edwards mine from Northern Ore Co. Along with Edwards, St. Joe acquired an option on mineral rights on the Balmat property, about 10 mi to the southwest, a site that had long been known to bear low grade zinc mineralization but that had frustrated previous attempts at commercial production.

The Balmat option subsequently proved to be a bonanza for St. Joe. The company's geologists have discovered three major deposits and several smaller satellite orebodies in the immediate Balmat area, and the Balmat-Edwards mines now account for 17% of US mined zinc production.

Balmat production has increased in stages since St. Joe became active in the district. St. Joe topped off its latest expansion in 1972 with completion of the No. 4 Balmat shaft and a new 4,300-tpd zinc concentrator that is among the most highly automated plants of its type in the world. Mined ore production of the Balmat-Edwards Div. has risen from 869,000 tons in 1972 to 1,247,000 tons in 1975. Zinc content of concentrates rose from 63,544 tons to 80,034 tons over the same time span, with all concentrates shipped to St. Joe's zinc smelter at Josephtown, Pa.

Expanded production has resulted in a substantial increase in the Balmat-Edwards Div. workforce. Many of the new miners lacked experience, and employee training has contributed to the success of the expansion, along with increased use of rubber-tired trackless equipment underground. The complex Balmat orebodies demand flexibility in mining methods and equipment, which range from jackleg slusher stopes to large room-and-pillar areas that allow use of three-boom, rubber-tired jumbos and 5-yd LHDs.

At the Balmat mill, a bank of lead roughers and a talc prefloat added to the flotation circuit have improved plant concentrate recovery and grade, and the plant will soon be using all of the mine water produced by the three Balmat mines in its processing circuit.

A revegetation program has successfully seeded the now inactive tailings pond of the previous Balmat No. 2 mill. Plantings in the spring of 1976 included Kentucky 31 Fescue, perennial rye grass, timothy, and alsike clover, and by midsummer, all planted areas showed good signs of growth, according to Marvin Lane, manager of the Balmat-Edwards Div.

New Balmat mill meets changing demands

Early in 1972, the new 4,800-tpd Balmat mill started operating to treat combined ore from the three Balmat mines. The old mill that was replaced had operated for over 40 years, starting at 600 tpd in 1930 and finally reaching 2,400 tpd by 1970.

The new mill incorporated all of the modern mill design concepts that could be economically justified, including an on-line X-ray analyzer for three elements in five streams. Even so, during only four years of operation, there have

been six major mill changes or additions, necessitated by new criteria that were not part of the original design concept. These changes include provision for receiving other outside ores, additions to the byproduct lead flotation circuit, installation of a talc prefloat circuit, incorporation of a third stage of cleaning in the zinc circuit, purchase of another large X-ray analyzer, and several major revisions of concentrate loadout and shipping.

Primary crushing of ore from the three Balmat mines is performed underground at the new central No. 4 shaft by a 36 x 48-in. jaw crusher set at 4 in. In the mill, a secondary stage of crushing to ¾ in. is done with an 84-in. hydrocone crusher in open circuit with a 6 x 14-ft screen, at a rate of 250-400 tph into two mill storage tanks with a combined capacity of 4,000 tons. Six variable-speed belt feeders under the storage bins deliver the crushed ore to the rod mill.

The grinding circuit consists of an 11½ x 16-ft rod mill and a 12-ft-dia x 14-ft ball mill. Each is powered by an identical 1,000-hp, direct coupled, 4,160-v motor. Using 4-in. rods, the rod mill discharges to the same variable-speed cyclone pump that is in closed circuit with the ball mill, which uses 2-in. balls. Actual horsepower averages 1,025 for the ball mill and 835 for the rod mill, but the latter can be speeded up if necessary. Steel consumption is 0.47 lb per ton of molycop rods and 0.54 lb per ton of balls.

The overflow from four operating 20-in. cyclones goes to flotation at 80% minus 65 mesh. The original design called for feeding a bank of only four 300-cu-ft lead roughers, producing a lead byproduct after four stages of lead cleaning. The zinc circuit also consisted of 300-cu-ft cells arranged as six roughers, seven scavengers, three cleaners, and two recleaners.

The large central control room is high enough to overlook all operations of crushing, grinding, flotation, thickening, filtering, and drying of concentrates. Besides the on-line X-ray analyzer, the control room is equipped with numerous indicators, alarms, strip chart recorders, and analog set point controllers. In addition to controlling pH, densities, feed rates, circulating loads and reagent additions, even the pulp levels in the flotation banks can be varied by the operator in the control room.

Mill tailings are pumped 6,000 ft through one of two tailings lines to either end of a mile-long valley. The two dams, now 20 ft high, will eventually reach a height of 50 ft. A decant tower and 2,000 ft of decant line allow 1,500 gpm to flow from the pond, of which 700 gpm is returned to the mill as reclaim water.

New equipment added

Soon after starting operations, Balmat's operators learned that considerable ore would be available from an open pit at No. 3 mine and from a small mine 120 mi away in Ontario. Accordingly, a jaw crusher was installed on the surface, with a ramp for truck dumping and a conveyor to allow simultaneous delivery of ore from the apron feeder under the mine bin and from the new surface crusher.

Although the No. 3 open pit and the Canadian mine no longer furnish ore, the surface crusher still provides over 10% of the ore milled. It receives ore trucked from five sources: from upper levels of the No. 2 mine, from an open pit at No. 2 mine, from the Hyatt mine decline 10 mi away, from a decline at No. 2 mine, and from ore stockpiled on surface during rod mill relining.

All the zinc concentrate produced is shipped to the St. Joe smelter at Monaca, Pa. During initial mill operations in 1972, problems at the zinc smelter were caused by Balmat zinc concentrates that assayed close to 1% lead instead of only 0.5%. Despite considerable blending, for extended periods the crude ore milled assayed much higher lead than the 0.3% that was anticipated. Accordingly, by April 1974, a bank of four lead scavengers was added to the original lead circuit. Doubling the flotation time not only reduced the lead content of zinc concentrates but also increased the overall lead recovery.

During 1973 and 1974, the zinc smelter received an increasing proportion of its concentrates from Balmat. Serious problems with furnace life were encountered, attributed to the relatively high level of gangue and insol in Balmat concentrates. After many partially successful efforts during 1974, such as using gangue depressants, a complete talc prefloat circuit was installed at Balmat during early 1975, consisting of four 300-cu-ft roughers, two cleaners, and a recleaner. During the last six months of 1975, concentrates shipped to the smelter assayed only 0.5% calcium and 0.4% magnesium—almost a 50% reduction. Unfortunately, zinc recovery in the mill, which had reached 94% in 1974, dropped to only 92%. The higher value of concentrates assaying 58% instead of 56% only partially offset this loss in recovery.

During the latter part of 1975 and early 1976, every effort was made to keep concentrate grade high while getting recovery back up. Fairly successful results were finally achieved in April 1976 with the addition of a third stage of cleaning, consisting of three deep cells with air control. Current operating results are 93.5% recovery with a concentrate grade of 59% zinc.

During 1973 and 1974, an additional use was made of the on-line X-ray analyzer. Dry briquets were produced instead of using wet methods of assaying mine samples, core samples, daily samples from Edwards mill, and weekly composites. The on-line analyzer was shut down, the briquets inserted into vacant positions, and simultaneous assays of Pb, Zn, and Fe were made.

Meanwhile, time-consuming procedures at both the smelter and mill were making it difficult to generate sufficient assays for calcium, magnesium, and silicon. With reduction of gangue being so important, it appeared justified to purchase a separate fluorescent X-ray analyzer, which assays a briquet for as many as 11 elements simultaneously. Installed in the summer of 1975, it has helped immeasurably in monitoring shift samples and daily shipments of concentrates, as well as performing all other routine assays without having to shut down the on-line analyzer.

The original design called for loading out concentrates from the dryer into any kind of railroad car—box cars, open gondolas, or covered hoppers—onto one of two tracks alternately, after going over a belt scale.

In 1973, a fleet of 80 specially built gondolas were leased for service between Balmat and Josephtown. However, many problems were caused by rain and ice in both loaded and empty cars, and wind losses averaged 1½% despite spray coatings. Finally, by 1975, one-piece fiberglass covers were designed, built and installed. These covers eliminated all ice and water problems and wind losses and have allowed the average moisture content from the dryer to be reduced from 7% to 4½%. □

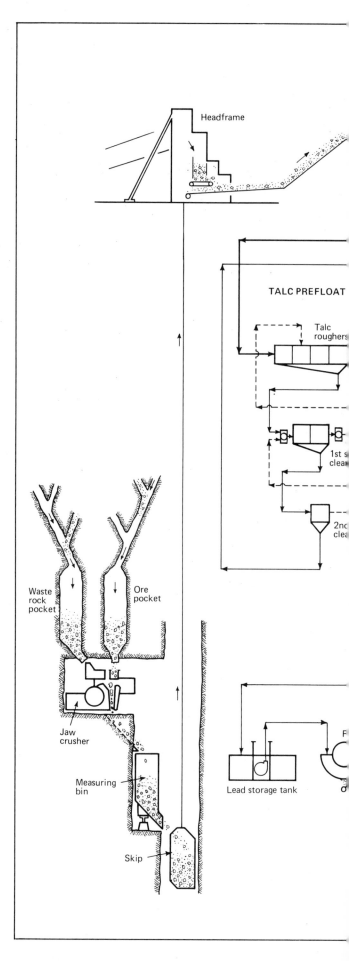

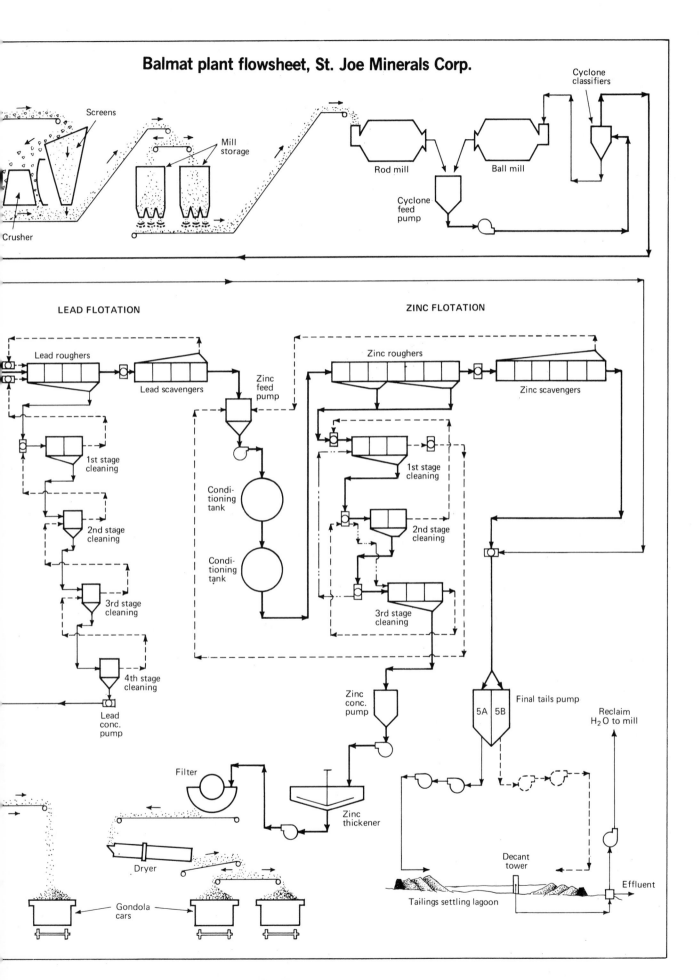

Balmat plant flowsheet, St. Joe Minerals Corp.

Screens

Mill storage

Crusher

Rod mill

Ball mill

Cyclone classifiers

Cyclone feed pump

LEAD FLOTATION

ZINC FLOTATION

Lead roughers

Lead scavengers

Zinc feed pump

Zinc roughers

Zinc scavengers

1st stage cleaning

2nd stage cleaning

3rd stage cleaning

4th stage cleaning

Lead conc. pump

Conditioning tank

Conditioning tank

1st stage cleaning

2nd stage cleaning

3rd stage cleaning

Zinc conc. pump

Final tails pump

5A 5B

Reclaim H₂O to mill

Filter

Zinc thickener

Dryer

Gondola cars

Decant tower

Tailings settling lagoon

Effluent

Theory, applications, and practical operation of hydrocyclones

Dr. Helmut Trawinski, director, Equipment Construction Div.,   Amberger Kaolinwerke GmbH

SEPARATION BY SETTLEMENT OF PARTICLES occurs in nature in any lake or pool into which turbid water is fed. The particles settle to the bottom and form a sediment that is thickened relative to the feed concentrations, while the remaining water, discharged as overflow, is clarified. Artificial basins fulfilling the same function are termed thickeners or clarifiers. If the flow rate of the water streaming through the pool or basin is so high that the finest particles do not have enough time to settle, but are discharged together with the overflow, a classification into fine and coarse fractions takes place. This type of wet classification is called stream classification. The force generating these three kinds of separation is gravity.

The same reactions occur in rotating suspensions, where the much higher centrifugal forces produce separation effects by increasing the rate of settling. Centrifuges with solid bowls are the usual equipment used for this purpose, and the hydrocyclone can be regarded as operating as a solid bowl centrifuge in which the casing is not rotated, but rotation of the suspension is produced by its being fed into the cyclone tangentially under pressure. Depending on the degree of solids recovery to the underflow, the cyclone can act either as clarifier or as classifier. The rejects are thickened in any case.

Theoretical considerations

Fig. 1 demonstrates schematically the working of a hydrocyclone. The suspension fed into it forms a primary vortex along the inside surface of the cylindrical and conical wall, aiming to leave the cone apex. As this is throttled, only part of the stream is discharged as underflow, carrying the coarse particles or even all of the solids with it. The bulk of the liquid — being cleaned by the settling of the solids in the primary vortex or carrying the residual fine particles with it — is forced to leave the cyclone through the overflow nozzle by forming an upward-spinning secondary vortex surrounding the core of the casing. Inside the core, a low pressure is generated, collecting all the air that has been carried in as bubbles or dissolved in the feed water. Even vapor will enter this visible air core. Because of the increase in circumferential speed in the secondary vortex, higher centrifugal forces are generated, resulting in a highly efficient secondary separation. The rejected fine particles settle radially and join the primary vortex, from which most of them are discharged finally through the spigot formed by the cone apex. The separation inside a hydrocyclone therefore takes place as a result of two process stages, the final cut point being determined mainly by the acceleration of the inner secondary vortex.

The flow pattern inside the cyclone may be described as a potential vortex generating an increase in tangential speed in the radial direction toward the core. (See Fig. 2.) The Helmholtz equation for the ideal vortex, uninfluenced by friction, is

$$v \cdot r = const \quad (1a)$$

or

$$v_o \cdot r = v_x \cdot x \quad (1b)$$

The speed at any radial distance x therefore would be

$$v_x = v_o \cdot \frac{r}{x} \quad (2a)$$

The angular velocity ω increases to a higher degree. With

$$v = r \cdot \omega$$

the Helmholtz vortex is described by the equation

$$\omega \cdot r^2 = const \quad (1c)$$

So we get

$$\omega_x = \omega_o \cdot \left(\frac{r}{x} \right)^2 \quad (2b)$$

We know from experience that the equation defining the vortex stream when frictional forces are taken into consideration is of the form

$$v \cdot r^n = const \quad (3a)$$

For clear water, Bradley[2] claimed that $n = 0.7$, and Krijgsman[3] determined that $n = 0.5$ for suspensions with average solids contents. Based on the latter approxima-

Fig. 1—Hydrocyclone flow diagram

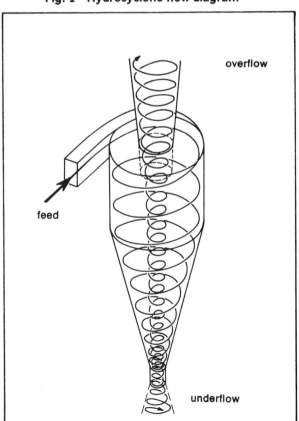

overflow

feed

underflow

Two 12-in.-dia hydrocyclones demonstrate how shape can be varied: left, a 20° cone with a short cylinder; right, a 30° cone with a long cylinder. Design: Amberger Kaolinwerke.

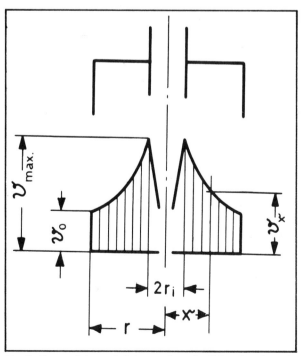

Fig. 2—Tangential speed diagram of a potential vortex shows increasing speed with decreasing diameter up to the overflow diameter, with decreasing speed in the central core.

tion, the vortex equation should be read as

$$v \cdot \sqrt{r} = const \tag{3b}$$

resulting in

$$v_x = v_0 \cdot \sqrt{\frac{r}{x}} \tag{4a}$$

or

$$\omega_x = \omega_0 \left(\frac{r}{x} \right)^{3/2} \tag{4b}$$

Along with increasing tangential speed or angular velocity, the centrifugal acceleration b increases too. This is defined by

$$b = r \cdot \omega^2 \tag{5a}$$

e.g., $b_0 = r \cdot \omega_0^2$ (5b) and $b_x = x \cdot \omega_x^2$ (5c)

Introducing Eq. 4b, we get

$$b_x = r \cdot \omega_0^2 \cdot \left(\frac{r}{x} \right)^3 \tag{6a}$$

Now, replacing ω_0^2 by Eq. 5b, we get

$$b_x = b_0 \left(\frac{r}{x} \right)^2 \tag{6b}$$

These equations show clearly that the centrifugal acceleration in the secondary vortex is higher than that in the primary vortex by the inverse ratio of respective radii, to the second power. It is obvious, therefore, that the inner vortex determines the separation cut. In addition, we may conclude that high shear forces are characteristic of cyclone flow, *preventing flocculation* and therefore limiting mass recovery. This is, however, compensated for by the sharpness of the size cut achieved by cyclones compared to hydroseparator settling tanks.

To determine the cut point of the separation from test results, one has to plot the Tromp curve.[4] (See Fig. 3). Diagram A shows the grain size distribution of a particle assembly plotted as cumulative screen residues R against particle diameter d in the Rosin-Rammler-Bennet net. If δ is the difference between two particle diameters x and $x-\delta$, we define the difference between the corresponding residues ΔR as $R_x - R_{(x-\delta)}$.

Pairs of such ΔR-values have to be taken from the grain size distributions of the overflow ΔR_F and underflow solids ΔR_c. In addition, we require the value of the mass recovery Θ, which may be obtained either by weighing the solids content of the feed (entrace) M_E and the underflow (coarse) M_c from samples taken simultaneously:

$$\Theta = \frac{M_c}{M_E} \tag{7}$$

or from the solids contents of feed, E, e, overflow F, f and underflow C, c (where the capital letters refer to figures in grams per liter, and the small letters in weight percent), by using the following calculations:

$$\Theta = \frac{E - F}{C - F} \cdot \frac{C}{F} \tag{8a}$$

or

$$\Theta = \frac{e - f}{c - f} \cdot \frac{\gamma_c - c}{\gamma_c - e} \tag{8b}$$

where γ_c equals the specific gravity of the solids.[5]

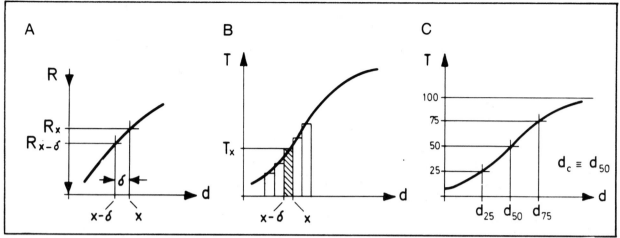

Fig. 3—Origin of Tromp curve: A) grain size distribution line (Rosin-Rammler-Bennett net); B) fractional mass recovery stair generates Tromp curve; C) points of Tromp curve determining separation mesh (cut point) and imperfection (Equation 10).

The Tromp curve is the plotting of the distribution numbers T_x (the differential mass recovery for the particle size range between x-δ and x) against the particle diameter d, calculated as follows:

$$T = \frac{\Theta \cdot \Delta R_c}{\Theta \cdot \Delta R_c + (1-\Theta) \cdot \Delta R_F} \tag{9}$$

The resulting step chart has to be approximated by a continuous curve. (See diagram B.)

The cut point (separation mesh) d_c is defined as that point on the Tromp curve for which T equals 0.5 or 50%, i.e., where the particles have an equal chance of going either with the overflow or the underflow. (See diagram C.) The sharpness of the cut depends on the particle diameters for $T = 0.75$ (d_{75}) and $T = 0.25$ (d_{25}), both of which may be taken from the Tromp curve. The so-called Imperfection I is calculated by the formula:[4]

$$I = \frac{d_{75} - d_{25}}{2 \cdot d_c} \tag{10}$$

Several formulas can be found in hydrocyclone literature for calculation of the separation mesh. The derivation of any such formula must start with Stokes' law describing the settling speed in laminar flow. Although the flow of the suspension in a hydrocyclone is turbulent (i.e., high Reynolds number), the flow surrounding the settling particle is laminar (small Reynolds number). The settling rate in a gravity field is

$$u_{so} = \frac{d^2 \cdot (\rho_s - \rho_1)}{18\,\eta} \cdot g \tag{11}$$

where ρ_s and ρ_1 are the densities of solids and liquids, η the dynamic viscosity of the liquid, and g the acceleration due to gravity. Within centrifugal fields, the gravitational acceleration g is replaced by the centrifugal acceleration b or the product of g and the acceleration factor z. Therefore, the increased settling rate in the hydrocyclone amounts to

$$u_s = \frac{d^2 \cdot (\rho_s - \rho_1)}{18\,\eta} \cdot b = u_{so} \cdot z \tag{12}$$

The settling speed of particles having the cut point diameter d_c (i.e., u_s of Eq. 12) determines the capacity of the classifier area[6] at that point

$$q_F = \frac{Q}{F} \tag{13}$$

We can therefore write

$$u_s = q_F \tag{14}$$

We may now introduce the following relations:
For the separating area

$$F = \frac{2}{3}\,D \cdot \pi \cdot L_e \backsim \lambda D^2 \quad \cdot$$

wherein the "slenderness" figure λ is defined as the ratio of the effective length L_e and the cyclone diameter D. For the acceleration factor z, using r for $D/2$ and $v = \sqrt{2gH}$, with H as "pressure height" (gauge reading divided by slurry density, in meters):

$$z = \frac{v^2}{g \cdot r} = 4 \cdot \frac{H}{D} \tag{15}$$

For the volume flow capacity (semi-empirical):

$$Q = X \cdot D^2 \cdot \sqrt{H} \tag{16}$$

X being the correction factor for the particular cyclone's geometry (cylinder length, cone angle, nozzle diameter, etc.). Finally, we get out for the cut point:[7]

$$d_c \backsim \sqrt{\frac{\eta}{g \cdot (\rho_s - \rho_1)}} \cdot \sqrt{\frac{X}{\lambda} \cdot \frac{\sqrt{D}}{\sqrt[4]{H}}} \tag{17}$$

The first term collects the characteristic data of the suspension, and the second, those of the individual cyclone geometry, while the third term demonstrates that the size at the cut point is influenced by the square root of the cyclone diameter, but only by the fourth root of the pressure drop, and that inversely.

We may conclude from this statement that lower cut points could, at least in theory, be achieved with big cyclones, provided high enough pressures are applied. The economic restriction (power consumption, abrasion, etc.) is, however, of major importance, and in practice the cut point is determined primarily by the size of the cyclones. Fine separation undoubtedly requires small cyclones. As these have only a small capacity, several

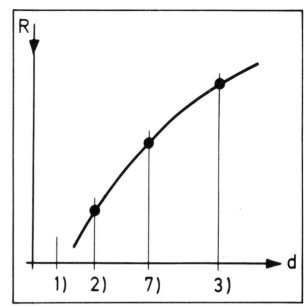

Fig. 4—Grain size distribution determines cyclone application: point 3 applies for degritting, point 7 for fractionation, point 2 for desliming, and point 1 for clarification.

Annular distributor with thirty-one 40-mm-dia hydrocyclones has an antiblocking filter in front. (See Fig. 20.)

cyclones have to be connected in parallel if high capacity or treatment rate is required.[8]

Hydrocyclone applications

There are 10 principal applications for hydrocyclones.

Thickening eliminates most of the water in a suspension to produce dewatered solids. True thickening aims at the recovery of all solids, resulting in the clarification of the liquid. However, flocculating agents cannot be used in hydrocyclones as settling aids, and in practice, the mass recovery is limited and a turbid overflow may be the result; i.e., desliming takes place in the cyclone. The building of tailing dams with hydrocyclones makes use of this phenomenon.

Desliming aims to eliminate fine particles from the overflow. This step is often necessary to improve the product for subsequent processes such as flotation, wet magnetic separation, filtration, etc. In chemical plants, desliming cyclones are often used for dewatering after a crystallization process, with the fine crystals being discharged with the overflow and recycled to the crystallizer, where they act as nuclei for crystal growth.

Degritting produces overflow as a product, and smaller amounts of oversize particles are rejected in the underflow. The difference between degritting and desliming is demonstrated graphically in Fig. 4 by using a grain size distribution line similar to that of Fig. 3A. Cut point 2 at the lower end of the curve refers to desliming, and cut point 3 at the upper end to degritting. Point 1, at the left of the curve, represents clarification or thickening, and point 7, in the middle, represents fractionation.

Closed circuit grinding processes often use cyclones for both degritting and desliming. Four possible circuits in which classifying hydrocyclones and wet mills can be employed together are illustrated in Fig. 7.

In case "a," the cyclone is installed ahead of the mill to deslime the feed. The fine fraction discharged with the overflow is blended with the ground mill product. The coarse underflow is ground in the mill and becomes the main component of the blended product. Such a circuit is called an "open" circuit.

In case "b," the feed goes directly to the mill, whose discharge is fed to a cyclone for degritting. The cyclone overflow is the product, and the underflow (oversize) goes back to the mill for more grinding, along with new feed. Such a circuit is called a "closed" circuit.

In case "c" (a combination of cases "a" and "b"), the circuit feed and the mill discharge are blended and classified together in the same cyclone. The cyclone deslimes the coarse feed and degrits the fine mill product. The cyclone overflow is the product, and the underflow is fed back to the mill. Because of the dual function of the cyclone, such circuits are called "double" circuits.

To optimize the performance of cyclones, desliming and degritting should be handled independently in separate cyclones of different sizes—as in case "d." Both overflows are then products and are fed to the mill. This is a more logical combination of cases "a" and "b" and is called an "improved" circuit.

Fig. 6 illustrates some further modifications of the four basic circuits in Fig. 5, which may be of advantage in certain applications.

To reduce mill loading still further, a closed circuit can be further modified by employing two-stage degritting, as in case "e." The primary grit is deslimed in the second cyclone, and the intermediate product is blended with the primary feed. Without reducing the size quality of the final product, the rejects to the mill carry less fine residues.

If the primary overflow still carries too much oversize, it can be cleaned up in a second cyclone stage, as in case "f." Because the underflow of the secondary cyclone will carry too many fines, it is returned to the primary feed for further desliming.

Case "g" is a modification of circuit "d" that can be

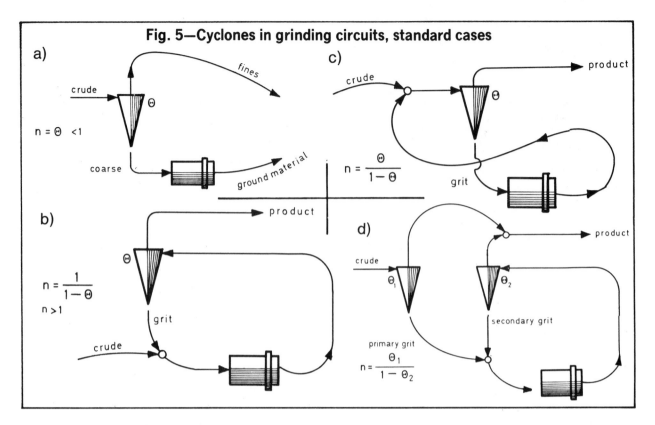

Fig. 5—Cyclones in grinding circuits, standard cases

a)

crude

$n = \Theta \quad <1$

coarse

fines

ground material

b)

Θ

$n = \dfrac{1}{1-\Theta}$

$n > 1$

grit

product

crude

c)

crude

product

$n = \dfrac{\Theta}{1-\Theta}$

grit

d)

crude

product

Θ_1

Θ_2

primary grit

$n = \dfrac{\Theta_1}{1-\Theta_2}$

secondary grit

used if the overflow of the primary cyclone is not of the required quality. In this case, the primary overflow is blended with the secondary feed for a second cleaning operation.

The circulating load factor *n* compares the tonnage fed to the mill with the feed required to produce final tonnage of product. It can be calculated by using the given formulas when the mass recovery figures for the cyclones are known.[9]

Selective classification. The sorting of nonhomogenous feeds into their mineral components can be based on differing characteristics of the minerals. Specific gravity

is used in heavy media separation, jigs, tables, and spirals; particle shape is used in tables and spirals; surface tension is used in flotation; electrical and magnetic properties are used in separators; and solubility is used in leaching processes. Sometimes, differences in grain size allow for a purely mechanical separation.

Antiparallel grain size distribution is illustrated in Fig. 7.[10] Kaolin is refined on the basis of such a grain distribution, with the finer product on the left being kaolin and that on the right being quartz. The cut at the size grain indicated in the diagram produces an enrichment of the fine kaolin in the cyclone overflow and of the coarse

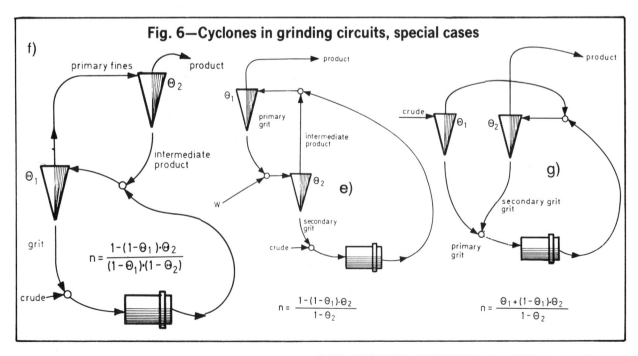

Fig. 6—Cyclones in grinding circuits, special cases

f)

primary fines

product

Θ_2

intermediate product

Θ_1

grit

crude

$$n = \dfrac{1-(1-\Theta_1)\cdot\Theta_2}{(1-\Theta_1)\cdot(1-\Theta_2)}$$

e)

Θ_1

primary grit

product

intermediate product

W

Θ_2

secondary grit

crude

$$n = \dfrac{1-(1-\Theta_1)\cdot\Theta_2}{1-\Theta_2}$$

g)

product

crude

Θ_1

Θ_2

secondary grit grit

primary grit

$$n = \dfrac{\Theta_1+(1-\Theta_1)\cdot\Theta_2}{1-\Theta_2}$$

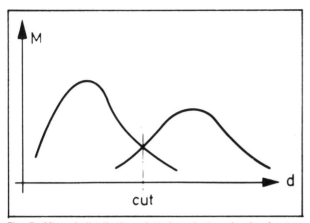

Fig. 7--Mineral distribution plotted against grain size for two minerals shows how selective classification works.

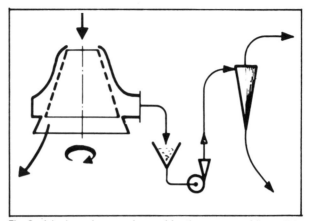

Fig. 8—A hydrocyclone can be used for the recovery of fine solids from the effluent of a screen-type centrifuge.

quartz in the underflow.

Solids recovery from turbid effluents (overflows or filtrates) of washing and dewatering equipment may prevent loss of fine product fractions. The recovery of these fine fractions from sand spirals, log washers, vibro screens and dewatering centrifuges (of the scroll discharge screen, vibro screen, or pusher type) is an attractive application of hydrocyclones.[12] A flowsheet for a scroll centrifuge and hydrocyclone combination is shown in Fig. 8.

Fractionation, which separates two fractions for further treatment in different processes, is another interesting application for hydrocyclones. Iron ore concentrate fractionation into sinter feed (coarse) and pellet feed (fine) is a typical example.

Preconcentration using hydrocyclones can be used to enrich the mineral components of ground ore if there are large differences in the specific gravity of the mineral components. This is a gravity concentration process—or perhaps more aptly, a centrifugal concentration process. No heavy medium is used in such cyclones.[13] Typical examples are the separation of heavy components such as metal sulphides (pyrite and zinc blende), metal oxides, and precious metals (gold, platinum, silver) from gangue.

Cyclones for such applications look different from standard cyclones; their flat bottoms and longer barrels have been proved to increase efficiency. Three cyclone configurations and typical applications are shown in Fig. 9.

Liquid recovery. If process water or parent liquids must be recycled, hydrocyclones may often produce satisfactory clarification. In coal washing plants, this is a major problem, especially when existing thickeners are overloaded. Hydrocyclones are often installed in parallel to keep the level of turbidity of the recycle water at a suitable value.

Countercurrent washing can eliminate adherent acids or lyes or fine particles from a product by periodical dilution and thickening in multiple cyclone stages. If X is the dilution factor of stage *i,* and *n* successive stages are used, the overall washing effect Ω amounts to

$$\Omega = \frac{1}{(1 - X_1)(1 - X_2)(1 - X_3) \cdots (1 - X_n)} \quad (18)$$

A total of *n* times the amount of diluting water used per stage is required. Countercurrent washing can achieve high efficiencies by adding fresh water once only: to the last cyclone stage. The overall washing effect is somewhat lower than when fresh water is added several times, of course, but relative to the amount of fresh water added, the countercurrent system is much more effective.

A flowsheet for a four-stage CCW plant is shown in Fig. 10.

If the splitting factor of the cyclone (for the liquid only and not the volume of the suspension) is τ_1 for stage number *i*, the following formula gives the overall washing effect:[14]

$$\Omega = \frac{1 - \tau_4(1 - \tau_3) - \tau_3(1 - \tau_2) - \tau_2(1 - \tau_1) + \tau_2\tau_4(1 - \tau_1)(1 - \tau_3)}{(1 - X_1)(1 - X_2)(1 - X_3)(1 - X_4)} \quad (19)$$

Practical hydrocyclone operation

The determination of cyclone size is dependent on either the required mass recovery or the requirements of particle size split. Even for gravity concentration, there is a connection between enrichment, yield, and mass recovery. In no case should the cyclone size be determined by the desired total capacity. As the cut point is dependent on a lot of variables in addition to the cyclone size, practical tests are the only way to achieve the final layout.

Amberger Kaolinwerke cyclone plant beneficiates kaolin, making selective classifications on the basis of particle size.

Before discussing the various parameters influencing the cut point of a given cyclone, the test possibilities should be described. Cuts at small particle diameters (i.e., in the fine particle range) are tested with full size cyclones by running several sizes simultaneously in parallel or one after the other, while varying the pressure and/or the nozzles. Equation 17a shows the influence of cyclone diameter and pressure:

$$d_c \backsim \frac{\sqrt{D}}{\sqrt[4]{H}} \qquad (17a)$$

A further approach would be the introduction of nozzle diameters using the characteristic factor, with d_o for overflow nozzle and d_e as equivalent diameter of the generally rectangular-shaped feed nozzle:

$$\psi = \frac{d_e \cdot d_o}{D^2} \qquad (20)$$

Multiplying Eq. 17a by $\sqrt{\psi}$ results in:[15]

$$d_c \backsim \sqrt{\frac{d_e \cdot d_o}{D} \cdot \frac{}{D}} \cdot \frac{\sqrt{D}}{\sqrt[4]{H}} = \frac{\sqrt{\dfrac{d_e \cdot d_o}{D}}}{\sqrt[4]{H}} \qquad (17b)$$

Because of the large numbers of other factors that influence the cut point, this equation cannot be used for numerical calculations, but it gives an idea of the direction in which one should continue to run tests after having obtained some preliminary results by arbitrary runs.

The real problem arises when coarse cutting cyclones are needed in the plant (for closed circuit grinding, etc.). Cutting at large particle sizes requires large diameter cyclones with consequent high capacities, but often only small amounts of material are available for the pilot plant or laboratory tests. Small test cyclones must therefore be employed, resulting—because of Eq. 17a/b—in lower cut points than desired. The limitations of such test work are very severe in terms of variations in the cyclone diameter. To fulfill the model law of Eq. 17a, we must consider, for constant cut d_c

$$\sqrt{D} \backsim \sqrt[4]{H} \text{ or } H \backsim D^2 \qquad (21)$$

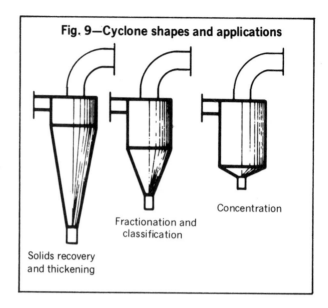

Fig. 9—Cyclone shapes and applications

Solids recovery and thickening

Fractionation and classification

Concentration

This means that when running a test with a cyclone of half the diameter D, the pressure loss H employed should be a quarter of that of the plant. If the diameter of the original unit is 700 mm (28 in.) and it is to be run with 6-m liquid head pressure, then a test cyclone of 350-mm (14-in.) diameter requires 1.5-m pressure, which is close to the limit of air core stability. A cyclone with a diameter of 175 mm (7 in.) would require a mere 0.4-m pressure, which is not possible. Here, the corrected form of Eq. 17b is of help. If the big cyclone has smaller nozzles (e.g., a ψ-factor of about 0.05), a test cyclone with big nozzles may be used—e.g., $\psi = 0.12$, thus obtaining a conversion factor of $\sqrt{2.4} = 1.55$. This reduces the pressure factor from 1/16 to 1/10 for a test cyclone of one-fourth the full scale diameter. It must be determined whether the cyclone is stable in its operation with 0.6-m liquid head; e.g., 0.06 bar pressure. (The capacities may be as follows: 300 cu m per hr for the 700-mm-dia unit, 40 cu m per hr for 350 dia, and 5 to 12 cu m per hr for 175 dia, depending on nozzle sizes.)

There is no possibility of running a test with 3-in. or

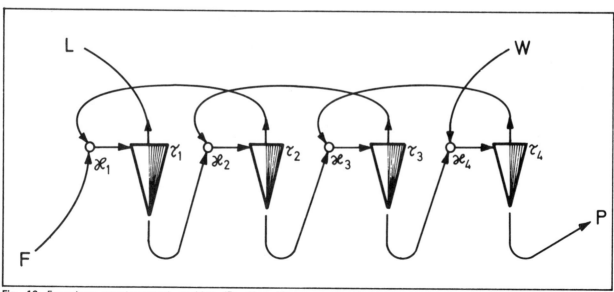

Fig. 10—Four-stage countercurrent washing (Equation 19): F = feed with lye content, P = washed product, L = residual washing liquid, W = wash water, τ = free liquid split ratio of cyclones, χ = wash liquid ratio at mix tank.

4-in.-dia cyclones—a mistake sometimes made in test institutes. For these cyclones, the equivalent pressure would be 0.1 to 0.15 m LH (equivalent to only 0.01-0.015 bar). No cyclone can function in this way. In addition, when the cyclone diameter is reduced by a factor of 8 (the cross sectional area by 64), the Reynolds Number will vary by the same factor, changing from transitional to laminar flow, and therefore disturbing any model law. In summary, satisfactory pilot plant tests can be made with a cyclone unit of half the diameter, using one-fourth of the pressure, and producing one-eighth of the throughput of a full scale plant. A reduction of 1:3 may be the optimum limit (1/10 of the pressure, approximately 1/30 of the capacity), but smaller cyclones will lead to incorrect results.

In addition to cyclone diameter, and feed and over-flow nozzle diameter and pressure, the cut point is influenced by further geometric factors—e.g., the effective cyclone length $L_e = \lambda \cdot D$, which is determined by cone angle and barrel length. This factor is incorporated in

Table 1—Influence of specific gravity and viscosity on cut point (separation mesh)

Solids	Liquid	ρ_s	ρ_L	η	Cutpoint factor
Sand	Water	2.6	1	1	1
Coal	Water	1.4	1	1	2
Iron ore	Water	5.0	1	1	0.63
Rock salt	Brine	2.1	1.2	6	3.26

Eq. 17a. Also important is the feed nozzle geometry. A rectangular-shaped feed duct in the cover plate, together with evolute entrance, has proved to be most satisfactory, but no data quantifying the influence of these design features are available.

The characteristics of the slurry that is fed to the cyclone also influence the cut point. The grain size distribution determines the relationship between the fractions plus and minus the separation mesh, and therefore the residual solids content in the overflow (the effective viscosity of the parent liquid). In the same way, the effective slurry viscosity, since it appears in the Stokes equation, influences the cut point. It is determined by the solids content in the feed. Higher slurry concentrations therefore generate coarser cuts than lower concentrations. This effect can also be described as hindered settling, because the movement of the coarser particles is hindered by the zone of smaller particles, through which the coarser ones must pass. The effect has also been measured in fluidized beds.[16] Fig. 11 explains the practical result of increasing separation mesh and imperfection by feeding slurries with a higher solids content.

The viscosity of the liquid itself acts in the same way. Furthermore, the difference in densities or specific gravity between the solids and the carrying liquid is important. Table 1 compares four examples, based on the assumption that the nominal cut at low solids content will be 100 microns. Again Eq. 17 should be considered —i.e., the first term of it:

$$d_c \sim \sqrt{\frac{\eta}{\rho_s - \rho_L}} \tag{22a}$$

or

$$d_c = d_o \sqrt{\frac{\eta_1}{\eta_2} \cdot \frac{\rho_{so} - \rho_{Lo}}{\rho_{s1} - \rho_{L1}}} \tag{22b}$$

The shape of the particles is also important. Very flat particles such as mica tend to go to the overflow even though they are relatively coarse. The definition of a shape factor based on specific surface is not of great help because the particle diameter itself is not sufficiently well defined. In any case, flat particles will become concentrated in the overflow. Surface-active fine particles will probably increase their diameter by hydration, and their density will decrease. Others will tend to float. Predictions of performance based solely on calculation are therefore not possible.

The separation mesh or cut point in terms of a formula such as Eq. 17 is the cut obtained inside the secondary vortex flow. Overflow and underflow of the cyclone may be influenced by outside forces that disturb the primary cut and make the simple formulas invalid. In most published work on separation mesh formulas, this point is ignored, but it is of such practical importance in the efficient operation of hydrocyclones that it

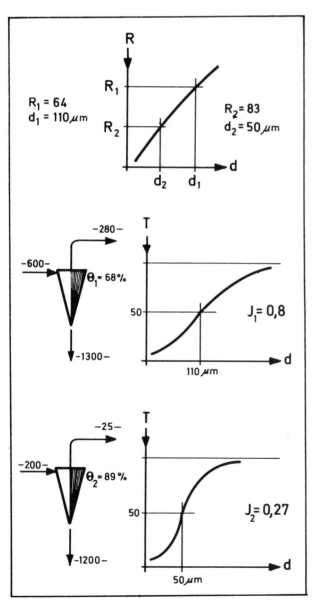

Fig. 11—Influence of feed solids content on separation mesh cut and imperfection: top, grain size distribution line (RRB); center and bottom, two Tromp curves.

Overflow discharge chambers of good design may be beneficial, especially on bigger cyclones such as this 24-in.-dia unit.

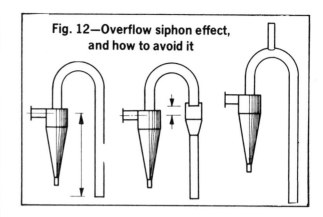

Fig. 12—Overflow siphon effect, and how to avoid it

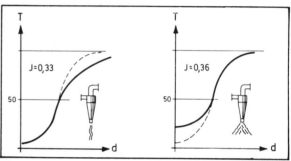

Fig. 13—Influence of underflow nozzle throttling on Tromp curve: left, rope discharge; right, umbrella discharge.

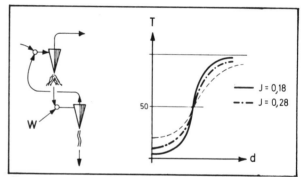

Fig. 14—Two stages in X-connection, with umbrella discharge on the first stage and rope discharge on the second stage, are applied to reach optimum Tromp curve, lowest imperfection.

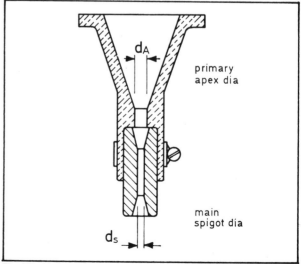

Fig. 15—Hydrocyclone spigot diameter can be controlled by the use of exchangeable apex stoppers.

is worthy of closer examination.

The overflow elbow of the cyclone should not be sharply curved or bent, because the rotation of the air core is continued inside the elbow.[17] Elbows of bigger radius are effective, as shown in Fig. 12. Overflow discharge chambers of good design are beneficial too, and are especially useful for bigger cyclone units. Leading the overflow from this chamber or from the hermetically closed elbow to lower levels, as shown on the left in Fig. 12, causes a siphon effect that disturbs the cut point. This is the case even when using the siphon for underflow regulation. To break the siphon effect, either the length of the elbow must be cut (Fig. 12, center), or a degassing pipe must be welded on (Fig. 12, right).

The throttling of the spigot causes other problems with cut point. High underflow concentrations are reached with a rope discharge, but in this case, some particles that have already been rejected inside the cyclone are returned to the overflow, disturbing the upper part of the Tromp curve (Fig. 13, left). A diluted underflow, called umbrella discharge, carries fine particles with the diluting water. This dead flux results in a disturbed lower part of the Tromp curve (Fig. 13, right). The imperfections of both cases are obvious. Improvement requires two cyclone stages if good degritting is required in the overflow simultaneously with good desliming of the underflow. For best results, as demonstrated in Fig. 14,

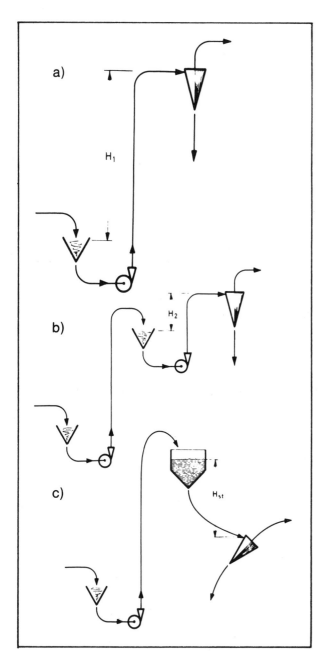

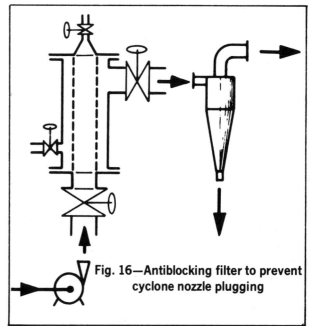

Fig. 16—Antiblocking filter to prevent cyclone nozzle plugging

the primary stage should be run with umbrella discharge and the secondary with rope discharge, with secondary overflow recycled to the main feed. This principle has been used with great success, as it also reduces the effect of fluctuating solids content and size distribution of the main feed. The result is an optimum Tromp curve with low imperfection (Fig. 14, right).

The medium Tromp curve in Fig. 14 refers to a single-stage operation where the cyclone spigot is regulated to optimize the underflow. Regulation can be done continuously by a hydraulic valve, which, of course, in-

Fig. 17 (below)—Sump level regulation: left, excess sump overflow; right, controlled partial hydrocyclone overflow recycle.

Fig. 18 (left)—Geodetic feed height and cyclone functioning: a) bad installation with too great a difference in height; b) good installation that makes use of intermediate pump; c) steady head generating gravity feed.

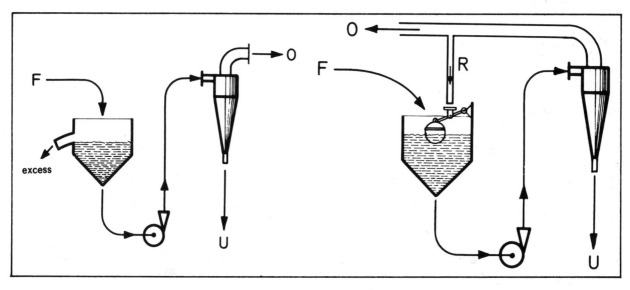

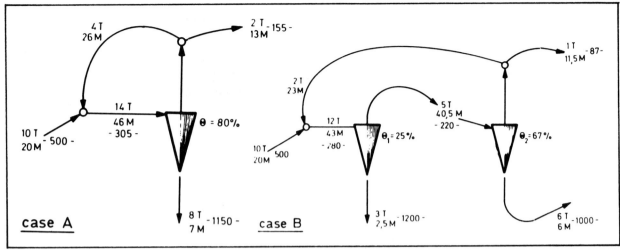

Fig. 19—Feed predilution by overflow recycle: case A, single stage installation (high mass recovery); case B, two-stage instal- lation (low mass recovery in first stage). M = cu m per hr, T = tph, numbers between dashes = gpl.

creases capital and maintenance costs. But it can also be carried out in stages by changing apex stoppers manually, as shown in Fig. 15—a foolproof method. Such spigots with reduced diameters for higher underflow concentrations are, however, somewhat prone to plugging. To prevent plugging, the size of the biggest particles fed into the cyclone should be below one-fourth of the definite spigot diameter (in no case bigger than one-third). The anti-blocking-filter shown in Fig. 16 is a simple device to solve the problem. It is fitted with a main cleaning valve on top and with a rinsing device that will clean the perforated barrel when both the main valves are closed.

Optimum functioning of a hydrocyclone depends on constant conditions in the feed, especially the volumetric flow rate. To assure steady conditions, the level of the pump sump must be kept constant, and—above all—the level must not fall to a point where air is sucked through the pump. Fig. 17 shows two possibilities for the regulation of the feed level. In the left-hand sketch, the pump sump has a simple overflow system for the excess feed, but in many operations this principle can not be used. Much better is the principle of partial recycle of the overflow, shown on the right. The bypass line R recycling overflow suspension is closed by a simple butterfly valve connected with a float. The capacity of the cyclone is selected to be 10% or 15% bigger than the original feed F to the system.

Even a pump with controlled sump level can cause trouble—e.g., when transporting the slurry over a longer pipe system or against a somewhat greater head than that for which it was designed. Fluctuations in feed concentration can cause variation of the friction losses in the pipeline, diminishing or increasing periodically the residual pressure that remains available for dissipation in the cyclone itself. Fig. 18a demonstrates an incorrect installation, and the intermediate pump in Fig. 18b solves the problem. The height difference H_2 should be smaller than the pressure loss of the cyclone ΔH_c—if possible, only 50% of it. The safest method, of course, is to use a steady-head tank instead of the intermediate pump (Fig. 18c). This tank's level has to be controlled, which happens automatically if the tank itself is high enough.

For the optimum operation of hydrocyclones, some practical hints may be given in the form of flowsheets. If necessary, the solids content of the feed may be re- duced, as shown in Fig. 11. Adding water is simple but generally impractical, as it increases the liquid load on the whole process, especially on any thickeners later in the operation. Recycling the overflow is often helpful. Fig. 19 demonstrates two possibilities. In case A, direct recycling of the overflow to the feed tank can be used where high mass recovery of the cyclone produces a dilute overflow. The recycle factor depends on the original feed concentration c_o, that of the expected overflow c_2, and the demand on maximum feed concentration c_1. The factor n of the recycling flow referred to the original feed can be calculated as follows:

$$n = \frac{c_o - c_1}{c_1 - c_2} \qquad (23)$$

In the example (case A), this results in

$$n = \frac{500 - 305}{305 - 155} = \frac{195}{150} = 1.3$$

Indeed, 26 M equals 1.3 × 20 M (in the flowsheet, M stands for cu m per hr, T for tph, and the numbers preceded and followed by dashes are gpl).

In cases of lower mass recovery, the installation of a thickening cyclone stage in the overflow of the main cyclone produces the required overflow with low solids content. Case B in Fig. 19 is an example. If c_2 is the overflow concentration of the thickening cyclone, Eq. 23 is valid for this case too. We calculate

$$n = \frac{500 - 280}{280 - 87} = \frac{220}{193} = 1.14$$

Here, 23 M recycle equals 1.14 times feed 20 M. In both cases, the regulation is done automatically by the float system shown in Fig. 17, provided that capacity of the cyclone stages has been determined correctly. The secondary cyclone stage in Case B produces a secondary underflow. This may be treated separately or remixed with the overflow, depending on the demand of the flowsheet.

Another possibility of reducing the solids content in the feed to the main cyclone stage is the installation of a scalping cyclone. Fig. 20 demonstrates an example of the refining of kaolin by hydrocyclones. The desired feed

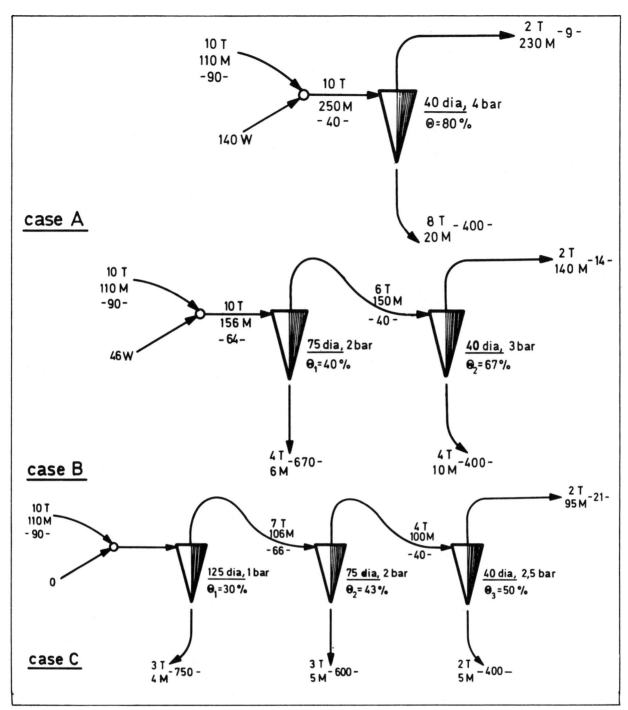

Fig. 20—Scalping cyclones reduce feed concentration: case A, diluting water is fed into a single cyclone stage; case B, a reduction in diluting water is accomplished with a scalping stage; case C, a three-stage installation avoids dilution.

concentration is 40 gpl. The feed coming from the blunger or log washer may have 90 gpl solids content. In case A, 125% fresh water is added. When one scalping stage is installed (case B), rejecting half of the coarse fraction, the water factor can be reduced to 42%. With two scalping stages (case C), 75% of the coarse fraction will be rejected. The desired feed concentration of the main (third) stage is reached without adding water at all.

A kaolin refining plant is usually operated as in case C. In addition to the reduction of solids content without adding water, there are other reasons for installing scalping stages. One is the reduction of the number of cyclones for the most expensive, main stage (in the ex-

ample, by a factor of 2.5). Altogether, 26% excess capacity must be treated. But because these cyclones are bigger, this part of the installation is cheaper. Another reason is that in case A, the single cyclone stage is fed with the complete spectrum of particle sizes. The refining effect is poor because the coarse particles hinder the fine separation by stratification. Case C, however, offers optimum conditions for good refining results. Finally, although 26% more capacity is pumped in case C, power consumption is less because the scalping stages are running at lower pressure.

Maintenance costs (wear) also must be considered. The first stage is built using bigger cyclones (125-mm

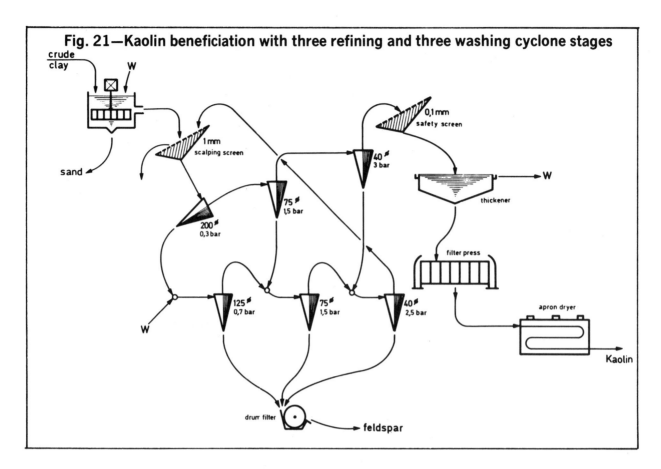

Fig. 21—Kaolin beneficiation with three refining and three washing cyclone stages

diameter) and is run at lower pressure (1 bar), generating low centrifugal forces (320 g). Therefore, there is little wear. The second stage, with 75-mm-dia cyclones and 2-bar pressure, generates 1,070 g (calculated using Eq. 15). As all coarser particles (plus 50 microns) have already been removed, there is little wear in the second stage, either. The main third stage handles only minus 25-micron particles. Therefore, even at the high acceleration of 2,500 g generated by 40-mm-dia cyclones under 2.5-bar pressure, the wear is not significant. Indeed, this is another big advantage of a three-stage refining plant.

In addition to three refining stages, a modern kaolin refining plant[8,11] incorporates three washing stages, each stage as shown in Fig. 14. The overflows from the first and second washing stages are blended with the underflows from the second and third refining stages, and the overflow of the third washing stage is recycled to the first feed (Fig. 21). The decision on optimum blending of intermediate product streams can be made by using so-called generation like numbers.[18] Ahead of the six-stage cyclone plant, a blunger or stirrer system is installed to disperse the crude clay and to discharge the sands (plus 0.5 mm). The subsequent 1-mm mesh screen eliminates fibers, wood, and leaves that come from the mine quarry. The final overflow passes through the 0.1-mm safety screen (mica screen) and then goes to the thickener. Sludge from the thickener is filtered in automatic filter presses and dried in apron-type dryers. The underflows from the three washing stages, being feldspar, are dewatered on vacuum drum filters.

In kaolin refining plants, hydrocyclones do the main job. In most other mineral treatment plants, they are auxiliary equipment, but, nevertheless, they may be important for achieving optimum results in product quality and yield. □

References

1) Trawinski, H., "Grouped Hydrocyclones for the Beneficiation of Raw Materials," INTERCERAM, Vol. 22, 1973, No. 3.
2) Bradley, D., and D. J. Pulling, "Flow Patterns in the Hydraulic Cyclone and their Interpretation in Terms of Performance," Trans. Inst. Chem. Engrs., Vol. 37, 1959, pp 34-45.
3) Krijgsman, C., "De Toepassing van de Centrifugaalkracht in Moderne Kolenwasserijen," Woordrachten Koninklijk Instituut van Ingenieurs Nederland, Vol. 1, 1949, No. 5, 691-907.
4) Eder, Th., "Probleme der Trennschärfe," AUFBER. TECHNIK, Vol. 2, 1961, pp 104-9, 36-48, 313-21, 484-95.
5) Trawinski, H., "A Calculation for Elutriation," INTERCERAM, Vol. 19, 1970, No. 1, pp 51-56.
6) Trawinski, H., "Behandlung fester Stoffe in Flüssigkeits-Suspensionen," CHEMIE-INGENIEUR-TECHNIK, Vol. 29, 1957, No. 5, pp 330-32.
7) Trawinski, H., "Näherungssätze zur Berechnung wichtiger Betriebsdaten für Hydrozyklone und Zentrifugen," CHEM.-ING.-TECHN., Vol. 30, 1958, pp 85-95.
8) Trawinski, H., "Die Aufbereitung von Kaolin," Handbuch der Keramik, 1973, Verlag Schmid, Freiburg/Br.
9) Trawinski, H., "Nassklassieren von feinkörnigem Gut, besonders in Mahlkreisläufen," TECHN. MITT., Vol. 59, 1966, No. 5, pp 249-57.
10) Trawinski, H., "The Wet Beneficiation of Kaolin (China-Clay)," INTERCERAM, Vol. 17, 1968, No. 4, and Vol. 18, 1969, No. 1.
11) Trawinski H., and F. Donhauser, "Der Hydrozyklon und seine Anwendungen in der Aufbereitung von Kaolin," SILIKAT-JOURNAL, Vol. 11, 1972, No. 8, pp 244-50.
12) Trawinski, H., "Kombinationsschaltungen von Apparaten zur mechan. Trennung fest-flüssiger Mischsysteme," CHEM. ING.-TECHN., Vol. 32, 1960, No. 9, pp 576-81.
13) Bath, M. D., A. J. Duncan, and E. R. Rudolph, "Some Factors Influencing Gold Recovery by Gravity Concentration," J. SOUTH AFRIC. MIN. MET., Vol. 73, 1973, No. 11, pp 363-84.
14) Trawinski, H., "Die Gegenstrom-Waschung von eingedickten Suspensionen durch Anwendung wiederholter Sedimentation," VERFAHRENSTECHNIK, Vol. 8, 1974, No. 1.
15) Trawinski, H., "Allgemeines über die Anwendungen des Hydrozyklons in der Erzaufbereitung," ERZMETALL, Vol. 7, 1954, No. 12, pp 537-40.
16) Trawinski, H., "Aufstromklassierer," Beitrag zu Bd. 11 in Ullmanns Enzyklopädie der Techn. Chemie, S. 70/80, Verlag Chemie, 1972.
17) Trawinski, H., "Practical Aspects of the Design and Industrial Application of the Hydrocyclone," FILTRATION & SEPARATION, Vol. 6, 1969, Jul/Aug., pp 361-67, and Nov/Dec., pp 651-57.
18) Trawinski, H., "Generationsgerechte Schaltungen bei der Vielstufenschlämmung mit Stromklassierern, insbesondere in der Kaolin-Industrie," KERAMISCHE ZEITSCHRIFT, Vol. 16, 1964, No. 1, pp 20-24, and No. 2, pp 74-77.

Tilden's major processing breakthrough capitalizes on selective flocculation and flotation of low grade, fine grained, nonmagnetic ores.

Cleveland-Cliffs takes the wraps off revolutionary new Tilden iron ore process

Robert Sisselman, Associate editor

HUGE TONNAGES OF fine grained, low grade hematite in the iron ranges of Michigan and Minnesota may now respond favorably to beneficiation, thanks to the development of a prototype hydrometallurgical process in use at the recently dedicated $200 million Tilden mine in National Mine, Mich. Twenty-five years of joint research and testing by the US Bureau of Mines and The Cleveland-Cliffs Iron Co. were required to perfect the process, which capitalizes on selective flocculation and froth flotation to efficiently remove siliceous slimes from iron ore.

Tilden's novel new technology consists essentially of fine grinding ore to liberate the iron fraction from the siliceous gangue, selective flocculation of the hematite, desliming of finely dispersed silica, and removal of the siliceous gangue from hematite via froth flotation. The predominantly nonmagnetic iron mineral fraction in the Tilden ore precludes the use of magnetic separation, as practiced "next door" at Cliffs' Empire mine in Palmer, Mich., and in many of Minnesota's Mesabi Range operations.

Selective flocculation-flotation is not just a technological breakthrough. It is equally important in the socioeconomic scheme, for the process promises to revitalize the iron mining industry of Michigan's Upper Peninsula. Moreover, according to officials of Cleveland-Cliffs, which is both manager of Tilden and part owner (20%), this nifty new twist in processing low grade iron ores is expected to apply, in equivalent fashion, to other low grade hematite, martite, goethite, and magnetite reserves on the Marquette Range of Michigan. Beyond this lies the vast, unexposed potential of the Mesabi, where an estimated reservoir of 10 to 15 billion tons of low grade, nonmagnetic material is thought to be amenable to Tilden-type processing. The tonnage is "perhaps much more than that if, in the future, these orebodies are followed downdip," surmised one Cliffs official.

Soaring project price tags spurred Tilden's backers to put together a financing package with the aid of 10 banks and four insurance companies. Cliffs put up 5% of the $200 million-plus in cash and took notes for the remainder with its partners: Algoma Steel Corp., 30%; Jones and Laughlin Steel Corp., 27%; The Steel Co. of Canada, 10%; Wheeling-Pittsburgh Steel Corp., 8%; and Sharon Steel Corp., 5%.

Tilden is expected to reach its budgeted production rate of 4 million ltpy in pellets late in 1975, drawing on reserves of more than 1 billion tons of hematite ore averaging 36% iron and 45% silica.

However, an even bigger role is envisioned for the newest North American iron mine. Management plans to expand pellet production by another 4 million ltpy in a second stage "Tilden II," due on line by January 1, 1979. Although formal announcement of Tilden II startup plans has yet to be made, excavation work began this past summer in preparation for an expansion of concentrating and pelletizing facilities. Tilden II will be at the top of the agenda when the partners assemble at their semiannual meeting next month, and a formal announcement on expansion plans is expected before the end of the year.

"The cost will be more than $300 million for Tilden II, in spite of the fact that we don't have to duplicate the primary crushers, crude ore conveyor, and other major items," said H. Stuart Harrison, chairman and chief executive officer of Cleveland-Cliffs, during dedication ceremonies at Tilden in mid-August.

Tilden's process is competitive with magnetic taconite operations, so even with higher costs at the mine, management is obtaining a higher-iron-content pellet (65% Fe), "for which we will receive 47.2¢ per iron unit, the highest iron unit pellet we have," Harrison added.

The principals in Tilden will carefully weigh the economics of expansion before pushing ahead. "Today the steel industry is in a period of delayed recession," observed Harrison. "Consequently, if one is operating an industry at 60% of capacity, no one is going to be all that enthusiastic about putting money into expansions."

In actuality, many steel companies are not cutting back on expansion programs, but instead are delaying them. The prospects down the road are reflected in Cliffs' plans for "Tilden III," the final expansion at Tilden, which Harrison refers to as "just a gleam in our eye." Tilden III may come to fruition sometime in the early 1980s, contributing another 4 million ltpy in pellet capacity and pushing the Tilden total to 12 million ltpy. The facility would then become Cliffs' largest property, outproducing both the Robe River project in Western Australia and the Empire mine in Michigan. Application of the Tilden process to low grade Michigan ores would transform the Marquette Range from an annual producer of an expected 14.5 million ltpy in 1975 to more than 26.5 million ltpy with the advent of Tilden III.

Tilden process prolongs life on the Marquette

The Marquette Range has seen few developments as exciting as the Tilden process since the introduction of pelletizing of nonmagnetic taconite ores in the late 1950s, a feat in which Cliffs shared. And nothing is soon likely to top the Tilden act, latest in a series of events that bode well for

Six 27½-ft-dia x 14½-ft autogenous mills grind ore at 226 tph per line, and discharge into 12 15½-ft-dia pebble mills.

the North American iron ore industry in general and that will, at the very least, prolong the life of the iron mining industry in the Upper Peninsula. With the opening of the Empire mine, the last of the Marquette Range major magnetic holdings were developed. Without a new and economic means of beneficiating the estimated 3 billion tons of nonmagnetic resources on the Marquette, there would likely have been a gradual phaseout of mining activity for Cliffs, which has mined the Range for 125 years and provides a livelihood for nearly one-third the residents of the Upper Peninsula.

Not an "overnight success" by any means, the Tilden process was the culmination of 25 years of research and pilot trials performed by Cliffs at its Ishpeming laboratory in Michigan and by the USBM at its Twin Cities Research Center in Minneapolis, Minn. The USBM holds the patents on the selective flocculation process, which are available to interested parties at no charge.

In tandem, desliming and froth flotation are unique to a system that begins when crushed ore is conveyed to the covered ore storage building, having a combined live and dead capacity of about 200,000 lt. Gravity feeds the crude into six lines of autogenous mills. Each of the mills accepts coarse feed at an average rate of 226 tph.

Cliffs does not attempt to crush fine ore in its 60 x 109-in. Allis-Chalmers gyratory unit; instead, it is trying to leave an ample supply of 10-in. chunks in the crude, essential to the effective operation of Tilden's fully autogenous milling system. In addition to maintaining size consistency, the pit staff of 190 is responsible for monitoring hardness and keeping a uniform iron analysis of 36% entering the crusher.

Prior to entry of ore into the grinding section, sodium hydroxide is added for pH control. Management wants to run the grind on the basic side, with a pH of about 10.8 be-

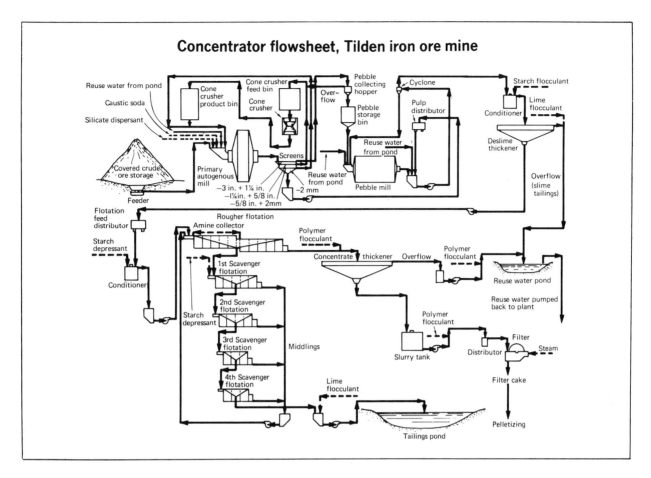

Concentrator flowsheet, Tilden iron ore mine

fore the pulp is run into deslime thickeners. Along with the sodium hydroxide, sodium silicate is added to disperse the fine silica particles in the desliming stage. The ore-reagent mixture is sent through the primary autogenous circuit at the rate of 29,000 tpd, and into 12 Nordberg secondary pebble mills. Each pair of pebble mills is driven by 2,520-hp electric motors. Primary autogenous grinding reduces the ore to minus 1/16 in., and some of the coarse oversize is recycled, while undersize is fed to the pebble circuit, where ore is further reduced to 80% minus 500 mesh. Pebbles, running up to 3-in., are screened from the autogenous mills and used as grinding media. As the pebbles wear out, they become part of the ore stream.

The pebble mills are operated in closed circuit with a total of 108 15-in. Krebs cyclones, each of the 12 mills paired with nine cyclones.

Cooked cornstarch is a key ingredient in process

Fine grind is sent to cyclones where overflow is channeled into 12 Eimco 55-ft-dia deslime thickener tanks, along with cooked cornstarch to flocculate the finely ground iron particles.

"What we're doing in this deslime thickener," explained Hugh Leach, vice president of research and development for Cleveland-Cliffs, "is to flocculate the iron-bearing particles. When the flocs are of sufficiently large size they will sink against a slowly rising column of water and report in the thickener underflow. The silica, on the other hand, is maintained as separate discrete particles, dispersed in the thickeners with the aid of the sodium silicate reagent added during primary grinding."

The bulk of the silica slime, substantially finer than 500 mesh, is removed in the deslime thickeners, where it is overflowed with the water stream and reports to tailings.

Approximately 20% of the material in the thickeners is rejected at 12.5% iron content, the loss being only approximately 7% of the iron in the crude ore.

Without the deslime and flocculation stage, flotation would not be very effective—as the presence of slimes creates a twofold problem: they interfere with the flotation process itself, and, because of their size, they require an excessive amount of reagent.

Underflow from the deslime tanks is sent through a conditioning step where additional starch is added to maintain flocculation and depress the iron during flotation.

Tilden's flotation machines are the largest used in the iron ore industry. Five stages of flotation (a total of 150 Wemco units spread over six plant lines) are required to produce an acceptable tailing and a final concentrate suitable for agglomeration. Conditioners send the ore into rougher flotation, where amine is added as a silica collector, plus additional cooked cornstarch. Tailings from the rougher flotation run through four stages of scavenging, from which middlings are recycled to the rougher circuit.

Concentrate discharging from the rougher flotation as underflow is dewatered to 60-70% solids in thickeners before steam filtration. Final tailings, flocced by lime, are sent by gravity to the tailings pond.

Tilden's clarification system recirculates 95% of process water. Nearly 6,200 gpm of makeup water are piped into the plant from the primary water source, the newly created Greenwood Reservoir, approximately 7 mi from Tilden.

Steam filtering: unique in iron ore industry

One unique feature of the Tilden plant is the use of steam in filtering. Thickener underflow at 30% moisture enters the filters—24 eight-disc units 8 ft 10 in. in diameter. Steam filtering dewaters the concentrate to 10-11%. Tilden's filter discs are all steam hooded. The steam raises water temperature in the filter cake and reduces its surface tension, thereby freeing two-thirds of the water content and producing a product suitable for either storage or balling.

The steam-assisted filtration was a calculated gamble for Cliffs and its partners, which elected to use the system after successful pilot scale trials.

"We had the alternatives of going to steam or to ordinary filtering methods, reducing moisture down to 15%, then to about 10% in some type of rotary dryer," explained Hugh Leach, "but decided this was effective, simpler, and more trouble-free."

Pellet operation is imposing in size

The scale of Tilden's pelletizing equipment is highly impressive—including the largest-diameter rotary pelletizing kiln in the world (160 ft long with an inner diameter of 25 ft). The grate feeding into the kiln is 18 ft 6 in. wide and 210 ft long, and has 3½ updraft drying wind boxes, 7½ downdraft drying wind boxes, and eight preheat wind boxes. A dust collector is positioned at the preheat section, and electrostatic precipitators remove more than 99% of the particulates from the kiln's waste gases.

Concentrate, mixed with 0.5-1.0% bentonite binder, is balled in seven 12-ft-dia x 33-ft-long balling drums, dried, and then preheated to 1,800°F on the grate and sent at 2,400°F through the kiln at 12,400 ltpd. Product—pellets of 65% iron and 5% silica—is cooled in a 66-ft-dia annular cooler, the largest of its type in the iron ore industry.

Tilden's kiln and steam boilers will be fueled with No. 4 fuel oil received by truck and stored prior to use in a 1.5-million-gal tank.

Finished product is sent either to the 1.3-million-ton pellet stockpile or to the 13,200-ton pellet load-out bin. The load-out bin discharges into 70- to 80-ton rail cars for shipment 14 mi to the port of Marquette, or 60 mi to Escanaba, and then to the partners.

In anticipation of power requirements for both the Empire expansion (1.3 million ltpy of pellets) and the coming on stream of Tilden, Cliffs and its partners constructed two 80-Mw power plants at Presque Isle, Mich. Two additional 80-Mw units will be built to accommodate Tilden II.

Manmade Greenwood Reservoir provides mill water

Cliffs and partners also spent about $17 million of the $200 million price tag of the project on environmental quality controls. The investment included equipment for air and water pollution abatement, with emphasis on dust control and water clarification systems.

The Greenwood Reservoir was also created as the source of water for Tilden. The Tilden operation requires 86,000 gpm water in the concentrator and pellet plant, of which about 6,200 gpm is makeup water. The present water supply was planned to accommodate the full 12 million tons of annual pellet production that may be realized during the early 1980s.

The 1,400-acre reservoir stores water from high flow periods and diverts authorized quantities to the Tilden plant. It impounds 22,000 acre-ft of water and has a shoreline of 26 mi, excluding 13 islands that provide an additional 11 mi of shoreline.

Water is released from the reservoir at the main dam through any or all of the four hydraulically controlled sluice gates, installed at different elevations on an inclined pipe placed in concrete against the north abutment of the main dam.

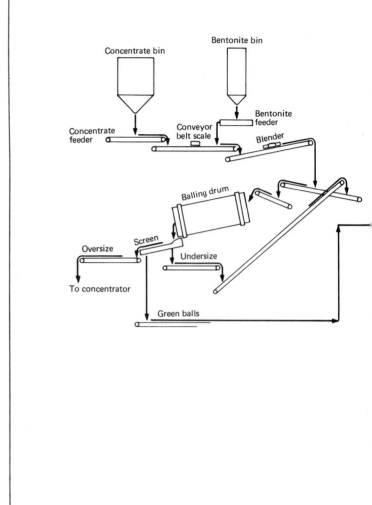

The water flows through the dam in a concrete-embedded 96-in.-dia pipe and into the afterbay. This four-part outlet permits the selection of optimum-temperature water for release and the conservation of colder water for release during the summer months.

A thermograph is installed at the discharge into the afterbay as an aid to water temperature management. The exact quantity of water released into the afterbay is controlled by a 24-in. butterfly valve and also by a float-operated 17-in. hollow cone valve that discharges in a circular pattern above the water surface to aerate the water. With the hollow cone valve in operation, a constant water surface elevation will automatically be maintained in the afterbay.

Both the 24-cu-ft-per-sec release of water to the Escanaba River and the diversion of process water to the plant will come from the afterbay. Process water is diverted by gravity from the lower arm of the afterbay through a 4,000-ft pipeline into Green Creek, which flows into the Schweitzer Reservoir. A pumping station and pipeline convey the water ½ mi from the Schweitzer to the re-use basin, and 1.5 mi to the Tilden mine.

The USGS maintains continuous-recording stream-gauging stations at four locations.

Water leaving the Tilden tailings basin enters Warner Creek, which flows into the East Branch of the Escanaba River. Thus, water diverted from the Middle Branch finds its way to the parent river downstream.

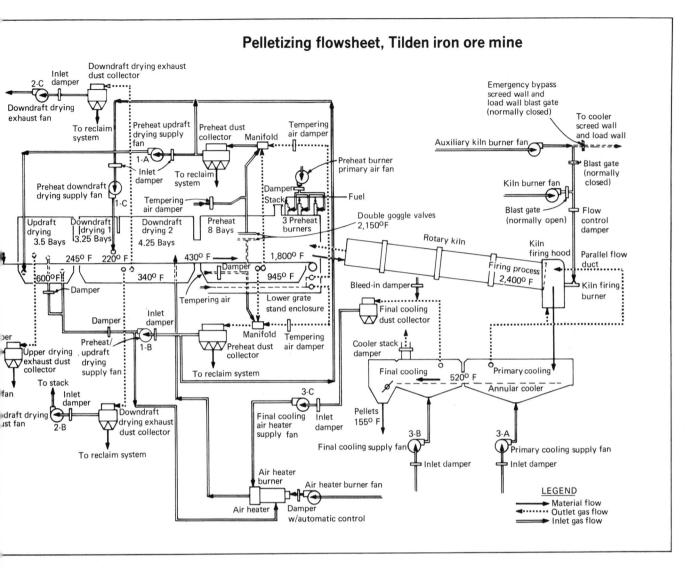

Pelletizing flowsheet, Tilden iron ore mine

Cliffs worked on Tilden process for 25 years

Research began in 1949 to "unlock" Marquette Range reserves of low grade, nonmagnetic material, the existence of which had been known for over 100 years. Laboratory scale work continued on an intermittent basis until 1963, when pilot plant trials were also conducted.

Pilot plant operations resumed in 1965, and in 1968 a larger pilot facility (5-8 tph) was erected. Over 45,000 lt of various crude ore samples from Tilden's land holdings were processed through the facility. In 1966 the USBM, in a cooperative agreement with Cleveland-Cliffs, began testing Tilden ore in a pilot plant at the Twin Cities Research Center in Minneapolis, Minn. Previous to this, the Bureau of Mines had successfully applied to low grade iron ores the principle of selective flocculation and desliming.

Under the direction of Cliffs, design and construction for the entire project was provided by Kaiser Engineers. Allis-Chalmers supplied design detail and pelletizing equipment, including the grate-kiln system.

Preliminary design work started in 1971, and construction commenced in February of 1972. At the peak of activity in the summer of 1973 and throughout most of 1974, up to 1,400 workers were engaged by contractors and subcontractors at the site.

On October 1, 1974, the first crude ore was fed to the primary crusher, and later in the month Tilden's initial two autogenous grinding lines were started up in the concentrator. Three additional circuits came on in November and by December 9, all six lines were operating in the concentrator.

The first pellets were produced on December 11, 1974, and on December 17, the initial trainload of product was railed from the mine to Marquette, Mich., for delivery to the Algoma Steel Corp. Ltd. at Sault Ste. Marie, Ont.

Billion-ton Tilden may be good for 90 to 95 years

Holding more than 1 billion tons of crude ore reserves, the Tilden orebody is essentially a martite chert, or a hematite after magnetite, striking 80° east and dipping 30° to 40° in a northwesterly direction. Intermittently throughout the ore zone, which grades 36% iron, intrusions of meta-diabase occur, greenish in color. The hanging wall in the ore zone is the diabase, whereas the footwall—both geologic and mining—consists of the Palmer gneiss.

Diamond drilling of 113,000 ft conducted at Tilden outlined the billion tons of low grade ore, and preproduction work began in March 1972 with stripping of 4.4 million cu yd of glacial overburden.

Proven and probable ore reserves, adequate to produce a total of over 360 million tons in pellets, would sustain mining for 90 to 95 years at current levels of production. Of course, projected life of the mine will be shortened considerably when Tilden II and III expansions come on line.

Ultimately, the Tilden pit will reach a maximum width

Ore pulp treated with sodium hydroxide, sodium silicate, and cooked corn starch is fed to twelve 55-ft-dia desliming tanks.

Six lines of 500-cu-ft flotation machines draw out iron fraction as underflow and send it to two 150-ft-dia thickeners.

Steam filtration—unique to the iron ore industry—reduces moisture in filter cake to preballing level of 10½%.

of 4,400 to 4,500 ft and a total east-west length of 1½ mi. Pit excavation began at an elevation of plus 1,600 ft and is planned to bottom out at 200 ft above sea level for an ultimate depth of 1,400 ft.

Five 45-ft-high benches are now being mined at the rate of 18,400 tpd. Haulage roads are roughly 100 ft wide, with a maximum 8% grade, and a downhill haulage distance of 2,800 ft to the primary crusher. The downhill grade will prevail for about six years at current mining rates.

Drilling is accomplished on 30- to 35-ft spacings by three 12¼-in. rotary drills. In blasting the ore, slurry and prills are loaded into 50-ft holes and triggered in 25-millisecond delays to prevent vibrations from disturbing neighboring communities. All blasts are recorded on seismographs in the towns of National Mine and Ishpeming to make certain that no disturbance results. Ore is carefully blasted to provide proper chunk availability for the fully autogenous grinding system, and crude ore blending in the pit is necessary to reach a uniform size and assay feed to the mill.

Six Bucyrus Erie electric shovels—five 10-yd 195B models and one 5-yd 150B model—are employed to load ore into a fleet of fifteen 75-ton Wabco and Dart trucks. Two 12-cu-yd Michigan rubber-tired front-end loaders are also used for loading ore into trucks and pellets into rail cars. Tilden maintains 10 of the haulage trucks in production on an 8-hr shift, with additional units either in backup or in repair.

The maintenance shop houses 20 work bays large enough to handle 200-ton trucks, and in view of imminent expansion under Tilden II, trucks of this size may be added. For the present, however, the 75-ton haulers are considered a definite plus in blending ore. In addition to facilities for handling drills, trucks, dozers, and loaders, the maintenance building also contains offices and dry facilities for the approximately 190 pit personnel.

Tilden produces ore on two shifts daily and removes overburden during three shifts, operating the mine around the clock, seven days a week, both on ore production and stripping.

The primary 60-in. gyratory crusher has a rock box capacity of 340 tons of crude ore. Truck boxes are heated by the vehicles' exhaust to prevent ore freezing during the winter months, when the temperature dips down to –30° to –40°F.

Crushed to minus 10 in., the ore is conveyed to the covered 200,000-ton-capacity ore storage building. There it awaits Tilden's novel new approach to beneficiation before being pelletized.

Today Tilden . . . tomorrow Cascade

The next logical development step for Cleveland-Cliffs is Cascade, an orebody similar in mineralogy to Tilden, located on the Marquette Range. According to chairman H. Stuart Harrison, Cascade "will undoubtedly be our next venture into iron ore."

The 160-million-ton orebody has "sufficient proven ore reserves to supply a 4-million-ltpy operation for 30 years, meeting our criterion for considering a new venture," revealed Hugh Leach. "And we have reason to believe that we may nearly double that reserve."

Cliffs officials have found that some portions of the Marquette Range's low grade iron resources will not respond adequately to the Tilden flow scheme—either recovery is too poor or grade of concentrate is too low, or both. The softer goethite ores of the Marquette, for example, do not respond well to this treatment, probably because of the fine-grained nature of the rock. There are "some very substantial quantities of that type of ore on the Marquette," according to Leach.

"On the whole, however, the Tilden process is a versatile one, and will work on hematite, martite, goethite, and even magnetite. . . .with, of course, the proper adjustments in the process chemistry." □

A simple equation for CCD calculations

P. M. Page, technical director, metallurgy, Holmes & Narver, Inc.

METALLURGICAL PROCESS ENGINEERS are familiar with the problems of running a material balance for a countercurrent decantation (CCD) system when a large number of stages are involved. A simple, generalized formula to eliminate the tedium and the potential for error is offered here as a new tool for the process metallurgist.

Material balance calculations are required for CCD systems, as such systems are a nearly inevitable part of agitated or Pachuca leaching plants. Fig. 1 shows a leach slurry successively diluted and rethickened, the dilution or wash water flowing countercurrent to the slurry. The concentration of valuable material in solution in the slurry is known from leaching. It is known also for the wash liquor flowing into stage Z, but nowhere else. Flow rates are also known, but the material balance equation for each thickener cannot be solved directly because it contains the concentration for at least one other stage.

The engineer's usual approach is to write a balance equation for each stage. Since the number of unknowns (the concentration in each stage) equals the number of equations, the equations are solved simultaneously. For operations of even three or four stages, this solution represents a moderate chore. For seven or eight stages—as may become typical of new uranium mills—hand calculations of the numerous simultaneous equations are tedious and prone to error.

In an attempt to determine whether a simple, generalized formula might be written in terms of wash ratio and number of stages, the first step was to limit consideration to the simplest but most common case. (The wash ratio is defined as the wash water flow divided by the slurry liquor flow.) Leaching is assumed to be complete prior to the CCD circuit; that is, no material passes into solution during washing. The mixing of slurry and wash liquor in each stage is assumed complete. The flow rate of solution in the incoming leach slurry is the same as in each of the thickener underflows, and the wash water flow equals each of the thickener overflows. There is no allowance for evaporation nor for any addition of extraneous streams. Finally, for convenience only, the concentration of valuable material in the incoming wash water was taken as zero, and the concentration in the feed slurry liquor as unity.

Table 1 shows the calculated concentration in the slurry liquor from the final thickener (the same as the concentration within the thickener) for wash ratios of 1, 2, and 3, as determined by a minicomputer program. The denominators are all exact integers to at least four decimal places, suggesting that a simple relationship must exist.

If we call the wash ratio *WR* and solve a generalized set of simultaneous equations for two stages, the concentration in stage Z is:

$$C_z = \frac{1}{1 + WR + WR^2}$$

For three stages, it is derived as:

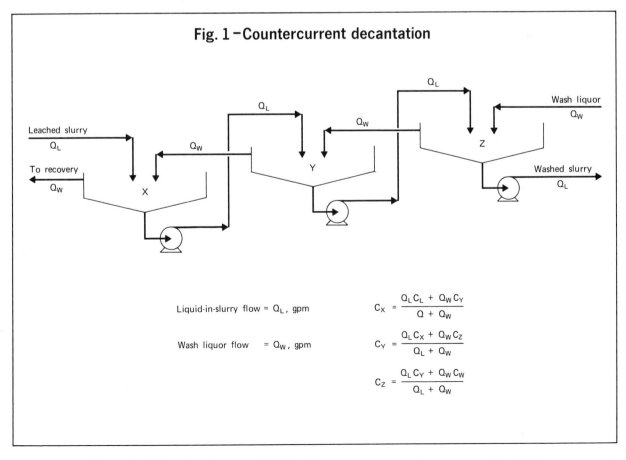

Fig. 1 – Countercurrent decantation

Liquid-in-slurry flow = Q_L, gpm

Wash liquor flow = Q_W, gpm

$$C_X = \frac{Q_L C_L + Q_W C_Y}{Q + Q_W}$$

$$C_Y = \frac{Q_L C_X + Q_W C_Z}{Q_L + Q_W}$$

$$C_Z = \frac{Q_L C_Y + Q_W C_W}{Q_L + Q_W}$$

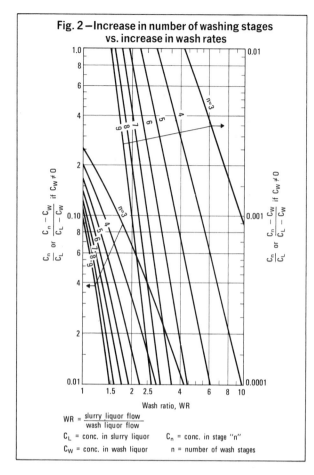

Fig. 2—Increase in number of washing stages vs. increase in wash rates

$$WR = \frac{\text{slurry liquor flow}}{\text{wash liquor flow}}$$

C_L = conc. in slurry liquor C_n = conc. in stage "n"

C_W = conc. in wash liquor n = number of wash stages

Table 1—Calculated concentration in slurry liquor from final thickener

(concentration in feed slurry liquor = 1.0)

Number of stages	Wash ratio 1	2	3
2	$1/3$	$1/7$	$1/13$
3	$1/4$	$1/15$	$1/40$
4	$1/5$	$1/31$	$1/121$
5	$1/6$	$1/63$	$1/364$

Table 2—Calculations for sample CCD problem, 11 stages

Inputs	Outputs	Thickener no
Wash ratio WR = Q_W/Q_L = 2.73	$C_n = 7.26 \times 10^{-5}$	11
C_L = 5.210 gpl	$C_n - 1 = 2.16 \times 10^{-4}$	10
$C_W = 2 \times 10^{-5}$ gpl	$C_n - 2 = 6.08 \times 10^{-4}$	9
No. of stages: 11	$C_n - 3 = 1.68 \times 10^{-3}$	8
	$C_n - 4 = 4.60 \times 10^{-3}$	7
	$C_n - 5 = 1.26 \times 10^{-2}$	6
	$C_n - 6 = 3.43 \times 10^{-2}$	5
	$C_n - 7 = 9.38 \times 10^{-2}$	4
	$C_n - 8 = 0.256$	3
	$C_n - 9 = 0.699$	2
	$C_n - 10 = 1.91$	1
	$C_n - 11 = C_L = 5.21$	

$$C_z = \frac{1}{1 + WR + WR^2 + WR^3}$$

And for four stages, it works out (very tediously) as:

$$C_z = \frac{1}{1 + WR + WR^2 + WR^3 + WR^4}$$

It appears that the general equation for n stages is:

$$C_z = \frac{1}{1 + WR + WR^2 + \ldots + WR^n}$$

The calculations were applied to five stages and the results were compared with those generated by a pocket calculator's simultaneous equation program. The results matched exactly.

If incoming wash liquor has a concentration other than zero, that concentration can be considered an additive to all solutions in the system—a sort of invariable property. For example, if the leach liquor contains 5.3 gpl and the wash liquor contains 0.14 gpl, it can be said that the leach liquor has a 0.14-gpl fixed property and 5.16-gpl effectively variable condition. If C_L equals the concentration of the leach liquor and C_W is the corresponding wash concentration, then the generalized version of our presumed relation is:

$$C_n = \frac{C_L - C_W}{1 + WR + WR^2 + \ldots + WR^n} + C_W$$

If C_n is thus determined, the balance around thickener Z

contains only one unknown, C_Y, which is thus determined. This permits, in turn, solution of the balance around thickener Y, yielding the value of C_X. This process can be continued back to the first thickener, which can be balanced to determine C_W, which must match the known value of C_W. If it does, C_n was obviously determined correctly.

As a test, two simple pocket calculator programs were written. The first determined C_n according to the above presumed formula. The second program successively balanced around each of the thickeners, giving C_Y, C_X, etc., and eventually the corresponding value of C_W. An arbitrary problem of 11 stages was run as shown in Table 2, and the calculated value of C_W matched exactly the input value.

While the proposed equation has not been rigorously derived by a mathematician's standards, it has been so proven through four stages and experimentally verified as exact through 11 stages. The equation should therefore be valid for CCD process calculations, particularly since calculation of the initial leach liquor concentration will always provide an almost automatic exact check.

It is obvious from the equation that increased recovery of values from the process can be obtained either by increasing the number of wash stages or by increasing the wash ratio. The latter choice requires a larger quantity of liquor to be processed, and therefore a more costly solvent (or other) extraction plant. To evaluate the relative merits of an additional thickener vs. a higher wash ratio, the equation has been plotted in Fig. 2. The graph conveniently shows that if it is desired that the slurry-liquor-to-tailings concentration be no more than 1/500th of the leach liquor concentration (C_n/C_L = 0.002), eight stages can be used at a wash ratio of 2.0, seven stages at a wash ratio of 2.25, or five stages at a wash ratio of 3.2. □

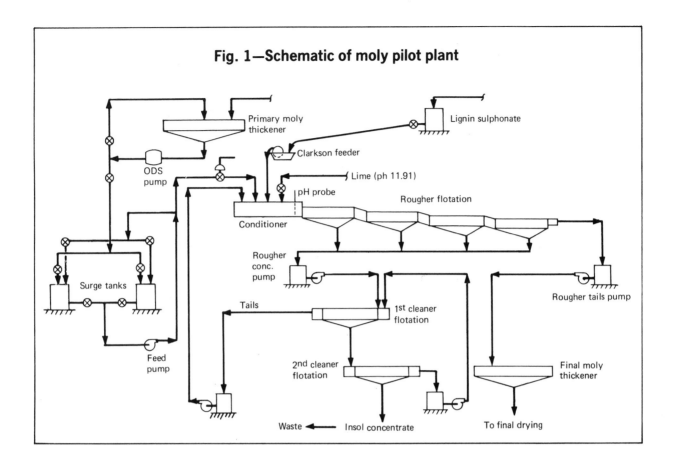

Fig. 1—Schematic of moly pilot plant

Use of lignin sulphonate as moly depressant boosts recovery at Twin Buttes

T. O. Hiscox, Caribou concentrator superintendent, Bathurst, N. B.; and **Dr. M. C. Kuhn,** manager, process technology Natural Resources Group, The Anaconda Co.

T. B. Buza, technical service metallurgist, Water Treating and Mining Chemicals Div., American Cyanamid Co.

A NEW SYSTEM USING LIGNIN SULPHONATE to depress molybdenum has allowed increased production of salable by-product molybdenum concentrates at the Twin Buttes complex in Arizona. In searching for reagents to separate insolubles—including clays and talc minerals—from molybdenum concentrates at Twin Buttes, The Anaconda Co.'s Metallurgical Research Department discovered that large quantities of lignin sulphonate, in combination with a high-pH milk-of-lime, depressed the molybdenite while allowing talcs and clays to float.

The Twin Buttes property is a typical porphyry copper operation now owned by Anamax, an Anaconda-Amax joint venture. Open-pit mining recovers ore for treatment in a 30,000-tpd flotation concentrator. As is common at most copper operations producing molybdenum, molybdenite (MoS_2) is recovered by flotation along with the copper minerals in the concentrator, resulting in a copper-moly concentrate. Molybdenum values are then separated from the copper in a concentrate by-products plant.

The use of lignin sulphonate to depress moly originated as a response to problems experienced in the operation of the Twin Buttes moly plant. After extensive laboratory testing and further testing and refinement on a pilot plant

scale (Fig. 1), this process is now a part of the installation.

The Twin Buttes moly plant consists of two circuits: a primary circuit, which separates molybdenite from the copper sulphides, and an insoluble circuit, which upgrades the moly concentrate.

Copper-moly concentrate is fed after thickening to the head of the primary circuit, where it is conditioned with sodium hydrosulphide (NaHS), then processed through a rougher and seven stages of countercurrent cleaner flotation. Here copper minerals are depressed, and moly is recovered as a primary concentrate. Tailings from this circuit are sent to the final copper spray dryer, while the molybdenite concentrate is either sent to final moly spray dryers or treated in the insol circuit for further upgrading.

The insol circuit as originally installed consisted of a thickener, a spray dryer, and two stages of flotation (Fig. 2). The pulp from the thickener was spray dried to remove the collectors from the sulphide mineral surfaces. The two flotation stages then floated the gangue and discarded it, while the moly tails were sent to the final dryers.

Although the original insol circuit produced good metallurgical results (Table 1), a problem developed in the capacity of the system to treat the volume of primary con-

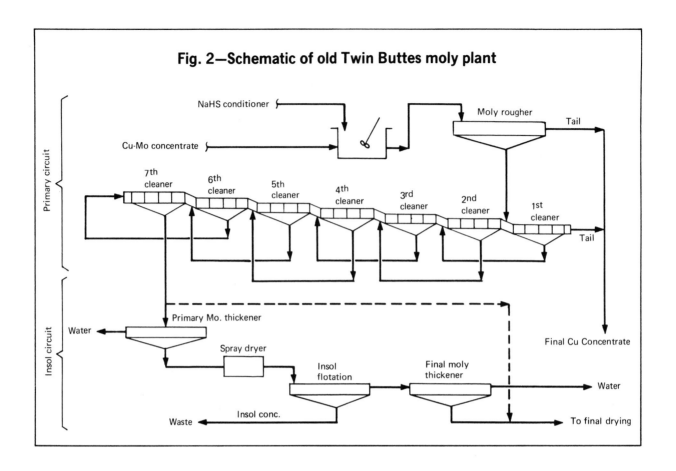

Fig. 2—Schematic of old Twin Buttes moly plant

Table 1—Average results, spray dryer insol circuit

	% Assay		% Distribution	
	Mo	Insol	Mo	Insol
Insol concentrate	11.52	61.04	14.49	76.86
Moly concentrate	51.10	7.44	85.51	23.14
Feed	38.20	25.63	100.00	100.00

Table 2—Typical open-circuit flotation test results

	% Assay			% Distribution		
	Mo	Insol	Cu	Mo	Insol	Cu
Sample 1						
First cleaner conc.	4.06	80.40	1.72	6.10	75.00	44.70
First cleaner tail	16.80	52.30	1.02	2.90	5.60	4.10
Rougher tail	46.20	15.90	0.84	91.00	19.40	51.20
Calculated head	27.37	44.40	1.21			
Sample 2						
Second cleaner conc.	1.62	74.00	1.49	0.78	63.02	26.20
Second cleaner tail	21.40	38.90	1.14	1.66	5.34	3.24
First cleaner tail	32.40	31.20	1.06	4.81	8.17	5.74
Rougher tail	49.50	7.10	0.95	92.74	23.47	64.82
Calculated head	38.72	21.95	1.06			
Sample 3						
First cleaner conc.	12.70	55.40	3.08	1.90	37.10	10.20
First cleaner tail	43.70	18.30	16.00	6.10	11.40	49.80
Rougher tail	51.30	6.30	1.00	92.00	51.50	40.00
Calculated head	48.10	10.50	2.15			

centrate produced. Due to the variable nature of the Twin Buttes ore, the gangue at times contains amounts of talc-type layered silicates and alumina clays, such as montmorillonite, in addition to the normal carbonates and silicates. The layered silicates and clays are naturally floating and report to the primary concentrate along with the molybdenite. When present, these gangues dilute the moly concentrate, increase the volume, and may cause the grade obtained to drop as low as 15% Mo.

The original design specifications at Twin Buttes provided for a 1,200-tpd feed of copper-moly concentrate containing 1% Mo. The primary circuit was expected to produce approximately 24 tpd of moly concentrate, and the insol circuit spray dryer was designed to handle this load. However, depending on ore type and concentrator performance, the feed to the primary circuit may contain up to 2% Mo at feed rates over 1,400 tpd. This increased production, along with increased bulk due to dilution of the primary concentrate, may deliver over 75 tpd to the insol circuit. At this production level, the insol circuit was overloaded, with the spray dryer being the bottleneck.

The problem, as presented to the Anaconda laboratories, was to develop a circuit that would produce final grade molybdenum concentrates from these higher tonnage, lower grade primary concentrates.

Lab work develops basic moly-insol circuit

Phase 1 of the laboratory test work centered on finding insol depressing mechanisms that could be employed in the primary circuit to depress the talc and clay minerals. The results were generally not good. Phase 2 centered on insol depressing schemes that would operate on the primary moly concentrate in the insol circuit. For a while these efforts also met with little success.

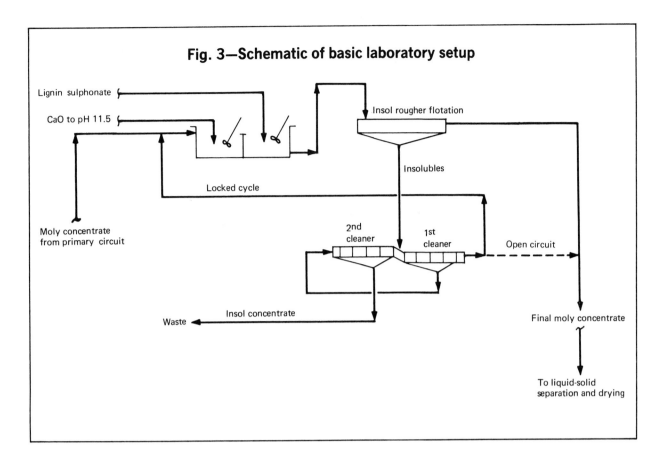

Fig. 3—Schematic of basic laboratory setup

During this second phase, it was discovered that lignin sulphonate, normally an *insolubles* depressant, tended to have the reverse effect when present in large quantities—it depressed molybdenite, which is naturally floatable. Lignin sulphonate, a common by-product of paper pulp mills, has been used on a limited basis in mineral processing as a binder material, dispersant, and emulsifier. The reagent is inexpensive (about 8¢ per lb) and is readily available under many trade names, such as "Orzan" and "Lignosite."

Further laboratory investigation produced very encouraging results using lignin sulphonate to depress the moly while allowing gangue to float. A basic circuit was developed (Fig. 3), in which the primary moly concentrate was conditioned at reduced percent solids with lignin sulphonate and milk-of-lime (CaO). The layered silicates and clays were then floated off in a three-stage countercurrent flotation circuit, which produced a throwaway second cleaner concentrate and a final moly concentrate from the rougher tails. Retention times used in the laboratory circuit were a 20-min conditioner stage, 20-min rougher flotation, 15-min first cleaner, and 10-min second cleaner.

Extensive batch flotation tests were conducted using daily samples from the moly plant's primary circuit. Feed ranging from 27.7% to 48.1% Mo was run through the open circuit, and recovery from the rougher tails was a consistently high 91% to 92.7%. Molybdenum grades obtained were good, ranging from 46.2% to 51.3% Mo (Table 2).

In addition, locked cycle tests were conducted to determine the effects of recirculating products. Locked cycle results show high overall recoveries of 96% to 99%, with moly grades of 47% to 48% obtained (Table 3). A comparison of locked cycle and open circuit results shows that the molybdenum concentrate is slightly lower grade in the locked cycle; however, a much higher recovery (approximately 4% to 8%) is obtained.

Data generated from the laboratory tests indicated that a pilot plant study was justified, and construction of the pilot circuit began in January 1973 at the Twin Buttes moly plant. Design of the pilot circuit was based on the expected feed rate from the high volume, low grade primary concentrates. The availability of salvage equipment from the previous Twin Buttes copper concentrator pilot plant made it advantageous to build the pilot circuit for the total expected feed from the primary circuit (1 to 3 tph), rather than split the flow of primary moly concentrate and use smaller equipment.

The pilot circuit, installed in place of the insol circuit, was started up in early March 1973. (See Fig. 1.) Underflow from the primary moly thickener was fed by ODS pumps to two surge tanks upstream from the conditioner. Feed to the circuit was bled off a recirculating feed loop from the surge tanks into the conditioner, which was constructed using cut-down Agitair No. 48 mechanisms in four compartments to minimize short-circuiting.

The conditioner overflow was fed by gravity to four banks of rougher cells consisting of a total of 20 Galigher No. 24 cells. The rougher tails were pumped directly to the final moly thickener, and the rougher concentrate was pumped to the first cleaner, consisting of eight Galigher No. 24 cells. First cleaner tails were pumped back to the conditioner, and the first cleaner concentrate was fed to the head of the second cleaner. The second cleaner, consisting of six No. 24 cells, produced a tail (pumped back to the first cleaner) and a throwaway concentrate.

Lignin sulphonate was metered to the conditioner by a Clarkson feeder, and milk-of-lime flow was controlled by a ball valve. Other reagents, if required, could have been added using a Clarkson feeder at any point in the circuit.

The pilot plant ran on a limited basis through the end of March, when it underwent circuit modification, including the installation of additional equipment and facilities. It was then restarted in June and ran through the end of July

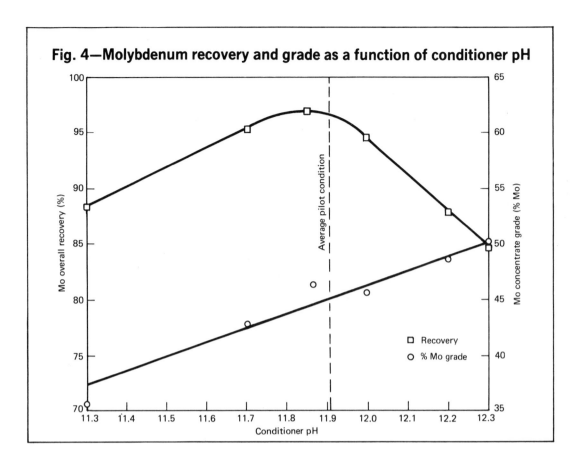

Fig. 4—Molybdenum recovery and grade as a function of conditioner pH

1973. An average feed of 35.21% Mo was treated, producing a 45.87% Mo concentrate at an overall recovery volume of 91.11%. (See Tables 4 and 5.) Since the prime objective in the development of the process was the treatment of tonnages up to 3 tph, a five-shift, continuous production run was made at an average of 3.1 tph, with several shifts running over 4 tph. Metallurgical results compared favorably with the average results of the original spray dryer-insol circuit.

Key variables determined from pilot data

The relationship of key variables (retention time, lignin sulphonate dose, pH level, gangue mineralogy) in the circuit to the grade and recovery achieved was determined from the pilot plant data. In general, the retention time in the conditioner does not appear to be critical above a minimum time of 8 min. The lignin sulphonate dosage is determined primarily by the feed grade to the circuit—lower grade feed requires lesser quantities. At too low a dosage, the flotation of molybdenite is readily apparent in the roughers. At an excessive dosage, a number of problems occur, the most apparent being the formation of a persistent, voluminous foamy froth which defies control. The amount of lignin sulphonate normally used was in the range of 4 to 6 lb per ton.

Data indicate that a maximum recovery is achieved at a pH of 11.91, with higher pH values producing lower recoveries but higher grades (Fig. 4). Froth characteristics are also pH-dependent. A pH below 11.7 produces a persistent, foamy froth, while a value above 12.1 produces a brittle, watery froth that tends to carry slime molybdenite. The desired froth for good differential flotation is a tight, brown, heavy froth with the insol well flocculated.

The gangue mineralogy was determined by the difference between the *calculated* insoluble content and the in-

Table 3—Typical test results, locked cycle flotation of primary molybdenum concentrate

	Wt. (%)	% Assay			% Distribution		
		Mo	Insol	Cu	Mo	Insol	Cu
Sample A							
Insol, second cleaner conc.	25.1	5.34	79.9	1.25	3.62	62.42	31.56
Moly tail.....................	74.9	47.58	15.5	0.90	96.38	37.57	68.43
Head grade.................	100.0	36.77	31.1	0.98	100.00	100.00	100.00
Sample B							
Insol, second cleaner conc	29.9	1.15	79.2	0.99	0.94	62.04	31.15
Moly tail.....................	70.1	48.45	19.4	0.88	99.06	37.96	68.85
Head grade.................	100.0	30.26	37.2	0.91	100.00	100.00	100.00

Table 4—Average pilot plant operating results

	Wt. (%)	% Assay			% Distribution		
		Mo	Insol	Cu	Mo	Insol	Cu
Insol concentrate........	29.95	10.41	64.52	2.08	8.89	65.75	46.14
Moly concentrate........	70.05	45.87	15.22	1.12	91.11	34.25	53.86
Feed	100.00	35.21	30.58	1.42	100.00	100.00	100.00

soluble content as determined by standard aqua regia digestion. This difference between the calculated and analytical assays is due to the presence of gangue minerals such as carbonates, sulphates, and chlorides, which will dissolve in the digestion and therefore not report as insol.

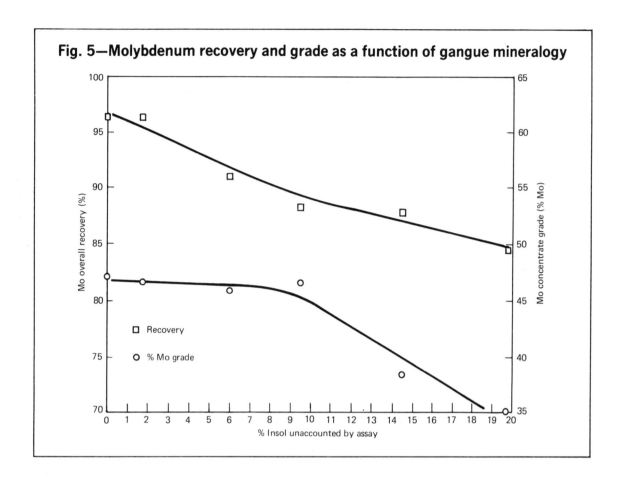

Fig. 5—Molybdenum recovery and grade as a function of gangue mineralogy

(See Fig. 5.) The circuit performs best on silicates and clays, and as the proportion of carbonates and sulphates increases, the recovery and grade both suffer. This is as expected, since the carbonates and sulphates are not naturally floatable. Their presence in the primary moly concentrate can normally be attributed to a physical entrapment in the froth during the primary flotation separation of moly and copper.

Laboratory work done on primary concentrate samples containing higher than average amounts of copper indicated that, with the moly depressed in the lignin sulphonate system, a xanthate collector could be added to activate the copper minerals and reduce the copper content of the final concentrate. While some activation of the moly occurred, preliminary results from laboratory and pilot tests were encouraging (Table 6). Use of the collector lowered the overall molybdenum recovery value; however, there were some offsetting increases in concentrate grade. The copper content in the moly concentrate is a major price penalty, and work is continuing to further test and develop this system.

Evaluating the success of the new system

The new process using lignin sulphonate at Twin Buttes has indeed met the requirements that initiated its development. The aqueous moly-insol flotation system will handle primary molybdenum concentrates ranging in feed grade from 20% to 40% Mo at capacities up to *four* times the original spray dryer circuit, while maintaining equivalent metallurgical results. With this circuit on line, it is now possible to utilize both spray dryers for treating final moly concentrates, thus greatly increasing the capacity of the by-products plant. The major disadvantage of the system is its inability to effectively separate carbonate gangue from the molybdenite. If a considerable volume of carbonates is carried over into the primary concentrate, a molybdenite-carbonate separation will become necessary. ☐

Table 5—Pilot plant average conditions

Lignin sulphonate	5.65 lb per ton
Conditioner density	14.50% solids
pH	11.91
Conditioning time	25.33 min
Rougher flotation	27.70 min

Table 6—Effect of xanthate collector, average results

Addition of 0.1 lb per ton of xanthate (approx.)	% Assay			% Distribution		
	Mo	Insol	Cu	Mo	Insol	Cu
Feed	34.89	30.89	1.30	100.00	100.00	100.00
Moly concentrate	47.47	14.80	0.79	88.60	31.64	39.13
Insol concentrate	11.40	62.13	2.23	11.40	68.36	60.87
Control—no addition of xanthate						
Feed	35.56	30.24	1.55	100.00	100.00	100.00
Moly concentrate	44.34	15.62	1.43	94.19	37.31	65.01
Insol concentrate	8.45	68.30	1.85	5.81	62.69	34.99

Continuous pilot plant testing confirms floatability of Duluth Complex sulphides

R. B. Schluter and **A. B. Landstrom**, metallurgists, Twin Cities Metallurgy Research Center

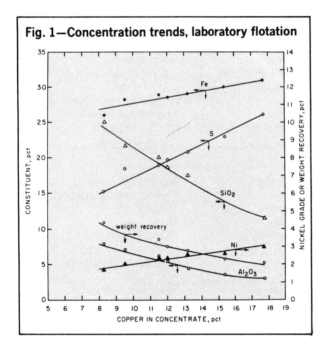

Fig. 1—Concentration trends, laboratory flotation

AS PART OF THE US BUREAU OF MINES' research program aimed at assuring an adequate US supply of minerals, the Twin Cities Metallurgy Research Center is investigating the recovery of copper, nickel, and precious metals from the sulphide deposits of northeastern Minnesota. The deposits occur in a large body of mafic igneous rock called the Duluth Complex, which extends in a great arc from Duluth to the northeastern point of the state. Most of the copper-nickel mineralization occurs along the northwestern contact of the Duluth Complex, between Hoyt Lakes and the South Kawishiwi River, just southeast of Ely, Minn. The Minnesota Geological Survey has estimated copper-nickel resources in the area at 2.2 billion tons of mineralized rock at a cutoff grade of 0.5% combined copper and nickel.[3] This mineralization represents 13.8 million tons of copper and 4.6 million tons of nickel.

Although the deposits have been known since 1899,[7] they did not receive much attention until after 1955.[2] Samples from the vicinity of the South Kawishiwi River were tested by the USBM in 1955[1]; the Mines Experiment Station at the University of Minnesota reported on the mineralogy and beneficiation of samples from the same area in 1968.[4] Both of these investigations involved only laboratory batch testing.

This paper presents the results of laboratory batch flotation and pilot plant continuous flotation tests on a 120-ton bulk sample of copper-nickel-bearing rock from the Duluth Complex. The objectives of this investigation were to

Editor's note: This article is based on a presentation made at the 37th Annual Mining Symposium in Duluth, Minn., during January 1976.

determine the bulk flotation response of the sample and to produce sufficient concentrates for subsequent pyrometallurgical and hydrometallurgical test work.

The Duluth Complex sample was part of a larger (10,000-ton) sample removed by International Nickel Co. from a test pit about 4 mi east of Minnesota State Highway 1, near the South Kawishiwi River. The rock was basically an altered troctolite consisting of large amounts of plagioclase, pyroxene, and olivine, plus lesser amounts of serpentine, talc, amphibole, and chlorite. The principal sulphide minerals were pyrrhotite, chalcopyrite, cubanite, and pentlandite.[5] The sulphide minerals were uniformly disseminated throughout the rock, with very few occurrences of coarse-grained sulphides; however, petrographic examination showed that a high proportion of the sulphides would be unlocked at 200 mesh. Table 1 details a partial chemical analysis of the Duluth Complex sample.

Lab work develops basic data

A 250-lb random sample was crushed to a nominal minus ¼-in. size for use in laboratory flotation studies. Several 1,500-g portions of this sample were ground to 200 mesh and processed in a 1,500-g Denver flotation cell. Various xanthate collectors were employed in 0.05- and 0.10-lb-per-ton quantities to evaluate Cu-Ni extractions on the basis of collector types. The xanthates included sodium ethyl, potassium ethyl, potassium sec amyl, potassium amyl, potassium isopropyl, potassium hexyl, sodium isopropyl, sodium sec butyl, and sodium isobutyl. Testing indicated no distinct superiority of one xanthate over another, and a 0.05-lb-per-ton dosage was sufficient to extract the liberated Cu-Ni sulphides. Sodium isobutyl xanthate and light alcohol frothers were used in the succeeding batch tests in amounts of 0.05 lb per ton each.

Primary separation products were a rougher flotation concentrate and a final tailing. The rougher concentrate was cleaned once, yielding a bulk Cu-Ni concentrate and a middling product. All tests used Minneapolis tap water, resulting in pulp having a pH of 8.2 to 8.7. No pH regulators were employed in the test work.

There was no appreciable difference in copper or nickel recovery with any of the collectors tested. A single cleaning of the rougher concentrates produced bulk concentrates with 85-91% Cu recovery, 60-71% Ni recovery, and 2-4% weight recovery (Table 2). The percentage recovery of several other concentrate elements is plotted in Fig. 1 in relation to concentrate copper grade.

Table 1—Analysis of Duluth sample by weight percentage

Cu	0.35	CaO	7.9
Ni	0.11	MgO	7.2
Fe	12.7	Al₂O₃	18.5
S	0.80	Co	0.015
SiO₂	43.1	TiO₂	1.0
	Cu/Ni ratio	3.18	

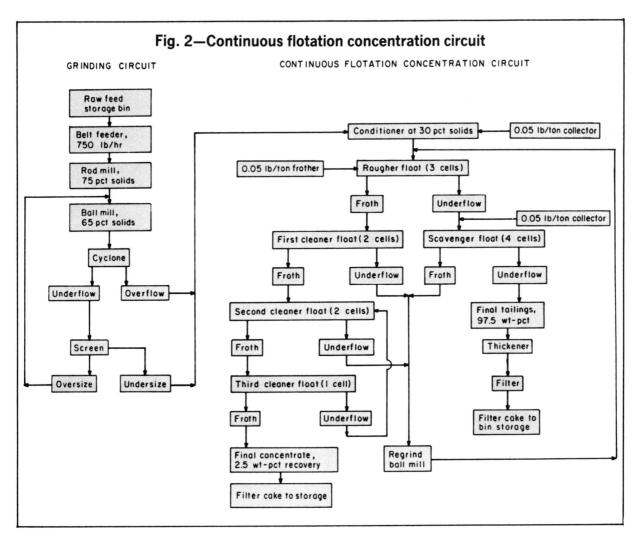

Fig. 2—Continuous flotation concentration circuit

GRINDING CIRCUIT   CONTINUOUS FLOTATION CONCENTRATION CIRCUIT

The loss of copper and nickel in the initial float was about 6% and 29%, respectively. The results of the rougher float were fairly consistent, with a spread of 3.3% in weight distribution in the rougher concentrates. However, reflotation of the rougher concentrates resulted in a rather wide range of Cu-Ni grades, possibly because of the small quantity of material being refloated.

Microscopic examination of the products showed that most of the sulphide minerals in the sample were liberated at a 200-mesh grind. In the form of bulk concentrates, laboratory copper and nickel extractions of 89.1% and 63.6%, respectively, were attainable at grades of 12.4% copper and 2.3% nickel. The gangue minerals in the concentrates were primarily plagioclase containing fine, unliberated sulphides, plus lesser amounts of naturally floatable talc and mica.

Continuous flotation performed at pilot plant

For pilot testing, the sample was crushed in a jaw crusher, followed by a Shorthead cone crusher, to a nominal minus 1½-in. size. The crushed material was stored in 55-gal drums to prevent exposure to the elements and minimize oxidation of the sulphides.

The flotation was done in the Twin Cities Metallurgy Research Center flotation process demonstration plant. The plant grinding circuit is equipped with a 2 x 4-ft rod mill and a 3 x 3-ft ball mill and has a nominal capacity of ½ tph. The ball mill was operated in closed circuit with a

cyclone, and an inclined rapped screen was positioned to deliver a nominal minus 200-mesh product. The flotation circuit consisted of a rougher float followed by three cleaner floats, plus a scavenger float on the rougher tails (Fig. 2). Fagergren-type flotation cells were used throughout the circuit.

The feed to rougher flotation was maintained at about

Table 2—Summary of analyses of batch flotation separation products

	Bulk Cu-Ni concentrates*		Middlings*		Rougher tailings	
	Analysis, %	Distribution, %	Analysis, %	Distribution, %	Analysis, %	Distribution, %
Weight						
Average	—	3.1	—	4.8	—	91.9
Range	—	2.1-	—	2.7-	—	89.6-
	—	4.2	—	6.0	—	92.9
Copper						
Average	12.4	89.1	0.31	4.3	0.026	5.9
Range	8.28-	84.8-	0.17-	2.3-	0.022-	5.5-
	17.60	91.4	0.37	6.4	0.029	6.6
Nickel						
Average	2.3	63.6	0.167	8.2	0.036	28.9
Range	1.77-	59.2-	0.087-	3.6-	0.030-	24.9-
	3.00	70.6	0.216	13.5	0.042	33.1
Sulphur						
Average	20.4	77.4	1.69	11.1	0.092	10.6
Range	15.25-	67.2-	0.090-	4.3-	0.067-	7.8-
	26.11	87.9	3.78	20.5	0.126	14.2

*Refloat of rougher concentrates.

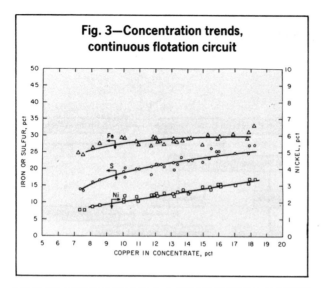

Fig. 3—Concentration trends, continuous flotation circuit

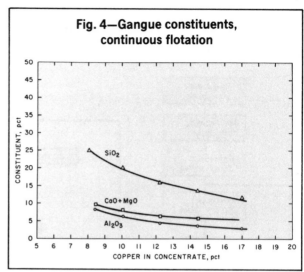

Fig. 4—Gangue constituents, continuous flotation

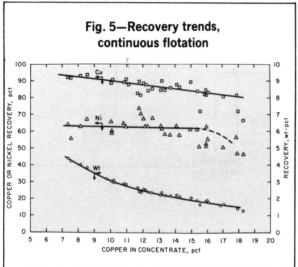

Fig. 5—Recovery trends, continuous flotation

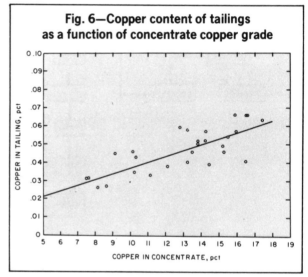

Fig. 6—Copper content of tailings as a function of concentrate copper grade

30% solids. There was no solids control in the cleaner cells, but by minimizing water dilution of the froth products, the solids were maintained near the 10% level. Float time was 20 min for the rougher and scavenger floats, and 15 to 20 min for the cleaner floats. Flotation reagents were sodium isobutyl xanthate collector (0.1 lb per ton) and "Aerofloat" 71R frother (0.05 lb per ton).

Half the collector was added to the conditioner prior to rougher flotation, and half was added directly to the scavenger flotation feed box to assure maximum sulphide recovery. All the frother was added to the rougher float, except when a low froth level required additional frother to

be added to the scavenger float. No additional reagents were added in any of the cleaner floats. Minneapolis city water was used throughout the test work, and flotation was carried out at the natural slurry pH of 8.5.

The final concentrate and a portion of the final tailings were thickened, filtered, and stored for future research studies. The flotation circuit was sampled hourly, and these samples were combined into 8-hr shift samples.

The bulk sample was processed in three five-day tests that continued around the clock. The feed rate to the demonstration plant was 750 lb per hr of minus 1½-in. ore. The grind was held uniform throughout the three tests. A typical size distribution for the feed is shown in Table 3.

Plant and lab responses were almost identical

The flotation circuit was initially operated to produce a bulk concentrate containing 10-12% copper while maintaining copper recovery near the 90% level. Information obtained from the bench-scale tests had indicated this to be a reasonable goal. Actual operations produced concentrates with daily average copper analyses ranging from 7.5% to 18% copper over the three test periods. Most of the low-grade concentrates (less than 10% Cu) were produced in the first test during the startup period, when mechanical upsets in the system resulted in periods of low concentra-

Table 3—Nominal size distribution for flotation feed

Screen size	Percent weight	Cumulative percent weight	Percent copper	Percent nickel	Percent sulphur
Plus 150	3.4	3.4	0.26	0.08	0.57
-150 + 200	6.7	10.1	0.25	0.10	0.58
-200 + 270	12.5	22.6	0.27	0.10	0.58
-270 + 325	22.3	44.9	0.33	0.11	0.73
Minus 325	55.1	100.0	0.44	0.13	0.96

Table 4—Analysis of composite* bulk Cu-Ni concentrates

Sample no.	Chemical analyses, percent								
	Cu	Ni	Fe	S	Co	SiO$_2$	Al$_2$O$_3$	CaO	MgO
1**	10.0	2.2	26.1	18.3	0.11	20.4	6.4	2.8	5.3
2	14.4	3.1	29.1	24.0	0.14	13.6	3.6	1.7	4.0
3	12.2	2.5	27.5	21.1	0.12	15.7	4.3	2.0	4.4

* Each sample represents the blending of all concentrates produced for the week's test period. ** Sample 1 includes reprocessed concentrates.

Table 5—Precious metals assay of flotation concentrates

(oz per ton)

Sample*	Au	Ag	Pt	Pd	Rh	Ir	Ru
1	0.04	1.1	0.036	0.120	0.003	0.001	0.002
2	0.04	1.5	0.030	0.128	0.002	0.001	0.001
3	0.04	1.4	0.021	0.122	0.003	0.002	0.004

* Numbers correspond to samples in Table 4.

Table 6—Analysis of bulk tailing sample by weight percentage

Fe	12.7	SiO$_2$	43.1
Cu	0.050	CaO	7.8
Ni	0.045	MgO	7.0
S	0.21	Al$_2$O$_3$	18.3

tion. These low-grade concentrates were stored separately and reprocessed later.

The shift average results, graphed in Figs. 3, 4, and 5, show that the continuous flotation responses were almost identical to the results of laboratory batch flotation (Fig. 1). The nickel content of the concentrates increased in direct proportion to the copper content (Fig. 3), and ranged from 1.5% to 3.5%. The sulphur content ranged from about 15% in the low-Cu concentrates to over 25% in the high-Cu concentrates. Iron content of the concentrates varied only from 24% to 29% over the full range of copper concentrations, partially because the gangue minerals carry an appreciable iron content (approximately 12%).

Excluding iron, the predominant gangue constituents in the concentrates were silica, magnesia, alumina, and calcia (Fig. 4). Above the range of 13-15% Cu, the decrease in gangue content of the concentrates began to level off, and further efforts to increase the concentrate grade by adjustment of the flotation circuit resulted in copper recoveries below 80% (Fig. 5).

At a 14% Cu grade, the average copper concentrate contained 22.5% sulphur. A sulphur balance indicated that the concentrate was comprised of about 70% by weight sulphide minerals. Chalcopyrite and cubanite (Cu-Fe sulphides) made up about 44% of the concentrate, while pyrrhotite (FeS) comprised 19% and pentlandite (Ni-Fe sulphide) about 7%.

Nickel recovery was consistent at the 60% level up to a copper grade of 15%. Above 15%, the recovery data are scattered, but there is probably a downward trend in nickel recovery. The low nickel recovery is typical of the results of other research on similar Duluth Complex samples and has been attributed to unrecoverable nickel occurring either as fine pentlandite inclusions or as nickel replacing magnesium in the olivine lattice.[1, 4]

The weight recovery in Fig. 5 is calculated from the copper balance. For the three tests, the total weight recovered in the concentrate amounted to about 2.5%, in close agreement with the calculated figures.

Concentrates from each of the test periods were blended and analyzed (Table 4). Sample 2 had the highest average copper and nickel grades. During the analyses, daily Cu grades were seen to range as high as 18%, with a corresponding decrease in copper recovery. The average Cu and Ni recoveries in the concentrate composite were 85% and 62%, respectively.

Sample 3 represents the most consistent operation of the continuous flotation circuit. The composite contained 12.2% Cu and 2.5% Ni, with recoveries of 87% and 62%, respectively.

Sample 1, a composite of the concentrates produced in the first test period, includes the portion of the concentrates that were reprocessed at the end of the period. This composite contains the lowest grade concentrates produced during startup and balancing of the grinding and flotation circuits.

The three concentrate composites were assayed for precious metals content (Table 5) by the USBM's Reno Metallurgy Research Center, using an emission spectrographic method.[6] Platinum group metals were predominant in dollar value, along with small amounts of gold and silver. The values ($25-30 per ton in Sample 2) were sufficient to make recovery of the precious metals attractive.

The copper content of the tailings ranged from 0.025% to 0.065%, with the higher value corresponding to an 18% Cu grade (Fig. 6). The nickel content of the tailings did not demonstrate an upward trend with increasing concentrate grade but remained constant at about 0.045% up to the 15% Cu level. The nickel analyses of the tailings were scattered when the Cu grade was above 15%, but probably show an upward trend. A partial chemical analysis of the bulk tailings composite appears in Table 6.

In summary, data obtained in the pilot plant flotation of the Duluth sample confirm the results of laboratory work on similar samples by the USBM and other investigators. Copper recoveries for the composite bulk concentrates ranged from 85% at a 15% Cu grade to 90% at a 10.7% Cu grade. Nickel recoveries remained at 60% over the same range of copper grades, with corresponding nickel grades of 3.1% and 2.1%, respectively. Nickel recovery will be limited by a minimum nickel content of 0.030% to 0.042% in the tailings.

Gangue content of the concentrates was about 30% at a 15% Cu grade. Bulk concentrate grades of 12% to 14% Cu and 2.4% to 2.7% Ni appear to give the optimum combination of grade and recovery, while copper grades above 15% do not appear practical because of increased copper and nickel losses to the tailings. □

References

1) Grosh, W. A., J. W. Pennington, P. A. Wasson, and S. R. B. Cooke, "Investigation of Copper-Nickel Mineralization in Kawishiwi River Area, Lake County, Minn.," USBM Report of Investigations 5177, 1955, 17 pp.
2) Sims, P. K., "Exploration for Copper-Nickel in Northeastern Minnesota," Proc. 28th Ann. Min. Symp., Univ. of Minn., 1967, pp 59-64.
3) Sims, P. K., and G. B. Morey, "Minnesota Mineral Resources: A Brief Overview," SKILLINGS' MINING REVIEW, Vol. 63, No. 16, April 6, 1974, 5 pp.
4) Vifian, A. R., and I. Iwasaki, "Mineralogical and Beneficiation Studies of the Copper-Nickel Bearing Duluth Gabbro," Proc. 29th Ann. Min. Symp. and 41st Ann. Meeting of Minn. Sec., AIME, Duluth, Minn., Jan. 15-17, 1968, pp 183-194.
5) Wager, R. E., "A Comparison of the Copper-Nickel Deposits of Sudbury and Duluth Basins," Proc. 30th Ann. Min. Symp. and 42nd Ann. Meeting of Minn. Sec., AIME, Duluth, Minn., Jan. 13-15, 1969, pp 95-96.
6) Whitehead, A. B., and H. H. Heady, "Emission Spectrographic Method for Platinum Fire Assay—Palladium, Rhodium, and Gold," APPLIED SPECTROSCOPY, Vol. 24, No. 2, March-April 1970, pp 225-228.
7) Winchell, N. H., "The Geology of Minnesota," Univ. of Minn. Final Report, Vol. 4, 1899, pp 344 and 490.

Research shows way to send Indian copper rougher concentrates directly to smelter

Dr. Arjun Raja, Pacific Chemicals, Bombay, India

Table 1—Flotation test results, ores from Singhbhum copper belt

Surda copper ore

Product	% Weight floated	Assay % Cu	% Cu distri-bution	% Cu cum. distri-bution
Rougher conc.	6.27	23.34	95.80	95.80
Scav. conc. 1	0.83	2.99	1.62	97.42
Scav. conc. 2	0.64	0.83	0.37	97.77
Tailings	92.26	0.037	2.23	

Calculated head assay: 1.508% Cu. Ore also contains about 0.062% Ni, which is being recovered.
Reagents used: Xanthate XL-15 ($C_4H_9OCSSNa$)—0.03 kg/ton.
Pine oil (frother)—0.03 kg/ton.

Mosabani copper ore

Product	% Weight floated	Assay % Cu	% Cu distri-bution	% Cu cum. distri-bution
Rougher conc.	5.73	27.30	86.50	86.50
Scav. conc. 1	1.34	8.70	6.50	93.00
Scav. conc. 2	1.01	3.81	2.18	95.18
Tailings	91.92	0.095	4.82	

Calculated head assay: 1.80% Cu.
Reagent used: Reagent-606PC ($(C_8H_{17}O)_2PSSH$)—0.03 kg/ton.
No xanthate or frother was used.

Rakha copper ore (Phase II)

Product	% Weight floated	Assay % Cu	% Cu distri-bution	% Cu cum. distri-bution
Rougher conc.	3.75	23.70	90.2	90.20
Scav. conc. 1	0.90	3.90	3.6	93.80
Scav. conc. 2 + 3.	1.00	1.20	1.4	95.20
Tailings	94.40	0.05	4.8	

Calculated head assay: 0.985% Cu.   **pH:** Natural.
Flotation reagents used: Reagent-606PC—0.035 kg/ton.
MIBC—0.005 kg/ton.
No xanthate was used.

Rakha copper ore (Phase I)
Bulk copper-molybdenite flotation

Product	% Weight floated	Assay % Cu	Assay % MoS₂	Distribution % Cu	Distribution % MoS₂
Concentrate	14.00	28.40	0.75	98.02	—
Tailings	86.00	0.083	—	1.98	—

Grind: 26.5% minus 250 mesh.   **Calculated head assay:** 4.047% Cu.
Reagents used: Xanthate XL-15—0.03 kg/ton.   **pH:** Natural
Frother-107PC—0.03 kg/ton.

Differential copper-molybdenite flotation*

Product	% Weight floated	Assay % Cu	Assay % MoS₂	Distribution % Cu	Distribution % MoS₂
Cleaner conc.	1.34	16.14	43.18	0.76	76.71
Cleaner tails	4.87	30.37	2.00	5.21	12.91
Rougher tails (copper conc.)	93.79	28.47	0.083	94.02	10.36

Reagents used: Reagent-22PC (depressant for chalcopyrite).
Kerosene oil (promoter for molybdenite).
MIBC frother.

*Differential copper-molybdenite flotation was done by conditioning with Reagent-22PC and kerosene oil for 3 min and floating with MIBC frother. Three-stage cleaning using the same reagents was done.

ALL OF INDIA'S COPPER ORE PRODUCTION comes from three copper belts, in the states of Bihar in the east, Rajasthan in the northwest, and Karnataka to the south. The three respective belts—Singhbhum, Khetri, and Chitradurga—are separated by more than 1,000 mi. While the major copper mineral in the ores from all three regions is chalcopyrite, the ore flotation characteristics differ for a given set of reagents and conditions. However, research on flotation of these ores suggests that a common flowsheet for flotation is practicable. The flowsheet consists of a rougher float followed by two scavenger floats. The ores from Chitradurga and Khetri would also require conditioning. The proposed flowsheet eliminates cleaning operations, yet laboratory tests showed copper recoveries of 95% to 97% in all cases.

Chemical control within the flotation process is a prerequisite for efficient operation. With proper chemical control, metallurgical grade concentrates can be obtained from the preliminary rougher float. Elimination of cleaner flotation stages can reduce both capital and operating costs. This finding is important for India, where many potentially economic deposits are known but exploitation is lacking, partly because many high grade, low tonnage deposits lack convenient concentrators. These deposits could be operated economically if efficient, low cost concentrators were suitably located to treat the ores on a toll basis.

In 1975, India consumed 45,000 mt of copper, of which 25,000 tons was supplied by Hindustan Copper Ltd. At present, only six copper concentrators operate in India: the Mosabani, the Surda, and the copper-molybdenum concentrator of Rakha, all in the state of Bihar; the Khetri in Rajasthan; the Chitradurga in Karnataka; and a concentrator near Hutti, also in the state of Karnataka. The Mosabani and Surda concentrators are operated by Hindustan Copper Ltd., and Rakha and Khetri are both owned and operated by that company. The Chitradurga concentrator is an undertaking of the state government, and the Hutti plant is owned and operated by Hutti Gold Mines Co. Ltd.

The effect of collector chain length on recovery

The flotation characteristics of Singhbhum, Khetri, and Chitradurga ores—and the effect of sulphydril collector chain length—were the subject of the study described here. Sulphydril collectors with the collector molecule ranging from $C_2H_5OCSS^-$ to $(C_8H_{17}O)_2PSS^-$ have been tested.

Ores from Singhbhum are readily amenable to flotation, with any sulphydril collector providing a high degree of selectivity of concentrate grade. No appreciable change in concentrate grade was observed when the length of the collector chain was increased.

By contrast, ores from Khetri and Chitradurga were found to be highly sensitive to the chain length of the collector, with poor grade recovery associated with use of long-chain collector molecules.

Singhbhum copper ores are readily floated

The nine mining properties within the Singhbhum copper belt have combined reserves estimated at 92 million tons grading 1.5% to 2.7% copper. Chalcopyrite is the major mineral in these ores, and some of the mines also recover small amounts of nickel and molybdenum. The host rock is a quartz-chlorite-biotite schist, with mineralization along the shear zones consisting mainly of chalcopyrite, pyrite, pyrrhotite, pentlandite, quartz, and magnetite. Small amounts of molybdenum occur at one location.

Flotation studies on copper ores from Mosabani, Surda, and Rakha—three of the nine properties of the range—show that the ores are readily amenable to flotation with any sulphydril collector—xanthate or dithiophosphate. The grade of the product is not changed appreciably by an increase in chain length or size of collector molecule. Use of the higher xanthates or dithiophosphates appears to improve recovery of nickel and sulphur—a consequence of floating the middling pentlandite and pyrrhotite, which is not easily floated with ethyl xanthate or isopropyl xanthate. Therefore, improvement in copper recovery would be associated with the middling copper connected with or enclosed in the pyrrhotite.

Flotation testing of these ores was done in a Denver Model D-1 laboratory flotation machine. The results, presented in Table 1, show that grade of copper concentrate is relatively unaffected either by use of the long-chain sulphydril collector $(C_8H_{17}O)_2PSS^-$ or by using xanthate XL-15 $(C_4H_9OCSS^-)$. Tests with potassium ethyl xanthate $(C_2H_5OCSS^-)$ and sodium isopropyl xanthate $(C_3H_7OCSS^-)$ have given similar concentrate grades. These tests clearly indicate the highly selective flotation characteristics of copper ores from the Singhbhum belt.

Chitradurga ores are sensitive to chain length

Flotation characteristics of Chitradurga ores have previously been described.[1] However, these ores are highly sensitive to an increase in chain length of the collector molecule. Use of reagent 606PC proved unsatisfactory, while grade of concentrates was much improved by use of lower alkyl xanthates (sodium isopropyl xanthate and potassium ethyl xanthate). Even so, the concentrate grade was only 14% to 15% copper, and repeated cleaning was necessary for grade improvement. Gangue flocculation and subsequent flotation was attributed to activating soluble salts in the ore, or perhaps to the presence of talcose minerals, which had smeared particle surfaces during the grinding stage.[2] Several gangue depressants were tried. Conditioning with sodium silicate gave the most satisfactory results (Table 2).

Khetri copper ores can be floated simply

The Khetri copper belt has four properties, with combined reserves exceeding 155 million tons. Some 143 million tons contain about 0.8% copper; the remaining tonnage grades up to 2.2% copper. Khetri copper ores are characterized by a high pyrrhotite content. Use of a sulphydril collector, xanthate, and pine oil provided an unsatisfactory grade of concentrate. Microscopic examination of the concentrates revealed that the poor grade was due not only to high pyrrhotite-pyrite but also to the existence of large amounts of highly flocculated gangue. Sodium silicate was used in an attempt to disperse the gangue but the results were not encouraging. Dextrine was used as a depressant—presuming the presence of talcose minerals—but the results were also unsatisfactory. It was suspected that the gangue had been activated by soluble salts, possibly iron. When "Paquest-100," a dequestrant, was tried as a complexing agent, the grade was much improved.

The Khetri copper smelter uses the Outokumpu Oy

Table 2—Flotation test results, Chitradurga copper ore

Product	% Weight Recovery	Assay % Cu	% Cu distribution	Cumulative % Cu Recovery
Test A*				
Rougher conc. ...	18.19	13.44	85.43	85.43
Scav. conc. 1.....	2.67	7.168	6.70	92.13
Scav. conc. 2.....	7.25	1.280	3.25	95.38
Tailings	71.89	0.179	4.62	
Calculated head assay: 2.86% Cu.				
Test B**				
Rougher conc. ...	10.99	25.152	92.19	92.19
Scav. conc. 1.....	1.01	2.560	0.87	93.06
Scav. conc. 2.....	5.40	1.206	2.17	95.22
Tailings	82.60	0.173	4.77	
Calculated head assay: 2.998% Cu.				

Reagents used: Sodium isopropyl xanthate—0.03 kg/ton. MIBC frother—0.02 kg/ton.
In second scavenger float, copper sulphate (0.45 kg/ton) was added as activator for copper-pyrrhotite coarse middlings.

*Without using sodium silicate. **Using 1.37 kg/ton sodium silicate; conditioning for 2½ min.

flash smelting process. Maximum recovery of copper and sulphur is desired because a sulphuric acid plant is being installed. About 10% to 12% copper grade is believed to be acceptable. The use of Paquest-100 achieved this grade in the rougher float alone, precluding the necessity of cleaning operations. Results of the testing are presented in Table 3.

The grades of concentrates shown in Table 3, in terms of chalcopyrite + pyrrhotite/pyrite $(CuFeS_2 + FeS_2)$, are 82.27%, 70.01%, and 52.69%, respectively, while the tailings are only 2.94%. This clearly shows the high degree of selective float and the high recoveries of sulphide minerals.

Results in Tables 2 and 3 show that, by proper control of the chemistry during flotation, it is possible to obtain a smelter-grade concentrate at the rougher stage without resorting to subsequent costly cleaning stages. With this in mind, a simplified process flowsheet has been drawn up. (See illustration.) The system should be highly economical

Table 3—Flotation test results, Khetri copper ore

Product	% Weight recovery	Assay % Cu	% S	Distribution % Cu	% S	Cum. recovery % Cu	% S
Rougher conc....	17.39	10.17	41.8	91.49	61.81	91.49	61.81
Scav. conc. 1.....	3.67	1.52	37.90	2.89	11.84	94.38	73.65
Scav. conc. 2.....	6.84	0.76	28.40	2.69	16.54	97.07	90.14
Tailings.............	72.10	0.079	1.60	2.93	9.81		

Calculated head assay: 1.93% Cu and 11.76% S.

Reagents used: Sodium isopropyl xanthate—0.035 kg/ton.
Frother, 107PC—0.03kg/ton.
Pacfloat-1395, $(C_4H_9O_2)PSSH$—0.025 kg/ton.
Paquest-100 (dequestrant).
pH: Natural. Pulp conditioned for 3 min with Paquest-100.
Flotation time: 3 min + 3 min + 5 min.

Note: Pacfloat-1395 was used in second scavenger float as auxiliary promoter for middling pyrrhotite.

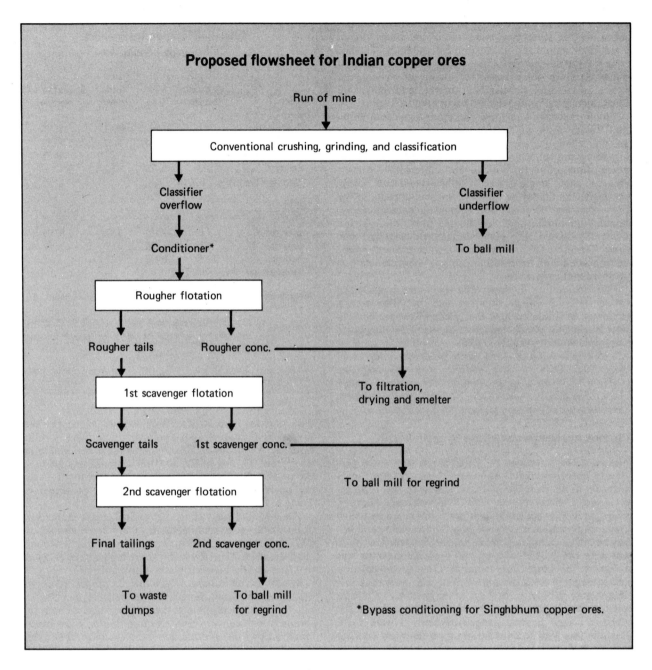

Proposed flowsheet for Indian copper ores

Run of mine

↓

Conventional crushing, grinding, and classification

Classifier overflow ↓   Classifier underflow ↓

Conditioner* ↓   To ball mill

Rougher flotation

Rougher tails ↓   Rougher conc. → To filtration, drying and smelter

1st scavenger flotation

Scavenger tails ↓   1st scavenger conc. → To ball mill for regrind

2nd scavenger flotation

Final tailings ↓   2nd scavenger conc. ↓

To waste dumps   To ball mill for regrind

*Bypass conditioning for Singhbhum copper ores.

and is applicable for copper ores from all three major copper belts of India.

Summary and conclusions

Results of detailed studies on flotation characteristics of copper ores from the three copper regions of India, and the effect of sulphydril collector chain length on these ores, lead to the following conclusions:

■ Singhbhum belt ores are characterized by a high degree of selectivity of concentrate grade with any sulphydril collector—an alkyl xanthate or di-alkyl di-thiophosphate.

■ No appreciable change in concentrate grade is observed by increasing the chain length of the collector molecule for Singhbhum ores.

■ Khetri and Chitradurga ores are characterized by gangue activation caused by the presence of activating soluble metal ions in the ores. Staged cleaning, believed to be the current plant practice, has been necessary to obtain metallurgical grade concentrates.

■ A common flotation flowsheet, incorporating a rougher and two scavenger floats, is proposed for all ores. In the case of Chitradurga and Khetri ores, provision for conditioning is proposed. Rougher concentrate is directed to the smelter, while scavenger concentrates go to regrind. Conditioning with sodium silicate is proposed for Chitradurga ores, and Paquest-100 dequestrant has been found satisfactory for Khetri ores.

Proper chemical control during this flotation study produced metallurgical grade concentrates in the rougher flotation stage, obviating the need for cleaning operations while reducing capital and operating costs. In all cases, recoveries on the order of 95% to 97% Cu were obtained. ☐

References

1) Raja, A., "Investigations on Flotation Behaviour of Ingaldhal Copper Ores, near Chitradurga (Karnataka)," INDIAN CHEMICAL JOURNAL, December 1974, p 23.
2) Arbiter, N., Fujjii, Y., Hansen, B., and Raja, A., "Surface Properties of Hydrophobic Solids," A.I.Ch.E. Symposium Series, Vol. 71, No. 150, 1975, p 176.

US flotation: cost of reagents averaged 21c per ton in 1975

AN ADVANCE SUMMARY of a nation-wide survey of froth flotation in the US mining industry was released last month by the Bureau of Mines. Containing 22 tables, the advance summary is a distillation of information to be published in the "Mining and Quarrying Trends" chapter of the forthcoming 1975 *Minerals Yearbook* (the volume entitled *Metal and Nonmetal Industries*).

According to the survey, 252 US flotation plants with a combined daily treatment capacity of 1,612,000 tons operated in 1975. Nearly 423 million tons of ore were processed, from which over 60 million tons of concentrate were recovered. Of the total ore treated, 66% was metal sulphides, 7% metal oxides and carbonates, 24% nonmetallic minerals, and 3% coal.

Energy requirements at flotation plants in 1975 totaled over 6.5 billion kwh, or an average of 15.8 kwh per ton of ore treated. Water use amounted to 527 billion gal, or 1,270 gal per ton processed. Steel consumption for rod, ball, and liners of grinding mills totaled 406

million lb, 73 million lb, and 36 million lb, respectively, or 1.31, 0.46, and 0.12 lb per ton processed.

Consumption of flotation reagents, as shown in the accompanying table, exceeded 1.7 billion lb, or an average of 4.2 lb per ton of ore treated. The value of reagents consumed was reported at $87.7 million, which reduces to an average cost of 21¢ per ton of ore fed to plants.

Tabular material presented in the survey also profiles mineral recovery by commodity groupings. For example, 18 US copper concentrators in 1975 processed over 2.1 million tons of concentrate containing an average 25.50% Cu, 0.0522 oz of gold, and 2.94 oz of silver per ton. Copper recovery was 80%, while gold and silver recoveries were 61% and 67%, respectively. The cost of flotation reagents consumed amounted to an average 15.7¢ per ton of feed material, which totaled slightly over 92 million tons in 1975.

Another 15 copper-molybdenum concentrators produced 2.6 million tons of copper concentrate and 30,323 tons of

molybdenum concentrate from a little more than 145.4 million tons of ore. The copper concentrates had an average grade of 24.82% Cu, 0.102 oz of gold, and 2.314 oz of silver per ton; recoveries of copper, gold, and silver were 84%, 61%, and 77%, respectively, in the copper concentrates. The molybdenum concentrates produced at these plants averaged 56.76% Mo at a recovery of 53% of the molybdenum in the molybdenum concentrate. The average reagent cost at these plants was 11¢ per ton of ore treated.

Other typical reagent costs per ton of feed at flotation plants in 1975 include: 21 lead-zinc concentrators, 49.8¢; 13 copper-lead-zinc concentrators, 24.7¢; three copper-zinc-iron sulphide plants, 60.4¢; 10 zinc concentrators, 17.9¢; 13 feldspar, mica, and quartz plants, 58.4¢; three fluorspar flotation plants, $2.068; five iron ore plants, 37.8¢; 19 phosphate flotation plants, 33.0¢; eight US potash plants, 19.6¢. □

(See chart, p 182)

(See chart, p 182)

Reprinted From E/MJ, December 1976

Brushy Creek — a tour de force in mining

Recognized as one of the mining industry's most modern operations, the Brushy Creek mine and mill complex is the newest of St. Joe's lead properties, having started up on November 1, 1973. The complex, located 10 mi north of Bunker, Mo., is near the center of the Viburnum Trend. Sized for 5,000 tpd, the complex required a capital investment of $24,155,000; today, the mine is producing 4,750 tpd of ore averaging 4.34% lead, 0.85% zinc, and 0.05% copper. Last year, mill output was 59,648 tons of concentrate with a metal content of 44,804 tons.

The Brushy Creek orebody, buried about 1,000 ft below the surface installation, measures 5 mi long, 50 to 1,000 ft wide, and 14 to 50 ft thick, and is enclosed in very gently dipping Bonneterre dolomite host rock. The deposit was discovered in 1959 using surface diamond drill coring techniques. The mine was developed through two circular, concrete-lined shafts that measure 12.5 ft in diameter. No.

33 shaft, used primarily for ore hoisting, is 1,394 ft in depth, intersecting the mine's two levels and the skip loading station below the crusher room. No. 34 shaft, used primarily for workers and materials, intersects only the higher level of the mine, at a depth of 1,085 ft. Headframes for the two shafts are open construction, and measure 130 ft and 80 ft tall, respectively.

Automated hoisting in the ore shaft is accomplished with a Nordberg single-drum, geared-drive hoist powered by a 600-hp General Electric dc motor. Ore is hoisted in two 8-ton, bottom-dump, 177-cu-ft skips that are run in balance for a maximum capacity of 245 tph.

The ore shaft is also the upcast side of the mine's ventilation system. Fresh air is downcast to the first mine level through the man/materials shaft at 200,000 cfm using Joy Axivane fans. It is fed to the outlying stopes, sucked to the second level through 96-in. ventilation holes located at the

E/MJ OPERATING HANDBOOK OF MINERAL PROCESSING *Reprinted From E/MJ, November 1976* **179**

lateral extremes of the mine, then upcast through the No. 33 shaft.

The mine is laid out in room-and-pillar fashion, essentially on one level at the elevation of the orebody. The second level, mostly inactive now, is used for drainage and ventilation. For the future, St. Joe envisions a need for 40- to 50-ton trucks or a combined truck and rail haulage system fed by transfer chutes when LHD haulage becomes uneconomical because of the tramming distance.

The mine is developed fairly symmetrically around the two shafts, using open stoping techniques that create 25-ft-dia support pillars and 35-ft-wide rooms. Haulage drifts are cut 32 ft wide and 18 ft high to accommodate the large mechanized equipment. Standard expansion shell rock bolts are used in 8-ft lengths where needed, but several areas in the mine require no support because of the competence of the overlying strata. Mining is planned to move either upgrade (so that hauling will be downgrade) or on the contour of the ore trend.

Like the other New Lead Belt mines, Brushy Creek must continuously pump subsurface ground water originating in the Lamotte sandstone out of the mine to maintain normal operating conditions. Brushy uses its lower level to house the drainage equipment—a 13-stage vertical Peerless sump pump with 500-hp motors, handling 1,900 gpm of inflow.

All drilling is done with Joy RPD Drillmobile jumbos and 1½-in. bits. A typical round at Brushy Creek consists of 68 holes with a burn cut of three 3-in. holes at the center, requiring a total drilling time of roughly 4 hr. Holes are then filled at the rate of one hole per minute with "Gelamite" 60% dynamite and shot. Rounds yield 580 tons of broken ore on the average, although some rounds yield 700 tons or more. The average powder factor is 0.6 lb per ton of ore; drilling footages average 0.7 tons of ore per ft of hole.

Broken ore is loaded and hauled to the dump circle by St. Joe's modified fleet of 988 Caterpillar front-end loaders. St. Joe builds the 10-ton buckets for the 988s and shortens the bucket linkages to keep the buckets both low and level while tramming.

Mucking a typical round with the 988s takes about 4 hr, with tramming distances between 200 and 1,250 ft. The maximum haul in the mine is now 3,000 ft, and according to one mine engineer, "That's already taxing the efficiency limits of this sort of system." All loaders at Brushy are equipped with wet injection-type exhaust scrubbers.

At the dump circle, ore is unloaded through grizzlies into a 5,000-ton ore storage pocket. From the pocket, ore is fed by 6 x 10-ft vibrating feeders into an Allis Chalmers 42 x 48-in. jaw crusher, which reduces all ore to minus 6 in. Crushed ore then falls into an automatic loading hopper that alternately fills the two ore skips. Skips are hoisted and dumped every 2 min.

Plant is compact and easily supervised

The Brushy Creek 5,000-tpd concentrator into which the ore now moves is an extraordinary study in plant design and automation. It is notable for its compactness, minimal amount of fine ore storage on the surface, ease of operation, and the integration of the secondary crusher into the grinding circuit. The past experience of St. Joe operators in the Old Lead Belt has led them to the conclusion that three-stage crushing is both expensive and unnecessary.

The mill abuts a 1,000-ton capacity skip bin housed in the headframe of the Brushy Creek ore hoisting shaft. The skip bin thus becomes the feed end of the plant in a unique architectural combination of underground primary crushing, ore hoisting, and concentration. Between the skip bin discharge and the secondary crusher, located inside the mill at the grinding bay, there is less than 40 ft of conveyor footage. In the entire mill, there is less than 150 ft of conveyor. Storage capacity for the plant is maintained underground.

The bulk reagent storage and mix room and a truck cargo receiving dock flank one side of the skip bin. The entire arrangement is highly utilitarian, resulting in a compactness of layout that is visually pleasing. More important, however, the layout lends itself to ease of supervision and control by mill operators. For example, secondary screening, secondary crushing, rod milling, ball milling, and all flotation circuits are grouped on a single floor. The central control room and console on the floor are positioned to provide operators with a panoramic view of the system, from secondary screening and crushing through flotation.

Ore from the 1,000-ton skip bin is crushed to minus 1 in. by an Allis Chalmers 1084 "Hydrocone" crusher, then conveyed directly to the open-circuit 11 x 16-ft Allis Chalmers rod mill and mixed with water to form a 73% solids slurry. (See flowsheet.) The rod mill discharge is then pumped to a battery of four Krebs D20L cyclones, where the underflow is routed to an A.C. 13 x 14-ft ball mill operating in closed circuit with the cyclones. The product of the grinding circuit is a slurry containing 50% minus 200-mesh and 5% plus 48-mesh ore.

The grinding circuit product flows by gravity to a bank of eight 120-in. Wemco roughers to bulk-float the lead and copper while depressing the zinc and gangue. (See reagent addition table.) These large flotation cells represent a significant advance over other St. Joe concentrators. "With the bigger float machines at Brushy, we get the same product using one-third the horsepower," says L. A. Weakly, director of mining research.

The Pb-Cu rougher froth is pumped to two further banks of four-cell, 66-in. cleaners, then to a lead/copper separation circuit, where lead is depressed and copper is recovered as froth. (In recent months, the copper circuit, containing a rougher, cleaner, and thickener, has been used for zinc flotation because ROM ore has not contained enough copper for economic recovery.) The lead concentrate is pumped to a thickener, then to 10-ft 6-in.-dia, eight-disc vacuum filters, and finally to a 5 x 35-ft, gas-fired Hardinge rotary dryer before it is conveyed to 10-ton containers on automatic indexing turntables. The lead concentrate, bound for St. Joe's Herculaneum smelter, contains about 5% water at this point.

Tailing from the Pb-Cu bulk flotation circuit is the primary feed for zinc flotation. Sphalerite is actuated with copper sulphate and conditioned in a 12-ft 3-in. x 12-ft Wemco conditioner. The zinc flotation circuit consists of a six-cell 120-in. Wemco rougher followed by three stages of three-cell 66-in. Wemco cleaners. Zinc concentrates from the final stage of cleaning are leached with sulphuric acid to reduce the MgO content to less than 0.5%. The zinc content averages 63%.

The final tailing from the zinc flotation circuit is pumped 4,000 ft through a 12-in. heavy-gauge pipe to a portable cyclone installation on the tailing dam. The sand fraction from the cyclone installation is used to build the dam, and the slimes are discharged behind the containment.

The underflow product of the zinc and copper concentrate thickeners (when operational) is dewatered to about 9% moisture on a single 10-ft 6-in.-dia, three-disc filter that operates alternately on one concentrate or the other as

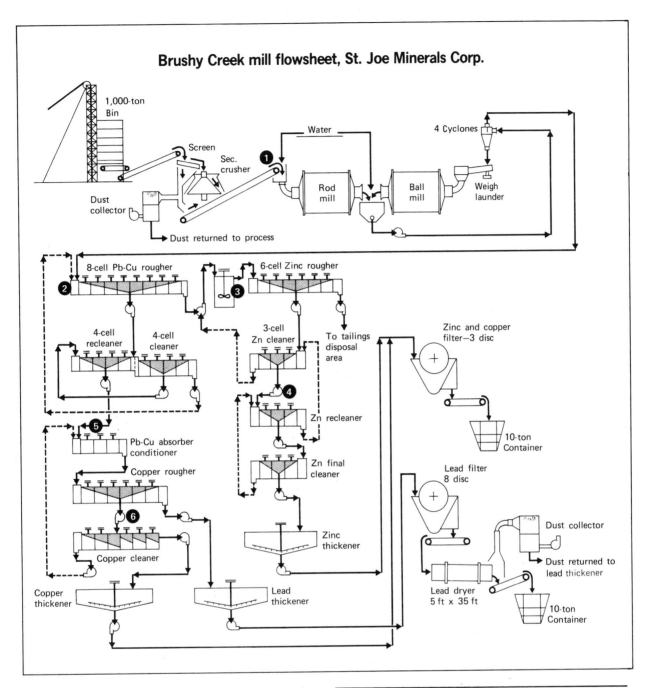

Brushy Creek mill flowsheet, St. Joe Minerals Corp.

necessary. The thickeners have adequate surge capacity for storage ahead of the filter. The zinc filter cake or copper cake is discharged into 10-ton containers on an indexing table similar to the one in the lead circuit.

The flotation circuits produce a 74% lead concentrate with 98% total lead recovery. Flotation parameters are adjusted in accordance with the readout of the mill's on-stream ARL X-ray analyzer, working with a 2114B analog computer. The analyzer continuously monitors seven different sample streams for data on the composition of the feed, concentrates, and tailings.

Power for the mill is provided at roughly 1.9¢ per kwh by the Arkansas-Missouri Power Co. Mill process water comes from clarified mine water and is recycled from the tailings pond. Tailings water is 100% reclaimed and stored in the mill reservoir. St. Joe plans to progressively stabilize the dewatered tailings by revegetation. The company has substantial experience in this area, gained primarily from studies done in the Old Lead Belt as far back as the 1930s. □

Reagent additions at Brushy Creek mill

Point*	Reagents added	Quantity (lb per ton ore)
1	Xanthate 343	0.06
	Zinc sulphate	0.35
2	Frother 71	0.03
3	Copper sulphate	0.05
	Z-200	0.02
	Frother 71	0.02
4	Cyanide (NaCn)	0.01
	Sodium dichromate	0.02
5	Sulphur dioxide	0.2
6	Sodium dichromate	0.06

*Points of reagent addition are shown on Brushy Creek mill flowsheet

Consumption and value of reagents in froth flotation in 1975

Function and name	Consumption, pounds Total	Per ton	Function and name	Consumption, pounds Total	Per ton
Modifier			**Collector** (continued)		
Alum	343,307	0.432	Kerosene	6,945,824	0,100
Ammonia	30,133,682	0.511	Minerec	1,114,611	0.018
Caustic soda	20,135,833	0.495	Petroleum sulphonate	764,079	0.884
Hydrochloric acid	436,765	0.063	Potassium amyl xanthate	1,736,593	0.022
Lignin sulphonate	393,401	0.132	Sodium Aerofloat	1,140,965	0.028
Lime	1,030,504,061	3.819	Sodium butyl xanthate,		
Nalco	787,949	0.010	sodium isobutyl xanthate	2,015,442	0.091
Phosphates	4,962,102	0.052	Sodium ethyl xanthate	1,640,463	0.046
Salt	3,365,022	12.259	Sodium isopropyl xanthate	1,676,650	0.021
Soda ash	4,371,392	1.761	Tall oil	24,097,510	1.711
Sodium silicate	21,433,039	0.331	Xanthates (unspecified)	1,067,386	0.057
Sulphur dioxide	3,512,873	0.493	Other	4,836,383	0.157
Sulphuric acid	132,465,271	1.139	**Total**		
Other (Barochem, Calgon,			Pounds	400,727,122	0.970
Tergitol, miscellaneous)	6,974,159	0.065	Value	$40,240,045	$0.097
Total					
Pounds	1,259,818,856	3.253	**Frother**		
Value	$25,320,137	$0.065	Aerofroths (unspecified)	404,591	0.235
			Aerofroth 65	362,809	0.020
Activator			Aerofroth 71	758,163	0.033
Copper ammonium chloride,			Aerofroth 73, 77	46,363	0.007
copper chloride	630,377	0.202	Barrett oil	2,370,699	0.251
Copper ammonium sulphate,			Cresylic acid	1,283,283	0.030
copper sulphate	9,316,627	0.616	Dowfroth 250	2,486,653	0.038
Sodium hydrosulphide,			Dowfroth 1012, 1263, 4082	202,176	0.026
sodium sulphide	1,779,371	0.331	Methyl isobutyl carbinol	11,884,790	0.061
Total			Nalco	511,549	0.407
Pounds	11,726,375	0.497	Pine oil	1,587,062	0.041
Value	$2,551,045	$0.108	UCON 23	270,830	0.034
			UCON 48, 55, 122	727,370	0.050
Depressant			UCON 133, 190	713,415	0.026
Aero Depressant 610, 633	71,859	0.007	Other	3,008,219	0.145
Caustic soda	195,927	0.011	**Total**		
Guar	332,704	0.070	Pounds	26,617,972	0.084
Hydrofluoric acid	1,201,594	1.025	Value	$7,705,165	$0.024
Phosphorus pentasulphide	883,832	0.016			
Quebracho	398,515	0.936	**Flocculant**		
Sodium cyanide	2,332,685	0.025	Aerofloc (unspecified)	208,892	0.094
Sodium dichromate	358,868	0.061	Aerofloc 30, 1202	17,288	0.001
Sodium ferrocyanide	2,183,795	0.034	Aerofloc 550	18,471	0.003
Sodium hydrosulphide	14,133,487	0.572	Alum	802,459	0.806
Sodium silicate	2,807,982	4.756	Calgon	169,391	0.019
Sodium sulphite	765,397	0.479	Dowell	492,239	0.138
Starch	16,657,178	0.935	Nalco	1,183,308	0.036
Zinc hydrosulphite	29,586	0.182	Polyhall	1,064,634	0.027
Zinc sulphate	7,715,512	0.682	Separan	1,971,671	0.077
Other (ammonium sulphide,			Superfloc 16	132,208	0.004
lignin sulphonate, sodium			Superfloc 20	12,890	0.010
siliofluoride, miscellaneous)	8,784,152	0.099	Superfloc 127	19,398	0.030
Total			Superfloc 206	25,774	0.001
Pounds	58,853,073	0.303	Superfloc 330, unspecified	38,654	0.032
Value	$7,269,290	$0.037	Other (lime and miscellaneous)	4,316,315	0.432
			Total		
Collector			Pounds	10,473,592	0.069
Aerofloat 25, 31	124,407	0.016	Value	$4,292,252	$0.028
Aerofloat 208	7,534	0.084			
Aerofloat 211	231,296	0.099	**Other**		
Aerofloat 238	795,108	0.016	Aerodri 100	539,051	0.018
Aerofloat 242	58,415	0.023	Carbon	149,439	0.025
Aero Promoter 404, 407	407,262	0.037	Miscellaneous	84,792	0.071
Aero Promoter 801, 825	143,409	0.425	**Total**		
Aero Promoter 899	4,579,030	0.919	Pounds	773,282	0.021
Aero Promoter 3302	801,225	0.014	Value	$303,692	$0.008
Amines	9,407,166	0.099			
Dow Z-200	1,067,792	0.026	**Total reagents**		
Fatty acids	130,919,928	1.607	Pounds	1,768,990,272	4.186
Fuel oil	205,148,644	1,011	Value	$87,681,626	$0.208

Source: US Bureau of Mines.

Cyprus develops moly-talc separation float

Gerald Parkinson, McGraw-Hill World News, Los Angeles

CYPRUS MINES CORP. IS OFFERING TO LICENSE other companies to use a moly flotation process developed at Cyprus Pima Mining Co. (50.01% owned) and patented in November 1975. The process at Pima is applied to a copper concentrate containing 27% Cu, 0.5% moly, and talc, which is difficult to separate from moly because the two minerals have similar flotation characteristics. The Cyprus process depresses the talc and floats the moly, eliminating an oxidizing roast that previously characterized the moly concentration flowsheet at Cyprus.

In the new process, moly and talc are floated from the copper concentrate, and the moly-talc float product advances directly to moly-talc separation cells. The cell feed is treated first with a water-soluble metallic salt of a weak base and a strong acid (aluminum sulphate), and then by a water-soluble salt of a weak acid (sodium silicate). These reagents depress the talc, permitting a moly float. Cyprus states that other chemicals could be substituted for aluminum sulphate and sodium silicate. Introduction of the new process raised average moly content in Pima moly concentrates to 43% in 1975, from a level of 40% for material processed by multiple-hearth roasting and talc flotation.

Before introduction of the new process, Pima had been using a Bartlett-Snow-Pacific seven-hearth roaster to oxidize the surface of the molybdenite and remove xanthate collector. The talc was not altered by roasting, and was subsequently floated while the moly was depressed.

"We had problems with uniformity using the old process," according to George A. Komadina, vice president and general manager of Cyprus Pima. "Molybdenum content often went below 40%. At times, it got down to 10-15%. We stored all of that material in drums, and we were able to reprocess it and bring it up to specifications with our new methods." Komadina notes that concentrate must contain at least 40% moly to be marketable.

The principal problem with the former process, Komadina states, was the difficulty in maintaining desired temperatures of about 500°F. The total volume of material varies because of variations in the amount of talc, and the temperature sensors were unable to adjust the heat input quickly enough. "We could have solved that problem by putting in a bigger roaster with more heating capacity," he says, "but that would have involved an additional investment." (Replacement costs for the roaster previously used by Pima would be about $250,000 at current prices. A filter to extract water prior to feeding material to the roaster would cost another $20,000 to $25,000.)

The new system uses the existing flotation plant, and no additional cells were needed. Though specific operating costs have not been calculated, Komadina believes the flotation process is less expensive, because the roaster required a substantial amount of energy for heat. The roasting process used natural gas, but if now operating, it would have to use fuel oil because no natural gas is available for that application.

The Cyprus plant has a capacity of 55,000 tpd of ore and in 1975 shipped about 150 million lb of copper in concentrates and about 1.8 million lb of molybdenum in concentrates. The ore grades 0.47% Cu and 0.015% moly. □

General mill flowsheet, Cyprus Pima Mining Co.

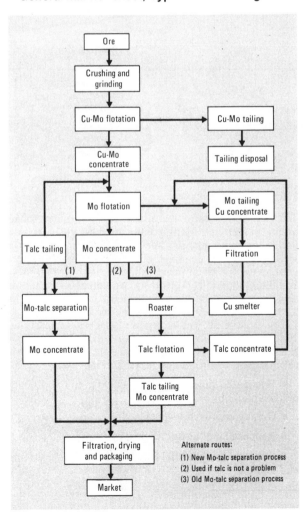

'Minexan 202': new on-stream isotope analyzer for small concentrators

A NEW CONCEPT IN SLURRY ANALYSIS—"Minexan 202"—is the latest addition to the range of analyzers offered to the process industries by Finland's Outokumpu. According to the company, the system represents a significant expansion of the field of application, especially in small concentrators requiring only a few assay points.

Based on isotope analysis technique, the system's advantages include:

- Low initial investment.
- Elimination of pipelines and pumps for slurry transfer.
- Use of a single probe to obtain simultaneous measurements of up to five elements and pulp density.
- Ease of installation—only one cable loop is needed to connect all probes.
- Expansion of the system by adding more probes.
- Stainless steel housing for the probes, which are designed to withstand the process environment.

If Minexan is not enough, its "big brother" Courier 300 is available for larger concentrator plants and for complicated processes, Outokumpu notes.

The Minexan system consists of probes placed at critical points in the process and linked together to form a loop. The loop establishes communication between the probes and a computer that controls the operation of the probes, converts the primary pulse data into element concentrations, and reports them by means of a typewriter or recorders.

The probes are self-sufficient; each one contains not only the excitation source, X-ray detector, and associated electronics, but also digital circuits for operation logics and pulse counting, as well as for data communication. Each probe is connected to the loop by a coupling unit that allows any probe to be bypassed if necessary.

The probes can be immersed directly in the slurry or solution, or supplied with a flow cell through which the sample stream passes. (The latter is recommended.) The minicomputer used with the system is normally equipped with a 32-kiloword core memory. The system permits the configuration of the computer and peripheral devices to be adapted to customers' needs.

Programming is performed primarily by using an automatic language. In normal operation, the programs are accessible through adjustable parameters for updating, checking, etc. Support programs are available for system maintenance.

Three probes are generally regarded as the practical minimum for system coverage; the maximum number is arrived at through economic comparison of the distributed and centralized analyzer systems. □

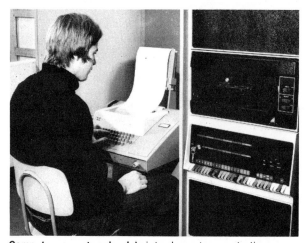

Computer converts pulse data into element concentrations.

Probes may be tipped up in their cradles for servicing.

Probes can be immersed directly in the slurry stream.

Chapter 3
Hydrometallurgical Processing

Crystallization in the copper sulphate-sulphuric acid-water system

The technology of handling copper sulphate solutions is becoming more important with today's increases in hydrometallurgical processing. Crystallization of $CuSO_4$ from solution is a key step in producing the most important industrial compound of copper.

David A. Milligan and **Henry R. Moyer III**, senior research engineers, The Anaconda Co.

COPPER SULPHATE IS THE MOST IMPORTANT industrial compound of copper. Of the copper sulphates $CuSO_4$, $CuSO_4 \cdot H_2O$, and $CuSO_4 \cdot 5H_2O$, the pentahydrate is the usual commercial form. Copper sulphate production in the US for the years 1968-1972 is estimated as follows[1] (in short tons):

1968	43,784
1969	50,568
1970	45,352
1971	34,648
1972	38,052

Copper sulphate pentahydrate crystallizes from an aqueous solution in large, blue, triclinic crystals. Upon heating, it loses water to form the white to greenish-white monohydrate at 110°C and the anhydrous salt at 250°C. Commercial uses for copper sulphate include soil additives, fungicides, and bulk preparation of other copper compounds.

Crystalline copper sulphate is manufactured from an aqueous solution of copper sulphate, primarily in cooling crystallizers or vats. Solutions are prepared commercially by circulating copper sulphate-sulphuric acid solutions through a tower containing metallic copper granules up to 2 in. in diameter while simultaneously passing air up through the tower.[2] Most of the impurities in the solution accumulate in a sludge that is filtered off for precious metal recovery. Fig. 1 is a flowsheet for production of large copper sulphate crystals in a cooling vat crystallizer coupled with a granular copper leach operation.

Alternate sources of concentrated solutions of copper sulphate include:

■ Discard solutions from electrowinning or electrolytic refinery operations.

■ Leach solutions from copper matte or cement copper.

■ Leach solutions from copper oxide or roasted concentrates.

■ Solvent ion-exchange stripping solutions.

Fig. 2 illustrates the production of small copper sulphate pentahydrate crystals in a continuous cooling crystallizer coupled with a heap leach operation.

Impurities often found in copper sulphate solutions include antimony, arsenic, calcium, cobalt, iron, nickel, sodium, and zinc. Various processes have been successful in removing these impurities, such as precipitation of iron and other metals by neutralization with cupric oxide.[3]

Impurities are also often separated from copper sulphate during crystallization by the inherent distribution coefficient between the solution and the crystal. Crystal purity can also be improved by changing the operating conditions of the crystallizer to prevent inclusion of the solution within the crystal.

Crystallization of copper sulphate

Production of commercial copper sulphate pentahydrate in a cooling crystallizer requires careful control of the feed solution and operating conditions while recycling the effluent solutions. There are three basic steps in the crystallization process: generation of supersaturation, formation of nuclei, and growth of nuclei into crystals. Numerous variables are known to affect crystallization, including:

■ Level of impurities in the aqueous phase.

■ Configuration and type of crystallizer.

■ History of solution prior to crystallizer processing.

■ Method of generating supersaturation.

■ Rate at which supersaturation is generated.

■ Seed bed of crystals for growth.

■ Residence time of seed bed.

Saturation and yields

Saturation and supersaturation may be generated in several ways. In the copper sulphate-sulphuric acid-water sys-

---

Equation 1

$$Y = \frac{1}{C_1} \ln \left[e^{C_1(A_1X+Y_0)} - e^{C_1(A_1X+B_1)} + e^{C_1B_1} \right]$$

Equation 2

$$\rho = \frac{1}{C_2} \ln \left[e^{C_2A_2} + e^{C_2(0.0093X+B_2)} \right]$$

Where:

Y = mass percentage of $CuSO_4 \cdot 5H_2O$ in saturated solution

ρ = density of saturated solution in g per cc

X = mass percentage of H_2SO_4 in solution

T = temperature in °C

$Y_0 = 20.37e^{0.01316T}$

= mass percentage of $CuSO_4 \cdot 5H_2O$ in saturated solution with no acid content

$A_1 = -0.6439e^{0.007361T}$

$B_1 = 12.82 \left[1 + e^{-0.08481(T-36.05)} \right]^{-1}$

$C_1 = 0.263 \left[1 + 0.0009775(T - 16.1)^2 \right]^{-1}$

$A_2 = 1.126e^{0.005511T^{0.8027}}$

$B_2 = 0.9257 + 0.001244T$

$C_2 = 14.7 \left[1 + 0.0007949(T - 32.38)^2 \right]^{-1}$

Fig. 1—Copper sulphate from a batch vat crystallizer

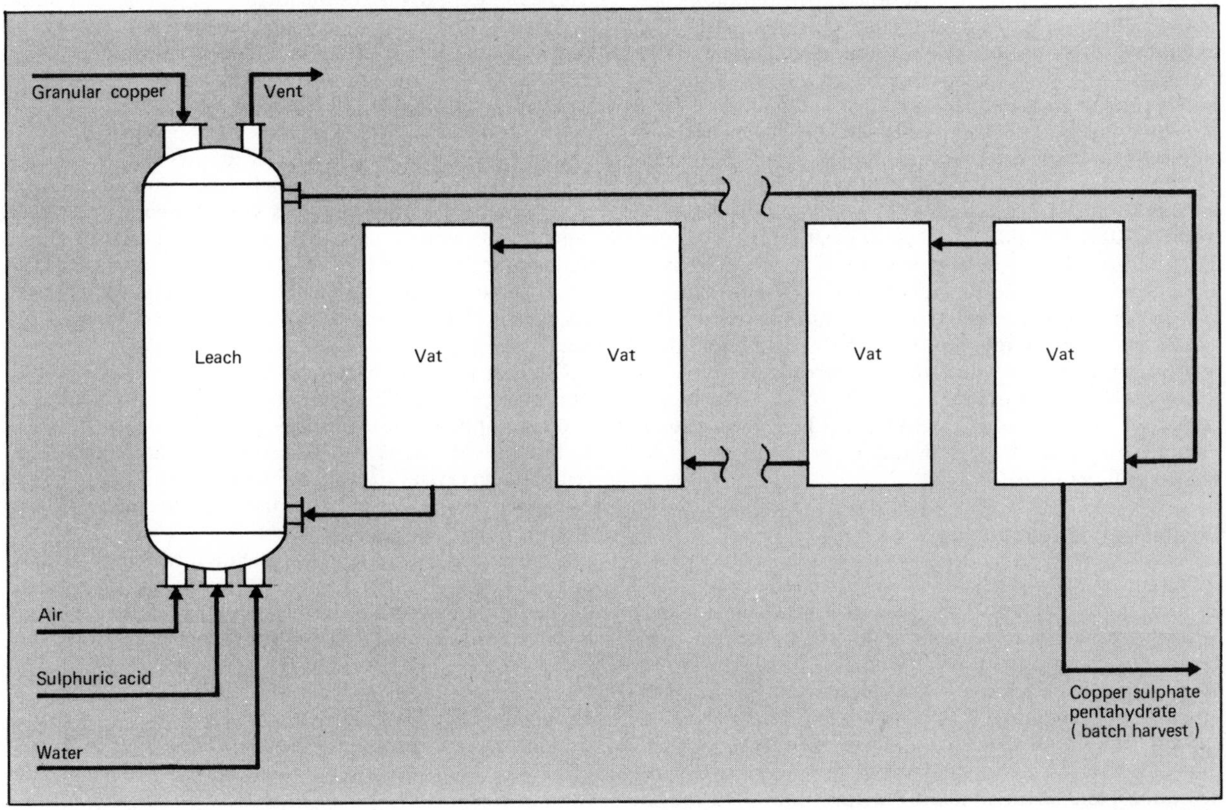

tem, adding sulphuric acid, removing water, or reducing the temperature will decrease the solubility of copper sulphate in the liquid phase. When the solution is already at the saturation point and solubility is decreased, the formation of crystalline copper sulphate pentahydrate may or may not occur. Control of the extent of supersaturation is one of the most important considerations in crystallization.

When a sulphuric acid-water solution saturated with copper sulphate is cooled, the crystallization of $CuSO_4 \cdot 5H_2O$ may be great enough to affect significantly the solution mass and therefore the sulphuric acid mass fraction. Complete determination of a crystallization system (i.e., crystal yield and mother liquor composition) requires data on both solution density and copper sulphate mass fraction at saturation, as functions of temperature and sulphuric acid mass fraction. Such a determination is made by trial and error, following these steps:

1) Assume a sulphuric acid mass fraction for the mother liquor at the desired temperature.

2) Obtain solution density and copper sulphate solubility data by interpolating the available data (difficult at best with two independent variables).

3) Calculate a new value for the sulphuric acid mass fraction based on a mass balance of the system.

4) Return to step 2 as necessary.

By finding suitable mathematical expressions for the available data, an iterative solution of the system can easily be programmed, which may be particularly helpful in process optimization and control. The isothermal curves in Figs. 3 and 4 were drawn from Equations 1 and 2, which in turn are fitted to the data of Agde and Barkholt as reported in Linke.[4] Data for solutions in equilibrium with solid phases other than the pentahydrate (i.e., the mono- and tri-hydrate) have been omitted since they occur at higher sulphuric acid levels on each isotherm, and are ac-

companied by drastic decreases in copper sulphate solubilities that do not plot as smooth curves.

Equations 1 and 2 provide an excellent basis for computing both supersaturation and the yields that occur under various operating conditions in a $CuSO_4 \cdot 5H_2O$ crystallizer. It may be shown that, within the ranges of temperature and sulphuric acid content covered by the systems in Figs. 1 and 2, crystal yield obtained with any specified temperature drop through crystallization will increase with increasing temperature of the feed solution, and decrease with increasing sulphuric acid content.

Nucleation of crystals

Crystal nuclei are formed in several ways. They may be introduced as particles of either copper sulphate or foreign matter, or they may be formed by the abrasion of existing crystals due to impact with other crystals or the crystallizer. They can also be formed by homogeneous nucleation within the solution when the supersaturation exceeds a maximum limit. A study by Nyult et al[5] describes the kinetics of homogeneous nucleation and the metastable supersaturation zone width. The zone width is a function of cooling rate. With no crystals present, this zone width is approximately 4.5°C wide at a cooling rate of 2°C per hr, and 10.7°C wide at a cooling rate of 20°C per hr. When crystals were present in Nyult's study, secondary nucleation in a magnetically stirred device generated crystals at one-third the supersaturation temperature required for nucleation without crystals. Nyult estimated the activation energy for nucleation to be 5-7 kcal per mole.

Factors affecting crystal growth

After nucleation, each nucleus grows and is either swept

out into the product stream or accumulates in the vat of a vat-type crystallizer. A study by McCabe[6] describes the kinetics of crystal growth under various supersaturation conditions. The process of growth under normal operating conditions is controlled by diffusion. McCabe observed that larger crystals grew faster, and growth was approximately proportional to the characteristic length of the crystal. When the relative velocity between the crystal and the solution exceeds a certain limit (approximately 3 cm per sec in the cases studied), the growth rate's dependence on velocity disappears. The rate of growth at zero velocity is approximately half that at velocities greater than 3 cm per sec. The growth rate at zero velocity is approximately a linear function of supersaturation, with a growth rate of 1 micron per min occurring at a supersaturation of 1.78°C (equal to a supersaturation of 1 g $CuSO_4 \cdot 5H_2O$ per 100 g free water), and a growth rate of 3 microns per min occurring at a supersaturation of 3.52°C (equal to a supersaturation of 2 g $CuSO_4 \cdot 3H_2O$ per 100 g free water). Tanimoto[7] estimated the activation energy for growth to be 12.3 kcal per mole.

Crystallization technology

Present crystallizer technology is illustrated in Fig. 5, after Randolph.[8] Expressed in differential form, this is an information flow diagram for a simple crystallizer. The diagram suggests how an output crystal size distribution from a crystallizer is determined by various system parameters. Inputs such as agitation level, amount of crystal deposited per unit volume of feed solution, average retention time, recycling of crystals through a dissolver, and various configuration parameters all affect the operation of an industrial crystallizer.

Fig. 5 gives the population balance equation, which summarizes the life cycle of all crystals in the crystallizer. This equation establishes the identity of a crystal based on a characteristic dimension. Also shown in Fig. 5 is the overall mass balance equation (input equals output).

Operation of industrial crystallizers

Control of nucleation is the key to industrial crystallizer operation. Most industrial crystallizers operate in an area of supersaturation that prevents homogeneous nucleation. Nucleation in these crystallizers is secondary nucleation, and results from the interaction of the crystal bed within the crystallizer. Secondary nucleation occurs through both crystal-to-crystal impacts and crystal-to-crystallizer impacts.

Changes in agitation significantly alter the size distribution of copper sulphate pentahydrate crystals. Studies of copper sulphate crystallization in fluidized bed crystallizers[9] and hydroclone crystallizers[10] illustrate a significant reduction in crystal size due to increases in nucleation rate. The rate increases result from increased secondary nucleation at higher agitation levels.

Other factors affecting the nucleation rate include presence of foreign solid material in the feed, use of a vacuum crystallizer, quantity of soluble impurities in the feed, and thermal gradients in the crystallizer. Nuclei are often generated outside the crystallizer and enter with the feed. This can become a problem when submicron dust particles or undissolved copper sulphate crystals appear in the crystallizer feed. Degassing the feed solution[11] improves crystal size by reducing nucleation in the crystallizer, as does the use of direct cooling instead of flash evaporation in a vacuum crystallizer.[12]

Fig. 2—Copper sulphate from a continuous crystallizer

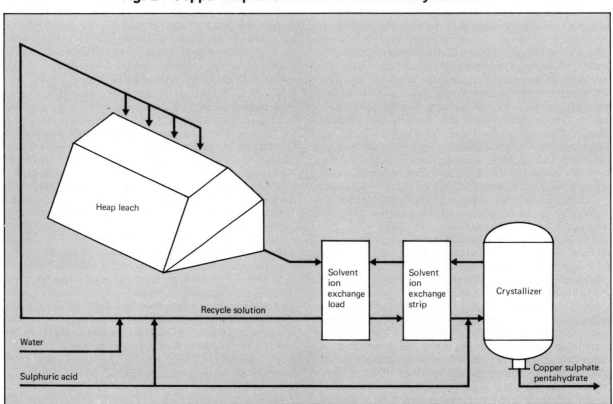

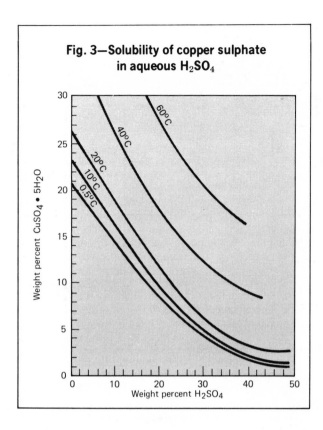

Fig. 3—Solubility of copper sulphate in aqueous H_2SO_4

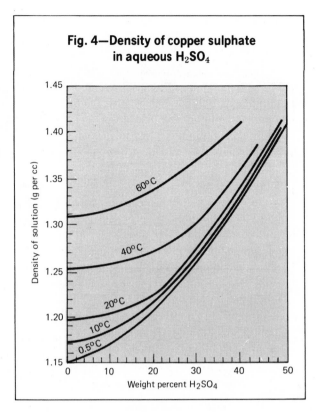

Fig. 4—Density of copper sulphate in aqueous H_2SO_4

Control of nucleation by reduction of supersaturation, removal of foreign nuclei, minimization of secondary nucleation, or destruction of nuclei normally provides some control over crystallizer operation. However, mechanically agitated crystallizers inevitably produce smaller crystals than those produced by vat crystallizers because of the generation of an increased number of nuclei.

Industrial crystallizer selection

For growing large $CuSO_4$ crystals, cooling vat crystallizers are still the only acceptable technology. However, agitated crystallizers have several advantages over vat crystallizers, including continuous automated operation, low labor cost per unit throughput, higher-purity product from a given feed solution,[13-17] and lower capital cost per unit of output.

The operation of existing continuous crystallizers can be improved by certain modifications, such as the use of pneumatic mixers, gas lift agitation, and the use of staged or sequential crystallizers. With either staged or sequential crystallizers, each successive crystallizer should operate on a fixed supersaturation differential between inlet and outlet that is low enough to prevent excessive nucleation, yet high enough to provide reasonable growth. At a typical growth rate of 1 micron per min, an average residence time of more than a day is required to grow crystals of acceptable quality and size. This time requirement suggests the use of a retained solids crystallizer.

Problems caused by impurities

Impurities are carried in the feed solution to the crystallizer through coextraction with copper from the leach feed material. In general, these impurities affect the size, crystal habit, and impurity level of copper sulphate pentahydrate through a series of complicated surface phenomena. Iron and sulphuric acid are the most common impurities in copper sulphate crystallizer circuits. Both tend to reduce the size, alter the habit, and increase the impurity level of $CuSO_4 \cdot 5H_2O$ crystals.[13, 15, 18-22] Both can be removed by extending the leaching process until nearly all the sulphuric acid has been consumed, or by neutralization with a base such as copper oxide or lime. The iron may also be left in solution if it is complexed with various agents, such as fluoride ions.[19-21]

Other impurities, such as Sb, As, Ca, Co, Ni, Na, and Zn, are normally allowed to build up in the recycle stream, and are then bled from the circuit or removed in a separate processing unit. Arsenic can be removed by adding ferrous iron, followed by oxidizing and neutralizing to precipitate the arsenic as a complex iron-arsenic compound.[22] Examples of impurity distribution coefficients are given by Matusevich[15] and Kafarova[18] for various impurities. Several authors[13-17] illustrate the exclusion of impurities from $CuSO_4 \cdot 5H_2O$ by adjusting crystallizer operation. These studies include data on how stirring affects the exclusion of impurities from the crystal and how it affects the entrapment of mother liquor in the crystal.

Conclusions

Crystallization of copper sulphate pentahydrate from aqueous sulphuric acid is the most important unit operation in the production of copper compounds. The growth of minus 30-mesh to plus 60-mesh copper sulphate pentahydrate crystals is relatively simple in a mildly agitated, single-stage continuous crystallizer. At elevated temperatures, these crystals require a residence time of approximately 2 hr. For growth of larger crystals, careful control of nucleation, growth rate, and average residence time is required. Elevated temperature with low sulphuric acid levels seems to be the most acceptable operating point for growing large crystals. □

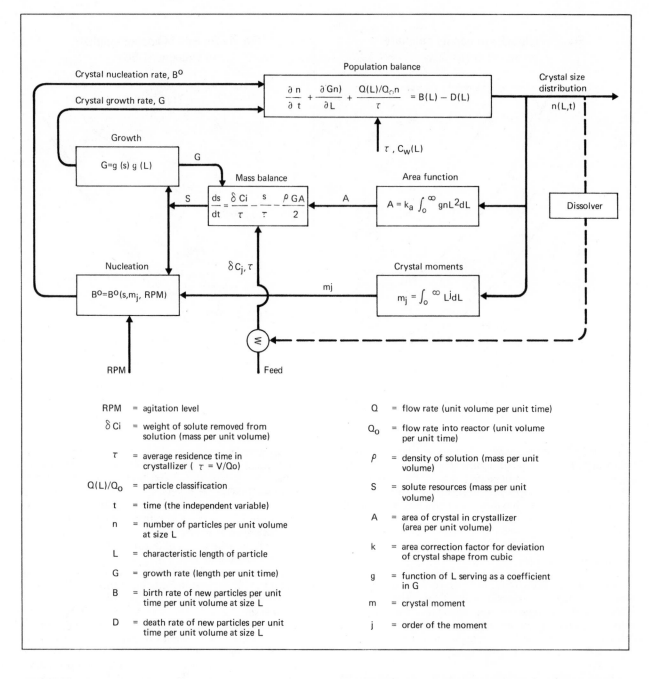

RPM = agitation level

δC_i = weight of solute removed from solution (mass per unit volume)

τ = average residence time in crystallizer ($\tau = V/Q_0$)

$Q(L)/Q_0$ = particle classification

t = time (the independent variable)

n = number of particles per unit volume at size L

L = characteristic length of particle

G = growth rate (length per unit time)

B = birth rate of new particles per unit time per unit volume at size L

D = death rate of new particles per unit time per unit volume at size L

Q = flow rate (unit volume per unit time)

Q_0 = flow rate into reactor (unit volume per unit time)

ρ = density of solution (mass per unit volume)

S = solute resources (mass per unit volume)

A = area of crystal in crystallizer (area per unit volume)

k = area correction factor for deviation of crystal shape from cubic

g = function of L serving as a coefficient in G

m = crystal moment

j = order of the moment

References

1) *Minerals Yearbook*, Vol. I; Metals, Minerals and Fuels (1972), US Department of Interior, BUREAU OF MINES, US Government Printing Office (1974).
2) Harike, G. E., US Patent 2,533,245, December 12, 1950.
3) Eissler, M., *The Hydrometallurgy of Copper*, Van Nostrand Co., New York (1902).
4) Linke, W. F., *Solubilities of Inorganic and Metal Organic Compounds, Fourth Ed.*, Vol. 1, pp 965-968, American Chemical Society, Washington, D.C. (1958).
5) Nyult, J., R. Rychly, J. Gottfried, and J. Wurzelova, "Metastable Zone-Width of Some Aqueous Solutions," JOURNAL OF CRYSTAL GROWTH, Vol. 6, No. 2 (1970), p 151-162.
6) McCabe, W. L., and R. P. Stevens, "Rate of Growth of Crystals in Aqueous Solutions," CHEMICAL ENGINEERING PROGRESS, Vol. 47, No. 4 (1951), p 168-174.
7) Tanimoto, A., K. Kobayashi, and S. Fujita, "Rate of Crystallization of Copper Sulfate Pentahydrate in Stirred Vessel," KAGAKU KOGAKU, Vol. 27, No. 6 (1963), p 424-428.
8) Randolph, A. D., and M. L. Larsen, *Theory of Particulate Processes*, Academic, New York (1971).
9) Razaumovskii, L. A., and V. V. Streltsov, "Size Distribution Characteristics of Crystals Grown in a Fluidized Bed," TEOR. OSN KHIM. TEKHNOL., Vol. 1, No. 3 (1967), p 360-361. (C.A. 68:33882w)
10) Molyneux, F., "Crystallization in a Hydroclone," CHEM. PROCESS ENG. Vol. 44 (1963), p 248-253.
11) Wawrzyczek, W., "Effect of Ultrasound on the Crystallization of Salts," NATURWISSENSCHAFTEN, Vol. 51, No. 1 (1964), p 9-10. (C.A. 60-9987e)
12) Nakai, T., Y. Aoyama, and K. Mikake, "Application of the Thermal History

of Copper Sulfate Solution to Industrial Crystallization, Part I, Crystallization with Pilot Plant," KRIST. TECH., Vol. 8, No. 11 (1973), p 1313-1324.
13) Matusevich, L. N., "Effect of Stirring a Solution on the Purity of the Crystals Obtained from It," UKR. KHIM. ZH., Vol. 29 (1963), p 7-11. (C.A. 59-2233c)
14) Chatterjee, G. S., "Experimental Studies in Crystallization II," Trans. Indian Inst. Chem. Engrs., Vol. 2 (1948-49), p 57-62.
15) Matusevich, L. N., "Effect of Conditions of Crystallization of Copper Sulfate on Size and Purity of Crystals Produced."
16) Matusevich, L. N., "Effect of Saturation, Temperature and Seed Crystals on Crystallization from Aqueous Solutions," KRIST. TECH., Vol. 1, No. 4 (1966), p 611-625. (C.A. 69-39296a)
17) Matusevich, L. N., "Crystallization by Precipitation in the Presence of Nonisomorphic, Isomorphic and Adsorbic Admixtures," KRIST. TECH., Vof. 1 (1966), p 127-136. (C.A. 69-62163)
18) Kaforova, I. A., "Fractionation of Trivalent Iron and Other Microimpurities in the Crystallization of Copper Sulfate from Aqueous Solutions," ZH. PRIKL. KHIM., Vol. 35 (1962), p 1934-1940. (C.A. 58-1958e)
19) Gorshtein, I. G., and I. A. Kiforva, USSR Patent 149,412, August 28, 1962. (C.A. 58-5292d)
20) Chervyakov, V. M., B. S. Kaunatskaya, and N. M. Shkolnik, "Removal of Iron Impurities from Reactive Copper Sulfate," KHIM. PROM., Vol. 48, No. 9 (1972), p 711. (C.A. 78-99792e)
21) Kaunatskaya, R. S., V. M. Cheryakov, and N. M. Shkolnik, USSR Patent 368,189, January 26, 1973. (C.A. 79-7524p)
22) Ivanova, E. S., "Apparatus for Removal of Iron and Arsenic at the Beginning of the Vitriol Shop Line," URAL. NAUCH-ISSLED. PROEKT. INST. MEDNOI PROM., No. 12 (1969), p 235-238. (C.A. 74-144818y)

ENGINEERING AND MINING JOURNAL

In-situ leaching opens new uranium reserves in Texas

This complex of pipes, valves, and wells—part of a less-than-3-acre pattern near George West, Tex.—does not <u>look</u> like a uranium mine. But since April it has been extracting U_3O_8 from sandstones at depths to 550 ft by in-situ leaching. The Atlantic Richfield-US Steel-Dalco joint venture may be only the first of several commercially scaled, in-situ leaching operations to successfully produce uranium concentrate from Texas ores.

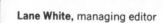

Lane White, managing editor

A COMMERCIAL IN-SITU URANIUM LEACHING OPERATION that is quite probably the largest ever built started up in April, 10 mi southwest of George West, Tex. Producing from a pattern of 66 injection wells and 46 extraction wells occupying an area of less than 3 acres, the Clay West mine and plant are expected to reach design capacity of 250,000 lb per year of yellowcake by the end of the summer. By late May, results were sufficiently favorable to make the owners think seriously about an early expansion.

Built at a cost of $7 million by joint venturers Atlantic Richfield (50% owner and operator), Dalco (25%), and US Steel (25%), the Clay West mine may be only the first of several mines to extract U_3O_8 from a uranium province that stretches from north of Houston to Brownsville, at the southernmost tip of the state. Westinghouse subsidiary Wyoming Minerals is building a 250,000-lb-per-year plant near Bruni, with startup planned before the end of 1975, and Mobil Oil is setting up a pilot-scale plant in the same area. A number of other companies are reported to be actively interested in development of in-situ uranium leaching in Texas.

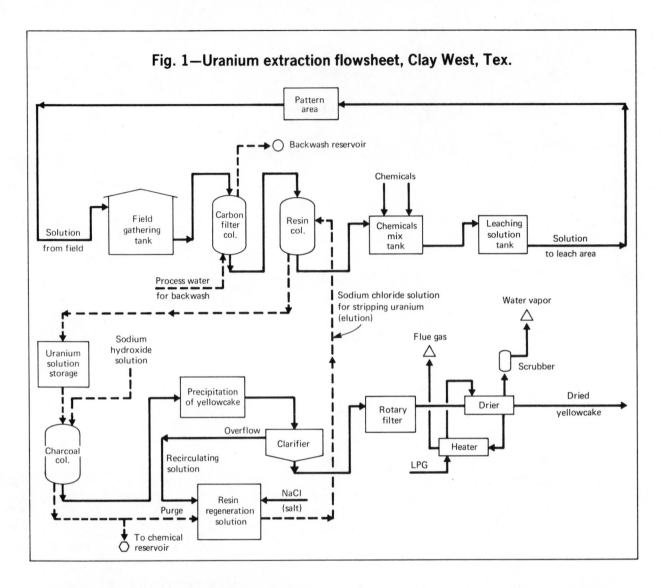

Fig. 1—Uranium extraction flowsheet, Clay West, Tex.

Chemicals mix tank in the Clay West plant area feeds leaching solution to a surge tank located at the in-situ mining pattern.

The Atlantic Richfield (Arco) Clay West operation will employ 45 people, supported by a staff of 12 at Arco uranium operations headquarters in Corpus Christi. Reserves are thought to be sufficient for at least 20 years' production, uranium operations manager Glen R. Davis said during E/MJ's visit to the property. The Arco-Dalco-US Steel partnership has access to 35-40 sections, and patterns of injection and production wells will eventually be operated up to 2 mi from the central processing plant.

The Clay West operation uses a proprietary alkaline leach solution developed during pilot testing by Dalco and US Steel. Solution is pumped into and out of uranium-bearing ore zones at equal rates to prevent loss of solution in the sandstone formation. The pregnant solution is collected at an 800-bbl field gathering tank and then pumped to the plant area. There the solution passes through one of six parallel trains, each consisting of a carbon column and an ion exchange column in series (Fig. 1). A commercial resin extracts U_3O_8 in the ion exchange column. Solution circulates through the leach pattern at 2,000 gpm.

New environmental control procedures were formulated by the Texas Water Quality Board to govern Clay West operations, as there was no precedent for the Arco request to pump a solution into and out of an aquifer. The company will be required to monitor the zones around producing patterns to assure that no leaching solution escapes the producing area, and when a pattern is exhausted, Arco

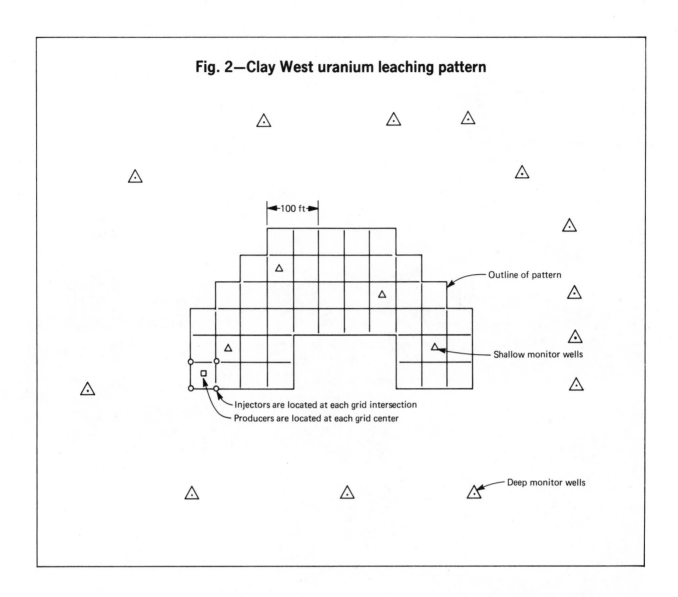

Fig. 2—Clay West uranium leaching pattern

←100 ft→

Outline of pattern

Shallow monitor wells

Injectors are located at each grid intersection
Producers are located at each grid center

Deep monitor wells

must restore the aquifer to the chemical condition that prevailed prior to operation.

A deep disposal well will be used to dispose of solution pumped from the patterns during aquifer renovation.

Oakville sandstone is source horizon of U_3O_8

The Clay West mine extracts uranium from a maximum depth of 550 ft in the Miocene Oakville sandstone—about 350 ft of interbedded sands, silts, and bentonitic clays. The ore occurs in zones 10 to 60 ft thick and grades from a low 0.05% U_3O_8 to as high as 0.5%—the latter being uncommon. Regionally, rock formations dip toward the Gulf of Mexico at about 79 ft per mi.

The Oakville is underlain by Catahoula clays—about 2,100 ft of clays and thin beds of sand that have a higher-than-normal background count of U_3O_8. The U_3O_8 in the Catahoula is thought to derive from volcanic ash deposited during Catahoula time, according to Arco geologist Charles Trimble. Percolating ground waters dissolve the U_3O_8 and transport it to neighboring rocks, where, in the presence of H_2S derived from oil-bearing formations, the U_3O_8 precipitates, sometimes in commercial concentrations.

The Clay West mine taps the Oakville deposits through a pattern of production wells spaced at 50-ft intervals (Fig. 2). The 46 extraction wells are interspersed at regular in-

tervals with a grid of injection wells and are surrounded by monitor wells.

The Oakville sandstone is a regional aquifer having a slow rate of flow—about 12 ft per year. Should the monitor wells detect leaching solution escaping from the production zone, the rate of production can be increased or the rate of injection decreased to pull the solution back.

A Midway drill of the type used for seismic blasthole drilling sinks the 4-in.-dia injection wells and the 6-in.-dia extraction wells (Fig. 3), the latter being larger to accommodate a submersible pump at the bottom of the well. Open screened sections of pipe in the ore zones permit production of leach solution with minimal extraction of entrained particulates.

Well piping, along with most other piping at the Clay West mine, is of PVC, to minimize corrosion and to keep corrosion products out of the system, Davis said. This protection will prevent plugging of injection wells and contamination of the yellowcake product. Two 12-in. mainline PVC pipes connect the plant and production areas.

The pregnant leach solution arrives at the processing plant carrying dissolved U_3O_8. It first passes through a carbon column, which removes any sand present in the solution, and then through an ion exchange column, which extracts the uranium. The carbon columns are backwashed periodically to remove trapped sand. A backwash reservoir provides clean water and acts as a settling pond. The water

View of the Clay West plant across one of two solution storage ponds: chemicals mix tank is shown at the right, storage and process facilities at center, and yellowcake processing building to the left.

is recirculated and evaporation losses are made up by water from a fresh water well.

A sodium chloride solution is used to extract U_3O_8 from the ion exchange column. The rich uranium-bearing solution (about 1% U_3O_8) passes through a charcoal column for removal of impurities, including molybdenum, and then reports to precipitation tanks, where yellowcake is precipitated with ammonia. Recovery of moly as a byproduct is a possibility in the future.

Chemical wastes from the plant are disposed of in reservoirs lined with highly resistant chlorinated polyethylene lining. The design of the reservoirs keeps net annual evaporation rate equal to the volume of chemical wastes generated each year. Reservoir capacity is sufficient to accommodate periods of high rainfall and low evaporation. During the first year of operation, a critical examination of waste streams is seeking opportunities for waste reduction.

After precipitation, yellowcake is allowed to settle in a clarifier, filtered, dried, and packed for shipping to the Allied Chemical uranium hexafluoride plant at Metropolis,

Ill. The dryer, the only source of air emissions in the plant, is a screw-conveyor unit based on indirect heat transfer between a recirculating heated oil and yellowcake solids. The heat-transfer oil is heated externally in a unit fueled with liquefied petroleum gas. The quantity of flue gas from the dryer is insufficient to require a permit from the Texas Air Control Board.

One of the advantages of the dryer is minimal dust problems, because of the absence of air contact. For added protection, however, exhaust gases will be scrubbed by a two-stage water scrubber. The exhaust from this scrubber will be virtually dust-free, releasing only water vapor to the air.

The Clay West operation is not energy-intensive, as circulating solutions all flow at ambient temperatures. Power draw for the entire operation is about 1,500 kw from San Patricio Electric, a small co-op producer at Sinton, Tex. The major costs of operation are labor and chemicals.

Mine manager Walter Ely noted that creation of jobs at the Clay West mine has provided a welcome injection of

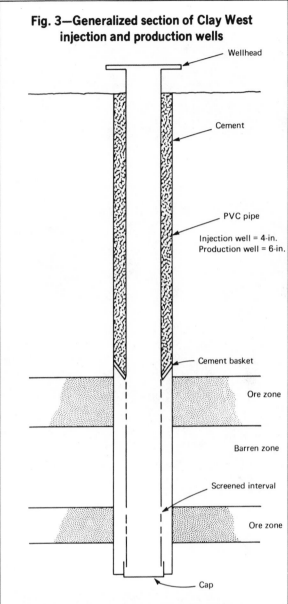

Fig. 3—Generalized section of Clay West injection and production wells

Wellhead

Cement

PVC pipe

Injection well = 4-in.
Production well = 6-in.

Cement basket

Ore zone

Barren zone

Screened interval

Ore zone

Cap

cash into the local economy. The mine is located in pleasant, rolling countryside that has produced well for farmers and ranchers but has provided few non-agricultural jobs. The Clay West mine offers an opportunity for some George West natives to secure long-term employment near home, and the $500,000 annual payroll will help support additional jobs in the George West community.

Arco has adopted a system of rotation for its employees that will regularly move each into a different job in various areas of mine and plant activity. The system is expected to create a more interesting work environment for the employees and more highly trained and valuable employees for Arco.

Controlling solution in the leaching zone

Waters present in the Clay West orebody are not now a source of potable water due to naturally-occurring high levels of radium. As noted above, the two primary environmental considerations will be to prevent contaminants

from leaking out of the ore zone during leaching and to restore the water in the orebody after conclusion of leaching. During leaching, injection and production rates will be balanced, with each injection and production line equipped with direct-reading flow meters. A central instrument panel in the pattern area monitors the flow meters, and a daily check is made to balance total 24-hr production against total 24-hr injection.

All injection and producing wells in the leach area are cased and cemented to the surface, preventing upward migration of injected solutions behind the casing. Four shallow monitor wells drilled in the pattern area are sampled and analyzed routinely to determine whether the leach solution moves upward.

A detailed program of water well sampling was formulated by Arco in consultation with the Texas Water Quality Board, and all water wells within a 5-mi radius of the pattern were sampled and analyzed prior to production. During production, one-eighth of these wells will be examined every three months to detect any change in the

Six pairs of carbon column and ion exchange column tanks are the heart of the Clay West plant site. Building in the background houses offices and a well-equipped laboratory. Farm country beyond the building is typical of the George West area.

Clay West clarifier is a wood-stave thickener-type unit.

Rich eluate tank provides surge capacity ahead of charcoal column.

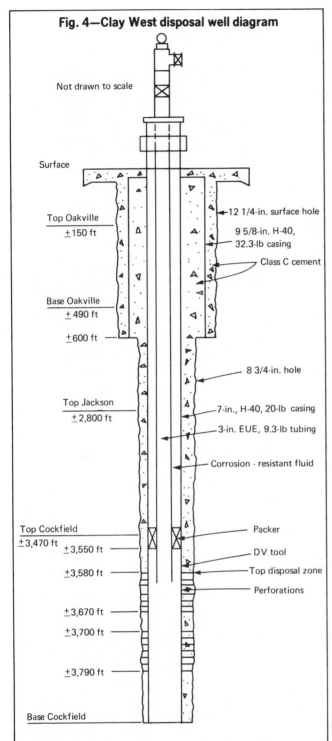

Fig. 4—Clay West disposal well diagram

Not drawn to scale

Surface

Top Oakville
±150 ft

Base Oakville
±490 ft

±600 ft

Top Jackson
±2,800 ft

Top Cockfield
±3,470 ft

±3,550 ft

±3,580 ft

±3,670 ft

±3,700 ft

±3,790 ft

Base Cockfield

12 1/4-in. surface hole

9 5/8-in. H-40,
32.3-lb casing

Class C cement

8 3/4-in. hole

7-in., H-40, 20-lb casing

3-in. EUE, 9.3-lb tubing

Corrosion - resistant fluid

Packer

DV tool

Top disposal zone

Perforations

The Clay West laboratory is equipped with a spectrophotometer, a Technicon, and an atomic adsorption apparatus for analyzing the many samples required both for process solutions and for regional water sampling. Monitor wells in the leach area are sampled regularly to detect any migration of injected solutions. If migration occurs, the material balance of reservoir fluids can be controlled, resulting in a net flow of native water into the leaching area, preventing any migration outside the leach area.

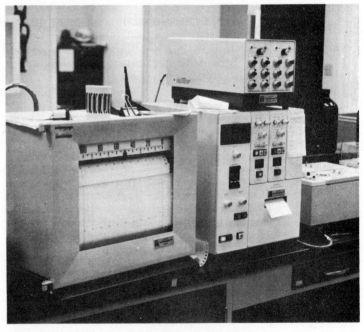

chemical analysis of the water. The wells will be analyzed for calcium, sodium, iron, molybdenum, bicarbonate, sulphate, chloride, nitrate, nitrite, ammonium, pH, and total dissolved solids (List A). The same wells will be analyzed for Gross Alpha and Gross Beta radiation. If Gross Alpha exceeds three picocuries per liter, a barium co-precipitation for radium 226 will be performed. If Gross Beta exceeds 50 picocuries per liter, a lead 210 determination will be performed. Every six months, the nearest six wells used for drinking water will be examined radiometrically and List A analyses will be run.

During development of the Clay West leach pattern, 28 operating wells were sampled and analyzed for List A ions. In addition, 10 of these wells were analyzed for radiation and heavy metals—magnesium, fluoride, arsenic, barium, boron, cadmium, copper, chromium, lead, manganese, mercury, nickel, selenium, silver, uranium, zinc, simple cyanide and P-alkalinity as $CaCO_3$, and total alkalinity as $CaCO_3$ (List B). As part of this program, some wells were sampled and analyzed as many as four times prior to operation.

To monitor surface drainage, Spring Creek is sampled

Clay West process building houses precipitation tanks, rotary filter, heater, dryer, and packaging and shipping facilities.

upstream of the Clay West plant site and downstream of the pattern area. The Nueces River, which provides drinking water for Corpus Christi, is sampled above and below its confluence with Spring Creek. Samples are analyzed radiometrically and chemically.

Arco also organized an in-house environmental task force to perform a baseline study of the Clay West environment prior to moving into the area. The task force included biologists, radiologists, chemical engineers, petroleum engineers, geologists, hydrologists, and zoologists. Among its subjects of study were fish, amphibia, birds, insects, bacteria, shrubs, grasses, roots, stems, soils, and streams.

The present plan for orebody restoration is to pump contaminated solutions out of the leached zone into a deep disposal well until ion concentrations are down to acceptable levels. Pilot tests conducted by Dalco and US Steel demonstrated that when injection is stopped but production maintained, there is a gradual decrease in ionic species in the produced solutions. These data are proprietary but were released on a confidential basis to the Texas Water Quality Board. Other alternatives to pumping the orebody will also be studied, and techniques for converting the aquifer back from an oxidized state to a reduced state are under investigation.

The Clay West disposal wells—two are planned—will be drilled to a total depth of 4,500 ft, down through the Cockfield sandstone of Upper Claiborne (Oligocene?) age. The

On a smaller scale, other mines have recovered U$_3$O$_8$ by in-situ leaching

While the new Clay West in-situ uranium leaching mine in Texas is the first of its type to produce on a commercial scale, limited quantities of uranium have been produced by other in-situ mines operating now or in the past. A number of these operations are described briefly in "Analysis of Non-coal Underground Mining Methods," prepared by Dravo Corp. for the US Bureau of Mines and published in 1974.

Mine water near Grants, N. Mex., was found to carry 2-10 ppm of dissolved uranium, the report states. The slightly basic water (7 to 8 pH) takes the uranium into solution as the tricarbonate ion, which is readily extracted by ion exchange. Oxidation of the insoluble tetravalent uranium to a soluble hexavalent uranium is accomplished by exposure to air and possibly by bacterial action. After passing through ion exchange, the water is returned to the mine and sprayed on drift and stope walls. It then drains back to a sump for return to the ion exchange columns. Production of 5,000 to 15,000 lb per month is dependent on the flow of water and the ground area being wetted.

The same procedure is used in the Elliot Lake district in Canada, the report states, except that an acid environment is generated by the oxidation of iron sulphides in the ore.

"The Pitch mine in Colorado was water leached by drilling injection wells from the surface into the abandoned and caved stoping areas," the Dravo report notes. "The water percolated through the old mine workings, collected in the main haulage tunnel, and passed through an ion exchange column. The stripped water was then returned to the injection wells. Later in the program, soda ash and bicarbonate were added to

the leach solution to improve extraction. This operation is now closed, but has potential for producing additional uranium by in-situ leaching."

Utah Mining and Construction Co. (now Utah International) experimented with a series of injection wells, usually three, around a production well. Based on groundwater flow, the injection wells were drilled upstream from the production well. Tracer dyes were used to study solution flow between injection wells and the production well. After flow patterns were established, an acid leach solution was injected. Withdrawal rate was slightly more than the injection rate. The pregnant solution was passed through ion exchange columns for uranium extraction, and then it was rejected because it contained soluble gypsum that would blind the leach area if reused.

"The area under leach from each set of wells was very small," according to the Dravo report, "seldom larger than 25-ft dia. The project never produced more than 7,000 or 8,000 lb per month of U$_3$O$_8$, even with as many as five well systems operating. Leaching was discontinued in 1968, when the operation was converted to an open pit."

Exxon (Humble Oil) is experimenting with the same leach method in the Powder River Basin in Wyoming, the report states, except that a carbonate system is used, permitting recirculation of the leach solution.

"With the depletion of higher grade deposits of uranium," the report concludes, "much of the future production may depend on successful in-situ leach extraction. This is particularly important for small, isolated deposits of lower grade values that will not economically support conventional . . . extraction."

Cockfield is the proposed disposal zone.

During aquifer renovation following leaching, Arco expects to pump an estimated 150 gpm of slightly saline water from the leach pattern, with a probable maximum of 2,000 mg per liter total dissolved solids. This water will be pumped to the disposal well after most of the uranium has been removed. The native water in Cockfield sands is much more saline than the disposal stream.

The surface hole will be drilled 12½-in. dia and 600 ft deep, through the Oakville aquifer and into the underlying Catahoula clays. H-40, 32.3-lb pipe with a diameter of 9⅝ in. will be set as casing to 600 ft, and Class C cement circulated to the surface. An 8¾-in. hole will then be drilled to 4,500 ft. Upon completion of drilling, electrical and bulk density logs will be run in the hole.

Casing—7-in.-dia, 20-lb, H-40 pipe—will be set on the bottom and cemented in two stages. The first stage will bring cement to the top of the Cockfield sand, a depth of about 3,500 ft. Utilizing a D-V tool, sufficient additional cement will be pumped to circulate to the surface.

Injection intervals will be determined from electric and gamma-ray logs. Proposed intervals are from 3,580 ft to 3,670 ft and from 3,700 ft to 3,790 ft. The balance of the Cockfield sand between the depths of about 3,790 ft and 4,500 ft is considered a reserve for future disposal, if volumes or pressure gradients exceed present estimates.

When the ore zone of a leaching pattern has been restored, Arco will turn the surface back to normal use. The area will need reseeding, but reclamation in the usually understood sense will be unnecessary. The leaching operations will leave the surface essentially undisturbed. Within a few years after leaching stops, it may be difficult to identify a leach pattern area as ever having been different from the surrounding countryside. □

Developers eye Texas potential for in-situ uranium leaching

Emmy Crawford, McGraw-Hill World News, Houston

IN ADDITION TO the Arco-US Steel-Dalco plant now in production near George West, Tex., several other in-situ uranium leaching projects are in various stages of planning, design, and construction in south Texas.

The most advanced project belongs to Westinghouse's wholly owned subsidiary, Wyoming Minerals, which is building a 250,000-lb-per-year plant near Bruni, Tex., about 40 mi east of Laredo. While Wyoming Minerals has not revealed any details of its process, a source at the Texas Water Quality Board states that the operation will use a weak ammonia leach and a proprietary ion exchange extraction system.

Wyoming Minerals also plans a second commercial uranium in-situ leach plant near Ray Point, north of George West in Live Oak County. The Texas Water Quality Board has received an application for this operation, but as of early June, no date had been set for a hearing.

In Duval County, Union Carbide is considering a pilot-scale in-situ leach operation, but for it too, no hearing date had been set by early June.

(While n t of direct interest to Texas uranium production, a Burlington Northern-Wyoming Minerals joint venture calls for Wyoming Minerals to conduct minerals exploration on 8.4 million acres of Burlington Northern railroad property in Oregon, Washington, Idaho, Wyoming, Montana, North Dakota, Minnesota and Wisconsin. The agreement, which includes gas, oil, and uranium as well as other minerals, will run five to eight years, and Wyoming Minerals will get up to 50% interest in discovered properties, depending on how much money it invests in the project. The joint venture company—called Bur-West—is headquartered in Billings, Mont.)

Mobil pilot plant is under construction

Southeast of Bruni, in Webb County, Tex., Mobil Oil Corp. is building a pilot plant to test the feasibility of a proprietary in-situ uranium leaching method. The plant is expected to start up around October 1 to leach U_3O_8 in place, at depths of 410 to 430 ft.

Present plans call for an initial 18-month test program, with an overlapping 15-month test at a nearby site if the first program is successful. The capacity of the pilot scale operation will not be determined until solution is actually put into the ground, and Mobil has no present timetable for commercial development.

The Mobil pilot operation will inject a leach solution into the uranium-bearing formation through 15 injection wells and extract it through seven production wells. The solution is identified as a dilute ammonium carbonate made by mixing gaseous ammonia and carbon dioxide with formation water treated with ordinary water softener. An unidentified oxidant is also added. Solution produced will be collected in a surge tank and then pumped to a holding tank at the recovery plant site, about 700 ft away.

A sand filter will remove suspended solids, and an ion exchange column will extract U_3O_8. The barren effluent from the ion exchange column will be pumped to a holding tank where an oxidant and leach chemicals are added, and the solution will be recycled to the injection wells.

Uranium will be extracted from the ion exchange resin by an unidentified chemical, and the U_3O_8-rich eluate will be pumped to a holding tank and then to a precipitation tank for uranium precipitation. Ammonia and carbon dioxide gases generated in the precipitation process will be vented to a 20-ft-high fume scrubber. Water spray in the scrubber will absorb the vapors, and the resulting solution will be recycled to the injection well stream.

Filters, ion exchange, and water softener tanks will be backwashed periodically and the water held in a 500-bbl tank. If backwash water is found to contain excess solid or radioactive material, it will be pumped to an evaporation pit.

A system of eight monitoring wells will determine if there is leakage of chemicals outside the planned injection production pattern.

This Mobil pilot, the new Arco plant at George West, Wyoming Minerals' active development program, and Union Carbide's interest in entering the in-situ development activity all point to future growth of uranium production by in-situ leaching in south Texas. This prospect is strengthened, of course, by recent improvement in yellowcake prices—now topping $20 per lb and expected to go still higher. ☐

How to extract uranium from refractory ores

Professor Alcidos Caldas, director of engineering chemistry, Federal University of Rio de Janeiro

A SOLID-PHASE TECHNIQUE of oxidizing-sintering has been developed for recovery of uranium from essentially insoluble ores, at lower temperatures than conventional methods, with minimum use of an oxidant.

A number of uraniferous minerals lock uranium in the tetravalent form, but U^{+4} is essentially insoluble in sulphuric acid, or in a solution of alkaline carbonate, when oxidizing agents are absent. To dissolve uranium, U^{+4} must first be oxidized to U^{+6} by means of topological reactions that take place on the surface of the solid particles of the ore. The usual method is to treat ground ore with a hot dilute solution of sulphuric acid and then add a suitable oxidizing agent.

In the new method, the oxidizing agent may be.added to ore during grinding. The mixture is then heated to an appropriate temperature determined by the nature of the oxidizing agent, so that an oxidizing sinter occurs in a solid state reaction. The presence of V_2O_5—either occurring naturally in certain uranium ores or added prior to calcination—improves the subsequent extraction of uranium.[1]

Even though the new method utilizes ordinary oxidizing agents, it differs from the conventional method in that oxidation is done prior to lixiviation instead of simultaneously. This technique offers better conditions for efficient oxidation and dissolution of uranium, while using less acid and dissolving fewer of the other constituents of the ore. Compared with current methods, the new process uses milder conditions of temperature with less corrosion of the equipment, shorter residence time, and a better extractive yield of uranium.

Without considering economics, some oxidizing reagents are well suited to this type of reaction, as they produce a dry oxidation.

Manganese dioxide (either the natural or the artificial product) is a highly insoluble and infusible material. Its efficiency, and consequently the reproducibility of the results, are very much dependent on the surface conditions of the particles, since this is really a reaction in the solid state, between insoluble and infusible reagents. MnO_2 is low in cost and can be recovered either by chemical precipitation or by an electrolytic process. The "formation of salt by sintering" reactions do not occur in a wet way between MnO_2 and WO_3 or MoO_3, nor with natural sulphides such as FeS_2. They can be realized very easily by sintering.[2]

Sodium nitrate, $NaNO^3$, is a very mild oxidizing reagent (except in the presence of a strong reducing agent), and a very soluble compound, allowing easy penetration into the pores of the ore. It also has a relatively low melting temperature ($310°C$), and by decomposition at a high temperature ($400°C$) it furnishes the correspondent nitrite, $NaNO_2$, which is both an oxidant and a solvent for the metallo-acid elements.[3] However, sodium nitrate cannot be recovered.

Chromium trioxide, CrO_3, is an extremely strong and easily soluble oxidizing agent whose oxidizing power increases with decreasing water content of the solvent.[3] It is the anhydride of chromic acid, H_2CrO_4, which in acid media forms higher condensed acids such as $H_2Cr_2O_7$.

The use of $Cr_2O_7^{-2}$ as an oxidizing agent in dilute acid (usually sulphuric) is well known:

$$Cr_2O_7^{-2} + 14H^+ + 6e^- \rightleftarrows 2Cr^{+3} + 7H_2O$$

This is a reaction between ions in solution. In the presence of insoluble iron mineral products, the corresponding oxidation does not take place easily unless Fe^{+2} is first put into solution. In hot concentrated sulphuric acid, the following reaction occurs:

$$2H_2Cr_2O_7 + 5H_2SO_4 \rightleftarrows 2Cr_2(SO_4)_3 + 8H_2O + 3O_2$$

On the other hand, the CrO_3 decomposes above its melting point ($197°C$) according to the reaction:

$$4CrO_3 \rightarrow 2Cr_2O_3 + 3O_2$$

Under these conditions, the oxidizing reaction would occur because the gaseous O_2 formed is not very soluble and not very efficient for the reaction with the insoluble minerals of U^{+4}.

The use of CrO_3, obtained by evaporation ($105°$ to $110°C$) of H_2CrO_4 solution added to the ore, is especially efficient since the solid that is formed does not decompose at this temperature and acts directly on the reducing agent:

$$3UO_2 + 2CrO_3 \rightarrow 3UO_3 + Cr_2O_3$$

In this way U^{+4} passes to U^{+6} and becomes easily soluble, requiring a minimum of acid for its extraction.[5]

The acid solution thus obtained, containing U^{+6} and Cr^{+3} sulphates, can be treated by conventional processes in the same way as the solution obtained when dichromate is used as the oxidizing agent. In this way the U^{+6} can be extracted by appropriate organic solvents, and the chromic and sulphuric acids can be recovered from the aqueous layer by electrolytic oxidation, according to the overall equation:

$$Cr_2(SO_4)_3 + 5H_2O + 1\frac{1}{2}O_2 \rightarrow 2H_2CrO_4 + 3H_2SO_4$$

The new process has been tested with good results for the extraction of uranium from low grade refractory uranium ores, such as uraniferous zirconium ores, and from pyrochlore concentrates. ☐

References

1) McClaine, L. A., E. P. Bullwinkel, and J. C. Huggins, Proceedings of International Conference on Peaceful Uses of Atomic Energy, United Nations, New York, 1968, Vol. 8, p 33.
2) Arnold, H. Z., INORG. CHEM., 88, 1914, p 74.
3) Feigl, F., L. I. Miranda, and H. A. Suter, J. CHEM. EDUC., 21, 1944, pp 18-24.
4) Fieser, L. F., Experiments in Organic Chemistry, Heath, London, 1955, p 309.
5) Brazilian patent No. 5095/74.

Renovated Atlas mill will produce uranium, vanadium, and copper

Lane White, Managing editor

ATLAS MINERALS' RENOVATED MOAB, UTAH, MILL—based on one of the more complex flowsheets now in use in the US uranium industry—is slated to go on stream during the first quarter of 1976. The mill will incorporate a new, strong acid uranium-vanadium circuit, and a new caustic precipitation alkaline leach circuit will replace the resin-in-pulp alkaline leach circuit first installed in the 1950s. The mill renovation and flowsheet modification program also includes provision for impoundment and evaporation of all liquid effluent not recycled to plant use, eliminating previous discharge into the Colorado River.

The Atlas mill, built during the 1950s uranium rush by Charles Steen to process the output of his famed Mi Vida mine, is expected to produce about 1 million lb per year of yellowcake and 3 million lb per year of vanadium when the new facilities are fully on stream, according to general superintendent William Badger. The new acid leach circuit, which replaces an acid circuit destroyed by fire in 1969, will permit the Atlas mill to process uranium-vanadium carnotite ores that characterize uranium deposits of the Morrison formation. The mill also has a flotation section for floating copper sulphide minerals ahead of the uranium leaching circuits. The mill flowsheet description here was drawn largely from the "Facility Design and Construction" section of Atlas' presentation to the Nuclear Regulatory Commission to obtain authority for the mill modification program.

Completion of the Atlas mill renovation has coincided opportunely with the revival of the uranium market. Atlas chairman and president Edward R. Farley Jr. reported in mid-November that the company has signed an agreement to supply Houston Lighting & Power Co. with 1.25 million lb of uranium concentrate during the next two years. Pricing will depend on the market price of uranium at the time of delivery, with a minimum price fixed by the agreement.

Farley also said Atlas has renegotiated its agreement to provide Boston Edison Co. with 2.3 million lb of uranium during the next four years. The revised agreement calls for "somewhat higher" prices to reflect increased costs for uranium mining and processing and a revised and stretched-out schedule for delivery of the uranium. Atlas was also expecting to renegotiate its agreement with Iowa Electric Power and Light Co., which is scheduled to buy 750,000 lb of Atlas uranium concentrate.

The stepped-up pace at the Atlas mill is expected to lift employment at the plant from 90-100 to the 120-130 range, Badger said. The Moab economy, of which the Atlas mill has been a mainstay over the past 20 years, will benefit through a bigger payroll and increased tax dollars. Furthermore, higher uranium prices are already drawing uranium hunters to the "hot spots" of the Moab area's 1950s uranium boom to check out the possibility of renewed production.

Ore preparation geared to two circuits

Atlas receives all of its ore by truck from its own mines

Ore storage bins dominate Atlas Minerals' mill yard.

and from the mines of 20 to 30 small shippers, who account for about 10% of the mill feed. The mill yard provides space for segregation of ore according to varying contents of uranium, vanadium, and copper and according to ownership. A front-end loader reclaims ore and feeds it onto a 12-in. grizzly. Grizzly oversize feeds to a jaw crusher, where it is broken to about minus 10 in., while undersize moves by conveyor to an 80-ton hopper.

Crusher discharge passes under a suspended magnet that removes tramp iron and then feeds to a screen having 3-in. openings. A secondary jaw crusher breaks the screen oversize to minus 3 in.; the broken ore rejoins the screen undersize; and the ore stream feeds to two ¾-in.-opening screens in parallel. A cone crusher in closed circuit with the screens reduces the oversize to minus ¾ in., and the screen undersize—the final product of the crushing plant—moves by conveyor to a sampling tower.

The sampling tower receives 10% of the ore throughput, which undergoes two reductions of particle size and quantity to produce a 1-lb sample for each ton of mill feed. After further manual reduction, rejected sample material returns to the main ore stream.

Four bag-type dry dust collectors control dust emission in the crushing and sampling area. Two of the collectors service points of dust emission at the crushers and at transfer points between them, a third collects dust from the fine ore storage feeders, and a fourth controls dust from the sampling equipment. A 16-nozzle spray system under 40 psig of water pressure also gives coverage at points of potential dust emissions and at times when especially dry ores are being processed.

Dusting of the ore is a function of grain size and moisture and varies from one lot of ore to the next. The Chinle ores in the Atlas mill feed tend toward fine grain sizes, while the Morrison ores tend toward coarser grain sizes

Flowsheet—Atlas Minerals uranium mill, Moab, Utah

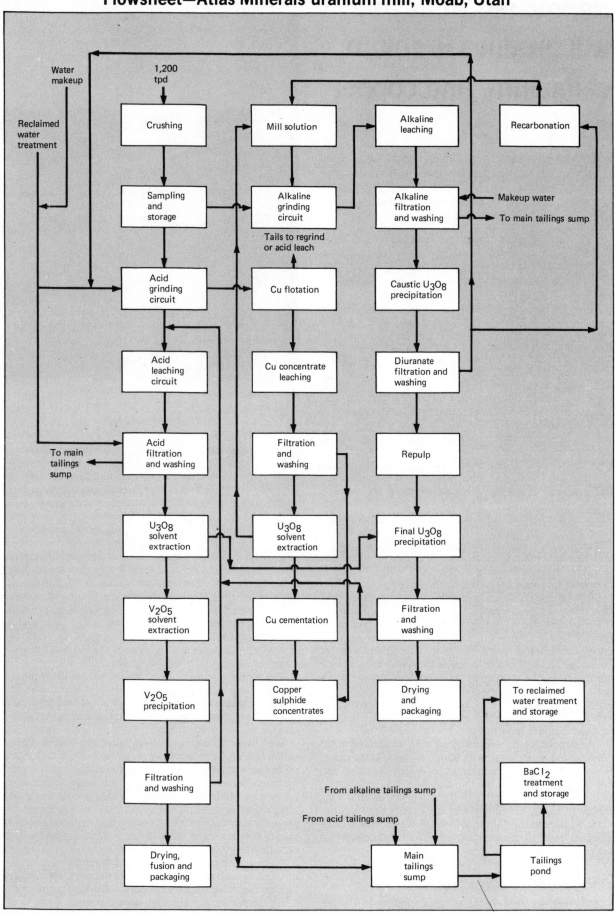

that are less susceptible to dusting. Ores of about 4% or more moisture content usually do not create dusting problems. At about 4% moisture or less in the ore—based on experience in handling the various ores in the Atlas mill feed—the crusher foreman activates the water sprays.

After sampling, crushed ore is stored in 10 cylindrical ore bins, 20 ft in diameter x 40 ft high and having a capacity of 300 tons each. Five bins feed to the acid grinding circuit and four to the alkaline grinding circuit. The tenth accepts reject material, which is subsequently transferred to stockpiles for resubmission to the grinding circuit.

Alkaline leaching through autoclaves at 50 psig

Alkaline process ore moves by conveyor from fine ore storage to the primary ball mill in a two-stage grinding circuit, where the ore is contacted with mill solution containing 50-60 gpl of Na_2CO_3. Primary ball mill discharge flows to a spiral classifier, where it is diluted with additional mill solution to about 20% solids in the classifier discharge (fine fraction). Classifier oversize returns to the ball mill for regrinding.

A bank of four cyclones makes another size separation, and the cyclone underflow (coarse fraction) feeds to a regrind ball mill in closed circuit with the cyclones. The cyclone discharge, which constitutes the finished grind product, is pumped to a grind thickener. Grind thickener overflow returns to the mill solution storage tank, where soda ash content is adjusted to 50-60 gpl, and then recycles to the grinding circuit. (The grind thickener also receives recycled liquor streams from later stages in the process.)

Pumps move thickener underflow through the cold side of four heat exchangers arranged in two banks of two units each, then through two preleach tanks in series to an autoclave-feed surge tank, and then to 14 autoclaves arranged in two banks of seven units in series. Steam coils supply added heat to the first two autoclaves in each bank, and compressed air is injected into each unit. Regulation of pressure in the autoclaves at 50 psig results in a temperature of about 250°F. Retention time of the ore in the circuit is about 6 hr.

Autoclave discharge passes through the hot side of the heat exchangers—thereby heating the grind thickener underflow before it enters the leaching section.

The leached pulp feeds from the heat exchangers to a filtration section via a first-stage filter feed tank. The filter section has six drum filters in two banks of three filters each. The filters function as a modified countercurrent washing system that separates leach liquor from leached solids in three stages:

1) Filtrate from the third stage washes first-stage filter cake and is collected in the unclarified pregnant storage tank. The filter cake is repulped with liquor from a recarbonation tower.

2) Liquor from the recarbonation tower washes second-stage filter cake and then goes to the grind thickener as makeup mill solution. The filter cake is repulped with water.

3) After washing with water and repulping with solvent extraction raffinate, third-stage filter cake is pumped to the main tailings sump, where it joins the acid circuit tailings for transfer to the tailings pond. As much of the third-stage filtrate as possible is used to wash the first-stage filter cake, and the remainder joins the first-stage filtrate as pregnant solution in the unclarified pregnant liquor storage.

After clarification through pressure filters, pregnant liquor is pumped to a storage tank. Clarified pregnant solution is used periodically to backwash the filter beds, and the backwash slurry recycles to the first-stage filter tank.

Clarified pregnant solution passes through four agitated precipitation tanks in series. Steam and sodium hydroxide added in the first tank produce a sodium diuranate $(Na_2U_2O_7)$ precipitate that is pumped first to a thickener and then to two drum filters in parallel. Water repulps the sodium diuranate filter cake, and sulphuric acid dissolves it in a resolution tank.

The diuranate filtrate and thickener overflow go to the recarbonation tower for contacting with high-carbon-dioxide boiler stack gas. The excess sodium hydroxide is thereby converted to sodium carbonate and bicarbonate—essential reagents for the leaching process.

Dissolution of the sodium diuranate may develop considerable heat of solution, which is detrimental to the subsequent hydrogen peroxide precipitation step, so the solution is cooled to 80° to 90°F by passing through a heat exchanger before it is mixed with pregnant uranium liquor from the acid circuit. The alkaline and acid pregnant solutions mix in the first of two carbon dioxide removal tanks operating in series, and carbonate decomposition is accomplished by addition of sulphuric acid.

The uranium is precipitated in one of three batch-operated precipitation tanks by raising the pH to 2.4 with anhydrous ammonia and adding hydrogen peroxide. The precipitate is filtered through pressure filters, and the filter cake is dried on a multiple-hearth dryer. The dryer discharge passes through a hammer mill that produces a minus ¼-in. product for packaging in 55-gal drums for shipment.

Strong acid leach extracts uranium and vanadium

Acid circuit ore feeds via conveyors to a ball mill operating in closed circuit with a spiral classifier. Water is used as ball mill and classifier diluent. In normal operation, a disc filter dewaters the classifier discharge, with filter cake dropping into the first-stage leach tank, and filtrate recycling to water storage. (Provision has been made for bypassing the disc filter by operating the classifiers at high density—50% solids in the overflow—and pumping this overflow directly to the first-stage leach.)

When copper-bearing ores are being processed, classifier discharge reports at about 20% solids to the copper flotation circuit. After removal of copper sulphides, flotation tails return to the alkaline leach regrind circuit or, alternately, to the acid leach section, depending on the nature of the ore.

Along with filtered grind product, the first-stage leach tank receives high grade, high acid leach liquor from the wash thickeners and a small 3-gpm stream of ferric hydroxide [$Fe_2(OH)_3$] slurry from the vanadium solvent extraction regeneration system. The first-stage leach utilizes, to the extent possible, the residual acidity of the acid leach pregnant liquors to neutralize alkaline constituents of the freshly ground ore stream, achieving reagent economies.

Pumps transfer first-stage leach discharge to a battery of three cyclones operating in parallel, and cyclone underflow is then directed to the first of four second-stage leach tanks in series. Sodium chlorate and sulphuric acid are added in the first tank, and all four are heated by steam lances. Retention time is about 21 hr.

Cyclone overflow discharges to a slimes thickener, and thickener underflow circulates back to the No. 1 second-stage leach tank. The slimes thickener overflows to a second thickener for additional clarification. Underflow from this second clarification is very small and is periodically pumped back to the slimes thickener. Thickener overflow flows to the unclarified pregnant storage tank.

Discharge from the fourth acid leach tank flows through

a cooling tower consisting of a baffled tank with a fan for air circulation to two Esperanza drag classifiers operating in parallel. Classifier oversize falls into the feed tank of the first stage of a three-stage filtration system, while undersize is pumped to two washing thickeners in parallel. Drag classifier diluent is filtrate from the first stage and a portion of the filtrate from the second stage of the three-stage countercurrent filtration system. Pumps transfer washing thickener overflow to the first-stage leach tank for neutralization of alkaline constituents in the ores, as described above. Underflow reports to the first-stage filter tank via a sump and a pump.

The filtration section has six drum filters in two parallel banks of three; the three filters in each bank operate in series. First-stage filter feed is split between the two banks. Second-stage filtrate is used to wash first-stage filter cake on the filters. The filtrate then transfers to the Esperanza classifiers, while the filter cake is repulped with third-stage filtrate. Second-stage filter cake is washed with third-stage filtrate and repulped with water. Second-stage filtrate not needed in washing first-stage filter cake reports to the Esperanza classifiers. Third-stage filter cake is washed with water, diluted with solvent extraction raffinate, and then pumped to the main tailings sump and on to the tailings pond. Filtrate is used as wash on the second stage filters and to repulp the first-stage filter cake.

Pregnant liquor is clarified through a bank of three vertical pressure filters in parallel and collected in a storage tank. Periodically, accumulated solids are backwashed from filter beds with clarified pregnant liquors, and backwash slurry reports to the slimes thickener.

Solvent extraction separates uranium and vanadium

The clarified pregnant liquor, after pH adjustment to 1.0-1.2, feeds from the storage tank to a bank of four uranium mixer-settlers in the solvent extraction circuit, becoming the aqueous phase of an aqueous-organic separation and concentration process. The aqueous phase enters the circuit at uranium extraction mixer No. 1, while the organic phase—consisting principally of No. 1 diesel oil (92.5%) and carrying tertiary amine (5%) and isodecanol (2.5%)—enters the system at the No. 4 uranium extraction mixer and flows countercurrently.

Uranium raffinate flows from the No. 4 settler to a trap tank, where some small additional phase separation takes place, and the accumulated organic is periodically decanted back to process.

The uranium-loaded organic is also pumped to a trap tank from the No. 1 uranium extraction settler for some small additional phase separation, with a small continuous bleed of settled aqueous taken back to settler No. 1. The loaded organic then enters the uranium strip circuit by gravity, flowing countercurrently to an aqueous strip liquor of 150-gpl sodium carbonate. Stripped organic flows to a storage tank, from which it is recircuited through the extraction cycle. The uranium-bearing aqueous moves to a trap tank for final phase separation and then to carbon dioxide removal tanks and uranium precipitation (described in the foregoing discussion of the alkaline leach process).

Uranium raffinate from the uranium extraction circuit becomes feed for a vanadium solvent extraction circuit of five mixer-settler units, with four added pH adjustment mixers between each of the mixer-settlers. Before entering the vanadium extraction circuit, the uranium raffinate flows through two EMF tanks (normally operating in parallel but with provision for bypassing one or the other), where the solution is contacted with metallic iron shavings and/or powder. EMF is reduced to –150 millivolts or lower, at which point the iron is almost completely reduced and the vanadium partially reduced. This condition minimizes loading of iron on the organic and promotes loading of the vanadium. The pH of the reduced solution is adjusted by addition of anhydrous ammonia to 2.0, and the solution then flows by gravity to the mixer of the No. 1 vanadium extraction mixer-settler.

The vanadium-bearing aqueous solution flows countercurrently to an organic, as described above for uranium extraction, except that the pH is adjusted back to 2.0 in each of the four pH adjustment mixers. (The pH tends to drop as the vanadium loads). The organic is No. 1 diesel oil (91%) carrying di-(2-ethylhexhy) phosphoric acid (6%) and isodecanol (3%). The organic bypasses the pH adjustment settlers.

The depleted aqueous from the settler of the No. 5 vanadium mixer-settler flows through a trap tank and is then pumped to both the alkaline and acid tailings sumps, where it is used to repulp the filter cakes prior to transfer to the main tailings sump.

The vanadium-loaded organic is pumped from the No. 1 vanadium settler to a trap tank and then flows by gravity to the vanadium strip circuit, consisting of four mixer-settler units. The organic enters the circuit at the No. 1 vanadium stripping mixer and flows countercurrently to a 15% sulphuric acid strip solution that enters the circuit at the No. 4 vanadium stripping mixer. The stripped organic recycles to the vanadium extraction circuit. The vanadium-bearing strip liquor is pumped to a trap tank and then to the vanadium precipitation section described below.

Iron not completely reduced in the EMF tanks or oxidized by contact with air during processing loads into the organic with the vanadium in the extraction circuit but is not stripped with the vanadium in the stripping circuit. This accumulation of iron in the organic must be controlled if the organic is to retain its ability to load vanadium. Control is accomplished in a regeneration step that first diverts about 30% of the organic flow from the storage tanks to two mixers in parallel, where ferric iron is precipitated as hydroxide by introduction of a soda ash solution. The solution flows from each mixer to a cone-bottom settling tank, and the decanted organic from these tanks rejoins the main organic flow in the No. 5 vanadium extraction mixer. The settled aqueous, containing a ferric hydroxide slurry, is pumped to another cone-bottom settling tank where three products are obtained: 1) a small quantity of organic that is periodically decanted to the No. 5 vanadium extraction mixer, 2) an aqueous fraction containing soda ash that is excess to the requirement for precipitating the iron, which is pumped to the soda ash solution makeup tanks, and 3) a thickened ferric hydroxide slurry containing a small amount of uranium, which will be withdrawn from the bottom of the cone and pumped to the first-stage acid leach tank.

Vanadium is precipitated in batches in three tanks in parallel by introduction of steam, sodium chlorate, and ammonia, which produces "red cake"—a complex compound composed principally of vanadium oxides. Contents of the precipitation tanks flow to a vanadium thickener as batches are completed. Thickener overflow returns to the second-stage acid leach, while underflow is pumped to a drum filter. Filtrate returns to the vanadium thickener, and filter cake drops into a three-hearth dryer. Dryer offgas is cleaned in a wet scrubber, with thickener overflow used as a scrubbing agent. Dryer discharge is collected in skips that are hoisted as filled to the feed hoppers of one of two hearth-type fusion furnaces. The molten

Atlas uranium and vanadium solvent extraction circuits incorporate Denver Equipment mixer-settler units. The settlers have a capacity of about 15,000 gal. An extensive network of piping over the solvent extraction area provides protection against fire.

vanadium oxide flows to rotating water-cooled casting wheels, where it solidifies into a flake about ⅛ in. thick. The flake is broken by a disc cylinder riding on the casting wheel prior to packaging in 55-gal drums.

Flotation produces byproduct Cu concentrate

Copper-bearing ores are processed through the Atlas plant when sufficient amounts have accumulated, beginning in the acid leach grinding circuit. Such ores are diverted ahead of the first-stage acid leach to a sump, then across a trash removal screen to two banks of flotation cells, each consisting of a fine rougher and two cleaners in parallel. Rougher concentrate flows to cleaner cells, and cleaner tails return to the roughers. Rougher tails are thickened and usually sent to the alkaline leach regrind mill—with provision for diverting them to acid leach if dictated by the nature of the ore. Thickener underflow recycles to the grinding circuit.

Extraction of uranium content in the copper sulphide concentrates is accomplished by a hot, highly oxidizing, highly acidic, extended-time leach. First, after thickening and filtering, the copper concentrate filter cake is repulped and sulphuric acid, sodium chlorate, and steam are added. The pulp then discharges to the first of a series of five leaching tanks. Leaching conditions are readjusted in the third leach tank by feeding additional steam, sulphuric acid, and sodium chlorate, and air is injected into all five leach tanks as well as the repulp tank.

A drum filter then separates the uranium pregnant liquor from the leached copper sulphides. The filter cake—the major copper product of the Atlas plant—is air-dried in heaps and loaded in bulk on trucks when sold.

The filtrate goes to a uranium solvent extraction section employing standard aqueous-organic countercurrent flow through three mixer-settler units.

The solvent extraction raffinate contains some copper dissolved during the uranium leach, which is recovered by cementation.

The uranium-loaded organic is contacted with 15% soda ash solution in two mixers in parallel, followed by two settlers. The aqueous solution strips the organic and is sent to the mill solution storage tank, with values subsequently recovered in the alkaline leach circuit.

Closed circuit eliminates mill effluent

Liquid and solid residues from the Atlas milling processes are pumped to the tailings pond via pipeline. The coarsest fractions settle near the discharge, and after such an area dries, this material is pushed to the periphery to heighten the berm as required. Fine fractions flow away from the periphery, and clear liquor is decanted from the settlement pool for recycling to the mill.

Makeup water is drawn from a pump station on the north bank of the Colorado River and treated with flocculants. Flocced solids settle and are impounded in one settling pond, and the clear overflow goes to another settling pond. Pumps mounted on a barge feed the clear water to a large storage tank, which supplies a water tower, a water filtration system, and a fire pump. The fire pump feeds a fire loop encircling the premises, with hydrants at regular, frequent intervals.

The filter section comprises three vertical pressure filters with sand beds, and filtered water is stored in a tank having a level control that maintains storage at capacity. A portion of the filtered water is pumped through two ion exchange columns for calcium removal, and thence to "culinary" storage. Though labeled culinary, this product is not considered potable, and drinking fountains in the plant are fed by a special system supplied by water hauled from the Moab water system. The plant thus has four water systems—the tower for bulk uncritical usages, filtered water for usages requiring clarity, filtered and softened water used mainly for boiler feed, and the potable system for usages requiring the highest quality—and redesign of the circuit has eliminated discharge to the Colorado River. □

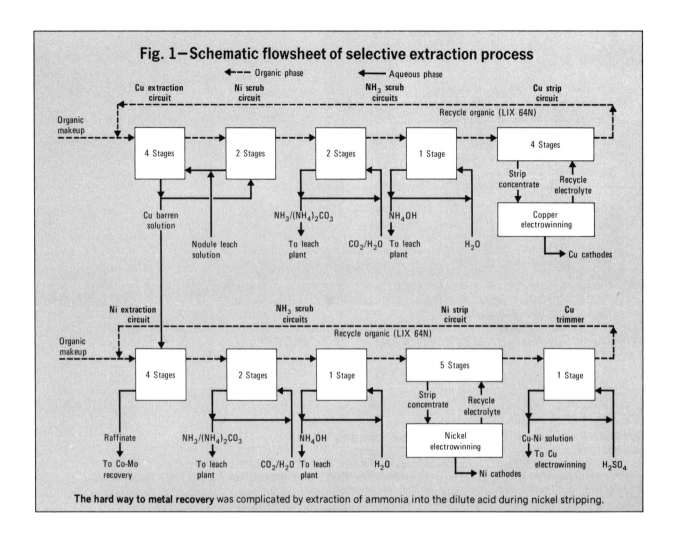

Fig. 1—Schematic flowsheet of selective extraction process

◀-- Organic phase   ◀— Aqueous phase

The hard way to metal recovery was complicated by extraction of ammonia into the dilute acid during nickel stripping.

A new FIX on metal recovery from sea nodules

KCC pilots fluid ion exchange technology for coextraction
of copper and nickel from leach solution, followed by
selective stripping of each into tankhouse electrolytes

Dr. Jagdish C. Agarwal, Dr. Norman Beecher, Dr. G. L. Hubred, David L. Natwig, and **Roald R. Skarbo,**
Ledgemont Laboratory, Kennecott Copper Corp.

WHEN KENNECOTT COPPER CORP. DECIDED to use an ammoniacal leach for recovery of copper, nickel, and cobalt from deep sea nodules, it faced the problem of developing a new technology. There was no commercially satisfactory process for the separation and production of these metal values from the pregnant liquor. Yet, an ammonium carbonate leaching system presented very attractive possibilities for regenerating the leach reagent.

KCC attacked the problem by both sponsored and in-house research. The product of this effort is a relatively nontoxic, fluid ion exchange process (FIX) whereby LIX 64N* in an organic carrier is used to coextract nickel and copper from the pregnant solution. These metals are then selectively stripped into a pair of acidified electrolytes—one for copper and the other for nickel electrowinning.

*LIX 64N is a trademarked reagent of General Mills Chemical Co.

Cobalt remains in a nickel-free raffinate, easily treatable and recoverable by chemical means.

The process has been piloted and the cost has been estimated from an engineering design view. Such studies have indicated capital expenses of about $320 per annual ton of metal recovered. Detailed equilibrium data have shown the dramatic effect of free ammonia on system performance.

The problem: nodules have similar Cu-Ni contents

Nodules from the bed of the Pacific Ocean typically contain nickel, copper, and cobalt in the ratios of 6:5:1.[1] Viewed as a nickel recovery problem, using Nicaro or Sherritt Gordon technology,[8] the copper and cobalt contents are too high for efficient operation. For recovery of

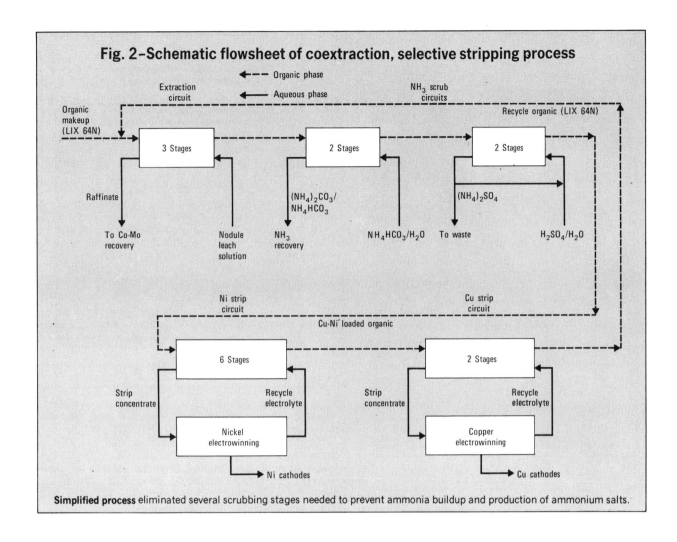

Fig. 2–Schematic flowsheet of coextraction, selective stripping process

Extraction circuit

NH₃ scrub circuits

- - → Organic phase
→ Aqueous phase

Organic makeup (LIX 64N)

Recycle organic (LIX 64N)

3 Stages

2 Stages

2 Stages

Raffinate

$(NH_4)_2CO_3/$
NH_4HCO_3

$(NH_4)_2SO_4$

To Co-Mo recovery

Nodule leach solution

NH_3 recovery

NH_4HCO_3/H_2O

To waste

H_2SO_4/H_2O

Ni strip circuit

Cu strip circuit

Cu-Ni loaded organic

6 Stages

2 Stages

Strip concentrate

Recycle electrolyte

Strip concentrate

Recycle electrolyte

Nickel electrowinning

Copper electrowinning

Ni cathodes

Cu cathodes

Simplified process eliminated several scrubbing stages needed to prevent ammonia buildup and production of ammonium salts.

copper, the nickel and cobalt contained in the nodules constitute overwhelming impurities.

Kennecott reviewed a number of chemical separation approaches, including sulphide precipitation, ammonia stripping to give carbonate precipitation, and carbonyl chemistry. Use of a sulphide reagent results in conversion of sulphur to ammonium sulphate—and the unhappy choice between entry into the fertilizer business or addition of an expensive recycling step. Carbonate precipitation uses excessive amounts of energy to produce steam for stripping the ammonia. Carbonyl chemistry requires processing some of the world's most toxic compounds.

Fluid ion exchange technology has been used extensively for recovery of copper from acid solutions, by Ranchers Exploration and Development Co. near Miami, Ariz., by Cyprus Bagdad at Bagdad, Ariz., and by others. Until recently, recovery of metal cations had not been practiced except at two small operations: Capital Wire and Cable Co. recovered copper from scrap, and SEC Corp., at El Paso, Tex., recovered nickel[2] from a copper tankhouse bleed stream.

Elsewhere, equilibrium data and process proposals were provided in several papers.[6,7,9,10] The Arbiter process, the first ammoniacal FIX system, was developed to extract only copper.

Against this background, it was apparent that development of new technology was needed. Kennecott initiated a screening of fluid ion exchange reagents, under a small research contract with the Colorado School of Mines Research Institute (CSMRI). Reagents examined included di-

2-ethyl hexyl phosphoric acids, carboxylic acids, and chelating reagents. A single reagent that could be used for both copper and nickel was sought because of possible deleterious interactions between two reagents. LIX 64N was found to be the best single reagent for the extraction of both copper and nickel.

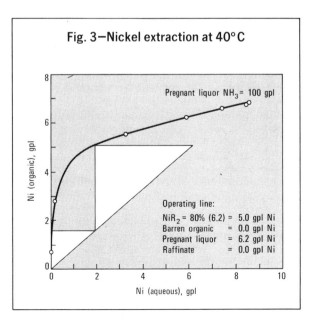

Fig. 3–Nickel extraction at 40°C

Pregnant liquor NH₃ = 100 gpl

Ni (organic), gpl

Operating line:

NiR_2 = 80% (6.2) = 5.0 gpl Ni
Barren organic = 0.0 gpl Ni
Pregnant liquor = 6.2 gpl Ni
Raffinate = 0.0 gpl Ni

Ni (aqueous), gpl

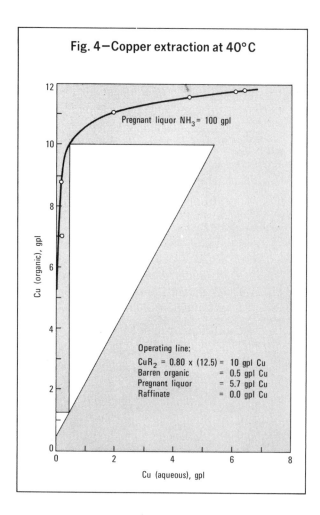

Fig. 4–Copper extraction at 40°C

Pregnant liquor NH$_3$ = 100 gpl

Cu (organic), gpl

Operating line:
CuR$_2$ = 0.80 x (12.5) = 10 gpl Cu
Barren organic = 0.5 gpl Cu
Pregnant liquor = 5.7 gpl Cu
Raffinate = 0.0 gpl Cu

Cu (aqueous), gpl

Selective extraction of Cu and Ni

The obvious approach to a fluid ion exchange process was selective extraction of nickel and copper. When this method was tried at CSMRI, the separation achieved with LIX 64N was surprisingly clean—with a nickel/copper ratio of 25,000 to 1 and a copper/nickel ratio of 350 to 1. Unfortunately, it soon became apparent that the extraction of ammonia into the organic, along with nickel and copper, was relatively high—up to 3 gpl. When nickel was stripped from the organic into dilute acid suitable as an electrowinning electrolyte, the extracted ammonia was converted into ammonium sulphate. Buildup of this salt in the nickel

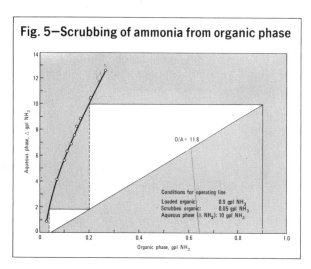

Fig. 5–Scrubbing of ammonia from organic phase

Aqueous phase, Δ gpl NH$_3$

O/A = 11.8

Conditions for operating line
Loaded organic: 0.9 gpl NH$_3$
Scrubbed organic: 0.05 gpl NH$_3$
Aqueous phase (Δ NH$_3$): 10 gpl NH$_3$

Organic phase, gpl NH$_3$

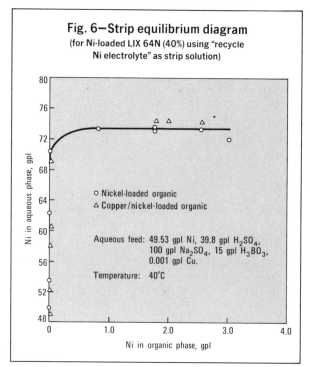

Fig. 6–Strip equilibrium diagram

(for Ni-loaded LIX 64N (40%) using "recycle Ni electrolyte" as strip solution)

Ni in aqueous phase, gpl

○ Nickel-loaded organic
△ Copper/nickel-loaded organic

Aqueous feed: 49.53 gpl Ni, 39.8 gpl H$_2$SO$_4$,
100 gpl Na$_2$SO$_4$, 15 gpl H$_3$BO$_3$,
0.001 gpl Cu.

Temperature: 40°C

Ni in organic phase, gpl

electrolyte resulted in rapid precipitation of the double salt nickel ammonium sulphate, NiSO$_4$(NH$_4$)$_2$SO$_4$ · 6H$_2$O.

Scrubbing stages were then added to remove ammonia from organic after the extraction, and the flowsheet became increasingly complex (Fig. 1). (Merigold[6] subsequently published a similar flowsheet.) Salt solutions for recoverable ammonia scrubbing and dilute sulphuric acid for a final scrub were found satisfactory.

Coextraction and selective stripping

Kennecott then moved the FIX research in-house and sought to simplify the process. The flowsheet was analyzed for ways to reduce its 26 stages. Ten stages were devoted to nickel and copper extraction, including two stages of nickel scrub required to give a clean separation in copper extraction. There were two three-stage ammonia scrub trains—one required after each contact between organic and aqueous. Stages could be eliminated in both areas if coextraction of nickel and copper were feasible.

Coextraction with selective stripping was tried and found practicable. The flowsheet was then simplified accordingly (Fig. 2).

Selective extraction of copper requires six stages because a separation between copper and nickel is being made. Nickel and copper load together, and then copper displaces nickel in the latter stages. In coextraction, only two stages are theoretically required. Since equilibrium is rapidly attained in the ammoniacal FIX system, actual stages correspond closely to the theoretical. Equilibrium curves and staging are presented in the McCabe/Thiele diagrams[11] of Figs. 3 and 4. Such diagrams have been used with success even though they do not take into account changes in the unreacted organic reagent and aqueous concentrations such as ammonia and hydrogen ion. Such factors can best be handled with a computer model—currently used for extraction system calculations.

Multicomponent extraction is even more difficult to deal with graphically. As an approximation to guide this process development, the nickel and copper extractions were considered independently. In concept, a certain amount of organic was provided for copper extraction and an additional amount provided for nickel extraction:

$$\frac{\text{Organic volume } O}{\text{Aqueous volume } A} = \frac{O}{A}_{\text{copper}} + \frac{O}{A}_{\text{nickel}}$$

$$1.8 = \frac{5.7}{10.0} + \frac{6.2}{5.0}$$

The flowsheet for coextraction with selective stripping requires contact between the organic phase and the ammoniacal aqueous phase only once—requiring only one train of ammonia scrubbing. Two actual scrubbing stages reduce the ammonia content to 0.1 gpl (Fig. 5), followed by an acid scrub stage for final cleanup.

The key advantage of the selective stripping process over selective extraction is that the copper-nickel separation is made in the acid conditions of the nickel stripping circuit. Because much sharper separation is obtained in acid conditions, fewer total stages are necessary to effect the copper-nickel separation. Nickel is stripped from its organic by feeding into the circuit the sulphuric acid equivalent of the organic nickel content, producing a concentrated nickel stream at pH 3.0, which is suitable for nickel electrowinning. (See Fig. 6.)

A more concentrated acid solution of 160 gpl H_2SO_4 is used to strip the copper. Equilibrium is reached much more rapidly than with nickel. Two stages are used, although residual copper is 0.6 gpl (Fig. 7). The residual copper slightly decreases the loading capacity of the LIX 64N that is recycled to extraction. The loss is more than offset by the economy of eliminating additional stages of copper stripping.

The acid strip solution for both nickel and copper is used directly as the electrowinning electrolyte, without pH modification. In turn, the depleted electrolytes are recycled after electrowinning directly to the FIX strip circuits.

Concentration of free ammonia is important

Concentration of free ammonia in the pregnant liquor is very important in influencing the equilibrium loading of nickel and copper on the fluid ion exchange reagent. The excess ammonia provides the driving force for formation of amine complexes that draw metal ions away from the FIX reagent, as indicated in the following equations:[3,5]

$$Me(NH_3)_x + 2RH \longleftrightarrow MeR_2 + 2H^+ + XNH_3$$

$$K = \frac{(MeR_2)\,(H^+)^2\,(NH_3)^x}{(Me(NH_3)_x)\,(RH)^2}$$

Nickel generally has a higher amine coordination number than copper. For that reason, its extraction is more strongly dependent upon the free ammonia content than copper (Fig. 8).

Pilot plant successfully operated

A pilot plant coextraction selective strip system has been operated successfully, including one run of 20 days. The circuit was operated by one man per shift, with no downtime for process reasons. Mixer-settlers with 4.5-liter mixer boxes were used for all cells. Pregnant liquor at a flow rate of 432 ml per min containing 6.2 gpl Ni, 5.7 gpl Cu, and 90 gpl NH_2 was treated. Tables 1, 2, and 3 provide a complete summary of the operating conditions. More than 99.9% of the copper and nickel was extracted. About 5% of the am-

Table 1—FIX pilot plant performance

Extracted	Percent
Cu	99.9
Ni	99.9
NH₃	5.5
NH₃ Scrubbed	
Primary	96.3
Secondary	3.4
Overall	99.7
Stripped	
Ni	98.8
Ni/Cu ratio	~25,000/1
Cu	99.9+
Cu/Ni ratio	~75/1

Table 2—FIX pilot plant operating parameters*

Block	No. of stages	External O/A (vol)	Contact time (min)	Settler flow (gpm/ft²)
Extraction	3	1.7	3.0	0.52
NH₃ Scrub				
Primary	2	3.3	3.75	0.42
Secondary	2	1.0	3.0	0.52
Nickel strip	6	7.6	3.75	0.42
Copper strip	2	3.1	3.75	0.42

*All stages at 40°C and internal organic: aqueous (O/A) volume = 1.

monia also was extracted. However, ammonia was nearly completely scrubbed in the ammonia wash circuits.

Kinetics are slow in nickel stripping, and long mixing time is needed to reach equilibrium. Because pilot plant cells were standardized with a fixed mixer holdup time, six

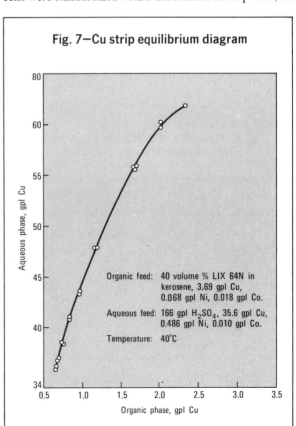

Fig. 7—Cu strip equilibrium diagram

Organic feed: 40 volume % LIX 64N in kerosene, 3.69 gpl Cu, 0.068 gpl Ni, 0.018 gpl Co.

Aqueous feed: 166 gpl H_2SO_4, 35.6 gpl Cu, 0.486 gpl Ni, 0.010 gpl Co.

Temperature: 40°C

(Aqueous phase, gpl Cu vs. Organic phase, gpl Cu)

Table 3—A steady-state profile of the FIX process in action

Products	Pregnant liquor	Raffinate	Barren organic	Loaded organic	Primary NH₃ scrub			Secondary NH₃ scrub			Nickel strip			Copper strip	
					Organic effluent	Aqueous feed	Aqueous effluent	Organic effluent	Aqueous feed	Aqueous effluent	Organic effluent	Aqueous feed	Aqueous effluent	Aqueous feed	Aqueous effluent
Grams per liter															
Cu	5.7	0.002	0.5	3.8	3.8	0	0	3.8	—	—	3.8	0.0008	0.0011	37.0	47.0
Ni	6.2	0.007	0.008	3.6	3.6	0	0	3.6	0.55	0.55	0.04	50.0	77.0	1.4	1.5
NH₃	90.0	85.0	0	2.49	0.09	17.0	25.0	0.005	27.0	27.0	0	0.31	0.39	0.15	0.16
CO₂	55.0	55.0	—	—	—	—	—	—	—	—	—	—	—	—	—
Co	0.2	0.194	0.07	0.07	0.07	0	0	0.07	—	—	0.07	0.0027	0.0042	0.012	0.012
Grams per min organic ...	432	432	746	746	746	224	224	746	746	746	746	98	98	237	237
Grams per min aqueous ..	453	447	625	631	631	230	232	631	783	783	627	119	121	277	279

stages were used in nickel stripping to achieve a total contact time of 22.5 min. The equilibrium nickel stripping data shown in Fig. 6 indicate that only one stage is theoretically required. However, one or two additional stages are desirable to ensure a sharp nickel-copper separation. The proposed commercial design is based upon three stages of 9-min mixer contact in each stage.

Spent electrolyte from nickel electrowinning—which constituted the feed to nickel stripping—is typically 50 gpl Ni and 42 gpl H_2SO_4 for nickel electrowinning diaphragm cells. Feed rate is controlled to provide acid equivalent to the nickel contained on the loaded organic. The resulting nickel concentrate electrolyte contains 75 gpl Ni and has a pH of 3.0. Small adjustments in the flow rate were made in nickel strip feed to maintain that pH. An excellent metal separation resulted, with the Ni/Cu ratio in the nickel electrolyte being 25,000 to 1. The nickel-barren organic, containing 3.8 gpl Cu and 0.04 gpl Ni, was sent to copper stripping. Copper was stripped in two stages, as is done in industrial LIX 64N copper circuits. Remaining nickel was also stripped, necessitating a bleed from the copper tankhouse to hold the nickel level below 20 gpl. Metal-barren

organic containing 0.6 gpl Cu was recycled to extraction.

KCC's engineering design estimate arrived at approximate capital costs of $320 per annual ton of metal—about 30% above the cost of a similar plant for extracting only copper. The higher tab reflects the greater difficulty of extracting nickel and the requirement for metal separation. □

References

1) Agarwal, J. C., Beecher, N., Davies, D. S., Hubred, G. L., Kakaria, V. K., and Kust, R. N., "Processing of Ocean Nodules—A Technical and Economic Review," 104th AIME Meeting, New York, 1975.
2) Eliasen, R. D., "The Operation of a Nickel Solvent Extraction and Electrowinning Circuit," AIChE Meeting, Tucson, 1973.
3) Haffenden, W. J., and Lawson, G. J., "Effect of Ammonium Salts on the Solvent Extraction of Metal Ions with Liquid Cation Exchangers," ADVANCES IN EXTRACTIVE METALLURGY, Inst. of Mining and Metallurgy, London, 1968, pp 678-85.
4) Kuhn, M. C., Arbiter, N., and Kling, H., "Anaconda's Arbiter Process for Copper," CIM BULL., Feb. 1974, pp 62-73.
5) Kust, R. N., "The NH₃-CO₂-H₂O Leaching System," 105th AIME Annual Meeting, Las Vegas, Feb. 1976.
6) Merigold, C. R., and Sudderth, R. B., "Recovery of Nickel by Liquid Ion Exchange Technology," International Symposium on Hydrometallurgy, edited by D. J. I. Evans and R. S. Shoemaker, AIME, New York, 1972, pp 552-88.
7) Merigold, C. R., and Jensen, W. H., "The Separation and Recovery of Nickel and Copper from a Laterite-Ammonia Leach Solution by Liquid Ion Exchange," Vol. II, Proceedings of International Solvent Extraction Conference, Soc. Chem. Ind., Lyon, 1974, pp 1231-63.
8) Queneau, P., Extractive Metallurgy of Copper, Nickel and Cobalt, Interscience, New York, 1961.
9) Ritcey, G. M., and Lucas, B. H., "Separation of Copper from Nickel and Cobalt by Liquid-Liquid Extraction from Ammoniacal Solutions," CIM BULL., May 1972, pp 46-9.
10) Siemens, R. E., Good, P. C., and Stickney, W. A., "Recovery of Nickel and Cobalt from Low-grade Domestic Laterites," USBM Report of Inv. 8027, 1975.
11) Treybal, R., Liquid Extraction, McGraw-Hill, New York, 1963.
12) Skarbo, R. R., "Selective Stripping Process," US Patent 3,853,725, Dec. 10, 1974.
13) Skarbo, R. R., "Process for Recovering Nickel Selectively," US Patent 3,855,090, Dec. 17, 1974.

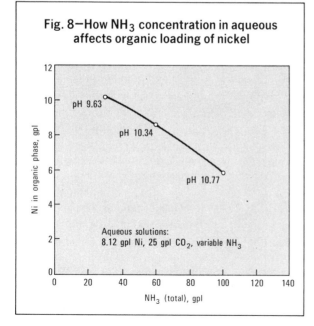

Fig. 8—How NH₃ concentration in aqueous affects organic loading of nickel

pH 9.63
pH 10.34
pH 10.77

Ni in organic phase, gpl

Aqueous solutions:
8.12 gpl Ni, 25 gpl CO₂, variable NH₃

NH₃ (total), gpl

Acknowledgement

The authors gratefully acknowledge the contributions of Hal D. Peterson and Edmond A. Morin, of the Colorado School of Mines Research Institute, to the initial work on fluid ion exchange development.

The novel concepts in the coextraction-selective stripping of nickel and copper from ammoniacal solutions are protected in two patents issued to R. R. Skarbo[12,13] and assigned to Kennecott. Patent applications also are pending in six foreign countries.

This article is based on a paper presented at the 105th Annual Meeting of AIME in Las Vegas, Feb. 22-26, 1976.

The $110,000 IMC phosphate chemical complex near New Wales, Fla., was completed in 1975. Capacity is 1.3 million tpy of concentrated phosphate products. This production is sufficient to fertilize 90 million acres of wheat.

From matrix to fertilizers:
Florida's phosphate industry
girds to produce over 50 million tpy

Richard Hoppe, Senior editor

THE HUB OF US PHOSPHATE PRODUCTION is central Florida, principally Polk County. Its 1975 output of 38 million tons supplied more than 75% of US needs and accounted for a third of the world's supply. Phosphate fertilizer is basic to agriculture. Scheduled plant expansions in Florida will increase capacity by two-thirds, from 30 million tpy in 1970 to over 50 million tpy by 1980.

Polk County is also one of the fastest growing population centers of the US. The county's Division of Development Coordination has predicted a half-million inhabitants by the year 2000, more than double the 228,000 of 1970. Such growth is bound to place pressures on the traditional economic mainstays of citrus farming, cattle raising,

Editor's note: This report on phosphate beneficiation and the production of acid and fertilizers in central Florida is based on an E/MJ field trip in February 1976. Operating companies and methods of mining and reclamation were described in the May *1976 issue of E/MJ.*

and the mining of phosphates for fertilizers.

Sections of Lakeland—Polk's major city, a few miles from Disneyworld—already show the blight of fast-food chains, motels, trailer parks, sprawling shopping centers, drive-in banks, and drive-in churches.

Some dozen miles to the south of this neon dazzle lies the town of Mulberry, the "phosphate capital of the world," but the drive from Lakeland to Mulberry is like a transition to the early 1900s. Typically, a late afternoon freight crosses the main streets, tying up all traffic in and out of this somnolent, sun-drenched town. A rural atmosphere surrounds the world's largest phosphate fertilizer operations. Ironically, the ponds that hold water, sands, and the clay residues from mining—labeled by some as ecological blights—offer one of the few temporary buffer zones against encroaching commercial development. The miles of ponds are tranquil, a haven for fish and waterfowl and the odd rattlesnake. Here, for a time, cattails whisper and a solitary white crane glides over sparkling waters.

Phosphate washing plant mimics aggregate plant

The preliminary beneficiation of mined phosphate is

Banks of flotation cells are installed at the W. R. Grace Hookers Prairie beneficiation plant, which will open late in '76.

similar to the production of sand and gravel aggregate for the construction industry. The principal function of the wash plant is to prepare a clean phosphate pebble product for market or for captive acid manufacture. To this end, the matrix is sent through a variety of machines for attrition, screening, scrubbing, and washing. Materials exiting the plant consist of the plus 16-mesh final pebble product; a preliminary deslimed product, nominally 16 to 150 mesh, requiring further beneficiation; and minus 150-mesh clay slimes, which are transported to holding ponds for settlement as waste.

The composition of slurried matrix entering the wash plant circuit is typically 9% phosphatic pebble, 21% phosphatic particles recoverable by flotation, and 70% sands and clay slimes, the latter two about equally divided in weight.[1] These proportions vary within the mining district,

IMC's 2,400-tph shiploader waits for ship to dock off the Port Sutton terminal in glistening Tampa Bay.

leading to minor variations in equipment selection and flowsheets. The aim of all producers is to maximize recovery of values while minimizing overall costs.

A typical circuit begins with pipeline discharge of the slurried matrix into a distribution tank. From the tank, the slurry is pumped onto flat, nonvibrating screens or trommels, where a ¾-in. size separation is made. The oversize material passes through a disintegrator, or hammermill, that breaks up clay balls containing pebbles. From the disintegrator, the material returns to the primary screens.

Minus ¾-in. material from the primary screens is sent to a series of water-sprayed vibrating screens and log-washers. This wash section produces a coarse, plus 6-mesh pebble, and a fine pebble, nominally 6 to 16 mesh. Scrubbed, sized pebble is conveyed to storage piles or bins, where it is segregated by size and BPL content. The pebble is used in captive acid plants or is shipped to market.

Minus 16-mesh material passes through cyclones to remove and waste all material—principally clays—that is nominally smaller than 150 mesh. Several stages of cyclones are used prior to flotation to remove the bulk of fines and clays that would inhibit flotation. Slimes are directed to gravity ditches for distribution to settling ponds. Plants such as Agrico's Fort Green, Brewster's Lonesome, and IMC's Kingsford utilize 500- to 550-ft-dia thickeners to bring the solids content of slimes slurries to 6% before discharging into gravity ditches. Thickening promotes speedy recovery of recycled plant water.

The fly in the ointment: the 16 to 35-mesh cut

All material from the wash plant, nominally 35 to 150 mesh, winds up as feed to the flotation plant. Prior to flotation, this feed requires normal preparation. But the nominal 16 to 35-mesh material—containing both sands and phosphatic values similar to the 35 to 150-mesh feed—presents a tricky separation problem. Because it is relatively fine, it is difficult to screen, and because it is also heavy, it is difficult to float. Specific gravity variations between sands and phosphatic particles are small. Treatment of the 16 to 35-mesh fraction varies widely from plant to plant, based largely on the predilections of plant engineers and management. Generally, plants use combinations that include some of the following: hydroclassifiers, screw classifiers, screens, shaking tables, belts or Humphrey spirals, and differential flotation. The goal of each plant is profitable recovery of values and elimination of waste. The 16 to 35-mesh fraction often presents problems of a tradeoff.

IMC's Kingsford plant employs screening and spirals to cope with the pesky 16 to 35-mesh fraction. After removal by screening of the 35 to 150-mesh material, which is sent to bins as feed for the "fine" rougher float, the 16 to 35-mesh fraction is separated, by screening, into 16 to 24-mesh and 24 to 35-mesh fractions. The latter is sent to bins as feed for the "coarse" rougher float, while the 16 to 24-mesh fraction is conditioned with soap, fuel oil, and water at 72% solids, diluted to 40% solids, and introduced to a bank of five-turn spirals. As the conditioned feed moves down the spiral race, differential segregation takes place. Treated phosphate particles move to the race's outer edge, complete the run, and are collected at the bottom of the spiral. The untreated sands remain along the inner part of the race, where protruding lips, located at intervals, catch the sands and discharge them to a separate line. Both the 16 to 24-mesh fraction and the tailings from the coarse rougher flotation section pass through this beneficiation process. The sand tails from the spirals are collected and treated in a scavenger float. Reject is mixed with the sands from the flotation sections and pumped to land reclama-

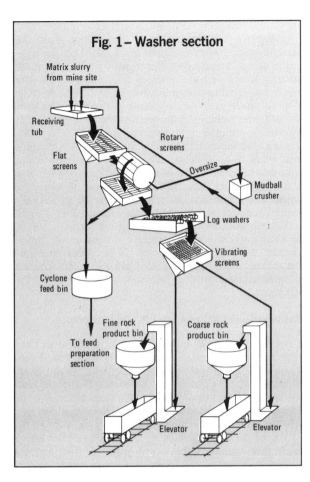

Fig. 1 – Washer section

Matrix slurry from mine site

Receiving tub

Flat screens

Rotary screens

Oversize

Mudball crusher

Log washers

Vibrating screens

Cyclone feed bin

Fine rock product bin

Coarse rock product bin

To feed preparation section

Elevator

Elevator

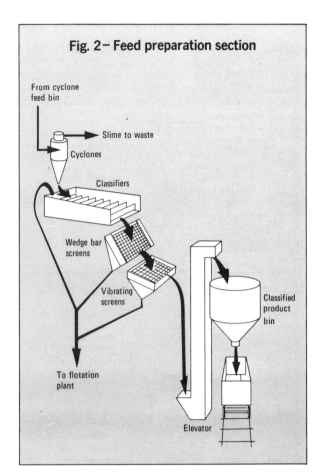

Fig. 2 – Feed preparation section

From cyclone feed bin

Slime to waste

Cyclones

Classifiers

Wedge bar screens

Vibrating screens

Classified product bin

To flotation plant

Elevator

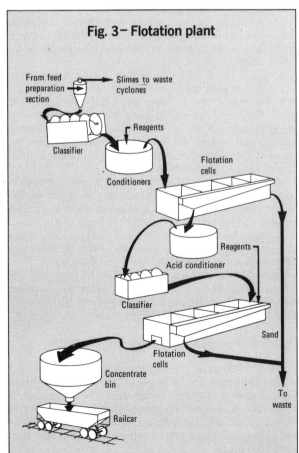

Fig. 3 – Flotation plant

From feed preparation section

Slimes to waste cyclones

Classifier

Reagents

Conditioners

Flotation cells

Reagents

Acid conditioner

Classifier

Flotation cells

Sand

Concentrate bin

To waste

Railcar

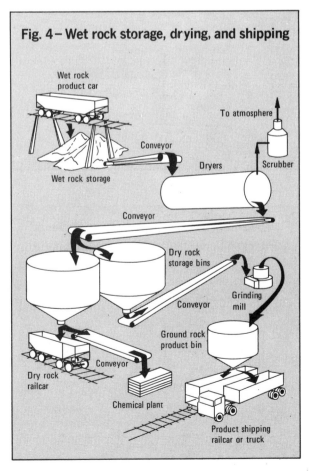

Fig. 4 – Wet rock storage, drying, and shipping

Wet rock product car

To atmosphere

Conveyor

Dryers

Scrubber

Wet rock storage

Conveyor

Dry rock storage bins

Grinding mill

Conveyor

Ground rock product bin

Dry rock railcar

Conveyor

Chemical plant

Product shipping railcar or truck

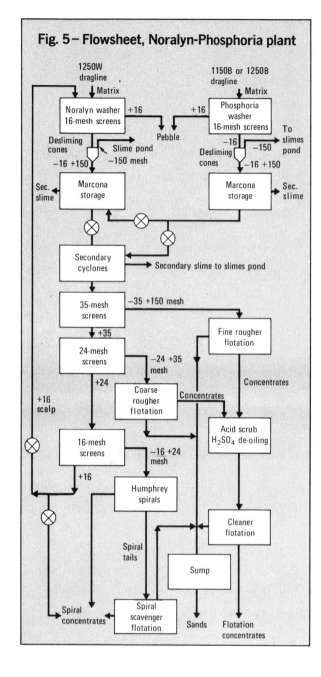

Fig. 5 – Flowsheet, Noralyn-Phosphoria plant

Fig. 6 – Simplified schematic of controls for Marconaflo system at Noralyn-Phosphoria

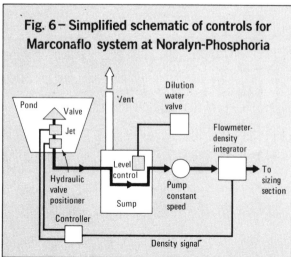

tion areas. The scavenger float is a product of value.

At Agrico's recently completed Fort Green plant, the two independent washer sections in the flowsheet are identical in design. Material smaller than 14 mesh is deslimed, dewatered, and sent to "unsized" feed storage bins. The bins are sampled to determine the grade of both the 14 to 28-mesh and 28 to 150-mesh fractions. If both are less than 12% BPL, the material in the bin is wasted. Otherwise, the material is pumped to hydrosizers for a 35-mesh split. Minus 35-mesh material becomes fine feed for the rougher float, while 14 to 35-mesh material is pumped to holding tanks and sampled. If the 14 to 35-mesh material is found to be lower than 12% BPL, it is wasted; if not, it is screened at a nominal 20-mesh, and the 20 to 35-mesh fraction becomes coarse feed for the rougher float. The 14 to 20-mesh fraction is again sampled for sand content. If the sand count is low, the material is used as an "intermediate" product; if not, it is sent to an amine float section, where sand is floated off, and sink material is directed to "intermediate" product piles for sale or use in captive acid plants.

Marconaflo at IMC plant feeds sizing section

Hoping to provide a steady flow of material at controlled density to the sizing section, IMC has installed dual Marconaflo systems at Noralyn-Phosphoria. Each system includes a 60,000-ton-capacity, 300-ft-dia, 25-ft-deep pond divided into two equal sections, allowing material to be drawn from one section while the other is being filled.

When activated, the Marconajet slowly oscillates at the bottom of the section, emitting a high pressure stream of water that undercuts the stored material. The material slumps to a sump that feeds a common pump station, where it is piped to the plant sizing section for final desliming before screening. (See Figs. 5 and 6.)

The feed rate for each system is 1,400 tph, dry basis. Major controls of the system determine the water pressure of the jet, the main valve openings, and the quantity of dilution water.

A density signal device located in the pipeline past the pump station actuates a controller, which is programmed to hydraulically raise or lower the main valve within the pond. The controller also actuates the pressure setting of the Marconajet. A level control within the enclosed sump actuates and controls the low pressure dilution water line ahead of the pump. The system is set to operate at a slurry flow of some 40% solids by weight.

Management found that "severe, cyclic size segregation occurs in the system, adversely affecting the sizing section of the plant." Unlike belt stockpiling—in which the largest particles fall farthest from the point of impact on a conical pile—single-point filling of the pond sections has resulted in coarse particle buildup near the point of discharge, while fines tend to migrate to the sides of the ponds. IMC believes that the problem can be solved by increasing the number of points for filling the pond. Once this is accomplished, management expects the systems will provide good control over feed to the sizing plant.

Flotation of phosphate: breakthrough in 1929

Before 1929, when the flotation process was introduced to phosphate recovery, more phosphate values were lost to waste than were recovered by processing. No technological breakthrough of equal importance has since taken place in phosphate processing, although important modifications and improvements of plant equipment and systems have since been made.

The breakthrough came when John Burrows, vice president of International Agricultural Corp. (IAC, forerunner of IMC), announced in 1929 that the flotation system had been perfected. The "reverse," double, or combination flotation process—as it was variously called—was developed in IAC's laboratory. The development team, headed by Arthur Crago, Hal Martin, and Francis Tartanon, included also Allen T. Cole, James A. Barr Jr., Charles Chapman, J. B. Duke, and Harry Motsinger.

Flotation accomplished the separation of phosphate rock from waste particles, chiefly sands, of approximately the same size and specific gravity by mixing the particles with water and reagents to form oil or soap films around the particles, and then applying forces to create bubbles to which the treated particles would adhere, forming a froth. Either sand particles or phosphate particles could be treated to cause them to float, while the untreated material sank. In the "reverse" process, two flotation stages are used. In the first, or rougher, stage, the particles floated are principally phosphate; in the second, or cleaner, stage, the retained particles from the rougher float are treated to float the sand remaining in the first product. Reagents used include fuel oil, pine oil, caustic soda, and soap or soap-forming materials, such as fatty acids or their derivatives, oleic acid and oleates.[2]

The present practice of phosphate flotation

The principle of reverse flotation allows preliminary beneficiation to selectively remove the lesser bulk of value from the greater bulk of gangue. The froth flotation product is obtained by preferentially coating the surfaces of the smaller amounts of valuable material, reducing expenditures for reagents. In the second float, the majority of gangue particles remaining in the rougher concentrate are conditioned for flotation; because they represent, in this case, the lesser quantity of surface to be treated, reagent use is minimized.

In a typical phosphate flotation plant in central Florida, rougher feed is dewatered to 65-70% pulp density, then conditioned with fatty acid in agitated tanks. The pH is controlled to between 9.0 and 9.5 by addition of ammonia, which also cleans the surface of phosphate particles to promote the absorption of the tall oil coating. (Proper conditioning is always required for efficient flotation.)

In the coarse and fine sections of the rougher (anionic) float, reagents used are crude fatty acid and fuel oil/kerosene. Coarse feed generally contains approximately 30% plus 35 mesh, while fine feed contains only about 10% plus 35 mesh. The conditioned feed is then sent to the flotation cells, where maximum recovery of phosphate is achieved at some sacrifice of grade. (Some gangue adheres to the float.) The bulk of the gangue (sands) sinks to the bottom of the cells and is removed as waste. The froth is collected for further treatment.

Before the second, cleaner (cationic) float, the float products from both coarse and fine rougher flotation sections are combined and washed with water and sulphuric acid to remove the anionic reagent from the surfaces of the feed. Cleaned rougher product is sent to the cleaner circuit, where an amine float removes the remaining sand. In this circuit, pH is set at 7.3 to 7.8 while cationic reagents (amines) and kerosene are added to the feed box. (Amines are derivatives of ammonia in which the hydrogen atoms have been replaced by radicals containing hydrogen and carbon atoms, e.g., methylamine—CH_3NH_2.) These reagents condition the surfaces of the remaining fine sand particles, causing them to adhere to the bubbles produced in the float cells. The gangue is removed on the froth,

Agrico's recently completed Fort Green beneficiation plant—part of the industry's capacity surge—has a 550-ft-dia thickener.

while the final concentrate sinks to the bottom of the cells and is removed, washed, and dewatered for storage and shipment.

Reagent consumption is influenced by the efficiency of desliming and surface preparation. Excessive use of reagent in the anionic flotation stage raises reagent consumption in cationic flotation as well. Ranges of reagent usage in rougher flotation, in pounds per ton of feed, are: ammonia, 0.3 to 1.5; fatty acid (tall oil), 0.75 to 1.25; and fuel oil, 1.0 to 3.0. Cleaning of the rougher product consumes 0.5 to 3.0 lb of sulphuric acid per ton, while the amine section uses 0.1 to 3.0 lb of amine and 0.25 to 0.50 lb of kerosene.

In the last few years, the phosphate industry has witnessed a dramatic scale-up in equipment size. As an example, in 1975, U. K. Custred of Brewster Phosphates presented a paper describing the benefits of giant 300-cu-ft flotation cells.[3] He noted that for a fixed floor space, replacement of small cells by the large units would increase rougher flotation capacity by up to 50%, while reducing the requirements for both pulp dilution—saving plant water—and power. In the same year, Agrico opened the Fort Green plant with a rougher flotation section incorporating 500-cu-ft Wemco cells, over 11.5 ft high.

There is speculation within the industry as to how far and how fast equipment scale-up can proceed before the adverse effects of size outweigh its benefits.

With the exception of size scale-up and minor modifications of equipment design and flowsheet layout, the basic design of wash, size, and flotation plants is not likely to change much from the processing that now produces pebble, intermediate product, and flotation product. All plants segregate their products by size and BPL content—for ultimate use within captive wet acid plants or for shipment and sale via the ports of Tampa, Boca Grande, and St. Petersburg. Rock ultimately bound for dry grinding mills is normally dried to 3% moisture in either rotary or fluosolids dryers before shipment. Trends toward wet grinding may alter final treatment of phosphate rock.

Many fertilizers made from Florida rock

By dominating the phosphate rock production of the US and much of the world, Florida producers of phosphate fertilizers are the commanding force in the domestic fertilizer industry. In 1973, Florida's phosphate fertilizer capacity amounted to 58% of total US capacity for wet-process phosphoric acid, 78% for concentrated superphosphate, and 31% for ammonia phosphate.[4]

Nearly all Florida rock destined for domestic consumption is first used to produce wet-process phosphoric acid. Rock is digested by sulphuric acid to produce a waste gypsum (presently too impure for commercial use) and phosphoric acid. Phosphoric acid is then used to produce both liquid and dry fertilizers, including normal superphosphate, triple superphosphate (TSP), diammonium phosphate (DAP), and the nitrogen-phosphorus-potassium (NPK) complete fertilizers. Aside from these primary products, secondary derivatives of the wet-process phosphoric acid industry include fluorine and uranium.

Agriculture accounts for nearly 85% of the US demand for phosphate rock. In 1973, the fertilizer market took more than 26 million tons of rock, of which 21 million tons went into production of wet-process phosphoric acid.[4] The two major fertilizers, DAP and TSP, consumed more than 16 million tons of rock production.

The US agricultural community would be in poor shape without phosphates. The major crops of corn, hay and pasture, wheat, cotton, oats, barley, and soybeans account for 82% of US phosphatic fertilizer consumption. Over 85% of the US corn crop is grown using phosphatic fertilizers.

Central Florida's major phosphate fertilizer producers are Agrico Chemical Co., Borden Chemical Co., CF Industries, Conserve Inc., W. R. Grace & Co., International Minerals & Chemical Corp., Occidental Agricultural Chemical Co., Royster Inc., SOPAG, and USS Agri-Chemicals Inc. Some of these producers also ship phosphate rock to fertilizer plants in other states, as do Brewster Phosphates, Mobil Oil, and Swift Agricultural Chemicals Corp.—which produce primary rock (but not fertilizers) in central Florida.

Phosphoric acid consumes 50% of US sulphur

Approximately 11 million tons of sulphur was produced in the US in 1975, of which nearly 6 million tons was consumed in the production of phosphoric fertilizers. Step number one in the production of wet-process phosphoric acid and fertilizers is the production of sulphuric acid. Liquid sulphur is received from the Gulf Coast in rail cars and trucks and loaded into storage tanks at the acid-fertilizer complex. Molten sulphur is pumped and burned at 1,800°F with compressed air to convert it to sulphur dioxide. This gas is passed through a waste-heat boiler to generate steam and then through a catalytic (vanadium pentoxide) converter, where the gas is converted to sulphur trioxide. The SO_3 is directed to an absorbing tower, where water is absorbed to produce sulphuric acid.

The process is nearly 100% efficient, with steam produced in burning sulphur used in the evaporation process of the phosphoric acid plant.

Producing wet-process phosphoric acid

Wet-process acid manufacture was developed in Belgium by Prayon. It is the starting point for all subsequent fertilizer manufacture, and while the process is simple, it requires accurate control of numerous interacting physical variables. Simply described, wet or dry phosphate rock is ground to 60% minus 200 mesh, then mixed with sulphuric acid in a series of digestion tanks. Chemical reaction within the tanks creates a slurry, consisting of calcium sulphate ($CaSO_4 \cdot 2\ H_2O$) and phosphoric acid (H_3PO_4). (As a fertilizer constituent, the latter is expressed as P_2O_5.) The slurry passes over a large rotating disc filter, where the cal-

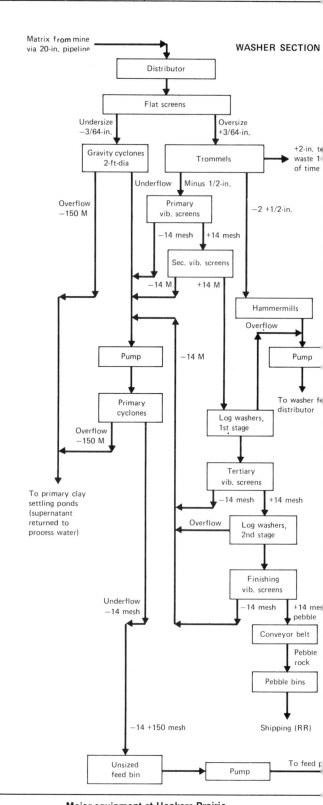

Major equipment at Hookers Prairie

Washing section	Size	HP	Manufacturer
Flat screens, 6*	7 ft x 20 ft long	—	Met-Pro Co.
Trommels, 6	7 ft x 16 ½ ft long	25	Met-Pro Co.
Log washers, 4	46 in. x 30 ft long	200	Eagle Iron Works
Wet cyclones, 38	2 ft dia	20	Met-Pro Co.
Hammermills, 2	36 in. x 42 in. dia	250	Koppers Co.
Vibrating screens, 16	6 ft x 16 ft	20	Deister Machine Co.
Pebble bins, 2	35 ft x 27 ft high	—	Reco Constructors

*Double

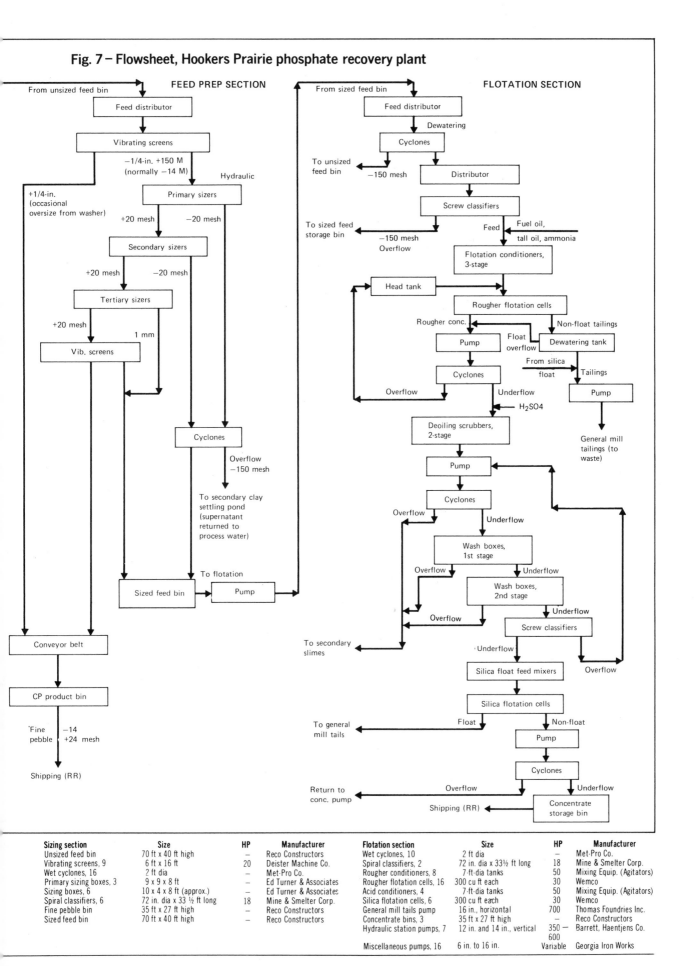

Fig. 7 – Flowsheet, Hookers Prairie phosphate recovery plant

FEED PREP SECTION

From unsized feed bin

Feed distributor

Vibrating screens

−1/4-in. +150 M (normally −14 M)

+1/4-in. (occasional oversize from washer)

Hydraulic

Primary sizers

+20 mesh / −20 mesh

Secondary sizers

+20 mesh / −20 mesh

Tertiary sizers

+20 mesh / 1 mm

Vib. screens

Cyclones

Overflow −150 mesh

To secondary clay settling pond (supernatant returned to process water)

To flotation

Sized feed bin → Pump

Conveyor belt

CP product bin

Fine pebble −14 +24 mesh

Shipping (RR)

FLOTATION SECTION

From sized feed bin

Feed distributor

Dewatering

Cyclones

To unsized feed bin

−150 mesh

Distributor

Screw classifiers

To sized feed storage bin

−150 mesh Overflow

Feed

Fuel oil, tall oil, ammonia

Flotation conditioners, 3-stage

Head tank

Rougher flotation cells

Rougher conc. / Non-float tailings

Pump / Float overflow / Dewatering tank

From silica float / Tailings

Cyclones

Overflow / Underflow

Pump

H_2SO4

Deoiling scrubbers, 2-stage

Pump

Cyclones

Overflow / Underflow

Wash boxes, 1st stage

Overflow / Underflow

Wash boxes, 2nd stage

Overflow / Underflow

Screw classifiers

Underflow / Overflow

To secondary slimes

Silica float feed mixers

Silica flotation cells

Float / Non-float

To general mill tails

Pump

Cyclones

Return to conc. pump / Overflow / Underflow

Concentrate storage bin

Shipping (RR)

General mill tailings (to waste)

Sizing section	Size	HP	Manufacturer
Unsized feed bin	70 ft x 40 ft high	—	Reco Constructors
Vibrating screens, 9	6 ft x 16 ft	20	Deister Machine Co.
Wet cyclones, 16	2 ft dia	—	Met-Pro Co.
Primary sizing boxes, 3	9 x 9 x 8 ft	—	Ed Turner & Associates
Sizing boxes, 6	10 x 4 x 8 ft (approx.)	—	Ed Turner & Associates
Spiral classifiers, 6	72 in. dia x 33 ½ ft long	18	Mine & Smelter Corp.
Fine pebble bin	35 ft x 27 ft high	—	Reco Constructors
Sized feed bin	70 ft x 40 ft high	—	Reco Constructors

Flotation section	Size	HP	Manufacturer
Wet cyclones, 10	2 ft dia	—	Met-Pro Co.
Spiral classifiers, 2	72 in. dia x 33½ ft long	18	Mine & Smelter Corp.
Rougher conditioners, 8	7-ft-dia tanks	50	Mixing Equip. (Agitators)
Rougher flotation cells, 16	300 cu ft each	30	Wemco
Acid conditioners, 4	7-ft-dia tanks	50	Mixing Equip. (Agitators)
Silica flotation cells, 6	300 cu ft each	30	Wemco
General mill tails pump	16 in., horizontal	700	Thomas Foundries Inc.
Concentrate bins, 3	35 ft x 27 ft high	—	Reco Constructors
Hydraulic station pumps, 7	12 in. and 14 in., vertical	350 — 600	Barrett, Haentjens Co.
Miscellaneous pumps, 16	6 in. to 16 in.	Variable	Georgia Iron Works

cium sulphate crystals (gypsum waste) are separated from the liquid phosphoric acid. The disc is subjected to a water spray to capture the acid. The gypsum is then slurried to 22% solids and pumped (at 120°F and 50 psig) through polybutylene pipe to holding ponds. The decant water is returned to the plant for reuse.

Portions of the dilute acid are returned to the digestion tanks, and the rest of the weak, filtered phosphoric acid is pumped to vacuum evaporators, where excess water is driven off and the acid reaches approximately 54% strength. The evaporator-condenser is equipped with a scrubber to capture hydrofluosilicic acid from the fumes. This byproduct acid is recirculated until it attains a strength of 25% and is then collected.

Concentrated phosphoric acid is clarified and sent to storage, for shipment or for use locally in the production of fertilizers. Not all acid removed from the Prayon filter is concentrated to 54%. Some is brought up only to a 30% concentration, for use in dry product fertilizers. Generally, three concentrations of acid are produced: 30%, 40%, and 54% (P_2O_5). The latter is principally a shipping acid. Sludge removed from these liquid acids is in many cases used to manufacture granular TSP.

Controversy over wet vs. dry grinding

In the past, most phosphate rock was dried to about 2% moisture before being sent to ball mills for grinding to a specified fineness for wet phosphoric acid plants. Recently, there has been a move toward wet grinding in the ball mills. New acid plants of Agrico, CF Industries, and Grace employ this technique. Advantages of wet grinding are:

■ If the acid plant is near the wash/flotation plant, wet rock can be transported inexpensively by pipeline.

■ Capital and operating costs for dryers are eliminated.

■ Air pollution from drying and dry grinding is eliminated, reducing equipment requirements for pollution control.

■ Other capital and operating costs (for covered storage, dry-rock feed systems, rock distribution, etc.) are eliminated, and distribution is simplified.

■ Classification of wet flotation fines can reduce the amount of material that must be sent to grinding mills.

According to one source, by wet grinding of phosphate rock, "overall operating costs at a Florida location can be reduced by a total of $3.00 to $4.25 per ton of P_2O_5."[5]

However, the old bromide about there being no such thing as a free lunch is still operative. Wet grinding and wet feed do create problems in controlling the feed rate of rock to the acid circuit, which can adversely affect operations down the line. Because grinding mills cannot tolerate acidic waters, plant water balance must be altered. Wet grinding can result in a tripling of the wear rate of balls and mill liners. Nevertheless, the advantages can include a 30% to 40% reduction of required horsepower in the grinding circuit and a corresponding reduction in mill size. The adverse effects of wet grinding can be mitigated by clean-cut plant design and effective use of process controls.

Some recent modifications of Prayon process

Davy Powergas Inc., of Lakeland, Fla., has introduced modifications of the Prayon wet phosphoric acid process. The rock is subjected to wet grinding. Then, phosphate pulp is pipelined to react with sulphuric acid in an attack volume in four to eight compartments in series. A modified agitation system is designed to achieve uniform particle dispersion and to prevent pockets of calcium and sulphate ions from forming, which would impede homogeneous crystallization.

The gypsum-phosphoric acid slurry is filtered, and the gypsum is washed countercurrently to collect acid. There is always a trade-off between efficient acid recovery from washing the crystals and dilution of the recovered acid. A portion of the acid from the filtration process is returned to the attack tanks for use with the new feed. Recirculation is accomplished through side openings in the tank, instead of the conventional over-and-under system. A newly designed flash cooler eliminates the necessity of diluting sulphuric acid feed to 55% strength before addition to the attack tank. The cooler also removes reaction heat more effectively and, functioning as a vacuum degasifier, makes slurry pumping easier by preventing pulsations in flow. The new Davy Powergas system is said to reduce rock grinding specifications to 40% minus 200 mesh, as opposed to the 60% minus 200 mesh that was required before modification.

Irrespective of the relative design merits of wet acid plants, tight controls over wet processing are needed throughout all systems. The main controls are rock feed controller, sulphuric acid flow recorder-controller, total water flow recorder-controller, filter feed slurry flowmeter, recycle acid flowmeter, and multipoint temperature recorder. Close supervision is required to maintain operations within a limited range of values for these parameters.

Grace's Bartow plant is a good example of fertilizer manufacture. Located between Mulberry and Bartow, the plant is being modernized and expanded. Presently, the complex produces 2,400 tpd of sulphuric acid, 1,000 tpd of phosphoric acid, 1,000 tpd of DAP (18-46-0), and 1,200 tpd of granular TSP. Two obsolete sulphuric acid plants have been replaced with one new one. As part of Grace's expansion program, two additional sulphuric acid plants and one new phosphoric acid plant will be constructed to produce an additional 380,000 tpy of phosphoric acid. (The production figures for all acids are based on 100% acid content, although most acids are diluted.) The expansion, a joint venture, will treat rock product from Grace's new Hookers Prairie plant, along with expanded production of USS Agri-Chem.

Some 50% of the phosphoric acid produced at Bartow is used in the production of DAP. Phosphoric acid is partially neutralized with ammonia, creating a slurry. The slurry is further neutralized by additional ammonia to form crystals within the blunger (an inclined paddle mixer). The crystals, or granules, are passed through a rotary dryer and then cooled and screened, with oversize returned to the blunger while the screened final product, nominally 6 to 16 mesh, is sent to storage. The storage building is kept under negative pressure in order to capture the ammonia fumes.

Production of TSP follows the processing scheme used for DAP, except that phosphoric acid is reacted with finely ground phosphate rock—no ammonia is used. TSP is produced in either pulverized or granular form. Granular TSP (0-46-0) is made by mixing 39%-strength phosphoric acid and 85% minus 200-mesh phosphate rock, normally 70-75% BPL. The ground rock and acid are mixed in steam-heated reaction tanks to form a thick slurry. The slurry passes into blungers, where phosphate rock fines are added and granular particles are formed. The mix passes through rotary dryers, where moisture content is reduced to 2%. From the dryers, material is elevated to vibrating screens, where fines are removed and returned to the blungers while product is conveyed to bulk storage. Production lines are readily converted to produce either TSP or DAP. Another product, "run-of-pile" TSP (0-46-0) is manufac-

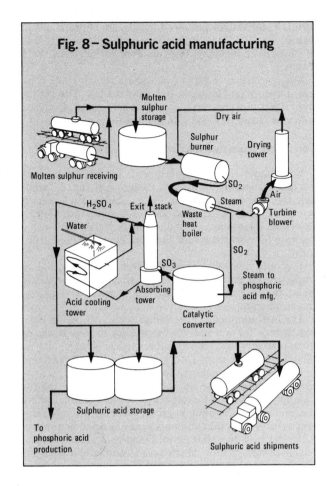

Fig. 8– Sulphuric acid manufacturing

Molten sulphur storage
Dry air
Molten sulphur receiving
Sulphur burner
Drying tower
SO_2
H_2SO_4
Exit stack
Steam
Air
Water
Waste heat boiler
Turbine blower
SO_2
SO_3
Steam to phosphoric acid mfg.
Acid cooling tower
Absorbing tower
Catalytic converter
Sulphuric acid storage
To phosphoric acid production
Sulphuric acid shipments

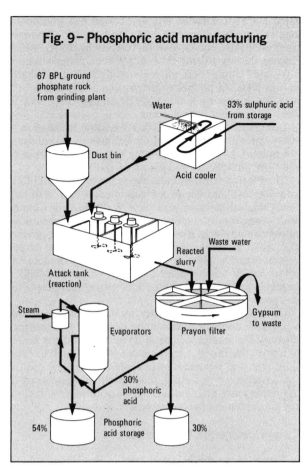

Fig. 9– Phosphoric acid manufacturing

67 BPL ground phosphate rock from grinding plant
Water
93% sulphuric acid from storage
Dust bin
Acid cooler
Attack tank (reaction)
Reacted slurry
Waste water
Steam
Evaporators
Prayon filter
Gypsum to waste
30% phosphoric acid
54%
Phosphoric acid storage
30%

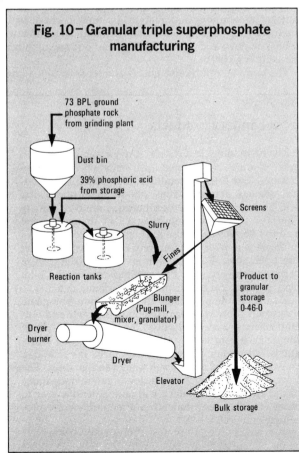

Fig. 10– Granular triple superphosphate manufacturing

73 BPL ground phosphate rock from grinding plant
Dust bin
39% phosphoric acid from storage
Slurry
Screens
Fines
Reaction tanks
Product to granular storage 0·46·0
Dryer burner
Blunger (Pug-mill, mixer, granulator)
Dryer
Elevator
Bulk storage

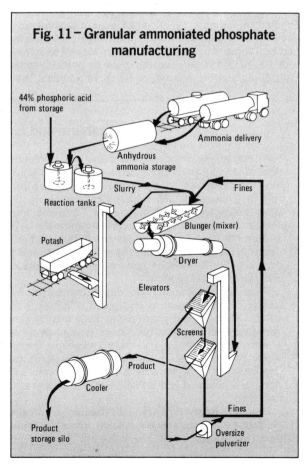

Fig. 11– Granular ammoniated phosphate manufacturing

44% phosphoric acid from storage
Ammonia delivery
Anhydrous ammonia storage
Slurry
Fines
Reaction tanks
Blunger (mixer)
Potash
Dryer
Elevators
Screens
Product
Cooler
Fines
Product storage silo
Oversize pulverizer

tured from a controlled mix of 54%-strength phosphoric acid and ground phosphate rock. Products are introduced proportionately into a cone (developed by TVA), which slurries the ingredients. The slurry is discharged onto a 5-ft-wide "setting" belt, where it quickly forms a semihard, porous mass. At the belt's discharge end, the mass is broken into lumps by a disintegrator before being sent to storage for curing and shipment.

Like most such plants, Grace's Bartow installation is equipped with potash handling facilities to manufacture "complete" fertilizers, containing varying percentages of nitrogen, phosphorus, and potassium (NPK).

The Florida fertilizer industry is now in a period of expansion. IMC has completed construction of a $110 million chemical complex near New Wales in Polk County, with a capacity of 1.3 million tons per year of concentrated phosphate products. Essentially all of the planned production has been committed under long term, take-or-pay agreements. The plant can supply sufficient phosphate fertilizer for 90 million acres of wheat, or about 3 billion bushels—equal to the grain needs of 450 million people for one year.

Government and the industry are studying new methods to improve undesirable conditions caused by fertilizer production. The studies include acid recovery by direct acidulation of the matrix, development of high-analysis fluid fertilizers, and treatment of calcareous phosphate ores. If these studies prove fruitful, they should alleviate some of the burgeoning problems associated with success, including the depletion of good reserves.

Tampa is major US fertilizer port

Tampa is the ninth largest port of the US in volume handled. Phosphate rock and related products account for over 95% of all exports and some 50% of the total tonnage handled by the port. In 1975, 11.5 million tons of phosphate rock was exported from Florida, about 90% from the port of Tampa. An additional 8 million tons of phosphate rock was barged from Tampa to domestic ports along the Gulf Coast and the Mississippi River. In addition, most fertilizer derivatives produced locally are shipped out of Tampa. In 1975, IMC shipped more than 11 million tons of phosphatic materials from its Port Sutton terminal in Tampa.

Major overseas buyers of phosphate rock include Canada, Japan, West Germany, Italy, and the UK. The Mississippi River provides direct access for barging of phosphate rock and fertilizers to the farming heartland of the US.

Terminals store and load rock and fertilizers

Four major shiploading terminals for phosphate rock are located within Tampa Bay: Eastern Associated Terminal, the Seaboard Coastline (SCL) Railroad's Rockport terminal, the IMC terminal at Port Sutton, and Agrico's Big Bend installation. At these four facilities, the storage capacity for phosphate rock (wet and dry) exceeds 750,000 tons.

Typically, phosphate rock and fertilizers are railed or trucked from producers in Bone Valley to the terminals, where they are stored, sampled, and stemmed aboard vessels and barges.

The IMC terminal at Port Sutton, which opened in 1965, has storage for wet and dry phosphate rock, a dockside drying facility and storage for various grades of fertilizers. Products from IMC's plants in Polk County are railed to Port Sutton. Dried rock and fertilizers are sent to covered storage, while wet rock is conveyed from the car dumper to a 200,000-ton-capacity wet-storage area, where it is segregated according to grade. Wet rock from the storage piles or from the car dumper may be dried at a rate of 6,250 tpd in a fluosolids dryer. Dried rock is conveyed to one of 16 storage silos, which have a combined capacity of 60,000 tons. Rock of various BPL grades can be blended for shipment from the silos. The tonnage loaded aboard ship and barge is recorded with a Merrick weightometer. Automated sampling and analysis are used to check rock quality during loading. The sampler makes a continuous cut of the flow, and up to 1% of the cargo passes through the sampling system.

The terminal can receive potash at a separate unloading

Uranium and fluorine: secondary products

All marine phosphorites contain uranium, in concentrations ranging from 0.005% to as much as 0.05%, and most US phosphate reserves contain 3% or more fluorine as fluor-apatite. Phosphate rock reserves in the Bone Valley formation, estimated at 1.2 billion tons, contain a minimum 150,000 tons of recoverable U_3O_8 and are the largest source of fluorine in the US. Fluorine is critical to the production of aluminum and is used also for fluoridation and in the manufacture of many chemical compounds.

Fluorine and uranium are now recovered as by-products from wet-process acid plants. Fluorine is recovered from the exit gases (steam, hydrogen-fluoride, and silica-fluoride) from phosphoric acid evaporators. These gases are directed into the wet scrubbing towers, where fluorine gases are absorbed by the water in the scrubber. The acid produced is recirculated until 25% strength is obtained and is then stored for shipment to customers.

Uranium Recovery Corp. (a subsidiary of United Nuclear Corp.) operates a full-scale primary uranium recovery module at Grace's Ridgewood plant. Two other modules are planned for installation at IMC operations. (See E/MJ, December 1975, p 80.) URC's module extracts uranium from 30%-strength phosphoric acid by interrupting the flow between the Bird-Prayon filter and the evaporation process that strengthens the acid to 54%. Westinghouse has conducted a cooperative pilot plant test for uranium recovery at the Gardinier Inc. operations. Gulf has been involved with Agrico in uranium recovery. And Freeport has developed a pilot plant program for its facilities in Louisiana.

One burgeoning problem for the Florida phosphate industry is concern by environmentalists, state and federal officials, and others over the radiation levels of some lands and water affected by phosphate operations. The major concern appears to be the radiation emission levels of certain well waters and landfills. The Environmental Protection Agency began investigations of radiation in 1975, which will take at least a year to complete. The study may affect some mining and processing practices.

The 'Backstacker' used at Eastern Associated's terminal in Tampa Bay is a significant innovation in stockpiling-reclaiming.

facility. Potash is conveyed to a 40,000-ton-capacity storage building to await shipment by rail or truck.

'Backstacker': a bright new idea in stockpiling

Back in 1970, Ed Schultz, manager of Eastern Associated Terminal at Tampa, came up with an idea for a better way to stack and reclaim piles of phosphate rock. After several years of experiments in modifying a conventional stacker-reclaimer, the design of the "Backstacker" was completed in December 1974. The concept of the machine is quite simple, using only a drag conveyor for stacking and reclaiming (see photo). The flights travel in opposite directions, depending on the function. Material is pushed up the pile from base to peak in stacking, as opposed to being dropped from a conventional conveyor head onto the pile. The elimination of free fall prevents dusting and segregation of sizes. The Backstacker increases the amount of material that can be stored over a given area by 20% to 40%. Further, the machine permits precise segregation of material whenever desired, as well as precise reclaim blending of such segregated materials. Having proved eminently successful at the EAT terminal, the Backstacker has been patented, and four 3,000-tph machines are now in operation at two of Tampa's largest phosphate terminals. Viewing the simplicity of operation makes one wonder why it took so long to think the machine into reality.

Barging fertilizers to the US farm heartland

In addition to the four major phosphate rock terminals in Tampa Bay, SCL operates a wet rock terminal on the Gulf Coast, at Boca Grande, 100 mi south of Tampa. While some phosphate rock from Bone Valley is shipped by rail for domestic use, abut 80% is barged from Tampa and the Gulf Coast to Louisiana for conversion to fertilizer, and then to markets up the Mississippi River and its tributaries. Agrico, for example, ships wet rock from Big Bend via a 450-mi barge run to its Faustina chemical plant at Donaldsonville, La.

Barges used by Agrico for the run from Big Bend to Louisiana are self-unloading. (See E/MJ, May 1974, p 94.) The barges measure 495 ft long by 85 ft wide and have an overall draft of 30 ft. Each barge carries a load of 22,500 lt. Designed and developed in Sweden, such barges were used successfully for years in the European pulp and paper industry. The parascrew unloaders used in the US were built by Orba Corp. for St. Phillip Towing and Transportation Co., which is contracted to haul Agrico's rock. The St. Phillip barges are the first application of the design in the US.

Wet phosphate rock weighs 93 lb per cu ft, containing 6% to 10% moisture. The material has a tendency to be sticky and to bridge. The parascrew handling system not only improves discharge capability to a rate of 3,000 tph, but also eliminates the wedge-shaped holds for gravity feed, thereby increasing barge capacity some 20%.

After rock processing at Faustina, a typical Agrico shipment of fertilizer up the river might include two barges of DAP and two barges of urea, destined for a 960-mi trip to Henderson, Ky. After the barges are loaded, an Agrico shift boat pulls them to midriver, where they meet a commercial tow. The tow is a train of barges, perhaps 35 in all, destined for various points upriver. When the tow reaches the Ohio River, it drops the Agrico barges at the river mouth, where another tow picks them up for delivery to Henderson.

From the peninsula of Florida, phosphate from Bone Valley finds its way up the main inland water artery of the US to help produce food from seed.

An overview of phosphate economics

In 1974, world production of phosphate rock totaled some 120 million tons, of which more than 45 million tons was produced in the US. The US, USSR, and Morocco dominated world supply, furnishing about 78% of total production. Principal producing areas of the world are Florida, the Kola peninsula and Kazakhstan in the USSR, and the Khouribga and Youssoufia areas of Morocco.[6]

At the production rates existing and foreseeable, world reserves of phosphate rock are relatively ample. In addition to the 17.7 billion tons of reserves listed in the accompanying table, another 66 billion tons of material are classified by the US Bureau of Mines as "resources." The figures for reserves and resources have risen over the past decades as new phosphate fields have been discovered, as technology has improved recoveries, and as knowledge of existing fields has been extended. There is every reason to expect that future increases will be recorded, at least over the next several decades.

Presently, major phosphate reserves of the US outside Florida are found in North Carolina, Idaho, Montana, Utah, Wyoming, and Tennessee. Overseas phosphate reserves are found in South America, Africa, Asia, and Australia, in addition to the major reserves of the USSR and Morocco.

The USBM forecasts an average annual growth rate of 3% for US consumption of phosphate products and 6% for the rest of the world during the period 1973-2000.[6] Similarly, Stanford Research Institute's *Chemical Economics Handbook* forecasts an average growth rate of 3-5% in the domestic consumption of phosphate fertilizers.

Florida remains phosphate's vital center

Outside the USSR, only Morocco exceeds the state of Florida in export of phosphate rock. No country exceeds Florida in export of phosphate products—nor comes close to it in production of phosphate rock, which in 1975 exceeded 38 million tons in Florida. Some 11.5 million tons of rock was exported, at a sales price close to $500 million. Another 8 million tons of rock was tied up in phosphatic products shipped abroad, a shot in the arm for the US balance of payments.

Within the US, the Florida phosphate industry has a substantial salutory impact on the US economy. According to USBM, "Throughout the nation, the Florida phosphate industry will account for approximately 91,000 jobs, and $3.3 billion of gross output, including $390 million in personal income, in 1975." In Florida alone, the industry accounts for 61,000 jobs and nearly $1.5 billion in gross output, of which $262 million is personal income. Estimated Florida state tax revenues from phosphate production for 1975 exceeded $23 million, with another $30 million in county tax assessments.[6]

Production of Florida phosphate rock began a decade before the 20th century, growing to 750,000 tpy in 1900, 3.7 million tpy in 1930, and 13 million tpy in 1960. Since then, production has taken off—topping 30 million tpy in 1970 and reaching nearly 40 million tpy in 1975. Projections suggest a zenith of about 55 million tpy in the 1980s, followed by a gradual decline as grade of the matrix declines and remaining reserves diminish. To everything, there is a season. For now, the production of Bone Valley phosphate rock is in full bloom. □

Major known reserves of phosphate rock*

(million tons)

US	2,500
USSR	800
Morocco	10,000
Spanish Sahara	1,700
Australia	1,000
Other countries	1,712
Total	**17,712**

Source: *Mineral Facts and Problems*, 1975 ed., USBM.
*Based on a value of $27.66 per ton, 70% BPL (the price effective July 1, 1974, f.o.b. Florida plant).

References

1) "The Florida Slimes Problem," USBM IC 8668, 1975.
2) Blakey, Arch Frederic, *The Florida Phosphate Industry*, Harvard University Press, Cambridge, Mass., 1973.
3) Custred, U. K., Degner, V. R., and Long, E. W., "Recent Advances in Coarse Particle Recovery Utilizing Large-Capacity Flotation Machines," TRANSACTIONS, SME, December 1975, p 324.
4) Wang, Kung-Lee, et al, "Economic Significance of the Florida Phosphate Industry," USBM IC 8653, 1974.
5) Houghtaling, Samuel V., "Wet Grinding of Phosphate Rock Holds Down Dollars, Dust, and Fuel," E/MJ, January 1975, p 94.
6) "Phosphate Rock," *Mineral Facts and Problems*, 1975 ed., USBM.

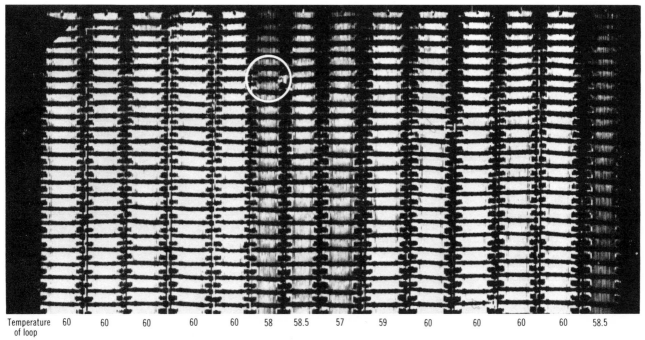

Temperature of loop	60	60	60	60	60	58	58.5	57	59	60	60	60	60	58.5

At Hoboken's Olen refinery, infrared photography shows three rows of cells at center with flow problems and a short in circled portion.

Infrared scanning spots tankhouse problems

James Smith, McGraw Hill Brussels Bureau

BELGIUM'S METALLURGIE HOBOKEN-OVERPELT is well into its third year of using infrared thermal mapping techniques to detect short circuits in its 5-acre copper refinery at Olen in north Belgium. The program, developed jointly with Sweden's Aga Aktiebolag, a producer of infrared equipment for military uses, substantially simplifies the job of manual inspection of some 80,000 cathodes in the refinery; it also improves cathode quality and gives the company the option of reducing tankhouse staff or using the same manpower over a larger capacity.

The heart of the Belgian system is an Aga infrared line scanner mounted on a succession of overhead cranes, which sweep over the tankhouse area. The apparatus produces a thermal map of the tankhouse cells on a photographic recorder. Temperature differences due to shorting show up as white spots on the map. Current bars and normal electrodes appear as black lines, and the surrounding electrolyte, being warmer, is registered as a light gray. The system can also detect cooling of the electrolyte due to faulty flow circuits in some cells.

The Olen refinery has about 2,000 cells, each containing 36 cathodes and 35 anodes which are electrically linked in parallel within each cell. The cells themselves are connected in series in two circuits. The plant can turn out about 270,000 mtpy of refined copper—the biggest refinery in Europe. The cells are served by three electrolyte flow circuits. Cathodes are normally pulled after 10 to 12 days.

Prior to the first experiments with the new system in 1970, manual inspection in the refinery consisted of pounding and parallel hanging of 3,500 new anodes and insertion of 7,000 starting sheets each day. In addition, the staff was required to finger-control the temperatures of 14,000 young cathodes and to mv-meter 80,000 cathodes, in addition to correcting all irregularities located.

The IRIPS (Infrared Industrial Process Supervision) system replaces the fingering and metering by a complete scanning run in the early morning hours, involving one man working about 2 hr, and a partial scanning at noon of young sections and sections to be corrected by the afternoon shift (about one manhour). Besides cutting inspection time, the system also reduces the number of shorts, thus cutting correction time. Hoboken estimates an overall manpower saving of about 10 men per day.

The IRIPS system thus makes it possible to work at a high current density, to form a longer anodic cycle, or to work with less distance between electrodes, the company says. (Hoboken, in fact, managed to increase the efficiency of its tankhouse and at the same time enlarge capacity by about 33% without increasing its inspection crews. Other advantages, the company reports, are more regular slime fallout, fewer nodules, and improved cathode surface as a result of better electrolyte flow and more regular temperature. Hoboken consulting engineer Jozef de Keyser says the improvement in efficiency has shown up mainly in more cathodes meeting the very high quality standard and in an improvement in current efficiency from 94% to about 95%.

The Aga revolving scanner uses a liquid-nitrogen-cooled germanium lens to pick up infrared rays. An indium antimonite crystal then converts the rays to electronic impulses which are amplified and fed to an oscilloscope. The image is recorded on photo-sensitive paper, which moves from the apparatus in a continuous printed black and white roll.

At Hoboken, the camera is basically portable and is successively mounted on overhead cranes serving the tankhouse. Controlled by a cable from the crane cabs, it moves at normal crane speeds of up to 100 m per min across the cell. Since the scanning angle of 80° covers about 4 m, the width of one cell, a complete bay needs four scanning runs. Sixteen sweeps are needed to cover the entire tankhouse. (There are four bays and four cranes in the tankhouse. Normally the camera is mounted successively on four cranes, each covering half a bay, but this may vary according to work load.)

The scanner in the prototype system installed at Olen in

(Continued on p 225)

Amarillo complex—"world's most modern copper refinery"

THE GOVERNOR OF TEXAS and the chairman of the board of Asarco Inc. symbolically opened Asarco's new Amarillo copper refinery late in June by cutting a strand of continuous-cast copper rod near the plant entrance. The ceremony marked the formal dedication of the plant, for which construction started in July 1973.

After severing the 5/16-in. copper rod, Charles F. Barber, Asarco chairman, hailed the $190 million plant as the most modern copper refinery in the world, and one of the largest. "This magnificent new plant is a significant contribution to the nation's copper-producing capacity and establishes Amarillo as one of the copper centers of the world," he said.

The refinery, located on a 250-acre site on a 3,000-acre tract northeast of Amarillo, has the capacity to refine 420,000 tpy of copper. When the Amarillo plant came on stream last fall, it marked the beginning of the end for Asarco's 75-year-old refinery in Perth Amboy, N.J. Production costs per ton of refined copper there had nearly tripled since 1966, and extreme difficulty was experienced in bringing the plant into compliance with environmental standards. These factors, coupled with the increased importance of the Midwest as a market for refined copper, prompted the phasing out of the Perth Amboy refining operation as the Amarillo facility is brought up to full production.

Copper arrives at the Amarillo plant in three forms: anodes from Asarco smelters at El Paso, Tex., and Hayden, Ariz.; blister copper from both domestic and foreign smelters; and No. 2 grade scrap.

Anodes from smelters and anodes cast at the refinery are transferred to the tankhouse for electrolytic refining. The tankhouse, which covers 11 acres, contains 2,400 plastic-lined concrete cells for electrolytic refining, each 15 ft 3 in. x 4 ft 2 in. x 5 ft. Operations in the tankhouse are almost completely automated, with four overhead cranes in each of the two long bays picking up blanks and anodes in full-cell loads and delivering the cathodes and used anodes for washing before further processing or recycle, respectively.

Starting sheets stay in the tanks for 14 days, slowly growing into 300-lb plates of copper cathodes. Cathodes are then removed from the tanks and replaced by new starting sheets. Anodes remain in the tank for 28 days, until they are almost completely dissolved, and are then replaced with new anodes.

At Amarillo, cathodes are melted at the refinery and cast into cake, billet, wirebars, and continuous-cast rod.

In addition to the electrolytic tankhouse, the Amarillo facility comprises a refined copper casting building to produce continuous-cast billet (one 5-tph melting furnace, one 15-ton holding furnace), continuous-cast cake (one 40-tph melting furnace, one 15-ton holding furnace), continuous-cast rod (one 40-tph melting furnace, one 15-ton holding furnace), and wirebar (one 20-mold casting wheel, one 60-tph melting furnace, and one 15-ton holding furnace).

In addition to copper, Amarillo will produce 60 million oz per year of silver from a parting plant for gold and silver; selenium and tellurium in another plant; and nickel sulphate.

Sulphuric acid for the electrolytic cells is supplied, at up to 500 tpm, from Asarco's El Paso smelter. Three wells at Amarillo provide the necessary 400 g per min. The electrical system is set up to handle up to 50 Mw from Southwestern Public Service Co., two of whose plants are visible from the Asarco site. Pioneer Natural Gas Co. supplies up to 7 million cu ft per day for heating electrolyte and melting copper.

Byproduct recovery at Amarillo is accomplished in three units that extract desired values from cell slimes. The gold-

Huge tankhouse, heart of Amarillo complex, covers almost 500,000 sq ft under one roof.

Cake is largest of the basic shapes of refined copper produced at Amarillo. The plant casts cake in several sizes, up to 38 ft long and weighing as much as 30 tons.

silver plant has the capacity to produce 60 million oz per year of refined silver.

In labeling the plant environmentally pure, Asarco engineers point out that several million dollars were invested in pollution control equipment. The tank-house area has a forced-air ventilation system to prevent buildup of contaminants. Air samplers near the plant continually monitor for particulates, and samples of soil and vegetation surrounding the plant are periodically analyzed for traces of metals.

Water from all refinery processes is sent to a lined, 4-acre pond, from which it is eventually injected into a mile-deep well for final disposal.

The Amarillo facility will employ 750, with an estimated annual payroll of $9.56 million. An additional $3.6 million per year will go for supplies and services.

In an address later in the dedication ceremonies, Barber said that the new copper refinery makes Texas the number one state in copper refining in the US. "It is the most complete such facility in the world," he stated. "Copper from Amarillo will be available in all the shapes used by industry—cathodes for melting and wirebars for drawing, cakes and billets, and continuous-cast rod. Silver and gold, selenium and tellurium are all found with copper in nature. Each of these elements will be recovered here—some will arrive in the copper blister and anodes; some in byproduct materials from other metallurgical plants. In each instance, the production of this plant will

Continuous-cast rod is shipped from the plant in coils of 5,000 lb and larger. The rod is becoming a popular shape of refined copper for use in manufacturing wire.

constitute a significant share of the nation's supply."

Barber praised the "very effective teamwork on the part of many people," which facilitated construction and startup of the refinery. He singled out the fine support given to Asarco by the Amarillo community, and said that Amarillo had to be "one of the most hospitable locations in the US." ☐

(Continued from p 223)

June 1970 operated at 16 revolutions (or lines) per sec. This was being upgraded to 32 lines per sec for better picture definition in a new model of IRIPS to be installed at the end of 1973. Since July 1971, Hoboken has relied fully on IRIPS for short circuit detection.

During the development stage, problems arose because infrared emission is influenced by the surface condition of the hanging bars, with the result that equal temperatures do not always give the same radiation. This situation required treatment of some bars.

In addition, it was necessary to avoid accidental cooling of bars due to opened windows, tankhouse ventilating fans, and condensation or leaks causing wet bars. Finally, considerable judgment had to be evolved in photo interpretation since large shorts often consist of many smaller ones. In addition, a

large number of shorts on a section reduces the intensity of each short, making detection on the photograph difficult. Therefore, interpretation of photos had to take into account the age of the section. A second inspection on new sections was instituted because of the likelihood of numerous shorts.

Successful use of IRIPS also requires a specially trained crew—at Olen it consists of three men. It also requires careful organization, first to avoid unnecessary walking on sections, which could cause shorts, and second, to minimize the time between detection and correction. At first, crews were hostile to the new system, but initial losses in current efficiency recovered after about five months. At Olen, short corrections are made on an organized schedule so that young sections get the most intensive work and so that work results may be personalized. Corrections are made only during the day shift except for

teams which have a section pulled.

One of the advantages of IRIPS is the photographic record of short detection, which improves control over inspection teams, facilitates training of young correctors, and provides a base for long-term studies on the origin of shorts and improvement of correction methods.

Instead of being installed on cranes, as at Olen, the system could be mounted on separate monorails from a central control unit placed in an instrument room. A variation on the Hoboken system is operating in American Smelting and Refining Co.'s "Baltimore groove" refinery at Tacoma, Wash., and it has been sold to Canadian Copper Refiners and to Rhokana in Zambia.

Hoboken notes that the accuracy of the system improves with higher current density, "the normal evolution in tankhouse practice," and that it is most suited to refineries using current reversal methods. ☐

Cementation-in-pulp of copper leach liquors— an attractive route to copper extraction

Improved through more effective slimes control, cementation-in-pulp of copper leach liquors can possibly add significant ore reserves to the US national inventory of recoverable copper. At the same time, the concept opens other attractive possibilities for copper processing—such as improved metal recoveries through a reduction in pregnant solution losses, or substantial reduction of settling and filtering area requirements, among other things, at hydrometallurgical copper operations.

Edmund C. Bitzer, Metallurgical engineer

ADAPTABLE TO A WIDE VARIETY of copper-oxide-bearing materials through highly flexible flowsheet arrangements, the cementation-in-pulp (CIP) system is little more than an extrapolation of precipitation-in-pulp procedures practiced elsewhere. Examples include charcoal-in-pulp recovery of gold from cyanide solutions or resin-in-pulp precipitation of U_3O_8 from acid leach liquors. CIP's simplicity has much to recommend it. The process makes use of familiar solution handling techniques and one of the oldest commercial copper precipitation methods known to man. It may even have the capability of competing with copper liquid ion exchange (LIX) systems, which are now enjoying a wave of popularity.

The key to CIP is the established fact that chemical reactions involved in precipitation occur just as well in a solution that contains suspended solids as in a relatively clear solution such as thickener overflow or filter effluent. This fact eliminates the necessity (and cost) of very large settling or filtering areas normally required for adequate washing of leached residue and pregnant solution recovery. Since precipitation involves the time-honored cementation reaction with shredded iron, the process was dubbed cementation-in-pulp.

Adequate sand-slime separation and washing of slimes to flush entrained pregnant solution is important to the success of the CIP system. Investigations indicate that mechanical classification in equipment such as spiral, Esperanza, or reciprocating rake classifiers—units that have been phasing out at most processing plants in favor of hydrocylones—can handle this problem effectively.

As noted in the accompanying background essay, the first leaching of copper in place was recorded five centuries ago, and the first large scale use of cementation occurred over 200 years ago. Since then, little improvement in leach and cementation systems has been documented, other than recent efforts centering around precipitation. Kennecott Copper Corp. has developed two types of vessels to replace iron launders. Both feature upward flow of solution through shredded iron. This technique requires considerably less iron than horizontal launders, with a marked saving in iron consumption. Others have experimented with vessels of kindred design with similar results.

Another major development in copper precipitation is LIX, which involves simultaneous purification and upgrading of pregnant solution so that cathode copper can be electrowon from the liquor. One limitation of LIX, however, is that it will not tolerate suspended solids in the feed solutions. Nevertheless, two such plants are in operation and one is in the design stage in the US. Another large LIX plant is presently starting up in Zambia.[3]

The biggest opportunity for process development lies in bettering metal extraction and solution recovery efficiencies. Vat leaching recoveries for which information is available range between 70% and 80%. Dump, heap, and in-situ leaching recoveries range from 40% downward. A significant portion of the losses from these operations is dissolved copper trapped in the slime fraction that never reaches the precipitation plant. By contrast, metal recovery rates in gold cyanide and uranium plants seldom fall below 90%.

Disregarding the unit operations of mining, crushing, and tailing disposal, most leach processes involve four steps: 1) exposure of the prepared ore to a solvent; 2) recovery of pregnant solution by simultaneous dewatering and washing; 3) clarification of the raw pregnant solution; and 4) precipitation.

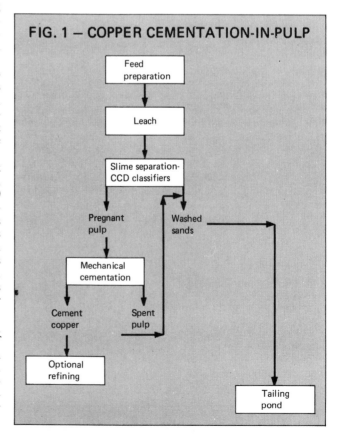

FIG. 1 — COPPER CEMENTATION-IN-PULP

The CIP concept greatly simplifies step (2), with considerable reduction in capital cost, and eliminates step (3), an item of appreciable operating cost. The system solves problems associated with treatment of slimy, sticky feed materials. It will permit the design of lower-cost and much more efficient copper leaching plants. With reduction in capital costs, small and medium size oxide deposits become more attractive for development. Finally, CIP opens opportunities for profitable recovery of copper from abandoned heap leach dumps, waste ore dumps, and old flotation tailings.

There has been speculation that LIX processing will ultimately replace cementation, but in the long range view this does not appear likely. The capital cost of an LIX plant is high and the process does not touch the heart of the matter—poor leaching recovery. Also, the potential of the simpler cementation process has yet to be fully explored.

Poor recoveries stem from two major problems which exist in varying degrees in conventional dump, heap, or vat leaching operations. In probable order of importance, the problems are: 1) insufficient crushing and incomplete exposure of minerals to leach solutions; and 2) slimes in the ore as mined or as formed during treatment. The slimes inhibit or completely prevent adequate percolation of solutions in static (dump or vat) leaching. Slimes also inhibit settling and filtration rates, with low efficiency of pregnant solution recovery, and they retain large amounts of pregnant solution because of their enormous surface area.

The crushing-exposure problem is controllable to the extent that adequate crushing and material handling equipment is available. It is with the slimes factor—a universal problem—that CIP technology is concerned.

Use of gold and uranium technology

Precipitation technology for uranium which evolved from the Chapman process (see background essay) can, with modifications, be adapted to copper cementation.

The flow diagram in Fig. 1 illustrates the simplicity that can be achieved. Detailed engineering estimates will demonstrate that dramatic savings in capital costs are possible by eliminating the enormous settling areas required for conventional solution recovery using CCD thickeners.

Adapting the basic flowsheet to specific applications makes feasible the exploitation of copper reserves tied up in old waste ore dumps (particularly those which are being leached by present methods), flotation tailings, or even tailings from vat leaching operations. Not the least of the advantages of the new technology lies in the exploitation of relatively small, virgin oxide deposits which will not support the large capital cost or poor recovery rate of conventional methods. A particular advantage in the use of classifiers, as shown in Fig. 1, is their ability to handle a wide range of sizes in the solids of the feed. Thickeners are restricted to relatively fine materials—a major limitation.

Sand-slime separation and washing

The Chapman and LPF processes were conducted in pulps originating as classifier overflows of wet grinding circuits. After preliminary thickening, the pulp was close to 50% solids, with a size of 48 to 65 mesh, meaning that 98-99% of the dry solids would pass a sieve of the specified size. Possibly 45-65% would pass a 200 mesh sieve. Precipitation was effected in this environment—the ultimate in simplicity of equipment.

Such simplicity was impossible in the transition to the RIP process for uranium ores, because the equipment used for contacting ion exchange resins with the pulp would not tolerate solid particles much coarser than 325 mesh. It was thus necessary to make a sand-slime separation of the pulps involved. The split was generally quite coarse by wet grinding

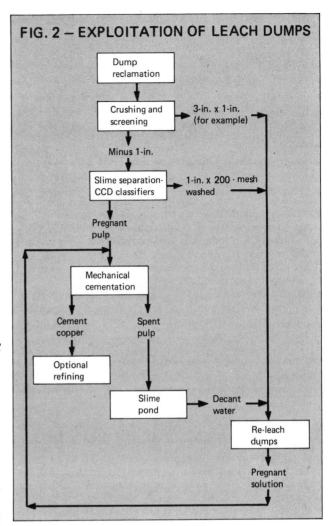

FIG. 2 – EXPLOITATION OF LEACH DUMPS

standards—in the range of 20 mesh—and the pulp was delivered for acid leaching at close to 50% solids. After leaching, the pulp was mechanically classified in a series of four units arranged for CCD washing. The overflow from the first classifier in the series contained solids in the range of 48 to 65 mesh. This slurry was further classified in cyclones which delivered an ion exchange feed at 325 mesh. In some cases, the coarse cyclone underflow was returned to the second mechanical classifier; sometimes a series of parallel CCD cyclones was used. After ion exchange treatment, the spent pulp was combined with the washed oversize from the last CCD classifier and pumped to tailing storage.

Following are details of pregnant solution handling by mechanical classification.

Overflow pulp characteristics. The consistency of the pulp ranged from 1.04 to 1.10 specific gravity—rarely approaching the higher figure. The pulps were very stable and behaved as a true heavy liquid, with no tendency toward sedimentation at any point in the ion exchange system. Specific gravity determinations for control purposes were normally made with a standard hydrometer, another indication of pulp stability. (A further discussion of pulp characteristics is included in the succeeding description of the cementation vessel.)

Washing efficiency. As noted, the efficiency of solution recovery using four stages of classifiers was nearly perfect—much better than could have been achieved with the same number of CCD thickeners. The reason is that the classifier sand products were in the same range of 70% solids. It would be difficult to approach—much less maintain—a 50% consistency in thickener underflows without mechanical problems.

There is no need to check washing efficiency in the classic fashion in view of this spread in moisture content of the products, but at least one additional stage of thickening would be required to approach the efficiency of mechanical classifiers.

Size of feed solids. An outstanding advantage of washing with classifiers is that they will accept a wide range of particle sizes—ranging from a conventional wet grind of 48 to 65 mesh (to which thickeners are largely restricted) to material as coarse as 1½-in. top size. This capability makes it possible to process ores which yield satisfactory recoveries in a coarse size range (see Fig. 2).

Area requirements. This is an overpowering advantage for the choice of classifiers over thickeners, since a pregnant pulp can be obtained with much less plant area than if thickeners were used to produce a nominally clear pregnant solution.

As a rough quantitative comparison, in one instance 650 ft of total classifier area were required to handle 1,000 tpd of dry plant feed.[6] A plant now being designed for copper leaching and solution recovery with CCD thickeners requires 60,000 sq ft of settling area to treat the same tonnage—over 90 times as much plant area.

Without going into details of comparative capital cost estimates, this wide discrepancy in area requirements for effective pregnant solution recovery (about 90 to 1) leads to three general conclusions:

1) The capital cost of the CIP process will be far below that of a plant using conventional solution recovery.

2) The feasibility of housing the compact arrangement makes it possible to consider operations where weather conditions are extreme.

3) The flexibility of classifiers with respect to feed size offers a unique advantage for treating materials effectively at coarse sizes, providing an adequate leach recovery rate is assured.

The present generation of mill operators and equipment vendors has little experience with the mechanical classifiers which once dominated the sizing in fine grinding circuits, since such units have been outmoded by very large mills. In any case, the classifier application for CIP is completely different from closed-circuit grinding.

Design and layout of mechanical classification

Closed-circuit grinding requires introduction of the feed to a side of the machine near the shallow end of the pool in the case of a spiral classifier, or across the width of the pool in the same location for a reciprocating rake machine. For best classification results, the drainage deck above the pool is designed to be as long as possible to promote elimination of fines that should report in the overflow lip at the deep end. The slope of the drainage deck is also made as steep as possible to promote drainage and gain sufficient elevation to obtain gravity flow of the classifier sand back to the feed end of the grinding mill.

Background essay: Evolution of CIP concept focuses on effective slimes control

The past few years have been marked by renewed interest in copper hydrometallurgy, for both oxide ores and sulphide concentrates. Such interest has been generated mainly by Federal air quality legislation, which prompted investigation of several sulphide leaching processes. Some of these have reached the pilot testing state. The ultimate objective is to eliminate conventional smelting operations as a source of pollution.

An alternate approach to meeting legislated air standards is to convert the principal pollutant to sulphuric acid during pyroprocessing—already evidenced by the expansion of acid-making facilities at smelters. Since it is unlikely that existing smelter capacity will be superseded by new processes in the foreseeable future, it appears that ample acid supplies will be availble for exploiting what would normally be considered marginally leachable materials, of which there are enormous reserves. One example is the billions of tons of waste dumps, many of which are being presently worked; these reserves are increasing year by year. Old flotation tailings and many abandoned heap leach operations may also become attractive targets for leaching.

Dump and in-situ leaching followed by precipitation of copper with scrap iron is probably one of the oldest of hydrometallurgical processes. The earliest large scale use of cementation took place around the middle of the 18th century at the Rio Tinto mine in Spain.[1] Leaching of copper ore in place was successful on a small scale in Hungary during the 15th century.[2]

Leaching followed by precipitation still accounts for a substantial portion of total copper production—between 15% and 20% of total domestic copper output.[1] However, for various reasons, leaching of copper has never developed the degree of sophistication or metallurgical extraction efficiency attained by kindred leaching treatments for gold and uranium ores. In both the latter ores, slime control technology was developed so that precipitation of metal values in pulps became possible.

The following history of the development of the cementation-in-pulp (CIP) concept will help to establish credibility for the process, while acknowledging past contributions to the art. Refractory slimes have always presented vexatious and expensive problems for mill operators, resulting in frontal assaults on this situation.

The first known commercial attempt to perform precipitation in pulp was a trial of what was known as the Chapman process in the Philippines, some 40 years ago.[4] This trial was based on the use of activated charcoal, an avid precipitant, in a cyanide solution containing gold. Most gold ores mined in the Philippines were characterized by a considerable slime content, which greatly inhibited settling and filtration rates. A considerable plant area was required to obtain reasonable treatment capacities. Weather was also a major factor in plant design, since the annual rainfall of close to 200 in. in most areas occurred in a relatively short season, and mill buildings had to be of tight, expensive construction. The promises of a sharp reduction in building costs, as well as economies incident to simplification of equipment, were undoubtedly major incentives for the experiment.

Details of this Philippine operation are somewhat fragmentary because the mine was on a remote island and communication facilities were poor. Fine activated charcoal was added to the cyanide agitators and subsequently recovered by froth flotation. The intent was apparently to recover the precipitated gold by burning the charcoal, which proved to be quite difficult because of the large volumes involved. With the elimination of thickeners and filters, the plant must have been quite compact. However, it is doubtful that a significant amount of gold was ever re-

All of the above conditions are inimical to the requirements of CCD washing. The aim here is to obtain very fine material in the overflow and to reject a maximum of the classifier feed in the settled product without regard for the amount of fine material. Thus it is necessary to reverse the customary feed and overflow points—introducing feed at the deep end of the pool and overflowing the fines near the shallow end. This reduces pool turbulence because the flow of feed and settled material is concurrent. The slope of the drainage deck should be as flat as layout conditions permit and its length should be as short as possible.

Many of the classifiers used in the uranium plants were of the Esperanza type, designed according to the criteria outlined. When the original pilot plant to treat Colorado uranium ores was constructed, time lag was a critical factor and small rake or spiral classifiers were not easily available in acid-proof construction. Accordingly, small Esperanza classifiers were designed and fabricated in a local machine shop. They performed so well in the pilot operation that the design was expanded to commercial capacity and made available for purchase. The price turned out to be lower than for other types of classifiers.

It may be necessary to handle relatively coarse feed sizes in copper operations. The Esperanza-type machine will very likely handle up to ¼-in. material with no problems (20-mesh feed was generally treated in uranium operations). For coarser sizes, reciprocating-rake types, preferably heavy duty,

should be considered because they can be fabricated of corrosion resistant materials with relative ease. Acid-proofing is not so feasible for spiral-type classifiers in sizes much larger than 30-in., although the spiral classifier has many other advantages over the rake type.

Upright vessels favored for cementation

Iron launders, which are designed and operated in analogous fashion to zinc boxes used during the dawn of the cyanide process, have several drawbacks. To compensate for erratic flow of pregnant solution, an excess of shredded iron must be used in the system, which permits time for the reaction of free acid and ferric iron in the solution. In addition to this unproductive consumption of iron, the reclamation of cement copper is cumbersome and time consuming.

These shortcomings are considerably alleviated by rising upright vessels, which permit the upward flow of pregnant solution evenly through the bed. The cementation reaction is practically instantaneous, and this type of vessel gives satisfactory results in a minimum of time with less consumption of iron by unproductive reactions. However, as with iron launders, upright vessel operation is static except for the rising current of solution. A point is soon reached where the iron in the lower part of the bed is completely coated with copper and cementation is inhibited.

To maintain a satisfactory level of copper in the spent solu-

covered, and Pearl Harbor subsequently dropped a historical curtain on the matter.

Work on the process continued in the US, however, and a viable operation resulted. When Golden Cycle Corp. moved its milling operation from Colorado Springs to Cripple Creek, Colo., the new Carlton mill was designed and operated with charcoal precipitation in pulp. In the nature and handling of the carbon, there were some significant differences from the Philippine experiment. The charcoal was of sufficient size and stability to permit recovery from the pulp by simple screening. The gold was recovered by chemical stripping, after which the charcoal was reactivated and reused.

The Carlton operation was in regular production as late as 1952, but was then shut down because of the unfavorable economic climate for gold mining. That operation, however, served as a basis for adapting the procedure to acid leaching of domestic uranium ores, leading to a considerable surge in uranium production on the Colorado Plateau.

As late as 1952, the bulk of uranium for US defense requirements was procured from Canada and the Belgian Congo (now Zaire). Concurrently, an extensive program, sponsored by the US Atomic Commission, was underway in South Africa to recover uranium from cyanide residues (tailings).

The South African operations are notable for being the first massive application of ion exchange processing to hydrometallurgical operations. The cyanided residues from gold leaching were generally free of refractory slimes. Although quite fine grinding was required for gold extraction, the pulps filtered with remarkable ease. The filtering rate was about four to five times that of Philippine gold ores ground to the same degree. Rotary filters were used on the acid uranium leach pulps, making it relatively easy to produce clear solutions for ion exchange treatment. This permitted that use of ion exchange columns and resins similar to those employed in water treatment plants.

Concurrently with the South African activities, exploration work in the US resulted in development of substantial uranium deposits on the Colorado Plateau. These ores in general responded well to acid leaching, but the application of ion exchange was quite another matter, because the pulps neither settled nor filtered at anything approaching economic rates. Laboratory tests, however, demonstrated that the ion exchange resins worked just as well in slime suspensions as in clear solutions—an obvious resemblance to the charcoal process at Cripple Creek, Colo.

To work out the problems involved in the transition from charcoal pellets to ion exchange resins, a pilot plant was constructed.[5] The pilot not only confirmed feasibility, but equipment devised by the staff to meet material handling problems proved susceptible to scale-up to commercial sizes. No major difficulties were encountered in this phase of the project. The pilot plant staff, some of whom were experienced in cyanide mill operation, deserve considerable credit for their ingenuity and perseverance.

The technique developed at the uranium pilot plant became known as the resin-in-pulp (RIP) process, and in a relatively short period after the completion and evaluation of pilot work, a number of leaching and RIP plants were constructed and placed into successful production: at Moab, Utah; Bluewater, N.M.; Edgemont, S.D.; Tuba City, Ariz.; and Jeffrey City, Wyo. The latter operation has been described in some detail.[6] The aggregate capacity of the plants was in the range of 5,000 to 6,000 tpd or more.

The history of precipitation in pulp suspensions would be incomplete without mention of the leach-precipitation-float (LPF) process developed by metallurgists of the Miami Copper Co. (now Miami Copper Operations, a unit of Cities Service Co.) in Arizona. LPF evolved at about the same time that the Chapman process was under development.

An excellent historical and technical account of the LPF process has been published by the Colorado School of Mines.[7]

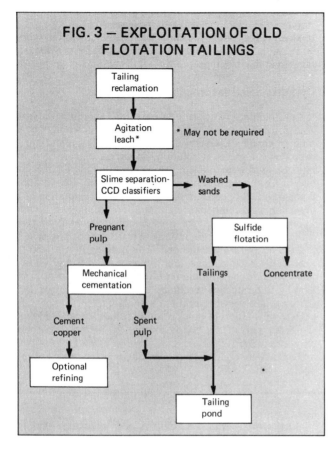

FIG. 3 — EXPLOITATION OF OLD FLOTATION TAILINGS

Tailing reclamation

Agitation leach* *May not be required

Slime separation-CCD classifiers → Washed sands

Pregnant pulp

Sulfide flotation → Tailings / Concentrate

Mechanical cementation

Cement copper / Spent pulp

Optional refining

Tailing pond

tion, it is necessary to dump the lower part of the iron bed and separate unreacted iron and copper. Upright vessels eliminate to a large degree the time-consuming manual sluicing and transfer of iron, but the intermittent cycle and labor cost of iron launder operation is not completely avoided.

A modification of the upright vessel has been designed for pregnant solutions containing slimes. The modification provided for mechanical agitation of the iron bed in the reaction zone and for liberation of coated copper *within* this zone. The cement copper is discharged to a separate compartment with a minimum of unreacted iron. Periodic or continuous discharge of copper, depending upon the grade of pregnant solution, can be accomplished without stopping the inflow of pregnant pulp. The separation of cement copper at a specific gravity of 5.0 in a stable pulp of 1.10 specific gravity presents no problems.

Details of the agitation mechanism are quite simple and it can be easily designed for corrosion resistance. A variety of construction materials are available for the tank and storage compartment of the vessel. Currently, wood stave tanks with a unit capacity of 10 tpd of copper are envisioned.

Exploiting the new technology

A recent survey[2] gives details of 4 billion to 5 billion tons of ore dumps that are being leached by conventional methods. The list is far from complete, and since its publication in 1968 the expansion of copper production has resulted in the accumulation of substantial additional dumps. Other leachable sources include abandoned heap-leach operations, old flotation tailings, and some vat leach tailings which could possibly be reworked with interesting results. The tonnage of copper economically recoverable from such materials would be very impressive. Within living memory, the economic grade of copper sulphide reserves has decreased from around 20 lb to less than 10 lb of copper per ton of ore. The overall grade of

leachable dumps of various types is probably close to the lower figure, and, in general, the unit operating cost of leaching should be lower than for recovering copper from sulphide deposits.

Several other factors make CIP attractive for recovery of the potential large national resources available in dump materials:

■ All of the materials have been mined and in most cases are readily available for rehandling and treatment. Corollary to this, large efficient material handling equipment is already developed.

■ Metallurgical processing, with prospective substantial improvement in recovery efficiency and precipitation techniques, seems to present no problems.

■ Cementation is presently the only method that will cope with the slime problem. The CIP method is simple, the capital costs are low, and the proximity of the deposits to large population centers, at least in the US, assures a ready supply of scrap iron.

Several unit process diagrams are reproduced here to illustrate various combinations for the application of CIP technology. No attempt has been made to prepare detailed flowsheets of the unit processes, since they will naturally vary considerably for individual conditions.

Dump leaching (Fig. 2) involves long periods of time, during which many complex reactions and changes occur in dump conditions, depending upon the manner in which the dump was constructed and the mode of application of leaching solutions. It is obviously impossible to predict exactly what the leaching results will be, but it may be safely assumed that recoverable copper will be present in two forms—undissolved minerals and dissolved copper that has been retained (mainly in the finer particle sizes and refractory fractions).

The complexity of chemical and physical changes in dump leaching was evident in an experimental 200,000-ton dump of pit-run material. At the conclusion of leaching tests under controlled conditions, a cut was made through the dump to expose faces from 20 to 30 ft in height. The upper half of each face had been well leached, at least visually, down to a well-defined layer of slime which was rich in dissolved copper. Below this slime layer, which had apparently been formed by downward migration of the fines, no leaching had been accomplished. On the contrary, some enrichment had occurred in the contact zone by the deposition of artificial chalcocite.

If the unit process arrangement in the Fig. 2 were applied in this instance, it might be advisable to strip and discard the upper layer. Treatment of the slime and lower layer would result in immediate recovery of dissolved copper in considerable amounts, followed by recovery at a good rate in the deslimed re-leach dumps. The simplicity of the treatment scheme speaks for itself. Modular design of the various units might also be advantageous, making it possible to move the plant site when justified by savings in material handling costs.

Reworking old flotation tailings

The leachable reserves in "old" flotation tailings were produced before and during World War II, when grinding and classification equipment was more primitive and flotation techniques were probably inferior to current practices. Weathering, chemical changes, and possibly bacterial action have taken place over considerable time periods. There is some interest now in moving and reworking some of these reserves for various reasons; Fig. 3 illustrates CIP possibilities.

Combined desliming and froth flotation of sulphides should give excellent results in the type of treatment shown in Fig. 3. Very fine, clean sulphides would tend to concentrate in cyclone underflows, and the absence of slimes in the flotation cells should make for sharp separations and low reagent consumption. Also, there is no reason why the grade of cement copper produced would not be close to that obtained by current methods, although this consideration may be of questionable importance.

Flotation and refining of cement copper

To date, the only viable technology for retreating flotation tails is the old LPF process, used with varying degrees of success. The cementation drums employed in LPF developed some peculiar problems that were encountered wherever the process was used. The quality of the final concentrate was poor due to inclusion of the slime fraction in the flotation feed, and the moisture content was understandably high. In comparison, the CIP concept offers obvious advantages.

A CIP agitation leach arrangement (Fig. 4) is capable of achieving maximum recovery and is applicable to virgin oxide deposits or other leachable materials of better than average grade. By suitable sizing of equipment, the scheme is applicable to deposits of moderate size because of relatively modest capital and operating costs.

The only other method that can approach the high metallurgical efficiency of CIP is vat leaching. Without delving into capital costs, which would require a great deal of detailed engineering, it is possible to make certain comparisons of operating details and probable metallurgical performance. The obvious disadvantage of vat leaching is its batch nature, as opposed to continuous agitation leaching.

Mechanical factors in leaching

One of the principal metallurgical limitations of vat leaching is the degree of crushing possible for suitable vat feed material. With an ore of favorable dry screening characteristics, the limit of crushing is ⅜-in. top size—depending on good weather and a low content of primary slime in the deposit. Since such ideal conditions cannot be realized all of the time, plant capacity can only be maintained by compromising on the degree of crushing, with consequent lower metal recovery.

The combination of partial crushing and wet grinding completely avoids handling problems incident to wet, sticky ore. The only limitation to the wet circuit is the maximum size that can be handled in mechanical agitators. However, some overgrinding could probably be justified by the advantages inherent in a continuous system if this is necessary to satisfy the requirement of the equipment.

Mechanical agitators are available for handling material as coarse as 10 mesh. Coarser material might be successfully processed if the primary slime content is high enough to lend stability to the pulp. It is in this department that capital and operating costs, especially the latter, would show decided advantages over vat operation. Some points to be considered are: 1) the extensive construction and large area required for vats; 2) the cost of massive vat charging and excavating equipment; and 3) intermittent charging and excavating, plus wear and tear on vats and equipment—unquestionably a more costly material handling method than gravity flow. Disposal of tailings by pumps from a continuous system is less costly than trucking or conveying coarse vat tailings.

The bonus in mechanical classifiers

The use of classifiers for slime separation and CCD washing operations is an overpowering advantage for the CIP concept from every standpoint. It is possible either to include desliming and washing equipment for vat operation at an additional cost or to exclude it and accept higher copper losses in the vat tailings. Of two vat leaching plants recently constructed in the Southwest in recent years, one made the choice for desliming and the other did not. Regardless of the method selected, the efficiency of solution recovery in vat operation

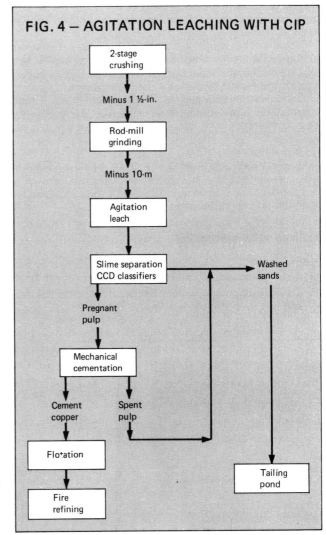

FIG. 4 — AGITATION LEACHING WITH CIP

leaves much to be desired. Vat tailings, if accessible, are a possible source of feed for retreatment and recovery of additional copper.

If desliming is adopted for vat operation, the conventional method of recovering pregnant solution from the slime fraction is CCD thickeners. This requires further comparison of the CIP method with a unit CCD thickening operation because it would be possible to design an agitation plant by replacing the classifiers with thickeners, to recover a clear pregnant solution. In addition to the enormous reduction in plant area possible with CCD classification, and the sharp limitation of thickeners with respect to the size of solids in the feed, other factors in the operation of thickeners constitute pitfalls of considerable magnitude.

Some pulps, even though within acceptable particle size limits, will cause jamming of the rake assembly with no particular warning. This was true of many Philippine ores, which appeared to form high density zones that would suddenly settle in the tank. The reasons were never clear, and such a pulp characteristic could not be detected by prior testing. A similar experience occurs with some South African gold ores.[8] In this instance, the difficulty is ascribed to sloughing of the thickener bed, and it is possible that the slope angle of the rake assembly is a critical factor. This sort of operating difficulty is not infrequent.

A plant that uses thickeners for solution recovery should include provisions for expeditious draining of the tanks and sufficient sump storage for the contents of one tank to prevent the loss of pregnant solution. It also follows that the use of very large thickening units involves considerable risk of major operational disruptions and variations in the metallurgical results.

High-lime ores will evolve gas during leaching. Thickener settling problems can occur unless all gas is dissipated before the pulp reaches the settling circuit. This factor may be of sufficient magnitude to preclude the use of thickeners.

Climate and weather may disturb thickener efficiency. Low temperatures affect settling rates adversely, and prolonged freezing weather can be disastrous to equipment which is installed in the open. High winds and heavy rains create obvious problems.

All of the foregoing risks can be avoided by using classification equipment that can be economically enclosed in a compact building if necessary. Massive clearing and foundation work is largely eliminated.

Refining of cement copper

Virtually all cement copper currently produced is delivered for final electrorefining combined with blister copper from the smelting of sulphide concentrates. Small amounts are marketed directly after processing by other means.

prepared.

The Cananea operation opens up speculation on the competition between cementation and LIX processing of leach liquors, which currently holds center stage in the US Southwest.

The simplicity and relatively low capital cost of cementation are potent advantages. One of the purported advantages of LIX processing—in the face of substantial capital costs—is the ability to produce cathode copper by electrowinning. It is not clear, however, whether all such production is marketable without further refining. Electrowinning does not necessarily guarantee this; at least one large operation in Arizona finds it necessary to fire refine the cathodes produced from vat leach liquors.

In summary

The 500-year-old cementation process still appears to be facing a long and productive life, providing some research and development therapy is supplied. It is the only process currently adaptable to direct recovery of dissolved copper from slimes, while at the same time delivering improved recoveries of leach solutions. In turn, this opens up exciting pos-

Edmund C. Bitzer

"The 500-year-old cementation process still appears to be facing a long and productive life, providing some research and development therapy is supplied. It is the only process currently adaptable to direct recovery of dissolved copper from slimes, while at the same time delivering improved recoveries of leach solutions."

The most notable example is the treatment developed by Cia. Minera de Cananea SA, in Sonora, Mexico. An unusually large proportion of total Cananea production is in the form of cement copper derived from dump leaching, and most of this is refined separately to a purity suitable for fabrication of copper tubing.[9]

The Cananea treatment starts with preliminary concentration of raw cement copper to 88.5% Cu and 1.5% Fe by froth flotation using a Minerec collector. It is reported that 92% of the copper is recovered in this step, and the concentrate is dewatered to 13% moisture in a plate and frame filter press. This damp material is smelted in a reverberatory and deoxidized in a refining vessel (both of local design). Bars or ingots of 825 lb are shipped to a fabricator of copper tubing in Mexico City. Further details are currently unavailable, but it is understood that a technical paper on the subject is being

sibilities for effective utilization of substantial reserves or resources of very low grade materials. □

References

1) Shaffer, Herman W., and Evans, LaMar G., "Copper Leaching Practices in the Western United States," Bureau of Mines Information Circular-8341, 1968.
2) Lidell, *Handbook of Non-ferrous Metallurgy*, McGraw Hill, 1926.
3) ——, "Large Chingola copper solvent extraction plant seen as major advance," E/MJ, July 1973.
4) US Patent No. 2,315,187; March 30, 1943.
5) American Cyanamid Co. and National Lead Co., contractors to US Atomic Energy Commission; R. F. Hollis, project manager. Circa 1952.
6) Bitzer, E. C., "Western Nuclear proves worth of resin-in-pulp ion exchange". E/MJ, May 1958.
7) Bean, J. J., "The leach, precipitation, flotation, concentration method at Miami Copper Company," COLORADO SCHOOL OF MINES QUART., Vol. 56, No. 3.
8) King, A., "Gold Metallurgy on the Witwatersrand," Transvaal Chamber of Mines, Johannesburg, 1949.
9) AIME Spring Smelter meeting, 1973; Cananea, Sonora, Mexico.

British strong-acid leach process targeted at refractory uranium ores

A STRONG-ACID LEACH PROCESS for uranium extraction developed by the UK Atomic Energy Authority (UKAEA) could reduce capital costs for uranium extraction plants by as much as 30%, according to the organization. The patented process makes use of an acid about six times as strong as that used in dilute-acid uranium processing.

UKAEA does not foresee rapid development of the commercially untried process as long as known uranium ore reserves can be worked at production costs of less than $10 per lb. However, UKAEA officials are confident that the process will make a significant contribution toward solving future extraction problems, when producers will be forced to work with more refractory ores. In about five years' time, conventional uranium technology at foreseeable prices will be uneconomic, UKAEA argues.

The concept of strong-acid leach of uranium ores has been known for some time; bench tests with low extraction results were performed in Oklahoma in the 1950s. However, the UKAEA system was the first such process to be patented. The process is now at the takeoff stage, and its commercial development should coincide with the exhaustion of currently viable reserves, according to John Gay, patents licensing officer for the Atomic Energy Research Establishment. Indeed, Gay feels, it is only the price boom of the last two years—with U_3O_8 prices rising from $8 per lb to $13 per lb—that has allowed marginal deposits to continue using dilute-acid processes. Gay added that an unnamed US mining company believes that bench test results using the UKAEA process are impressive enough to obviate the need for a pilot plant before moving on to commercial operation.

The reported potential economies for a 3,000-tpd ore processing plant based on the UKAEA process include a capital savings of 20% to 30% on investment that now runs about $12 million to $14 million. Savings in operating costs are projected at 30¢ to 50¢ per lb.

Acid usage in the UKAEA process is projected at about the same rate as required in dilute sulphuric acid processes—between 60 lb and 80 lb per ton of ore. Ore can reportedly be processed at larger grind sizes in the UKAEA process, reducing crushing and grinding investment by about 10%.

The results of lab-scale testing

Working under laboratory conditions with ore from Elliot Lake, Ont., using six-normal sulphuric acid, the UKAEA process reportedly obtained uranium extraction of 94-96% after 12 to 14 hr of leaching at 75°C.

Using conventional dilute-acid processing with process acid concentration maintained at 50 g per liter, extraction of 95% uranium required 48 to 72 hr of leaching at 70°C. Liquid-acid content of the slurry was held to 30-40%.

While the two processes were comparable in uranium extraction achieved, iron extraction was much lower with the UKAEA process. Only 4% of the iron in the ore was dissolved during UKAEA processing.

Removal of solubilized uranium in the UKEA process was accomplished by percolation, which was found to be as effective as reslurrying and which produced only about 0.2% of fine solids in the liquor.

Because the acid-ore mixture is only about 10% liquid in the UKAEA process, less effluent is produced. In a commercial operation, this reduction would result in additional processing economies.

Since leaching accounts for 35% to 50% of direct operating costs, the difference in leach times between the two processes suggests that the UKAEA process offers important savings, according to a paper by UKAEA engineers, S. E. Smith and K. H. Garret.

Plant requirements for UKAEA's strong-acid leaching differ from dilute-acid processing at the feed preparation, acid mixing, curing, and washing stages. Elsewhere in the circuit, conventional equipment and practice can be used.

Crushed and ground ore to be fed into the UKAEA strong-acid circuit should be essentially dry, because the ore-acid mix in leaching is only 10-12% liquid. To avoid drying the ore before it is fed into the circuit, milling is done in a dry rod mill.

Because of the dryness of the UKAEA process, the acid can be sprayed onto a moving bed of ore in a rotary drum. High shear mixing is not necessary. Granulation can be controlled and improved by fitting lifting bars in the drum and varying the acid strength.

Removal of the solubilized uranium is most simply done by percolation of liquor through the ore, either by direct percolation through a deep bed in a curing silo or by washing through a shallow bed. Alternative washing methods are feasible by storing ore in above-ground vats and transferring it to separate equipment for washing. This approach would make possible large scale throughput by minimizing mechanical handling problems, since the vats could be emptied by gravity.

Washing through a thin bed in a filter pan would reduce the importance of the percolation rate, and the liquor flow rate would be increased.

(As a footnote to this report on the UKAEA process, Pechiney has reportedly patented a similar process using a six-normal acid, which it is using for commercial uranium extraction at a plant in Niger.)

Apart from its strong-acid leach process, UKAEA has also worked on a bacterial leaching system for uranium. Similar bacterial leaching is commercially viable for copper ores, but with uranium the process is more complex, because the ores are not sulphides that can be directly attacked by the bacteria.

UKAEA is trying to optimize particle size and achieve cost savings in liquid-solid separation and agitation for bacterial leaching by experimenting with a static bed of crushed ore, upon which is introduced a solution, air, and bacteria from a bacterial fermenter.

The work so far has produced 95% extraction of uranium in a matter of days, according to UKAEA, vs. the several months required for heap leaching. Although the process may be cost-competitive with other uranium extraction techniques, it would probably not be as cost efficient as the UKAEA strong-acid leach process. UKAEA officials do not now foresee commercial development of bacterial leaching for uranium.

In another UKAEA development, the organization has obtained patents in most uranium producing countries to protect its work on the use of ion exchange columns to process 20% uranium slurries. UKAEA is continuing research to establish the merits of the process. □

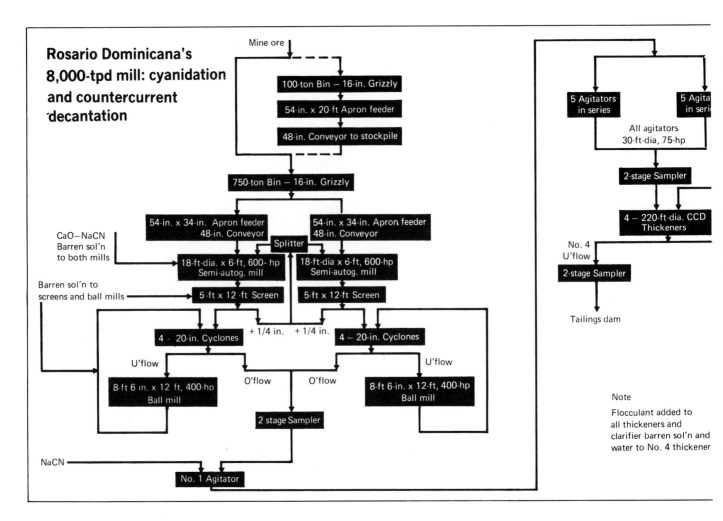

Rosario Dominicana's 8,000-tpd mill: cyanidation and countercurrent decantation

Rosario Dominicana launches Latin America's largest gold mine

Robert Sisselman, Associate editor

LUCRATIVE AND TIDY, the Dominican Republic's recently dedicated $45 million open-cut complex at Pueblo Viejo is the second largest gold producer in the Western Hemisphere and fifth largest in the Free World. Later this year, when the mill—utilizing cyanidation followed by countercurrent decantation—achieves rated throughput of 8,000 tpd ore, it will be pouring 350,000 oz of gold and 1.5 million oz of silver annually in the form of Doré bullion destined for Switzerland.

Pueblo Viejo is mining proven reserves of 30 million tons of oxidized ore averaging 0.126 oz gold and 0.76 oz silver per ton. The complex is owned and operated by Rosario Dominicana SA, a joint venture of Rosario Resources (40%), Simplot Industries (40%), and the Central Bank of the Dominican Republic (20%). Rosario Resources is managing the property.

Those who stand to benefit most from Pueblo Viejo are the Dominicans, who will realize 65% of the anticipated $20 to $30 million in annual profits from the sale of the precious metals. Moreover, the injection of US dollars into the developing Dominican economy is expected to provide a substantial shot in the arm for

the nation's balance of payments.

Economics and technology played the key roles in shaping Pueblo Viejo. Low production costs (Pueblo Viejo was conceived based on $35 gold), the simplicity of mining and processing, the tempting prospect of finding a metallurgical means of tapping the rich underlying complex sulphides, and the ultimate blessing of the Dominican government combined to give rise to the progressive venture. Behind this success story is a rich and varied history that enabled a 450-year-old mine to regain prominence in the 20th century, ulti-

Cyanide, mill solution added to grinding system

During the work week (two shifts at the mine, three shifts at the mill), ore is stockpiled and dumped directly into a 750-ton double drawer bin. Ore is taken from the stockpile on the graveyard shift only. From the hopper, ore is conveyed 322 ft on a 48-in. belt to the plant, offloading into the semi-autogenous mill feed hopper. Here, barren solution, sodium cyanide, and pebble quicklime (for the necessary safety margin of alkalinity) are intro-

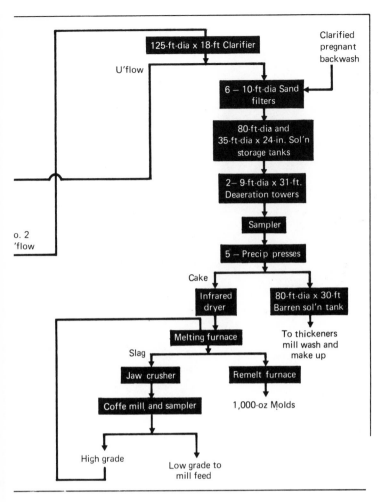

Clarified pregnant backwash

125-ft-dia x 18-ft Clarifier

U'flow

o. 2 'flow

6 – 10-ft-dia Sand filters

80-ft-dia and 35-ft-dia x 24-in. Sol'n storage tanks

2– 9-ft-dia x 31-ft. Deaeration towers

Sampler

5 – Precip presses

Cake

Infrared dryer

80-ft-dia x 30-ft Barren sol'n tank

To thickeners mill wash and make up

Melting furnace

Slag

Jaw crusher

Remelt furnace

Coffe mill and sampler

1,000-oz Molds

High grade

Low grade to mill feed

2.0 lb per st sodium cyanide and 1.5 lb per st lime to achieve a pH of 11.5. Flowing into the initial agitation tank, the pulp splits off into two parallel lines of five tanks each; agitation in the leach tanks is accomplished with axial flow-type propellers. Total retention time in the tanks is 16½ hr, most of which is required to leach the silver values; gold is leached within the first 1½ hr.

Continuous countercurrent decantation

Countercurrent decantation takes place in four thickeners, 220 ft in diameter and 14 ft deep, with a combined capacity of 4 million gal. Overflow from No. 1 thickener is mixed with flocculant and allowed to settle in a 125-ft-dia x 18-ft clarifier tank with a holding capacity of 1,650,000 gal. No. 4 thickener overflow is pumped to an 82-ft-dia x 42-ft barren solution tank. The washed underflow is pumped to tailings.

After retention for 5½ hr, overflow from the clarifier is pumped at 70 ppm solids to six Baker sand filter units. The resulting filtrate—clarified, pregnant solution containing a maximum 5 ppm solids—is held in a 900,000-gal, 80-ft-dia x 25-ft storage tank for 3 hr. It is then pumped to another storage tank of 166,000-gal capacity for 30-min residence time. The solution is then taken to the top of two 28-ft-high, 9-ft-dia deaeration towers, where the flow is split in half. Four vacuum pumps reduce the oxygen contents below 0.05 ppm as a prelude to gold-silver precipitation.

Zinc injection precipitates gold and silver

Precipitation occurs when zinc dust (3,000 lb per day) as dry reagent is mixed with lead nitrate (300 lb per day) as wet reagent used to speed up reaction time, and the two are injected into the solution on its way to the precipitation presses.

A predetermined decrease in flow into any press caused by caked precipitate will force that unit to discharge the caked concentrate onto the precipitate buggy positioned under the press.

The refining process begins when the buggy is moved under a 120-kw infrared drying hood, where the cake is dried at 600°F. Removed on a precipitate tray car to the flux bin, the cake is weighed and assayed, and the following fluxing materials are added: sodium nitrate, potassium permanganate, borax, silica, fluorspar, and soda ash. Cake is loaded into furnace charging buckets and then into one of two 2,200-lb-capacity reverberatory melting furnaces. Gold-silver "buttons" are poured, solidified, and remelted in a 1,600-lb-capacity furnace to produce 75-lb bricks of Doré bullion, each valued in the neighborhood of $100,000. Slag is stored for future shipments to a refinery.

From mining through milling, in solution in the various leach and thickener tanks, and at the point where it emerges from the precipitation filters, all gold content is carefully monitored. Assays are performed on the initial gold pour as well as on the final brick of Doré bullion, which is stamped, numbered, and sent on its way to Switzerland via New York's Kennedy airport.

Originally presented as an 8-page report in the October 1975 issue of E/MJ, this article has been shortened to include only those portions dealing with hydrometallurgy.

---

duced into the ore stream.

Ore is ground to 65% minus 200 mesh in a pair of 600-hp Koppers Hardinge semi-autogenous mills that are designed as crusher-scrubbers because of the quantity of clay contained in the crude. The mills are fed with 4-in. balls. Ore and worn balls are subsequently discharged into a single deck 48-mesh vibrating screen, the surface of which is sprayed with barren solution. Oversize is collected by a 24-in., 108-ft-long conveyor, equipped with magnetic head pulley to segregate metal chips or broken balls. A 24-in. cross belt, 43 ft long, recycles oversize ore to the semi-autogenous feed hopper. Grinding media consumption is about 1.5 lb per ton milled, and liner steel consumption about 0.15 lb per ton milled.

Meanwhile, undersize is diluted with barren solution and pumped at 80% minus 48 mesh by two 40-hp feed pumps to a bank of four 24-in. Krebs cyclones—three in operation and one on standby. Underflow reports to a ball mill feeder and then to one of two 400-hp Marcy ball mills, 8½ ft in diameter and 12 ft long. The mills are fed with about 2½-in. balls. Ore is retained in the mills for a maximum of 30 sec, then discharged into a grind sump pump common to the undersized screenings.

Leaching section: eleven 30-ft-dia tanks

Cyclone overflow at 65% minus 200 mesh is fed by pump into the leach section, consisting of 11 tanks, 30 ft in diameter, 30 ft high, each with a 165,000-gal capacity.

The pulp at this stage—about 45% solids—is adjusted to

Alunite deposits to be mined as feed for Earth Resources' alunite-alumina project are located on a mountain that rises several hundred feet above the valley floor where the plant will be located. Drill-proved reserves exceed 100 million tons.

Golden pilot plant points way to 500,000-tpy alumina-from-alunite mine and plant in Utah

Gerald Parkinson, McGraw-Hill World News, Los Angeles

A PILOT PLANT PRODUCING ALUMINA FROM ALUNITE at Golden, Colo., could be the forerunner of a substantial future US alunite-alumina industry. The plant could also lead to a greater degree of self-sufficiency in alumina for the US, which is now heavily dependent on imported bauxite.

The alumina-from-alunite project is a joint venture of Earth Sciences Inc., of Golden (50%), and National Steel Corp., of Pittsburgh, and Southwire Co., of Carrollton, Ga. (25% each). National and Southwire jointly operate an aluminum smelter at Hawesville, Ky., that consumes approximately 360,000 tpy of alumina.

Alunite is a complex basic hydrous sulphate of alumina and potassium, containing roughly one-third alumina, one-third sulphur trioxide, and a final third about equally divided between potassium sulphate and water. The ore being processed at the Golden pilot plant is brought in from Utah, where it occurs as an acid volcanic rock grading about 40% alunite in a rather uniform distribution. Quartz accounts for

about 50% of the remainder of the mineral, and iron and other constituents account for about 10%.

Alumina makes up 37% of the alunite and averages 14.8% in the overall rock structure.

Until recently, alunite has not been considered an economic alternative to bauxite as a source of alumina. However, the Soviet Union has been operating an alunite processing plant at Kirovabad, near the Caspian Sea, and Guanos y Fertilizantes de Mexico SA is building an alunite plant at Salamanca, Mexico. The Russians use a caustic leach process, while the Mexican plant will use an acid reaction process developed at the University of Guanajuato (E/MJ, June 1971; CHEMICAL ENGINEERING, April 19, 1971; CHEMICAL WEEK, June 9, 1971; and METALS WEEK, July 5, 1971).

The process developed by Earth Sciences and its associates is also caustic based, the latter part of the technique being a modified Bayer process.

Like the Mexican and Russian technology, the Earth Sci-

Pilot plant potassium sulphate leach tanks: Commercially, potassium sulphate recovered during the alumina extraction process will be used to manufacture byproduct fertilizers.

ences process yields fertilizers as byproducts. A potassium sulphate fraction is recovered, and SO_2 reduced from SO_3 is combined with phosphate rock to produce phosphatic fertilizers.

Briefly, the ore is crushed, dehydrated, and reduced with hot gases to drive off SO_2 for conversion to sulphuric acid. It is then water-leached to dissolve out potassium sulphate, and treated by a modified Bayer process to obtain alumina.

Patents have been applied for on the overall process and on specific steps of the operation.

The drive to unlock resources

Earth Sciences has obtained or is negotiating for permits, leases, and mining claims on 10 to 15 alunite properties in Utah, Arizona, Nevada, Colorado, and California, and more than half of these look promising, the company states.

In Beaver County, Utah, near Cedar City, the company has drill-proved a deposit of more than 100 million tons. Exploratory drilling at four other peripheral locations in the county has established the presence of ore zones over an area of more than 25 sq mi. (The Beaver County deposits are located in the Wah Wah Mountains at altitudes of 6,300 to 7,300 ft.) Total resources in the five explored locations are estimated at 680 million tons, and the inference is that there is much more ore in the area. Earth Sciences does not even feel that the explored zones are necessarily the richest of those that may eventually be found.

In Golden, the $3 million alunite pilot plant began operating in November 1973 at a capacity of about 10 tpd of ore. Earth Sciences stresses that the extraction process had already been proved in a mini-plant. The pilot plant is being built to define engineering details for a prototype commercial scale plant in Utah now being planned at a capacity of 500,000 tpy of alumina.

By the end of 1974, the pilot plant will provide necessary data for engineering of the commercial plant, and construction on the commercial plant is expected to begin in mid-1975.

The prototype commercial plant will be built on the site of the drill-proved Utah alunite deposit, and production is scheduled to begin in late 1977 or early 1978. Cost estimates for the alumina plant alone run to slightly more than $100 million. Additional facilities could cost as much as $100 million, depending on the types of fertilizers produced.

The Utah plant will serve primarily as a supplier of alumina to the National-Southwire smelter in Kentucky, but its alumina output will also be marketed to other aluminum producers. Earth Sciences anticipates that successful development of its project will encourage other aluminum companies to further develop the extensive alunite deposits in the West, creating a major US alunite-alumina industry in the future.

The knock on alunite

Past arguments against the use of alunite as a possible source of alumina have been based on the mineral's low alumina content. This low grade, it was argued, would prohibit economic recovery.

Earth Sciences feels that alumina grade in alunite is a relatively minor factor. More important, the company asserts, is the fact that alunite of uniform quality is readily available in large quantities in the western US. Earth Sciences claims that the new process will be competitive with production of alumina from bauxite—based on alumina production alone. Production of fertilizer byproducts will be an added bonus.

The main advantage of bauxite, according to Earth Sciences, is its high grade. However, the disadvantages are that the grade varies widely, disposing of tailings is a problem, and bauxite deposits are usually found in remote parts of the world, which increases the costs of mining and processing.

The existence of large uniform alunite deposits in the western US was not fully understood until recently, Earth Sciences points out, and development of an alunite process was not encouraged.

As recently as December 1970, a report on a panel study, published by the National Materials Advisory Board, stated:

"This panel did not consider alunite to be a source of aluminum with economic potential, because no large pure deposits are known to exist in this country. Although the total alunite in the western US may eventually be found to amount to hundreds of millions of tons, all known deposits occur in such form that large tonnages of uniform grade could not be mined. The beneficiation of disseminated alunite would be too costly to compete with other aluminous materials.

"Alunite has little potential for being a major raw material of aluminum in this country because all known deposits are either small or scattered or have the mineral disseminated through volcanic rock. Alumina extracted from such material would not be competitive in price."

Pilot plant probes the recovery system

Ore for the pilot plant at Golden is trucked from the Utah mine site to the Union Pacific Railroad, 23 mi away, and crushed to 1 in. prior to shipment. After receipt of the ore at Golden, it is crushed to about ⅛ in. and then fed into a rotary kiln for dehydration. The dehydration temperature is being tested through a range from 400°C to 700°C, about the maximum before beginning to drive off sulphur.

The ore moves pneumatically from the kiln to a standard fluidized bed reactor, where reducing gases drive off sulphur contained in the ore's aluminum sulphate. (It has been contended also that this sulphur is not present as a sulphate but as sulphur in the alunite lattice.)

Currently, reducing gases for test purposes are being obtained from ammonia reformed with natural gas and steam. The main objective of the tests is to determine the thermodynamics and kinetics of the process and not the gases to be used in the prototype plant. It is anticipated that a coal gasification plant will produce gas for the prototype alumina plant.

Gaseous SO_2 produced at the pilot plant is collected in a wet scrubber; however, roaster effluent is being analyzed to facilitate design of a sulphuric acid unit for the prototype plant.

Following sulphur removal, the calcine is wet ground. Tests of particle sizes ranging from 14 to 60 mesh are being conducted to determine the optimum size for downstream processing. A ball mill and a rod mill have been used for grinding, and other methods may be tested on a batch basis before a decision is made on milling methods to be used at the prototype commercial plant.

After milling, the ground slurry, still hot from the fluidized bed reactor, flows through a pipe into a series of three agitators for water leaching of the potassium sulphate. Pilot plant leach tanks are open with top-mounted propeller-type agitators. The potassium sulphate is readily soluble, and after it has been dissolved in water, a solid-liquid separation is made. The K_2SO_4 solution is drawn off to a drying-crystallizer-compaction circuit for testing purposes. At the commercial plant, the potassium sulphate will be available for fertilizer.

(As a processing alternative, a potassium sulphate leach may be made by a weak solution of ammonia following dehydration in the rotary kiln. For the present, however, Earth Sciences feels there are minor advantages to using a fluidized bed for the second stage, followed by water solution of the potassium sulphate.)

Various equipment componentry is being evaluated for use in the solid-liquid separation on a commercial scale, with pan, drum, and disk filters, screw classifiers, thickeners, cyclones, and filter presses now receiving consideration.

Quartz-and-alumina filter cake produced during the solid-liquid separation is collected in a hopper and weighed to obtain a material balance. In the commercial scale plant, this cake will become feed for a modified Bayer process.

Low pressure caustic leach looks attractive

The quartz-and-alumina filter cake passes through a series of six tanks in which a sodium hydroxide solution leaches the alumina from the quartz. Because the bulk of the alunite structure has already been removed, the alumina dissolves readily. In contrast to the normal Bayer process for bauxite, which requires steam pressure of nearly 200 psi for several hours, the Earth Sciences process requires no pressure, and the sodium hydroxide is kept at a temperature of only about 95°C. As a result, the process is less corrosive—although the Bayer process is not considered to be particularly corrosive, either.

Another advantage claimed for alunite is that silica is present only in the form of quartz, which is not as highly reactive as the silica clays frequently found in bauxite. These clays consume caustic solution during leaching, according to Earth Sciences, and add to bauxite processing costs.

Following the alumina leach, the pregnant solution is separated from the quartz tails. Various solid-liquid separative approaches are also being tested in this area.

Any silica taken into solution is removed by a reaction with a desilication product (DSP) seed, as is standard in the Bayer process. The clean liquor is then transferred to four precipitation tanks, where it is seeded with alumina hydrate. The alumina in the solution attaches itself to the seeds and settles

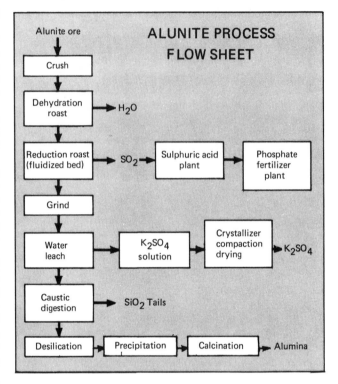

to the bottom of the tanks. The alumina is drawn off as a slurry, washed, and calcined to remove water. The caustic solution is re-used. Calcining at the pilot plant is done on a batch basis.

Pilot plant alumina production is being shipped to the Hawesville, Ky., smelter for processing to determine its metallurgical characteristics. Earth Sciences feels that as a result of using a modified Bayer process, its alumina should be similar to that produced at other alumina facilities and therefore acceptable to any US smelter.

Fertilizer byproducts will also be made up on a batch basis at the pilot plant and shipped to prospective customers for evaluation. The joint venture partners plan to develop advance-sale contracts to secure ready customers for the fertilizers when the prototype commercial plant goes onstream.

Pilot testing has so far produced no problems of note, Earth Sciences states. The company points out that the process is relatively straightforward and that mild steel is used for most of the pilot plant and will also be used in the commercial plant.

Earth Sciences has deliberately mined several samples of "oddball rock" that it plans to run through the pilot plant to learn what effect variable feed might have on the operation. These samples all contain alunite but have unusual amounts of iron, silica, clay, sodium, or other materials. It has been difficult to obtain sufficient amounts of some of these rock types to make worthwhile tests, according to a company spokesman, so even if they prove unacceptable to the processing circuit, they should be easy to avoid in mining.

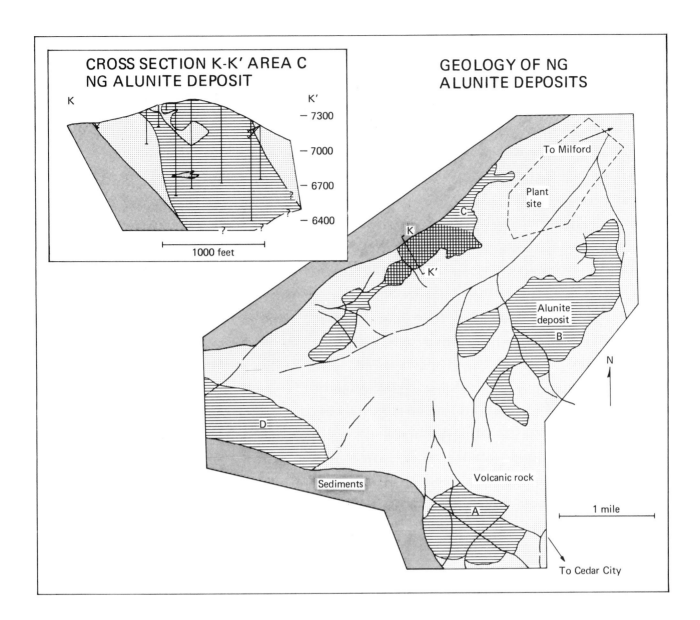

CROSS SECTION K-K' AREA C NG ALUNITE DEPOSIT

K   K'

— 7300

— 7000

— 6700

— 6400

1000 feet

GEOLOGY OF NG ALUNITE DEPOSITS

To Milford

Plant site

C

K

K'

Alunite deposit

B

N

D

Sediments

Volcanic rock

1 mile

A

To Cedar City

Marshalling the raw materials

As noted above, the Utah plant is planned for an alumina production capacity of 500,000 tpy. If this figure is adopted in the final design, the plant will also produce 250,000 tpy of potassium sulphate and 450,000 tpy of sulphuric acid for phosphate fertilizer.

The commercial plant is to be located in a valley below a drill-proved alunite deposit of more than 100 million tons in Beaver County, Utah. Test drillings have penetrated the deposit to depths of 1,000 ft and have still been in alunite, according to Earth Sciences. There is practically no overburden.

A study of the actual mining plan is still in progress, but it is probable that the alunite deposit will be bench mined. Haul roads will be built to truck the ore to the plant.

It is likely that the ore will be drilled, blasted, and loaded by shovel or front-end loader into haulers, but a mobile crusher and conveyor is also a possibility. A 23-mi railroad will be built from the plant to the Union Pacific railhead.

Earth Sciences plans to develop its own phosphate mine near Soda Springs, in the southeastern part of Idaho. Production will be used in the fertilizer manufacturing operations at the alumina plant. The deposits are described as a 15-ft layer of phosphate rock overlaying a vanadium-bearing coal shale.

Earth Sciences also plans to mine the vanadium to produce vanadium pentoxide for the steel industry. An underground test program is in progress at the site, and a few pounds of vanadium per hour are being processed in a bench plant.

Site work for the Idaho mine is expected to be finished in 1975, and a vanadium plant of about 10 million lb per year is planned for startup in 1977. An open-pit mine will be developed initially, with vanadium and phosphate rock being mined selectively in the same pit. Later, a drift mine may be developed.

Earth Sciences states that the vanadium shale deposit, with reserves at about 75 million tons, is significant because very little vanadium is presently mined in the US, which relies heavily on imported South African ores.

All three of the alunite project joint venture partners participated in the design and engineering of the pilot plant in Golden. Alumet (Alunite Metallurgical Center), a joint company formed at the outset of the project, built part of the plant. National-Southwire was project manager for plant construction. Other firms involved were Hazen Research Inc., of Golden, which fabricated and installed most of the equipment and Barnes Engineering, also of Golden.

Ralph M. Parsons Co., of Los Angeles, and Chapman, Wood and Griswold, Inc., of Albuquerque, are consultants for the proposed commercial alunite mine and plant—Parsons working mainly on the plant and Chapman on the mine. ☐

Uranium recovery from phosphoric acid nears reality as a commercial uranium source

Richard C. Ross, technical specialist, United Nuclear Corp.

MOST OF THE WORLD'S PRODUCTION of phosphate comes from marine phosphorites, of which there are large deposits in Florida, the western US (particularly Idaho), Morocco, and Spanish Sahara. These deposits generally contain 50 to 200 ppm uranium (0.005% to 0.02%, or 0.1 to 0.4 lb per ton). Although such concentrations are only 5% to 10% as high as those of commercially mined uranium ores, the vast extent of the phosphate deposits has made them targets of considerable interest as uranium sources for many years. At the 1958 Geneva Conference, for example, mineable reserves of phosphate rock in the US alone were reported to contain more than 1 billion lb of uranium.[1]

The uranium content of marine phosphorites is believed to be derived from seawater or from later percolating solutions. Since the uranium concentration in phosphorites is a factor of 10^4 to 10^5 higher than in seawater, these minerals clearly have a significant affinity for uranium—a factor that affects the recoverability of uranium from this source.

During the early 1950s, considerable effort was directed at developing methods for selectively leaching uranium from phosphate rock. Alkaline leach methods were found to be completely ineffective, and acid leaching required complete dissolution of the phosphate rock, consuming several tons of sulphuric acid per pound of U_3O_8 recovered. By contrast, uranium ores in the western US are primarily sandstone deposits containing 2-5 lb of U_3O_8 per ton of rock. Since these ores are essentially insoluble in acid, the uranium can be dissolved selectively by a relatively mild acid or alkaline digestion.

Fortunately, a large and increasing proportion of commercial phosphate production is being converted first to a relatively dilute phosphoric acid by the "wet process" (as distinguished from the furnace process, which produces elemental phosphorus by direct reduction of ore). A phosphoric acid producer first manufactures sulphuric acid, then uses it to digest the rock (Fig.1). The chemical reaction forms phosphoric acid and calcium sulphate. The latter is filtered out, providing enormous quantities of waste gypsum, and leaving an impure acid stream typically containing about 30% P_2O_5. Most of the uranium in the original rock shows up in this acid, and various solvent extraction processes have been developed to recover it.

This "30% acid" is generally evaporated to a "merchant acid" containing about 54% P_2O_5, which is used to manufacture a variety of products, chiefly fertilizers. The higher the P_2O_5 concentration, the harder it is to extract uranium, so the 30% stage is the point at which uranium extraction must take place. If uranium is not extracted, it ends up as a minor impurity in the various end products.

The 30% acid can be either "black" or "green." All phosphate rock contains certain amounts of organic material. If the organic content is not excessive, it is left in, and the digestion process produces a black-colored acid. The organic content creates problems in the extraction process.

If the original organic content of the rock is too high to be tolerated, the rock is calcined before digestion to burn out the organic matter, and the resultant acid has a greenish tint. Such acid is easier to process. Unfortunately, most

> **Editor's note:** This article is based on a presentation made by the author at the annual meeting of the American Nuclear Society in New Orleans, June 8-13, 1975.

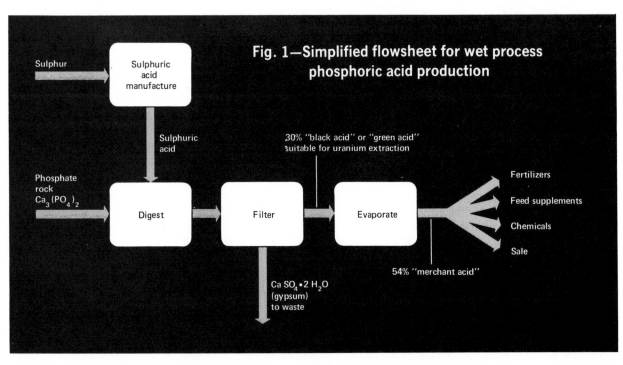

Fig. 1—Simplified flowsheet for wet process phosphoric acid production

Fig. 2—Locations of wet process phosphoric acid plants in the US

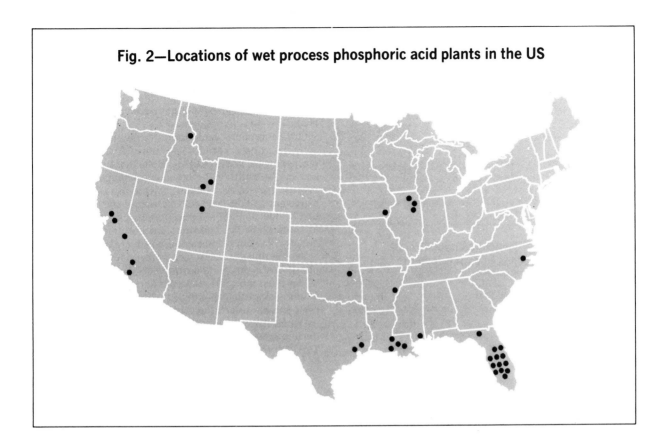

central Florida rock—which has the highest uranium content—is processed to black acid.

Production of phosphoric acid in the US

A cluster of 12 wet process phosphoric acid plants is located in central Florida, and another seven are on the Gulf Coast in Texas, Louisiana, and Mississippi.[2] (See Fig. 2.) The Gulf Coast plants all use central Florida rock, which is transported in the same vessels used to ship sulphur to the Florida plants. In addition, there are a number of plants in the West (which use western rock), a few up the Mississippi River (which use central Florida rock), and one plant each in northern Florida and North Carolina.

Total wet process phosphoric acid production capacity of the US is summarized in Table 1. Acid from central Florida rock contains about 1 lb of U_3O_8 per ton of P_2O_5—meaning that as much as 4.7 million lb of potentially recoverable U_3O_8 is lost each year from the plants in this area. The other US plants are generally much smaller in capacity and process material with only one-half to one-third the uranium concentration, making uranium recovery less attractive economically. Total uranium content in all wet process phosphoric acid produced per year in the US is probably between 5.5 and 6 million lb U_3O_8.

Because of growing demand for fertilizers, two new plants and a number of plant expansions are under construction. By 1976 total wet process acid capacity is projected to increase by more than 35%. Although this spurt of growth is likely to lead to temporary overcapacity, the potential for uranium recovery is obviously increasing substantially.

In the late 1940s and early 1950s, a great deal of work was done on the recovery of uranium from phosphoric acid, and three commercial scale plants were built and operated successfully.[3] Two of these used solvent extraction and the third used a chemical precipitation method that

was applicable only to the unique conditions of that plant. These plants operated for a few years but were shut down when uranium became available at a lower cost from mines in the western US. However, work continued to improve the process, and rising uranium prices have provided additional stimulus.

Today at least four uranium extraction programs are at various stages of development toward commercialization, and one commercial plant is nearing completion. All of these programs are based on liquid-liquid solvent extraction processes. In such a process, the acid is contacted with an organic liquid consisting of an extractant that has an affinity for uranium dissolved in a kerosene-type solvent. The organic and acid streams are mixed thoroughly, causing some of the uranium to transfer into the organic phase. The organic and the acid are then allowed to settle and separate as a result of their differing densities, with the organic rising and floating on the aqueous liquid.

The uranium is only partially transferred to the organic in a single contact—it becomes distributed between the two phases in accordance with an equilibrium coefficient. A number of stages in countercurrent flow are needed to approach complete extraction of uranium and obtain a usefully high concentration of uranium in the final organic solution.

Variables associated with uranium recovery

Typical values of some of the constituents and properties of wet process phosphoric acid are shown in Table 2. The P_2O_5 content varies from 28% to 31%, and as mentioned before, this variability affects uranium extraction. Uranium content may also vary widely, although for acid from a given source, the uranium content will be within much narrower limits than is indicated in the table. Most of the Florida acids in work done by United Nuclear Corp. have contained approximately 0.15 gpl uranium.

Table 1—US wet process phosphoric acid capacity

(000 tpy P_2O_5)

Location	1974 Number of plants	1974 Total capacity	1976 Number of plants	1976 Total capacity
Central Florida	11	3,200	12	4,570
Gulf Coast	6	1,540	7	1,940
Subtotal	17	4,740	19	6,510
Other	16	2,010	16	2,650
Total US	33	6,750	35	9,160

Source: "Fertilizer Trends, 1973," Tennessee Valley Authority.

Table 2—Typical composition of wet process phosphoric acid

P_2O_5	28-31%
U	0.1-0.2 gpl
Fe (total)	6-12 gpl
Fe (+2)	0.1-1 gpl
Total F	20-30 gpl
Al	2-3 gpl
Specific gravity	1.3
emf	280-330 mv

Table 3—Possible solvent extractants of uranium

Uranium condition	emf (mv)	Solvents
Reduced—U^{+4}	<300	Pyrophosphoric acids Orthophosphoric acids
Oxidized—UO_2^{+2}	>420	Solvent pairs: D_2EHPA—TOPO (D_2T)

Total iron content and iron oxidation state are both important variables: iron can interfere with uranium extraction, and the oxidation state of the iron tends to control the oxidation state of the uranium. The uranium in phosphoric acid can be in either the tetravalent or hexavalent state, and extraction solvents are specific for one state or the other. To reduce or oxidize the uranium, it is necessary to reduce or oxidize some or all of the iron in solution—and iron content is about 60 times the uranium content. Only a small amount of the iron is in the reduced (divalent) state. The emf of the solution (its oxidation potential measured against a standard calomel electrode) is a measure of the oxidation state of both iron and uranium, and typically is slightly over 300 mv.

The high fluorine content of the acid necessitates careful selection of construction materials, and aluminum content of the acid can interfere with uranium extraction. Not shown in Table 2 is the organic content of the acid or the fact that the acid is supersaturated with gypsum, which tends to crystallize out at any opportunity. Since the density of the acid is high, fairly rapid separation of organic and acid phases during solvent extraction might be expected. However, both the gypsum and the wax content of the acid tend to promote emulsion formation and hinder phase separation.

Uranium can be extracted under either reduced or oxidized conditions, as indicated in Table 3. Various pyrophosphoric acids and orthophosphoric acids have good ex-

traction coefficients for tetravalent uranium. For these extractants, the solution emf should be below 300 mv. On the other hand, a number of synergistic solvent pairs can be used to extract hexavalent uranium at emf values above 420 mv. The most developed of such solvents is a mixture of di (2-ethylhexyl) phosphoric acid, otherwise called D_2EHPA, and trioctyl phosphine oxide, or TOPO; the mixed solvent is referred to as D_2T.

Orthophosphoric acids consist of phosphoric acid molecules with organic groups substituted for one or more of the hydrogen atoms (Fig. 3). Both the molecular weight and the structure of the organic grouping are important, because they affect uranium extraction, solubility of the extractant in both acid and kerosene, and phase separation. Production of orthophosphoric acids yields a mixture of "mono" and "di" substituted acids. Fortunately, such a mixture is a better extractant than either pure compound.

Pyrophosphoric acids are anhydrides of orthophosphoric acids—that is, two orthophosphoric acid molecules with a water molecule removed. They are extremely strong uranium extractants but unfortunately tend to hydrolize to orthophosphoric acids in acid solutions.

D_2EHPA is a specific di-orthophosphoric acid, with the organic grouping as one particular branched octyl group. TOPO at first glance resembles the orthophosphoric acids, but the organic octyl groups have replaced the oxygen as well as the hydrogen in phosphoric acid, giving rise to significantly different properties.

Fig. 4 shows how extraction coefficients for typical extractants tend to vary with solution emf.[4, 5] The data for the different extractants are not directly comparable, since temperatures and acid concentrations used in testing were different, but trends are consistent. The extraction coefficient is the ratio of uranium concentration in the organic phase to that in the acid (or aqueous) phase. As long as the extraction coefficient is greater than zero, some extraction will take place. However, extraction coefficients need to be at least three or four, and preferably higher, to get suitable uranium recoveries and useful concentrations.

As indicated, pyrophosphoric acids give good extraction coefficients even at fairly high emf's, but are much better at low emf's. At the emf of fresh plant acid, neither orthophosphoric acids nor D_2T gives very good extraction, and reduction or oxidation of the acid is therefore desirable. There are other orthophosphoric acids better than the one shown, and since both temperature and acid concentration affect extraction, there may be circumstances under which extraction will be practical without emf modification.

A look at three actual recovery processes

The main process employed during the 1950s was developed under the auspices of the Atomic Energy Commission (Fig. 5). Wet process acid was "borrowed," cooled, and its emf reduced by iron addition. The uranium was then extracted with a 5% solution of capryl pyrophosphoric acid, and the 30% acid was returned to the acid plant.

Note that metallic iron is an effective reducing agent in this situation. It is not necessary to reduce *all* the iron in solution but merely to obtain an Fe^{+2} to Fe^{+3} ratio in the neighborhood of 0.2:1 to 0.3:1. Since each atom of metallic iron added can reduce two atoms of Fe^{+3} to produce three atoms of Fe^{+2}, the necessary iron addition is only about 10% or less of the iron initially present.

After extraction, the uranium was precipitated from the organic solvent as an impure UF_4 (green salt) by treatment with HF. Since about one-third of the pyrophosphoric acid hydrolized in each cycle, additional solvent had to be

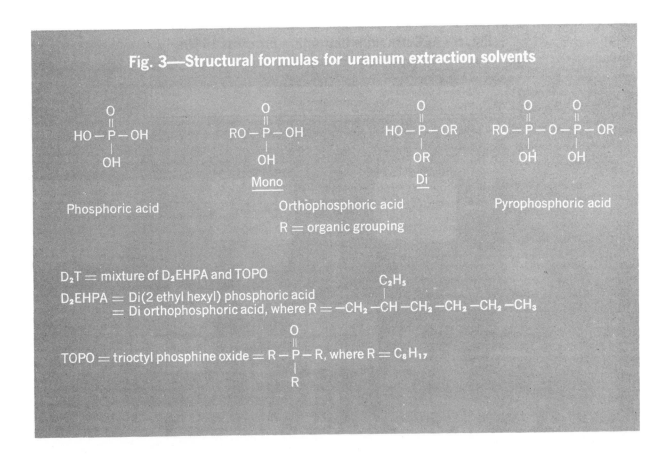

Fig. 3—Structural formulas for uranium extraction solvents

Phosphoric acid

Orthophosphoric acid
R = organic grouping

Mono

Di

Pyrophosphoric acid

D_2T = mixture of D_2EHPA and TOPO

D_2EHPA = Di(2 ethyl hexyl) phosphoric acid
= Di orthophosphoric acid, where R = $-CH_2-CH-CH_2-CH_2-CH_2-CH_3$

TOPO = trioctyl phosphine oxide = $R-P-R$, where R = C_8H_{17}

added continuously. The solvent extracted significant amounts of iron from the acid, and much of this iron was precipitated along with the UF_4.

The process had the advantage of simplicity, and it worked. The principal disadvantages were solvent decomposition, additional solvent loss by carryover with the acid stream (in spite of the use of centrifuges to separate the phases after each contacting), and impurity of the product. Cost of uranium by this process was higher than the AEC purchase price established for uranium from commercial mines, so the plants were shut down in the late 1950s.

In 1969, workers at Oak Ridge National Laboratory (ORNL) published some results of their work on solvent extraction of uranium[4] using D_2T, and later proposed a more complicated but elegant flowsheet for uranium recovery.[6] (See Fig. 6.) This system takes advantage of the selectivity of extraction toward the uranium oxidation state to concentrate and purify the uranium by several phase transfers. I believe that at least some elements of this flowsheet are used in all of the work being done by other agencies; however, the elements may have been developed independent of ORNL research.

The uranium in the plant acid is first oxidized and extracted with D_2T. The uranium is then stripped from the D_2T and further concentrated by contacting with a 30% acid stream containing a reducing agent such as divalent iron. As noted previously, at low emf's, the extraction coefficient for uranium is much less than 1, which means that the uranium concentrates in the acid phase. This acid is then reoxidized and the uranium is re-extracted into a second D_2T solvent. The hexavalent uranium could then be stripped into an ammonium carbonate solution and precipitated as ammonium uranyl tricarbonate (AUT), which is easily calcined to a pure U_3O_8 product. Each stripping and extraction step tends to purify and concentrate the uranium content above that of the previous step.

Although more complex than that of the early AEC process, the ORNL process has a number of advantages. Besides producing a pure product, it uses stable solvents, which greatly reduces solvent makeup requirements. Also, by highly concentrating the uranium before precipitation, chemical consumption is reduced. (The reason is that ammonia reacts also with the solvent, so that ammonia consumption depends on the amount of solvent treated in the precipitation stage.) Finally, the more complex process

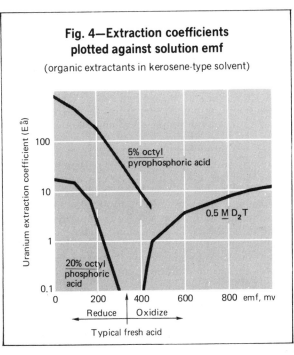

Fig. 4—Extraction coefficients plotted against solution emf

(organic extractants in kerosene-type solvent)

Fig. 5—AEC uranium extraction process, 1950s

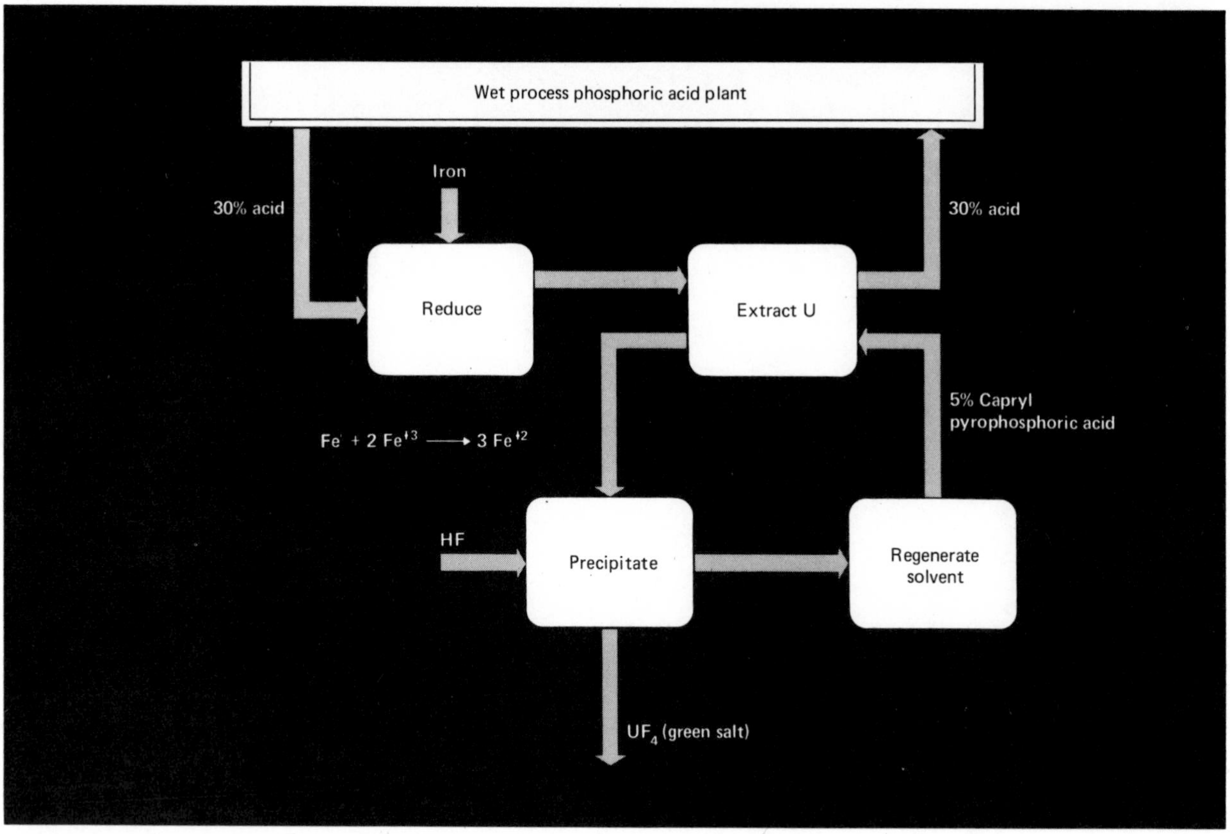

makes possible uranium recoveries in excess of 90%.

Each of the extraction and stripping steps in Fig. 6 constitutes a number of countercurrent stages, so the process is considerably more complex than shown. Many variations on the flowsheet are possible, including manipulations of temperature, strip acid concentration, and switchover to a reductive extraction with an orthophosphoric acid solvent instead of the oxidative extraction with D_2T in the first circuit.[7]

Uranium Recovery Corp. (URC), a subsidiary of United Nuclear Corp., will be using a "module" concept in its acid plant in Florida. A portion of the process to be employed is illustrated in Fig. 7. The most obvious feature is that the process has been split into two parts, with only the initial extraction and stripping operations taking place at the phosphoric acid plant site; the concentrated strip solution is trucked to a central processing plant a few miles away. Using this approach, a simplified module can be erected at each phosphoric acid plant. Each module will have only the larger-scale front end processes, while the somewhat more complex but smaller-scale downstream processes (including all yellowcake handling) will be concentrated in a single, centrally located plant.

As indicated in the flowsheet, the first operation is cleaning up the acid to remove emulsion-forming materials. All the programs working with fresh black acid are believed to have found such a step essential. The exact nature of the valence adjustment, extraction, and stripping chemistry at the module are proprietary. However, it is permissible to say that oxidation with sodium chlorate has been avoided because of the possibility of corrosion caused by residual chloride. At the central processing plant, URC plans to use essentially the rest of the ORNL flowsheet to prepare a pure U_3O_8 product.

URC has just completed its first full scale module at the W. R. Grace & Co. plant near Bartow, Fla. The plant is now in the startup testing phase and is expected to be in full scale operation sometime during the first quarter of 1976. The URC central processing plant has also been completed, near Mulberry, Fla., 6 mi from the Grace module.

URC has also contracted to install two modules at a new phosphoric acid plant owned by a subsidiary of International Minerals and Chemical Co., which has just come on line about 10 mi west of Mulberry, and to install another module at the Grace plant during an expansion planned for completion in 1977. When all four of these modules are on line, the production capacity should be about 1.3 million lb of uranium per year.

Other recovery programs underway

In addition to the URC work, three other programs have been conducted in the Florida area. Westinghouse has carried out a cooperative pilot plant program with Gardinier Inc. at Gardinier's Tampa plant. The program is completed but no definite commitments for a commercial plant have been made.

Gulf Oil Chemicals has been operating a mobile pilot plant at the Agrico Chemical Co. phosphoric acid plant in South Pierce, Fla. The project was scheduled for completion during the third quarter of this year, but again there is no commitment for construction of a commercial plant.

Freeport Minerals is in the advanced stages of a uranium pilot plant program at its phosphoric acid plant at Uncle Sam, La. Freeport has concluded that its process is

Fig. 6—ORNL uranium extraction process, 1970

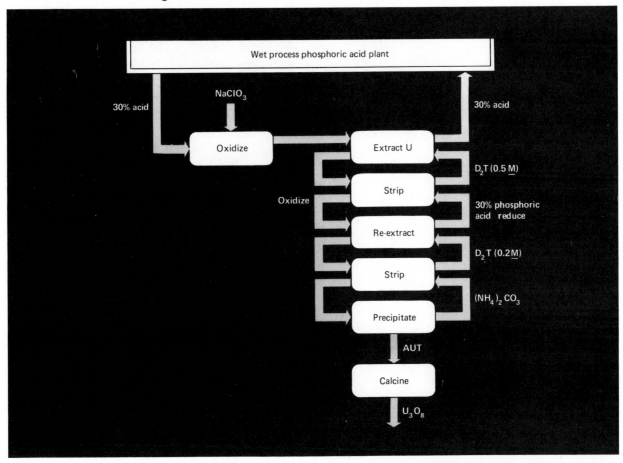

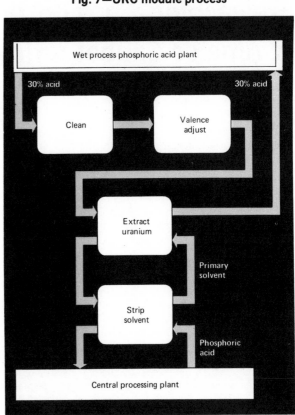

Fig. 7—URC module process

feasible and economic but has not announced any details of the program nor any plans for commercial operation.

All of these programs are believed to be based on processes similar to the ORNL flowsheet, although various modifications have been made, both to overcome specific problems and to introduce potential improvements.

In conclusion, large scale uranium recovery from phosphoric acid is apparently nearing reality. Phosphoric acid producers have expressed a great deal of interest in the pilot projects, and if URC can demonstrate successful operation at its first module at W. R. Grace, a number of other acid producers will probably install uranium recovery units. Much of the uranium now lost in processing Florida phosphates will then be recovered. ☐

References

1) Nininger, R. D., "Geologic Distribution of Nuclear Raw Materials," Proc. Intern. Conf. on Peaceful Uses of At. Energy, Geneva, P/862, No. 2, pp 7-10 (1958).
2) "Fertilizer Trends—1973," Bulletin Y-77, National Fertilizer Development Center, Tennessee Valley Authority, Muscle Shoals, Ala. (1974).
3) Kennedy, R. U., "Recovery of Uranium from Low-Grade Sandstone Ores and Phosphate Rock," *Processing of Low-Grade Uranium Ores*, pp 220-26, Int At. Energy Agency, Vienna (1967).
4) Hurst, F. J., D. J. Crouse, and K. D. Brown, "Solvent Extraction of Uranium from Wet-Process Phosphoric Acid," ORNL-TM-2522 (1969).
5) Ellis, D. A. "The Recovery of Uranium from Industrial Phosphoric Acids by Solvent Extraction—Summary Status Report," DOW-81 (1952).
6) Hurst, F. J., D. J. Crouse, and K. D. Brown, "Recovery of Uranium from Wet Process Phosphoric Acid," IND. ENG. CHEM. PROC. DES. AND DEV., January 1972, No. 11, p 122.
7) Hurst, F. J., and D. J. Crouse, "Recovery of Uranium from Wet-Process Phosphoric Acid by Extraction with Octyphenylphosphoric Acid," *ibid.*, July 1974, No. 13, p 286.

Filter cake is discharged at a nominal 500 tpd from string discharge filter equipped with a monofilament polypropylene filter cloth.

Preleaching zinc concentrates
at Amax's Sauget refinery

James E. Gorman, plant manager, and **Richard F. Pagel,** chief metallurgist, Amax Zinc Co. Inc.
Emil H. Nenniger, associate, Hatch Associates Ltd.

INCREASED EMPHASIS ON HYDROMETALLURGICAL PROCESSES for the production of metallic zinc from its ores, both in the US and abroad, has compelled the development of procedures to treat a wide variety of zinc minerals, especially those associated with dolomitic limestones. A large portion of zinc ore mined in the US at present—particularly in Tennessee and Missouri—originates in dolomitic orebodies. Concentrates from these deposits may contain 0.25% to 1.25% magnesium, along with 0.5% to 2.5% calcium.

When Amax acquired the former American Zinc Co. refinery at Sauget, Ill., in 1972, the company planned to use ores from southeast Missouri as the main source of feed material for Sauget. While such Missouri zinc concentrates are satisfactory for use in pyrometallurgical operations, where magnesium is removed in the slag, attempts to treat the concentrates by conventional roasting and leaching methods in an electrolytic refinery result in a gradual buildup of magnesium in the circulating electrolyte. A large magnesium buildup in the electrolyte can displace zinc and reduce current efficiency. Buildup can also increase the electrolyte's specific gravity, hindering settle-

ment and filtration in the leaching and purification operations.

Most electrolytic plants have been able to accept small percentages of total feed from dolomitic ores by controlling the magnesium buildup through normal electrolyte bleeding. Higher percentages of total feed require methods for either increasing electrolyte bleeding or pretreating the concentrate for magnesium removal.

Borrowing an idea from Bunker Hill

The Bunker Hill Co. in 1958 had developed a process for removing large quantities of magnesium from zinc ores in the form of dolomite or other carbonates. This process, a batch operation, was described by Bunker Hill's Walter Schmittroth at the 1958 annual meeting of AIME.

Since it was known that the southeast Missouri zinc concentrates would introduce an undesirable amount of magnesium into the circuit, Amax Zinc Co. started work in conjunction with Hatch Associates Ltd. to determine if the concentrates could be treated to lower their magnesium content. Using the same principles employed by Bunker

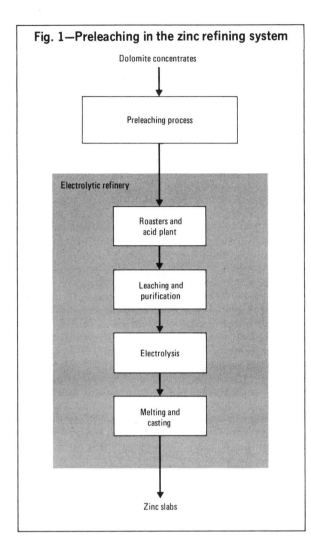

Fig. 1—Preleaching in the zinc refining system

Dolomite concentrates

↓

Preleaching process

↓

Electrolytic refinery

Roasters and
acid plant

↓

Leaching and
purification

↓

Electrolysis

↓

Melting and
casting

↓

Zinc slabs

Hill, it was quickly established that the magnesium and calcium present were soluble in relatively weak sulphuric acid solutions, and that the zinc was relatively insoluble under these leaching conditions. The production process now used by Amax Zinc at Sauget is based on data and design information from both laboratory and pilot plant tests of the preleaching process. The process removes magnesium before the concentrates are roasted. Fig. 1 shows the preleach process in the framework of the overall electrolytic refining system. The zinc-sulphide concentrates are leached continuously by dilute sulphuric acid:

$$MgCO_3 + H_2SO_4 \rightarrow MgSO_4 + CO_2 + H_2O$$

$$CaCO_3 + H_2SO_4 + H_2O \rightarrow CaSO_4 \cdot 2H_2O + CO_2$$

Magnesium sulphate is readily soluble; calcium sulphate is partially soluble.

Water conservation first, then plant construction

Before determining the design parameters for a preleach plant, an overall water conservation study was made for the zinc plant. Material and solution flows were calculated and a water balance for the operation was established. From these data, and an established maximum level of 12 g per l of magnesium desired in the electrolyte solution, it was apparent that about 0.1% magnesium could be toler-

ated in the leached concentrates—i.e., 90% of the magnesium must be removed.

Using these parameters, a series of bench-scale tests were then conducted to obtain data on the chemistry, physical behavior, and reaction rate. Initially, tests were performed on a batch basis in a 4-l beaker. Similar vessels were later used to obtain data for continuous leaching tests.

Preliminary capital estimates indicated that there was considerable economic incentive to leach at high-solids concentration on a continuous basis to reduce reactor size. In addition, a final moisture level in the concentrate in the vicinity of 10% would eliminate the need for a drying kiln, with its additional energy requirements.

Bench-scale testing showed that the reaction rates were essentially independent of solids concentration in the range of 30% to 60% solids, and that the reactions were virtually complete in 2 hr. During the tests, it was not possible to produce enough leached concentrate to establish realistic filtration rates at higher solids concentrations. Also, the question of reagent acid concentration remained open during the tests.

Results of the bench-scale batch tests were taken from the "batch curves" to determine the "smoothed reaction curve" (Fig. 2). A quantitative estimate based on the reaction curve indicated that the continuous reaction rate should be about 10% of the initial batch leaching rate after equilibrium was established. It was further projected that a line of three reactors in series, each having a 1-hr retention time, would yield the percentages of the 2-hr batch reaction rates shown in Table 1. Continuous bench-scale tests confirmed these projections.

During bench-scale testing, it became apparent that a larger test should be conducted to provide a more accurate appraisal of the filtering characteristics of the leached concentrate, its soluble magnesium content, and the moisture content of the filter cake.

Pilot plant scaled up by factor of 90

Following the bench-scale tests, a pilot plant was designed to verify the results and to obtain further design information. A scale-up factor of approximately 90 was used. This factor was fixed by the size of the available pilot plant filter.

In the pilot plant, three leaching tanks with gravity flow carried slurry through the system to the filter vat. Slurry with a density of 65% solids was delivered to the first leach tank by a metering pump. Acid, at either 50% or 93% concentration, was introduced by another metering pump. Agitation was created in each tank by propeller-type agitators with variable-speed drives.

Some foaming problems were encountered at startup, but additions of a silicone-based defoamer controlled them. Once steady-state conditions were reached, foaming was no longer a problem. A single mechanical foam-breaker gave good results.

The feed rate in the pilot plant was varied to produce filtration rates ranging from 51.4 to 98.6 lb per sq ft per hr of dry, leached concentrate over the filter. At these rates, the moisture content of the leached material ranged from 6.8% to 9.7%, increasing as the feed rate increased. With 3.6 displacement washes, soluble magnesium content was reduced to 0.025%.

During periods of good operation, total magnesium concentration in the leached product reached an average of 0.10%. Zinc losses were about 0.5%, an acceptable figure for that concentrate. There was some leaching of the minor elements chlorine, fluorine, sodium, and potassium,

Table 1—Reaction rates projected from bench-scale tests

Continuous reactor	Cumulative retention time (min)	Percent completion (vs. 120-min batch)
1	60	70.0
2	120	91.0
3	180	97.7

and about 70% of the manganese was leached, indicating that it was probably present as the carbonate.

The filter cake discharged readily from the polypropylene-twill cloth filter that was used. String discharge was selected for the filter because it was felt that a drier cake could be produced, and experience at the mill that produced the concentrate showed the string discharge filter to be very satisfactory.

Hydrogen sulphide emissions, while present, were not a problem if the acid concentration in the reactors was kept within reasonable limits. An independent laboratory measured the maximum concentration of hydrogen sulphite in the reactors as less than 0.16 ppm.

The temperature rise due to exothermic reactions occurred as expected. Maximum temperature reached about 46°C when the slurry feed temperature was 19°C, using 93% acid. When 50% acid was used, maximum temperatures were lower.

The 93% sulphuric acid concentration was usable as long as the amount of excess acid was kept under control. As the excess acid was increased up to about 5 g per l, the amount of undissolved magnesium remaining in the concentrate decreased. Acid concentration above this value did not lower the magnesium content appreciably. Table 2 summarizes the salient results obtained from the pilot plant operation. Calculated materials balances for the pilot operation proved to be excellent.

Design and plant construction proceed in 1973

Based on the successful laboratory and pilot plant tests, Amax Zinc in 1973 proceeded with the design and construction of a commercial plant. (See Fig 3.) Hatch Associates, which had been heavily involved in the bench and pi-

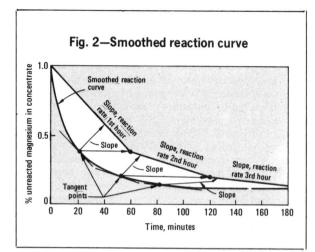

Fig. 2—Smoothed reaction curve

lot-scale testing, was selected to design the process equipment and structure. Amax provided the general contractor, construction supervision, and final equipment selection.

The commercial plant, which started up in January 1975, is designed to treat 150,000 tpy of zinc concentrate with a magnesium content of about 1.0%, reducing the magnesium content to 0.1% or less. Based on an 86% duty factor, the daily rate of concentrate output is 471 tons.

To make maximum use of the waste water available in the electrolytic plant and roaster circuits, the preleach plant uses fresh water only where it is absolutely necessary—for example, at pump seals and for filter wash water. Water from the wet scrubbing system at the roasters is used to repulp the concentrates as they are received and is further utilized to dilute the slurry from the storage tank before leaching. Water from this source is very corrosive. Therefore, a considerable effort was made to select materials that would be relatively inert in hostile environments.

The preleach plant receives concentrates either from storage or from railroad cars. Concentrates are received on belt conveyors and are stored in a 70-ton bin. Tramp iron in the concentrates is removed by a magnet before entering the bin. A weigh-belt conveyor withdraws concentrates from the bottom of the surge bin and discharges them into

Table 2—Pilot plant operating results

Concentrate heads	
H_2O	7.5%
Zn	55.3% total
	0.068% H_2O soluble
Mg	0.97% total
	0.025% H_2O soluble
Ca	2.01%
Leached concentrate	
H_2O	7.2%
Zn	55.6% total
Mg	0.107% total
Ca	2.01%
Magnesium removal	89.0%
Zinc loss (total)	Less than 0.5%
Washing efficiency	Soluble Mg reduced to 0.025% with 3.5 displacement washes (based on final cake moisture).

Table 3—Commercial plant operating efficiency

Throughput (tpd)	Magnesium extracted	Magnesium eliminated
560	91.5%	86.2%
478	92.7	86.5
396	94.6	89.6

Table 4—Magnesium and calcium in leached concentrate from commercial plant

Throughput (tpd)	Magnesium total	Water-Soluble magnesium	Calcium total
560	0.13%	0.05%	2.15%
478	0.13	0.06	2.46
396	0.10	0.05	2.19

the first of two repulp tanks. There, scrubber water is added to form a slurry of about 80% solids. Top-overflow discharges slurry from this tank. The slurry then passes over a screen to remove tramp material that might damage equipment or clog lines further downstream. A second repulp tank receives the screened slurry, which is then pumped to the slurry holding tank by a rubber-lined transfer pump. Both repulp tanks are rubber-lined and have rubber-covered agitators.

The slurry holding tank, constructed of unlined carbon steel, has a capacity of 91,000 gal. Agitation in the tank maintains a uniform slurry density. The large capacity is designed on the premise that slurry will only be made on the day shift, from freshly unloaded concentrates. A design capacity of 32 hr of storage was selected because the concentrate handling equipment is also used to reclaim concentrates for the roasters. With this capacity, it is possible to delay slurry-making for up to two shifts.

From the slurry holding tank, the repulped concentrate is pumped to elevated constant-head tanks that provide a uniform slurry flow to the metering section. Excess slurry from the constant-head tanks is returned to the slurry holding tank by gravity flow. In the metering section, slurry is diluted to the desired density with either fresh water or water recycled from the roasting plant scrubbers.

The plant throughput rate, measured in the metering section, must be determined for proper acid concentration adjustments. Acid is added to the first and second leach tanks at a rate calculated to dissolve the dolomite and thus solubilize the magnesium. At the same time, the amount of acid remaining in the filtrate must be minimized. The density of the dilute slurry is measured by a nuclear gauge whose output controls the addition of dilution water.

The leach tanks are constructed of polyester-fiberglass with a bonded lining. Agitation is created by axial-flow impellers, sized to provide complete solids suspension. Horsepower is sufficient for startup of the agitators under "sanded-in" conditions. There are three leach tanks in series, with a fourth tank of identical size to provide surge capacity during periods of filter washing. Top-overflow is used through the reactor system, with the fourth tank emptying by bottom discharge to the filter feed pumps that discharge to the filter.

A blower system that vents all four tanks in the leaching

circuit also maintains a negative pressure in these tanks. At the designed leaching rate, about 100 cfm of carbon dioxide is liberated from the circuit. In addition, there is a potential for hydrogen sulphide evolution through the vents.

The fourth tank in the series discharges into the filter feed pumps, which maintain a constant level in the filter vat. An overflow weir returns excess slurry to the filter feed tank. The conventional drum-type filter is equipped for string discharge of the leached concentrate. Both filter cloth and strings have ample chemical resistance to the solutions.

Filtrate from the filter pump passes over a clarifier designed to trap concentrate particles that may get into the filtrate through cloth damage. Clarifier underflow is pumped back to the slurry holding tank. Clarifier overflow discharges to a lined holding pond before being pumped to the waste water treatment plant.

Leached concentrate is discharged from the filter to a conveyor and returned to storage. The same conveyor can recycle concentrate through the repulp circuit if the leaching is not complete, or if the filter cake is too wet for return to storage.

Daily production rates are flexible

Although the preleach plant is designed to operate at a nominal capacity of 471 tpd of concentrate, the design provides enough flexibility to permit operation at rates either above or below this level. As the electrolytic plant does not operate on a feed that requires leaching 100% of the feed concentrates, there are opportunities to run the preleach plant at both high and low throughput rates. Data were collected at these rates to determine how well the process functions. Table 3 lists some typical results, obtained while treating incoming concentrates that averaged 0.96% magnesium. The calcium assay averaged 2.32% in the feed. The magnesium assay of the outgoing leached concentrates and the corresponding calcium assays are given in Table 4.

Variations in the amount of water-soluble magnesium in the results reflect differences in washing efficiency. Using wash water equivalent to ±3.5 displacement washes has, on occasion, given water-soluble magnesium assays as low as 0.03%. Acid used during this period averaged about

Reaction tanks slurry zinc concentrate and sulphuric acid in continuous preleaching process. Tanks hold 5,200 gal each.

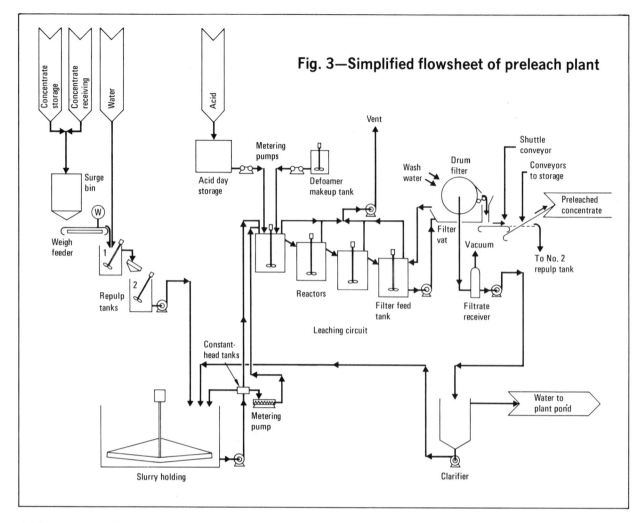

Fig. 3—Simplified flowsheet of preleach plant

0.07 tons per ton of concentrates leached.

The preleaching operation, using 93% sulphuric acid, proceeds very rapidly and is accompanied by a violent evolution of carbon dioxide. Therefore, if an excess of flotation reagent is present, or if the acid is added too rapidly, the leach tanks behave like large flotation cells, carrying large quantities of unreacted dolomite from tank to tank. In addition, large amounts of acid are retained in the froth. Both conditions are undesirable.

Excess acid reacting with the residual dolomite generates gas in the pulp, which produces cavitation in the filter feed pumps. Further, strong acid carryover reacts with the zinc sulphides to liberate hydrogen sulphide, which is highly corrosive to the stainless steel equipment. The chlorides and fluorides present when scrubber water is used instead of fresh water are much more corrosive under highly acidic conditions.

Keeping down corrosion rates

During the early phase of plant operation, it was noted that severe attack had been made on areas adjacent to welds and on the weld beads themselves. Accordingly, every effort is made to minimize acid concentration in any pulps that contact metal portions of the leaching system. Measurement of corrosion potentials by potentiostatic means has shown that corrosion rates can be held to an acceptable rate of ±0.001 in. per year.

Initially, the circuit used only fresh water and acid in both the repulping and leaching systems. As operating experience grew, scrubber water from the roaster gas scrub-

bing section was introduced into the system. Neither potential measurements nor visual observation indicates any increase in corrosion from the change. Typical changes in the concentration of corrodents are:

	Chlorine (mg per l)	Fluorine (mg per l)
Before scrubber water	56.0	5.80
After scrubber water	200.0	10.30

These levels are expected to rise as changes are made in the gas cleaning circuit.

Periodic analysis of the preleach filtrate indicates that only trace levels of hydrogen sulphide are present in the pulp as it enters the filter vat, but only if acid concentrations are kept low.

Filtration of the leached product presents difficulties unless the proper filter cloth is used. Calcium sulphate crystals, in the shape of long needles, form a felt-like mat that effectively blocks off the face of the filter. For this reason, the filter is washed frequently to maintain full flow.

Use of the string discharge filter gives a cloth life of about four months before change is necessary. The monofilament cloth in use has little tendency to blind if kept clean.

Suspended solids in the filtrate tend to be higher in the commercial plant than those in the pilot operation. They are largely removed by the clarifier, from which underflow is periodically pumped to the slurry holding tank.

In all, actual production results compare favorably with those anticipated from the performance of the pilot plant. ☐

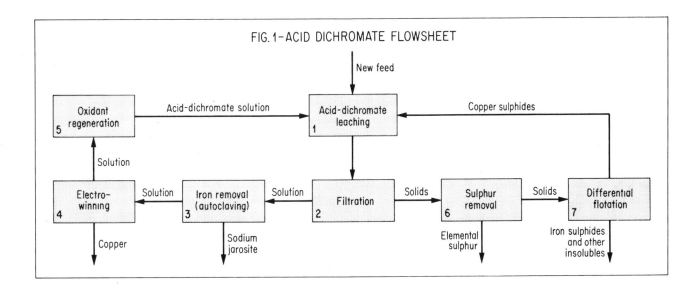

FIG. 1-ACID DICHROMATE FLOWSHEET

Dichromate process demonstrated for leaching of copper sulphide concentrates

Robert Shantz, graduate student, and **T. M. Morris,** professor of Metallurgical Engineering, University of Arizona, Tucson, Arizona

A SULPHURIC ACID SOLUTION OF SODIUM DICHROMATE is a powerful oxidizing medium with a pH-dependent oxidation potential of about −1.3v. Consequently, copper sulphides leached with such a solution are rapidly oxidized to cupric ion, elemental sulphur, and sulphate ion. For example, 42% of the copper in a chalcopyrite concentrate was leached in 7 min with leach conditions adjusted to give a 50% final extraction (for reasons discussed below).

Similarly, 86% extraction in 10 min was obtained with a chalcocite concentrate.

The overall reactions for chalcopyrite are as follows:

$$3\,CuFeS_2 + 5\,CrO_3(OSO_3)^{2-} + 30\,H^+ \rightarrow$$
$$3\,Cu^{2+} + 5\,Cr^{3+} + 6\,S + 15\,H_2O + 3\,Fe^{3+} + 5\,SO_4^{2-}$$

$$3\,CuFeS_2 + 17\,CrO_3(OSO_3)^{2-} + 54\,H^+ \rightarrow$$
$$3\,Cu^{2+} + 17\,Cr^{3+} + 3\,Fe^{3+} + 23\,SO_4^{2-} + 27\,H_2O$$

The dichromate and acid consumed during the leach can be electrolytically regenerated, thus reducing the complexity of the circuit. The straightforward regeneration of the oxidant and the rapid leaching of chalcopyrite are the chief advantages of the system. The major problems are high oxidant consumption caused by competing reactions (especially the oxidation of sulphide to sulphate) and the difficulty in removing ferric iron from the leach solution without excessive loss of chromium.

The proposed process, as shown in Fig. 1, consists of the following steps:

1) Leaching the concentrate with a sulphuric acid solution of sodium dichromate.

2) Filtering the unreacted solids from the solution.

3) Removing most of the dissolved iron and sulphur from the solution by autoclaving.

4) Electrowinning the copper from solution with concurrent regeneration of dichromate and acid in a diaphragm cell.

5) Regenerating the dichromate consumed above that produced in step 4.

6) Removing elemental sulphur from unreacted solids.

7) Using differential flotation to reject gangue and pyrite from the unreacted solids, returning the concentrate to step 1.

The interlocking of these steps places several restraints on the conditions used in the process. First, the Fe^{+3} produced during the leach must be removed prior to electrowinning to achieve acceptable current efficiencies, and consequently must be separated from the chemically similar Cr^{+3}. Since dichromate would react with the copper cathode, its concentration must be essentially zero at the start of electrowinning. To effect iron removal by hydrolysis at elevated temperatures, the end pH of the leach cannot be lower than 1-2, but this pH must be sufficiently low to prevent the precipitation of the gelatinous hydrated ferric oxide. Finally, since the major operating expense is the energy consumed in regenerating the dichromate, the leach conditions must be adjusted to minimize sulphate formation and oxidation of iron minerals.

(The electrolytic regeneration of dichromate and acid is being further investigated at The University of Arizona, and the results will be published as an M.S. thesis.)

Editor's note

Use of sulphuric acid solution of sodium dichromate to leach copper concentrates was investigated at the University of Arizona, and the results were published as an M.S. thesis in 1972. Testing demonstrated that typical concentrates leached readily, and a means of removing iron from solution was demonstrated.

More comprehensive testing is being done by Inspiration Consolidated Copper Co., to which a patent has been issued. (A review of Inspiration's work follows this article.) The process description by Shantz and Morris here is based solely on work supported by the University of Arizona.

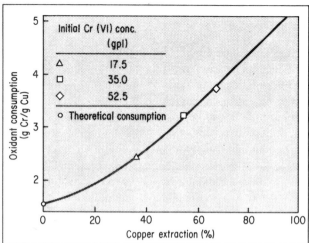

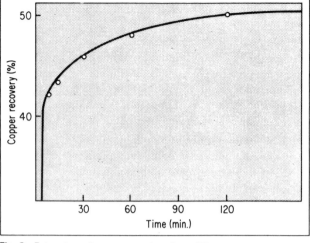

Fig. 2—Oxidant consumption as a function of extraction for a chalcopyrite concentrate

Fig. 3—Extraction of copper as a function of time

Good current efficiencies have been obtained during testing. Separation of the unreacted solids and differential flotation of them are standard unit operations, while the removal of elemental sulphur can be accomplished in several ways, including solvent extraction and volatilization.

Leaching tests yield high extraction rates

Most of the tests were run with a chalcopyrite concentrate since it is the most difficult to treat hydrometallurgically. When higher initial chromium concentrations were used to increase extraction, the dichromate consumption per unit weight of copper extracted increased (Fig. 2). Hence, an extraction of 50% was considered reasonable for investigating the process variables. The chalcopyrite concentrate leached rapidly, as shown in Fig. 3, with over 80% of the final extraction occurring in the first 10 min. The effects of other process variables can be summarized as follows:

1) Higher sulphuric acid concentration increases copper extraction and lowers the dichromate consumption, but it also lowers the pH of the off-solution.

2) Higher sulphate ion concentration lowers the dichromate consumption slightly.

3) Higher temperature gives more rapid extraction and slightly lower dichromate consumption. Temperatures above boiling were not investigated in order to avoid the use of pressure vessels.

4) Chalcocite concentrates leach very rapidly, but those with a high iron content have comparatively high dichromate consumptions and high iron off-solutions (see Table 1).

A copper-nickel concentrate was also tested and was found

to leach readily. While the development of an elemental sulphur film on the mineral surfaces during the leach was not demonstrated, such a film might develop and have serious effects during a high extraction-low agitation leach.

Removal of iron and excess sulphate

The large amounts of ferric and sulphate ions which are produced during the leach must be removed from the circuit. Direct neutralization produces a gelatinous precipitate which is not only difficult to filter but which also entraps a considerable amount of chromium and copper. Consequently, hydrolysis of the ferric iron at elevated temperatures was attempted. Good extractions were finally obtained by adding sodium sulphate to cause the precipitation of sodium jarosite, $Na_2O \cdot 3Fe_2O_3 \cdot 4SO_3 \cdot 6H_2O$, at 170°C (approximately 100 psig). Successive simulated redissolution-reprecipitation steps improved the Fe:Cr ratio of the precipitate by about 3:1 (see Table 2), and thus the chromium losses could be tolerated after three stages. Little copper was lost in the final precipitate.

The other significant results of these tests were:

1) Higher temperature increases iron extraction but results in markedly higher pressure.

2) High Cr^{+3} concentration inhibits iron precipitation.

3) Time is not a major factor, at least in laboratory batch autoclaves.

Since high-pressure, acid-resistant vessels are required for this step, the removal of iron from solution is probably the most serious problem with the process.

This preliminary investigation has shown that leaching copper sulphide concentrates with a sulphuric acid-dichromate solution should be investigated further. More work is necessary on the removal of iron from the leach solution, as well as on the optimization of leach conditions for the particular concentrate. Current work at The University of Arizona indicates that fairly high current efficiencies can be obtained during the regeneration of dichromate; hence the electrowinning and regeneration steps should not present major problems. An investigation must also be made to determine the materials required for handling the solutions.

Subsequent to the work reported above, tests made by Inspiration Consolidated Copper Co. have demonstrated that an extraction of 97% to 99% of the copper from a chalcopyrite concentrate can be obtained in a one-step leach if desired. A procedure was also developed for the precipitation of iron as a jarosite at a temperature of 95°C, eliminating the need for pressure vessels. The leach solutions are not corrosive and stainless steel and PVC have been used in equipment. □

Table I—Results of leach tests

Concentrate type	Iron sulphide content	Copper extraction	Cu:Fe ratio (solution)	Cr(VI) consumption (g Cr/ g Cu)
Chalcopyrite	nil	48	1.1	2.4
Chalcocite	low	93	5.0	1.0
Chalcocite	medium	94	2.7	1.7
Chalcocite	high	81	1.0	3.0

Note: These tests were not made for maximum extraction of copper.

Table 2—Simulated stages in iron removal

Stage number	Initial concentration(gpl)				Extraction	Precipitate composition			
	Na	Cr	Fe	Cu	Fe	Cr	Fe	Cu	So₃
1	20	21	11	33	71	6.3	28	2.5	33
2	18	5	20	2	90	3.2	30	0.44	32
3	0.4	1.7	20	nil	57	1.1	34	nil	33

Inspiration aids in development of dichromate leach processing steps

In 1971, at the University of Arizona and at Inspiration Consolidated Copper Co., Inspiration, Ariz., research was initiated on hydrometallurgical recovery of copper from copper sulphides using chromic acid. Robert Shantz at the U. of A. and Frank Christman at Inspiration performed the initial test series, evaluating leaching characteristics of chromic acid and the problems during subsequent processing of leach liquors.

Results were favorable, and on May 1973, US patent No. 3,730,860 was issued for the process.

The chromic acid process is primarily divided into four interrelated steps: 1) chromic acid leaching, 2) iron removal, 3) copper electrowinning, and 4) chrome regeneration.

Leaching is performed at atmospheric pressure in open vessels, with optimum temperature being the boiling point of the chromic acid solution. At such conditions, required leaching time for 97% dissolution of the copper is 1 hr.

Elemental sulphur forms on the particle surfaces during dissolution, retarding reaction rate and subsequently efficiency. However, it was determined that relatively vigorous agitation during the leaching cycle physically abraded elemental sulphur from the particle surfaces, allowing the leaching reactions to continue to completion without sulphur removal and without sacrificing the copper recovery.

Optimum temperature for the leaching reaction varies with the type of feed. For chalcopyrite ($CuFeS_2$), the temperature must be near the boiling point of the solution. For chalcocite (Cu_2S) and covellite (CuS), excellent recoveries can be obtained at 50° to 60°C. Native copper dissolved very rapidly at room temperature.

The leaching solution contains about 40 gpl total chromium with 25 gpl chrome VI. The acid content is 80 to 100 gpl free H_2SO_4 with roughly 25 gpl recycled copper. Following the leach, the pregnant leach liquor contains 35 to 50 gpl Cu at a pH of 1.5 to 2.0.

The leaching reactions are as follows:

Chalcopyrite: $5\,Na_2Cr_2O_7 + 6\,CuFeS_2 + 35\,H_2SO_4 \rightarrow$
$$5\,Na_2SO_4 + 3\,Fe_2(SO_4)_3 + 5\,Cr_2(SO_4)_3 + 6\,CuSO_4 + 12\,S° + 35\,H_2O$$

Chalcocite: $2\,Na_2Cr_2O_7 + Cu_2S + 14\,H_2SO_4 \rightarrow$
$$2\,Na_2SO_4 + 2\,Cr_2(SO_4)_3 + 6\,CuSo_4 + 3\,S° + 14\,H_2O$$

Covellite: $Na_2Cr_2O_7 + 3CuS + 7\,H_2SO_4 \rightarrow$
$$Na_2SO_4 + Cr_2(SO_4)_3 + 3\,CuSO_4 + 3\,S° + 7\,H_2O$$

Theoretical Cr/Cu consumption ratios can be calculated from these equations: for chalcocite and covellite, the ratio is 0.546 g of Cr VI reduced per g of Cu dissolved; for chalcopyrite, 1.364. Comparisons of the theoretical and the actual ratios indicate the amount of iron dissolved—such as pyrrhotite—and the amount of sulphate formed during the leach.

Following leaching, the slurry is filtered. Separated solids contain any undissolved copper, elemental sulphur, pyrite, molybdenum and insoluble waste, as well as any precious metals present in the concentrate. The filtrate, containing the copper, is ready for purification.

To remove iron dissolved during the leach, the filtered pregnant leach liquor is subjected to an autoclave step. The autoclave temperature is maintained between 150° and 200°C at equilibrium pressure, and iron is removed as a natrojarosite precipitate—$Na_2Fe_6(OH)_{12}(SO_4)_4$.

The removal of iron also generates sulphuric acid:

$$Na_2SO_4 + 3\,Fe_2(SO_4)_3 + 12\,H_2O \rightarrow$$
$$Na_2Fe_6(OH)_{12}(SO_4)_4 + 6\,H_2SO_4$$

It is possible for as much as 30% of the iron in natrojarosite to be replaced by the chrome in the solution, and sufficient replacement of this type occurs to demand recovery of the chrome. The recovery method used is the standard chromite treatment process, consisting of a sodium carbonate roast followed by water dissolution of the chromium. During the roast, the chrome III is oxidized to water-soluble chromate, which is then crystallized from solution as sodium dichromate following acidification.

Since the natrojarosite is a basic ferric sulphate, the iron must be in the ferric state to insure optimum removal during hydrolysis. To insure that all of the iron in solution is in the ferric state, the solution fed to the autoclave should contain about 1 gpl chrome VI.

The autoclave step also insures that intermediate sulphur-oxygen ions, such as thiosulphate (S_2O_3), that may form during the leach are decomposed prior to electrolysis. These ions complex with chrome III and are not reactive at leach temperatures. If allowed to pass to electrolysis with the solution, they decompose at the cathode, producing high sulphur contents in the copper. The elevated temperatures of the autoclave decompose the sulphur-oxygen ions to elemental sulphur and sulphate.

Following hydrolysis and filtration, electrolysis is performed in a typical electrowinning facility, with the exception that diaphragms separate the anodes and cathodes. The diaphragms assure that electrical current is not consumed by continued oxidation and reduction of chromium at the anodes and cathodes. The hydrolysis filtrate first passes through cathode compartments for removal of copper and then through anode compartments for chrome regeneration.

Additional chrome VI regeneration is necessary to maintain a balance, because chrome VI is consumed not only in dissolving copper but also in dissolving iron and in the formation of elemental sulphur and sulphates. The additional chrome regeneration is accomplished in electrowinning cells as described above, utilizing dilute sulphuric acids as a catholyte from which electrolysis produces hydrogen at the cathode and chrome IV regeneration at the anode.

The first electrowinning step involves the deposition of copper and regeneration of chrome VI:

$$Na_2SO_4 + 3\,CuSO_4 + Cr_2(SO_4)_3 + 7\,H_2O \rightarrow$$
$$3\,Cu° + Na_2Cr_2O_7 + 7\,H_2SO_4$$

During the second electrowinning step, hydrogen is produced the cathode and chrome VI is regenerated at the anode:

$$Na_2SO_4 + Cr_2(SO_4)_3 + 7\,H_2O \rightarrow$$
$$Na_2Cr_2O_7 + 3\,H_2 + 4\,H_2SO_4$$

If an alternate source of copper solution is available, it can be substituted as the catholyte, depositing copper rather than generating hydrogen.

The initial catholyte following copper deposition and chrome VI regeneration is recycled to the leaching circuit as the leach liquor. The cathode copper is removed as a finished cathode of excellent quality. Since all impurities, such as iron, are reduced to low levels during hydrolysis and since electrol-

(Continued on p 256)

Leaching chalcocite with cyanide

Robert Shantz metallurgist, New Mexico Bureau of Mines & Mineral Resources,
and **Walter W. Fisher,** metallurgist, Arizona Bureau of Mines

THE NEED TO MINIMIZE ENVIRONMENTAL DEGRADATION has caused several copper producers to seek alternatives to conventional smelting of copper sulphide concentrates. Several new smelting techniques are receiving attention, and many copper producers are considering or have recently implemented hydrometallurgical extraction processes.

Chalcopyrite is both the most abundant and most difficult to leach of the copper minerals, and the majority of research and development efforts have focused on chalcopyrite concentrates. However, there is a need for processes that are limited in application to other copper minerals.

For example, a brief survey of copper producers in the Southwest indicates that about 5,000 tons of chalcocite concentrates are produced daily. These concentrates often contain up to 75% pyrite, which leads to high slag losses and problems with SO_2 removal during smelting. Because chalcocite leaches much more readily than chalcopyrite, the development of a leach process using milder leach conditions than those required for chalcopyrite—with a resultant cost savings in construction materials—could be attractive. Thus, a hydrometallurgical extraction process developed specifically for chalcocite concentrates would be justified.

Several proposals have been offered for leaching copper-bearing materials with cyanide solutions.[1,2,4] Laboratory studies confirm that most copper minerals, with the notable exception of chalcopyrite, leach rapidly in cyanide solution.[4] Minerals that contain Cu(I) will leach without oxidation to form cuprocyanide ions and bisulphide ions. Copper minerals containing Cu(II), or the existence of oxidizing conditions in the solution, cause loss of cyanide by cyanate and thiocyanate formation.

Chalcocite (CuS_2) is leached rapidly without oxidation in cyanide solution to produce cuprocyanide and bisulphide ions. Because the pyrite that is frequently associated with chalcocite is not attacked, cyanide leaching would be an attractive method for extracting copper from chalcocite concentrates if an economical means of recovering copper from the solution were available.

Dissolution of chalcocite in cyanide solution under nonoxidizing conditions was studied to obtain basic data on such a leaching system.[7] While the principal objective of the study was the determination of an empirical rate equation, the extraction data yielded a good indication of the effects of the major process variables. (It should be noted that coarse size fractions of a mineral containing less than 10% impurities were leached at 1% solids. Consequently, the following results should be interpreted as indicating trends, rather than as results directly applicable to actual operating conditions.)

Solution chemistry for leaching

The three cyanide complexes of Cu(I) are described elsewhere in the literature.[3,5,6] The concentration of free cyanide ion, CN^-, which dominates the reaction rate, is dependent on the dissociation of hydrocyanic acid and is thus also dependent on the sulphide ion-bisulphide ion

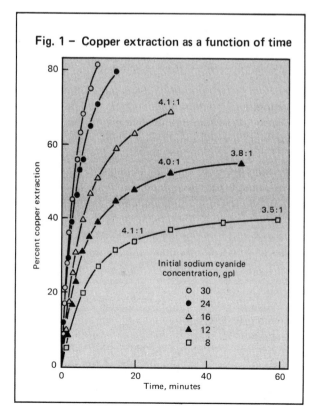

Fig. 1 – Copper extraction as a function of time

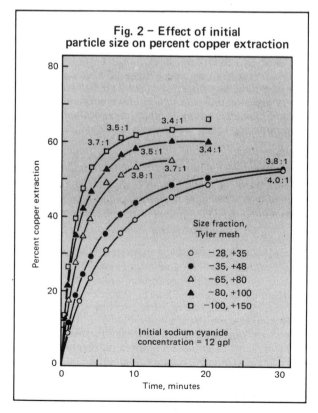

Fig. 2 – Effect of initial particle size on percent copper extraction

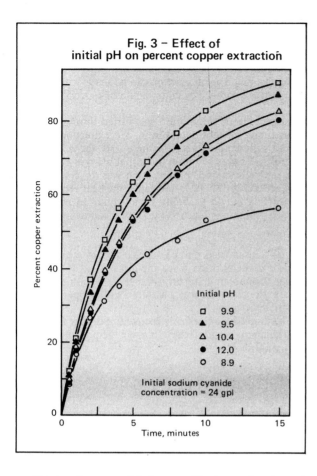

Fig. 3 – Effect of
initial pH on percent copper extraction

Initial pH
□ 9.9
▲ 9.5
△ 10.4
● 12.0
○ 8.9

Initial sodium cyanide
concentration = 24 gpl

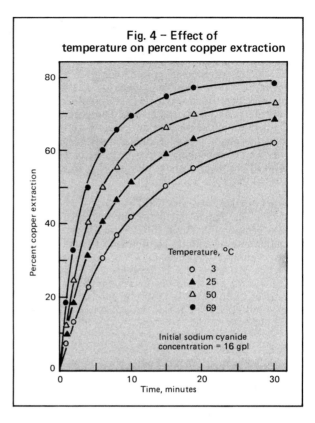

Fig. 4 – Effect of
temperature on percent copper extraction

Temperature, °C
○ 3
▲ 25
△ 50
● 69

Initial sodium cyanide
concentration = 16 gpl

equilibrium because of their mutual hydrogen ion dependence.

The concentrations of ionic species formed during the leaching of chalcocite can be described by a series of chemical equilibrium and mass balance equations. The stepwise dissociation of the cupro-tetracyanide and cupro-tricyanide complexes is given by the following reactions:

$$Cu(CN)_4^{3-} \overset{K_{4,3}}{=} Cu(CN)_3^{2-} + CN^- \qquad (K_{4,3} \sim 10^{-1})$$

$$Cu(CN)_3^{2-} \overset{K_{3,2}}{=} Cu(CN)_2^- + CN^- \qquad (K_{3,2} \sim 10^{-5})$$

The interaction between the $H_2S/HS^-/S^{2-}$ and HCN/CN^- systems is illustrated by the following reactions:

$$H_2S \overset{K_1}{=} HS^- + H^+ \qquad (K_1 \sim 10^{-7})$$

$$HS^- \overset{K_2}{=} S^{2-} + H^+ \qquad (K_2 \sim 10^{-14})$$

$$HCN \overset{K_A}{=} H^+ + CN^- \qquad (K_A \sim 10^{-10})$$

Mass balance equations can be written for the cyanide, sulphur, and copper species and for hydrogen ion. Simultaneous solution of the equilibria and mass balance equations by numerical methods gives the concentrations of the individual ionic species. The results of these calculations indicate that under the test conditions used, the principal copper species are $Cu(CN)_4^{3-}$ and $Cu(CN)_3^{2-}$. The distribution between the two species is dependent primarily on the CN:Cu ratio. The sulphide ion produced by the reac-

tion is largely hydrolized to bisulphide ion. Except in the lower pH range (less than 9), the hydrogen cyanide concentration is negligible.

The pH effects are especially interesting. Because of the difference in the bisulphide ion and hydrogen cyanide dissociation constants, there is an initial pH below which hydrogen ions are released from hydrocyanic acid faster than they are consumed by the sulphide ions formed during the reaction. Thus, at a relatively low pH (8 to 10), the solution becomes more acidic during the leach, while at a higher pH it becomes more basic. The overall reactions for these two cases can be approximated by the following:

$$Cu_2S + 6CN^- + H_2O \rightarrow 2Cu(CN)_3^{2-} + HS^- + OH^-$$
(higher pH)
$$Cu_2S + 3CN^- + 3HCN \rightarrow 2Cu(CN)_3^{2-} + HS^- + 2H^+$$
(lower pH)

The opposing effects on the reaction rate caused by the lowering of both the free cyanide ion and sulphide ion concentrations as the pH decreases lead to a maximum reaction rate in relation to pH. Under the test conditions used, this maximum occurred at a pH of about 9.9.

Test procedure and results

Size fractions containing about 75% copper were made from a massive chalcocite sample whose principal impurity was quartz. Leach tests were run in a closed, 2.5-liter batch reactor. After purging oxygen from the solution, the mineral sample was introduced and 10 samples taken for copper analysis. The solutions were prepared from reagent grade sodium cyanide. Sodium hydroxide and glacial acetic acid were used to adjust the initial pH. A complete description of experimental procedure is given by Shantz.[7]

The results of the kinetic study indicate that the reaction rate is directly proportional to the free cyanide ion concentration and surface area and inversely proportional to the sulphide ion concentration to a low power (~ 0.1). (The effects of the major process variables are described below and in the accompanying graphs in terms of percent extraction rather than reaction rates in order to give values that are of more general interest.)

Initial cyanide concentration. The effect of cyanide concentration was demonstrated by a test series with a minus 28 plus 35 mesh fraction at 25°C. As shown in Fig. 1, the extraction rate is rapid in the presence of high concentration of cyanide. However, as the CN:Cu ratio decreases to the 4:1 to 3:1 range, the free cyanide ion is largely consumed and the extraction rate decreases sharply. The molar ratio of CN:Cu is given at several points on Fig. 1 to illustrate this effect. The initial pH is 12.0 and the final pH about 12.5.

Initial particle size. Several size fractions of chalcocite were tested, ranging from minus 28 plus 35 mesh to minus 150 plus 200 mesh. Only the results from tests having the same initial pH are given in Fig. 2. In this test series, the initial pH was 12, the temperature was 25°C, and the total sodium cyanide concentration was 12 gpl. The sharp leveling of the curves results mainly from the near exhaustion of the free cyanide at CN:Cu ratios less than about 4:1.

Initial pH. Results of a series of tests with different initial pH values are given in Fig. 3. As explained above, a maximum extraction occurs at a pH of 9.9 as a consequence of the HCN/CN$^-$ and the HS$^-$/S^{2-} equilibria. The size fraction was minus 28 plus 35 mesh, the temperature was 25°C, and the total sodium cyanide concentration was 24 gpl.

The fact that a batch reaction can go acidic with possible evolution of hydrogen cyanide should be especially noted.

Temperature. Temperature was varied through a series of tests, and as shown in Fig. 4, the extraction rate increased with temperature. For these tests, the size fraction was minus 28 plus 35 mesh, the initial pH was 12, and the total sodium cyanide concentration was 16 gpl. Because the reaction is exothermic and rapid, the heat generated by the reaction would probably be adequate to maintain a high temperature in leach vessels under commercial conditions.

Tests thus showed that chalcocite leaches rapidly in alkaline cyanide solution when the molar ratio of CN:Cu is greater than about 4:1. Further, cyanide leaching does not affect pyrite and produces a solution with copper in the -1 oxidation state.

A method of economically recovering copper from such leach solutions is still needed to make the process economically viable. □

References

1) Chamberlain, C., Newton, J., and Clifton, D., "How Cyanidation Can Treat Copper Ores," E/MJ, Vol. 170, No. 10, pp 90-91 (Oct. 1969).
2) "Copper Leaching With Cyanide—a Review of Five Inventions," E/MJ, Vol. 168, No. 9, pp 123-127 (Sept. 1967).
3) Izatt, R., Johnston, H., Watt, G., and Christensen, J., "Thermodynamics of Metal Cyanide Coordination. VI. Copper (I) and Silver (I) Cyanide Solutions," INORGANIC CHEMISTRY, Vol. 6, No. 1, pp 132-135 (Jan. 1967).
4) Lower, G. W., and Booth, R. B., "Recovery of Copper by Cyanidation," MINING ENGINEERING, Vol. 17, No. 11, pp 56-60 (Nov. 1965).
5) Penneman, R. A., and Jones, L. H., "Infrared Absorption Studies of Aqueous Complex Ions. II. Cyanide Complexes of Cu(I) in Aqueous Solutions," THE JOURNAL OF CHEMICAL PHYSICS, Vol. 24, No. 2, pp 293-296 (Feb. 1956).
6) Rothbaum, H. P., "The Composition of Copper Complexes in Cuprocyanide Solutions," JOURNAL OF ELECTROCHEMICAL SOCIETY, Vol. 104, No. 11, pp 682-685 (Nov. 1957).
7) Shantz, R., Cyanide Leaching of Chalcocite, Ph.D. dissertation, University of Arizona, 1976.

(Continued from p 253)
ysis occurs in diaphragmed cells where cathodic copper is free from anodic contamination, the copper produced is of sufficient quality to compete with electrorefined products.

Research on the chromic acid process in the past year has been concentrated primarily on: 1) development of a single stage leach, 2) optimization of elemental sulphur produced during leaching, and 3) optimization of iron removal techniques.

The single stage co-current leach is now standard procedure. With sufficient agitation, recoveries of 97% can consistently be attained with any feedstock at indicated temperature and retention time.

The production of elemental sulphur has been optimized at a minimum of 70%, minimizing the chrome VI consumption. The SO_4^{--} that is inevitably produced can be removed by combination in the natrojarosite formation.

The iron removal step has proven to be quite effective with autoclave hydrolyzation. Temperatures as low as 150°C effectively hydrolyze iron with an initial hydrolysis pH of 2.0 As the pH is lowered, however, the temperature for hydrolysis must increase. Also important: lower hydrolysis temperatures will lower the quantity of chromium substitution during natrojarosite formation.

Another major improvement was contributed by John Rodgers at the University of Arizona, in work involved with the chrome VI regeneration. Under typical conditions, the anode current efficiency for chrome VI was 60% when regenerating 70% of the total chrome. However, by improving anode characteristics, the current efficiency can be maintained at 90% through 70% regeneration of the chrome. The improvement in efficiency significantly improves the operating costs.

The dichromate leaching scheme is very versatile. One application which has received considerable attention and proven quite effective is purification of moly concentrates from typical concentrator operations. This procedure was developed to improve total moly recoveries by reducing the flotation cleaning stages and leaving a 5% to 15% copper content in the moly concentrate. The moly concentrate is then subjected to chromic acid leaching, which reduces copper content below penalty levels.

In summary, the chromic acid process as currently developed offers a scheme for treatment of all copper sulphide minerals. The process will recover 97% of the contained values in a concentrate with a maximum 1-hr retention time and temperatures not exceeding the boiling point of the leach solution.

Operating costs should be competitive with those of conventional pyrometallurgical processes. □

Polish refinery designed to streamline handling of copper anodes and cathodes

Ralph A. Bengtsson, product manager, C J Wennberg AB, Karlstad, Sweden

THE NEW GLOGOW II COPPER REFINERY in Poland is carefully designed to avoid problems commonly encountered in handling anodes and cathodes. The 300,000-mtpy installation will start up after C J Wennberg of Sweden delivers a complete line of handling machines in mid-1976.

Design criteria at Glogow II stressed optimizing of space utilization and minimizing of operating costs. To meet these criteria, technicians worked out a design concept that places the starting sheet preparation machines, anode spacing machine, scrap anode washing machines, and cathode washing machines on the ground floor. The tanks, starting sheet stripping, and starting sheet pre-trimming are on the first floor. With this design configuration, the space required around the handling machines does not infringe on the space required for the tanks.

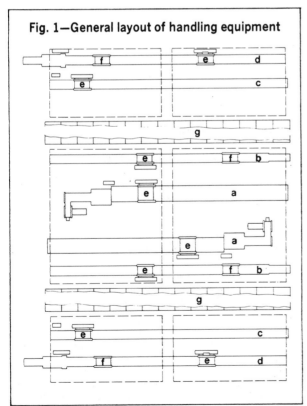

Fig. 1—General layout of handling equipment

a) Starting sheet machine, b) cathode washing machine, c) anode spacing machine, d) scrap anode washing machine, e) manual straddle carrier, f) automatic straddle carrier, g) electrolytic tanks.

To transport starting sheets—anodes and cathodes—between the different levels, openings were designed directly above the machines for loading and unloading (Fig. 1).

Outlining the problems to be solved

One problem apparent in many refineries is handling defective anodes delivered to the tankhouse for processing, which must then be returned to the anode foundry for re-casting. The job of transporting the heavy rejected anodes is costly and time consuming.

In addition, there is a strong possibility of mixing faulty anodes with production anodes, either by accident or to save personnel time in the tankhouse. Faulty anodes in the tank create a risk of short circuits, which interrupt production and increase costs. These problems will be avoided at Glogow by placing the anode straightening machine in the anode foundry and making the foundry manager responsible for delivering acceptable anodes to the tankhouse.

As planned at Glogow, the anode straightening machine in the anode casting area receives a batch of anodes on a chain conveyor. The lugs are ram-straightened both horizontally and vertically. The anode is weighed and checked to see if it hangs plumb. The weight is displayed on the control panel. Anodes having broken lugs, out-of-plumb anodes, and those that are over or under weight are rejected automatically and then recast without leaving the foundry.

The accepted anodes are transported to the tankhouse ground floor, to be loaded onto the receiving conveyor of the anode spacing machine, which produces the correct tank spacing. A straddle carrier places the spaced anodes on storing beams, from which a tank-set of anodes will be lifted up to the first floor by an overhead crane and placed in a tank.

In the tankhouse, the two anode spacing machines will be placed so that the storing beams of the machines stretch into both crane bays. Furthermore, the machines are situated so that the storing beams are parallel to the receiving beams of the scrap anode washing machines. In this way, when the crane discharges a batch of scrap anodes for washing, it need travel only a short distance to pick up a tank-set of fresh anodes. (See Fig. 2.)

The scrap anode washing machines handle scrap anodes by straddle carriers running on rails. The straddle carrier travels slowly through the wash tank, where the scrap anodes are washed three times by spray nozzles mounted on three spray headers placed in line inside the wash tank. The straddle carrier then discharges its load of scrap anodes onto a chain conveyor. From the chain conveyor, the scrap anodes are down-ended three at a time onto the ro-

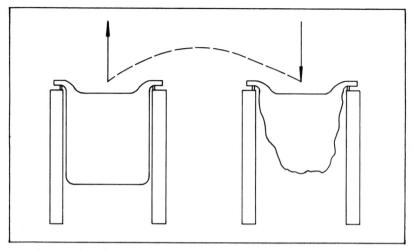

Fig. 2—Crane travels only a short distance when discharging spent anodes and picking up fresh anodes.

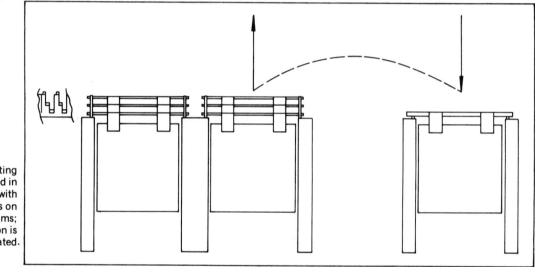

Fig. 3—Starting sheets are stored in three tiers, with cathodes on receiving beams; crane motion is indicated.

tating lowering-table, which enables the anode lugs to be placed in all four corners of the stack for stability. The stack is then transported to the anode casting building for recasting.

Two starting sheet preparation machines and two cathode washing machines will also be situated on the ground floor. The starting sheet machines are placed so that the storing beams of each one stretch into two different crane bays. The receiving beams of the cathode washing machines stretch into both crane bays (Fig. 1).

The starting sheet assembly machines are completely automatic with the exception of the straddle carriers for transporting assembled starting sheets to the storing beams. The straddle carrier is partially automatic—it picks up a load of starting sheets from the starting sheet machine unassisted. The operator then takes over and runs the carrier along the storing beams, deposits its load in a convenient position, and then runs it back again for a new load.

The storing beams are divided into two parallel aisles. Next to the starting sheet machine is a transfer station where the operator chooses the aisle in which to unload the starting sheets. The storing beams are designed so that starting sheets are discharged into three tiers, with each tier having the correct tank spacing. In other words, the straddle carrier will be carrying three tank-sets at a time from the starting sheet machine to the storing beams. The overhead crane picks up one tier at a time when charging a tank. Since he has two aisles to choose from, the operator can, in cooperation with the crane operator, make opti-

mum use of the storing beams.

The starting sheet machines and cathode washers, like the anode spacing machines and scrap anode washers, are situated so that the cranes, when discharging a load of cathodes onto the receiving beams of the washer, have to travel only a short distance to pick up a tank-set of starting sheets. This optimizes crane usage (Fig. 3).

The cathode washing machines are, in principle, the same as the scrap anode washers except for the down-ender. The bars are removed manually from the cathodes as they enter the down-ender, which places batches of 22 cathodes horizontally on the storing conveyor.

The starting sheet stripping area is on the first floor. Here, the blanks will be stripped manually until an acceptable automatic stripping machine can be found. It was decided from the beginning that automatic handling of sheets in the starting sheet machine would require a uniform stack of sheets. The best way of achieving this is to trim and stack the sheets before they enter the starting sheet machine. Therefore, the design concept called for a pre-trimming machine in each of the two stripping areas. The pre-trimming machines trim, pre-straighten, and stack the sheets on pallets for transport to the starting sheet machine. Pre-trimmed sheets eliminate many stops in the automatic feed to the starting sheet machine. As the loop slitting machine is also situated in the stripping area, all of the scrap copper strips will be collected in the same vicinity, and no scrap will accumulate in the starting sheet machine area. □

Chapter 4
Pyrometallurgical Processing

Dwight-Lloyd downdraft sinter machines agglomerate calcines, return fines, bag filter dust, furnace residues, sand, and oxidics to produce high grade, intermediate, and prime western feed for the Josephtown smelter's electrothermic furnaces.

Josephtown smelter provides process flexibility

ACQUISITION OF Balmat, N.Y., zinc properties in the late 1920s spurred St. Joe research in basic zinc metallurgy that led to development of its electrothermic zinc smelting process—the basis of the company's 250,000-tpy Josephtown smelter at Monaca, Pa. The plant is one of the world's largest zinc producers, with a workforce of 1,600. Its flexible electrothermic circuitry permits St. Joe to produce a variety of zinc grades, tailor-made alloys, and both American and French process zinc oxide from plant feed that includes zinc concentrates from up to a dozen different sources, plus up to 20% secondary materials, primarily customer returns.

The Josephtown smelter is also the site for the bulk of St. Joe's current research in extractive metallurgy and new products. St. Joe researchers are giving special attention to a new "low energy" pyrometallurgical zinc process, according to Joseph G. Sevick, St. Joe vice president for smelting. Energy now accounts for about one-quarter of the Josephtown smelting costs, up from 12-13% a few years ago, even though St. Joe operates its own steam-coal power generating plant on the smelter site. St. Joe is working with Lurgi on the low energy zinc process and is seeking patents on some aspects of the system. A pilot plant to test the process is planned, with construction to begin soon. Apart from lowering energy costs, St. Joe hopes to develop a process that is environmentally sound and not labor-intensive.

Environmental controls have absorbed a large share of the Josephtown capital spending budget in recent years, with financing coming from $22.5 million in tax-free Beaver County Industrial Development Authority bonds issued at 5.6% interest. Part of recent spending for pollution

control went into installation of a large pair of electrostatic precipitators at the power plant, in series with existing collectors, to raise fly ash removal from 95% to 99.5%.

Upcoming projects include construction of a demonstration plant to test the US Bureau of Mines citrate process for control of SO_2 in power plant stack gases; installation of a new bag house in place of existing electrostatic precipitators, to improve particulate recovery at the sinter plant; and construction of a new add-on interpass adsorption unit to capture fugitive sulphur emissions in the tail gases of the current acid plant. Beginning in 1976, St. Joe planned to spend about $30 million for pollution controls at the zinc smelter over the next four years—which does not imply that the St. Joe smelter is not a clean plant overall. Recovery of sulphur from roaster plant offgases already runs to 97%. With the new interpass adsorption unit, recovery will increase to 99.8%, according to division manager, Charles Henderson.

Flexible flowsheet aids smelter operation

Roasting, sintering, furnacing, and refining are the four main steps in the St. Joe electrothermic smelting process. (The description of the process offered here draws primarily on "Extractive Metallurgy of Lead and Zinc," Vol. 2 of the proceedings of the 1970 AIME World Symposium on Mining and Metallurgy of Lead and Zinc.)

The Josephtown roasting plant utilizes multiple hearth furnaces for de-leading zinc concentrate smelter feed, and fluid-bed and suspension roasters for desulphurization. A sinter plant agglomerates the calcine produced by the roasters to form a hard, porous furnace feed. Sinter and

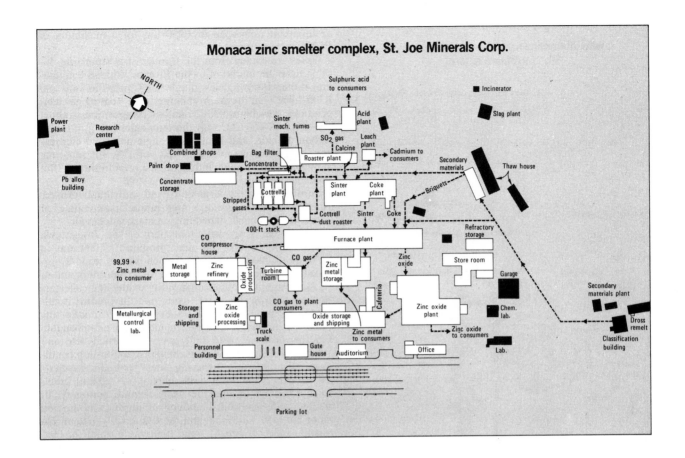

Monaca zinc smelter complex, St. Joe Minerals Corp.

coke then feed to the top of resistance-type electric shaft furnaces, and the flow of current through the charge develops the temperatures required for smelting at the reaction sites.

To produce metal, the furnace offgases bubble through a large "U"-tube filled with molten zinc, condensing the zinc gas to liquid, which is cast into slabs. To produce zinc oxide, the furnace vapors are burned in a combustion chamber with air additives, and the resultant powders are collected.

The Josephtown plant makes use of three distinct circuits to produce the variety of end products sold to zinc metal and zinc oxide buyers; one circuit produces high grade metal and American process zinc oxide, a second produces intermediate grades and "tailor-made" alloys of controlled lead and cadmium content, and the third circuit produces prime western metal and feedstock for refining to French process oxide.

Extensive residue treatment keeps overall zinc recovery high, and smelter byproducts include sulphuric acid, cadmium, mercury, lead cake, and low grade ferrosilicon.

Five modified Nichols-Herreshoff multiple-hearth roasters are used for de-leading in the roaster plant, with 95% of the lead eliminated as sublimed PbS by heating the concentrates to 950-980°C in a low-oxygen atmosphere. Concentrates in the high grade and intermediate circuits are then desulphurized in fluidized bed roasters of St. Joe design. In the prime western circuit, lead elimination is not a key consideration, and a suspension roaster of Cominco design is used for desulphurizing.

A modest amount of natural gas or carbon monoxide gas is burned on the fourth, sixth, and tenth hearths of the multiple-hearth roasters to maintain desired temperature distribution. The hearth furnace product is "partially desulphurized," typically containing about 22% S.

Three fluid bed roasters operate at 950°C, with twin screws injecting feed 30 cm below the surface of the fluidized bed at a feed rate of about 250 tpd. Fluidizing air enters the roasters through tuyeres positioned on 20-cm centers, with the feed-air ratio regulated by monitoring the oxygen content of cyclone exit gases, which ranges from 2% to 5% O_2. Before entering waste heat boilers, offgases pass directly to hot cyclones for dedusting. Each of the fluid roasters and the flash roaster have individual waste heat boilers that cool offgases from about 950°C to 400°C. Electrostatic precipitators dedust the roaster gases before they enter the acid plant, where five Leonard-Monsanto contact acid units convert the sulphur in the offgases to sulphuric acid. The Josephtown engineering department is now working on the design of the $9.4 million add-on acid plant previously mentioned, to capture the approximately 1,600 ppm of SO_2 in acid plant tail gases. The new unit may be on stream in 1977.

Calcine produced at the roaster plant is ground to 50% minus 0.044 mm to improve the pelletizing characteristics of the charge for sintering. Revolving drum and inclined disc pelletizers are used for pelletizing.

The sinter plant uses Dwight-Lloyd downdraft machines to agglomerate high grade, intermediate, and prime western feed for the electrothermic furnaces. A silica content of 8-10% is required to produce a strong sinter of relatively uniform particle size. Two-stage sintering in the high grade circuit promotes elimination of impurities.

Sinter feed, in addition to calcine, includes return fines (48-60% of feed depending on the circuit), bag filter dust, furnace residue, coke breeze (up to 5%), sand, and oxidics, which originate from both in-plant and purchased high-zinc fines. Three electrostatic precipitators and a bag house filter now clean the sinter gases. Installation of new bag filter facilities is planned, to replace the precipitators and improve dust collection.

A leach plant treats about 19 tpd of sinter plant fume

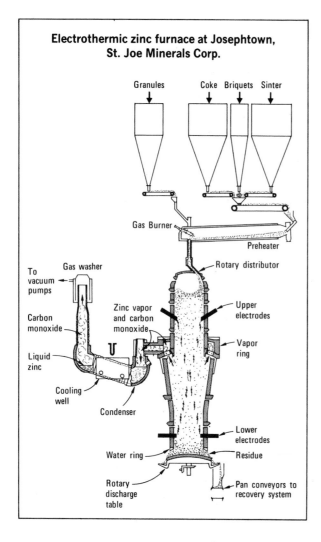

Electrothermic zinc furnace at Josephtown, St. Joe Minerals Corp.

Granules   Coke Briquets Sinter

Gas Burner

Preheater

To vacuum pumps

Gas washer

Carbon monoxide

Zinc vapor and carbon monoxide

Liquid zinc

Cooling well

Condenser

Water ring

Rotary discharge table

Rotary distributor

Upper electrodes

Vapor ring

Lower electrodes

Residue

Pan conveyors to recovery system

and 125 cu m per day of scrubber liquor from the acid plant purification circuit to produce about 525 tpy of cadmium and 1,650 tpy of lead cake, a lead sulphate residue that contains small but significant quantities of gold, silver, and indium. The lead cake is sold. Zinc reports in zinc sulphate solution, which is used in pelletizing the sinter mix.

The sinter fume typically contains 38% Zn, 9% Pb, and 10% Cd. The scrubber liquor, which supplies much of the acid required for leaching, contains 30 gpl Zn, 0.2 gpl Cd, and 15 gpl H_2SO_4.

The furnace plant is equipped with 17 St. Joe-designed electrothermic smelting furnaces, five of them used to produce American process zinc oxide and 12 used to produce metal. (See accompanying drawing.) Three of the metal furnaces are "small" (1.75 m ID and 11.3 m high) and nine are "large" (2.44 m ID and 15 m high). The large furnaces can produce as much as 100 tpd of zinc.

Furnace charge heated to about 750°C in a gas-fired preheater enters the furnace through a rotary distributor. The principal feed is sinter and coke, but as much as 25% of total zinc input may be other zinc-bearing materials, including briquettes, granules, metallic screenings, and slab dross. The nominal coke rate is 44% of sinter weight and about 300% stoichiometric carbon relative to zinc in sinter. Retention time of charge in the furnace is about 22 hr.

Eight pairs of electrodes, each connected to its individual single-phase transformer and voltage regulator, introduce power into the furnace, forming a resistance path about 9 m long through the furnace. Power input per elec-

trode circuit ranges up to 1,250 kw, for a maximum of 10,000 kw per furnace.

Gases are vented from the furnace at a vapor ring, located near the midpoint of the furnace. Charge temperature at the vapor ring elevation is 900°C near the walls and 1,200-1,400°C in the main smelting zone. Venting gas temperatures are about 850°C, and gas composition is about 45% Zn and 45% CO, with the remainder being nitrogen, carbon dioxide, and hydrogen. Single-pass zinc elimination in the furnaces averages 92%, with 7% zinc reporting to recirculating residue and 1% to discarded residue. After condensation, single-pass recovery is 85%.

Furnace circuiting is flexible, and individual furnaces can be utilized to produce high grade, intermediate, or prime western metal, depending on market demand.

Zinc oxide is an important part of the Josephtown smelter product mix; the plant produced 67,000 tons in 1974 and 47,000 tons in 1975. French process oxide is produced by burning zinc metal vapor in a combustion unit of St. Joe design to produce high purity oxide. Bag collectors filter oxide from the carrier gases, and the product is collected and bagged. Several grades of French process zinc oxide are produced to meet "regular" and photoconductive specifications, with differences in particle size and properties being achieved by changing combustion conditions. Electrothermic furnacing directly produces American process oxide, with gases passing to vertical, brick-lined manifolds around the oxide furnace periphery. In the manifolds, controlled amounts of air mix, and the zinc vapor burns to zinc oxide and the CO to CO_2. Use of low volatile cokes for smelting and high grade sinter for feed produces a product of high chemical purity, which is collected in bag filters and bagged for shipping. St. Joe also produces organic coated oxides. The coating, dispersed over the surface of the oxide, increases its rate of incorporation into rubber and prevents adsorption of CO_2 and H_2O on the oxide surface.

Furnace residues are treated physically to recover coke and unsmelted zinc and to segregate slag and low grade ferrosilicon byproducts. Magnetic separators remove the ferrosilicon, which is sold as a foundry material. Pneumatic tables recover free coke. A heavy media circuit separates the remaining residue into zinc-rich and zinc-lean fractions. The former becomes a sinter plant feed; the latter is sized and sold as ballast.

To further diversify its product line, St. Joe is installing a small plant to produce about 6,000 tpy of zinc dust for sale to the paint and coating market. Design work for the $1.5 million unit began during the summer of 1976.

A 110,000-kw, St. Joe-owned coal-burning power station commissioned on the Josephtown smelter site in 1957 supplies the bulk of the plant's power requirement. Planning is under way for a $12.7 million demonstration plant for the US Bureau of Mines citrate process as a means of removing SO_2 from the power station's flue gas. St. Joe and USBM will share the cost of the plant, and St. Joe anticipates that a variety of high and low sulphur coals will be processed in the power station during one year of testing to determine the effectiveness of the process. Construction of the plant, which will produce elemental sulphur from SO_2, is expected to take two years. USBM has run pilot tests on the process at smelters in Arizona and Idaho, and a modification of the process was used to process flue gas from a small power station at an Indiana chemical plant.

Support groups contribute to smelting efficiency

The Josephtown smelter's metallurgical laboratory and the design engineering and maintenance groups provide indispensable support for the plant's smelting process. The metallurgical control laboratory, housed in a new building that opened in 1970, is one of the most advanced control labs in the industry. The design engineering and maintenance personnel are key elements in sustaining the continued efficient operation of a plant that produced its first zinc oxide in 1930.

The primary function of the metallurgical control laboratory is to support the smelting process with analyses of plant feed and intermediate process products, including concentrates, cokes, breeze, secondary materials, and sinters. The new laboratory building, which combined the functions of several lab and assay sites at the smelter, has made it possible to reduce the time lapse between sampling and assay readout to 6 hr from 48 hr (real time) previously. Investment in the new facility totaled $1.5 million, not including the cost of some major equipment that was moved in from existing facilities. The lab made more than 1.4 million determinations in 1975, including analyses for environmental controls, and urine and blood analyses for plant biological monitoring.

Between 2% and 3% of the laboratory's effort goes toward monitoring of plant hygiene, and the chief chemist, Dr. James H. Kanzelmeyer, is pursuing a program that will lead to accreditation of the laboratory by the American Industrial Hygiene Association. Criteria for accreditation include a review of the educational credentials of the laboratory staff and assurance that routine quality control procedures are an integral part of lab procedure, that equipment meets certain minimum standards, and that files and records are maintained in accordance with AIHA standards. The Josephtown lab already applies 5% to 10% of its effort toward monitoring its own procedures, Kanzelmeyer said. A minicomputer in the lab is programmed to compare assay results with established standards, and three development chemists on the staff devote the bulk of their time to developing chemical procedures for use within the company.

Analysis of local streams, including the Ohio River, is an ongoing part of the laboratory's work schedule.

Major engineering projects total 49

The Josephtown design engineering staff, headed by chief engineer William Steele, was working on 49 major projects and an additional 78 "class two" projects when E/MJ visited the plant during the summer of 1976. The design engineering staff—17 engineers and 14 draftsmen—produced between 500 and 600 drawings in 1975, and it supervised work on as many as 200 other drawings done under contract.

Over the past few years, environmental controls have taken an increasingly larger share of the Josephtown engineering staff's time. In 1975, environmental projects accounted for about half of the $5.2 million in capital expenditures closed out by the engineering staff; in 1976 the portion will exceed $3 million. In 1977, a new Monsanto-Leonard unit will be installed to reduce sulphur in the existing acid plant's tail gas. Cost of the project will be about $9.4 million. Other environmental control projects now supervised by the engineering department include installation of new bag collectors for improved control of sinter plant offgases and construction of a demonstration plant to test the USBM citrate process at the smelter's power plant.

Construction of a small plant to produce marketable zinc dust and installation of a residue crushing system are among other large projects now in progress under the supervision of the engineering staff.

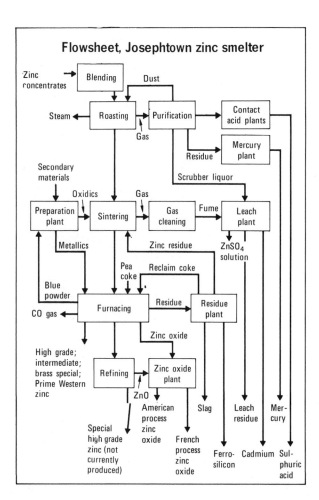

Flowsheet, Josephtown zinc smelter

Maintenance budgeted at $20 million per year

Maintaining the 10,000 units of moving equipment and machinery in use at the Josephtown smelter is a $20 million per year job. The maintenance department, headed by plant engineer James R. Kester, uses a card file that now runs to more than 16,000 entries to keep tabs on the maintenance history of all equipment in the plant, and plans are being developed to computerize the data. The file system uses an eight-digit code for identifying the entries, with the first two digits representing the plant in which the equipment is located; the second two digits, the department; the third two, the piece of equipment in question; and the last two, subassemblies in the equipment.

About half of the Josephtown maintenance work is done by regularly assigned crews located at the various plants and departments throughout the smelter. The central maintenance shops—which include separate instrument, electrical, machine, structural, sheet metal, pipe fitting, and paint shops—handle work that cannot be done by the department crews.

The Josephtown maintenance department has benefited over the years from an apprentice program established in 1936 in cooperation with the US Department of Labor. The St. Joe apprentice training program spans about four years, leading to certification as a journeyman by the Commonwealth of Pennsylvania in the various crafts offered. The program covers apprenticeships in 10 crafts: auto mechanic, carpenter, pipe fitter, structural iron worker, tinner, machinist, electrician, instrumentation, lead burner, and mill wright.

Plant engineer Kester graduated from the St. Joe apprentice program.

Nichols-Herreshoff multiple-hearth roasters are used to de-lead concentrates prior to desulphurizing in fluid bed roasters.

Zinc oxides are an important part of the Josephtown smelter's production: 46,914 tons in 1975 and 67,217 tons in 1974.

Research encompasses broad field of activity

St. Joe spent about $3.3 million in 1975 for research on new product development, improvement of existing products, development of new extractive processes for lead and zinc, improvement of plant operating procedures, environmental controls, and a number of other developmental activities. The bulk of the research was conducted at the Josephtown smelter.

The Josephtown research group is headquarters for long range corporate programs as well as for projects related directly to current smelting practice at existing plants. Such research includes investigation of new pyro- and hydrometallurgical processes for producing lead metal; the pre-

viously described intensive investigation of a "low energy" zinc smelting system; and systems for extracting copper from copper oxides, concentrates, and mattes. Other long range work has included a study of means for removing heavy metal ions from aqueous systems and for documenting the sources of trace metals in process streams.

The research group also has an eye out for potential markets for solid wastes generated at St. Joe operations. The company's goal is to develop markets for all solid materials produced at its plants. "We don't want to leave anything on the ground," asserts vice president for smelting, Joe Sevick.

The Josephtown researchers, headed by the director of research, Robert E. Lund, are also looking for ways to improve data monitoring and handling. A special services section has "built" a computer model of the smelter, based on 800 monitorable variables, that can track all of the plant's circuits, including those for recirculating residues, and 500 constraint equations. The goal is to optimize smelter operation for any combination of plant feed, product mix, and operating rate.

In new product research and market development, St. Joe is now concentrating on lead-calcium-tin alloys for use in the grids of maintenance-free batteries, on a metal coating system that can apply a thin coating of lead or other metals to almost any substrate without changing the physical properties of the substrate, and on high strength zinc-aluminum alloys that develop very favorable "plastic" forming properties at about 500°F. The research group also is working to improve the position of St. Joe zinc oxides as a coating for paper used in copying machines—a competitive market.

Commercial use of St. Joe-developed lead-calcium-tin alloys in maintenance-free batteries is still on a modest scale. However, the market has potential for rapid growth over the next few years. One major US battery manufacturer predicts that by 1980 all new cars will be equipped with maintenance-free batteries. Such a development would allow St. Joe, a supplier of primary lead, to enter the market for battery grids, which is currently supplied largely by secondary smelters.

St. Joe's metal coating technology has a number of potential applications. Of particular interest to St. Joe is lead coating of building materials for improved sound attenuation.

Formet Corp., a St. Joe subsidiary, is working to develop markets for the company's high-strength zinc-aluminum alloys. Formet was organized as an independent enterprise, with the goal of making it a new St. Joe profit center.

The research group is responsible also for providing technical service to users of St. Joe metals. The technical service lab maintains an extensive file of past problems encountered and solved in galvanizing, and when a customer is having difficulty, St. Joe is usually able to offer a solution to the problem by reference to physical metallurgy and the file.

The Josephtown research facilities include a corrosion lab that is used both for customer service and for St. Joe research, a test cell for batteries, and a variety of mechanical devices for testing the properties of materials.

When possible, the Josephtown smelter is used as the research group's test facility, a practice that is encouraged by the number and variety of the smelter's circuits. Aspects of smelter operations that are of interest to the research group include control of sulphur in sinter plant feed, optimization of fuel consumption at the sinter plant, and reduction of cadmium and lead that is retained in the sinter product. □

Target: new technology to improve economics of iron ore beneficiation

COMMERCIALIZATION OF THE IRON ORE PELLETIZING process and construction of large pelletizing plants has over the past 20 years been the most obvious technical advance in iron ore processing. Now, after many years of research and development, direct reduction of iron ore is capturing a growing share of the capital being invested in ore processing plants. Other important research, directed at fuel economization at pelletizing plants and separation of iron from nonmagnetic taconites, may hold the key to future technical breakthroughs by the iron ore industry.

As of November 1974, North American direct reduction capacity—installed, operating, and committed—totaled 4,084,000 net tpy of sponge iron. Mexico was the leader with a capacity of 2,134,000 net tpy, the US had exactly 1 million net tpy, and the Canadian share was 950,000. The HyL process accounted for 2,134,000 net tpy of this capacity, followed by the Midrex process with 1.6 million net tpy and the Armco process with 350,000. It is estimated that North American demand for metallized iron ore might grow to 27 million net tpy by 1985 (E/MJ, September 1974, p 116).

One problem in achieving projected demand for reduced iron ore is the production of pellets or ore of adequate quality to feed direct reduction facilities. Gangue limitations for such plants ($SiO_2 + Al_2O_3$) fall below 3%, while US pellet production currently averages about 6.6% gangue and Canadian production more than 5%. About 95% of US ore and pellet production is unacceptable for direct reduction. Unless an economic beneficiation method of reducing these gangue percentages is developed—magnetic, flotation, or otherwise—foreign ores must of necessity provide the major source of feed for future North American direct reduction plants. (An exception is found in pellet production at Pea Ridge, Mo., which averages 69% Fe and 2.1% gangue.)

A number of direct reduction processes are now in the process of evaluation and development. The currently dominant processes are described briefly here.

HyL—four-stage, fixed bed reduction

In the HyL process, a carbon monoxide and hydrogen reducing gas—generated by the steam reforming of natural gas or other hydrocarbons such as LPG or naphtha—reduces iron ore or oxide pellets to sponge iron in four fixed bed reactors. To economize utilization of reducing gas, the gas flows from one reactor to the next through four reduction stages: **initial reduction,** in which the charge is heated and partially reduced by hot gases from the reactor in the primary reduction stage; **primary reduction,** in which further reduction takes place using gas from the cooling stage reactor; **cooling,** in which fresh, cool reformed gas is passed through the charge of reduced iron to complete the reduction and to add carbon; and **unloading and reloading,** in which the reduced sponge iron is removed from the bottom and a fresh charge is loaded through the top.

HyL process: static bed reduction with four reactors

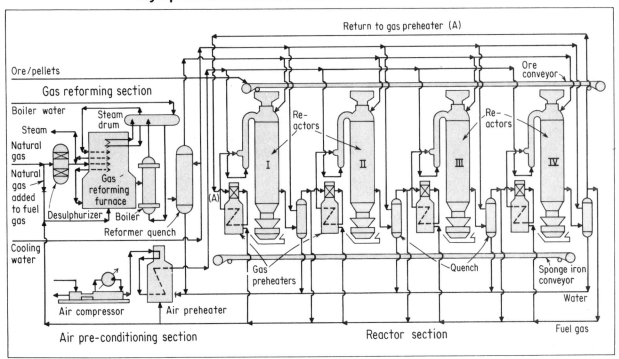

Midrex process: cylindrical furnace with countercurrent gas flow

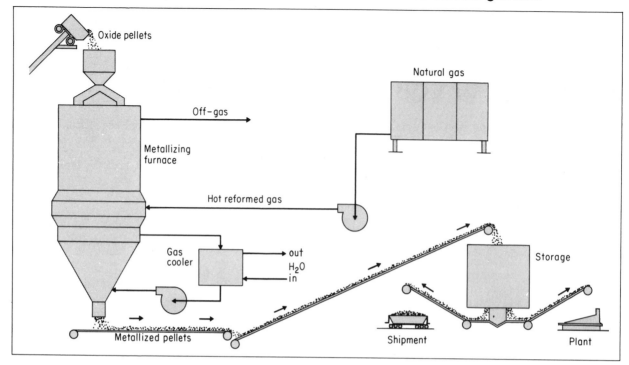

Each step requires 3 hr, for a total cycle time of 12 hr. Reducing temperatures are in the range of 1,600°F to 1,900°F, depending on ore reducibility and pyroplastic limits.

The HyL process can handle lump ore in the range of minus 1½ in. plus ¼ in. and pellets in a gradation that provides suitable bed permeability. Metallization for ore ranges from 82% to 87%, and pellets are reported to be 92%-plus, consuming approximately 15 million Btu per net ton of sponge.

Midrex—a vertical, cylindrical-shaft furnace

The Midrex process furnace is a cylindrical shaft about 15½ ft ID and 125 ft high (exclusive of charging superstructure) and is divided into separate zones for reduction and cooling. Material is conveyed to the top of the reducing vessel by skip or conveyor, and the reducing gas is supplied by a gas reforming system.

The charge is fed into the top of the shaft through a large number of distributor pipes and moves downward through the shaft as the gas moves upwards. The hydrogen-rich reducing gas, exceeding 95% combined H_2 and CO, is introduced into the shaft at mid-height through a system of tuyéres, not unlike those of a blast furnace. Reduction temperatures are about 850°C and reduction is accomplished in the top half of the shaft.

The bottom half of the shaft, conically shaped on the inside, contains a separate cooling gas circuit with an internal gas distributor and collection system. The reduced product is cooled to near-ambient temperatures before the sponge iron is discharged through a dynamic gas seal to the exit conveyor and screening operation. Cooling gas from this zone is kept out of the reduction zone by a series of baffles.

A unique aspect of the Midrex process is the system for recycling furnace offgas. After cooling to remove most of the contained water, offgas containing about 20% CO_2 is mixed with raw natural gas and fed to the reformers, where the CO_2 and residual water provide the necessary oxygen to reform the natural gas. This feature eliminates external steam or oxygen systems required for other types of reformers, with the additional benefit of reducing capital costs and overall energy consumption.

The Midrex process produces a 92% metallized sponge iron with an energy consumption of about 12 million Btu per net ton and a power usage of about 122 kwh per net ton. Midrex claims impressive sponge iron passivity with minimal oxidation. Passivation is accomplished by a patent-pending technique.

Armco process enters commercialization

Like the Midrex process, the Armco process uses a vertical-shaft furnace, with solids descending against rising gases fed to the shaft through 12 symmetrically spaced tuyeres. The cooling gas injected at the bottom rises to the top for exit along with the spent reducing gas. About 60% of this gas becomes reformer fuel and the remainder is further cooled and compressed for reuse as cooling gas and for blending with fresh reducing gas to attain reaction temperatures of 1,420°F.

Armco uses steam-methane catalytic reforming to produce reductant at 1,750°F from natural gas. Top-gas provides the entire fuel demand.

Pilot operations at the rate of 350,000 net tpy have produced an 88-90% metallized product with a consumption of 11.8 million Btu per net ton and 35 kwh per net ton.

Solid reductant processes are undeveloped

Although the extensive coal reserves of North America represent a large potential fuel source, solid reductant processes for direct reduction have not been successfully implemented. However, the present short supply of gaseous reductants calls for a reassessment of solid reductants.

Krupp direct reduction process

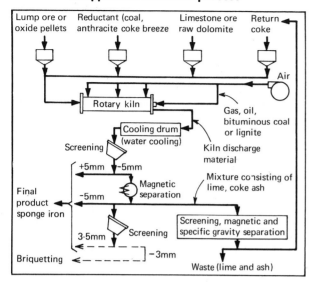

Armco direct reduction process

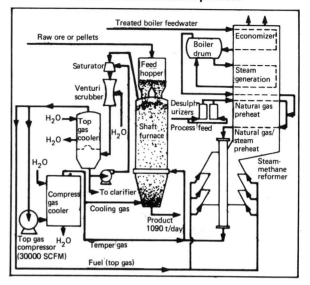

The 150,000-tpy Krupp direct reduction plant of Dunswart Iron and Steel Works Ltd. in South Africa, which can be charged with either coal or lignite or a mixture of these fuels, has reportedly met all specifications and is producing a 92% metallized product from a 67% Fe feed. Moreover, the Krupp organization claims that a 65% Fe ore or pellet feed can be handled, putting a sizable portion of North American pellet production into the acceptable category.

The Krupp direct reduction process evolved from experience gained in the earlier Krupp-Renn and Waelz processes. Using a rotary kiln charged with coal or lignite and fluxes, the process reduces iron ore to metallic iron. Ore and recycled char are introduced at the entrance to the kiln while the kiln is being fired by blowing fresh solid carbon or any available fuel under reducing conditions. Reduction is accomplished by the action of both the reducing gases and the solid reductant in contact with the charge. Nozzles are provided throughout the entire length of the kiln to control the temperature profile, which ranges from 950°C to 1,050°C over three-fourths of the length.

The mixture discharged from the kiln consists of sponge iron, char, fluxes, and ash. Following cooling in a rotary cooler, the mixture is separated into usable sponge and other materials such as char for recycling. Separation is by means of screens, magnetics, and gravity.

Metallization up to 92%-plus is claimed, depending upon the ore or pellet quality.

Bridging the fuel gap in pelletizing

According to the Process Evaluation Group of the US Bureau of Mines, the energy consumed at a typical 2 million-ltpy magnetic taconite plant is distributed as follows (in percent):

	Electric power	Natural gas	Both
Mining	7%	—	2%
Crushing	7	—	3
Concentrating	67	—	26
Pelletizing	15	88	60
Utilities	4	12	9
	100	100	100
Percent of total	39	61	100
Total consumption, Btu per long ton pellets			1.03×10^6

Worries over the availability of natural gas for pellet plants have sparked testing of fuel alternatives for concentrates produced in Minnesota, Michigan, western Ontario, Missouri, and elsewhere. There is a very real possibility that natural gas supplies will be inadequate to support budgeted expansion programs, and supplies may well become interruptible for current installed capacity. The obvious solutions lie in Bunker C—now used by pelletizers on the Labrador Trough and Cleveland Cliffs' new Tilden plant, and an alternative option in Missouri—or sub-bituminous coals or lignites of western origin—the Dakotas, Montana and Wyoming.

At the US Bureau of Mines Twin Cities Metallurgy Research Center, 120-hr test runs on Minnesota magnetic concentrates have been conducted since June 1964 in an 850-lb-per-hr grate-kiln module. While results discussed during E/MJ's September visit can only be considered tentative, some findings were beginning to surface then.

Concentrates from four Minnesota taconite plants have been tested at solid fuel Btu additive rates about twice the indicated 670,000 Btu per long ton of magnetic concentrate, with a balancing input of natural gas to maintain a 1,300°C kiln induration temperature in simulation of actual heat requirements in a commercial scale plant.

Ash input to the kiln at these feed rates was approximately 13 lb per long ton of pellets, and 50% to 70% of this input was picked up by the finished pellets. Thus the finished pellets were gaining ash at rates of 6 to 10 lb per lt. At 10 lb per lt, the ash might degrade the iron content of the finished pellet by close to 0.5%, but it is debatable whether this should be counted as a debit or credit at the blast furnace since part of the ash may contribute fluxing properties. In general, however, tests have indicated that sulphur introduced from coal combustion is not picked up by the pellets.

The USBM coal firing system involves pulverizing coal to 60% minus 200 mesh. This product, fed through a venturi with 2-3 lb of air per lb of coal, is piped at 6,000 ft per min into the hood of the kiln, creating a flame 8 to 10 ft long. At the pulverizer, preheated air from the cooler at 400°F is tempered with ambient air, exhausting a gas stream at 120° for transport of the pulverized coal. The 34-in. x 34-ft kiln has been run with about 35% excess air. Outside air is blended with natural gas at the grate to duplicate commercial practice.

At indicated fuel consumption rates of 670,000 Btu per lt of pellets, each ton of magnetite pellets would require about 75 lb of sub-bituminous coal and 100 lb of lignite for induration. Fuel rates for pellets of hematitic-geothitic origin could be expected to range from 50% to 100% higher than for magnetic pellets. If the entire 40 million-ltpy Minnesota taconite industry converted to solid fuel firing of pellet lines, the theoretical need for supplies would be about 1.5 million stpy of sub-bituminous coal or 2 million stpy of lignite. The 50% expansion now underway in Minnesota taconite capacity would raise the supply requirement proportionately.

Additional details of experimental work involving solid fuel firing of several pelletizing systems will be discussed at the 48th Annual Meeting of the Minnesota Section of AIME and 36th Annual Mining Symposium at Duluth in January 1975.

A breakthrough in particle size monitoring

With the enormous power input to grinding systems employed at iron ore processing centers—particularly those handling the flinty ores on the eastern half of the Mesabi—reliable sensors to continuously monitor particle size could provide a valuable tool for process engineers. At the 1974 Mining Symposium in Duluth, Autometrics' Robert E. Hathaway discussed in optimistic terms a prototype system under trial at a prominent taconite plant. Hathaway supplied the following comments for E/MJ.

"An instrument system for continuous, real-time measurement of iron ore slurry particle size has recently been developed and field tested by Autometrics Co. of Boulder, Colo. Called the PSM System-200 (for Particle Size and Percent Solids Monitor), the instrument will provide two analog output signals: one calibrated to read particle size directly in terms of the desired screen fraction and the other calibrated to read percent solids by weight or volume. The System-200 is patterned after the PSM System-100 developed by Autometrics for the base metals industry. PSM System-100's are now operating in more than 35 plants in the US, Canada, Africa and the Philippines.

"The particle size measurement is made by accurately sensing the attenuation (or loss) of two ultrasonic signals as they pass through a flowing slurry sample drawn from the process flowstream. These two ultrasonic signals are at different frequencies, selected to yield maximum sensitivity to changes in particle size for one, and minimum sensitivity to particle size changes for the other. The attenuation of both signals is affected by the solids content of the slurry. The two signals are compared electronically to eliminate the percent solids dependency and yield an output which is a function of particle size distribution only. The solids content information is used to provide the other output signal which indicates slurry percent solids.

"The real test of the value of this new instrument system will be its ability to increase profits by increasing overall plant throughput and/or plant operating efficiency. This information should be forthcoming soon, as Autometrics plans to deliver the first production PSM Systems-200's to iron ore companies late this year."

High intensity wet magnetic separation

In tracing the theory and development of wet high intensity magnetic separators, J. E. Lawver and D. M. Hopstock of University of Minnesota's Minerals Resources Research Center offered pertinent comments on applications for iron ore.

Potentially large supplies of ore in the US are contained in the oxidized or nonmagnetic taconites of Minnesota, and it is reasonable to expect that in the future these ores will be beneficiated at least in part with high intensity wet magnetic separators. MRRC began to test this concept in 1964. It was found that the most promising flowsheet consisted of preliminary concentration by high intensity wet magnetic separation followed by regrinding and flotation to produce the final concentrate.

The results showed that the costs of treating nonmagnetic taconite could be comparable to those of treating unaltered taconite if improvements were made in flotation to increase recovery and reduce consumption of reagents. One of the problems in flotation of iron ore is that the quartz particles tend to have fine coatings of submicron size goethite or hematite slimes.

Recent developments in high intensity magnetic separation technology have made possible improvements in the oxidized taconite flowsheet. One possibility mentioned by Lawver and Hopstock is to use a powerful fine-matrix high intensity wet magnetic separator to concentrate material that has been reground to flotation size—a size previously considered too small for recovery by magnetic means. This tactic would simplify subsequent flotation—or possibly eliminate the need for flotation entirely. A second possibility would be to pass the reground product through a very intense magnetic field such as that produced by a superconducting solenoid. Such treatment might aid selective flocculation of hematite in the same manner in which low intensity magnetic fields are used to selectively flocculate magnetite. An upgraded and deslimed material would show a better response to flotation. Experimental tests of these ideas are underway at MRRC.

The full Lawver-Hopstock paper on wet high intensity magnetic separation is scheduled for publication in MINERALS SCIENCE AND ENGINEERING, published by the National Institute for Metallurgy, Private Bag 7, Aukland Park, South Africa. The text of the paper, without accompanying drawings and illustrations, is available from the Department of Conferences, Continuing Education and Extension at the University of Minnesota.

Process model simulation and computer control

Other fundamental work underway at MRRC includes a project jointly sponsored by the National Science Foundation and a taconite producer to apply computer control techniques developed in Australian copper ores to taconite processing. MRRC's R. L. Wiegel discussed this work with E/MJ.

The objectives of this project are to improve control of product size, and to increase capacity of present grinding circuits. If these goals are realized, the result would be to reduce problems encountered in pelletizing because of swings in product size, and to improve efficiencies in the use of energy in grinding operations.

A related project is aimed at generating more fundamental knowledge of the various unit operations employed in taconite processing, as a basis for developing general purpose mathematical models of these operations. Such models can then be used in computer simulation either of the individual unit process or of the integrated process system.

These process simulation capabilities offer development engineers a quick way to examine process changes or alternatives which could be too costly or too innovative to permit full scale plant trials without prior guarantees of success. Work on process simulation is being done with the cooperation and partial direction of a similar group in Australia, which has successfully developed similar models and control techniques in copper ore processing plants. □

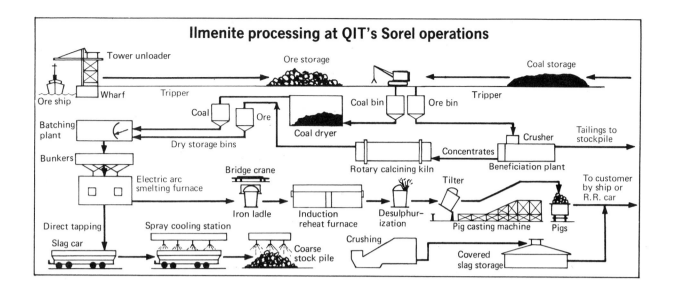

Ilmenite processing at QIT's Sorel operations

QIT—innovative, aggressive, a leader in ilmenite smelting

The Quebec Iron and Titanium Corp., owned two-thirds by Kennecott Copper Corp. and one-third by New Jersey Zinc Co., has pursued a technologically innovative and aggressive development program for the past quarter-century. It has led the way in ilmenite extractive technology to produce high titania slags for pigment manufacture, and low residual pig iron. At Sorel, 50 mi from Montreal, almost 2.0 million ltpy of ilmenite ore is processed to produce 850,000 lt of 70% titania slag and 600,000 lt of high quality pig iron.

The world's largest ilmenite mine is operated by QIT at Lac Tio, 27 mi by rail from Havre St. Pierre, 600 mi downstream from Montreal on the north shore of the St. Lawrence. Production is at the rate of 2.0 million ltpy for processing at Sorel and 300,000 ltpy for use in heavy aggregate. The mine at Lac Tio covers 134 acres. The deposit at the surface measures 3,600 x 3,400 ft and is considered to consist of three orebodies—the Main, the Northwest, and the Cliff. Mining is concentrated in the Main orebody at present. The ore is a massive ilmenite (FeO, TiO_2) and hematite (Fe_2O_3) in the ratio of 2:1, with anorthosite as the principal gangue mineral, along with some pyroxene, biotite, pyrite, and magnetite. Specific gravity ranges from 4.4 to 4.9

The present open pit is horseshoe-shaped, measuring 1,800 x 1,600 ft. Mining is carried out in nine 35-ft benches, with ultimate berms 35 ft wide. Waste to ore ratio is about 0.75:1. Percussion drilling uses four Ingersoll-Rand "Crawlmaster" down-the-hole drills to put down 6-in. holes in a 13 x 17-ft pattern. Metallized slurry is employed. Canadian Industries Ltd.'s M-4 is loaded in the bottom, M-2 in the center, and M-3 in the upper part, with stemming for the top 8-10 ft, depending on rock conditions. Blasts generally range from 75,000 to 175,000 lt and are carried out once a week. The powder factor is estimated at 0.52 lb per cu yd for ore. If secondary breaking is necessary, a drop ball is used.

Ore is loaded by three electric shovels—two P&H 1400s, and one Marion 4160—all with 4- to 5-yd buckets. A Marion 151 with a 7-yd bucket is used on waste. The haulage fleet is 15 diesel trucks of 45- to 50-ton capacity—seven Terex and eight Euclid. Haulage distance is 3,000 ft to the crusher, and 1,800 ft to the waste dump.

Ore is crushed to minus 9 in. in a primary Traylor 48 x 72-in. jaw crusher, then to minus 3 in. in a 7-ft Symons cone crusher. Sized ore is loaded directly into 60-ton hopper type cars. Unit trains of 45 cars each transport the ore over the Romaine River Railroad to the shiploading facilities at Havre St. Pierre, 27 mi away. Two 1,600-hp Alco diesel locomotives pull the ore trains. Six unit trains per day deliver 14,000 lt of ore to the docks, where it is loaded onto two 30,000-ton bulk carriers chartered for the April 1 to December 1 shipping season.

Sorel—center of unique extractive facilities

Vessels arriving at QIT's facilities at Sorel are unloaded by two 10-ton tower unloaders at the rate of 1,100 tph, with the ore going into stockpile or directly to the preparation system. The first step in ore preparation is crushing in 4-ft Symons cone crushers in closed circuit with 6 x 14-ft loose rod vibrating screens. The minus ⅜-in. product is discharged onto 20 mesh, 5 x 14-ft step-deck vibrating screens which make a split at about 14 mesh. The coarse fraction, representing about 85% of the total feed, is upgraded in 10-in. Dutch State Mines cyclones using magnetite as the heavy medium. The remaining 15%—the fine fraction—is deslimed in a thickener and processed in Humphrey spirals.

The feed to the cyclones is 86 grade (combined titanium and iron oxides), which is raised to 94 grade. The combined concentrate averages out to 93 grade with a final analysis of 36.8% TiO_2 and 41.8% Fe. Plant capacity is 150-200 ltph of concentrate, with about 90% recovery.

The presence of pyrite necessitates calcination, which is accomplished in four rotary kilns fired by smelter offgases. The kilns are 11 x 200 ft, rated at 50 tph. The roasted ore is cooled in rotating drum coolers, batch weighed, and mixed with dried anthracite in an automated proportioning system. The blend is fed to the smelting operation.

The smelting operation is an exclusive QIT development that evolved as a consequence of highly innovative and persistent R&D efforts. QIT's pioneering work carried over from the beneficiation flowsheet to smelting, which utilizes 50 x 20 x 20-ft rectangular electric furnaces with six 24-in.-dia. electrodes-in-line, to achieve selective reduction in an open bath, coupled with the very difficult technique of containing highly corrosive titania slag at 2,850°F. Some nine furnaces, with power input ranging from 40,000 kw to almost 90,000 kw, produce a high titania slag (70-72% TiO_2) and a low residual pig iron. Slag for the pigment market is cooled, crushed, and sized. Titania is marketed under the trade name "Sorelslag."

The pig iron is processed further to meet carbon and sulphur specifications for ductile iron manufacture and other applications requiring low residuals. The metal product is called "Sorelmetal." A continuously cast grade of ductile iron—"Sorelbar"—is produced for special applications. "Sorelflux"—a carefully sized raw ilmenite ore—is marketed as a steelmaking slag conditioner.

Continuing R&D efforts at QIT are the keystone of operations improvement and new product development. Out of a total of 1,350 employees, approximately 100 are assigned to R&D, with 10 of that staff working on quality control problems.

The QIT operation has given birth to two satellite operations: Quebec Metal Powders Ltd. (powdered iron), and Great Lakes Carbon (Canada) Ltd. (which supplies electrodes to the QIT smelter and to other operations). The metal powder operation is a wholly owned subsidiary of QIT.

In addition to being a technological pioneer in the mining and extractive metallurgical industries, QIT was also the first of several industries to headquarter at St. Joseph de Sorel, Que. Industrial developments in the Sorel-Tracy area now include a 600-Mw thermal plant, a stainless steel plant owned by Atlas Steel, and a pigment plant owned by Tioxide of Canada.

The QIT operation is significant in the overall North American iron picture because it has demonstrated a way to process titania-bearing materials for the recovery of iron. Heretofore, such materials could not be counted on to supply acceptable iron. Now, the vast resources of titaniferous magnetite of the St. Lawrence and other parts of Canada may be included in the total of potential iron ore resources. □

Meramec: an exercise in quality iron ore output

When Meramec first went into production, E/MJ reported in April 1964 the following primary objectives of the beneficiation plant:

1) To produce high quality pellets high in iron and low in silica, phosphorus, and sulphur.

2) To operate a grinding system capable of freeing phosphorus-bearing apatite from the ore (requiring a minus 200-mesh grind) and of achieving a 65% minus 325-mesh size for the iron units presented to the balling and pelletizing plant.

3) To scalp off nonmagnetic waste ahead of the grinding circuit with magnetic cobbers when losses of hematite are not excessive.

4) To maintain grinding at an optimum mesh, with an effective system of automatic controls in grinding and classification.

5) To remove magnetite, comprising most of the mill feed, in the form of clean concentrates ahead of flotation.

6) By differential selective flotation, to first float a clean pyrite concentrate so that an acceptable apatite concentrate could be recovered from the tailing, and then treat the phosphate tails for production of a hematite concentrate.

7) To pump magnetite and specular hematite to the pelletizing plant to be blended as feed for balling drums.

These general objectives prevail today, although the original circuitry has undergone modifications to keep the flowsheet in step with recovery requirements and with changing ore characteristics as the mine matures. For example, specular hematite was found in the predominantly magnetite orebody near the footwall and in the upper reaches of the deposit. Recovery of this iron component assumed a high level of importance in the earlier stages of mining. As mining went deeper, the proportion of hematite contained in plant feed tended to decline. However, with the advent of pillar mining, hematite recovery has required renewed attention.

The byproduct recovery systems occupy miniature circuits in both the beneficiation plant and the feed preparation section of the pellet plant. Major changes in the original flowsheet include the placement of primary crushing underground rather than on the surface. In the plant, a single regrind circuit was installed to assist the four original lines of grinding mills, each line consisting of an open circuit KVS rod mill followed by a KVS ball mill in closed circuit with 20-in. Krebs cyclones. Addition of the regrind circuit provided better control of particle size and the capture of magnetics escaping the primary magnetic separators as tailing, for byproduct processing and hematite recovery. It was also necessary for quality control as recovery of the heavy media product, M-25, and apatite assumed added importance.

The concentrate flowsheet

Primary magnetic recovery of the Meramec plant is arranged in four processing lines, which receive a minus ⅜-in. product prepared in a three-stage crushing and screening circuit. This product is rescreened at ⅛-in. for a coarse cobbing step that produces a quick reject of nonmagnetic oversize to waste. The minus ⅛-in. fines undergo a sand-slime separation in spiral classifiers.

The pinned cobber magnetics and classifier sands travel through an open circuited rod mill to a cyclone feed sump, where they join the mechanical classifier slimes. The sumped cyclone feed is pumped through 20-in. cyclones in closed circuit with the four ball mills. The primary cyclones produce an underflow for the ball mills and a 60-70% minus 325-mesh overflow for the primary magnetic separators.

In each mill line, the primary separators consist of eight three-drum Jeffrey units equipped with Alnico permanent magnets. Each of the eight is fed in parallel, and the magnetic product of each drum is repulped for downstream cleaning. The magnetic fraction is processed through the regrind circuit and the nonmagnetic portion is pumped to a 100-ft hydroseparator.

Regrinding

The regrind circuit contains cyclones, an elaborate battery of DSM screens, a KVS 11½ x 15-ft regrind ball mill, dewatering magnets, and a set of eight three-pass magnetic separators.

At the upstream end of this circuit is a set of four Krebs 10-in. cyclones, which produce a heavy media separation effect during cycloning. Thus, DSM screens with an 0.01-in. deck opening can screen out an undersize from the un-

derflow, producing a high grade magnetic fraction. This is sumped for pumping to the pellet plant. Some oversize is pumped to the regrind mill.

The cyclone overflow is processed through a two-stage set of DSM screens equipped with decks having 0.004-in. openings. The screens split a first-stage undersize for the magnetic concentrate pumping system. The second-stage fine screens yield an undersize which is cleaned on the regrind magnetic separators.

The secondary DSM oversize is pumped through two dewatering magnets to the regrind mill. This unit, charged with ⅞-in.-dia balls, operates in a closed circuit with two stages of DSM screening. Both stages contain decks having 0.004-in. openings. Regrind screen undersize is pumped to regrind magnetic separation. Regrind screen oversize is returned to the regrind mill.

Primary magnetic tailing, regrind magnetic tailing, and dewatered magnetics are the feed for flotation. Pyrite is floated in a xanthate system. The sulphide flotation tailing is conditioned with sodium silicate, fatty acid, and fuel oil for phosphate flotation.

When hematite was recovered by flotation, both fatty acid and amine systems were used. Fatty acid flotation was abandoned in favor of amine flotation because the residual reagent caused problems in the balling and pelletizing circuit. Hematite recovery has been reactivated in a Reichert cone followed by a DSM screen—a circuit producing a 62% iron concentrate of hematite.

The pellet plant is equipped with five Bethlehem-designed shaft furnaces, each measuring 15 x 7 ft in the upper horizontal cross section and equipped with bottom coolers.

The lower part of the induration section is equipped with chunk breakers (a roller bar device) to break up clumps of pellets before discharge from the furnace. The firing zone of the furnace reaches a maximum temperature of about 2,350°F. Each furnace produces 1,100 tpd of pellets with a 93 tumble test and a 90 "Q" index. ☐

Groveland pelletizing at 2 million-tpy rate

Producing 2 million tpy of 63.1% Fe, 6.95% Si pellets, Hanna Mining Co.'s Groveland open-pit mining and pelletizing operation near Iron Mountain, Mich., was the company's first US pellet producer and has been a mainstay of its pellet production since the plant came onstream in 1963. The 100%-Hanna-owned property started up in 1959 as a producer of concentrates and achieved its present capacity in 1968 as the result of successive expansions in mine output and the addition in 1963 of a pelletizing operation. Pelletizing features six balling circuits (five of them having 10-ft-dia x 31-ft balling drums and the sixth a 12-ft-dia x 32-ft drum), and a 235-ft-long Dravo-Lurgi traveling grate indurating machine.

The Groveland operation extracts a Michigan jasper-type ore grading about 35% Fe from a 600-ft-wide orebody that dips at about 70° to the north. Magnetite is the predominant iron mineral, accounting for about 60% of the iron content, with the remainder split between hematite (38%) and silicate (1-2%). However, pit ore ranges from

zero to 100% magnetite and requires blending to achieve a mill feed that operating personnel try to maintain in a 50-60% magnetite range.

Groveland recently switched from jet piercers to rotary drills for blasthole drilling, general superintendent George Kotonias said when E/MJ visited the property. Blastholes are drilled to 15-in-dia., and some experimenting has been done with 17½-in. holes. Ore is blasted once or twice a month, and blasts range up to 500,000 tons in size. Five- and 6-yd-capacity shovels load ore into a haulage fleet that includes four 54-ton, seven 75-ton, one 85-ton, and three 120-ton haulage trucks. Eight- and 9-yd shovels are used for loading out overburden, which is moved at a ratio of about 0.7 tons per ton of ore. The pit has reached a depth of 350 ft, and with at least 25 years of reserves at current operating rates, eventual depth is projected in the neighborhood of 1,000 ft.

Haul roads grade about 10%, and in the pit Groveland uses crushed tertiary grind product to line the road bed.

Three crushing stages—through a 54-in. gyratory, a newly installed 7-ft standard secondary, and three 7-ft Shortheads—reduce ore to 82% minus ½ in. for concentrator feed.

There are four concentrator lines: two installed at the time of the mine's 1959 startup, a third added when the pellet plant came onstream in 1963, and a fourth added when present capacity was achieved in 1968. There are some variations in equipment on the four lines, but the basic flow common to all is through conventional rod and ball mill grinding, classifying cyclones, cobber magnetic separators to produce a magnetite concentrate, and flotation circuits that float out the tails, primarily silica, and produce a flotation concentrate. Both the magnetic and flotation concentrate report to a common thickener, and following filtration, the concentrate moves via conveyor to the pellet plant.

Flotation reagents are petroleum sulphonate 899, sodium silicate depressant, fuel oil frother, fatty acid, and sulphuric acid. The pH is held at 5.6.

At the pellet plant, four ball mills regrind the concentrate, which then reports to an 85-ft-dia elutriator where silica content is reduced from about 9% to 6.3%. Elutriator underflow concentrate reports to a slurry agitator tank that distributes it to the six balling lines, each having disc filters, a concentrate surge bin, bentonite feed and mixing, a balling drum, and screens ahead of the 54-in. belt conveyor that moves green balls to the indurating machine.

The 35 windboxes in the machine function as follows: five updraft drying, three downdraft drying, two preheat zone, nine firing zone, three after-firing zone, nine first cooling, and four second cooling.

After cooling, pellets move via conveyor to a stacker and rail loadout for shipment to the Lake Michigan port of Escanaba.

Experimental planting is being carried out on tailings dikes to develop the plant types that will be used on tailings basins when the time comes. Among the trees tested to date are cottonwoods, jackpine, locust, and yellow willow.

As a 100%-Hanna-owned property, the Groveland operation will supply the company with pellets for sale for years to come at its current operating rate of 2 million tpy. □

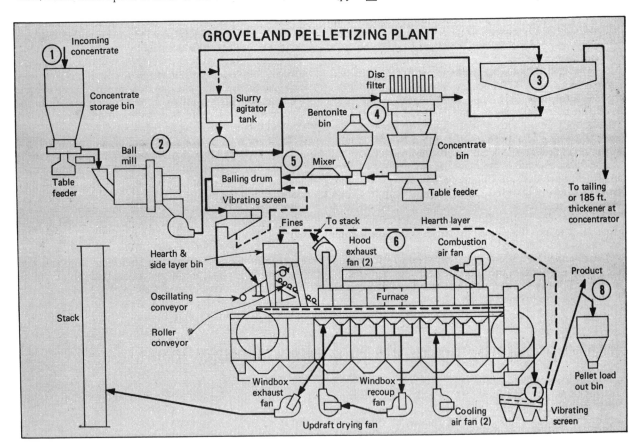

GROVELAND PELLETIZING PLANT

GROVELAND PELLETIZER

1. Regrind surge bins, capacity 1,000 lt.
2. Four ball mills; two are 12½ × 27-ft with 2,000 hp drive and two are 9 × 15-ft with 650 hp drive.
3. One elutriator, 85-ft dia; 20,000 spray nozzles.
4. Six disc filters.
5. Six balling drums.
6. Travelling grate indurating machine, 9 ft 10⅛-in. wide × 254 ft 10¼-in. long; 35 windboxes with total useable area of 2,258 sq ft. Furnace is fed from 54-in. belt and roller conveyor. Latter is equipped with 28 rolls, 5 ft 9/16-in. dia × 9 ft 8-in. long, of stainless steel. Each is individually driven by 2 hp motors. Process functions are updraft drying, down-draft drying, pre-heat, firing, after-firing and two stage cooling.
7. Pellet screen, 7 × 20 ft.
8. Stacker and load-out system; stockpile capacity at plant is 600,000 lt.

Production: 2.1-million ltpy 62.8% Fe and 6.90% SiO_2.

Direct reduction heats up in steelmaking

Jack Robert Miller, E/MJ special correspondent

NO LONGER A TECHNOLOGICAL CURIOSITY, direct reduction of iron ore is gathering momentum in international steelmaking operations. The growing acceptance and use of prereduced products was widely documented during the second Bucharest Seminar on Direct Reduction. The meeting, at the end of May, attracted 300 steelmakers from 35 countries.

The five-day gathering, organized by the Steel Committee of the UN Economic Commission for Europe and hosted by Rumania's Ministry of the Metallurgical Industry, included an inspection tour of the recently completed Special Steel Works at Trigoviste, approximately 50 mi northwest of Bucharest. Dimitru Nita, Manager of the Ministry of the Metallurgical Industry, served as president of the seminar.

How capacity will multiply

When the UN's first direct reduction (DR) meeting was held in Bucharest in September 1972, there were only seven sponge iron plants in operation and 15 others in various stages of startup or construction. As the second seminar opened 45 months later, the total number of DR plants in production had increased to 20, with 14 more scheduled for completion before the end of 1976. When these 34 facilities are on line, the world steel industry will be equipped with a total sponge iron capacity of over 12 million mt scattered in 13 countries.

Moreover, sponge iron producers will be able to meet global demands of up to 30 million mt from 50 plants in 19 nations by the end of the present decade. By 1985, prereduced iron capacity will be approximately 55 million tons at 90 operations in 35 countries around the world. (See accompanying table for more details.)

In presenting these figures, the author observed that the DR scenario for 1980 was *not* a forecast. The numbers are a tabulation of capabilities of prereduction facilities already in operation worldwide, plus the demonstrated capacities of plants now under construction and the planned outputs from well-publicized projects for which firm legal

and financial commitments have been made. Global DR production of 70 million to 100 million mt per year in 1990 and 250 million to 450 million mt in 2000 was projected in a paper by C. Scortea and A. Olteanu, of Rumania.

The considerable advance of DR during the past four years was reflected by the subjects covered in 48 technical papers presented and reviewed during the meetings. The main thrust of this year's discussions was the utility of the directly reduced product, in contrast to the 1972 focus on the technical and economic validity of the available processes. In the relatively short span of 45 months, questions about the feasibility and viability of DR practice had been resolved, and in a decisive number of cases, the resolutions were strongly positive.

Three-fourths of the papers were concerned with prereduced materials, their use in electric arc furnaces, and related factors such as reoxidation, storage, transport, mechanical properties, and weldability. These topics were presented during two full-day discussions chaired by Dr. A. Palozzi (Italy), Dr. Hans Graf (Federal Republic of Germany), and C. Rizescu (Rumania). During another session, directed by F. Fitzgerald (UK) and Paul Nilles (Belgium), participants discussed the design and operation of electric furnaces to facilitate processing of prereduced charges, and the use of directly reduced iron in installations other than electric arc furnaces. The fourth working period, with Jacques Astier (France) in the chair, reviewed seven documents dealing mostly with economic considerations.

In general, the papers reflected a high level of sophisticated knowledge of the R&D background of direct reduction development, and some awareness of practical operating conditions in the field. (See box.)

No less than 10 papers cited laboratory tests and/or field trials that supported the use of directly reduced iron in blast furnaces, foundry cupolas, induction furnaces, open hearths, and basic oxygen converters. In all cases, the documents reported that sponge iron can be used (melted) "without any great technical difficulties." The comparative advantages and disadvantages of such applications were described in considerable detail.

Can DR pump new flexibility into steel plants?

In the opinion of the author, such results are sufficiently encouraging to suggest the general use of sponge iron as a balancing iron-bearing material for the overall steel operation. The author proposed "for serious consideration by every iron and steel plant official and operator who is concerned about rising material prices, runaway construction costs, limited availability of natural gas, coking coal and steel scrap, that each integrated steelworks include a direct reduction unit as an important supplementary process facility. . . . The direct reduction plant will be not only an effective means of recovering waste oxide and waste gas values but also a supporting source of prereduced raw material at all conventional integrated plants with blast furnaces and oxygen-blown converters. This, of course, is in addition to the established use of sponge iron in small and large electric furnace steel plants, and as a feed to foundry cupolas."

Seminar delegates tour the No. 2 meltshop of Rumania's highly modern Special Steel Complex at Trigoviste.

Direct reduction plants and projects scheduled for operation

(capacities in thousand metric tons per year)

| | Yearend 1976 | | | Yearend 1980 | | | Yearend 1985 | | |
	No.*	Mt	%	No.*	Mt	%	No.*	Mt	%
North America.....	8	2,850	23.3	10	4,250	14.1	13	6,400	11.7
South America	17	5,750	46.9	22	11,275	37.3	32	17,840	32.4
Western Europe...	2	390	3.2	4	1,790	5.9	8	4,830	8.8
Eastern Europe ...	—	—	—	1	5,000	16.5	4	6,500	11.8
Asia....................	4	2,250	18.4	4	2,250	7.4	12	4,480	8.2
Africa.................	2	870	7.2	3	1,120	3.7	7	3,760	6.8
Middle East	—	—	—	5	4,430	14.7	11	9,630	17.5
Oceania..............	1	120	1.0	1	120	0.4	3	1,560	2.8
Total...............	34	12,205	100.0	50	30,235	100.0	90	55,000	100.0

* = Number of plants. Source: J. R. Miller, June 20, 1976.

The old and new at Trigoviste

Approximately 200 of the seminar participants toured the Special Steel Complex at Trigoviste on May 27. The city, which dates back to the 14th century, is described as "one of the oldest towns of Rumania," but the steelworks now in operation is so recent that it is described by less than 10 lines in the 1974 edition of *Iron and Steel Works of the World.* Construction began in 1971 and the plant has been put into production progressively since 1974.

Output in 1975 was approximately 350,000 mt of medium and large forgings, high quality bars and sections, and alloy steel sheet and strip, including grain-oriented silicon sheets. Production this year is expected to reach 600,000 mt, and a 1-million-mtpy output is planned before 1980. Stainless steel operations, with an initial annual capacity of 30,000 mt, are scheduled to start in 1977 and later increase to 120,000 mtpy.

The main electric furnace shop (No. 2) includes five melting units: four 50-ton furnaces powered from 25-mva and 30-mva transformers and one 100-ton furnace connected to a 50-mva source. The meltshop and crane runway designs are very heavy and are obviously planned to accommodate larger melting units in the future. The layout of numerous bins for raw materials suggests that the use of directly reduced iron is included in such plans.

Like the forging and rolling mill departments, the structures and equipment of the steel meltshop are installed according to modern concepts of steel plant layout and design. Most of the facilities have been supplied from socialist countries (USSR, Czechoslovakia, People's Republic of Germany), but many units from Western European countries (Sweden, Federal Republic of Germany, and Italy) were also in evidence. One of the tour guides stated, in reply to a question, that the Trigoviste Works had already cost 4 billion leis—about $500 million at the official exchange rate, if his remark was correct.

At the closing session on May 28, the delegates approved a recommendation that the UN sponsors of the seminar prepare a consolidated report based on the papers and discussions at the meeting. The interest of the steel industry in the general use of prereduced materials in iron- and steelmaking is now so great that it was further proposed that the report be published in English, French, and Russian—the three working languages of the Economic Commission for Europe—for widespread distribution. □

Direct reduction of iron ore gathers strength in Brazil

Jack Robert Miller, Iron and steel consultant

THE CAPACITY OF BRAZIL'S STEEL INDUSTRY, which produced 5.4 million mt of raw steel ingots in 1970 and 7.5 million mt in 1974, is programmed to reach 22.4 million mt in 1980 and 32.0 million mt in 1985. Ironmaking capabilities in 1980 and 1985 are projected at 15.3 million and 23.8 million mt, respectively. According to official government plans, the iron producing installations are to include direct reduction (DR) facilities that will provide 1.25 million mt in 1980 and 1.6 million mt in 1985. In actuality, each of these DR capacity projections will be exceeded.

Two DR plants are already being operated, by Usiba in Bahia and by Piratini at Charqueadas. Together, they produced approximately 140,000 mt of sponge iron in 1974. Each plant produced at about half the rated capacity, which is 200,000 mtpy at the Usiba HyL unit and 60,000 mtpy at Piratini's SL/RN kiln. For 1975, sponge iron production at the two plants is likely to be around 225,000 mt, or better than 80% of the combined design capacity.

Sponge iron production in Brazil will rise sharply after mid-1976. Scheduled for startup in 1976 are two 350,000-mtpy Purofer plants now under construction for Consigua near Rio de Janeiro and for Jose Mendez Junior at Juiz de Fora, about 80 km north of Rio. In addition, a 400,000-mtpy Midrex plant will be put onstream in 1977 by Ikosa (Fiel-Korf) at Sao Jose dos Campos, 50 km east of Sao Paulo. These plants will push the country's installed DR capacity well beyond the 1.25 million mt called for by the National Steel Industry plan for 1980.

Within the full 1975-1985 time frame, a number of additional direct reduction projects are likely to materialize. Midrex reports inquiries and negotiations in Brazil that are expected to result in capacity additions of no less than 8 million mt by 1985. HyL confirms new DR capacity of the same magnitude based on its contacts and discussions in Brazil. Even if there is full overlapping in these estimates, it is evident that a 1.6-million-mt projection for sponge iron capacity in Brazil by 1985 is extremely conservative. The accompanying table and map draw a more realistic picture of the 1975-1985 DR scenario for Brazil.

The information in Table 1 is not complete. Several proposed undertakings have not been entered and some anticipated capacities have been altered, on the basis of personal judgment after discussions with sponsors, planning authorities in Brazil, and DR plant suppliers and operators. Furthermore a number of the "study" and "planned" entries will certainly be subjected to revision.

Gaseous reduction processes dominate the listings in Table 1, but there is a very definite probability that much of the reduction fuel will be derived from coal. Both coal and oil gasification are to be used. For the Usiminas, Cosipa, and CSN projects, cleaned coke oven gas is to be the primary reducing medium. Of course, where natural gas is readily available (Usiba and Siderbras), it will probably be the primary fuel. Piratini and Sta. Catarina are situated near domestic coal sources. There will undoubtedly be opportunities for use of all currently available DR processes, and some new suppliers may be expected to enter the field soon.

To translate the anticipated capacities in Table 1 into an acceptable forecast for direct reduction production in Brazil in 1980 and 1985, reasonable probabilities may be assigned to each of the five groups listed. Personal on-site observations during mid-1975 suggest that the likelihood of realization is 100% for the operating plants and projects under construction (A and B); 80% for the programmed installations (C); and 40% for the facilities under study and in early planning stages (D and E). From this evaluation, Brazilian DR capacity can be estimated at 280,000 mt in 1975; 2.5 million mt in 1980, and 6.5 million mt in 1985. On the basis of these capacities, I expect sponge iron production in Brazil to be 2.3 million mt in 1980 and 5.5 million mt in 1985. □

Iron ore: direct reduction sites

(see table)

Table 1—Brazilian direct reduction capacity, actual and projected

(000 mtpy)

Company	(A) Operating 1973-1974	(B) Construction 1976-1977	(C) Programmed 1976-1980	(D) Under study 1976-1982	(E) Planned 1976-1985	Total
1. Acesita	–	–	–	400	–	400
2. Anhanguera	–	–	–	400	–	400
3. Cofavi	–	–	400	–	–	400
4. Consigua	–	350	–	–	–	350
5. Cosipa	–	–	–	800	–	800
6. CSN	–	–	–	–	800	800
7. Eldorado	–	–	–	–	400	400
8. Ikosa	–	400	–	400	–	800
9. Jose Mendez Jr.	–	350	–	–	–	350
10. Mannesmann	–	–	–	400	–	400
11. Piratini	60	–	240	–	–	300
12. Siderbras	–	–	–	–	2,000	2,000
13. Sidersol	–	–	–	400	–	400
14. Sta. Caterina	–	–	–	–	2,000	2,000
15. Talsa	–	–	–	400	–	400
16. Usiba	220	–	400	–	–	620
17. Usiminas	–	–	400	–	1,600	2,000
18. Villares	–	–	–	400	–	400
Totals	**280**	**1,100**	**1,440**	**3,200**	**7,200**	**13,220**

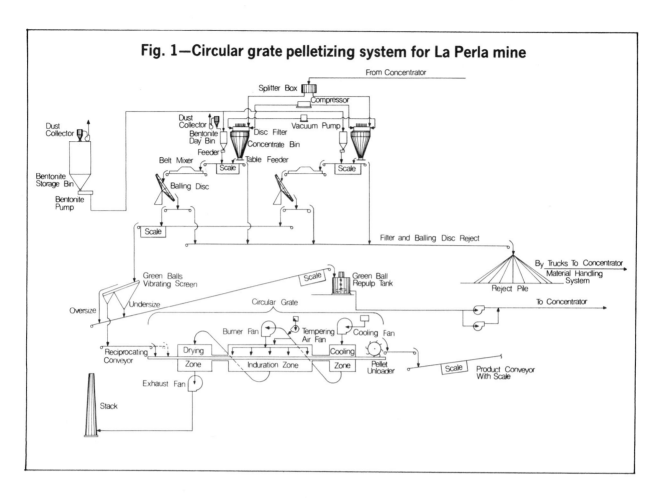

Fig. 1—Circular grate pelletizing system for La Perla mine

Circular grate pelletizing of iron ore is commercial success at Altos Hornos

S. S. Sephton, assistant division vice president and technical manager, Arthur G. McKee & Co.

THE FIRST COMMERCIAL CIRCULAR GRATE PLANT for pelletizing iron ore concentrates is successfully producing at the La Perla mine of Altos Hornos de Mexico and has heightened industry interest in this new process. Operating at rates of more than 100 tph, the La Perla plant has demonstrated the validity of claims respecting low operating costs and high product quality. It has reinforced the confidence with which a circular grate installation can be sized to produce guaranteed tonnages of quality product at lower fuel, power, maintenance, and labor requirements than either the straight grate or grate kiln systems.

The La Perla plant incorporates a quite conventional filtering-balling circuit (Fig. 1). Incoming concentrates are fed through a splitter box to two disc filters, and filter cake is then mixed with bentonite and fed to two 18-ft-dia balling discs. Green balls are screened, with the on-size material dropping onto a reciprocating conveyor and the off-size material being recycled back into the process.

Reciprocating conveyors are used as a feed mechanism in most pellet plants employing a wide grate. However, the circular grate posed a special problem, because the inner circumference requires fewer green balls than the outer circumference to obtain a uniform bed depth of green balls. The problem was overcome by modifying the hy-

draulic unit that moves the reciprocating conveyor (Fig. 2). This unit for feeding green balls onto the grate is a conveyor-carrier assembly on a wheeled track. The entire unit is moved forward and then retracted by a hydraulic ram.

The forward stroke of the conveyor carriage matches the actual speed of the conveyor, preventing any green balls from being deposited on the grate during the forward stroke. On the retracting stroke, green balls are discharged to the grate, and by gradually decelerating the retracting stroke, a decreasing amount of green balls is deposited on the inner portion of the grate. The speed of the conveyor and ram and the position and duration of the ram stop at the end of each stroke are fully adjustable. This arrangement permits automatic deposition of a perfectly level bed on the grate.

The total amount of green balls fed to the grate is weighed, and the grate speed is adjusted automatically to maintain a set bed height. Mean diameter of the grate is 60 ft, and the grate is 9 ft wide.

How circular grate processing works

Processing green balls into fired pellets of high quality requires close control of airflow time and airflow temperature. Processing should also be accomplished with a minimum expenditure of manpower, electrical energy, fuel, and spare parts, and a minimum of downtime.

At the La Perla plant, an 8-in. bed of green balls is placed on top of a 2-in. hearth layer. Drying, preheating, indurating, recuperation, and cooling are accomplished in one pass around the grate. The push-pull system of airflow used at La Perla is shown in Fig. 3.

After firing, pellets are cooled by a forced-draft fan that takes outside ambient air and forces it downward through the hot pellet bed. The cooling air strips heat from the hot pellets, rising in temperature to more than 1,000°F. The air is under sufficient pressure to force it to the recuperation, ignition, and preheat zones through a large diameter duct. The temperature is then further raised to approximately 2,400°F for induration zone processing. The hot process gases are induced through the bed of dry green balls, through a second large-diameter duct, and then through the drying zone by an induced-draft fan. A 100-hp hot fan is used to divert some of the hot gases recuperated from the cooling zone, which are used in the North American hot air burners along with No. 6 fuel oil and atomizing steam.

The two main process fans provide a simple but very effective control over process air. The static pressure control of the induced-draft fan is set to maintain a constant pressure drop across the drying zone. The air moves via duct work from the drying zone to the ignition zone, where a pressure sensor picks up any variation in pressure caused by modification of the induced-draft fan louvers. The pressure sensor is also a controller-transmitter set to maintain the ignition zone at atmospheric pressure. If pressure in the ignition zone changes from atmospheric, the ignition zone pressure controller actuates the inlet louvers of the forced-draft fan to maintain a correct balance between the two fans.

Temperatures of the preheat and ignition zones are preprogrammed and automatically maintained by control over multiple burners to give an optimum time-temperature profile.

A bucket unloader removes the cooled pellets from the grate (Fig. 4). The buckets are nominally the width of the grate bed and travel through a cam track to scoop up a uniform depth of product. The unloader is equipped with a lift mechanism that allows the depth of the hearth layer to be varied. In normal operation, a hearth layer of fired pellets is left to cover the grate, but the unloader can be lowered to remove the hearth layer for maintenance or lifted out of the bed to recycle the full pellet bed under idling conditions. A new hearth layer is formed by simple delivery of green balls to the grate. After one revolution or process cycle, the bucket unloader is lifted approximately 2 in. off the grate, and the fired pellets remain on the grate to form the new hearth layer. Pellets discharge from the unloader onto a variable-speed belt conveyor synchronized to produce a uniform belt load from the bucket surges.

The circular grate system minimizes operating expense, because costs of fuel, power, manpower, and maintenance are low.

How the circular grate saves money

Four main factors contribute to lower fuel consumption in the circular grate system than in straight grate or grate kiln systems. First, only one exhaust stack is required. The temperature and volume of exit gases in the circular grate system are about the same as those of the drying exhaust gases in grate kiln and straight grate systems for compa-

Fig. 2—Reciprocating conveyor has been adapted to feed green balls evenly onto circular grate pelletizing bed.

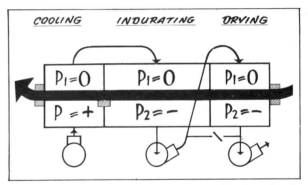

Fig. 3—Schematic of push-pull airflow shows location of main fans and areas of positive, zero, and negative pressure.

Fig. 4—Bucket unloader discharges La Perla grate. Bucket rides up cam tracks and unloads after topping the curvature.

Fig. 5—This 1-tph pilot plant proved circular grate's technical feasibility prior to construction of the La Perla plant.

rable tonnages. However, both the grate kiln and straight grate systems have a second exhaust stack that runs at a higher exit temperature, with consequent waste of heat units.

Second, the circular grate has no return strand, and the elimination of this radiating surface further reduces heat losses.

Third, for units of comparative capacity, the grate kiln has a proportionately larger area of hot radiating surface. The circular grate has the smallest area, and the straight grate falls somewhere in between.

Fourth, water seals and labyrinth-type, over-bed seals prevent all leakage into and out of the circular grate, ensuring a minimal thermal loss, a dust-and-gas-free envi-

ronment, and uniform pellet quality.

The low power requirements anticipated for circular-grate pelletizing have been fully proven at the La Perla plant. The power requirement for the circular grate is 10.8 kwh per mt of product. For the shaft furnace, straight grate, and grate kiln, power requirements are 40, 25, and 20 kwh per mt, respectively. The remarkable power saving with the circular grate is achieved by the fans, which operate at low static pressures and comparatively low temperatures.

Static pressure in a pelletizing system is approximately proportional to the depth of the pellet bed. The shallower, wider bed of the circular grate system results in a substantially lower pressure drop than for either a straight grate or the cooler of a grate kiln. The process air, time, and temperature requirements per ton of pellets are the same, but gas velocity is reduced in proportion to the active grate area. The pressure drop across the bed is reduced by an amount equal to the square of the velocity ratio. The shallow bed and low air velocities of the circular grate result in pressure drops of about 8 in. for each pass through the pellet bed—compared with 20 in. for the straight grate—with proportionate power savings.

The compact arrangement of the circular grate, with the feed and discharge points located next to each other, permits visual monitoring of the area from the control room, reducing manpower requirements. In addition, only one piece of equipment is operating instead of the three pieces of the grate kiln cooler, and no hearth layer screening and recycle system is required, as on the straight grate—for a further reduction in operating personnel.

While it is too early in the operating life of the first circular grate to be definitive about maintenance costs; indications are that they could be as low as half the maintenance costs of other pelletizing systems. Reasons for the lower costs include:

- Less heat and abrasion.
- One point of pellet discharge.
- Stationary bed of pellets.
- Moving parts remote from heat.
- Grate supported by water-cooled struts.

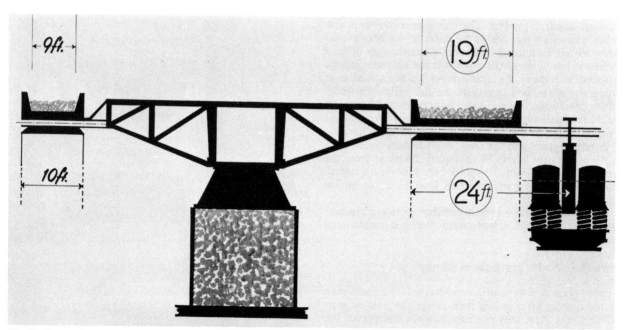

Fig. 6—Composite schematic of the circular grate shows how a small machine of the type installed at La Perla without peripheral support of the grate (left) could be scaled up to 1 to 4 million tpy of capacity by widening the overall diameter of the machine, widening the grate, and adding a track around the outside circumference of the grate to increase structural support.

The evolution of pelletizing systems

Blast furnaces producing basic pig iron are the main source of supply for continually increasing worldwide steel demand. The use of pelletized iron ore concentrates as blast furnace feed began 20 years ago, and the improvements they yielded in blast furnace productivity and reduced operating costs encouraged rapid development of the pelletizing process. Pellets are now being made from high grade ores as well as from various iron ore concentrates.

The trend toward pelletizing was forced on iron ore producers by the gradually diminishing supply of high grade ores and the corresponding need to beneficiate lower grade ores. Beneficiation produces a concentrate that is usually between 70% and 100% minus 325 mesh in size—too fine for direct charging into a blast furnace and also a cause of problems in sintering. Pelletizing plants solve this problem by converting the finely ground concentrates to nominal ½-in.-dia, heat-hardened pellets that are most suitable for subsequent smelting in a blast furnace.

Three pelletizing systems account for most oxide pellets produced today: the shaft furnace, the straight grate, and the grate kiln.

The shaft furnace can be considered the first generation of pelletizing equipment. A typical furnace is of simple construction, about 7 ft x 21 ft, open at the top, refractory lined, and about 60 ft high. A pantographic feeder distributes unfired pellets evenly across the top

of the furnace. Combustion air at 2,400°F is introduced into the furnace via a bustle pipe from combustion chambers on each side of the furnace. Cooling air introduced at the bottom of the furnace strips the sensible heat from the pellets as they descend, and the heated air then joins the hot air entering from the bustle pipe.

This system is very economical in heat recovery and capital costs but has certain major disadvantages. Pellets are not uniformly treated because of gas stratification in the deep bed. Of the two major types of iron ore—magnetite and hematite—only magnetite can be successfully treated. Magnetite oxidizes to hematite in an exothermic reaction. With hematite, this exothermic reaction does not occur, so all heat must be externally introduced. Furthermore, because of the shaft furnace configuration, it is very difficult to subject the total cross section of the furnace to the full heat requirement in a uniform manner.

The development of straight grate pelletizing was an offshoot of sintering technology. The process treats the pellet burden more uniformly and can successfully process all types of iron ores and concentrates.

The rotary kiln of the cement industry served as the basis for the grate kiln system.

Each of the three systems has advantages. But developers of the circular grate feel that until its advent, there was no one system that could incorporate the advantages of all three.

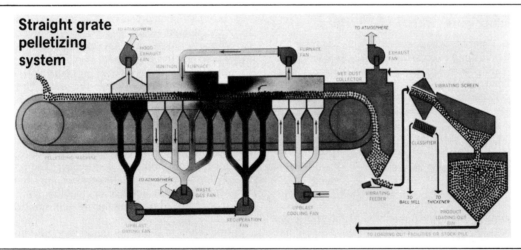

Straight grate pelletizing system

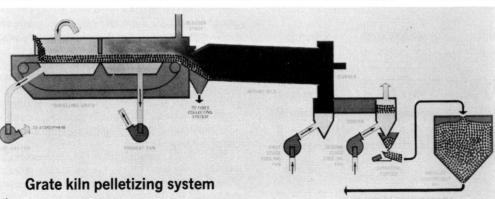

Grate kiln pelletizing system

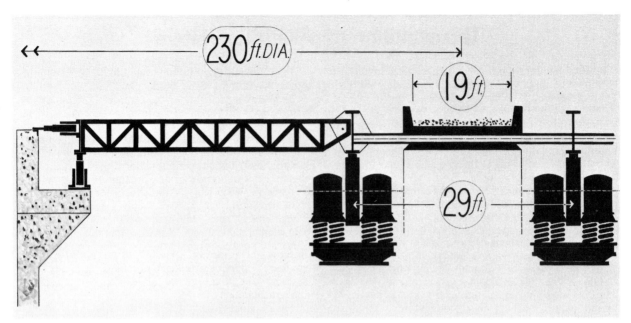

Fig. 7—Expansion of the circular grate to a maximum of 8-million-tpy capacity may be achieved by adding support to the grate both inside and outside the grate periphery. A machined, 72-ft-dia pedestal face is proposed to ensure concentricity.

- Maximum use of refractory.
- Minimum number of moving parts.

In comparison with North American pellet plants now producing between 2 and 3 million tons of product annually, the circular grate should save about $1 million per year in operating costs.

Development for large-capacity operations

The circular grate has been proven on a pilot scale at 1 tph (Fig. 5), and the first commercial plant is rated in excess of 100 tph. Basic designs for larger machines have been completed. The largest is designed to produce 8 million tpy of pellets from a magnetite feed.

Three basic designs have been developed for incremental machine sizes, to maintain a minimum capital cost from the smallest to the largest production size. Each design is a logical outgrowth of the preceding size, with a minimum of changes. All designs retain the three principal features contributing to the success of the circular grate: water seals, a center pedestal, and water-cooled grate-support structure.

The first basic design, which was used in the pilot plant and at La Perla, is a table feeder configuration without any peripheral support. This simple concept will be used for plants producing up to 1 million tpy. Using this principle, it is now possible to build mini-pelletizing plants that previously would not have been economical.

For plants in the 1-million-tpy to 4½-million-tpy range, a set of outside support rollers is added. The rollers are remote from the heat and similar to those used on deep-bed sinter coolers for many years. The minimal design changes from the smaller to the larger machine are illustrated in the composite drawing of two machines in Fig. 6. Further expansion to the maximum 8-million-tpy capacity is shown in Fig. 7. In this design, support rollers have been added both inside and outside the grate. The machine is connected to the center pedestal, which will have a 72-ft-dia machined face to ensure concentricity.

Processing of pellets on a circular grate is similar to processing on a straight grate in that the feed must pass through various temperature zones and be subjected to air and gas flows to produce a good pellet. The push-pull airflow system is easy to understand and easy to operate. As an alternative to this method, the cooling fan may be used in a more conventional manner to cool the pellets by updraft.

Introduction of a hot fan under the ignition zone to assist in transfer of pressure between the forced-draft fan and induced-draft fan is shown in Fig. 8. This system, which is similar to the straight grate system, would allow more exact control over the various zones, and with each zone close to atmospheric pressure, it would permit elimination of over-bed seals between the processing zones. It is therefore possible for the circular grate to have the same processing times and airflow directions as the straight grate and yet use drastically less power because the bed is shallower and wider. The mechanical concept of a water-cooled structure permits use of a wider grate without danger of sagging.

The idea of using a circular grate for metallurgical processing is not new. Nor is the pelletizing process itself new. However, application of sound basic engineering principles and mechanical innovations to the circular grate has made a fourth-generation pelletizing plant available to the iron ore industry. □

Fig. 8—Alternate airflow system introduces updraft fan for cooling and a hot fan under the pellet ignition zone.

Non-polluting autogenous desulphurizing process recovers metals, elemental sulphur

Telfer E. Norman, president, Norman Research Inc.

CAREFULLY CONTROLLED REACTION of iron, nickel, and copper sulphide concentrates at elevated temperatures in the presence of steam-oxygen will convert contained metals into their respective oxides and liberate all contained sulphur in the elemental form. This technique will avoid the air pollution problems caused by sulphur dioxide production in conventional smelting. The metallic oxides can be reduced by one or more of the conventional reduction processes as a prelude to metals recovery. Elemental sulphur, produced in the gaseous state, may be collected as a liquid or solid by cooling and condensation. The overall reactions are exothermic and may be carried out autogenously in a suitably designed reactor.

Process pluses include clean air, cheap energy

The autogenous desulphurization process offers a number of advantages for treating chalcopyrite, pyrrhotite, pyrite, and other copper-, nickel-, or iron-bearing sulphide concentrates.

The process recovers sulphur in the elemental form, with low energy requirements. The present availability of low-cost oxygen and the fact that most or all of the steam used in the process can be generated in a combined waste-heat boiler and sulphur condenser make recovery of the sulphur from sulphide concentrates both economically and environmentally attractive.

The oxide product of autogenous desulphurizing can readily be smelted or otherwise reduced in a non-polluting process to produce copper or nickel and possibly iron oxide as a byproduct. For example, after treatment in the desulphurizing reactor, chalcopyrite concentrates could be processed in an electric or fuel-fired reduction furnace to produce anode grade copper containing any precious metal values present in the original concentrate. Alternately, the oxidized concentrates would lend themselves well to copper recovery in a sulphuric acid leach-electrowinning circuit, or in one or more of the new processes for recovering copper from roasted copper concentrates.

For pyrite and pyrrhotite concentrates, which have had limited commercial value to date, the desulphurization process offers an economical means of producing both elemental sulphur and high-grade iron oxide. Presumably, much of the pyrite and pyrrhotite now discarded in tailings from many ore concentrating operations could be concentrated and treated profitably in the desulphurizing process. The pyrite recovered from cleaning high-sulphur coal might also be treated for sulphur and iron recovery by this method.

Search for pollution-free process began in 1972

The autogenous desulphurizing process is an outgrowth of a search started by the author in 1972 for a copper concentrate smelting process that would liberate all of the contained sulphur in sulphide concentrates as elemental sulphur, thus eliminating the air pollution problems of conventional smelting. To conduct a search of this type, it appeared advisable to start with thermochemical and thermodynamic studies of the many known chemical reactions

that occur during roasting and smelting of sulphide concentrates of iron, copper, and nickel. The use of oxygen or oxygen-enriched air to achieve the desired reaction temperatures, thermal balances, and low fuel costs also appeared to have considerable promise.

In 1936, a similar approach had been used to demonstrate the technical and economic feasibility of smelting copper concentrates autogenously with oxygen or oxygen-enriched air to produce molten matte, slag, and a rich SO_2 gas.[1] This process, as further developed by Inco, Outokumpu, and others, has withstood the test of time—demonstrating the reliability of the data and calculations used in the 1936 paper. It appeared that a similar approach might lead to a process or processes in which all of the sulphur in copper-iron sulphide concentrates would be liberated as elemental sulphur rather than as sulphur dioxide.

A search of the literature on processes to produce elemental sulphur from sulphide ores or concentrates unearthed some old but pertinent information. Between 1892 and 1897, C. W. Stickney[2,3] obtained three US patents on a method of producing elemental sulphur from pyritic ores by reacting them with a steam-air mixture and maintaining the reaction temperature at the required "red heat" by burning carbonaceous or hydrocarbon fuel in the reaction chamber. While there was little, if any, commercial production of sulphur by the Stickney process, it did demonstrate as early as 1892 that steam and oxygen from air, when suitably proportioned, would react with "red-hot" iron sulphides to produce elemental sulphur.

From 1911 to 1914, W. A. Hall developed a roasting process that was very similar to Stickney's but that called for more specific operating conditions.[4] Hall obtained several patents covering his roasting process,[5] which was tested on a pilot-plant scale by H. F. Wierum[6] at the Balaklala smelter in California in 1914. In spite of many handicaps during the few months of testing, Wierum ably demonstrated that by suitably proportioning a mixture of air, fuel, and steam in a McDougall multi-hearth roasting furnace, a pyritic ore could be desulphurized to produce an iron oxide calcine and an effluent gas in which practically all of the sulphur was in elemental form. Wierum's tests, discontinued when the smelter was shut down in 1914, were apparently never resumed.

The fact that steam-oxygen mixtures will react at significantly rapid rates with metal sulphides, especially iron sulphide, to produce metal oxides and elemental sulphur, appeared to be well confirmed by Stickney's, Hall's, and Wierum's tests. The basic reactions are as follows:

$$2FeS + 2H_2O = 2FeO + 2H_2S \qquad (A)$$
$$FeS + 1\tfrac{1}{2}O_2 = FeO + SO_2 \qquad (B)$$
$$2H_2S + SO_2 = 2H_2O + 1\tfrac{1}{2}S_2 \qquad (C)$$

In summary,

$$3FeS + 1\tfrac{1}{2}O_2 + 2H_2O = 3FeO + 1\tfrac{1}{2}S_2 + 2H_2O \qquad (D)$$

A number of additional reactions occur, such as the reaction of FeO with O_2 to form Fe_3O_4 and Fe_2O_3 in a roasting operation, or the reaction of FeO with SiO_2 flux to form molten slag in the smelting operation.

While H_2O reacts with FeS to produce H_2S as an inter-

Fig. 1—Flowsheet of non-polluting autogenous desulphurization process

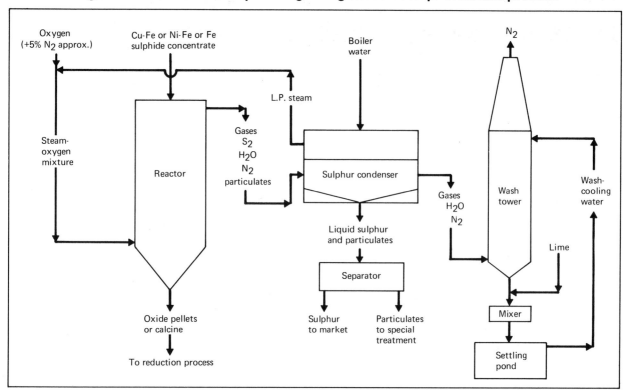

mediate product, in the final result (equation D) there is no permanent consumption of H_2O. However, tests performed by the author have confirmed that the presence of H_2O is necessary for the reactions to proceed at a significantly rapid rate. The reaction kinetics are such that the amount or concentration of H_2O should be substantially greater than that indicated by the stoichiometric proportions in equation (D).

In view of the results obtained by Stickney, Hall, and Wierum, together with the author's thermochemical and heat balance calculations, it was decided to pursue the steam-oxygen route in the search for a smelting process that would liberate the sulphur in sulphide concentrates in the elemental form.

Heat balance studies indicated that it would be more practical and economical to use oxygen of about 95% purity rather than air as the source of oxygen.

The first approach investigated—smelting the concentrates to molten matte and slag, followed by converting the matte to blister copper—has shown considerable promise. This process of smelting to molten products is not autogenous and requires a carbonaceous fuel in addition to the steam-oxygen mixture. However, the amount of fuel required is relatively small, and total cost of fuel plus oxygen is estimated to be less than that for conventional reverberatory smelting of copper concentrates. Various means of carrying out this smelting process commercially are described in a recently issued US patent specification.[7]

To investigate this fuel-steam-oxygen smelting process experimentally, a small furnace consisting of a smelting shaft set on an enclosed gas-tight forehearth was constructed using space and facilities provided by the Colorado School of Mines Research Institute (CSMRI), in Golden, Colo.

Smelting experiments in this furnace demonstrated that it was possible to carry out complete desulphurization of

sulphide concentrates autogenously by reacting the concentrates in their solid state with a steam-oxygen mixture. This approach appeared to offer several advantages. Specifically, it could avoid conversion of a copper-iron matte to copper and slag—a rather expensive and environmentally troublesome step in conventional copper smelting. The technique could also avoid the dilution by carbon dioxide of both the reacting gases and exit gases in the desulphurizing reactor—simplifying the recovery of elemental sulphur in the exit gas. The exit gas consists principally of elemental sulphur vapor and water vapor, both of which can be condensed, leaving only a small amount of nitrogen to be discharged to the atmosphere.

Furthermore, since the process is autogenous, its energy requirements are low, consisting mainly of the electric energy required to produce tonnage oxygen for the process. The accompanying flowsheet (Fig. 1) shows the essential parts of the autogenous desulphurizing process, as applied to typical iron, copper, or nickel sulphide concentrates.

Testing the autogenous desulphurizing process

In the experimental refractory-lined vertical-shaft type furnace, the shaft, or reaction chamber, was 22 in. high and the diameter of the inside of the refractory lining was 9 in. This served as a batch-type stationary bed reactor. A preheating chamber with a natural gas burner was attached to the bottom of the shaft, separated from it by a steel mesh screen to retain a bed of concentrate briquettes or pellets in the shaft and permit entry and upward flow of the steam-oxygen mixture into the bed. Effluent gases from the top of the bed were carried by a short flue at the top of the shaft to a sampling station, then on to a water-spray gas washer. An electrically heated boiler capable of generating steam at constant and predetermined rates was

Table 1—Composition of sulphide concentrates studied in heat balances

	Chalcopyrite	Pyrite	Pyrrhotite
Fe	28	46.0	60.0
S	30	51.3	37.5
Cu	25	–	–
SiO_2	10	2.0	2.0
CaO*	3	–	–
Al_2O_3	2	0.7	0.5
Combined H_2O	2	–	–
Totals	100	100.0	100.0
Moisture	2	2.0	2.0

* All basic oxides are calculated as CaO.

used to supply process steam for the tests. The steam was mixed with a regulated flow of oxygen from oxygen cylinders, and the mixture was introduced into the preheat chamber. There it was preheated to about 500°C by residual heat from the refractory lining prior to its entry into the bottom of the bed of concentrates.

To determine the preheat temperatures prior to each test and the reaction temperatures in the bed of concentrates during the progress of each test, a thermocouple was inserted through the sidewall of the shaft to measure the temperature of the bed at a point about midway between the top and bottom of the shaft.

For these tests it would have been preferable to use a descending bed reactor with continuous feed and discharge. However, the more expensive and complicated installation could not be practically justified for initial tests.

The tests were run on a chalcopyrite flotation concentrate having a composition approximately the same as that listed under "chalcopyrite" in Table 1. The concentrate was fashioned into small briquettes about 1 x 1 x ½ in., using a lignone binder to form a relatively hard, dense briquette. (In retrospect, it probably would have been preferable to pelletize this concentrate to provide a more porous and somewhat smaller agglomerate.)

For each test run, the preheat chamber and shaft of the furnace were preheated to about 550°C with the gas burner. The gas burner was then shut off, the shaft was charged to its full height with about 40 lb of the concentrate briquettes, and the flow of steam-oxygen mix into the furnace was started. Average flow rate of the mixture into the bed of briquettes was about 3 scfm, and oxygen content of the mixture ranged from 24% down to 18% by volume in the tests, with the 18% mixture yielding the best results. It was judged that for a larger furnace, where the proportion of heat loss to the walls would be substantially less, a steam-oxygen mixture containing about 15% by volume of oxygen (equivalent to 23% by weight) would be about right.

Ignition of the reaction between the steam-oxygen mixture and the green briquettes occurred almost immediately at the start of each test run. The temperature at the thermocouple placed midway between the top and bottom of the column of briquettes rose steadily for the first 3½ hr of the test period to a maximum of 885°C, then began to drop slowly as the heat generating reactions progressed upward toward the top of the bed. The exit gases contained only elemental sulphur and water vapor for the first 2 hr of each 5-hr test. No SO_2 or H_2S odor could be detected in these gases during the first 2 hr. The wash water

from the gas washer was heavily laden with particles and agglomerates of bright yellow sulphur.

During the third hour of the test some sulphur dioxide odor could be detected in the exit gases as the reaction zone progressed toward the top of the shaft. The sulphur dioxide odor increased during the fourth and fifth hour of the 5-hr test.

The changes in exit gas composition can be explained on the basis of reaction kinetics. As the steam-oxygen mixture enters the column of briquettes at the bottom of the bed, the oxygen reacts rapidly with any sulphides present to form sulphur dioxide. The water reacts more slowly to form hydrogen sulphide. When the sulphur dioxide rises through a high column of sulphide briquettes, it is reduced by the hydrogen sulphide and to some extent by iron sulphide to form elemental sulphur. However, when the column of sulphide briquettes is short, as toward the end of the test period, the hydrogen sulphide formed is insufficient to reduce all of the sulphur dioxide. For this reason, sulphur dioxide appears in the exit gases.

The tests indicate that a countercurrent flow of gases and solids is necessary in the reactor, and that the contact time between gases and solids should be sufficient to permit a series of reactions to occur, whether in sequence or concurrently.

The oxidized briquettes formed during the 5-hr runs showed considerable evidence of sintering together, especially near the bottom of the shaft, where their temperature probably exceeded the maximum of 885°C indicated at the thermocouple location. In a continuous moving-bed reactor, where oxidation of the briquettes or pellets would occur more slowly and in less concentrated reaction zones, the sintering effect probably would not occur.

Many of the oxidized briquettes contained a core of magnetic sulphides (probably iron sulphide and copper sulphide). A retention time longer than the 5 hr in the test reactor appeared to be needed for complete oxidation of the briquettes. If ½-in. pellets had been used in place of the larger and rather dense briquettes, complete desulphurization and oxidation of the pellets might have occurred with a 5-hr retention time. However, for a commercial moving-bed reactor, a retention time of at least 8 hr should probably be planned to obtain complete desulphurization and oxidation of the pellets.

While total desulphurization was not obtained in the 5-hr tests, selective sampling of the oxidized portions of the briquettes indicated that sulphide-sulphur contents could readily be reduced from their original value of about 30% down to less than 1% and that sulphate sulphur could also be held below 1% by keeping the maximum reaction temperature above 850°C. Additional tests in a moving-bed reactor would be very helpful in establishing the required operating parameters.

The oxidized portions of the briquettes contained mostly Fe_2O_3 and CuO, though some magnetic iron oxide (Fe_3O_4) and some red copper oxide (Cu_2O) were present. However, for thermochemical calculations, it appears safe to assume that the sulphide concentrates will oxidize completely to Fe_2O_3 and CuO.

Reactor calls for counterflow of solids, gases

In designing the reactor for autogenous desulphurization, it is necessary to plan for counterflow of solids and gases. Counterflow produces complete desulphurization of the solids and permits the reactor to operate with high thermal efficiency, since incoming solids are preheated by heat exchange with exit gases, and outgoing solids preheat the steam-oxygen mixture prior to its reaction with the sulphides.

For the typical chalcopyrite concentrate listed in Table 1, the heat of reaction provides about 1 million Btu per net ton of solid charge. Experience with iron ore pellet-hardening furnaces indicates that this amount should be ample to heat the charge up to the desired temperatures, though the comparison is not strictly parallel since autogenous desulphurization also involves heating up relatively large amounts of steam to these same temperatures.

However, heat balance studies indicate that with counterflow of solids and gases, typical chalcopyrite, pyrite, and pyrrhotite concentrates can all be desulphurized autogenously without any extraneous fuel. In addition, most and possibly all of the process steam required can be produced from the heat in exit gases from the reactor, although an auxiliary steam boiler would be required at least for startup purposes.

With minor modifications, the furnace designs for hardening or prereduction of iron ore pellets appear well suited for commercial desulphurization of sulphide concentrates. Suitable designs include several of the vertical-shaft type and also probably the rotary-kiln type furnaces, which normally require feed in pelletized form. There is also a good possibility that multistage, fluid bed roasters would work well on certain concentrates fed to the reactor as a thickened slurry or as a partially dried powder.

A fluid bed reactor generally operates in closed circuit with one or more hot cyclones, which would be necessary in autogenous desulphurization to prevent excessive carryover of suspended particulates into the combination waste-heat boiler and sulphur condenser. In spite of the requirement for hot cyclones or other means of dust collection, a multistage, fluid bed reactor appears to offer several advantages for the desulphurizing process. No physical preparation of the concentrate by pelletizing would be necessary, required retention time of the concentrate in the reactor would be considerably reduced, control over the rate and means of solids discharge would be simplified and, in the case of copper concentrates, the resultant calcine from a fluid bed reactor would be in the desired physical condition for chemical leaching to recover copper, or for treatment to recover copper and precious metals by the solid state segregation process recently developed by W. R. Opie et al.[8]

Defining the operating parameters

The vertical-shaft, continuously-descending-bed type of reactor lends itself well to thermochemical and heat balance studies of the autogenous desulphurizing process, and also permits calculation of temperature with a reasonable degree of accuracy. Consequently, the author's heat balance studies assumed a commercial-size reactor of the vertical-shaft type, fed with pelletized concentrates, and a pellet retention time of 8 hr. A furnace of this type should desulphurize 1,000 to 1,200 tons of concentrate per day when its inside dimensions are about 6 ft wide, 30 ft long, and about 50 ft high.

Thermochemical and heat balance calculations were made for the desulphurization of typical chalcopyrite, pyrite, and pyrrhotite concentrates using the flowsheet in Fig. 1. To simplify calculations, it was assumed that all of the iron was oxidized to Fe_2O_3 and all of the copper was oxidized to CuO, even though in practice small amounts of Fe_3O_4 and Cu_2O would normally be present. All of the sulphur in the exit gases was assumed to leave as sulphur vapor. The molecular state of this sulphur can have a considerable influence on the heat balances, since if it leaves the reactor as S_6 or S_8 instead of S_2, it would give up a sub-

Table 2—Summary of data from material and heat balances

(Per metric ton of concentrate)

	Chalcopyrite	Pyrite	Pyrrhotite
Concentrate composition			
Fe, %	28	46	60
S, %	30	51.3	37.5
Cu, %	25	–	–
Oxygen in steam-oxygen mix (weight percent)	23	23	23
Concentrate dry weight (kg)	1,000	1,000	1,000
Oxygen used (kg)	183	198	258
Oxide pellets produced (kg)	863	685	883
Sulphur produced (kg)	300	513	375
Process steam used (kg)	606	653	852
Process steam produced in waste heat boiler (kg)	495	688	1,007
Heat of reaction (k-cal)	276,140	267,990	625,420
Total heat input to reactor (k-cal)	318,240	313,380	684,620
Heat in reactor exit gases (k-cal)	228,500	240,180	504,030
Heat in oxide pellets (k-cal)	44,960	34,630	86,210
Heat to wall loss (k-cal)	44,780	38,570	94,380
Total heat output (k-cal)	318,240	313,380	684,620
Temperature of steam-oxygen mix into reactor (°C)	150	150	150
Temperature of exit gases from reactor (°C)	600	600	1,000
Temperature of exit gases from waste heat boiler (°C)	150	150	150
Maximum reaction temperature, approximate (°C)	900	850	1,300
Temperature of oxide pellets at discharge (°C)	300	300	500

stantial number of heat units to the solid charge in the reactor. The reaction $3S_2 \rightarrow S_6$ becomes significant when the sulphur vapor cools down to about 600°C. This reaction tends to hold the temperature of the exit gas between about 500° and 600°C.

The author's calculations assumed that there was no sulphur dioxide or hydrogen sulphide in the exit gases when they left the sulphur condenser. In actual operation, this "balanced" condition would be maintained by adjusting the ratio of steam to oxygen in the incoming steam-oxygen mixture. While tests at CSMRI indicated that the steam-oxygen mixture should contain about 15% oxygen by volume (23% by weight), this steam-oxygen ratio would probably be adjusted in practice so that a small amount of sulphur dioxide would be present in the exit gas from the sulphur condenser. The sulphur dioxide would be collected and neutralized by wash water in the gas washing tower. Fig. 1 shows a lime addition to maintain an alkaline condition in the wash water. Under these circumstances, the exit gas from the wash tower would be nitrogen saturated with water vapor.

For material and heat balance purposes, the overall reaction when desulphurizing chalcopyrite is:

$$2CuFeS_2 + 2\frac{1}{2}O_2 + X\ H_2O \rightarrow$$
$$2CuO + Fe_2O_3 + 2S_2 + X\ H_2O \quad (1)$$

However, there are many intermediate reactions; the

Telfer E. Norman, president of Norman Research Inc., has spent most of the past three years on a project aimed at developing a low-energy pyrometallurgical process to recover copper and elemental sulphur from copper-sulphide concentrates.

In 1972, Norman retired as manager of abrasion-resistant alloy development for Climax Molybdenum Co. During his 35 years with Climax, he directed and coordinated a program of research, testing, and development on new or improved abrasion-resistant steels and irons for crushing, grinding, and handling ores and other abrasive materials.

Norman, who was born in Canada, attended the University of British Columbia and the University of Toronto. During his schooling he gained metallurgical experience at the Cominco smelter in British Columbia and the Inco smelter at Copper Cliff, Ont. After receiving a degree in metallurgical engineering from the University of Toronto in 1936, he served as research associate at the Ontario Research Foundation until late 1937, when he joined the Climax organization.

most important (in their succession from top to bottom of the reactor) probably are:

$$2CuFeS_2 + heat \rightarrow Cu_2S + 2FeS + \tfrac{1}{2}S_2\uparrow \quad (2)$$
$$2H_2S + SO_2 \rightarrow 2H_2O\uparrow + 1\tfrac{1}{2}S_2\uparrow \quad (3)$$
$$FeS + H_2O \rightarrow FeO + H_2S\uparrow \quad (4)$$
$$Cu_2S + H_2O \rightarrow Cu_2O + H_2S\uparrow \quad (5)$$
$$2FeS + SO_2 \rightarrow 2FeO + 1\tfrac{1}{2}S_2\uparrow \quad (6)$$
$$6FeO + SO_2 \rightarrow 2Fe_3O_4 + \tfrac{1}{2}S_2\uparrow \quad (7)$$
$$3FeS + 5O_2 \rightarrow Fe_3O_4 + 3SO_2\uparrow \quad (8)$$
$$Cu_2S + 2O_2 \rightarrow 2CuO + SO_2\uparrow \quad (9)$$
$$Cu_2O + \tfrac{1}{2}O_2 \rightarrow 2CuO \quad (10)$$
$$2Fe_3O_4 + \tfrac{1}{2}O_2 \rightarrow 3Fe_2O_3 \quad (11)$$

Similar intermediate reactions occur during desulphurization of pyrite and pyrrhotite, except that no copper compounds are involved. The overall reaction for pyrite is:

$$2FeS_2 + 1\tfrac{1}{2}O_2 + X\ H_2O \rightarrow$$
$$Fe_2O_3 + 2S_2 + X\ H_2O \quad (12)$$

For pyrrhotite, which may be considered to be FeS even though its actual Fe-to-S ratio varies somewhat, the reaction is:

$$2FeS + 1\tfrac{1}{2}O_2 + X\ H_2O \rightarrow$$
$$Fe_2O_3 + S_2 + X\ H_2O \quad (13)$$

If nickel is present as a partial replacement for iron or copper in any of these sulphide concentrates, it will be oxidized to NiO or (Ni, Fe)$_2$O$_3$ in the desulphurizing process.

Runaway reaction is improbable

Since steam in excess of the stoichiometric amounts required by equations (4) and (5) is always present in the re-

actor, the possibility of a runaway reaction between steam and metal sulphides should be considered. Thermodynamic balances indicate that such a runaway reaction cannot occur, since reactions (4) and (5) are somewhat endothermic and will only proceed to the extent that heat is supplied by hot-gas transfer from the major oxidizing reactions (8) through (11), which are exothermic. Thermodynamically, the operation is quite similar to the continuous production of water-gas in a coke-filled gas producer, where the oxygen in a steam-oxygen mixture reacts exothermically with carbon to produce carbon monoxide plus carbon dioxide, while the steam reacts endothermically to produce carbon monoxide and hydrogen. The desired reaction temperature is maintained by adjusting the ratio of steam to oxygen.

Oxygen efficiency in the desulphurizing process may, by definition, be considered to be 100% when it produces only metal oxides during the desulphurizing process. If sulphates occur in the solid product or if sulphur dioxide is present in the exit gas from the sulphur condenser, additional oxygen would be consumed, and oxygen efficiency would then be somewhat less than 100%. Since the reaction temperatures will normally be above 800°C, practically no sulphate sulphur will be produced, and oxygen efficiencies near 100% should be obtained. An oxygen efficiency of 100% was assumed in the material and heat balances.

Zinc may also be won from copper concentrates

Copper concentrates frequently contain significant quantities of zinc, lead, and sometimes arsenic or antimony. Sulphides of these four metals are volatile enough to tend to leave the reactor in the exit gases and be collected in the liquid sulphur in the sulphur condenser. Under such circumstances, the volatile sulphides could be collected and removed from liquid sulphur by settling, filtration, or possibly by distillation of the sulphur. The process thus provides for recovering zinc from copper concentrates. In conventional copper smelting, zinc is normally lost in the slag. However, to simplify calculations in this report, it was assumed that the concentrates contained no zinc or other volatile sulphides.

Calculating material and heat balances

The heat balances in this study are based on the heats of formation and enthalpy of the substances involved in equations (1), (12), and (13). Accurate data on these properties—essential for a reliable heat balance—are now available from various sources. The enthalpy of steam, at the temperatures involved in the reactor, was a major factor in these heat balances.

Table 2 summarizes data derived from detailed calculations of the material and heat balances for desulphurization of the three sulphide concentrates listed in Table 1. In desulphurizing the chalcopyrite concentrates with a steam-oxygen mixture containing 15% by volume of oxygen (23% by weight), the maximum reaction temperature is 900°C—quite close to the 885°C obtained in test runs at CSMRI. The calculated maximum reaction temperature with pyrite concentrates is a little lower, due to the relatively large amount of sulphur that must be volatilized. On the other hand, when pyrrhotite concentrates are desulphurized, a relatively high reaction temperature of about 1,300°C is indicated, due to the large amount of iron oxidized to Fe$_2$O$_3$. A 1,300°C temperature is probably excessively high and could cause problems from fusion or excessive sintering of the pellets in the reactor. To reduce the temperature to the desired range of about 800° to 950°C, the oxygen in the steam-oxygen mixture could be diluted with air, or possibly the oxygen content in the steam-oxygen mixture could be reduced to about 10% by volume. If the oxygen is diluted with air, it would reduce requirements for manufactured oxygen, probably down to about 0.20 tons of manufactured oxygen per ton of concentrate, or about the same as required for chalcopyrite and pyrite concentrates.

Heat of reaction ample to maintain reaction

Table 2 indicates that total heat input to the reactor is about 318,000 k-cal per mt of chalcopyrite concentrates, equivalent to about 1.15 million Btu per short ton. Most of this heat is obtained from the heat of the reactions, with a relatively small additional amount from the enthalpy of the steam-oxygen mixture, which was assumed to enter the reactor at 150°C. Even when a rather liberal allowance is made for heat loss through the reactor walls, there appears to be ample heat left to maintain the desired reaction temperatures. The same conclusion can be drawn for desulphurization of pyrite and pyrrhotite concentrates. It appears that a small proportion of process steam will have to be generated in an auxiliary boiler when chalcopyrite concentrates are desulphurized, while an excess of process steam is produced by the waste-heat boiler when pyrite or pyrrhotite concentrates are desulphurized.

Oxygen consumption (Table 2) amounts to slightly less than 0.20 tons per ton of chalcopyrite or pyrite concentrates desulphurized. For pyrrhotite concentrates, indicated consumption is 0.258 tons per ton of concentrate.

However, as previously discussed, it will probably be desirable to obtain a portion of the oxygen by diluting the incoming steam-oxygen mixture with air, to lower the maximum reaction temperature. Consequently, only about 0.2 tons of manufactured oxygen may be required for pyrrhotite desulphurization. A reactor capable of treating 1,000 tpd of concentrates would require an oxygen plant capable of delivering 200 tpd of oxygen about 95% pure. A plant of this size should produce oxygen at a cost of $15-20 per ton, consuming about 350 kwh per net ton of oxygen. Oxygen cost per ton of concentrate should be $3-4, and energy consumption for oxygen production should be about 70 kwh per net ton of concentrate.

Further development of the desulphurization process appears to be well justified. The next step should preferably be tests on a small pilot plant scale to study the operation in various types of reactors and to determine physical requirements of the pelletized or powdered concentrates fed to the reactors. □

References

1) Norman, T. E., "Autogenous Smelting of Copper Concentrates with Oxygen-Enriched Air," E/MJ, Vol. 137, October and November 1936.
2) Stickney, C. W., US Patents 475,824, May 1892; 512,235, January 1894; and 587,068, July 1897.
3) Stickney process description, E/MJ, Vol. 65, June 4, 1898, pp 674-75.
4) Hall, W. A., "The Hall Ore Desulphurizing Process," E/MJ, Vol. 96, July 5, 1913, pp 35-36.
5) Hall, W. A., US Patents 1,076,763; 1,083,246; 1,083,247; 1,083,248; 1,083,251; 1,083,252; 1,083,253; 1,133,636.
6) Wierum, H. F., "Experimental Development of the Hall Process," Proc. of Mining and Metall. Soc. of America, Vol. 7, Sept. 30, 1914, pp 134-46.
7) Norman, T. E., US Patent 3,849,120, Nov. 19, 1974.
8) Opie, W. R., and L. D. Coffin, US Patent 3,799,764, March 26, 1974.

Hysla boosts pellet production to 1.5 million mtpy

The Hylsa Steel Group has operated its own iron ore mine in the state of Jalisco since 1955, with a pellet plant in production since 1970. The plant has a design capacity of 3,334 mtpd for an annual production of 1.1 million mt, but Hylsa is now producing 4,400 mtpd and expects to produce 1.5 million mt in pellets in 1974, against 1.36 million tons in 1973.

The mine operator is the company Las Encinas SA. The conventional open-pit operation utilizes rotary drilling (9⅛ in.), supplemented by track drilling. Ore is hauled from the pit by truck to an on-site crushing plant. The ore, primarily a magnetite, averages 60% iron. Hylsa presently mines 6,000 tpd ore at an ore-to-waste ratio of 1:2.

Following two stages of crushing, the ore is transported by aerial tramway to the concentrator and pellet plant at Alzada, about 14 mi away, in the neighboring state of Colima. The tramway, employed because of the mountainous terrain, was designed and installed by Germany's Pohlig-Heckel-Bleichert Vereinigte Maschinenfabriken AG. Each bucket holds 1.5 mt, with the entire system handling a total of 309 tph.

The magnetic separation plant has a capacity of 5,000 mtpd. Hylsa is currently adding five more drums in the second section, for a total of 12 in that section, to increase the pellet grade from 67% to 67.5%.

Pellets are produced in a plant designed and built by Lurgi, employing four 2-ft-dia pellet disks, one of which is on standby. Indurated product is shipped by rail to steelmaking facilities at Monterrey and Puebla. Ore is processed by the firm's patented direct reduction system, which is fired by natural gas.

The company has found that the use of pellets has cut gas consumption from 1,500 to 1,100 cu m per ton of ore in the sponge iron process. In addition, the 67% iron pellets are of higher grade than the 62-63% ore formerly fed to the sponge iron plants.

Initially, Hylsa used bentonite as pellet binder but subsequently switched to hydrated lime. While the lime costs only about one-third as much as bentonite, a more important advantage with lime as a binder is the self-fluxing pellet which results.

Bentonite is a better agglomerate than lime, but Hylsa has been able to control pellet quality by making adjustments to the ball and rod mills, filters, and disks. About

Hylsa's open-pit mine (left), operated by Las Encinas SA, sends 6,000 tpd of 50% magnetite ore to an on-site crushing plant. An aerial tramway (right) then takes material to a concentrator and pellet plant at Alzada, about 14 mi away.

0.5% lime is required for agglomeration. However, 1.2-1.5% is added to provide a basicity of 1.15 for steelmaking.

In other changes at the pellet plant, Hylsa has switched from steel to polyethylene filters, which are less expensive and easier to handle, and from nylon to polyurethane bags. The latter are less porous than nylon, have reduced the loss of solids from about 3% to less than 0.5%, and have also decreased humidity. ☐

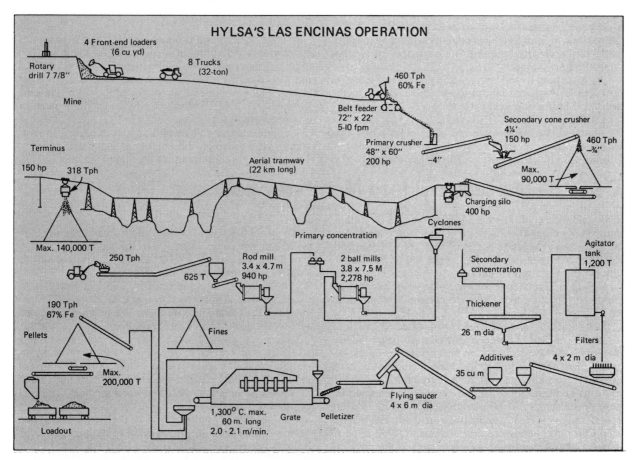

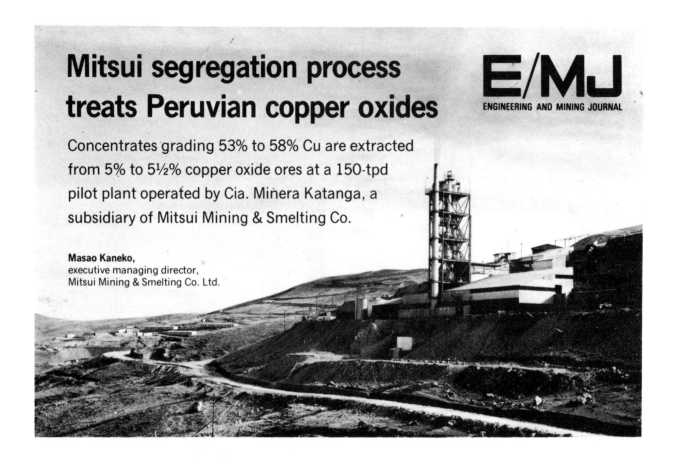

Mitsui segregation process treats Peruvian copper oxides

E/MJ ENGINEERING AND MINING JOURNAL

Concentrates grading 53% to 58% Cu are extracted from 5% to 5½% copper oxide ores at a 150-tpd pilot plant operated by Cia. Minera Katanga, a subsidiary of Mitsui Mining & Smelting Co.

Masao Kaneko,
executive managing director,
Mitsui Mining & Smelting Co. Ltd.

THE RECOVERY BY FLOTATION OF OXIDE COPPER minerals such as malachite, chrysocolla, and cuprite is difficult, and the usual method employed for their treatment is sulphuric acid leaching. However, if an ore contains carbonate minerals and considerable amounts of precious metals, it is not amenable to acid leaching because of both high acid consumption and the loss of precious metals.

The segregation method for treatment of oxide copper ores was developed in 1923 to overcome the defects of acid leaching. The Mitsui Mining & Smelting Co., after many years of research to find a method for treating copper oxide ores, has successfully developed a new segregation technique, patented as the "Mitsui Segregation Process."

Construction of a segregation plant using the new process was started in December 1972 at the Katanga mine, located at Provincia de Chunbivilca, Departamento de Cuzco, southern Peru. Situated on a plateau of about 4,000 m elevation above sea level, the mine is approximately 90 km air distance from the ancient Inca capital of Cuzco. The Katanga segregation plant was completed in November 1973 at a rated capacity of 150 tpd, and a trial run began the following month.

The Katanga copper deposit occurs on the eastern slope of the Andes Mountain chain, which is composed mainly of rocks of Mesozoic age. Widely distributed rocks of the region are Cretaceous limestone and shale which have been intruded by Cretaceous and Tertiary granodiorite and quartz porphyry.

The Katanga deposit is of the contact metasomatic type, but vein and disseminated types are also observed locally. The deposit has undergone such strong oxidation that the copper minerals present now are mostly malachite and chrysocolla. Sulphide copper minerals are almost nonexistent at Katanga.

The four orebodies—the Katanga, the Congo, the Fundicion, and the Quivio—have ore grades averaging 5% to 5½% Cu. The gangue minerals are mainly limestone and quartz.

Several companies conducted exploration programs at the Katanga property at various times from 1900 to 1968, when the property was purchased by Mitsui Mining & Smelting.

What is segregation processing of copper ore?

In the segregation process, copper ore is ground to the proper size and then mixed with a small amount of salt and cokes. When this mixture is heated to over 650°C, the copper minerals react with the salt to form copper chloride, which vaporizes. In turn, the copper chloride comes in contact with the cokes, thereby being reduced to metallic copper, which is deposited on the surface of the remaining cokes. The metallic copper, with cokes, is then recovered by flotation to produce high grade copper concentrate.

There have been numerous reports on the reactions involved in the segregation process for copper oxides. These reactions can generally be grouped in three categories.

1) Decomposition of salt. When the temperature reaches more than 650°C, the salt reacts with the clay minerals or silica and produces HCl:

$$4\,NaCl + Al_2O_3 \cdot 2\,SiO_2 \cdot 2\,H_2O \rightarrow$$
$$4\,HCl + Na_4Al_2O_3 \cdot 2\,SiO_2$$
$$2\,NaCl + SiO_2 + H_2O \rightarrow 2\,HCl + Na_2SiO_3$$

2) Vaporization of copper chloride:

$$2\,CuO + 2\,HCl \rightarrow Cu_2Cl_2 + 2\,H_2O + Cl_2$$
$$2\,(CuSiO_3 \cdot 2\,H_2O) + 4\,HCl \rightarrow$$
$$Cu_2Cl_2 + 6\,H_2O + Cl_2 + 2\,SiO_2$$

Fig. 1—Mitsui segregation plant at Katanga

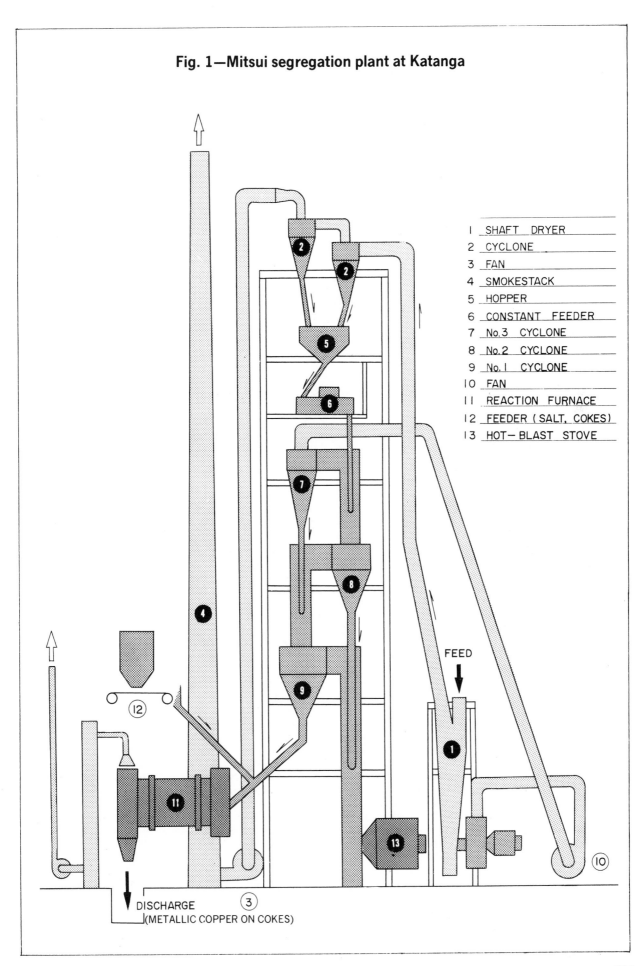

1	SHAFT DRYER
2	CYCLONE
3	FAN
4	SMOKESTACK
5	HOPPER
6	CONSTANT FEEDER
7	No.3 CYCLONE
8	No.2 CYCLONE
9	No.1 CYCLONE
10	FAN
11	REACTION FURNACE
12	FEEDER (SALT, COKES)
13	HOT—BLAST STOVE

FEED

DISCHARGE
(METALLIC COPPER ON COKES)

$$CuCO_2 \cdot Cu(OH)_2 + 4\,HCl \rightarrow$$
$$Cu_2Cl_2 + 3\,H_2O + CO_2 + Cl_2$$

3) Decomposition of metallic copper. The vaporized chloride copper is reduced immediately to metallic copper by the cokes and steam and is deposited on the surface of the remaining cokes:

$$Cu_2Cl_2 + C + H_2O \rightarrow 2\,Cu + 2\,HCl + CO$$
$$2\,Cu_2Cl_2 + C + 2\,H_2O \rightarrow 4\,Cu + 4\,HCl + CO_2$$

The HCl produced in these reactions is reused in the process, which is evidenced by the lower consumption of salt as compared with the ordinary chloridizing process.

Furnace demands maximum thermal efficiency

In the segregation process, the ore being treated does not contain any element that serves as a source of heat. Consequently, an outside source must be used to heat the ore to more than 650°C. After the reactions are completed, the copper is cooled and floated. Because of these procedures, the thermal efficiency of the furnace is of utmost importance. Various types of furnace designed for use in the segregation process have all aimed at achieving maximum thermal efficiency.

The furnace in the Mitsui Segregation Process has also been designed with maximum thermal efficiency as a primary objective, while at the same time maintaining the proper atmosphere for the reactions and minimizing the corrosion of the various parts of the furnace by the HCl gas produced during the reaction process.

The furnace erected at the Katanga mine is made up of a suspension preheater composed of three stages of cyclones and incorporates an exclusive hot-blast stove and a rotary type reaction furnace.

The 1,100°C hot blast produced in the stove ascends through the first stage cyclone at the bottom of the preheater (Fig. 1) and then through second and third stages of cyclones, preheating the ore coming down from the third stage cyclone at the top. Ore is discharged from the first stage cyclone at the bottom of the preheater at a temperature high enough for the necessary reactions. The preheated ore is then charged into the reaction furnace, together with a small amount of salt and cokes.

The Mitsui Segregation Process has a number of noteworthy features:

1) Inside the preheater, the ore is in suspension within the hot blast, so the heat exchange between the ore and the hot blast takes place in a very short time. By proper selection of the number of cyclone stages, it is possible to lower the discharged hot blast to 200°C, thereby increasing the thermal efficiency of the process.

2) In the segregation process, it is very important that the reactions take place in a neutral or slightly reducing atmosphere. In the Mitsui Process, maintenance of the proper atmosphere is easy, because no burner is used for the reaction furnace and because special provision is made to prevent free air from entering the reaction furnace.

3) Special devices are used to prevent HCl gas from the reaction furnace from entering the preheater. With the HCl gas removed from the reaction furnace and treated separately, corrosion in the reaction furnace is confined to a very small part of the furnace.

4) Since the amount of ore in process at any given time inside the preheater and the reaction furnace is small, stopping and restarting is easy.

5) Limestone in the ore is not a problem, because the preheating time is too short for limestone to decompose.

6) Because the hot blast stove is separate from the

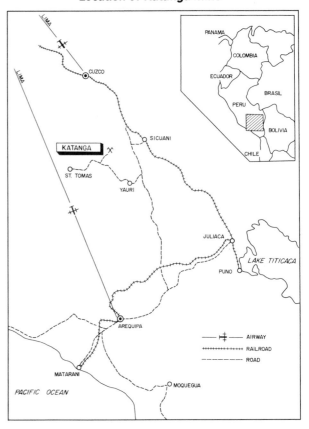

Location of Katanga mine

preheater, the choice of fuel for the stove is flexible. Any fuel available in the locality can be used to advantage.

Extraction of Katanga ores

Katanga ore is mined by open-pit methods from the 4,100-m level and dropped through a raise to the 4,000-m level, where it is loaded into mine cars and hauled by a locomotive to the coarse ore bin located on the uppermost level of the plant.

Crushing is open circuited through two stages. The primary crusher, a 30 x 20-in. jaw crusher, is followed by a 3 x 8-ft screen and a secondary 3-ft cone crusher. The ore is crushed to minus 15 mm and is stored in a 200-ton fine ore bin (Fig. 2).

Ore from the fine ore bin is ground through the closed circuit of a 6 x 6-ft ball mill and a 10-in. cyclone to minus 65 mesh. These steps are followed by an 8-in. cyclone and a 32-ft thickener. The thickened pulp is filtered through an 8 x 12-ft drum filter.

Filter cake is fed to a shaft dryer, and the resulting dried ore is brought to the top of the suspension preheater by air current. The ore, separated from the air current by means of eight units of 1-m cyclones, is then dropped into a hopper. Air separated from the ore passes to a 37-m-high smokestack and is released to the atmosphere.

From the hopper, the dried ground ore is fed with a constant feeder to the topmost cyclone (No. 3) of the preheater, subsequently dropping by gravity through the No. 2 and No. 1 cyclones. While passing through the three cyclones, the ore is heated by the ascending 1,100°C hot blast from the stove. The ore remains in the preheater for only 20 to 30 sec. Upon reaching the No. 3 cyclone, the hot blast is discharged at about 400°C and conducted by

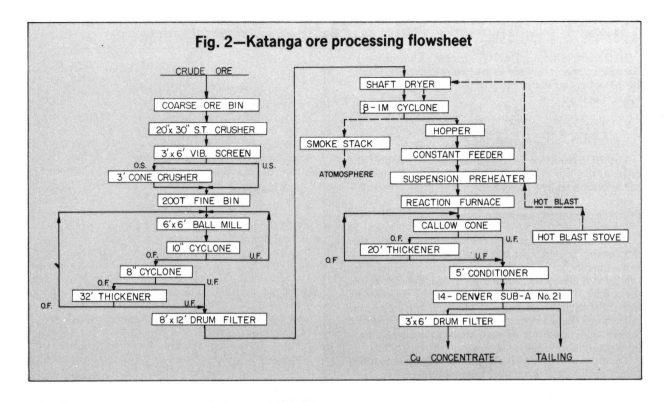

Fig. 2—Katanga ore processing flowsheet

CRUDE ORE
→ COARSE ORE BIN
→ 20" x 30" S.T. CRUSHER
→ 3' x 6' VIB. SCREEN
O.S. → 3' CONE CRUSHER ← U.S.
→ 200T FINE BIN
→ 6' x 6' BALL MILL
→ 10" CYCLONE (O.F. / U.F.)
→ 8" CYCLONE (O.F. / U.F.)
O.F. → 32' THICKENER (U.F.)
→ 8' x 12' DRUM FILTER

SHAFT DRYER
→ 8-IM CYCLONE
→ SMOKE STACK → ATMOSPHERE
→ HOPPER
→ CONSTANT FEEDER
→ SUSPENSION PREHEATER
→ REACTION FURNACE ← HOT BLAST
→ CALLOW CONE
O.F. → 20' THICKENER (U.F.) ← HOT BLAST STOVE
O.F → 5' CONDITIONER
→ 14- DENVER SUB-A No. 21
→ 3' x 6' DRUM FILTER
→ Cu CONCENTRATE   TAILING

Control panel at Katanga plant
monitors production of
copper concentrates by the
Mitsui segregation process.

means of a fan to the shaft dryer, where it is used to dry the filter cake.

The preheated ore is discharged from the lowest cyclone at the proper reaction temperature of 800°C and is charged into a rotary-type 1.9 x 5.0-m reaction furnace, along with powdered salt and cokes. The reaction is completed in about 20 min. Ore discharged from the furnace is immediately quenched with water and then thickened by means of a callow cone and a 20-ft thickener. The thickened pulp is pumped to the flotation section.

The flotation of the metallic copper deposited on cokes is done with 14 cells of Denver Sub-A No. 21 flotation machines. In the three stages of cleaning, the reagents used are KAX, pine oil, and a small amount of Z-200. The final froth is filtered through a 3 x 6-ft drum filter and then weighed and bagged before being sent to storage.

The results of six months of plant operation beginning in December 1973 were an average 75% to 80% recovery treating a crude ore grading from 5% to 5½% Cu. Concentrates produced graded from 53% to 58% Cu. After six months of trial operation, the process has been stabilized, and the operators are now trained, leading to expectations of achieving 90% recovery and 60% concentrates in the near future.

In addition to the 15 years of research on its segregation process for copper, Mitsui has also spent five years researching a similar process for nickel at the Mitsui Tokyo Central Laboratory. Pilot plants of 1-tpd and 10-tpd capacities are in continuous operation at these laboratories.

The Mitsui Segregation Process is patented in the company's name in several countries, including the US, Canada, Zambia, Chile, France, the Philippines, Peru, England, and Morocco, and a few other patent applications have been made.

The furnace used in the process at the Katanga plant was manufactured by Kawasaki Heavy Industries.

The 150-tpd capacity of the Katanga plant is still pilot plant scale; however, based on the performance of this facility, Mitsui plans to build a much bigger plant based on its segregation process in the near future. □

Direct reduction using coal gasification

Gabriele G. Carinci and **David C. Meissner**, Midrex Corp.

DIRECT REDUCTION OF IRON ORE is one of the most important recent developments in the steel industry worldwide. Midrex Corp. successfully developed and commercially demonstrated the first continuous direct reduction process and has studied the concept of adapting coal gasification technology to the process. Engineering studies and process interfacing have been completed, concentrated in the area of partial-oxidation-based coal gasification. (See Figs. 1 and 2.) This technology has been fully developed and commercially proven using a wide variety of coals. Midrex Corp. is now capable of marketing a modified coal-based Midrex* direct reduction process that equals the reliability and availability of existing direct reduction plants based on natural gas. Two coal gasification processes—dilute-phase partial-oxidation gasification and fluid-bed gasification—are in commercial operation in many locations in the world and can be integrated wih the Midrex direct reduction process.

Dilute-phase partial-oxidation coal gasification

A coal preparation plant performs primary crushing and drying and subsequent simultaneous drying and pulverization in a wind-swept closed system using a ball or rod mill. Coal is pulverized to 70% minus 74 microns and dried to approximately 1% moisture.

Coal is then piped with nitrogen to bunkers above the gasifiers. In the gasifier, oxygen of 98% purity and steam are mixed with the coal dust (Fig. 3). Partial oxidation of coal dust takes place at temperatures greater than 1,400°C, forming a flame in the gasifier. As a result, coal is converted from a solid to a gaseous phase at a relatively uniform high temperature through concurrent gasification in an empty chamber.

The high gasifier temperatures convert hydrocarbons in the coal to carbon monoxide (CO), carbon dioxide (CO_2), and hydrogen (H_2) according to equilibrium conditions. The resulting gas contains only traces (less than 0.1% vol.) of methane (CH_4), with no long-chain and condensable hydrocarbons or phenols. Sulphur contained in the coal is transferred to the gas, 90% as hydrogen sulphide (H_2S),

*Registered trademark of Midrex Corp.

and the remainder as carbonyl sulphide (COS).

The ash content of the coal is important because it is fed to the gasifier as ballast and must be heated to the gasification temperature, which is somewhat higher than the ash melting temperature. Approximately 50% of the ash is withdrawn as molten slag, and 50% is discharged dry with the hot gas stream. Molten slag is granulated in a water bath.

The double-shell gasifier is designed as a low pressure boiler. In the boiler, saturated steam is produced for external use, as well as for internal use in the gasifier.

The hot offgas, produced by partial oxidation, flows through a waste heat boiler system, which cools the hot gas and produces a high pressure saturated steam. The steam supplies part of the heating requirements for CO_2 stripping and acid gas stripping.

After leaving the waste heat boiler, crude gas flows to the cooler-washer, where it is cooled by direct spraying with water. Banks of sprays remove approximately 90% of the entrained ash. The clean, raw gas is then compressed and is ready for acid gas removal.

Fluid-bed gasification of coal

For fluid-bed gasification, coal is crushed to minus 8 mm. Fluid-bed dryers can be used if predrying of surface moisture is required to prevent plugging and buildup.

Coal feed is conveyed by lock hoppers and screw conveyors to the gasifier, where a fluidized bed of coal is maintained (Fig. 4). In fluid-bed gasification, the proposed operating pressure is approximately 4 atmospheres absolute (ATA). A mixture of steam and oxygen is injected into the bed at several levels to gasify the coal. Only steam is injected into the lowest level of the gasifier, to fluidize the coal and to cool the ash particles discharged from the bottom of the gasifier.

The ratio of oxygen and steam to coal is controlled to maintain the desired bed temperature. Optimum bed temperature is a compromise between product gas (carbon monoxide plus hydrogen content) and carbon efficiency, but is limited by the ash softening temperature. If bed temperature exceeds the ash softening temperature, the ash may fuse and agglomerate—upsetting the fluidization

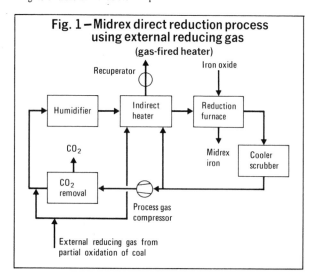

Fig. 1 — Midrex direct reduction process using external reducing gas
(gas-fired heater)

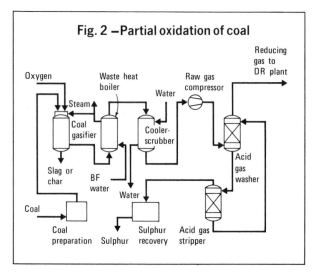

Fig. 2 — Partial oxidation of coal

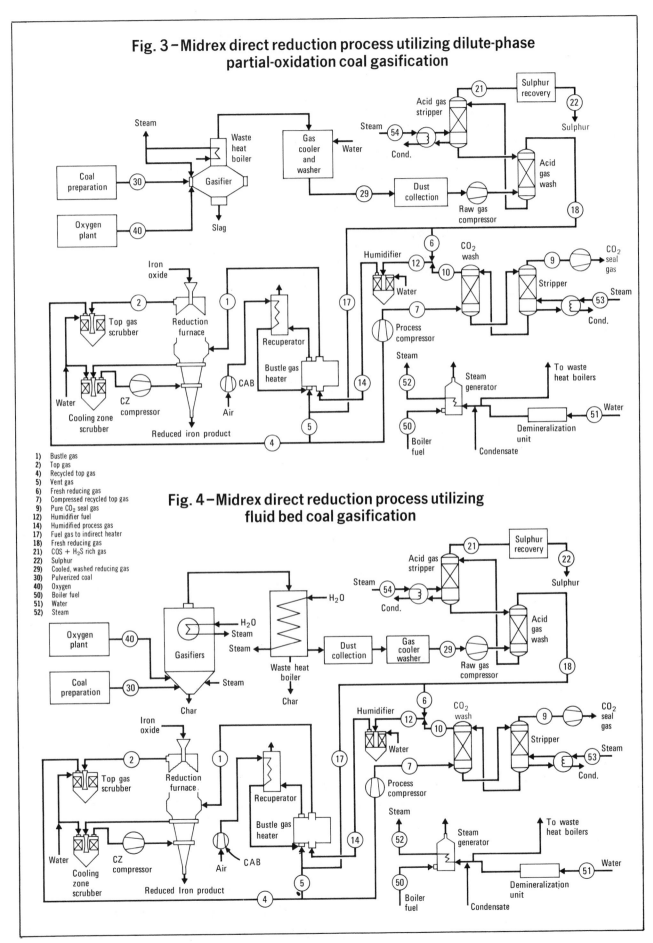

Fig. 3 – Midrex direct reduction process utilizing dilute-phase partial-oxidation coal gasification

1) Bustle gas
2) Top gas
4) Recycled top gas
5) Vent gas
6) Fresh reducing gas
7) Compressed recycled top gas
9) Pure CO_2 seal gas
12) Humidifier fuel
14) Humidified process gas
17) Fuel gas to indirect heater
18) Fresh reducing gas
21) COS + H_2S rich gas
22) Sulphur
29) Cooled, washed reducing gas
30) Pulverized coal
40) Oxygen
50) Boiler fuel
51) Water
52) Steam

Fig. 4 – Midrex direct reduction process utilizing fluid bed coal gasification

characteristics of the bed and possibly plugging the gasifier.

Bed temperatures are typically 925° to 1,100°C, obtained by the partial oxidation of the carbon and hydrocarbons contained in the coal. Such gasification temperatures assure that the tars, gaseous hydrocarbons, and carbon present in the coal are converted to carbon monoxide, hydrogen, and carbon dioxide. A small percentage of methane remains in the raw product.

Fluidization causes ash particles and their contained carbon to segregate according to size and specific gravity. Heavier particles fall through the fluidized bed and pass into the ash discharge unit at the bottom of the gasifier. Lighter particles are carried up through the bed by the raw product gas. Some 50-75% of the incoming ash is entrained in the hot product gases leaving the top of the gasifier.

The portion of the gasifier above the bed further gasifies any entrained carbon particles and separates any heavier solid material. This two-fold function is accomplished by adding steam and oxygen near the upper limit of the fluid bed, producing maximum reaction temperature in the space above the bed. Within this area, ash particles may be exposed to temperatures above their softening point. A radiant boiler is installed in the gasifier above the secondary gasification zone to prevent molten particles from forming deposits on the refractory, and possibly blocking the exit duct. The boiler cools the gas by 150-200°C before it leaves the gasifier—thus resolidifying molten particles. Hot gases containing ash leave the gasifier and pass through the waste heat recovery train, generating high pressure steam and preheating boiler feed water.

The heavier char particles leaving the bottom of the gasifier are crushed and conveyed to the ash bunker. The remaining char and ash are carried out of the gasifier in the product gas. Most of these solids are removed in the waste heat recovery train and are conveyed to the ash bunker by a transfer screw conveyor. Additional char and ash are removed in cyclones. The waste heat recovery train and cyclones are designed to remove at least 85% of the entrained solids. Char is pneumatically conveyed from the ash bunker for disposal or for use as supplemental fuel in a solid fuel boiler.

Gas from the cyclones passes through a venturi-type scrubber that removes the residual solids.

The process of acid gas removal

Clean raw gas from either of the two coal gasification processes can be used as a source of fresh reducing gas for the Midrex direct reduction process after being passed through an acid gas wash. The clean raw gas may require further compression, depending upon the pressure requirements of the acid gas wash system.

Either a physical absorption wash, a chemical absorption wash, or a combination of the two can be used for acid gas removal. For example, a combination Benfield and DEA (diethanolamine) wash will clean the raw gas to the desired levels of 1% CO_2 and 50 to 100 ppmv of H_2S + COS. The rich solution from the acid gas washer is regenerated by stripping the CO_2, H_2S and COS out through flash evaporation and reboiling with steam. The regenerated solution is then recycled to the acid gas washer. The sulphur contained in the acid gas stream can be recovered as elemental sulphur by Claus technology. The CO_2 in the acid gases is discharged to the atmosphere.

Fresh reducing gas discharged from the acid gas washer is piped to the reduction plant, at a pressure of 2.5 ATA and at ambient temperature. The gas is divided into two streams. One stream is sent to the bustle gas heater as sup-

plemental fuel for the burners, and the other is mixed with recirculated top gas from which CO_2 has been removed. The combined stream of fresh reducing gas and CO_2-free recirculated top gas flows through a humidifier where the water vapor content is adjusted. The humidified gas enters the bustle gas heater, where a water gas shift reaction occurs: portions of the CO and H_2O react to produce CO_2 and H_2. From the bustle gas heater, the hot reducing gas (approximately 760°C) flows to the Midrex reduction furnace. Hot reducing gas entering the furnace is approximately 41% CO, 42% H_2, 5% CO_2, 4% H_2O, and the balance N_2.

The Midrex direct reduction process

Iron oxide is fed to the top of the reduction furnace, and as it descends by gravity through the furnace, it is contacted countercurrently by hot reducing gas. Iron oxide is reduced to metallic iron and carburized during 6 hr of residence time in the reduction zone. In the lower portion of the furnace, the directly reduced iron is cooled to ambient temperature by a closed-loop recirculating gas system. Cooling-zone gas leaving the furnace is cooled, washed, and recycled. The Midrex reduction furnace operates at moderate pressure. Gas seals on both the furnace feed leg and the product discharge leg prevent escape of process gases to the atmosphere. The gas seals, which eliminate the need for mechanical seals, ensure that only inert gas is released to the atmosphere.

Spent reducing gas, or top gas, leaves the furnace at approximately 400°C and passes through a scrubber, where it is cleaned and dehumidified. Clean gas is then divided into two streams. One stream is mixed with fresh gas from the coal gasification plant and used with preheated air to fire the bustle gas heater burners. Flue gas from the bustle gas heater and combustion air from the bustle gas heater burner undergo heat exchange in a recuperator. The purpose of venting this portion of the top gas to the burners is to prevent an increase in nitrogen content in the recirculating gas system.

The major portion of the top gas is compressed to approximately 3 ATA before flowing to the CO_2 washer. The top gas flows upward through a tower countercurrent to an amine solution that absorbs CO_2, reducing the CO_2 content of the gas to 1% by volume. The top gas is then mixed with fresh reducing gas. The CO_2-rich wash solution passes through a stripper, where the amine solution is regenerated by reboiling with steam. Tail gas from the stripper is essentially pure CO_2, which is compressed and used as seal gas in the reduction plant.

Steam generated in a free-standing boiler supplements the steam produced in the waste heat boiler system of the gasification plant to supply the steam requirements of the CO_2 stripper reboilers.

The accompanying table lists the expected utility requirements for operation of a Midrex direct reduction

Acknowledgement

The authors wish to acknowledge the assistance of Herman F. Staege, manager of business development for coal and gas, Krupp-Koppers GmbH; Howard F. Leonard, senior project engineer, Koppers Co. Inc.; and I. Norman Banchik, manager of commercial development, Davy Powergas Inc.

Projected operating requirements of Midrex direct reduction plant using coal gasification

(per mt of product; plant capacity 420,000 mtpy)

	Dilute-phase partial-oxidation system	Fluid bed system
Power	560 kwh	310 kwh
	(includes 170 kwh for O_2 plant)	(includes 130 kwh for O_2 plant)
Coal	5.0 Gcal*	5.8 Gcal**
Oxygen	500 kg	370 kg
Water (make-up)	4.4 cu m	3.1 cu m
Boiler feed water	1.2 cu m	0.8 cu m
Manpower...	0.7 manhours	0.7 manhours
External steam.....	400 kg	–

*Based on a coal with 28.0% ash and a higher heating value of 5,750 Kcal per kg (dry). **Based on a coal with 23% ash and a higher heating value of 5,735 Kcal per kg (dry).

---

plant having an annual capacity of 420,000 mt of directly reduced product, using either of the two coal gasification processes described here. The expected range of capital costs for a facility to produce 420,000 mtpy of directly reduced product based on either of the coal gasification processes with the Midrex direct reduction process is $210 to $230 per annual metric ton.

The role of coal in direct reduction plants

The direct reduction process is based on the inherent thermal and chemical efficiency of the shaft furnace. The Midrex process has the flexibility to produce a high quality product, with a uniform metallization controllable to any desired level within the range of 85-95% and a carbon content controllable to the desired level within the range of 1.0% to 3.0%.

By 1979, Midrex direct reduction plants in operation will have a combined annual production capacity in excess of 10 million mt. Experts predict that worldwide steel production will increase to 900 million mt by 1980—30% above the 1975 level. It is also predicted that 30 million mtpy of directly reduced iron will be required by 1980—almost a 600% increase over 1975, when total worldwide installed production capacity for directly reduced iron was approximately 7 million mtpy.

The Midrex direct reduction process using coal gasification is an important development in an era of dwindling and costly fuel sources. The vast majority of coal reserves available throughout the world can be used in direct reduction-coal gasification plants but are not of sufficiently high quality to be used in making coke for blast furnace operation. The use of coal gasification for direct reduction of iron appears to be an important technological breakthrough. □

USBM investigates potential for indurating iron pellets with low-rank coals

TESTING PULVERIZED COAL—lignite and subbituminous varieties—as a substitute for natural gas for indurating iron oxide pellets is the focus of ongoing research at the US Bureau of Mines' Twin Cities Metallurgy Research Center. The immediate objective of the test program was to assess the degree of pellet contamination and accretion buildup on the lining of an induration furnace caused by deposition of low-fusion-temperature ash released during combustion of solid fuels. Commercial operation was simulated in a pilot-scale traveling grate rotary kiln, as described in a paper presented by Robert S. Kaplan and Ralph C. Kirby at the Lignite Symposium in Grand Forks, N. Dak., May 1975.*

Tests conducted with solid fuels at the Twin Cities Metallurgy Research Center have shown that:

■ When coal is fired directly into the rotary kiln of a grate-kiln unit, the major problem is formation of coalescent masses or rings in the kiln interior. The severity of ring formation has not been traced to any one source, but the best performance can be expected from coals having an ash-fusion temperature above the range of temperatures at which induration occurs. Dust deposition in constricted passages, as in grate-to-kiln transfer chutes, may also be expected when using Montana subbituminous coal.

■ Pellet contamination from coal combustion products and residues, including sulphur pickups, is not a serious problem.

■ Pellets made in the pilot plant from commercial magnetite concentrates and indurated in a grate-kiln system with bituminous coal, subbituminous coal, or lignite had mechanical properties equal to or better than their commercial counterparts.

■ Pellet contamination from the alkalies Na_2O and K_2O in the fuel is less than that contributed to the green pellet by bentonite additions.

■ Temperature profiles with coal firing show steeper descent from burner to feed end of the kiln than with natural gas firing. Because of the localized luminous flame obtained with coal, temperature control based on kiln exit gases—as practiced in natural gas firing—may result in excessively high temperatures at the hot end.

■ Fluxing interaction of coal or lignite ash with iron ore-bentonite mixtures plays an important role in promoting ringing at or near the induration temperature. Fuel selection must include consideration of ash fluxing behavior as well as fusion temperatures.

■ If fuel selection cannot control ringing, cyclone burners, other external coal combustion chambers, or coal gasification may be required, but costs would be expected to be higher than those for direct firing.

■ There are strong indications that magnetite pellets undergo some reversion from their partially oxidized state as they pass through the coal flame. This condition may require some adjustments in standard operating procedures to insure that the required degree of pellet oxidation is reached and maintained.

*Robert S. Kaplan is staff metallurgist in the division of solid wastes, and Ralph C. Kirby is chief of the division of metallurgy, USBM, Washington, D.C.

Reprinted From E/MJ, August 1975

USBM natural gas-coal fired grate-kiln pelletizing plant

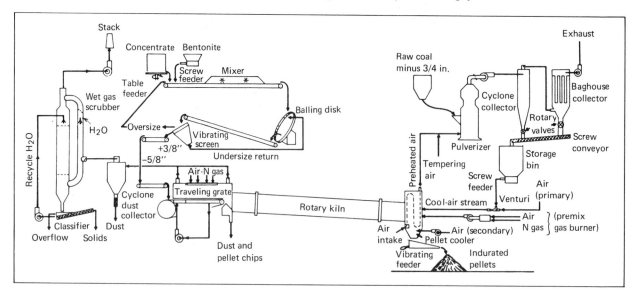

Lignite and subbituminous coals were included in the USBM study for two reasons. First, they are low cost, readily available fuels. Second, they are located predominantly in the Rocky Mountains and North Great Plains—relatively close to the iron ore mining center of the US. Another advantage is that more than 90% of these fuels are low in sulphur content (less than 1.0%).

Rotary kiln: main piece of equipment

The central item of equipment used in the USBM study is the 34-in.-ID, 35-ft rotary kiln (see flowsheet). Its slope, for the tests performed, was ¼ in. per ft for countercurrent flow. A 4½-in. dam at the discharge end allowed a maximum pellet loading of 11%. The discharge end of the kiln had a stainless steel hood containing both the coal burner and the supplemental natural gas-air premix burner. Firing of supplemental natural gas was required because of the pilot kiln's high heat losses. The hood was cooled by a flow of air, and the resultant heated air was directed to the coal pulverizer to dry and classify the coal.

Half the kiln was lined with 70% alumina refractory brick for the hot zone, and the other half was lined with heavy duty fireclay brick.

The green pellets were sized and conveyed to a 12-in.-wide by 10-ft-long traveling grate for drying, partial hardening, and oxidation. In the 4-ft downdraft preheat section, supplementary heat was supplied by natural gas burners to maintain a temperature consistent with commercial practice. The preheat section exhaust gases flowed through a 2-ft updraft drying section. Preheated pellets flowed through a transfer chute equipped with a ¼-in. grizzly to remove fines before discharging into the kiln.

Offgases from both grate and kiln were drawn into a cyclone dust collector and a wet scrubber before venting to the atmosphere.

A 30-in. bed of hot pellets leaving the kiln was retained in a refractory-lined shaft, where flowing ambient air cooled the pellets and then entered the kiln hood to be used as preheated, secondary combustion air for burning the pulverized coal.

The pilot plant is monitored and controlled through a master control room, and data on process temperatures,

gas flows, gas pressures, and offgas analysis are recorded continuously.

Trying out a variety of coals

The solid fuels tested at the Twin Cities Metallurgy Research Center ranged from lignite through western subbituminous coal to bituminous coals. However, the more pronounced tendency toward kiln ringing when firing with lower rank western coals instead of natural gas—as well as industry interest—also prompted tests with high-volatile bituminous coals from Kentucky and Colorado. The Kentucky coal had a high ash-fusion temperature and a moderate ash content, while the Colorado coal had both a low ash-fusion temperature and low ash content.

Commercial concentrates from three different Mesabi Range magnetic taconite plants were used. The materials were similar in chemical and physical properties, and are considered typical of magnetite concentrates produced in the Lake Superior district.

Six tests staged in pilot plant

Six simulation trials were scheduled for 120 hr in five-day blocks, with the fourth and fifth tests being duplicates using Montana subbituminous coals. Commercial concentrates were formed into pellets on a balling disc, closely simulating industry practices. Bentonite was added to the concentrates at a rate of 18.9 lb per lt. Following thorough mixing of the concentrate with the bentonite and the required amount of water, the green balls were formed on a disc rotating at 14 rpm and inclined at 45°, sized at minus ⅜ in., plus ⅜ in., and transported to the grate at a rate of 830 dry lb per hr. Drying and preheating of green pellets on the grate were accomplished with 5 and 10 min retention time, respectively, with the maximum average above-the-bed temperature of 860°C being maintained in the downdraft preheat zone. Bed depth was 3.5 in., and grate speed was 5.0 in. per min.

High heat losses encountered in the pilot plant kiln required a heat input of approximately 3.3 million Btu per hr to maintain maximum pelletizing temperatures of 1,300°C and a kiln offgas temperature of 900°C. This requirement was established during the base line test using only natural gas for firing. At pellet feed rates of about 800 lb per hr, the heat input was equivalent to about 9 million Btu per lt of pellets—in contrast to commercial heat consumption of about 700,000 Btu per lt. This inordinate heat requirement was a determining factor in the decision to operate the kiln using a dual firing system—burning natural gas plus a set amount of coal.

Sufficient coal was introduced to yield an average of 1.2 million Btu per hr under these conditions. The premix gas system then automatically supplied enough natural gas to maintain a temperature of 1,300°C in the hot zone. It should be emphasized that these coal rates represented a highly exaggerated condition in introducing ash and other deleterious constituents, because the coal rates furnished nearly five times the normal heat required for commercial induration of magnetite pellets.

Coal fed to the pulverizer was a nominal minus ¾ in. size. The coal pulverizer was an oversized unit that could not be throttled down to operate continuously at the lower coal rates needed for the investigations. Hence, after intermittent pulverization to about 60% minus 200 mesh, the coal was collected in a dry cyclone and a baghouse, and stored in a bin made inert with carbon dioxide gas. Indirectly heated air from the kiln hood was used to reduce the moisture content of the coal during the grinding operation, which increased heats of combustion by about 1,500 to 2,000 Btu per lb. The pulverized coal was then fed from the bin by a volumetric feeder to a venturi, where the coal was picked up and transported to the burner pipe by an air stream equivalent to 15-18% of stoichiometric requirements. The coal was injected into the kiln through a simple 1-in.-dia stainless burner pipe.

The coals were pulverized so that about 10% was retained on a 100-mesh sieve, and about 60% passed through a 200-mesh sieve.

Problems resulting from the presence of coal ash (kiln ringing, pellet quality, and fouling of the grate-to-kiln transfer points) did occur as expected. Other characteristics determined were kiln temperature gradients and sulphur distributions.

Kiln ringing occurred after 24 to 36 hr

In test No. 1 in the pilot plant kiln, with 100% natural gas firing, a uniform coating about ½ in. thick was formed on the kiln lining. No evidence of ring buildup was observed during this 120-hr test period. However, during pellet induration tests with solid-fuel firing, signs of ring formation began to show within 24 to 36 hr of steady state operations. The rings continued to grow at a comparatively slow rate but, except for Colorado coal, they did not affect pellet flow during the relatively short runs. Ring growth was most severe with Colorado coal, less severe with lignite, still less with subbituminous coal, and least with Kentucky coal.

The Colorado coal produced a pronounced buildup, averaging about 9 in. in height, with irregular accretions almost blocking the kiln's interior in 80 hr. The kiln ringing had so effectively blocked passage of pellets that the test had to be terminated at that time. Lignite firing caused a buildup about 2.5 ft in length and 5 in. deep. The less severe ringing problems that occurred with subbituminous coal firing (average thickness 3 in., with irregular accretions reaching 6 in.) could be attributed to the lower calcia and soda contents of that coal's ash. The fact that the ring accretion contained mostly iron oxide and only a small percentage of ash is an indication that the fluxing action of these particular ash elements may be more important to ring formation than the ash-fusion temperature.

An additional factor that may also have contributed to the less severe ringing was the higher burner tip velocity used in the test with subbituminous coal. The higher velocity subbituminous flame was more compact and intense than the lignite flame, and the ash particles may have been propelled further from the kiln hot zone, where they would be less likely to contribute to ring buildup. Future tests will determine whether the burner tip velocity is an important factor in ring formation.

It might be expected that some indicator—such as sodium content, ferrous iron content, or basicity of ash—could be found to help in screening out coals that would be poor performers in terms of buildup. However, at this

Net contributions of alkalies and sulphur from bentonite, subbituminous coal, and lignite

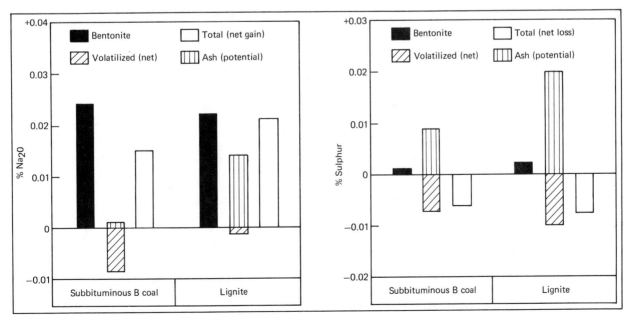

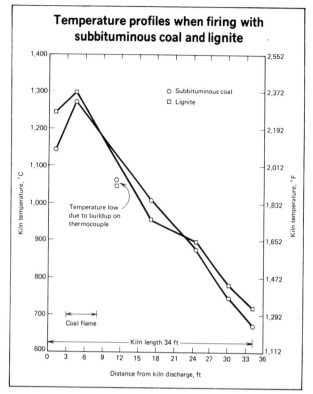

Temperature profiles when firing with subbituminous coal and lignite

Kiln temperature, °C / Kiln temperature, °F

○ Subbituminous coal
□ Lignite

Temperature low due to buildup on thermocouple

Coal flame

Kiln length 34 ft

Distance from kiln discharge, ft

point there is no single indicator that can be pinpointed—except that the highest ash-fusion temperature obtainable appears to be preferable. Even in this instance, however, present evidence is not conclusive because of differences in behavior noted in the Montana and Colorado coals, which are closely matched in ash-fusion temperatures. Still more confusing is the lesser amount of kiln ringing caused by Montana coal compared with lignite—in spite of the lignite's higher ash-fusion temperature.

Pellets suffer no chemical degradation

Pellets discharging from the kiln were of moderate strength and abrasion resistance. Crushing strengths ranged from 550 lb for pellets fired with natural gas down to 360 lb for those fired with Kentucky coal. The variation seems to reflect the degree of pellet oxidation, as measured by ferrous iron content, and the degree of pellet oxidation, in turn, is indicative of different stoichiometric requirements of oxygen for burning each of the fuels.

Since one of the concerns over coal firing is that pellets will suffer chemical degradation, it is gratifying to note that such effects with coal firing were insignificant except for 0.20-0.25% increase in silica content. Sulphur pickup from coal gases, which had been considered a potential problem, did not occur. In fact, sulphur contained in the green pellets was partially oxidized and carried out of the system with the main effluent gas stream. Data from tests 5 and 6 (subbituminous coal and lignite firing) give detailed support to the conclusion regarding pellet contamination.

Visual examination of the pellets produced from both the subbituminous and lignite firing tests showed irregular, dark, raised blotches on the pellet surface. Scanning electron microscope photographs revealed that the blotches consisted of iron oxide grains cemented together by a slag matrix, while the uncontaminated or non-blotch areas consisted simply of sintered iron oxide grains. Chemical analysis of material from the contaminated area indicated that it was similar in composition to the ring material and was apparently picked up by the pellets en route through

the kiln.

Preliminary calculations at normal magnetite induration heat consumption rates indicated that even if all the coal ash were picked up by the pellets, contamination with either lignite or subbituminous coal ash would not significantly affect pellet analysis. The analyses from test 1 (subbituminous coal) indicate that about 40% of the ash input to the kiln, or about 5 lb ash per lt of pellets, was picked up by the pellets and accounted for less than 0.2% of the weight of the fired pellets. In test 2, nearly 80% of the ash, or about 10 lb ash per lt of pellets, generated from lignite combustion was picked up by the pellets, adding 0.2% silica-plus-alumina, and 0.15% calcia-plus-magnesia.

It is difficult to assess the amount of alkalies (Na_2O + K_2O) and sulphur that may have been absorbed by the pellets from coal combustion since these constituents were erratically volatilized during the high-temperature induration process. The chief source of alkalies retained in the pellets seems to be bentonite, rather than coal. Sulphur from either the bentonite or the coal was apparently completely volatilized, with a net retained sulphur content in the pellet lower than the initial sulphur content of the concentrates. The composition of fired pellets from both tests was well within the range of acceptable levels. These results show that pellet composition will not be affected significantly by coal firing, even under exaggerated conditions.

Fly ash in lining: only small part of total ash

Although molten ash accumulating on the kiln lining or contributing to ring formation was a major concern, only a small proportion of total ash was accounted for in this manner. The preponderant amounts of ash left the system either in the exhaust gases or adhering to the pellets.

The more volatile elements in the ash particles (sodium, potassium, and sulphur) will largely be in the gas phase, with the preponderance of the sulphur reacting to form sulphur dioxide. Nearly all the reaction paths of sodium lead to sodium sulphate, possibly through the reaction of sulphur dioxide and sodium oxide in the gas phase. This is evidenced by the fact that much of the sodium found in electrostatic precipitator ash is in the form of sodium sulphate. The remaining extraneous or inherent ash constituents (SiO_2, Al_2O_3, CaO, MgO, and Fe_2O_3) become free to coalesce and deposit onto the pellets or kiln lining.

Deposition of fly ash in the grate-to-kiln transfer chute was observed when firing with Montana subbituminous coal. Partial fusion of fly ash particles was also noted.

The effect of coal firing on flame length

In tests 2 and 3, using Kentucky and Colorado coals, substantially less total heat input (less natural gas required) gave a temperature profile at the hot end similar to that of baseline test 1, but the kiln exit gas temperatures were more than 100°C lower than for all-gas firing. This resulted because the control thermocouple in the hot zone sensed the localized high temperature coal flame and automatically reduced the heat input from the gas burner. In test 4, the localized coal-flame hot zone was forward of the control thermocouple so that more natural gas was automatically introduced, while maintaining coal input at about the same Btu-per-hr level. In this way, the total thermal input was raised to approximate that of the baseline test. The net effect was to flatten the temperature profile and to raise the temperature of kiln exit gases. Although both tests were run under similar conditions, somewhat higher temperatures were sustained in test 6. □

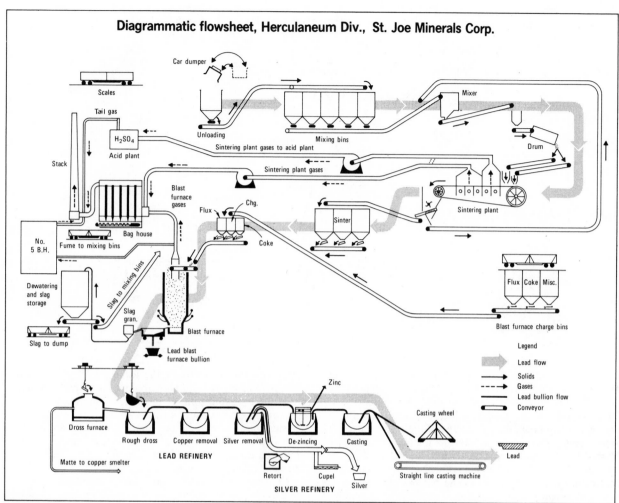

Diagrammatic flowsheet, Herculaneum Div., St. Joe Minerals Corp.

Flowsheet adapted from *Extractive Metallurgy of Lead and Zinc*, Vol. II, AIME; copyright 1970.

Herculaneum: tops in US refined lead output

ST. JOE MINERALS CORP. HAS EXPANDED the Herculaneum lead smelter and refinery to a level that makes it the largest producer in the US and puts it in a standoff position with Broken Hill's Port Pirie plant as the biggest producer of refined lead in the world. (This stature is based solely on plant output, since there are several installations that may claim to be larger on the basis of total charge material handled.)

Located on the western bank of the Mississippi River, about 25 miles south of St. Louis, Mo., the Herculaneum installation is a classic smelter of the 20th century. It processes 72% lead-bearing concentrates from St. Joe's Missouri Mining and Milling Div., taking in little or no purchased or toll feed from other sources.

Carrying roughly 0.8% to 2.9% zinc, 0.9% Cu, and roughly 1 oz of silver per ton, the concentrates are sintered with smelter returns and slag-forming materials into a self-fluxing blast furnace charge containing 45-50% lead. The agglomeration roast, carried out on a 10 x 100-ft Dwight Lloyd updraft sintering machine built by McDowell Wellman, yields a clinker with an approximate 1.4% S content.

The furnace charge is layered intermittently by shuttle conveyors on top of the burden in two of three blast furnaces. The shuttle conveyors also alternately spread coke on top of the freshly layered sinter in a weight proportion of about 9% of the sinter charge.

The blast furnace bullion is first decopperized at a drossing plant, and the dross yields copper and nickel-bearing mattes after treatment in a reverberatory furnace. The drossed lead is then desilverized in a refinery that features zinc precipitation of silver and vacuum dezincing of lead by the well-known Isbell process—a St. Joe development.

The major output of the plant amounts to approximately 225,000 tpy of refined lead, of which about 80% is a corroding grade and 20% is tailored to alloy grades meeting customer specifications.

The smelter is also equipped with a small silver refinery that produces about 200,000 oz annually; a Chemico contact sulphuric acid plant that manufactures 6,000 to 7,000 tpm of 66° Be acid from offtake metallurgical gas pulled from the Dwight Lloyd machine; automatic casting equipment; slag granulation facilities; an extensive gas handling and dust collection system; and a wide assortment of additional support units.

Development benchmarks

The Herculaneum plant is nearing its 85th year of continuous service, having been placed on line in 1892. In the intervening period, the smelter has been completely rebuilt, overhauled, and expanded a number of times—a task that occasionally called for near-heroic efforts, consid-

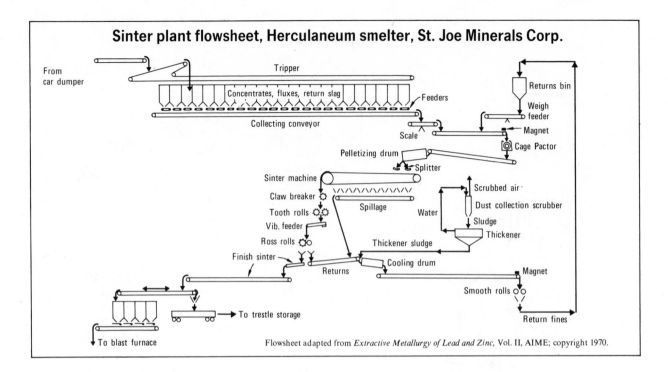

Sinter plant flowsheet, Herculaneum smelter, St. Joe Minerals Corp.

Flowsheet adapted from *Extractive Metallurgy of Lead and Zinc*, Vol. II, AIME; copyright 1970.

ering the boxed-in site. The plant now bears little resemblance to the original installation. During its lifetime, the plant and St. Joe personnel have made significant contributions to basic knowledge of lead extractive metallurgy. Herculaneum now operates on one of the highest lead sinter contents in the US—a feature which substantially reduces blast furnace volume and materials handling requirements. St. Joe personnel have also been particularly active in the development of lead-based alloys, especially the calcium-lead and tin systems. As a result, the plant is now equipped with a small alloy casting section.

Since 1970, the smelter was supplemented with a 550,000-cfm Wheelabrator baghouse, which joined a family of three existing Wheelabrator baghouses that had a combined capacity of 525,000 cfm. These units have a total filter area of about 14 acres. All are equipped with synthetic acrylic bags, which must periodically be washed, inspected, and patched for reuse. The dust load captured by the baghouses has a lead content of 50-60%.

The post-1970 gas handling project, with attendant flues and fans, represented an investment of approximately $6 million in clean air and product recovery. The plant is presently in conformance with Missouri air quality standards.

Marshalling the feed

The smelter receives inbound concentrates from the mines via the Missouri Pacific Railroad, in 100-ton cars. The smelter site is laced with about 9 mi of track for materials handling and transfer of intermediate products. Major equipment includes two diesel-electric locomotives and 23 side-dump cars of 70-ton capacity. The in-plant rail system is also equipped with cranes, flatcars, and gondolas. Inbound cars are weighed and sampled immediately upon arrival.

Concentrate is unloaded in a side car tippler designed by Strachan & Henshaw and built by Stephens Adamson. This unit rotates single cars through an arc of about 160° to empty them into a four-compartment bottom-discharge hopper. The entire cycle takes about 6 to 8 min, including the time necessary for car positioning and dumping. The system normally handles about 10 to 14 concentrate cars per day, plus four or five miscellaneous carloads of flux or other recycled smelter products. These products, all processed through the unloading system on day shift only, are belt-conveyed to a set of 23 V-bottom concrete storage bins in the mixing room. A tripper conveyor distributes sinter charge products to the storage system.

The 23-bin proportioning system provides storage for granulated blast furnace slag, lead concentrates, silica sand, crushed limestone, crushed iron ore, plant residues, and baghouse dust. Concentrate storage capacity is about 3,000 tons and slag capacity is 850 tons.

Feed preparation and proportioning

Each of the 23 bins is equipped with an apron feeder at the bottom and with manually operated, preset gates. The apron feeders load a single collector belt, which terminates in the sintering department. The amount of new feed delivered to the sintering department through the proportioning system can be varied by remote control of the drive speed on each of the apron feeders. The weight of new feed entering the sintering department, in turn, proportionately controls the amount of recycled undersize sinter that is collected in a separate 150-ton bin in the sintering circuit.

Control is accomplished by a belt scale that weighs the new feed and electronically controls a weigh feeder below

Lead smelting

(short tons)

Year	Lead and lead alloy production	Lead metal equivalent sold	Sulphuric acid sold
1971	222,213	224,321	48,800
1972	207,877	223,230	54,844
1973	215,012	284,018	54,870
1974	230,873	281,424	30,422
1975	185,889	182,340	39,915

the sinter returns bin according to a ratio set by the control room operator.

New feed and sinter returns are joined on a common belt, which feeds a Gundlach Cage-Paktor where they are mixed and crushed to about 85% minus ¼ in. The Cage-Paktor discharge is moistened to about 4-4.5% and balled in a 9 x 30-ft Allis Chalmers drum. The discharge of the pelletizing drum is split by a flop gate and two chutes into two hoppers. The first batch (10% of the total) is used as an ignition hearth layer on the sintering machine. It is laid down and leveled directly on the pallets to a depth of about 1¼ in. at the head of an 84-in. downdraft section. The bulk of the pelletized feed is introduced at the start of the updraft section of the machine and is leveled to a depth of 10 to 12 in.

The updraft burn occurs within the next 30 ft of machine length, while the remaining travel is used for cooling the clinker. Acid-strength gas of 5-7% SO_2 is pulled from the first 30 ft of the machine. The remaining gas from the cooling section of the sintering machine is filtered through a baghouse unit.

As sintered cake exits the Dwight Lloyd machine, it falls to a crash deck and grizzly, which feeds a claw breaker and tooth rolls. Here, the material is crushed to minus 5 in. and the downstream discharge is size-split by means of a Ross Rolls screen featuring a remote-controlled setting that is normally 2 in. The oversize fraction is conveyed to three 300-ton bins supplying the blast furnace department, while the undersize is recycled through a cooling drum to a sinter returns bin.

The sinter plant conveyors are hooded at transfer points. These points and other dust generating sections are vented to a scrubbing system. The sludge recovered during scrubbing is thickened for return to the sinter returns bin. The sinter machine is fed at a nominal rate of 170 tph, producing roughly 75 tph of finished product for blast furnacing. During the process, incoming lead concentrate containing approximately 72% lead and 16% S is blended with charge components and converted into a clinker containing about 45-50% lead and 1.6% sulphur for the blast furnace.

Blast furnacing: no matte, no speiss

The antimony, arsenic, and copper content of the feed is low, making the furnace operation largely one of reducing the lead and melting the burden. The zinc content of the slag is not high enough to warrant zinc fuming. The bullion produced by the furnace contains over 90% Pb. The slag may have a lead content of 2.5%.

Herculaneum is equipped with three Port Pirie-type blast furnaces of differing dimensions—a reflection of continual efforts at improving furnace design and operating characteristics. The furnaces are water-jacketed to within 5 ft of the charging floor, and above that level they are lined with a 13½-in. thickness of fire-clay brick. All are equipped with centerline offtakes for the gas stream. There is very little bosh zone, and the vertical jackets slope steeply to the basic crucible dimension.

A yard storage system having a capacity of 1,600 tons of sinter, 350 tons of coke, and 500 tons of miscellaneous materials is located below a railroad highline. The storage system is positioned between the sintering department and the blast furnace department to provide added capacity if blast furnace and sintering rates become unbalanced.

The furnace charge floor is equipped with three small bins containing 150 tons of sinter, 30 tons of coke, and 30 tons of gravel. Each furnace is fed from the charge bins via a conveyor system that terminates at each furnace in a pair of shuttle conveyors—one on each side of the center gas offtake. Coke and sinter are alternately layered on the burden. Because of the degree of quality control of the charge preparation, corrective additions of materials are rarely required at the blast furnace charge floor.

Coke and sinter are proportioned through preprogrammed weighing systems. The furnace feed belts shuttle the long dimension of the furnace, depositing coke and charge. The distribution rate normally follows an automatic timing and travel sequence, although an operator can override the system to handle irregular burden descent.

The crucibles are fitted with a continuous Roy tapper at one end, which permits reacted and melted charge to flow into a gas-fired 9 x 3.5 x 3-ft settler where the slag and bullion separate. The slag overflows the settler and is treated in a granulation system. The bullion exits the settler through a siphon-type lead well. The hot metal, at about 1,000°F, is collected in a 10-ton ladle for movement by overhead crane to the drossing department.

Blast air for the furnaces is supplied by three Roots

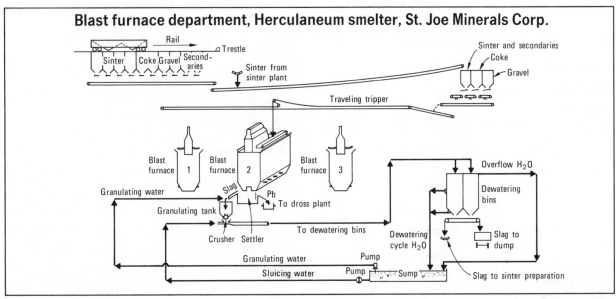

Blast furnace department, Herculaneum smelter, St. Joe Minerals Corp.

Flowsheet adapted from *Extractive Metallurgy of Lead and Zinc*, Vol. II, AIME; copyright 1970.

Connersville centrifugal blowers, each rated for 15,000 cfm.

Slag handling: unique and clean

All furnaces are equipped with granulation tanks that taper to conical bottoms. A toothed, disc-type crusher mounted in the bottom of the tank feeds a venturi system. Overflow slag from the settler is shock-chilled with 60-psig water jets, and the granulated product settles into the tank and disc crusher system. High pressure sluicing water conveys the granulated slag in a thin slurry through a venturi to one of two conical elevated dewatering bins.

Supplied by United Conveyor Corp., the granulation system provides for batch settling and drainage of water from the bins. The conical bin bottoms are equipped with a number of drain ports, which allow the water to settle to a concrete sump when a drain valve is automatically opened. Following drainage, a hydraulically operated seal gate can be opened to reclaim the solids by means of a reversible conveyor. The granular product is then returned to the charge proportioning system, or it can be loaded in railroad cars for disposal on the slag dump.

Molten slag can also be drawn from the settler into wheeled slag pots for transport to the dump by a locomotive.

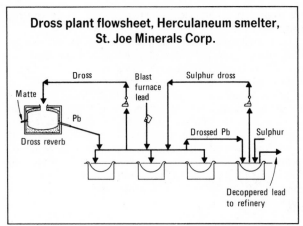

Dross plant flowsheet, Herculaneum smelter, St. Joe Minerals Corp.

Flowsheet adapted from *Extractive Metallurgy of Lead and Zinc*, Vol. II, AIME; copyright 1970.

Drossing: mainly a copper removal exercise

The drossing section is equipped with four 250-ton hemispherical steel kettles. One is used for stirring out copper, and the remaining three are used to receive lead blast furnace bullion. The bullion from the blast furnace

---

Typical operating data at Herculaneum smelter

Inbound concentrate (approx.) .72.0% Pb, 2.9% Zn, 2% Cu, 1.0 oz Au per ton
Annual capacity ....220,000-235,000 st

Sintering department

Sinter plant feed (analysis)	%Pb	% S
Inbound conc.	40-45	9-11
Recycled material........................	43-45	1.2-1.7
Machine feed..............................	40-45	4.7-7.0
Finished sinter............................	45-50	1.4-1.8

Typical final sinter (analysis) .... 48% Pb, 1% Cu, 10% insol, 9% SiO₂, 15% FeO, 5% CaO, 1.4%S

Sinter plant feed........................... Inbound 50%, recycled 50%
Balling machine dimensions........... 9 x 30 ft
Sinter machine dimensions .... 10 x 100 ft
 Machine feed .... 160-180 stph
 Finished sinter
 (to blast furnace) .... 75-100 stph
Sinter pallet speed .... 40-48 in. per min
Sinter ignition bed
 depth (approx.)....................... 1¼ - 1½ in.
Sinter total bed
 depth (approx.)....................... 10-14 in.
Sinter windbox area
 Updraft................................... 1,020 sq ft, 13 boxes
 Downdraft .... 70 sq ft, 1 box
 Air volume.............................. 106,700 cfm total
 7,200 downdraft
Sinter fuel (nat. gas per ton
 finished sinter)......................... 85,000 Btu

Blast furnace department

Dimensions	Furnace 1	2	3
Crucible depth (in.)............................	18	24	24
Width at top tuyeres (ft)...................	10.5	10.5	10.5
Width at bottom tuyeres (ft)	5.5	5.5	5.5
Length (ft-in.).....................................	28-1	28-1	28-1
Height (ft-in.)	18-3	16-9	15-3
Number of tuyeres............................	44	44	44
Tuyere diameter (in.).........................	4.75	4.75	4.75
Furnace area (sq ft at bottom tuyeres)...............................	155	155	155
Sinter smelted (stpd)............................	900	900	
Sinter size (in.)..............................	+2-5	+2-5	
Sinter charge (st per batch).................	10.0	10.0	
Coke on charge (%).............................	9-10	9-10	
Coke size (in.)..............................	+1-4	+1-4	
Air (cfm).............................	9,000-10,500	9,000-10,500	
Air blast (oz per sq in.)........................	30-45	30-45	
Sinter melted (stpd per sq ft)................	5.8	5.8	
Sinter melted (per 1,000 cfm)	90	90	

Drossing department

Charge material, per week	Short tons	% of charge
Dross.....................................	835	92
Soda ash	45	5
Coke breeze............................	16	2
Silica sand	10	1

Tap product, per week		
Lead bullion............................	590	65
Copper matte	164	18
Slag..	81	9
Ni-bearing material..................	10	1

Dross plant analyses	Pb	Cu	S	Ni	Insol	FeO	Zn
Reverb bullion........	—	1.4	—	—	—	—	—
Copper matte........	10	50	20	2	—	7	1
Nickel matte..........	35	35	20	15	—	2	—
Dross.....................	60	13	4.5	3.0	3.0	1.5	4.3
Lead......................	—	0.01	—	0.004	—	—	0.001

Refinery flowsheet, Herculaneum smelter, St. Joe Minerals Corp.

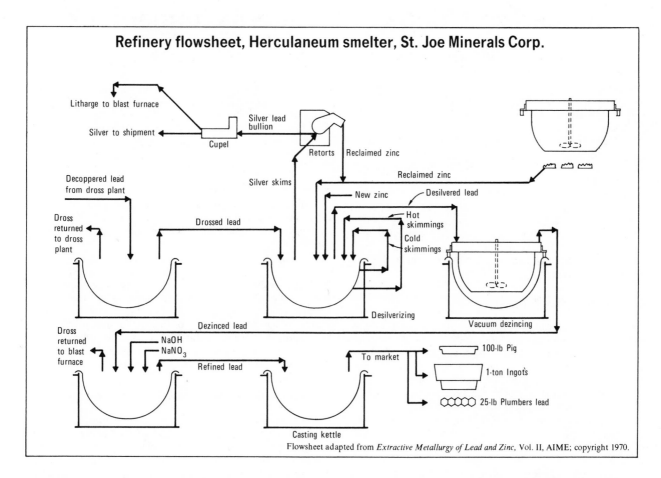

Flowsheet adapted from *Extractive Metallurgy of Lead and Zinc*, Vol. II, AIME; copyright 1970.

contains some dissolved matte and a little reduced copper, silver, and zinc. As the bullion cools, the copper and any nickel compounds begin to freeze from solution, forming a dross, which is skimmed by a perforated scoop and charged to one of a pair of 12 x 25-ft reverberatory furnaces. Only one furnace is in use at any time.

The dross is melted and fluxed in the reverberatory with soda ash, producing a soda matte containing roughly 10% lead and 45-48% copper. This product is the smelter outlet for copper and nickel. The rough drossed lead in the receiving kettles is transferred to a final decoppering kettle, where it is stirred with sulphur, and the final dross is returned to the reverberatory furnace.

The drosses smelted in the reverberatory yield a matte, bullion, and occasionally a small amount of nickel matte at the bullion-matte interface. Reverberatory bullion is tapped into one of the drossing kettles. Time is important in achieving a low copper content during drossing. The lower the copper content of the bullion transferred to the refining department, the less zinc is consumed in desilverizing.

Refining: a batch process

Lead is pumped and laundered to the refining department, which is equipped with eleven 250-ton kettles. Each of the kettles is heated by three burners, which are normally fired using natural gas. Provision has been made, however, to use fuel oil.

The charge in the kettles is stirred by four-bladed impellers suspended from a shaft. Framing for the assembly is supported by the kettle rim. The propellers, driven by 40-hp motors, are encased in a basket.

The kettles are serviced by centrifugal pumps for advancing bullion through the kettles in a batch operation.

Another pump system is used to deliver bullion to the casting machines. Silver is removed by adding zinc metal, which produces an Ag-Zn skim that is collected for silver refining and recovery and return of zinc to the circuit. Since zinc is soluble in lead to the extent of about 0.6%, desilvered lead must go through a vacuum distillation process.

In oversimplified terms, the St. Joe-designed dezincers consist of a submerged bell and a water-cooled condensing top. The bells contain impellers driven by 60-hp motors. By application of process heat and vacuum, metallic zinc is fumed from the melt for collection on the condensing top.

Herculaneum produces a fire-refined silver. Silver skims from the refining kettles are charged to four tilting furnaces containing graphite retorts and cast iron condensers for capturing fumed zinc. Each of the retorts is fired by two natural gas burners.

The cupellation furnace contains a 7-in.-deep pan that is 44 x 132 in. in horizontal dimensions, enclosed in a firebrick-lined furnace fired by natural gas. Silver bullion is sidecharged to the pan through a trough. A Sturtevant blower supplies about 2,500 cfm of cupellation air.

Refined lead bullion is pumped to a casting department, equipped to produce 1-ton ingots, 100-lb pigs, and plumbers lead, which is cast in links by a Sheppard straight-line machine. The 1-ton ingots are cast on a 26-ft-dia wheel. The pigs are cast either by a wheel nearly 20 ft in diameter or by a Treadwell-designed straight-line machine that casts four pigs at a time.

St. Joe is capable of producing 99.996% to 99.999% refined lead—possibly the purest lead available anywhere.

Samples of each batch of refined lead and alloy lead are analyzed for As, Sn, Cu, Zn, Fe, Cd, Ag, and Ca, and the analyses are stored for at least two years as a customer service. □

Submerged smelting of lead merits longer look

T. A. A. Quarm, principal engineer, Mining and Metals Div., Bechtel Corp.

"SUBMERGED SMELTING" IS a process originally designed to produce zinc metal by injecting roasted sulphide concentrate, flux, fuel, and air into a bath of molten slag.[1] A review of efforts to devise a lead production process that would be simpler and less expensive than conventional blast furnace smelting suggested that the submerged smelting technique could solve many of the problems encountered. A preliminary study was thus undertaken on the submerged smelting of lead.

In this study, only the basic heat and material balances were calculated; no attempt was made to evaluate obvious improvements, such as oxygen enrichment, or to specify equipment design. Nevertheless, the indicated savings in capital and operating costs of submerged smelting of lead as compared with conventional lead smelting is such that further investigation is warranted.

Lead smelting a metallurgical paradox

Smelting lead in a blast furnace entails the metallurgical paradox that concentrate, which commonly contains 70-80% lead, has to be diluted to 40-45% lead with flux and recirculated slag before it can be sintered to prepare a suitable furnace feed. Furthermore, an acceptably low sulphur content in finished sinter, about 1.5%, can be achieved in one pass only if the diluted concentrate is mixed with at least an equal weight of crushed, recirculated sinter before it is charged onto the sinter machine. Not only is this procedure costly, but the coke required for smelting—about 10% of the sinter weight—is also expensive.

Before the introduction of sintering, most of the world's supply of lead was extracted directly from concentrate or rich ore via roast-reaction on a hearth. In this process, which probably has been known to man since time immemorial, part of the lead sulphide was allowed to roast in air to form lead oxide that reacted with the remainder of the sulphide to liberate lead metal and sulphur dioxide. Unfortunately, about one-fifth of the lead remained in a rich slag containing about 50% lead, which had to be smelted by other methods. This, among other factors, led to the predominance of blast furnace smelting. The reaction, though undoubtedly more complex, was usually described by the following equations:

$$2\,PbS + 3\,O_2 = 2\,PbO + 2\,SO_2$$
$$2\,PbO + PbS = 3\,Pb + SO_2$$

In spite of the demise of this process, the principle continues to attract attention, and many attempts have been made to devise a technique that would permit its application without producing rich slag.

About 20 years ago, Boliden[2] developed a process in which concentrate was partly roasted with flux and then smelted in an electric furnace to produce lead bullion. The sulphur content of the roast was so controlled that a small excess of lead sulphide remained in solution in the bullion, thereby ensuring essentially complete reaction of lead oxide that would otherwise report in the slag. Although the slag was sufficiently low in lead to be discarded, the sulphur in the bullion had to be removed by blowing it with air in a converter.

Outokumpu Oy combined roasting and smelting

In a later experiment, Outokumpu Oy combined roasting and smelting by blowing a mixture of lead concentrate and flux with preheated air into the reaction shaft of a pilot flash smelting furnace.[3] Most of the heat required was provided by the strongly exothermic reaction; the remainder was supplied by burning butane. Ideally uniform conditions could not be maintained, however, and the slag contained lead oxide while the bullion contained lead sulphide. This problem was solved by tapping both lead and slag into a furnace with a deep hearth cooled at the bottom to a temperature just above the melting point of lead. Under these conditions, lead sulphide migrated to the surface of the bullion, where it came into contact with the slag and reacted with the lead oxide, producing additional metal. After about two hours in the separation furnace, the slag was tapped and discarded.

In another pilot plant program, conducted by St. Joe Minerals Corp.,[4] lead concentrate and air were blown through tuyeres into a bath of molten lead in a converter. Although lead was produced successfully, the gangue did not fuse at the temperature of operation, and in order to dissolve it, lead oxide had to be produced by overblowing. Consequently, about one-eighth of the lead in concentrate reported in rich slag. There was also the problem of severe erosion of the refractory lining of the converter, particularly in the vicinity of the tuyeres.

How submerged smelting would work for lead

In the submerged smelting technique, concentrate, flux, and air would be blown through tuyeres into a bath of molten slag at 1,200°C, whereupon lead and sulphur dioxide would be liberated by roast-reaction, as in the St. Joe process. The gangue and flux, however, would be dissolved. Moreover, if the furnace were constructed with water jackets in the manner of a slag fuming furnace, a layer of frozen slag on the inner surfaces would act as a self-regenerative refractory, and erosion would pose no problem. To maintain working temperature in such a furnace, the supplementary heat needed would be supplied by adding pulverized coal to the charge. Then, in contrast to the Outokumpu process, lead metal and slag

---

Table 1—Analyses of concentrate, flux, and coal

		Percent
Lead concentrate:	Pb	74.2%
	S	15.6
	Fe	3.0
	Zn	5.3
	SiO_2	1.1
	CaO	1.9
	MgO	0.5
	CO_2	6.0
Flux:	SiO_2	90.0
Pulverized coal		
Proximate analysis:	Fixed carbon	73.2
	Volatile matter	19.1
	Ash	7.7
Ultimate analysis:	C	81.0
	H	4.5
	O	4.0
	N	1.8
	S	1.0
Ash analysis:	Fe	10.0
	SiO_2	30.0
	CaO	15.0

Fuel value: 7,890 k cal per kg (14,190 Btu per lb)

---

would be kept in intimate association by the violent agitation induced by submerged combustion of the coal. As a result, the reaction would proceed in spite of minor fluctuations in feed composition. Iron oxide in the slag, credited with a major role in slag fuming,[5] would then be expected to play a similar part in this process.

At convenient intervals, the slag accumulated in the furnace would be tapped into a settler, where entrained lead would separate. After settling, the slag would be discarded or, if it contained sufficient zinc, transferred to a fuming furnace.

Air would be admitted to the smelting furnace above the slag bath to ensure oxidation of metal vapor in the gas before it flowed to a waste-heat boiler. Fume would be recovered from the cool gas in conventional equipment and would be added to the incoming concentrate to provide part of the lead oxide required for reaction. Clean gas, rich in sulphur dioxide but free of the volatile carbonaceous compounds that contaminate sinter gas, would then be sent on to an acid plant.

For purposes of calculation, the furnace was assumed to be 6.5 m long by 2.5 m wide, and to be supplied with air at the rate of 500 N cu m per min (17,650 scfm). Heat and material balances were computed by constructing and solving an equation for the heat balance in a slag bath at 1,200°C from which the heat loss to the water jackets was taken to be 1,650 million cal per hour (6.5 x 10⁶ Btu per hr). Analyses of concentrate, flux, and coal are shown in Table 1, and the results of the calculation in Table 2.

The quantity of lead carried from the bath as fume was estimated from the vapor pressure of lead metal at 1,200°C. Although the system probably would be more complex, the computed fume load, about 20% of the lead in the concentrate, was in agreement with data given for the St. Joe process. For reasons of simplicity, recirculated fume was assumed to be lead oxide.

Conservatively speaking, the slag was assumed to contain 4% lead. However, the quantity produced would be too small for its lead content to have any appreciable effect on lead recovery.

Calculations predicted a favorable smelting rate

At the assumed rate of air flow, the calculations predicted that a smelting rate of 33.2 mtph concentrate would produce 24.6 mt of lead metal. Coal consumption would be 1.5 mtph. For comparison, a conventional smelter of this capacity would require an updraft sinter machine with an area of about 80 sq m, and a blast furnace roughly 11 m long by 3 m wide (at the top of the shaft). The furnace would consume about 5.5 mtph of metallurgical coke.

Cooling the gas leaving the smelting furnace to 350°C in a waste heat boiler would recover about 10,000 million cal per hr (40 x 10⁶ Btu per hr) in steam, the equivalent of about 85% of the fuel value of the coal. Clean gas flowing to the acid plant, 34,000 N cu m per hr (20,000 scfm), would contain about 11% sulphur dioxide.

Although an effort was made to be conservative in the calculations for submerged smelting of lead, some optimism in the assessment of details may have escaped notice. Nevertheless, the indicated advantages in capital and operating costs are significant enough to warrant further investigation of the submerged smelting technique. □

References

1) Quarm, T. A. A., "Preliminary calculations for zinc extraction by submerged smelting," TRANS. INSTIT. MIN. METALL., Vol. 81, 1972, pp 669-73.
2) Herneryd, O., "Large metallurgical units featured at Boliden's Ronnskar Works," E/MJ, Vol. 156, 1955, pp 78-83.
3) Bryk, P. et al, "Flash smelting of lead concentrates," JOURNAL OF METALS, December 1966, pp 1298-1302.
4) Fuller, F. T., "Process for direct smelting of lead concentrates," JOURNAL OF METALS, December 1968, pp 26-30.
5) Quarm, T. A. A., "Slag fuming–kinetic or thermodynamic?" E/MJ, January 1968, pp 92-93.

MATERIAL BALANCE FLOW DIAGRAM FOR SUBMERGED SMELTING

Table 2—Calculated results of submerged smelting

Charge composition	Mtph
Lead concentrate	33.2
Fume	5.3
Silica flux	0.6
Pulverized coal	1.5

Slag analysis	Percent
Fe	25.3
SiO₂	23.0
CaO	16.3
Zn	10.8
Pb	4.0

Heat balance:

	M cal/h	Btu X 10⁻⁶/h		M cal/h	Btu X 10⁻⁶/h
Heat of reaction	7,570	30.0	Heat of bullion	1,100	4.4
			Heat of slag	1,630	6.5
Heat of combustion	11,840	47.0	Heat of gas and fume	15,030	59.6
			Heat loss to jackets	1,650	6.5
	19,410	77.0		19,410	77.0

Lead balance:

	Mtph		Mtph
Concentrate	24.6	Bullion	24.4
Fume	4.9	Fume	4.9
		Slag	0.2
	29.5		29.5

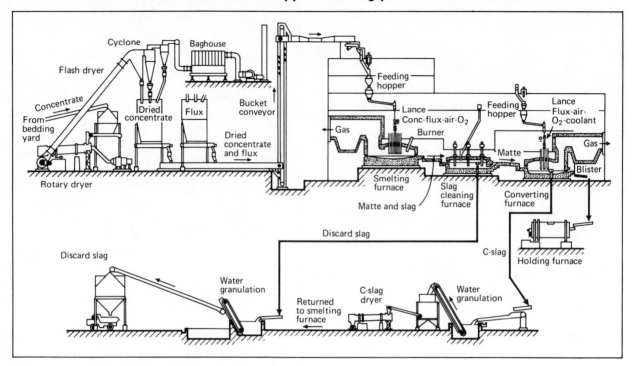

Mitsubishi Metal previews its promising new continuous copper smelting process

Peter Rutledge, McGraw-Hill World News, Tokyo

CONTINUOUS COPPER SMELTING as devised by Mitsubishi Metal Corp. may provide all the edge the metals producer needs to survive future government attempts to thin the ranks of the Japanese copper smelting fraternity. The Japanese are growing increasingly concerned about the viability of the copper smelting business—now deep in the red because of the government-imposed ban on exports of copper metal, sagging domestic demand, and soaring production costs. However, Mitsubishi may escape such a fate, thanks to its new, cost-efficient, relatively clean process. The Mitsubishi process has been licensed to Texasgulf for use at its 130,000-tpy smelter in Timmins, Ont. But even more promising, company insiders hint, is the additional interest in the process that has been expressed by other companies.

Mitsubishi recently let E/MJ take a brief look at the new process it has been using on a small but commercial scale on tiny Naoshima Island, in Japan's Seto Inland Sea. Many questions went unanswered, but it was clear that the Mitsubishi version of continuous copper smelting holds great promise.

The heart of the Mitsubishi process is a system of three small furnaces: a smelting furnace, a slag-cleaning furnace, and a converting furnace. All are controlled by an IBM System 7 computer. The melt overflows the furnaces and moves through a series of launders. Since the melt overflows, there is no need for skimming or other manual work associated with conventional batch-type smelters.

Nor is there any need for ladles, buckets, or furnace-tilting devices to transfer the melt from one furnace to another.

Elimination of ladles and buckets and the use of small furnaces saves 20% to 30% in capital costs compared with conventional reverberatory or flash systems, according to Mitsubishi officials.

An even greater saving in manpower is reportedly possible. A total of 50 workers is assigned to the new smelter at Naoshima, which has a capacity of 4,000 mtpm. By comparison, 160 workers were assigned by Mitsubishi to the 50-year-old, 4,000-mtpm reverberatory smelter that was replaced by the new facility in March 1974.

In the first step of the Mitsubishi process, concentrates—typically, dry unroasted charge—and air are injected through a series of pneumatically operated lances directly into the bath of the smelting furnace. This overhead injection technique creates agitation in the bath, speeding up smelting of concentrate and fluxes and minimizing release of mechanical flue dust.

The lances are installed in the center of the smelting furnace, with the outlet tips directly over the bath. Injection charging produces "relatively large" matte particles, making it easier to separate matte and slag in the slag-cleaning furnace, company officials say.

Computer control permits Mitsubishi to achieve a copper matte grade as high as 65% at a temperature as low as 1,210° to 1,230°C without increasing copper loss in the slag. The process can maintain a slag factor of 0.7 to 1.0, vs. a slag factor of 1.0 to 1.5 in a conventional system.

Slag and matte overflow into the electric slag-cleaning furnace, where the large matte particles drop to the bottom and are siphoned off into another launder. The slag is cleaned by adding pyrite and coke, and copper content in the slag is cut to the 0.4-0.5% range. Slag then overflows through the slag hole and is discarded.

Matte in the converting furnace is converted to blister copper by the addition of limestone flux and oxygen-enriched air, both of which are charged in through another series of overhead lances. The oxygen mixture is said to aid in controlling temperature in the converting furnace. Sulphur content in the blister is under 0.05% and copper content in the revert slag ranges from 13% to 18%. Mitsu-

bishi says sulphur content in the blister can be reduced by adjusting the oxygen mixture, but this raises the copper content in the revert slag.

Blister is stored in a holding furnace before delivery to the anode plant. Revert slag is granulated, dried, and returned for later charging into the smelting furnace.

Another factor that contributes to economical operation is sulphur dioxide collection, the company says. Gas collected from all three furnaces averages 12-15% SO_2 when it reaches the sulphuric acid plant. By contrast, SO_2 content in gases collected from the reverberatory smelter on Naoshima was only 1-2%. Officials say that high fuel consumption in the reverb smelter explains why SO_2 content there is so low. □

Alcoa saves energy on the way to aluminum with fluid flash calciners

ALUMINUM CO. OF AMERICA'S fluid flash calcining process—now used at seven Alcoa and affiliated bauxite refining operations—has been authorized for an eighth alumina refinery at Mobile, Ala. This proprietary process, which drives off water of crystallization from precipitated aluminum hydroxide in the Bayer process, reportedly reduces fuel requirements by 30-40%, decreases capital and investment costs, and yields a better quality product.

Alcoa first used fluid flash calcining in a 300-tpd unit at its Bauxite, Ark., alumina refinery in 1963. This was followed with 600-tpd calciners in Surinam and at Kwinana, Australia in 1965 and 1966, and new, 1,500-tpd Mark III systems in Jamaica and at Pinjarra, Australia, and Port Comfort, Tex. Alcoa's William M. Fish, manager of equipment development for the Alumina and Chemical Div., reported on the process late in February.

The starting material for aluminum electrolytic potlines is alumina (Al_2O_3), which is recovered from bauxite by means of a caustic digestion, followed by the clarification, cooling, and precipitation of $Al(OH)_3$ (gibbsite). It is necessary to drive off combined water from the precipitate by calcining before reduction at the smelter. During decomposition, the hydroxide passes through a series of intermediate hydroxide forms or phases before arriving at the final alpha alumina or corundum phase. The alpha phase is essentially anhydrous and inert. The lower crystalline forms contain some water and will adsorb water in humid atmospheres.

Calcination of aluminum hydroxide requires about 1,600 Btu per lb of combined water removed, which corresponds to 850 Btu per lb of alumina. If the calcination is continued to the alpha form, an exothermic reaction occurs which releases about

120 Btu per lb of alumina. Historically, calcination was carried on in rotary kilns, and kiln and cooler improvements in the mid-1940s had reduced heat requirements from early figures of 4,000 Btu per lb of alumina to about 2,100 Btu per lb. While this figure was still about 2½ times the theoretical requirement for calcining alumina, it was approaching the practical limit imposed by rotary kiln design.

The Mark III system of fluid flash calcination evolved from a pressurized, multiple, fluid-bed system with limited capacity, through a dispersed phase contacting method with only a single hearth in the combustion reactor, to the current design (see illustration). In the current system, the combustion zone has been eliminated entirely and the furnace takes the shape of a vertical cylinder with conical ends.

Heated combustion air enters at the bottom of the furnace. Fuel is introduced at several points around the periphery of the lower portion of the cylindrical section. Partially calcined alumina from a cyclone heat exchanger is fed to the combustion zone through an inclined conduit aimed to spout the alumina into the central portion of the furnace.

The calcined alumina and combustion products leave the top of the furnace and enter a cyclone where the solids separate from the gas stream and fall into a fluid bed in the lower portion of the cyclone vessel. Complete combustion and maximum calcining temperature are achieved in the dispersed phase (flash) calcination stage. The holding period in the fluid bed, at the calcining temperature or slightly below due to radiation losses and fluidizing air, provides control of loss of ignition (LOI) and surface area.

The Mark III process combines advantages of dense-phase fluidization and di-

lute-phase techniques. All of the high-volume combustion products and released water vapor are handled in high-velocity, low-density suspension systems to keep vessel diameters and pressure drops at a minimum. Dense-phase fluidized beds provide high heat transfer rates for indirect heat exchange and thermal and mass capacity for close process control.

In the fluid flash calciner, moist filter cake is fed into a flash drying section where surface moisture is removed by contact with combustion products. The dried hydroxide is held in a fluidized bed dryer, which provides a "thermal fly wheel" to allow for feed variations and to insure dryness. Dry hydroxide is conveyed from the dryer to the calcining section at a controlled rate to maintain constant calcining temperature. Calcined alumina leaving the combustion zone is retained in a fluidized bed for the desired period of time by control of the bed level. The combination of calcining temperature and retention time determines the physical characteristics of the product alumina.

The calcined product is first cooled by direct contact with combustion air in a series of cyclone heat exchangers and finally in a two-deck fluid bed cooler. A tubular heat exchanger in the upper deck heats air for the fluid dryer, and water-cooled tube bundles provide the final cooling on the lower deck.

Fuel requirement for the Alcoa calciner is approximately 1,400 gross Btu per lb of alumina, and, due to the high heat exchange efficiency, is practically independent of the calcining temperature. About 100 Btu per lb of alumina is available for heating process water. Power consumption is about 20 kwh per ton. The Mark III is 90 ft in height and occupies a building area of 50 ft x 106 ft. □

Isa Oxy Probe advances quality control and automation in copper refining

'The Isa Oxy Probe system has proven a reliable industrial monitoring device for the continuous on-line analysis of oxygen in molten copper over a normal operating range of 0.003% to 0.10% oxygen and 1,115°C to 1,150°C.'

William A. Scholes, McGraw-Hill World News

THE ISA OXY-PROBE SYSTEM for continuous monitoring of the oxygen content of molten copper is an important new quality control tool that offers increased opportunity for automation.

The system was developed jointly by the Div. of Tribophysics of Australia's Commonwealth Scientific and Industrial Research Organization and Copper Refineries Pty. Ltd. (CRL), of Queensland, a subsidiary of MIM Holdings Ltd. The development was based on fundamental studies at the School of Metallurgy, University of New South Wales.

The measuring probe used in the system contains a small, solid-electrolyte oxygen-sensing cell which is cheap and readily replaceable. CRL has been operating the system since October 1970 at its copper refinery; it now monitors the oper-

ations of a 70-tpd Asarco shaft furnace and associated wirebar casting system with oxygen concentration in the range of 0.004% to 0.008%, and two 440-ton reverberatory furnaces and associated anode casting system with oxygen concentration in the range of 0.01% to 0.1%.

The control of oxygen is critical in production of cast refinery products since oxygen content affects the physical properties (especially the conductivity of cast shapes), the occurrence of casting defects (especially cracks and low set and rolled edges in wirebar casting), and the properties of anodes for economical electrolytic refining.

In standard refinery practice, oxygen content is usually determined visually, by the appearance of the 'set' surface of the

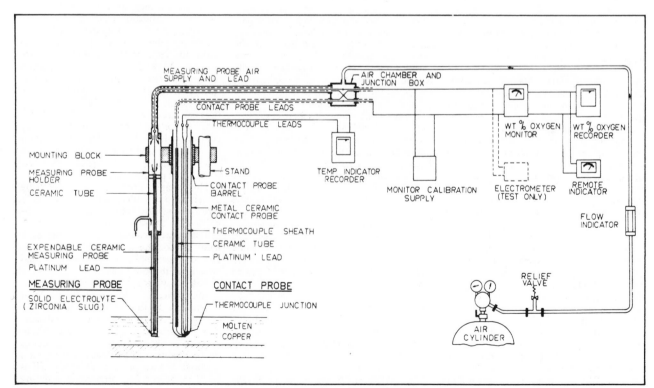

Fig. 1—Schematic diagram of Isa Oxy Probe system.

Reprinted From E/MJ, October 1974 **E/MJ OPERATING HANDBOOK OF MINERAL PROCESSING**

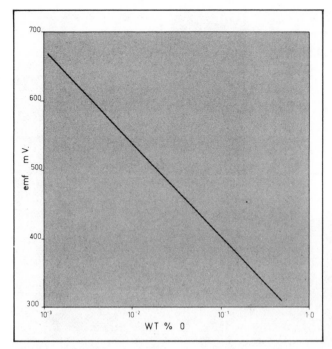

Fig. 2—Relationship between e.m.f. (mV) and wt% O in pure copper.

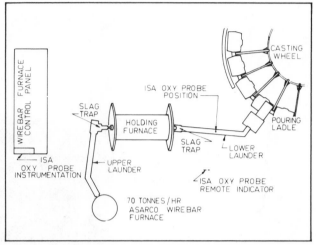

Fig. 3—Wirebar casting layout.

casting and by the amount of gas evolution during solidification. Oxygen content can also be accurately determined by chemical analysis.

The obvious drawbacks are that visual observations rely on the skill of the operators, and both visual and chemical methods involve time delays in taking corrective action. The principal objective in developing the Isa Oxy Probe was to overcome these drawbacks. Additionally, the increasing use of the continuous melting furnace and continuous rod casting processes pointed to the need for a monitoring system.

The Isa Oxy Probe system consists of the measuring probe assembly, contact assembly, wiring and instrumentation system, and ancillary equipment such as the mounting block raising and lowering mechanism, heat shielding, and air supply. (Fig. 1.)

Two expendable parts are the 19-in.-long, 8-mm-OD ceramic probe in the measuring probe assembly, and the outer metal ceramic sheath (24-in.-long, ⅞-in.-OD) of the contact probe assembly. The life of these two expendable parts is: assembly probe—six to twelve 7-hr casts in wirebar, and one to two 6½-hr casts in anode; outer sheath—55 7-hr casts in wirebar, and 28 6½-hr casts in anode.

How the probe works

The Isa Oxy Probe operates on the principle of a galvanic concentration cell, giving an electromotive force (e.m.f.) output directly related to the difference in oxygen chemical potential between the oxygen dissolved in the copper and a convenient, accurately-known reference oxygen potential. On the basis of the known relationship between oxygen chemical potential and oxygen concentration in liquid copper, a direct conversion from e.m.f. output to oxygen concentration can be made.

The basic feature of the oxygen cell is a solid electrolyte which conducts electric current by the migration of oxygen ions. Cubic stabilized zirconia is generally used for the electrolyte.

A constant potential is maintained by flowing air over one face of the electrolyte, and a platinum wire contacting this face acts as the current collector. A variable potential is obtained due to the variation in oxygen content of the liquid

copper in contact with the other face of the electrolyte. Liquid copper acts as the current collector for this face, and the circuit is completed by using a suitable inert electronically conducting material.

The voltage, E, developed by the cell may be established by the following formula:

$$E = \frac{RT}{nF} \, , ln_e \left[\frac{pO_2 \text{ (air)}}{pO_2 \text{ (liquid metal)}} \right]$$

where R = the gas constant, T = the absolute temperature

Fig. 4—Wirebar probe installation.

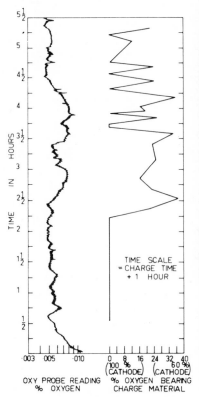

Fig. 6—Probe oxygen, and oxygen in charge material, vs. time.

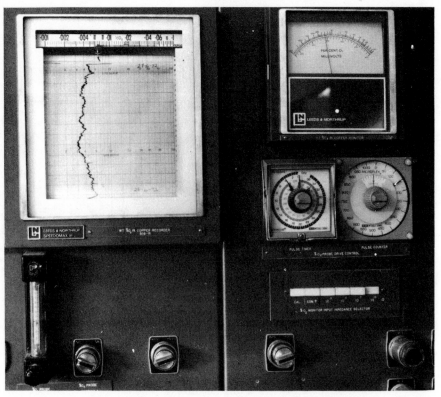

Fig. 5—Instrument panel for oxygen and temperature monitoring.

°K, n = the number of electrons transferred per oxygen molecule = 4, F = the value of a Faraday, p = the partial oxygen pressure.

To produce a calibration for liquid copper requires information relating oxygen partial pressure to dissolved oxygen content in the copper. The system at CRL uses recently determined data of K. A. Johnson and D. R. Young. The calibration, calculated for a temperature of 1,125°C at sea level, is illustrated in Fig. 2.

The theoretical principles of the cell have been understood for many years, and the cell has been used in various ways for over 10 years in laboratory studies. Difficulties with the ther-

mal stock sensitivity of the electrolyte and the lack of stability of its conductive properties at high temperatures have retarded the industrial application of the oxygen measuring cell. In the present cell construction, these problems are overcome by using small discs of zirconia to ensure thermal shock resistance, with the discs being of a selected composition which exhibits time-stable conductivity properties.

Oxy probe installation at CRL

In wirebar casting at CRL, the probe is located in the lower launder between the holding furnace and the casting ladle. The wirebar casting system layout is shown in Fig. 3 and the actual probe installation in Fig. 4.

The instrumentation for oxygen and temperature monitoring and recording is housed in the furnace control room, with remote indicators for both temperature and oxygen content conveniently located (Fig. 5). The melting furnace, holding furnace, both launders, and the pouring ladle bowl systems are naphtha fired with manual fuel-air ratio control on all systems to maintain a protective reducing atmosphere from melting to casting. There are no facilities for 'poling' or adding charcoal to the holding furnace or ladle bowl to adjust the oxygen content after melting.

The continuous melting furnace does not alter the composition of the charge material, but simply melts the charge at about 60 tph to correspond to the casting speed of the wheel. Blending of high-oxygen charge material, such as casting splash, molds, and revert wirebar, with electrolytically refined cathode is controlled to maintain the oxygen content between 0.005% and 0.008%. A typical oxygen variation is illustrated in Fig. 6, compared with the variation of the content of oxygen-bearing charge material. The average oxygen content of the oxygen-bearing charge material is about 0.03%. There is about a 1-hr time lag between charging and melting at the taphole, and the charge material graph is time corrected.

If the probe readings are higher than 0.008% and increasing, and the ratio of oxygen bearing charge to cathode is nor-

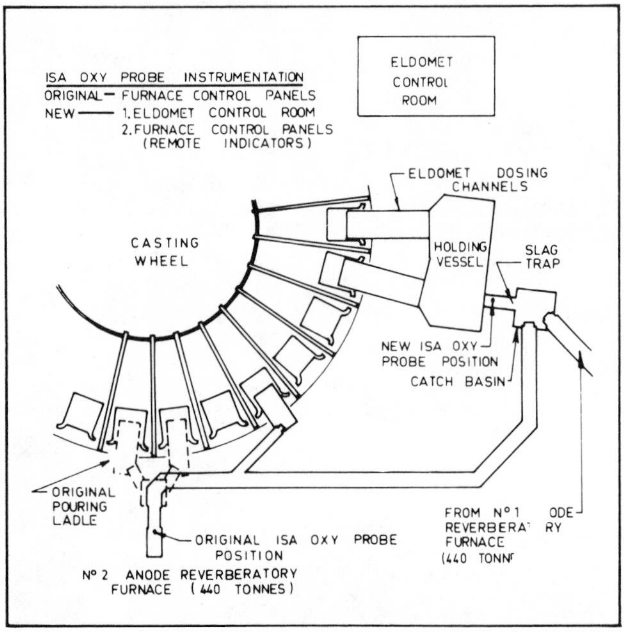

Fig. 7—Anode casting layout.

Relationship between Oxy Probe reading, average wirebar content, and casting defects

Oxy Probe reading (% O)	Temperature at Oxy Probe position (°C)	Wirebar content, cross section sample (% O)	Casting defects associated with oxygen and temperature
0.004-0.005	1,120 1,110-1,115	0.021-0.022	Nil cracks.
0.006-0.008	1,120	0.023-0.026	Nil—normal casting.
0.009	1,125-1,130	0.027	Rolled edges (approx. 5%).
>0.010	1,120	>0.028	Low set and rolled edges.

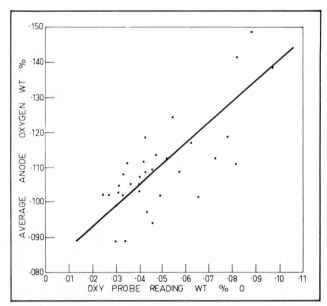

Fig. 8—Relationship between Oxy Probe reading and anode oxygen content.

mal, immediate checks are made of fuel-air ratios of the furnace burners, and appropriate adjustments are effected immediately to maintain the reducing conditions. Under normal rotational analysis of fuel-air ratios, a period of approximately 20 min elapses between checks.

During startup periods, oxygen contents are on the order of 0.010% and decrease as the oxidized charge remaining in the furnace from the previous shutdown is melted. If a forced shutdown occurs with a full charge in the furnace, the initial startup oxygen will be on the order of 0.015% to 0.020%, but decreasing. The probe will monitor the decrease and indicate the point at which good production can be expected.

In the case of monitoring a casting operation, although the probe is situated in the middle of the lower launder, the readings at this point can be related to the oxygen content of the cast wirebar, and the casting defects that can be expected. Variations in oxygen content of the wirebar will occur due to pouring practice, and only average values are quoted. This relationship is shown in the accompanying table.

The control of oxygen content between 0.006% and 0.008% with temperature between 1,116°C and 1,124°C eliminates the cracking problem and restricts the occurrence of rolled edges to the pouring operation. Oxygen contents at the probe position above 0.011% result in total rejection of the wirebars.

In the case of gas cover on the holding furnace and launders—as in the melting furnace—checks of the fuel-air ratio are undertaken when the oxygen content exceeds 0.008% under normal charging conditions. In addition, when the oxygen is less than 0.005% and the temperature below 1,115°C, an oxidizing atmosphere is required on several lower launder burners to raise the oxygen content slightly and avoid the occurrence of cracks.

At the CRL operations, anode casting features a new automatic electromagnetic dosing system. The basic layout of the system is shown in Fig. 7.

Monitoring and control of oxygen content is important to ensure that the oxygen content of the cast anodes best suits the tankhouse operation. The furnace atmosphere and the degree of poling are controlled to produce an oxygen content at

the probe site of 0.03% to 0.05%. Once this oxygen level is achieved by vigorous poling, it is controlled within this range by the control of furnace pressure and the protective reducing gas atmosphere on the launder between the furnace and the dosing ladles.

The relationship between the oxy probe reading and the final anode oxygen is shown in Fig. 8. The upper limit of anode oxygen for economical tankhouse operation is approximately 0.10%. Oxygen contents above 0.10% increase the amount of copper taken in solution in the electrolyte and result in increased recovery costs.

Conclusion

"The Isa Oxy Probe system has proved a reliable industrial monitoring device for the continuous on-line analysis of oxygen in molten copper over a normal operating range 0.003% to 0.10% oxygen and 1,115°C to 1,150°C," according to its developers. Data are available to allow the accurate use of the probe up to 0.4% oxygen. In addition, the accuracy of determination of ±2.5% of the scale reading is an improvement on current laboratory methods, especially in the range 0.003% to 0.01% oxygen.

In wirebar casting, defects associated with oxygen and temperature conditions have been minimized by the Isa Oxy Probe, while in anode casting the oxygen content of the anode is controlled to suit economical tankhouse practice.

The application of this system to continuous rod casting processes would allow better control of the melting furnace, especially in scrap retreatment, and would provide the only method of continuously monitoring oxygen content of the cast rod. □

Editor's note

This article is based on a paper presented at the IFAC Symposium on Automatic Control in Mining and Metal Processing, Sydney, Australia, in 1973; the paper, "The Development, Construction and Operation of the Isa Oxy Probe," is the work of Dr. K. A. Johnson, G. R. McKean, and Dr. D. R. Young.

References

1) Estell. T. H., and Flengas, S. N., CHEMICAL REVIEW, Vol. 70, 1970, pp 339-376.
2) Rapp, R. A., and Shores, D. A., *Physiochemical Measurements in Metals Research.* Part 2. (R. A. Rapp, editor). Wiley-Interscience, New York, 1970, pp 123-192.
3) Patterson, J. W., J. ELECTROCHEM. SOC., Vol. 118, 1971, pp 1033-1039.
4) Osterwald, J., Reimann, G., and Stichel, W., Z PHYS. CHEM., Vol. 66, 1969, pp 1-7.
5) Johnston. K. A., *An Electrochemical Study of Oxygen in Molten Copper,* PhD Thesis, University of New South Wales, 1970.
6) Fruehan. R. J., and Richardson, F. D., TRANS. MET. SOC. AIME, Vol. 245, 1969, pp 1721-1726.
7) Jacob, K. T., and Jeffes, J. H. E., TRANS. IMM (London), Vol. 80, 1971, pp C32-C41 and C181-C189.
8) Fitterer, G. R., J. METALS, Vol. 19, 1967, pp 92-96.
9) Fruehan, R. J., Martonik, L. J., and Turkdogan, E. T., TRANS. MET. SOC., Vol. 245, 1969, pp 1501-1509.

Mineral dressing and chemical metallurgy combine to process difficult-to-treat ores

I. Iwasaki, Mineral Resources Research Center, University of Minnesota

DIFFICULTY IN TREATING many ferrous and nonferrous ores may arise when liberation size for an ore is so fine or properties of the constituent minerals are so similar that conventional mineral processing techniques are ineffective. In such cases, either pyro- or hydrometallurgical pretreatments may facilitate subsequent application of mineral dressing techniques. Conversely, use of mineral dressing methods at some appropriate stage in pyro- or hydrometallurgical processing may simplify a treatment scheme and lower the overall cost.[1, 2] Thus, difficult-to-treat ores are converted to readily concentratable artificial minerals by applying clever combinations of chemical processes and mineral dressing techniques. Several of these processes are reviewed here.

Magnetizing roasting of nonmagnetic iron ores

Low grade, nonmagnetic iron ores can be upgraded by conventional mineral dressing techniques without pretreatment, or they can be upgraded by magnetizing roasting or direct reduction followed by magnetic separation. Mineralogical and textural characteristics, as well as overall economics, dictate the method to be used. Flotation is sometimes used, but it is highly sensitive to the nature and amount of slimes in ores. The application of flotation is therefore limited at present to specularite and martite ores. For nonmagnetic iron oxides and carbonates, conversion to either magnetite, maghemite, or metallic iron has definite operational advantages, not only in the concentration step but also in grinding and filtration. Recent developments in wet high-intensity magnetic separators, however, may offer some economic advantages for certain ores over the combination processes discussed here.

To convert nonmagnetic iron oxides to magnetite, iron ores are roasted in a weakly reducing atmosphere at 600° to 700°C. Rotary kilns,[3] shaft furnaces,[4] fluid-bed roasters,[5] traveling-grate roasters,[6] and a pneumatic conveyor roaster[7] have been tested. A heat requirement of 1 billion to 1.5 billion Btu per ton is commonly thought to be the major deterrent to wide acceptance in commercial applications, but a treatment scheme further incorporating oxidation of the magnetite to maghemite—thereby utilizing the exothermic heat and achieving an overall reduction in the heat requirement—has been reported.[8] In addition, the use of scrap iron as a reductant[9] appears to provide a unique approach to recycling waste materials.

In spite of the energy requirement in roasting, magnetic separation in general is technically simpler and also more selective and more effective than flotation. Furthermore, roasting results in a lower grinding cost and better filtration characteristics. The availability of the heat of oxidation during pelletizing is sometimes cited as an additional point in favor of magnetizing roasting, but artificial magnetite reoxidizes at somewhat lower temperatures than natural magnetite, so the actual advantage arising from the exothermic heat may be doubtful.

In dealing with ores containing finely disseminated iron oxides, cationic flotation of magnetic concentrates may be helpful in removing locked siliceous gangue,[10] and a detailed re-evaluation of the overall economics of magnetizing-roasting may be warranted, at least under certain specific conditions.

Some associated minerals or impurities may be converted to ferrites during roasting and recovered in magnetic concentrates. However, much of the manganese present in low grade manganiferous iron ores is lost in the magnetic separation stage, perhaps because of the low roasting temperature and only partial conversion to manganese ferrite. This particular point may be used to advantage in the treatment of low grade, high-iron manganese ores by converting the iron oxides into magnetite and the manganese minerals into manganous oxide. The reduced ores can be readily crushed and separated into iron-rich, magnetic products and manganese-rich nonmagnetic products by magnetic separation.[11]

Direct reduction processes using beneficiation

The Krupp-Renn[12, 13, 14] and the SL/RN processes[15] incorporate the beneficiation step in direct reduction flowsheets, thereby producing, respectively, luppen and sponge iron briquettes. The processes require 12 million to 19 million Btu per ton of reduced iron products, and certain geographic and economic conditions are therefore necessary to make them attractive.

In the Krupp-Renn process, crushed ores are reduced in a rotary kiln, and the reduced iron is agglomerated into luppen at 1,250° to 1,350°C in semi-fused slag. The mixture of luppen and slag is quenched in water, crushed, and concentrated by magnetic separation. Luppen, analyzing 88% to 97% iron, may be recovered, with iron recoveries exceeding 90%. This process, therefore, may be applied to low grade siliceous ores that are so fine-grained that neither conventional mineral dressing methods nor magnetizing-roasting are effective. The process is also able to use low grade, noncoking coal. Luppen may be used not only as a scrap substitute in steelmaking but also as a raw material in blast furnaces and electric furnaces. Low desulphurization and high maintenance costs are disadvantages. The process has been applied to the treatment of titaniferous beach sands[14] and oxidized nickel ores.[16]

One major difference between the SL/RN and Krupp-Renn processes is in the rotary kiln burner design. The SL/RN process allows a closer control of both atmosphere and temperature. Because operating temperatures are kept well below the fusion points of the raw materials during reduction—at 1,100° to 1,200°C—the iron is reduced to the metallic state without grain growth. As a result, very few impurities combine with the metallic iron, so the ground concentrates may be used in powder metallurgy and the briquetted concentrate may be used as a scrap substitute. The SL/RN process can also operate at a relatively low capacity, perhaps 200,000 tpy, and low grade coke breeze and char may be used as reductants. The process is therefore ideally suited for geographic locations where demand for steel is too small to warrant an integrated steel mill. Several commercial plants are reported to be in operation in New Zealand, Korea, Brazil, India, and Canada.[12]

Direct reduction may accomplish the separation of a discrete oxide phase from a mineral in which iron is a major constituent and is chemically associated with another element in the mineral crystal. For example, titanium may be separated from ilmenite or from a mixture of ilmenite and magnetite or hematite by direct reduction followed by fine grinding and magnetic separation.[15] The addition of soda ash during roasting is said to facilitate the separation of sodium titanate slag from metallic iron.[17] The possibility of separating manganese from manganiferous iron ores is also reported.[18]

Pyro pretreatments aim at grain growth

Flotation is the primary method of concentrating base metal sulphide ores, and flotation technology for sulphide ores is fairly well developed. Consequently, numerous attempts have been made to convert difficult-to-treat ores, either pyro- or hydrometallurgically, to forms more amenable to conventional flotation procedures. Other processes aim at promoting grain growth, thereby circumventing the principal treatment problems commonly encountered in flotation: complex and sometimes intimate associations of various sulphide minerals; presence of refractory oxides, carbonates, and silicates; recovery of precious metals from oxidized ores; and partial oxidation in sulphide ores.

Nonferrous metal oxides, carbonates, and silicates can be readily sulphidized with gaseous sulphur, hydrogen sulphide, or pyrite at relatively low temperatures (150°-600°C).[19, 20] However, the application of this process may be limited to well-liberated minerals, since very little grain growth occurs in the stated temperature range. Furthermore, only surficial conversion to sulphides is necessary for flotation.

For more finely disseminated ores, grain growth is essential in effecting concentration. Introduction of a small amount of sodium chloride along with pyrrhotite or pyrite and a slightly higher temperature of 500° to 800°C in roasting could promote the grain growth of some oxidic base metal ores,[21] as in the segregation mechanism described below.

Roast-flotation aids grain growth of oxides

Excessive oxidation of sulphide minerals adversely affects their floatability with sulphhydryl collectors. The roast-flotation process makes use of differing susceptibilities to oxidation of various sulphides to achieve selective flotation. The process was originally proposed by Horwood in 1912 for the differential flotation of bulk flotation concentrates of galena and sphalerite.[22]

The process is applied in the Magna-Arthur concentrator, where molybdenite is floated selectively from a copper scavenger concentrate.[23] Apparently, flotation reagents on mineral surfaces are removed by roasting at 260° to 290°C, thereby allowing the collection of the molybdenite in a subsequent flotation step using fuel oil as a collector.

The US Bureau of Mines has reported the application of this process to the separation of cobaltite from iron sulphides in a copper-cobalt ore from Blackbird, Ida., by roasting at 425° to 450°C.[24] The USBM has also reported the application of this process to differential flotation of cobalt and nickel from iron sulphides in the copper-lead flotation tailings of a complex copper-lead-cobalt-nickel sulphide ore from Madison, Mo., by roasting at 420° to 500°C.[25]

Segregation process a plus for gold, silver ores

Oxidized copper ores are commonly treated by leaching or by conventional flotation processes, but some ores do not respond to these treatments satisfactorily because of the presence of excessive slimes and clay minerals. The presence of calcareous gangue makes the consumption of acid prohibitively high. The segregation process[26, 27] may be applied to such ores, with particular advantages for those ores that contain gold and silver, which are ordinarily lost in leaching. In this process, ore is heated, together with a small amount of salt (0.1% to 1.0%) and solid reductant (1.0% to 1.5%), to about 750°C. Copper in the ore vaporizes as cuprous chloride and migrates toward the surface of the solid reductant, where it is reduced to metallic copper. The segregated copper particles are then recovered by flotation.

The segregation process was developed in 1923 by Moulden and Taplin while attempting to apply the Perkins ammonia leaching process to an oxidized copper ore from Chile that contained sodium chloride. Several attempts have been made to operate pilot scale and commercial scale plants since 1931.[27] Two large scale plants have been reported in operation: a 4,000-tpd plant at Akjoujt, Mauritania, using the Torco process,[29] and a 150-tpd experimental plant at the Katanga mine in Peru, which uses the Mitsui process.[30]

The segregation process may be applied to mixed oxide-sulphide ores, and it has been suggested that antimony, bismuth, cobalt, gold, lead, nickel, palladium, silver, and tin may be treated in this manner. In recent years, considerable interest has been directed toward the application of the segregation process for recovery of nickel from garnierite ores and laterites.[31] For nickel ores, however, considerable development work is needed to overcome less favorable thermodynamics, higher operating temperatures, and greater reagent consumption.

Matte separation pairs smelting, mineral dressing

Matte separation, a method of separating copper and nickel, was adopted in 1944 by International Nickel Co. at its plant at Copper Cliff, Ont.[32, 33] The nickel-rich flotation concentrate consists of pentlandite, pyrrhotite, chalcopyrite, and various silicate minerals in intimate mixtures. Their liberation and separation by conventional mineral dressing is virtually impossible. At Copper Cliff, the concentrate is smelted by passing it through a multiple-tray roaster, a reverberatory furnace, and a converter. Iron and silica are removed in slags, and sulphur content is reduced.

The resulting matte of copper, nickel, precious metals, and sulphur is cast in molds and slowly cooled from 980° to 480°C over a period of three days to promote the growth of copper sulphide grains and nickel-copper alloy grains in a nickel sulphide matrix. The slow-cooled matte is ground, the nickel-copper alloy containing the precious metals is removed with a wet magnetic separator, and the nonmetallic fraction is then separated by floating the copper sulphide particles. Perhaps because of unliberated nickel sulphide particles, the copper sulphide concentrate is reported to analyze 73% copper and 5% nickel and is fed directly to the converters treating copper flash furnace matte. The nickel sulphide concentrate, containing 73% nickel and as little as 0.6% copper, is used to produce nickel metal. This process is a unique way of treating difficult ores with a combination of smelting and mineral dressing techniques. Similar procedures have been reported to show promise in separating cobalt-copper matte, copper sulphide-zinc sulphide matte, and lead sulphide-zinc sulphide matte.[32]

LPF process treats highly altered copper ores

Highly altered copper ores containing both acid-soluble oxidized copper minerals and sulphide copper minerals may be treated by a process consisting of sulphuric acid leaching of oxidized copper minerals, precipitation of dissolved copper with metallic iron, and recovery of cemented copper and sulphide copper minerals by flotation.[34, 35] The leach-precipitation-float (LPF) process was originally developed during the years 1929-1934 by Miami Copper Co. Several different types of flowsheets use the LPF process.

In one approach, mixed ores are ground and classified into sand and slime fractions; the sand fraction is concentrated by conventional lime-xanthate flotation and the slime fraction by the LPF process. This approach was used in the Butte[36] and Hayden[37] concentrators. A later modification at Butte used hydrogen sulphide precipitation and flotation.

A second approach is to apply conventional lime-xanthate flotation to the entire ground ore first, followed by LPF processing of the flotation tailings. The Miami concentrator[39] used this type of flowsheet. Separate sulphide and cement copper flotation permitted recovery of molybdenum contained in the sulphide concentrate. The process currently operating at Morenci[40] involves crushing and acid leaching of ore, followed by precipitation of the dissolved copper as CuS with a sulphide precipitant. Then the slurry is made alkaline and ground, and the sulphide minerals—both natural and precipitated—are recovered by flotation to minimize requirements for costly corrosion-proof equipment.

Similar approaches have been reported for oxidized lead ores[41] and nickel laterites.[42] Lead ores may be metallized with scrap iron in hot aqueous pulp, and the sponge lead may then be floated in the same manner as metallic copper. A process for nickel laterites involves pressure leaching and cementation with iron powder, followed by magnetic separation of the cemented nickel.

A process for gold ores consisting of dissolution with cyanide, adsorption on charcoal, and flotation of the gold-rich charcoal may be regarded as an LPF process. This procedure, proposed by Chapman in 1939,[43] can be applied to the treatment of difficult gold ores—ores containing large amounts of fines with settling rates too slow for practical countercurrent decantation, gold ores containing graphite, or mixed ores with part of the gold intimately associated with sulphides. The carbon-in-pulp process, currently in operation at Homestake,[44] uses a coarse, sized fraction of activated carbon (10 x 20 mesh), and the gold-rich carbon is removed by screening. Another variation of this method makes use of ion exchange resins.[45] Since ion exchange resins are available with widely different sorption characteristics, leach-ion exchange-flotation processes may be adaptable to a wider range of ores and difficult-to-treat waste liquors.

Ion flotation applied to very dilute solutions

Removal of heavy metal ions from mine and industrial effluent streams is of much current interest. Precipitation of heavy metal ions with a typical collector and removal of the precipitate by flotation provide not only the extraordinary concentration factor that permits application to extremely dilute solutions, but also a high degree of selectivity.[46] The effectiveness of sulphhydryl collectors on the precipitation of various heavy metal ions has been investigated, and a few reports of its application in Japan on a commercial scale are available.[47, 48] Automatic control of reagent addition to minimize the residual heavy metal ions or the collector, design of the flotation cells for precipitate recovery, and recycling of sulphhydryl collectors appear to be in need of further development. An additional refinement of the method has been proposed[49] in separating various metal ions in aqueous solutions by using xanthates as selective precipitants (e.g., nickel and cobalt ions from ferrous and/or zinc ions). Furthermore, the separation of nickel and cobalt xanthates by selective dissolutions of nickel xanthate with ammonia is described.

Heavy metal ions may be removed by precipitating them as sulphides. A method has been reported for treating waste mine water containing free sulphuric acid and copper, zinc, ferric, and ferrous ions with hydrogen sulphide, with recovery of the precipitated copper sulphide by sedimentation.[50] Apparently, flotation may also be applied to recover such precipitates, as mentioned previously. Precipitation as metal hydroxides, followed by flotation of the precipitates, has been reported.[51] A similar technique that precipitates heavy metal ions by neutralization and oxidation, thereby removing the precipitates by magnetic separation, was also reported recently.[52] This method appears to be capable of reducing such heavy metal ions as copper, nickel, tin, lead, chromium, and mercury from several thousand ppm to a fraction of 1 ppm. □

References

1) Spedden, H. R., "Concentration of Materials Other Than Natural Ores," MINING MAGAZINE, Vol. 93, 1955.
2) Yonezawa, T., "Cooperation of Mineral Dressing and Metallurgy," Nippon Kogyo Kaishi, Vol. 76, 1961.
3) Meyer, K., "The Lurgi Process of Magnetizing Roasting, a Possible Method of Processing Iron Ore," Sixth International Mineral Processing Congress, Cannes, 1963.
4) Davis, E. W., "Magnetic Roasting of Iron Ore," University of Minnesota, Mines Experiment Station Bulletin No. 13, 1937.
5) Boucraut, M., Guyot, R., Ivanier, L., and Toth, I., "Grillage Magnetisant en Fluidisation a l'Echelle Semi-industrielle," Eighth International Mineral Processing Congress, Leningrad, USSR, 1968.
6) Wade, H. H. and Schulz, N. F., "Magnetic Roasting of Iron Ores in a Travelling Grate Roaster," MINING ENGINEERING, Vol. 12, 1960.
7) King, R. E., "Magnetic Oxide Conversion by the Iron Ore Research Process," 27th Annual Mining Symposium, University of Minnesota, 1966.
8) Stephens, F. M. Jr., Lanston, B., and Richardson, A. C., "The Reduction-Oxidation Process for the Treatment of Taconites," Blast Furnace, Coke Oven and Raw Materials Committee Proceedings, Vol. 12, 1953.
9) Fine, M. M. and Melcher, N. B., "Ore-Scrap Magnetic Roasting," JOURNAL OF METALS, Vol. 16, 1964.
10) Bunge, F. H., Rule, W. T., and Trainor, L. W., "Upgrading of Magnetic Roasted Concentrates by Cationic Flotation," 25th Annual Mining Symposium, University of Minnesota, 1964.
11) Subramanya, G. V. and Narayanan, I. A., "Beneficiation of Low-Grade Manganese Ores with Particular Reference to Semi-Pilot-Plant Studies on a Low Temperature Magnetizing Reduction Process for Ferruginous Manganese Ores," International Mineral Processing Congress, Westminster, England, 1960.
12) Dolezil, M. and Reznicek, J., "Pelletization and Direct Reduction Trends in 1973," WORLD MINING, Vol. 27, No. 9.
13) Johannsen, F., "The Krupp-Renn Process, a Direct Process for Silicious Iron Ores," Blast Furnace, Coke Oven, and Raw Materials Committee Proceedings, Vol. 11, 1952.
14) Kennard, M. J., "Krupp-Renn Direct Reduction Process," MINING CONGRESS JOURNAL, Vol. 47, January 1961.
15) "The SL/RN Process for Production of Sponge Iron," Lurgi Gesellschaft fur Chemie und Huttenwesen MbH.
16) Ito, T., "Ferronickel Smelting at Oeyama Plant," Nippon Kogyo Kaishi, Vol. 84, 1968.
17) MacMillan, R. T., Heindl, R. A., and Conley, J. E., "Soda Sinter Process for Treating Low Grade Titaniferous Ores," US Bureau of Mines RI 4912, 1952.
18) Schulz, N. F. and Lex, H. A., "Reduction and Magnetic Separation of Manganiferous Iron Ores by the R-N Process," Trans. AIME, Vol. 241, 1968.
19) Bautista, R. G. and Sollenberger, C. L., "Conversion of Metallic Oxide Mineral Surfaces to Sulphides," E/MJ, Vol. 163, No. 11, 1962.
20) Balberyszski, T., Cooke, S. R. B., and Dorenfield, A. C., "Flotation of Artificial Sulfide Minerals," Trans. AIME, Vol. 241, 1968.
21) Bechand, L. J. and Hartjens, H., "Heat Treatment and Concentration of Oxide Ores," US Patent 2,989,394, 1961.
22) Horwood, E. J., "Separating Zinc Sulfide from Other Sulfides by Heating and Flotation," US Patent 1,020,353, 1912.
23) Gaudin, A. M., Flotation, McGraw-Hill Book Co. Inc., New York, N.Y., 1957.
24) Zimmerley, S. R. and Ravitz, S. F., "Pilot-Plant Investigation of Concentration of Blackbird Cobalt Ores by Roast-Flotation Process," Trans. AIME, Vol. 187, 1950.

25) Fine, M. M., Vahrenkamp, G. J., Lankenau, A. W., and Moreland, O. N., "Upgrading Cobalt-Nickel Stockpiles by the Roast-Flotation Process," US Bureau of Mines RI 5388, 1958.
26) Iwasaki, I., Malicsi, A. S., and Jagolino, N. C., "Segregation Process for Copper and Nickel Ores," *Progress in Extractive Metallurgy*, Vol. 1, Gordon & Breach, New York, N.Y., 1973.
27) Wright, J. K., "The Segregation Process," MINER. SCI. ENG., Vol. 5, 1973.
28) Rey, M., "Early Development of the Copper Segregation Process," Trans. Instit. Mining Met., Sect. C, Vol. 76, 1967.
29) Pinkney, E. T. and Plint, N., "Treatment of Refractory Copper Ores by the Segregation Process," JOURNAL SOUTH AFRICAN INST. MIN. MET., Vol. 67, 1967.
30) Kaneko, M., "Mitsui Segregation Process Treats Peruvian Copper Oxides," E/MJ, Vol. 175, No. 12, 1974.
31) Dor, A. A., ed., *Nickel Segregation*, Metallurgical Society of AIME, 1972.
32) Sproule, K., Harcourt, G. A., and Renzoni, L. S., "Treatment of Nickel-Copper Matte," JOURNAL OF METALS, Vol. 12, 1960.
33) Boldt, J. R. Jr., and Queneau, P., *The Winning of Nickel*, Van Nostrand, Princeton, N.J., 1967.
34) Sheffer, H. W. and Evans, L. G., "Copper Leaching Practices in the Western United States," US Bureau of Mines IC 8341, 1968.
35) Beall, J. V., "Southwest Copper, a Position Survey," MINING ENGINEERING, Vol. 17, No. 10, 1965.
36) Huttl, J. B., "How New Leach-Float Plant Handles Greater Butte's Ore," E/MJ, Vol. 154, No. 6, 1953.
37) Last, A. W., Stevens, J. L., and Eaton, L. Jr., "L-P-F Treatment of Ray Ore," MINING ENGINEERING, Vol. 9, No. 11, 1957.
38) Kuhn, M. C., Noakes, M. J., and Rovig, A. D., "H_2S Precipitation and Flotation of Copper in the Weed Concentrator, Butte, Montana," AIME Fall Meeting, 1974.
39) Bean, J. J., "LPF at Miami, Analysis of Latest Operations," MINING ENGINEERING, Vol. 12, No. 12, 1960.
40) Bolles, J. L., "The Morenci L-P-F Process," AIME Annual Meeting, 1971.
41) Zimmerley, S. R., "Flotation of Oxidized Silver-Zinc Ores as Influenced by Modified Grinding," US Bureau of Mines RI 3364, 1937.
42) "Republic's New Nickel Process Digests Laterites, Silicates, or Sulphides," E/MJ, Vol. 174, No. 5, 1973.
43) Chapman, T. G., "A Cyanide Process Based on the Simultaneous Dissolution and Adsorption of Gold," Trans. AIME, Vol. 134, 1939.
44) Hall, K. B., "Homestake Uses Carbon-in-Pulp to Recover Gold from Slimes," WORLD MINING, Vol. 27, No. 12, 1974.
45) Bhappu, R. B., "Froth Flotation of Ion Exchange Resins and its Applications," QUARTERLY OF THE COLORADO SCHOOL OF MINES, Vol. 56, No. 3, 1961.
46) Sebba, F., *Ion Flotation*, Elsevier, New York, N.Y., 1962.
47) Ishii, G. and Sugimoto, I., "Flotation Treatment of Effluents Containing Cadmium Using Xanthate," Nippon Kogyo Kaishi, Vol. 88, 1972.
48) Nagahama, T., "Treatment of Effluent from Kamioka Concentrator by the New Application of Flotation Techniques," Nippon Kogyo Kaishi, Vol. 88, 1972.
49) Ohyama, T., Shimoiizaka, T., Baba, I., and Ikeuchi, S., "Utilization of Xanthate as a Selective Precipitant for Nickel and Cobalt Ions," Nippon Kogyo Kaishi, Vol. 78, 1962.
50) Yamada, M., "Mine Water Treatment by Hydrogen Sulfide at Akita Mine," Nippon Kogyo Kaishi, Vol. 81, 1965.
51) Baarson, R. E. and Ray, C. L., "Precipitate Flotation—a New Metal Extraction and Concentration Technique," *Unit Processes in Hydrometallurgy*, Gordon & Breach, New York, N.Y., 1964.
52) "New Technique Removes Heavy Metals from Wastewaters," CHEMICAL ENGINEERING, Vol. 80, No. 17, 1973.

McDowell Wellman develops electric ironmaking process to yield refined metal

DEVELOPMENT OF A PATENTED electric ironmaking plant and process that can be economically operated either continuously or on a one-shift-per-day basis has been announced by the McDowell Wellman Engineering Co. According to the company, the new process is a radical departure from conventional blast furnace iron production, as well as from existing direct reduction processes.

The significance of the McDowell Wellman process lies in four major characteristics, according to the company:

■ It is an industry-ready process combining proven equipment with advanced metallurgical concepts to yield high-quality hot metal of either foundry or basic pig iron grade.

■ It is simple and practical, free of many of the constraints of traditional blast furnaces.

■ Its flexibility opens up new options in ironmaking, and offers capital and operating cost savings.

■ It is environmentally compatible and uses a variety of plentiful materials, consuming far less oil or natural gas than alternate processes.

The electric ironmaking process uses self-fluxing, self-reducing pellets made of ore and carbon particles mixed in the proper proportion. The pellets, about ½ in. in diameter, are fed continuously into a traveling grate where they are dried, heated, and prereduced. From the traveling grate, they are continuously charged, hot, into a submerged arc electric furnace where reduction is completed.

Commenting on the future impact of the process, company president Roger L. Hulette said, "With the earth's limited resources, we face a future of growing scarcity and rising costs. We don't see our process competing with the blast furnace for high volume production except in special circumstances. Electric ironmaking can, however, provide a very practical and economic answer in many other instances. One outstanding advantage is the fact that capacity can be added in increments as market conditions warrant."

Hulette also pointed out that the new process differs from other direct reduction processes in two key aspects: it produces a *refined*, liquid iron ready for casting or steelmaking without further processing, and it requires far less oil or natural gas.

The company sees three markets for the process that show immediate promise: medium to large-size foundries, where it would be feasible to produce hot metal with minimal dependence on scrap; specialty steelmakers, where production volume could not justify installation of a blast furnace or coke plant; and integrated steelmaking facilities, where waste materials could be recycled into useful product.

The process uses electricity as the primary energy source, eliminating problems in cost and availability of hydrocarbon fuels. "With the advances we have made in metallurgical technology, we have also freed the process from the need for high grade or highly beneficiated ores," noted Thomas E. Ban, vice president of research. "Instead, our process includes a form of beneficiation as an integral part of the cycle," he added.

The company recently completed a 30-day economic evaluation of the process at its Dwight-Lloyd Research Laboratories pilot plant. According to the company, results indicated good profitability at a throughput of only 4 tpd.

Projected capital cost for a 500- to 1,000-tpd facility is between $25 million and $50 million. The plant can be built on a relatively small parcel of land, and construction costs are correspondingly reduced by eliminating a coke plant, sinter plant, or extensive water treatment facilities.

"The new McDowell Wellman electric ironmaking process is the culmination of an 18-year investment of time, effort, ingenuity, and foresight," said company chairman and chief executive officer Robert C. McDowell. □

New drying-calcining unit cuts yellowcake processing costs

PROCESSING OF AMMONIUM DIURANATE (yellowcake) to produce uranium oxide is a new application for the stainless steel "Turbo-Heat-Treater" unit made by Wyssmont Co. Inc. The Turbo-unit may be used to continuously dry and calcine approximately 10 tpd of yellowcake at a reduced processing cost, stemming from the very close temperature profile and the elimination of refractory requirements, the manufacturer reports.

Wyssmont Co., based in Fort Lee, N.J., was recently awarded a major contract by Fluor Utah for a high-temperature unit to be used at a new uranium facility near Albuquerque, N. Mex. The design and associated scale-up of the unit were based on small-scale tests conducted at Wyssmont's laboratory. Delivery is scheduled for the latter part of 1975, with startup targeted for 1976.

The basic component of the Turbo-unit is a slowly rotating vertical stack of trays housed in a 10-ft-high x 9½-ft-dia insulated shell. The yellowcake containing 30-40% moisture is fed to the top tray, then transferred continuously to each succeeding lower tray in a plug-flow fashion, with the help of stationary wiper blades and leveler arms. Intimate gas-solids contact in the unit is facilitated by the vertical cross-flow introduction of hot air through the housing, coupled with fans rotating inside the tray stack. The unit may reach operating temperatures of 1,000-1,200°F, and the uranium oxide product is continuously discharged from the bottom at temperatures up to 750°F.

Dust carryover to secondary collectors is reportedly minimized by the inherently low velocity and low turbulence in both the tray stack and the specially designed air exhaust system breeching at the top of the unit. In addition, the bottom trays (where final drying and subsequent calcining take place) incorporate the proprietary "over the rim" design developed many years ago by Wyssmont. The design is said to aid material flow by precluding solids entrainment in the exhaust gas.

The overall construction material for the Turbo-unit will be AISI 304 stainless steel. Equipment features include an external direct-fired air heater using No. 2 fuel oil, and automatic instrumentation.

Approximately 300 Turbo-units are already operating throughout the world, and a substantial number of them have been installed for combined processing operations such as the Albuquerque installation, Wyssmont reports. Wyssmont also supplies equipment systems to chemical process industries for cooling, subliming, regeneration, activation, and feeding of particulate materials. □

Stainless steel houses the vertically stacked, rotating trays.

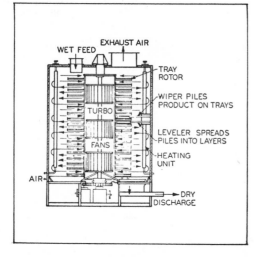

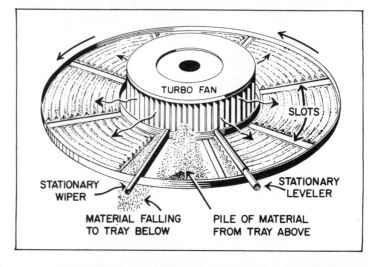

Chapter 5
Energy and the Environment

Environmental protection and energy conservation go hand-in-hand

SINCE THEY PROTECT OUR HEALTH and the environment, pollution controls are undoubtedly a big plus for society. But environmental goals have both real and "hidden" costs associated with them, costs that the public might not be aware of until their impact reaches the pocketbook. Just what are the costs and their benefits? It is difficult or impossible to place a dollar value on the benefits of environmental protection. On the other hand, control costs are better-documented.

Take water pollution. In mid-1973, EPA took a survey that found that industry will have to invest about $12 billion within the next few years to meet standards set by the Federal Water Pollution Control Act of 1972. This is an estimate of what polluters must pay to install the "best practicable treatment control technology" by the 1977 deadline; it does not include the cost of controlling thermal pollution, which might be another $2 billion to $9 billion depending upon the number of plants exempted from thermal standards.

Estimates for controlling pollution within specific industries are equally high. The Council on Environmental Quality (CEQ) says that electric utilities must invest $10.7 billion between 1972 and 1976 if they are to meet air and thermal pollution control restrictions. Of this total, $7.5 billion will cover air pollution control expenses, the remaining $3.2 billion going into thermal control. Even so, CEQ thinks the final cost might actually run as high as $17.8 billion, or nearly twice the original estimate, by the time inflation and other factors are taken into account. If the consumer foots the entire bill, he will pay an additional 0.22 to 1.52 mills per kwh, depending upon the region of the country in which he lives. These costs, by the way, exclude outlays for controlling nitrogen oxide emissions from thermal plants and low-level, residual radiation from atomic power stations, should this become a requirement in the future.

Environmental challenges facing the mining industries

The mining sector is particularly susceptible to environmental problems, in that mineral resources must be shipped from areas where they are mined to areas where they are needed, and often must be converted into more convenient or useful forms before being consumed. Each step in the process—extraction, transportation, conversion and distribution—represents a direct interaction with the environment. Each step also requires an expenditure of energy that sets off another environmental interaction. Some type of study is needed to pinpoint key environmental problems in each step. One such study is shown for fuels, with the environmental hazards associated with each step clearly identified. The study shows, at a glance, those energy-environmental "interfaces" which are targets for pollution legislation.

Base metal producers—aluminum, copper, lead, zinc, and others—are viewed by EPA as major sources of industrial pollution. As such, EPA feels they must meet admittedly tough restrictions on air and water pollution. Not even the producers can predict the future cost of controls with any accuracy, in part because adequate data does not exist on all the ways a given level of control will affect a particular refining, smelting or manufacturing process. With this in mind, here are some estimates made by the Council on Environmental Quality:

For the copper industry, CEQ predicts that the capital investment needed from 1972 to 1976 for air and water pollution control will total from $300 million to $690 million, with a most likely estimate of $341 million. Costs are projected to increase from $6 million annually in 1972 to a high of $95 million in 1976. For other base metal industries over the same period, CEQ made these estimates: aluminum, $935 million; lead, $70 million; and zinc, $62 million. The actual impact of pollution control on product prices, meaning that portion of cost actually passed on to the consumer, was placed at $0.020-0.032 per lb of refined aluminum, $0.025-0.05 per lb of refined copper, $0.012-0.017 per lb of lead, and $0.012-0.027 per lb of zinc. CEQ concluded that for most industries the impact of pollution control costs would not be severe and would not seriously threaten their long-run economic viability. Aluminum and copper producers probably have the necessary financial resources to pay for controls, CEQ stated, but in the case of lead and zinc, the high-cost, marginal producer undoubtedly will find it difficult and perhaps impossible to stay in business.

Steel industry must also spend more

Like other base metal producers, the steel industry has its share of problems in fighting pollution. According to McGraw-Hill's Economics Department, steelmakers were expected to pay out $276 million for controls in 1973. But within the next three years the annual rate of expenditures will hit $520 million, if the department's forecast is accurate. A better picture of the impact of controls is seen by looking at one company within the industry: Armco Steel Corp.

Armco Steel spent $125 million on pollution controls over the past 14 years. Now Armco says it will have to come up with another $100 million over the next decade, as legislated standards become more stringent. And all steel producers, including Armco, may have to replace coke ovens and other facilities which are too old to comply with new laws.

As with any other construction project, pollution abatement costs are extremely sensitive to inflationary pressures. At one open hearth furnace where Armco decided to install wet scrubbers, the original estimated cost was $6.5 million. But by the time the project was finished four years later, actual costs had climbed to nearly $12 million. Like other producers, Armco complains about limitations on available pollution control technology, and radical changes in standards which could easily make a brand-new anti-pollution unit completely obsolete in a short time.

Federal agencies differ over sulphur regulations

Utilities have spent more than $300 million searching for a

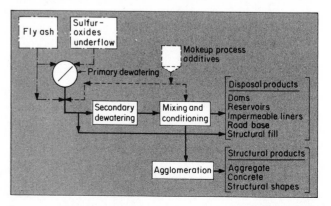

Conversion process turns fly ash and sludge into salable products.

Major Energy-Environmental Interfaces

	Fuel Production				Fuel Consumption	
	Extraction	Transportation	Conversion	Distribution	Mobile	Stationary
Air pollution	Gas leaks / Evaporative losses from petroleum products / Emissions from transportation equipment				Internal combustion engine emissions	Stack gas emissions
Water pollution	Oil spills at wells / Acid mine drainage	Oil spills	Product spills / Process and cooling water contamination	Products spills	Waste oil and lubricants	Boiler water contamination / Wet-process stack gas cleaning
Solid waste disposal	Mine spoil banks / Drilling mud disposal		Process sludge disposal		Discarded automobiles	Ash disposal / Nuclear byproducts
Thermal pollution	Gas flares		Low-grade heat in cooling water			Waste heat from power plants
Other health problems	Deep mining hazards / Surface subsidence	Marine sanitation / Ballast disposal	Sewage disposal / Nuclear radiation			Nuclear radiation
Aesthetic, including land use	Flares / Fumes / Mine and well siting	Siting for terminals and pipelines	Plant Construction noise	Transportation noise / Siting for terminals and service stations	Vehicle noise and odors	Smoke and odors

solution to the sulphur emission problem, without finding a method they feel is both practical and reliable. More time, money and research is needed before utilities will buy such systems. In that case, will thermal plants adhere to existing air quality standards? The Federal Power Commission doesn't think so. Strict adherence to the 1975 clean air standard could severely cripple the nation's power reserves, the Commission says, leaving the nation "critically deficient in seven of the nine electric reliability areas." FPC argues that variances must be granted to burn available fuels or to use some form of supplemental control.

EPA is in flat disagreement with this view on scrubbers. According to EPA, fuel gas desulphurization units are ready now, and no plant needs to be shut down for nonconformity. While a long legal battle is in the making over enforcement of EPA regulations, some utilities feel that scrubbers are not the only alternative. American Electric Power advocates the "tall stack" approach to protecting air quality, an approach some officials within EPA are privately backing. The tall stack disperses flue gas at high level while a continuous monitoring system measures ground-level concentrations of sulphur dioxide. Coupled with careful furnace control, AEP feels its approach will fully comply with EPA ambient-air standards, giving utilities an immediate if only temporary solution to the sulphur emission problem.

Ironically, there is evidence to suggest that land pollution from stack gas cleaning systems might pose an even worse problem than sulphur dioxide. Second-generation cleaning systems now under development will produce sulphuric acid, elemental sulphur or liquid SO_3, some of which will find a ready market. The remainder, plus wastes from limestone scrubbing systems, will lack market outlets and will wind up at disposal sites unless something else is done with it. But help for this problem is on the way. Researchers have found that sulphur sludge and boiler ash is convertible into structural materials such as bricks and blocks, a promising new development indeed. And in one study, the cost evaluation revealed that converting waste to a salable product was competitive with the cost of simply transporting the waste to dumps or lined lagoons for final disposal.

The coal industry is watching all these developments with keen interest. Since current air-quality regulations preclude burning most Eastern coals, further development of high-sulphur coal mines in the Appalachian region may have to await the arrival of stack gas cleaning equipment, pre-combustion sulphur removal, coal gasification, or some other environmental clean means for using coal.

Environmental impact of new energy sources

In the years ahead, production of synthetic natural gas will grow in importance. With this new technology will come a new waste disposal problem. A typical 250-million-cu ft-per-day coal gasification plant will yield tremendous tonnages of waste products over one year—38,000 tons of crude phenol, 40,000 tons of sulphur, 553,000 bbl of naphtha, 1,210,000 bbl of tar, etc. These wastes probably will be sold, whenever possible, as byproducts to petrochemicals processors. But for those chemicals lacking markets, disposal becomes an environmental problem of some proportion. Realizing the seriousness of the problem, the Office of Coal Research started a 30-month study last summer to examine all aspects of siting coal-based industrial complexes. Information will be developed on a number of refinery locations to better define the relationship of geologic, topographic and other characteristics of these massive complexes, which would place coal mines, a coal refinery and a large power plant within a relatively close geographic setting.

Even such "clean" energy sources as geothermal steam have an environmental price attached to them. In geothermal power generation, hot steam or fluids flow to the surface and power an electric generator. While entailing only local environmental problems, the steam plant will still require access roads and wells, a pipeline system for conveying steam to the power plant, and a disposal mechanism for waste liquids. In contrast to geothermal steam, oil production from shale or tar sands poses an immense disposal problem. By some calculations, every 100,000 bbl of oil produced will require mining from 150,000 to 200,000 tons of material, 90% of which is waste that must be disposed of.

Cutting auto emissions 90% by 1976

By far, one of the most controversial issues facing the public is the question of automobile emission standards. It is one of few environmental issues that has a direct and immediate impact on the pocketbook of practically every American. Perhaps the most noticeable effect of a cleaner automobile engine is a cut in gasoline economy. Indeed, steps taken in 1973 to reduce nitrogen oxide emissions reportedly came at a cost of about 30% in fuel economy for family-size autos. And under standards set to become law in 1976, all lead must be removed from gasoline as part of the drive to make the internal combustion engine a negligible polluter. Some sources say this will cut mileage another 10-35%. For new cars alone, these sources claim, the "lead-out" ban will create an incremental gasoline demand of 300,000 bbl per day. And gasoline prices will rise as more expensive components are used in gasoline blending. One critic estimates that implementation of the 1976 automotive standards will cost the consumer nearly $20 billion per year and will add $314 to the cost of the 1975 models.

EPA, on the other hand, thinks it is about time the public learned to accept environmental controls on the automobile by realizing that it is an inherently "dirty" mode of transportation. Moreover, EPA feels the public tends to forget its own role in the environmental arena. As one EPA staff member discovered, the consumer could achieve fuel savings of up to 6% by simply tuning his car regularly. And as a matter of fact, mandatory tune-ups are included in EPA's proposals to the states, as one method of making older cars less of a pollution problem.

Power needs for pollution control

As the use of stationary environmental controls grow, so does the need for electricity to power them. Electric consumption for this need was measured in an Edison Electric Institute survey of 87 utilities. Customers served by these companies consumed 8.8 billion kwh of electricity in 1971 for pollution control. This usage represented 7.3% of their total electric requirements that year. Several customer groups stood out as requiring significantly higher percentages of electricity for pollution control: sewage treatment (52.5%), waste disposal (50.5%), and waste recycling (53.7%). In the survey, specific power users most frequently cited were dust collec-

Electric energy for pollution control

SIC classification	Customer annual kwhr use (000)	Est.kwhr required for pollution control			
		1971 Kwhr (000)	% of total	1972 Kwhr (000)	1973-1977 Kwhr (000)
(01) Agriculture	336	147	43.8	147	147
(10) Metal mining	114,813	5,500	4.8	6,000	7,500
(12) Coal & lignite mining	1,391,782	105,598	7.6	148,469	155,857
(13) Oil & gas extraction	191,901	23,475	12.2	24,270	25,150
(14) Mining, non-metallic minerals	209,164	19,520	9.3	24,440	28,495
(19) Ordnances & accessories	130,771	2,690	2.1	2,890	2,970
(20) Food & kindred products	2,537,370	181,488	7.2	229,935	349,991
(21) Tobacco manufactures	80,543	5,625	7.0	5,625	4,056
(22) Textiles mill products	1,323,482	51,117	3.9	89,761	106,178
(23) Apparel & related products	53,127	3,439	6.5	5,645	6,422
(24) Lumber & products	675,069	69,376	10.3	76,198	125,854
(25) Furniture & fixtures	208,287	18,058	8.7	19,427	24,609
(26) Paper & allied products	9,942,803	623,014	6.3	1,198,737	2,082,366
(27) Printing & publishing	175,189	18,174	10.4	19,974	23,728
(28) Chemicals & allied products	27,274,339	1,042,437	3.8	1,465,076	2,473,771
(29) Petroleum & coal products	10,402,361	353,523	3.4	593,080	1,433,127
(30) Rubber & plastic products	1,948,235	61,955	3.2	90,687	120,400
(31) Leather & leather products	25,027	2,881	11.5	2,923	3,215
(32) Stone, clay & glass products	5,427,263	307,051	5.7	475,271	600,189
(33) Primary metal products	36,891,652	3,239,702	8.8	4,056,683	6,039,986
(34) Fabricated metal products	3,170,350	136,284	4.3	215,170	714,471
(35) Machinery, except electrical	2,296,337	117,423	5.1	147,009	265,031
(36) Electrical equipment supplies	4,643,895	871,778	18.8	876,895	1,162,994
(37) Transportation equipment	7,826,845	251,561	3.2	391,273	584,722
(38) Instruments & related products	284,456	4,274	1.5	4,931	7,420
(39) Miscellaneous manufactures	804,613	182,105	22.6	185,979	200,181
(49) Sewage treatment	1,894,316	993,677	52.5	1,306,866	3,596,401
(59) Retail stores	17,400	229	1.3	229	229
(xx) Waste disposal	28,047	14,156	50.5	11,439	13,597
(xx) Waste recycling	82,927	44,557	53.7	63,186	219,051
(99) Nonclassifiable	327,718	935	0.3	1,006	13,606
Total	120,380,418	8,751,749	7.3	11,739,221	20,391,714

tors, sewage treatment units, industrial waste water treatment units, scrubbers, and precipitators. Utilities in the survey did not include their own power needs for air and water pollution control.

What about the future?

As the short-term energy squeeze pushes the US toward a

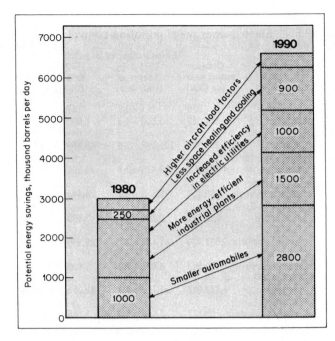

US has five most likely ways to conserve energy

deed, it is forecasted that the potential energy savings in the residential and commercial sector amounts to about 7% of total energy use. Actual savings might be even greater because as insulation is added, air conditioners and other cooling losses are cut while waste heat from lights, appliances and other sources becomes a substantial part of total heating requirements. Finally, by turning to heat pumps for space heating in the residential and commercial sectors, the nation might save energy equivalent to 1.5 billion bbl of oil per year.

As for industry, the use of more economical processes could cut industrial energy demand by at least 35%. Energy savings might also spring from recycled materials. Production of steel from scrap requires one-fourth the energy of steel from ore, while recycled aluminum takes one-twentieth the energy of original raw material. Solid wastes also hold vast energy potential. By burning two-thirds of the nation's municipal trash, the US could supply heat equivalent to 1.5% of our total energy demand.

Just how does industry go about saving energy? Industrial savings come about by using such devices as heat exchangers to capture waste heat, and by installing "oxygen analyzers" on boiler stacks to closely control air intake for better boiler efficiency. Indeed, one large consulting group claims that almost any industrial plant with an annual energy bill over $500,000 can cut its energy costs by 7-15% or more.

hurried attempt at self-sufficiency, there probably will be less time and money available for correcting environmental problems. As such, environmental goals planned by EPA and state regulatory agencies may prove unrealistic. Too many blocks already exist in working out environmental problems. Some ecological goals are stymied by poor communication between regulators and industry, by conflicting regulations and procedures between Federal, state and local agencies, and by lack of adequate technical know-how and capacity to build and install pollution-control equipment.

Implementation delays, if not accompanied by an equal delay in the final target date, tend to increase the rate at which changes must be finally made. Even worse, the US may already be at the point where the necessary resources simply aren't available. Even with a massive injection of Federal funds, with environmental investment incentives, and with consumer willingness to pay the price of a cleaner environment, the country may still fall far short of environmental goals. This has led to proposals that the US limit itself to no more than a 2% growth in energy demand, or less than half the 4.8% growth rate experienced between 1968 and 1972. A 2% growth level would keep the country within reach of its available energy supply, these sources say, and would provide time for perfecting new, lower-cost cleanup technologies.

Energy conservation—making less do more

Since energy production and utilization causes environmental damage, it follows that conserving energy lessens the impact on the environment. Unfortunately, energy abundance has become synonymous with a high standard of living in the US, and changing consumer preferences and attitudes is no easy task.

Energy studies all agree that fantastic savings are possible in the residential and commercial sectors. These authorities suggest that the largest energy savings and, perhaps in the long run, the easiest to accomplish, could come in homes and commercial buildings, which until recently were not designed to conserve energy. Additional insulation in walls and ceilings, weather stripping, foil insulation in floors, and other energy-saving techniques often are economically justified, both in new and old construction. These improvements might save as much as 42% of the energy used for space heating. In-

Shifting patterns in electricity use

Energy conservation measures will certainly bring about a shift in the composition of the market for electricity. One study made by a major oil company concluded that the residential market, which today accounts for almost one-third of electricity sales, is expected to fall 22% by 1990 because of energy conservation measures. Ironically, electric resistant heaters now being installed in over one-third of all new homes and perhaps one-half of all new buildings are virtually 100% efficient. But based on the fact that 1 kwh of electricity requires about 3 kwh of heat equivalent, and since about 10% of the electricity is lost in transmission and distribution, the real efficiency of electric heating falls to less than 30%.

Looking at the problem from the other end, electric utilities historically have attempted to improve efficiency of fuel use, since fuel is a major part of operating expense. But now it looks as though utilities have done all they can to conserve energy, at least for the present. In a study of the potential for energy conservation in the utility industry, the Office of Emergency Preparedness discovered that no reasonable economic incentive could bring about efficiency improvements in nuclear plants or fossil fuel steam turbine plants in the near future. "Hence," said the report, "conservation measures in the electric utility industry in the short run must be based on more effective use of existing facilities and accelerated replacement of outmoded equipment still in service."

Congressional action will boost conservation

It is impossible to predict with certainty just how much the demand for energy will moderate in the years ahead because of energy conservation measures. But conservation will get a big boost indirectly from Congress where drastic changes in the energy-cost structure and the tax system have been proposed as a means of slowing energy development and consumption. Some members of Congress are calling for an end to depletion allowances, capital gains shelters, and specific tax deductions for energy-producing industries. All these steps will have the effect of making energy and raw mineral commodities more dear to consumers, and will stimulate the trend to conservation. Whatever policies are followed, the net effect on industry is higher prices for energy and raw materials and hence greater incentives for their conservation. □

An energy profile of the US primary copper industry

IF THE 1963 TO 1973 TREND is any indication, the energy consumed in total US primary copper production could more than triple by the year 2000. As it is, the cost of energy to produce a pound of copper jumped by a factor of 2.4 during the 1963-73 time span. And while figures are lacking on the energy cost picture since the Arab oil embargo, it is probable that the 1973 energy costs to recover a pound of metal from newly mined ore have doubled again.

Energy consumed in copper production in 1963 and 1973

	1963	1973
Mining-beneficiation.		
Btu consumed (billions)	46,035	87,603
Copper produced (million lb)	2,426	3,436
Btu per lb copper	18,973	25,497
Smelting-refining		
Btu consumed (billions)	64,768*	87,773
Copper produced (million lb)	2,991	3,667
Btu per lb copper	21,654	23,935
Total energy consumed (Btu per lb copper)	40,627	49,432

*Estimated from 1962 data.

A recent survey by the US Bureau of Mines* highlighted some disturbing facts about energy trends in the US primary copper industry. For example, the energy required to produce a pound of copper grew almost 22% and the total energy consumption of the US primary copper industry rose nearly 60% during the period 1963 to 1973. Data from the USBM survey are abstracted in this article.

Specifically, the published survey indicated that the energy consumed per pound of metal increased from nearly 41,000 Btu to almost 50,000 Btu in 1973. Most of the greater energy investment in each pound of copper was attributed by USBM to mining lower grade ores and to strict environmental controls.

The industrial sector has accounted for nearly 40% of US energy consumption, and more than 20% of the industrial share is used in the production of primary metals—primarily aluminum, iron, and copper. Energy consumed in copper production totaled approximately 110 trillion Btu in 1963, when copper output totaled 2.426 billion lb. By 1973 the energy requirement reached 175 trillion Btu for the 3.667 billion lb of copper produced in that year—an annual growth rate of 4.75%.

Data for the USBM report were gathered by question-

*"Energy Consumption in Domestic Primary Copper Production," by Rodney D. Rosencranz (US Bureau of Mines Information Circular 8698).

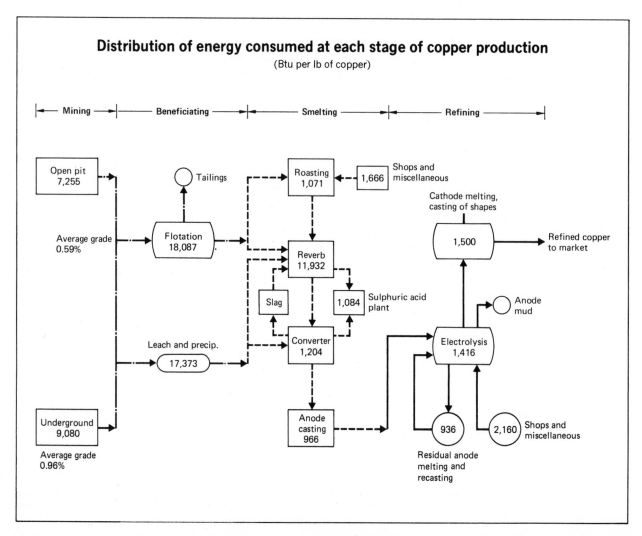

Distribution of energy consumed at each stage of copper production
(Btu per lb of copper)

shows little to cheer about

naires, visits to copper plants, and conversations with industry officials. Electrical energy was converted to equivalent Btu's by assuming an averaged efficiency of 33% at fossil-fueled steam-electric plants. Thus, 10,239 Btu is equivalent to 1 kwh.

The USBM report also assumed that all energy consumed in the industry went into the production of copper alone. Therefore, any energy used in byproduct production was included in copper production figures. Where this occurred, the energy consumption was overstated somewhat.

The copper processing flowsheet shows the distribution of average energy consumption among various unit operations, from mine to product. From 1963 to 1973, energy costs per pound of copper increased from 2¢ to 4.8¢ (current dollar value). Higher fuel and energy prices are prompting many producers to improve efficiency and to seek alternative processing steps.

The energy picture in mining and milling

Domestic mine production of copper has been increasing at an average rate of 2.1% a year for the last 10 years. During this period, the average yield has declined from 15 lb to 11 lb of copper per ton of ore, while the energy required to mine and beneficiate the lower grade ores has increased nearly 3% per year—from 18,973 Btu per lb of copper in 1963 to 25,497 Btu in 1973.

The average grade of copper ore mined by open-pit operations in 1973 was 0.59%, while underground copper mines averaged 0.96%. The operations canvassed accounted for 97% of the 3.4 billion lb of copper mined in the US in 1973. Electricity is the major form of energy used in mining and beneficiation. Nearly $30 million was spent on energy by copper mines in 1973, resulting in an average cost of 0.858¢ per lb.

Almost 2.7 billion lb of copper was produced from US open pits in 1973. They consumed an average 7,255 Btu per lb of copper produced, for a total energy consumption of 19 trillion Btu. Diesel oil and electricity were the dominant energy sources in open-pit mining, accounting for nearly 96% of the energy used.

Underground copper mines produced about 756 million lb of copper in 1973, resulting in a net energy consumption of 9,080 Btu per lb of metal and a total energy requirement of 6.9 trillion Btu. Most of the energy used in underground mining is in the form of electricity. The cost of energy used in underground mining during 1973 was about $1.31 per million Btu (1.19¢ per lb of copper mined); the cost for open pits in the same year amounted to $1.08 per million Btu (0.78¢ per lb of copper mined).

Most of the copper mined in the US is processed by flotation, although about 6% of the 1973 tonnage was treated by leaching and precipitation. The energy consumed at copper flotation plants averaged about 18,087 Btu per lb of copper, while leaching and precipitation averaged an estimated 17,373 Btu per lb of metal. Total energy consumed in copper beneficiation was approximately 62 trillion Btu. The cost of the energy for beneficiation averaged 2.46¢ per lb of copper.

The energy costs for beneficiation are higher per unit of copper recovered because of the extensive use of electricity, the most expensive form of energy. The copper industry spent nearly $85 million on energy for beneficiating mined ores.

How energy was used for US primary copper output in 1973

Mining[5]	Quantity	Btu (billions)	Cost ($1,000)
Electricity[1]	1,163,655	11,915	17,024
Heavy fuel[2]	463	69	33
Diesel or light fuel[2]	92,212	12,789	11,287
Gasoline[2]	4,320	540	842
Other petroleum[2]	368	48	44
Natural gas[3]	545	562	230
Coal[4]	2	52	26
Coke[4]	–	–	–
Other energy[1]	–	–	–
Total mining		**25,975**	**29,486**
Beneficiation[6]			
Electricity[1]	5,608,773	57,428	82,050
Heavy oil[2]	200	30	14
Diesel or light fuel[2]	5,300	735	649
Gasoline[2]	1,590	199	310
Other petroleum[2]	181	24	22
Natural gas[3]	3,117	3,213	1,317
Coal[4]	–	–	–
Coke[4]	–	–	–
Other energy[1]	–	–	–
Total beneficiation		**61,629**	**84,362**
Smelting[7]			
Electricity[1]	223,545	2,289	3,218
Heavy oil[2]	47,316	7,083	3,393
Diesel or light fuel[2]	4,180	580	512
Gasoline[2]	354	44	69
Other petroleum[2]	81	11	10
Natural gas[3]	48,228	49,722	20,673
Coal[4]	182	4,383	2,145
Coke[4]	42	1,104	1,552
Other energy[1]	8,796	90	140
Total smelting		**65,305**	**31,712**
Refining[8]			
Electricity[1]	1,369,659	14,024	19,653
Heavy fuel[2]	6,739	1,009	483
Diesel or light fuel[2]	6,934	962	849
Gasoline[2]	459	57	90
Other petroleum[2]	72	9	9
Natural gas[3]	6,124	6,314	2,674
Coal[4]	–	–	–
Coke[4]	4	93	130
Other energy[1]	–	–	–
Total refining		**22,468**	**23,888**
Total energy, all unit operations			
Electricity[1]	8,365,633	85,656	121,945
Heavy fuel[2]	54,719	8,191	3,923
Diesel or light oil[2]	108,626	15,065	13,297
Gasoline[2]	6,724	840	1,311
Other petroleum[2]	702	92	85
Natural gas[3]	58,013	59,811	24,894
Coal[4]	184	4,435	2,171
Coke[4]	46	1,197	1,682
Totals		**175,377**	**169,448**

1) Thousand kwh. 2) Thousand gal. 3) Million cu ft. 4) Thousand st. 5) Based on production of 3,435,880,000 lb. 6) Based on production of 3,435,800,000 lb. 7) Based on production of 3,643,556,000 lb. 8) Based on production of 3,736,976,000 lb.
Source: US Bureau of Mines Information Circular 8698, "Energy Consumption in Domestic Primary Copper Production."

The total energy consumed in smelting and refining rose from an estimated 65 trillion Btu in 1963 to 88 trillion Btu in 1973—an annual increase of 3%. The higher energy requirements are the result of greater production and an increase in the amount of energy needed to smelt and refine

Distribution of energy consumption and cost in 1973

	Energy consumed (Btu per lb copper)	Energy cost (¢ per lb contained copper)
Mining		
Underground mines............	9,080	1.19
Open pit mines..................	7,255	0.78
Average	**7,560**	**0.86**
Beneficiation		
Flotation	18,087	2.46
Leaching and precipitation.	17,373	2.45
Average	**17,937**	**2.46**
Smelting................................	17,923	0.87
Refining................................	6,012	0.64
Grand total or average ...	**49,432**	**4.83**

each pound of copper. Annual copper production rose from nearly 1.5 million tons in 1963 to 1.8 million tons in 1973. The energy required to smelt and refine a pound of copper increased 11% between 1963 and 1973, to 23,935 Btu.

Recently enacted legislation and emission control standards are partly responsible for increased energy consumption at smelters. Many operators have added sulphuric acid plants and other systems to reduce SO_2 and other effluents.

About 76% of the energy used in smelting was supplied from natural gas. Most reverberatories covered by the USBM report were fired by natural gas, although many have been converted to heavy fuel oil. The energy required for smelting copper averaged 17,923 Btu per lb of copper produced in 1973, including 1,666 Btu used by sup-

porting shops, plants, and other miscellaneous applications.

In 1973, energy costs in smelting averaged 49¢ per million Btu, or an average 0.87¢ per lb of copper smelted. The extensive use of natural gas, the lowest-cost energy form, helped keep these costs down.

If concentrates are roasted, the energy requirement amounts to about 1,071 Btu per lb of copper. At green feed smelters, concentrates are charged directly to the reverberatory furnace, which consumes about 11,932 Btu per lb of copper—the most energy-intensive operation in the smelting process. Although no energy is required to heat the charge in copper converters, about 1,204 Btu per lb of copper is required to keep these units hot between charges.

Copper precipitates can enter the smelting process at the reverberatory, the converter, or the casting stage.

In 1973, US refineries produced 3.737 billion lb of copper from domestic and foreign ores. The energy requirements for refining then averaged 6,012 Btu per lb of copper produced. The USBM energy estimates for US refineries were based on data from plants accounting for 25% of US refinery production. Energy costs for refining copper in 1973 averaged about $1.06 per million Btu (0.64¢ per lb of refined metal). Electricity accounted for 62% of the energy consumption and 82% of the energy cost at refineries in 1973.

About the future

A recent USBM forecast predicts that domestic demand for copper in the year 2000 will be 2.5 times the current consumption. Based on an annual increase of 3.5%, demand is expected to range between 4.1 million and 7.5 million tons by the year 2000, with a probable demand of 6.0 million tons. An estimated 4.2 million tons will likely be supplied by primary copper, with the remaining 1.8-million-ton requirement coming from secondary copper.

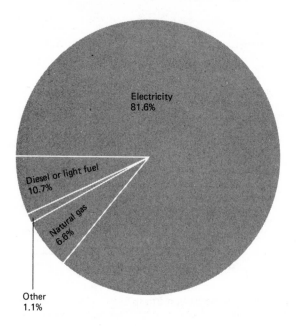

Energy forms used in underground mining in 1973
Average requirement: 9,080 Btu per pound copper

Electricity 81.6%
Diesel or light fuel 10.7%
Natural gas 6.6%
Other 1.1%

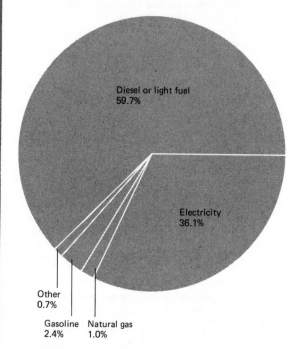

Energy forms used in open-pit mining in 1973
Average requirement: 7,255 Btu per pound copper

Diesel or light fuel 59.7%
Electricity 36.1%
Other 0.7%
Gasoline 2.4%
Natural gas 1.0%

Estimated 1973 energy costs to copper producers[1]

Area	Electricity[2] (¢/kwh)	Heavy fuel[3] (¢/gal)	Diesel or light fuel[4] (¢/gal)	Gasoline[5] (¢/gal)	Other petroleum[6] (¢/gal)	Natural gas[7] (¢/1,000 cu ft)	Coal[8] ($/ton)	Coke[9] ($/ton)	Other energy[2] (¢/kwh)
East North-Central (Michigan)	1.624	7.17	12.24	19.5	12.0	66.577	11.77	–	1.624
East South-Central (Tennessee)	1.053	7.17	12.24	19.5	12.0	48.580	–	–	1.053
West South-Central (Oklahoma and Texas).	1.297	7.17	12.24	19.5	12.0	33.978	–	–	1.297
Mountain (Montana, Idaho, New Mexico, Arizona, Utah, Nevada)	1.458	7.17	12.24	19.5	12.0	42.245	11.77	36.55	1.458
Pacific (Washington)	1.305	7.17	12.24	19.5	12.0	54.783	–	–	1.305

1) Since actual energy costs are dependent on the duration of the contract, quantity purchased, locality, and transportation charges, energy costs vary from operation to operation. 2) Edison Electric Institute, Yearbook of the Electric Utilities, tables 22S and 36S. 3) Oil and Gas Journal, average midcontinent price, No. 6 (max. 1% S), various months. 4) Oil and Gas Journal, average midcontinent price, diesel oil 58 di and above, various months. 5) Platts Oil Price Handbook. 6) Estimated. 7) Bureau of Mines Yearbook 1973, Natural Gas chapter, table 13. 8) Bureau of Mines Yearbook 1973, Coal Chapter, table 1. 9) Bureau of Mines Yearbook 1973, Coke chapter, table 18.

The US is expected to supply 90% of the estimated 4.2 million tons of primary copper required for domestic demands. Because copper recovered from secondary sources requires only one-third to one-seventh of the energy needed for primary production, there is a significant potential for scrap copper.

If domestic copper demand reaches 6.0 million tons by the year 2000, an estimated 375 trillion Btu will be required to produce a domestic primary supply of 3.8 million tons. This estimate is considered low because the assumption is made that energy requirements per ton will remain constant in future years. Energy requirements, however, will probably increase because of the continuing trend to lower grades ores and the need to capture pollutants. It is probable that increasing energy demands will more than offset any energy reduction through improved technology.

If the average grade of domestic ore were to drop to 0.2% copper by the year 2000, nearly 60 million Btu would be required to mine each ton of copper. This would raise the total energy consumption by an estimated 135 trillion Btu per year at that time. □

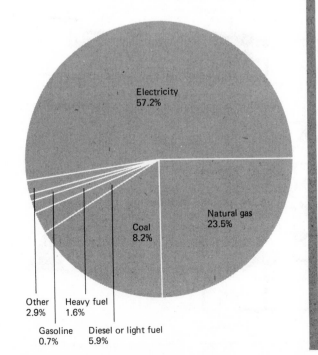

1963 energy mix used in mining and beneficiation

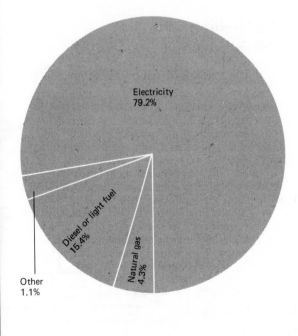

1973 energy mix used in mining and beneficiation

Merchant iron plants: the case for importing energy in the form of direct reduced iron

M. J. Greaves, vice president and technical director, Iron and Steel Div., Arthur G. McKee & Co.

IRON ORE PLUS ENERGY EQUALS STEEL. The commercial availability of direct reduction processes, with their flexible energy requirements, and prevailing nationalistic desires to upgrade raw materials prior to export will combine to create new merchant producers of iron metallics in energy-rich areas of the world. Industrial nations lacking iron ore and fuel will become importers of directly reduced iron metallics in lieu of iron ore, coking coal, and oil.

In 1973 world steel production totaled about 700 million mt, of which about 85% was produced by the classic method of converting blast furnace hot metal into steel in either open hearth or basic oxygen furnaces. Most of the remainder was produced by electric arc furnace steelmaking.

In the 1980s, world steel production is projected to increase to approximately 1 billion mtpy, with electric arc furnace steelmaking accounting for about 25% of the total. If this estimate proves correct, 25% more steel will be made via the coke oven-blast furnace-hot metal route, and 150% more steel will be made by the electric furnace route. Since sufficient scrap may not be available for these expanded needs, it may be necessary to produce large amounts of directly reduced iron as a scrap alternative.

Producing directly reduced metallics for the steel industry requires significant amounts of energy. Fuel expended near the energy source to produce prereduced iron briquettes is a substitute for fuel consumption in the possibly energy-short country receiving the briquettes. Therefore, metallics stockpiled as briquettes (as iron ore and scrap are stockpiled) represent a compact equivalent of energy—

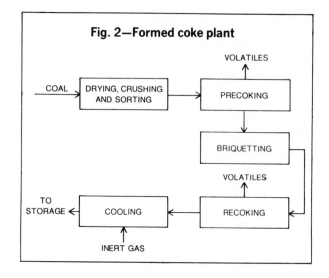

which must also be imported and stored. The key element needed for imports of "energy in iron" to become a commercial reality is the merchant plant concept.

Merchant concept ties plant site to fuel supply

The current popular concept for a direct reduction plant calls for integration with an on-site steelmaking operation—a "mini" steel plant. However, increasing demand for metallized products is expected to throw the spotlight

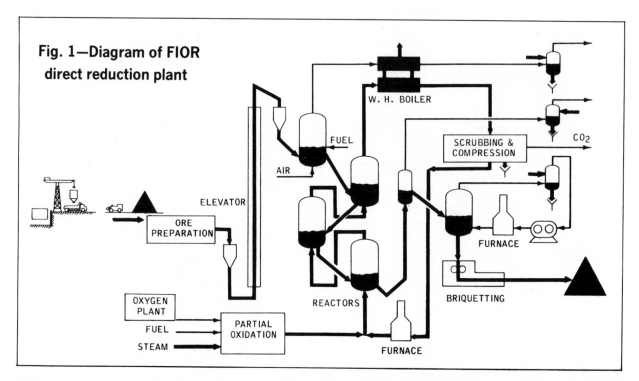

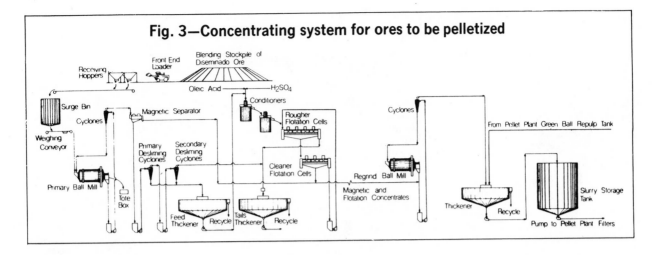

Fig. 3—Concentrating system for ores to be pelletized

on the merchant concept for direct reduction, which involves siting the plant in an area having the necessary long term availability of fuel. The metallized product will be shipped to existing steelmaking facilities in highly industrialized areas of the world. Currently, gas- and oil-rich locations such as Venezuela, the Middle East, and northern Africa are considered to be among the prime candidates for the location of merchant direct reduction plants. Eventually, areas in the world rich in coal will serve a similar function. The steelmaking centers of Western Europe and Japan, where fuel is in relatively short supply, are among the areas logically expected to use the merchant product.

A dense, highly compacted, low porosity, readily shippable metallized briquette is the most desirable form for such a merchant product. The FIOR direct reduction process produces briquettes that admirably meet these requirements. To date, over 45,000 tons of FIOR briquettes have been shipped throughout the world in conventional dry-bottom ocean vessels, as well as by all other standard modes of transportation.

Metallized briquettes exhibit high density, which minimizes back-oxidation during transportation and storage. They also float at the interface between liquid iron and slag, and they are high in thermal conductivity, which promotes rapid melting. Furthermore, briquettes are consistent in analysis and low in tramp elements, making them an ideal charge for steelmaking. They are also uniform in size, which facilitates continuous charging.

Other forms of metallized products, such as metallized pellets and metallized ore, are also produced by direct reduction processes.

Energy requirements for direct reduction

The reducing media used in most direct reduction processes is a hydrogen-rich gas that can be produced from a wide range of hydrocarbon feedstocks, including heavy crude oils, fuel oils, naphtha, LPG, natural gas, and coal. Several proven processes, such as partial oxidation and catalytic steam reforming, can be used to convert the selected feedstock into reducing gas. To produce a gas with a high hydrogen content, the products from the gas generator are normally passed through a shift converter, followed by an absorption tower to remove carbon dioxide.

Reducing gas from any source, including coal, can be utilized in the production of direct reduction briquettes. Several coal gasification processes can be considered commercial by today's standards. All these processes utilize steam, coal, and oxygen to produce a gas with a heating value of 200-300 Btu per cu ft The CO and H_2 ratios are adjusted with steam in shift reactors, similar to those commonly used in petroleum plants. The gas produced in the shift reactors may contain 95% hydrogen and is well suited for utilization in direct reduction plants.

Coal gasification will release direct reduction processes from their dependency upon natural gas as the source of reductant, and the use of coal as a reducing gas feedstock will ultimately become commonplace as coal gasification processes become more common.

In a typical direct reduction process, hydrogen-rich gas from the gas generating system is mixed with recycle gas from the reduction reactors, preheated to a temperature above 550°C, and then allowed to flow countercurrent to the ore in the reduction reactors. The spent reducing gas leaving the reactors is cooled and scrubbed to remove water and entrained solids. It is then compressed for recycle. (See Fig. 1.)

Where the reduction is accomplished in fluidized bed reactors, as many as four reactors, operating at elevated pressure, may be used in series. The first reactor preheats the ore to reduction temperature by direct contact with hot combustion gases. The preheated ore then flows by gravity to the first of the three reduction vessels. As the ore moves downward through the three reactors, it is in contact with the countercurrent flow of reducing gas. The use of three separate reactors in series results in the production of a highly metallized, chemically consistent product.

Metallization can be closely controlled, at a desired value, through straightforward operating procedures. In general, reduced product for use as feed in steelmaking should be 90% to 95% metallized. For ironmaking in a blast furnace, the optimum range is 80% to 85%. Most plants will have the flexibility to vary the metallization of the product over a wide range.

The carbon content of the metallized product can be varied between 0% and 2%, with the carbon analysis controllable within ±0.05% of the control point. Controlled variations in the carbon content of the product, to accommodate preferred steelmaking practices, are another advantage of the metallized product.

The chemical composition of the ore has a negligible effect on the metallization process. However, since most gangue constituents, including phosphorus, are not removed during mineral processing, the ore controls the chemical analysis of the metallized product.

In the electric furnace, volume occupied by slag reduces steelmaking capacity. In addition, deep slag blankets reduce the efficiency of the electrode-steel regime and increase the batch time, further reducing the unit's steelmaking ability. Therefore, if metallized product is to be

Fig. 4—System for ore balling and induration

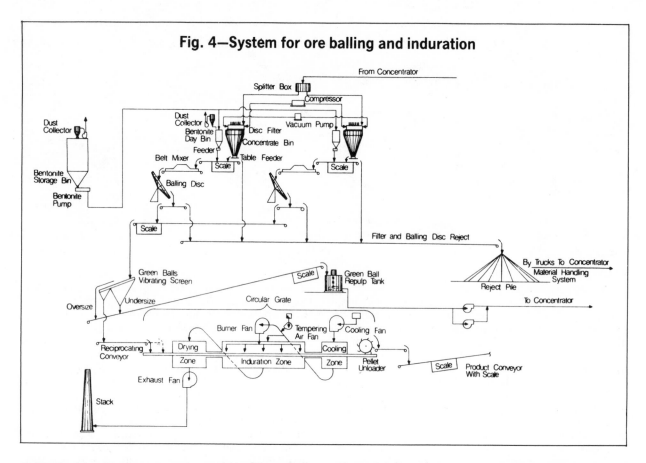

used as feed for electric steelmaking, certain ore impurities must be maintained at a minimum. This situation should ultimately lead to new ore concentration processes, prior to direct reduction, to permit the utilization of lower grade ores. A whole new industry may eventually be required, to cope with this problem.

Table 1—Cost factors used in evaluations

RAW MATERIALS ($ per mt)

Ore pellets*		Coal		Scrap	
US	28.76	US	45.00	US	90.00
Venezuela...(NA)	17.39	Australia	45.00		
Brazil	25.12				
Australia	21.20				
Goa	21.20				

*65% lump ore assumed to cost $8 per ton less than pellets; fines cost 15% less than lump ore.
NA—Pellets not available; synthesized cost.

SHIPPING ($ per mt)

Ore		Briquettes	
Within US	0.46	Venezuela to US	9.32
Brazil to US	9.32	Venezuela to Japan	18.69
Australia to Japan	12.35		
Goa to Saudi Arabia	5.75		

Coal		Scrap	
Australia to Japan	12.35	US to Japan	8.00

ENERGY

Electricity	$ per kwh	Gas or oil	$ per mm Btu
US	0.015	US	0.83
Japan	0.038	Japan	2.07
Venezuela	0.0055	Venezuela	0.15
Saudi Arabia	0.0055	Saudi Arabia	0.05
Australia	0.01	Australia	0.55

In US, classic technology will dominate

In the US and other countries where indigenous ores contain more than about 5% silica plus alumina after concentration, the classical coke oven-blast furnace technology will continue to dominate iron production. If economical methods are developed to further beneficiate these ores to significantly lower the slag forming materials, the direct reduction-electric furnace technology could become predominant. In some cases, a direct reduction product may be advantageously used to increase the capacity of existing blast furnaces, and high gangue would not be a problem since a minimum slag volume is required for good results. In some cases, slag forming minerals are added to rich ores to achieve a satisfactory blast furnace practice.

In addition, formed coke will in the future permit the utilization of currently nonusable coal to make metallurgical coke. World reserves of easily accessible, low-volatile coals, suitable for metallurgical coke, are sufficient to serve as a basis for all of the large scale steel expansions which are projected. However, since world reserves of high-volatile coals are significant, considerable effort is underway to develop methods for producing metallurgical coke from these materials. Formed coke must have the following desirable characteristics, which are inherent in metallurgical coke: strength to resist crushing, abrasion resistance, low packing density (voidage), and high specific surface area (reactivity and heat exchange).

Most formed coke processes consist of two parts: heat treatment and shaping. The order of these two steps varies from process to process. A typical process might include precoking, hot briquetting, and recoking. The raw material—high bituminous lignite, or caking coal—is dried, crushed, and sorted. It is conveyed to a hot-briquetting plant where the feed is carbonized at 700-800°C in a fluidized bed, and then pressed into pillow-shaped briquettes. Next, the hot briquettes are re-coked. Upon exit from the coker, the formed coke is cooled with inert gas. Fig. 2 is a diagram of a formed coke plant.

Modern US blast furnace feed is primarily iron oxide pellets. Pellets are used not only because they are made from concentrated ore, but also because they represent a superior shape which permits increased blast furnace capabilities.

Typical concentrating and pelletizing systems are illustrated in Figs. 3 and 4. The concentration plant shown is unique in that it treats a mixture of rich ore fines and various types of concentrates. The pelletizing system is also the first of its kind.

In taconite plants as many as 9 tons of raw ore are processed to provide 1 ton of oxide pellets containing 60-65% iron. Energy usage is about 1.4 million Btu per ton for mining, crushing, grinding, and concentrating, plus 800,000 Btu per ton for pellet induration. Even after expending this quantity of energy, the pellets still contain over 5% silica.

None of the treatments presently in use can remove the remaining percentage of silica compounds from domestic US ores more economically than the blast furnace. This means that unless radical new processes are developed for the removal of silica during ore beneficiation, high-silica iron ores, which are typical in the US, cannot be utilized successfully in direct reduction processes.

Large, single-unit plants offer sound economics

Large blast furnaces designed to produce as much as 4 million mtpy of hot metal have materially improved the economics of blast furnace technology. The same is true of direct reduction units. Plant capacities of 2 million mtpy can now be reached with a single direct reduction unit. Large capacity, single-unit direct reduction plants will provide worthwhile capital and manufacturing cost advantages over multi-unit plants, as has been the case with blast furnaces and other process plants.

The following analyses are based on data obtained in January 1975. Table 1 is a summary of cost factors used in these analyses. The battery limit capital requirement for a 2 million-mtpy plant producing 92% metallized briquettes is about $100 million, based on January 1975 costs. Basically, this figure represents erected costs for equipment and systems within the direct reduction process, from ore preparation through cooled and passivated briquettes ready for shipment or storage. In some cases, a direct reduction complex may be integrated into existing facilities with savings in off-site investments and costs. A corresponding 400,000-mtpy plant would cost about $30 million.

The manufacturing costs for hypothetical 400,000-mtpy and 2 million-mtpy FIOR plants located in Venezuela are presented in Table 2. An advantage of about $10 per ton in manufacturing costs is indicated for the large single unit. Even though local demand may not justify more than a small plant, the larger size plant can be advantageously operated in many fuel-rich areas of the world as a merchant producer of metallized briquettes, serving both a domestic steel industry and an export market consisting of the industrialized nations of the world. Briquettes are suggested as the form of metallized product for reasons previously enumerated, the most important being the ability to be shipped to remote locations.

The manufacturing costs for direct reduction production presented in Table 2 include amortization, interest, and insurance, but they do not include local taxes, selling expenses, or charges for return on capital. These cost figures were based on steam reforming of natural gas for producing the reducing gas requirements and the use of steam turbine drives on major rotating equipment. If natural gas is not available in the area selected for a direct reduction plant, steam reforming of naphtha can be used for producing the reducing gas without affecting the capital investment. However, manufacturing costs would vary, depending upon the cost of naphtha and conversion costs. As an

---

Table 2—Relative production costs for direct reduction steel using FIOR process

(US $ per ton of total iron in briquettes)

	2,000,000	2,000,000	400,000	2,000,000	2,000,000
Plant capacity (mtpy)	US	Venezuela	Venezuela	Saudi Arabia	Australia
Location	US	Venezuela	Venezuela	Saudi Arabia	Australia
Raw materials:					
Ore	23.01	12.66	12.66	17.83	17.83
Shipping	15.09	0.00	0.00	11.43	0.00
(Source)	(Brazil)	(Local)	(Local)	(Goa)	(Local)
Ironmaking conversion:					
Electricity	0.68	0.25	0.25	0.25	0.45
Gas (cost per mm Btu)	12.12 (0.83)	2.19 (0.15)	2.40 (0.15)	0.73 (0.05)	–
Oil (cost per mm Btu)	–	–	–	–	8.03 (0.55)
Labor	2.24	0.90	3.76	0.90	2.24
Other costs	6.07	6.07	6.09	6.07	6.07
General works services:					
Operating costs and OH	2.30	2.30	2.30	2.30	2.30
Total operating cost	61.51	24.37	27.44	39.51	36.92
Capital charges:					
Iron making*	7.52	7.52	14.17	7.52	7.52
Total cost	69.03	31.89	41.61	47.03	44.44

*15% of capital cost.

Table 3—Relative cost of semifinished steel production

($ per mt)

Country	US	US	US	US	US
Rate (mtpy)	2,000,000	2,000,000	2,000,000	2,000,000	2,000,000
Process	BF-BOF	EF	DR-EF	EF	BF-BOF
Source	US ore US scrap	US scrap	Brazil ore	Venezuelan briquettes	US ore Venezuelan briquettes
Manufacturing cost	$151	$133	$126	$ 98	$140
Capital charges	19	8	8*	8*	19
Total cost	$170	$141	$134	$106	$159

Country	Japan	Japan	Venezuela	Venezuela	Australia	Saudi Arabia
Rate (mtpy)	2,000,000	2,000,000	2,000,000	400,000	2,000,000	2,000,000
Process	BF-BOF	EF	DR-EF	DR-EF	DR-EF	DR-EF
Source	Australian ore, US scrap	Venezuelan briquettes	Venezuelan ore	Venezuelan ore	Australian ore	Goa ore
Manufacturing cost	$162	$122	$ 78	$104	$ 87	$ 92
Capital charges	19	8 *	8 *	8 *	8 *	8 *
Total cost	$181	$130	$ 86	$112	$ 95	$100

*EF plant only; briquettes in "Manufacturing Cost" have capital charge of 15% + 20% profit.

example, in Brazil, with naphtha or some other available fuel at $0.55 per million Btu, the manufacturing costs of FIOR briquettes produced in a 2 million-mtpy plant would be about $48 per mt. Areas such as Brazil and Bolivia that anticipate natural gas availability in the future can build direct reduction plants using naphtha and convert to natural gas at a later date with only minor modifications to the gas reforming system.

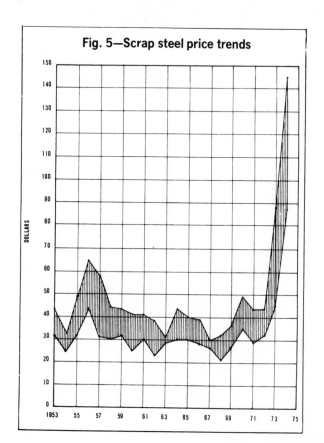

Fig. 5—Scrap steel price trends

The current upward trend of scrap prices throughout the world (Fig. 5), along with manufacturing costs (Table 3), indicate the overall economic attractiveness of large capacity direct reduction plants in several areas of the world, producing merchant briquettes to replace or supplement scrap in steelmaking charges.

Steelmaking in the US

In the US, most of the steel industry is using coke oven-blast furnace-open hearth-basic oxygen furnace technology to produce steel. With ecological demands closing down some existing facilities and with demand for steel increasing, new sources of iron metallics must be developed. At the same time, many existing plants are very old by world standards and may have to be replaced, due to obsolescence or uneconomical scale. In this respect, the US and Canada have no operating blast furnaces with a capacity of over 6,000 mtpd, whereas Japan has recently built units with capacities exceeding 10,000 mtpd. Nevertheless, by virtue of having significant coking coal reserves and indigenous ores with high silica contents, the most practical approach in the US appears to be continued utilization of blast furnace-basic oxygen processes for a long time to come. High-silica ores are not economically practical in the direct reduction-electric furnace process since excess silica wastes time and materials during the electric smelting step.

Modern blast furnace technology is reducing the amount of coke required per unit of steel production (Fig. 6). This, coupled with the increasing interest in coke oven byproducts to replace petroleum base raw materials, makes coking coal an important source of energy in the US, where it is plentiful, further reinforcing the economic utilization of blast furnaces.

Direct reduction requires less water

Water, used for ore processing in the mining operation and cooling in subsequent operations, must be considered when locating steel plants. Typical, average water con-

E/MJ OPERATING HANDBOOK OF MINERAL PROCESSING

sumption per ton of semi-finished steel is as follows:

Mining	1 ton	(can vary by order of magnitude)
Coke oven....................	3 tons	
Blast furnace................	12 tons	
Subtotal.....................	16 tons	(4,200 gal)
Basic oxygen furnace..	10 tons	
Total........................	**26 tons**	**(6,900 gal)**
FIOR process	4 tons	(1,100 gal)
Electric furnace...........	2 tons	
Total........................	**6 tons**	**(1,600 gal)**

Normally, the availability of low cost water has been a factor in the location of ore processing plants and steel plants. The advent of direct reduction plants, however, reduces the significance of cooling water in steelmaking, and permits the location of steel plants in new areas of the world.

In assessing the impact of energy availability, raw material availability, and national policy, it is necessary to choose specific locations and make an economic evaluation of the production of semifinished steel based on existing conditions and various scales of operation. Many combinations of conditions have been examined; following are illustrations of salient cases:

- Coking coal and blast furnace ore both plentiful—US.
- Neither indigenous fuel nor ore available—Japan.
- Natural gas, petroleum, and high grade ore all plentiful—Venezuela.
- Natural gas and petroleum plentiful, but no available iron ore suitable for concentration and use in the direct reduction process—Saudi Arabia.
- High grade ore plentiful, but natural gas not available—Brazil.

Table 3 indicates the relative cost of semifinished steel under these varying conditions.

Impact of energy sources on steelmaking

The US is a large importer of ore. By utilizing direct re-

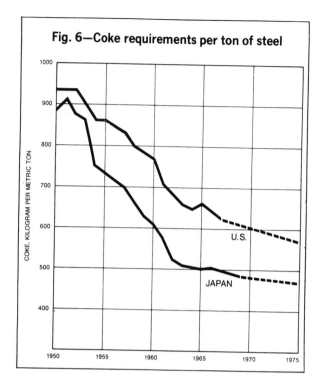

Fig. 6—Coke requirements per ton of steel

duction-electric furnace technology, it may be economically desirable to import reduced ore briquettes from fuel-rich countries and utilize them in place of costly scrap in electric furnaces. Alternatively, rich ore and fuel for metallization could be imported.

Countries lacking coal and iron ore, such as Japan, may in the future import direct reduced briquettes or semifinished steel rather than expand their current coke oven-blast furnace-basic oxygen facilities. The increasing reluctance of natural resource-rich countries to provide basic raw materials without upgrading to more valuable products leads one to question the recent intensive blast furnace building program in Japan. A more rational solution might be to build electric furnaces only and import direct reduced briquettes. This, of course, may also prove uneconomical, since Japan's electrical energy is derived from imported fuels, and is expensive. Low cost electricity derived from nuclear fuel could change this situation.

Energy relationships in the production of iron and semifinished steel are shown in Table 4.

Since most countries would be reluctant to base their economies on massive importation of semifinished steel, the importation of reduced iron briquettes should be considered more likely. Each ton of reduced iron briquettes imported into a country eliminates the need to import 19.0 million Btu of energy. If steel manufacturers in the US imported one quarter of their current requirements (30 million tpy) as briquettes, it would save the economy the equivalent of 96 million bbl of oil. This quantity represents approximately 7% of the current oil import requirement.

The energy-saving potential of briquettes is further emphasized by the fact that 1 mt of reduced iron briquettes occupies 11 cu ft—less than the volume required to store an energy-equivalent amount of oil.

In addition, FIOR briquettes, being relatively inert, could be stored in open piles rather than the costly tank farms required for oil. Consequently, in the near future, piles of briquettes may supplement oil tank farms. National policy aimed at reducing oil imports could further encourage briquette stockpiling. □

Table 4—Energy utilization in steelmaking

Energy required per metric ton of semifinished steel (mm Btu)

Process	CO-BF-BOF	Electric furnace
Coal	18.7	—
Gas...	—	—
Oil	2.0	—
Electricity*...............................	2.7	6.6
Subtotal	23.4	6.6
Mining		
Oil or gas	0.8	—
Electricity*...............................	1.4	—
Subtotal	2.2	0.0
Grand total............................	**25.6**	**6.6**

Energy savings by importing 1 mt of reduced
iron briquettes: 25.6 million Btu - 6.6 million Btu = 19.0 million Btu.

Energy savings by importing 1 mt of semifinished steel: 25.6 million Btu.

Volume of 1 ton of FIOR briquettes: 11 cu ft.

Volume of oil equal to energy savings
in 1 ton of briquettes: 15.3 cu ft or 3.0 bbl.

*10,000 Btu required to generate 1 kwh of electrical power.

Commercial development of oil shale: forecast goes from cloudy to bleak

Unless the Federal government removes restraints and provides incentives, construction of a full-size Paraho module is threatened and the move to commercialize shale oil is sure to lose steam.

Harry Pforzheimer, program director, Paraho Oil Shale Demonstration

PREPARATIONS FOR OIL SHALE DEVELOPMENT in the US, with one major exception, advanced on schedule during 1975. The single exception came in December, when two adverse actions initiated by the Federal government changed the future viability of shale oil production from "uncertain" to "unattractive."

In mid-December 1975, the US House of Representatives struck Sections 102 and 103 from the funding bill for the Energy Research and Development Administration (ERDA). Section 102 would have made an oil shale lease available for commercial development by in-situ techniques. Section 103 would have provided loans totaling up to $6 billion to encourage development of synthetic fuel, mainly from coal and oil shale. The second adverse action was the passage of the Energy Policy and Conservation Act of 1975, which rolled back the price of domestic crude to an average of $7.66 per bbl and imposed a continuation of price controls on domestic crude for an additional 40-month period.

The side-tracking of commercial oil shale development programs may only be temporary, however, if new Federal legislation is passed. New legislation should provide the emerging oil shale industry with:

■ Grants to encourage construction and operation of modules. Although they are unprofitable investments, modules are essential to the orderly development of oil shale.

■ Government assurance, through an exemption from price controls, that synthetic crude, products, and by-products will be able to compete in the marketplace.

■ Assurance that Federal funds will be available for socioeconomic projects in the communities to be affected by construction of oil shale facilities and by their production.

Until such legislation is passed, the Federal oil shale leasing program is vulnerable because the government changed the rules after four leases were auctioned off in 1974, for bonus bids totaling $450 million. The bids are payable in five equal installments, of which the fourth (1977) and the fifth (1978) are optional. To avoid surrender of leases next year, a moratorium or suspension of the lease terms should be granted, to delay the due dates of the fourth and fifth payments. Assurances are required to protect a lessee who has diligently pursued development through the fourth and fifth bonus payments until conditions justifying commercial development are established or the initial term of the lease has expired.

Of the four oil shale projects under development at present, the one that stands the best chance of bringing the dream of a large-scale shale oil industry to fruition is the Paraho Oil Shale Demonstration program at the Anvil Points Experimental Station near Rifle, Colo.

The project is a privately financed program to prove the feasibility of the Paraho retorting process and hardware in the extraction of oil from shale. The program was launched in late 1973 under the sponsorship of 17 participants,* many of whom were active in earlier oil shale research. In 1975, the participants increased funding for the project to $9 million.

Two new Paraho retorts, a pilot plant and a semiworks size unit, were installed and put into operation during 1974. The pilot plant is used to explore operating parameters to define conditions for demonstration in the larger semiworks retort. The results of Paraho operations to date have been encouraging, demonstrating the feasibility of the process, the durability of the equipment, and the environmental soundness of the operation on a pilot and semiworks scale.

Successful operation of Paraho's 10½-ft-dia semiworks retort has prompted a proposal for a $76 million expansion.

*Atlantic Richfield, Carter Oil (Exxon), Chevron Research (Standard Oil of California), Cleveland-Cliffs Iron, Gulf Oil, Kerr-McGee, Marathon Oil, Arthur G. McKee, Mobil Research, Phillips Petroleum, Shell Development, Sohio Petroleum, Southern California Edison, Standard Oil Co. (Indiana), Sun Oil, Texaco, and the Webb-Chambers-Gary-McLoraine Group.

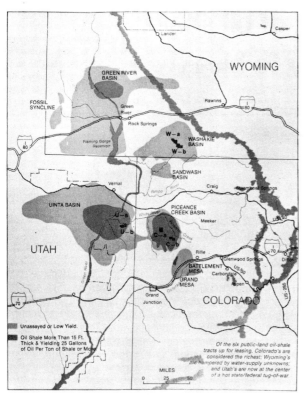

Oil shale deposits mapped here are estimated at 1.8 trillion bbl. Present technology can recover up to 600 million bbl.

- Paraho's retort consumes no water.
- The lumps of retorted shale produced do not create serious dust problems.
- Water requirements—primarily for revegetation—are small.
- Emissions of sulphur, nitrogen oxide, and particulates have been found acceptable under the strict Colorado standards.
- High thermal efficiencies—in the 84% to 92% range—are indicated for the Paraho retort in the direct-heated mode of operation. Rather than discarding the residual carbon on the retorted shale, the Paraho direct-heated process consumes much of it to fuel and power the process. The retort yields enough low-Btu gas to produce all the electricity required to operate a commercial plant and supply the community needed to staff such a facility.

Early in 1976, successful operations in Paraho's indirect-heated mode were begun in the large, semiworks retort. The objective of the process is to obtain a higher liquid yield (100% of the Fischer Assay) and to produce a high-Btu gas, which is particularly valuable in subsequent processing to upgrade the crude shale oil. Thermal efficiencies in the range of 70-75% were obtained.

Paraho has also conducted preliminary tests in a combination mode of operation. It is hoped that this mode will embody the overall advantage of both the direct method (high thermal efficiency) and the indirect (100% liquid yield plus a high-Btu gas).

Based on the success of the Paraho oil shale project, the next logical step would be the construction and operation of a single full-size retort or module at Anvil Points. This step would reduce industry's concern about the ability to successfully scale up proven technology to a commercial plant requiring 10 or more retorts that would meet standards of the Environmental Protection Act.

Although major additional risks would be involved in the subsequent commercialization of oil shale, successful operation of a full-size Paraho module should accelerate the development of an oil shale industry. If justified by future economic conditions, the module could encourage the simultaneous construction of several "first" commercial plants by competitive enterprise, with minimal governmental involvement and support. Such plants could be in operation before the year 1985.

A 56-day operability run was completed on the semiworks retort in March 1975, following which 10,000 bbl of the shale oil produced were refined into seven different fuels for use by the US Navy—the largest such conversion of shale oil into military products.

Nationwide testing of Paraho's shale oil is being conducted by industry and government, coordinated by the Navy's Energy and Natural Resource Research and Development Office, for the Department of Defense, ERDA, the Department of Interior, and other Federal agencies. The tests have shown that crude shale oil can be refined into high grade military and commercial products.

In addition to laboratory tests, the synthetic fuels have undergone major operational tests. An Air Force T-39 jet flew from Wright-Patterson Air Force Base near Dayton, Ohio, to Carswell Air Force Base, Fort Worth, Tex., powered by Paraho JP-4 jet fuel. A Cleveland-Cliffs Iron Co. ore carrier successfully tested Paraho heavy fuel oil in a seven-day Great Lakes cruise. Paraho's 92 octane unleaded motor gasoline and diesel fuel have been subjected to intensive operational testing by the US Army and by Paraho in its own fleet of vehicles. During 1975, Paraho crude shale oil was successfully used to fuel a Southern California Edison electric generating plant. This last test indicates another potential—though not yet commercially competitive—use for shale oil.

Why Paraho looks like the way to go

The Paraho retort offers certain advantages in design and construction:
- The equipment has few moving parts and costs less to build and operate.
- The system utilizes countercurrent flow and gravity transport; it does not require a separate circuit for solid, heat-carrying bodies.

But progress at Paraho is stymied

However, at this time it is highly unlikely that a Paraho commercial-scale module would be built without Federal assistance. The reasons are clear.

In May 1975, Paraho announced its proposal to construct and operate a commercial-scale retort at Anvil Points, near Rifle, Colo. The proposal included a full-scale Paraho retort, an expanded mine, and all auxiliary equipment. The $76 million project for a full-size Paraho module would be the next logical step after Paraho's successful ongoing semiworks demonstration.

Considerable interest and support was evidenced by industry and government in Paraho's proposal for a full-size module. The chairmen of the Armed Services Committees in the US House of Representatives and the Senate granted the right to mine the additional shale required from the Naval Reserve. The Navy, in turn, authorized the Paraho demonstration to proceed when ready. ERDA extended Paraho's lease on the Anvil Points Oil Shale Experiment Station and the Bureau of Mines completed an environmental assessment of the module proposal.

Meanwhile, at the Interior Department, the solicitor's office issued guidelines for the Federal Prototype Oil Shale

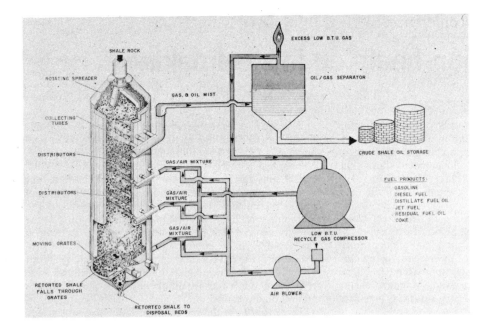

Paraho's retort employs countercurrent flow and burns most of the carbon in the retorted shale, achieving a high thermal efficiency. In addition, the Paraho hardware consumes no water in retorting and is, therefore, ideal for operation in the water-scarce region where oil shale occurs.

Leasing Program. The guidelines provided, among other specifications, that expenditures by lessees for patented or demonstrated technology, such as Paraho's, would be creditable against the fourth and fifth lease bonus payments. As a result, while any of the 17 participants in the Paraho Oil Shale Demonstration (and qualified outsiders) would be logical candidates to join the full-size module project, the Paraho participants that are also lessees under the Federal oil shale leasing program now have more compelling reasons for doing so.

In July 1975, the $6 billion Synthetic Fuels Amendment was added to the ERDA appropriations act and was approved by the US Senate. With this Federal assistance in the offing, it looked as if everything Paraho needed to move ahead with joint government-industry financing would be available for the full-size Paraho module.

In August 1975, President Ford toured the Anvil Points operation with energy chief Frank Zarb. Ford reported favorably to the media on the size, productivity, and environmental acceptability of Paraho's operation. The President then said that oil shale must play a bigger part in this nation's energy program, and shortly after his visit he spoke in favor of the subsequently defeated Synthetic Fuels Amendment.

How the problems emerged

Then the questions of jurisdiction and expediency began to develop in Washington. Paraho was advised that another environmental impact statement would have to be prepared before the Paraho participants could build a full-size model at Anvil Points. ERDA has jurisdiction in the matter of an impact statement, which if expeditiously handled, could be completed in nine to 13 months. As a result, instead of the prospect of initial operation of a full-size Paraho module in early 1977, it now appears that the project will be no further along than August 1975.

In October 1975, the Committee on Science and Technology started hearings on the ERDA appropriations act, particularly Sections 102 and 103. In spite of an excellent job performed by Congressman T. Wirth (D-Colo.) in chairing the oil shale portions of the hearings and the constructive input provided by Senator F. Haskell (D-Colo.) and Governor R. Lamm (D-Colo.), Sections 102 and 103

in the Conference Committee's compromise act were defeated in the House of Representatives.

This defeat was compounded by the passage of the Energy Policy and Conservation Act, rolling back the price of domestic crude oil. While the defeat of the $6 billion Synthetic Fuels Amendment eliminated a potential incentive for the creation of an oil shale industry, the subsequent rollback in the price of domestic crude oil to an average of $7.66 per bbl made commercial development of synthetic fuels impossible. At this time, incentives—not restraints—are needed to encourage energy production and conservation.

Even with nonrecourse, guaranteed loans, it is estimated that oil produced from oil shale—while less expensive than liquids or gas from coal—would have to sell for approximately double the newly legislated average price of $7.66 per bbl to be commercially attractive. As a result, lessees under the Federal oil shale leasing program now have a new concern: the likelihood of losing their leases after completing their fourth and fifth bonus payments. Congress has legislated conditions which make expeditious lease development commercially unattractive. The lessee's alternative is not to make expenditures to offset the fourth and fifth bonus payments, but to surrender the leases before those payments are due.

The future conditions required to encourage commercialization of shale oil cannot be determined at this time. Therefore, Federal oil shale lessees who have covered their fourth and fifth bonus payments should be permitted to hold leased properties until conditions conducive to commercialization are established. When such conditions do arise, any Federal funding assistance needed should be available for the construction of the first commercial plants and for socioeconomic projects needed by the communities to be affected by such plants.

The US is sitting on the largest known oil shale deposits in the world. Potential reserves exceed all those in the Middle East. Development of these deposits should be orderly and gradual. In any event, the commercialization of shale oil production will be a slow process. Major financial commitments will be required for energy and related investments. The restraints which have been created must be eliminated, and the incentives required to move ahead must be provided now. □

Occidental's Logan Wash shale oil deposits are located far above the valley floor. Road to the Oxy mine is at left.

Oxy to ignite 5,000-bbl-per-day in-situ shale oil retort this year

Dan Jackson, *Western editor*

AFTER INVESTING FIVE YEARS and more than $30 million of its own money on a process that combines mining and underground retorting to extract oil from shale, Occidental Petroleum expects to have a 5,000-bpd commercial underground retort in operation by the end of 1976. In the two-step process, about 15% to 20% of the retort volume is removed by conventional mining, and the remainder of the retort volume is blasted into the resulting void with conventional explosives. The rubbleized shale is then retorted in place.

The Oxy DA shale property is located on a mountainside at Logan Wash, Colo., near De Beque, where the company has been field testing its process since August 1972. Since then, it has successfully constructed and retorted three small in-situ retorts and one larger retort rated at 500 bpd. The Occidental shale oil process leaves the spent shale underground, uses almost no water, and does not require a large work force. By contrast, conventional above-ground methods of extracting oil from shale require construction of massive retorts on the surface, transport of mined shale to the retorts, and use of large quantities of scarce water. Disposal of spent shale creates major environmental problems, which boost production costs for surface plants.

Uncertainties about future financing, which in many cases hinged on government support, have forced most developers of surface shale oil projects to move their plans to the back burner. Occidental, which brought its process to the current stage of development without aid from the government, is proceeding full steam ahead. "Provided our preliminary economics continue to be substantiated," Occidental executive vice president Donald Baeder said recently, "we are prepared to spend more to prove and improve our technology. Recent congressional actions denying government-guaranteed loans to pioneers of synthetic fuel technologies have in no way deterred us from going forward with our program.

"If we are successful in operating the 5,000-bpd plant, we would bring our shale oil operation to commercial proportions as soon as possible without the need for Federal subsidies or loan guarantees, although Federal support could help speed up the commercialization process."

Occidental estimates the cost of its project at about $250 million, and total cost per barrel produced is estimated at $5 to $6, including amortization of investment over 15 years. Capital costs per barrel of installed capacity are estimated at about half those for above-ground plants.

Occidental's 5,000-bpd plant is the next logical step

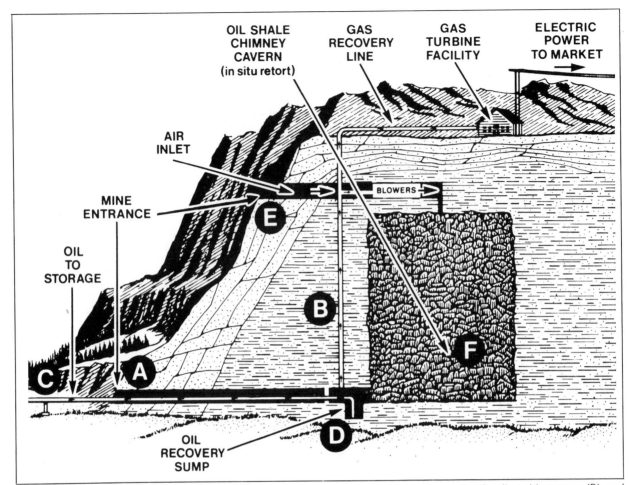

A simplified cross section of the Oxy shale oil recovery process shows an underground chimney retort (F) filled with shale crushed by conventional explosives. Air enters the air inlet hole (E) and feeds an underground combustion previously started by natural gas. Shale oil is produced, collected in a sump (D), and pumped through the mine tunnel to the mine entrance (A). Oil storage is at (C). The process also produces gas, which can be returned to the surface (B) and used to produce electricity.

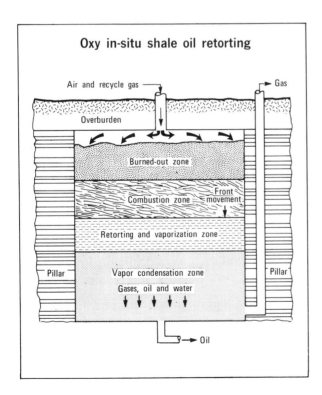

toward proving advanced mining techniques and use of in-situ retorts, the company states. The new plant is expected to prove conclusively the economics of the process, provide a practical demonstration that the process is environmentally acceptable, and show the extent to which it will be applicable to lower quality shale on a large scale.

Tests thus far indicate that the Occidental process does not create subsidence problems, and material removed by the mining operation has proved itself capable of supporting vegetation. Virtually all plant operations are located inside the mountain—even oil storage—and the exterior appearance of the operation does not materially affect the environment.

Occidental states that it can and does process substantially the entire thickness of an oil shale seam, in contrast to above-ground projects, which involve selective mining of high grade shale, taking perhaps only 60-80 ft from a total thickness of up to 1,500 ft.

Mining equipment at the Occidental operation now includes Caterpillar 988 front-end loaders and Eimco 920 LHDs, both equipped with 9-cu-yd dippers. Isco 20-cu-yd dump trucks transport mined material to a special land-use dump near the mine adits, where the company has permission to discharge waste.

Future mining plans have not been finalized and will depend partly on results achieved with the retort now being prepared for ignition. The largest heading driven to date measures 20 x 30 ft. Headings are drilled with an Atlas Copco hydraulic jumbo (see box).

Although AN/FO is the standard blasting agent, Occidental has experimented with other types of explosives. The company expects that standard belt conveyors will eventually be installed for the main haulage system.

How the Oxy retorts work

Once an Occidental retort has been formed and properly connected to processing facilities, retorting is initiated by heating the rubble to more than 900°F at the top of the retort, using an outside energy source. At this temperature, the retort begins to produce oil, combustible gas, and residual carbon. When a predetermined amount of shale has been retorted, the outside source of energy is discontinued, and the combustion process is maintained by injecting air into the retort for reaction with the residual carbon. A portion of the offgas is recycled to control oxygen concentration of the inlet gas, which can also be controlled by using other diluents.

There are four distinguishable zones within the retort: a burned-out zone at the top, a combustion zone, a retorting zone, and a vapor condensation or cooling zone. The combustion zone moves slowly downward, with movement controlled by the amount of air injected. Oil produced in the retorting zone flows by gravity to the bottom of the retort, where it is collected in a sump and then pumped to an underground storage area.

Offgas not recycled goes to a combustion turbine to generate electricity for the entire operation. The process also produces an excess of offgas that could be used commercially elsewhere.

Each of Oxy's first three retorts was 30 ft x 30 ft in horizontal dimensions, and the heights of the retorts were successively extended from 60 ft to 90 ft to 120 ft. The fourth retort was 120 ft x 120 ft in horizontal dimension and 280 ft high. Dimensions of the fifth retort have not been released.

Data gained from operation of the first four retorts is influencing the design of the No. 5 unit. The No. 4 retort produced 300 to 400 bpd during operations in the first half of 1976. □

Hydraulic drill boosts Oxy penetration rates

An Atlas Copco Boomer H132 with two COP 1038 HD hydraulic percussive drills mounted on BUT 14 ER booms has produced excellent results at Occidental's Logan Wash shale oil mine, achieving penetration rates from 50% to 100% higher than those achieved with pneumatic drills.

The Atlas Copco unit has been under test at the Occidental operation for 1½ years, operating two shifts per day and drilling as many as four 12-ft rounds per shift. A typical round at the Occidental mine has 24 holes on 8-ft centers.

The faster penetration rates have not reduced drill steel life because impacts are lighter with the hydraulic drill. Rods and bits drill an average of 15,000 ft without regrinding, using Sandvik Coromant 14-ft lengths of 1½-in. light drifter rods with carbide insert cross bits.

Maintenance characteristics have been excellent, and availability has been 90%. The hydraulic rig also has a favorable operator environment—noise is as much as 10 to 15 dBA lower than with pneumatic drills, and because there is no moisture fog, visibility is greater.

Power consumption for the hydraulic drills is low—less than one-third that needed for pneumatic equipment. The rig carries a 45-kw electric motor with a hydraulic pump for each drill, and current is supplied through a cable that is brought to the rig over a cable reel having a reach of 410 ft.

The carrier is diesel powered. Four-wheel drive and hydromechanical gear box without clutch make the rig easy to drive, and central articulation permits smooth advances in narrow spaces. The booms and feeds can be maneuvered during traveling. A two-circuit brake system with inverted compressed air brakes assures full safety even on steep inclines and tunnel entrances.

Each drill has its own hydraulic power and electronic control systems. When under electronic control, drilling is a semiautomatic operation actuated by a single lever. After the feed has been positioned, the operator moves the lever forward to collar the hole, initiating impact mechanism, rotation, flushing, and feeding. A push but-ton on the lever permits reduction of the impact energy during collaring. When the hole is collared, the operator moves the lever forward to place the drill under automatic control.

An automatic feed-control monitors progress in the hole and prevents the steel from sticking. When the correct drilling depth has been reached, the impact mechanism is turned off, the drill is returned to the rear position on the feed, and rotation and flushing are stopped.

It is also possible to perform the complete sequence manually.

The two hydraulic booms feature automatic parallel vertical holding and feed rollover. Since the feed can be rotated about its axis, contour holes are easier to drill.

The roomy operator's platform on the Atlas Copco drill is suspended on vibration-absorbing rubber elements. A hydraulic adjustable-height protective roof over the driller's position and a fixed protective roof over the driver's seat are other standard features.

A typical round of 24 holes, drilled on 8-ft centers, is completed in 1½ to 2 hr by Oxy's Atlas Copco hydraulic drills.

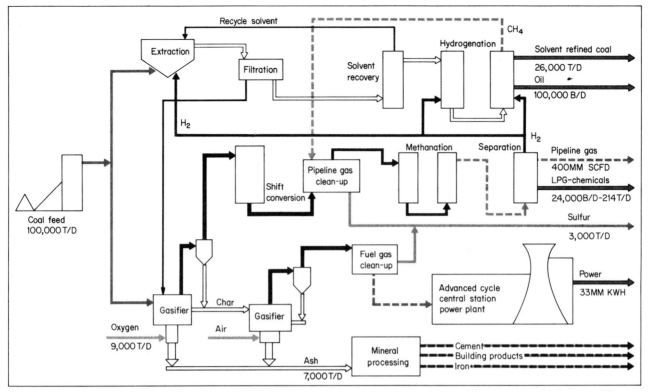

Wide spectrum of useful products is expected to pour out of a high-sulphur coal conversion plant. The COG plant would take 100,000 tons of coal (per day) and produce 26,000 tons of solvent refined coal, 100,000 bbl of oil, 400 million cu ft of pipeline gas, 24,000 bbl of butane/propane, 214 tons of chemicals for plastics and petro-chemicals—plus 33 million kwh of electric power. Yet, as one OCR official said, "We got the money for it—why aren't people beating down our door to co-sponsor such a plant?"

New processes brighten prospects of synthetic fuels from coal

THE SEARCH FOR PROCESSES AND TECHNIQUES for converting coal to more usable forms of energy, such as gas and oil, has markedly increased in pace during the past few years. Most of the efforts and programs are still aimed at the gasification of coal, and utilities, impatient with the snail-like progress along these lines, are turning to the older "first-generation" techniques, such as the Lurgi process, to fill voids created by shortages in natural gas. Such plants may be in operation by 1977 or 1978—but none are under construction as yet.

Coal gasification is also the committed goal of the American Gas Association. A joint OCR/AGA program is backing the development of several "second-generation" processes, including the HYGAS, BI-GAS and CO₂ Acceptor techniques (the Office of Coal Research [OCR] is a government agency in the Department of the Interior).

Pilot plants of these processes are already in operation, and if the results are favorable, the next step will be the construction of a demonstration plant (a smaller-size commercial plant), which may be initiated sometime next year and take about three years to be completed—which brings us to 1978, or thereabouts.

But in the opinion of knowledgeable researchers in the government, the optimum path to be pursued is not one of coal gasification—nor even coal liquefaction, although for many reasons liquefaction is more attractive than gasification—but that of multiproduct production, such as a "COG" process in which coal, perhaps high-sulfur coal, is fed into the COG plant to produce clean Coal-Oil-Gas or Coke-Oil-Gas products. This type of plant is expected to really pay off; for to make oil from coal, one must also have to make a gas—and it's not too difficult to make a coke or refined coal too. In a

plant of that type, the entire potential chemical energy of the coal would be employed usefully down to the last bit.

Although the COG concept is considered a "third-generation" plant, it may be further along than many realize. Actually, several companies, notably FMC Corp., with its COGAS process, and US Steel Corp., with its Clean-Coke process, are already thinking along the COG lines.

This, then, is the overall picture—although it is not quite so simple as it sounds. There are now scores of good techniques that have been proposed or are in the process of being tried out, either for the direct conversion of coal or for supporting operations, such as the methanation of coal-derived gases. Most of these processes have some components that are unique and worthwhile, and battle lines are being drawn as to which will be selected for commercial use.

Artist's rendering of COG plant shows compactness of operation.

"You got all the components of a big jig-saw puzzle," one OCR researcher says, "and when a company starts planning a coal conversion plant, it has to put together the best of the various pieces of the overall operation in order to optimize the spectrum of end-products. By adding component A or component B, you can change the product spectrum and em- phasize either a gas or a liquid, and the gas can be either high-Btu or low-Btu for long-distance pipelining or on-site power consumption.

"The next 12 months to two years are the critical ones be- cause industry, or the government, or both are going to make commitments to fairly large commercial plants."

First-generation synthetic-fuel plants . . .
Lurgi criticisms and go-ahead signs

THE MOST SUCCESSFUL commercial gasification process to date is the Lurgi fixed-bed process. Lurgi Oil Techniques, Ltd., in Frankfort, West Germany, began development of its gasifier in Germany about 40 years ago, and since that time at least 58 units have been built in Europe and in other parts of the world, with the largest installation comprising 13 gasifiers at the Sasol synthesis plant in Sasolburg, South Africa. But, so far, no Lurgi plant has been built in the US. Why?

Critics of the process say that it requires too high an invest- ment cost per unit of capacity. For example, a commercial Lurgi plant for producing SNG (synthetic natural gas), which recently was pronounced scheduled to be built in this country, has been estimated as requiring 25 to 30 Lurgi gasifiers to produce 250 million cu ft/day of pipeline gas from about 700 to 800 tph of coal. On the other hand, recent estimates based on anticipated gas yields from second-generation gasification processes, such as the Synthane and HYGAS processes, indicate that as few as three fluidized-bed gasifiers would be needed to make the same amount of gas. Thus the newer gasification concepts will involve lower plant-investment costs.

Other drawbacks with the Lurgi process include that it can- not operate well with the caking coals of the East nor with run-of-mine coals containing fines. The coal has to be very carefully sized, which causes severe operating problems. Lurgi engineers counter by pointing out that 59 different grades of coal from all over the world have been successfully processed.

But in spite of a lack of enthusiasm for the Lurgi process by many researchers in this country, the first commercial US SNG plants using coal as a raw material will use the Lurgi process. Announcements of plans to build Lurgi plants have been made by El Paso Natural Gas Co., by a consortium of Pacific Lighting Corp. and Texas Eastern Transmission Corp., by Commonwealth Edison with the support of the Electric Power Research Institute, and by Panhandle Eastern Pipe Line Co.

Panhandle Eastern says its proposed $400-million plant would be able to produce 90 billion cu ft of pipeline-quality gas annually and would process about 25,000 tpd of coal. It has commitments for substantial coal reserves to serve such a plant under an agreement with Peabody Coal Co., and antici- pates the plant to be operational before 1980, assuming timely government authorizations. The OCR now is trying to determine just what the limits are in a Lurgi gasifier, and un- der an AGA/OCR program, a single Lurgi gasifier is being operated in the Westfield coal plant in Scotland. The gasifier has been modified to try to overcome the obstacles mentioned previously.

How the Lurgi process works

Basic operations of the Lurgi process are fairly simple. Coal is heated in the presence of steam in a gasifier. This causes some of the hydrogen in the steam (H_2) to unite with carbon in the coal to form methane, CH_4 (methane is the main constituent of natural gas). Besides producing methane, the coal gasifier also generates carbon monoxide and hydrogen. These two gases can be made to react to form more methane in a step called methanation.

The heat necessary for the reaction in the Lurgi process is furnished by burning some of the coal in an oxygen atmo- sphere, so oxygen is a necessary ingredient. If air is used in place of oxygen, the nitrogen from the air would dilute the end product, thus lowering its Btu value. Even using oxygen, however, carbon dioxide is produced as a waste product. Gasification yields other waste products—ash and sulphur (the latter can be stored or sold). Gasification's obvious ad- vantage is that it removes these impurities.

The off-gas then goes through a crude gas shift conversion step and a cleaning process for the production of low-Btu gas. If high-Btu gas is desired, the gas goes to a methane synthesis step which brings together CO and H_2.

High-Btu gas, commonly referred to as SNG, has a heating value of about 1,000 Btu/cu ft and is completely interchange- able with natural gas. Low-Btu gas, with a heating value in the range of 100 to 200 Btu/cu ft, is valuable too. It can be used directly in power generation close to the gasifier, either in gas turbines or in conventional burners for steam gener- ation.

K-T—another commercially proven process

The Koppers-Totzek (K-T) process for coal gasification had been developed back in 1948 in cooperation with a German

Feed coal

Coal lock

Recycle tar

Drive

Steam

Distributor

Scrubbing cooler

Gas

Grate

Grate drive

Water jacket

Steam + oxygen

Ash lock

Lurgi, a German method, got the jump on newer American methods.

company. There are 16 K-T plants operating around the world, but none in the US. Koppers claims its K-T plants are more pollution-free and efficient than the Lurgi process, and are quicker and less expensive to build. A plant could be in operation within 2½ years. It would have neither complicated mechanical equipment nor pressure sealing devices. The only moving parts at the gasifier are screw feeders for solids or pumps for liquid feedstock.

Furthermore, Koppers claims that a mine's entire output is usable: Coal size is not a limiting factor, and coking coals can be handled without pretreatment.

The K-T process employs the partial oxidation of pulverized coal in suspension with oxygen and steam. The gasifier is a refractory lined steel shell equipped with a steam jacket for producing low-pressure process steam. A two-headed gasifier is capable of gasifying over 400 tpd of coal. Coal, oxygen and steam are brought together in opposing gasifier burner heads spaced 180° apart. Reaction temperature at the burner discharge is 3,300-3,500F, and operating pressure within the gasifier is slightly above atmosphere. The coal is gasified almost completely and instantaneously. Carbon conversion is a function of the reactivity of coal, approaching 100% for lignites.

Gaseous and vaporous hydrocarbons emanating from the coal at medium temperatures are passed through a zone of very high temperature in which they decompose so rapidly

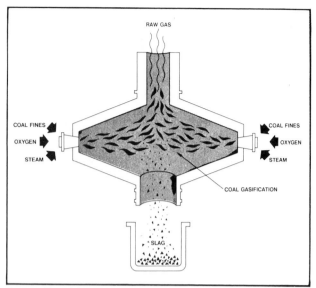

Koppers-Totzek is another good first-generation European process.

that coagulation of coal particles during the plastic stage does not occur. Thus any coal can be gasified irrespective of caking property, ash content or ash fusion temperature.

Second-generation plants . . . multi-directional crash programs for high-energy fuel gas

FOUR PROCESSES for converting coal to high-Btu gas— synthane, HYGAS, BI-GAS and CO₂ Acceptor—are being tested in pilot plants by the Department of the Interior with the objective of having at least one economically sound process in operation commercially by 1980.

Data obtained from the four plants will help draw up the engineering design of a demonstration plant which will use commercial-scale equipment to produce about 80 million cu ft/day of high-Btu gas from 5,000 tons of coal. If successful, this demonstration plant will provide the basis for industry by the end of the 1970s to begin building and operating full-scale, commercial plants producing SNG from coal.

In addition to the "big four," several other gasification techniques are gaining momentum, sponsored in most cases by both industry and OCR.

HYGAS—a leading US process

The HYGAS process, sponsored by OCR (2/3 of funds) and AGA (⅓ of funds), is said to be the most advanced American coal-to-gas conversion scheme under development. A HYGAS pilot plant has been built at Chicago by Procon, Inc. at a cost of over $7 million and has a daily capacity of 80 tpd of coal, or 1.5 million cu ft of pipeline-quality gas. Plant construction began in 1969 and was completed in 1971. It has operated successfully for over 100 hr, producing 900- to 1,000-Btu gas from Montana coal. However, the gas was not cleaned of nitrogen, so the Btu was 900 to 1,000 "corrected for nitrogen content." Also, no shift conversion was carried out. Hydrogen requirements are met by reforming methane, so the process is still very much a pilot research project and not a demonstration unit.

HYGAS has many advantages. It can accept any type of coal; furthermore, the hydrogasifier yields an off-gas relatively high in methane, thereby minimizing the need for further methanation. Finally, the process, from gasification through meth-

anation, operates at pipeline pressure (1,000 psi). The final product thus can enter a pipeline without additional compression.

The HYGAS process begins with raw coal being crushed into particles about the size of grains of table salt with all moisture

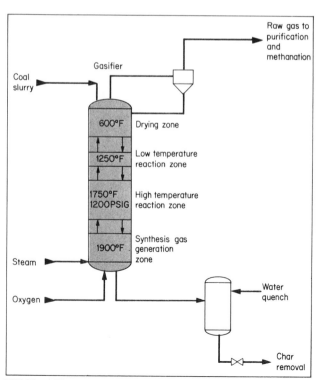

HYGAS gasifier accepts any type coal to yield gas high in methane.

removed from it. Air heated to about 800°F is blown through the particles to prevent the coal from becoming sticky at high temperature.

Addition of light oil—a byproduct of gasification—produces a mud-like mixture or slurry. In this form the coal can be fed into the system's gasification reactor—the heart of the operation—which is at high pressure (1,000 psi) and high temperatures (1,500° to 1,800°F). Injected into the top of a 135-ft-tall hydrogasification reactor, the coal drops downward and is subjected to heat and hydrogen that causes a chemical reaction to take place. This produces methane, the major component of natural gas.

The newly produced gas is cooled after leaving the top of the reactor, and rinsed in a water quench that removes the light oil, the steam and the coal fines. The oil is separated, and part of it is returned to the stage of the process in which it again is mixed with crushed coal to form more of the slurry mixture.

BI-GAS—complete conversion of coal

Key item in Bituminous Coal Research's BI-GAS process (sponsored by OCR and AGA), is a two-stage, high-pressure gasifier which produces a very high yield of methane directly from coal. Subsequent processing of the output gas thus is minimized. There are other advantages too. Because BI-GAS is an entrained rather than a fixed or fluidized-bed system, all types of coal should be amenable without prior treatment. Furthermore, all feed coal is consumed in the process (principal byproducts are slag for disposal and sulphur for sale), and the two-stage gasifier, being an integral unit, is relatively simple in design and amenable to scale-up to almost any size.

In the two-stage process, coal and steam are fed into the upper stage of the gasifier, and oxygen and steam are fed with char into the lower stage. The volatile portion of the coal in-

troduced with steam into the upper stage is converted into methane-rich gas by reaction with the hot synthesis gas coming up from the lower stage.

The raw product gas is withdrawn from the top of the gasifier and passes through a cyclone which separates the char for return to the gasifier. The remaining gas, still uncleaned, moves downstream for processing. The char is recycled to the gasifier and helps to make the process a continuous one.

Development work on the BI-GAS process has proceeded from batch-type experiments in rocking autoclaves, through continuous-flow experiments in a 5-lb/hr externally heated reactor, to operation of a 100-lb/hr internally fired process and equipment development unit (PEDU). Using North Dakota lignite, Wyoming subbituminous C coal, and Pennsylvania high-volatile A bituminous coal, the research has confirmed the basic assumption that high yields of methane could be obtained from coal at elevated temperatures and pressures.

With the completion of the test program, a larger-scale, fully integrated, 5-tph gasification pilot plant at Homer City, Pa. is now under construction. Completion of construction of the plant is scheduled for early 1975. The final objective is to provide sufficient design data for construction of a commercial plant.

CO₂ Acceptor—a novel way to supply heat

The CO₂ Acceptor process developed by Consolidation Coal is a significant technological advance in coal-to-gas conversion—both in the equipment and the method used to apply and sustain heat to the reactors to produce synthetic gas.

In the process, lignite is ground, dried and fed into a gasifier where, under pressure of 150 to 300 psi, it is heated in the presence of steam to a temperature of 1,500°F. Dolomite (crushed limestone), preheated to 1,900°F in the regenerator,

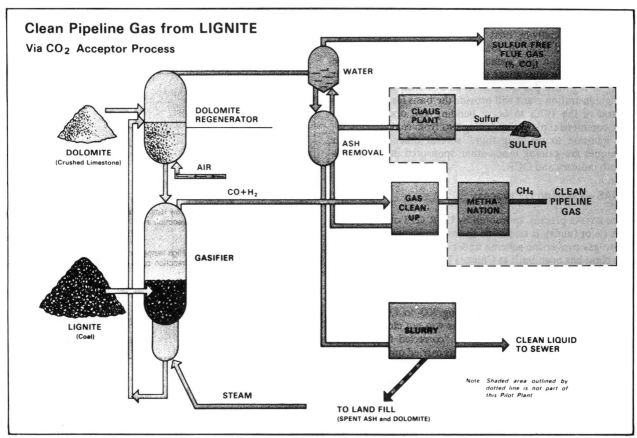

Consolidation Coal's CO₂ Acceptor method is typical of more efficient second-generation American techniques for gasifying coal.

is fed into the top of the gasifier. The limestone particles filter down through the gasifier, furnishing the heat because of its high temperature and by a unique chemical reaction, in which the dolomite absorbs carbon dioxide (a desirable step by itself). In other words, when dolomite (CaO) combines with CO_2 to form $CaCO_3$, a great deal of heat is given off—and it is mainly this heat which is used in gasification.

The spent dolomite and carbon residue are circulated to the regenerator where the dolomite is regenerated, using heat from the burning of the carbon. The gases released by heat and chemical reaction between steam and coal in the gasifier represent the final product containing all the ingredients needed to make pipeline gas.

Consol's CO_2 Acceptor pilot plant at Rapid City, S.D. has been operating about a year-and-a-half, and Consol has made 13 runs using lignite char as feedstock. Consol also has achieved a 100-hr integrated run in which all elements of the process were working. The shutdown of that run was semi-voluntary; the run could have been longer.

Synthane—a simple way to make gas

Beginning with laboratory and small pilot-plant research, the Bureau of Mines has come up with a relatively simple process for converting bituminous coal, subbituminous coal, and lignite to SNG. The process involves gasifying coal in a fluidized bed—up to 1,000 psi—to a raw gas containing methane, carbon monoxide, hydrogen, carbon dioxide, water vapor and impurities such as dust, tars and sulphur compounds. The raw gas is purified to a mixture of methane, hydrogen

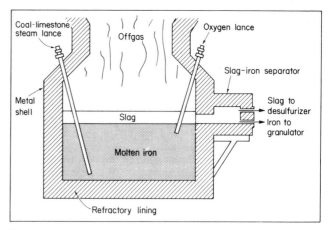

Molten-iron gasification shows high degree of American ingenuity.

and carbon monoxide and finally converted catalytically (methanated) to nearly 100% methane, or SNG.

The Synthane process claims many appealing features:
• Caking coals can be used directly, as can a wide range of other coals including lignite.
• Considerable methane is made in the gasifier, and external coal pretreatment is avoided.
• Minimum oxygen and lower oxygen plant investment is required, and fluid-bed technology is utilized.

The Bureau has commissioned Lummus Co. to design and

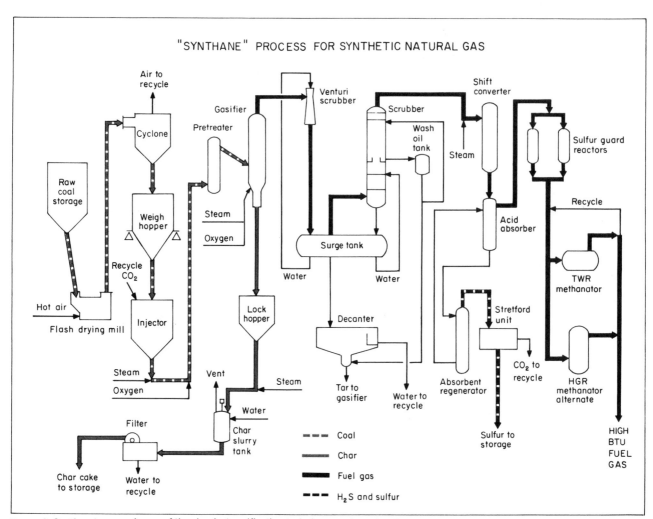

Bureau's Synthane process is one of the simplest gasification techniques, yet requires lower plant investment than most others.

build a 3- to 5-tph pilot plant at Bruceton, Pa. Completion of the $12-million pilot plant is expected by mid-1974.

Atgas—dissolving coal in molten iron

The strong affinity that exists between iron and sulphur is the basis of a novel gasification technique developed by Applied Technology Corp. (Pittsburgh, Pa.). All types of coal can be gasified because coal properties, such as sulphur content, caking characteristics and ash fusion have no influence on the process.

Crushed coal with steam is injected directly into a molten iron bath. Steam dissociation and thermal cracking of coal volatile matter generates hydrogen, carbon monoxide and methane. The coal sulphur is captured by the iron and transferred to a lime slag from which elemental sulphur is recovered as a byproduct. The fixed carbon of the coal is dissolved in the iron from which it is removed by oxidation to carbon monoxide, with oxygen injected near the molten iron surface. The product gas is treated by conventional shift conversion and methanation.

Much of the technology pertinent to the process already exists as discrete commercial steps in the iron and steel industry. However, the combination of these steps into simultaneous ones remains to be demonstrated on a large scale.

Kellogg Process—purging coal in molten salt

Gasification of coal in a bath of molten sodium carbonate through which steam is passed is the basis of a system developed by M.W. Kellogg Co. (Houston, Tex.).

The technique offers several important advantages. First, sodium carbonate strongly catalyzes the basic steam-coal reaction permitting essentially complete gasification of coal at reduced temperature. Second, the molten salt can be used to supply heat to the coal undergoing gasification. Third, the molten bath serves to disperse coal and steam throughout the reactor, which permits direct gasification of caking coals and eliminates the need for carbonization of such coals. Fourth,

the bath of salt operates at a uniform temperature in the gasification range and, combined with the catalytic effect of sodium carbonate on steam-carbon gasification, yields a raw gas that is free of tars as well as tar acids and tar bases.

Kellogg had OCR funding from 1964 through 1967, at which time such support was dropped because of problems arising from corrosion produced by the molten salt. However, the company has received a new grant from OCR because of promising results that indicate the process can be used as a method for generating a fuel gas suitable for magnetohydrodynamic (MHD) systems. The residual ash and sulphur are retained in the molten ash during gasification and subsequently removed as a component of a purge stream. Also, the clean CO-rich gas is an ideal fuel for MHD generator systems.

Battelle/Union Carbide self-agglomerator for turbines

A self-agglomerating, fluidized-bed technique is said to be so effective for collecting ash contained in coal that the resulting gas is essentially free of fly ash and therefore can be used directly in gas turbines to drive electric generators.

Originally developed by Union Carbide Corp., the Agglomerated Ash process gasifies coal in a bottom-fed, steam-fluidized bed gasifier. Coal is injected near the base of the gasifier into a bed of hot, sintered ash agglomerates. As the coal flows up through the bed, it is heated to the carbon-steam reaction temperature and converted to char and gas.

The char concentrates at the top of the unit where some additional gasification takes place. The gas then is piped off for purification and methanation.

The agglomerates enter the gasifier just below the top of the char bed at a temperature of about 2,000°F, and the gasification reactions cool this material to about 1,000°F by the time it is withdrawn at the bottom. An "agglomerating bed combustor" reheats the agglomerates, using the residual char as fuel. The char particles produce an essentially ash-free flue gas as they burn. This gas is cleaned and fed to an open-cycle turbine compressor for energy recovery.

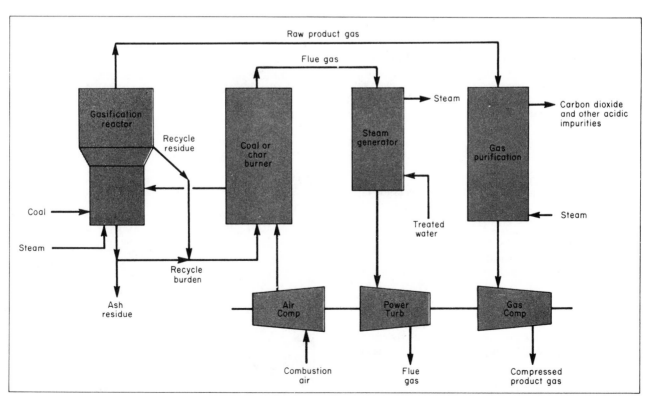

Self-agglomerating technique produces steam and clean gas for feeding directly to a combined turbine-compressor power unit.

Battelle Memorial Institute (Columbus, Ohio) has been awarded a contract by OCR and AGA to build a PEDU unit of 80,000 ft/hr of synthesis gas (CO, H_2).

The process is said to have substantial capital cost savings over single-stage systems requiring an oxygen plant, and over systems with char-fed steam generation facilities. In addition, caking coals are not pretreated, and the relatively "clean" product gas eliminates expensive water treatment of raw gas scrubber effluent.

Exxon's high-Btu, nitrogen-thwarting process

Exxon recently revealed it has already spent $20 million on a novel high-Btu gasification process that uses air instead of the oxygen that most of the other processes use. This eliminates need for an oxygen plant. Furthermore, the process can handle all types of coal.

In gasification, part of the coal is combusted to provide the necessary heat to combine coal with steam, but if air is used for the combustion, nitrogen from the air is entrapped in the final gas, diluting it. Keeping the two reactions separate usually causes heat transfer difficulties. Exxon's method, being kept under wraps, is said to involve removing pulverized coal from the gasification reactor, partially burning it in a second vessel, letting the flue gases escape, and then taking coal which did not burn, but of which the temperature was raised by the burning, and recycling it back to the reactor where it combines with steam.

Thus a continuous stream of solids circulates from combustion vessel to gasification vessel and back again, never giving nitrogen a chance to mix with the combustible ingredients of coal gas. Exxon says this is less complex and expensive than other gasification methods. A small pilot plant at Baytown, Tex. is already in operation, and Exxon plans a larger pilot plant at a cost of $80 million to convert 500 tpd of coal into gas. □

Coal liquefaction . . . a better route than gasification?

LIQUEFACTION has not yet received the high level of research effort that has been going into coal gasification. One reason is that the AGA frankly is committed to its members who have put up at least $40 million so far for the development of a commercial system to make synthetic pipeline gas. AGA feels it must have a demonstration plant going by 1980 or earlier.

Cost data, however, from the National Petroleum Council on liquefaction, and the Federal Power Commission show that the cost of producing either coal gas or coal liquids is essentially the same, about $1.70 to $1.75 per million Btu, based on 1973 costs. In fact, liquefaction came out slightly less costly. And there are other advantages to liquefaction too, when compared with gasification:

• Liquefaction requires less chemical transformation and hydrogenation than gasification and has higher energy-conversion efficiency—78% for liquefaction vs 60-70% for gasification.

• Synthetic fuel oil is much easier to store and cheaper to pipeline than SNG. It is also more economically pressurized to fire industrial power turbines.

• Liquefaction does not require as much water as gasification and thus creates less severe water pollution problems.

And those advocates of multiproduct plants in which coal will be converted to liquid, gas, and coke or solvent-refined coal, say there is an added discount cash flow of 10% by following this route rather than one in which only gas or only liquids are produced.

Bureau's SYNTHOIL process

In liquefaction coal must be hydrogenated to be liquefied because it has only half as much hydrogen as crude oil. Hydrogenation also partially removes oxygen, sulphur and nitrogen which are present. Secondly, crude contains almost no ash whereas coal can contain roughly 10%, and this too must be removed.

The Bureau of Mines has developed a process for converting high-sulphur coals to fuel oil that has very low sulphur and ash contents. Its pilot plant is very successfully converting ½ tpd of coal into 1.5 bbl of clean fuel oil (3 bbl per ton). The process works on any kind of coal; five different grades have been processed. Typically, an inexpensive Kentucky coal having 5.5% sulphur and 17% ash has been converted to clean fuel oil having only 0.17% sulphur and 0.7% ash. Carbon conversion was 98% and energy conversion efficiency was 78%.

In the SYNTHOIL operation, pulverized coal is slurried with some of its own product oil and then pumped into the reactor with hydrogen at high velocity to create turbulence. The reactor is filled with immobilized catalyst pellets. The combined effect of the hydrogen, turbulence and catalyst is to liquefy and desulphurize the coal at high yields and high throughput. Sulphur is removed as hydrogen sulphide which is easily converted into a preferred product, elemental sulphur for immediate use by industry or for storage. The unused hydrogen is recycled for reuse in the process. The raw oil is centrifuged to remove ash, providing an immediately usable low-sulphur, low-ash fuel oil. This oil can also be easily refined to gasoline or diesel oil if desired.

Oil from coal by the SYNTHOIL process appears to be less costly than current petroleum-derived fuel oils, providing incentive for the current plans to build a larger, 24 bbl/day (bpd) pilot plant.

FMC's COED and COGAS techniques

FMC's pilot plant at Princeton, N.J., sponsored by OCR, has a capacity of 36 tpd of coal, yielding about 30 bpd of refinery feedstock plus char. The COED process (Char Oil Energy Development) employs multiple fluidized beds, and the plant has operated on Illinois, Colorado and Wyoming coals. FMC has installed also an oil-absorber system which is expected to enhance oil yield and permit coal solids to be recovered from the gas stream to be cycled back into the pyrolysis reactors.

The COGAS process is an outgrowth of COED. As originally conceived, it was thought that the char would be a desirable boiler fuel. However, with the demand for pipeline-quality

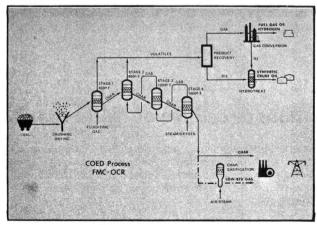

Changes in FMC's COED process will produce gas as well as oil.

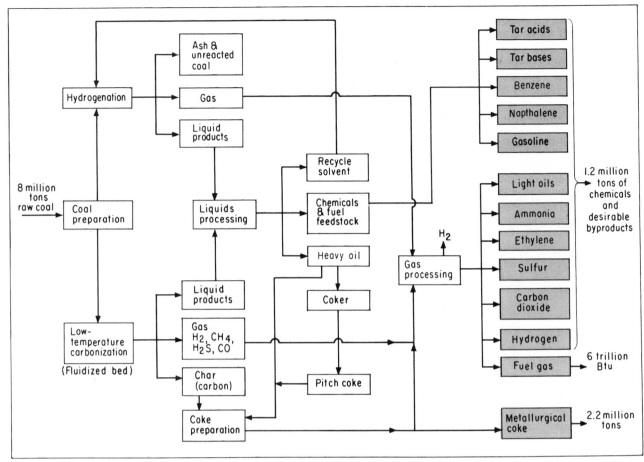

Most-advanced multiproduct technique is US Steel's Clean Coke. High-sulphur coal is converted to gasoline, oils, chemicals, gas and coke.

gas, COED is being modified in a separate project to include gasification of the char. The process has been renamed COGAS and produces both oil and pipeline gas.

Exxon's put-and-take technique

Exxon is also successfully converting high-sulphur coal to synthetic crude oil by using a "donor" technique. Oil is first made from coal, and hydrogen added to it through a hydrogenation step. The solvent (the oil), now loaded with hydrogen molecules, is brought together with more coal and fed to a reactor where, with enough pressure and heat, the hydrogen in the solvent donates the extra hydrogen to the coal to liquefy it. The solvent is thus a transfer mechanism. A high yield, about 2 to 3 bbl of oil per ton of coal, is expected.

Exxon has operated a small pilot plant and is designing a large, 200-to-300-tpd unit. The Federal government is being asked to participate in the development.

US Steel's Clean Coke Process

Sponsored by OCR, Clean Coke is a multiproduct process that combines carbonization and hydrogenation to convert non-metallurgical-grade coals to low-sulphur metallurgical coke, chemical feedstocks, and liquid and gaseous fuels.

According to the process design, raw coal from the mine is processed first in a preparation section, where it is cleaned, dried and sized, and then split into two approximately equal portions. One portion of coal is processed in the carbonization section, where it is converted to low-sulphur char, chemicals-rich tar, and gas rich in hydrogen.

The other portion of coal is processed in the hydrogenation section where it is converted to a chemicals-rich liquid and gas rich in light paraffins. These products are separated from a residue of unconverted coal and ash minerals by a novel method of vapor stripping with hot process gases.

Construction of process-development units should be completed this year to permit evaluation tests. □

Improved methods provide
more direct use of high-sulphur coal

ASIDE FROM GASIFYING OR LIQUEFYING high-sulphur coal, there are better ways now to convert such coal to a refined solid, or to clean the sulphur out of it more effectively—or, if everything else fails, to scrub out the sulphur emissions from stack gases.

Solvent refined coal

Developed by Pittsburg & Midway Coal Mining Co., a subsidiary of Gulf Oil Co., and sponsored by OCR, the SRC (Solvent Refined Coal) process produces low-sulphur (less than 0.5%), low-ash solids from high-sulphur coal.

The process consists of dissolving coal in a coal-based solvent (derived from the process) under moderate hydrogen pressure. All of the pyritic sulphur and 60-70% of the organic sulphur are removed as H_2S, and the sulphur is removed as elemental sulphur. The solvent is recovered by distillation. The product, liquid during the process, may be cooled and formed into small BB-like particles or lumps of brittle, pitch-like material.

A 50-to-70-tpd pilot unit has been built at Fort Lewis, Wash., and is about ready to operate.

More effective coal cleaning

Sulphur occurs in coal as particles of pyrite (iron sulphide) and as organic sulphur intimately tied to the chemical structure of coal itself. Cleaning by gravity techniques, for example, utilizes the difference in the specific gravities of the pyrite and the coal to separate the two. Typically, about half the sulphur in coal is in the form of pyrite, half of which might be removed by normal cleaning procedures.

Two-stage flotation. An effective new process, which has proven successful in removing pyritic sulphur from coal before the coal is burned, is expected to reduce greatly the pollution-limitations of many bituminous coals. The process, developed by the Bureau of Mines and funded by EPA, involves two-stage froth flotation, in which special chemicals are added in the second stage to remove sulphur left in the coal by conventional flotation.

One of the chemicals, xanthate, picks up pyritic sulphur particles as it bubbles to the surface of a flotation tank; the other chemical, a colloid, makes the coal sink to the bottom of the tank. The two-stage process has been tested successfully. In one laboratory test, pyritic sulphur content of a sample of coal was reduced from 2.31% to 0.28% in two stages.

Stack gas scrubbing

Numerous conflicting statements have been issued regarding the capability and reliability of techniques and equipment for removal of SO_2 in stack gases. Some manufacturers advertise that they have proved equipment available, and some electric utilities have spent large sums for installations of desulphurization devices, only to find that they failed to perform adequately and reliably.

There are literally a hundred or more processes for taking dilute SO_2 and making concentrated SO_2. The only acceptable process in the long run, however, is one in which elemental sulphur is produced so that it can be stored or sold. The Bureau of Mines' citrate process appears highly promising along these lines.

Citrate system. The Bureau's new process consists of four basic steps. First, the waste gas is washed to remove particulate matter and the small amounts of sulphur trioxide the gas contains. Then the SO_2 is absorbed in a citric acid solution. Next, the absorbed SO_2 is reacted with hydrogen sulphide to produce elemental sulphur. In the last step, the sulphur is separated from the citrate solution, and the solution is regenerated to absorb more SO_2.

Hydrogen sulphide for the third step is made from part of the sulphur produced by the process. A copper smelter using the Bureau process could control SO_2 emissions for less than 3¢/lb of copper produced, or less than 2¢ if the smelter already is converting part of its SO_2 to sulphuric acid. Coal-burning power plants could control SO_2 emissions for under 1½ mills/kwh of electricity generated, or $4.10 per ton of coal burned. These costs could be reduced by selling the recovered sulphur.

Improved fluidized beds

Much work is going on to perfect the fluidized-bed boiler, in that it permits more efficient burning of coal while also controlling emissions of SO_2. In a fluidized bed, air required for combustion is blown up through a thick layer, or bed, of inert granular particles. The gas flow-rate approximates 10 to

SOLVENT REFINED COAL PROCESS

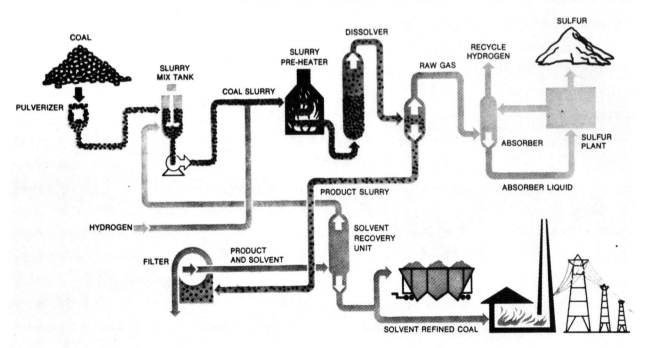

Small BB-like particles of coal with less than 0.5% sulphur will be made from high-sulphur coal in pilot plant at Fort Lewis, Wash.

15 ft/sec, which is sufficient to cause the granular particles to be suspended and the bed to behave as though it were a boiling liquid. Coal added to a hot fluidized-bed burns rapidly, and the generated heat is transferred quickly and efficiently to the boiler tubes.

A major improvement has been the "cell" concept for large fluidized-bed furnaces. The furnace is divided into a series of cells using boiler tubes as dividers. The cells share a common bed material which flows between the cells via specially placed gaps in the tube wall barriers. Cells may be shut down independently to accommodate changes in the steam demand. To carry out special functions, cells would be operated at different temperatures and with different levels of excess air. OCR has awarded a $5.8-million contract to Pope, Evans and Robbins to design a multicell fluidized boiler at the Rivesville, W.Va. plant of Monongahela Power Co.

Another innovation that is coming with respect to fluidized beds is the use of limestone particles to make up much of the bed. This produces large amounts of heat while reducing emissions of sulphur dioxides.

OCR is planning to combine the fluidized-bed technique with gas turbines. Efficiency of such a combined cycle will be about 50%, as opposed to the conventional boiler cycle of about 36%. ☐

Underground coal gasification . . . still a long way to go

ONE OF THE MOST UNORTHODOX CONCEPTS for gasifying coal involves underground (in-situ) burning of coal beds to develop a low-Btu gas. Until recently, the idea was considered technically feasible but not economically competitive with other fuel sources. But this might change now. According to the Bureau of Mines, considerable advancement in technology makes underground gasification more efficient, and tests are now going on at a gasification site near the town of Hanna, Wyo.

The Bureau's method is to drill a series of holes penetrating the coal bed—in the Hanna case, the seam is 30 ft thick and lies under a 400-ft overburden. Hydraulic or explosive shock waves then are induced in the holes to fracture the coal horizontally, thus creating passages for the gasification process and for the resulting gases to escape.

To ignite the coal, the Bureau inserted propane burners down the holes, lit them and pumped air down to furnish oxygen for combustion. Heat of combustion causes coal to react with steam (from underground moisture) to form gas. The gas is created all along the fracture planes and vented to the surface by a pipe system.

Because air is employed for the combustion, there will be considerable amounts of nitrogen and carbon dioxide in the gas, thus producing a gas of low-Btu quality. But conceivably the gas can be fed directly to a power plant near the site to generate electricity and thus avoid both the reclamation problems connected with surface mining, and the safety and health problems connected with underground mining.

While flow rates exceeding 2 million cu ft/day of gas containing generally a heating value of 100 to 200 Btu were achieved, it is still too early to assess completely the Hanna test results because gas volumes and heating values fluctuated widely. Future flow rates should exceed 5 million cu ft/day, a flow rate more representative of that required to support a small power station.

Future experiments will include oxygen injection to determine if the combustion reaction can be accelerated or if the gas Btu content can be increased or stabilized. Furthermore, to stimulate better gas flow, directional horizontal holes will be drilled through the coal bed. These horizontal holes, called "longwall generators," increase coal utilization in direct proportion to their length. The coal will be burned between parallel horizontal holes drilled in the butt cleat direction. This preferred direction would enable the injected air and product gases to move along the face cleats for maximum permeability, perhaps eliminating the need to fracture the coal prior to injection.

Both the use of oxygen and the directional drilling will be tried by the Bureau this year. Results of these experiments may help determine whether underground gasification can compete economically with conventional technology for mining and utilizing coal. ☐

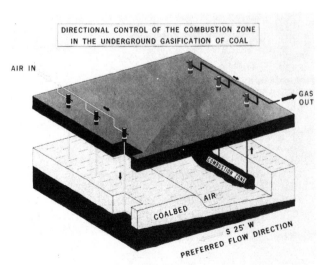

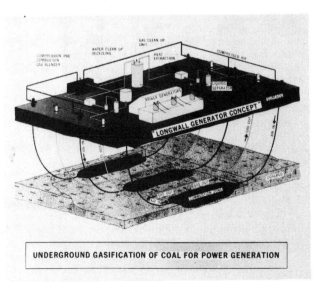

Just light the fuse and go, said one researcher about Bureau's method (left) to convert coal beds to low-Btu gas. Possible: on-site turbines.

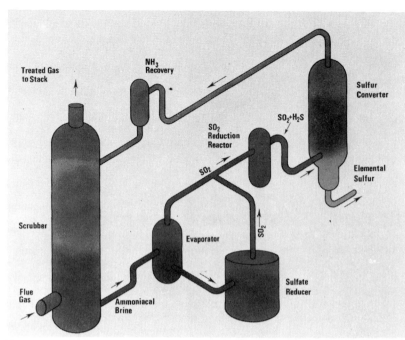

New process merges sulphur recovery technology with plumeless ammonia scrubbing.

SO_2 cleanup: IFP joins the systems chase

THE FRENCH PETROLEUM INSTITUTE (Institut Francais du Petrole) has unveiled a sulphur recovery process which it is prepared to license to utilities, smelters, coke oven operators, and others emitting large volumes of stack gases.

The IFP system has been demonstrated on a stack gas slip-stream that was the equivalent of a 30-Mw portion of a 250-Mw oil-fired power plant equipped with two electrical generating units. The demonstration took place from March through July 1976. IFP officials say that, after debugging and a three-month continuous run, "we knew our process was ready to be put on the market."

The IFP system consists of two separate sections, which may be located close to each other or far apart. The first is the scrubbing section, which captures SO_2 in an aqueous ammonia liquor. The second is the reactor section, where sulphur values in the ammoniacal brine are converted to a molten elemental state, and the ammonia is recycled to the scrubbing system.

Ammonia scrubbing is based on reliable technology, but it can produce stack problems—for example, a blue plume that develops when submicron particles of ammonium salts escape the scrubber. IFP formed an association with several US companies, including Air Products, which has a patented ammonia scrubbing process said to produce no opacity in the plume. As offered today, the IFP system includes "a fumeless Air Products scrubbing section."

In the French process, the effluent liquor from the scrubber contains ammonium sulphite, ammonium bisulphite, and a small amount of ammonium sulphate. IFP stresses that widely varying concentrations of sulphur oxides can be handled without difficulty and that the SO_2 content of cleaned flue gas can be reduced to 100 ppm.

In the conversion section, the liquor is decomposed into ammonia, SO_2, and water in a two-stage operation that uses IFP submerged combustion technology to reduce sulphates. IFP spokesmen say they spent heavily on this.

Two-thirds of the SO_2, they say, is transformed to H_2S using any sort of reducing gas. A gasifier can be used to produce this gas, and IFP notes that the process can use gas with hydrogen and carbon monoxide in any proportion. H_2S and SO_2 are fed in the proper 2:1 stoichiometric proportion to the tower, where they react according to the Claus equation to form elemental sulphur. Commercial-quality sulphur is withdrawn in a molten state from the boot of the tower, according to IFP spokesmen. They also point out that the Claus reaction takes place in the presence of the same solvent used in their TGT-1500 process—a Claus tailgas cleanup method, with which IFP claims to have enjoyed "some of its greatest success" in sulphur oxide systems. The group reports that 30 plants are licensed to use the TGT-1500 process.

Overheads from the reaction tower are condensed, and ammonia is recycled to the scrubber. IFP personnel say the process produces no significant amounts of waste and that the system appears economically attractive. Part of the attractiveness, they say, is that the heats of reaction of sulphur compounds being recovered produce steam utilized in various parts of the process; other advantages include simplicity of design, lack of corrosion problems, and low labor requirements.

The demonstration system was installed at a power plant owned by Electricite de France, the French national electric utility, at Champagne-sur-Oise, near Paris. Data gathered during the demonstration run are shown in the above table. IFP notes that the approximate $14.7 million investment (including the first charge of catalyst and solvent) is equivalent to $58.50 per installed kw for a 250-Mw plant. Operating costs at such an installation would be about 3.3 mils per kwh. These values correspond to an increase of about 20% in investment and 15% in operating costs over those of a plant without environmental controls.

IFP has also developed cost analyses indicating that the investment may drop to about $30 per installed kw and 1.5 mils per kwh for a 1,000-Mw plant. □

Two-stage process chemically treats mine drainage to remove dissolved metals

H. Peter Larsen and **Laurence W. Ross**, University of Denver

TREATMENT OF MINE DRAINAGE WATERS has fast become a necessity for all mining operations, and regulations governing discharge into local waterways can be expected to become even more stringent. One aspect of mine water treatment—removal of dissolved metals—can be accomplished by a two-stage process developed at the Denver Research Institute (DRI). The first stage of the process treats the waters by lime neutralization to eliminate Fe and Al. A second stage then removes Cu, Zn, Mn, and heavy toxic metals (Hg, Cd, As) by adding sulphide to the waters.

The quantitative effect of both stages of treatment can be predicted by a mathematical description based on the equilibrium relations involved:

$$mM^{+d} + dD^{-m} \rightarrow M_m D_d \downarrow \qquad (1)$$

where M is the metallic cation of charge $(+d)$ and D is the anion of charge $(-m)$.

The removal of dissolved metals by neutralization (stage 1) is predicted quantitatively. Total sulphide addition to achieve removal of specific metals is predicted for stage 2.

Table 1 provides the set of numerical constants used to describe the system mathematically. These values were selected from the literature as yielding the best approximation to measured results. Butler[1] has pointed out that K_{sp} values are often so small that they are outside the realm of realistic measurement. Therefore, a set of values that gives consistent results is all that is needed.

DRI process successful in field studies

Field investigation for the DRI process included erection of a treatment pond beside Mineral Creek in the

---

Fig. 1—Field treatment system for mine drainage

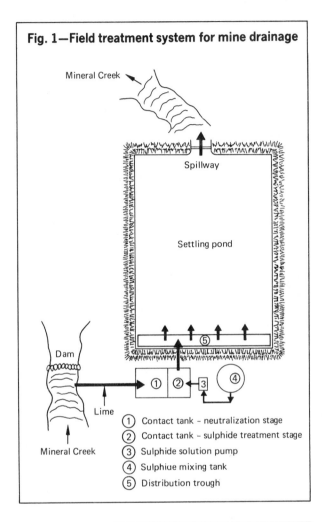

① Contact tank - neutralization stage
② Contact tank - sulphide treatment stage
③ Sulphide solution pump
④ Sulphide mixing tank
⑤ Distribution trough

Fig. 2—Results of sulphide addition to Idaho drainage sample

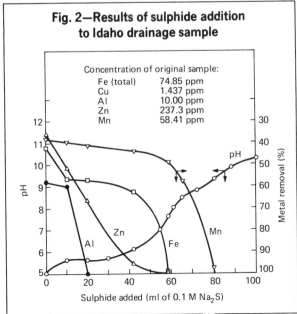

Concentration of original sample:
Fe (total)	74.85 ppm
Cu	1.437 ppm
Al	10.00 ppm
Zn	237.3 ppm
Mn	58.41 ppm

Sulphide added (ml of 0.1 M Na₂S)

Fig. 3—Results of sulphide addition to Montana drainage sample

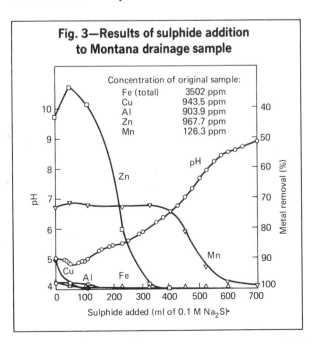

Concentration of original sample:
Fe (total)	3502 ppm
Cu	943.5 ppm
Al	903.9 ppm
Zn	967.7 ppm
Mn	126.3 ppm

Sulphide added (ml of 0.1 M Na₂S)

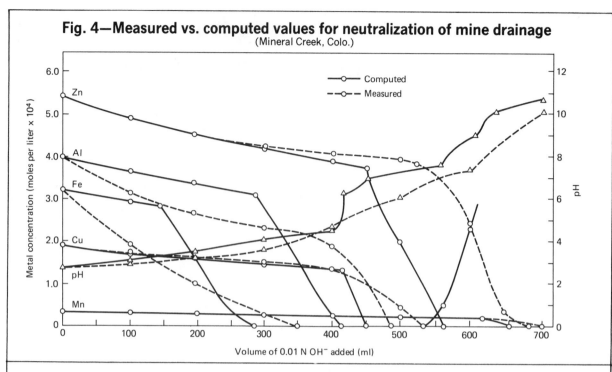

Fig. 4—Measured vs. computed values for neutralization of mine drainage
(Mineral Creek, Colo.)

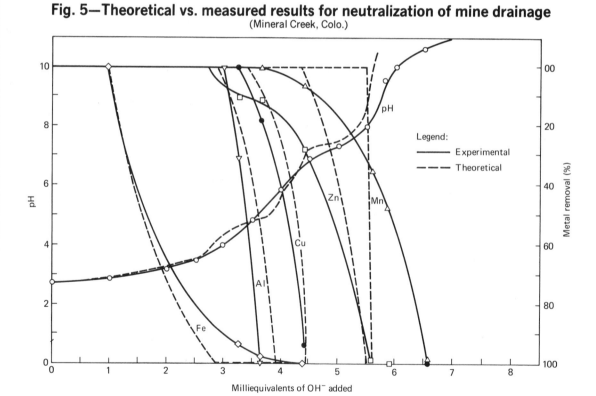

Fig. 5—Theoretical vs. measured results for neutralization of mine drainage
(Mineral Creek, Colo.)

Table 1—Solubility-product constants for hydroxides and sulphides of heavy metals in mine drainage

	Hydroxide	Sulphide
Ferric iron	1.1×10^{-36}	2.0×10^{-88}
Aluminum	1.2×10^{-32}	—
Cupric copper	6.0×10^{-20}	7.7×10^{-36}
Zinc	7.1×10^{-18}	1.6×10^{-24}
Manganese	1.6×10^{-13}	2.5×10^{-13}

Rocky Mountains, west of Denver, Colo. Fig. 1 shows the design of the pond. A single pond can be used to separate the minerals of potential economic value (e.g., Cu and Zn) from Fe and Al, because $Fe(OH)_3$ and $Al(OH)_3$ will not settle when a pond is even slightly agitated by surface breeze. The sulphides, on the other hand, precipitate almost immediately after being introduced into the settling pond.

Control of pH in the two stages of the process was quite simple, requiring only good mixing for 3 to 5 min in the contact chambers (1 and 2 in Fig. 1). Neutralization of the influent from pH 2.6 to pH 5.0 was achieved in the first stage, and sulphide addition in the second stage brought the pH to 6.5—the ambient regional pH.

Fig. 2 is an experimental plot of the behavior of metals in a drainage water sample from an Idaho mine tunnel after treatment by the DRI process. Mn was completely removed, although previously reported dual processes had removed Mn only partially.[2] The DRI process also succeeded in completely removing the toxic metals As, Cd, and Hg.

Fig. 3 shows the pattern of metal removal from a sample of drainage water taken in Montana. All Cu was apparently removed by neutralization before pH 3 was achieved.

Simulation of two-stage DRI process

Equation 1 is the basis for mathematical simulation. For example, the precipitation of ferric iron occurs as

$$Fe^{+3} + 3OH^- \rightarrow Fe(OH)_3 \downarrow$$

and the terms in equation 1 now become: $d = 3$, $m = 1$, $M = Fe^{3+}$, and $D = OH^-$.

The dissociation of water must also be considered:

$$H^+ + OH^- \rightarrow HOH$$

Finally, when the anion is sulphide ion, two additional equilibria must be expressed:

$$H^+ + S^{-2} \rightarrow HS^-$$
$$H^+ + HS^- \rightarrow H_2S$$

With the values reported in Table 1, equilibrium for the five metals of interest can be computed as a function of their concentration, the solution pH, and the amount of sulphide added. The two-stage DRI process was simulated by assuming a starting mixture consisting of typical Mineral Creek water, then raising the pH to 5.0, after which a given amount of sulphide was added.

Fig. 4—a set of curves for neutralization alone—illustrates the most difficult case to compute, because the liquid volume is changing. The plot in Fig. 4 suggests the presence of an unreported metal. The lag of pH rise and the delay in Zn precipitation indicate that another cation may be consuming OH^- ion. The unreported metal could be Mo, common in the Rocky Mountains but never reported in state or Federal routine sampling. Alternately, the metal could be As, which has been found in waters of this region in concentrations up to 20 ppm.

Computation is simpler when the sample of mine drainage water doesn't undergo a volume change. This is the case when solid chemicals, such as lime and sulphide, are added. Fig. 5 shows the results of such a computation for neutralization, and Fig. 6 shows the results of sulphide addition alone. The neutralization plot (Fig. 5) is fairly satisfactory at all points, but the plot for sulphide addition (Fig. 6) appears useful mainly as a predictive tool for Cu and Zn precipitation. □

References

1) Butler, J. M., "*Ionic Equilibrium: A Mathematical Approach*, Addison-Wesley, New York, 1964.
2) Zawadzki, E. A. and Glenn, R. A., "Sulphide Treatment of Mine Drainage," Bituminous Coal Research Inc., BCR Report L-290, Monroeville, Pa., July 1, 1968.

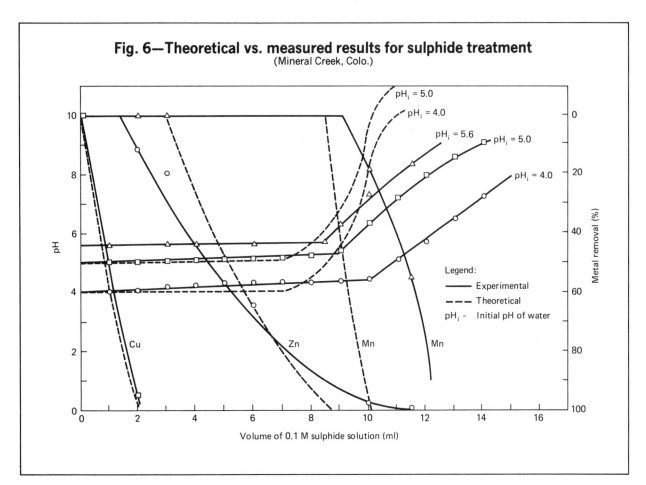

Fig. 6—Theoretical vs. measured results for sulphide treatment
(Mineral Creek, Colo.)

Resident agronomist at Pima's reclaimed tailings project in Arizona examines a desert tobacco indigenous to the area.

Pima studies tailings soil makeup as prelude to successful revegetation

K. L. Ludeke, agronomist, Pima Mining Co.
A. D. Day, agronomist; **L. S. Stith,** plant breeder; and **J. L. Stroehlein,** associate agricultural chemist; Arizona Agricultural Experimental Station, University of Arizona.

SOIL MATERIALS IN COPPER MINE TAILINGS contain nutrients for plant growth but require the addition of varying amounts of nitrogen, phosphorus, and potassium for successful revegetation. Replanting of tailings structures results in stabilization of the slopes and control of wind and water erosion, as exemplified by a Pima Mining Co. project at its Arizona copper mining operations.

Based on a detailed study of the characteristics of copper mine tailings, Pima's use of plants to revegetate and stabilize tailings is effectively blending these structures into the desert environment. This initial success, however, represents only one phase of a broad-based program designed to ultimately reclaim once-active mining properties in Arizona.

The importance of stabilizing mine wastes is reflected in figures released by the US Department of Health, Education, and Welfare. HEW documents the fact that over the past 30 years more than 20,000 million tons (670 million tpy) of solid mineral wastes have been generated in the US. Moreover, US mineral wastes are now accumulating at a rate of 2,000 million to 4,000 million tons annually. In the light of passage of the 1973 US Surface Mine Reclamation Act, which requires that all mine areas be revegetated within two years of abandonment, a successful program of reclamation of mineral wastes is critical for the mining industry.

Mine tailings may take the form of solids, liquids, gases, or a combination of any of the three, but for the most part they are comprised of barren overburden or submarginal-grade ore extracted from open-pit or surface mines. This waste material not only detracts from the appearance of the natural landscape, but contributes to air pollution as well, through dispersement of the finely ground tailings fraction.

How Pima analyzed mine tailings

The tailings beautification project piloted by Pima near Tucson, Ariz., undertook to compare differences in average content of organic matter, bulk density, pH, total soluble salts, nitrate-nitrogen, phosphorus, sodium, and acid-extractable potassium in soil materials found in copper mine tailings. Since it was assumed that the presence of acid-extractable iron, magnesium, zinc, manganese, and copper might prove toxic to plant growth, the amounts of available iron, magnesium, and copper in copper tailings were also recorded.

The water retention capacity of fresh wet tailings, fresh oven-dried tailings, and old natural-weathered tailings (approximately six to eight months old) was studied by recording moisture percentages at five different levels of tension: 0.3, 1, 5, 10, and 15 atmospheres. In 1972, samples were taken from four soil materials designated as tailings, tailings-overburden, overburden, and desert soil (undisturbed for three to 11 years), and evaluated with respect to the foregoing characteristics. All data were analyzed using the Student-Newman-Keul Test as described by Steel and Torrie.[8]

Average organic matter, bulk density, pH, total soluble salts—nitrogen (NO_3–N), phosphorous (P), sodium (Na), and potassium (K)—for each of the four soil materials are shown in Table 1.

Organic content proved higher at the 6-in. depth than at the 35-in. depth, suggesting that breakdown of organic matter is rapid. The presence of organic matter in tailings has not been previously recorded in the literature. The low content of organic matter in all four soil materials indicates that it may be necessary to incorporate straw or other forms of organic materials into the surface of tailings slopes to obtain satisfactory plant growth.

The bulk densities of the four soil materials studied were representative of those normally found for mineral soils and were not influenced by the depth from which the samples were taken. The average bulk density of tailings-overburden (1.37) was slightly higher than the bulk densities of the other three soil materials (tailings, overburden, and desert). However, with the exception of tailings-overburden at 35 in., the bulk densities did not vary sufficiently to indicate any serious change in the amount of air, water, or root growth within the waste materials tested.

The pH of the desert soil was found to be lower than the pH of the other soil materials. An increase in pH in tailings at the 35-in. depth suggested that some leaching had occurred.

Significant differences found in soluble salts

Total soluble salts differed significantly in the four materials tested. Desert soil material contained the highest concentration of soluble salts, and tailings material had the lowest. Disregarding sample depth, this suggested that leaching was slower in desert soil material than in the mill waste. Preliminary observations also indicated that grass plants grew best in desert soil material. Therefore, it may be assumed that the total soluble salt content in each of the waste materials tested was low enough to permit satisfactory plant growth of relatively non-salt-tolerant plants.

Nitrogen content was higher in tailings at the surface level than it was in the other waste materials studied, and desert soil contained the least nitrogen. The NO$_3$-N levels in all waste materials tested, however, were too low for normal plant growth; therefore, it is suggested that fertilizer be supplied for grass planting in the revegetation of copper mine wastes.

No significant differences in phosphorus were observed at different soil depths. However, differences in P were evident between soil materials. No reports were found in the literature to suggest that sodium had been a problem in revegetating mineral tailings, and, generally, the quantity of Na found in the waste materials tested was not high enough to be detrimental to plant growth. Both the surface and subsurface of tailings berms contained similar concentrations of potassium, but the K content was slightly higher in tailings material than in other soil materials tested.

Comparison of acid-extractable mineral concentrations

It was assumed that the concentration of acid-extractable mineral elements may be indicative of a number of problems, including toxicity. Therefore, data were accumulated to compare extractable concentrations with available concentrations. Acid-extractable iron (Fe) content was highest at the surface in all soil materials (see Table 2). The concentration of Fe was particularly high in tailings.

Quantities of Fe found in tailings and tailings-overburden may appear excessive when compared to desert and overburden soil materials, the reason being that ore removed from open-pit copper mines contains high concentrations of pyrite, along with other minerals containing lesser quantities of iron. As for tailings-overburden, the mixing of the two would dilute the Fe ion, but would still keep Fe content relatively high. Tailings soil material also contained more acid-extractable Fe at both soil depths than did the other soil materials tested. Acid-extractable Fe was higher in desert soil material at the 6-in. depth than it was in overburden.

Acid-extractable magnesium was also higher in the surface layer of all soil materials. Tailings soil material contained the

highest concentration of acid-extractable Mg at the 6-in. depth. At the 35-in. depth, overburden contained less extractable Mg than did the other soil materials tested.

Tailings soil material recorded the highest concentration of zinc at the 6-in. depth and contained the most acid-extractable quantity of the metal. High concentrations of the metal found in tailings may be explained by the fact that zinc is present in copper ore in the form of sphalerite. The remaining soil materials were found to have similar quantities of extractable zinc.

Concentrations of manganese in tailings and desert soil materials were similar at the surface levels, and higher than in tailings-overburden and overburden. Acid-extractable copper proved higher in tailings and tailings-overburden than in overburden and desert soil materials.

Table 1—Organic matter, bulk density, pH, soluble salts, NO$_3$-N, P, Na, K in four soils

Potential soil material	Depth of sample (in.)	Organic matter (%)	Bulk density (g/cm^3)	pH	Total soluble salts (ppm)	Elements (ppm)			
						NO$_3$-N	P	Na	K
Tailing	6	0.21 a	1.35 b	7.75 a	355 c	22 a	31 b	66 b	51 a
	35	0.18 a	1.31 b	7.88 a	271 c	7 a	48 a	55 b	35 a
Tailing and overburden	6	0.11 b	1.34 b	7.78 a	2869 b	7 b	26 b	189 a	25 b
	35	0.11 b	1.40 a	7.55 b	2808 b	8 b	1 b	104 a	39 a
Overburden	6	0.14 b	1.29 b	7.85 a	2452 b	7 b	2 b	135 a	15 b
	35	0.14 b	1.28 b	7.56 b	2896 b	8 b	2 b	107 a	20 b
Desert	6	0.18 a	1.37 b	7.45 b	3182 a	6 b	1 b	63 b	17 b
	35	0.13 b	1.27 b	7.44 b	5540 a	3 b	1 b	55 b	21 b
C.V. (%)		26	4	19	73	57	59	47	43

Significance of differences:
1. Between soil depths		*	ns	*	**	**	ns	**	ns
2. Between soil materials		**	*	**	**	**	**	**	**

Legend: ns = not significant at 5%, * = significant at 5%, ** = significant at 1%.
Means followed by the same letter, within soil depths, are not different at the 5% level of significance (Student-Newman-Keul test).

Table 2—Acid-extractable, available minerals at two depths in four soil types

Potential soil material	Depth of sample (in.)	Acid extractable (ppm)					Available (ppm)		
		Fe	Mg	Zn	Mn	Cu	Fe	Mg	Cu
Tailing	6	16215 a	7028 a	187 a	178 a	761 a	823 a	718 b	39 a
	35	14678 a	3758 c	74 b	54 b	709 a	1021 a	832 a	68 a
Tailing and overburden	6	13013 b	6016 b	110 b	116 ab	689 b	619 b	686 b	25 b
	35	11188 b	3520 c	63 bc	54 b	521 b	565 b	541 b	24 b
Overburden	6	6113 d	3131 d	67 c	145 b	22 c	15 c	438 c	4 c
	35	5828 c	2938 d	54 bc	72 b	9 c	12 c	371 c	2 c
Desert	6	7255 c	3984 c	64 c	178 a	16 c	21 c	338 c	3 c
	35	4683 d	3555 c	40 c	159 a	13 c	18 c	354 c	2 c
C.V. (%)		43	34	55	43	99	103	33	109

Significance of differences:
	Fe	Mg	Zn	Mn	Cu	Fe	Mg	Cu
1. Between soil depths	**	**	**	**	**	**	*	**
2. Between soil materials	**	**	**	**	**	**	**	**

Legend: ns = not significant at 5%, * = significant at 5%, ** = significant at 1%.
Means followed by the same letter, within soil depths, are not different at the 5% level of significance (Student-Newman-Keul test).

Table 3—Organic matter, bulk density, pH, soluble salts, NO₃-N, P, Na, K in tailings soils

Treatments of a soil material	Depths of sample (in.)	Organic matter (%)	Bulk density (g/cm³)	pH	Total soluble salts (ppm)	Elements (ppm)			
						NO₃-N	P	Na	K
Fresh, wet	6	0.89 b	1.51 a	10.39 a	3427 a	1 b	1 b	196 b	75
tailing	35	1.29 b	1.61 a	10.20 a	2165 b	1 b	1 b	72 a	45 b
Fresh, oven-	6	1.71 a	1.08 a	8.19 b	4059 a	1 b	2 ab	158 a	138 a
dried tailing	35	2.36 a	1.18 a	8.20 b	3483 b	1 b	3 ab	114 a	71 b
Old, natural-	6	0.21 c	1.35 a	7.75 b	355 b	22 b	3 a	66 c	51 b
weathered tailing	35	0.18 c	1.31 a	7.88 b	271 b	7 a	5 a	55 a	35 b
C.V. (%)		74	18	13	84	169	84	105	63

Significance of differences:

1. Between soil depths		**	ns	ns	ns	**	ns	*	**
2. Between soil treatments	**		**	**	**	**	**	**	*

Legend: ns = not significant at 5%, * = significant at 5%, ** = significant at 1%.
Means followed by the same letter, within soil depths, are not different at the 5% level of significance (Student-Newman-Keul test).

Available iron found in tailings and tailings-overburden was significantly higher at both depths than in the other soil materials. As was explained for acid-extractable Fe, the amount of available Fe in tailings may be related to the Fe present in high-Fe pyrite. Acid-extractable and available Fe appear to be immobile and are not leached in soil materials. Tailings and tailings-overburden possessed higher concentrations of available magnesium at the surface than did overburden and desert soil materials. Tailings material has the highest available Mg content at the 35-in. depth. Predictably, total available copper was higher in tailings than in the other soil materials tested.

Available magnesium appears to be more readily leachable from copper milling wastes than available iron and manganese, because it is found in similar concentrations at both surface and subsurface soil depths. The remaining two extractable ions evaluated, zinc and manganese, were not studied from the standpoint of their availability because they were present in low concentrations. This was particularly true for the Mn ion, since its low concentration was relatively constant in all soil materials evaluated.

Tailings soil analyzed under three conditions

In a separate study involving only tailings soil material, the average organic matter, bulk density, pH, and total soluble salts at two depths were measured for three conditions (see Table 3).

Organic matter was highest in fresh, oven-dried tailings. The addition of organic matter to any soil material decreases its bulk density and increases its capacity for water retention. Organic matter can be provided by transporting plant residue to the soil material site, and is increased by the plant growth which it supports.

Bulk density of tailings was decreased by the addition of organic matter and was not changed by depth of sample or pH. Fresh, wet tailings had a higher pH value than the other materials tested because lime was added during the copper milling operation. As tailings material is left to weather under natural environmental conditions, its pH is gradually decreased, probably as a result of leaching.

Highest concentrations of total soluble salts were contained in fresh, oven-dried tailings. Old, natural-weathered tailings were low in total soluble salts, probably because leaching had occurred.

In tailings waste material, the elements N, P, Na, and K were present in such low concentrations as to be of little value as plant nutrients. Therefore, they were not considered to be important in this study.

The three different tailings treatments did not alter the general concentrations of acid-extractable and available mineral elements in tailings present in copper mine disposal berms (Table 4).

Average atmospheres of tension, percent moisture, and available water for four waste materials in copper mine tailings disposal slopes are reported in Table 5. The amount of residual water was higher in tailings soil material than it was in the other waste materials studied.

Organic matter is essential for improving tailings waste material to support plant growth, and the growth of annual and perennial vegetation itself supplements the organic content of the tailings slopes. The goal should be to mix these plant materials into the tailings when the tailings are rich in organic material.

As the total soluble salt concentration in tailings waste decreases through leaching and natural weathering, the amount of available water for plant growth increases. In this experiment, the average moisture content from field capacity to five atmospheres tension decreased much more rapidly in tailings soil material than it did in the other soil materials which were studied at Pima. □

Table 4—Acid-extractable, available minerals at two depths in three tailings soils

Treatments of a soil material	Depth of sample (in.)	Acid extractable (ppm)					Available (ppm)		
		Fe	Mg	Zn	Mn	Cu	Fe	Mg	Cu
Fresh, wet	6	1896 c	2123 c	29 c	56 b	100 c	1214 b	1091 b	76 b
tailing	35	1538 c	2279 c	24 c	33 b	85 c	1320 b	1522 b	82 b
Fresh, oven-	6	3560 b	4000 b	56 b	104 a	185 b	2285 a	2100 a	145 a
dried tailing	35	2745 b	3800 b	43 c	100 a	165 b	2010 a	2009 a	125 a
Old, natural-									
weathered	6	16215 a	7028 a	185 a	178 a	761 a	823 b	718 c	39 c
tailing	35	14678 a	3758 h	74 b	54 ab	709 a	1021 b	832 c	68 c
C.V. (%)		94	44	83	60	88	40	42	42

Significance of differences:

1. Between soil depths		**	**	**	**	ns	ns	ns	ns
2. Between soil treatments		**	**	**	**	**	**	**	**

Legend: ns = not significant at 5%, * = significant at 5%, ** = significant at 1%.
Means followed by the same letter, within soil depths, are not different at the 5% level of significance (Student-Newman-Keul test).

References

1) Aynes, Q. C., and Coates, D. C., *Land Drainage and Reclamation*, McGraw-Hill Inc., New York, 1939.
2) Donaldson, G. W., "The stability of slime dams in the gold industry," JOURNAL OF THE SOUTH AFRICAN INSTITUTE OF MINING AND METALLURGY, Vol. 60, pp 183-199.
3) Frey, Donald N., "Policies for solid waste management," US Department of Health, Education, and Welfare, Bureau of Solid Waste Management Bulletin No. 75, 65 pp.
4) Jones, W. L., "Stabilizing mine dumps with vegetation," ENDEAVOUR, Vol. 11, pp 1-10.
5) Keen, P. R., "Vegetation to stabilize mine dumps," MINING MAGAZINE, No. 3, pp 157-159.
6) Knabe, W., "Strip-mine reclamation in Germany," OHIO JOURNAL OF SCIENCE, Vol. 64, pp 75-105.
7) Peterson, Howard B., and Monk, Ralph, "Vegetation and metal toxicity in relation to mine and mill wastes," Utah Agricultural Experiment Station (1967), Circular 148, 75 pp.
8) Steel, R. G. D., and Torrie, J. H., *Principles and Procedures of Statistics*, McGraw-Hill Book Co. Inc. New York, 1960.
9) Vaughn, Richard D., "Solid waste management: the federal role," JOURNAL OF HEALTH AND EDUCATION, Vol. 46, pp 1-22.

Inspiration's design for clean air

Stan Dayton, Editor-in-chief

New copper smelting technology introduced to US weds a Norwegian electric matte furnace with Belgian siphon converters. All units pipe metallurgical gas to a West German double absorption acid plant in lower foreground. Electric furnace is housed in building under precipitators and discharge end of elevated dryer. New converter aisle is normal to the furnace structure and joins the older smelter.

ALREADY EQUIPPED WITH ONE OF THE WORLD'S most complete copper metallurgical installations, Arizona's fully integrated Inspiration Consolidated Copper Co. plunged deeply into air pollution abatement with a $54 million expenditure for a new electric smelter and double absorption sulphuric acid plant—both containing some of the largest componentry of their type anywhere.

For Inspiration, which ranks on the lower end of the size scale among US primary copper producers, the drive for absolute and final compliance with air standards was one more in a long list of bold and heady maneuvers that have characterized the company since it sprang to life in 1911. The dollars poured into the project (the equivalent of over three times the company's 1973 net income, and 60% of the year's gross income) were essentially chasing clean air—not an immediate return on investment.

As financially painful as this may seem, the new plants are also a solid hedge against the future and are expected to yield hidden benefits. Such accrual, however, will depend on management ingenuity—a "long suit" at Inspiration—and the shape of future events in the smelter-short US copper economy, which could also soon be facing a shortage of mined copper.

Last month the new smelter, equipped with an Elkem 51-mva furnace and five siphon converters of Hoboken-Overpelt design, started phasing in the production line as a replacement for an older, reverberatory, Peirce-Smith converter installation handling a green charge. The latter, built in 1915, modernized, and acquired from The Anaconda Co.'s former

Editor's note: This report drew freely on the experience of many past and current Inspiration staff members, their reports, and their contributions to the literature. Top management has been generous in releasing information and lending encouragement in publication. If E/MJ has overlooked due acknowledgment of sources in the rush to get into print, the editors apologize for any oversight.

International Smelting and Refining Co., was an efficient, low-cost producer of anode copper. However, it presented a near-hopeless prospect for meeting a Federal 90% sulphur recovery goal, even with extensive modification and tightening of the gas handling system—not to mention the expense for an add-on SO_2 recovery plant.

Coupled to the new smelter—which handles 1,500 tpd of copper concentrates and copper precipitates of Inspiration and toll origin—is a "showcase" 1,330-tpd Lurgi acid train fed from an elaborate collection system that "dry cleans and launders" electric furnace and siphon converter offgases.

The new project places Inspiration first among western US copper smelters in the race to meet the Federal Environmental Protection Agency's idealistic 90% sulphur recovery goal for stationary plants. The replacement system will enable mothballing of the present smelter as a reserve asset.

An investment in the future

What has Inspiration gained from its efforts (other than empty praise from a fickle public for being socially responsive to environmental demands)?

■ It has stretched its oxide and sulphide ore reserves at In-

Clamps and slip ring gear for the six self-baking electrodes on the furnace control the feed rate to compensate for daily consumption of 6 to 10 in. of casing and carbon. Floor level of the photo is about 25 ft above arched furnace roof.

spiration Div. mines in porphyry ore formation by providing a source of low cost acid supply that more than meets its needs.

■ Inspiration is creating future copper reserves from rock in its holdings which today is worthless because it is submarginal for recovery.

■ The acid supply increases the productive potential of the company, and makes development more feasible for new properties now under investigation (such as one at Safford, Ariz.).

■ The company has gained an "antiseptically" clean new smelting system which theoretically should achieve production costs comparable to the old plant, and which lends itself to closer automatic control of matte smelting and matte conversion conditions.

■ Inspiration has moved in the direction of relatively stable energy costs for metal making, becoming more dependent on electric power and less reliant on natural gas or fuel oil.

■ Perhaps most important, the financial commitment to clean air is part of the company's past, and Inspiration can now turn its efforts to solidifying and expanding its resource base without the distraction of shooting at erratically moving targets for air emissions. During the process, it has established a tight matte smelting installation from which a 4-6% SO_2 gas can be pulled to blend with a 6-9% gas from the converters—products rich enough for acid making. In-plant emission of sulphur dioxide will also be dramatically lowered, making the total working environment more pleasant.

It is expected that the plant will experience normal startup difficulties because it involves new systems, more sophisticated than those employed in the old smelter. The technology is new in this country, and of course there is the matter of gaining practical operating and trouble-shooting experience by crews that have received theoretical training in the technology, systems, and procedures, as well as the basics of copper smelting. In the wings, however, is the present smelter, which can function as a production line safety valve during possible emergencies in the new plant.

How Inspiration settled on the new system

At the present smelter, roughly 10% of the sulphur comes off a 32-ft-wide by 110-ft-long reverberatory at 265,000 scfm in a dilute gas stream of 0.5-0.8% SO_2. The remaining 90% is contained in 160,000 scfm of 1.5% SO_2 converter gases.

Before air quality legislation, Inspiration was examining a sulphur removal method under an agreement with Golden Cycle Corp. The work had been nursed along through bench scale to a mini-pilot scale using an SO_2 absorbing reagent swept by a weak gas stream. The process had a potential for concentrating sulphur dioxide into a manageable gas volume of sufficient strength for acid making. When air quality control rules were dropped on the copper smelting industry, it was apparent that this investigation, through January of 1971, left far too little time for development to commercial scale within the time frame allowed for compliance.

Alternatives were scanned on an increasingly urgent basis, including tightening the current plant to minimize air infiltration and using undershot oxygen, or combustion air enrichment. Other, newer methods were considered, such as the Worcra and Noranda processes, but in 1970 both of these had to be considered not fully proven. Other possibilities included fluid bed roasting, flash smelting and oxygen smelting in converters, and electric matte smelting with downstream converters. Because Inspiration's production of cement copper is growing, and because a portion of the sulphide mineralization is made up of chalcocite, it was thought that even with toll input of chalcopyrite concentrates, the sulphur content of the charge would be deficient for flash smelting or fluid bed roasting prior to electric smelting.

A breakthrough occurred when Inspiration negotiated a large block of interruptible electric power from the Salt River Project at an acceptable price, lying between the cheap but deteriorating supply of natural gas and the more expensive fuel oil substituted during natural gas shortages. By March 1971 the company had committed itself to the pursuit of the electric matte smelting option using a dried green feed.

Electric furnace interior was lined by Harbison-Walker with 292,571 bricks. The 38-ft sprung arch roof contains concentrate feed ports and openings for electrode casing over coke cans on floor. Endwall port is for converter slag return.

Next came an evaluation of the converter system. The electric furnace could have been installed to deliver matte to the existing converter aisle. This is equipped with three 13 x 23-ft and one 12 x 20-ft Peirce Smith units and two Great Falls 12-ft-dia converters, a 13 x 20-ft natural-gas-fired refining furnace, and a 21-ft-dia casting wheel for 1,200-lb copper anodes. The old converter building was inadequate for support of the massive hooding that would have been required for tightening of the gas recovery system.

The expense of beefing up the old structure, which would have considerably lengthened the flue run to the acid plant, began to make an extension of the old converter aisle toward the acid site look more attractive. There were also obvious advantages in separating construction work from active metal making operations.

Figuring strongly in the logic were natural advantages of the Belgian Metallurgie Hoboken-Overpelt siphon converters, which had the capability of limiting extraneous air dilution of exit gases. They offered potential savings in capital and operating costs for gas handling and cleaning systems. Furthermore, the gas production would be more consistent because silica flux, matte, and cold dope (converter slag, shells, etc.) could be fed without interrupting the converter blow. By October of 1971 it was agreed to go with the siphon converter concept.

It had been decided early to use acid making to strip the sulphur from the gas stream. In this respect, Inspiration enjoys a somewhat unique tactical advantage. The company consumes large quantities of acid in its ore recovery operations—currently about 600 tpd. Since not many other copper producers have a need for acid in such proportions, those with smelters find themselves in an awkward position. If they rely upon acid recovery, currently considered the most reliably proven system for fixing sulphur in a metallurgical gas stream, they may face either a surplus of acid or perhaps no market at all for the product. This sorry state of affairs begins to take on some ridiculous dimensions because all excess acid must be neutralized with lime or limestone and wasted as gypsum. In essence, this trades an air pollution problem for a solid waste disposal problem—solid waste that exacts a toll of over a ton of mined limestone per ton of acid to be wasted.

Therefore, the two fundamental items that shaped Inspiration's attack on air quality were the availability of reasonably priced electric power and the ability to absorb internally a large portion of the acid produced. In adopting its new game plan, Inspiration abandoned some $7 million in capital improvements to the old smelter during the early 1970s.

Fitting the new facilities to the existing system

The new plant makes use of existing facilities for materials receiving and crushing, as well as the fire refining and anode casting section in the converter aisle of the old smelter. New construction occupies an offset blocked T, oriented so that the wing housing the new converter aisle extends that of the old smelter. The remaining wing, normal to the converter aisle, houses the electric furnace, transformers, electrode paste handling, and furnace feed from the dryer. The control room, located on the furnace feed floor, affords a panoramic view of the converter aisle.

The new plant will be operating about 40% on Inspiration feed and 60% on toll-processed material. The electric matte furnace is designed for a daily diet of 1,821 tons of feed composed about as follows: 1,500 tpd of concentrate, 148 tpd of cold dope, 123 tpd of silica flux, and 50 tpd of limestone.

Inspiration feed and toll concentrate (with copper precipitates) are bedded in an enclosed building on a concrete slab in two parallel 6,000-ton piles by means of an overhead tripper conveyor system. Lime is needed for the electric furnace and is added as minus ¼-in. material in the bedding plant. The bed mixture is reclaimed by front-end loaders which deliver it to a 24-in. wet charge belt equipped with a continuous weighing system. Wet concentrate with silica flux, as required, and reverts are conveyed to a 550-ton wet charge bin.

A screening installation is used to provide the converters with sized plus ¼ in., minus 2-in. cold dope and silica. This

Converters are slanted 37.5° from long axis of aisle, putting mouths under craneway for matte charging and slag skimming. Retractable chutes feed both flux and reverts. Aisleway for the old smelter is visible in the background, far right.

system also handles and sizes matte smelter reverts to minus ¼-in. for the electric furnace. The feed preparation used for the new plant varies somewhat from the mix blended for the reverberatory system. Formerly, flux, concentrates, and precipitates were interlayered in the bedding building, and the old furnace was fed a wet charge. Reverts were recycled directly to the converters.

The mix delivered to the wet charge bin in the new system has a moisture content of 9% to 12%. It must be taken to a bone-dry condition, largely to prevent explosions that may range from a mild bump to something of a damaging proportion. Experience elsewhere has shown that serious eruptions can occur in an electric furnace when the charge contains free moisture. For efficient operation, electric matte furnaces run best with the bath completely covered with solid charge. If moist charge caves or sloughs into the bath, an eruption may follow.

Considered only from the aspects of the material and moisture load, Inspiration invested in a rather large 16-ft-dia by 80-ft-long Fuller rotary dryer with a fully insulated, but unlined, stainless 316L steel shell. It is designed to reduce the moisture content to 0.1% to 0.3%. Fired by either natural gas or heavy fuel oil, the dryer helps conserve power consumption in the electric furnace. However, the main factor considered in its sizing was relief from the dust load carryover.

Most materials handled by the smelter are finely divided and become very dusty when dried. They are easily swept by a fast-moving stream of gases. In order to hold the particulate load of dryer gases within reasonable limits, the unit was designed to keep gas velocities low while taking advantage of dryer residence time. It has been calculated that 20%, or less, of the solids will be entrained in the gas stream.

The dryer is concurrently fired from Peabody burners. The exit gas is maintained above the dew point for a cleaning system consisting of a pair of Dracco cyclones and a high-efficiency baghouse before it is vented to the atmosphere. The

dried charge is a very abrasive mixture that can become aerated to form a fluid, free-flowing mass. To minimize problems in handling this difficult material, the dryer was elevated on a concrete pier to bring the discharge point as close as possible to a pair of 700-ton-capacity furnace feed bins, located on the charging floor above the slag tapping endwall of the furnace. Both are totally enclosed structures vented into the dryer dust collection system.

The Elkem electric furnace is the largest copper matting furnace in the world. Measuring 34 ft wide by 117 ft long (ID), the furnace is equipped with six in-line, self-baking carbon electrodes, 71 in. in dia, that enter the furnace along the centerline of the sprung arch roof. They dip into the molten slag layer. Heat for smelting is generated by resistance of the slag to the submerged arc between electrode pairs.

On the charging floor, a twin system is employed. Dried feed is reclaimed from each 700-ton bin by a 6-ft-long variable speed screw feeder which augers the charge to a 22-in.-wide, four-speed drag conveyor extending 114 ft, nearly the length of the furnace. Each bin features this arrangement, one serving the east and the other the west side of the electrode line. Each totally enclosed drag conveyor delivers the charge to a series of 15 feed spouts that enter the furnace roof. Seven of these spouts are near the line of electrodes, and the other eight are near the furnace sidewall. The charge in the spout enters the furnace through an arc gate and then a weighted tilt gate, sequenced so that a seal is maintained on the furnace. The end spout is open at all times. Most of the charge will be introduced in the line of spouts nearest the electrodes; the remaining 10% to 20% will enter the line near the furnace sidewalls.

About the world's largest electric copper furnace

The inverted, double-arch bottom of the furnace and the end and sidewalls, to a point above the bath line, are of basic

E/MJ OPERATING HANDBOOK OF MINERAL PROCESSING

Tuyere puncher clears ports for introduction of blast air at 20 psi from bustle. Puncher is Gaspe-type, mounted on rails. This view is photographed from side opposite the photo at left. Siphon housing for converter gas is shown at right.

brick construction. Above the bath, the upper-side and endwalls and the sprung arch roof contain firebrick. The furnace is supported on concrete piers. Vertical steel columns and tie rods clamp the sidewalls and provide additional structural support. The unit operates with 30 in. of matte and a 60-in. slag layer.

The endwalls of the furnace are water cooled. The sidewalls and bottom are air cooled from a set of three blowers, rated at 118,000 cfm each, on each side of the furnace at the ground level. Normally, two operate on each side and one is on standby. Air sweeps under the furnace, up the sidewalls and exhausts through the roof, changing the atmosphere once a minute.

Electric power is delivered to Inspiration at 115 kv and stepped down to 22.9 kv in a new substation rated at 56,000 kva. The transformer vault, located on the furnace charging floor, takes 22.9-kv power on the primary side of three single-phase transformers with a total rating of 51,000 kva.

The electric furnace transformers reduce the voltage to the operating level required for slag resistance operation. They are connected to the furnace electrodes by means of a bus bar and flexible cable arrangement leading to a copper contact

All Inspiration ore is surface mined—most by shovels and trucks, such as this 10-yd P&H and 75-ton Dart hauler. Several types of ore with variable mineral content are treated.

Vat leaching plant is first recovery step for two ore types. High oxide ore is leached and discarded. Mixed oxides and sulphides are leached, and residue then goes to sulphide flotation.

Inspiration Div. producing mines include: 1) Thornton, 2) Live Oak, 3) Red Hill, and 4) Willow Springs. Leach vats are at far rim of Thornton, near the electrowinning and electrolytic refineries and associated wash water and cementation launders.

shoe below the electrode slip ring. The slip ring permits automatic adjustment of the electrode position according to the desired power input. A full range of operating voltages is available, and the power input will not exceed 11.5 kw per sq ft of hearth area. The bus bars are contained in an enclosed duct, which is under pressure to maintain a dust free atmosphere. If the transformers should develop a leak, the oil is drained out of the building and away from the electrical atmosphere.

Electrode paste for the Soderberg self-baking electrodes is delivered to the smelter in 1-ton blocks having the following specifications: fixed carbon 75.4%, volatile matter 11-12%, and ash 7.6%. The blocks have a density of approximately 1.6 gm per cc, and become fluid at 80° to 100°C. The electrode clamps and slipping mechanisms, which act on the steel casing housing the carbon, are the reverse of the arrangement used elsewhere. At Inspiration, the clamps are spring loaded in a closed position and can be opened only by the application of hydraulic power to 100-ton jacks for purposes of positioning. The slip rate, based on power input requirements, is normally handled automatically, but the system is equipped with a manual override from a remote station.

The upper floor of the furnace building is arranged for electrode paste handling and the assembly of steel casing for the carbon blocks. The floor is serviced from an elevator for delivery of carbon blocks and flat 12-gauge steel plates. New casing is assembled in sections standing 5 ft 11 in. in height by first punching the sides of 18 plates to shape fins pointing inward, then rolling them to the proper radius. The shaped and punched sections are then joined into a finished cylindrical section by an automatic welding machine. As casing and carbon are consumed, a new casing section is mounted and welded to the shortened assembly. A hoist then loads the carbon blocks into the empty casing.

The big dividend: an enriched exit gas

Electric furnace matte smelting eliminates the dilution of reaction gases by the large volume of combustion products associated with fuel-fired furnaces. This makes it possible to pull a 4-6% SO_2 gas stream from the furnace into the uptake positioned in the furnace roof near the matte tap endwall—a marked contrast to the weak 0.5-0.8% SO_2 coming off the reverberatory furnace.

The furnace endwall panels, two slag tap blocks, four matte tap blocks, and six electrode contact clamps are water-cooled from a 1,200-gpm pumping, distribution, and return system. The six electrode compression rings are water cooled by a separate 300-gpm pumping and circulation network.

Slag and matte tapping

Slag is skimmed from one of two tap holes in the endwall of the furnace. A pair of launders, sloped close to 19%, delivers the slag to a set of 600-cu-ft pots, and at the rated capacity, the slag handling will amount to about 980 tpd. The pots will be hauled to the dump by trucks of special design. The slag end of the furnace is equipped with a Joy tapping machine with a mud gun assembly for opening and replugging the slag skimming hole.

The matte endwall faces the converter aisle, parallel to the longitudinal axis of the latter. This endwall contains four holes for drawing off matte into two pairs of launders that take a modified V-shape in plan.

At the two junctions, the matte flows into one of two swivel spoons. Four 300-cu-ft ladles are positioned in a sand pit at the matte end. As a ladle is filled, the swivel spoon is tilted to a slight reverse slope, accumulating matte in the spoon. It is then pivoted to a new position over an empty ladle and down-tilted. Rotation and tilt of the swivel spoon is handled by air-actuated cylinders.

The converter is equipped with two 75-ton, two-hook P&H overhead bridge cranes. A clever leap-frog winch arrangement, installed near the junction of the two buildings, allows the position of the new cranes to be interchanged on the same track connecting the two converter aisles. The converter aisleway serving the reverberatory furnace contains cranes with a 40-ton main hoist and two 20-ton auxiliary hoists for the 175-cu-ft ladles in use there.

At the nominal rated capacity of the new smelter, over 1,200 tpd of matte will be tapped through the endwall. Converter slag is returned through the matte tap endwall from ladles that empty into two launders entering the furnace on 10 ft 6 in. centers about 10 ft above the matte tap holes.

Siphon converters tightly sealed

The siphon converters, 14 ft dia by 38 ft long, are considered the equivalent of 14 × 32-ft Peirce Smith converters. The five Hoboken-Overpelts are equipped with automatic draft control, 52 tuyeres on 6-in. centers, a tight converter flue and gas cleaning system, and a charge mouth of 20 to 25 sq ft. This opening is small by comparison with standard converters. The reaction end of the vessel, measuring 32 ft long, is extended by the siphon which is totally enclosed and dammed from the reaction zone to contain the bath. The casing for this extension contains a raised roof to siphon off the gases. It is also equipped with a counterweight to compensate for the asymmetry of the vessel.

A horizontal 9-ft-dia concentric cylinder taps the siphon on the rotary centerline of the converter unit, conducting the offgases to a dust settling chamber and the gas uptake. A proprietary gas-tight seal and joint links the rotating portion of the vessel assembly with a stationary section which enters the dust chamber. The entire converter assembly from endwall to the dust chamber and uptake measures about 75 ft long.

It is anticipated that each siphon converter, equipped with 1½-in. tuyeres, will be unable to take an air blast in the bath much in excess of 20,000 scfm without tending to plug the siphon.

The Hoboken-Overpelt converters are installed on 55-ft centers in a unique "en echelon" pattern slanted at 37.5° from the converter aisle craneway. This arrangement places each converter mouth under the crane aisle for ladle servicing. The siphon end and gas uptake system of each converter extends outside the craneway in a lateral extension of the building. By freeing the exit gas handling system from the path of crane travel, it has been possible to use a simpler and more desirable design for the gas uptake and initial cooling system since

Ball mill line at Inspiration concentrator takes direct-fed higher sulphide ore and leached dual process ore from vats.

Southwire continuous cast plant turns out 5/16-in.-dia rod from electrowon and electrorefined Inspiration cathodes.

it has unencumbered headroom. The converter platforms are equipped with Gaspe-type Heath & Sherwood tuyere punching machines.

Individual dampers installed in the flue system behind each

Clean air project panorama shows elevated dryer, furnace building, and acid plant with emergency and tail gas stacks.

converter are automatically controlled. Regulation of the dampers maintains an approximate zero pressure across the mouth of the converter. The Hobokens will, in fact, hardly tend to puff at the mouth, thus preventing gas escape and minimizing the intrusion of dilution air. The latter two effects are among the big advantages claimed for the siphon converter. Reduced gas escape will obviously improve in-plant working conditions, and SO_2, concentrated in a manageable gas stream, is a more desirable acid plant feed.

How copper conversion is handled

Each Inspiration converter is equipped with separate 80-ton capacity cold dope and silica bins. Both bins are equipped with variable-speed feeder belts which deliver sized, plus ¼-in., minus 2-in. products to an adjustable downspout. This system is able to feed flux or cold dope to the converter while the tuyeres are submerged and the converter is blowing. Matte can also be ladled into the converter during a blow. Such flexibility assists in achieving an optimum gas grade for delivery to the acid plant.

Since the converters must now be geared to efficient acid making, as well as blister copper recovery, the operating strategy of Inspiration's seasoned converter crews will require some reorientation. A new objective is in effect at the operation—to maintain as smooth a gas flow as possible in a volume that has a concentrated SO_2 content for the acid plant.

The latter will run more efficiently if surging volumes and SO_2 grades are reduced.

Of the five converters, four will be in service while one is down for repairs. The converters will be cycled so that one hot converter will be on standby, and the other three will be in operation and blowing a large percentage of the time. The three on blows are staggered so that one is on its copper or finishing blow while the other two are at differing stages of slag blowing. Matte is tapped from the electric furnace for the hot standby converter as the unit on the copper blow nears its end point. The fourth converter can then start a slag blow, and the finished converter can be down-turned for pouring blister copper. The hot blister can be transferred via the craneway to the existing anode refining furnace at the near end of the old converter aisle. Alternatively, the blister can be cast into 6,000-lb cakes.

The converters on slag blows are periodically turned down to skim slag for return to the electric furnace. When the smelter is at its nominal rated capacity, about 600 tpd of converter slag will be returned to the electric furnace. A fan of 40,000-cfm capacity ventilates the matte tap end of the furnace.

From a materials handling view, the converter aisleway, the reaction vessels and their work platforms, the associated gas handling equipment, and the feed arrangements for fluxing and reverts present a clean, uncluttered design which lends a feeling of spaciousness to the interior. The ground floor of the aisle is concreted, but contains appropriate gravel pits under splash areas, such as the converter mouths and the matte tap and slag return area of the electric furnace. The aisleway also contains a preheat station that can accommodate three ladles along the wall to the west of gravel pit at the matte tap section. Between the preheat and matte tap pits, a ladle crust breaker ram has been mounted.

Gas handling: a two-part excercise

Electric furnace and converter gases are processed in separate hot cleaning systems designed for high-efficiency recovery of particulates. The final exhaust from the hot gas cleaning system is drawn through a 90-in.-dia flue to the acid plant where the stream enters a cold gas cleaning installation.

The electric furnace generates an approximate average of 30,000 scfm of gas at 1,300°F. It leaves the furnace through an uptake hood serving an American Schack Co. model, 14 ft sq by 65 ft high, vertical radiation and shot-cleaned convection cooler. The radiation section features water-wall construction. On leaving the convection cooler, the gas has a temperature of about 850°F. A coupled flue on the furnace building roof delivers the gas to one of two Ducon dust cyclones arranged in parallel. It is estimated that a peak 6,700 lb per hr of particulates can reach the cyclones, which are designed to drop 80% of the dust load. Cycloned gas enters a high-velocity flue linked with a Research Cottrell electrostatic precipitator, which has a design specification of 98% collection efficiency.

On entering the Cottrell, the gas has been cooled to about 750°F. With some air infiltration in the system up through the electrostatic precipitator, an estimated volume of 38,000 scfm of gas from the electric furnace hot gas cleaning system is delivered through a 48-in. flue to the insulated duct leading to the acid plant.

Converter gases are handled in much the same way. At peak volume, each converter will produce about 23,000 scfm of gas at 2,200°F, which is swept from the dust chamber to a vertical American Schack water-wall radiation and shot-cleaned convection cooler. The gas leaves the radiation section at about 1,200°F and exits the convection cooler at about 900°F. It is then cleaned in a Ducon cyclone (one per converter), and five 46-in. flues deliver the cycloned converter gases to a mixing plenum chamber which serves three Research Cottrell electrostatic precipitators in parallel.

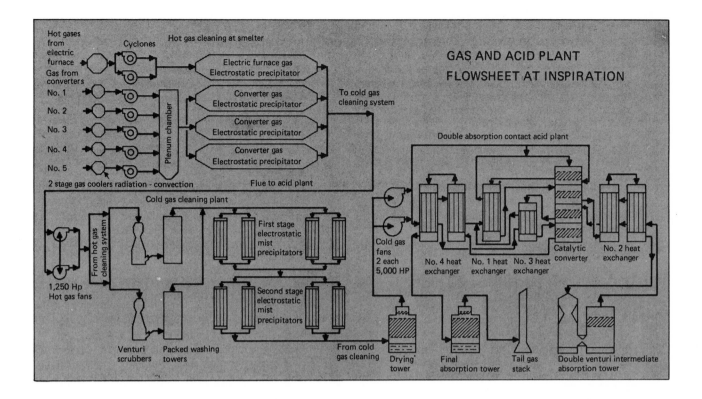

The converter cyclones are also designed to separate 80% of the dust carryover in the gas stream. The electrostatic precipitators on the converter system are each designed to handle 34,000 scfm of gas with a maximum temperature of 750°F at 95% collection efficiency. All electrostatic precipitators for the furnace and converters are ganged on the roof of the furnace building. Electrostatic precipitator gases from the converter system are ducted in 48-in. insulated lines into the 90-in. main delivering gas to the acid plant.

Dust from the precipitators and plenum chamber is collected by screw conveyors and transported to a bin at ground level next to the furnace building or to the furnace feed bins.

The draft to pull electric furnace and converter gases through the hot cleaning system is created by two 1,250-hp hot gas fans, each rated for 70,000 scfm. A total of about 140,000 scfm of gas will be drawn to the acid plant from the hot gas cleaning system of the electric furnace and the three converters that are on-line. All flues in the hot gas handling installation are high-velocity ducts which convey gas at speeds of 4,000 to 7,000 fpm to minimize the settling of dust in the flues. The gas delivered to cold gas cleaning at the acid plant should be about 550°F.

Cold gas cleaning

The merged gas streams from the smelter are piped 430 ft in the 90-in. main to the cold gas cleaning system at the acid plant. Here, the gas is split between a pair of venturi scrubbers, flowing concurrently with 25% sulphuric acid solution down through the units into the lower end of two packed washing and cooling towers.

A bleed stream from the acid wash solution goes through a set of settling tanks to remove sludge so that the circulating acid can be adjusted to about 0.5% solids content. Some of the acid is bled to SO₂ strippers. Stripper gas joins the smelter gas stream entering the packed towers. The 25% acid from the stripper is recovered for use in an agitation leach and CCD circuit for slimes at the Inspiration concentrator.

A 1% washing acid circulates through the packed towers countercurrently to the gas flow. This solution passes through graphite tube and shell coolers. The condensed water from the gases is ducted from the washing tower overflow to the sump of the venturi scrubber.

Cooled gases from the packed towers at about 104°F are combined and enter eight electrostatic mist precipitators, furnished by Plastic Design and Engineering. They are arranged in two stages, with four units in parallel composing each stage. This final gas cleaning renders an optically clear stream for the adjacent acid plant.

Making acid in a quality plant

To attain the desired degree of SO₂ recovery, a more expensive double-absorption contact system, furnished by American Lurgi, was selected for acid making. Clean gas from the cold cleaning system contains about 7% SO₂. It is pulled through a drying tower countercurrently to a flow of 93-96% sulphuric acid by a pair of downstream, 5,000-hp Allis Chalmers blowers in parallel.

From the blowers, the gas enters the conversion and absorption system. The Lurgi plant is equipped with a total of four V₂O₅ catalyst beds for converting SO₂ to SO₃. Four Cyclotherm heat exchanger installations, two of them containing two vessels in series, maintain proper gas temperatures for conversion and absorption. Top bed gases from the catalytic converter are cooled in one heat exchanger. Gases leaving the second bed are cooled by two heat exchangers in series before going to the intermediate double venturi type absorber. With over 80% of the SO₂ converted to SO₃, the heat-exchanged, second-bed gases flow concurrently with acid from the top of the intermediate absorber down through the unit. This helps conserve heat required for the catalytic reaction in the third state of conversion.

The weak offgas from the absorber returns to the catalytic converter after it is further heated in the shell of the set of exchangers handling second-bed gases. Containing less than 2% SO₂, this weak gas passes through the third and fourth catalyst beds, with a single heat exchange taking place between them. The gas from the fourth bed enters two heat exchangers in series and then the final absorption tower. Off-gas from the final absorption tower goes to the 200-ft-high tail gas stack.

Nominal monohydrate acid production, without allowances for losses, will be 1,330 tpd in the plant, which has the capability of producing either 93% or 98% acid. The final product will be delivered to a 10,000-ton storage system.

Steam plant recovers waste heat

An ingenious system recovers waste heat from furnace and converter gas cooling stages and utilizes it to generate steam in a plant designed by Treadwell Corp. as part of its overall engineering contract.

High pressure, high temperature water ($500°F$ at 1,000 psi) circulates in a closed loop system through the water jackets on the American Schack radiation coolers handling electric furnace and converter offgases. Heat is removed from this closed recirculation system and converted to steam in steam generators. A peak total of 126,000 lb per hr of steam will be generated. The steam is used to drive turbines supplying blast air to the converters and to drive the pumps which recirculate the high pressure water through the radiation coolers. Any excess steam can be fed to the Inspiration power plant.

Maintaining the cooling water at $500°F$ will keep the offgases above the dew point and out of the corrosion range. The system includes water treatment facilities to supply treated water to the steam plant.

In conclusion

The new smelter-acid installation is a highly sophisticated system with two control centers. The nerve center for the smelter commands a sweeping view of the converters and furnace. This control room houses the instruments which monitor and control furnace and converter operating conditions. Temperature indicator and recorder panels track sensitive points in the system, including concentrate feed, hot gases, and cooling water. Functioning of equipment, which is operated either automatically or manually by local operators, is also monitored in the smelter control room.

A Du Pont 460 photometric analyzer monitors the SO_2 content of effluent gases at seven locations. A paging system links the smelter control center, the acid plant control center, and the smelter cranemen for telephone communications.

Inspiration's engineers and management have launched a modern new recovery system and introduced new technology to the US. They are joined by the contractors and suppliers in a justifiable feeling of pride in this achievement. □

References

1) Rodolff, D. W., and Marble, E. R. Jr., "Air Pollution Abatement at the Inspiration Smelter," 1972 AIME meeting.
2) Gonzales, J., Lira, M., and Vargas, E., "The Paipote Copper Smelter of Empresa Nacional de Mineria," 1972 AIME meeting.
3) Salat, S. J., Treadwell Corp., unpublished description of Inspiration's new copper smelter.

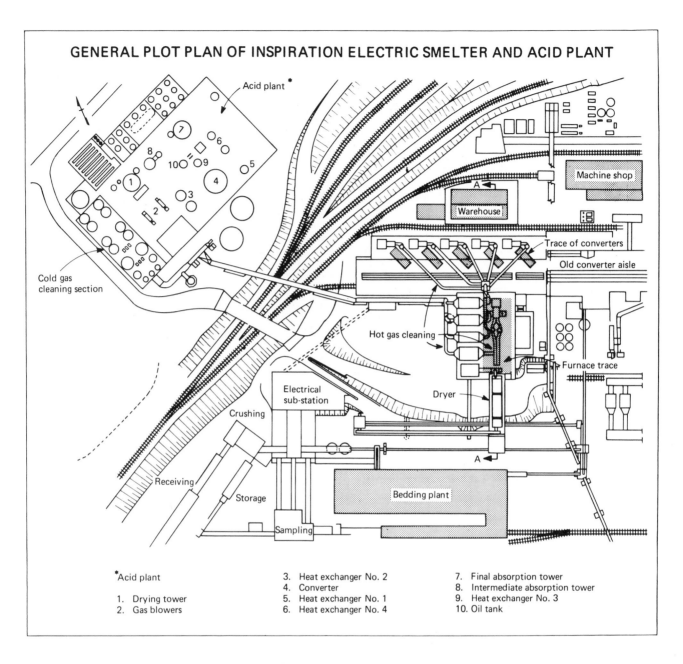

GENERAL PLOT PLAN OF INSPIRATION ELECTRIC SMELTER AND ACID PLANT

Acid plant *

Cold gas cleaning section

Machine shop

Warehouse

Trace of converters

Old converter aisle

Hot gas cleaning

Furnace trace

Dryer

Electrical sub-station

Crushing

Receiving

Storage

Sampling

Bedding plant

*Acid plant

1. Drying tower
2. Gas blowers
3. Heat exchanger No. 2
4. Converter
5. Heat exchanger No. 1
6. Heat exchanger No. 4
7. Final absorption tower
8. Intermediate absorption tower
9. Heat exchanger No. 3
10. Oil tank

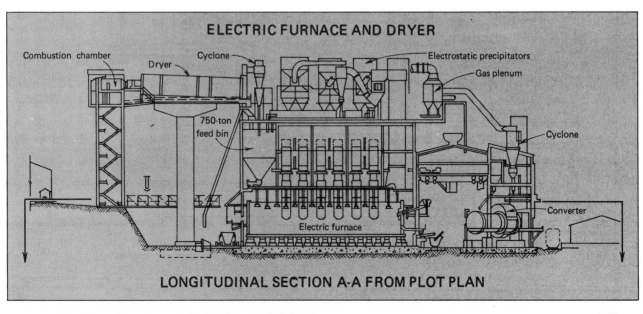

ELECTRIC FURNACE AND DRYER

Combustion chamber

Dryer

Cyclone

Electrostatic precipitators

Gas plenum

750-ton feed bin

Cyclone

Converter

Electric furnace

LONGITUDINAL SECTION A-A FROM PLOT PLAN

CROSS SECTION, ELECTRIC FURNACE BUILDING AT INSPIRATION

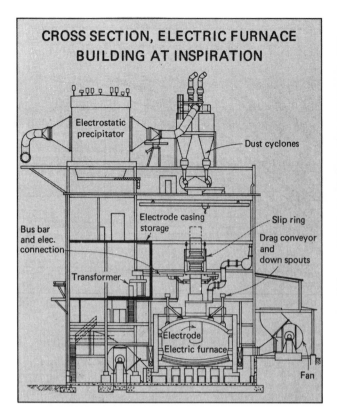

TYPICAL CONVERTER INSTALLATION AT INSPIRATION

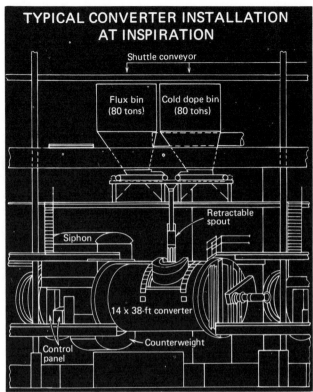

SLAG AND MATTE TAP DETAILS ON INSPIRATION ELECTRIC FURNACE

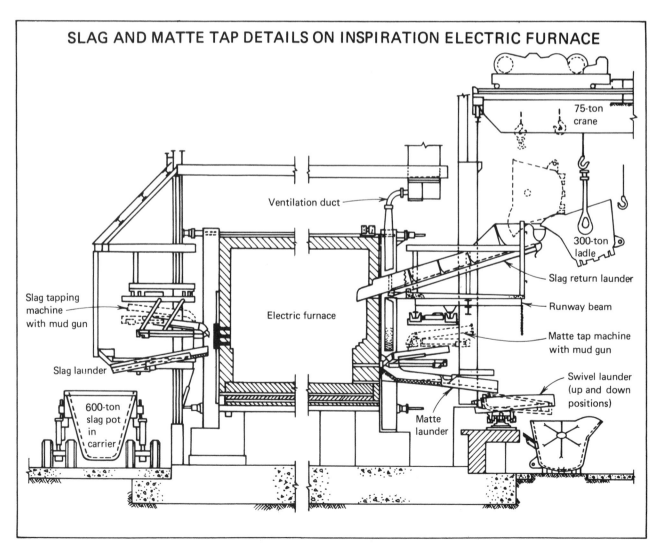

Bunker Hill's second tall stack: a gamble on reasonable SO₂ rules

THE ANNOUNCEMENT on June 1 of Bunker Hill Co.'s decision to proceed with construction of a 715-ft-tall stack at its lead smelter represents a major gamble by the company on an uncertain future. The company had begun construction of a 610-ft stack at its zinc plant in April. In making the announcement at news conferences in Kellogg and Spokane, Bunker Hill president James H. Halley said that construction of the two stacks will permit the company to meet Federal clean air standards for sulphur dioxide, as well as the existing Idaho state regulation—but therein lies the gamble.

Decision based on long study

The decision to use tall stacks followed four years of intensive investigation into all possible means for complying with clean air standards. The company tested the existing acid plants and equipment, investigated the availability of all other types of sulphur dioxide recovery equipment, and conducted meteorological studies of the Kellogg valley.

In early 1975, after consulting Arthur G. McKee, Monsanto Corp. (sulphur dioxide control equipment design), and North American Weather Consultants, Bunker Hill concluded that the equipment already installed at its operation was the best commercially available and that the only method left for complying with ambient air standards by mid-1977 was to erect taller stacks so that the SO₂ that could not be captured would be dispersed at a higher level above the surrounding terrain.

However, EPA rejection of the state plan for SO₂ control, and substitution of its own plan, created a serious dilemma for the company. The EPA regulation threatened to close the plant in mid-1977 if the company did not meet the EPA emission limitation of 82%, a degree of control that the company believes to be technically impossible. The company deferred construction of the stacks pending in-depth studies.

An assessment completed in April 1976 indicated that stack construction at the zinc plant should proceed at once, and work began in mid-April. The decision to construct the second stack was made following an evaluation of the lead smelter's long-term financial viability. The study was conducted by the company's financial personnel with the assistance of Arthur D. Little Inc.

"While the decision to proceed was based on the results of the economic study," Halley said, "we had to consider much more than just the economics. We had to attempt to evaluate the long term effects of both present and future possible regulations imposed on us by a

Bunker Hill's first tall stack—at the zinc plant—here had reached about 60 ft of its total 610-ft height. It will replace the 200-ft stack in the background.

number of regulatory agencies. The Federal EPA, for example, has already promulgated regulations which apply only to Bunker Hill and which we believe are both technically impossible and economically unreasonable. This regulation was the reason for the long deferral of the stack construction. We are appealing this regulation in the courts. The state is supporting our appeal on the basis of violation of state's rights.

"In spite of present and future uncertainties, we are proceeding on the basis of the belief that we can meet any reasonable present or future regulations and that the courts will protect us from regulations which are technically impossible or economically unreasonable."

In the case of the tall stacks, the gamble on future EPA rulings requires a major expenditure by the company—the

lead smelter stack and its ancillary facilities will cost a total of about $8 million. With a combined cost of nearly $11 million, the Bunker Hill stacks will rank as one of the largest single expenditures for environmental control ever undertaken in Idaho.

Smelter stack uses slip-forms

Site preparation for the new smelter stack, to be located 125 ft south of the existing 200-ft stack, began on June 1. Water lines under the new stack site were disconnected and relocated. The base and supporting pillar for the stack were slated for completion on Aug. 1, to be followed immediately by column construction, using the German-developed continuous-pour slip-form method.

Workers on a platform suspended from the stack columns continually adjust the slip-forms as the stack rises, to produce the desired wall thickness and taper. Concrete will be poured around the clock, and pouring will be finished in only 42 days.

Excavation for the zinc plant stack began on April 20, the base and supporting pillar were completed in 30 days, and pouring of the stack column began June 17. The zinc plant stack is being constructed using the more conventional jump-form technique, which is slower but less expensive than slip-forming.

Both stacks are scheduled for completion by Thanksgiving, when fiberglass-reinforced plastic liners will be installed. To ensure quality control of the concrete for the stacks, Pittsburg Testing Laboratories has set up a trailer near the batch plant to sample each batch for stress ability. The concrete is being mixed for a stress capacity of 5,000 lb per sq in.

Before construction of either stack began, a geological consulting firm tested the ground stability at each location, penetrating down to 100 ft under the surface to determine the suitability of the subsurface for supporting the heavy columns. Stack height was determined by North American Weather Consultants, which examined existing meteorological

Tall stack facts

	Smelter	Zinc plant
Height	715 ft	610 ft
Outside diameter at base	53 ft 1 in.	45 ft 8 in.
Outside diameter at top	21 ft 10 in.	21 ft 6 in.
Wall thickness at base	31¼ in.	30 in.
Wall thickness at top	9 in.	9 in.
Concrete for stack column	6,974 tons	4,800 tons
Reinforcement bar in stack	300 tons	70 tons
Width of base	83 ft	68 ft
Depth of base	7 ft	6 ft
Concrete in base	3,000 tons	977 tons
Column completion date	—	Nov. 25, 1976
Diameter of liner	13 ft 6 in.	6 ft
Composition of liner	—	Fiberglass-reinforced plastic
Length of flue	300 ft	1,000 ft
Diameter of flue	13 ft 6 in.	5 ft
Composition of flue	—	Fiberglass-reinforced plastic
Air rise velocity	—	75 ft per sec.
Project completion date	—	July 1, 1977
Contractor	—	M. W. Kellogg Co.

information and gathered additional data by inserting tracer gas into the existing stacks and tracking the gas with airplanes to determine dispersal and air fume patterns in the area.

In opting for the second tall stack, Bunker Hill is taking a closely calculated risk on the degree of judicial reason in applying EPA regulations and decisions to specific situations. □

Geothermal steam supplies added power for Mitsubishi's Akita zinc plant

Peter Rutledge, McGraw-Hill World News

JAPANESE PRODUCERS OF PRIMARY NONFERROUS METALS have been squeezed by power shortages this winter, and the prospect of continued shortages is a threat to the island industry's long-term growth. A partial solution to this problem may be found in geothermal steam power generating stations. Mitsubishi Metal Corp. is starting up such a power plant at its 8,100-tpm electrolytic zinc plant at Akita, and if all goes according to plan, the zinc operation will be able to rely on geothermal steam for about 20% of its 40 million-kw power requirement by the end of 1974.

Other Japanese smelting operations are lending Mitsubishi moral support in its effort to harness geothermal steam. A subcommittee of the Japan Mining and Metallurgical Association is preparing an estimate for the government on the future of geothermal power for the nonferrous industry. And if the Mitsubishi experience at Akita proves successful, which now seems likely, it is expected that the government will pitch in with subsidies for other geothermal generating stations. Such government assistance would not only add to available power supplies but could also bring an important reduction in smelting power costs, which in the case of electrolytic zinc currently account for one-third of all production costs.

The Mitsubishi geothermal generating plant is the third geothermal station to be built in Japan but the first to be used in nonferrous production. This plant will not of itself yield Mitsubishi a savings in power costs, since the company

invested $7 million in research and construction costs. But, Mitsubishi says, it is expected that knowhow developed during construction of the present plant will pay off in lower power costs when future plants are built.

In late 1973, Mitsubishi was testing three geothermal steam production wells capable of generating 6,500 kw in the mountains of Akita Prefecture on the Sea of Japan coast. Barring unforeseen developments, these three wells will be supplying power to the Akita zinc plant by the second quarter of 1974. A fourth production well was being drilled, and if it proves out, it will be tied into the zinc plant power supply in the fall. The combined output of the four wells will provide about one-fifth of the zinc plant's total electric power requirement.

Why did Mitsubishi decide to tap the Akita area's subterranean steam reserves?

"It was known for many years that there was a potential for geothermal power generation in the Akita area," a Mitsubishi engineer explained. "Mitsubishi had two copper mines in the area, and for many years we had been supplying power to the mines from hydro stations operated by the company in the same area. So Mitsubishi had knowledge not only of the area's geothermal power potential, but it also had experience in supplying its own power. In 1965, the company started investigations into ways to use the geothermal steam."

The generator shack at the Mitsubishi geothermal steam station houses 10,000-kw condensed twin-turbine generators.

Test wells precede production facilities

Six test wells were bored into the Akita area's Tertiary volcanic and pyroclastic rock formations, and the results from these wells formed the basis for the decision to move into a practical production phase. For operating wells, the production casing is 9⅝ in. OD and 8⅛ in. ID.

One of the findings made during the sinking of test wells was that the steam-water reserves located at depths from 1,400 to 1,700 m below the surface were relatively salt-free.

"Our findings so far suggest that once or twice a year we may have to scrape the turbine blades to remove accumulated salts, but this is not a serious problem," the Mitsubishi engineer said. The presence of relatively salt-free steam also means that it will not be necessary to build desalting facilities for the steam before it is piped to the generating turbines.

The Mitsubishi geothermal steam wells are sited in a national park, which created a few special problems. Among other things, this led to a decision to drill two of the production wells from a single surface location—one well drilled vertically to one steam "pool" and another drilled on an angle to reach a second "pool." Under ordinary conditions, it would have been more reasonable to put the second well directly over the second pool, but that would have meant installing a second wellhead, with additional piping and extra scarring of the forest, Mitsubishi said.

"Out of consideration for nearby villagers, we are also studying ways to utilize the waste steam for their benefit—perhaps in a regional heating system or for heating greenhouses," the Mitsubishi engineer reported.

The wells for the geothermal station are paired in two groups of two each, about 200 m from the generator shack which houses the turbines. The turbines were supplied by Mitsubishi Heavy Industries.

Power from the generators is fed to a Mitsubishi hydro station about 30 km away, where it is tied into existing lines running an additional 70 km to the Akita plant. The hydro

Two of the production wells (left) and a separator form part of geothermal generating station, slated for startup this spring.

station has supplied electricity to the zinc plant and to Mitsubishi copper mines for years.

The steam-water combination from the Mitsubishi wells—"about half and half," the engineer said—reaches the wellhead at a temperature of about 150°C. It is first fed into separators, where pressure is maintained at about 2 kg per sq cm. Separated steam is piped to the generators, and water is piped to a silencer at the wellhead, where ambient pressure is maintained. Because the altitude is about 950 m above sea level and the water reaches the silencer at 96°C, the water boils, creating additional steam. While this steam is currently vented into the air, Mitsubishi feels that it may be put to some future use in the region of the wells. □

Chemical agent stabilizes dust at Climax tailings ponds and dams

CLIMAX MOLYBDENUM CO. HAS CONDUCTED extensive tests on tailings dust stabilization at its Climax, Colo., operations. A number of chemical stabilizers were tested to determine the least toxic, most efficient, and most economical product for controlling dust from tailings ponds and on tailings dam faces. The results of these tests led to the first phase of the dust control program reported here.

Problems involved in the Climax tailings dust stabilization program include cost, terrain, and high-altitude climatic conditions. Climax, an operating division of American Metal Climax Inc., employs a full-time environmental control engineer, and tailings stabilization testing was carried out under his direction.

Reports of successful use of "Coherex"—an emulsion of petroleum oils and resins—for control of wind erosion at tailings sites elsewhere suggested that this stabilization agent might offer a solution to the problem of airborne tailings dust at Climax. Supplied by Witco Chemical's Golden Bear Div., of Bakersfield, Calif., Coherex was tested at Climax and found successful on a number of counts.

Applied in a dilution of 9:1 (water to agent), one application of the dust retardant proved sufficient to hold down fugitive dust for the duration of the annual dry season.

In the most difficult test, the dust retardant was sprayed on a dam face with a slope of 2½ to 1. The slope presented both an application and a retention problem. Water flows over the slope, wind blows over it, and rainwater and melted snow run down the face. After four years, the dam face surface treated with Coherex dust retardant is still holding up, with only slight peeling away noted from the action of rain and snow.

The dust retardant is drawn from a storage tank and mixed with waste water, 5.5 to 7.0 pH, in a 3,000-gal distributor tank. The tank and sprayer system were designed and built by Climax and mounted on a Flextrac Nodwell body manufactured in Canada. The boom has three spray nozzles, with a fourth nozzle added for spraying roads.

So far, Climax crews have sprayed 50,000 gal of Coherex dust retardant mixed with 450,000 gal of industrial water from the retention ponds.

During the first phase of the testing, crews have been spraying the dam crest and the surface of an inactive pond that currently serves as a backup to an active pond. A single pass has proven to be sufficient for one season, but Climax reports that it is too early to tell how well dust will be controlled after several winters. Snow depth reaches 100 in. in some areas of Climax operations, and snow furnishes 74% of the area's 25-in.-per-year precipitation. Average annual temperature is less than 32°F, with high temperatures in the mid-70s and lows near −30°F.

In addition to tailings pond treatment, Climax is also testing the dust retardant on open-pit haul roads and for dust control in its underground operations.

Climax has also used Coherex at older tailings ponds now being reclaimed by seeding with native grasses. The chemical agent reportedly helps in reseeding by holding surface sand (crushed rock) in place while the seeds germinate. The area, at 11,300-ft altitude, has a very short growing season—45 to 60 days—so reclamation proceeds slowly. Climax is cooperating

Waste water from one of Climax's active tailings ponds is drawn off by water intake unit and pumped to Coherex mixing area.

Track-mounted dust retardant spray vehicle has a forward speed of 1½ mph. One tank load covers 40-ft swath 0.55 mi long.

with Dr. Bill Berg of Colorado State University in studies to determine the best grasses, shrubs, and trees for the land reclamation project.

Though not substantiated by Climax, there have been indications elsewhere that Coherex dust retardant may promote growth by enhancing the chemistry of arid soils. Dean and Havens of the US Bureau of Mines reported that germination is promoted and wilting minimized by a dark heat-absorbing surface created by chemical stabilization agents. For Coherex, a 64% germination rate and 61% survival rate were reported for leached tailings. For unleached tails, the Coherex germination rate was 30.5% and the survival rate 16.0%. It is expected that the Colorado State University studies may furnish more data on this in the future.

Meanwhile, Climax is encouraged by results so far in using Coherex dust retardant. Summing up its effect on the two tailings ponds, the firm's environmental control engineer commented, "At times the airborne dust used to be so bad that you couldn't see across the pond. But this year, since spraying most of the ponds with Coherex, we've had very little dust." □

Guidelines for designing, constructing, and operating tailings dams and ponds

Arthur B. Chafet, Arthur B. Chafet and Associates, Denver, Colo.

CERTAIN SOUND ENGINEERING PRINCIPLES must be applied to the design and construction of tailings dams and ponds, regardless of the geologic, hydrologic, or climatologic setting. The guidelines offered here are not intended to restrict the design of dams and ponds to standardized structures, but to outline the universal engineering concepts to be applied.

Such concepts become even more critical because, in time, governmental controls are expected to be imposed on the construction and operation of mine tailings facilities. The Environmental Protection Agency already controls effluent discharges from tailings ponds and dams and has determined, with the aid of state environmental agencies, limitations on the concentrations of various dam waters.

Eventually, perpetual containment of tailings ponds may be required. This would permit complete compatibility of the disposal area with the surrounding environment when the structures are abandoned. Allocation of funds, or a bond to insure proper abandonment, may then be required to accompany the initial filing of construction plans and specifications with the regulatory agency.

The need to consider abandonment and final stabilization of the pond and dam area at the time of filing the original design criteria should be stressed. Many factors must be considered during original design and filing, including provision for rapid runoff without causing erosion, bypassing rainfall or snow without causing stream contamination, stabilizing solids to eliminate dust problems, and avoiding harmful slides.

Pointers on good tailings practice

Required design data should be filed with appropriate state and regional regulatory agencies, such as the state water pollution control agency, the regional branch of the Environmental Protection Agency, and the state engineer's office. The following criteria and procedures are important.

■ Toxic or other serious pollutants present in tailings ponds necessitate further storage considerations. Membrane sealing of the pond area may be required.

■ Lack of an effluent treatment plan at a proposed property, or failure of effluents to meet state or EPA standards, necessitates special design considerations.

■ No discharges will be allowed into streams that fail to meet EPA effluent standards, or state water quality standards, whichever are more stringent.

■ Site location, if near a stream or river, should be above the maximum known flood level. In some cases, where available sites are limited, riprapping may be required to protect against erosion.

■ Site location should never be near a heavily traveled road or thoroughfare.

■ Tailings ponds and dams should never be eyesores. They should be made to blend in with the environment. When near civilization, the area should be screened by using trees, shrubbery, and grasses.

■ A registered professional engineer proficient in soil mechanics should be retained for design of the tailings dam, or a registered professional engineer and licensed soil consultant should be used. All findings and data, including design data, should be filed with regulatory agencies for a permanent record.

■ Topographic or photogrammetric mapping is an aid and guide to good engineering analysis, and should form a part of the permanent record on file.

■ Complete geologic and hydrologic studies, including underground and stream chemical water analyses and soil analyses, should be made at the site location and filed with regulatory agencies.

■ Foundation and construction soils investigations should include—but not be limited to—grain size and distribution, density, permeability, shear strength, moisture content, and plasticity.

■ No tailings ponds should be constructed over old mine workings, water bearing geologic faults, or outcrops. The study of soil in the area can determine closeness of ponds to workings. Deep mining in competent rock usually presents no problem.

■ Up-to-date files should be maintained by owners, showing constant changes in shape and elevation of the dam and pond, even though all original data have been filed with regulatory agencies.

■ Provisions for continuous inspection of construction should be included in design specifications to ensure that construction conforms with specifications.

■ No foundation or starter dams should be built with permeable clay-type materials, or where the material is in shear and subject to saturation.

■ Possibility of earth tremors and liquefaction caused by sonic or other forces must be considered in design of structures. The possibility of foundation subsidence and the stability of surrounding slopes must be investigated. Leaching and erosion to streams, or ground water contamination, must be avoided. Measures to prevent wave and wind erosion are also necessary.

■ Permanent water diversions or bypasses or interceptors for storms, rain, and snow runoff must be provided in perpetuity. Where ground water is extremely high, drains up-gradient of the site, prior to construction, may avoid future leaching of the tailings.

■ Drain lines, filter blankets, french drains, etc., should be designed for non-plugging operation and for perpetual use.

■ Decant towers and collector lines should be geared for total saturated loading for compression, shear, and tension. They should have water-tight joints to avoid "sucking" fines out of the dam and pond. If decant towers are used, a minimum of two should be required.

■ If decant collector lines are not large enough for annual visual inspection, television cameras should be used. A record of inspections should be maintained in the owner's file.

■ No piping or other structures should be allowed through the dam face, foundation, or toe dam, unless the location precludes the use of side decant lines or structures, or unless the line cannot be placed under the dam.

- If pump barges or siphons are used for water reclamation, a concrete or grouted riprap spillway should be provided to avoid overtopping caused by loss of power or loss of siphon.

- Water detention time should be long enough to oxidize the more common mill reagents used in the process of mineral recovery.

- The higher the dike and the finer the material, the greater are the chances for failure. Cyclones, therefore, should be used to grade out the coarser tailings fraction for construction.

- For small volume ponding, a dam built from borrow material may be most economical for construction and operation.

- Deposition of any waste material undergrowth or debris in the area should be at a distance from the tailings pond site. These materials should not be placed in the dam structure. If the topsoil in the area to be covered can be used for future stabilization, it should be stockpiled.

- Effluent recycling should be practiced whenever possible, as a matter of good water management.

- Solid tailings might be recycled into old mine workings as backfill. In some difficult mining locations, this may be the method of economical disposal.

- All installations should be inspected regularly.

- Piezometer wells should be maintained in all dams to measure ground water levels and pore pressures for ongoing analysis.

- The slope of the downstream embankments should be designed for eventual planting of vegetation—preferably 1:4 for machine maintenance. A slope of 1:3 is sufficient for low growth not requiring machine maintenance.

- Stabilization of surfaces should use regional flora wherever possible. To aid in stabilization of surfaces with vegetation, the local soil conservation service, forest service, or highway department should be consulted.

- Where vegetation cannot be sustained, geologic cover materials, chemical agents, or dust palliatives should be used to stabilize surfaces.

At all times, it is important for the owner to observe and comply with federal, state, and local laws, ordinances, and regulations that in any manner affect the contract or the work to be done on tailings dams and ponds. ☐

References

1) Kealy, C. D., and Soderberg, R. L., "Design of Dams for Mill Tailings," Inf. Circ. 8410, US Bureau of Mines, 1969.
2) "Spoil Heaps and Lagoons," National Coal Board, *Technical Handbook*, second draft, London, 1970.
3) "Tentative Design Guide for Mine Waste Embankments in Canada," prepared for the Mines Branch Mining Research Center, Department of Energy, Mines and Resources, Ottawa.
4) "Northeastern New Brunswick Mine Water Quality Program," *Mineral Resources and Waste Management*, Vol. 3, Part 4, Montreal Engineering Co. Ltd., 1972.
5) Windolph, Frank, "Tailing Pond Design," MINING ENGINEERING, November 1961.
6) Smith, Edwin S., "Tailing Disposal and Liquefaction," TRANSACTIONS, SME, June 1969.
7) "Hydrocyclones," CANADIAN MINING JOURNAL, June 1970.
8) MacIver, Bruce N., "How the soils engineer can help the mill man in the construction of proper tailing dams," E/MJ, May 1961.
9) Shikaze, K., "Mine Tailing Dam Construction in Ontario," CANADIAN MINING JOURNAL, June 1970.
10) "Inorganic Fertilizer and Phosphate Mining Industries—Water Pollution and Control," Batelle Memorial Institute, Environmental Protection Agency Report 12020 FPD, September 1971.
11) Kealy, C. D., and Busch, R. A., "Determining Seepage Characteristics of Mill Tailing Dams by the Finite-Element Method," RI No. 7477, US Bureau of Mines, 1971.
12) Smalley, I. J., "Boundary Conditions for Flowslides in Fine-Particle Mine Waste Tips," TRANSACTIONS, INST. OF MIN. AND MET., Sect. A., Vol. 81, London, 1972.
13) Rumble, R. V., Coughlin, P. M., and Harris, D. P., "Slimes Dams for C.A.S.T. Ltd., Diamond Mine, Ghana," *ibid.*, Vol. 75, 1966. (Also discussion in Vol. 76, 1967.)
14) Finn, A. A. T., "Tailing Dam Construction at Mufulira Copper Mines, Ltd., Zambia," *ibid.*, Part 12, Vol. 74, 1965. (Also discussion in Vol. 75, 1966.)
15) Berg, William A., "Vegetative Stabilization of Mine Wastes," MINING YEARBOOK, 1972, Colorado Mining Association, Denver, Colo.
16) Dean, Karl C., and Havens, Richard, "Stabilization of Mineral Wastes from Processing Plants," MINING YEARBOOK, 1970, Colorado Mining Association.
17) Barrett, C. J., "Application of Impermeable Membranes for Seepage Prevention," *ibid.*
18) Toland, George C., "About Tailing Dams—Construction, Sealing and Stabilization," MINING ENGINEERING, December 1971.
19) Webb, Stephen L., and Smith, Edwin S., "Tailing Dams Sealed by Slime Slurry," *ibid.*
20) "Cyanamid shoots for instant reclamation of mined land," E/MJ, January 1970.
21) *Design of Small Dams*, US Department of the Interior, Bureau of Reclamation, first edition, 1960.
22) Peele, *Mining Engineers Handbook*, Wiley Handbook Series, third edition, Vols. I and II.
23) *American Civil Engineering Practice*, Robert W. Abbett, ed., Wiley Handbook Series.
24) Young, George J., *Elements of Mining*, McGraw-Hill Book Co., 1946.
25) Krynine, Dimitri P., and Judd, Wilbam R., *Principles of Engineering, Geology and Geotechnics*, McGraw-Hill Book Co., 1957.
26) "Mining Practices and Environmental Impacts in Colorado," Rocky Mountain Center on Environment, MINING YEARBOOK, 1973, Colorado Mining Association.
27) Wahler, W. A., "Availability of Engineering Technology for Design and Construction of Tailing Structures," International Tailing Symposium, sponsored by WORLD MINING, 1973.
28) Burke, Harris H., "Structural Characteristics Resulting from Construction Methods," Int. Tailing Symp., 1973.
29) Sazanov, G. T., "Design, Construction and Operation of Tailing Systems," Int. Tailing Symp., 1973.
30) Ludeke, Kenneth L., "Vegetative Stabilization of Copper Mine Tailing Disposal Berms of Pima Mining Co.," Int. Tailing Symp., 1973.
31) Smith, Edwin S., "Tailing Disposal!—Failures and Lessons," Int. Tailing Symp., 1973.
32) Dean, Karl C., and Havens, Richard, "Comparative Costs and Methods for Stabilization of Tailing," Int. Tailing Symp., 1973.
33) D'Appolonia, E., Ellison, R. D., and Gormley, J. D., "Abandonment of Tailing Facilities," Int. Tailing Symp., 1973.
34) Steiner, Wesley E., "Arizona's Dam Safety Program and its Implications for Tailing Dams," Int. Tailing Symp., 1973.
35) Rigg, John B., "Technology, Reality, and Availability," Int. Tailing Symp., 1973.
36) Swaisgood, James R., and Toland, George C., "Control of Water in Tailing Structures," Int. Tailing Symp., 1973.
37) Stearns-Roger Corp., Denver, Colo., private correspondence.
38) R. V. Lord & Assoc., Boulder, Colo., private correspondence.
39) Arthur B. Chafet and Assoc., Denver, Colo., private studies from files.
40) Environmental Protection Agency, National Field Investigations Center, Denver, Colo., private correspondence.
41) "Design and Construction of Tailing Dams," CANADIAN MIN. & MET. BULL., Vol. 65, No. 720, April 1972.
42) "Design, Construction and Initial Operation of the Tailing System at Brenda Mines Ltd.," *ibid.*, Vol. 64, No. 712.
43) "Gibraltar comes on stream in B.C.," E/MJ, July 1972.
44) "Waste Problems Relative to Mining and Milling of Molybdenum," PURDUE INDUSTRIAL WASTES, Vol. 22, 1967.

Chapter 6
Laboratory Research
and Techniques

New technique improves sample briquettes used in microscopy

A NEW TECHNIQUE for creating improved mineral grain sample briquettes has been developed by Fernando Greene of the Microscopy Department of Chile's Centro de Investigacion Minera y Metalurgica. The briquettes, used in granule examinations with petrographic microscopes, can now be made faster, at lower cost, and with improved sampling characteristics—without sacrificing polishing quality.

Formerly, briquettes at CIMM were prepared by mixing 5 g of sample material with 8 g of plastic mounting powder. ("Transoptic Powder," a product of Illinois-based Buehler Ltd., was used.) The mixture was heated and pressed in a mold to form a briquette 31.7 mm in diameter and 9-14 mm thick, depending on the density of the sample material.

The surface of the briquette was then ground flat using silicon carbide powder or carborundum papers on steel laps. Final polishing was done by using levigated alumina or chromium oxide powder on a cloth lap. The whole briquetting and polishing process required 45-50 min.

Using the new method, a thin wafer-type briquette is produced and mounted on a base to facilitate handling in the grinding and polishing operations. The wafer is made using a solution of mounting powder in chloroform, in a ratio of 75 g of Transoptic to 500 cc chloroform. About 0.5 g of sample material is stirred into 3-4 cc of the solution, and the mixture is stirred thoroughly on a watch-glass to allow all the chloroform to evaporate.

Stirring has two beneficial effects: 1) it ensures that all grains are well coated with plastic, which improves particle adhesion in the finished briquette, and 2) it randomizes the orientation of sample grains and reduces sedimentation and segregation of minerals with widely differing densities.

Stirring is continued until the plastic is almost solid. The mixture is then dried with gentle heat (a lamp is recommended as a heat source) for approximately 10 min, or until completely dry. (It is important that all the chloroform be evaporated at this stage, since traces of chloroform in the finished wafer make it soft and unpolishable.) The sample now resembles a thin paper sheet, and it must be torn or broken to put into the mold.

The pressing process is the same as in the traditional method, but the resulting briquette is very thin (about 1-1.5 mm). One-inch-diameter molds are normally used. The wafer must be mounted on a 1-in.-dia base about 10-20 mm high. Originally, the bases were produced by making "blank" briquettes from the Transoptic-chloroform mixture, and the wafers were simply fixed to the bases with a plastic cement. The results were entirely satisfactory, but to reduce costs, the plastic bases have been replaced by varnished wood bases cut from broom handles or similar wooden doweling. Large numbers of these bases are made in advance, and when required for use, the identification tickets are stuck to the side and varnished over.

The grinding process is the same as in the old method, but the polishing stage has been improved by using two grades of diamond paste (1 m and 3 m) on cloth or nylon laps. The improved particle adhesion and the use of diamond paste have been found to significantly reduce the total process time—31 to 40 min being the average for a sample.

The wafer briquettes are lower in density-segregation and orientation errors than their predecessors; however, results can be improved still further by making two briquettes for each sample and polishing the top surface of one and the bottom surface of the other (top and bottom referring to the position of the briquette as it lies in the press).

Production cost is also lowered appreciably with the new method. Discounting the cost of polishing, which is the same for both methods, the net savings using the new method with wooden bases is 5.7¢ per sample. □

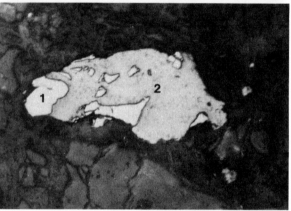
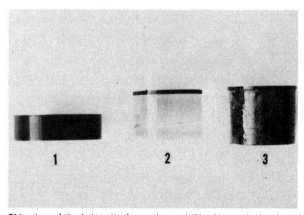

New wafer briquettes (bottom) exhibit quality comparable to briquettes made with traditional methods (top). In both cases, mineral No. 1 is pyrite and No. 2 is chalcocite.

Side view of the briquette formerly used (No. 1); newly developed wafer with plastic base (No. 2) and wooden base (No. 3).

Fighting metals corrosion and abrasion: two techniques push toward wider acceptance

US Bureau of Mines metallurgy research staff

STOPPING CORROSION AND ABRASION of metal parts are the goals of ongoing research in ion implantation and chemical vapor deposition (CVD). Although ion implantation has yet to hit its stride in industrial applications, its acceptance as a corrosion inhibitor is expected to parallel developments in the semiconductor industry 10 to 15 years ago. CVD, too, has yet to become prominent in commercial applications, although research and development have been extensive.

With critical shortages of materials expected in the near future, metallurgists will have to turn to innovative techniques like ion implantation and CVD to produce high quality alloys.

Formation of surface alloys by ion implantation has good potential for reducing US dependence on imports of critical alloying elements such as chromium and nickel. Ion implantation—which causes alterations in the physical properties of a solid target by bombarding the target with a flux of energetic atomic particles—is a versatile technique. It can be used either as a research tool to evaluate alternative alloys or as an economic coating process for metallic surfaces.

Serious industrial interest in ion implantation dates from the early 1960s, a time of pioneering research—most notably at the Ion Physics Corp. In the mid-'60s, fabrication of large-scale devices became possible, and almost all US producers of semiconductor devices are now equipped for production use of ion implantation. Implanted integrated circuits have been most successfully exploited in such systems as pocket calculators, computers, communications systems, and digital wristwatches.

The current status of applying ion implantation to inhibit corrosion in metals is similar to the status of semiconductor research in the early '60s. Some research has been conducted at laboratories in England and the US, but thus far there has been no industrial application, although the technology exists for ion accelerators capable of delivering high intensity ion beams of different metals.

Ion implantation influences range of properties

Surface properties already shown to be influenced by ion implantation include corrosive resistance, electrochemical behavior, wear resistance, coefficient of friction, and bonding ability. These properties are controlled by the composition within a depth of a few microns below the surface—the region accessible to ion implantation. Surface requirements are often met by a coating applied by painting, electroplating, diffusion, spraying, hot dipping, or cladding, but such techniques prove inadequate in some instances, usually because of interfacial corrosion or bonding failure (adherence problems).

Ion implantation can produce a surface that is coherent with the substrate, with no interfacial weakness and negligible dimensional change. It is, in principle, more versatile and more accurate than diffusion techniques. The absence of any dimensional change during the implantation offers an obvious advantage: a component may be given a fine mechanical finish, then implanted to control its surface composition.

Ion implantation equipment undergoes adjustment for the formation of surface alloys at USBM center in College Park, Md.

Much of the research on the effects of ion implantation on the surface properties of metals and alloys has been performed at the Atomic Energy Research Establishment at Harwell, England. One example is the application of yttrium ion implantation to the high-temperature oxidation of a 20% chromium, 25% nickel, niobium-stabilized austenitic stainless steel. It was demonstrated that a shallow layer of ion-implanted yttrium can be just as effective as yttrium alloyed throughout the steel, even though the total implanted dose is equivalent to only a single monolayer in terms of surface density. As for mechanical properties imparted to hard surfaces, it was demonstrated at Harwell that the implantation of tin into the surface regions of steel drastically reduced the surface coefficient of friction. Apparently, ion implantation can modify the tendency for surfaces to adhere during friction, providing a means of dry lubrication.

USBM research aimed at chromium conservation

Research at the USBM's College Park Metallurgy Research Center in Maryland has been directed at conserving chromium in the fabrication of chromium steels by forming surface alloy regions rather than bulk alloys. In most early studies, low-energy chromium ions have been implanted into the surface regions of pure iron samples, fol-

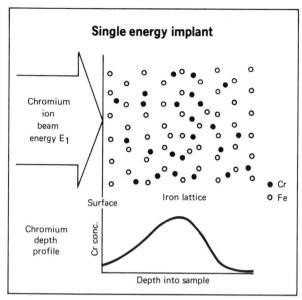

Single energy implant

Chromium ion beam energy E_1

Surface

Iron lattice

● Cr
○ Fe

Chromium depth profile

Cr conc.

Depth into sample

Model of iron lattice after implantation using chromium ions.

lowed by studies of corrosion behavior in gaseous and aqueous environments. It was demonstrated that the surface alloys had corrosion characteristics similar to bulk iron-chromium alloys, while chromium requirements were decreased by many orders of magnitude.

Corrosion problems tackled in geothermal brines

Problems with corrosion are also being tackled in systems for mineral recovery from geothermal brines. In this type of recovery, the tendency has been to use the ordinary, inexpensive structural materials. However, such materials corrode rapidly in contact with brines, which may contain as much as 28% salts, as well as hydrogen sulphide, carbon dioxide, and air. Furthermore, the brines come from the well at temperatures of 350° to 700°F and at pressures up to 450 psi. Another problem is the severe scaling that often occurs in brine processing systems, which may result in clogged piping systems and/or im-

paired heat transfer. The need to cope with scaling will require detailed knowledge of the chemical composition of the brines, and probably some phase studies.

CVD makes inroads as anti-abrasion technique

Chemical vapor deposition (CVD) of highly pure tungsten metal, pioneered in the mid-1950s by the Bureau of Mines, has not yet gained wide acceptance as a commercial process. However, research has led to extensive use of tungsten CVD in some rather exotic applications—for example, tubing and fixtures for nuclear and aerospace applications, where chemical resistance is critical, and tungsten-rhenium alloys formed as thermocouple wells for nuclear apparatus.

The USBM's Rolla, Mo., research center plans to apply a tungsten facing on steel ring seals for large ball valves used in feeding coal into gasification reactors, in experiments to overcome erosion of the valve seals.

CVD has begun to make its mark in the metals industry, which may lead to extensive commercial production. Some examples:

■ A conventional sintered carbide tool insert apparently achieves greatly improved performance and life when the cutting edge has a coating of TiN, TiC, or titanium carbonitride, and toll producers are doing extensive investigations of the possibilities.

■ Pyrolytic carbon, a CVD product, is being used in composite materials to meet high temperature, high strength criteria.

■ There is widespread interest in CVD of nitrides and carbides of titanium and silicon for corrosion- and abrasion-resistant surfaces (bearings, valves, and tools).

■ Pipe and chamber linings produced by CVD of tantalum, tungsten, and other inert metals are reportedly being developed for corrosion resistance.

■ Production of Nb_3Sn and Nb_3Ge superconducting ribbon by a continuous CVD process was recently announced. Work on CVD is widespread in solid state electronics, to apply semiconductors, thermionic materials, super-conductors, and tungsten and other metal attachments to miniature electrical devices.

■ The USBM research center at Rolla, Mo., will investigate the application of TiN to valve ring surfaces for abrasion resistance in coal-hopper valves. □

Reclaiming and recycling secondary metals

US Bureau of Mines metallurgy research staff

THE PAST TWO DECADES HAVE SEEN STEADY GROWTH in the reclamation of secondary metals from new and used scrap, smelting residues and drosses, and numerous metallic waste solutions. The US industry is now remelting and refining more than 3 million tpy of nonferrous scrap metals. More lead is recovered from scrap than from ores, more than half of US copper and steel requirements are supplied by scrap, and greater than 30% of domestic aluminum is recycled. Improvements in recycling rates will require expansions of processing facilities and innovations in processing technology.

Introduction of new technology during the past 20 years was overshadowed by expansion of plant facilities to handle the increasing volume of secondary metals to be processed. However, it is new technology that has enabled the secondary metals industry to help meet the growing needs of the US. Technologic achievements in the last 20 years include improved cleanup procedures and processes

for gaseous and liquid effluents; improved methods for treating and recovering metal values from unusual fumes and byproducts; improved smelting techniques for treating fine scrap and dusts; and development of low-temperature, low-energy hydrometallurgical, pyrometallurgical, and electrometallurgical processes and equipment.

Environmental control influences new technology

The push toward new or improved technology during the 1970s has come largely from the enactment of strict environmental standards for industrial emissions. The impact of these regulations on the nonferrous industry has been great, particularly in the area of smelting. The copper industry is making a major effort to develop and commercialize hydrometallurgical processes to reduce the sulphur dioxide emissions characteristic of conventional smelting processes. This same trend is beginning to surface in the

Metals are reclaimed from urban refuse in a ½-tph pilot plant operated by the USBM in College Park, Md.

lead industry, which reprocesses thousands of tons of lead batteries annually. The US Bureau of Mines recently developed a combination hydrometallurgical and low temperature smelting process for reprocessing scrap lead from batteries without producing sulphur dioxide emissions. The process is being tested commercially by one company.

In the zinc industry, existing or proposed air pollution standards are shifting the emphasis from pyrometallurgical toward electrometallurgical processing of many scrap and waste materials.

The aluminum industry, which generates fluoride and chloride emissions, is spending millions to improve reduction and smelting operations. The Bureau of Mines has developed a hydrometallurgical method aimed at recycling chloride fluxes to reduce disposal problems, and an inert-gas fluxing method that would eliminate chloride fluxes in smelting.

Trend in steel to recover values from flue dusts

One technologic trend in the steel industry is to treat more of plant-generated byproducts such as pickle liquors to recover marketable products such as iron oxide and hydrochloric acid. The industry is also integrating into plant operations the recovery of resources from low-valued wastes—flue dusts, residues, and sludges.

Increasing quantities of flue dusts containing zinc, copper, lead, iron, and other metals are generated at steel mills, brass mills, secondary smelters, galvanizers, and other facilities. At a time when the US is rapidly becoming more dependent on foreign sources for zinc metal, 200,000 to 235,000 tpy are lost in flue dusts at domestic operations.

Disposal of these dusts on land is customary, although storage sites are becoming scarce. Furthermore, the untreated wastes cause more dusting problems during transportation and storage, and they can contaminate streams and groundwaters.

In steelmaking, a significant amount of each furnace charge is converted to dust and collected in scrubbers or baghouses. Although these dusts are a potentially rich source of iron, zinc, and lead, very little of them re-enter the industrial cycle. However, the combination of stricter pollution regulations and the shortage of domestic zinc has generated widespread industrial interest in zinc recovery processes. Direct recycling of these dusts to steel furnaces is inadvisable, but a number of other processes have been proposed for separating the zinc and lead from the iron.

The Bureau of Mines studied a sulphuric acid leach, followed by pyrometallurgical methods to recover separate zinc, lead, and iron products. M. F. Munoz has investigated a sulphuric acid leach for separating the metals. Flue dusts that contain 40% or more zinc can be leached in sulphuric acid, and the impure zinc sulphate solution is used as a fertilizer additive. At least one company has converted zinc-bearing steel furnace flue dust into a frit that is subsequently crushed and added to fertilizer for soils deficient in zinc and iron. Mineral beneficiation methods, however, have not been effective.

M. D. Holowaty and the Bureau of Mines have recently studied reduction-volatilization methods for separating the metals. Holowaty suggested a large regional plant to serve several steel companies, which would greatly improve the economics of the process. However, his proposal has not been accepted by the industry.

In Japan, Kawasaki Steel Corp. recently brought on stream a plant for treating 40,000 tpm of flue dust and sludge, recycling the iron to the steelmaking process. In another project, 25 ferrous and nonferrous producers organized Sohtetsu Metal Co. to process 60,000 tpy of steelmaking flue dust.

Utilization of flue dust from brass smelters depends to a large extent on the availability of zinc. When zinc is readily available, metal recovery from dust is economically noncompetitive. The Bureau of Mines has developed both hydrometallurgical and pyrometallurgical processes for recovering zinc, copper, lead, and lead-tin from brass smelter dusts. A substantial fraction of brass and bronze flue dusts is consumed in production of pigments and zinc chemicals and for agricultural purposes.

In new steel technology, the Bureau of Mines has done extensive research on the smelting and chemistry of rebar metal made from incinerated can scrap recovered from municipal waste. A sodium sulphate treatment has been developed to remove or control the copper content in smelting ferrous scrap.

Steady growth for electroslag refining

Developed nearly 40 years ago, the electroslag process is a secondary technique in which a consumable electrode is melted through an appropriate flux. Applications of the process grew slowly but steadily through 1968, then expanded rapidly. Reluctance to accept the process, now used chiefly for specialty steels and superalloys, has hinged on difficulties in evaporative removal of impurities, extensive capital investments already made in proven conventional secondary melting techniques, and general unavailability of reliable cost comparisons.

However, plants employing the electroslag process have increased in number from 20 to 85 since 1968, not including installations in the USSR. This recent, relatively rapid growth in electroslag installations is attributed to their potential for extensive refining reactions, improved ingot surfaces, improved cleanliness, lack of segregation, greater yields, use of inexpensive electrical power, and the relative ease with which ingot shapes can be prepared.

Electroslag melting appears to be demonstrating the viability of producing larger ingots at reasonable costs. While it is considered unlikely that the electroslag process will replace vacuum-arc melting, especially in the US, there is no reason to doubt that the two processes will effectively complement each other in the future. Considerable growth of the electroslag process is anticipated as new secondary melting facilities are constructed and producers become better acquainted with the unique capabilities of the process.

Removing metals from electroplating wastes

Removal of metals and cyanides from electroplating wastes via numerous procedures is summarized in reports of the Environmental Protection Agency (EPA).

One method for destroying cyanides in water, developed at Karlesruhe University in Germany, involves heating the solution to 160° to 200°C, causing the cyanide to decompose into ammonia and a salt of formic acid. Solid cyanide wastes, such as the cyanide-chloride mixtures used in case-hardening of steel, can be treated with steam at 600° to 700°C. The products are carbon monoxide, ammonia, sodium carbonate, and hydrogen.

The Cyanil Co. of Kitchener, Ont., has developed an electrochemical method for destroying cyanides in solution. No chemicals are used, and the process is claimed to be less expensive than conventional methods, such as treatment with chlorine or hypochlorite. As an alternative approach, a cyanide-free zinc plating process has been developed and tested.

In a new Bureau of Mines process for recycling metals and cyanides in electroplating wastes, the cyanides can either be recovered as sodium cyanide for recycling, or burned off. One electroplating plant is already using this process, a second plant has requested permission from state pollution control authorities to start using it, and other plants are considering integrating the process into their waste treatment systems to reduce reagent consumption.

Copper, zinc taken from etching solutions

Recovery of copper and zinc values from spent chromium etching solutions has been given very little attention. Solutions of chromic acid and sulphuric acid are used to etch and brighten brass and zinc parts and to etch copper from printed circuits. The etching of brass dissolves copper and zinc and reduces some of the hexavalent chromium to trivalent chromium. The spent solutions are usually discarded.

In a Bureau of Mines process, hexavalent chromium is reduced to trivalent chromium by a low cost reagent such as waste paper, methyl alcohol, or formaldehyde, and the metal values are recovered by a variety of methods.

Electrochemical machining sludge recovered

Very little work has been done on recovery of electrochemical machining sludge wastes despite the magnitude of the waste disposal problem. These wastes result from the machining of nickel-base and cobalt-base alloys used in the manufacture of aircraft engines. The wastes consist of very finely divided metal hydroxide particles in an aqueous electrolyte solution, usually containing sodium chloride or sodium nitrate.

Filtration of the sludge to separate the electrolyte solution and the metal hydroxides is an obvious approach, but the filtration rate is much too slow to be practical. The Bureau of Mines has developed a recovery process whereby the sludge is first evaporated to dryness to agglomerate the metal hydroxide particles, and water is then added to redissolve the electrolyte. After this treatment, the filtration rate is 20 to 120 times faster than that of the original sludge. The slurry is filtered to recover the electrolyte solution for recycling to the machining operation, and the metal hydroxides are heated to convert them to oxides, which are subsequently reduced to metal.

Metallurgical wastes recycled from foundries

Improving the efficiency of domestic foundries by recycling waste products and finding domestic substitutes for imports such as chromite and zircon has been studied by the USBM.

One phase of the study, recently concluded, involved development of methods to recover brass and molding sand suitable for recycling from phenolic-bonded brass foundry waste. The material tested—a combination of phenolic-bonded shell mold and residue from deburring operations—was composed of 3% copper as a high-copper brass, 2% phenolic resin, 3% iron oxide, and about 90% molding sand. Brass was recovered by a combination of screening and gravity concentration on a standard concentrating table. The final concentrate recovered 75% of the brass copper at a grade of 45.5% copper. Eighty-three per-

Extracting copper from blast furnace slag

The Bureau of Mines has also studied the feasibility of recovering a recyclable copper product from granulated blast furnace slag from Southwire Corp. The slag contained 5-7% total copper and 3-4.5% metallic copper. Bench scale tests showed that tabling of minus 35-mesh material recovered 57% of the total and 83% of the metallic copper in a concentrate that graded 47% copper. Flotation of material ground through 65 mesh with a di-xanthogen collector produced a concentrate analyzing 40% copper, with recovery of 82% of total Cu and more than 98% of the metallic copper. Under a cooperative program with Southwire, small-scale continuous testing emphasized only gravity separation techniques. A 40-hr test was made with a circuit that included rod mill grinding and Humphrey's spirals and shaking tables. A coarse (plus 35 mesh) and a fine concentrate analyzed 68% and 72.5% copper, respectively; the composite analysis was 68.6% copper. The composite concentrate recovered 60% of the total and 88% of the metallic copper.

Zircon reclaimed from waste foundry molds

The advent of greatly increased zircon prices has generated interest by the casting industries in reclaiming zircon from waste foundry molds. The Bureau of Mines has been studying the recoverability of zircon flour from spent investment casting molds in cooperation with Sherwood Refractories Inc. The USBM has also been working with Esco Corp. to reclaim zircon and sand from spent molds.

Recycling resources from urban refuse

The Bureau of Mines has been very active in development of continuous mechanical systems for separating materials from mixed refuse, and the agency was the first to demonstrate that the key to solving the problem was the application of minerals processing technology. For several years the USBM's College Park Metallurgy Research Center in Maryland has been operating a ½-tph pilot plant for reclaiming metals and minerals from municipal incinerator residues. The plant is assembled entirely of conventional minerals engineering equipment. It uses continuous screening, crushing, grinding, magnetic separation, gravity concentration, and froth flotation to produce metallic iron

Hydrometallurgical process for treating aluminum oxide slags is among the USBM recycling projects now in the research stage.

cent of the original waste was then reclaimed as sand by burning in a rotary kiln. Foundry evaluation of brass and sand showed both to be suitable for recycling.

USBM mini-plant flowsheet for recovering products from high-salt aluminum slag

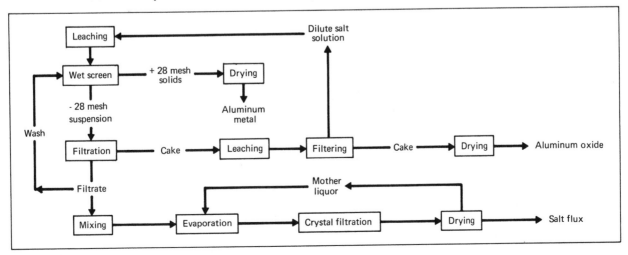

concentrates, high-quality aluminum, clean heavy non-ferrous metal composites, pure glass, fine carbonaceous ash, and slag tailings. Ground breaking for a commercial-size plant based on this process was scheduled for early 1975 in Lowell, Mass., by the contractor, Raytheon Service Co. This demonstration project is being funded by EPA, the State of Massachusetts, and the city of Lowell.

More recently, the Bureau of Mines has been operating a 5-tph pilot plant for continuous separation of materials contained in raw refuse. This patented system utilizes multistage processing in a variety of unit operations, including shredding, air classification, magnetic separation, screening, gravity concentration, electrostatic separation, and froth flotation. The system recovers a light-gauge iron fraction that includes tin cans, massive iron, massive heavy nonferrous metals, aluminum, pure glass, and combustibles in a form suitable for use as fuel. All processing is conducted on dry material except for the glass recovery section, which employs jigging and froth flotation.

Bureau of Mines technology is the basis of a commercial-size plant to treat 400 tpd of refuse in Baltimore County, Md., for which ground was broken in August 1974. Teledyne National is the contractor for this project, with funding provided by Baltimore County and Maryland Environmental Services. A 2,000-tpd, $25 million plant to be built in Monroe County, N.Y., by Raytheon Service Co. will also use the patented USBM process.

Even though prices for secondary materials declined markedly during the latter part of 1974 from early record peaks, markets are highly encouraging for products reclaimed from both incinerator residues and raw refuse. Many potential customers have evaluated the products recovered in both of the USBM pilot plants, reporting that these materials are perfectly acceptable.

Two major detinners have processed the ferrous fractions from raw refuse, each recovering 6.5 lb of tin per ton and steel scrap equivalent to a No. 1 bundle containing less than 0.03% tin. Major secondary aluminum smelters consider products from both plants to be of very high quality. Mixed nonferrous metals are chemically similar to automobile radiator scrap and presumably could enter the same recycling channels, although verification will require tests using large tonnages of these products, which are not yet available.

Processing junk autos for metal values

In the scrap processing industry, the shredder has replaced the baler and the shear as the major producer of prepared scrap from junk automobiles. Shredder installations are now being equipped with efficient dust control systems, and the trend is toward increasingly heavy construction for all parts of the shredder auxiliary systems to prevent damage from explosions, which still occur at intervals. Another trend is toward shredding of the entire automobile, including engine, transmission, gas tank (punctured), and seats. Even such items as tires, batteries, and radiators are run through the shredder if they are still in place on a junked car.

Scrap processors are becoming more aware of the potential value of the nonferrous components of junk automobiles. Only a few years ago, most of the nonmagnetic fraction of a shredded car was disposed of in landfill areas after hand-picking to recover some of the copper, zinc, and aluminum.

The Bureau of Mines has developed a system involving air classification and water elutriation for recovering a mixed nonferrous metal concentrate from auto shredder non-magnetic rejects. The system is used by some shredder operators. In addition, several large commercial plants are operating on rejects shipped in from surrounding shredders. Most of these plants use processes similar to those developed by the USBM, with the addition of heavy media or other systems to separate the mixed nonferrous metals.

One steadily mounting problem for shredder operators is disposal of the nonmetallic portion of shredder residues. At present, all of this material is disposed of by landfill. Disposal costs average about $5 per ton and are rising rapidly as hauling and labor costs increase and available landfill areas become scarcer.

In an effort to recover still more of the constituents of junk automobiles, the Bureau of Mines has entered into cooperative agreements with Ford Motor Co. and General Motors Corp. to investigate recovery of plastics from shredder residues. The USBM will develop physical recovery methods, and the auto companies will furnish raw materials and evaluate the recovered plastics for recycling potential. □

References

AIME, World Symposium on Mining and Metallurgy of Lead and Zinc, New York, N.Y., 1970.

Barnard, P. G., A. G. Starliper, W. M. Dressel, and M. M. Fine, "Recycling of Steelmaking Dusts," BuMines Report TPR-52, February 1972.

Council on Environmental Quality, Fifth Annual Report, December 1974, pp 134-136.

Environmental Protection Agency, "An Investigation of Techniques for Removal of Cyanide from Electroplating Wastes," EPA Report No. 12010 EIE, November 1971.

———. "Resource Recovery and Source Reduction," Second Report to Congress, prepared by Office of Solid Waste Management Programs, EPA SW-122, March 26, 1974, p 38.

———. "Resource Recovery Systems Marketed in the United States," EPA AW-563, January 1975.

Fukubayashi, H., and L. W. Higley, "Recovery of Zinc and Lead from Brass Smelter Dust," BuMines Report of Investigations 7880, 1974.

George, L. C. and A. A. Cochran, "Recovery of Metals and Other Materials from Chromium Etching and Electrochemical Machining Wastes," Proc. of Fourth Mineral Waste Utilization Symposium, IIT Research Institute, Chicago, Ill., May 7-8, 1974, pp 346-53.

Higley, L. W., and H. Fukubayashi, "Method for Recovery of Zinc and Lead from Electric Furnace Steelmaking Dusts," Proc. of Fourth Mineral Waste Utilization Symposium, 1974, pp 295-302.

Hogan, J. C., "Physical and Chemical Characterization of Refining Furnace Flue Dusts," Symposium on Waste Oxide Recycling, McMaster University, May 16-17, 1974.

Holowaty, M. D., "A Process for Recycling Zinc-Bearing Steelmaking Dust," Chicago Regional Technical Meeting of AISI, October 14, 1971, 23 pp.

Iron and Steelmaking, "Steel via Direct Reduction," January 1975, pp 10-16.

Jackson, F. R. Recycling and Reclaiming of Municipal Solid Wastes, Noyes Data Corp., Park Ridge, N.J., 1975, pp 90-141.

Journal of Metals, "Japan Watching," July 1973, p 4.

Martin, John J. Jr., "Chemical Treatment of Plating Waste for Removal of Heavy Metals," EPA Report No. R2-73-044, May 1973.

Munoz, Maximo F., "Investigations on Recovery of Metal Values from Steel Furnace Dusts," Final Report, Project A-1349, Georgia Institute of Technology, June 1972.

Powell, H. E., H. Fukubayashi, L. W. Higley, and L. L. Smith, "Recovery of Zinc, Copper, and Lead-Tin Mixtures from Brass Smelter Flue Dusts," BuMines Report of Investigations 7637, 1972.

Sitting, Marshall, Pollution Removal Handbook, Noyes Data Corp., Park Ridge, N.J., 1973.

Stanczyk, M. H., P. M. Sullivan, and M. J. Spendlove, "Continuous process for mechanically separating materials contained in urban refuse," US Pat. No. 3,848,813, November 19, 1974.

Sullivan, P. M. and M. H. Stanczyk, "Economics of Recycling Metals and Minerals from Urban Refuse," BuMines TPR 33, 1971, 19 pp.

Sullivan, P. M. and H. V. Makar, "Bureau of Mines Process for Recovering Resources from Raw Refuse," Proc. of Fourth Mineral Waste Utilization Symposium, May 1974, pp 128-41.

USBM, "Technologic and Related Trends in the Mineral Industries," BuMines IC 8643, 1974, 52 pp.

Watson, Michael R., Pollution Control in Metal Finishing, Noyes Data Corp., Park Ridge, N.J., 1973.

Blaine tube measurements made easy

Eugene W. Price, consultant to Allis-Chalmers

THE BLAINE AIR-PERMEABILITY TUBE—long used by the cement industry for determining specific surface (cm²/gm) of finished portland cement—is now an effective tool for laboratory work and production control for iron ores and elsewhere in the minerals industry. However, cumbersome formulas have tended to inhibit the use of the Blaine tube outside the cement industry. There is a need, especially in the iron ore industry's control of pellet plant and magnetic separator feed, for a Blaine tube procedure that will satisfy several requirements.

■ The system must adhere to ASTM standards of procedure.

■ The procedure should be rapid, simple, and precise.

■ The system must encompass the ranges of specific gravities and surface areas of the material tested.

■ The system should allow construction of easy-to-use, comprehensive tables for a given Blaine instrument.

A method to meet these requirements is outlined here. It can be extended to cover any material, any range of specific gravities, any range of sample weights, and any range of times of air flow.

Blaine tube use is simple for cement

The accepted method of testing with the Blaine tube follows ASTM Procedure C204-68. In the basic equation used for expressing the surface area of cement, two of the terms—specific gravity and porosity of bed—have been standardized throughout the industry. Standardization of these terms has made possible the use of the following equation:

$$S = \frac{Ss\sqrt{T}}{\sqrt{Ts}} \qquad (1)$$

where
S = specific surface of test sample,
Ss = specific surface of NBS (National Bureau of Standards) Standard Sample of portland cement,
T = time of air flow in seconds for test sample, and
Ts = time of air flow when calibrating a particular Blaine instrument against an NBS standard cement sample.

The Blaine air tube is used to determine fineness of grinds in terms of specific surface (cm²/gm). The apparatus is a means of drawing a definite quantity of air through a prepared bed of material of definite porosity. The number and size of the pores in a bed of definite porosity is a function of the size of the particles and determines the rate of air flow through the bed. (See ASTM Designation C204-68.)

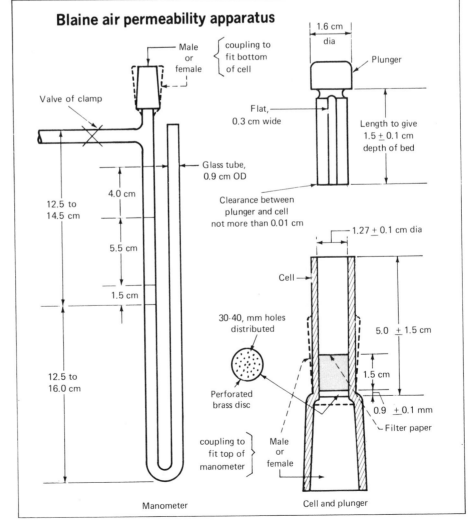

Blaine air permeability apparatus

Male or female — coupling to fit bottom of cell

1.6 cm dia

Plunger

Valve of clamp

Flat, 0.3 cm wide

Length to give 1.5 ± 0.1 cm depth of bed

Glass tube, 0.9 cm OD

Clearance between plunger and cell not more than 0.01 cm

12.5 to 14.5 cm

4.0 cm

5.5 cm

1.5 cm

1.27 ± 0.1 cm dia

Cell

5.0 ± 1.5 cm

30-40, mm holes distributed

1.5 cm

12.5 to 16.0 cm

Perforated brass disc

0.9 ± 0.1 mm

Filter paper

coupling to fit top of manometer

Male or female

Manometer

Cell and plunger

For a given instrument, Eq. 1 may be simplified:

$$S = K \sqrt{T} \qquad (2)$$

where S = same as in Eq. 1,
$K = Ss \div \sqrt{Ts}$ (from Eq. 1), and
T = same as in Eq. 1.

Using Eq. 2, the operator need only determine the time of fall for a test sample, then multiply the square root of that time by the K value. Comprehensive tables may be constructed for a *particular* Blaine instrument to allow rapid determinations of surface areas of cement test samples.

Formulas more complex outside cement industry

The ease and simplicity of operation of the Blaine tube in the cement industry led to its use in other fields. In the iron ore industry, the Blaine instrument is widely used to control grinds used for pelletizing.

Problems occur under the ASTM procedure when the Blaine tube is used for materials other than portland cement because the two terms—specific gravity and porosity of bed—cannot be standardized. The ASTM procedure states, "When this method is used for materials other than portland cement . . . the weight of sample shall be adjusted so that a firm, hard bed is produced by the compacting process. In no case, however, should more than thumb pressure be used to secure the proper bed. Nor should such thumb pressure be used that the plunger 'rebounds' from the cell top when pressure is removed."

Calculation of specific surface now becomes complicated, as shown by the following equation (actually Eq. 7 of the ASTM procedure, condensed into a working form that can be related to a *given* Blaine instrument):

$$S = \frac{K_1 \sqrt{e^3} \sqrt{T}}{(\text{sp. gr.}) (1-e)} \qquad (3)$$

where S = specific surface, in cm²/gm,
K_1 = a constant relating a particular Blaine instrument to an NBS standard cement sample,
e = percent porosity of compacted bed,
T = time of air flow (in seconds) for the test sample,
sp. gr. = specific gravity of the test sample, and
$(1-e)$ = percent of the compacted bed occupied by the solids.

To follow the prescribed ASTM procedure, the proper weight of sample required to give a firm, compacted bed must be determined experimentally. The $(1-e)$ term and the bed porosity can then be calculated from the equation:

$$(1-e) = \frac{\text{Wt.}}{(\text{sp. gr.}) (V)} \qquad (4)$$

where $(1-e)$ = same as in Eq. 3,
sp. gr. = same as in Eq. 3, and
V = volume (in cm³) occupied by the compacted sample in sample tube.

Once the $(1-e)$ term has been found, bed porosity (e) can be determined and Eq. 3 completed. Most users of the Blaine tube in the iron ore industry have been reluctant to use these cumbersome formulas. In violation of ASTM procedure, they have sought to simplify the formulas by standardization of specific gravity and porosity of bed, as done in the cement industry. These attempts at simplifica-

Table 1—K₂ numbers for selected sample weights and specific gravities

(applicable to a specific test)

Sample wt. (gm)	Specific gravity of ore					
	4.72	4.75	4.78	4.81	4.84	4.87
4.62	(213)	(216)	(219)	(220)		
3	211	214	217	219	220	
4	(210)	(213)	(216)	(217)	(218)	(220)
5	208	211	214	215	217	219
6	(206)	(209)	(212)	(214)	(216)	(218)
7	205	208	211	213	215	217
8	(204)	(207)	(210)	(212)	(214)	(216)
9	203	206	209	211	213	215
4.70	(202)	(205)	(208)	(210)	(212)	(214)
1	200	203	206	208	211	213
2	(199)	(202)	(204)	(206)	(209)	(211)
3	198	201	203	205	208	210
4	(197)	(200)	(202)	(204)	(207)	(209)
5	196	198	201	203	206	208
6	(195)	(197)	(200)	(202)	(205)	(207)
7	194	196	199	201	204	206
8	(193)	(195)	(198)	(200)	(202)	(205)
9		194	197	199	201	204
4.80			(196)	(198)	(200)	(201)

tion have usually resulted in spurious modifications of the basic ASTM equations and have led to widespread confusion and lack of agreement between various laboratories.

Attempts to standardize specific gravity and porosity of bed fail because specific gravity of iron ore can vary widely, affecting the terms $(1-e)$ and (e) for the compacted bed. Furthermore, porosity of the bed will be directly influenced by the relative fineness of the ore. The coarser the grind, the lower the porosity of the bed and conversely, the finer the grind, the higher the porosity of the bed. Porosity of the bed is also influenced profoundly by particle shape and particle size distribution.

How to simplify measurements for all materials

The following example of a procedure to determine rapidly the specific surfaces of iron ores was developed in response to the needs of an iron ore pellet plant. At this plant, the specific gravity of the filter cake varied from week to week, from 4.72 to 4.86; the specific surface varied between 1,690 cm²/gm and 2,290 cm²/gm. Furthermore, the available technicians lacked the skills to properly handle ASTM procedures outlined in Eqs. 3 and 4.

The example cited here provides a method that rigorously follows ASTM procedure. Once the basic computations and tables are completed, no further calculations are required.

Specific sets of tables can be constructed only for individual Blaine instruments. Once constructed, recalculation of the tables would be required only if significant changes occurred in the Blaine instrument. The constructed tables would include only the range of variables encountered for a particular installation.

The K_1 number relating the Blaine instrument used in this investigation to NBS Standard Cement Sample 114k was 1740. The volume occupied by the compacted sample bed was 1.81 cm³.

Step 1 of the procedure was to calculate the K_2 numbers

shown in Table 1. K_2 values represent the following sets of terms taken from Eqs. 3 and 4:

$$K_2 = \left[\frac{K_1 \sqrt{e^3}}{(\text{sp. gr.}) \, (1\text{-}e)} \right] \qquad (5)$$

Once the proper K_2 values have been determined—over the desired range of sample weights and specific gravities—they can be multiplied by the $\sqrt{T}$ measured for the test samples.

How to compute K_2 numbers

As an example, a given sample weight of 4.62 gm and a specific gravity of 4.72 are applied to Eq. 4 to determine the (1–e) and the (e) values:

$$(1\text{-}e) = \frac{4.62}{(4.72)\,(1.81)} = 0.540 \qquad (6)$$

Therefore, (e) = 1.000–0.540 = 0.460.

The values of 0.540 and 0.460 are substituted in Eq. 5:

$$K_2 = \frac{(1740)\,(0.312)}{(4.72)\,(0.540)} = 213 \qquad (7)$$

The K_2 number 213 appears in the upper left-hand corner of Table 1.

Continuing the computations for a sample weight of 4.62 gm and a specific gravity of 4.75, the K_2 number is 216. All other K_2 numbers for any sample weight and any specific gravity are calculated in similar fashion.

Note that for Table 1, no calculations of K_2 numbers need be made for the specific gravities of 4.71 and 4.73. These K_2 values can be interpolated from the K_2 value of 213—calculated for a specific gravity of 4.72. The K_2 number for the specific gravity of 4.71 would be 212, while the K_2 number for the specific gravity of 4.73 would be 214.

Nor is it necessary to calculate all of the K_2 numbers relating *weight* changes to different specific gravities. For example, the K_2 numbers for sample weights of 4.63 gm, 4.65 gm, and 4.67 gm can be interpolated. For Table 1, the only K_2 values that required calculation are shown in parentheses. Determinations of these K_2 values by calculation and interpolation are well within the accuracy stipulated by the ASTM procedure.

Step 2 of the procedure is to calculate the necessary spread of Blaine numbers, as shown in Table 2. These Blaine numbers are the product of the K_2 numbers multiplied by the square root of the times of air flow. Numbers shown in Table 2 are the final answers—in cm^2/gm (Blaine surfaces)—for sample weights ranging from 4.62 gm to 4.80 gm, specific gravities from 4.71 to 4.88, and times of air flow from 70 to 79 sec. (The particular filter cake for which this method was developed required sets of tables that covered times of air flow from 70 to 110 sec. Table 2 is one of these tables.) As in Table 1, parentheses indicate the only

Table 2—Required spread of Blaine numbers ($K_2\sqrt{T}$)

(applicable to a specific test)

K_2 Nos.	Time of air flow (sec)									
	70	71	72	73	74	75	76	77	78	79
193	(1615)	1630	(1640)	1650	(1660)	1670	(1680)	1695	(1705)	1715
4	1625	1635	1645	1655	1670	1680	1690	1700	1710	1720
5	(1635)	1645	(1655)	1665	(1675)	1685	(1700)	1710	(1720)	1730
6	1640	1650	1665	1675	1685	1695	1710	1720	1730	1740
7	(1650)	1660	(1670)	1680	(1690)	1700	(1715)	1725	(1735)	1745
8	1660	1670	1680	1690	1700	1710	1725	1735	1745	1755
9	(1670)	1680	(1690)	1700	(1710)	1720	(1735)	1745	(1755)	1765
200	1675	1685	1695	1710	1720	1730	1745	1755	1765	(1780)
1	(1680)	1690	(1705)	1715	(1730)	1740	(1750)	1760	(1770)	(1785)
2	1690	1705	1715	1725	1735	1750	1760	1770	1780	(1795)
3	(1700)	1710	(1720)	1735	(1745)	1755	(1770)	1780	(1790)	1800
4	1710	1720	1730	1745	1755	1765	1780	1790	1800	1810
5	(1720)	1730	(1740)	1750	(1760)	1775	(1790)	1800	(1810)	1820
6	1725	1735	1745	1760	1770	1785	1795	1810	1820	1830
7	(1730)	1745	(1755)	1765	(1780)	1795	(1805)	1815	(1825)	1835
8	1740	1755	1765	1775	1790	1805	1815	1825	1835	1845
9	(1750)	1760	(1770)	1780	(1795)	1810	(1820)	1830	(1840)	1850
210	1755	1765	1780	1790	1805	1820	1830	1840	1850	1860
1	(1765)	1775	(1785)	1800	(1810)	1825	(1840)	1850	(1860)	1870
2	1775	1785	1795	1810	1820	1835	1850	1860	1870	1880
3	(1780)	1795	(1805)	1820	(1830)	1840	(1855)	1865	(1880)	1890
4	1790	1805	1815	1830	1840	1850	(1875)	1885	(1900)	1910
5	(1800)	1810	(1825)	1835	(1850)	1860	1870	1895	1910	1920
6	1810	1820	1835	1845	1860	1870	1885	1895	1910	1920
7	(1815)	1830	(1840)	1850	(1865)	1880	(1890)	1905	(1920)	1930
8	1825	1835	1850	1860	1875	1890	1900	1910	1925	1940
9	(1830)	1840	(1855)	1870	(1880)	1900	(1910)	1920	(1930)	(1945)
220	(1840)	1850	(1865)	1875	(1890)	1905	(1920)	1930	(1940)	(1955)

Fig. 1—Test results illustrating 'plateau principle'

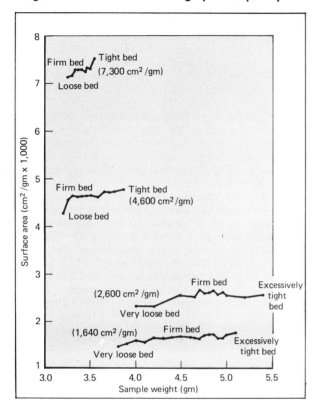

Fig. 2—Relationship of bed porosity to surface area

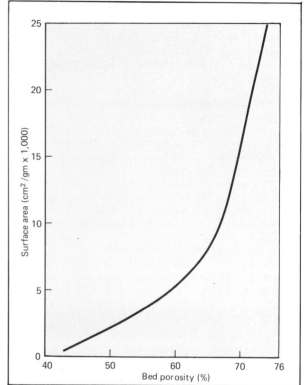

values that need be calculated; the rest may be interpolated. Values for 0.5-sec differences in time can also be interpolated and will fall within the range of accuracy stipulated by the ASTM procedure.

Putting the simplified method into practice

As an example, for a given sample of 4.71 gm having a specific gravity of 4.75 and an air flow time of 74 sec, Table 1 shows the K_2 value to be 203. In Table 2, the column for K_2 number 203 and the column for 74 sec of air flow intersect at the answer 1,745 cm^2/gm.

By setting up tables similar to Tables 1 and 2 for those ranges of values encountered at a particular plant, operators can avoid the time-consuming requirement of repeatedly solving the basic ASTM Eq. 7 (Eq. 3 in this article). The tables can be used by personnel having rudimentary mathematical skills, reducing the chance of error because no calculations are required.

How to arrive at proper weight of the sample

There is controversy about the method of determining the proper weight of a test sample. Experience with thousands of Blaine determinations indicates that the operator will have a properly weighted test sample when he experiences the same feel of compaction as when calibrating the Blaine instrument against an NBS standard sample of cement. This will approximate the "firm, hard bed" prescribed in the ASTM procedure.

These observations are confirmed by a new method that eliminates operator subjectivity. The method involves calculating surface areas over a range of sample weights that include those required to produce the desired compaction. When surface areas are calculated for this range of sample weights, it is found that not one, but several, successive incremental weight changes will produce close, if not identi-

cal maximum surface areas.

Weights outside this range—both lower and higher—provide lower Blaine numbers. This "plateau principle" is illustrated in Fig. 1, in which all points are plotted from actual test data. If enough additional weight of material is used, the Blaine numbers will rise, but excessive pressure must then be used to seat the plunger.

It has been found that coarse material will produce a broad plateau and fine material a narrow plateau. For coarse, strong ores with a Blaine surface of some 1,000 cm^2/gm, the plateau is broad (Fig. 1) and determination of a proper sample weight is easy. Care must be exercised when working with soft ores having high surface areas—6,000 to 7,000 cm^2/gm—because the range of sample weights producing similar maximum surface areas is small and the plateau is narrow.

Porosity of bed is an important factor in determining the choice for weight of the test sample. It is axiomatic that—for irregular particles—the lower the surface area, the lower the bed porosity and conversely, the higher the surface area, the higher the bed porosity. (See Fig. 2.) These relationships are helpful when making a first estimate of the weight of sample to be used.

A good rule-of-thumb for approximating the sample weight of iron ore pellet feeds is that the sample weight in grams should be about the same number as the specific gravity. Using a typical Blaine instrument, this weight should produce a porosity of about 45%.

For low-surface-area grinds, the bed porosity will often drop to around 40%. High-surface-area grinds will have a bed porosity of 60% or more. When determining proper sample weights, incremental changes to arrive at a satisfactory weight need not be smaller than 1.0%. For example, a series of sample weights might be taken at 4.80, 4.85, and 4.90 gm, with no need for samples at intermediate weights. □

Lab researchers at the University of Wisconsin monitor a micro-hy-drocyclone (left) and a commercial unit (right). The project, partly funded by the Federal Sea Grant Office, has so far focused on basic hydrocyclone operation above and below water.

Researchers look for payoff in hydrocyclone processing of marine heavy mineral sand deposits

A. Hayatdavoudi, research assistant; **R. W. Heins**, professor of Mineral Engineering; and **T. D. Tiemann**, associate chairman, Dept. of Metallurgical and Mineral Engineering, University of Wisconsin.

MANY COASTAL AREAS OF THE CONTINENTS have underwater sand deposits at varying depths, containing valuable minerals such as tin, platinum, gold, rutile, magnetite, zircon, ilmenite, and barite. Some of these may be recovered by dredging operations, bringing all of the material, mineral and gangue, to the surface for processing. In many instances, however, recovery by dredging or similar methods may cause extensive water pollution.

For this reason, application of hydrocyclones to successful underwater processing of heavy mineral-bearing sand deposits is being explored by the Department of Metallurgical and Mineral Engineering at the University of Wisconsin. This research is supported by the Department of Commerce through the Sea Grant Program.

The Wisconsin program calls for pumping heavy minerals to the surface after concentration in the submerged hydrocyclone, while the tailings would be returned to the deposit area, thus avoiding widespread water pollution. The tailings comprise by far the greater portion of the original deposits.

The immediate objective of the program was to study the mechanisms of hydrocyclone operation and to determine the difference between normal and underwater operation. The preliminary findings, derived principally from these basic operational studies of the hydrocyclone, above and below water, are presented here. Studies have been conducted with both a laboratory "micro-hydrocyclone" and a commercial unit.

Theory behind the machine

Use of the hydrocyclone for separation on the basis of size or density has been the subject of thorough investigation for many years, both in the US and abroad. A great deal of effort has gone into understanding and optimizing the constituent parameters of the hydrocyclone, such as shape of feed inlet, diameter and length of vortex finder, diameter of cylinder section, angle of cone section, and apex diameter. The effect of these variables on hydrocyclone performance, with some theories on separation dynamics, is discussed at great length by F. J. Fontein et al,[1,2] Reitema,[3] and others.

Other fundamental studies related to the internal dynamics of the hydrocyclone have been carried out by D. F. Kelsall.[4] The mathematical work by M. I. G. Bloor and D. B. Ingham[5] has confirmed Kelsall's experimental work. In practically all of these studies some consideration has been given to the balance of forces: centrifugal in equilibrium with drag force neglecting the gravitational force. On the matter of gravity, Kelsall[4] reported in his third series of tests that at 40-psi feed pressure, a tangential velocity of 3,600 ft per min at a radius of 0.2 in. was developed, which is equivalent to 7,000 g. As a result of this equilibrium, Stokes' Law for radial velocity is applicable:

$$U = \frac{(V^2)}{R}\,\frac{d^2(P_s - P)}{18\,\mu}$$

in which U = instantaneous radial velocity of the particle.
$\quad d$ = particle diameter.
$\quad R$ = radius at any point.

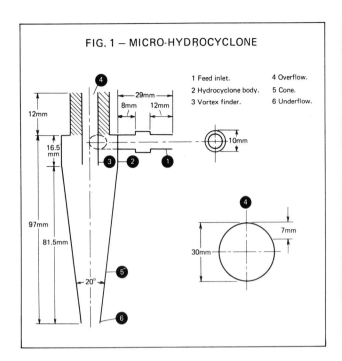

FIG. 1 — MICRO-HYDROCYCLONE

1 Feed inlet. 4 Overflow.
2 Hydrocyclone body. 5 Cone.
3 Vortex finder. 6 Underflow.

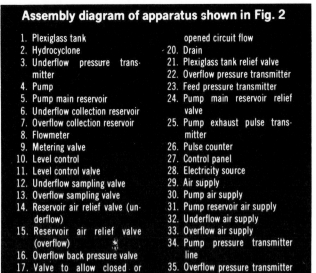

Assembly diagram of apparatus shown in Fig. 2

1. Plexiglass tank
2. Hydrocyclone
3. Underflow pressure transmitter
4. Pump
5. Pump main reservoir
6. Underflow collection reservoir
7. Overflow collection reservoir
8. Flowmeter
9. Metering valve
10. Level control
11. Level control valve
12. Underflow sampling valve
13. Overflow sampling valve
14. Reservoir air relief valve (underflow)
15. Reservoir air relief valve (overflow)
16. Overflow back pressure valve
17. Valve to allow closed or opened circuit flow
18. Valve to allow closed or opened circuit flow
19. Valve to allow closed or opened circuit flow
20. Drain
21. Plexiglass tank relief valve
22. Overflow pressure transmitter
23. Feed pressure transmitter
24. Pump main reservoir relief valve
25. Pump exhaust pulse transmitter
26. Pulse counter
27. Control panel
28. Electricity source
29. Air supply
30. Pump air supply
31. Pump reservoir air supply
32. Underflow air supply
33. Overflow air supply
34. Pump pressure transmitter line
35. Overflow pressure transmitter line
36. Underflow pressure transmitter line

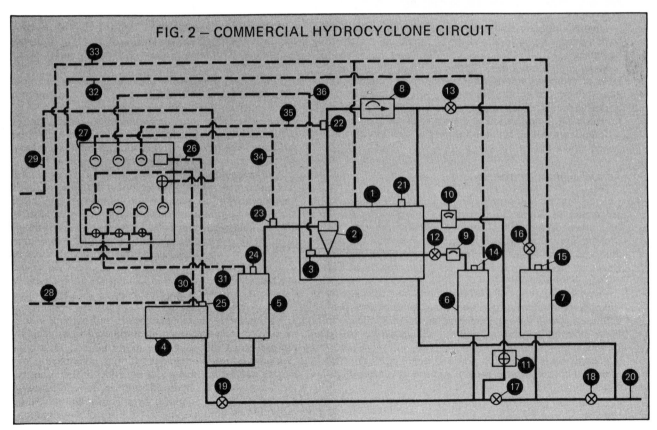

FIG. 2 — COMMERCIAL HYDROCYCLONE CIRCUIT

V = peripheral velocity.
μ = viscosity.
P_s = density of solids.
P = density of liquid.

Differentiating the above expression with respect to radius and integrating between two radius limits, keeping peripheral velocity constant, the result for a mean radial velocity will be:

$$U = \frac{K(2.3)\log\dfrac{R_2}{R_1}, R_1 \div 0}{R_2 - R_1}$$

and $K = \dfrac{V^2 d^2 (P_s - P)}{18\,\mu}$

Knowing the velocity distribution, it is possible to determine the size distribution at any point in the hydrocyclone.

The theoretical values, however, as calculated from the above relationship, can be expected to vary more or less from the actual data. This is due primarily to the complexity of the internal mechanics of the hydrocyclone, secondly to the assumption that the settling velocity is equal to the centrifugal velocity (which may not be true), and finally to the assump-

FIG. 3—MICRO-HYDROCYCLONE, UNDERFLOW AND OVERFLOW RATIOS

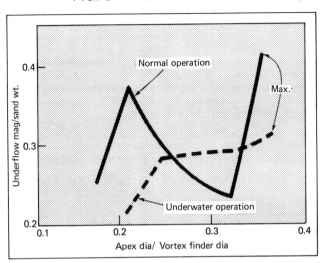

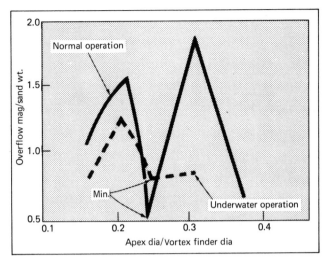

tion that all particles have the same resistance time in the hydrocyclone.

Theoretically, for optimum separation the liquid should have a density between that of the two materials which are to be separated.

Many investigators have written in detail about the operation of hydrocyclones in either open or closed circuits, under atmospheric conditions. However, F. J. Fontein[1] et al reported some excellent results in studying the effect of back pressures on the operation of a hydrocyclone. No significant difference was found between the normal open circuit and the system under back pressure.

Test equipment and procedure

The principal equipment used in preliminary work at the University of Wisconsin consisted of a laboratory size unit (the micro-hydrocyclone) and a commercial-size hydrocyclone. The micro-hydrocyclone, equipped with five replaceable apex nozzles and three exchangeable vortex finders, is shown in Fig. 1. The circuit employing the commercial hydrocyclone is shown in Fig. 2.

The versatile design of the large apparatus permits study of separate characteristics of underflow, overflow, and feed in conjunction with closed loop circulation or in open circuit. Flow rates and operating pressures are indicated and controlled.

Closely sized (minus 100 plus 150 mesh) mixtures of sand and magnetite in varying proportions and at various dilutions

Acknowledgements

The authors thank the staff of the Sea Grant Program for their assistance, particularly Dr. J. Robert Moore, director, Geo-Environmental and Mineral Resources.

The help of Dr. S. R. Balajee, Inland Steel Co., and Dr. Rodney L. Stone, Bethlehem Steel Corp., in furnishing samples of magnetite is appreciated.

This project was partially funded by the National Oceanic and Atmospheric Administration's Office of Sea Grant, Department of Commerce, through an institutional grant to the University of Wisconsin.

have been used throughout. The investigation is controlled by a two-level fractional factorial design.

Preliminary study has been directed toward determining the basic operating characteristics of the hydrocyclone and comparing its operation above and below water at atmospheric pressure.

Two distinct phenomena occur in the hydrocyclone operating above the surface: the presence of a stationary or oscillating inner air core, and the spraying action at the hydrocyclone apex. The latter is absent under water, the former present only if air is purposely introduced or present by entrainment. The relative effect of these phenomena is shown in Fig. 3, which confirms the work of F. J. Fontein et al.[1,2] The ratio of magnetite to sand in either the underflow or overflow is a function of apex-to-vortex finder diameters. Obviously, for concentration we seek the maximum magnetite in the underflow and a minimum in the overflow. It should be noted that the numerical values of the apex-to-vortex diameters are different for underflow and overflow.

Underwater operation, as indicated in Fig. 3, gives curves somewhat similar to those of normal above-water operation, but considerably compressed. This is, in all probability, related to the absence of the air core and vortex spray in underwater operation.

With properly chosen parameters and perhaps with some modification, the hydrocyclone is believed to be adaptable to the processing of underwater heavy mineral sand deposits. Continuing research envisions further investigation of controlling parameters, a study of the effect of fluid density, and the application of hydrocyclones in series. Operation is planned at depth, simulated by a pressurized tank environment, and the combination of the principles of flotation with those of the hydrocyclone will be investigated. ☐

References

1) Fontein, F. J., Vavkooy, J. G., and Leniger, H. A., "The Influence of Some Variables Upon Hydrocyclone Performance," BRITISH CHEMICAL ENGINEERING, Vol. 7, June 1962.
2) Fontein, F. J., and Dyksman, C. "The Hydrocyclone, Its Application and Its Explanation."
3) Reitema, K., and Verver, C. G., Cyclones in Industry, Elsevier Publishing Co., 1961.
4) Kelsall, D. F., "A Study of the Motion of Solid Particles in a Hydraulic Cyclone," Institution of Chemical Engineers, TRANSACTIONS, Vol. 30, 1952.
5) Bloor, M. I. G., and Ingham, D. G., "Theoretical Investigation of the Flow in a Conical Hydrocyclone," Institution of Chemical Engineers, TRANSACTIONS, Vol. 51, 1973.

University of California process recovers copper from leach liquor

A POTENTIALLY LOW-COST, non-polluting process for copper recovery from a liquor resulting from the leaching of copper ore and scrap metal has been patented by two University of California engineers.

The process, which would yield high concentrations of copper through electrochemical action, also has potential application in the recovery of mercury, lead, cadmium, silver, and gold, according to the inventors.

A concentrating cell is the heart of the method developed by Professor Douglas N. Bennion of the UCLA Energy and Kinetics Department and Professor John Newman of the UC Berkeley Chemical Engineering Department. Robert S. Wenger, an engineering graduate student at UCLA, carried out the test work.

The cell, 2 ft x 9 in. x 2 ft deep, consists of two compartments separated by an AMF ion exchange membrane. The two compartments are filled with granular carbon to act as electrodes—one compartment being charged negatively and the other positively.

In a commercial process, fresh solution would be pumped into one compartment and recycled solution from the electrowinning plant would be pumped into the other. Each solution passes through the carbon to an outlet on the opposite side of its compartment.

The electrodes are charged so that copper from the fresh solution is deposited on the carbon, while in the recycled solution compartment, copper is released into the solution and the resulting concentrate is fed into the electrowinning plant. After about five days the polarity is reversed, and the flow of solutions is switched, so that copper collected from the fresh solution is released into the pregnant electrolytic solution which is then flowing through that compartment. The membrane allows electrical current flow, but keeps the solutions separate.

In this process, about one molar (63 gm of Cu per liter) or more can be concentrated for the electrowinning plant, as compared with about 0.7 molar for liquid extraction, based on preliminary work. Dr. Bennion states that the electrical driving force used by the process is powerful and can be accurately controlled, whereas in the case of liquid extraction, an immediate competitive process, process control is limited to pH or difference in acid concentrations. According to Dr. Bennion, his process recovers about 99% of the copper in solution.

A commercial cell would probably measure 8 ft long, 9 in. wide, and 4 ft deep. Approximately 1,000 cells of this size would process 1 to 2 million gal of dilute solutions daily, to yield 5 to 10 tons of copper per day, according to Dr. Bennion. The next step seen by Dr. Bennion is one in which several cells will demonstrate, on a larger scale, the further technical viability of the process, as well as gather data for capital and operating costs. Several companies have expressed an interest in the process, Dr. Bennion reports. □

Reprinted From E/MJ, August 1974

On the technology front: chloride chemistry and pollution-free metal winning

SULPHUR IN COPPER SULPHIDE CONCENTRATES can be converted into insoluble anhydrite ($CaSO_4$) by roasting the concentrate with lime (CaO) to fix the element in a harmless throwaway product in a hydrometallurgical copper recovery approach suggested by US Bureau of Mines research. Following the roast, the calcine is leached with hydrochloric acid to take metal oxides into solution. Molybdenum is stripped by adsorption on activated carbon, and copper is precipitated on sponge iron.

USBM research made use of rougher flotation concentrates, which opens a pair of attractive options—the potential for cost saving by elimination of cleaner flotation steps and a possible reduction in metal loss to tailings during cleaner concentration.

Rougher flotation concentrates were pelletized with theoretical amounts of lime and roasted at 700°C for an hour in a 6½-in. x 11-ft-long rotary kiln. Sulphur retention in the calcine was about 97%. The roasted feed was then leached with a 20% HCl solution which extracted 99% of the copper, 73% of the iron, and 91% of the molybdenum. After stripping of molybdenum from solution, copper of 99% purity was obtained by cementation on sponge iron. The barren solution was then spray roasted at 500°C to recover HCl for recycle and Fe_2O_3 as a by-product. Details are given in RI 8006.

Back in 1971, USBM reported on a method to recover copper and elemental sulphur using a ferric chloride leach, according to the reaction:

$$CuFeS_2 + 3FeCl_3 \rightarrow$$
$$CuCl + 4FeCl_2 + 2S$$

Since that time further work has been done to improve procedures, including recovery of sulphur from leach residues, recovery of copper and iron from leach solution, and the regeneration of the leach solution.

It was found that more than 99% of the elemental sulphur in the leach residue could be extracted at ambient temperature with an ammonium sulphide solution. Heating the pregnant solution precipitated crystals of rhombic sulphur (99.5% pure) and liberated ammonia and hydrogen sulphide for recycle.

Copper with a purity in excess of 99% was recovered by electrowinning, using a diaphragm cell with an energy requirement of less than 0.7 kwh per lb of metal. The cathode deposit was composed of a weakly adhering powder that could be easily dislodged and continuously withdrawn from the cell in a slurry. During electrolysis, some of the ferrous iron was oxidized to the ferric state at the anode so there was no chlorine evolution.

The leach solution was regenerated by direct oxidation of the spent electrolyte with air or oxygen in a turboaerator at 80°C. This precipitated the iron, dissolved during leaching, in an easily filterable form—$Fe_2O_3 \cdot xH_2O$, and converted the remaining ferrous iron to ferric iron. RI 8007 reports more on results.

The USBM also recently studied the chlorination kinetics of selected metal sulphides, including iron, copper-iron, nickel, lead, zinc, silver, bismuth, arsenic, rhenium, molybdenum, and tungsten at temperatures up to 600°C. Copper-iron, lead, and zinc sulphides showed at least some product-controlled (parabolic) kinetics at the lower end of the temperatures studied, but only nickel and silver sulphides had chlorination rates controlled by parabolic reaction kinetics in the commercially important temperature range of 450° to 600°C. USBM RI 8002 contains details.

All publications cited here may be obtained from the Publications Distribution Branch, Bureau of Mines. □

Columbia professors study treatment of metal sulphides

STUDIES ARE UNDERWAY at Columbia University on the basic chemistry of three different potential processes for treatment of metal sulphide emissions, based on either retaining the sulphur in solid form or emitting only concentrated sulphur dioxide that can be converted to byproduct acid. A group of professors at the Mineral Engineering Div. of Columbia's Henry Krumb School of Mines are working under a contract with the National Science Foundation, a special grant from Amax Inc., and a fellowship grant from the Asarco Foundation.

In one hydrometallurgical method, sulphur dioxide would oxidize zinc sulphide in acid solution according to the reaction:

$$2ZnS + 2H_2SO_4 + SO_2 \rightarrow$$
$$2ZnSO_4 + 3S° + 2H_2O$$

The sulphur from zinc sulphide and that from SO_2 would be converted to elemental sulphur, the easiest form to store or transport. The zinc sulphate solution would be electrolyzed to produce zinc metal and to regenerate the acid needed for dissolution. The factors influencing the rate of this reaction are being studied to find the most practical conditions of operation.

Another process for recovery of copper from copper-iron sulphides, recently patented by Amax Inc., is also under study. The sulphide is first oxidized by air (roasted) to produced concentrated SO_2 for conversion to acid. The resultant copper-iron oxides are then subjected to "segregation"—a process in which small amounts of common salt and finely ground coal are added to the metal oxides and the mixture heated to 700-800°C. Volatile copper chloride forms, diffuses to the coal particles, and is there reduced to metallic copper. The study is concentrating on the basic mechanism of segregation and means to optimize the recovery of copper. The final study concerns the direct reduction of zinc sulphide with carbon, in the presence of lime, according to the reaction:

$$ZnS(c) + C(c) + CaO(c) \rightarrow$$
$$Zn(g) + CO(g) + CaS(c)$$

In this system, the sulphur is retained as solid calcium sulphide, while zinc vapor and carbon monoxide pass out of the reactor to a condenser for zinc recovery. The reaction has been found to be relatively rapid at 1,000-1,100°C and can be accelerated by addition of about 1% of certain catalysts. Under study are reactions whereby the calcium sulphide byproduct can be converted to elemental sulphur with regeneration of the lime needed for the main reduction reaction. Several methods to accomplish this by processing the calcium sulphide in aqueous solution are also being researched. □

Reprinted From E/MJ, March 1975

Anglo studies new methods to boost gold recovery

AT ANGLO AMERICAN CORP.'S research laboratories in Johannesburg, a program is underway to boost the company's gold recovery by 3% to 4%. The two approaches to recapture the elusive percentage of gold that escapes the recovery process are construction of computer models designed to optimize current procedures without plant changes or capital expenditures, and development of new equipment through the use of pilot plants at the mines.

Using computerization, a model of a mine's metallurgical processes was constructed that saved $44,000 in reagents and increased profits by $740,000. The cyanide plant had been using too much of one reagent and too little of another.

Another project underway is an attempt to find a method of removing the coating that protects minute gold particles from recovery by preventing their going into solution. This covering is usually pyrite, quartz, uraninite, or thucholite—the carbonized remnants of primordial plant matter, resembling a plastic. While there is a primary coating on the gold in most of the reefs mined in South Africa, the stubborn plastic-like coating starts forming only when the gold particle has been released from the ore by crushing and milling, and is lying in a wet environment—particularly in the presence of fine iron. The contact with iron in the drilling and grinding processes results in free gold grains in the plant tailings becoming covered with hydrated iron oxide.

Another line of investigation at Anglo American involves development of an instrument that can instantaneously measure particle size in a mill through ultrasonic waves. Milling is the most expensive single operation in the recovery plant, and final gold recovery depends on the crushed ore being reduced to a precisely suitable particle size. The new instrument is being tested at the Welkom mine.

Once the gold ore in Anglo American's plants has been milled, it goes either to a low-grade cyanidation circuit or to a gravity concentration circuit. Metallurgists believe treating a greater proportion of the gold through gravity concentration will offer a better opportunity for complete recovery. Theoretically, it should be possible to treat 70% to 75% of the gold ore by gravity concentration, and Anglo's laboratories are working on new methods to achieve at least 99.7% efficiency, thereby eliminating the need for using the cyanide process on tailings. Among methods explored have been flat-cone hydrocyclones, wet shaking tables, and vibrating strakes to replace other gravity separation methods.

Traditionally, gold collected on the gravity side has been treated by amalgamation with mercury, but experiments to replace this process with cyanidation are being conducted.

Another stage at which gold losses occur is in inadequate washing after filtration on the cyanidation circuit—yet another reason for putting more gold ore through the high-grade gravity concentration circuit. Anglo American scientists have confirmed that activated charcoal will "scavenge" the soluble gold lost at the filtration stage, which can then be collected, along with gold particles in thucholite in the tailings residue. Charcoal adsorption towers at a pilot plant have absorbed the bulk of gold and silver in mine effluents, and the effect of powdered charcoal is to be tested at the President Brand mine. □

Microbe leaching
of copper and molybdenum ores

THE TECHNIQUE OF BIOEXTRACTIVE METALLURGY has been known for some time and has been used in leaching copper from waste dumps and other areas formerly termed "economically unfavorable" under conventional methods. Corale L. Brierley, of the New Mexico Bureau of Mines and Mineral Resources, went on to explain that the organisms associated with copper leaching have been identified as "Thiobacillus thiooxidans" and "Thiobacillus ferrooxidans," whose functions in the leaching process are to oxidize sulphides to polythionates, and sulphate and ferrous iron to ferric iron. The combination of the oxidized metals and the increased level of acidity created by the biogenic activity results in a chemical lixiviant which produces an accelerated chemical alteration of the minerals.

The ability of these organisms to grow and perform their specific function is limited only by the availability of an energy source and nutrients and by environmental changes, particularly temperature, pH, and oxygen availability.

While the organisms mentioned and their relationship to bioextractive mining have been relatively well-studied, there have been no attempts to discover or study other microorganisms which may be more compatible with the high temperatures, low-oxygen environment, and heavy metal concentrations at leach dumps and in-situ mining operations.

An unidentified, high-temperature microbe, which oxidizes reduced inorganic sulphur and iron in an acid medium between 45° and 75°C at a pH of 2.0, has been the subject of further lab studies, according to Brierley. The morphology is unlike that of the thiobacilli, being pleomorphic rather than rod-shaped (Fig. 1). The organism ranges in size from 1 to 1½ μin.-dia.

In tests of reactions with copper sulphide minerals, the microbe leached a chalcopyrite concentrate in a batch reactor using an acid medium (pH 2.5), with 0.02% yeast extract at 60°C. The copper is solubilized at a rate of 10-16 mg per liter per day from a chalcopyrite concentrate (27.6% copper—74-105 microns in particle size) over a 30-day period. The solubilization of copper in uninoculated flasks occurs at a rate of 1.0-1.8 mg per liter per day over the same period. Preliminary results indicate that about 50% of the copper in a low-grade ore (0.32% copper, -16 to +50 mesh, from the Chino mine of Kennecott Copper Corp.) is leached from the ore in 60 days at 60°C in an acid medium containing the organism. About half of this copper is solubilized by the acid medium.

The ability of the organism to tolerate soluble copper is essential to successful leaching of copper sulphide minerals. The tolerance of the organism to copper is ascertained by comparing the oxygen uptake of the organism when it is suspended in varying concentrations of soluble copper to the oxygen uptake when no copper is present. Although the organism can tolerate more than 10.0 gpl copper, it is not able to grow when the concentration of copper exceeds 1.0 gpl. Growth tolerance is ascertained by suspending the organism in acid medium containing varying concentrations of soluble copper, 0.02% yeast extract as a growth enhancement factor, and elemental sulphur, an oxidizable energy source. The absence of microscopically observable microbes, protein production, and pH decline indicate the absence of growth.

A 98.5% molybdenite concentrate with a particle size of 12 to 62 microns is oxidized by the microbe at 60°C. Over a 30-day period, 3.3% of the molybdenum is solubilized from the

Reprinted by permission of Canadian Journal of Microbiology.

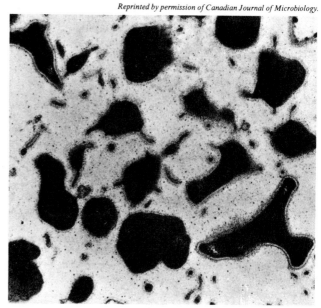

Fig. 1—Electron micrograph of a thin section of microorganism.

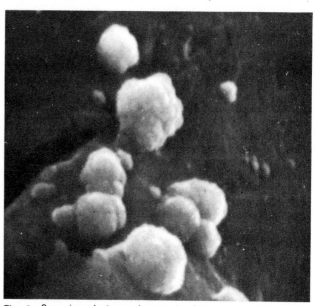

Fig. 2— Scanning electron micrograph of high temperature microorganism on molybdenite fines.

molybdenite, according to Brierley, when it is suspended in an inoculated medium (pH = 2.5). It was also found that this yield can be increased to 8.3% in 30 days when 0.02% yeast extract is added. The addition of 0.02% yeast extract and 1% $FeSO_4 \cdot 7H_2O$ increases the yield to 13.3% in 30 days. In all cases, the leaching of molybdenite in uninoculated controls yields 0.1% molybdenum solubilized in 30 days (Fig. 2).

Structural and physiological studies had indicated that the high-temperature microbe is unrelated to the thiobacilli and is probably another type of microorganism that has neither

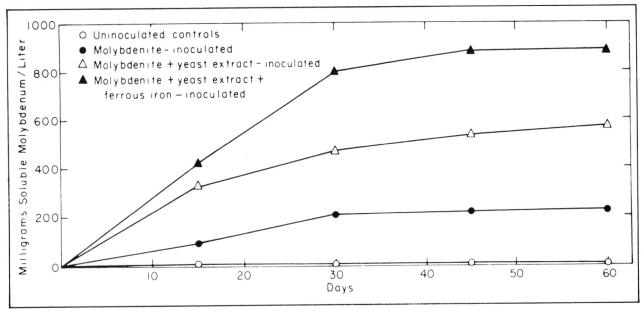

Fig. 3—Solubilization of molybdenum from molybdenite concentrate for 60 days.

been previously isolated nor considered for leaching purposes. Field studies indicated that temperatures within low-grade copper ore dumps may reach 80°C. These elevated temperatures probably inhibit the leaching activity of strains of sulphur- and iron-oxidizing bacteria whose optimum temperatures range from 25°C to 45°C. Brierly concluded that the economic implication of this new study, at least initially, is that it is technically feasible for the new microbe to biogenically extract copper at temperatures exceeding 45°C and that molybdenite can now be biogenically extracted. □

Effect of particle size on microbiological leaching

TO ASSESS THE LEACHABILITY of a particular waste ore, a representative sample is usually subjected to a series of column tests, to determine the maximum possible extraction, and to get some idea about the rate at which this extraction can be carried out. A. Bruynesteyn and D. W. Duncan, of the Mineral Microbiology Section of British Columbia Research, reported on one test performed in 6-ft-high by 6-in.-dia PVC columns, to determine the effect of particle size on the microbiological leaching of chalcopyrite bearing ore. They noted: "The information developed from such tests is of distinct value in assessing whether or not the material is leachable; the rate of extraction, and possibly the extent of extraction, are strongly influenced by the particle size of the material under test."

To further understand this relationship, tests were conducted on a 1,000-lb sample of minus 2 in. ore from the Britannia Beach operation of the Anaconda Co. in British Columbia. The ore consisted of a mixture of chalcopyrite, sphalerite, and pyrite, and was separated into six fractions. Each fraction was assayed for copper and zinc values (see

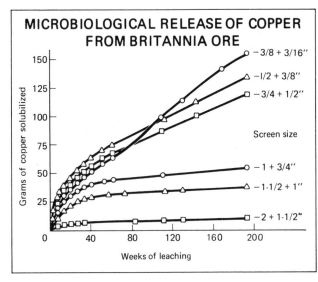

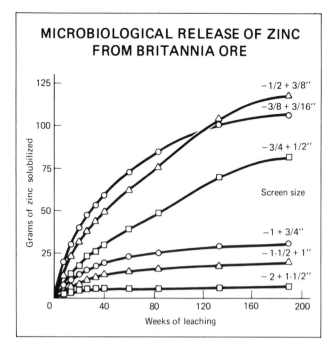

MICROBIOLOGICAL RELEASE OF ZINC FROM BRITANNIA ORE

Table 1 —Assays of head samples

Screen Size (in.)			% Cu	% Zn
-2	+1½	inch	0.53	1.48
-1½	+1	inch	1.00	0.46
-1	+3/4	inch	0.81	0.36
-3/4	+½	inch	0.95	0.42
-½	+3/8	inch	0.81	0.42
-3/8	+3/16	inch	0.82	0.33

Table 2—Theoretical and actual zinc to copper release ratios

Screen Size		Grams Metal Released per 100 Weeks		Actual Ratio Zn/Cu	Theoretical Ratio Zn/Cu
		Cu	Zn		
-3/8	+3/16 inch	65.1	51.8	0.80	0.40
-½	+3/8 inch	49.0	58.4	1.19	0.52
-3/4	+½ inch	39.2	48.0	1.22	0.44
-1	+3/4 inch	9.3	8.2	0.88	0.44
-1½	+1 inch	6.2	6.8	1.10	0.46
-2	+1½ inch	2.0	1.02	0.51	2.70

Table 1), after which 100-lb portions were leached in duplicate columns, utilizing a one-week leach, four-week rest cycle. Each column was inoculated with an active strain of thiobacillus ferrooxidans grown in shake flasks on finely ground chalcopyrite concentrate. All the columns were installed in a specially built room, where the temperature was maintained at 35°C. A total of 20 liters of leach solution, contained in a 50-liter plastic bucket placed underneath each column, was used to leach the charge in the column, with the aid of an air-lift water recycling system.

The data obtained, according to the authors, indicate that the relationship between extraction rate and particle size is a hyperbolic function. If the relationship was based solely on surface area, the results from the column studies would have given a straight line, since reducing the particle size of a fixed weight of mineralization results in an increase in the actual number of particles, proportional to the cube of the diameters, but also results in a reduction in surface area of the individual particle, proportional to the square of the diameter. The actual increase in surface area of a fixed weight of material is inversely proportional to the decrease in the diameter of the particles involved.

The authors concluded that the rate of microbiological leaching of a fixed weight of mineralization is not directly proportional to the surface area, but rather is influenced by the actual volume of the material which is exposed to the leaching environment. This exposed volume consists of the actual surface area plus the depth of penetration of both the leach liquors and the leaching bacteria.

The configuration of the zinc and copper rate curves obtained with this particular sample suggested that little improvement in leach rate can be effected by crushing, unless the ore is crushed to less than 2 in. At 2 in., the copper extraction rate was 0.15% per week, so that even with the ideal environment and physical conditions of the lab column test, it still would take 1,000 weeks or 19.2 years to get 15% extraction after the initial soluble copper has been removed. Most important, leach dumps of considerable height would have to be built in order to produce pregnant solutions, based on the results of the metal recovery rate curves.

These tests have shown that an evaluation of leaching rates for different particle sizes can yield valuable information about the actual performance of this material in a commercial leaching dump. The authors cautioned that if a column test is performed on only one particle size, the information obtained could result in erroneous scale-up to a dump-size operation. However, if the information obtained from a test at various particle sizes indicates that leaching rates are substantial even at 2-in. particle sizes, then commercial dump performance could be reasonably predicted by extrapolating this rate curve. Finally, the particle size tests will yield information not only on the performance of the ore under test but also on leach liquor characteristics. □

The editors of E/MJ express their appreciation to the Society of Mining Engineers of AIME and its Executive Secretary, Claude L. Crowley, for permission to summarize selected articles from the Dallas Solution Mining Symposium.

A special word of thanks is also due to: F. F. Aplan, chairman, Penn State University; W. A. McKinney, US Bureau of Mines; and A. D. Pernichele, Dames and Moore. It was their monumental task to compile and edit the large number of technical papers presented.

The entire text of the proceedings, bound in a single volume, is available at a price of $15.00 to non-AIME members, $10.00 to AIME members, and a special rate of $6.00 to student AIME members. Write to: Society of Mining Engineers, AIME, 540 Arapeen Drive, Salt Lake City, Utah 84108.

Chapter 7
Products and Ideas

Stainless steel: effective corrosion control for copper recovery operations

E. S. Kopecki, Committee of Stainless Steel Producers, American Iron and Steel Institute

STAINLESS STEEL OFFERS MANY ADVANTAGES for containing strongly acidic leaching reactions in copper recovery operations. Hydrometallurgical techniques for copper extraction have been known probably since 1752, but the dissolution of copper by leaching and the recovery from solution by precipitation or electrowinning did not become significant in the US until the mid-1960s. Today, hydrometallurgy accounts for a large percentage of US primary copper production—perhaps more than 300,000 tons annually—and virtually all copper producers now use or plan to install some form of leaching and recovery operation.

The environment of principal concern in copper leaching is a solution containing up to 20% sulphuric acid (by weight) and various concentrations of copper sulphate and other metal sulphates. Temperatures range from ambient to boiling. Acid corrosion in this environment can demand constant maintenance—one of the largest plant operating costs. Failure of components through corrosion can render a substantial portion of any plant temporarily inoperative. As a result, a growing number of leach plant engineers are expressing a preference for the use of stainless steel in leach plant pumps, piping, valves, heat transfer equip-

ment, tanks, and various other structures because of its proven success in handling corrosion problems. Table 1 shows the compositions of the AISI stainless steels most important in these applications.

Table 1—Effect of copper sulphate on corrosion by sulphuric acid
(10% H_2SO_4 at 150°F)

Metal	Corrosion rate in inches per year	
	Cupric sulphates present (40 gpl)	Air free, no oxidizing salts
Type 304 stainless steel	0.0023	2.6
Type 316 stainless steel	0.0001	0.084
Silicon bronze	Specimen destroyed	0.015
Monel nickel-copper alloy	0.203	0.007
Chemical lead	0.0024	0.0019

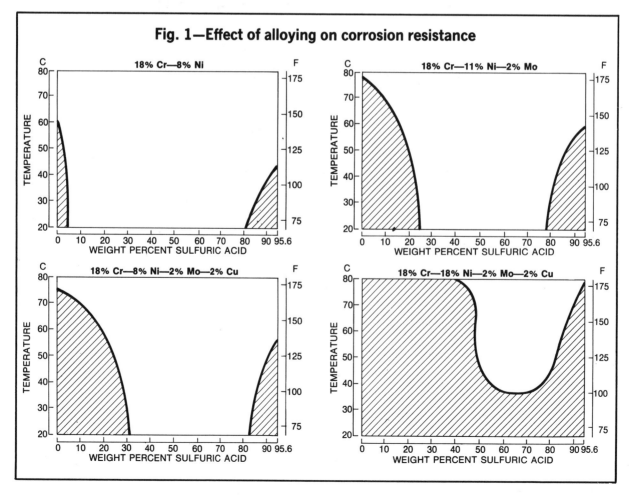

Fig. 1—Effect of alloying on corrosion resistance

Table 2—Percentage compositions of selected AISI stainless steels

AISI type	Chromium	Nickel	Molybdenum	Carbon (Maximum)	Other
410.........	11.5-13.5	–	–	0.15	
430.........	16-18	–	–	0.12	
446.........	23-27	–	–	0.20	
304.........	18-20	8-10.5	–	0.08	
304L........	18-20	8-12	–	0.03	
309.........	22-24	12-15	–	0.20	
310.........	24-26	19-22	–	0.25	
316.........	16-18	10-14	2.0-3.0	0.08	
316L........	16-18	10-14	2.0-3.0	0.03	
317.........	18-20	11-15	3.0-4.0	0.08	
321.........	17-19	9-12	–	0.08	Titanium 5xC min.
347.........	17-19	9-13	–	0.08	Columbium + tantalum 10xC min.

Corrosion resistance of stainless steels

The chromium in stainless steels imparts a passive chromium oxide film to the metal surface, with an accompanying resistance to corrosion. As service conditions become more severe, successively higher chromium percentages are required to promote formation of this passive film and preserve its integrity under a broad range of conditions. The addition of molybdenum to stainless steel also improves corrosion resistance, while addition of nickel improves both fabricability and corrosion resistance.

An especially useful property of stainless steels is that they withstand those oxidizing conditions that are most harmful to ordinary steel and to many nonferrous metals. However, some concentrations of relatively pure sulphuric acid, and reducing environments in general, are not conducive to the formation and retention of the passive film.[1] The data in Fig. 1 show how an increased percentage of nickel and the addition of copper will increase the range of concentrations and temperatures within which stainless steel will exhibit satisfactory resistance to sulphuric acid.

Oxidizing salts, such as cupric and ferric salts, when dissolved in significant amounts in sulphuric acid solutions, exert a corrosion-inhibiting effect on the solubility of stainless steels in that acid. Such salts also help maintain the passive film past the normal range of resistance.[2] To illustrate the effect, a laboratory test exposed specimens to a cupric sulphate/sulphuric acid solution at 150°F. The results of this test are shown in Table 2.

Kiefer and Renshaw[3] investigated the inhibiting effect of metal sulphates on the solubility of stainless steels in sulphuric acid. Various amounts of ammonium, sodium, manganese, iron (ferrous), nickel, tin (stannous), and copper (cupric) sulphates were added to 5% and 30% sulphuric acid. AISI steel types 304 and 316 were tested in these solutions at 100°, 150°, 175°, and 200°F. Figs. 2 and 3 show typical data obtained in 5% sulphuric acid at 175°F. Some of the findings:

■ The presence of any of the sulphates materially lowers the corrosion rate.

■ As temperature increases, the inhibiting effect of the sulphates becomes less pronounced.

■ The sulphates of metals above nickel in the Standard Electromotive Series vary only slightly in their inhibiting effect, and none provides complete inhibition. Sulphates of metals above iron have little effect.

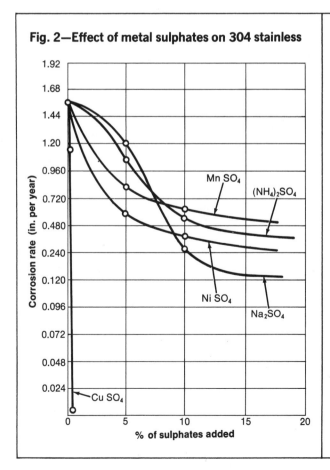

Fig. 2—Effect of metal sulphates on 304 stainless

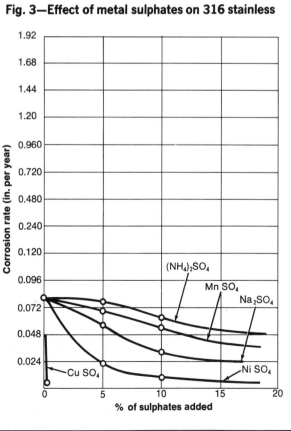

Fig. 3—Effect of metal sulphates on 316 stainless

■ The valence state of the sulphate is very important; higher valence sulphates are extremely effective even at low concentrations.

Such laboratory data is well supported by extensive, successful use of stainless steels in leach and recovery plants throughout the western US. One plant uses equipment constructed of about 300,000 lb of AISI 316L stainless steel in leaching, solvent extraction, and electrowinning operations, and the plant manager reports no problems with stainless after three years of almost continuous operation. Such reports are typical among operating and maintenance engineers in many areas.

Picking the right stainless steel

Pitting corrosion may occur in stainless steel equipment even though its general corrosion resistance is excellent. Pitting results from a highly localized breakdown in the passive oxide film, and may occur in the presence of chlorides. (Unless chloride levels are relatively high, such attack is not likely.) In addition, accumulation of solids on metal surfaces is conducive to pitting and should be avoided where practical. In general, AISI 316 stainless, which contains 2-3% molybdenum, is more resistant to pitting attack than AISI 304, and its greater cost is frequently justified for copper recovery applications.

Intergranular corrosion is another problem. When some 300 series stainless steels are heated to 800-1,500°F, some of the chromium and carbon in the metal combine to form chromium carbide, which precipitates at the grain boundaries. Chromium carbide formation causes localized depletion of chromium at the grain boundaries, which can lead to intergranular corrosion in acidic environments. Hot copper sulphate/sulphuric acid solutions, for example, strongly promote intergranular corrosion. Stainless steel in which chromium carbide has formed is referred to as having been "sensitized." This condition most commonly occurs when heat treatment of the material is not performed after weld fabrication.

Intergranular corrosion can be avoided by heat treating equipment after weld fabrication, by using low-carbon stainless steels (such as types 304L and 316L), or by employing stabilized stainless steels. In low-carbon grades containing a maximum 0.03% carbon, there simply is not enough carbon available to produce a damaging amount of chromium carbide. In stabilized stainless steels, the carbon preferentially combines with the stabilizing agent (titanium or columbium), thereby preventing precipitation of chromium carbide.

Crevice corrosion may occur at contact surfaces of flanged joints and incompletely welded attachments. In these areas, corrosive media penetrate between the surfaces to form a stagnant area or pocket, resulting in a depletion of inhibiting copper salts and entrapment of corrosion products. The contact area may become sufficiently anodic to adjacent areas to cause localized breakdown of the passive film and active corrosion. This typically results in failures under gaskets at flanged joints, and under sludge or slimes settling in tanks.

Type 316 stainless is more resistant to crevice corrosion than type 304. However, metallurgical composition is not the only factor influencing crevice corrosion. Design and fabrication details are important, and attention to a few fundamentals can avoid crevice corrosion:

■ Provision should be made for free and complete drainage of equipment, avoidance of crevices, and ease of cleaning and inspection.

■ Butt joints with complete weld penetration should be

Copper precipitate settles through type 304 stainless screen.

Type 316 stainless rake is used in leach tank at copper plant.

Leach area now uses stainless valves and piping exclusively.

used wherever possible.

■ If lap joints with fillet welds are necessary, the welds should be continuous on the process side.

Specific uses of stainless in copper recovery

In the precipitation recovery method, copper is precipitated from solution by contact and cementation with metallic iron, such as shredded scrap detinned cans, and the spent solution is reused for further leaching. The precipitation reaction is:

$$Cu^{++} + SO_4^{--} + Fe \text{ (metal)} \rightarrow$$
$$Cu \text{ (metal)} + Fe^{++} + SO_4^{--}$$

One western plant uses cone-type precipitators developed by Kennecott Copper Corp. Into each tank, 14-ft dia and 20 ft high, an inverted 10 x 10-ft cone is mounted. The annular space between the inner cone and the tank is covered by a heavy-gauge type 304 stainless screen and holds about 15 tons of iron scrap. Pregnant leach solution is pumped up through the scrap, while the copper precipitate settles down through the stainless screen into the annular space, to be discharged intermittently.

Precipitates from the cones are pumped to a filter plant where they are dewatered in a 48-in. all-stainless filter press equipped with stainless steel filter screens. The tanks containing the cones are wood, reinforced with ¾-in.-dia type 304 stainless bar hoops. A 4-in.-dia type 304 stainless pipe carries 92% sulphuric acid from the acid plant to the point where it enters the tailing water from the precipitation plant.

The plant has 34 multiple-stage, vertical turbine pumps handling leach water. Pump bodies and impellers are AISI 304 (cast), and the 11-ft-long pump shafts are precipitation-hardened stainless steel. Except for some minor erosion-corrosion problems with the pumps, the plant has had very little trouble with the type 304 steel.

Good copper recoveries can also be achieved by vat leaching of copper oxides and silicates with dilute sulphuric acid. In one vat leaching plant, crushed ore is placed in 110 x 100 x 18-ft concrete vats and leached with up to 10% sulphuric acid solution. Most piping, pumps, valves, clarifier arms, and even the 8-yd clamshell bucket at the plant are fabricated of AISI types 316 and 316L stainless steels. According to the maintenance superintendent, service has been virtually trouble-free.

In the slimes leach tank and clarifier at the plant, fine particles of silicate are leached and settled. The steel "rake" that scrapes the tank bottom is constructed of type 316 stainless structural shapes. The slimes are so abrasive that, for the most part, rubber-lined pumps are used here—even the valves are rubber pinch valves. However, stainless gate valves back up the pinch valves.

This plant originally used PVC-lined piping to a great extent, until leaks developed at the pipe ends. Since the PVC pipe cost $16 per ft for 12-in.-dia, 40-ft-long sections, every effort was made to salvage end-damaged pipe. However, the $150-per-end repair cost was prohibitive, so as the pipe failed, replacement was made with type 316 stainless pipe. All pumps and valves in the leach area are now stainless.

The clamshell bucket used for loading leach vats was originally mild steel, requiring wear-plate replacement every week and complete rebuilding every 60 days. After success in extending wear-plate life to five weeks by switching to type 304 stainless plate, the plant purchased a new bucket made entirely of stainless steel. Now repairs are needed only twice a year, at a fraction of the original cost.

Liquid ion exchange, otherwise known as solvent extraction, is not a new process; however, its application in copper leaching is relatively new. The process utilizes a special reagent that has an affinity for copper ions in a weak acid solution and a low affinity for other metal ions. The reagent operates on a hydrogen ion exchange cycle, which proceeds as follows: The reagent, carried by an organic medium (kerosene), is intimately contacted with aqueous leach solution in the extraction system. Hydrogen ions are exchanged for copper ions, thus regenerating the sulphuric acid in the leach solution, while the copper is extracted. The copper-containing organic medium passes to the stripping system where it is contacted with aqueous copper sulphate in the presence of sulphuric acid. Copper ions are

All-stainless clamshell bucket, used to load leach vats, offers much lower repair costs than original mild steel construction.

exchanged for hydrogen ions, thus regenerating the reagent, while the enriched copper sulphate solution is essentially free of impurities and ideally suited for electrowinning.

One of the first solvent extraction plants in the US, in operation since 1970, produces about 40,000 lb per day of 99.9% pure copper via this method. The plant was built using types 316 and 316L stainless for all wetted surfaces in the extraction area. There have reportedly been no problems with corrosion. Mix tanks at the plant are constructed of 3/16-in. type 316L stainless plate, while the 8 x 9-ft extraction tanks and the 7 x 9-ft strip tanks, plus all interconnecting pipes, are constructed of 0.1406-in. type 316L stainless sheet. All valves are ball or butterfly type made of 316L stainless with Teflon seats. Turbine pumps are single- or multiple-stage with stainless bowls and internal parts. Many smaller fittings, such as pipe tees, are forged from type 316 steel bar.

The enriched copper sulphate solution produced by solvent extraction must undergo electrowinning to produce high purity copper. Common practice in electrowinning is to electroplate starting sheets on 3/16-in.-thick hard-rolled copper or titanium blanks. However, titanium is expensive and copper blanks are subject to both corrosion at the solution line and mechanical damage from tools used to pry loose the starting sheets. In addition, copper blanks require the application of a release agent to facilitate sheet removal.

To avoid these problems, plants are using AISI 304 or 316 stainless steel for starting blanks, and most expect a 20- to 30-year service life. These blanks have an AISI 2B surface finish.

Stainless steels have also been used extensively in electrolytic copper refining equipment in tankhouses, cell acid purification and recovery, sulphate production, and in the handling of slimes. Most miscellaneous equipment, such as tankhouse tools, sheet flopping racks, anode and cathode wash boxes, and crane hooks—plus a multitude of fasteners everywhere—can be made of type 304 stainless.

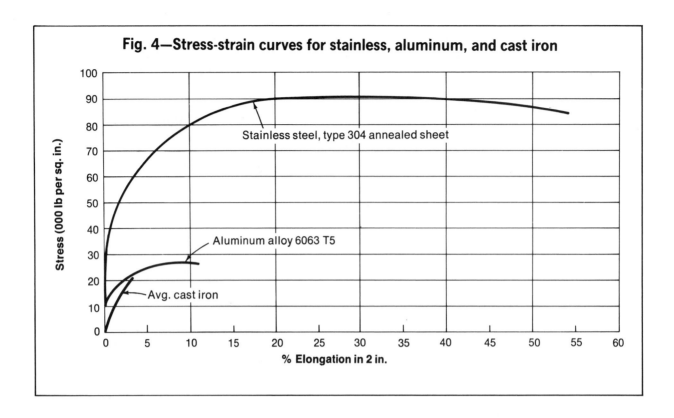

Fig. 4—Stress-strain curves for stainless, aluminum, and cast iron

Stainless steel, type 304 annealed sheet

Aluminum alloy 6063 T5

Avg. cast iron

Stress (000 lb per sq. in.)

% Elongation in 2 in.

However, types 316 and 316L are specifically indicated for surfaces in contact with hot solutions (200°F and higher), some of which have acid contents of up to 15% by weight. It bears repeating that low-carbon grades should be used in welding construction.

Considerable data are available showing the resistance of stainless steels to various solution conditions in electrolytic copper refining. Operating conditions that must be considered include temperature, velocity, aeration, galvanic action, and stray currents. The paper by Schillmoller and LaQue[2] provides information on many of these subjects; however, in the absence of specific information, corrosion tests should be conducted to permit selection of the proper alloy.

Strength and hardness factors

Stainless steels are by far the strongest of the metals

used in copper hydrometallurgy, a fact suggested by the stress-strain curve in Fig. 4, comparing stainless with cast iron and aluminum. Note that the curve for stainless steel continues beyond the breaking point of the other metals, emphasizing its superior strength and ductility.

Stainless steels do not exhibit a distinct yield point; their stress-strain curves show a gradual transition from a straight line to a curve. It has become customary to consider the yield strength of stainless as the point where the stress-strain curve intersects the "0.2% offset" line (Fig. 5).

The AISI series 300 stainless steels are hardenable by cold working. This is usually done in the steel mill by cold rolling, a process that not only hardens the metal but also increases both its yield strength and tensile strength.

In addition to the standard annealed condition, some AISI series 300 steels are available in four standard tempers—¼-hard, ½-hard, ¾-hard, and full-hard. As an example of the increase in strength resulting from cold rolling, type 301 annealed has a yield strength of 40,000 psi; at ¼-hard temper, the yield strength is 75,000 psi; and at ½-hard temper, the yield strength is 110,000 psi. Type 304 stainless also work hardens, but to a lesser extent than type 301.

Even at high strengths, stainless steel retains sufficient ductility to permit forming, although additional allowance for springback is required. A recently introduced "dead soft" fully annealed stainless steel, which has a maximum yield strength of 35,000 psi, is also available for use where ease of forming is of prime importance. ☐

Fig. 5—Yield strength as determined by offset

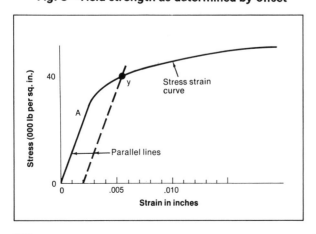

Stress (000 lb per sq. in.)

Stress strain curve

Parallel lines

Strain in inches

References

1) Anon., "Stainless Steel—Improved Resistance to Sulfuric Acid," IRON AND STEEL, Vol. 23, 1950, pp 309-311.
2) Schillmoller, C. M., and F. L. LaQue, "Factors in the Choice of Corrosion-Resisting Materials of Construction," Interscience Publishers Inc., 1961.
3) Kiefer, G. C., and W. G. Renshaw, CORROSION, Vol. 6, 1950.
4) Evans, L. G., and H. W. Sheffer, "Dump and Heap Leaching Practices in the Western United States," MINING CONGRESS JOURNAL, September 1968, pp 96-100.

Giant air classifier reclaims saleable fraction from high grade Rouessa mine iron ore tailings

WHAT IS BELIEVED TO BE THE LARGEST CLASSIFIER system in existence is now in operation deep in the Sahara desert on the west coast of Africa. Located at the Rouessa mine, the pneumatic classifier, supplied by Combustion Equipment Associates Inc. (CEA) of New York, processes some 1,200 tph of iron ore tailings. The mine, near the lower reaches of the north-south boundary separating Rio de Oro (Spanish West Africa) and Mauritania, is operated by Soc. Anonyme des Mines de Fer de Mauritanie (Miferma).

The gravitational-inertial classifier separates undesirable minus 100 mesh fines from the minus ½-in. ore that remains after three crushing and screening operations. The plus 100 fraction is sold to Japan. At present, the fines are a waste product.

FIG. 1—SIMPLIFIED SECTION THROUGH AIR CLASSIFIER SEGMENT

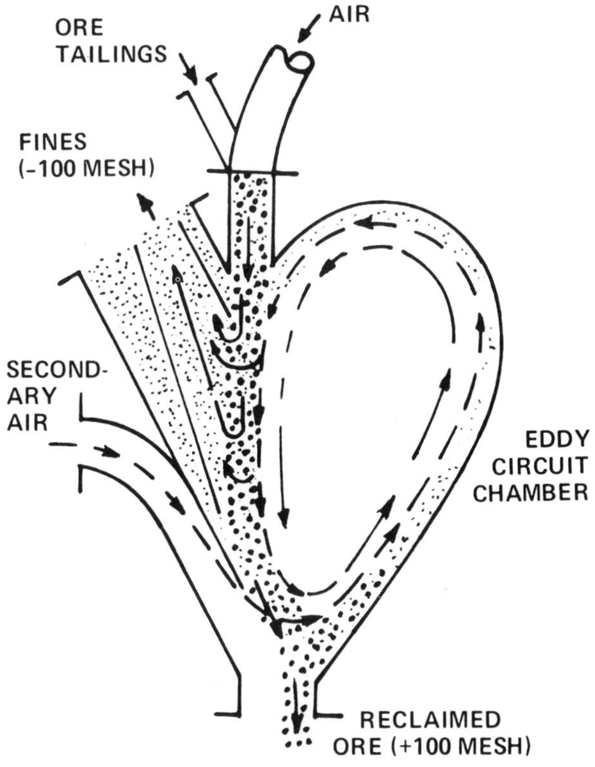

Ore at the Rouessa mine grades about 64% Fe. Of the minus ½-in. tailings, approximately 72% are plus 100 mesh, for which there is a market if the fines are removed. The CEA classifier makes it economically worthwhile to salvage this sizeable plus 100 mesh fraction of rich iron ore.

The classification system, which features a minimum of moving parts, consists of: 1) a feed conveyor, 2) a feed hopper and feed regulator, 3) a 24-segment classifier, 4) a plus 100 mesh take-away conveyor, 5) a classifier exhaust plenum, 6) a plenum exhaust duct, 7) four cyclones, 8) a minus 100 mesh conveyor, and 9) a 450-hp fan.

Tailings are moved to the classifier from final screening operations by conveyor, the last section of the conveyor being inclined and discharging into the classifier feed hopper.

The conical feed hopper contains an inverted truncated cone that distributes tailings uniformly into a shallow inverted-cone container that feeds directly into the classifier segments. Inlet gates are uniformly regulated by three level sensors embedded in the feed material. The gates open and close automatically in relation to fluctuations in tailings from the screening operation.

Classifier segments in radial arrangement

Tailings feed through spouts into the 24-classifier segments arranged radially around the feed hopper. The feed enters air inlet ducts (Fig. 1), and within each segment the entering airstream makes a sharp U-turn into an air outlet duct. The entering airstream also establishes a recirculating air current in an eddy current chamber opposite the outlet duct.

Tailings particles larger than 100 mesh fall directly through the classifier segments to outlets at the bottom. Centrifugal force overcomes gravitational and inertial forces on the particles smaller than 100 mesh as the airstream makes its U-turn into the air outlet duct. These fine particles discharge through the outlet duct with the airstream.

The "cut point" at which fine particles are separated from coarse particles is determined by inlet air velocity. This in turn depends on the air flow through the secondary air inlet. Varying the secondary air flow while maintaining constant exhaust flow varies primary air inlet velocity, and this varies the centrifugal force that carries the fines into the exhaust duct.

The secondary airstream and exiting eddy current scrub fine particles from coarse particles as these air currents cross through the falling tailings. The eddy current provides a moving wall of air that contains the descending curtain without introducing frictional forces as would a solid wall.

The coarse fraction discharges from the classifier segments into a hopper that feeds onto a take-away conveyor. The take-away conveyor services rail cars that carry the reclaimed ore to the seaport of Nouadibou, about 450 mi away. The railroad was completed some 10 years ago specifically to transport ore to Nouadibou from Rouessa and two other nearby mines.

Air and entrained fines exhausted from the classifier segments enter a common plenum chamber. Tailings that settle out are discharged through two airlock valves and diverted to the plus 100 mesh take-away conveyor to the extent that ore specifications permit the presence of fines. The remainder of the settlings are diverted to the minus 100 mesh conveyor.

Air and entrained fines leave the plenum via a 7-ft-dia exhaust duct and are conveyed to four cyclones that separate the fines from the airstream.

The plenum exhaust duct is located directly above a conveyor that carries fines to a disposal area. The horizontal duct has four airlock outlets along the bottom. Low velocity fines discharge by gravity through the airlocks onto the fines conveyor below, decreasing duct and cyclone abrasion. The duct divides near the discharge end, delivering the airstream and entrained fines equally to the four CEA cyclones.

The 160,000-cfm cyclone cluster separates remaining fines from the airstream and discharges them into a hopper that feeds the minus 100 mesh conveyor. The cleaned airstream exhausts through the tops of the cyclones to the fan. Cyclones are lined with cast refractory material for abrasion resistance.

The minus 100 mesh conveyor is totally enclosed to prevent

dispersal of the fines by the wind and carries the fine residue some 600 ft for disposal in the desert.

Analysis shows that the fines average 68% Fe, vs. 64% Fe for the ore as a whole. It is thus felt that, now that the plus 100 micron fraction of the tailings is being recovered, attention may be given to agglomerating the extra-rich fines to make them saleable.

Air for the classifying system is drawn through the system by a 450-hp fan. The air enters the system through classifier segment inlets and travels through the classifier segments, plenum chamber, plenum chamber exhaust duct, cyclones, fan, and back to the atmosphere.

With the exception of the classifier-segment gates and conveyor motors, the fan is the only moving part of the classifier system—an important consideration in the 130°F desert, where both skilled mechanics and spare parts are rare and where normally minor mechanical difficulties can cause serious production problems.

Because of this problem of isolation, extra efforts were made to simplify equipment maintenance. For example, classifier segments are unlined to avoid relining operations. They are fabricated of ½-in.-thick, abrasion-resistant plate. When a section finally wears thin, the entire section is unbolted, hoisted out using lifting lugs provided for the purpose, and replaced with a new section. □

New conveyor drive with feedback circuit: soft starts for loaded mine belts

A NEW CONVEYOR BELT DRIVE SYSTEM that provides "soft start ups" through controlled acceleration has been developed by Synchrotorque, a division of Philadelphia Gear Corp. The "Synchrodrive" variable speed drive uses a set of oil-immersed clutch discs that are squeezed together at precise pressures through a feedback system to impart smooth acceleration to both heavily loaded and completely empty conveyors. Without a speed and acceleration control system that modulates motor output, conveyors can easily be overstrained, resulting in damaged lacing or belt snapping, the manufacturer points out.

The new drive can also be coupled easily to a set of flywheels to provide coasting capabilities, thus preventing possible belt damage when a conveyor is stopped quickly by a power failure or an emergency. In addition, the Synchrodrive's controller is substantially smaller than typical rheostat controllers, and the motor used with the drive is less complex than standard motors.

"A conventional way to start heavily loaded conveyors is to use a wound-rotor motor, typically controlled by a liquid rheostat," says John Liu, manager of Synchrotorque. "Such rheostats occupy at least a 5-ft square, and are 4 to 5 ft high. This is approximately 100 times the cubic space that a Synchrodrive controller takes. A wound-rotor motor is also considerably more complex than the simple squirrel-cage motor used with a Synchrodrive—it has slip rings, while the squirrel-cage does not." Liu also states that a Synchrodrive is lower in initial cost than other drives, and its controller makes starting procedures fully automatic. "In wound-rotor installations, the operator usually has to cut in various resistors to pick up the belt speed, and this can create a problem because of the human element," Liu says.

How the Synchrodrive works

The key component in a Synchrodrive unit is its "disc pack"—two sets of discs interspersed with each other (see simplified schematic). One set is attached to the input (driven by the motor), and the other is attached to the output (coupled to the load). Both disc sets ride on splines so that they can be shifted axially and clamped together to transmit torque from the input to the output.

The torque, however, is *not* transmitted by contact friction between the two sets of discs, as is the case with a friction clutch. Instead, oil is continuously passed between the surfaces of the discs, which are grooved and contain oil pockets. It is these oil films that actually transmit the torque when combined with the hydraulically-supplied clamping force that squeezes the disc sets together.

An increase in the clamping force increases the oil film's resistance to shear, thus raising the output speed. This "hydroviscous" principle is used in Synchrodrives to produce controlled variable output speed in motors with capacities up to 20,000 hp running at 3,600 rpm.

To control drive output, the operator initially sets the desired speed setpoint and acceleration time, after which the process is automatic when the controller is turned on. The Synchrodrive uses an electric-hydraulic control system that responds to the command signal linearly through a

Dual drive schematic

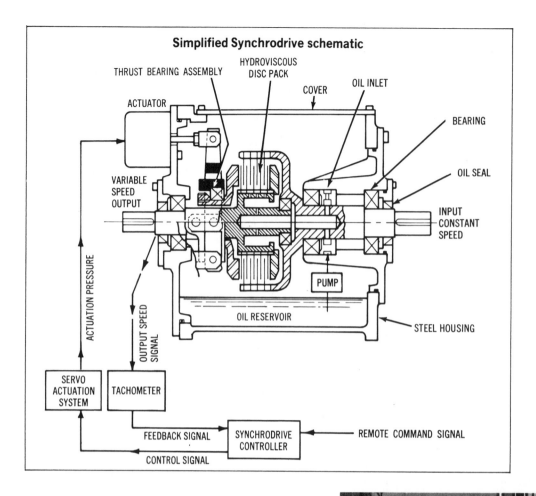

Simplified Synchrodrive schematic

THRUST BEARING ASSEMBLY

HYDROVISCOUS DISC PACK

COVER

OIL INLET

ACTUATOR

BEARING

OIL SEAL

VARIABLE SPEED OUTPUT

INPUT CONSTANT SPEED

ACTUATION PRESSURE

PUMP

OUTPUT SPEED SIGNAL

OIL RESERVOIR

STEEL HOUSING

SERVO ACTUATION SYSTEM

TACHOMETER

FEEDBACK SIGNAL

SYNCHRODRIVE CONTROLLER

REMOTE COMMAND SIGNAL

CONTROL SIGNAL

speed feedback mechanism. A comparator circuit in the controller measures the difference between the setpoint and the actual output speed, then feeds back an error signal to a high-gain amplifier.

The amplifier output energizes a servo valve, which in turn establishes a proportional hydraulic actuation pressure. This pressure operates the clamping piston that varies the force on the disc pack. As the driven load increases or decreases in speed, the speed feedback signal goes through the loop, then stabilizes at the set point.

This modulation may seem to be a lengthy process, but the response time is actually extremely fast. Full torque modulation usually occurs within 50 milliseconds, even for units in the 10,000- to 20,000-hp range. There is, of course, slippage between the driving and driven discs when a Synchrodrive is producing a reduced output speed; however, there is no metal-to-metal contact during the slippage because of the oil film, and wear is negligible.

The servo control system is available in both a simple, highly responsive, hydropneumatic version and an electronic version. The latter includes an electronic box using either dc or digital-tachometer feedback signals.

Two Synchrodrives were recently installed on a conveyor system used to haul copper ore from a large mine to a crushing station. Each drive is coupled to a 700-hp motor on either side of the head pulley, and drives the belt through gear reducers (see dual drive schematic). The Synchrodrives at this installation are designed to lock up automatically in the event of a power failure—the clamping mechanism locks all the discs solidly together so that the input rotates with the output on a one-to-one basis. If such a lockup occurs, a flywheel coupled to the drive output will keep the conveyor going for about 100 ft, to avoid an abrupt stop that might overstrain the belt. □

Synchrodrives, coupled to a loader, are set up on a testing stand, where their ability to control acceleration is checked.

New particle size analyzer uses optics and electronics

LEEDS & NORTHRUP CO. UNVEILED its new "Microtrac" particle size analyzer for laboratory use and on-line monitoring at the SME-AIME fall meeting in Denver early in September.

The new instrumentation system facilitates swift, reproducible measurements of dry powders or wet slurries without special techniques for handling samples, according to Leeds & Northrup, while providing numerical data on particle size and particle size distribution. Measured and calculated values read out on a large illuminated digital display. Installation can be mobile or permanent, with a minimum of utility connections.

The Microtrac is designed to assure operator safety, Leeds & Northrup says, with no special precautions required. It is self-calibrating. No zero or span adjustments are needed, and a computer corrects data for background signals.

Cost of the laboratory analyzer is $19,500, and base price for the on-line monitor is $22,500. With the most expensive optional features, total cost for the on-line unit can reach a maximum of $24,300.

How the Microtrac works

The new analyzer and monitor make use of optics and electronics to provide faster analysis than conventional sieve analysis, specific-surface analysis, interval counting, or microscopic determination, according to the manufacturer.

A small representative sample is introduced into the sample-handling equipment, either dry or as a slurry. Wide loading tolerance eliminates the need for precise weighing of samples, which typically range from 1 to 6 g. The sampling equipment automatically supplies debubbled dilution water, agitates the mixture to maintain representative particle distribution, and circulates it to the sample cell for measurement. After measurement, a push-button initiates a programmed drain-and-refill cycle to prepare for the next sample.

All measured and calculated values for each cycle are stored in the microcomputer memory and are available for individual display. Switch-selected types of data can be logged automatically by the printer for a permanent record.

Particle size range for the new instrument system is from zero to 200 microns. Particles larger than 250 microns provide negligible response, and the practical minimum size is 2 microns.

Rotating filter and drive: the only moving parts

Measuring equipment for the Leeds & Northrup system comprises an optical bench on which are mounted a laser light source, sample cell, high-quality optics, Leeds & Northrup's proprietary 'Compumask' optical filter, and a solid state photo detector.

Electronic components include solid state modules for input-output and analog-to-digital conversion, self calibration, memory, and computation, and for control of a microcomputer for timing. A Leeds & Northrup digital printer is provided for logging data on paper tape.

The sampling system includes an input filter, pressure regulator, pumps, and appropriate gauges for debubbling, sample circulation, and system drain.

Both systems—the analyzer and the on-line monitor—use the same measurement principle. The analyzer can be used to complement the monitor for quality control, process development, or research applications.

Data reported includes average diameters, surface areas, volumes, and standard deviations for area and volume.

Descriptive literature is available from Leeds & Northrup Co., North Wales, Pa. 19454. □

'Microtrac' particle size analyzer

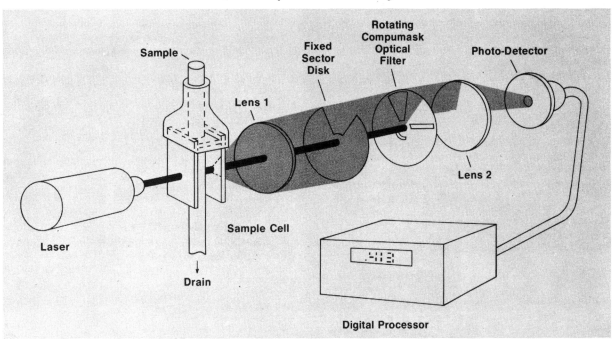

The **Drager BG-174A self-contained breathing apparatus** is distributed in the US by National Mine Service Co. Known world-wide for its use in fire fighting and mine rescue, this compressed oxygen SCBA was the first to receive a 4-hr MESA approval.

A fresh look at industrial respirators— new laws, new equipment, old problems

Richard A. Thomas, Assistant editor

THE CONCEPT OF PERSONAL RESPIRATORY PROTECTION has been understood since the time of Roman miners, who covered their mouths and noses with swatches of wet cloth. However, the concept has gained special attention only in recent years, as a result of numerous Federal acts and agencies focused on creating safe environments for workers in the mining and processing industries. Non-emergency respirators are being used to perform various functions in the industries that mine coal, lead, limestone, gypsum, asbestos, silica, mercury, and uranium; in the processing of chromates, chlorides, lead, and zinc; in blasting dust applications; and wherever acid fumes or mists pose hazards to the health of personnel. Emergency respirators are now a part of every US underground miner's personal protection equipment, and all mine rescue units incorporate some type of self-contained breathing apparatus (SCBA).

The term "respirator" has expanded in scope over the years. Initially restricted to filter-type devices that remove gases or particulates from the air, the term now includes SCBAs, air-line equipment, and other supplied-air devices. A respirator is now defined legally as "any device designed to provide the wearer with respiratory protection against inhalation of a hazardous atmosphere."

Knee-deep in Federal agencies

In making an attempt to understand the laws governing

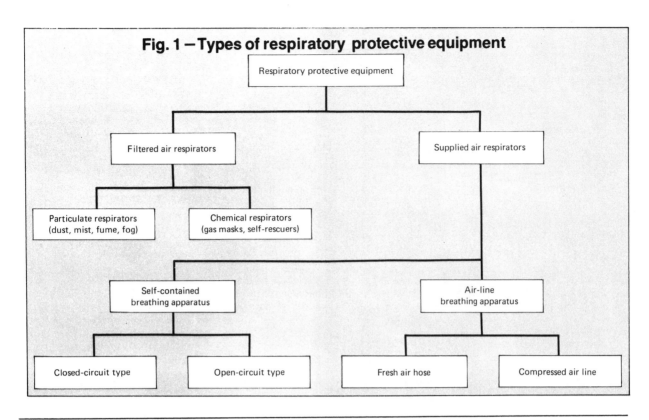

Fig. 1 — Types of respiratory protective equipment

Respiratory protective equipment
- Filtered air respirators
  - Particulate respirators (dust, mist, fume, fog)
  - Chemical respirators (gas masks, self-rescuers)
  - Self-contained breathing apparatus
    - Closed-circuit type
    - Open-circuit type
- Supplied air respirators
  - Air-line breathing apparatus
    - Fresh air hose
    - Compressed air line

Table 1 — Guide for selection of respirators

Hazard	Respirator
Oxygen deficiency	Self-contained breathing apparatus. Hose mask with blower. Combination air-line respirator with auxiliary self-contained air supply or an air-storage receiver with alarm.
Gas and vapor contaminants Immediately dangerous to life or health.	Self-contained breathing apparatus. Hose mask with blower. Air-purifying, full facepiece respirator with chemical canister (gas mask). Self-rescue mouthpiece respirator (for escape only). Combination air-line respirator with auxiliary self-contained air supply or an air-storage receiver with alarm.
Not immediately dangerous to life or health.	Air-line respirator. Hose mask without blower. Air-purifying, half-mask or mouthpiece respirator with chemical cartridge.
Particulate contaminants Immediately dangerous to life or health	Self-contained breathing apparatus. Hose mask with blower. Air-purifying, full facepiece respirator with appropriate filter. Self-rescue mouthpiece respirator (for escape only). Combination air-line respirator with auxiliary self-contained air supply or an air-storage receiver with alarm.
Not immediately dangerous to life or health.	Air-purifying, half-mask or mouthpiece respirator with filter pad or cartridge. Air-line respirator. Air-line abrasive-blasting respirator. Hose mask without blower.
Combination gas, vapor, and particulate contaminants Immediately dangerous to life or health.	Self-contained breathing apparatus. Hose mask with blower. Air-purifying, full facepiece respirator with chemical canister and appropriate filter (gas mask with filter). Self-rescue mouthpiece respirator (for escape only). Combination air-line respirator with auxiliary self-contained air supply or an air-storage receiver with alarm.
Not immediately dangerous to life or health.	Air-line respirator. Hose mask without blower. Air-purifying, half-mask or mouthpiece respirator with chemical cartridge and appropriate filter.

Source: ANSI Z88.2-1969.

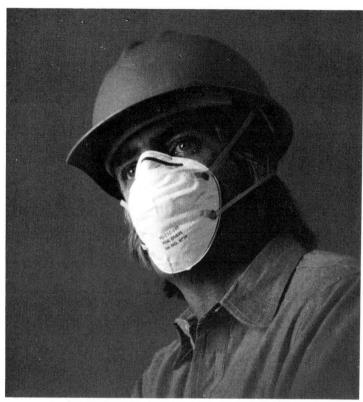

The Model 8710 respirator, made by 3M Co., is disposable and MESA/NIOSH approved. It is reportedly 99% effective against particles having a mean diameter of 0.4-0.6 microns.

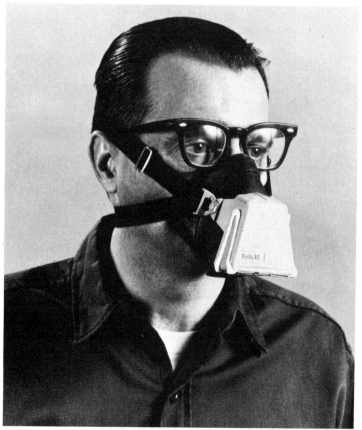

The new "Dustfoe 88" respirator from Mine Safety Appliances features a streamlined filter holder, lots of room for eyewear, and an inturned lip construction that adjusts to facial contours.

the use of respirators, the uninitiated may find themselves struggling in a bog of acronyms. MNMSAC, NFPA, AIHA, ANSI, NIOSH, USBM, MESA, and OSHA* all have their fingers in the pie somewhere. Furthermore, the shift of responsibility from USBM to MESA and the 1974 Memorandum of Understanding between OSHA and MESA have made keeping abreast of up-to-date standards a study in itself. For example, although Federal laws dictate the use of MESA-approved respirators, there is no list of equipment that is "MESA-approved." The relationship between MESA and NIOSH results in "NIOSH-certified" respirators that are, in fact, MESA-approved.

The agencies governing respirator usage take authority from three basic acts: the Federal Metal and Nonmetallic Mine Safety Act of 1966, the Federal Coal Mine Health and Safety Act of 1969, and the Occupational Safety and Health Act of 1970. The first two laws govern working conditions in mining and milling processes (including comminution, pelletizing/sintering/briquetting, calcining, and retorting), while the third act dictates all other industry-related working conditions (including smelting, refining, and electrowinning).

The crux of Federal regulations pertaining to respirator usage in the mining industry is found in Title 30—Mineral Resources. (Title 29 defines OSHA's role.) Part 11 of the title establishes and consolidates testing fees, approval procedures, and performance requirements for respirators, and is essentially a guide for manufacturers of respiratory protection equipment. Parts 55, 56, and 57, promulgated in accordance with the Metal and Nonmetallic Safety Act, contain standards for respirator usage in open pits, sand/gravel/crushed stone operations, and underground mines, respectively. Parts 70, 71, 75, and 77, promulgated in accordance with the Coal Mine Safety Act, establish similar standards for respirator usage in the coal industry.

Standards 55.5-5, 56.5-5, and 57.5-5 all contain the following passages:

Mandatory. Control of employee exposure to harmful airborne contaminants shall be [accomplished], insofar as feasible, by prevention of contamination, removal by exhaust ventilation, or by dilution with uncontaminated air. However, where accepted engineering control measures have not been developed or when necessary by the nature of work involved . . . employees may work for reasonable periods of time in concentrations of airborne contaminants exceeding permissible levels if they are protected by appropriate respiratory protective equipment. Whenever respiratory protective equipment is used, a program for selection, maintenance, training, fitting, supervision, cleaning, and use shall meet the following minimum requirements:

(a) [MESA] approved respirators which are applicable and suitable for the purpose intended shall be furnished, and employees shall use the protective equipment in accordance with training and instruction. [List is available from Office of Technical Publications, NIOSH, Post Office Bldg., Cincinnati, Ohio 45202.]

(b) A respirator program consistent with the requirements of ANSI Z88.2-1969 . . . entitled American National Standards Practices for Respiratory Protection . . . is hereby incorporated by reference and made a part hereof. [Z88.2 is available from ANSI Inc., 1430 Broadway, New York, N.Y. 10018.]

(c) When respiratory protection is used in atmospheres immediately harmful to life, the presence of at least one other person with backup equipment and rescue capability shall be required in the event of failure of the respiratory equipment.

*Metal and Nonmetal Mine Safety Advisory Committee, National Fire Protection Association, American Industrial Hygiene Association, American National Standards Institute, National Institute of Occupational Safety and Health, US Bureau of Mines, Mining Enforcement and Safety Administration, and Occupational Safety and Health Administration.

This respirator hood, made by US Safety Services, is intended for use where there is a combined hazard of contaminated atmosphere and harmful liquids or solids that may contact the skin.

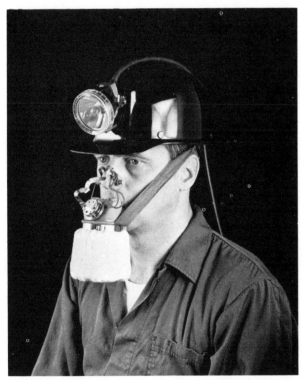

MSA's W65 self-rescuer is one of only two such devices approved for use in the US. The unit weighs 2.2 lb, is normally carried on the hip, and exceeds MESA service life requirements.

Situations where respirators are acceptable include: performance of routine operations while engineering controls are being instituted, evaluated, or repaired ("transient and interim conditions"); operations where controls have been instituted but contaminants are still above legal standards; non-routine operations that occur so infrequently that the application of engineering controls is highly impractical; and emergencies.

In addition to the above regulations, standards 57.15-30 and 57.15-31 were promulgated in September 1974, to apply only to underground mines:

57.15-30 *Mandatory.* A 1-hr self-rescue device approved by [MESA] shall be made available by the operator to all personnel underground. Each operator shall maintain self-rescue devices in good condition.

57.15-31 *Mandatory.* (a) Except as provided in paragraph (b) and (c) of this section, self-rescue devices meeting the requirements of 57.15-30 shall be worn or carried by all persons underground.

(b) Where the wearing or carrying of self-rescue devices . . . is hazardous to a person, such self-rescue devices shall be located at a distance no greater than 25 ft from such person.

(c) When a person works on or around mobile equipment, self-rescue devices may be placed in a readily accessible location on such equipment.

A number of suggested standards, under consideration by MNMSAC since January 1975, would also require respiratory protection against radon daughters [^{218}Po(RaA), ^{214}Po(RaC'), ^{214}Bi(RaC), ^{214}Pb(RaB)] in environments exceeding 1.0 WL, and protection against radon gas itself in accordance with certain daughter measurements. Sources in the American Mining Congress say these suggested standards were still under consideration as of December 1975, but have not yet reached the level of proposals.

The cost of compliance

The "feasibility" concept as used in the pertinent standards requires engineering controls for the elimination of hazardous atmospheres where *technically* feasible. Walter E. Ruch, program director of NIOSH, notes that the requirements are not based on economic feasibility. "This implies that the employer must be able to prove that he is using respiratory protection because technical knowledge for the application of engineering controls does not exist," Ruch says.

Where respirator use is permissible, initial costs vary widely with the application—4-hr breathing devices can cost as much as $1,500-1,700, while filter-type respirators approved for dusty atmospheres can be obtained for $7.00 or less. (Completely disposable respirators are considerably less expensive.) Maintenance costs vary with application and frequency of use; the average per-person cost of a respirator program complying with Z88.2 could not be obtained for this article.

Cost of compliance with the self-rescuer law is easier to estimate. Complete self-rescue devices are priced around $40-50 per unit—representing a considerable increase over the last few years. These units are "one-shot deals," and theoretically require no maintenance.

Respirators for any atmosphere

A comprehensive examination of all the different generic types of respirators is far beyond the scope of this article—or any single book, for that matter. Technology has diversified respiratory equipment to the point where protection against almost any atmosphere is possible for almost any period of time. The major generic difference in equipment is between filtered air (or air purifying) respirators and supplied air respirators. Filtered air respirators remove particulates, gases, or both from inspired (inhaled) air; supplied air respirators, which are less common, provide the user with an uncontaminated atmosphere that is completely independent of input from the surrounding environment.

A general breakdown of respirator generic types is illustrated in Fig. 1. This breakdown is fairly limited. It does not account for respirators that provide protection in multiple-hazard environments (e.g., gas-particulate units like self-rescuers); it does not include respirators that have combined operation modes (e.g., supplied air/filtered air units); and it does not account for further subdivisions (e.g., continuous-flow vs. demand-type, half-facepiece vs. full-facepiece). By comparison, NIOSH divides respirators into the following categories: chemical cartridge respirators, dust/fume/mist respirators, "supplied air respirators" (air-line), "gas masks" (self-rescuers), and SCBAs.

The respirator type for a given task should be selected in accordance with ANSI Z88.2. General considerations include the nature and extent of the hazard, working requirements and conditions, and characteristics and limitations of available respirators. Table 1, reproduced from Z88.2, is "a quick reference guide for the selection of respiratory protection appropriate to the type and degree of hazard. [This list] provides minimal guidance, however, and shall be used along with other information such as that given in [Z88.2] and in directions provided by respirator manufacturers," ANSI says. Once the equipment type is ascertained, selection may be made from the MESA/NIOSH-approved list.

There are fewer than 20 manufacturers of approved respirators (Table 2), and many of them are primarily geared to supplying the needs of the chemical and aviation industries. Of the companies responding to E/MJ inquiries, Mine Safety Appliances offers by far the largest line of respirators for the mining and ore processing industries. MSA's line includes numerous particle- and gas-filtering respirators; a full line of industrial gas masks; air-line devices with and without demand-flow valving; the famous "McCaa" oxygen rebreathing apparatus; and several specialized protection systems, such as the "Blastfoe" abrasive helmet, the "Leadfoe" hood, the "Welder's Adapter," pesticide respirators, and even a rocket propellant mask.

National Mine Service Co. supplies two important devices to the mining industry: the Drager BG-174A rescue unit and the FSR-810 self-rescuer. Both are products of Dragerwerk AG, of Lubeck, Germany.

Other respondents included the 3M Co., which offers both filter-type and supplied-air respirators, and American Optical Corp., which carries filter-type units with cartridges for chemicals or dust.

As for unapproved respirators, the AIHA notes that the reason for lack of approval is not always readily apparent. Lack of approval may be explained by a lack of suitable standards (for more esoteric devices and hazards), by failure of a device to meet the approval standards, or by failure to submit the device for approval. If a qualified individual selects an unapproved device for a particular situation, the device can be used safely under certain circumstances, AIHA says. Unapproved respirators usually fall into one of two main groups: "nuisance dust" respirators and respirators for special materials significantly more toxic than lead.

The two most common types of respirators in mining and processing are particulate-filtering devices (mainly dust respirators) and carbon monoxide-blocking self-rescuers. Particulate respirators usually have packaged or cartridged throw-away filters made of felt, paper, or other fibrous materials, and numerous chemical sorbents. The majority of such respirators are highly efficient. The AIHA reports that in a test performed on 100 commercially available respirator filters, 95% of the filters exhibited efficiencies in excess of 99.97% (Fig. 2).

The self-rescuers that all underground mine personnel must carry are compact 2- to 3-lb emergency devices usually mounted on a waist belt. Their primary function is to protect users from hazardous concentrations of carbon

Table 2—Manufacturers and distributors of approved respirators

American Optical Corp., Safety Products Div., 100 Cannal St., Putnam, Conn. 06260.

BioMarine Industries Inc., 303 W. Lancaster Ave., Devon, Pa. 19333.

Cesco Safety Products, Parmalee Industries Inc., PO Box 1237, Kansas City, Mo. 64141.

DeVilbiss Corp., Toledo, Ohio 43601.

Drägerwerk AG, D-24 Luebeck 1, Postfach 1339, Germany.

Globe Safety Products Inc., 125 Sunrise Place, Dayton, Ohio 45407.

Lear Siegler Inc., 714 North Brookhurst St., Anaheim, Calif. 92803.

Lockheed Missiles & Space Co., 1111 Lockheed Way, Sunnyvale, Calif. 94088.

Mine Safety Appliances Co., 201 N. Braddock Ave., Pittsburgh, Pa. 15208.

Safeline Products, PO Box 550, Putnam, Conn. 06260.

Scott Aviation, Division of ATO Inc., Lancaster, N.Y. 14086.

Siebe Gorman Ltd., Chessington Surrey, England.

SurvivAir, Division of US Divers Co., 3323 W. Warner Ave., Santa Ana, Calif. 92702.

3M Co., 3M Center, St. Paul, Minn. 55101.

United States Safety Service, Parmalee Industries Inc., PO Box 1237, Kansas City, Mo. 64141.

Welsh Manufacturing Co., 9 Magnolia Street, Providence, R.I. 02909.

Willson Products Div., ESB Inc., PO Box 622, Reading, Pa. 19603.

Fig. 2—Efficiency of respirator filter cartridges

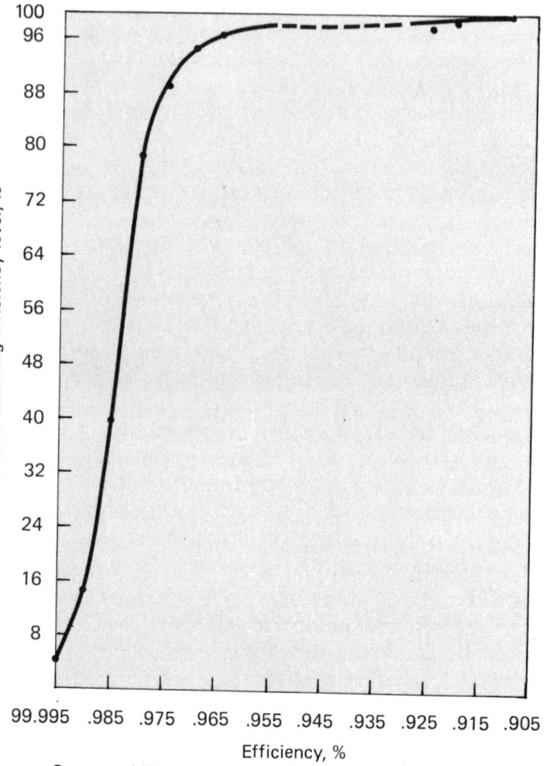

Source: AIHA

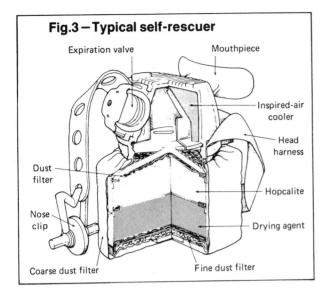

Fig. 3 — Typical self-rescuer

- Expiration valve
- Mouthpiece
- Inspired-air cooler
- Head harness
- Dust filter
- Hopcalite
- Nose clip
- Drying agent
- Coarse dust filter
- Fine dust filter

monoxide (CO) gas that sometimes result from underground fires or explosions. However, they also contain particulate filters that eliminate the dust often associated with these emergency conditions.

Self-rescuers contain a catalyst ("Hopcalite") that converts CO, which is toxic in 0.5% concentrations, into CO_2, a nontoxic respiration exchange gas. During an emergency, a user must breathe through a mouthpiece inserted past the teeth, and integral clips must be employed to block the inspiration of CO through the nose (Fig. 3).

At present, the only two self-rescuers approved for use in the US are the Drager Model 810 and the MSA Model W-65.

It's not all easy breathing

Although many respirators are readily available for protection against a wide spectrum of hazards, respirator use is unfortunately not a simple matter of selecting the appropriate generic type at the right price and then training personnel in proper use. Problems such as correct fitting, impediments to communication and vision, temperature extremes, maintenance, bulkiness, and personnel acceptance demand serious consideration, since any of these factors can result in failure of a respiratory program and/or possible exposure to hazardous conditions.

A properly fitted facepiece is probably the most important factor in respiratory protection, since the point at which most respirators are likely to fail is the seal between the facepiece and the user's face. Failure at the seal is most common in filtering devices because substantially all of them operate under a negative pressure in the facepiece; by contrast, supplied air respirators often have positive pressure in the facepiece. ANSI lists various types of respirators according to the increasing amount of inward leakage to be expected during routine use. (See Table 3.)

Impediments to a good face-to-mask seal include facial hair, eyeglasses, denture problems, widely varying racial characteristics, and skin irregularities. An additional problem here can be inhalation resistance, as devices with higher inhalation resistance will magnify any leakage that stems from poor fit. (This is not to say that low-resistance devices are necessarily better. Very low inhalation resistance probably indicates some form of malfunction.)

Impediments to vision and communication can sometimes be difficult to surmount. Full-face masks restrict peripheral vision in varying degrees and preclude the use of normal eyeglasses; half masks reduce these problems somewhat. Where frequent verbal communication is necessary for job performance, most respirators are not satisfactory. Respirators with "speaking diaphragms" are available to assist speech intelligibility.

Personnel acceptance of respirators is, surprisingly, a noticeable problem in numerous plants where protection is required. Personnel acceptance is essentially a reflection of the degree of comfort afforded by a device and the degree of interference with normal job functions. Too often a worker can be seen performing some function that requires the use of a dust respirator while the respirator is resting at the back of his neck or on a ledge beside him. Such problems are bound to occur when workers have been at their tasks for 20 years or more without the respirator, as they will resist change.

Personnel confidence in respirators also plays a role in overall acceptance. With certain demand-flow units, there is a perceivable time lag between inhalation, which creates negative facepiece pressure, and valve actuation, which reestablishes pressure balance and supplies air. Such units can be slightly disconcerting at first, and until the wearer gains confidence in the device, he tends to continually reassure himself that the air supply is in fact "there" at his every breath.

Although high or low temperature extremes are not a frequent occurrence in respirator operation, they can cause difficulties. The major problems created by low temperatures are fogging of full-face masks (correctible with antifog agents) and freezing of exhalation valves (deterred by using dry respirable air). The one instance where high temperatures are commonly encountered in respirators is in the use of self-rescuers. Self-rescuer catalysts are exothermic in their conversion of CO to CO_2, and temperature of the inspired air rises in proportion to the amount of CO being converted. Where CO concentrations are in the 1% to 2% range (as is possible in smoldering fires), the inspired air temperature can be in the neighborhood of 150°F, even with proper functioning of the integral heat exchangers on each device.

After the disastrous Sunshine mine fire of May 1972, the testimonies of miners and engineers bore out the difficulties with self-rescuers. One miner said he had to keep removing the mouthpiece because "it burned like a piece of dry ice in my mouth." A spokesman for the manufacturer of the self-rescuers used during the fire said that when breathing hot air, there is a tendency to cough, and a person might think that smoke is being inhaled. "Yes, it's hot," he said, "but the alternative is quick death."

Trends in research and laws

Apparently the bulk of research dollars in the field of respiratory protection is going toward improvements and modifications of self-rescuers. Research in self-rescuer design is being conducted by MSA, Lockheed, USBM, Dragerwerk, and other organizations, based on the need to protect workers against additional gases and the need to lower heat production of the devices. With the new and varied materials being used in mine construction, engineers now realize that protection against CO alone is not sufficient. Numerous other possibly hazardous gases can result from mine emergencies.

The focus of continuing research is the elimination of filter devices for emergency situations and the employment of small O_2-generating SCBAs. According to industry spokesmen, two avenues of attack are being explored: 1-hr SCBAs that are fully as portable as current self-rescuers, and 10-min SCBAs that will enable a worker to get

Table 3—Respirators ranked by degree of inward leakage

1) Supplied-air suit (least leakage).
2) Pressure-demand full facepiece open-circuit and air-line devices.
3) Pressure-type full facepiece closed-circuit self-contained breathing apparatus.
4) Continuous-flow full facepiece air-line respirator.
5) Air-line respirator with loose-fitting hood gathered around the waist.
6) Hose-mask with blower and full facepiece mask.
7) Demand-type full facepiece open-circuit self-contained breathing apparatus.
8) Demand-type full facepiece air-line respirator.
9) Pressure-demand half-mask air-line respirator.
10) Continuous-flow half-mask air-line respirator.
11) Demand-type half-mask air-line respirator.
12) Air-line respirator with loose-fitting hood gathered around the neck.
13) Air-purifying respirator with blower and with full facepiece or hood gathered around the waist.
14) Air-purifying respirator with blower and with half-mask facepiece or hood gathered around the neck.
15) Hose mask without blower.
16) Air-purifying full facepiece respirator without blower.
17) Air-purifying half-mask respirator without blower.
18) Mouthpiece respirator (most leakage).

Source: ANSI Z88.2-1969.

---

safely to a 1-hr unit. The 1-hr SCBA concept is being explored by Lockheed and Dragerwerk, and one Lockheed design has already been approved. The 10-min unit is MSA's development. Although approval has been granted, the device is not by itself a sufficient self-rescue system under the law. It must be backed up by longer term devices in close proximity to a miner's work area. The USBM has provided funds for several of these private company research endeavors.

Other ongoing research includes the exploration of unconventional personal breathing protection mechanisms, such as the helmet-mounted "air curtain" of Donaldson Co. Inc.; extension of the operation time for the larger SCBAs (the Drager BG-17A and the Scott Aviation "Rescue Pak" now have 4-hr approvals); development of respirators in combination with other body protection devices, such as acid suits and abrasion helmets; and closer inspection of respirator technology as it applies to nucleonics (Dragerwerk is involved in this phase of research).

On the legal side, the trend is toward increased restriction of the quantities of hazardous respirable substances to which personnel may be exposed. Numerous Threshold Limit Values (TLV) are decreasing or threatening to do so; these changes will not only cost industry more "compliance dollars" but will in some cases require industry to go hunting for new compliance techniques. Such temporary lapses in ventilation technology could easily call more respirators into play on an interim basis.

Examples of the trend toward tighter standards include the curbs on respirable asbestos slated for July 1976; MESA's new suggested standards for protection against radon and its daughters; the recent NIOSH criteria document suggesting a 50% reduction in the free silica TLV; and OSHA's new proposals to reduce both the sulphur dioxide and ammonia TLVs

With constantly dropping TLVs, respirators must continue to become more efficient if they are to maintain proportional safe limits for workers. Happily, the numerous advertisements surfacing monthly for "new and improved" protection devices support the belief that increases in efficiency and other improvements are well within the growing technological scope of the respirator industry. □

References

1) "Practices for Respiratory Protection," ANSI Z88.2-1969, American National Standards Institute Inc.
2) "NIOSH Certified Personal Protective Equipment," US Department of Health, Education and Welfare, Publication No. 75-119, July 1974 (plus cumulative supplement to January 1975).
3) *Respiratory Protective Devices Manual*, American Industrial Hygiene Association and American Conference of Governmental Industrial Hygienists, 1963.
4) Ruch, Walter E., and Bruce J. Held, *Respiratory Protection—OSHA and the Small Businessman*, Ann Arbor Science Publishers Inc., 1975.
5) *Medicine in the Mining Industries*, John M. Rogan, ed., F. A. Davis Co., 1972.
6) "Metal and Nonmetal Mine Health and Safety Standards and Regulations," Mining Enforcement and Safety Administration, Stock No. 024-019-00010-5, October 1974.
7) "Government Reviews Sunshine Disaster," E/MJ, October 1972, pp 92-95.
8) "Threshold Limit Values for Chemical Substances and Physical Agents in the Workroom Environment," American Conference of Governmental Industrial Hygienists, 1973.
9) "Memorandum of Understanding Between MESA and OSHA," FEDERAL REGISTER, Vol. 39, No. 145, July 26, 1974.
10) "Safety Guide for Respiratory Protection against Radon Daughters," ANSI Z88.1-1969, American National Standards Institute Inc.
11) "Draft MESA Standards to Advisory Committee," American Mining Congress, Dec. 2, 1974.

This dual-element respirator, which may be used with 10 interchangeable filter cartridges, is available from American Optical Corp. The Model R6000 shown here is designed for large faces.

Sonic level monitors automate storage system at Pinto Valley

NON-CONTACT LEVEL MEASUREMENT instruments and fully automated tripper control systems are improving material conveyance and storage in the mining industry. Cities Service Co. recently installed two such systems in its new Pinto Valley ore handling facility near Miami, Ariz. Western Marine Electronics (Wesmar) in Seattle, Wash., provided the level measurement devices and designed a material handling control system for Pinto Valley.

The major component in the level measurement system is Wesmar's level monitor, which uses a non-contact sonar principle to measure the amount of air space between a sensor and the stored material. The time span required for bursts of sound to travel roundtrip between the sensor and the material is converted into a representative electrical signal, which is displayed on level indicators and used for the logic circuitry's control functions. The monitors can be used for nearly any material, Wesmar says. Cities Service is using them for copper ore and powdered lime.

Wesmar designed the level monitors and tripper systems to function in two material handling operations at the Pinto Valley installation: fine ore storage and tertiary surge storage. Each of the six tertiary bins is equipped with one ultrasonic sensor, while each fine ore bin has two sensors. Since each fine ore bin has two withdrawal points, averaging the outputs of two sensors in each bin provides a more accurate picture of the bin level.

The level monitor sensors are interrogated sequentially at a predetermined rate by a scanner-programmer. Level information acquired from each sensor is sent to the control system's logic circuitry, which programs the two belt-traveling tripper cars. In addition, the logic circuitry receives tripper position data from Wesmar magnetic proximity switches, and it directs the trippers to move forward, move in reverse, or stop to fill one of the bins. Switches at the main control panel also allow the operator to modify tripper movement.

The ore level of each bin is electronically compared with the average level. If the level of a particular bin is below the average, the tripper stops and fills the bin for a time proportional to the distance of the ore level below the average level. In this manner, the tripper control system maintains a uniform ore level above each of the withdrawal points in the bins.

The tripper ordinarily traverses the storage area and changes direction at each end. However, tripper direction can be reversed at any position by throwing either a lockout switch on the main control panel or an active high-level tilt switch at the next bin. When the tripper system is operating in the automatic mode and a malfunction occurs, a trouble signal will automatically activate a backup control system that causes the tripper to continually traverse bins one through six without stopping to fill them. (The lockout and tilt switches can still be utilized at this time.) Once the backup control is activated, it will function until the operator resets the system, thus preventing the system from switching back and forth between automatic and backup should an intermittent malfunction occur.

The tripper control system at Pinto Valley uses CMOS solid state logic circuitry because of its low power drain and good noise rejection. Such integrated circuits also save space and are more reliable than the relay logic circuits previously used, Wesmar says.

Wesmar suggests that potential applications of the level monitor and tripper control system in the mining industry are "boundless." Additional applications for the systems include elimination of bin overflow, starting or stopping a conveyor, prevention of plugged chutes and hoppers, and synchronization of material flow with other processing equipment.

For more information on these systems, write to: Level Monitor Div., Western Marine Electronics, 905 Dexter Ave. North, Seattle, Wash. 98109. □

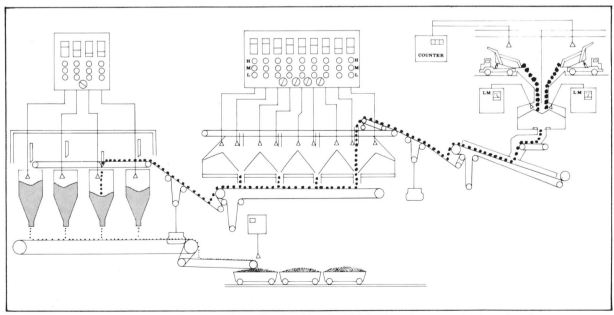

Level monitors are used in both fine ore storage bins and tertiary bins. An additional monitor counts trucks as they dump ore.

The burner head, shown open here, is only 9 m long.

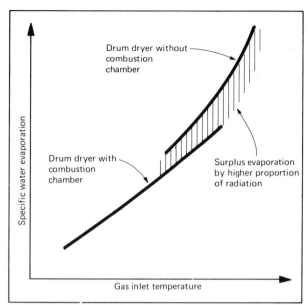

Specific water evaporation as function of gas inlet temperature.

Burner head dryer cuts costs, saves space

A NEW FURNACE GAS ROTARY DRYER with a rigorously simplified design has been showing its advantages for treating bulk material that is unaffected or minimally affected by heat. In a departure from conventional design for rotary dryers, the large, costly combustion chamber that confines gas flames has been replaced by a short burner head that allows flames to enter the drum compartment freely. The design change makes the entire unit shorter, hence cheaper. Refractory requirements have been minimized—the burner head, by comparison with the combustion chamber, needs hardly any brick lining. In addition, the higher proportion of radiation reaching the material pays off in higher specific water evaporation.

The dryer with burner head is manufactured by KHD Industrieanlagen AG Humboldt Wedag, which also makes combustion chamber dryers. The latter are being manufactured only for heat-sensitive materials where it is necessary to avoid local overheating caused by the greater intensity of the open flame, Humboldt says. The burner head dryer is now being used in the chemical industry, in cement factories, in parts of the nonmetallic ore dressing industry, and—increasingly—to dry iron ore concentrates in preparation for classification and pelletizing.

It's easy to see the difference in design between the earlier combustion chamber dryers and the burner head dryers. The combustion chamber usually occupies a quarter to a third of the length of the entire drum, whereas the burner head occupies only about one tenth of the total drum length.

Among other advantages of the new design, the foremost is increased drying ability. The above graph of specific water evaporation for both designs shows that at equivalent inlet temperatures, evaporation is substantially higher in the burner head dryer. The open flame imparts a higher proportion of radiation per unit of bulk material, intensifying and accelerating drying.

The burner head design is much less susceptible to material encrustations than the conventional design, Humboldt reports, even when the material is difficult to dry. The flow of heating gases through the drum is thus facil-

itated, and cleaning costs are reduced.

Humboldt also says several years of industrial use have proved that the open flame of the new design does not increase the wear rate over that of the combustion chamber dryer. In addition, drying can be started up more quickly with the burner head, and the dryer may be stopped in a shorter time without damage because of the lesser amount of brick used in the lining.

New design proves a success

Numerous examples illustrate industry's acceptance of the new design. In one Eastern European iron ore dressing plant, a burner head dryer has been processing 1- to 100-mm iron ore particles since 1969. The unit receives material containing up to 30% water and dries it to a residual moisture content below 10%. The drum compartment of the dryer is 22 m long and 3.4-m dia, with a throughput of 180 tph. Because the installation has proved so valuable, the company has chosen to use a second dryer of the same design, but with an even larger drum compartment.

The largest Humboldt burner head dryer now in operation is used in a Turkish cement factory to dry granulated blast furnace slag containing 35% water. The unit processes 85 tph of material using a 22-m-long, 4-m-dia drum compartment. Heating capacity is 28,500 kilocalories per hr.

In one German metallurgical plant, the new rotary unit dries approximately 23 tph of very fine zinc leaching residues containing 45% water to a residual moisture content of 15-18%. The unit is 20 m long and has a 2.6-m diameter. Similarly, an Italian ironworks has used the burner head dryer for several years to reduce water content of precipitated converter dusts from 25% to 8-10%. This unit measures 16 m x 2.2-m dia.

Humboldt reports that it will soon supply an Algerian cement factory with the largest burner head unit so far. The dryer will be 24 m long and 4.8-m dia, with a natural gas-generated heating capacity of 34,000 kilocalories per hr. The installation will dry 170 tph of calcareous marl containing up to 25% adherent moisture. □

'Hopper-Popper' cures frozen coal problem using air pressure

Three augers with pneumatic shells ride over holding tracks.

FROZEN, COMPACTED COAL in railroad hopper cars was a longstanding and expensive problem at US Steel Corp.'s Lorain-Cuyahoga steelmaking complex—until a new bulk breaking system was put into operation. The "Hopper-Popper" system, designed and manufactured by Long-Airdox Co., is significantly reducing the unloading time for frozen hopper cars and has substantially reduced the quantities of natural gases previously used in this operation.

Before the advent of the new system, it was time-consuming and costly to maintain a constant flow of coal from hopper cars to the coke oven charging bins. Moisture in hopper cars tends to freeze the contents, especially during the winter months, making cars impossible to empty. Coal in a car can become "like a giant ice cube," and the only way to break it loose was to heat the outside of the car or break up the contents by chipping.

Thawing required lots of gas

In a previous attempt to solve the freezing problem, gas lines carrying coke oven gas were laid between the hopper car holding tracks near the dumping area. When trains containing frozen coal were spotted on the tracks, the lines were ignited, and the burning gas was applied to the car bottoms to thaw the contents. Hand-held propane torches were required to apply additional heat to the sides of cars to break the frost bond between metal and coal.

Once the coal was thawed, the cars were pulled into a rotary dumper and emptied. Any chunks of coal too large to fit through the grating at the dumper bottom had to be broken by hand.

While this conventional thawing method was effective, it required nearly 4 million cu ft of oven gas and 7,000 cu ft of propane per day, and the time needed to thaw one car averaged about 4 hr. In periods of prolonged cold weather, the thawing time was extended, putting a strain on the coke production schedule. USS was thus required to assign four- to six-man crews to the torching operation, and costly railroad demurrage charges were incurred.

Search for a new system

In 1971, USS began to search for an automated, economical method of breaking up frozen coal in hopper cars. After exploring several possible solutions, USS officials selected a modified "Ladco" bulk breaker system, which operates by releasing high pressure air through pneumatic cartridges to break up compacted material along natural lines of cleavage.

The system was originally developed by Long-Airdox as a non-explosive method for mining coal in gassy mines. High pressure air tubes are placed into holes drilled in a mine face, and air is discharged at up to 10,000 psi, shattering the coal without using a chemical explosive.

The system was later adapted for breaking up compacted materials in storage bins and silos, using pneumatic shells permanently installed in bin sides. The Ladco installation at the Lorain-Cuyahoga Works in Ohio is a hybrid of these two systems. Nicknamed the "Hopper-Popper," it was designed to meet USS specifications and has been in operation since January 1975.

The Hopper-Popper consists of three 3⅛-in.-OD augers mounted on a rubber-wheeled frame, which sits atop a 75-ft-long runway straddling the holding tracks. Pneumatic shells are permanently mounted at the top of the augers, which have hollow stems (1⅝ in. ID) that permit high pressure air to be released into the holes created by the augers in the frozen coal.

Air is supplied by three 60-hp, six-stage compressors capable of developing up to 12,000 psi. The compressors are housed in a separate building 300 ft from the main unit.

Other components of the system, located between the compressors and the pneumatic cartridges, include: 1) a receiver unit for storing compressed air to avoid discharge delays, 2) steel, copper, and polyester tubing to move air from the receiver unit to the cartridges, and 3) valve hardware.

The Hopper-Popper trams hydraulically, and can move a distance of 50 ft along the runway—the length of one hopper car. By moving the device to various positions above a hopper car, frozen coal can be "shot" with compressed air any number of times at a single spotting. One person located in the control house at the end of the runway can operate the system without assistance. Pushbutton controls are used to tram the unit into position, drill into the coal, and fire cartridges at the desired pressure.

Frozen coal can be broken up in a hopper car within 6 to 8 min after the car has been spotted under the main unit, Long-Airdox says. This compares very favorably with the 4 hr needed for thawing. Although a small section of the gas line is still being used by USS to preheat cars before coal is broken up, the number of cubic feet of gas used in this process has been reduced by 80%. □

High efficiency motors cut energy costs and trim power factor penalties

A NEW LINE OF HIGH EFFICIENCY, high power factor electric motors designed to use substantially less electricity has been developed by the Century Electric Div. of Gould Inc. A typical industrial motor user (300-500 motors) could, after payback, save as much as $10,000 annually by switching to these motors, Gould claims, and payback for the higher initial cost of the units should take less than two years for all models. Available in 10 different models ranging from 1 to 25 hp, the motors are designed for a minimum power factor rating of 85%, and may allow the user to avoid paying a power factor penalty to the utility company.

Although the new motors have the same NEMA frame diameters as current Gould models, numerous modifications have been made to increase unit efficiency and power factor. Stator and rotor cores have been lengthened, the air gap has been reduced, winding material has been added to the rotor and stator, the slot configuration has been altered, and core steel with improved core loss properties has been added. Reduction of the air gap directly reduces the amount of current needed to magnetize the core, while the addition of copper and aluminum to the magnetic core reduces the flux density and core resistance, further reducing current requirements and increasing motor efficiency. Leakage resistance has also been minimized by optimizing the geometry of the stator and rotor slots, Gould reports.

Increased motor prices resulting from these modifications are more than justified by the energy saved in motor operation, according to Gould. For example, payback of the price premium for a 3-hp drip-proof motor of the new design is less than one year at an energy cost level of 2-3¢ per kwh and an in-service time of 4,000 hr annually. After payback, the same unit will save approxi-

mately $100 in the next 20,000 hr of operation, according to the manufacturer's calculations. Since higher-horsepower motors normally have higher efficiencies and better power factors initially, payback of the price premium will be proportionally slower at the same energy cost; however, even the 25-hp unit has a payback of less than two years at today's energy costs.

All of the new motors are four pole/three phase, available in both drip-proof and totally enclosed, fan-cooled designs. Besides the energy savings, a number of other benefits are claimed for the units. Magnetic noise is considerably reduced because of the lower magnetic density in the motor cores. The motors also run cooler (as much as 10°C cooler in some instances) because they have fewer current losses to dissipate. Cooler operation extends insulation life and allows use of smaller, quieter ventilation fans. In addition, sensitivity to line voltage variations is much reduced. Although voltage fluctuation itself does not have a large effect on motor efficiency, it can have a sizable effect on power factor.

Although it might be hoped that motors greater than 25 hp would be produced in the new design, Gould representatives note that 90% of all motors used in industry are in the 1- to 25-hp range, and high-hp motors already have fairly good efficiency and power factors. As for the future of the new models, H. S. Burker, director of marketing for Century Electric, says, "Skyrocketing electricity costs and possible future shortages virtually dictate evolution of high efficiency and high power factor motors. As energy costs continue to escalate in coming years, the value of energy-saving motors will be further reinforced."

For more information about high efficiency motors, write to Ray Jokerst, Gould Inc., Century Electric Div., 1831 Chestnut St., St. Louis, Mo. 63166. □

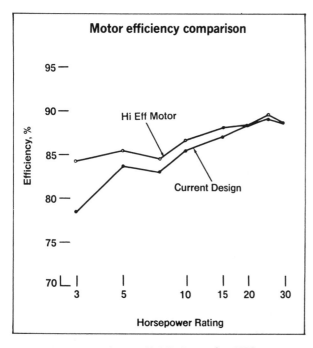

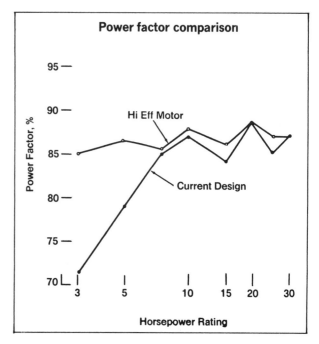

Space-saving controls get alumina plant out of tight squeeze

THE 1971 EXPANSION of Reynolds Metals Co.'s alumina plant in Gregory, Tex., posed an interesting puzzle in space economy. The addition of four new evaporation units to the plant's spent-liquor concentration system caused a problem in the use of control room space: the addition of four control cabinets to a room that could not handle them comfortably. Instead of opting for a costly expansion of floor space, Reynolds engineers elected to install the space-saving "ac²" analog control systems manufactured by Fisher Controls Co.

Basic to liquor recovery in the plant's spent-liquor concentration system are two kinds of multistage evaporators: multi-effect evaporators, in which steam is used to effect water removal from the liquor, and salting-out process (SOP) evaporators, in which spent liquor is concentrated to the point of precipitating out undesirable products picked up by the values-containing solution during earlier stages in the process.

In 1971, construction began on two new caustic evaporators and two new SOP units. Engineering plans called for analog control functions for each new unit. The control room had been designed for each existing evaporator to be supplied with its own control cabinet, which brought together all input and output signals, analog controllers, and recorders.

The original control room layout contained seven control cabinets, each 94 in. wide, for the caustic evaporators, and three more cabinets for the SOP units, each 56 in. wide (see diagram). It was immediately apparent to the engineers that incorporating four new control cabinets would necessitate either lengthening the room or closing off the door at one end and rearranging some existing panels to generate more wall space.

Neither solution was appealing. Lengthening the building would take up roadway space and involve considerable expense, and closing off a door was considered unsafe. There was only one other alternative: If the building didn't fit the equipment, then the equipment would have to fit the building.

Reynolds engineers investigated various analog control systems on the market to find one that would handle all the necessary functions in the limited space available. Several systems were checked out at the Instruments and Controls Evaluation Laboratory of Reynolds' Lister Hill plant in Alabama. The lab finally recommended Fisher Controls' ac² system as the best space-saving dollar value. The system was ordered in January 1971, delivered in July, and went into operation a few months later.

Each of the Fisher control cabinets is 24 in. wide. Four of them take up 8 ft—close to the amount of room required by the operator's desk. In the caustic evaporator cabinets, five control panels are stacked vertically to handle all functions. In the top panel are 10 ac² modules that indicate levels in five process stages, pressures in stages 2 through 5, and pressure in the barometric condenser. In the next row down are controllers for steam feed pressure and flow, total feed, and flow of intermediate levels.

In the third panel from the top are six recorders fed with square root signals for stream flow, total feed, and flows for three intermediate stages. The fourth panel is a row of linear signal recorders that handle header stream pressure, chest pressure, fourth stage density, output density, and

Four compact ac² control cabinets now occupy the space that was formerly reserved for an operator's desk.

conductivity of recovered condensate. On the lowest level is a multipoint temperature recorder.

The SOP cabinets are arranged in a fashion similar to that of the caustic evaporators but are only two-stage units. The control panels housing the caustic evaporator ac² modules were designed to hold 12 modules in all, thus leaving room for two additional modules in the top panel and five in the next lower panel if more controllers become desirable. The top panels of the SOP cabinets are currently unused.

Reynolds engineers are very pleased with the ac² systems—they do everything the old systems did, and they do it in a lot less space. ☐

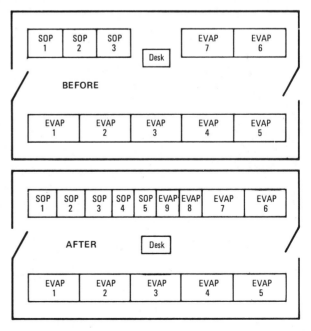

MOD III—a major new advance in control technology for the process industries

A NEW PROCESS CONTROL/DATA DISPLAY SYSTEM, billed as "a years-ahead breakthrough in control technology for the process industries," has been developed by the Taylor Instrument Process Control Div. of Sybron Corp. The "MOD III" system consists of an operator's command console and a control rack connected by a bus (a single plug-in, multiconductor cable). It "condenses 1,000 ft of conventional control board into 10 ft," according to Taylor. One operator using MOD III can acquire process information from and manipulate signals to more than 500 control loops.

Besides the total centralization of information displays, alarms, and controls, several other features of the MOD III set it apart from other process control systems. The user has a choice of dedicated analog or time-shared digital control on a loop-by-loop basis, and single-loop integrity is assured. MOD III is designed to interface simply and effectively with the Taylor 1010 computer but will also accept I/O from other computers.

The operator's command console is a marvel of "Star-Trek" type technology; it includes:

■ A status display CRT (cathode ray tube) that can alphanumerically show the status and alarm condition, plus analog deviation indication, of up to 30 loops simultaneously. Thirty "pages" of 30 loops each may be accessed using the page selector keyboard.

■ A loop display CRT that shows alphanumeric data and graphic trend lines for individual loops (up to three at a time). The keyboard directly below this CRT allows the operator to manipulate loops individually.

■ A digital controller panel with a format keyboard to set up display data and a system memory tape transport with a process variable tape recorder.

■ An optional Taylor "Colorgraphics" display terminal—a computer-driven, full-color CRT that shows a process flow diagram of the instrumentation systems and loops under control.

The system control rack contains all the individual modules that communicate with a particular loop or function, such as analog and digital controllers that include auto/manual station, switch I/O, and other functions. The rack also houses the electronic equipment needed to send and receive data throughout the system.

Other equipment is available as extensions of the console, including a hard-copy recorder, remote monitors, and uninterruptible power supplies. The cost of the basic system is in the neighborhood of $80,000-100,000, and it reportedly begins to become economical when 50 or more process loops are involved.

One major international chemical company is already using the MOD III for a 50-loop process, and "reports exceed our highest level of expectations," Taylor spokesmen say. As for maintenance, one Taylor representative explains that there is relatively little data available: "The system simply hasn't failed enough."

For more information on MOD III, write to Taylor Instruments, Sybron Corp., 95 Ames St., Rochester, N.Y. 14601. □

An operator seated at the MOD III console has immediate access to process information, displayed alphanumerically and graphically, for as many as 512 control loops. Thirty loops may be scanned at a glance to spot deviations from setpoints.

Nomograph simplifies valley angle calculation

A "VALLEY ANGLE"—formed by the intersection of two side walls of a storage bin, hopper, or chute—must be greater than the angle of repose of the material in the receptacle or the material won't flow. The valley angle is always less than either wall angle, and may be calculated mathematically using the following equation:

$$\cot^2 V = \cot^2\alpha + \cot^2\beta$$

where V is the valley angle and α and β are the side angles, all measured in degrees.

A new nomograph created by F. Caplan, a professional engineer from Oakland, Calif., permits rapid solution of the equation and eliminates the need to refer to trigonometric tables. Example: What is V if α and β are 63° and 70°, respectively? Align 63 on the left scale with 70 on the right scale and read $V = 58°$ on the middle scale. □

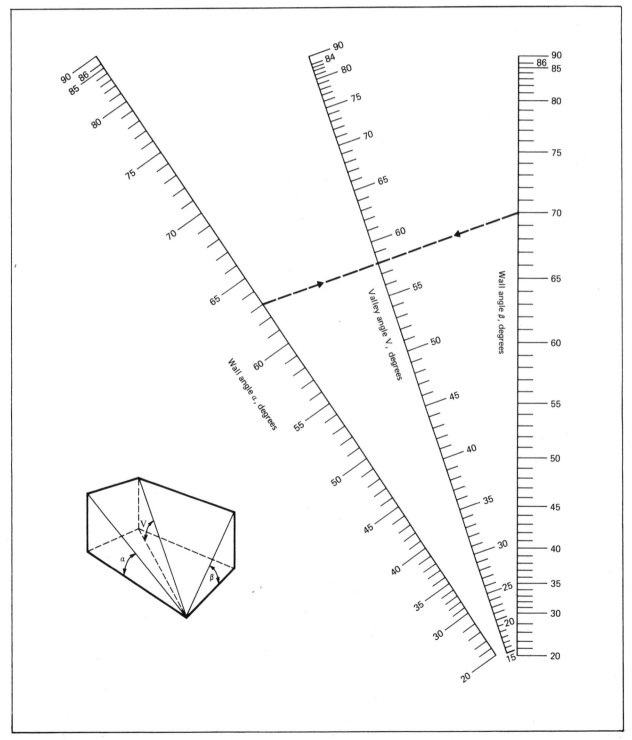

Nomograph simplifies power factor evaluation

WHEN A LARGE ELECTRIC MOTOR is to be added to a system that already has a low power factor, it may be desirable to select a synchronous motor or an induction motor, or to install capacitors. By using the power factor improvement nomogram developed by electrical engineer Glenn Stangland, of St. Petersburg, Fla., it is possible to predict what the final power factor will be after installation, or to determine what the power factor rating of the added motor should be in order to adjust the final power factor to a desired value.

Today's energy problems and the penalty clauses for poor power factor require that plant engineers consider carefully the impact of adding power capacity. The Stangland nomogram provides a simpler method for evaluating power factors than the reactive kva method or the complex number method.

For each load (original and added) two of the following four variables must be known: kilowatts (kw), kilovolt-amperes (kva), reactive kilovolt-amperes (kvar), and power factor (PF). Any two variables will establish a single point on the chart, from which the other two variables may also be read.

What will be the new power factor of your plant when you add another motor? Here's how to use the nomogram to find out:

Example 1

Assume that a plant carries 790 kw at 1,000 kva. In the Plant Quadrant of the nomogram, mark point A where a vertical line from 7.9 on the Original Load kw scale intersects 10 on the Load kva circle. The synchronous motor to be added is rated 0.8 PF and 250 kw. In the Synchronous Motor Quadrant, mark point B where a vertical line from 2.5 on the Added Load kw scale intersects the 0.8 PF radial line.

To find the final power factor of the plant, draw the dashed line from A to B; then draw another line through the bullseye, parallel to A-B. Where this line intersects the perimeter, read the final PF—in this case, it is 0.92 lagging in the Plant Quadrant.

How can you determine what the power factor of the added load must be in order to raise the total plant PF to a desired value? Like this:

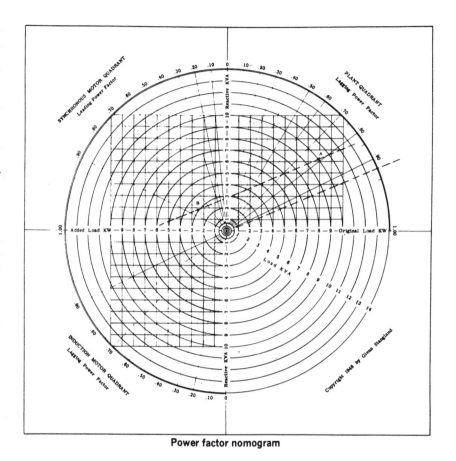

Power factor nomogram

Example 2

Assume that a plant carries the same 790 kw at 1,000 kva. Establish point A in the Plant Quadrant using the same procedure as before. The final desired power factor of the plant is to be 0.92. In the Plant Quadrant, draw a line through the bullseye intersecting the perimeter at 0.92 PF.

To find the necessary PF of a 250-kw synchronous motor, draw a line parallel to the first line through point A. Mark point B where this line intersects a vertical line from 2.5 on the Added Load kw scale in the Synchronous Motor Quadrant. Then draw a radial line through point B.

Where the radial line intersects the perimeter, read 0.8 PF leading as the required power factor rating of the new motor.

Note that each point established on the chart has four values. For point A, the kw is 7.9 (790), the kva is 10 (1,000), the kvar is 6.15 (615), and a radial line through A indicates a PF of 0.79 (lagging). Likewise, for point B, the kw is 2.5 (250), the kva is 3.1 (310),

the kvar is 1.9 (190), and a radial line through B indicates a PF of 0.8 (leading).

A few short rules will guide the use of the nomogram in determining values for other loads:

- When the added load has a lagging power factor, work in the Induction Motor Quadrant.
- When the added load is a capacitor, work along the upper Reactive kva scale.
- When the added load is pure resistance, work along the left-hand kw scale.

Stangland's nomogram is not a new idea—having been copyrighted in 1948—but energy consciousness is making many old ideas timely today. □

To order E/MJ reprints
Please address all orders for E/MJ editorial reprints—both single copies and in bulk—to: Otto Smith, Promotion Manager, E/MJ Reprint Dept., P.O. Box 689, Hightstown, N.J. 08520. (Telephone: (609) 448-1700, ext. 5366.)

General Index

Authors Index

Flowsheet and Cross-section Index